STUDIES IN LOGIC

AND

THE FOUNDATIONS OF MATHEMATICS

VOLUME 103

ELSEVIER

AMSTERDAM – LONDON – NEW YORK – OXFORD - PARIS – SHANNON - TOKYO

THE LAMBDA CALCULUS

ITS SYNTAX AND SEMANTICS

H. P. BARENDREGT

Rijksuniversiteit Utrecht
The Netherlands

revised edition

ELSEVIER

AMSTERDAM – LONDON – NEW YORK – OXFORD - PARIS – SHANNON - TOKYO

ELSEVIER SCIENCE B.V.
Sara Burgerhartstraat 25
P.O. Box 211, 1000 AE Amsterdam, The Netherlands

First edition: 1981
Revised edition: 1984
Second impression: 1985

Paperback edition: 1985
Second impression: 1990
Third impression: 1994
Fourth impression: 1998
Fifth impression: 2001

ISBN 0 444 86748 1 (Hardbound)
ISBN 0 444 87508 5 (Paperback)

Library of Congress Cataloging in Publication Data

Barendregt, H. P. (Hendrik Pieter)
The lambda calculus.
(Studies in logic and the foundations of mathematics ; v. 103)
Bibliography: p.
Includes indexes.
1. Lambda calculus. I. Title. II. Series.
QA9.5.B36 1984 511.3 84-5966
ISBN 0-444-87508-5

The paper used in this publication meets the requirements of ANSI/NISO Z39.48-1992 (Permanence of Paper).
Printed in The Netherlands.

La musique est une mathématique mystérieuse, dont les éléments participent de l'infini.

Claude Debussy [1903]

This book is dedicated to two women:

Dolly Barendregt-Kessing

and

Maria Montessori.

The first gave birth to me and showed me the use of mindfulness; the second taught me without teaching and introduced me to the experience of truth.

PREFACE

Around 1930 the type free lambda calculus was introduced as a foundation for logic and mathematics. Due to the appearence of paradoxes, this aim was not fulfilled, however. Nevertheless a consistent part of the theory turned out to be quite successful as a theory of computations. It gave an important momentum to early recursion theory and more recently to computer science. Moreover, in spite of the paradoxes, the possibility of using the lambda calculus as an alternative foundation is still open. This question recently received a good deal of renewed attention.

As a result of these developments, the lambda calculus has grown into a theory worth studying for its own sake. This *pure* lambda calculus is the subject matter of this book. Readers interested in applications may also find the book useful, since these applications are usually heuristic rather than direct. Constructions in the lambda calculus give the right intuition for constructions in, for example, the semantics of programming languages. Thus the book is written for logicians, mathematicians, computer scientists and philosophers.

Acknowledgements. This book was written at the suggestion of Anne Troelstra, one of the editors of the series "*Studies in Logic*". Einar Fredriksson of the North-Holland Publishing Company, remained patient after the deadline of delivering the manuscript had passed.

During the year 1974/1975 I had an inspiring seminar with Jan Bergstra, Jan Willem Klop and Henri Volken. With Gordon Plotkin and Dana Scott I had several useful conversations. Jan Willem Klop was always willing to discuss lambda calculus. Not all of his ideas relevant to the subject are in this book; these can be found in Klop [1980]. The following persons read parts of the manuscript and gave critical comments: Mariangiola Dezani, Roger Hindley, Karst Koymans, Jean-Jacques Lévy, Giuseppe Longo, Gerd Mitschke, Albert Visser and Chris Wadsworth.

Special thanks are due to Joseph Quinsey for reading the whole manuscript and making many stylistic improvements in the English and mathematical language; to Adrian Rézus for preparing the indices and references; and to Jan Willem Klop for drawing the figures.

The main part of the book was written at the Rijksuniversiteit Utrecht, where Dirk van Dalen kindly provided excellent working conditions. Other support came from the Netherlands Organization for the Advancement of Pure Science (Z.W.O.); from the Mathematisches Forschungsinstitut at the E.T.H. Zürich; and finally from the Mathematisches Forschungsinstitut Oberwolfach where I finished the manuscript.

This book could not have been printed if it had not been typed. Ninety per cent of this was done by Do Breughel-Vollgraff (who typed faster than I could write); the remaining ten per cent was typed by Ans, Ellwyn, Joke, Marianne, Renske, Sineke and Sophie. To all my heartfelt thanks.

Budapestlaan 6, 3508 TA Utrecht
The Netherlands

February, 1980 Henk Barendregt

Added in print

The main part of the proof checking was done in Cogne (Italy) at the mountain resort of Mariangiola Dezani-Ciancaglini. She, and also Simonetta Ronchi della Rocca, provided valuable support.

August, 1980 H. B.

Preface to the second edition

In the first edition of this book the notions of lambda algebra and lambda model were introduced in a correct but somewhat elaborate way. Recent work of others made it possible to give an elegant categorical description of both kinds of models. This lead to the main changes in this edition: a complete rewriting of chapter 5 introducing models with some consequent changes in chapter 18 constructing models. Moreover, some additional material was included at the end of the book and several corrections were made.

May, 1983 H. B.

Added in print

The following persons suggested several corrections after reading the first edition: Tetsuo Ida, Marly Roncken and Yoshihito Toyama.

February, 1984 H. B.

CONTENTS

HINTS FOR THE READER

Prerequisites

This book is essentially self contained. Occasionally some elementary parts of first order logic, topology, set theory, recursion theory and category theory are needed. For these topics the reader may consult the following books if necessary.

First order logic: Enderton [1972], Barwise [1977a].
General topology: Kelly [1955].
Set theory: Halmos [1960], van Dalen et al. [1978].
Recursion theory: Rogers [1967].
Category theory: Arbib and Manes [1975], MacLane [1972].

Notation

The following notation is used in this book.

$\mathbb{N}$: set of natural numbers.
$P(\mathbb{N})$ or $P\omega$: set of subsets of $\mathbb{N}$.
$\lambda x. \cdots$: (meta lambda abstraction) the set theoretic function f such that $f(x) = \cdots$ for all x (e.g. $(\lambda x.x^2+1)(3) = 10$).
$\mu x \cdots$: the least $x \in \mathbb{N}$ such that $\cdots$
Seq: Set of coded sequence numbers, i.e.

$$\text{Seq} = \{\langle n_1, \ldots, n_k\rangle \in \mathbb{N} \mid k \in \mathbb{N}, n_1, \ldots, n_k \in \mathbb{N}\}.$$

If $\alpha = \langle n_1, \ldots, n_k\rangle \in \text{Seq}$, then $\text{lh}(\alpha) = k$. By convention $\langle\ \rangle \in \text{Seq}$ and $\text{lh}(\langle\ \rangle) = 0$. If $\alpha = \langle n_1, \ldots, n_p\rangle$, $\beta = \langle m_1, \ldots, m_q\rangle$, then $\alpha * \beta = \langle n_1, \ldots, n_p, m_1, \ldots, m_q\rangle$ and $\alpha \leqslant \beta$ iff $p \leqslant q$ and $n_i = m_i$ for $1 \leqslant i \leqslant p$. Write $\alpha < \beta$ if $\alpha \leqslant \beta$ but not $\beta \leqslant \alpha$.

The logical connectives are $\neg$ (not), $\vee$ (or), $\wedge$ (and), $\Rightarrow$ (implies), $\Leftrightarrow$ (if and only if, iff), $\forall$ (for all) and $\exists$ (there exists). These are usually used in the informal metalanguage. $\exists! x$ denotes that there is a unique x.

Often some "category theoretic" pictures are used to denote statements. For example, let R be a binary relation on a set X, then

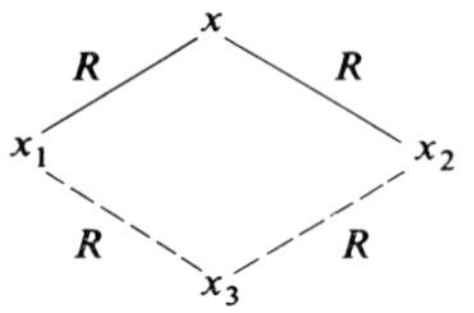

expresses

$$\forall x, x_1, x_2 \in X \quad [xRx_1 \wedge xRx_2 \Rightarrow \exists x_3 \in X[x_1Rx_3 \wedge x_2Rx_3]].$$

Others uses will be self explanatory.

Presentation of the material

The main subjects within the pure lambda calculus are: *conversion*, *reduction*, *theories* and *models*. These topics are systematically treated in the main parts of this book. Moreover there is an initial part that gives an introduction to each of the other ones: chapter i (with the last section giving a survey) is an introduction to part i for $2 \leqslant i \leqslant 5$. Chapter 1 is a general introduction and also presents the prerequisites of the less familiar theory of complete partial orders.

The following table roughly indicates the interdependence of the chapters. The broken arrows indicate that some results of a later chapter are stated without proof in an earlier one.

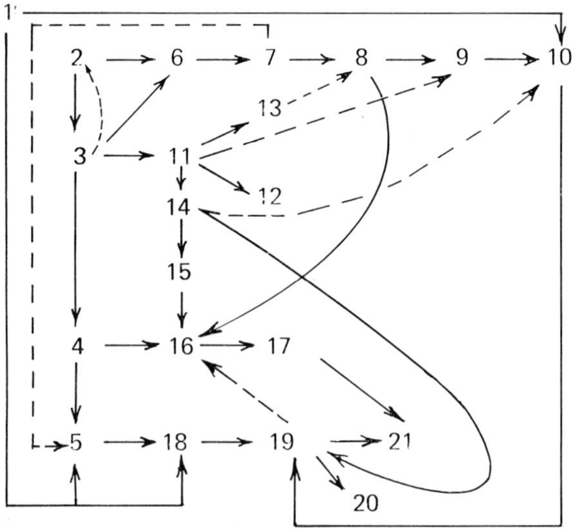

(I hope the reader will find it easier to follow the book than this diagram.)

Each chapter is followed by a section with exercises. The more difficult ones are marked with an asterisk (∗).

Since this is a systematic rather than didactical treatise, let me indicate how one might present (or read) the material. A very short course would consist of §§ 2.1, 3.1, 3.2, chapter 6, §§ 1.2, 5.1, 5.2, 5.3 and 5.4. This gives insight into the recursive power of the language and proves consistency in both a model-theoretic and a syntactic way.

To this basic course one might add at first §§ 7.1, 7.2, 8.1, 8.2, 8.3, 10.1, 11.1, 11.2, 13.1, 13.2, 18.1 and 18.2, dealing with 1. the theory of combinators; 2. solvability, Böhm trees, special reductions; 3. the models $P\omega$, D_∞.

Then one could add §§ 10.2, 10.3, 14.1, 14.3, 16.1, 16.2, 19.1 and 19.2, giving an analysis of the values of terms inside models.

Other topics of interest, depending on the reader's taste, can be found using the last sections of chapters 2, 3, 4 and 5, which give an overview of the rest of the book. The author's favorites are the following: §§ 13.4, 15.3, 17.1, 20.4; and also: §§ 9.4, 10.4, 17.2 and chapter 21, although the latter are somewhat more technical.

PART I

TOWARDS THE THEORY

Schönfinkel (1922)
(Courtesy of
Mrs. N. Courant)

Curry (1932)
(With daughter Anne;
courtesy of Mrs. V. Curry)

Church (1965)

Rosser (photo by
T. Hirano, 1935)

Kleene (photo by
T. Hirano, 1935)

Turing (1951)

CHAPTER 1

INTRODUCTION

1.1. Aspects of the lambda calculus

The lambda calculus is a type free theory about functions as *rules*, rather than as graphs. "Functions as rules" is the old fashioned notion of function and refers to the process of going from argument to value, a process coded by a definition. The idea, usually attributed to Dirichlet, that functions could also be considered as graphs, that is, as sets of pairs of argument and value, was an important mathematical contribution. Nevertheless the λ-calculus regards functions again as rules in order to stress their *computational* aspects.

The functions as rules are considered in full generality. For example, we may think of functions as given by definitions in ordinary English applied to arguments also expressed in English. Or, more specifically, consider functions as given by programs for machines applied to, that is, operating on, other such programs. In both cases we have a type free structure, where the objects of study are at the same time function and argument. This is the starting point of the *type free* λ-calculus. In particular a function can be applied to itself. For the usual notion of function in mathematics (as in Zermelo-Fraenkel set theory), this is impossible (because of the axiom of foundation). (See also exercise 18.5.30.)

There are three aspects of the λ-calculus:

I. Foundations of mathematics.

II. Computations.

III. Pure lambda calculus.

These aspects will be described in the following pages. Some other views on the foundations of lambda calculus are expressed in Scott [1975b], [1980] and [1980a].

I. Foundations and lambda calculus

The founders of the λ-calculus and the related theory of combinatory logic had two aims in mind:

(1) To develop a general theory of functions (dealing, for example, with formula manipulations).

(2) To extend that theory with logical notions providing a foundation for logic and (parts of) mathematics.

The first point was explicitly stressed by Schönfinkel and Curry, the founders of combinatory logic, and it was also implicit in the work of Church founding the λ-calculus.

Unfortunately all attempts to provide a foundation for mathematics failed. Church's original system [1932/33] was inconsistent as shown by Kleene and Rosser [1935]. As was pointed out in Aczel [1980], Frege's well known inconsistent theory [1893, 1903] essentially contains the λ-calculus; so that was in fact another failure.

Curry [1930] did provide a consistent theory fulfilling the first point above (pure combinatory logic), but the logical part of his theory is too weak to be adequate as a foundation.

After the discovery of the Kleene–Rosser paradox Church was discouraged in his foundational program. Church [1941] gave a consistent (as shown by the Church-Rosser theorem) subtheory of his original system dealing only with the functional part. This theory is the λI-calculus.

Curry on the other hand did not want "to run away from the paradoxes". He proposed to extend pure combinatory logic by so-called illative notions in order to fulfil the second aim and to give at the same time an analysis of the paradoxes; see Curry et al. [1958], [1972]. Although Curry's program has not been completed, some progress has been made: see Fitch [1974], Scott [1975a], Seldin [1976/77] and Aczel [1980].

There are other foundational approaches related to the λ-calculus. Feferman [1975], [1980] develops systems based on a partial application function as a foundation for constructive mathematics. The underlying sets of partial functions are related to Uniformly Reflexive Structures of Wagner [1969] and Strong [1968], (see also Barendregt [1975]). It is an open question how these URS's relate to the λ-calculus models where application is always defined (see addendum 1 at the end of the book).

Then there are relations between the λ-calculus, proof theory and category theory. The λ-calculus used in this context is, however, the typed λ-calculus; see appendix A, in particular §A.3.

II. Computations and lambda-calculus

Recursion theory

The part of the λ-calculus dealing only with functions turned out to be quite successful. Using this theory Church proposed a formalization of the notion "effectively computable" by the concept of λ-definability. Kleene [1936] showed that λ-definability is equivalent to Gödel–Herbrand recursiveness and in the meantime Church formulated his thesis (stating that recursiveness is the proper formalization of effective computability). Turing [1936], [1937] gave an analysis of machine computability and showed that the resulting notion (Turing computable) is equivalent to λ-definability.

After the discovery of the paradoxes, Kleene translated results on λ-definability and obtained several fundamental recursion theoretic theorems (see Crossley [1975], p. 4–7). The enumeration theorem for partial recursive functions, the s-m-n theorem and the recursion theorem were all inspired by the λ-calculus.

Computer Science

The rise of the computer in the last few decades resulted in an extensive development of programming languages. The λ-calculus possesses several features of programming languages and their implementations. For example, bound variables in the λ-calculus correspond to formal parameters in a procedure; and the type free aspect corresponds to the fact that for a machine a program and its data are the same, namely a sequence of bits.

By the analysis of Turing it follows that in spite of its very simple syntax, the λ-calculus is strong enough to describe all mechanically computable functions. Therefore the λ-calculus can be viewed as a paradigmatic programming language. This certainly does not imply that one should use it to write actual programs. What is meant is that in the λ-calculus several programming problems, specifically those concerning procedure calls, are in a pure form. A study of these can bear some fruits for the design and analysis of programming languages.

For example, several programming languages have features inspired by λ-calculus (perhaps unconsciously so). In Algol '60, '68 or Pascal, procedures can be arguments of procedures. In LISP the same is true and moreover a procedure can be the output of a procedure. The language GEDANKEN, see Reynolds [1970], is explicitly founded on the λ-calculus. For relations between λ-calculus and programming languages, see McCarthy [1962], Landin [1965, 1966, 1966a], Morris [1968], Reynolds [1970], Gordon [1973] and Burge [1978].

Because of the similarities of λ-calculus and some programming languages, ideas for the semantics of the former may be applied to the latter.

Landin [1965] gave a semantics of Algol by translating this language in λ-calculus and by describing an *operational semantics* for the latter. For further work on this kind of semantics, see Wegner [1972], Ollongren [1975], Plotkin [1975], O'Donnell [1977] and Burge [1978].

In the mean time there was a need for a *denotational semantics* of programming languages (in order to express what is the functional meaning of a program). A similar problem had occurred in a pure form in the λ-calculus. Due to the type free character it was not clear how to construct models for that theory. One would want a set X in which its function space $X \to X$ can be inbedded; for cardinality reasons this is impossible. The difficulty was overcome by Scott in 1969, who constructed λ-calculus models by restricting $X \to X$ to *continuous* functions on X (with a proper topology). Only then did it become clear how to develop a denotational semantics for programming languages. This is because Scott's method is powerful enough to give also a meaning to the following two features of programming languages: recursion (least fixed points) and data types (integers, lists, arrays etc.). See Scott–Strachey [1971], Milne–Strachey [1976], Stoy [1977] and Gordon [1979].

What kind of computations are captured by λ-calculus? Berry showed that these must be essentially sequential: see theorem 14.4.8. Not being able to deal with parallel computations may seem at first to be a severe restriction. This is not so, however, since most programming languages do not deal with parallel processes either. On the other hand, in the Scott–Strachey approach to semantics, there is a natural place for functions like the "parallel or", i.e.

$$f(x,y) = \text{if } x \text{ or } y \text{ is defined and true, then true else undefined.}$$

Therefore the semantics of the λ-calculus has a place for this kind of parallelism. See also Plotkin [1977].

III. Pure lambda calculus

Lambda calculus as treated in this book is not directed towards applications as above, but is studied for its own interest.

The formal (type free) λ-calculus, a theory denoted by **λ**, studies functions and their applicative behaviour and not, as in category theory, functions under composition. Therefore *application* is a primitive operation of **λ**. The function f applied to the argument a is denoted by fa. Complementary to application there is *abstraction*. Let $t(\equiv t(x))$ be an expression possibly containing x. Then $\lambda x.t(x)$ is the function f that assigns to the argument a the value $t(a)$. That is

$$(\beta) \qquad (\lambda x.t(x))a = t(a).$$

That one considers only application and abstraction for unary functions is reasonable, following an observation of Schönfinkel [1924]. He remarked that functions of several variables could be reduced to unary functions. If $f(x,y)$ is e.g. a binary function, then define $f_x = \lambda y.f(x,y)$ and $a = \lambda x.f_x$. Then one has $(ax)y = f_x y = f(x,y)$.

This is an important principle in the λ-calculus. It corresponds to the equation

$$X^{Y \times Z} = (X^Y)^Z$$

in the category of sets. This equation holds in all cartesian closed categories and in fact all models of the λ-calculus are objects in such a category.

The theory **λ** has as terms the set Λ (λ-*terms*) built up from variables using application and abstraction. The statements of **λ** are equations between λ-terms and **λ** has as its only mathematical axioms the scheme (β). [Some trivial identifications like $\lambda x.x = \lambda y.y$ have to be made however.]

As was mentioned above, the λ-calculus studies functions as rules. Because of this intensional character, the linguistic means to describe these functions–the λ-terms–play a central role. By the theory **λ** some of these λ-terms are identified (so called *convertible* terms). But it is important to note that the theory **λ** is itself not the focus of interest; it is just a way to generate the principal objects, namely the *terms modulo convertibility*. Only then does the real λ-calculus start: the study of these objects using all possible mathematical tools.

The following questions show how these objects are studied.

(1) What kind of functions (on terms) are definable (as term)?

(2) Let M, N be non-convertible terms. Is it reasonable to identify M and N (taking a less intensional view)?

(3) What is the correspondence between the applicative behaviour and the syntactic form of terms?

Some typical answers to these questions are as follows. First consider (1).

(i) Restricted to numerals exactly the recursive functions are definable (theorem 6.3.13).

(ii) The range of a definable function on terms is always infinite or a singleton (theorem 17.1.16).

(iii) There is a natural topology on terms, the so-called tree topology. With respect to this topology all definable functions are continuous.

Result (iii) is non-trivial and has several interesting consequences. The topology is obtained by associating to terms so called Böhm trees and then translating the Scott topology on these trees to terms.

The second question can be approached by either giving consistency proofs of natural extensions of **λ** or by constructing models $\mathfrak{M}$ for **λ** and considering the set of equations true in $\mathfrak{M}$. The theory **λη** (extensional λ-calculus) is obtained by the first method. The theories $\mathcal{B}$ (which identifies terms with the same Böhm tree) and $\mathcal{H}^*$ (the unique maximally consistent extension of $\mathcal{H}$) are formed by the second method ($\mathcal{B} = \mathrm{Th}(P\omega)$; $\mathcal{H}^* = \mathrm{Th}(D_\infty)$).

With regard to (3), let F be a λ-term. One has e.g. the following.

(iv) F is solvable iff F has a head normal form (theorem 8.3.14). This relates the syntactic notion of head normal form, i.e. $F = \lambda x_1 \ldots x_n . x_i M_1 \ldots M_m$, to solvability, which indicates applicative behaviour: $\forall Q\ \exists n\ \exists P_1 \ldots P_n\ FP_1 \ldots P_n = Q$.

(v) F is $\beta\eta$-invertible iff F is a finite hereditary permutation (theorem 21.2.21). Here $\beta\eta$-invertibility means that there exists a λ-term G such that in the extensional λ-calculus

$$F \circ G = G \circ F = \lambda x.x,$$

where $\circ$ denotes the composition of functions. The finite hereditary permutations are some syntactically defined class.

Now that we have seen the questions and some results, let us indicate how the subject is treated. There is some connection between pure λ-calculus and number theory. The connection is superficial, in that the methods and results are totally different, but it is nevertheless good to indicate it in order to obtain some feeling of how the subject matter of the pure λ-calculus is organized.

If $\mathcal{T}$ is a consistent extension of $\boldsymbol{\lambda}$, write $\mathfrak{M}_{\mathcal{T}}$ for the term model consisting of open or closed (i.e. with or without free variables) λ-terms modulo $\mathcal{T}$. The principal object of study is $\mathfrak{M}_{\boldsymbol{\lambda}}$ (in number theory this is, say, the ring of integers $\mathbb{Z}$). One considers various extensions $\mathcal{T} \supseteq \boldsymbol{\lambda}$ and the corresponding $\mathfrak{M}_{\mathcal{T}}$ (in number theory $\mathbb{Z}/(m)$). If $\mathcal{T} \subseteq \mathcal{T}'$, then there is a canonical homomorphism of $\mathfrak{M}_{\mathcal{T}}$ onto $\mathfrak{M}_{\mathcal{T}'}$ (in number theory $\mathbb{Z}/(m) \to \mathbb{Z}/(m')$ if m' divides m, i.e. for the ideals $(m) \subseteq (m')$). Some $\mathfrak{M}_{\mathcal{T}}$ (e.g. $\mathfrak{M}_{\mathcal{H}}$ and $\mathfrak{M}_{\mathcal{B}}$) have a unique homomorphic image that is simple (in number theory $\mathbb{Z}/(p)$, with p prime, is simple; $\mathbb{Z}/(p^k)$ is of the second kind, a so-called *local* ring). In number theory the field $\mathbb{Q}$ (rationals) is extended in a topological way to $\mathbb{R}$ (reals) and also to the $\mathbb{Q}_p$ (p-adic field). Similarly in the λ-calculus the models $\mathfrak{M}_{\mathcal{B}}$ and $\mathfrak{M}_{\mathcal{H}^*}$ are embedded in $P\omega$ and D_∞ respectively, models which are constructed via topological notions. Figure 1.1 shows some of the parallels (and differences).

An interesting aspect of number theory is that results about $\mathbb{Z}$ and $\mathbb{Q}$ are sometimes proved via results about $\mathbb{R}$, the p-adic numbers $\mathbb{Q}_p$ or $\mathbb{C}$ (complex numbers). Similarly results about λ-terms are sometimes proved via the "continuous" models $P\omega$ and D_∞, e.g. theorem 21.2.21 mentioned above. In this context the Böhm trees play an important role. These possibly infinite trees may be compared to the continued fractions of the reals. Each tree is the limit of finite trees. A natural topology on λ-terms can be defined using the Böhm trees. With respect to this topology the λ-calculus operations are continuous (theorem 14.3.22). This continuity theorem has several applications. Thus we agree with a remark of Scott that the introduction of models and continuity considerations make the theory really λ-*calculus*.

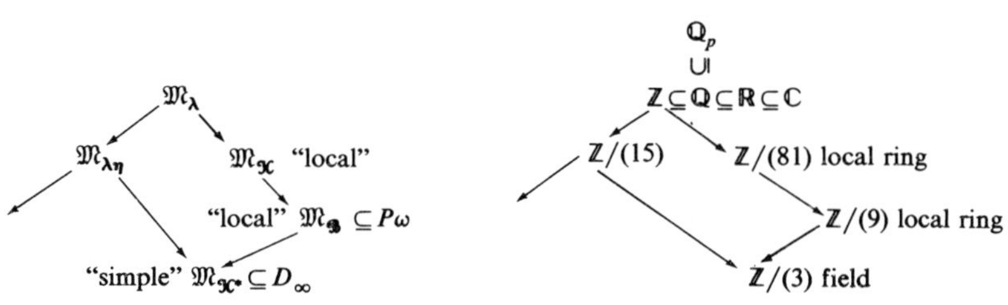

FIG. 1.1.

So far we have indicated roughly what happens in parts II, IV and V of this book. Part III, which is about reduction, is of a different nature. This group of results is about the λ-terms themselves (i.e. not modulo convertibility). The main purpose is to give a proof theoretic analysis of convertibility and some extensions by Church–Rosser theorems–a method analogous to cut elimination in proof theory.

Finally we list some topics that belong to the pure λ-calculus (or are closely related) but are not treated in this book.

(1) Already mentioned was the typed λ-calculus. This theory is rather different from the type free theory, see Appendix A. For alternative type theories, see Coppo et al. [1980] and the references there.

(2) Relations with higher type recursion theory; see Kleene [1961/62].

(3) Ordinal notations in the λ-calculus; see Church and Kleene [1937].

(4) Embeddings of the λ-calculus in first order logic; see Barendregt [1973] and Bel [1977].

(5) Optimal reductions; see Lévy [1980].

1.2. Complete partial orders and the Scott topology

This section is an introduction to the category of complete partial orders with continuous maps. The material is needed in §10.2, §14.3 and in part V for the construction of λ-calculus models. The reader may skip this section until necessary while reading the text.

Originally Scott defined his topology on complete lattices, see Scott [1972], Gierz et al. [1980]. The definition generalizes immediately to complete partial orders. This more general situation will be treated here, since it has some advantages to work with the latter structures (there is a natural interpretation of λ-terms as certain trees and they form a complete partial order, not a complete lattice; complete partial orders are more abundant).

Another setting in which constructions for λ-calculus models can take place, is Ershov's category of f_0-spaces (and various of its subcategories); see Ershov [1975]. These categories have the advantage to be cartesian closed in which each object is a topological space, such that the topology on a product is the product topology and on a function space the topology of pointwise convergence. This is not true for the category of complete partial orders. We will treat nevertheless these latter structures, since they are somewhat easier to describe than f_0-spaces (see exercise 1.3.19).

1.2.1. Definition. Let $D = (D, \sqsubseteq)$ be a poset, i.e. a partially ordered set (with reflexive $\sqsubseteq$).

(i) A subset $X \subseteq D$ is *directed* if $X \neq \emptyset$ and

$$\forall x, y \in X \ \exists z \in X \ [x \sqsubseteq z \text{ and } y \sqsubseteq z].$$

(ii) D is a *complete partial order* (cpo) if

(1) There is a least element $\bot \in D$, i.e. $\forall x \in D\ \bot \sqsubseteq x$. The element $\bot$ is called *bottom*.

(2) For every directed $X \subseteq D$ the supremum $\bigsqcup X \in D$ exists.

A *complete lattice* is a poset D where *every* $X \subseteq D$ has a supremum. Each complete lattice is a cpo, since $\bot = \bigsqcup \emptyset$.

1.2.2. Examples. (i) Let X be a set and $P(X)$ its power set. Then $(P(X), \subseteq)$ is a cpo (even a complete lattice).

(ii) Let $\mathbb{T} = (\{\bot, t, f\}, \sqsubseteq)$ with $\bot \sqsubseteq t$, $\bot \sqsubseteq f$ (no other relations). Then $\mathbb{T}$ is a cpo.

1.2.3. Definition. Let $(D, \sqsubseteq)$ be a cpo. The *Scott topology* on D is defined as follows.

$O \subseteq D$ is *open* if

(1) $x \in O \wedge x \sqsubseteq y \Rightarrow y \in O$,
(2) $\bigsqcup X \in O$, with $X \subseteq D$ directed $\Rightarrow X \cap O \neq \emptyset$.

Clearly $\emptyset$ and D are open and open sets are closed under arbitrary unions; if O_1, O_2 are open, then $O_1 \cap O_2$ is open by the fact that in (2) above, X is directed. Therefore definition 1.2.3 indeed determines a topology.

Unless stated otherwise, cpo's will always be considered with the Scott topology. From now on in this section $D = (D, \sqsubseteq), D = (D', \sqsubseteq'), \ldots$ will range over cpo's.

1.2.4. Lemma. *Let $U_x = \{z \in D \mid z \not\sqsubseteq x\}$. Then U_x is open.*

Proof. Easy. □

1.2.5. Corollary. *D is a T_0 space which is generally not T_1.*

Proof. Let $x, y \in D$ with $x \neq y$, say $x \not\sqsubseteq y$. Then $x \in U_y$, $y \notin U_y$ and U_y open. Hence D is T_0.

If $x \sqsubseteq y$, then every neighborhood of x contains y. Therefore D does not need to be T_1. □

The following characterization of continuous functions is the main reason for introducing the Scott topology.

1.2.6. PROPOSITION. *Consider a map* $f\colon D \to D'$. *Then*

$$f \text{ is continuous iff } f(\bigsqcup X) = \bigsqcup f(X) \text{ for all directed } X \subseteq D,$$

where $f(X) = \{f(x) | x \in X\}$ *and the second supremum is in* D'.

PROOF. ($\Rightarrow$) Let f be continuous. Suppose $x \sqsubseteq y$ in order to show $f(x) \sqsubseteq' f(y)$. If not, then $f(x) \in U_{f(y)}$, so $x \in f^{-1}(U_{f(y)})$ which is open. Therefore $y \in f^{-1}(U_{f(y)})$, i.e. $f(y) \in U_{f(y)}$, a contradiction. This shows that f is monotonic. Therefore $\forall x \in X\ f(\bigsqcup X) \sqsupseteq f(x)$, hence $f(\bigsqcup X) \sqsupseteq \bigsqcup f(X)$. If $f(\bigsqcup X) \not\sqsubseteq \bigsqcup f(X)$, then $f(\bigsqcup X) \in U_{\bigsqcup f(X)}$ and a contradiction can be obtained as above, using condition (2) for open sets.

($\Leftarrow$) Again it follows that f is monotonic, since if $x \sqsubseteq y$, then $y = x \sqcup y$, hence $f(y) = f(x) \sqcup f(y)$, so $f(x) \sqsubseteq f(y)$. Therefore if $O \subseteq D'$ is open, so is $f^{-1}(O) \subseteq D$: e.g. if for directed $X \subseteq D$ one has $\bigsqcup X \in f^{-1}(O)$, then $f(\bigsqcup X) = \bigsqcup f(X) \in O$; but $f(X)$ is directed, hence $f(X) \cap O \neq \emptyset$ and it follows that $X \cap f^{-1}(O) \neq \emptyset$. □

1.2.7. COROLLARY. *Continuous maps on* cpo's *are always monotonic.* □

The direct product of two cpo's can be considered again as a cpo.

1.2.8. PROPOSITION. *Given* D, D', *let* $D \times D'$ *be the cartesian product partially ordered by*

$$\langle x, x' \rangle \sqsubseteq \langle y, y' \rangle \quad \text{iff} \quad x \sqsubseteq y \text{ and } x' \sqsubseteq' y'.$$

Then $D \times D'$ *is a cpo with for directed* $X \subseteq D \times D'$

$$\bigsqcup X = \langle \bigsqcup X_0, \bigsqcup X_1 \rangle,$$

where

$$X_0 = \{x \in D | \exists x' \in D'\ \langle x, x' \rangle \in X\}$$

and

$$X_1 = \{x' \in D' | \exists x \in D\ \langle x, x' \rangle \in X\}.$$

PROOF. Easy. $\langle \bot, \bot' \rangle$ is the bottom of $D \times D'$; moreover, note that if $X \subseteq D \times D'$ is directed, then so are X_0, X_1. □

The following is somewhat unexpected.

FACT. The topology on $D \times D'$ is in general not the product of the topologies on D and on D'; see exercise 1.3.12. See also proposition 1.2.27.

1.2.9. DEFINITION. Let D, D' be given. Define

$$[D \to D'] = \{f: D \to D' \mid f \text{ continuous}\}.$$

This set can be partially ordered pointwise:

$$f \sqsubseteq g \quad \Leftrightarrow \quad \forall x \in D \; f(x) \sqsubseteq' g(x).$$

Clearly $[D \to D']$ is a poset.

1.2.10. LEMMA. *Let $\{f_i\}_i \subseteq [D \to D']$ be a directed family of maps. Define*

$$f(x) = \bigsqcup_i f_i(x).$$

Then f is well defined and continuous.

PROOF. Since $\{f_i\}_i$ is directed, $\{f_i(x)\}_i$ is directed for all x and hence f exists. Moreover for directed $X \subseteq D$

$$f(\bigsqcup X) = \bigsqcup_i \bigsqcup_{x \in X} f_i(x) = \bigsqcup_{x \in X} \bigsqcup_i f_i(x) = \bigsqcup f(X). \quad \square$$

1.2.11. PROPOSITION. *$[D \to D']$ is a cpo with the supremum of a directed $F \subseteq [D \to D']$ defined by*

$$(\bigsqcup F)(x) = \bigsqcup \{f(x) \mid f \in F\}.$$

PROOF. $\lambda x.\bot'$ is the bottom element of $[D \to D']$. By lemma 1.2.10 the map $\lambda x.\bigsqcup\{f(x) \mid f \in F\}$ is continuous. Clearly it is the supremum of F. $\square$

1.2.12. LEMMA. *Let $f: D \times D' \to D''$. Then f is continuous iff f is continuous in its arguments separately, that is, iff $\lambda x.f(x, x_0')$ and $\lambda x'.f(x_0, x')$ are continuous for all x_0, x_0'.*

PROOF. (⇒) Let $g = \lambda x. f(x, x_0')$. Then for directed $X \subseteq D$

$$\begin{aligned} g(\bigsqcup X) &= f(\bigsqcup X, x_0') \\ &= f(\bigsqcup \{(x, x_0') \mid x \in X\}) \\ &= \bigsqcup \{f(x, x_0') \mid x \in X\}, \quad \text{since } f \text{ is continuous and } \{(x, x_0') \mid x \in X\} \text{ is directed,} \\ &= \bigsqcup g(X). \end{aligned}$$

Hence g is continuous and similarly $\lambda x'. f(x_0, x')$.

(⇐) Let $X \subseteq D \times D'$ be directed. Then

$$\begin{aligned} f(\bigsqcup X) &= f(\bigsqcup X_0, \bigsqcup X_1) \\ &= \bigsqcup_{x \in X_0} f(x, \bigsqcup X_1) \quad \text{by assumption,} \\ &= \bigsqcup_{x \in X_0} \bigsqcup_{x' \in X_1} f(x, x') \\ &= \bigsqcup_{\langle x, x' \rangle \in X} f(x, x') \quad \text{since } X \text{ is directed,} \\ &= \bigsqcup f(X), \end{aligned}$$

and so f is continuous. □

1.2.13. PROPOSITION (Continuity of application). *Define application*

$$\mathrm{Ap} : [D \to D'] \times D \to D'$$

by Ap$(f, x) = f(x)$. *Then* Ap *is continuous (with respect to the Scott topology on the product* $[D \to D'] \times D$).

PROOF. $\lambda x. f(x) = f$ is continuous. Let $h = \lambda f. f(x)$. Then for directed $F \subseteq [D \to D']$

$$\begin{aligned} h(\bigsqcup F) &= (\bigsqcup F)(x) \\ &= \bigsqcup \{f(x) \mid f \in F\} \quad \text{by proposition 1.2.11,} \\ &= \bigsqcup \{h(f) \mid f \in F\} = \bigsqcup h(F). \end{aligned}$$

Hence h is continuous. Now lemma 1.2.12 applies. □

1.2.14. PROPOSITION (Continuity of abstraction). *Let* $f \in [D \times D' \to D'']$. *Define* $\hat{f}(x) = \lambda y \in D' f(x,y)$. *Then*

(i) $\hat{f}$ *is continuous, i.e.* $\hat{f} \in [D \to [D' \to D'']]$;

(ii) $\lambda f.\hat{f} : [D \times D' \to D''] \to [D \to [D' \to D'']]$ *is continuous.*

PROOF. (i) Let $X \subseteq D$ be directed. Then

$$\begin{aligned}\hat{f}(\sqcup X) &= \lambda y.f(\sqcup X, y)\\ &= \lambda y. \bigsqcup_{x \in X} f(x,y)\\ &= \bigsqcup_{x \in X} (\lambda y.f(x,y)) \quad \text{by proposition 1.2.11,}\\ &= \sqcup \hat{f}(X).\end{aligned}$$

(ii) Let $L = \lambda f.\hat{f}$. then for $F \subseteq [D \times D' \to D'']$ directed

$$\begin{aligned}L(\sqcup F) &= \lambda x \lambda y.(\sqcup F)(x,y)\\ &= \lambda x \lambda y. \bigsqcup_{f \in F} f(x,y)\\ &= \bigsqcup_{f \in F} \lambda x \lambda y.f(x,y) = \sqcup L(F). \quad \square\end{aligned}$$

1.2.15. DEFINITION. **CPO** is the category of cpo's with continuous maps.

1.2.16. THEOREM. **CPO** *is a cartesian closed category, see definition* 5.5.1.

PROOF. It is easy to show that $D \times D'$ is a product in **CPO**. Moreover the singleton cpo is a terminal object. By propositions 1.2.13 and 1.2.14 for each $f: D \times D' \to D''$ there exists a unique $\hat{f}: D \to [D' \to D'']$ such that

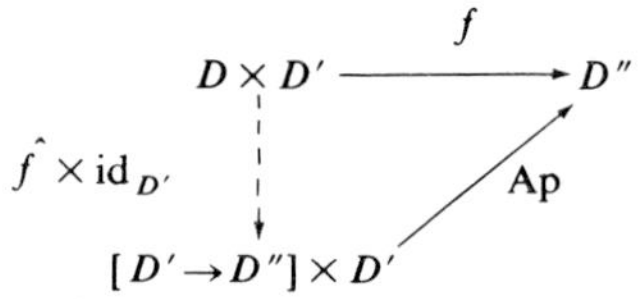

commutes. This is the required adjointness condition. $\square$

The following theorem (for complete lattices) is due to Tarski [1955]; see also Knaster [1928].

1.2.17. THEOREM. (*Fixed point theorem for* cpo's)

(i) *Every* $f \in [D \to D]$ *has a fixed point.*

(ii) *Moreover there exists a* Fix $\in [[D \to D] \to D]$ *such that for all* $f \in [D \to D]$ Fix(f) is the least fixed point of f.

PROOF. (i) Since $\bot \sqsubseteq f(\bot)$ it follows by monotonicity that $f(\bot) \sqsubseteq f(f(\bot)) = f^2(\bot)$, $f^2(\bot) \sqsubseteq f^3(\bot)$ etc. Therefore

$$x_f = \bigsqcup_n f^n(\bot)$$

exists. Now by continuity

$$f(x_f) = \bigsqcup_n f^{n+1}(\bot) = x_f,$$

i.e. x_f is a fixed point of f.

(ii) First note that x_f constructed in (i) is the least fixed point of f: if $f(y) = y$, then it follows by monotonicity that

$$f^n(\bot) \sqsubseteq f^n(y) = y,$$

hence

$$x_f = \bigsqcup_n f^n(\bot) \sqsubseteq y.$$

Now define

$$\text{Fix} = \lambda f.x_f = \lambda f.\bigsqcup_n f^n(\bot).$$

Then by proposition 1.2.13 and lemma 1.2.10 Fix is continuous. □

Now it will be shown that in **CPO** projective limits exist.

1.2.18. DEFINITION. Let $D_0, D_1, \ldots$ be a countable sequence of cpo's and let $f_i \in [D_{i+1} \to D_i]$.

(i) The sequence (D_i, f_i) is called a *projective* (or *inverse*) *system* of cpo's.

(ii) The *projective* (or *inverse*) *limit* of the system (D_i, f_i) (notation $\varprojlim(D_i, f_i)$) is the poset $(D_\infty, \sqsubseteq_\infty)$ with

$$D_\infty = \{\langle x_0, x_1, \ldots \rangle \mid \forall i\, x_i \in D_i \wedge f_i(x_{i+1}) = x_i\}$$

and

$$\langle \vec{x} \rangle \sqsubseteq_{\infty} \langle \vec{y} \rangle \quad \text{iff} \quad \forall i\; x_i \sqsubseteq y_i \quad (\text{in } D_i).$$

REMARKS. (i) As usual an infinite sequence $\langle x_0, x_1, \ldots \rangle$ is identified with a map $x : \mathbb{N} \to \bigcup_i D_i$ such that $x(i) = x_i \in D_i$ for all i.

(ii) Often $\varprojlim (D_i, f_i)$ is written as $\varprojlim D_i$.

1.2.19. PROPOSITION. *Let* (D_i, f_i) *be a projective system. Then* $\varprojlim (D_i, f_i)$ *is a cpo with*

$$\bigsqcup X = \lambda i. \bigsqcup \{x(i) \mid x \in X\}.$$

for directed $X \subseteq \varprojlim D_i$.

PROOF. If X is directed, then $\{x(i) \mid x \in X\}$ is directed for each i. Let

$$y_i = \bigsqcup \{x(i) \mid x \in X\}.$$

Then by the continuity of the f_i

$$\begin{aligned} f_i(y_{i+1}) &= \bigsqcup f_i\{x(i+1) \mid x \in X\} \\ &= \bigsqcup \{x(i) \mid x \in X\} = y_i. \end{aligned}$$

Therefore $\langle y_0, y_1, \ldots \rangle \in \varprojlim D_i$. Clearly it is the supremum of X. □

1.2.20. DEFINITION. Let D be a cpo and let $X \subseteq D$.

(i) $f \in [D \to D]$ is a *retraction* (*map*) of D onto X if $X = \text{Range}(f)$ and $f = f \circ f$.

(ii) X is a *retract* of D if there is a retraction map f of D onto X.

1.2.21. PROPOSITION. *Let* D *be a* cpo *with retract* X. *Then* X *is a* cpo *whose directed subsets have the same supremum as in* D *and whose topology is the subspace topology.*

PROOF. Let f: $D \to X$ be the retraction map. Let $Y \subseteq X$ be directed. Then Y is also directed as subset of D and $\bigsqcup Y = y$ exists in D. Now

$$\begin{aligned} f(y) &= f(\bigsqcup Y) \\ &= \bigsqcup f(Y) \quad \text{since } f \text{ is continuous,} \\ &= \bigsqcup Y \quad \text{since } Y \subseteq X, \\ &= y. \end{aligned}$$

Therefore $y \in X$ and hence is clearly the supremum of Y in X. □

1.2.22. DEFINITION. (i) $x \in D$ is *compact* if for every directed $X \subseteq D$ one has

$$x \sqsubseteq \bigsqcup X \quad \Rightarrow \quad x \sqsubseteq x_0 \text{ for some } x_0 \in X.$$

(ii) D is an *algebraic* cpo if for all $x \in D$ the set $\{y \sqsubseteq x \mid y \text{ compact}\}$ is directed and

$$x = \bigsqcup \left\{ y \sqsubseteq x \mid y \text{ compact} \right\}.$$

1.2.23. EXAMPLE. Let $D = (P\omega, \subseteq)$. Then $x \in D$ is compact iff x is finite. Therefore D is algebraic.

1.2.24. PROPOSITION. *Let D be algebraic and $f: D \to D$. Then f is continuous iff $f(x) = \bigsqcup\{f(e) \mid e \sqsubseteq x, e \text{ compact}\}$.*

PROOF. (⇒) Let f be continuous. Then

$$\begin{aligned} f(x) &= f\left(\bigsqcup \left\{ e \sqsubseteq x \mid e \text{ compact} \right\}\right) \\ &= \bigsqcup \left\{ f(e) \mid e \sqsubseteq x, e \text{ compact} \right\} \end{aligned}$$

by proposition 1.2.6.

(⇐) First notice that f is monotonic. If $x \sqsubseteq y$, then

$$\left\{ e \sqsubseteq x \mid e \text{ compact} \right\} \subseteq \left\{ e \sqsubseteq y \mid e \text{ compact} \right\},$$

hence

$$\begin{aligned} f(x) &= \bigsqcup \left\{ f(e) \mid e \sqsubseteq x, e \text{ compact} \right\} \\ &\sqsubseteq \bigsqcup \left\{ f(e) \mid e \sqsubseteq y, e \text{ compact} \right\} = f(y). \end{aligned}$$

Now let $X \subseteq D$ be directed. Then

$$\begin{aligned} f(\bigsqcup X) &= \bigsqcup \{ f(e) \mid e \sqsubseteq \bigsqcup X, e \text{ compact} \} \\ &\sqsubseteq \bigsqcup \{ f(x) \mid x \in X \}, \quad \text{by compactness,} \\ &\sqsubseteq f(\bigsqcup X), \quad \text{by monotonicity.} \end{aligned}$$

Therefore $f(\bigsqcup X) = \bigsqcup f(X)$. By proposition 1.2.6 we are done. □

1.2.25. PROPOSITION. *Let D be algebraic. Define $O_e = \{x \in D \mid e \sqsubseteq x\}$. Then $\{O_e \mid e$ compact$\}$ is a basis for the topology on D.*

PROOF. By the compactness of e the set O_e satisfies the second condition to be Scott open. The first condition is trivial.

Now let $x \in O$, O open. Since $x = \bigsqcup\{e \sqsubseteq x \mid e \text{ compact}\}$ is a directed sup one has

$$\exists e \sqsubseteq x \quad e \in O, e \text{ compact},$$

hence $x \in O_e \subseteq O$. Therefore each open O is the union of basis opens. □

1.2.26. LEMMA. *Let D, D' be* cpo's.

(i) *$(x,y) \in D \times D'$ is compact $\Leftrightarrow$ x and y are compact.*

(ii) *D and D' are algebraic $\Rightarrow$ $D \times D'$ is algebraic.*

PROOF. Easy; do exercise 1.3.9. □

It is easy to show that if $O \subseteq D \times D'$ is open w.r.t. the product of the Scott topologies on D and D', then O is Scott open in the product cpo $D \times D'$. The converse is not true in general: see exercise 1.3.12. However for products of algebraic cpo's the two topologies on $D \times D'$ coincide.

1.2.27. PROPOSITION. Let D, D' be algebraic cpo's. Then the Scott topology on $D \times D'$ is the product of the Scott topologies on D and D'.

PROOF. $D \times D'$ is algebraic by lemma 1.2.26. Hence by proposition 1.2.25 the family

$$\{O_{(e,f)} \mid e, f \text{ compact}\}$$

is a basis for the Scott topology on $D \times D'$. But $O_{(e,f)} = O_e \times O_f$. Hence each Scott open set of $D \times D'$ is the union of product open sets and therefore itself product open. □

It follows that since we work mainly with algebraic cpo's, there will be no confusion as to what topology to take on $D \times D'$. Cf. exercise 1.3.16.

Several natural cpo's have other nice properties.

1.2.28. DEFINITION. Let D be a cpo.

(i) $X \subseteq D$ is *consistent* if $\forall x,y \in X\ \exists z \in D\ [x \sqsubseteq z$ and $y \sqsubseteq z]$.

(ii) D is *coherent* if each consistent $X \subseteq D$ has a supremum.

1.2.29. DEFINITION. (i) Let $x,y \in D$. Then x is *way below* y (notation $x \ll y$) if y is in the topological interior of $\{z \mid x \sqsubseteq z\}$.

(ii) A *continuous lattice* is a complete lattice in which $x = \bigsqcup\{z \mid z \ll x\}$ for every x.

(iii) An *algebraic lattice* is a complete lattice that is algebraic as a cpo.

In exercise 1.3.7 it is shown that an algebraic lattice is always a continuous one. For extensive information on continuous lattices, see Gierz et al. [1980].

The following examples of special cpo's are important.

1.2.30. EXAMPLES. (i) Let $P(X)$ be the power set of a set X partially ordered by inclusion.

(ii) A partial map $\varphi: X \to Y$ is a map φ with $\mathrm{Dom}(\varphi) \subseteq X$. For $x \subset X$ the notation $\varphi(x)\downarrow$ means that $\varphi(x)$ is defined, i.e. $x \in \mathrm{Dom}(\varphi)$. Similarly $\varphi(x)\uparrow$ means that $\varphi(x)$ is undefined, i.e. $x \notin \mathrm{Dom}(\varphi)$. Let

$$X \rightharpoonup Y = \{\varphi \mid \varphi \text{ is a partial map from } X \text{ to } Y\}.$$

Partial functions as sets of ordered pairs are partially ordered by inclusion. Clearly $(X \rightharpoonup Y, \subseteq)$ is a cpo.

1.2.31. PROPOSITION. (i) *$P(X)$ is an algebraic lattice with $A \in P(X)$ compact iff A is finite.*

(ii) *$X \rightharpoonup Y$ is a coherent algebraic cpo with $\varphi \in X \rightharpoonup Y$ is compact iff φ is finite (as a set of ordered pairs).*

PROOF. Easy, do exercise 1.3.10. □

1.3. Exercises

1.3.1. Show that in a cpo $\{z \mid x \sqsubseteq z\}$ is not necessarily open.

1.3.2. Let $X \subseteq D \times D'$. Show that in general

$$X_0, X_1 \text{ directed} \;\not\Rightarrow\; X \text{ directed},$$

where X_0, X_1 are defined as in proposition 1.2.8.

1.3.3. Let $f: D \to D'$.

(i) Show that in general

$$f \text{ monotonic} \;\not\Rightarrow\; f \text{ continuous}.$$

(ii) Show that if in the definition of the Scott topology on a cpo clause (2) is omitted, then one still obtains a topology and

$$f \text{ monotonic} \;\Leftrightarrow\; f \text{ continuous}.$$

1.3.4. Let $e \in D$, $e' \in D'$ be compact. Define $f_{e,e'}(x) = \text{if } e \sqsubseteq x \text{ then } e', \text{ else } \bot$. Show that $f_{e,e'} \in [D \to D']$ is compact.

1.3.5. (i) Show that for $x \in D$

$$x \text{ is compact} \quad \Leftrightarrow \quad \{z \mid x \sqsubseteq z\} \text{ is open.}$$

(ii) Show that an algebraic lattice is a continuous lattice.

1.3.6. Let f, g be retractions of D. Write $f < g$ for $f = f \circ g = g \circ f$. Show that $<$ is a partial order. Does one have $f < g$ iff Range(f) $\subseteq$ Range(g)?

1.3.7. Show that

$$\begin{aligned} \text{algebraic lattices} &\subseteq \text{continuous lattices} \\ &\subseteq \text{complete lattices} \\ &\subseteq \text{cpo's.} \end{aligned}$$

and that the inclusions are proper.

1.3.8. Show that in a complete lattice D the infimum $\sqcap X$ exists for every $X \subseteq D$.

1.3.9. Prove lemma 1.2.26.

1.3.10. Prove proposition 1.2.31.

The following two exercises are due to Hyland.

1.3.11. For a topological space X, let $\mathcal{O}(X)$ be the collection of open sets in X, partially ordered by $\subseteq$.

For a cpo D, let TD be the topological space consisting of D with the Scott topology. Write $\mathcal{O}(D)$ for $\mathcal{O}(TD)$.

Let $\mathbf{0} = \{\bot, \top\}$ with $\bot \sqsubseteq \top$ be the complete lattice with two elements.

(i) Show that $\mathcal{O}(X)$ is a complete lattice. What is $\sqcap$?

(ii) Show that $\mathcal{O}(D) \cong [D \to \mathbf{0}]$, where $\cong$ denotes isomorphism.

(iii) Show that for compact $K \subseteq X$ the set

$$\mathfrak{U}_K = \{O \in \mathcal{O}(X) \mid K \subseteq O\}$$

is Scott open in $\mathcal{O}(X)$.

(iv) Let D be a complete lattice and let $D' = \mathcal{O}(D)$. Show that the $\in$-relation

$$\mathcal{E} = \{\langle d, O \rangle \in D \times D' \mid d \in O\}$$

is Scott open in $D \times D'$.

1.3.12*. Show that in general (see exericse 1.3.11)

$$TD \times TD' \neq T(D \times D').$$

[*Hints.* Let $\mathbb{N}$ be equipped with the discrete topology and let $\mathbb{B} = \mathbb{N}^{\mathbb{N}}$ with the product topology be Baire space. Take $D = \mathcal{O}(\mathbb{B})$, $D' = \mathcal{O}(D)$. Consider the set $\mathcal{E}$ defined in the previous exercise. Suppose $\mathcal{E}$ were open in $TD \times TD'$ in order to derive a contradiction.

For $f \in \mathbf{B}$ $\mathfrak{U}_f = \mathfrak{U}_{\{f\}}$ is a Scott open set in D, see previous exercise. Let $f \in O \in D$ be arbitrary. Then $\langle O, \mathfrak{U}_f \rangle \in \mathcal{E}$, hence by assumption for some $\mathfrak{U}_0$ open in D, $\mathfrak{W}_0$ open in D',

$$\langle O, \mathfrak{U}_f \rangle \in \mathfrak{U}_0 \times \mathfrak{W}_0 \subseteq \mathcal{E}.$$

(i) Show

$$f \in O \in \mathfrak{U}_0, \tag{1}$$

$$\mathfrak{U}_f \subseteq \mathfrak{U} \in D' \quad \Rightarrow \quad \mathfrak{U} \in \mathfrak{W}_0, \tag{2}$$

$$\mathfrak{U} \in \mathfrak{W}_0 \quad \Rightarrow \quad \mathfrak{U}_0 \subseteq \mathfrak{U}. \tag{3}$$

(ii) Prove $\forall n \in \mathbb{N}\ \exists O' \in \mathfrak{U}_0\ \exists g \in \mathbb{B}\ \left[f \in O' \wedge g \notin O' \wedge \bar{f}(n) = \bar{g}(n) \right]$,

(where $\bar{f}(n)$ is the sequence number $\langle f(0), \ldots, f(n-1) \rangle$).
[*Hint*. For a sequence number α, let $O_\alpha = \{g \in \mathbb{B} | \exists n\, \bar{g}(n) = \alpha\}$. By (1), for m sufficiently large $f \in O_{\bar{f}(m)} \subseteq O$. Then, writing $\alpha = \bar{f}(m)$ and

$$O = (O - O_\alpha) \cup \bigcup_{i=0}^{\infty} O_{\alpha * \langle i \rangle} \in \mathfrak{U}_0,$$

use the fact that $\mathfrak{U}_0$ is Scott open in D.]

(iii) Construct a sequence $g_n \in \mathbb{B}$ such that $\lim_{n\to\infty} g_n = f$ and

$$\forall n \in \mathbb{N}\ \exists O_n \in \mathfrak{U}_0\ [f \in O_n \wedge g_0, \ldots, g_n \notin O_n].$$

(iv) Conclude from (i) and (iii) that

$$\bigcup_{i=0}^{\infty} \mathfrak{U}_{g_i} \in \mathfrak{W}_0 \quad \text{but} \quad \bigcup_{i=0}^{n} \mathfrak{U}_{g_i} \notin \mathfrak{W}_0,$$

contradicting that $\mathfrak{W}_0$ is Scott open in D'.]

1.3.13. (i) Let $e, e' \in D$ be compact. Show that if $e \sqcup e'$ exists, then it is compact.

(ii) Show that even in an algebraic cpo $e \sqcup e'$ does not need to exist.

(iii) Show that if D is a complete lattice, then $e \in D$ is compact iff for *all* $X \subseteq D$

$$e \sqsubseteq \bigsqcup X \quad \Rightarrow \quad e \sqsubseteq \bigsqcup X_0 \text{ for some finite } X_0 \subseteq X.$$

1.3.14. Does the theory of continuous lattices generalize to continuous cpo's?

1.3.15. Let $(X, \sqsubseteq)$ be a coherent algebraic cpo. Show that the set of compact elements of X is dense in X.

1.3.16. (i) Show that if D, D' are algebraic cpo's, then so is $[D \to D']$. *Hint*. Use exercise 1.3.4.] Conclude that the algebraic cpo's form a cartesian closed category.

(ii) If D, D' are coherent algebraic cpo's, then the Scott topology on $[D \to D']$ coincides with the (trace of the) product topology (on D'^D).

(iii) Show that the coherent algebraic cpo's form a cartesian closed category.

1.3.17.* (Scott [1972]). Let D be a continuous lattice. Show that D is an injective topological space, i.e. for arbitrary topological spaces X and Y with X subspace of Y, every continuous f: $X \to D$ can be extended to a continuous f: $Y \to D$.

1.3.18. Define $f: \mathbb{R}^2 \to \mathbb{R}$ by

$$f(x, y) = \begin{cases} \dfrac{xy}{x^2 + y^2} & \text{if } (x, y) \neq (0,0), \\ 0 & \text{else.} \end{cases}$$

Show that f is continuous in its two arguments separately, but not continuous.

1.3.19.* (Ershov). An f_0-*space* is a structure $\langle X, X_0, \leqslant, \perp \rangle$ such that

1. $\langle X, \leqslant \rangle$ is a partial ordering with least element $\perp$;
2. $\perp \in X_0 \subseteq X$, the elements of X_0 are called "*finite*";
3. $\forall x, y \in X\, [x \nleqslant y \Rightarrow \exists x_0 \in X_0\ x_0 \leqslant x \wedge x_0 \nleqslant y]$;
4. $\forall x, y \in X_0\, [\exists z \in X\ x, y \leqslant z \Rightarrow x \sqcup y$ (in X) exists and $x \sqcup y \in X_0]$.

(i) Show that $\{y | x_0 \leqslant y\}$ with x_0 finite, is a base for a topology on X.

(ii) Show that f_0-spaces with continuous functions form a ccc.

(iii) Show that the topology of a product of two f_0-spaces is the product of the topologies.

CHAPTER 2

CONVERSION

2.1. Lambda terms and conversion

The principal object of study in the λ-calculus is the set of lambda terms modulo convertibility. These notions will be introduced in this section.

2.1.1. DEFINITION. (i) *Lambda terms* are words over the following alphabet:

$v_0, v_1, \ldots$	variables,
λ	abstractor,
(,)	parentheses.

(ii) The set of λ-terms Λ is defined inductively* as follows:

(1) $x \in \Lambda$;

(2) $M \in \Lambda \Rightarrow (\lambda x M) \in \Lambda$;

(3) $M, N \in \Lambda \Rightarrow (MN) \in \Lambda$;

where x in (1) or (2) is an arbitrary variable.

2.1.2. NOTATION. (i) $M, N, L, \ldots$ denote arbitrary λ-terms.

(ii) $x, y, z, \ldots$ denote arbitrary variables.

(iii) Outermost parentheses are not written.

(iv) The symbol $\equiv$ denotes syntactic equality.

The following notation is used constantly. It results from Schönfinkel's reduction of functions of many variables to those of one variable.

2.1.3. NOTATION. (i) Let $\vec{x} \equiv x_1, \ldots, x_n$. Then

$$\lambda x_1 \cdots x_n . M \equiv \lambda \vec{x} . M \equiv \lambda x_1 (\lambda x_2 (\cdots (\lambda x_n (M))..)).$$

(ii) Let $\vec{N} \equiv N_1, \ldots, N_n$. Then

$$MN_1 \cdots N_n \equiv M\vec{N} \equiv (\cdots((MN_1)N_2) \cdots N_n)$$

(*association to the left*).

(iii) $\| M \|$ is the *length* of M, that is, the number of symbols in M.

*If an inductive definition is given, it will always be understood that the class defined is the *least* class satisfying the conditions.

EXAMPLES. The following are λ-terms:

(i) xx,

(ii) $\lambda x.xx$,

(iii) $\lambda xy.yx(\equiv \lambda x(\lambda y(yx)))$,

(iv) $\lambda xy.yx(\lambda z.z)(\equiv \lambda x(\lambda y((yx)(\lambda z.z))))$.

It will not always be necessary to rewrite terms like (iii), (iv) above in their unabbreviated form. Once lemma 2.1.23 is proved the applicative behaviour of such terms is immediate.

The basic equivalence relation on λ-terms is that of *convertibility*. This relation will be generated by axioms. In order to formulate these axioms, a substitution operator is needed. $M[x:=N]$ denotes the result of substituting N for x in M. As in the case of predicate logic (or of programming), some care is needed in defining this operation in order to avoid confusion between free and bound variables. This care will be postponed for a moment.

2.1.4. DEFINITION. The theory **λ** has as formulas

$$M = N$$

where $M, N \in \Lambda$ and is axiomatized by the following axioms and rules:

(I)	$(\lambda x.M)N = M[x:=N]$,	(β-conversion);
(II.1)	$M = M$;	
(II.2)	$M = N \Rightarrow N = M$;	
(II.3)	$M = N,\ N = L \Rightarrow M = L$;	
(II.4)	$M = N \Rightarrow MZ = NZ$;	
(II.5)	$M = N \Rightarrow ZM = ZN$;	
(II.6)	$M = N \Rightarrow \lambda x.M = \lambda x.N$,	(rule ξ).

Provability in **λ** of an equation is denoted by $\boldsymbol{\lambda} \vdash M = N$ or often just by $M = N$. If $\boldsymbol{\lambda} \vdash M = N$, then M and N are called *convertible*. Note that $M \equiv N \Rightarrow M = N$, but not conversely.

The names "β-conversion" and "rule ξ" are historical. In the literature the theory **λ** appears under various names:

λ-calculus,

λβ-calculus,

λ*K*-calculus,

λ*K*β-calculus.

The K is to distinguish **λ** from a restricted theory **λ*I*** introduced in §2.2.

Note that **λ** is logic free: it is an equational theory. Connectives and quantifiers will be used in the informal metalanguage discussing about **λ**. For example,

$$\forall M \quad (\lambda x.x)M = M,$$

$$M = N \Rightarrow MM = NN \wedge MN = NM$$

the meaning being

$$\forall M \in \Lambda \quad \boldsymbol{\lambda} \vdash (\lambda x.x)M = M,$$

$$\boldsymbol{\lambda} \vdash M = N \Rightarrow \boldsymbol{\lambda} \vdash MM = NN \text{ and } \boldsymbol{\lambda} \vdash MN = NM.$$

The following quite useful theorem gives an illustration of what can be proved in $\boldsymbol{\lambda}$.

2.1.5. Fixed point theorem. $\forall F\, \exists X\; FX = X$.

Proof. Let $W \equiv \lambda x.F(xx)$ and $X \equiv WW$. Then

$$X \equiv WW \equiv (\lambda x.F(xx))W = F(WW) \equiv FX. \quad \square$$

Some syntactic notions and notations

2.1.6. Definition. A variable x occurs *free* in a λ-term M if x is not in the scope of a λx; x occurs *bound* otherwise.

For example in $M \equiv x(\lambda y.xy)$ the variable x occurs free (twice) and y occurs bound. A variable may occur both free and bound in a λ-term: $y(\lambda y.y)$.

In this respect λx has the same binding properties as $\forall x$ in predicate logic or $\int_0^1 \cdots \mathrm{d}x$ in calculus.

2.1.7. Definition. (i) $\mathrm{FV}(M)$ is the set of free variables in M and can be defined inductively as follows:

$$\mathrm{FV}(x) = \{x\},$$

$$\mathrm{FV}(\lambda x.M) = \mathrm{FV}(M) - \{x\},$$

$$\mathrm{FV}(MN) = \mathrm{FV}(M) \cup \mathrm{FV}(N).$$

(ii) M is *closed* or a *combinator* if $\mathrm{FV}(M) = \emptyset$.

(iii) $\Lambda^0 = \{M \in \Lambda \mid M \text{ is closed}\}$.

(iv) $\Lambda^0(\vec{x}) = \{M \in \Lambda \mid \mathrm{FV}(M) \subseteq \{\vec{x}\}\}$.

(v) A *closure* of $M \in \Lambda$ is $\lambda\vec{x}.M$, where $\{\vec{x}\} = \mathrm{FV}(M)$.

E.g. $\lambda xy.xy \in \Lambda^0$; $\lambda xy.xyz \in \Lambda^0(z)$.

Note that a closure of M depends on the order of the $\vec{x}$.

2.1.8. Definition. (i) M is a *subterm* of N(notation $M \subset N$) if $M \in \mathrm{Sub}(N)$, where $\mathrm{Sub}(N)$, the collection of subterms of N, is defined inductively as follows:

$$\text{Sub}(x) = \{x\},$$
$$\text{Sub}(\lambda x.N_1) = \text{Sub}(N_1) \cup \{\lambda x.N_1\},$$
$$\text{Sub}(N_1N_2) = \text{Sub}(N_1) \cup \text{Sub}(N_2) \cup \{N_1N_2\}.$$

(ii) A subterm may *occur* several times; e.g. $M \equiv \lambda x.x\mathbf{I}(x\mathbf{I})$ has two *occurrences* of the subterm $\mathbf{I} \equiv \lambda y.y$.

(iii) Let N_1, N_2 be subterm occurrences of M. Then N_1, N_2 are *disjoint* if N_1 and N_2 have no common symbol occurrences.

(iv) A subterm occurrence N of M is *active* if N occurs as $(NZ) \subset M$ for some Z, otherwise N is *passive*.

EXAMPLE. (i) Let $M \equiv \lambda x.xy(\lambda z.y)$. Then $xy \subset M$, but $z \not\subset M$ and $y(\lambda z.y) \not\subset M$, since $M \equiv \lambda x.((xy)(\lambda z.y))$.

(ii) The occurrences of x and $(\lambda z.y)$ in M are disjoint. So are the first occurrences of y and $(\lambda z.y)$.

(iii) x, xy are active subterms of M; y, $\lambda z.y$ are passive ones.

2.1.9. DEFINITION. Let F, $M \in \Lambda$. Then

(i) $F^0M \equiv M$; $F^{n+1}M \equiv F(F^nM)$,

(ii) $FM^{\sim 0} \equiv F$; $FM^{\sim n+1} \equiv FM^{\sim n}M$.

Terms modulo a change of bound variables

Now it will be shown why some care is needed for substitution.

2.1.10. FALLACY. $\forall MN\ M = N$.

PROOF. Let $F \equiv \lambda xy.yx$. Then for all M,N

$$FMN \equiv ((\lambda x(\lambda y.yx))M)N = (\lambda y.yM)N = NM.$$

In particular $Fyx = xy$. But

$$Fyx = ((\lambda x(\lambda y.yx))y)x = (\lambda y.yy)x = xx.$$

Hence $xy = xx$. From this it is not difficult to derive any equation. See exercise 2.4.2 (iii). □

REFUTATION. The apparent contradiction results from the step

$$(\lambda x(\lambda y.yx))y = \lambda y.yy.$$

The free variable y becomes bound after substitution for x in $\lambda y.yx$. This should not be allowed. In predicate logic one expresses this by "y is not substitutable for x in $\lambda y.yx$", and in programming by "confusion of local and global variables." □

This problem will be avoided in 2.1.11–2.1.14 along the following lines. See appendix C for the details.

(1) Identify two terms if each can be transformed to the other by a renaming of its bound variables.

(2) Consider a λ-term as a representative of its equivalence class.

(3) Interpret substitution $M[x:=N]$ as an operation on the equivalence classes of M and N. This operation can be performed using representatives, provided that the bound variables are named properly as formulated in the variable convention below.

2.1.11. Definition. (i) A *change of bound variables* in M is the replacement of a part $\lambda x.N$ of M by $\lambda y.(N[x:=y])$, where y does not occur (at all) in N. (Because y is fresh there is no danger in the substitution $N[x:=y]$).

(ii) M is *α-congruent* with N, notation $M \equiv_\alpha N$, if N results from M by a series of changes of bound variables. For example

$$\lambda x.xy \equiv_\alpha \lambda z.zy \not\equiv_\alpha \lambda y.yy,$$

$$\lambda x.x(\lambda x.x) \equiv_\alpha \lambda x'.x'(\lambda x.x) \equiv_\alpha \lambda x'.x'(\lambda x''.x'').$$

In Church [1941] the renaming of bound variables was built into the conversion rules: there the theory $\boldsymbol{\lambda}$ was extended by the axiom scheme

$$\lambda x.M = \lambda y.M[x:=y] \qquad (\alpha\text{-conversion})$$

where y is not free or bound in M.

We prefer to identify α-congruent terms on a syntactic level.

2.1.12. Convention. Terms that are α-congruent are identified.

So now we write $\lambda x.x \equiv \lambda y.y$, etcetera.

2.1.13. Variable convention. If $M_1, \ldots, M_n$ occur in a certain mathematical context (e.g. definition, proof), then in these terms all bound variables are chosen to be different from the free variables.

Examples of the use of the variable convention.

(1) Already in the proof of the fixed point theorem 2.1.5 the variable convention was implicitly used. In defining $W \equiv \lambda x.F(xx)$, it is essential that $x \notin \mathrm{FV}(F)$.

(2) Let $\mathbf{K} \equiv \lambda xy.x$. Then

$$\mathbf{K}M \equiv (\lambda x(\lambda y.x))M = \lambda y.M.$$

Hence

$$(*) \qquad \forall M \quad \mathbf{K}M = \lambda y.M.$$

But

$$\mathbf{K}y \neq \lambda y.y.$$

This is so, because by the variable convention $(*)$ has to be interpreted as

$$\forall M \quad \mathbf{K}M = \lambda y.M, \quad \text{where } y \notin \mathrm{FV}(M).$$

Hence by the identification of α-congruent terms

$$\mathbf{K}y = \lambda y'.y.$$

2.1.14. MORAL. Using conventions 2.1.12 and 2.1.13 one can work with λ-terms in the naive way.

Naive means that substitution and other operations on terms can be performed without questioning whether they are allowed. The moral will be proved in appendix C.

Substitution

2.1.15. DEFINITION. The result of substituting N for the free occurrences of x in M (notation $M[x := N]$) is defined as follows.

$$\begin{aligned}
&x[x:=N] \equiv N;\\
&y[x:=N] \equiv y, \quad \text{if } x \not\equiv y;\\
&(\lambda y.M_1)[x:=N] \equiv \lambda y.(M_1[x:=N]);\\
&(M_1 M_2)[x:=N] \equiv (M_1[x:=N])(M_2[x:=N]);
\end{aligned}$$

In the third clause it is not needed to say "provided that $y \not\equiv x$ and $y \notin \mathrm{FV}(N)$". By the variable convention this is the case.

2.1.16. SUBSTITUTION LEMMA. If $x \not\equiv y$ and $x \notin \mathrm{FV}(L)$, then

$$M[x:=N][y:=L] \equiv M[y:=L][x:=N[y:=L]].$$

PROOF. By induction on the structure of M.

Case 1. M is a variable.

Case 1.1. $M \equiv x$. Then both sides equal $N[y:=L]$ since $x \not\equiv y$.

Case 1.2. $M \equiv y$. Then both sides equal L, for $x \notin \mathrm{FV}(L)$ implies $L[x:= \cdots] \equiv L$.

Case 1.3. $M \equiv z \not\equiv x,y$. Then both sides equal z.

Case 2. $M \equiv \lambda z.M_1$. By the variable convention we may assume that $z \not\equiv x,y$ and z is not free in N, L. Then by the induction hypothesis

$$\begin{aligned}(\lambda z.M_1)[x:=N][y:=L] &\equiv \lambda z.M_1[x:=N][y:=L]\\ &\equiv \lambda z.M_1[y:=L][x:=N[y:=L]]\\ &\equiv (\lambda z.M_1)[y:=L][x:=N[y:=L]].\end{aligned}$$

Case 3. $M \equiv M_1 M_2$. Then the statement follows again from the induction hypothesis. □

2.1.17. PROPOSITION. (i) $M = M' \Rightarrow M[x:=N] = M'[x:=N]$.
(ii) $N = N' \Rightarrow M[x:=N] = M[x:=N']$.
(iii) $M = M'$, $N = N' \Rightarrow M[x:=N] = M'[x:=N']$.

PROOF. (i) By induction on the length of proof of $M = M'$. Since this kind of proof occurs often, this one will be spelled out in detail. Later on such details will be left to the reader.

Case 1. $M = M'$ is an axiom $(\lambda y.A)B = A[y:=B]$. Then

$$\begin{aligned}M[x:=N] &\equiv (\lambda y.A[x:=N])(B[x:=N])\\ &= A[x:=N][y:=B[x:=N]]\\ &\equiv A[y:=B][x:=N]\\ &\equiv M'[x:=N]\end{aligned}$$

by the substitution lemma 2.1.16 (by the variable convention $y \not\equiv x$, $y \notin \mathrm{FV}(N)$).

Case 2. $M = M'$ is an axiom because $M \equiv M'$. Then the result follows immediately.

Case 3. $M = M'$ is $ZM_1 = ZM_1'$ and is a direct consequence of $M_1 = M_1'$. Hence

$$\begin{aligned}M[x:=N] &\equiv Z[x:=N]M_1[x:=N]\\ &= Z[x:=N]M_1'[x:=N] \quad \text{by the induction hypothesis},\\ &\equiv M'[x:=N].\end{aligned}$$

The other derivation rules are treated similarly.

(i) Alternative proof.

$$M = M' \Rightarrow \lambda x.M = \lambda x.M'$$
$$\Rightarrow (\lambda x.M)N = (\lambda x.M')N$$
$$\Rightarrow M[x:=N] = M'[x:=N].$$

(ii) Use induction on the structure of M.

(iii) By (i) and (ii)

$$M[x:=N] = M'[x:=N] = M'[x:=N']. \quad \square$$

Is the following true?

$$N = N' \Rightarrow \lambda x.x(\lambda y.N) = \lambda x.x(\lambda y.N').$$

It is, but this does not follow from proposition 2.1.17 (ii) since $(\lambda x.x(\lambda y.N))$ cannot be written as $(\lambda x.x(\lambda y.z))[z:=N]$ if x or y is free in N. Therefore the following notion of context is useful.

2.1.18. DEFINITION. (i) A *context* $C[\ ]$ is a term with some holes in it. More formally:

x is a context,
$[\ ]$ is a context,
if $C_1[\ ]$ and $C_2[\ ]$ are contexts, then so are $C_1[\ ]C_2[\ ]$ and $\lambda x.C_1[\ ]$.

(ii) If $C[\ ]$ is a context and $M \in \Lambda$, then $C[M]$ denotes the result of placing M in the holes of $C[\ ]$. In this act free variables of M may become bound in $C[M]$.

EXAMPLE. $C[\ ] \equiv \lambda x.x(\lambda y.[\ ])$ is a context. If $M \equiv xy$, then $C[M] \equiv \lambda x.x(\lambda y.xy)$

Contexts are *not* considered modulo α-congruence. The essential feature of a context $C[\ ]$ is that a free variable in M may become bound in $C[M]$. *Par abus de langage* we write $C[\ ] \in \Lambda$ to indicate that $C[\ ]$ is a context.

2.1.19. PROPOSITION. *Let* $C[\ ] \in \Lambda$. *Then*

$$N = N' \Rightarrow C[N] = C[N'].$$

PROOF. Use induction on the structure of $C[\ ]$. $\square$

2.1.20. LEMMA. (i) $\forall C[\ ]\ \forall \vec{x}\ \exists F\ \forall M \in \Lambda^0(\vec{x})\ C[M] = F(\lambda \vec{x}.M)$.

(ii) $\forall C[\ ]\ \forall M\ \exists \vec{x}\ \exists F\ C[M] = F(\lambda \vec{x}.M)$.

PROOF. (i) Use induction on the structure of $C[\ ]$.
(ii) By (i). □

Sometimes simultaneous substitution is needed.

2.1.21. DEFINITION. (i) Let $\vec{N} \equiv N_1, \ldots, N_m$; $\vec{x} \equiv x_1, \ldots, x_n$. Then $\vec{N}$ *fits in* $\vec{x}$ if $m = n$ and the $\vec{x}$ do not occur in $\text{FV}(\vec{N})$.
(ii) Let $\vec{N} \equiv N_1, \ldots, N_m$; $\vec{L} \equiv L_1, \ldots, L_n$. Then

$$\vec{N} = \vec{L} \quad \text{if} \quad n = m \text{ and } N_i = L_i \text{ for } 1 \leqslant i \leqslant n.$$

Similarly $\vec{N} \equiv \vec{L}$ is defined.
(iii) Let $\vec{N}$ fit in $\vec{x} \equiv x_1, \ldots, x_n$. Then

$$M[\vec{x} := \vec{N}] \equiv M[x_1 := N_1] \cdots [x_n := N_n].$$

[Here it is needed that the $\vec{x}$ do not occur in $\text{FV}(\vec{N})$. For an alternative definition, see exercise 2.4.8.]
(iv) Let $M \in \Lambda$. As in predicate logic sometimes we write $M \equiv M(\vec{x})$, to indicate substitution:
if $M \equiv M(\vec{x})$ and $\vec{N}$ fits in $\vec{x}$, then $M(\vec{N}) \equiv M[\vec{x} := \vec{N}]$.

2.1.22. PROPOSITION. *Let $\vec{N}_i$ fit in $\vec{x}$. Then*

$$M_1(\vec{x}) = M_2(\vec{x}) \wedge \vec{N}_1 = \vec{N}_2 \Rightarrow M_1(\vec{N}_1) = M_2(\vec{N}_2).$$

PROOF. By proposition 2.1.17 (iii). □

Combinatory completeness

2.1.23. LEMMA. *Let $\vec{x} \equiv x_1, \ldots, x_n$. Then $(\lambda \vec{x}.M)\vec{x} = M$.*

PROOF. If $n = 1$, then

$$(\lambda x_1.M)x_1 = M[x_1 := x_1] \equiv M.$$

If $n = 2$, then

$$\begin{aligned}(\lambda \vec{x}.M)\vec{x} &\equiv ((\lambda x_1.(\lambda x_2.M))x_1)x_2 \\ &= (\lambda x_2.M)x_2 \quad \text{by the case } n = 1 \text{ for } \lambda x_2.M \\ &= M.\end{aligned}$$

The general case follows similarly (by induction on n). □

2.1.24. COROLLARY (Combinatory Completeness). *Let* $M \equiv M(\vec{x})$. *Then*:

(i) $\exists F\ F\vec{x} = M(\vec{x})$.

(ii) $\exists F\ \forall \vec{N}\ F\vec{N} = M(\vec{N})$, *where* $\vec{N}$ *fits in* $\vec{x}$.

(iii) *In* (i), (ii) *one can take* $F \equiv \lambda\vec{x}.M$.

PROOF. By the lemma, using proposition 2.1.22. □

EXAMPLE. $\exists F\ \forall MN\ FMN = \lambda z.zNM$. Indeed, take

$$F \equiv \lambda xy.(\lambda z.zyx) \equiv \lambda xyz.zyx.$$

Three combinators are of particular importance.

2.1.25. DEFINITION.

$$\mathbf{I} \equiv \lambda x.x, \qquad \mathbf{K} \equiv \lambda xy.x,$$

$$\mathbf{S} \equiv \lambda xyz.xz(yz).$$

2.1.26. COROLLARY. *For all* $M,\ N,\ L \in \Lambda$

(i) $\mathbf{I}M = M$,

(ii) $\mathbf{K}MN = M$,

(iii) $\mathbf{S}MNL = ML(NL)$.

PROOF. By Corollary 2.1.24. □

It will be shown that **I**, **K**, **S** generate the set Λ^0 using only application, see §8.1. Note that **SKK** = **I**, hence just **K**, **S** generate Λ^0.

Extensionality

Lambda terms denote processes. Different terms may denote the same process. For example, $\lambda x.Mx$ and M both yield the same result MN when applied to a term N. Therefore the following rule is introduced.

2.1.27. DEFINITION. (i) Extensionality is the following derivation rule

$$Mx = Nx \Rightarrow M = N \qquad (\boldsymbol{ext})$$

provided that $x \notin \mathrm{FV}(MN)$.

(ii) The theory $\boldsymbol{\lambda}$ extended by this rule is denoted by $\boldsymbol{\lambda} + \boldsymbol{ext}$.

The question rises what can be proved in $\boldsymbol{\lambda} + \boldsymbol{ext}$ but not in $\boldsymbol{\lambda}$. We have seen the example $\lambda x.Mx = M$. The following shows that this is essentially the only difference.

2.1.28. DEFINITION. Consider the following axiom scheme $\boldsymbol{\eta}$

$$\lambda x.Mx = M \qquad (\eta\text{-conversion})$$

provided that $x \notin \mathrm{FV}(M)$. $\boldsymbol{\lambda\eta}$ is the theory $\boldsymbol{\lambda}$ extended with $\boldsymbol{\eta}$.

2.1.29. THEOREM (Curry). *The theories* $\boldsymbol{\lambda} + \boldsymbol{ext}$ *and* $\boldsymbol{\lambda\eta}$ *are equivalent.*

PROOF. First we show $\boldsymbol{\lambda} + \boldsymbol{ext} \vdash \boldsymbol{\eta}$. Indeed

$$(\lambda x.Mx)x = Mx$$

Hence if $x \notin \mathrm{FV}(M)$, then by ***ext***

$$\lambda x.Mx = M.$$

Conversely, $\boldsymbol{\lambda\eta}$ is closed under the rule ***ext***. Let

$$Mx = Nx,$$

with $x \notin \mathrm{FV}(MN)$. Then by rule $\boldsymbol{\xi}$

$$\lambda x.Mx = \lambda x.Nx.$$

Hence by $\boldsymbol{\eta}$ one has $M = N$. □

Note that the rule $\boldsymbol{\xi}$ plays an essential role in the equivalence between $\boldsymbol{\lambda} + \boldsymbol{ext}$ and $\boldsymbol{\lambda\eta}$. Therefore rule $\boldsymbol{\xi}$ is sometimes referred to as the rule of *weak extensionality*.

The extensional λ-calculus will usually be denoted by $\boldsymbol{\lambda\eta}$. The following other names appear in the literature:

$\lambda\eta$-calculus,
$\lambda\beta\eta$-calculus,
$\lambda K\eta$-calculus,
$\lambda K\beta\eta$-calculus.

One of the reasons for considering $\boldsymbol{\lambda\eta}$ is that it enjoys a certain completeness property, see theorem 2.1.40.

Consistency

Since the theory $\boldsymbol{\lambda}$ is logic free, the notion of consistency has to be taken in the following sense

2.1.30. DEFINITION. (i) An *equation* is a formula of the form $M = N$ with $M, N \in \Lambda$; the equation is *closed* if $M, N \in \Lambda^0$.

(ii) Let $\mathfrak{T}$ be a formal theory with equations as formulas. Then $\mathfrak{T}$ is *consistent* (notation Con($\mathfrak{T}$)) if $\mathfrak{T}$ does not prove every closed equation. In the opposite case $\mathfrak{T}$ is *inconsistent*.

(iii) If $\mathfrak{T}$ is a set of equations, then $\boldsymbol{\lambda} + \mathfrak{T}$ is the theory obtained from $\boldsymbol{\lambda}$ by adding the equations of $\mathfrak{T}$ as axioms. $\mathfrak{T}$ is called *consistent* (notation Con($\mathfrak{T}$)) if Con($\boldsymbol{\lambda} + \mathfrak{T}$).

The reader may be worried by the fallacy 2.1.10. Moreover the proof of the fixed point theorem 2.1.5 is in fact a diagonal argument often leading to inconsistencies. Therefore it is not obvious that the theory $\boldsymbol{\lambda}$ is consistent.

The concept of reduction, introduced in chapter 3, will provide an important proof theoretic tool for the theory $\boldsymbol{\lambda}$ and some extensions. Using this one can prove the following.

2.1.31. FACT. The theories $\boldsymbol{\lambda}$ and $\boldsymbol{\lambda\eta}$ are consistent.

PROOF. See theorems 3.2.10(ii) and 3.3.11(ii). See also corollary 2.1.38. □

The theory $\boldsymbol{\lambda}$ extended by a single axiom may become inconsistent.

2.1.32. DEFINITION. Let $M, N \in \Lambda$. Then M and N are *incompatible*, notation $M \# N$, if $\neg$Con($M = N$).

2.1.33. EXAMPLE. $\mathbf{K} \# \mathbf{S}$.

PROOF. Reason in $\boldsymbol{\lambda} + \mathbf{K} = \mathbf{S}$: for all $X, Y, Z \in \Lambda$

$$\mathbf{K}XYZ = \mathbf{S}XYZ;$$

hence

$$XZ = XZ(YZ).$$

Take $X \equiv Z \equiv \mathbf{I}$. Then for all $Y \in \Lambda$

$$\mathbf{I} = Y\mathbf{I}.$$

By taking $Y \equiv \mathbf{K}M$, M arbitrary, it follows that for all M

$$\mathbf{I} = M.$$

Therefore $\boldsymbol{\lambda} + \mathbf{K} = \mathbf{S} \vdash M = \mathbf{I} = N$ for arbitrary M, N, in other words, $\neg$Con($\mathbf{K} = \mathbf{S}$). □

Normal forms

Consider a term like

$$(\lambda x.xa)\mathbf{I}.$$

This term can be "computed" to yield

$$\mathbf{I}a$$

and this gives

$$a.$$

The term a is called a normal form, for it does not "compute" any further. This notion is made precise as follows.

2.1.34. DEFINITION. Let $M \in \Lambda$.

(i) M *is a β-normal form* (abbreviated as β-nf or just nf) if M has no subterm $(\lambda x.R)S$.

(ii) M *has a* β-nf if there exists an N such that $N = M$ and N is a β-nf.

If M is a nf, it is also said that M is *in* nf.

EXAMPLES. (i) $\mathbf{I}$ is in nf.

(ii) $\mathbf{KI}$ has a nf (namely $\lambda y.\mathbf{I}$).

(iii) Let $\mathbf{\Omega} \equiv (\lambda x.xx)(\lambda x.xx)$. Then $\mathbf{\Omega}$ has no nf as will be proved in chapter 3.

In the extensional theory $\boldsymbol{\lambda\eta}$ the notion of nf is a bit different, since there also terms such as $\lambda x.ax$ "want to be computed".

2.1.35. DEFINITION. Let $M \in \Lambda$.

(i) M is a $\beta\eta$-nf if M has no subterm $(\lambda x.P)Q$ or $(\lambda x.Rx)$ with $x \notin \mathrm{FV}(R)$.

(ii) M has a $\beta\eta$-nf if

$$\exists N[\lambda\eta \vdash M = N \text{ and } N \text{ is a } \beta\eta\text{-nf}].$$

EXAMPLES. (i) $\mathbf{K}$, $\mathbf{S}$ are $\beta\eta$-nf's.

(ii) $\lambda x.x(\lambda z.xz)$ is not a $\beta\eta$-nf, but has as $\beta\eta$-nf the term $\lambda x.xx$.

2.1.36. FACT (Curry et al. [1972]). M has a $\beta\eta$-nf $\Leftrightarrow M$ has a β-nf.

PROOF. See Corollary 15.1.5. $\square$

Normal forms and consistency are connected as follows.

2.1.37. FACT. (i) If M, N are different β-nf's, then

$$\lambda \nvdash M = N.$$

(ii) Similarly for $\beta\eta$-nf's and provability in $\lambda\eta$.

PROOF. By theorems 3.2.10 and 3.3.11 and propositions 3.2.1 and 3.3.2. □

2.1.38. COROLLARY. *The theories* $\boldsymbol{\lambda}$ *and* $\boldsymbol{\lambda\eta}$ *are consistent.*

PROOF. By fact 2.1.37 one has $\boldsymbol{\lambda\eta} \nvdash \mathbf{K} = \mathbf{S}$, since both $\mathbf{K}$ and $\mathbf{S}$ are in $\beta\eta$-nf. □

On the other hand one has the following.

2.1.39. FACT (Böhm [1968]). If M, N are different $\beta\eta$-nf's, then $M \# N$.

PROOF. See corollary 10.4.3. □

It follows that for terms having a nf the theory $\boldsymbol{\lambda\eta}$ is Hilbert-Post complete, cf. definition 4.1.22.

2.1.40. THEOREM. *Suppose* M, N *have a* nf. *Then either* $\boldsymbol{\lambda\eta} \vdash M = N$ *or* $\boldsymbol{\lambda\eta} + M = N$ *is inconsistent.*

PROOF. By fact 2.1.36 the terms M, N have $\beta\eta$-nf's, say M', N'.
Case 1. $M' \equiv N'$. Then

$$\boldsymbol{\lambda\eta} \vdash M = M' = N' = N.$$

Case 2. $M' \not\equiv N'$. Then by fact 2.1.39 one has $\neg\text{Con}(M' = N')$, hence $\neg\text{Con}(\boldsymbol{\lambda\eta} + M = N)$. □

2.2. Some variants of the theory

In this section two variants of the theory λ are considered: combinatory logic and the λI-calculus. The technical development of these systems is given in chapters 7 and 9 respectively. Also a discussion is made about 'significance' of terms.

Combinatory logic

Independently of the λ-calculus a related theory, combinatory logic, was initiated by Schönfinkel [1924] and Curry [1930].

Curry developed combinatory logic with the intention of providing an alternative foundation for mathematics. His theory is divided into two parts: *pure combinatory logic*, concerning itself with notions like substitution and other (formula) manipulations; and *illative combinatory logic*, concerning itself with logical notions such as implication, quantification, equality and types.

As was mentioned before, Church had a similar aim with an extended version of the theory $\boldsymbol{\lambda}$. After the proposed system was shown to be inconsistent, Church abolished his program. Curry tried to be more careful with his theories and wanted to provide consistency proofs whenever possible. This was done for several systems of combinatory logic (see appendix B). But these systems are all very weak and hence inappropriate for a foundation of mathematics. In spite of this there are several interesting aspects of the theories that did come out.

The illative theories do not belong to the scope of this book. They are briefly discussed in appendix B. Pure combinatory logic is treated in chapter 7. *Par abus de language* the adjective "pure" is often suppressed.

The starting point of the theory is that the general scheme of combinatory completeness, corollary 2.1.24, follows from two of its instances. It suffices to assume that there are objects $\boldsymbol{K}$ and $\boldsymbol{S}$ satisfying

$$(*) \qquad \boldsymbol{K}MN = M, \qquad \boldsymbol{S}MNL = ML(NL)$$

for all M, N and L. Combinatory logic, $\boldsymbol{CL}$, is the formal equational theory with operation application and primitive constants $\boldsymbol{K}$ and $\boldsymbol{S}$, satisfying the axioms ($*$). In presence of the rule of extensionality the theories $\boldsymbol{CL}$ and $\boldsymbol{\lambda}$ become equivalent.

In $\boldsymbol{CL}$ it is not necessary to have a variable binding operation. Abstraction can be defined in terms of $\boldsymbol{K}$ and $\boldsymbol{S}$. This has several important applications to the λ-calculus itself. For example a term $\mathsf{E} \in \Lambda^0$ that enumerates all closed λ-terms is constructed via $\boldsymbol{CL}$. Moreover a proof-theoretic analysis is often more easy to give for extensions of $\boldsymbol{CL}$ than for extensions of $\boldsymbol{\lambda}$. This is especially useful if extensionality is present, since then the theories are equivalent.

In the λ-calculus the terms K, S satisfy ($*$). It will be indicated briefly how abstraction in Λ can be defined using these terms.

2.2.1. PROPOSITION. *In* $\boldsymbol{\lambda}$ *one has*:

(i) $\mathsf{I} = \mathsf{SKK}$.

(ii) (a) $\lambda x.x = \mathsf{I}$;

(b) $\lambda x.M = \mathsf{K}M$ if $x \notin \mathrm{FV}(M)$;

(c) $\lambda x.MN = \mathsf{S}(\lambda x.M)(\lambda x.N)$.

PROOF. (i) $\mathbf{SKK} = \lambda c.\mathbf{K}c(\mathbf{K}c) = \lambda c.c \equiv \mathbf{I}$.

(ii) (b) $\mathbf{K}M = \lambda x.M$ with $x \notin \mathrm{FV}(M)$.

(c) $\mathbf{S}(\lambda x.M)(\lambda x.N) = \lambda x.(\lambda x.M)x((\lambda x.N)x) = \lambda x.MN$. □

Therefore in each term in Λ the λ's can be eliminated successively in favor of **K** and **S**. Example:

$$\begin{aligned}\lambda xy.yx &\equiv \lambda x(\lambda y(yx))\\ &= \lambda x(\mathbf{SI}(\mathbf{K}x))\\ &= \mathbf{S}(\mathbf{K}(\mathbf{SI}))(\mathbf{S}(\mathbf{KK})\mathbf{I})\\ &= \mathbf{S}(\mathbf{K}(\mathbf{S}(\mathbf{SKK})))(\mathbf{S}(\mathbf{KK})(\mathbf{SKK})).\end{aligned}$$

Using this method, standard translations can be defined from λ-terms to CL-terms and back. These translations do not yet constitute an isomorphism between the two theories. The λ-terms have a fine structure that is not visible from the corresponding CL-terms. For example,

$$\boldsymbol{\lambda} \vdash \mathbf{SKK} = \mathbf{SKS} = \mathbf{I}$$

but

$$\boldsymbol{CL} \nvdash \boldsymbol{SKK} = \boldsymbol{SKS}.$$

Curry succeeded in constructing a finite set $\boldsymbol{A}_\beta$ of equations between CL-terms such that the theories $\boldsymbol{CL} + \boldsymbol{A}_\beta$ and $\boldsymbol{\lambda}$ are equivalent via the standard translations. Similarly there is a set $\boldsymbol{A}_{\beta\eta}$ such that $\boldsymbol{CL} + \boldsymbol{A}_{\beta\eta}$ and $\boldsymbol{\lambda\eta}$ are equivalent. See §7.3.

The λI-calculus

Church [1941] originally defined a restricted class of λ-terms.

2.2.2. DEFINITION. (i) The set of λI-terms (notation Λ_I) is defined inductively by

$$x \in \Lambda_I;$$

$$M \in \Lambda_I,\ x \in \mathrm{FV}(M) \Rightarrow \lambda x.M \in \Lambda_I;$$

$$M, N \in \Lambda_I \Rightarrow (MN) \in \Lambda_I.$$

(ii) The theory $\boldsymbol{\lambda I}$ ("the $\boldsymbol{\lambda I}$-calculus") consists of equations between λI-terms provable by the axioms and rules of $\boldsymbol{\lambda}$ restricted to Λ_I.

To emphasize the difference, the theory **λ** is sometimes called **λK**. Similarly the set Λ is sometimes denoted by Λ_K. Indeed, the essential difference between Λ_I and Λ_K is the term **K**: one has $\mathbf{K} \in \Lambda_K - \Lambda_I$ and in fact all λ*K*-terms are definable from **K** and λ*I*-terms.

The following names for the theory **λI** appear in the literature:

λ*I*-calculus,

λ*Iβ*-calculus.

Similarly the theory **λIη**, equivalent with **λI** + ***ext***, is denoted by the following:

λ*Iη*-calculus,

λ*Iβη*-calculus.

In Curry et al. [1958] Ch. 3 §3 Church is cited as giving the following arguments for his preference of the λ*I*-calculus over the λ*K*-calculus.

(1) What Church wanted to do with the λ-calculus could be done with the λ*I*-version; e.g. the representation of the (partial) recursive functions.

(2) If one—like Church—considers as significant only terms having a nf*, then significant λ*K*-terms may have non-significant parts (e.g. **KIΩ** with **Ω** without nf). This is not so for λ*I*-terms.

2.2.3. Fact. Let $M \in \Lambda_I$ and $N \subset M$. Then

$$M \text{ has a nf} \Rightarrow N \text{ has a nf}.$$

Proof. See corollary 9.1.6. □

(3) The *K*-calculus might lead to inconsistencies.

Let us discuss the three points.

The reason behind argument (1) can be explained by the existence of several approximations of **K** definable in the λ*I*-calculus. In the first place there exists a $\mathbf{K}_1 \in \Lambda_I^0$ such that

$$\mathbf{K}_1 x \mathbf{c}_n = x$$

for all numerals $\mathbf{c}_n \equiv \lambda fz.f^n z$. Take, say, $\mathbf{K}_1 \equiv \lambda xy.y\mathbf{II}x$. Moreover in corollary 9.4.24 it will be shown that for a finite set $\mathfrak{N}$ of nf's

$$\exists K_{\mathfrak{N}} \in \Lambda_I^0 \ \forall M \ \forall N \in \mathfrak{N} \ \ K_{\mathfrak{N}} MN = M.$$

Such a $K_{\mathfrak{N}}$ is said to be a *local K for* $\mathfrak{N}$.

The fact that all recursive, and hence by Church's thesis all computable, processes can be represented in the λ*I*-calculus has, however, a restricted value. The representation in **λI** is not the most efficient one since a

* On several occasions Scott disagreed with this position e.g. in his [1973], p. 159, 165. Below it will be shown that the views of Church and Scott are nevertheless compatible.

λI-computation of $0 \cdot 2^{100}$ first has to evaluate 2^{100} and only then is it able to multiply the result by 0. In the λK-calculus $0 \cdot 2^{100}$ can reduce immediately to 0. Moreover, in $\boldsymbol{\lambda K}$ a program (e.g. **KI**) may successfully act on another piece of program (e.g. $\boldsymbol{\Omega}$) even if the latter has no value when executed. Therefore argument (2) works rather in favour of the full λK-calculus.

As to argument (3), we know that $\boldsymbol{\lambda K}$ is consistent. Church probably had in mind the following. If one considers terms without nf as unsignificant, then it is natural to identify them. This is consistent in the λI-calculus (see theorem 16.1.13) but not in the λK-calculus.

2.2.4. Proposition. *Let* $\mathfrak{T} = \{M = N \mid M, N \in \Lambda_K$ *without* nf$\}$. *Then* $\neg\mathrm{Con}(\mathfrak{T})$.

Proof. Let $M \equiv \lambda x.x\mathbf{K}\Omega$, $N \equiv \lambda x.x\mathbf{S}\Omega$. Then $M = N \in \mathfrak{T}$. Hence

$$\mathfrak{T} \vdash \mathbf{K} = M\mathbf{K} = N\mathbf{K} = \mathbf{S}.$$

Since $\mathbf{K} \# \mathbf{S}$ by example 2.1.33, it follows that $\neg\mathrm{Con}(\mathfrak{T})$. □

Below it will be argued, however, that in the λK-calculus not all terms without a nf should be considered as meaningless.

In view of this discussion we choose to call the λK-calculus *the* λ-calculus. Therefore, unless stated otherwise, by λ-calculus is meant λK-calculus. In spite of this, Λ_I is an interesting subset of Λ_K. Moreover there are applications of the λI-calculus to the full theory. See, for example lemma 17.2.16.

Representing recursive functions

In the λ-calculus some sequence $\ulcorner 0 \urcorner, \ulcorner 1 \urcorner, \ldots$ of terms in nf is selected to represent the natural numbers. These λ-terms are called numerals. Relative to such a numeral system the notion of definability of functions can be given.

2.2.5. Definition. Let $f: \mathbb{N}^k \to \mathbb{N}$. Then f is λ-definable if for some $F \in \Lambda^0$ and all $n_1, \ldots, n_k \in \mathbb{N}$ one has

$$F \ulcorner n_1 \urcorner \cdots \ulcorner n_k \urcorner = \ulcorner f(n_1, \ldots, n_k) \urcorner .$$

2.2.6. Fact (Kleene [1936]). Let f: $\mathbb{N}^k \to \mathbb{N}$. Then

$$f \text{ is definable} \Leftrightarrow f \text{ is recursive}.$$

PROOF. See theorem 6.3.13 for λK and theorem 9.2.16 for λI. □

In order to represent a partial function by a λ-term, one has to choose how to represent "undefined". The question is this. If F is going to λ-define a partial function φ, what should $F\ulcorner n \urcorner$ be whenever $\varphi(n)$ is undefined. The classical proposal by Church (see his [1941], p. 29) is to represent undefined by terms without nf.

2.2.7. DEFINITION. Let φ: $\mathbb{N}^k \to \mathbb{N}$ be a partial function. Then φ is called *λ-definable* if for some $F \in \Lambda^0$ and for all $\vec{n} \in \mathbb{N}^k$

$$F\ulcorner n_1 \urcorner \cdots \ulcorner n_k \urcorner = \ulcorner m \urcorner \quad \text{if } \varphi(\vec{n}) = m$$
$$F\ulcorner n_1 \urcorner \cdots \ulcorner n_k \urcorner \text{ has no nf} \quad \text{if } \varphi(\vec{n}) \text{ is undefined.}$$

This definition has—at least for the λK-calculus—the following disadvantages.

(a) The concept of having a nf is not preserved under the translations between **λ** and ***CL***. It therefore does not follow automatically that if a class of partial functions can be defined by λ-terms, then this can be done also by CL-terms. In fact in Curry et al. [1972], p. 236 footnote 37, separate arguments are given for the proof of the definability in **λ** and in ***CL*** of the partial recursive functions.

(b) The notion of normal form is too syntactical. For example, it is not clear that it makes sense for elements of a model of the λ-calculus. In fact Wadsworth has shown the following.

2.2.8. FACT. Let D_∞ be one of Scott's lattice theoretic models of the λ-calculus. Then for *no* subset $\mathfrak{N} \subseteq D_\infty$ one has

$$M \text{ has a nf} \Leftrightarrow [\![M]\!]^{D_\infty} \in \mathfrak{N}.$$

Here $[\![M]\!]^{D_\infty}$ denotes the value of M in D_∞.

PROOF. See exercise 19.4.2. □

The disadvantage mentioned under (a) is in fact another aspect of the syntactic feature of the notion of nf.

(c) One is tempted to identify terms whose intended meaning is "undefined." This, however, is not possible by proposition 2.2.4.

(d) The partial λ-definable functions are closed under composition, but not intensionally so. That is, the λ-defining term of a composition is not necessarily the composition of the λ-defining terms.

2.2.9. EXAMPLE. For all n let $f(n) = 0$ and let $g(n)$ be undefined. Then $f(g(n))$ is undefined for all n. Now f and g can be λ-defined by $F \equiv \mathbf{K}\ulcorner 0 \urcorner$

and $G \equiv \mathbf{K}\Omega$ respectively. But then

$$F \circ G \equiv \lambda x.F(Gx) = \lambda x.\ulcorner 0 \urcorner$$

does not λ-define $f \circ g$.

The mentioned difficulties all result from the identification

$$\text{undefined} = \text{not having a nf}.$$

In the next subsection a different approach is proposed.

Solvable and unsolvable terms

A proper subclass of the class of terms without a nf will be introduced. The elements of this class are called unsolvable terms. It is proposed that these terms represent the notion of 'undefined'. This was first done in Barendregt [1971]. Independently Wadsworth [1971] introduced a class of terms 'without a head normal form'. He gave arguments that elements of this class should be considered as the meaningless terms in the λK-calculus.

2.2.10. Definition. (i) Let $M \in \Lambda^0$. Then M is *solvable* if

$$\exists n\ \exists N_1 \cdots N_n \in \Lambda \quad MN_1 \cdots N_n = I.$$

(ii) An arbitrary $M \in \Lambda$ is *solvable* if the closure of M, that is $\lambda \vec{x}.M$ with $\{\vec{x}\} = \mathrm{FV}(M)$, is solvable.

(iii) $M \in \Lambda$ is *unsolvable* if M is not solvable.

In this definition one can take everywhere $\Lambda = \Lambda_K$ or $\Lambda = \Lambda_I$. In the first case one speaks about K-solvability, in the second, I-solvability. If it is clear from the context which notion is meant, one simply speaks about solvability. Usually this will be K-solvability.

Examples. (i) $\mathbf{S}$ is I-solvable: $\mathbf{SIII} = \mathbf{I}$.

(ii) $x\mathbf{I}\Omega$ is K-solvable: $(\lambda x.x\mathbf{I}\Omega)\mathbf{K} = \mathbf{I}$.

(iii) Ω is both I- and K-unsolvable.

2.2.11. Definition. (i) M is a *head normal form* (hnf) if M has the form $M \equiv \lambda \vec{x}.y\vec{N}$

(ii) M *has* a hnf if $\exists N\ M = N$ and N is a hnf.

Example. $\lambda x.\mathbf{I}x\Omega$ has no nf, but has as hnf $\lambda x.x\Omega$. It is not hard to show that each nf is a hnf.

2.2.12. Fact. (i) (Wadsworth) In the λK-calculus:

$$M \text{ is unsolvable} \Leftrightarrow M \text{ has no head normal form}.$$

(ii) (Barendregt) In the λI-calculus:

$$M \text{ is unsolvable} \Leftrightarrow M \text{ has no normal form.}$$

PROOF. (i) Theorem 8.3.14. (ii) Corollary 9.4.21. □

Below the following identification will be proposed for λ-terms:

$$\text{'undefined' (or 'meaningless')} \Leftrightarrow \text{unsolvable.}$$

Using fact 2.2.12, this reconciles the positions of Church and Scott. Church had in mind the λI-calculus, hence

$$\text{meaningless} \Leftrightarrow \text{unsolvable} \Leftrightarrow \text{no nf.}$$

Scott on the other hand considered the λK-calculus, hence

$$\text{meaningless} \Leftrightarrow \text{unsolvable} \Leftrightarrow \text{no hnf} \overset{\not\Leftarrow}{\Rightarrow} \text{no nf.}$$

It turns out to be possible to λ-define the partial recursive functions when undefined is represented by unsolvable. This avoids the difficulties mentioned above when non-normalizing terms are used (definition 2.2.7).

(a) (Un)solvability is a notion that is preserved under the standard translations between **λ** and ***CL***, see proposition 8.3.22. Also the notion is not changed when extensionality is added to the theory, see proposition 15.1.7.

(b) The concept '(un)solvable' is not syntactic. It refers to the applicative behaviour of a term and therefore makes sense also in models of the λ-calculus.

Indeed, the images of unsolvable terms in Scott's models D_∞ and the graph model $P\omega$ are the least elements $\perp$ and $\emptyset$ respectively. Moreover solvability is a useful tool for the analysis of the structure of D_∞ and $P\omega$, see chapter 19.

(c) Both for the λI- and λK-calculus it is consistent to identify all unsolvable terms, see §16.1.

(d) The λ-defining term for a composition can be found uniformly from the λ-defining terms of the factors (by a kind of generalized composition).

Therefore the λ-definability of the partial recursive functions can be proved in such a way that a definition of a μ-recursive partial function is transformed into a λ-term defining that function. This intensional aspect would be lost if a partial recursive function φ were first to be expressed in Kleene's normal form

$$\varphi(\vec{n}) = U(\mu m\, T(e, \vec{n}, m)), \text{ for some } e,$$

and then the term defining φ constructed via the terms U and T.

It has been stressed by Kreisel [1971], p. 177, 178 that in connection with the so-called "superthesis", Church's thesis expresses less than we know. When we say that all partial recursive functions are λ-definable, we merely speak of the results of computation, of their graphs. But we have in mind that λ-terms correspond to our procedures for defining these functions. Thus as far as the μ-recursive and the λ-definable functions are concerned, the equivalence is proved not only in the sense of Church's thesis, but also of the superthesis.

In general, evidence for Church's superthesis is provided by the *proofs* of the equivalence between the various formalizations of the notion effective computability. See Rogers [1967], p. 19, Basic Result III.

This discussion strongly pleads for the identification of the unsolvable terms with undefined. A final argument is the following genericity property.

2.2.13. FACT. Let M be unsolvable and N be a nf. Then

$$C[M] = N \Rightarrow \forall X \; C[X] = N.$$

PROOF. See proposition 14.3.24. □

Therefore we will accept the following heuristic principle.

2.2.14. PROPOSAL. The unsolvable terms should be considered as representing the notion undefined.

By fact 2.2.12 (i) this implies the proposal of Wadsworth [1971] to identify in the λK-calculus terms without a hnf with undefined.

2.3. Survey of part II

Chapter 6. Classical lambda calculus

This is about λ-terms modulo (provability in) **λ**, sometimes modulo **λη**.

6.1. Fixed point combinators

DEFINITION. $Y \in \Lambda^0$ is called a *fixed point combinator* if

$$\forall F \quad YF = F(YF).$$

As a corollary to the fixed point theorem 2.1.5 it is proved that such terms exist. The following is a consequence of combinatory completeness and the fixed point theorem:

THEOREM.

$$\forall M \in \Lambda^0(\vec{x}, y)\ \exists F\ \forall \vec{A}\quad F\vec{A} = M(\vec{A}, F).$$

6.2. Standard combinators

Combinators are defined representing truth values ($\mathbf{T} \equiv \lambda xy.x \equiv \mathbf{K}$; $\mathbf{F} \equiv \lambda xy.y = \mathbf{KI}$), a pairing operation ($[M, N] = \lambda z.zMN$) numerals ($\ulcorner 0 \urcorner \equiv \mathbf{I}$, $\ulcorner n+1 \urcorner \equiv [\mathbf{F}, \ulcorner n \urcorner]$). The term $\Omega \equiv (\lambda x.xx)(\lambda x.xx)$ will play in later chapters the role of "undefined".

6.3. Lambda definability

DEFINITION. Let f: $\mathbb{N} \to \mathbb{N}$. Then f is *λ-definable* if

$$\exists F\ \forall n \in \mathbb{N}\quad F\ulcorner n \urcorner = f(n).$$

THEOREM. Let f: $\mathbb{N} \to \mathbb{N}$, then

$$f \text{ is } \lambda\text{-definable} \Leftrightarrow f \text{ is recursive.}$$

6.4. Numeral systems

The definition of numerals in §6.2 was chosen so that λ-definability of the recursive functions is easy to show. Some other numeral systems are defined on which this class of functions can be represented. Included is the system of Church in which $\boldsymbol{n} \equiv \lambda fx.f^n(x)$.

6.5. More about fixed points; Gödel numbers

Some alternative fixed point combinators are constructed.

MULTIPLE FIXED POINT THEOREM.

$$\forall F_1 \cdots F_n\ \exists X_1 \cdots X_n\quad X_1 = F_1\vec{X} \wedge \cdots \wedge X_n = F_n\vec{X}.$$

Let $\ulcorner X \urcorner$ be the numeral corresponding to the Gödel number of X.

SECOND FIXED POINT THEOREM.

$$\forall F\ \exists X\quad F\ulcorner X \urcorner = X.$$

6.6. Undecidability results

DEFINITION. A set $\mathcal{A} \subseteq \Lambda$ is *closed under equality* if

$$M \in \mathcal{A},\ M = N \Rightarrow N \in \mathcal{A}.$$

THEOREM. *Let* $\mathcal{A}$, $\mathcal{B} \subseteq \Lambda$ *be disjoint non-empty sets, closed under equality. Then* $\mathcal{A}$, $\mathcal{B}$ *are (after coding) recursively inseparable.*

COROLLARY. *Let* $\mathcal{A} \subseteq \Lambda$ *be closed under equality and nontrivial* ($\neq \emptyset$, $\neq \Lambda$). *Then* $\mathcal{A}$ *is not recursive.*

COROLLARY. *The set* $\{M \mid M$ *has a* nf$\}$ *is* r.e. *but not recursive.*

COROLLARY. *The theory* **λ** *has no recursive models.*

6.7. Digression: Self-referential sentences and the recursion theorem

Both are interpreted as an application of the fixed point theorem.

6.8. Exercises

Chapter 7. The theory of combinators

7.1. Combinatory logic

Combinatory logic (***CL***) is a formal theory with as primitive terms ***K*** and ***S*** and as primitive operation application (no abstraction). The axioms for ***CL*** are

$$\boldsymbol{K}PQ = P, \qquad \boldsymbol{S}PQR = PR(QR).$$

It is shown that in ***CL*** an abstractor λ^* can be defined such that β-conversion holds. It follows that all closed λ-terms can be defined in terms of **K**, **S** $\in \Lambda$, using application only.

*7.2. Reduction for **CL***

Provable equality in ***CL*** can be generated by a notion of reduction satisfying the Church–Rosser theorem.

*7.3. The relation between **CL** and **λ***

Using the defined abstraction λ^* in ***CL***, there is a canonical way of translating λ-terms in *CL*-terms and vice versa. There is a finite set $\boldsymbol{A}_\beta$ of equations between CL-terms such that $\boldsymbol{\lambda}$ and $\boldsymbol{CL} + \boldsymbol{A}_\beta$ become equivalent. Similarly there is a finite set of axioms $\boldsymbol{A}_{\beta\eta}$ such that the theories

$$\boldsymbol{\lambda\eta},\ \boldsymbol{\lambda} + \boldsymbol{ext},\ \boldsymbol{CL} + \boldsymbol{ext},\ \boldsymbol{CL} + \boldsymbol{A}_{\beta\eta}$$

are equivalent.

7.4. Exercises

Chapter 8. Classical lambda calculus (continued)

8.1. Applications of $\boldsymbol{CL}$ *to* $\boldsymbol{\lambda}$

It is shown that Λ^0 is generated by the λ-terms **K**, **S** using application only. Λ^0 can even be generated by a single element.

A term $\mathbf{E} \in \Lambda^0$ is constructed which enumerates Λ^0:

$$\forall M \in \Lambda^0\ \exists n \in \mathbb{N}\quad \mathbf{E}\ulcorner n \urcorner = M.$$

8.2. Uniformity; infinite sequences

DEFINITION. A sequence $M_0, M_1, \ldots \in \Lambda$ is called *uniform* if $\exists M \in \Lambda\ \forall n \in \mathbb{N}$ $M\ulcorner n \urcorner = M_n$. An intrinsic coding of uniform infinite sequences of λ-terms is defined.

8.3. Solvability; head normal forms

DEFINITION. (i) $M \in \Lambda^0$ is *solvable* if $\exists \vec{N}\ M\vec{N} = \mathbf{I}$.

(ii) M has a *head normal form* if M is convertible to a term of the form $\lambda\vec{x}.y\vec{N}$.

THEOREM *In the* λK*-calculus*

$$M \text{ is solvable} \Leftrightarrow M \text{ has a hnf.}$$

8.4. Definability of partial functions

DEFINITION. A partial function $\psi : \mathbb{N} \hookrightarrow \mathbb{N}$ is called λ-*definable* if for some $F \in \Lambda^0$

$$F\ulcorner n \urcorner = \begin{cases} \psi(n), & \text{if } \psi(n) \text{ is defined} \\ \text{unsolvable}, & \text{else.} \end{cases}$$

THEOREM. *ψ is λ-definable iff ψ is partial recursive.*

8.5. Exercises

Chapter 9. The $\boldsymbol{\lambda I}$-calculus

This theory is about the restricted class of λI-terms modulo convertibility.

9.1. Generalities

THEOREM. *$\boldsymbol{\lambda K}$ is conservative over $\boldsymbol{\lambda I}$.*

THEOREM. *$M \in \Lambda_I$ has a* nf *iff each subterm of M has a* nf.

Several notions about Λ_K relativize to Λ_I. For example $M \in \Lambda_I^0$ is I-solvable iff

$$\exists \vec{N} \in \Lambda_I \quad M\vec{N} = \mathbf{I}.$$

9.2. Definability

It is proved that the partial recursive functions can also be λ-defined by λI-terms.

9.3. Combinators

A theory $\boldsymbol{CL_I}$ is introduced which corresponds to $\boldsymbol{\lambda I}$ in the same way that $\boldsymbol{CL}$ corresponds to $\boldsymbol{\lambda}$.

9.4. Solvability

The notion of I-solvability is analysed.

THEOREM. *M is I-solvable $\Leftrightarrow M$ has a* nf.

Using the method of proof one can show that there exists a λI-term $\mathbf{K}^*$ that locally acts like $\mathbf{K}$, i.e.

$$(+) \qquad \mathbf{K}^* MN = M \quad \text{all } M \text{ and all } N \in \mathfrak{N},$$

where $\mathfrak{N}$ is some given finite set of normal forms. The construction of $\mathbf{K}^*$ can be made impredicative: one may assume $(+)$ for a set $\mathfrak{N}$ containing $\mathbf{K}^*$ and some terms containing $\mathbf{K}^*$ as subterm.

9.5. Exercises

Chapter 10. Böhm trees

10.1. Basics

For each $M \in \Lambda$ a certain tree BT(M) is constructed, the so called *Böhm tree* of M. BT(M) may be finite or infinite; it can be compared to the continued fraction of a real. The essential computational behaviour of a term M can be read off from BT(M).

The set of all possible trees (not necessarily the Böhm tree of a term) is denoted by $\mathfrak{B}$.

Characterizations are given of when an element of $\mathfrak{B}$ is the Böhm tree of a $\lambda(I)$-term.

10.2. Comparing Böhm trees; the tree topology on Λ

On the set $\mathfrak{B}$ a partial ordering is introduced: $A \subseteq B$ iff A results from B by deleting some subtrees.

PROPOSITION. $(\mathfrak{B}, \subseteq)$ *is an algebraic* cpo.

DEFINITION. The *tree topology* on Λ is the least topology such that the map $\mathrm{BT}: \Lambda \rightarrow \mathfrak{B}$ is continuous, where $\mathfrak{B}$ has the Scott topology. (In §14.3 it will be proved that the λ-calculus operations are continuous with respect to the tree topology.)

A kind of η-reduction is defined on $\mathfrak{B}$. By composing the relations $\subseteq$ and $\twoheadrightarrow_\eta$ on $\mathfrak{B}$ several other relations are obtained. In chapter 19 it is proved that these correspond to inequality in the models D_∞ and $P\omega$.

10.3. Böhm out technique

Given a tree A and a subtree A', a technique is developed to isolate A' from A. In general this will leave some traces on A'.

10.4. Separability of terms

DEFINITION. Let $\mathfrak{F} = M_1, \ldots, M_n$ be a finite sequence of closed terms. Then $\mathfrak{F}$ is *separable* if $\forall N_1, \ldots, N_n \, \exists F \, FM_1 = N_1 \wedge \cdots \wedge FM_n = N_n$.

A characterization is given for the separability of such $\mathfrak{F}$.

COROLLARY. *Let* $\mathfrak{F} = M_1,\ldots,M_n \in \Lambda^0$ *have distinct* $\beta\eta$–nf's. *Then* $\mathfrak{F}$ *is separable*.

10.5. Separability for the λI-calculus

The notation of separability relativizes to the λI-calculus.

THEOREM. *Let* $\mathcal{F} = M_1, \ldots, M_n$ *be closed. Then in the* λI*-calculus* $\mathcal{F}$ *is separable iff* $M_1, \ldots, M_n$ *have distinct* $\beta\eta$–nf's.

10.6. Exercises

This completes the survey of part II.

2.4. Exercises

2.4.1. Show that the following terms have a nf.

(i) $(\lambda y.yyy)((\lambda ab.a)\mathbf{I}(\mathbf{SS}))$.

(ii) $(\lambda yz.zy)((\lambda x.xxx)(\lambda x.xxx))(\lambda w.\mathbf{I})$.

(iii) $\mathbf{SSSSSSS}$.

(iv)* $\mathbf{S(SS)(SS)(SS)SS}$.

2.4.2. Show that

(i) $\mathbf{I} \# \mathbf{K}$.

(ii) $\mathbf{I} \# \mathbf{S}$.

(iii) $xy \# xx$.

2.4.3. Construct closed terms $M_0, M_1, \ldots$ such that $M_i \# M_j$ for all $i \neq j$.

2.4.4. Show that application is not associative; in fact, $x(yz) \# (xy)z$.

2.4.5. (C. E. Schaap) Let $X \equiv \mathbf{SI}$. Show that $XXXX = X(X(XX))$. Does $X^nX = XX^{\sim n}$ hold for all $n \in \mathbb{N}$?

2.4.6. Show that $\neg\exists F\, \forall MN\; F(MN) = M$. [*Hint.* Show that $F(xy) \# x$.]

2.4.7. Show $\exists M\, \forall N\; MN = MM$. [*Hint.* Use the fixed point theorem.]

2.4.8. Let $M \in \Lambda$, $\vec{x} \equiv x_1, \ldots, x_n$ and $\vec{N} \equiv N_1, \ldots, N_n$. If some of the x occur in $\mathrm{FV}(\vec{N})$, then $M[\vec{x} := \vec{N}]$ (simultaneous substitution) is defined as follows:

$$y[\vec{x} := \vec{N}] \equiv N_i \quad \text{if } y \equiv x_i \in \{\vec{x}\},$$
$$\equiv y \quad \text{if } y \notin \{\vec{x}\},$$

$$(M_1M_2)[-] \equiv M_1[-]M_2[-],$$

$$(\lambda y.M_1)[-] \equiv \lambda y.M_1[-].$$

Show that proposition 2.1.22 and corollary 2.1.24 remain valid.

2.4.9. Show that $(\lambda y.(\lambda x.M))N = \lambda x.((\lambda y.M)N)$.

2.4.10. (i) Construct an $M \in \Lambda^\circ$ such that $M = M\mathbf{S}$.

(ii) Idem with $M\mathbf{ISS} = M\mathbf{S}$. [*Hint.* Use the fixed point theorem.]

2.4.11. Construct an $F \in \Lambda$ such that $F\mathbf{I} = x$ and $F\mathbf{K} = y$. [*Hint.* Use the proof to be found in exercise 2.4.2 (i).]

2.4.12. (Jacopini). Let $\omega_3 \equiv \lambda x.xxx$ and $\mathbf{\Omega}_3 \equiv \omega_3\omega_3$. Show

(i) $\mathbf{I} \# \omega_3$.

(ii) $\mathbf{I} \# \mathbf{\Omega}_3$.

2.4.13. Show that for all terms M starting with a λ one has $\lambda x.Mx = M$.

2.4.14. Let $M \equiv \lambda x.x(\lambda y.yy)(\lambda y.yy)$; show that M is I-solvable.

2.4.15. Suppose a symbol of the λ-calculus alphabet is always 0.5 cm wide. Write down a λ-term with length less than 20 cm having a nf with length at least $10^{10^{10}}$ lightyear. The speed of light is $c = 3.10^{10}$ cm/sec.

CHAPTER 3

REDUCTION

There is a certain asymmetry in the defining equation for λ-abstraction. The statement

$$(\lambda x.x^2+1)3=10$$

can be interpreted as "10 is the result of computing $(\lambda x.x^2+1)3$", but not vice versa. This computational aspect will be expressed by writing

$$(\lambda x.x^2+1)3 \twoheadrightarrow 10,$$

which reads "$(\lambda x.x^2+1)3$ *reduces to* 10".

Apart from this conceptual aspect, reduction is also useful for an analysis of convertibility. The Church–Rosser theorem says that if two terms are convertible, then there is a term to which they both reduce. In many cases the inconvertibility of two terms can be proved by showing that they do not reduce to a common term.

3.1. Notions of reduction

The convertibility relation on Λ introduced in §2.1 is not the only equality relation that can be analyzed by reduction. Therefore this latter concept will be introduced in a general setting.

3.1.1. DEFINITION. (i) A binary relation $\boldsymbol{R}$ on Λ is *compatible* (with the operations) if

$$(M,M')\in\boldsymbol{R}\Rightarrow(ZM,ZM')\in\boldsymbol{R},\ (MZ,M'Z)\in\boldsymbol{R}$$
$$\text{and } (\lambda x.M,\lambda x.M')\in\boldsymbol{R},$$

for all $M,M',Z\in\Lambda$.

(ii) An *equality* (or *congruence*) *relation* on Λ is a compatible equivalence relation.

(iii) A *reduction relation* on Λ is one which is compatible, reflexive, and transitive.

Note that a relation $\boldsymbol{R} \subseteq \Lambda^2$ is compatible if

$$(M, M') \in \boldsymbol{R} \Rightarrow (C[M], C[M']) \in \boldsymbol{R}$$

for all $M, M' \in \Lambda$ and all contexts $C[\ ]$, with one hole.

3.1.2. DEFINITION. (i) A *notion of reduction* on Λ is just a binary relation $\boldsymbol{R}$ on Λ.

(ii) If $\boldsymbol{R}_1$, $\boldsymbol{R}_2$ are notions of reduction, then $\boldsymbol{R}_1\boldsymbol{R}_2$ is $\boldsymbol{R}_1 \cup \boldsymbol{R}_2$.

Many important examples of a notion of reduction are given by the graph of a partial recursive function on Λ. For example, this holds for the classical notion of reduction $\boldsymbol{\beta}$.

3.1.3. DEFINITION. $\boldsymbol{\beta} = \{((\lambda x.M)N, M[x:= N]) | M, N \in \Lambda\}$.

3.1.4. DEFINITION. If $\succ\!\!-$ is a binary relation on a set X, then the *reflexive closure* of $\succ\!\!-$ (notation: $\succ\!\!\overline{\overline{\ }}$) is the least relation extending R that is reflexive. The *transitive closure* (notation: $\succ\!\!-^{*}$) and the *compatible closure* (no notation) are defined similarly.

3.1.5. DEFINITION. Let $\boldsymbol{R}$ be a notion of reduction on Λ.

(i) Then $\boldsymbol{R}$ induces the binary relations

$\rightarrow_R$ *one step R-reduction*,

$\twoheadrightarrow_R$ *R-reduction* and

$=_R$ *R-equality* (also called *R-convertibility*),

inductively defined as follows. $\rightarrow_R$ is the compatible closure of $\boldsymbol{R}$:

(1) $(M, N) \in \boldsymbol{R} \Rightarrow M \rightarrow_R N$,

(2) $M \rightarrow_R N \quad \Rightarrow ZM \rightarrow_R ZN$,

(3) $M \rightarrow_R N \quad \Rightarrow MZ \rightarrow_R NZ$,

(4) $M \rightarrow_R N \quad \Rightarrow \lambda x.M \rightarrow_R \lambda x.N$.

$\twoheadrightarrow_R$ is the reflexive, transitive closure of $\rightarrow_R$:

(1) $M \rightarrow_R N \Rightarrow M \twoheadrightarrow_R N$,

(2) $M \twoheadrightarrow_R M$,

(3) $M \twoheadrightarrow_R N,\ N \twoheadrightarrow_R L \Rightarrow M \twoheadrightarrow_R L$.

$=_R$ is the equivalence relation generated by $\twoheadrightarrow_R$:

(1) $M \twoheadrightarrow_R N \Rightarrow M =_R N$,

(2) $M =_R N \Rightarrow N =_R M$,

(3) $M =_R N,\ N =_R L \Rightarrow M =_R L$.

(ii) The basic relations derived from $\boldsymbol{R}$ are pronounced as follows:

$M \twoheadrightarrow_R N$: *M R-reduces to N* or N is an *R-reduct* of M;

$M \rightarrow_R N$: *M R-reduces to N in one step*;

$M =_R N$: M is *R-convertible to N*.

The relations $\to_R$, $\twoheadrightarrow_R$ and $=_R$ are introduced inductively. Therefore properties about these relations can be proved inductively.

3.1.6. LEMMA *The relations* $\to_R$, $\twoheadrightarrow_R$ *and* $=_R$ *are all compatible. Therefore* $\twoheadrightarrow_R$ *is a reduction relation and* $=_R$ *is an equality relation.*

PROOF. For $\to_R$ this is immediate. For $\twoheadrightarrow_R$ and $=_R$ it follows by induction on the generation of these relations. This kind of proof occurs quite often; usually the details will be omitted, but here we shall give the proof for $\twoheadrightarrow_R$ explicitly.

Case 1. $M \twoheadrightarrow_R N$ because $M \to_R N$. Then by the result for $\to_R$ one has $C[M] \to_R C[N]$ and hence $C[M] \twoheadrightarrow_R C[N]$.

Case 2. $M \twoheadrightarrow_R N$ because $M \equiv N$. Then trivially $C[M] \twoheadrightarrow_R C[N]$.

Case 3. $M \twoheadrightarrow_R N$ is a direct consequence of $M \twoheadrightarrow_R L$ and $L \twoheadrightarrow_R N$. By the induction hypothesis $C[M] \twoheadrightarrow_R C[L]$ and $C[L] \twoheadrightarrow_R C[N]$. Therefore $C[M] \twoheadrightarrow_R C[N]$. □

3.1.7. REMARKS. (i) By the compatibility of $\twoheadrightarrow_R$ it follows (by induction on the structure of M) that

$$N \twoheadrightarrow_R N' \quad \Rightarrow \quad M[x:=N] \twoheadrightarrow_R M[x:=N'].$$

For $\to_R$ this is in general not true, since N, N' may be substituted for several x's in M.

(ii) The notion of compatible relation can be generalized directly to any set X with some operations on it. Also then one can speak of equality and reduction relations. In particular, this will be done to define on combinatory terms or on some extended λ-terms (like labelled λ-terms) reduction and equality relations via a notion of reduction.

(iii) Notions of reduction will be denoted by boldface letters; e.g. $\boldsymbol{\beta}$, $\boldsymbol{\eta}$, $\boldsymbol{\Omega}$. The derived relations will be written using the corresponding lightface symbols; e.g. $\to_\beta$, $\twoheadrightarrow_\beta$ etc.

EXAMPLE. $(\lambda x.xx)(\lambda y.y)z \to_\beta (\lambda y.y)(\lambda y.y)z$
$\qquad\qquad \to_\beta (\lambda y.y)z \to_\beta z.$

Hence

$$(\lambda x.xx)(\lambda y.y)z \twoheadrightarrow_\beta z$$

and if one is interested only in equality,

$$(\lambda x.xx)(\lambda y.y)z =_\beta z.$$

For the remainder of this section $\boldsymbol{R}$ is a notion of reduction on Λ.

Often a notion of reduction is introduced as follows. "Let $\boldsymbol{R}$ be defined by the following *contraction rules*

$$\boldsymbol{R} : M \to N \text{ provided } \cdots \text{"}.$$

This means that $\boldsymbol{R} = \{(M, N) | \cdots\}$. E.g. $\boldsymbol{\beta}$ could have been introduced by the contraction rule

$$\boldsymbol{\beta} : (\lambda x . M) N \to M[x := N].$$

3.1.8. Definition. (i) An *R-redex* is a term M such that $(M, N) \in R$ for some term N. In this case N is called an *R-contractum* of M.

(ii) A term M is called an *R-normal form* (*R-nf*) if M does not contain (as subterm) any R-redex.

(iii) A term N *is* an *R-nf of M* (or *M has the R-nf N*) if N is an *R-nf* and $M =_R N$.

The process of stepping from a redex to a contractum is called *contraction*. Instead of "M is an *R-nf*" one often says "M is *in R-nf*", thinking of a machine that has reached its final state.

Example. $(\lambda x.xx)(\lambda y.y)$ is a β-redex. Therefore $(\lambda x.xx)(\lambda y.y)z$ is not in β-nf; however this term has the β-nf z.

3.1.9. Lemma.

$$M \to_R N \quad \Leftrightarrow \quad M \equiv C[P], N \equiv C[Q] \text{ and } (P, Q) \in \boldsymbol{R}$$

for some $P, Q \in \Lambda$, $C[\;]$ *with one hole.*

Proof. By definition of $\to_R$. □

3.1.10. Corollary. *Let M be an R*-nf. *Then*

(i) *For no N one has $M \to_R N$.*

(ii) $M \twoheadrightarrow_R N \Rightarrow M \equiv N$.

Proof. (i) Immediate by the lemma and the definition of R-nf.

(ii) By (i), since $\twoheadrightarrow_R$ is the reflexive transitive closure of $\to_R$. □

It is not true in general that if

$$\forall N \quad [M \twoheadrightarrow_R N \Rightarrow M \equiv N],$$

then M is in R-nf. Take for example $\boldsymbol{R} = \boldsymbol{\beta}$ and $M \equiv \boldsymbol{\Omega}$.

3.1.11. Definition. (i) Let $\succ\!\!-$ be a binary relation on Λ. Then $\succ\!\!-$ satisfies the *diamond property* (notation $\succ\!\!- \models \Diamond$) if

$$\forall M, M_1, M_2 \quad [M \succ\!\!- M_1 \wedge M \succ\!\!- M_2 \Rightarrow \exists M_3 [M_1 \succ\!\!- M_3 \wedge M_2 \succ\!\!- M_3]]$$

see figure 3.1.

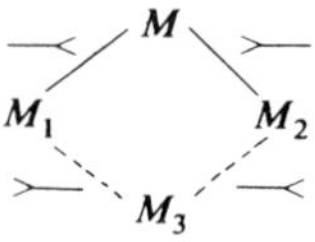

FIG. 3.1.

(ii) A notion of reduction $\boldsymbol{R}$ is said to be *Church–Rosser* (CR) if $\twoheadrightarrow_R$ satisfies the diamond property.

3.1.12. THEOREM. *Let* $\boldsymbol{R}$ *be* CR. *Then*

$$M =_R N \Rightarrow \exists Z[M \twoheadrightarrow_R Z \wedge N \twoheadrightarrow_R Z].$$

PROOF. By induction on the definition of $=_R$. If $M =_R N$ is a direct consequence of $M \twoheadrightarrow_R N$, then take $Z \equiv N$. If $M =_R N$ is a direct consequence of $N =_R M$, Z can be found by the induction hypothesis. If $M =_R N$ is a direct consequence of $M =_R L$, $L =_R N$, Z can be found using the induction hypothesis and the assumption that $\twoheadrightarrow_R$ satisfies the diamond property, see figure 3.2.

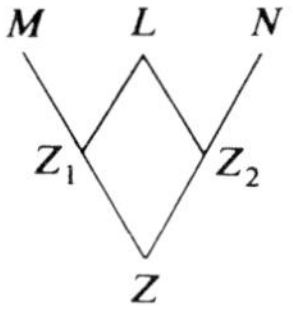

FIG. 3.2. □

3.1.13. COROLLARY. *Let* $\boldsymbol{R}$ *be* CR. *Then*

(i) *If* N *is an* R-nf *of* M, *then* $M \twoheadrightarrow_R N$.

(ii) *A term* M *can have at most one* R-nf.

PROOF. (i) Let $M =_R N$ and N be an R-nf. By theorem 3.1.12 for some Z one has $M \twoheadrightarrow_R Z$ and $N \twoheadrightarrow_R Z$. But since N is an R-nf, one has $Z \equiv N$ by corollary 3.1.10(ii). Therefore $M \twoheadrightarrow_R N$.

(ii) Suppose N_1, N_2 are both R-nf's of M. Then $N_1 =_R N_2$ $(=_R M)$. By theorem 3.1.12 one has $N_1 \twoheadrightarrow_R Z$, $N_2 \twoheadrightarrow_R Z$ for some Z. But then by corollary 3.1.10 (ii) it follows that $N_1 \equiv Z \equiv N_2$. □

In the next section it will be shown that $\boldsymbol{\beta}$ is CR.

Note that for any $\boldsymbol{R}$ one has

$$N \twoheadrightarrow_R N' \Rightarrow M[x := N] \twoheadrightarrow_R M[x := N']$$

but *not* always

$$M \twoheadrightarrow_R M' \Rightarrow M[x:=N] \twoheadrightarrow_R M'[x:=N].$$

Therefore the following notion is useful.

3.1.14. DEFINITION. A binary relation $\boldsymbol{R}$ on Λ is *substitutive* if for all $M, N, L \in \Lambda$ and all variables x one has

$$(M, N) \in \boldsymbol{R} \Rightarrow (M[x:=L], N[x:=L]) \in \boldsymbol{R}.$$

3.1.15. PROPOSITION. *If $\boldsymbol{R}$ is substitutive, then so are $\rightarrow_R$, $\twoheadrightarrow_R$ and $=_R$.*

PROOF. By induction on the definition of $\rightarrow_R$, $\twoheadrightarrow_R$, $=_R$. □

3.1.16. PROPOSITION. *$\boldsymbol{\beta}$ is substitutive.*

PROOF. Let $(M, N) \in \boldsymbol{\beta}$. Then $M \equiv (\lambda y.P)Q$ and $N \equiv P[y:=Q]$. Hence

$$M[x:=L] \equiv (\lambda y.(P[x:=L]))(Q[x:=L]),$$

$$N[x:=L] \equiv P[y:=Q][x:=L]$$

$$\equiv P[x:=L][y:=Q[x:=L]],$$

by the substitution lemma 2.1.16 and the variable convention 2.1.13. It follows that $(M[x:=L], N[x:=L]) \in \boldsymbol{\beta}$. □

3.1.17. DEFINITION. (i) Let Δ be a subterm occurrence of M, that is, $M \equiv C[\Delta]$. Write

$$M \overset{\Delta}{\rightarrow}_R N$$

if Δ is an R-redex with contractum Δ' and $N \equiv C[\Delta']$.

(ii) An *R-reduction* (*path*) is a finite or infinite sequence

$$M_0 \overset{\Delta_0}{\rightarrow}_R M_1 \overset{\Delta_1}{\rightarrow}_R M_2 \rightarrow_R \cdots .$$

3.1.18. CONVENTIONS. (i) $\sigma, \tau, \ldots$ range over reduction paths.

(ii) The reduction path σ in definition 3.1.17 (ii) *starts* with M_0. If there is a last term M_n in σ, then σ *ends* with M_n. In that case one also says that σ is a reduction path *from* M_0 to M_n. If $n=0$, then σ is called the *empty reduction* and is denoted by $\emptyset$: $M_0 \twoheadrightarrow_R M_0$. If $n \neq 0$, then σ is a *proper* R-reduction and one writes $(\sigma:)\ M_0 \underset{\neq\emptyset}{\twoheadrightarrow}_R M_n$.

(iii) Sometimes the Δ_0, Δ_1 are left out in denoting a reduction path.

(iv) We often write σ: $M_0 \to M_1 \to \cdots$ to indicate that σ *is* the path $M_0 \to M_1 \to \cdots$.

(v) If $\sigma : M_0 \to \cdots \to M_n$ and $\tau : M_n \to \cdots \to M_m$, then

$$\sigma + \tau : M_0 \to \cdots \to M_n \to \cdots \to M_m.$$

(vi) If Δ is an R-redex occurrence in M with contractum Δ', then (Δ) denotes the one step reduction $M \xrightarrow{\Delta}_R N$. That is

$$(\Delta) : C[\Delta] \xrightarrow{\Delta}_R C[\Delta'].$$

(vii) If σ is an R-reduction path, then $\|\sigma\|$ is its *length* i.e. the number of $\to_R$ steps in it. Note that $\|\sigma\| \in \mathbb{N} \cup \{\infty\}$.

3.1.19. Examples. (i) Let Δ be an R-redex with contractum Δ' and let $M \equiv (\lambda x.xx)\Delta$. Then

$$M \xrightarrow{\Delta}_R (\lambda x.xx)\Delta', \qquad M \xrightarrow{M}_\beta \Delta\Delta.$$

(ii) Let $\omega_3 \equiv \lambda x.xxx$. Then the following is an infinite β-reduction

$$\omega_3\omega_3 \xrightarrow{\omega_3\omega_3}_\beta \omega_3\omega_3\omega_3 \xrightarrow{\omega_3\omega_3}_\beta \omega_3\omega_3\omega_3\omega_3 \xrightarrow{\omega_3\omega_3}_\beta \cdots$$

(iii) In examples (i) and (ii) one could recover the Δ from the M and N in $M \xrightarrow{\Delta}_R N$. The following example of Lévy shows that this is not always so:

$$\mathbf{I}(\mathbf{I}x) \xrightarrow{\mathbf{I}x}_\beta \mathbf{I}x, \qquad \mathbf{I}(\mathbf{I}x) \xrightarrow{\mathbf{I}(\mathbf{I}x)}_\beta \mathbf{I}x.$$

For each $M \in \Lambda$ one can draw all the R-reducts of M with connecting arcs representing $\to_R$. These objects are called 'pseudo digraphs' in Harary [1969] and 'directed multigraphs' in Bollobás [1979]. We will simply call them graphs.

3.1.20. Definition. The R(reduction) *graph* of a term M (notation $G_R(M)$) is the set

$$\{N \in \Lambda \mid M \twoheadrightarrow_R N\}$$

directed by $\to_R$: if several redexes give rise to $M_0 \to_R M_1$, then that many directed arcs connect M_0 to M_1 in $G_R(M)$.

3.1.21. EXAMPLES. (i) $G_\beta(\mathbf{I}x) = \mathbf{I}x \to x$ or simply $\cdot \to \cdot$

(ii) $G_\beta(\mathbf{I}(\mathbf{I}x)) = \mathbf{I}(\mathbf{I}x) \rightrightarrows \mathbf{I}x \to x$

(iii) $G_\beta(\Omega) =$ 

(iv) $G_\beta(\mathbf{WWW})$ with $\mathbf{W} \equiv \lambda xy.xyy$ is 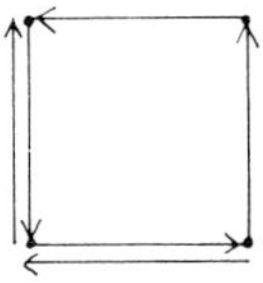

(v) $G_\beta(MM)$ with $M \equiv \lambda x.(\lambda y.yy)x$ is 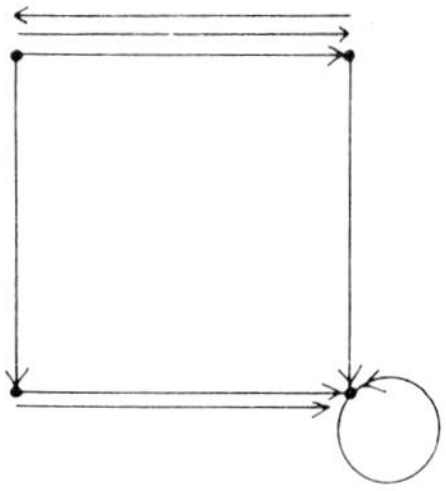

(vi) $G_\beta(\omega_3\omega_3)$ with $\omega_3 = \lambda x.xxx$ is

$\cdot \to \cdot \to \cdot \to \cdot \to \cdot \cdots$

3.1.22. DEFINITION. Let $M \in \Lambda$.

(i) M *R-strongly normalizes* (notation R-SN(M)) if there is no infinite R-reduction starting with M.

(ii) M is *R-infinite* (notation R-$\infty(M)$) if not R-SN(M).

(iii) R is *strongly normalizing* (SN) if $\forall M \in \Lambda$ R-SN(M).

3.1.23. FACT. (i) M having a β-nf neither implies nor is implied by $G_\beta(M)$ being finite.

(ii) β-SN(M) implies $G_\beta(M)$ is finite and M has a β-nf, but not conversely.

PROOF. (i) ($\not\Rightarrow$) Let $\omega_3 \equiv \lambda x.xxx$ and $M \equiv (\lambda x.\mathbf{I})(\omega_3\omega_3)$. Then M has the nf $\mathbf{I}$ but $G_\beta(M)$ is

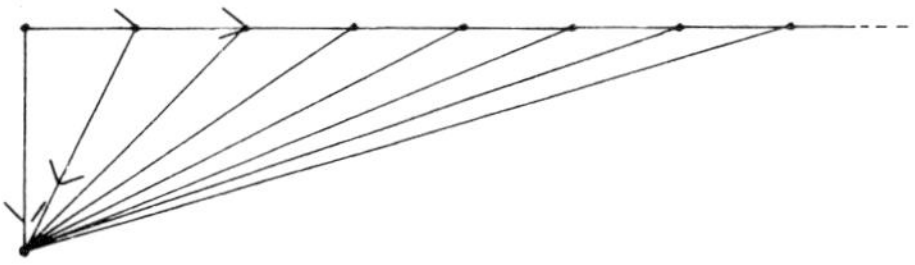

($\not\Leftarrow$) Note that $G_\beta(\Omega)$ is finite but Ω has no nf.

(ii) ($\Rightarrow$) Trivial, by König's lemma.

($\not\Leftarrow$) Consider $M \equiv (\lambda x.\mathbf{I})\Omega$. This term has as β-nf the term $\mathbf{I}$ and a finite β-graph:

But M has also an infinite β-reduction (loop around). □

3.1.24. Definition. (i) A binary relation $\succ\!\!-$ (on a set X) satisfies the *weak diamond property* if

$$\forall x, x_1, x_2 \quad [x \succ\!\!- x_1 \wedge x \succ\!\!- x_2 \Rightarrow \exists x_3[x_1 \overset{*}{\underset{=}{\succ\!\!-}} x_3 \wedge x_2 \overset{*}{\underset{=}{\succ\!\!-}} x_3]],$$

where $\overset{*}{\underset{=}{\succ\!\!-}}$ is thc transitive reflexive closure of $\succ\!\!-$.

(ii) A notion of reduction $\boldsymbol{R}$ is *weakly Church-Rosser* (WCR) if $\rightarrow_R$ satisfies the weak diamond property.

It is not true that WCR$\Rightarrow$CR, see exercise 15.4.7. But one has the following result of Newman [1942].

3.1.25. Proposition. *For notions of reduction one has*

$$\text{SN} \wedge \text{WCR} \Rightarrow \text{CR}.$$

Proof. By SN each term R-reduces to an R-nf. It suffices to show that this R-nf is unique. Call M *ambiguous* if M R-reduces to two distinct R-nf's. For such M one has $M \rightarrow_R M'$ with M' ambiguous (use WCR, see figure 3.3). Hence by SN ambiguous terms do not exist.

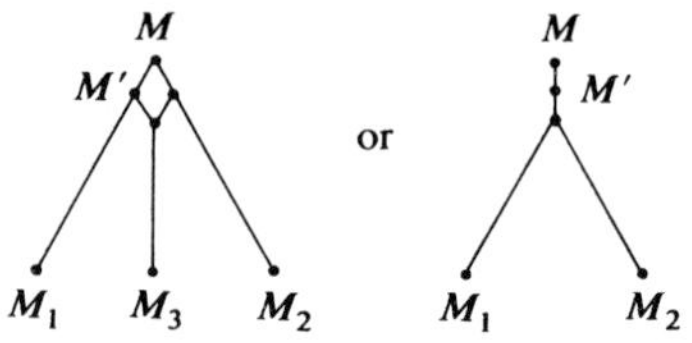

FIG. 3.3. □

3.1.26. Notation. (i) R-NF $= \{M \in \Lambda \mid M \text{ is in } R\text{-nf}\}$, R-NF$^0 = R$-NF $\cap\, \Lambda^0$.

(ii) If $\mathcal{X} \subseteq \Lambda$, then $M \in_R \mathcal{X}$ iff $M' =_R M$ for some $M' \in \mathcal{X}$.

In this notation, $M \in_\beta \beta$-NF iff M has a β-nf.

Finally the notion of solvability is relativized to a notion of reduction $\boldsymbol{R}$.

3.1.27. DEFINITION. (i) $M \in \Lambda^0$ is *R-solvable* if $\exists \vec{P} \in \Lambda\ M\vec{P} =_R I$.

(ii) $M \in \Lambda$ is *R-solvable* if some closed substitution instance of M is R-solvable.

3.2. Beta reduction

In this section the notion of reduction $\boldsymbol{\beta}$ will be studied more closely. This notion is quite useful, since on the one hand it characterizes provability in $\boldsymbol{\lambda}$ and on the other hand it is Church–Rosser.

3.2.1. PROPOSITION. $M =_\beta N \Leftrightarrow \boldsymbol{\lambda} \vdash M = N$.

PROOF. ($\Leftarrow$) Use induction on the length of proof of $M = N$.

($\Rightarrow$) Show by induction on the definition of the relations involved that

$$M \rightarrow_\beta N \Rightarrow \boldsymbol{\lambda} \vdash M = N,$$

$$M \twoheadrightarrow_\beta N \Rightarrow \boldsymbol{\lambda} \vdash M = N,$$

$$M =_\beta N \Rightarrow \boldsymbol{\lambda} \vdash M = N. \quad \square$$

Now a proof will be given that $\boldsymbol{\beta}$ is CR. This proof is due to W. Tait and P. Martin-Löf and is quite short. A somewhat longer but more perspicuous proof is given in §11.1. Sections 11.2 and 14.2 contain other conceptually important proofs of the Church–Rosser theorem.

3.2.2. LEMMA *Let* $\succ\!\!-$ *be a binary relation on a set and let* $\succ\!\!-^{*}$ *be its transitive closure. Then*

$$\succ\!\!- \models \diamond \quad \Rightarrow \quad \succ\!\!-^{*} \models \diamond .$$

PROOF. By a simple diagram chase suggested by figure 3.4.

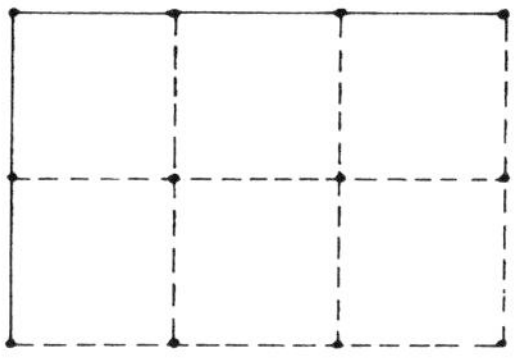

FIG. 3.4.

$\square$

Now a binary relation $\underset{1}{\twoheadrightarrow}$ on a Λ will be defined such that (1) $\underset{1}{\twoheadrightarrow}$ satisfies the diamond property, (2) the transitive closure of $\underset{1}{\twoheadrightarrow}$ is $\twoheadrightarrow_\beta$. Then it follows by lemma 3.2.2 that $\twoheadrightarrow_\beta$ satisfies the diamond property, i.e. $\boldsymbol{\beta}$ is CR.

3.2.3. DEFINITION. Define a binary relation $\underset{1}{\twoheadrightarrow}$ on Λ inductively as follows:

$$M \underset{1}{\twoheadrightarrow} M;$$

$$M \underset{1}{\twoheadrightarrow} M' \Rightarrow \lambda x.M \underset{1}{\twoheadrightarrow} \lambda x.M';$$

$$M \underset{1}{\twoheadrightarrow} M',\ N \underset{1}{\twoheadrightarrow} N' \Rightarrow MN \underset{1}{\twoheadrightarrow} M'N';$$

$$M \underset{1}{\twoheadrightarrow} M',\ N \underset{1}{\twoheadrightarrow} N' \Rightarrow (\lambda x.M)N \underset{1}{\twoheadrightarrow} M'[x:=N'].$$

3.2.4. LEMMA. *If* $M \underset{1}{\twoheadrightarrow} M'$ *and* $N \underset{1}{\twoheadrightarrow} N'$, *then* $M[x:=N] \underset{1}{\twoheadrightarrow} M'[x:=N']$.

PROOF. By induction on the definition of $M \underset{1}{\twoheadrightarrow} M'$.

Case 1. $M \underset{1}{\twoheadrightarrow} M'$ is $M \underset{1}{\twoheadrightarrow} M$. Then one has to show $M[x:=N] \underset{1}{\twoheadrightarrow} M[x:=N']$. This follows by induction on the structure of M, as is done in the following table.

M	LHS	RHS	Comment
x	N	N'	o.k.
y	y	y	o.k.
PQ	$P[\ ]Q[\ ]$	$P[\ ']Q[\ ']$	use induction hypothesis
$\lambda y.P$	$\lambda y.P[\ ]$	$\lambda y.P[\ ']$	idem

Case 2. $M \underset{1}{\twoheadrightarrow} M'$ is $\lambda y.P \underset{1}{\twoheadrightarrow} \lambda y.P'$ and is a direct consequence of $P \underset{1}{\twoheadrightarrow} P'$. By the induction hypothesis one has $P[x:=N] \underset{1}{\twoheadrightarrow} P'[x:=N']$. But then $\lambda y.P[x:=N] \underset{1}{\twoheadrightarrow} \lambda y.P'[x:=N']$, i.e. $M[x:=N] \underset{1}{\twoheadrightarrow} M'[x:=N']$.

Case 3. $M \underset{1}{\twoheadrightarrow} M'$ is $PQ \underset{1}{\twoheadrightarrow} P'Q'$ and is a direct consequence of $P \underset{1}{\twoheadrightarrow} P'$, $Q \underset{1}{\twoheadrightarrow} Q'$. Then

$$
\begin{aligned}
M[x:=N] &\equiv P[x:=N]Q[x:=N] \\
&\underset{1}{\twoheadrightarrow} P'[x:=N']Q'[x:=N'], \quad \text{by the induction hypothesis,} \\
&\equiv M'[x:=N'].
\end{aligned}
$$

Case 4. $M \twoheadrightarrow_1 M'$ is $(\lambda y.P)Q \twoheadrightarrow_1 P'[y:=Q']$ and is a direct consequence of $P \twoheadrightarrow_1 P'$, $Q \twoheadrightarrow_1 Q'$. Then

$$\begin{aligned} M[x:=N] &\equiv (\lambda y.P[x:=N])(Q[x:=N]) \\ &\twoheadrightarrow_1 P'[x:=N'][y:=Q'[x:=N']], \quad \text{by the induction hypothesis,} \\ &\equiv P'[y:=Q'][x:=N'], \quad \text{by the substitution lemma 2.1.16,} \\ &\equiv M'[x:=N']. \quad \square \end{aligned}$$

3.2.5. LEMMA. (i) *$\lambda x.M \twoheadrightarrow_1 N$ implies $N \equiv \lambda x.M'$ with $M \twoheadrightarrow_1 M'$.*
(ii) *$MN \twoheadrightarrow_1 L$ implies either*

$$L \equiv M'N' \quad \text{with } M \twoheadrightarrow_1 M', N \twoheadrightarrow_1 N',$$

or

$$M \equiv \lambda x.P, L \equiv P'[x:=N'] \quad \text{and} \quad P \twoheadrightarrow_1 P', N \twoheadrightarrow_1 N'.$$

PROOF. By an easy induction on the definition of $\twoheadrightarrow_1$. □

3.2.6. LEMMA. *$\twoheadrightarrow_1$ satisfies the diamond property.*

PROOF. By induction on the definition of $M \twoheadrightarrow_1 M_1$ it will be shown that for all $M \twoheadrightarrow_1 M_2$ there is an M_3 such that $M_1 \twoheadrightarrow_1 M_3$, $M_2 \twoheadrightarrow_1 M_3$.

Case 1. $M \twoheadrightarrow_1 M_1$ because $M \equiv M_1$. Then we can take $M_3 \equiv M_2$.

Case 2. $M \twoheadrightarrow_1 M_1$ is $(\lambda x.P)Q \twoheadrightarrow_1 P'[x:=Q']$ and is a consequence of $P \twoheadrightarrow_1 P'$, $Q \twoheadrightarrow_1 Q'$. By lemma 3.2.5 one can distinguish two subcases.

Subcase 2.1. $M_2 \equiv (\lambda x.P'')Q''$ with $P \twoheadrightarrow_1 P''$, $Q \twoheadrightarrow_1 Q''$. By the induction hypothesis there are terms P''', Q''' with $P' \twoheadrightarrow_1 P'''$, $P'' \twoheadrightarrow_1 P'''$ and similarly for the Q's. Then by lemma 3.2.4 one can take $M_3 \equiv P'''[x:=Q''']$.

Subcase 2.2. $M_2 \equiv P''[x:=Q'']$ with $P \twoheadrightarrow_1 P''$, $Q \twoheadrightarrow_1 Q''$. Then, using the induction hypothesis, one can take again $M_3 \equiv P'''[x:=Q''']$.

Case 3. $M \twoheadrightarrow_1 M_1$ is $PQ \twoheadrightarrow_1 P'Q'$ and is a direct consequence of $P \twoheadrightarrow_1 P'$, $Q \twoheadrightarrow_1 Q'$. Again there are two subcases.

Subcase 3.1. $M_2 \equiv P''Q''$ with $P \twoheadrightarrow_1 P''$, $Q \twoheadrightarrow_1 Q''$. Then, using the induction hypothesis in the obvious way, one can take $M_3 \equiv P'''Q'''$

Subcase 3.2. $P \equiv (\lambda x.P_1)$, $M_2 \equiv P_1''[x:=Q'']$ and $P_1 \twoheadrightarrow_1 P_1''$, $Q \twoheadrightarrow_1 Q''$. By lemma 3.2.5 one has $P' \equiv \lambda x.P_1'$ with $P_1 \twoheadrightarrow_1 P_1'$. Using the induction hypothesis in the obvious way one can take $M_3 \equiv P_1'''[x:= Q''']$; see figure 3.5.

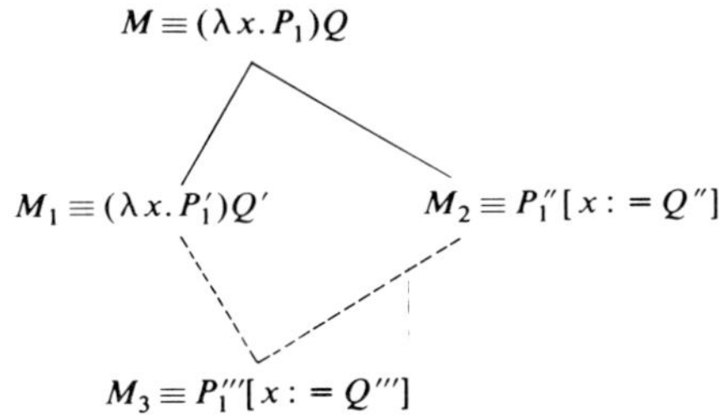

FIG. 3.5.

Case 4. $M \underset{1}{\twoheadrightarrow} M_1$ is $\lambda x.P \underset{1}{\twoheadrightarrow} \lambda x.P'$ and is a direct consequence of $P \underset{1}{\twoheadrightarrow} P'$. Then $M_2 \equiv \lambda x.P''$. By the induction hypothesis one can take $M_3 \equiv \lambda x.P'''$. □

3.2.7. LEMMA. *$\twoheadrightarrow_\beta$ is the transitive closure of $\underset{1}{\twoheadrightarrow}$.*

PROOF. Note that (for relations as sets of pairs) one has

$$\underset{=}{\to}_\beta \ \subseteq \underset{1}{\twoheadrightarrow} \subseteq \twoheadrightarrow_\beta$$

Since $\twoheadrightarrow_\beta$ is the transitive closure of $\underset{=}{\to}_\beta$, so it is of $\underset{1}{\twoheadrightarrow}$. □

3.2.8. THEOREM (Church–Rosser theorem).
(i) $\boldsymbol{\beta}$ *is* CR.
(ii) $M =_\beta N \Rightarrow \exists Z[M \twoheadrightarrow_\beta Z \wedge N \twoheadrightarrow_\beta Z]$.

PROOF. (i) By lemmas 3.2.2, 3.2.6, and 3.2.7.
(ii) By (i) and theorem 3.1.12. □

3.2.9. COROLLARY. (i) *If M has N as β-nf, then $M \twoheadrightarrow_\beta N$.*
(ii) *M can have at most one β-nf.*

PROOF. By corollary 3.1.13. □

For example it follows that $\boldsymbol{\Omega} \equiv (\lambda x.xx)(\lambda x.xx)$ does not have a β-nf. The only possible reduction path is

$$\boldsymbol{\Omega} \to_\beta \boldsymbol{\Omega} \to_\beta \cdots;$$

and as $\boldsymbol{\Omega}$ is not in β-nf, it does not have one.

Similar applications of corollary 3.2.9 will be frequently made.

3.2.10. THEOREM. (i) *Let* $M, N \in \beta$-NF *be distinct. Then* $M \neq_\beta N$.
(ii) *The theory* $\boldsymbol{\lambda}$ *is consistent.*

PROOF. (i) If $M =_\beta N$, then M would have two nf's, itself and N.
(ii) By proposition 3.2.1 one has $\boldsymbol{\lambda} \nvdash M = N$ for M, N as in (i). □

3.2.11. CONVENTION. The notion of reduction $\boldsymbol{\beta}$ will be used throughout this book. Therefore to simplify notation the subscripts will often be suppressed. That is

$$\to_\beta,\ \twoheadrightarrow_\beta,\ =_\beta,\ G_\beta(M),\ \beta\text{-NF},\ \beta\text{-}\infty(M)\ \text{and}\ \beta\text{-solvable}$$

will be denoted by

$$\to,\ \twoheadrightarrow,\ =,\ G(M),\ \text{NF},\ \infty(M)\ \text{and solvable.}$$

In this notation one has

$$\boldsymbol{\lambda} \vdash M = N \Leftrightarrow M = N$$

which is consistent, since one likes to suppress the $\boldsymbol{\lambda}\vdash$ anyway. The new notion solvable is the same as the old one by proposition 3.2.1.

The notation $\in_\beta$ will however not be replaced by $\in$ for obvious reasons.

3.3. Eta reduction

Another important notion of reduction is the following.

3.3.1. DEFINITION. (i) $\boldsymbol{\eta}: \lambda x.Mx \to M$ provided $x \notin \text{FV}(M)$; that is $\boldsymbol{\eta} = \{(\lambda x.Mx, M) | x \notin \text{FV}(M)\}$.
(ii) $\boldsymbol{\beta\eta} = \boldsymbol{\beta} \cup \boldsymbol{\eta}$.

The point of $\beta\eta$-reduction is that it axiomatizes provable equality in the extensional λ-calculus and it is CR.

3.3.2. PROPOSITION. $M =_{\beta\eta} N \Leftrightarrow \boldsymbol{\lambda\eta} \vdash M = N \Leftrightarrow \boldsymbol{\lambda} + \boldsymbol{ext} \vdash M = N$.

PROOF. By theorem 2.1.29 it is sufficient to prove only the first equivalence.
(⇐) By induction on the length of proof.
(⇒) Clearly $M \to_{\beta\eta} N \Rightarrow \boldsymbol{\lambda\eta} \vdash M = N$. Since $=_{\beta\eta}$ is the equality relation generated by $\to_{\beta\eta}$ and provability in $\boldsymbol{\lambda\eta}$ is an equality relation, the result follows. □

3.3.3. PROPOSITION. $\boldsymbol{\eta}$ *is substitutive.*

PROOF. Clearly $(\lambda x.Mx, M) \in \boldsymbol{\eta} \Rightarrow (\lambda x.M'x, M') \in \boldsymbol{\eta}$, where $M' \equiv M[y{:=}N]$ (by the variable convention $x \notin \mathrm{FV}(N)$). $\square$

To show that $\boldsymbol{\beta\eta}$ is CR we will use a method of Hindley [1964] and Rosen [1973].

3.3.4. DEFINITION. Let $\succ\!\!-_1$ and $\succ\!\!-_2$ be two binary relations on a set X. Then $\succ\!\!-_1$ and $\succ\!\!-_2$ *commute* if

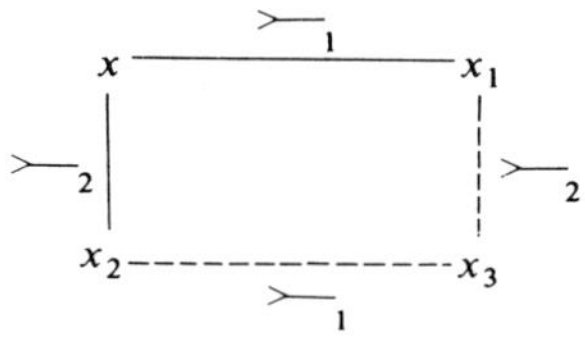

FIG. 3.6.

$\forall x, x_1, x_2 \in X[x \succ\!\!-_1 x_1 \wedge x \succ\!\!-_2 x_2 \Rightarrow \exists x_3 \in X[x_1 \succ\!\!-_2 x_3 \wedge x_2 \succ\!\!-_1 x_3]]$, see figure 3.6.

Note that $\succ\!\!- \models \Diamond$ iff $\succ\!\!-$ commutes with itself.

3.3.5. PROPOSITION (Lemma of Hindley–Rosen) (i) *Let* $\succ\!\!-_1$ *and* $\succ\!\!-_2$ *be two binary relations on a set* X. *Suppose*

(1) $\succ\!\!-_1 \models \Diamond$, $\succ\!\!-_2 \models \Diamond$.

(2) $\succ\!\!-_1$ *commutes with* $\succ\!\!-_2$.

Then $(\succ\!\!-_1 \cup \succ\!\!-_2)^* \models \Diamond$.

(ii) *Let* $\boldsymbol{R}_1$, $\boldsymbol{R}_2$ *be two notions of reduction. Suppose*

(1) $\boldsymbol{R}_1$, $\boldsymbol{R}_2$ *are* CR.

(2) $\twoheadrightarrow_{R_1}$ *commutes with* $\twoheadrightarrow_{R_2}$.

Then $\boldsymbol{R}_1\boldsymbol{R}_2$ *is* CR.

PROOF. (i) By a diagram chase suggested by figure 3.7.

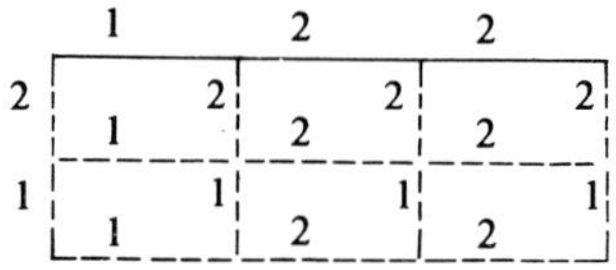

FIG. 3.7.

(ii) By (i), since $\twoheadrightarrow_{R_1R_2} = (\twoheadrightarrow_{R_1} \cup \twoheadrightarrow_{R_2})^*$. $\square$

3.3.6. LEMMA. *Let* $\succ\!-_1$, $\succ\!-_2$ *be two binary relations on a set* X. *Suppose*

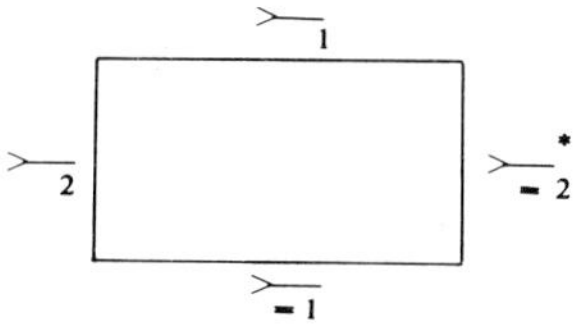

Then $\underset{=}{\succ\!-}^*_1$ *and* $\underset{=}{\succ\!-}^*_2$ *commute.*

PROOF. By a simple diagram chase. □

3.3.7. LEMMA. η *is* CR.

PROOF. Note that $\twoheadrightarrow_\eta = (\underset{=}{\rightarrow}_\eta)^*$, hence by lemma 3.2.2 it suffices to show that $\underset{=}{\rightarrow}_\eta$ satisfies the diamond property. For this proof write $\rightarrow$ for $\underset{=}{\rightarrow}_\eta$.

By induction on the definition of $M \rightarrow M_1$ it will be shown that for all $M \rightarrow M_2$ there is a common $\rightarrow$ reduct M_3 of M_1 and M_2.

If $M_1 \equiv M$, then one can take $M_3 \equiv M_2$. If $M_2 \equiv M$ or $\equiv M_1$, then one can take $M_3 \equiv M_1$. Therefore we may assume that $M_1 \not\equiv M$, $M_2 \not\equiv M$ and $M_2 \not\equiv M_1$.

Case 1. $M \rightarrow M_1$ is $\lambda x.Px \rightarrow P$. Then $M_2 \equiv \lambda x.P'x$ with $P \rightarrow P'$. Take $M_3 \equiv P'$.

Case 2. $M \rightarrow M_1$ is $ZP \rightarrow ZP'$ and is a direct consequence of $P \rightarrow P'$.

Subcase 2.1. $M_2 \equiv Z'P$ with $Z \rightarrow Z'$. Take $M_3 \equiv Z'P'$.

Subcase 2.2. $M_2 \equiv ZP''$ with $P \rightarrow P''$. By the induction hypothesis there is a P''' such that $P' \rightarrow P'''$, $P'' \rightarrow P'''$. Then take $M_3 \equiv ZP'''$.

Case 3. $M \rightarrow M_1$ is $PZ \rightarrow P'Z$. This case is treated as case 2.

Case 4. $M \rightarrow M_1$ is $\lambda x.P \rightarrow \lambda x.P'$ and is a direct consequence of $P \rightarrow P'$.

Subcase 4.1. $M_2 \equiv \lambda x.P''$ with $P \rightarrow P''$. Take $M_3 \equiv \lambda x.P'''$ by the induction hypothesis.

Subcase 4.2. $P \equiv P_0x$, $M_2 \equiv P_0$. Then $P' \equiv P_0'x$ and we can take $M_3 \equiv P_0'$. □

ALTERNATIVE PROOF. The above is all very well, but what really is going on is seen in figure 3.8.

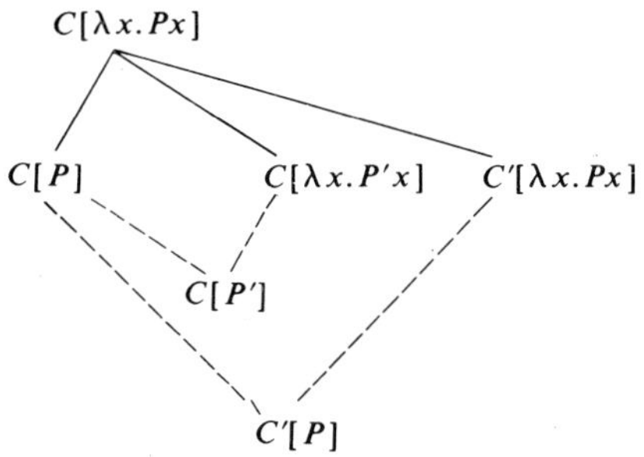

FIG. 3.8.

3.3.8. Lemma. $\twoheadrightarrow_\beta$ *commutes with* $\twoheadrightarrow_\eta$.

Proof. By lemma 3.3.6 it suffices to show

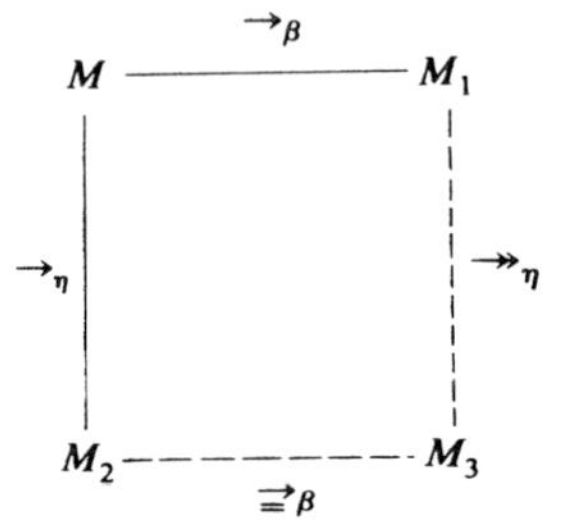

Again, what is really going on can be seen from the following three pictures:

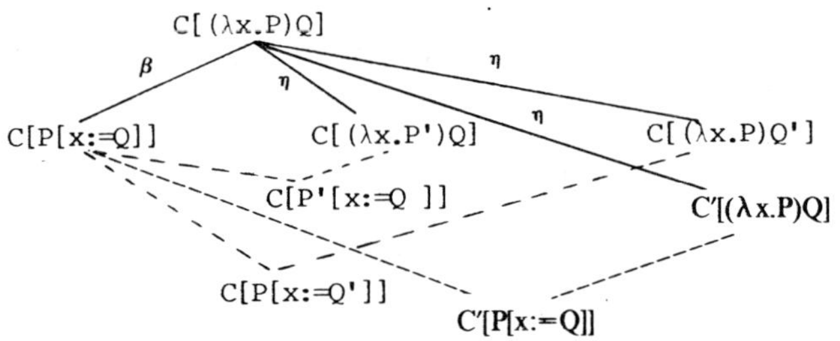

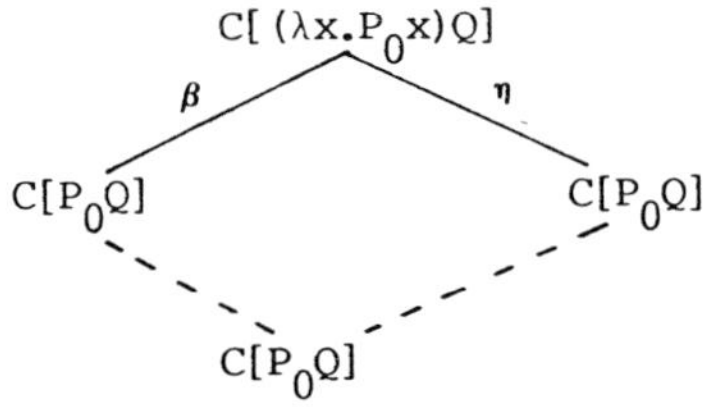

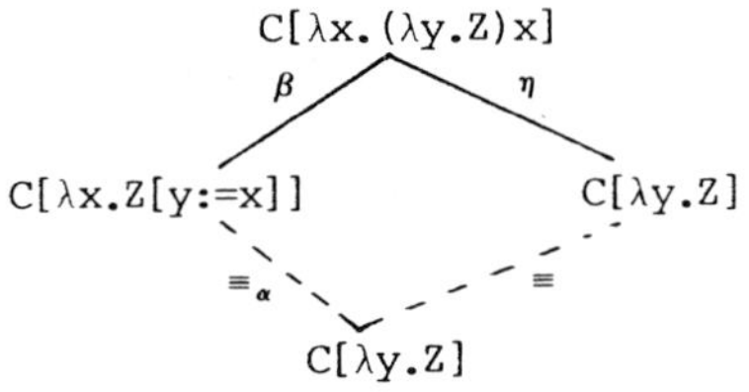

□

The following was first proved in Curry and Feys [1958] by a more complicated proof.

3.3.9. Theorem (*Church–Rosser theorem for βη-reduction*).

(i) *The notion of reduction* **βη** *is* CR.

(ii) $M =_{\beta\eta} N \Rightarrow \exists Z[M \twoheadrightarrow_{\beta\eta} Z \wedge N \twoheadrightarrow_{\beta\eta} Z]$.

PROOF. (i) By lemmas 3.3.7 and 3.3.8 using proposition 3.3.5.
(ii) By corollary 3.1.12. □

3.3.10. COROLLARY. (i) *If* M *has* N *as* $\beta\eta$-nf, *then* $M \twoheadrightarrow_{\beta\eta} N$.
(ii) *Each* M *has at most one* $\beta\eta$-nf.

PROOF. By corollary 3.1.13. □

In corollary 15.1.5 it will be proved that

$$M \text{ has a } \beta\text{-nf} \Leftrightarrow M \text{ has a } \beta\eta\text{-nf}.$$

3.3.11. THEOREM. (i) *Let* $M, N \in \beta\eta$-NF *be distinct. Then* $M \neq_{\beta\eta} N$.
(ii) *The theory* $\boldsymbol{\lambda} + \boldsymbol{ext}$ *is consistent.*

PROOF. As for theorem 3.2.10. □

Remember that for distinct $M, N \in \beta\eta$-NF one even has $M \# N$; see corollary 10.4.3.

The following is so obvious, that often it is not quoted explicitly: free variables cannot be created during a $\beta\eta$-reduction.

3.3.12. PROPOSITION. *Let* $M \twoheadrightarrow_{\beta\eta} N$. *Then*

$$x \in \mathrm{FV}(N) \Rightarrow x \in \mathrm{FV}(M).$$

PROOF. By induction on the definition of $\twoheadrightarrow_{\beta\eta}$. □

3.4. Survey of part III

Chapters 11, 12 and 13 are mainly about β-reduction on λ-terms. Chapter 14 studies reduction on a set of so called labelled λ-terms. This has applications on β-reduction itself and on the analysis in part V of several λ-models. Chapter 15 studies other notions of reduction in order to analyze λ-theories different from **λ**.

Chapter 11. Fundamental theorems

11.1. The Church–Rosser theorem

Although the CR theorem has been proved already in §3.2, a more perspicuous proof is given here. The technique involved is useful for the rest of the chapter.

11.2. The finiteness of developments

DEFINITION. Let M be a term and $\mathscr{F}$ a set of redexes in M. A *development* (relative to $\mathscr{F}$) of M is a reduction starting with M in which only redexes in $\mathscr{F}$ and their 'residuals' are contracted.

THEOREM. *Given M and $\mathscr{F}$ as above, then all developments of M are finite. All maximal developments of M end in the same term.*

Using this theorem still another proof of the CR theorem is given. In fact the proofs in §3.2 and §11.1 are both particular cases of this new proof.

11.3. Conservation theorem for $\boldsymbol{\lambda I}$

DEFINITION. An *I-redex* is a term $(\lambda x.M)N$ with $x \in FV(M)$.

THEOREM. *Let $M \overset{\Delta}{\rightarrow} N$ where Δ is an I-redex. Then $\infty(M) \Rightarrow \infty(N)$.*

COROLLARY. *If a λI-term has a* nf, *then each subterm has a* nf *as well.*

11.4. Standardization

DEFINITION. A reduction $\sigma\colon M \twoheadrightarrow N$ is *standard* if all contractions proceed from left to right, i.e. no redex is ever contracted which is a residual of a redex to the left of one already contracted. E.g.

$$\mathbf{I}((\lambda y.yy)a) \rightarrow \mathbf{I}(aa) \rightarrow aa$$

is not standard, but the following reduction is:

$$\mathbf{I}((\lambda y.yy)a) \rightarrow (\lambda y.yy)a \rightarrow aa.$$

THEOREM. *If $M \twoheadrightarrow N$, then there is a standard reduction from M to N.*

A short proof of this theorem is given, using §11.2.

11.5. Exercises

Chapter 12. Strongly equivalent reductions

12.1. Reduction diagrams

THEOREM. *Given* $\sigma: M \twoheadrightarrow N_1$, $\tau: M \twoheadrightarrow N_2$, *then there is a canonical way to obtain*:

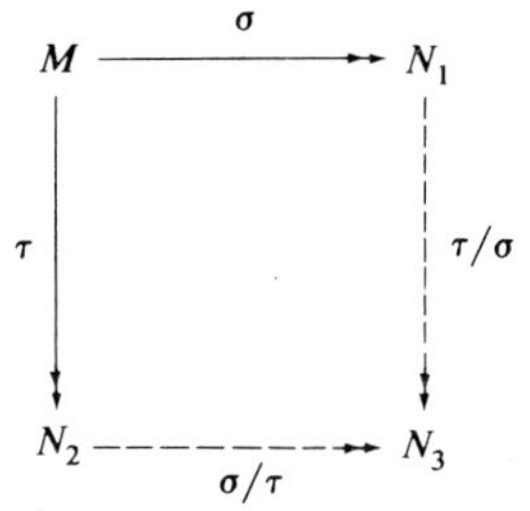

τ/σ (σ/τ *respectively*) *is called the projection of* τ *over* σ (σ *over* τ)

12.2. Strong versions of CR *and* FD!

DEFINITION. Let $\sigma: M \twoheadrightarrow N$ and $\tau: M \twoheadrightarrow N$. Then σ is *strongly equivalent* with τ (notation $\sigma \cong \tau$) if $\sigma/\tau = \tau/\sigma = \emptyset$ (the empty reduction).

THEOREM.

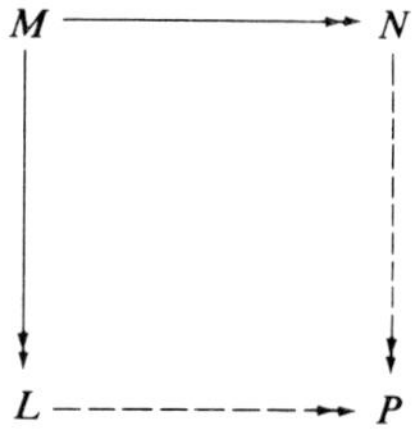

and the two reductions from M to P are strongly equivalent.

THEOREM. *Let M be given with a set* $\mathfrak{F}$ *of subredexes. Then all maximal developments of M are strongly equivalent.*

12.3. Strong version of standardization

THEOREM. *Let* $\sigma: M \twoheadrightarrow N$. *Then there is a unique* $\sigma_S \cong \sigma$ *such that* $\sigma_S: M \twoheadrightarrow N$ *is a standard reduction.*

12.4. Exercises

Chapter 13. Reduction strategies

13.1. Classification of strategies

DEFINITION. (i) A *reduction-strategy* F is a map F: $\Lambda \to \Lambda$ such that $M \twoheadrightarrow F(M)$ for all $M \in \Lambda$.

(ii) F is a *one step* strategy if for all M not in nf one has $M \to F(M)$.

(iii) F is *recursive* (respectively *effective*) if F is recursive (relatively simple to compute) after some coding to integers.

13.2. Effective normalizing and cofinal strategies

DEFINITION. A strategy F is *normalizing* if

$$M \text{ has a nf} \Rightarrow \exists n\ F^n(M) \text{ is a nf.}$$

THEOREM. *There exists an effective normalizing one step strategy.*

DEFINITION. A strategy F is *cofinal* if for all M, $N \in \Lambda$

$$M \twoheadrightarrow N \Rightarrow \exists n\ \ N \twoheadrightarrow F^n(M);$$

i.e. $\{F^n(M) | n \in \mathbb{N}\}$ is cofinal in $(G(M), \twoheadrightarrow)$.

THEOREM. *There exists an effective cofinal strategy.*

13.3. A recursive Church–Rosser strategy

DEFINITION. A strategy is *Church–Rosser* if

$$M = N \Rightarrow \exists n, m\ F^n(M) \equiv F^m(N).$$

THEOREM. *There exists a recursive* CR-*strategy.*

13.4. An effective perpetual strategy

DEFINITION. A strategy F is *perpetual* if

$$\infty(M) \Rightarrow M \underset{\neq\emptyset}{\twoheadrightarrow} F(M) \underset{\neq\emptyset}{\twoheadrightarrow} F^2(M) \underset{\neq\emptyset}{\twoheadrightarrow} \cdots$$

is an infinite reduction path.

THEOREM. *There exists an effective perpetual strategy.*

13.5. Optimal strategies

DEFINITION. (i) Let F, G be normalizing strategies. Then G is *t-better* than F if

$$\forall M \in_\beta \mathrm{NF} \quad \mu n[\,F^n(M) \text{ is a nf}\,] \geqslant \mu n[\,G^n(M) \text{ is a nf}\,],$$

but not conversely.

(ii) A one step strategy F is called *t-optimal* if F is normalizing and no one step strategy G is t-better than F.

THEOREM. *There is no recursive t-optimal one step strategy.*

13.6. Exercises

Chapter 14. Labelled reduction

14.1. Strong normalization

The set of labelled λ-terms is obtained by adding a constant $\perp$ and labels $\in \mathbb{N}$ to ordinary λ-terms. Labelled reduction is as ordinary β-reduction, except that labels are decreased and redexes with label 0 are contracted as follows: $(\lambda x.M)^0 N \to (M[x := \perp])^0$.

THEOREM. *All labelled reductions starting from a term M terminate.*

14.2. Applications

Using the results in §14.1 there are very fast proofs of the CR-, FD- and standardization-theorems. Some new results are proved as well.

14.3. Continuity

The following theorem has several applications. It is proved using the strong normalization theorem for labelled reduction.

CONTINUITY THEOREM. *Define* $f: \Lambda \to \Lambda$ *by* $f(M) = C[M]$ *for some context* $C[\ \ ]$. *Then f is continuous* w.r.t. *the tree topology on* Λ.

14.4. Sequentiality

It is proved that the λ-calculus computations are essentially sequential. A consequence is the following.

THEOREM. *Let* $P \approx Q$ *iff* $\mathrm{BT}(P) = \mathrm{BT}(Q)$. *Suppose* $\exists M_{ij}, P_i\ \forall M$

$$FMM_{12}M_{13} \approx P_1,$$

$$FM_{21}MM_{23} \approx P_2,$$

$$FM_{31}M_{32}M \approx P_3.$$

Then

$$\forall M_1M_2M_3 \quad FM_1M_2M_3 \approx P_1(\approx P_2 \approx P_3).$$

If P_1, P_2, P_3 are assumed to be in nf, then $\approx$ may be replaced by $=_\beta$.

14.5. Exercises

Chapter 15. Other notions of reduction

15.1. BH-reduction

THEOREM. $M \in \Lambda$ *has a* β-nf *iff* M *has a* $\beta\eta$-nf.

COROLLARY. M *is* β*-solvable* iff M *is* $\beta\eta$*-solvable*.

THEOREM. (postponement of η-reduction). *If* $M \twoheadrightarrow_{\beta\eta} N$, *then for some* L

$$M \twoheadrightarrow_\beta L \twoheadrightarrow_\eta N.$$

15.2. BHΩ-reduction

DEFINITION. Ω-reduction is defined by the contraction rule

$$\mathbf{\Omega} : M \to \mathbf{\Omega} \quad \text{if } M \text{ is unsolvable and} \not\equiv \mathbf{\Omega}.$$

THEOREM. $\boldsymbol{\beta\eta\Omega}$*-reduction is* CR.

THEOREM. $M \twoheadrightarrow_{\beta\eta\Omega} N \Rightarrow \exists L_1, L_2\ \ M \twoheadrightarrow_\beta L_1 \twoheadrightarrow_\Omega L_2 \twoheadrightarrow_\eta N.$

THEOREM. *Let* σ *be a cofinal reduction path in* $G_\beta(M)$ *such that infinitely many terms on* σ *are in* $\eta\Omega$-nf. *Then* σ *is cofinal in* $G_{\beta\eta\Omega}(M)$.

15.3. Δ-reduction

Delta reduction is not a particular notion of reduction but a collection of these. They are introduced in order to make some external functions φ on Λ definable. This is done by adding a new constant δ and postulating

$$\delta M \to \varphi(M).$$

A typical case is the following.

DEFINITION. Add to Λ a constant δ_C. Define on the extended set of terms the following notion of reduction.

$$\boldsymbol{\delta}_C: \begin{cases} \delta_C MM \to \mathbf{T} & \text{if } M \text{ is closed and in } \beta\delta_C\text{-nf}, \\ \delta_C MN \to \mathbf{F} & \text{if } M, N \text{ are closed and different } \beta\delta_C\text{-nf's}. \end{cases}$$

THEOREM. $\boldsymbol{\beta\delta}_C$ *is Church–Rosser.*

Some notions of delta reduction are not Church–Rosser in an unexpected way.

THEOREM. *Add to Λ constants δ, ε. Define on the extended terms the following notion of reduction*

$$\boldsymbol{\delta} : \delta MM \to \varepsilon .$$

Then $\boldsymbol{\beta\delta}$ is not Church-Rosser.

15.4. Exercises

This concludes the survey of part III.

3.5. Exercises

3.5.1. Draw $G(M)$ with
(i) $M \equiv (\lambda x.\mathbf{I}xx)(\lambda x.\mathbf{I}xx)$.
(ii) $M \equiv (\lambda x.\mathbf{I}(xx))(\lambda x.\mathbf{I}(xx))$.
(iii) $M \equiv \mathbf{WI}(\mathbf{WI})$, with $\mathbf{W} \equiv \lambda xy.xyy$.
(iv) $M \equiv \mathbf{KI}\Omega$.
(v) $M \equiv \mathbf{II}(\mathbf{III})$.

3.5.2. Find terms with the following β-graphs:
(i)

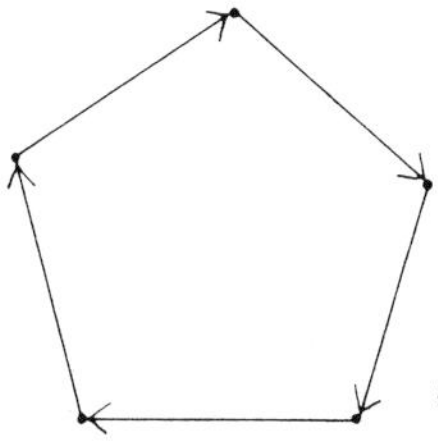

; generalize to n.

(ii)

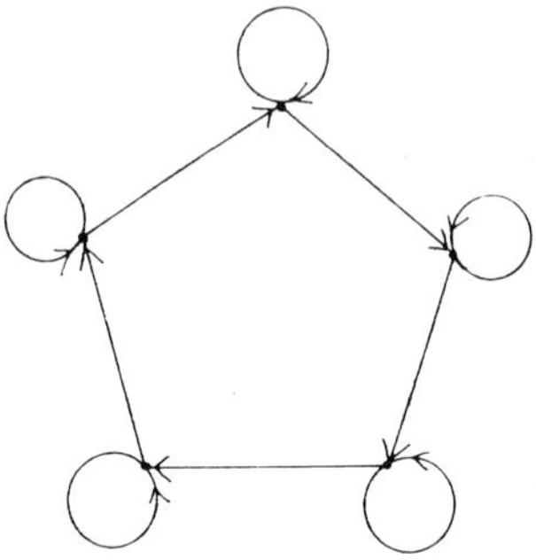

(iii)

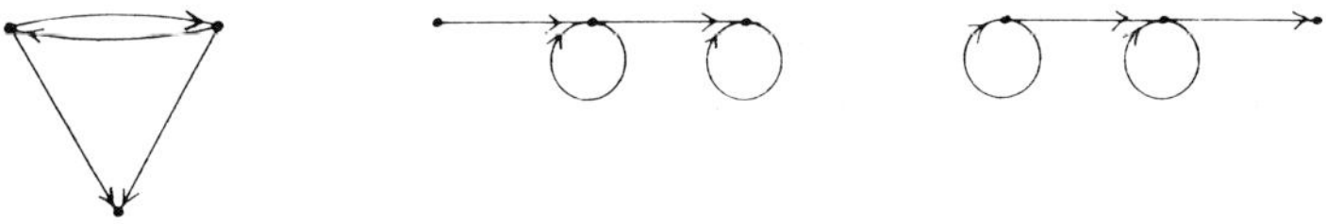

(iv)

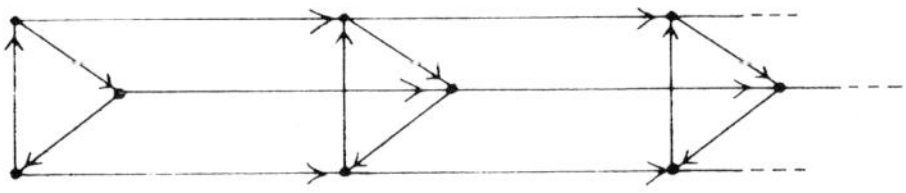

3.5.3. Construct a term M_0 such that

$$M_0 \twoheadrightarrow_\beta M_1 \rightarrow_\eta M_2 \twoheadrightarrow_\beta M_3 \rightarrow_\eta M_4 \twoheadrightarrow_\beta \cdots$$

*3.5.4. Let $M \equiv (\lambda bxz.z(bbx))(\lambda bxz.z(bbx))x$. Construct $G(M)$. Note that this graph has for each n as subgraph the n-dimensional cube. [*Hint.* Make systematic abbreviations.]

*3.5.5. (Böhm). Draw $G(M)$ with

(i) $M \equiv H\mathsf{I}H$ and $H \equiv \lambda xy.x(\lambda z.yzy)x$

(ii) $M \equiv LL\mathsf{I}$ and $L \equiv \lambda xy.x(yy)x$

(iii) $M \equiv PQ$ and $P \equiv \lambda u.u\mathsf{I}u$, $Q \equiv \lambda xy.xy\mathsf{I}(xy)$.

*3.5.6. (Visser). (i) Show that there is essentially only one term M such that $G(M)$ is

(ii) Show that there is no term M with $G(M)$

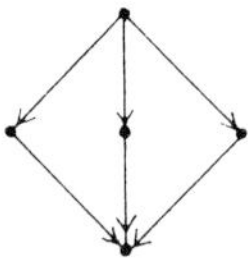

[*Hint.* Consider the relative positions of redexes.]

3.5.7. (i) Show that if G_1 and G_2 are the β-graphs of some term, then so is their cartesian product (see e.g. Harary [1969] for the definition).

(ii) If G is the β-graph of a term, then so is $G \leftrightarrow K_1$ (add one point that is below each point of G).

3.5.8. Show that if $\rightarrowtail_1$ and $\rightarrowtail_2$ are two commuting binary relations on a set X, then $\rightarrowtail^*_1$ and $\rightarrowtail^*_2$ commute.

3.5.9 Let $\boldsymbol{R}$ be a notion of reduction. Show that if R-SN(M) and each R-redex has only finitely many contracta, then $G_R(M)$ is finite.

3.5.10. (Hindley; Rosser; Staples). (i) Give an example of a binary relation $\succ\!\!-$ on a set X such that

(1) $\succ\!\!-$ satisfies the weak diamond property;

(2) $\succ\!\!\underline{-}^*$ does not satisfy the diamond property.

(ii) As (i) but with the extra condition

(3) X is finite.

3.5.11. Write $M\uparrow N$ if $L\twoheadrightarrow M$ and $L\twoheadrightarrow N$ for some L. Show:

(i) **KIK**$\uparrow$**KIS**.

(ii) $(\lambda x.ax)b\uparrow(\lambda y.yb)a$.

(iii) $(\lambda x.xc)c\uparrow(\lambda x.xx)c$.

(iv) $(\lambda x.bx)c\uparrow(\lambda x.x)bc$.

(v) $(\lambda x.bx(bx))c\uparrow(\lambda x.xx)(bc)$.

(vi) $(\lambda x.bx)c\uparrow(\lambda x.x)(bc)$.

*(vii) (Plotkin).$(\lambda x.bx(bc))c\not\uparrow(\lambda x.xx)(bc)$. Conclude that the "upside down CR property" does not hold.

3.5.12. (Klop). Let $\mathfrak{A} = (X, \succ\!\!-)$ where $\succ\!\!-$ is a binary relation. Define

(1) $x\succ\!\!-_n y$ if $\exists x_1, \ldots, x_n\ x = x_1\succ\!\!-x_2\succ\!\!- \cdots \succ\!\!-x_n = y$.

(2) $x\succ\!\!\underline{-}^* y$ if $\exists n\ x\succ\!\!-_n y$;

(3) $\mathfrak{A}\models \mathrm{WCR}(n, m)$ if

$$\forall x, x_1, x_2\quad [x\succ\!\!-_n x_1\wedge x\succ\!\!-_m x_2\Rightarrow\exists x_3[x_1\succ\!\!\underline{-}^* x_3\wedge x_2\succ\!\!\underline{-}^* x_3]].$$

(4) $B\subseteq \mathbb{N}^2$ is *closed* if $(n, m)\in B\Rightarrow(m, n)\in B$ and $(n+1, m)\in B\Rightarrow(n, m)\in B$.

(5) $\mathrm{WCR}(\mathfrak{A}) = \{(n, m)|\mathfrak{A}\models \mathrm{WCR}(n, m)\}$.

(i) Show that $\mathrm{WCR}(\mathfrak{A})$ is closed and that

$$\succ\!\!\underline{-}^*\models\Diamond\Leftrightarrow \mathrm{WCR}(\mathfrak{A}) = \mathbb{N}^2$$

$$\Leftrightarrow \mathrm{WCR}(\mathfrak{A}) \text{ is infinite}$$

$$\Leftrightarrow\forall n(1, n)\in \mathrm{WCR}(\mathfrak{A}).$$

(ii) Let $B\subseteq\mathbb{N}^2$ be a finite closed set. Construct an $\mathfrak{A} = (X, \succ\!\!-)$ such that $\mathrm{WCR}(\mathfrak{A}) = B$.

3.5.13. Let $\boldsymbol{R}$ be a notion of reduction such that if M has N as R-nf, then $M\twoheadrightarrow_R N$. Show that each term has at most one R-nf.

3.5.14 (D. Isles, Klop). Define

$$\mathrm{SN}_0 = \{M\in\Lambda|\mathrm{SN}(M)\},$$

$$\mathrm{SN}_{n+1} = \left\{M\in\Lambda|\forall\vec{N}\in\mathrm{SN}_n M\vec{N}\in\mathrm{SN}_n\right\}.$$

Show that $\mathrm{SN}_0\supsetneq\mathrm{SN}_1 = \mathrm{SN}_2 = \cdots$.

3.5.15. Let $\boldsymbol{R}$ be a notion of reduction. Write $x\in_R M$ if

$$\forall N =_R M\ x\in \mathrm{FV}(N).$$

Note that if $x\in_R M$ and $x\notin \mathrm{FV}(N)$, then $M\neq_R N$.

(i) Show that if $\boldsymbol{R}$ is CR and does not create variables (i.e. $M\twoheadrightarrow_R N\Rightarrow \mathrm{FV}(N)\subseteq \mathrm{FV}(M)$), then $x\in_R M$ iff

$$\forall N[M\twoheadrightarrow_R N\Rightarrow x\in \mathrm{FV}(N)].$$

(ii) Let $A_x = \lambda p.ppx$, $B_x = A_xA_x$. Show that $B_x\neq_{\beta\eta}B_y$ for $x\not\equiv y$.

CHAPTER 4

THEORIES

4.1. Lambda theories

Lambda theories are consistent extensions of the λ-calculus that are closed under derivations. They are studied because of their own interest and because there are applications to ordinary λ-conversion.

Remember that a (closed) equation is a formula of the form $M = N$ (with $M, N \in \Lambda^0$). If $\mathfrak{T}$ is a set of equations, then the theory $\boldsymbol{\lambda} + \mathfrak{T}$ is obtained by adding to the axioms and rules of the λ-calculus the equations in $\mathfrak{T}$ as new axioms.

4.1.1. Definition. Let $\mathfrak{T}$ be a set of closed equations.

(i) $\mathfrak{T}^+$ is the set of closed equations provable in $\boldsymbol{\lambda} + \mathfrak{T}$.

(ii) $\mathfrak{T}$ is a $\boldsymbol{\lambda}$-*theory* if $\mathfrak{T}$ is consistent and $\mathfrak{T}^+ = \mathfrak{T}$.

By corollary 2.1.38 both $\boldsymbol{\lambda}$ and $\boldsymbol{\lambda\eta}$ are $\boldsymbol{\lambda}$-theories.

4.1.2. Remarks. (i) Since the rule ξ is in $\boldsymbol{\lambda}$, each λ-theory $\mathfrak{T}$ is closed under ξ and hence $\mathfrak{T} \vdash M = N \Leftrightarrow \mathfrak{T} \vdash \lambda x.M = \lambda x.N$. The $\Leftarrow$ follows since $(\lambda x.M)x = M$ in $\mathfrak{T}$.

(ii) By (i) it follows that it does not matter to restrict ourselves in 4.1.1 to sets of closed equations.

(iii) Clearly $\mathrm{Con}(\mathfrak{T}) \Leftrightarrow \boldsymbol{\lambda} + \mathfrak{T} \nvdash \mathsf{T} = \mathsf{F}$.

For the λI-calculus one has $\mathrm{Con}(\mathfrak{T}) \Leftrightarrow \boldsymbol{\lambda} + \mathfrak{T} \nvdash \mathsf{I} = \mathsf{S}$; this follows from Böhm's theorem 10.5.31 for $\boldsymbol{\lambda I}$.

(iv) Each λ-theory is identified with the set of closed equations provable in it. In particular, $\boldsymbol{\lambda} = \{M = N \mid M, N \in \Lambda^0 \text{ and } \boldsymbol{\lambda} \vdash M = N\}$.

4.1.3. Proposition. *Let* $\mathfrak{T}$ *be a* λ-*theory. Then*

(i) $\mathfrak{T} \vdash M = M' \Rightarrow \mathfrak{T} \vdash C[M] = C[M']$,

(ii) $\mathfrak{T} \vdash M = M',\ \mathfrak{T} \vdash N = N' \Rightarrow \mathfrak{T} \vdash M[x := N] = M'[x := N']$.

Proof. (i) By induction on the structure of $C[\ \ ]$.

(ii) Assume $\mathfrak{T} \vdash M = M'$. Then by (i) $\mathfrak{T} \vdash (\lambda x.M)N = (\lambda x.M')N$ hence

$$\mathfrak{T} \vdash M[x := N] = M'[x := N].$$

If moreover $\mathcal{T} \vdash N = N'$, then by (i) $\mathcal{T} \vdash M'[x:= N] = M'[x:= N']$ and we are done. □

4.1.4. NOTATION. Let $\mathcal{T}$ be a λ-theory.

(i) $\mathcal{T} \vdash M = N$ stands for $\boldsymbol{\lambda} + \mathcal{T} \vdash M = N$; this is also written as $M =_{\mathcal{T}} N$.

(ii) $\mathcal{T} + M = N$ stands for $(\mathcal{T} \cup \{M = N\})^+$.

(iii) $\mathcal{T}\boldsymbol{\eta}$ stands for $(\boldsymbol{\lambda\eta} + \mathcal{T})^+$.

(iv) If $\mathcal{T} = (\mathcal{T}_0)^+$, then $\mathcal{T}$ is said to be axiomatized by $\mathcal{T}_0$.

(v) Write $x \in_{\mathcal{T}} M$ if $\forall N =_{\mathcal{T}} M\ x \in \mathrm{FV}(N)$; see exercise 3.5.15.

(vi) $M \in_{\mathcal{T}} \mathcal{X}$ if $\exists N =_{\mathcal{T}} M\ N \in \mathcal{X}$.

(vii) $\mathbf{1} \equiv \lambda xy.xy$, Church's numeral 1.

4.1.5. LEMMA. *For a λ-theory $\mathcal{T}$ one has $\mathcal{T}\boldsymbol{\eta} = \mathcal{T} + (\mathsf{I} = \mathbf{1})$.*

PROOF. Clearly $\boldsymbol{\lambda\eta} \vdash \mathsf{I} = \mathbf{1}$, hence $\mathcal{T}\boldsymbol{\eta} \vdash \mathsf{I} = \mathbf{1}$. Conversely

$$\begin{aligned}\boldsymbol{\lambda} + (\mathsf{I} = \mathbf{1}) \vdash \lambda y.My &= \mathbf{1}M \quad \text{if } y \notin \mathrm{FV}(M)\\ &= \mathsf{I}M = M.\end{aligned}$$

Hence $\boldsymbol{\lambda} + (\mathsf{I} = \mathbf{1}) = \boldsymbol{\lambda\eta}$. □

An important λ-theory is obtained following proposal 2.2.14 to identify unsolvable terms.

4.1.6. DEFINITION. (i) $\mathcal{H}_0 = \{M = N \mid M, N \in \Lambda^0, \text{ unsolvable}\}$.

(ii) $\mathcal{H} = \mathcal{H}_0^+$.

In §16.1 the consistency of $\mathcal{H}$ and $\mathcal{H}\boldsymbol{\eta}$ will be proved via the CR property for an appropriate notion of reduction. In chapter 19 model theoretic proofs of these facts will be given.

Although

$$\boldsymbol{\lambda},\ \boldsymbol{\lambda\eta},\ \mathcal{H},\ \mathcal{H}\boldsymbol{\eta}$$

are all λ-theories, in general

$$\mathrm{Con}(\mathcal{T}) \not\Rightarrow \mathrm{Con}(\mathcal{T}\boldsymbol{\eta});$$

see corollary 15.3.7. If $\mathcal{T}$ is semi-sensible, to be defined below, then the implication does hold, however; see corollary 17.1.2.

4.1.7. DEFINITION. Let $\mathcal{T}$ be a λ-theory.

(i) $\mathcal{T}$ is *r.e.* if after coding $\mathcal{T}$ is a recursively enumerable set of integers.

(ii) $\mathcal{T}$ is *sensible* if $\mathcal{H} \subseteq \mathcal{T}$.

(iii) $\mathcal{T}$ is *semi sensible* (*s.s.*) if $\mathcal{T}$ does not equate a solvable and an unsolvable term.

Clearly both $\boldsymbol{\lambda}$ and $\boldsymbol{\lambda\eta}$ are r.e. theories. Moreover both $\boldsymbol{\lambda}$ and $\boldsymbol{\lambda\eta}$ are s.s. as will be proved in §17.1.

Remember that $M \# N$ stands for $\neg\text{Con}(M=N)$. $M \#_I N$ stands for $\neg\text{Con}(\boldsymbol{\lambda I}+M=N)$.

4.1.8. LEMMA. (i) *Let* $\mathbf{K}^\infty$ *be a fixed point of* $\mathbf{K}$. *Then* $\mathbf{I} \# \mathbf{K}^\infty$.

(ii) (*Jacopini* [1975]). *Let* $\omega_3 \equiv \lambda x.xxx$ *and* $\boldsymbol{\Omega}_3 \equiv \omega_3\omega_3$. *Then* $\mathbf{I} \#_I \boldsymbol{\Omega}_3$.

PROOF. (i) First note that $\mathbf{K}^\infty x = \mathbf{K}\mathbf{K}^\infty x = \mathbf{K}^\infty$. Hence

$$\mathbf{I}=\mathbf{K}^\infty \vdash M = \mathbf{I}M = \mathbf{K}^\infty M = \mathbf{K}^\infty = \mathbf{K}^\infty N = \mathbf{I}N = N.$$

(ii) Note that $\boldsymbol{\Omega}_3 \equiv \omega_3\omega_3 = \omega_3\omega_3\omega_3 \equiv \boldsymbol{\Omega}_3\omega_3$. Hence

$$\mathbf{I}=\boldsymbol{\Omega}_3 \vdash \mathbf{I} = \boldsymbol{\Omega}_3 = \boldsymbol{\Omega}_3\omega_3 = \mathbf{I}\omega_3 = \omega_3.$$

Since $\mathbf{I}$ and ω_3 are different $\beta\eta$-nf's, one has by Böhm's theorem for $\boldsymbol{\lambda I}$, theorem 10.5.31, that $\mathbf{I} \#_I \omega_3$; hence we are done. □

4.1.9. COROLLARY. $\mathcal{T}$ *sensible* $\Rightarrow \mathcal{T}$ *semi sensible*.

PROOF. Suppose $\mathcal{T}$ is not s.s., i.e. for some solvable M and unsolvable N $\mathcal{T} \vdash M=N$. By taking closures it may be assumed that $M, N \in \Lambda^0$. Hence $M\vec{P}=\mathbf{I}$ and still $N\vec{P}$ is unsolvable for some $\vec{P}$. Therefore

$$\mathcal{H} \vdash N\vec{P} = \square$$

where $\square$ is $\mathbf{K}^\infty$ or $\boldsymbol{\Omega}_3$ (clearly $\square$ is unsolvable). It follows that

$$\mathcal{H} \subseteq \mathcal{T} \vdash \mathbf{I} = M\vec{P} = N\vec{P} = \square$$

and hence by lemma 4.1.8 $\mathcal{T}$ is inconsistent, a contradiction. □

Rules

The rule of extensionality (***ext***) and the rule ξ were introduced in chapter 2:

$$\textbf{\textit{ext}}: Mx = Nx, x \notin \text{FV}(MN) \Rightarrow M = N.$$

$$\xi: M = N \Rightarrow \lambda x.M = \lambda x.N.$$

The following rules are introduced to study models consisting exclusively of the interpretation of the closed terms.

4.1.10. DEFINITION. (i) The ω-*rule* is

$$\boldsymbol{\omega}: \forall Z \in \Lambda^0\, MZ = NZ \quad\Rightarrow\quad M = N.$$

(ii) The *term rule* is

$$\boldsymbol{tr}: \forall Z \in \Lambda^0 MZ = NZ \quad \Rightarrow \quad Mx = Nx, \quad \text{for arbitrary } x.$$

4.1.11. DEFINITION. Let $\mathfrak{T}$ be a λ-theory.

(i) $\mathfrak{T}$ is *closed under the ω-rule* notation $\mathfrak{T} \vdash \boldsymbol{\omega}$ if

$$\forall Z \in \Lambda^0 \quad \mathfrak{T} \vdash MZ = NZ \quad \Rightarrow \quad \mathfrak{T} \vdash M = N.$$

(ii) Similarly one defines $\mathfrak{T} \vdash \boldsymbol{R}$ for the other rules.
Note that, by definition, for every λ-theory $\mathfrak{T}$ one has $\mathfrak{T} \vdash \boldsymbol{\xi}$.

(iii) $\mathfrak{T}$ is *extensional* if $\mathfrak{T} \vdash \boldsymbol{ext}$.

4.1.12. LEMMA. (i) $\mathfrak{T} \vdash \boldsymbol{\omega} \Leftrightarrow \mathfrak{T} \vdash \boldsymbol{tr}$ *and* $\mathfrak{T} \vdash \boldsymbol{ext}$.

(ii) $\mathfrak{T} \vdash \boldsymbol{ext} \Leftrightarrow \mathfrak{T} \vdash \mathsf{I} = \mathbf{1} \Leftrightarrow \mathfrak{T} = \mathfrak{T}\boldsymbol{\eta}$.

PROOF. Trivial. (i) (⇐)

$$\forall Z \in \Lambda^0 \quad \mathfrak{T} \vdash MZ = NZ$$

$$\Rightarrow \mathfrak{T} \vdash Mx = Nx \quad \text{by } \boldsymbol{tr} \ (x \text{ fresh}),$$

$$\Rightarrow \mathfrak{T} \vdash M = N \quad \text{by } \boldsymbol{ext}.$$

(⇒)

$$\boldsymbol{tr}: \forall Z \in \Lambda^0 \mathfrak{T} \vdash MZ = NZ$$

$$\Rightarrow \mathfrak{T} \vdash M = N \quad \text{by } \boldsymbol{\omega},$$

$$\Rightarrow \mathfrak{T} \vdash Mx = Nx.$$

$$\boldsymbol{ext}: \ \mathfrak{T} \vdash Mx = Nx, \quad x \text{ fresh},$$

$$\Rightarrow \mathfrak{T} \vdash MZ = NZ \quad \text{for all } Z \in \Lambda^0, \text{ by proposition 4.1.3(ii)},$$

$$\Rightarrow \mathfrak{T} \vdash M = N \quad \text{by } \boldsymbol{\omega}.$$

(ii) By lemma 4.1.5 and theorem 2.1.29. □

4.1.13. NOTATION. For a λ-theory $\mathfrak{T}$ and a rule $\boldsymbol{R}$ let $\mathfrak{T} + \boldsymbol{R}$ or $\mathfrak{T}\boldsymbol{R}$ be

$$\{M = N \mid M, N \in \Lambda^0 \text{ and } \boldsymbol{\lambda} + \boldsymbol{R} + \mathfrak{T} \vdash M = N\}$$

in the obvious sense.

In general $\mathfrak{T}\boldsymbol{R}$ does not need to be a λ-theory; corollary 15.3.7 shows that $\neg\ \mathrm{Con}(\mathfrak{T}\boldsymbol{\eta})$ for some λ-theory $\mathfrak{T}$.

4.1.14. Definition. Let $\boldsymbol{R}^0$ be the rule $\boldsymbol{R}$ restricted to closed terms. E.g. $\boldsymbol{ext}^0$ is

$$Fx = F'x,\ F,\ F' \in \Lambda^0 \text{ and } x \notin \mathrm{FV}(FF') \quad \Rightarrow \quad F = F'.$$

4.1.15. Proposition. *Let* $\mathfrak{T}$ *be a λ-theory. Then*
(i) (*Hindley and Longo* [1980]). $\mathfrak{T} \vdash \omega^0 \Leftrightarrow \mathfrak{T} \vdash \omega$,
(ii) $\mathfrak{T} \vdash \boldsymbol{tr}^0 \Leftrightarrow \mathfrak{T} \vdash \boldsymbol{tr}$,
(iii) $\mathfrak{T} \vdash \boldsymbol{ext}^0 \not\Leftrightarrow \mathfrak{T} \vdash \boldsymbol{ext}$.

Proof. (i) ⇐. Trivial. ⇒. Suppose $\mathfrak{T} \vdash \omega^0$ and for $M, N \in \Lambda$ assume

$$(1) \qquad \forall Z \in \Lambda^0 \quad \mathfrak{T} \vdash MZ = NZ.$$

Let $\{\vec{x}\} = \mathrm{FV}(MN)$. Then $M \equiv M(\vec{x})$, $N \equiv N(\vec{x})$ and
$\forall \vec{P} \in \Lambda^0\ \forall Z \in \Lambda^0 \quad \mathfrak{T} \vdash M(\vec{P})Z = N(\vec{P})Z$, by (1),
$\Rightarrow \forall \vec{P} \in \Lambda^0 \quad \mathfrak{T} \vdash M(\vec{P}) = N(\vec{P})$ by ω^0,
$\Rightarrow \forall \vec{P} \in \Lambda^0 \quad \mathfrak{T} \vdash (\lambda\vec{x}.M(\vec{x}))\vec{P} = (\lambda\vec{x}.N(\vec{x}))\vec{P}$
$\Rightarrow \mathfrak{T} \vdash \lambda\vec{x}.M(\vec{x}) = \lambda\vec{x}.N(\vec{x})$ by ω^0,
$\Rightarrow \mathfrak{T} \vdash M = N$.
(ii) Similarly.
(iii) In exercise 16.5.2 it is shown that $\mathcal{H} \vdash \boldsymbol{ext}^0$ but $\mathcal{H} \nvdash \boldsymbol{ext}$. □

Term models

Although models will be treated in detail in chapter 5, it is useful to introduce already now the so called term models. These consist of the set of (closed) λ-terms modulo some λ-theory $\mathfrak{T}$ and reflect the properties of such a theory.

4.1.16. Definition. (i) A *combinatory algebra* is a structure

$$\mathfrak{M} = \langle X, \cdot, k, s \rangle$$

such that $\mathrm{Card}(X) > 1$ and $kxy = x, sxyz = xz(yz)$ are valid in $\mathfrak{M}$.
(ii) Moreover such a structure is *extensional* if in $\mathfrak{M}$

$$(\forall x\ ax = bx) \to a = b.$$

4.1.17. Definition. Let $\mathfrak{T}$ be a λ-theory.
(i) The (*open*) *term model* of $\mathfrak{T}$ is the structure

$$\mathfrak{M}(\mathfrak{T}) = \langle \Lambda / =_{\mathfrak{T}}, \cdot, [\mathbf{K}]_{\mathfrak{T}}, [\mathbf{S}]_{\mathfrak{T}} \rangle,$$

where for $M, N \in \Lambda$

$$M =_{\mathfrak{T}} N \Leftrightarrow \mathfrak{T} \vdash M = N,$$

$$[M]_{\mathfrak{T}} = \{N \in \Lambda | M =_{\mathfrak{T}} N\},$$

$$\Lambda / =_{\mathfrak{T}} = \{[M]_{\mathfrak{T}} | M \in \Lambda\},$$

$$[M]_{\mathfrak{T}} \cdot [N]_{\mathfrak{T}} = [MN]_{\mathfrak{T}}.$$

(ii) Similarly one defines the *closed term model*

$$\mathfrak{M}^0(\mathfrak{T}) = \langle \Lambda^0 / =_{\mathfrak{T}}, \cdot, [\mathbf{K}]_{\mathfrak{T}}, [\mathbf{S}]_{\mathfrak{T}} \rangle.$$

4.1.18. PROPOSITION. *Let $\mathfrak{T}$ be a λ-theory. Then*
(i) *$\mathfrak{M}(\mathfrak{T})$ and $\mathfrak{M}^0(\mathfrak{T})$ are combinatory algebras.*
(ii) *$\mathfrak{T} \vdash$ **ext** $\Leftrightarrow \mathfrak{M}(\mathfrak{T})$ is extensional.*
(iii) *$\mathfrak{T} \vdash \omega \Leftrightarrow \mathfrak{M}^0(\mathfrak{T})$ is extensional.*

PROOF. (i) Note that $[\mathbf{S}]_{\mathfrak{T}}, [\mathbf{K}]_{\mathfrak{T}} \in \mathfrak{M}(\mathfrak{T})$ satisfy the axioms for s and k Similarly for $\mathfrak{M}^0(\mathfrak{T})$.
(ii) ($\Rightarrow$) Suppose $[F]_{\mathfrak{T}}, [F']_{\mathfrak{T}} \in \mathfrak{M}(\mathfrak{T})$ and

$$\forall a \in \mathfrak{M}(\mathfrak{T}) \quad [F]_{\mathfrak{T}} a = [F']_{\mathfrak{T}} a.$$

In particular for some fresh variable x
$[F]_{\mathfrak{T}} [x]_{\mathfrak{T}} = [F']_{\mathfrak{T}} [x]_{\mathfrak{T}}$
$\Rightarrow [Fx]_{\mathfrak{T}} = [F'x]_{\mathfrak{T}}$
$\Rightarrow \mathfrak{T} \vdash Fx = F'x$
$\Rightarrow \mathfrak{T} \vdash F = F'$ since $\mathfrak{T} \vdash$ ***ext***,
$\Rightarrow [F]_{\mathfrak{T}} = [F']_{\mathfrak{T}}$.
($\Leftarrow$) Suppose for some fresh x

$$\mathfrak{T} \vdash Fx = F'x.$$

Then
$\mathfrak{T} \vdash FZ = F'Z$ for all $Z \in \Lambda$,
$\Rightarrow [F]_{\mathfrak{T}} [Z]_{\mathfrak{T}} = [F']_{\mathfrak{T}} [Z]_{\mathfrak{T}}$ for all $[Z]_{\mathfrak{T}} \in \mathfrak{M}(\mathfrak{T})$,
$\Rightarrow [F]_{\mathfrak{T}} = [F']_{\mathfrak{T}}$ since $\mathfrak{M}(\mathfrak{T})$ is extensional,
$\Rightarrow \mathfrak{T} \vdash F = F'$.
(iii) ($\Rightarrow$) As in (ii).
($\Leftarrow$) As in (ii) one can show $\mathfrak{T} \vdash \omega^0$. But then by proposition 4.1.15 (i) $\mathfrak{T} \vdash \omega$. □

REMARK. In general

$$\mathfrak{T} \vdash \boldsymbol{ext} \not\Rightarrow \mathfrak{M}^0(\mathfrak{T}) \text{ is extensional.}$$

This is so since $\boldsymbol{\lambda\eta} \vdash \boldsymbol{ext}$ but $\boldsymbol{\lambda\eta} \nvdash \omega$, as will be proved in §17.3. The ω-rule was introduced to study this situation.

4.1.19. DEFINITION. Let $\mathfrak{T}$ be a λ-theory. Then the *canonical map*

$$\varphi_{\mathfrak{T}} : \Lambda \to \mathfrak{M}(\mathfrak{T}) \text{ is defined by } \varphi_{\mathfrak{T}}(M) = [M]_{\mathfrak{T}}.$$

(ii) If $\mathfrak{T}_1$, $\mathfrak{T}_2$ are λ-theories with $\mathfrak{T}_1 \subseteq \mathfrak{T}_2$, then the canonical map

$$\varphi_{\mathfrak{T}_1,\mathfrak{T}_2} : \mathfrak{M}(\mathfrak{T}_1) \to \mathfrak{M}(\mathfrak{T}_2) \text{ is defined by } \varphi_{\mathfrak{T}_1,\mathfrak{T}_2}([M]_{\mathfrak{T}_1}) = [M]_{\mathfrak{T}_2}.$$

(iii) Similarly one defines canonical maps

$$\varphi^0_{\mathfrak{T}} : \Lambda^0 \to \mathfrak{M}^0(\mathfrak{T}) \quad \text{and} \quad \varphi^0_{\mathfrak{T}_1,\mathfrak{T}_2} : \mathfrak{M}^0(\mathfrak{T}_1) \to \mathfrak{M}^0(\mathfrak{T}_2).$$

4.1.20. LEMMA. *For the canonical maps one has the following commutative diagram*

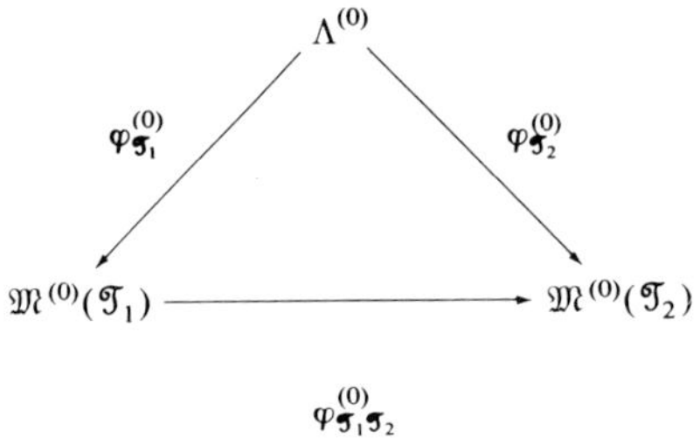

PROOF. Trivial. □

The canonical maps will be used to transfer topologies defined on Λ to term models.

Lambda theories are in fact non degenerate congruence relations on $\mathfrak{M}(\boldsymbol{\lambda})$. Next remark shows that these are less orderly than one would hope for.

4.1.21. REMARK. Combinatory algebras (allowing the trivial one point structure as a degenerate one) form an algebraic variety. Such a variety is called a *Mal'cev variety* if for each two congruence relations $\sim_1$, $\sim_2$ on a structure one has $\sim_1 \cdot \sim_2 = \sim_2 \cdot \sim_1$ ($\cdot$ denotes the product operation for binary relations). In exercise 16.5.8 it is shown that the combinatory algebras do *not* form a Mal'cev variety.

Completeness of theories.

4.1.22. DEFINITION. An equational theory $\mathfrak{T}$ is called *Hilbert Post* (HP)-*complete* if for every equation $M = N$ in the language of $\mathfrak{T}$

$$\mathfrak{T} \vdash M = N \quad \text{or} \quad \mathfrak{T} + (M = N) \text{ is inconsistent.}$$

The notion applies in particular to λ-theories. HP-complete theories correspond to maximally consistent theories in first order model theory. Note however the following difference. If $\mathfrak{A}$ is a first order structure then $\text{Th}(\mathfrak{A})$ is maximally consistent. But if $\mathfrak{M}$ is, say, a combinatory algebra, then

$$\text{Th}(\mathfrak{M}) = \{M = N \mid \mathfrak{M} \models M = N, \; M, N \in \Lambda^0\}$$

is not necessarily HP-complete. For example $\text{Th}(\mathfrak{M}(\boldsymbol{\lambda})) = \boldsymbol{\lambda}$ and this theory has many proper extensions.

By Zorn's lemma every λ-theory can be extended to a HP-complete one. It will be proved in §17.2 that $\mathcal{H}$ has a quite natural *unique* HP-complete extension $\mathcal{H}^*$.

4.2. Survey of part IV

Chapter 16. Sensible theories

This chapter is about λ-theories equating all unsolvable λ-terms.

16. The theory $\mathcal{H}$

In several ways it is shown that $\mathcal{H}$ and $\mathcal{H}\boldsymbol{\eta}$ are consistent. By relativizing to the λ*I*-calculus one obtains the consistency of

$$\boldsymbol{\lambda I} + \{M = N \mid M, N \in \Lambda_I^0 \text{ have no nf}\}.$$

It is proved that $\mathcal{H}$ is Σ_2^0-complete.

16.2. The theory $\mathcal{H}^*$

It will be proved that $\mathcal{H}$ has a unique maximal consistent extension $\mathcal{H}^*$. This theory is Π_2^0-complete. Moreover one has

$$\mathcal{H}^* \vdash M = N \Leftrightarrow M \simeq_\eta N.$$

In the λ*I*-calculus $\mathcal{H}^*$ is simply $\mathcal{H}\boldsymbol{\eta}$.

16.3. $2^{\aleph_0}$ sensible theories

An infinite set of combinators is constructed that is independent over $\mathcal{H}$. It follows that there are continuum many sensible theories.

16.4 The theory $\mathfrak{B}$

The continuity theorem implies that the theory $\mathfrak{B}$ identifying terms with equal Böhm tree is consistent.

A general scheme for defining λ-theories is given: if $\mathcal{P} \subseteq \Lambda$ is non trivial and closed under equality, then

$$\mathcal{T}_{\mathcal{P}} = \{ M = N \mid M, N \in \Lambda^0 \text{ and } \forall C[\ ][C[M] \in \mathcal{P} \Leftrightarrow C[N] \in \mathcal{P}]\}$$

is a λ-theory. One has $\mathcal{T}_{\mathrm{SOL}} = \mathcal{H}^*$ and $\mathfrak{B}\boldsymbol{\eta} \subseteq \mathcal{T}_{\mathrm{NF}} \subseteq \mathcal{H}^*$.

16.5. Exercises

Chapter 17. Other lambda theories

17.1. Semi-sensible and r.e. *theories*

It is shown that s.s. theories behave nicely:

$\mathcal{T}$ s.s. λ-theory $\Rightarrow \mathcal{T}\boldsymbol{\eta}$ s.s. λ-theory;

$\mathcal{T}, \mathcal{T}'$ s.s. λ-theories $\Rightarrow \mathcal{T} \cup \mathcal{T}'$ s.s. λ-theory;

$\mathcal{T}$ s.s. $\Leftrightarrow \mathfrak{M}(\mathcal{T})$ with its tree topology is not indiscrete.

For each r.e. theory $\mathcal{T}$ there is a term $\boldsymbol{\Omega}^*$ such that

$$\forall M \in \Lambda \quad \mathrm{Con}(\mathcal{T} + \boldsymbol{\Omega}^* = M).$$

Moreover r.e. theories are dense. As a consequence it follows that the reals can be embedded in the λ-theories partially ordered by $\subseteq$.

By defining a topology on term models of r.e. theories it is proved that all definable functions have as range a singleton or an infinite set.

17.2. Omega theories

It is shown that $\mathcal{H}^* \vdash \omega$. Alternatively, by an ordinal analysis the consistency of $\boldsymbol{\lambda\omega}$ is shown. As a consequence one obtains

$$\boldsymbol{\lambda\omega} \vdash M = \mathbf{I} \Rightarrow \boldsymbol{\lambda\eta} \vdash M = \mathbf{I}.$$

17.3. Partial validity of the ω-rule

It is shown that the ω-rule for M, N holds in $\boldsymbol{\lambda\eta}$ provided that M or N is not a $\beta\eta$-universal generator. The ω-rule for M, N holds in $\mathcal{H}\boldsymbol{\eta}$ provided that M or N has a $\beta\Omega$-nf.

17.4. Omega incompleteness

The ω-rule does not hold in general in $\lambda\eta$ or $\mathcal{H}\eta$, nor does the term rule in λ or $\mathcal{H}$.

It is shown that there is a term $\mathbf{\Pi}$ representing in $\mathcal{H}\omega$ universal quantification over $\mathbb{N}$:

$$[\forall n \in \mathbb{N}\ \mathcal{H}\omega \vdash F\mathbf{n} = F'\mathbf{n}] \Leftrightarrow \mathcal{H}\omega \vdash \mathbf{\Pi} F = \mathbf{\Pi} F'.$$

An argument is given for the conjecture that the theory $\mathcal{H}\omega$ is Π^1_1-complete.

17.5. Exercises

This completes the survey of part IV.

4.3. Exercises

4.3.1 Show that $\lambda x.x \# \lambda x.xxx$.

4.3.2 (Visser). $M \in \Lambda^0$ is called *easy* iff $\forall N \in \Lambda^0$ Con$(M = N)$. (In proposition 15.3.9 it is shown that Ω is easy) Suppose M is easy. Show

(i) $\forall N \in \Lambda^0 MN$ is easy.

(ii) M is unsolvable.

(iii) $\forall P_0, \ldots, P_n \in \Lambda^0$ Con$(M \ulcorner 0 \urcorner = P_0, \ldots, M \ulcorner n \urcorner = P_n)$.

(iv) For an arbitrary sequence $(P_n)_{n \in \mathbb{N}}$ of closed λ-terms Con$(\{M \ulcorner n \urcorner = P_n | n \in \mathbb{N}\})$. {*Hint*. Use (iii) and a compactness argument.]

(v) Con$(\{M = N | M, N \text{ easy}\})$.

4.3.3 Let $(\lambda)_C$ (respectively $(\lambda)_I$) be the classical (intuitionistic) first order theory, with Λ as terms and equations as atomic formulas, having as axioms

$$\neg \mathbf{K} = \mathbf{S},$$
$$(\lambda x.M)N = M[x := N],$$
$$(\forall x M = N) \to \lambda x.M = \lambda x.N.$$

(i) Show that $(\lambda)_C$ is conservative over λ, i.e.

$$(\lambda)_C \vdash M = N \Rightarrow \lambda \vdash M = N.$$

[*Hint*. Use that $\mathfrak{M}(\lambda)$ is a model of $(\lambda)_C$.]

(ii) Let ***TR*** be the rule

$$A(Z) \text{ for all } Z \in \Lambda^0 \Rightarrow \forall x A(x),$$

where A is any first-order formula. Show that $(\lambda)_C$ + ***TR*** is conservative over λ + ***tr***.

(iii) Let AC, the axiom of choice, be the scheme

$$\forall x\ \exists y\ A(x, y) \to \exists z\ \forall x\ A(x, zx).$$

Show that $(\lambda)_C + \boldsymbol{AC}$ is inconsistent. [in Barendregt [1973] it is shown that $(\lambda)_I + \boldsymbol{AC}$ is consistent and conservative over λ.]

(iv) Show that $(\lambda)_I + \boldsymbol{AC} \vdash \neg \forall x\ (x = I \vee x \neq I)$.

4.3.4. Show that $\neg\ \exists M\ \forall N$ Con$(\mathcal{H} + M = N)$.

CHAPTER 5

MODELS

In the type free λ-calculus the objects serve both as arguments and as functions to be applied to these arguments. Therefore one would like that a semantics for the λ-calculus consists of a domain D such that its function space D^D is isomorphic to D. By Cantors theorem this is impossible.

In 1969 Scott solved this problem by restricting D^D to the set of continuous functions with respect to some convenient topology on D. Because of Schönfinkels identification of $D^{D\times D}$ with $(D^D)^D$ it is natural to work with a class of topological spaces that form a cartesian closed category (ccc). For this reason Scott worked within the category of *complete lattices* with continuous maps and constructed an object D_∞ isomorphic to $D_\infty^{D_\infty}$, thus yielding an extensional model of the λ-calculus. Later it was found that for the construction of a λ-calculus model it is sufficient to have an object D in a ccc such that D^D is a retract of D. The graph model $P\omega$ is an example of this.

Some related cartesian closed categories are also of importance. First, the *continuous lattices* have a more natural relation between their lattice structure and topology. E.g. the topology of a product is the product of the respective topologies; this is false for complete lattices. Then there are the *complete partial orders* (cpo's) of which there are many more than the complete lattices. Plotkins [1978] model $\mathbb{T}^\omega$ is a cpo and not a complete lattice. Another useful category is that of *f_0-spaces* as defined by Ershov [1975]. These objects have the advantage of not having to be complete, e.g. the set of r.e. sets partially ordered by inclusion is an f_0-space. Scott [1982] gives an interesting alternative description of this category.

It took some time after Scott gave his model construction for consensus to arise on the general notion of a model of the λ-calculus. See Koymans [1982] for the history. Presently one considers two kinds of models, viz. the λ-algebras and the λ-models. The λ-algebras satisfy all provable equations of the λ-calculus and form an equational class (axiomatized by $kxy = x$, $sxyz = xz(yz)$ and the five combinatory axioms of Curry). Therefore the λ-algebras are closed under substructures and homomorphic images. The λ-models on the other hand satisfy all provable equations and moreover the axiom of weak extensionality

$$\forall x(M=N) \rightarrow \lambda x.M=\lambda x.N.$$

It turns out that λ-models can be described by first order axioms, but not by equations. Indeed λ-models are not closed under substructures nor under homomorphic images.

Besides the first order definition of λ-algebras and λ-models, there is a syntactical and also a categorical description of these classes. The syntactical description is convenient when calculating the interpretation of terms in a model. The categorical description of λ-algebras is rather natural and unifies the two concepts. It consists of a cartesian closed category $\mathbb{C}$ together with a so called reflexive object $U \in \mathbb{C}$, i.e. U^U is a retract of U: there are maps $F: U \rightarrow U^U$ and $G: U^U \rightarrow U$ such that $F \circ G = \mathrm{id}_{U^U}$. As shown in Koymans [1982], in this context a λ-model is a λ-algebra that arises from a category $\mathbb{C}$ with an object U that has "enough points".

Using the categorical description of the λ-calculus models, Scott [1980] makes the following philosophical remarks.

(1) The models for the type free λ-calculus come from ccc's with a reflexive object. The ccc's themselves correspond to the *typed* λ-calculus. (This connection was emphasized several times by Lambek, see e.g. his [1980].) Therefore the typed λ-calculus has priority over the type free theory.

(2) Let $\mathbb{C}$ be a ccc with reflexive object U. By the Yoneda lemma $\mathbb{C}$ can be embedded into a topos $\mathbb{D} = \mathrm{Set}^{\mathbb{C}^{\mathrm{op}}}$. Using the Kripke–Joyal semantics, inside $\mathbb{D}$ one has that U^U is the *full* function space of U and therefore the axiom of weak extensionality is satisfied by U in $\mathbb{D}$. The price one has to pay is to use intuitionistic logic, since classical logic is not sound for the Kripke–Joyal interpretation.

Some comments. As to (1), there are certainly nice results in the typed λ-calculus, for instance Statman [1980], [1982]. However, we disagree with Scott's conclusion that the typed λ-calculus has priority over the type free theory. Anyway not from a computational viewpoint: the typed λ-calculus (even in the presence of the recursor) can represent only a proper subset of the recursive functions, whereas the type free theory represents them all. As to (2), Scott's suggestion to make true the old dream of Church and Curry, namely $U^U \cong U$, inside a topos is very interesting indeed. In spite of not being weakly extensional, λ-algebras are worth studying; they are e.g. precomplete numbered sets in the sense of Ershov, see Visser [1980]. So now inside a proper topos these structures can be considered also as consisting of real functions.

5.1. Combinatory algebras

5.1.1. DEFINITION. (i) $\mathfrak{M} = (X, \cdot)$ is an *applicative structure* if $\cdot$ is a binary operation on X.

(ii) Such a structure is *extensional* if for $a, b \in X$ one has

$$(\forall x \in X\, a \cdot x = b \cdot x) \Rightarrow a = b.$$

Notation. (i) As in algebra, $a \cdot b$ is usually written as ab. If $\vec{b} = b_1, \ldots, b_n$, then $a\vec{b} = ab_1 \cdots b_n = (\cdots((ab_1)b_2) \cdots b_n)$.

(ii) If $\mathfrak{M} = (X, \cdot)$ then we write $a \in \mathfrak{M}$ instead of $a \in X$.

5.1.2. DEFINITION. Let $\mathfrak{M}$ be an applicative structure.

(i) The set of *terms over* $\mathfrak{M}$, notation $\mathfrak{T}(\mathfrak{M})$, is inductively defined as follows.

$$v_0, v_1, v_2, \ldots \in \mathfrak{T}(\mathfrak{M}), \qquad \text{(variables)}$$

$$a \in \mathfrak{M} \Rightarrow c_a \in \mathfrak{T}(\mathfrak{M}), \qquad \text{(constants)}$$

$$A, B \in \mathfrak{T}(\mathfrak{M}) \Rightarrow (AB) \in \mathfrak{T}(\mathfrak{M}).$$

Notation. $A, B, \ldots$ denote arbitrary terms and $x, y, \ldots$ arbitrary variables in $\mathfrak{T}(\mathfrak{M})$.

(ii) A *valuation* in $\mathfrak{M}$ is a map ρ: variables $\to \mathfrak{M}$. For a valuation ρ in $\mathfrak{M}$ the *interpretation* of $A \in \mathfrak{T}(\mathfrak{M})$ in $\mathfrak{M}$ under ρ (notation $(A)_\rho^{\mathfrak{M}}$ or $(A)_\rho$ or $(A)^{\mathfrak{M}}$ if $\mathfrak{M}$ or ρ is clear from the context) is inductively defined as usual:

$$(x)_\rho^{\mathfrak{M}} = \rho(x); \qquad (c_a)_\rho^{\mathfrak{M}} = a;$$

$$(AB)_\rho^{\mathfrak{M}} = (A)_\rho^{\mathfrak{M}}(B)_\rho^{\mathfrak{M}}.$$

(iii) $A = B$ is *true in* $\mathfrak{M}$ *under the valuation* ρ (notation $\mathfrak{M}, \rho \models A = B$) if $(A)_\rho^{\mathfrak{M}} = (B)_\rho^{\mathfrak{M}}$.

(iv) $A = B$ is *true* in $\mathfrak{M}$ (notation $\mathfrak{M} \models A = B$) if $\mathfrak{M}, \rho \models A = B$ for all valuations ρ.

(v) The relation $\models$ is also used for first order formulas over $\mathfrak{M}$. The definition is as usual.

FV(A) is the set of (free) variables in A. Clearly $(A)_\rho$ depends only on the values of ρ on FV(A). In particular for closed A (i.e. FV(A) $= \emptyset$) the interpretation $(A)_\rho$ is independent of ρ and may be denoted by (A).

5.1.3. DEFINITION (Curry). An applicative structure $\mathfrak{M}$ is a *combinatory complete* if for every $A \in \mathfrak{T}(\mathfrak{M})$ and $x_1 \cdots x_n$ with FV(A) $\subseteq \{x_1, \ldots, x_n\}$

one has in $\mathfrak{M}$

$$\exists f\ \forall x_1 \cdots x_n\ \ f x_1 \cdots x_n = A.$$

Note that an extensional applicative structure is combinatory complete iff for all $A \in \mathfrak{T}(\mathfrak{M})$ one has

$$\exists! f\ \forall \vec{x}\ \ f\vec{x} = A(\vec{x}).$$

5.1.4. NOTATION. (i) Let ρ be a valuation in $\mathfrak{M}$ and let $a \in \mathfrak{M}$. Then $\rho(x := a)$ is the valuation ρ' with

$$\rho'(x) = a,$$

$$\rho'(y) = \rho(y) \quad \text{if } y \not\equiv x.$$

(ii) If $\vec{x} = x_1, \ldots, x_n$ are distinct and $\vec{a} = a_1, \ldots, a_n$, then

$$\rho(\vec{x} := \vec{a}) = \rho(x_1 := a_1) \cdots (x_n := a_n).$$

(iii) $A[x := B]$ is the result of substituting the term B for x in A.

5.1.5. LEMMA. *Let $\mathfrak{M}$ be an applicative structure and $A, A', B, B' \in \mathfrak{T}(\mathfrak{M})$. Then*

(i) $(A[x := B])_\rho = (A)_{\rho(x := (B)_\rho)}$

(ii) $\mathfrak{M} \models A = A' \wedge B = B' \ \Rightarrow\ \mathfrak{M} \models A[x := B] = A'[x := B']$.

PROOF. (i) Induction on the structure of A.

(ii) By assumption $(A)_\rho = (A')_\rho$ and $(B)_\rho = (B')_\rho$ for all ρ. It follows that

$$(A[x := B])_\rho = (A)_{\rho(x := (B)_\rho)}, \qquad \text{by (i)},$$

$$= (A')_{\rho(x := (B')_\rho)} = (A'[x := B'])_\rho,$$

and we are done. □

5.1.6. DEFINITION. Let $\mathfrak{M} = (X, \cdot)$ be an applicative structure and let $\varphi : X^n \to X$ be a map.

(i) φ is *representable* over $\mathfrak{M}$ if

$$\exists f \in X \quad \forall \vec{a} \in X^n \ \ f\vec{a} = \varphi(\vec{a}).$$

(ii) φ is *algebraic* over $\mathfrak{M}$ if there is a term $A \in \mathfrak{T}(\mathfrak{M})$ with $\mathrm{FV}(A) \subseteq \{x_1, \ldots, x_n\}$ such that

$$(1) \qquad \forall \vec{a}\ \ \varphi(\vec{a}) = (A)_{\rho(\vec{x} := \vec{a})}.$$

(Clearly (1) does not depend on ρ).

Combinatory completeness says that all algebraic functions are representable. The converse is trivial. Schönfinkel showed that combinatory completeness follows from two of its instances.

5.1.7. DEFINITION. A *combinatory algebra* is an applicative structure $\mathfrak{M} = (X, \cdot, k, s)$ with distinguished elements satisfying

$$kxy = x, \qquad sxyz = xz(yz).$$

5.1.8. DEFINITION. Let $\mathfrak{M}$ be a combinatory algebra.

(i) Extend $\mathfrak{T}(\mathfrak{M})$ with new constants $\boldsymbol{K}$ and $\boldsymbol{S}$ denoting k, s respectively. Moreover define $\boldsymbol{I} = \boldsymbol{SKK}$.

(ii) For $A \in \mathfrak{T}(\mathfrak{M})$ and a variable x, define $\lambda^*x.A \in \mathfrak{T}(\mathfrak{M})$ inductively as follows:

$$\lambda^*x.x = \boldsymbol{I},$$

$$\lambda^*x.P = \boldsymbol{K}P, \quad \text{if } P \text{ does not contain } x,$$

$$\lambda^*x.PQ = \boldsymbol{S}(\lambda^*x.P)(\lambda^*x,Q).$$

(iii) Let $\vec{x} = x_1, \ldots, x_n$. Then $\lambda^*\vec{x}.A = (\lambda^*x_1 \cdots (\lambda^*x_n.A) \cdots)$.

5.1.9. PROPOSITION. (i) $\mathrm{FV}(\lambda^*x.A) = \mathrm{FV}(A) - \{x\}$.

(ii) $(\lambda^*x.A)x = A$, *in every combinatory algebra.*

(iii) $(\lambda^*\vec{x}.A)\vec{x} = A$, *in every combinatory algebra.*

PROOF. (i), (ii). Induction on the structure of A. Note that $\boldsymbol{I}x = \boldsymbol{SKK}x = \boldsymbol{K}x(\boldsymbol{K}x) = x$.

(iii) By (ii). $\square$

5.1.10. THEOREM. *An applicative structure $\mathfrak{M}$ is combinatory complete iff it can be expanded to a combinatory algebra (by choosing k, s). Hence every combinatory algebra is combinatory complete.*

PROOF. By proposition 5.1.9(iii). $\square$

5.1.11. REMARKS. (i) Note that a combinatory algebra $\mathfrak{M} = (X, \cdot, k, s)$ is nontrivial (i.e. $\mathrm{Card}(\mathfrak{M}) > 1$) iff $k \neq s$. Indeed, $k = s$ implies $a = s(ki)(ka)z = k(ki)(ka)z = i$ for all a, so $\mathfrak{M}$ is trivial.

(ii) When considering combinatory algebras, we usually tacitly assume that they are nontrivial.

5.1.12. DEFINITION. (i) Let $\mathfrak{M}_i = (X_i, \cdot_i, k_i, s_i)$, $i = 1, 2$, be two combinatory algebras. Then $\varphi: X_1 \to X_2$ is a *homomorphism* (notation $\varphi: \mathfrak{M}_1 \to \mathfrak{M}_2$) if φ

preserves application and k and s, i.e. $\varphi(x \cdot_1 y) = \varphi(x) \cdot_2 \varphi(y)$, $\varphi(k_1) = k_2$ and $\varphi(s_1) = s_2$.

(ii) $\mathfrak{M}_1 \to \mathfrak{M}_2$ if $\varphi : \mathfrak{M}_1 \to \mathfrak{M}_2$ for some φ.

(iii) $\mathfrak{M}_1$ is *embeddable* in $\mathfrak{M}_2$ ($\mathfrak{M}_1 \subsetneq \mathfrak{M}_2$) if $\varphi : \mathfrak{M}_1 \to \mathfrak{M}_2$ for some injective φ.

$\mathfrak{M}_1$ is a *substructure* of $\mathfrak{M}_2$ ($\mathfrak{M}_1 \subset \mathfrak{M}_2$) if $\varphi : \mathfrak{M}_1 \to \mathfrak{M}_2$ with φ the identity.

(iv) $\mathfrak{M}_1$ is *isomorphic* to $\mathfrak{M}_2$ ($\mathfrak{M}_1 \cong \mathfrak{M}_2$) if $\varphi : \mathfrak{M}_1 \to \mathfrak{M}_2$ for some bijective φ.

5.1.13. DEFINITION. (i) $\mathcal{C}$ is the set of terms of combinatory logic, i.e. applicative terms built up from variables and $\boldsymbol{K}, \boldsymbol{S}$ only.

$$\mathcal{C}^0 = \{ P \in \mathcal{C} | FV(P) = \emptyset \}.$$

(ii) Let $\mathfrak{M}$ be a combinatory algebra. Then

$$\mathrm{Th}(\mathfrak{M}) = \{ P = Q | \mathfrak{M} \models P = Q,\ P, Q \in \mathcal{C}^0 \}.$$

5.1.14. PROPOSITION. *Let $\varphi : \mathfrak{M}_1 \to \mathfrak{M}_2$. Then for $P, Q \in \mathcal{T}(\mathfrak{M}_1)$*

(i) $\varphi([\![P]\!]_\rho^{\mathfrak{M}_1}) = [\![\varphi(P)]\!]_{\varphi \circ \rho}^{\mathfrak{M}_2}$, *where $\varphi(P)$ results from P by replacing the constants c_a by $c_{\varphi(a)}$.*

(ii) $\mathfrak{M}_1 \models P = Q \;\Rightarrow\; \mathfrak{M}_2 \models \varphi(P) = \varphi(Q)$, *provided $P, Q \in \mathcal{C}^0$ or φ is surjective.*

(iii) $\mathrm{Th}(\mathfrak{M}_1) \subseteq \mathrm{Th}(\mathfrak{M}_2)$.

(iv) $\mathrm{Th}(\mathfrak{M}_1) = \mathrm{Th}(\mathfrak{M}_2)$, *provided that φ is injective.*

PROOF. (i) Induction on the structure of $P \in \mathcal{T}(\mathfrak{M})$.

(ii)
$$\begin{aligned} \mathfrak{M}_1 \models P = Q &\Rightarrow [\![P]\!]_\rho = [\![Q]\!]_\rho \quad \text{for all } \rho, \\ &\Rightarrow [\![P]\!]_{\varphi \circ \rho} = [\![Q]\!]_{\varphi \circ \rho} \quad \text{for all } \rho \text{ by (i)}, \\ &\Rightarrow [\![P]\!]_{\rho'} = [\![Q]\!]_{\rho'} \quad \text{for all } \rho' \text{ if } \varphi \text{ is surjective}, \\ &\Rightarrow \mathfrak{M}_2 \models P = Q. \end{aligned}$$

If $P, Q \in \mathcal{C}^0$ then their values do not depend on a ρ.

(iii) By (ii).

(iv) As for (ii). □

The axioms for combinatory algebras are suggested by the analysis of recursive processes, not by algebra. The following shows that these structures are in fact algebraically pathological.

5.1.15. PROPOSITION. *Combinatory algebras (except the trivial one) are*

(i) *never commutative,*

(ii) *never associative,*

(iii) *never finite,*

(iv) *never recursive.*

PROOF. (i) Suppose $ik = ki$. Then $k = ik = ki$, hence $a = kab = kiab = ib = b$ for all a, b and the algebra is trivial.

(ii) Similarly triviality follows from $(ki)i = k(ii)$.

(iii) Define $k_1 = k$, $k_{n+1} = kk_n$. Then the $k_1, k_2, \ldots$ are all distinct.

(iv) See exercise 7.4.14(iii). □

5.2. Lambda algebras and lambda models

Since in a combinatory algebra $\mathfrak{A}$ abstraction can be simulated by k and s, it is possible to interpret λ-terms in $\mathfrak{A}$.

NOTATION. Let C be a set of constants. $\Lambda(C)$ is the set of λ-terms possibly containing constants from C. The λ-calculus axioms and rules extend in the obvious way to equations $M = N$ with $M, N \in \Lambda(C)$. For these M, N we still write $\lambda \vdash M = N$. If $\mathfrak{M}$ is an applicative structure, then $\Lambda(\mathfrak{M})$ is $\Lambda(\{c_a | a \in \mathfrak{M}\})$.

5.2.1. DEFINITION. Let $\mathfrak{M}$ be a combinatory algebra.

(i) Define maps

$$CL: \Lambda(\mathfrak{M}) \to \mathfrak{T}(\mathfrak{M}),$$

$$\lambda: \mathfrak{T}(\mathfrak{M}) \to \Lambda(\mathfrak{M})$$

as follows; write M_{CL} for $CL(M)$ and A_λ for $\lambda(A)$.

$$x_{CL} = x, \qquad x_\lambda = x,$$

$$c_{CL} = c, \qquad c_\lambda = c,$$

$$(MN)_{CL} = M_{CL}N_{CL}, \qquad (AB)_\lambda = A_\lambda B_\lambda,$$

$$(\lambda x.M)_{CL} = \lambda^* x.M_{CL}, \qquad \mathbf{K}_\lambda = \lambda xy.x,$$

$$\mathbf{S}_\lambda = \lambda xyz.xz(yz).$$

We write $A_{\lambda,CL}$ for $(A_\lambda)_{CL}$ etcetera.

(ii) For $M, N \in \Lambda(\mathfrak{M})$ one defines

$$[\![M]\!]^{\mathfrak{M}}_\rho = [\![M_{CL}]\!]^{\mathfrak{M}}_\rho,$$

$$\mathfrak{M}, \rho \models M = N \iff [\![M]\!]^{\mathfrak{M}}_\rho = [\![N]\!]^{\mathfrak{M}}_\rho,$$

$$\mathfrak{M} \models M = N \iff \mathfrak{M}, \rho \models M = N \text{ for all } \rho.$$

If $\mathfrak{M}$ is a combinatory algebra and $a \in \mathfrak{M}$, then we write e.g. $\lambda x.xa$ for $[\![\lambda x.xc_a]\!]^{\mathfrak{A}}$.

Not all equations provable in λ-calculus are true in every combinatory algebra. E.g. if $\mathfrak{M}$ is the term model of $\boldsymbol{CL}$, then

$$\mathfrak{M} \not\models \lambda z.(\lambda x.x)z = \lambda z.z$$

since $((\lambda z.(\lambda x.x)z))_{CL} \equiv \boldsymbol{S}(\boldsymbol{KI})\boldsymbol{I}$ and $(\lambda z.z)_{CL} \equiv \boldsymbol{I}$; but $\lambda \vdash \lambda z.(\lambda x.x)z = \lambda z.z$.

5.2.2. DEFINITION. (i) A combinatory algebra $\mathfrak{M}$ is called a *λ-algebra* if for all $A, B \in \mathfrak{T}(\mathfrak{M})$

$$\lambda \vdash A_\lambda = B_\lambda \Rightarrow \mathfrak{M} \models A = B.$$

(ii) A λ-algebra *homomorphism* is just a combinatory algebra homomorphism.

5.2.3. LEMMA. *Let $\mathfrak{M}$ be a combinatory algebra. Then $\mathfrak{M}$ is a λ-algebra iff for all $M, N \in \Lambda(\mathfrak{M})$*

1. $\lambda \vdash M = N \Rightarrow \mathfrak{M} \models M = N$;
2. $\mathfrak{M} \models \boldsymbol{K}_{\lambda, CL} = \boldsymbol{K}, \qquad \mathfrak{M} \models \boldsymbol{S}_{\lambda, CL} = \boldsymbol{S}$.

PROOF. (⇒) First note that by induction on $M \in \Lambda(\mathfrak{M})$ one has $\lambda \vdash M_{CL, \lambda} = M$. Then

1. $$\begin{aligned} \lambda \vdash M = N &\Rightarrow \lambda \vdash M_{CL,\lambda} = N_{CL,\lambda} \\ &\Rightarrow \mathfrak{M} \models M_{CL} = N_{CL}, \qquad \text{since } \mathfrak{M} \text{ is a } \lambda\text{-algebra}, \\ &\Rightarrow \mathfrak{M} \models M = N, \qquad \text{by definition of } \models . \end{aligned}$$

2. Moreover for all $A \in \mathfrak{T}(\mathfrak{M})$ we have

$$\lambda \vdash A_{\lambda, CL, \lambda} = A_\lambda.$$

Therefore $\mathfrak{M} \models A_{\lambda, CL} = A$.

(⇐) First note that by induction on $A \in \mathfrak{T}(\mathfrak{M})$ it follows from 2 that $\mathfrak{M} \models A_{\lambda, CL} = A$. Hence

$$\begin{aligned} \lambda \vdash A_\lambda = B_\lambda &\Rightarrow \mathfrak{M} \models A_{\lambda, CL} = B_{\lambda, CL}, \qquad \text{by } 1, \\ &\Rightarrow \mathfrak{M} \models A = B. \quad \square \end{aligned}$$

5.2.4. PROPOSITION. (i) *If $\varphi : \mathfrak{M}_1 \to \mathfrak{M}_2$, then $\varphi[\![M]\!]^{\mathfrak{M}_1}_\rho = [\![\varphi(M)]\!]^{\mathfrak{M}_2}_{\varphi \circ \rho}$ for $M \in \Lambda(\mathfrak{M})$. In particular $\varphi[\![M]\!]^{\mathfrak{M}_1} = [\![M]\!]^{\mathfrak{M}_2}$ for $M \in \Lambda^0$.*

(ii) *Let* $\mathfrak{M}_1 \to \mathfrak{M}_2$. *Then* $\mathrm{Th}(\mathfrak{M}_1) \subseteq \mathrm{Th}(\mathfrak{M}_2)$. *Thus if* $\mathfrak{M}_1$ *is a* λ*-algebra, so is* $\mathfrak{M}_2$.

(iii) $\mathfrak{M}_1 \subset \mathfrak{M}_2 \;\Rightarrow\; \mathrm{Th}(\mathfrak{M}_1) = \mathrm{Th}(\mathfrak{M}_2)$.

PROOF. By proposition 5.1.14. □

By using Curry's combinatory axioms $\boldsymbol{A}_\beta$ one can axiomatize the class of λ-algebras.

5.2.5. THEOREM. *Let* $\mathfrak{M}$ *be a combinatory algebra. Then* $\mathfrak{M}$ *is a* λ*-algebra iff* $\mathfrak{M}$ *satisfies the following set of equations* $\boldsymbol{A}_\beta$:

(A.1) $\boldsymbol{K} = \boldsymbol{S}(\boldsymbol{S}(\boldsymbol{KS})(\boldsymbol{S}(\boldsymbol{KK})\boldsymbol{K}))(\boldsymbol{K}(\boldsymbol{SKK}))$,

(A.2) $\boldsymbol{S} = \boldsymbol{S}(\boldsymbol{S}(\boldsymbol{KS})(\boldsymbol{S}(\boldsymbol{K}(\boldsymbol{S}(\boldsymbol{KS})))$
$(\boldsymbol{S}(\boldsymbol{K}(\boldsymbol{S}(\boldsymbol{KK})))\boldsymbol{S})))(\boldsymbol{K}(\boldsymbol{K}(\boldsymbol{SKK})))$

(A.3) $\boldsymbol{S}(\boldsymbol{S}(\boldsymbol{KS})(\boldsymbol{S}(\boldsymbol{KK})(\boldsymbol{S}(\boldsymbol{KS})\boldsymbol{K})))(\boldsymbol{KK}) = \boldsymbol{S}(\boldsymbol{KK})$,

(A.4) $\boldsymbol{S}(\boldsymbol{KS})(\boldsymbol{S}(\boldsymbol{KK}))$
$= \boldsymbol{S}(\boldsymbol{KK})(\boldsymbol{S}(\boldsymbol{S}(\boldsymbol{KS})(\boldsymbol{S}(\boldsymbol{KK})(\boldsymbol{SKK})))(\boldsymbol{K}(\boldsymbol{SKK})))$,

(A.5) $\boldsymbol{S}(\boldsymbol{K}(\boldsymbol{S}(\boldsymbol{KS})))(\boldsymbol{S}(\boldsymbol{KS})(\boldsymbol{S}(\boldsymbol{KS})))$
$= \boldsymbol{S}(\boldsymbol{S}(\boldsymbol{KS})(\boldsymbol{S}(\boldsymbol{KK})(\boldsymbol{S}(\boldsymbol{KS})(\boldsymbol{S}(\boldsymbol{K}(\boldsymbol{S}(\boldsymbol{KS})))\boldsymbol{S}))))(\boldsymbol{KS})$.

PROOF. By the fact that the theories λ and $\boldsymbol{CL} + \boldsymbol{A}_\beta$ are equivalent, in the sense that

$$\lambda \vdash A_\lambda = B_\lambda \;\Leftrightarrow\; \boldsymbol{CL} + \boldsymbol{A}_\beta \vdash A = B,$$

see theorem 7.3.10(iv) and corollary 7.3.15. □

The lambda algebras usually arise as substructures of a more natural class of λ-calculus models, the so called lambda models. For these structures there is a uniform method to find the elements representing algebraic functions, independently of the way these functions are given (by terms); cf. theorem 5.5.8.

5.2.6. DEFINITION. Let $\mathfrak{M}$ be a combinatory algebra. $\mathfrak{M}$ is called *weakly extensional* if for $A, B \in \mathfrak{T}(\mathfrak{M})$

$$\mathfrak{M} \models \forall x(A = B) \rightarrow \lambda x.A = \lambda x.B.$$

The condition of weak extensionality is rather syntactical. Meyer [1980] and Scott [1980] replace it as follows.

5.2.7. DEFINITION. (i) In a combinatory algebra define $\mathbf{1} = \boldsymbol{S}(\boldsymbol{KI})$.

(ii) A λ-*model* is a λ-algebra $\mathfrak{M}$ such that the following Meyer–Scott axiom holds in $\mathfrak{M}$

$$\forall x(ax = bx) \rightarrow \mathbf{1}a = \mathbf{1}b.$$

5.2.8. LEMMA. *Let $\mathfrak{M}$ be a combinatory algebra. Then in $\mathfrak{M}$*

(i) $\mathbf{1}ab = ab$;

If moreover $\mathfrak{M}$ is a λ-algebra, then

(ii) $\mathbf{1} = \lambda xy.xy$, hence $\mathbf{1}a = \lambda y.ay$;

(iii) $\mathbf{1}(\lambda x.A) = \lambda x.A$, *for all $A \in \mathfrak{T}(\mathfrak{M})$*;

(iv) $\mathbf{11} = \mathbf{1}$.

PROOF. (i) $\mathbf{1}ab = \boldsymbol{S}(\boldsymbol{KI})ab = \boldsymbol{KI}b(ab) = ab$.

(ii) $\mathbf{1} = \boldsymbol{S}(\boldsymbol{KI}) = (\lambda xyz.xz(yz))(\boldsymbol{KI}) = \lambda yz.\boldsymbol{KI}z(yz) = \lambda yz.yz$.

(iii) $\mathbf{1}(\lambda x.A) = \lambda x.(\lambda x.A)x = \lambda x.A$, by (ii).

(iv) By (iii) and (ii). ☐

5.2.9. PROPOSITION. *$\mathfrak{M}$ is a λ-model $\Leftrightarrow$ $\mathfrak{M}$ is a weakly extensional λ-algebra.*

PROOF. ($\Leftarrow$) Let $\mathfrak{M}$ be weakly extensional. Then

$$\forall x\, ax = bx \;\Rightarrow\; \lambda x.ax = \lambda x.bx$$

$$\Rightarrow\; \mathbf{1}a = \mathbf{1}b, \qquad \text{by lemma 5.2.8(ii).}$$

($\Rightarrow$) Let $\mathfrak{M}$ be a λ-model. Then

$$\forall x\, A = B \;\Rightarrow\; \forall x(\lambda x.A)x = (\lambda x.B)x$$

$$\Rightarrow\; \mathbf{1}(\lambda x.A) = \mathbf{1}(\lambda x.B)$$

$$\Rightarrow\; \lambda x.A = \lambda x.B, \qquad \text{by lemma 5.2.8(iii).}\ ☐$$

5.2.10. PROPOSITION. *Let $\mathfrak{M}$ be a λ-algebra. Then*

$\mathfrak{M}$ is extensional $\Leftrightarrow$ $\mathfrak{M}$ is weakly extensional and satisfies $\boldsymbol{I} = \mathbf{1}$.

PROOF. ($\Rightarrow$)

$$A = B \;\Rightarrow\; (\lambda x.A)x = (\lambda x.B)x$$

$$\Rightarrow\; \lambda x.A = \lambda x.B, \qquad \text{by extensionality.}$$

Moreover $\boldsymbol{I}xy = xy = \mathbf{1}xy$, so by extensionality (twice) $\boldsymbol{I} = \mathbf{1}$.

($\Leftarrow$) By proposition 5.2.9 $\mathfrak{M}$ is a λ-model. Hence

$$\forall x\ ax = bx \ \Rightarrow\ \mathbf{1}a = \mathbf{1}b$$

$$\Rightarrow\ a = b \qquad \text{since } \mathbf{1} = \boldsymbol{I}. \ \square$$

An extensional combinatory algebra is automatically a λ-algebra. This is because $\lambda \vdash A_\lambda = B_\lambda \Rightarrow \boldsymbol{CL} + \boldsymbol{ext} \vdash A = B$, see theorem 7.3.14.

Term models, interiors

5.2.11. Definition. Let $\mathfrak{T}$ be a λ-theory.

(i) Define

$$M =_{\mathfrak{T}} N \ \Leftrightarrow\ \mathfrak{T} \vdash M = N; \qquad \text{this is a congruence relation on } \Lambda.$$

$$[M]_{\mathfrak{T}} = \{N \in \Lambda \mid M =_{\mathfrak{T}} N\}.$$

$$\Lambda/\mathfrak{T} = \{[M]_{\mathfrak{T}} \mid M \in \Lambda\}.$$

$$[M]_{\mathfrak{T}} \cdot [N]_{\mathfrak{T}} = [MN]_{\mathfrak{T}}; \qquad \text{this is well-defined.}$$

The *open term model* of $\mathfrak{T}$ is

$$\mathfrak{M}(\mathfrak{T}) = \langle \Lambda/\mathfrak{T}, \cdot, [\boldsymbol{K}]_{\mathfrak{T}}, [\boldsymbol{S}]_{\mathfrak{T}} \rangle.$$

(ii) By restricting everything to closed terms one defines the *closed term model* of $\mathfrak{T}$

$$\mathfrak{M}^0(\mathfrak{T}) = \langle \Lambda^0/\mathfrak{T}, \cdot, [\boldsymbol{K}]^0_{\mathfrak{T}}, [\boldsymbol{S}]^0_{\mathfrak{T}} \rangle.$$

Clearly if $\mathfrak{T}$ is consistent, i.e. does not prove every equation, then $\mathfrak{T} \nvdash \boldsymbol{K} = \boldsymbol{S}$, so $\mathfrak{M}(\mathfrak{T})$ and $\mathfrak{M}^0(\mathfrak{T})$ are nontrivial. In particular $\mathfrak{M}(\lambda)$ and $\mathfrak{M}^0(\lambda)$ are nontrivial since it follows from the Church–Rosser theorem that the theory λ is consistent.

5.2.12. Proposition. *Let $\mathfrak{T}$ be an extension of the λ-calculus and let $\mathfrak{M}$ be $\mathfrak{M}(\mathfrak{T})$ or $\mathfrak{M}^0(\mathfrak{T})$.*

(i) *For M with* $\mathrm{FV}(M) = \{x_1, \ldots, x_n\}$ *and ρ with $\rho(x_i) = [P_i]^{(0)}_{\mathfrak{T}}$ one has*

$$[\![M]\!]^{\mathfrak{M}}_{\rho} = [M[\vec{x} := \vec{P}]]^{(0)}_{\mathfrak{T}},$$

where $[\vec{x} := \vec{P}]$ denotes simultaneous substitution, see exercise 2.4.8.

(ii) $\mathfrak{T} \vdash M = N \ \Rightarrow\ \mathfrak{M} \vDash M = N$.

(iii) $\mathfrak{T} \vdash M = N \ \Leftrightarrow\ \mathfrak{M} \vDash M = N$, *provided that $\mathfrak{M} = \mathfrak{M}(\mathfrak{T})$ or that M, N are closed.*

PROOF. (i) Show by induction on $A \in \mathfrak{T}(\mathfrak{M})$ that $[\![A]\!]_\rho = [A_\lambda[\vec{x} := \vec{P}]]$ and use $\mathfrak{T} \vdash M_{CL,\lambda} = M$.

$$
\begin{aligned}
\text{(ii) } \mathfrak{T} \vdash M = N &\Rightarrow \forall \vec{P}\ \mathfrak{T} \vdash M[\vec{x} := \vec{P}] = N[\vec{x} := \vec{P}] \\
&\Rightarrow \forall \vec{P}\ [M[\vec{x} := \vec{P}]]_{\mathfrak{T}} = [N[\vec{x} := \vec{P}]]_{\mathfrak{T}} \\
&\Rightarrow \forall_\rho\ [\![M]\!]_\rho = [\![N]\!]_\rho \\
&\Rightarrow \mathfrak{M} \models M = N.
\end{aligned}
$$

(iii) For $\mathfrak{M} = \mathfrak{M}(\mathfrak{T})$. Let $\rho_0(x) = [x]_{\mathfrak{T}}$. Then

$$
\begin{aligned}
\mathfrak{M} \models M = N &\Rightarrow [\![M]\!]_{\rho_0} = [\![N]\!]_{\rho_0} \\
&\Rightarrow [M]_{\mathfrak{T}} = [N]_{\mathfrak{T}}, \qquad \text{by (i)}, \\
&\Rightarrow \mathfrak{T} \vdash M = N.
\end{aligned}
$$

For M, N closed.

$$
\begin{aligned}
\mathfrak{M} \models M = N &\Rightarrow [\![M]\!]_{\rho} = [\![N]\!]_{\rho} \\
&\Rightarrow [M]_{\mathfrak{T}} = [N]_{\mathfrak{T}}, \qquad \text{by (i)}, \\
&\Rightarrow \mathfrak{T} \vdash M = N. \quad \square
\end{aligned}
$$

5.2.13. COROLLARY. (i) $\mathfrak{M}^0(\mathfrak{T})$ *is a* λ*-algebra.*
(ii) $\mathfrak{M}(\mathfrak{T})$ *is a* λ*-model.*

PROOF. Write $\mathfrak{M} = \mathfrak{M}(\mathfrak{T})$.
(i) By 5.2.12(ii), the fact that $\mathfrak{T} \vdash \boldsymbol{K}_{\lambda,CL} = \boldsymbol{K}, \boldsymbol{S}_{\lambda,CL} = \boldsymbol{S}$ and lemma 5.2.3.
(ii)

$$
\begin{aligned}
\mathfrak{M} \models \forall x\ ax = bx &\Rightarrow \mathfrak{M} \models \forall x [M]x = [N]x, \quad \text{where } a = [M] \text{ and } b = [N], \\
&\Rightarrow \mathfrak{M} \models [M][z] = [N][z], \quad \text{for some fresh variable } z, \\
&\Rightarrow \mathfrak{T} \vdash Mz = Nz \\
&\Rightarrow \mathfrak{T} \vdash \lambda z.Mz = \lambda z.Nz \\
&\Rightarrow \mathfrak{T} \vdash \mathbf{1}M = \mathbf{1}N \\
&\Rightarrow \mathfrak{M} \models \mathbf{1}a = \mathbf{1}b. \quad \square
\end{aligned}
$$

Remarks. (i) (Jacopini [1975a]). $\mathfrak{M}^0(\mathfrak{T})$ is in general not a λ-model. Consider $\mathfrak{T} \supseteq \lambda$ axiomatized by $\{\boldsymbol{\Omega K}Z = \boldsymbol{\Omega S}Z | Z \in \Lambda^0\}$ where $\boldsymbol{\Omega} \equiv (\lambda x.xx)(\lambda x.xx)$. Then $\forall Z \in \Lambda^0 \mathfrak{T} \vdash \boldsymbol{\Omega K}Z = \boldsymbol{\Omega S}Z$, hence $\mathfrak{M}^0(\mathfrak{T}) \models \forall x \mathfrak{T} \boldsymbol{\Omega K}x = \boldsymbol{\Omega S}x$. But $\mathfrak{M}^0(\mathfrak{T}) \not\models \mathbf{1}(\boldsymbol{\Omega K}) = \mathbf{1}(\boldsymbol{\Omega S})$, since otherwise $\mathfrak{T} \vdash \boldsymbol{\Omega K}x = \boldsymbol{\Omega S}x$, which is false.

(ii) Plotkin [1974] shows, see corollary 20.1.2(i), that even $\mathfrak{M}^0(\lambda)$ and $\mathfrak{M}^0(\lambda\eta)$ are not λ-models.

(iii) By (i) it follows that proposition 5.2.12(iii) does not hold in general for $\mathfrak{M}^0(\mathfrak{T})$: take $M \equiv \boldsymbol{\Omega K}x$, $N \equiv \boldsymbol{\Omega S}x$.

5.2.14. Definition. Let $\mathfrak{A}$ be a combinatory algebra.

(i) The *interior* of $\mathfrak{A}$ (notation $\mathfrak{A}^0$), is the substructure of $\mathfrak{A}$ generated by k, s.

(ii) $\mathfrak{A}$ is *hard* if $\mathfrak{A}^0 = \mathfrak{A}$.

Note that up to isomorphism $\mathfrak{M}^0(\mathfrak{T})$ is the interior of $\mathfrak{M}(\mathfrak{T})$.

5.2.15. Proposition. *Let* $\mathfrak{A}$ *be a λ-algebra.*

(i) $\mathfrak{M}^0(\text{Th}(\mathfrak{A})) \cong \mathfrak{A}^0$

(ii) *Let* $\text{Th}(\underset{\sim}{\mathfrak{A}}) = \{M = N | M, N \in \mathfrak{T}(\mathfrak{A}),\ M, N \text{ closed and } \mathfrak{A} \vDash M = N\}$. *Then* $\mathfrak{M}^0(\text{Th}(\underset{\sim}{\mathfrak{A}})) \cong \mathfrak{A}$.

Proof. (i) $\varphi([M]_{\text{Th}(\mathfrak{A})}) = [\![M]\!]^{\mathfrak{A}}$ is a well defined isomorphism onto $\mathfrak{A}^0$.

(ii) Similarly. □

It follows that all λ-algebras arise as a substructure of a λ-model.

5.2.16. Proposition. (i) (Barendregt, Koymans [1980]). *Every λ-algebra can be embedded into a λ-model.*

(ii) (Meyer [1982]). *Every λ-algebra is the homomorphic image of a λ-model.*

Proof. (i) $\mathfrak{A} \cong \mathfrak{M}^0(\text{Th}(\underset{\sim}{\mathfrak{A}})) \subset \mathfrak{M}(\text{Th}(\underset{\sim}{\mathfrak{A}}))$.

(ii) Moreover $\mathfrak{M}(\text{Th}(\underset{\sim}{\mathfrak{A}})) \to \mathfrak{M}^0(\text{Th}(\underset{\sim}{\mathfrak{A}})) \cong \mathfrak{A}$ by the surjective map that replaces every free variable by say $\boldsymbol{K}$. □

The following is shown in Barendregt and Koymans [1980]. We state the result without proof.

5.2.17. Theorem. (i) *There is a λ-model that cannot be embedded into an extensional λ-model.*

(ii) *There is a combinatory complete applicative structure that cannot be made into a λ-algebra (by choosing k, s).*

(iii) *There is a λ-algebra that cannot be made into a λ-model (by changing k, s).*

(iv) *There is a λ-model that cannot be made into an extensional one (by collapsing it).*

The term models make it possible to give the following completeness proofs.

5.2.18. THEOREM. *Let* $M, N \in \Lambda$. *Then*

(i) $\boldsymbol{\lambda} \vdash M = N \Leftrightarrow M = N$ *is true in all* λ*-models (or* λ*-algebras).*

(ii) *Let* $\mathcal{T}$ *be an extension of the* λ*-calculus. Then*

$$\mathcal{T} \vdash M = N \quad \Leftrightarrow \quad M = N \text{ is true in all } \lambda\text{-models satisfying } \mathcal{T}.$$

(iii) *Let* $(\boldsymbol{\lambda})_c$ *be the classical first order theory axiomatized by the universal closure of*

$$\boldsymbol{K}xy = x,$$

$$\boldsymbol{S}yxz = xz(yz),$$

$$\boldsymbol{K} \neq \boldsymbol{S},$$

$$\forall x(ax = bx) \to \mathbf{1}a = \mathbf{1}b,$$

$$\boldsymbol{A}_\beta.$$

Then

$$(\boldsymbol{\lambda})_c \vdash M = N \quad \Leftrightarrow \quad \boldsymbol{\lambda} \vdash M = N.$$

PROOF. (i) ($\Rightarrow$) By lemma 5.2.3. ($\Leftarrow$) If $M = N$ is true in all λ-models, then it is true in $\mathfrak{M}(\boldsymbol{\lambda})$; hence $\boldsymbol{\lambda} \vdash M = N$ by proposition 5.2.12(iii).

(ii) Similarly.

(iii) ($\Rightarrow$) Note that $\mathfrak{M}(\boldsymbol{\lambda}) \vDash (\boldsymbol{\lambda})_c$. Therefore

$$(\boldsymbol{\lambda})_c \vdash M = N \;\Rightarrow\; \mathfrak{M}(\boldsymbol{\lambda}) \vDash M = N \;\Rightarrow\; \boldsymbol{\lambda} \vdash M = N.$$

($\Leftarrow$) Trivial. □

Models and rules

Let $\boldsymbol{R}$ be one of the rules for the λ-calculus considered in § 4.1. Then $\boldsymbol{R}$ has the form

$$R_1 \Rightarrow R_2,$$

where R_2 is always an equation and R_1 is either an equation (e.g. as for ***ext***) or a set of equations (e.g. as for ω).

There are two different ways in which a λ-algebra $\mathfrak{M}$ can "satisfy" such a rule $\boldsymbol{R}$:

(1) Th($\mathfrak{M}$) can be closed under the rule $\boldsymbol{R}$; or

(2) $\mathfrak{M}$ can satisfy roughly speaking the axiom corresponding to $\boldsymbol{R}$. ('Roughly' because it is not always immediate what the precise formulation of the corresponding axiom is.)

In the first case one writes $\mathfrak{M} \vDash \boldsymbol{R}$-rule, in the second $\mathfrak{M} \vDash \boldsymbol{R}$-axiom.

5.2.19. DEFINITION. Let $\boldsymbol{R} = R_1 \Rightarrow R_2$ be one of the rules $\boldsymbol{ext}$, ξ, ω, $\boldsymbol{tr}$. Let $\mathfrak{M}$ be a λ-algebra.

(i) $\mathfrak{M}$ satisfies the $\boldsymbol{R}$-rule (notation $\mathfrak{M} \models \boldsymbol{R}$-rule) if $\mathfrak{M} \models R_1 \Rightarrow \mathfrak{M} \models R_2$.

(ii) $\mathfrak{M}$ satisfies the $\boldsymbol{R}$-axiom (notation $\mathfrak{M} \models \boldsymbol{R}$-ax) is defined for each of the rules separately.

$$\mathfrak{M} \models \boldsymbol{ext}\text{-ax} \;\Leftrightarrow\; \mathfrak{M} \models (\forall x Mx = Nx) \rightarrow M = N,$$

$$\mathfrak{M} \models \xi\text{-ax} \;\Leftrightarrow\; \mathfrak{M} \models (\forall x M = N) \rightarrow \lambda x.M = \lambda x.N,$$

$$\mathfrak{M} \models \omega\text{-ax} \;\Leftrightarrow\; \mathfrak{M} \models (\forall x \in \mathfrak{M}^0 Mx = Nx) \rightarrow M = N$$

in the obvious sense,

$$\mathfrak{M} \models \boldsymbol{tr}\text{-ax} \;\Leftrightarrow\; \mathfrak{M} \models (\forall x \in \mathfrak{M}^0 Mx = Nx) \rightarrow \forall x Mx = Nx.$$

In the above $M, N \in \lambda$ are arbitrary and $x \notin \mathrm{FV}(MN)$ in the first and last two cases.

(iii) The notions of $\mathfrak{M}$ satisfying $\boldsymbol{R}^0$-ax or $\boldsymbol{R}^0$-rule are defined similarly by restriction to closed terms.

Note that ξ-ax = w.e.

5.2.20. FACT. (i) $\mathfrak{M} \models \boldsymbol{R}\text{-ax} \Rightarrow \mathfrak{M} \models \boldsymbol{R}$-rule, but the converse does not necessarily hold.

(ii) $\mathfrak{M}^0 \models \boldsymbol{R}\text{-ax} \Leftrightarrow \mathfrak{M}^0 \models \boldsymbol{R}$-rule; therefore one writes for hard models simply $\mathfrak{M} \models \boldsymbol{R}$.

(iii) $\mathfrak{M}^0 \models \boldsymbol{R} \Leftrightarrow \mathfrak{M}^0 \models \boldsymbol{R}^0$.

(iv) $\mathfrak{M} \models \boldsymbol{R}$-ax neither implies nor is implied by $\mathfrak{M}^0 \models \boldsymbol{R}$.

PROOF. (i) ($\Rightarrow$) Trivial. ($\not\Leftarrow$) Take $\mathfrak{M} = D_\infty$, $\boldsymbol{R} = \omega$; see exercise 19.4.6.

(ii) ($\Leftarrow$) Let $\mathfrak{M}^0 \models \boldsymbol{R}$-rule with $\boldsymbol{R}\text{-ax} = R_1 \Rightarrow R_2$. To show $\mathfrak{M}^0 \models \boldsymbol{R}$-ax, suppose $\mathfrak{M}^0, \rho \models R_1$. Let $R^*_{1,2}$ be the result of substituting in $R_{1,2}$ for $\vec{x}$ terms corresponding to $\rho(\vec{x})$. Then $\mathfrak{M}^0 \models R^*_1$, hence $\mathfrak{M}^0 \models R^*_2$, i.e. $\mathfrak{M}^0$, $\rho \models R_2$. Therefore $\forall \rho\, \mathfrak{M}^0, \rho \models R_1 \rightarrow R_2$, i.e. $\mathfrak{M}^0 \models \boldsymbol{R}$-ax.

(iii) Trivial.

(iv) ($\not\Rightarrow$) Take $\mathfrak{M} = \mathfrak{M}(\lambda\eta)$, $\boldsymbol{R} = \boldsymbol{ext}$; see theorem 20.1.1.

($\not\Leftarrow$) Take $\boldsymbol{R} = \boldsymbol{ext}$; see exercise 20.6.3. □

5.2.21. PROPOSITION. *Let $\mathfrak{M}$ be a λ-algebra. Then*

(i) $\mathfrak{M} \models \boldsymbol{ext} - \text{ax} \Leftrightarrow \mathfrak{M}$ *is extensional.*

(ii) $\mathfrak{M} \models \xi\text{-ax} \Leftrightarrow \mathfrak{M} \models \xi$*-rule* ($\Leftrightarrow \mathfrak{M}$ *is weakly extensional*).

(iii) $\mathfrak{M} \models \omega$*-rule* $\Leftrightarrow \mathfrak{M}^0 \models \omega \Leftrightarrow \mathfrak{M}^0$ *is extensional.*

PROOF. (i) Trivial.

(ii) By corollary 5.2.23.

(iii) $\mathfrak{M} \models \omega\text{-rule} \Rightarrow \mathfrak{M}^0 \models \omega$
$\Rightarrow \mathfrak{M}^0 \models \omega^0$
$\Rightarrow \mathfrak{M} \models \omega^0\text{-rule}$
$\Rightarrow \mathfrak{M} \models \omega\text{-rule}$ by the proof of theorem 4.1.15(i). □

5.2.22. PROPOSITION. *Let $\mathfrak{T}$ be a λ-theory and $\boldsymbol{R}$ one of the rules. Then*

$$\mathfrak{T} \vdash \boldsymbol{R} \Leftrightarrow \mathfrak{M}(\mathfrak{T}) \models \boldsymbol{R}\text{-rule}$$

$$\Leftrightarrow \mathfrak{M}(\mathfrak{T}) \vdash \boldsymbol{R} \text{ ax}.$$

PROOF. Let $\boldsymbol{R} = R_1 \Rightarrow R_2$ and suppose $\mathfrak{T} \models \boldsymbol{R}$. Then

$$\mathfrak{M}(\mathfrak{T}) \models R_1 \Rightarrow \mathfrak{T} \vdash R_1, \text{ by theorem 5.2.12(ii)},$$

$$\Rightarrow \mathfrak{T} \vdash R_2, \text{ by assumption},$$

$$\Rightarrow \mathfrak{M}(\mathfrak{T}) \models R_2.$$

Therefore $\mathfrak{M}(\mathfrak{T}) \models \boldsymbol{R}$-rule. Similarly one shows $\mathfrak{M}(\mathfrak{T}) \models \boldsymbol{R}\text{-rule} \Rightarrow \mathfrak{T} \vdash \boldsymbol{R}$. To show that $\mathfrak{M}(\mathfrak{T}) \models \boldsymbol{R}$-rule iff $\mathfrak{M}(\mathfrak{T}) \models \boldsymbol{R}$-ax is similar to the proof of fact 5.2.20(ii). □

5.2.23. COROLLARY. (i) *If $\mathfrak{T}$ is an extensional λ-theory, then $\mathfrak{M}(\mathfrak{T})$ is an extensional λ-model.*

(ii) *If $\mathfrak{T} \vdash \omega$, then $\mathfrak{M}^0(\mathfrak{T})$ is an extensional λ-model.*

PROOF. By propositions 5.2.21 and 5.2.22. □

5.3. Syntactical models

In this section a syntactical description of the λ-algebras and λ-models will be given, which is equivalent to the first order description in § 5.2. For some models, in particular the filter model of Barendregt et al. [1983], this syntactical description is more convenient than the first order one. The method is due to Hindley and Longo [1980].

5.3.1. DEFINITION. Let $\mathfrak{M} = \langle X, \cdot \rangle$ be an applicative structure.

(i) Val($\mathfrak{M}$) is the set of valuations in $\mathfrak{M}$.

(ii) A *syntactical interpretation* in $\mathfrak{M}$ is a map $I: \Lambda(\mathfrak{M}) \times \text{Val}(\mathfrak{M}) \to X$ satisfying the following conditions; $I(M, \rho)$ is written as $[\![M]\!]_\rho$.

(1) $[\![x]\!]_\rho = \rho(x)$,
(2) $[\![c_a]\!]_\rho = a$,
(3) $[\![PQ]\!]_\rho = [\![P]\!]_\rho \cdot [\![Q]\!]_\rho$,
(4) $[\![\lambda x.P]\!]_\rho \cdot a = [\![P]\!]_{\rho(x:=a)}$,
(5) $\rho \restriction \mathrm{FV}(M) = \rho' \restriction \mathrm{FV}(M) \;\Rightarrow\; [\![M]\!]_\rho = [\![M]\!]_{\rho'}$.

Note that by the variable convention, (4) implies that for $y \notin \mathrm{FV}(M(x))$ one has

(4′) $[\![M(x)]\!]_{\rho(x:=a)} = [\![\lambda x.M(x)]\!]_\rho a = [\![\lambda y.M(y)]\!]_\rho a = [\![M(y)]\!]_{\rho(y:=a)}$.

(iii) A *syntactical applicative* structure is of the form $\mathfrak{M} = \langle X, \cdot, [\![\ ]\!]\rangle$ where $[\![\ ]\!]$ is a syntactical interpretation in $\mathfrak{M}$.

5.3.2. Definition. Let $\mathfrak{M}$ be a syntactical applicative structure.

(i) The notion of satisfaction in $\mathfrak{M}$ is defined as usual:

$$\mathfrak{M}, \rho \models M = N \;\Leftrightarrow\; [\![M]\!]_\rho = [\![N]\!]_\rho$$

$$\mathfrak{M} \models M = N \;\Leftrightarrow\; \forall\rho\ \mathfrak{M}, \rho \models M = N$$

and this is extended to arbitrary first order formulas over the λ-calculus.

(ii) $\mathfrak{M}$ is a *syntactical λ-algebra* if

$$\lambda \vdash M = N \;\Rightarrow\; \mathfrak{M} \models M = N.$$

(iii) $\mathfrak{M}$ is a *syntactical λ-model* if

$$(\xi) \qquad \mathfrak{M} \models \forall x(M = N) \rightarrow \lambda x.M = \lambda x.N,$$

i.e.

$$\forall a\ [\![M]\!]_{\rho(x:=a)} = [\![N]\!]_{\rho(x:=a)} \;\Rightarrow\; [\![\lambda x.M]\!]_\rho = [\![\lambda x.N]\!]_\rho.$$

5.3.3. Lemma. *Let $\mathfrak{M}$ be a syntactical λ-model. Consider the statement*

$$\varphi(M, N) \equiv \forall\rho [\![M[x:=N]]\!]_\rho = [\![M]\!]_{\rho(x:=[\![N]\!]_\rho)}.$$

Then for $M, N \in \Lambda(\mathfrak{M})$

(i) $z \notin \mathrm{FV}(M) \;\Rightarrow\; \varphi(M, z)$;
(ii) $\varphi(M, N) \;\Rightarrow\; \varphi(\lambda y.M, N)$;
(iii) $\varphi(M, N)$.

Proof. (i) Write $M \equiv M(x)$. Then

$$[\![M(z)]\!]_\rho = [\![M(z)]\!]_{\rho(z:=\rho(z))} = [\![M(x)]\!]_{\rho(x:=\rho(z))} \qquad \text{by (4′)}.$$

(ii) First assume $x \notin \mathrm{FV}(N)$. By the variable convention $y \not\equiv x$, $y \notin \mathrm{FV}(N)$. Then for $\rho^* = \rho(x:=\llbracket N \rrbracket_\rho)$ and arbitrary $a \in \mathfrak{M}$

$$\begin{aligned} \llbracket M[x:=N] \rrbracket_{\rho^*(y:=a)} &= \llbracket M[x:=N] \rrbracket_{\rho(y:=a)} \\ &= \llbracket M \rrbracket_{\rho(y:=a)(x:=\llbracket N \rrbracket_\rho)}, \qquad \text{since } \varphi(M, N), \\ &= \llbracket M \rrbracket_{\rho^*(y:=a)}; \end{aligned}$$

(note that $\llbracket N \rrbracket_\rho = \llbracket N \rrbracket_{\rho(y:=a)}$). Therefore by ($\xi$)

$$\llbracket \lambda y.M[x:-N] \rrbracket_{\rho^*} - \llbracket \lambda y.M \rrbracket_{\rho^*}$$

and hence

$$\llbracket \lambda y.M[x:=N] \rrbracket_\rho = \llbracket \lambda y.M[x:=N] \rrbracket_{\rho^*} = \llbracket \lambda y.M \rrbracket_{\rho(x:=\llbracket N \rrbracket_\rho)}.$$

If $x \in \mathrm{FV}(N)$, then let z be a fresh variable. We have for $\tilde{M} \equiv \lambda y.M$

$$\begin{aligned} \llbracket \tilde{M}[x:=N] \rrbracket_\rho &= \llbracket \tilde{M}[x:=z][z:=N] \rrbracket_\rho \\ &= \llbracket \tilde{M}[x:=z] \rrbracket_{\rho(z:=\llbracket N \rrbracket_\rho)} \\ &= \llbracket \tilde{M} \rrbracket_{\rho(z:=\llbracket N \rrbracket_\rho)(x:=\llbracket N \rrbracket_\rho)}, \qquad \text{by (i)}, \\ &= \llbracket \tilde{M} \rrbracket_{\rho(x:=\llbracket N \rrbracket_\rho)}. \end{aligned}$$

(iii) Now $\varphi(M, N)$ follows by a simple induction on the structure of M □

5.3.4. THEOREM. *Let $\mathfrak{M}$ be a syntactical λ-model. Then*

$$\boldsymbol{\lambda} \vdash M = N \;\Rightarrow\; \mathfrak{M} \vDash M = N,$$

i.e. $\mathfrak{M}$ is a syntactical λ-algebra,

PROOF. By induction on the length of proof.

The axiom $(\lambda x.M)N = M[x:=N]$ is sound:

$$\begin{aligned} \llbracket (\lambda x.M)N \rrbracket_\rho &= \llbracket \lambda x.M \rrbracket_\rho \llbracket N \rrbracket_\rho, \qquad \text{by (3)}, \\ &= \llbracket M \rrbracket_{\rho(x:=\llbracket N \rrbracket_\rho)}, \qquad \text{by (4)}, \\ &= \llbracket M[x:=N] \rrbracket_\rho, \qquad \text{by lemma 5.3.3(iii)}. \end{aligned}$$

Soundness of the rule $M = N \Rightarrow \lambda x.M = \lambda x.N$ follows from (ξ). The other rules are trivial. □

5.3.5. DEFINITION. A *homomorphism* between syntactical λ-algebras is a map $\varphi: \mathfrak{M}_1 \to \mathfrak{M}_2$ such that for all $M \in \Lambda(\mathfrak{M})$ one has

$$\varphi[\![M]\!]^1_\rho = [\![\varphi(M)]\!]^2_{\varphi\circ\rho}$$

where in $\varphi(M)$ the c_a are replaced by $c_{\varphi(a)}$.

5.3.6. THEOREM. *The category of syntactical λ-algebras and homomorphisms and that of λ-algebras and homomorphisms are isomorphic. Moreover syntactical λ-models correspond exactly to λ-models under this isomorphism.*

PROOF. Easy. For a syntactical λ-algebra $\mathfrak{M} = \langle X, \cdot, [\![\ ]\!] \rangle$ define $F\mathfrak{M} = \langle X, \cdot, [\![K]\!], [\![S]\!] \rangle$; for $\varphi: \mathfrak{M}_1 \to \mathfrak{M}_2$ let $F\varphi = \varphi: F\mathfrak{M}_1 \to F\mathfrak{M}_2$. Then one has $[\![M]\!]^{F\mathfrak{M}}_\rho = [\![M]\!]^{\mathfrak{M}}_\rho$ for $M \in \Lambda(\mathfrak{M})$. Conversely for a λ-algebra $\mathfrak{A} = \langle X, \cdot, k, s \rangle$ define $G\mathfrak{A} = \langle X, \cdot, [\![\ ]\!]^{\mathfrak{A}} \rangle$ and $G\varphi = \varphi$ as above. Then F, with inverse G, is the required isomorphism. □

5.3.7. REMARK. In view of theorem 5.3.6 we say that $\mathfrak{M} = (X, \cdot, [\![\ ]\!])$ is a λ-algebra (λ-model) if $\mathfrak{M}$ is a syntactical λ-algebra (λ-model).

5.3.8. CONVENTION. When working inside a λ-algebra $\mathfrak{M}$, we write equations valid in $\mathfrak{M}$ informally, e.g. for $a \in \mathfrak{M}$ one writes

$$(\lambda x.xx)a = aa$$

rather than the formal $[\![(\lambda x.xx)y]\!]_{\rho(y:=a)} = [\![yy]\!]_{\rho(y:=a)}$ or $[\![\lambda x.xx]\!]a = aa$.

5.4. Models in concrete cartesian closed categories

In this section the framework will be explained in which Scott constructed his non-syntactical λ-models. We will use the category of cpo's. But the method works for arbitrary concrete cartesian closed categories.

Recall that if D is a cpo, then $[D \to D]$ is the set of continuous maps considered as cpo by pointwise ordering.

5.4.1. DEFINITION. A cpo D is called *reflexive* if $[D \to D]$ is a retract of D, i.e. there are continuous maps

$$F: D \to [D \to D], \qquad G: [D \to D] \to D$$

such that $F \circ G = \mathrm{id}_{[D \to D]}$.

It will be shown that every reflexive cpo defines in a natural way a λ-model.

5.4.2. DEFINITION. Let D be a reflexive cpo via the maps F, G.
(i) For $x, y \in D$ define

$$x.y = F(x)(y).$$

(ii) Let ρ be a valuation in D. Define the interpretation $[\![\ ]\!]_\rho : \Lambda \to D$ by induction as follows.

$$[\![x]\!]_\rho = \rho(x), \qquad [\![c_a]\!]_\rho = a,$$

$$[\![MN]\!]_\rho = [\![M]\!]_\rho\ [\![N]\!]_\rho,$$

$$[\![\lambda x.M]\!]_\rho = G(\boldsymbol{\lambda} d.[\![M]\!]_{\rho(x:=d)}).$$

5.4.3. LEMMA. $\boldsymbol{\lambda} d.[\![M]\!]_{\rho(x:=d)}$ *is continuous; hence* $[\![\lambda x.M]\!]_\rho$ *is well-defined.*

PROOF. By induction on M one shows that $[\![M]\!]_{\rho(x:=d)}$ depends for all ρ continuously on d. The only nontrivial case is $M \equiv \lambda y.P$. Then

$$\begin{aligned}[\![\lambda y.P]\!]_{\rho(x:=d)} &= G(\boldsymbol{\lambda} e.[\![D]\!]_{\rho(x:=d)(y:=e)}) \\ &= G(\boldsymbol{\lambda} e.f(d,e)), \qquad \text{say} \\ &= g(d), \qquad \text{say.}\end{aligned}$$

By the induction hypothesis f is continuous in d and e separately, hence by lemma 1.2.12 continuous. Therefore, by proposition 1.2.14(i) and the continuity of G, the map $g = G \circ \hat{f}$ is continuous. □

5.4.4. THEOREM. *Let D be a reflexive cpo via F, G and let $\mathfrak{M} = (D, \cdot, [\![\ ]\!])$. Then*
(i) *$\mathfrak{M}$ is a λ-model.*
(ii) *The functions representable are exactly the continuous functions.*
(iii) *$\mathfrak{M}$ is extensional iff $G \circ F = \mathrm{id}_D$, i.e. $G = F^{-1}$ and $D \cong [D \to D]$ via F, G.*

PROOF. (i) We verify the conditions in definition 5.3.1. (1), (2) and (3) are trivial. As to (4)

$$\begin{aligned}[\![\lambda x.P]\!]_\rho.a &= G(\boldsymbol{\lambda} d.[\![P]\!]_{\rho(x:=d)}).a \\ &= F(G(\boldsymbol{\lambda} d.[\![P]\!]_{\rho(x:=d)}))(a) \\ &= (\boldsymbol{\lambda} d.[\![P]\!]_{\rho(x:=d)})(a) = [\![P]\!]_{\rho(x:=a)}\end{aligned}$$

Condition (5) follows by an easy induction on M.

Therefore $\mathfrak{M}$ is a syntactical applicative structure. Moreover $\mathfrak{M}$ satisfies (ξ):

$$\begin{aligned}\forall d\ [\![M]\!]_{\rho(x:=d)} = [\![N]\!]_{\rho(x:=d)} &\Rightarrow \boldsymbol{\lambda} d.[\![M]\!]_{\rho(x:=d)} = \boldsymbol{\lambda} d.[\![N]\!]_{\rho(x:=d)} \\ &\Rightarrow G(\boldsymbol{\lambda} d.[\![M]\!]_{\rho(x:=d)}) = G(\boldsymbol{\lambda} d.[\![N]\!]_{\rho(x:=d)}) \\ &\Rightarrow [\![\lambda x.M]\!]_\rho = [\![\lambda x.N]\!]_\rho .\end{aligned}$$

It follows that $\mathfrak{M}$ is a λ-model; see remark 5.3.7.

(ii) Application $\cdot$ is continuous, since F is; therefore all representable functions are continuous. Conversely, a continuous $f: D \to D$ is represented by $G(f)$:

$$G(f)a = F(G(f))(a) = f(a).$$

In general, a continuous $f: D^n \to D$ is represented by

$$\lambda^G d_1 \cdots \lambda^G d_n . f(d_1, \ldots, d_n)$$

where

$$\lambda^G d. \cdots = G(\boldsymbol{\lambda} d. \cdots).$$

(iii) If $G \circ F = \mathrm{id}_D$, then

$$\begin{aligned}\forall e\ de = d'e &\Rightarrow \forall e F(d)(e) = F(d')(e) \\ &\Rightarrow F(d) = F(d') \\ &\Rightarrow d = d', \qquad \text{by applying } G.\end{aligned}$$

Therefore $\mathfrak{M}$ is extensional.

Conversely, suppose $\mathfrak{M}$ is extensional. Let $d \in D$ and $d' = G(F(d))$. Then for all $e \in D$

$$d'e = F(d')(e) = F(G(F(d)))(e) = F(d)(e) = de.$$

Hence $d' = d$ i.e. $G \circ F = \mathrm{id}_D$. □

To give an idea of how a reflexive cpo can be defined, we will describe the models D_A introduced by Engeler [1981] as a simplification of the graph model $P\omega$ introduced in § 18.1.

5.4.5. DEFINITION. Let A be a set.

(i) $B \supseteq A$ is the least set such that

$$\beta \subseteq B,\ \beta \text{ finite and } b \in B \ \Rightarrow\ (\beta, b) \in B.$$

(Assume that A does not contain such pairs).

(ii) $D_A = P(B)$, the powerset of B partially ordered by inclusion. This is a cpo (even an algebraic lattice).

(iii) For $x, y \in D_A$ and $f \in [D_A \to D_A]$ define

$$x \cdot y = \{ b \in B | \exists \beta \subseteq y (\beta, b) \in x \},$$

$$\lambda^G x.f(x) = \{ (\beta, b) \in B | \beta \text{ finite } \subseteq B \text{ and } b \in f(\beta) \}.$$

5.4.6. THEOREM. *D_A becomes a reflexive cpo by defining $F(x) = \lambda\!\!\!\lambda y.xy$, $G(f) = \lambda^G x.f(x)$. Therefore D_A defines a λ-model.*

PROOF. The continuity of F, G follows easily from propositions 1.2.24 and 1.2.31(i).

$$\begin{aligned} F \circ G(f) &= F(\{ (\beta, b) | b \in f(\beta) \}) \\ &= \lambda\!\!\!\lambda y.\{ b | \exists \beta \subseteq y\, b \in f(\beta) \} \\ &= \lambda\!\!\!\lambda y. \bigcup \{ f(\beta) | \beta \subseteq y \} \\ &= \lambda\!\!\!\lambda y. f(y), \qquad \text{by continuity of } f, \\ &= f. \ \square \end{aligned}$$

See exercises 5.7.7, 18.5.29 and 18.4.31 for more information on D_A.

5.5. Models in arbitrary cartesian closed categories

In this section it will be shown that in arbitrary cartesian closed categories reflexive objects give rise to λ-algebras and to all of them. The λ-models are then those λ-algebras that come from categories "with enough points". The method is due to Koymans [1982] and is based on work of Scott. In exercise 5.8.9 a categorial description of combinatory algebras is given.

5.5.1. DEFINITION. Let $\mathbb{C}$ be a category. The identity map on an object $A \in \mathbb{C}$ is denoted by id_A.

(i) $\mathbb{C}$ is *a cartesian closed category* (ccc) iff

(1) $\mathbb{C}$ has a *terminal object* T such that for every object $A \in \mathbb{C}$ there exists a unique map $!_A : A \to T$.

(2) For $A_1, A_2 \in \mathbb{C}$ there is an object $A_1 \times A_2$ (*cartesian product*) with maps $p_i: A_1 \times A_2 \to A_i$ (*projections*) such that for all $f_i: C \to A_i$ $(i=1,2)$ there is a unique map $\langle f_1, f_2 \rangle : C \to A_1 \times A_2$ with $p_i \circ \langle f_1, f_2 \rangle = f_i$, see figure 5.1.

Notation. If $g_i: A_i \to B_i$ $(i=1,2)$, then $g_1 \times g_2 = \langle g_1 \circ p_1, g_2 \circ p_2 \rangle : A_1 \times A_2 \to B_1 \times B_2$, see figure 5.1.

(3) For $A, B \in C$ there is an object $B^A \in \mathbb{C}$ (*exponent*) with map $\mathrm{ev} = \mathrm{ev}_{A,B}: B^A \times A \to B$ such that for all $f: C \times A \to B$ there is a unique $\Lambda f: C \to B^A$ satisfying $f = \mathrm{ev} \circ (\Lambda f \times \mathrm{id}_A)$, see figure 5.1.

(ii) Let $\mathbb{C}$ have a terminal object T. A *point* of $A \in \mathbb{C}$ is a map $x: T \to A$. The set of points of A is denoted by $|A|$. An object A *has enough points* if for all $f, g: A \to A$ one has

$$f \neq g \quad \Rightarrow \quad \exists x \in |A| \quad f \circ x \neq g \circ x.$$

It then follows that the same holds for all $f, g: A \to B$.

Note that in a ccc one has

$$\Lambda(h \circ g \times \mathrm{id}_A) = \Lambda(h) \circ g,$$
$$\langle f, g \rangle \circ h = \langle f \circ h, g \circ h \rangle,$$
$$f \times g \circ \langle h, k \rangle = \langle f \circ h, g \circ k \rangle.$$

5.5.2. Definition. Let $\mathbb{C}$ be a ccc. An object $U \in \mathbb{C}$ is *reflexive* if U^U is a retract of U, i.e. there are maps $F: U \to U^U$ and $G: U^U \to U$ such that

$$F \circ G = \mathrm{id}_{U^U}.$$

5.5.3. Definition. Let $\mathbb{C}$ be a ccc with reflexive object U (via the maps F, G). Then these data determine a syntactical applicative structure $\mathfrak{M}(\mathbb{C})$

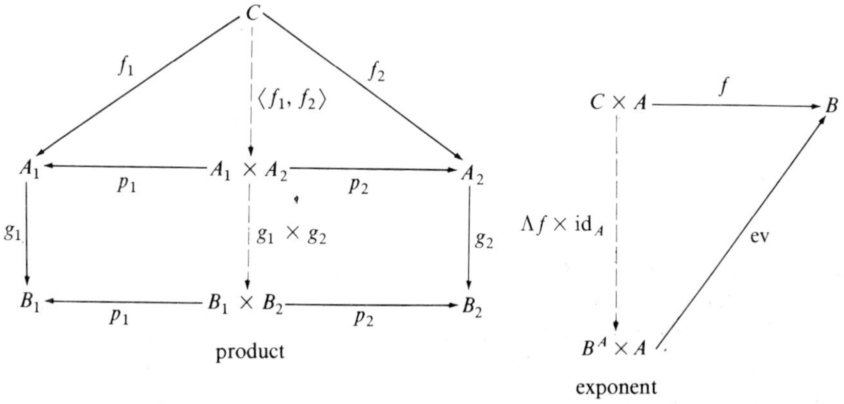

Fig. 5.1

($= \mathfrak{M}(\mathbb{C}, U, F, G)$) as follows:

(i) The domain of $\mathfrak{M}(\mathbb{C})$ is $|U|$.

(ii) Let $\mathrm{Ap}: U^2 \to U$ be the map $\mathrm{ev}_{U,U} \circ F \times \mathrm{id}_U$.
For $f, g: A \to U$ define $f \cdot_A g = \mathrm{Ap} \circ \langle f, g \rangle$. In particular for $x, y \in |U|$

$$x \cdot y = x \cdot_T y = \mathrm{Ap} \circ \langle x, y \rangle.$$

As applicative structure $\mathfrak{M}(\mathbb{C})$ is $\langle |U|, \cdot \rangle$.

(iii) $U^0 = T$, $U^{n+1} = U^n \times U$. Let $\Delta = x_1, \ldots, x_n$ be a sequence of distinct variables. Write $U^\Delta = U^n$.

(iv) $\pi^\Delta_{x_i}: U^\Delta \to U$ is the canonical projection on the ith coordinate.

(v) If $f_1, \ldots, f_n : A \to U$, then $\langle f_1, \ldots, f_n \rangle : A \to U^n$ is defined by

$$\langle\ \rangle = !_A,$$

$$\langle f_1, \ldots, f_{n+1} \rangle = \langle \langle f_1, \ldots, f_n \rangle, f_{n+1} \rangle.$$

Clearly

$$\pi^\Delta_{x_i} \circ \langle f_1, \ldots, f_n \rangle = f_i$$

(vi) Let $\Gamma = y_1, \ldots, y_m$ with $\{\vec{y}\} \subseteq \{\vec{x}\}$.
Define

$$\Pi^\Delta_\Gamma = \langle \pi^\Delta_{y_1}, \ldots, \pi^\Delta_{y_m} \rangle : U^\Delta \to U^\Gamma.$$

This is the canonical "thinning", i.e. "$\lambda \langle x_1, \ldots, x_n \rangle . \langle y_1, \ldots, y_m \rangle$".

(vii) For $\{\Delta\} \supseteq \mathrm{FV}(M)$ define inductively $[\![M]\!]_\Delta : U^\Delta \to U$ (with intended interpretation of e.g. $[\![M(x, y)]\!]_{x,y}$ being "$\lambda \langle x, y \rangle . [\![M(c_x, c_y)]\!]$") as follows.

$$[\![x]\!]_\Delta = \pi^\Delta_x;$$

$$[\![c_a]\!]_\Delta = a \circ !_{U^\Delta} \qquad (\text{for } a \in |U|);$$

$$[\![PQ]\!]_\Delta = [\![P]\!]_\Delta \cdot_{U^\Delta} [\![Q]\!]_\Delta;$$

$$[\![\lambda x . P]\!]_\Delta = G \circ \Lambda([\![P]\!]_{\Delta, x}),$$ where by the variable convention we assume $x \notin \{\Delta\}$.

(viii) For a valuation ρ in $|U|$ let

$$\rho^\Delta = \rho^{x_1, \ldots, x_n} = \langle \rho(x_1), \ldots, \rho(x_n) \rangle.$$

$$[\![M]\!]_\rho = [\![M]\!]_\Delta \circ \rho^\Delta \quad \text{with } \Delta = \mathrm{FV}(M).$$

Clearly $[\![M]\!]_\rho \in |U|$.

(ix) Finally $\mathfrak{M}(\mathbb{C})$ is the structure $\langle |U|, \cdot, [\![\ ]\!] \rangle$.

5.5.4. LEMMA. (i) *Let* $\{\Delta\}\supseteq\{\Gamma\}\supseteq \mathrm{FV}(M)$. *Then* $[\![M]\!]_\Delta=[\![M]\!]_\Gamma\circ\Pi^\Delta_\Gamma$.

(ii) *Let* $\{\Delta\}=\{\vec{x}\}\supseteq \mathrm{FV}(M)$, $\vec{N}$ *fit in* $\vec{x}$ *and* $\{\Gamma\}\supseteq\mathrm{FV}(\vec{N})$. *Then*

$$[\![M[\vec{x}:=\vec{N}]]\!]_\Gamma=[\![M]\!]_\Delta\circ\langle[\![N_1]\!]_\Gamma,\dots,[\![N_n]\!]_\Gamma\rangle.$$

(iii) *Let* $\{\Delta\}\supseteq\mathrm{FV}(\lambda x.M)$, $\{\Gamma\}\supseteq\mathrm{FV}((\lambda x.M)N)$ *and* $\{\Gamma\}\supseteq\{\Delta\}$. *Then*

$$[\![M[x:=N]]\!]_\Gamma=[\![M]\!]_{\Delta,x}\circ\langle\Pi^\Gamma_\Delta,[\![N]\!]_\Gamma\rangle.$$

PROOF. (i), (ii) Induction on the structure of M. We only treat $M=\lambda y.P$.

(i)
$$\begin{aligned}[\![\lambda y.P]\!]_\Gamma\circ\Pi^\Delta_\Gamma &= G\circ\Lambda([\![P]\!]_{\Gamma,y})\circ\Pi^\Delta_\Gamma\\ &= G\circ\Lambda([\![P]\!]_{\Gamma,y}\circ\Pi^\Delta_\Gamma\times\mathrm{id}_U), \qquad\text{by 4.1(1)},\\ &= G\circ\Lambda([\![P]\!]_{\Gamma,y}\circ\Pi^{\Delta,y}_{\Gamma,y})\\ &\underset{\mathrm{IH}}{=} G\circ\Lambda([\![P]\!]_{\Delta,y})=[\![\lambda y.P]\!]_\Delta.\end{aligned}$$

Here IH denotes "by the induction hypothesis".

(ii)
$$\begin{aligned}[\![(\lambda y.P)[\vec{x}:=\vec{N}]]\!]_\Gamma &= [\![\lambda y.P[\vec{x},y:=\vec{N},y]]\!]_\Gamma\\ &= G\circ\Lambda([\![P[\vec{x},y:=\vec{N},y]]\!]_{\Gamma,y})\\ &\underset{\mathrm{IH}}{=} G\circ\Lambda([\![P]\!]_{\Delta,y}\circ\langle[\![\vec{N}]\!]_{\Gamma,y},[\![y]\!]_{\Gamma,y}\rangle)\\ &\underset{*}{=} G\circ\Lambda([\![P]\!]_{\Delta,y}\circ\langle[\![\vec{N}]\!]_\Gamma\rangle\times\mathrm{id}_U), \qquad\text{see below},\\ &= G\circ\Lambda([\![P]\!]_{\Delta,y})\circ\langle[\![\vec{N}]\!]_\Gamma\rangle\\ &= [\![\lambda y.P]\!]_\Delta\circ\langle[\![\vec{N}]\!]\rangle_\Gamma.\end{aligned}$$

Now $*$ is shown as follows.

$$\begin{aligned}\langle[\![\vec{N}]\!]_{\Gamma,y},[\![y]\!]_{\Gamma,y}\rangle &\underset{(\mathrm{i})}{=} \langle[\![\vec{N}]\!]_\Gamma\circ\Pi^{\Gamma,y}_\Gamma,\pi^{\Gamma,y}_y\rangle\\ &= \langle[\![\vec{N}]\!]_\Gamma\circ p_1,\mathrm{id}_U\circ p_2\rangle\\ &= \langle[\![\vec{N}]\!]_\Gamma\rangle\times\mathrm{id}_U\circ\langle p_1,p_2\rangle=\langle[\![\vec{N}]\!]_\Gamma\rangle\times\mathrm{id}_U.\end{aligned}$$

(iii) Apply (ii) to $\Delta'\equiv\Delta,x$ and Γ, writing $\Delta\equiv\vec{y}$ and $M[x:=N]\equiv M[\vec{y},x:=\vec{y},N]$. $\square$

5.5.5. PROPOSITION. *Let* $M,N\in\Lambda(\mathfrak{M}(\mathbb{C}))$ *and* $\{\Delta\}\supseteq\mathrm{FV}(MN)$. *Then*

$$\lambda\vdash M=N\ \Rightarrow\ [\![M]\!]_\Delta=[\![N]\!]_\Delta.$$

PROOF. Induction on the length of proof of $M=N$. We treat the essential axiom (β) and rule (ξ).

Axiom $(\lambda x.P)Q = P[x:=Q]$.

$$
\begin{aligned}
[\![(\lambda x.P)Q]\!]_\Delta &= (G \circ \Lambda([\![P]\!]_{\Delta,x})) \cdot_{U^\Delta} [\![Q]\!]_\Delta \\
&= \mathrm{ev} \circ \langle F \circ G \circ \Lambda([\![P]\!]_{\Delta,x}), [\![Q]\!]_\Delta \rangle \\
&= \mathrm{ev} \circ \Lambda([\![P]\!]_{\Delta,x}) \times \mathrm{id} \circ \langle \mathrm{id}, [\![Q]\!]_\Delta \rangle \\
&= [\![P]\!]_{\Delta,x} \circ \langle \mathrm{id}, [\![Q]\!]_\Delta \rangle \\
&= [\![P[x:=Q]]\!]_\Delta, \qquad \text{by lemma 5.5.4(iii).}
\end{aligned}
$$

Rule $P = Q \;\Rightarrow\; \lambda x.P = \lambda x.Q$.

$$
\begin{aligned}
&[\![P]\!]_\Delta = [\![Q]\!]_\Delta, \qquad \text{by the induction hypothesis,} \\
&\Rightarrow\; [\![P]\!]_\Delta \circ \Pi_\Delta^{\Delta,x} = [\![Q]\!]_\Delta \circ \Pi_\Delta^{\Delta,x} \\
&\Rightarrow\; [\![P]\!]_{\Delta,x} = [\![Q]\!]_{\Delta,x} \\
&\Rightarrow\; [\![\lambda x.P]\!]_\Delta = [\![\lambda x.Q]\!]_\Delta. \quad \square
\end{aligned}
$$

5.5.6. THEOREM. *Every ccc* $\mathbb{C}$ *with reflexive object* U *determines a* λ*-algebra* $\mathfrak{M}(C) = \langle |U|, \cdot, [\![\ ]\!] \rangle$.

PROOF. Immediate from proposition 5.5.5 and the definition of $[\![\ ]\!]_\rho$. $\square$

5.5.7. PROPOSITION. *Let* $\mathfrak{M} = \mathfrak{M}(\mathbb{C}, U, F, G)$.

(i) *Let* $\{\Delta\} \supseteq \mathrm{FV}(M)$. *Then* $[\![\mathbf{1}M]\!]_\Delta = G \circ F \circ [\![M]\!]_\Delta$ *in* $\mathbb{C}$.

(ii) *U has enough points* $\Leftrightarrow$ $\mathfrak{M}$ *is a* λ*-model.*

(iii) $U \cong U^U$ *via* F, G $\Leftrightarrow$ $\mathfrak{M} \models \mathbf{1} = \boldsymbol{I}$.

(iv) $U \cong U^U$ *via* F, G *and U has enough points* $\Leftrightarrow$ $\mathfrak{M}$ *is extensional.*

PROOF. (i)
$$
\begin{aligned}
[\![\mathbf{1}M]\!]_\Delta &= [\![\lambda y.My]\!]_\Delta \\
&= G \circ \Lambda(\mathrm{ev} \circ \langle F \circ [\![M]\!]_{\Delta,y}, [\![y]\!]_{\Delta,y} \rangle) \\
&= G \circ \Lambda(\mathrm{ev} \circ \langle F \circ [\![M]\!]_\Delta \circ \Pi_\Delta^{\Delta,y}, \pi_y^{\Delta,y} \rangle) \\
&= G \circ \Lambda(\mathrm{ev} \circ \langle F \circ [\![M]\!]_\Delta \circ p_1, p_2 \rangle) \\
&= G \circ \Lambda(\mathrm{ev} \circ (F \circ [\![M]\!]_\Delta) \times \mathrm{id}) \\
&= G \circ F \circ [\![M]\!]_\Delta.
\end{aligned}
$$

(ii) ($\Rightarrow$) Let U have enough points. Then the same is true for U^1 ($\cong U$). Now for $a, b \in \mathfrak{M}$

$$
\begin{aligned}
&\forall x \in \mathfrak{M}\ ax = bx \;\Rightarrow\; \mathrm{ev} \circ \langle F \circ a, x \rangle = \mathrm{ev} \circ \langle F \circ b, x \rangle \\
&\Rightarrow\; \mathrm{ev} \circ (F \circ a) \times \mathrm{id} \circ \langle \mathrm{id}, x \rangle = \mathrm{ev} \circ (F \circ b) \times \mathrm{id} \circ \langle \mathrm{id}, x \rangle \\
&\Rightarrow\; \mathrm{ev} \circ (F \circ a) \times \mathrm{id} = \mathrm{ev} \circ (F \circ b) \times \mathrm{id}, \qquad \text{since } U^1 \text{ has enough points,} \\
&\Rightarrow\; \mathbf{1}a = \mathbf{1}b, \qquad \text{since by (i) } \mathbf{1}c = G \circ F \circ c = G \circ \Lambda(\mathrm{ev} \circ (F \circ c) \times \mathrm{id}).
\end{aligned}
$$

Hence $\mathfrak{M}$ is a λ-model.

(⇐) Suppose $\mathfrak{M}$ is a λ-model and let $f, g: U \to U$. Then

$$\forall x \in |U| \quad f \circ x = g \circ x \ \Rightarrow$$

$$\Rightarrow \ \forall x \hat{f} \cdot x = \hat{g} \cdot x, \quad \text{where } \hat{f} = G \circ \Lambda(f \circ p_2) \text{ and satisfies } \hat{f} \cdot x = f \circ x$$

$$\Rightarrow \ \mathbf{1} \cdot \hat{f} = \mathbf{1} \cdot \hat{g}$$

$$\Rightarrow \ G \circ F \circ \hat{f} = G \circ F \circ \hat{g}$$

$$\Rightarrow \ \Lambda(f \circ p_2) = \Lambda(g \circ p_2), \qquad \text{since } F \circ G = \text{id},$$

$$\Rightarrow \ f \circ p_2 = g \circ p_2$$

$$\Rightarrow \ f = g.$$

Therefore U has enough points.

(iii) (⇒) If $U \cong U^U$ via F, G, then $G \circ F = \text{id}_U$, hence by (i)

$$[\![\mathbf{1}M]\!]_\Delta = [\![M]\!]_\Delta,$$

in particular $[\![\mathbf{1}x]\!]_\Delta = [\![x]\!]_\Delta$. Then as in the proof of proposition 5.5.5 it follows that

$$[\![\mathbf{1}]\!]_\Delta = [\![\lambda x.\mathbf{1}x]\!]_\Delta = [\![\lambda x.x]\!]_\Delta = [\![\boldsymbol{I}]\!]_\Delta,$$

i.e. $\mathfrak{M} \models \mathbf{1} = \boldsymbol{I}$.

(⇐) Assume $\mathfrak{M} \models \mathbf{1} = \boldsymbol{I}$. Now

$$[\![\mathbf{1}]\!] = [\![\lambda xy.xy]\!] = G \circ \Lambda([\![\lambda y.xy]\!]_x)$$

$$= G \circ \Lambda(G \circ F \circ [\![x]\!]_x), \qquad \text{by (i)},$$

$$= G \circ \Lambda(G \circ F \circ p_2);$$

and $[\![\boldsymbol{I}]\!] = G \circ \Lambda(p_2)$. Therefore

$$G \circ \Lambda(G \circ F \circ p_2) = G \circ \Lambda(p_2)$$

$$\Rightarrow \ \Lambda(G \circ F \circ p_2) = \Lambda(p_2) \qquad (\text{use } F)$$

$$\Rightarrow \ G \circ F \circ p_2 = p_2 \qquad (\Lambda h \text{ uniquely determines } h)$$

$$\Rightarrow \ G \circ F = \text{id}_U \qquad (\text{use } \langle !, \text{id}_U \rangle).$$

(iv) By proposition 5.2.10 and (ii), (iii). □

Let $\mathfrak{A}$ be a λ-algebra that arises from a category that is "concrete", i.e. roughly one that is based on sets. Then $\mathfrak{A}$ is a λ-model and the interpretation in $\mathfrak{A}$ has a simple form.

5.5.8. DEFINITION. A ccc $\mathbb{C}$ is *strictly concrete* if there is a functor Φ: $\mathbb{C} \to \text{Set}$ such that

(1) Φ is faithful (i.e. injective on arrows).
(2) Φ is full (i.e. surjective) on $\text{Hom}_{\mathbb{C}}(T, A)$ for $A \in \mathbb{C}$.
(3) Φ preserves the terminal object, products and projections.
(4) For all $A, B \in \mathbb{C}$

$$\Phi(B^A) \subseteq \Phi(B)^{\Phi(A)},$$

$$\Phi(\text{ev}_{A,B}) = \text{ev}_{\Phi A, \Phi B} \upharpoonright \Phi(B^A) \times \Phi(A).$$

Note that this implies that every object in $\mathbb{C}$ has enough points. Moreover

$$\Phi(\Lambda_{\mathbb{C}} f) = \Lambda_{\text{Set}}(\Phi f),$$

where $\Lambda_{\text{Set}} g(a_1, \ldots, a_n) = \lambda\!\!\lambda d.g(a_1, \ldots, a_n, d)$ for $g: X^n \times Y \to Z$ in Set. Write $\{*\}$ for the terminal object in Set.

Complete partial orders or complete lattices with continuous maps are strictly concrete ccc's.

5.5.9. DEFINITION. Let $\mathbb{C}$ be a strictly concrete ccc with reflexive object U.

(i) $\varphi: |U| \to \Phi(U)$ is the bijection $\varphi(x) = \Phi(x)(*)$.
(ii) $\square: \Phi(U^U) \to \Phi(U)$ is the map $\square = \Phi(G)$.
(iii) $a \cdot b = \Phi(F)(a)(b)$ for $a, b \in \Phi(U)$.
(iv) $[\![M]\!]^{\Phi}_{\rho} = \varphi([\![\varphi^{-1}(M)]\!]^{\mathbb{C}}_{\varphi^{-1} \circ \rho})$ for $M \in \Lambda(\Phi(U))$.
(v) $\mathfrak{M}^{\Phi} = \langle \Phi(U), \cdot, [\![\ ]\!]^{\Phi} \rangle$.

5.5.10. THEOREM. (Koymans [1982]). (i) *The map* $[\![\ ]\!]^{\Phi}$ *in definition* 5.5.9 *satisfies*

(1) $[\![x]\!]^{\Phi}_{\rho} = \rho(x)$,
(2) $[\![c_a]\!]^{\Phi}_{\rho} = a$, *for* $a \in \Phi(U)$;
(3) $[\![PQ]\!]^{\Phi}_{\rho} = [\![P]\!]^{\Phi}_{\rho} \cdot [\![Q]\!]^{\Phi}_{\rho}$;
(4) $[\![\lambda x.P]\!]^{\Phi}_{\rho} = \square(\lambda\!\!\lambda d.[\![P]\!]^{\Phi}_{\rho(x:=d)})$.

(ii) $\mathfrak{M}^{\Phi}$ *is a* λ*-model isomorphic to* $\mathfrak{M}(\mathbb{C})$.

PROOF. (i) As an example we show (4). Let $\rho_0 = \varphi^{-1} \circ \rho$ and $\Delta = \text{FV}(\lambda x.P)$.

$$[\![\lambda x.P]\!]^{\Phi}_{\rho} = \Phi\big(G \circ \Lambda_{\mathbb{C}}([\![P]\!]_{\Delta,x}) \circ \rho_0^{\Delta}\big)(*),$$

where for simplicity we assume $\varphi^{-1}(P) = P$,

$$= \square\big(\Lambda_{\text{Set}}(\Phi([\![P]\!]_{\Delta,x}))(\rho^{\Delta})\big)$$

$$= \square\Big(\lambda\!\!\lambda d.\Phi([\![P]\!]_{\Delta,x})\big(\rho(x:=d)^{\Delta,x}\big)\Big)$$

$$= \square\Big(\lambda\!\!\lambda d.\Phi\big([\![P]\!]_{\Delta,x} \circ \rho_0(x:=\varphi^{-1}(d))^{\Delta,x}\big)(*)\Big)$$

$$= \square\Big(\lambda\!\!\lambda d.\varphi\big([\![P]\!]_{\varphi^{-1} \circ \rho(x:=d)}\big)\Big)$$

$$= \square\Big(\lambda\!\!\lambda d.[\![P]\!]^{\Phi}_{\rho(x:=d)}\Big).$$

(ii) The map $\varphi: \mathfrak{M}(\mathbb{C}) \to \mathfrak{M}^{\Phi}$ is by definition 5.5.9(iv) an isomorphism. By condition (4) it follows that $\mathfrak{M}^{\Phi}$ is a λ-model. □

$\mathfrak{M}^{\Phi}$ is called the *concrete version* of $\mathfrak{M}(\mathbb{C})$ *via the functor* Φ.

Now it will be proved that every λ-algebra can be obtained from a ccc with a reflexive object.

5.5.11. DEFINITION. Let $\mathfrak{A}$ be a λ-algebra. The *Karoubi envelope* of $\mathfrak{A}$, notation $\mathbb{C}(\mathfrak{A})$, is the category defined as follows. Let $a \circ b = \lambda x.a(bx)$, for $a, b \in \mathfrak{A}$:

Objects: $\{a \in \mathfrak{A} | a \circ a = a\}$.

Arrows: $\text{Hom}(a, b) = \{f \in \mathfrak{A} | b \circ f \circ a = f\}$.

Identity: $\text{id}_a = a$.

Composition: $f \circ g$.

It is easy to verify that $\mathbb{C}(\mathfrak{A})$ is indeed a category.

Karoubi [1978] defined the envelope for additive categories under the name "derived pseudo abelian category". This can be generalized to arbitrary categories. The notion then applies to a λ-algebra $\mathfrak{A}$ by introducing the monoid

$$\mathfrak{M}(\mathfrak{A}) = (\{a \in \mathfrak{A} | a = 1a\}, \circ, \boldsymbol{I})$$

considered as category with one object and as arrows the $a \in \mathfrak{M}(\mathfrak{A})$ with composition.

We need some notation from the λ-calculus. Let $[M, N] = \lambda z.zMN$ be pairing in the λ-calculus with projections $\pi_i = \lambda y.y(\lambda a_1 a_2.a_i)$, for $i = 1, 2$. Let $[M_1] = M_1$, $[M_1, \ldots, M_{n+1}] = [[M_1, \ldots, M_n], M_{n+1}]$ with π_i^n the canonical λ-terms such that $\pi_i^n[M_1, \ldots, M_n] = M_i$ for $1 \leqslant i \leqslant n$. $[\pi_1^1 = \boldsymbol{I}, \pi_{n+1}^{n+1} = \pi_2, \pi_i^{n+1} = \pi_i^n \circ \pi_1$ for $1 \leqslant i \leqslant n$.]

5.5.12. PROPOSITION. (Scott [1980]). (i) $\mathbb{C}(\mathfrak{A})$ *is a ccc.*

(ii) $\boldsymbol{I}$ *is a reflexive object in* $\mathbb{C}(\mathfrak{A})$ *via the arrows* $F = G = \mathbf{1}$.

PROOF. (i) 1. *Terminal object*. This is $t = \lambda xy.y$. Note that $f: a \to t \Leftrightarrow f = t$.

2. *Products*. Let $a_1, a_2 \in \mathbb{C}(\mathfrak{A})$. Then $a_1 \times a_2 = \lambda z.[a_1(\pi_1 z), a_2(\pi_2 z)]$ is the cartesian product with projections

$$p_i^{a_1 a_2} = a_i \circ \pi_i;$$
$$\langle f, g \rangle = \lambda z.[fz, gz].$$

3. *Exponents*. Let $a, b \in \mathbb{C}(\mathfrak{A})$. Then

$$b^a = \lambda z.b \circ z \circ a$$

$$\mathrm{ev}_{a,b} = \lambda z.b(\pi_1 z(a(\pi_2 z)))$$

$$\Lambda(f) = \lambda xy.f[x, y].$$

The calculations which show that everything works are straightforward and are left to the reader.

(ii) Note that $\boldsymbol{I}^{\boldsymbol{I}} = \mathbf{1}$. Moreover $\mathbf{1}: \mathbf{1} \to \boldsymbol{I}$, $\mathbf{1}: \boldsymbol{I} \to \mathbf{1}$ and $\mathbf{1} \circ \mathbf{1} = \mathbf{1} = \mathrm{id}_{\mathbf{1}}$. □

5.5.13. THEOREM. (Koymans [1982]). $\mathfrak{M}(\mathbb{C}(\mathfrak{A}), \boldsymbol{I}, \mathbf{1}, \mathbf{1}) \simeq \mathfrak{A}$.

PROOF. Let $\mathfrak{M} = \mathfrak{M}(\mathbb{C}(\mathfrak{A}))$. By induction on the structure of $M \in \Lambda$ one can show

$$(+) \qquad [\![M]\!]^{\mathfrak{M}}_{\vec{x}} = \lambda z.M[x_1, \ldots, x_n := \pi^n_1 z, \ldots, \pi^n_n z].$$

As an example we treat $M \equiv \lambda y.P$.

$$[\![\lambda y.P]\!]_{\vec{x}} = G \circ \Lambda([\![P]\!]_{\vec{x},y})$$

$$\underset{\mathrm{IH}}{=} \mathbf{1} \circ \lambda pq.(\lambda z.P[x_1, \ldots, x_n, y := \pi^{n+1}_1 z, \ldots, \pi^{n+1}_{n+1} z][p, q]$$

$$= \lambda pq.P[x_1, \ldots, x_n, y := \pi^n_1 p, \ldots, \pi^n_n p, q]$$

$$=_\alpha \lambda p.(\lambda y.P)[x_1, \ldots, x_n := \pi^n_1 p, \ldots, \pi^n_n p]$$

$$=_\alpha \lambda z.M[x_1, \ldots, x_n := \pi^n_1 z, \ldots, \pi^n_n z].$$

Let $\odot$ be application in $\mathfrak{M}$. Note that

$$a \odot b = \mathrm{Ap} \circ \langle a, b \rangle$$

$$= \mathrm{ev}_{\boldsymbol{I},\boldsymbol{I}} \circ \langle \mathbf{1} \circ a, b \rangle$$

$$= \lambda z.\mathrm{ev}_{\boldsymbol{I},\boldsymbol{I}}[\mathbf{1}(az), bz]$$

$$= \lambda z.az(bz) = \boldsymbol{S}ab.$$

Now define $\varphi: \mathfrak{A} \to \mathfrak{M}$ by $\varphi(a) = \boldsymbol{K}a$. Then φ is clearly injective. If $x \in |\boldsymbol{I}| = t \to \boldsymbol{I}$, then x is constant so $x = \boldsymbol{K}(x\boldsymbol{I}) = \varphi(x\boldsymbol{I})$; therefore φ is surjective. Finally φ is a homomorphism:

1. $\varphi(xy) = \boldsymbol{K}(xy)$
$= \boldsymbol{S}(\boldsymbol{K}x)(\boldsymbol{K}y)$, since $\mathfrak{A}$ is a λ-algebra,
$= \varphi(x) \odot \varphi(y)$.

2. $\varphi(\boldsymbol{K}) = \boldsymbol{KK} = [\![\boldsymbol{K}]\!]^{\mathfrak{M}}$ by $(+)$ and similarly for $\boldsymbol{S}$.
Therefore φ is an isomorphism and $\mathfrak{A} \cong \mathfrak{M}$. □

It follows that every λ-algebra (λ-model) can be obtained from a ccc with reflexive object U (having enough points).

Remarks. (i) It is not hard to show that if $\mathfrak{A}$ is a λ-model, then every object of $\mathbb{C}(\mathfrak{A})$ has enough points, see Koymans [1982].

(ii) It is not true that $\mathbb{C}(\mathfrak{M}(\mathbb{C}, U)) \cong \mathbb{C}$. The category $\mathbb{C}$ may have many more objects.

The notion of λ-algebra homomorphism can be characterized in a categorical way.

5.5.14. DEFINITION. A functor Φ between two ccc's is *cartesian* if Φ preserves the terminal object, products and exponents.

5.5.15. PROPOSITION. (i) *For $i = 1, 2$ let $\mathbb{C}_i$ be a ccc with reflexive objects U_i via the maps F_i, G_i. Let $\Phi : \mathbb{C}_1 \to \mathbb{C}_2$ be a cartesian functor with $\Phi(U_1) = U_2$, $\Phi(F_1) = F_2$, $\Phi(G_1) = G_2$. Then Φ induces a homomorphism $\Phi^* : \mathfrak{M}(\mathbb{C}_1) \to \mathfrak{M}(\mathbb{C}_2)$.*

(ii) *If $\varphi : \mathfrak{A}_1 \to \mathfrak{A}_2$ is a homomorphism, then φ induces a cartesian functor $\varphi^+ : \mathbb{C}(\mathfrak{A}_1) \to \mathbb{C}(\mathfrak{A}_2)$ preserving the reflexive elements $\boldsymbol{I}$ and retraction map $\mathbf{1}$. Moreover $\varphi^{+*} = \varphi$ up to isomorphism.*

PROOF. (i) For $x \in |U_1|$ define $\Phi^*(x) = \Phi(x) \in |U_2|$. This is a homomorphism since Φ preserves F, G and the cartesian structure.

(ii) For a an object of $\mathbb{C}(\mathfrak{A}_1)$ define $\varphi^+(a) = \varphi(a)$ and for $f \in \mathrm{Hom}_{\mathbb{C}(\mathfrak{A}_1)}(a, b)$ define $\varphi^+(f) = \varphi(f)$. Since φ preserves all closed λ-terms, this is a cartesian functor preserving $\boldsymbol{I}$ and $\mathbf{1}$. Clearly $\varphi^{+*} = \varphi$ on $\mathfrak{M}(\mathbb{C}(\mathfrak{A})) \cong \mathfrak{A}$. □

5.6. Other model descriptions; categorical models

Lambda models were defined as lambda algebras satisfying the Meyer–Scott axiom. Since the combinatory axioms describing λ-algebras are not memorable, one may wonder whether these can be simplified in presence of the new axiom. This is indeed the case; the result is due independently to Meyer and Scott.

5.6.1. DEFINITION. Define the following combinatory terms.

$$\mathbf{1}_1 = \mathbf{1} = \boldsymbol{S}(\boldsymbol{KI}); \qquad \mathbf{1}_{n+1} = \boldsymbol{S}(\boldsymbol{K}\mathbf{1})(\boldsymbol{S}(\boldsymbol{K}\mathbf{1}_n)).$$

Remark. Using the simpler definition $\mathbf{1}_1 = \mathbf{1}, \mathbf{1}_{n+1} = \boldsymbol{S}(\boldsymbol{K}\mathbf{1}_n)$ the results 5.6.2, 5.6.3 and 5.6.6(i) remain valid.

5.6.2. LEMMA. (i) *If* $\mathfrak{M}$ *is a combinatory algebra, then*

$$\mathfrak{M} \models \mathbf{1}_n a b_1 \cdots b_n = a b_1 \cdots b_n .$$

(ii) *If* $\mathfrak{M}$ *is a* λ*-algebra, then*

$$\mathfrak{M} \models \mathbf{1}_n = \lambda a b_1 \cdots b_n . a b_1 \cdots b_n .$$

PROOF. (i) (ii). Induction on n, e.g. in a λ-algebra

$$\mathbf{1}_1 = \boldsymbol{S}(\boldsymbol{KI}) = (\lambda xyz.xz(yz))(\boldsymbol{KI}) = \lambda yz.\boldsymbol{KI}z(yz) = \lambda yz.yz. \quad \square$$

5.6.3. THEOREM. (Meyer [1982]; Scott [1980]). *Let* $\mathfrak{M} = \langle X, \cdot, k, s \rangle$. *Then* $\mathfrak{M}$ *is a* λ*-model iff* $\mathfrak{M}$ *satisfies*

(1) $\boldsymbol{K}xy = x$,
(2) $\boldsymbol{S}xyz = xz(yz)$,
(3) $\forall x\ ax = bx \Rightarrow \mathbf{1}a = \mathbf{1}b$,
(4) $\mathbf{1}_2\boldsymbol{K} = \boldsymbol{K}$,
(5) $\mathbf{1}_3\boldsymbol{S} = \boldsymbol{S}$.

PROOF. ($\Rightarrow$) If $\mathfrak{M}$ is a λ-model, then by definition (1), (2), (3) hold. Moreover $\mathfrak{M}$ is a λ-algebra, hence satisfies (4), (5) since these equations are provable in $\boldsymbol{\lambda}$.

($\Leftarrow$) First show that for all $a, b \in \mathfrak{M}$ $\mathbf{1}(\boldsymbol{K}a) = \boldsymbol{K}a$ and $\mathbf{1}(\boldsymbol{S}ab) = \boldsymbol{S}ab$. Indeed, $\boldsymbol{K}a = \mathbf{1}_2\boldsymbol{K}a = \boldsymbol{S}(\boldsymbol{K}\mathbf{1})\boldsymbol{K}a = \mathbf{1}(\boldsymbol{K}a)$ and similarly for $\boldsymbol{S}$.

Since $\lambda x.A$ is always of the form $\boldsymbol{KP}$ or $\boldsymbol{SPQ}$ it follows that

$$(*) \qquad 1(\lambda x.A) = \lambda x.A.$$

Therefore $\mathfrak{M}$ is weakly extensional:

$$\begin{aligned} \forall x A = B &\Rightarrow \forall x (\lambda x.A)x = (\lambda x.B)x \\ &\Rightarrow \mathbf{1}(\lambda x.A) = \mathbf{1}(\lambda x.B), \qquad \text{by } 3, \\ &\Rightarrow \lambda x.A = \lambda x.B, \qquad \text{by } (*). \end{aligned}$$

It remains to show that $\mathfrak{M}$ is a λ-algebra. By lemma 5.2.3 it suffices to show that

(a) $\boldsymbol{\lambda} \vdash M = N \Rightarrow \mathfrak{M} \models M = N$,
(b) $\mathfrak{M} \models \boldsymbol{K} = \boldsymbol{K}_{\lambda, CL}$, $\mathfrak{M} \models \boldsymbol{S} = \boldsymbol{S}_{\lambda, CL}$.

Now, (a) follows by induction on the proof of $M = N$, weak extensionality taking care of the rule $P = Q \Rightarrow \lambda x.P = \lambda x.Q$. As to (b), we will prove this in several steps.

Step 1. $\forall x_1 \cdots x_n \quad ax_1 \cdots x_n = bx_1 \cdots x_n \Rightarrow \mathbf{1}_n a = \mathbf{1}_n b$.

Proof. Induction on n. If $n = 1$, then this is 3. If $n = p + 1$, then

$$\begin{aligned} ax_1 \cdots x_{p+1} = bx_1 \cdots x_{p+1} &\underset{\text{IH}}{\Rightarrow} \mathbf{1}_p(ax_1) = \mathbf{1}_p(bx_1) \\ &\Rightarrow \boldsymbol{S}(\boldsymbol{K}\mathbf{1}_p)ax_1 = \boldsymbol{S}(\boldsymbol{K}\mathbf{1}_p)bx_1 \\ &\Rightarrow \mathbf{1}(\boldsymbol{S}(\boldsymbol{K}\mathbf{1}_p)a) = \mathbf{1}(\boldsymbol{S}(\boldsymbol{K}\mathbf{1}_p)b) \\ &\Rightarrow \boldsymbol{S}(\boldsymbol{K}\mathbf{1})(\boldsymbol{S}(\boldsymbol{K}\mathbf{1}_p))a = \boldsymbol{S}(\boldsymbol{K}\mathbf{1})(\boldsymbol{S}(\boldsymbol{K}\mathbf{1}_p))b \\ &\Rightarrow \mathbf{1}_{p+1}a = \mathbf{1}_{p+1}b. \quad \Box_1 \end{aligned}$$

Step 2. $\mathbf{1}(\mathbf{1}_n a) = \mathbf{1}_n a$.

Proof. First note $\mathbf{1}ax = ax$, hence $\mathbf{1}(\mathbf{1}a) = \mathbf{1}a$, by 3. So we are done for $n = 1$. If $n = p + 1$, then $\mathbf{1}_n a = \mathbf{1}(\cdots)$, hence $\mathbf{1}(\mathbf{1}_n a) = \mathbf{1}(\mathbf{1} \cdots) = \mathbf{1} \cdots = \mathbf{1}_n a$. $\Box_2$

Step 3. $1_n(\lambda x_1 \cdots x_n.A) = \lambda x_1 \cdots x_n.A$.

Proof. Induction on n. If $n = 1$, then this is $(*)$. If $n = p + 1$, then

$$\begin{aligned} \mathbf{1}_n(\lambda x_1 \cdots x_n.A)x_1 &= \boldsymbol{S}(\boldsymbol{K}\mathbf{1})(\boldsymbol{S}(\boldsymbol{K}\mathbf{1}_n))(\lambda x_1 \cdots x_n.A)x_1 \\ &= \mathbf{1}_n(\lambda x_2 \cdots x_n.A) \\ &\underset{\text{IH}}{=} \lambda x_2 \cdots x_n.A \\ &= (\lambda x_1 \cdots x_n.A)x_1. \end{aligned}$$

Hence $\mathbf{1}(\mathbf{1}_n(\lambda x_1 \cdots x_n.A)) = \mathbf{1}(\lambda x_1 \cdots x_n.A)$ and therefore $\mathbf{1}_n(\lambda x_1 \cdots x_n.A) = \lambda x_1 \cdots x_n.A$ by $(*)$ and step 2. $\Box_3$

Finally let $\boldsymbol{K}' = \boldsymbol{K}_{\lambda, CL} = \lambda xy.x$. Then we have $\boldsymbol{K}xy = x = \boldsymbol{K}'xy$,

$$\mathbf{1}_2\boldsymbol{K} = \mathbf{1}_2\boldsymbol{K}', \qquad \text{by step 1,}$$

$$\boldsymbol{K} = \boldsymbol{K}', \qquad \text{by 4 and step 3.}$$

Similarly $\boldsymbol{S} = \lambda xyz.xz(yz)$. $\Box$

The following definition of Meyer [1982] simplifies even further the description of the essence of a λ-model.

5.6.4. DEFINITION. (i) A *combinatory model* is a structure $\mathfrak{M} = \langle X, \cdot, k, s, \varepsilon \rangle$

satisfying

(1) $\boldsymbol{K}xy = x,$

(2) $\boldsymbol{S}xyz = xz(yz),$

(3) $\varepsilon xy = xy,$

(4) $\forall x\ ax = bx \ \rightarrow\ \varepsilon a = \varepsilon b.$

(ii) A combinatory model is *stable* if moreover

(5) $\varepsilon\varepsilon = \varepsilon,$

(6) $\varepsilon_2 \boldsymbol{K} = \boldsymbol{K},$

(7) $\varepsilon_3 \boldsymbol{S} = \boldsymbol{S},$

Here, of course, $\varepsilon_1 = \varepsilon$ and $\varepsilon_{n+1} = \boldsymbol{S}(\boldsymbol{K}\varepsilon)(\boldsymbol{S}(\boldsymbol{K}\varepsilon_n))$.

5.6.5. Lemma. *Let* $\mathfrak{M} = \langle X, \cdot, k, s, \varepsilon\rangle$ *be a combinatory model.*

(i) $\varepsilon_{n+1}a = a \ \Leftrightarrow\ \varepsilon a = a \wedge \forall x\ \varepsilon_n(ax) = ax.$

(ii) $\varepsilon_n a = a \ \Leftrightarrow\ \forall x_1 \cdots x_i\ \varepsilon(ax_1 \cdots x_i) = ax_1 \cdots x_i, \quad 0 \leqslant i < n.$

(iii) $\mathfrak{M}$ *is stable* $\Leftrightarrow$ $\varepsilon, k, ka, s, sa, sab$ *are for all* a, b *fixed points of* ε.

Proof. (i) ($\Rightarrow$) By assumption

(1) $a = \boldsymbol{S}(\boldsymbol{K}\varepsilon)(\boldsymbol{S}(\boldsymbol{K}\varepsilon_n))a = \varepsilon(\boldsymbol{S}(\boldsymbol{K}\varepsilon_n)a).$

Hence by definition 5.6.4(3)

$$ax = \boldsymbol{S}(\boldsymbol{K}\varepsilon_n)ax = \varepsilon_n(ax);$$

therefore by 5.6.4(4) and (1)

$$\varepsilon a = \varepsilon(\boldsymbol{S}(\boldsymbol{K}\varepsilon_n)a) = a.$$

($\Leftarrow$) In a combinatory model one has $\varepsilon ab = ab$, therefore

(2) $\varepsilon(\varepsilon a) = \varepsilon a$

Now $\varepsilon_{n+1}a = \varepsilon(\boldsymbol{S}(\boldsymbol{K}\varepsilon_n)a)$, therefore by (2)

(3) $\varepsilon(\varepsilon_{n+1}a) = \varepsilon_{n+1}a,$

but also

$$\varepsilon_{n+1}ax = \varepsilon_n(ax) = ax.$$

Hence by definition 5.6.4(4) and assumption

$$\varepsilon(\varepsilon_{n+1}a) = \varepsilon a = a.$$

Together with (3) this implies $\varepsilon_{n+1}a = a$.

(ii) By induction on n, using (i).

(iii) ($\Rightarrow$) As to $\boldsymbol{S}ab$:

$$(4) \qquad \boldsymbol{S}ab = \varepsilon_3 \boldsymbol{S}ab = \varepsilon(\boldsymbol{S}ab).$$

As to $\boldsymbol{S}a$:

$$\boldsymbol{S}a = \varepsilon_3 \boldsymbol{S}a = \boldsymbol{S}(\boldsymbol{K}\varepsilon)(\boldsymbol{S}a),$$

and it follows by (4) and (2) that $\boldsymbol{S}a$ is a fixed point of ε. Similarly it follows that $\boldsymbol{S}$, $\boldsymbol{K}a$ and $\boldsymbol{K}$ are fixed points. By assumption ε is a fixed point of ε.

($\Leftarrow$) By assumption and (ii). □

5.6.6. PROPOSITION. (i) *Let* $\mathfrak{M} = \langle X, \cdot, k, s, \varepsilon \rangle$ *be a stable combinatory model. Then* $\varepsilon = 1$ *and* $\langle X, \cdot, k, s \rangle$ *is a* λ*-model. Moreover* k, s *are uniquely determined by* ε.

(ii) *If* $\mathfrak{M} = \langle X, \cdot, k, s, \varepsilon \rangle$ *is a combinatory model, then* $\mathfrak{M}' = \langle X, \cdot, k', s', \varepsilon' \rangle$ *is a stable combinatory model, where* $k' = \varepsilon_2 k$, $s' = \varepsilon_3 k$ *and* $\varepsilon' = \varepsilon\varepsilon$.

PROOF. (i) Note that

$$\begin{aligned} & xy = \mathbf{1}xy \\ \Rightarrow\ & \varepsilon x = \varepsilon(\mathbf{1}x), && \text{by definition 5.6.4(4)}, \\ & \quad\ = \mathbf{1}x, && \text{by lemma 5.6.5(iii) since } \mathbf{1}x = \boldsymbol{S}(\boldsymbol{KI})x, \\ \Rightarrow\ & \varepsilon\varepsilon = \varepsilon\mathbf{1}, && \text{by definition 5.6.4(4)}, \\ \Rightarrow\ & \varepsilon = \mathbf{1}, && \text{by stability and lemma 5.6.5(iii)}. \end{aligned}$$

Therefore $\langle X, \cdot, k, s \rangle$ is by theorem 5.6.3 a λ-model.

As to uniqueness, let $\langle X, \cdot, k_0, s_0, \varepsilon \rangle$ be also a stable combinatory model, in order to show $k = k_0$, $s = s_0$. Then

$$\begin{aligned} kxy = x = k_0xy \ &\Rightarrow\ \varepsilon(kx) = \varepsilon(k_0x) \\ &\Rightarrow\ s(k\varepsilon)kx = s(k\varepsilon)k_0x \\ &\Rightarrow\ \varepsilon(s(k\varepsilon)k) = \varepsilon(s(k\varepsilon)k_0) \\ &\Rightarrow\ \varepsilon_2 k = \varepsilon_2 k_0 \\ &\Rightarrow\ k = k_0. \end{aligned}$$

Similarly $s = s_0$.

(ii) Now let $x \in \{\varepsilon', k', k'a, s', s'a, s'ab\}$. By lemma 5.6.5(iii) it suffices to show that $\varepsilon x = x$ since then $\varepsilon' x = \varepsilon\varepsilon x = \varepsilon x = x$. But $x = \varepsilon y$ for some y, e.g.

$$x = k' = \varepsilon_2 k = s(k\varepsilon)(s(k\varepsilon))k = \varepsilon(s(k\varepsilon)k).$$

Then by 5.6.5(2) it follows that $\varepsilon x = \varepsilon(\varepsilon y) = \varepsilon y = x$. □

Although in λ-models k, s are uniquely determined by $1 = s(ki)$, a map that preserves application and 1 is not necessarily a homomorphism: take e.g. the constant map $\lambda\!\!\!\lambda x.1' : \mathfrak{M} \to \mathfrak{M}'$.

5.6.7 DEFINITION. (i) Let $\mathfrak{M} = (X, \cdot)$ be a combinatory complete applicative structure. An *expansion* of $\mathfrak{M}$ is of the form $(\mathfrak{M}, k, s) = (X, \cdot, k, s)$ which is a combinatory algebra.

(ii) $\mathfrak{M} = (X, \cdot)$ is a *categorical* λ-model (λ-algebra, combinatory algebra) if there is a unique expansion $(\mathfrak{M}, k, s)$ making $\mathfrak{M}$ into a λ-model (λ-algebra, combinatory algebra).

(iii) An element ε of $\mathfrak{M}$ is called a *stable* ε if

$$\varepsilon\varepsilon = \varepsilon \wedge \varepsilon ab = ab \wedge (\forall x\; ax = bx \to \varepsilon a = \varepsilon b).$$

5.6.8. THEOREM. (i) *Let* $\mathfrak{M} = (X, \cdot)$ *be combinatory complete. Let* $[X \to X] = \{f : X \to X \mid f \text{ representable}\}$ *and define* $F: X \to [X \to X]$ *by* $F(x)(y) = xy$. *Then* $\mathfrak{M}$ *can be expanded to a λ-model iff there exists a* $G : [X \to X] \to X$ *such that*

(1) $F \circ G = \mathrm{id}_{[X \to X]}$;

(2) $G \circ F \in [X \to X]$.

(ii) *The* G*'s satisfying* 1, 2 *in* (i) *correspond exactly to stable* ε*'s.*

(iii) $\mathfrak{M}$ *is a categorical λ-model iff the* G *in* (i) *is unique iff there is a unique stable* ε.

PROOF. (i) (⇒) Let $(\mathfrak{M}, k, s)$ be a λ-model. Define

$$G(f) = \mathbf{1}a_f$$

for some a_f representing f. G is well-defined: if $ax = f(x) = a'x$ for all x, then $\mathbf{1}a = \mathbf{1}a'$ by the Meyer–Scott axiom. Clearly $F(\mathbf{1}a_f) = F(a_f) = f$, so $F \circ G = \mathrm{id}$. Moreover $G \circ F(a) = \mathbf{1}a$, since a represents $F(a)$; hence $G \circ F$ is representable.

($\Leftarrow$) Let $k_0, s_0 \in X$ satisfy the k, s axioms. Define $\varepsilon_0 = G(G \circ F)$. Then $(X, \cdot, k_0, s_0, \varepsilon_0)$ is a combinatory model:

$$\begin{aligned}\varepsilon_0 ab &= G(G \circ F)ab \\ &= F(F \circ G(G \circ F)(a))(b) \\ &= F(a)(b), \qquad \text{since } F \circ G = \text{id}, \\ &= ab.\end{aligned}$$

$$\begin{aligned}\forall x\; ax = bx \;&\Rightarrow\; F(a) = F(b) \\ &\Rightarrow\; G \circ F(a) = G \circ F(b) \\ &\Rightarrow\; \varepsilon_0 a = \varepsilon_0 b, \qquad \text{since } \varepsilon_0 \text{ represents } G \circ F.\end{aligned}$$

It follows by proposition 5.6.6(ii) that $\mathfrak{M}$ can be expanded to a λ-model.

(ii) As in (i) define $G_\varepsilon(f) = \varepsilon a_f$ and $\varepsilon_G = G(G \circ F)$. First note that ε_G is actually stable:

$$\varepsilon_G \varepsilon_G = F(\varepsilon_G)(\varepsilon_G) = F(G(G \circ F))(G(G \circ F)) = \varepsilon_G.$$

Moreover $\lambda\!\!\!\lambda G.\varepsilon_G$ and $\lambda\!\!\!\lambda \varepsilon.G_\varepsilon$ are inverse of each other:

$$G_{\varepsilon_G}(f) = \varepsilon_G a_f = F \circ G(G \circ F)(a_f) = G \circ F(a_f) = G(f);$$

$$\begin{aligned}\varepsilon_{G_\varepsilon} &= G_\varepsilon(G_\varepsilon \circ F) = \varepsilon a_{G_\varepsilon \circ F} \\ &= \varepsilon\varepsilon, \qquad \text{since } \varepsilon \text{ represents } G_\varepsilon \circ F: \quad G_\varepsilon \circ F(b) = \varepsilon a_{F(b)} = \varepsilon b, \\ &= \varepsilon.\end{aligned}$$

(iii) $\mathfrak{M}$ is a categorical λ-model $\Leftrightarrow$
- $\Leftrightarrow$ there are unique k, s making $\mathfrak{M}$ into a λ-model
- $\Leftrightarrow$ there are unique k, s, ε making $\mathfrak{M}$ into a stable combinatory model
- $\Leftrightarrow$ there is a unique stable ε
- $\Leftrightarrow$ there is a unique G satisfying 1, 2 in (i). □

5.7. Survey of part V

Chapter 18. Constructions of models

18.1. The graph model $P\omega$

THEOREM. *Let $f: P\omega \to P\omega$ be continuous with respect to the Scott topology on the* cpo $(P\omega, \subseteq)$. *Then f is completely determined by*

$$graph(f) = \{(n, m) | m \in f(e_n)\} \in P\omega,$$

where $e_0, e_1, \ldots$ *is an enumeration of the finite elements of* $P\omega$ *and* (n, m) *is a pairing on* $\mathbb{N}$.

THEOREM. *The map*

$$graph: [P\omega \to P\omega] \to P\omega$$

is an embedding of $[P\omega \to P\omega]$ *as a retract into* $P\omega$. *Hence* $P\omega$ *can be considered as a* λ*-model by the theorem in* § 5.4.

18.2. The models D_∞

DEFINITION. Let D be a cpo. Define $D_0 = D$, $D_{n+1} = [D_n \to D_n]$

THEOREM. *There are maps* $\psi_n \in [D_{n+1} \to D_n]$ *such that for the projective limit* $D_\infty = \underleftarrow{\lim}\, D_n, \psi_n$ *one has* $D_\infty \cong [D_\infty \to D_\infty]$.

In particular D_∞ is an extensional λ-model by § 5.4.

18.3. The model $\mathfrak{B}$

$\mathfrak{B}$ is the set of Böhm-like trees considered as a cpo.

DEFINITION. For $A, B \in \mathfrak{B}$ let $A \cdot B = \cup_n \mathrm{BT}(M_{A^n} M_{B^n})$ where M_{A^n} is the term corresponding to the nth approximation of A.

THEOREM. $A \cdot B$ *is well defined and continuous on* $\mathfrak{B}$. *Moreover* $\mathrm{BT}(MN) = \mathrm{BT}(M) \cdot \mathrm{BT}(N)$.

THEOREM. $(\mathfrak{B}, \cdot)$ *is a* λ*-model such that for all* $M, N \in \Lambda$

$$\mathfrak{B} \models M = N \Leftrightarrow \mathrm{BT}(M) = \mathrm{BT}(N).$$

18.4. Exercises

Chapter 19. Local structure of models

19.1. Local structure of $P\omega$

THEOREM (*Characterization theorem for* $P\omega$).

$$P\omega \models M = N \Leftrightarrow \mathrm{BT}(M) = \mathrm{BT}(N),$$

$$P\omega \models M \subseteq N \Leftrightarrow \mathrm{BT}(M)^{\eta} \subseteq \mathrm{BT}(N).$$

The main tool in proving this is the following approximation theorem which states in fact that the interpretation map $[\![\ ]\!]_\rho : \Lambda \to P\omega$ is continuous (w.r.t. the Scott topology on $P\omega$ and the tree topology on Λ).

THEOREM. *If* $M \in \Lambda$, *then* $M = \cup_k M^{(k)}$ *in* $P\omega$.

19.2. Local structure of D_∞

THEOREM (*Characterization theorem for* D_∞).

$$\begin{aligned} D_\infty \vDash M = N &\Leftrightarrow M = N \in \mathcal{H}^* \\ &\Leftrightarrow \mathrm{BT}(M) =_\eta \mathrm{BT}(N) \\ &\Leftrightarrow \infty\eta\mathrm{BT}(M) = \infty\eta\mathrm{BT}(N), \\ D_\infty \vDash M \sqsubseteq N &\Leftrightarrow \mathrm{BT}(M)^\eta \subseteq {}^\eta\mathrm{BT}(N) \\ &\Leftrightarrow \infty\eta\mathrm{BT}(M) \subseteq \infty\eta\mathrm{BT}(N). \end{aligned}$$

Again the main tool is the following approximation theorem.

THEOREM. *In* D_∞ *one has* $M = \sqcup_k M^{(k)}$.

As a corollary to the characterization theorem one obtains

THEOREM. $D_\infty \vDash \omega$; *in particular the interior* D_∞^0 *is extensional.*

19.3. Continuous λ*-models*

DEFINITION. A *continuous* λ*-model* is a structure $\mathfrak{M} = (X, \cdot, \lambda)$ which is a cpo that is also a λ-model in which $\cdot$ is continuous and the approximation theorem holds.

THEOREM. $P\omega$, D_∞ *and* $\mathfrak{B}$ *are all continuous* λ*-models.*

THEOREM. *If* $\mathfrak{M}$ *is a continuous* λ*-model, then*

$$BT(M) = BT(M) \Rightarrow \mathfrak{M} \vDash M = N.$$

THEOREM. *Let* $\mathfrak{M}$ *be a continuous* λ*-model and let* $Y \in \Lambda$ *be a fixed point operator. Then* Y *represents in* $\mathfrak{M}$ *the least fixed point operator of the* cpo $\mathfrak{M}$.

Chapter 20. Global structure of models

20.1. Extensionality; categoricity

THEOREM. (i) $\mathfrak{M}(\lambda\eta)$ *is extensional, but* $\mathfrak{M}^0(\lambda\eta)$ *is not.*
$\mathfrak{M}(\lambda)$ *is weakly extensional, but* $\mathfrak{M}^0(\lambda)$ *is not.*
(ii) *Similar statements hold when in* (*i*) λ *is replaced by* $\mathcal{H}$ *or* **B**.

THEOREM. (i) *Neither* $P\omega$ *nor* $P\omega^0$ *are extensional.*
(ii) D_∞ *and* D_∞^0 *are both extensional.*

THEOREM. $P\omega$ *is a categorical* λ*-model, but* D_A *is not.* $P\omega$ *is not a categorical combinatory algebra.*

20.2. The range property

DEFINITION. A λ-algebra $\mathfrak{M}$ satisfies the *range property* iff every definable function on $\mathfrak{M}$ has either an infinite range or a singleton range.

THEOREM. (i) *Each open term model* $\mathfrak{M}(\mathfrak{T})$ *satisfies the range property.*
(ii) *If* $\mathfrak{T}$ *is r.e., then* $\mathfrak{M}^0(\mathfrak{T})$ *satisfies the range property.*
(iii) *If* $\mathfrak{M}$ *is a continuous* λ*-model, then* $\mathfrak{M}$ *and* $\mathfrak{M}^0$ *satisfy the range property.*

20.3. Nondefinability results

THEOREM. (*Nondefinability of Church's* δ). *There is no* $\delta \in \Lambda$ *such that for all closed* nf's

$$\begin{aligned} \delta MN &= T \quad \text{if } M \equiv N, \\ &= F \quad \text{if } M \not\equiv N. \end{aligned}$$

THEOREM. *A definable map on* $\mathfrak{M}(\mathfrak{T})$ (*or, for* $\mathfrak{T}$ r.e., *on* $\mathfrak{M}^0(\mathfrak{T})$) *with range included in the numerals is constant.*

20.4. Local is global representability

DEFINITION. (i) A map $\varphi: \mathfrak{M} \to \mathfrak{M}$ is *locally representable* if for each $b \in \mathfrak{M}$ the function ψ_b defined by $\psi_b(a) = \varphi(a) \cdot b$ is representable.
(ii) A λ-algebra $\mathfrak{M}$ is *rich* if all locally representable $\varphi: \mathfrak{M} \to \mathfrak{M}$ are representable.

THEOREM. $\mathfrak{M}$ *is rich* $\Rightarrow \mathfrak{M}$ *is extensional.*

THEOREM. $\mathfrak{M}(\lambda\eta)$, $\mathfrak{M}(\mathcal{H}\eta)$ *and* D_∞ *are rich.*

THEOREM. *If* $\mathfrak{M}$ *is hard and satisfies* $\mathfrak{B}$, *then* $\mathfrak{M}$ *is not rich.*

20.5. The tree topology on models

DEFINITION. Let $\mathfrak{M}$ be an open (or closed) term model. The *tree topology* on $\mathfrak{M}$ is the largest topology that makes $[\![\ ]\!]: \Lambda \to \mathfrak{M}$ continuous (when Λ has the tree topology).

PROPOSITION. *Let* $\mathfrak{M}$ *be an open or closed term model.*

(i) $\mathfrak{M}$ *is semi-sensible* $\Leftrightarrow$ $\mathfrak{M}$ *is not indiscrete.*

(ii) *If* $\mathfrak{M}$ *is semi-sensible, then for* $M \in \Lambda$
M is unsolvable $\Leftrightarrow$ *M in* $\mathfrak{M}$ *has as only neighborhood the whole space.*

PROPOSITION. *Let* $\mathfrak{M}$ *be* $M(\mathfrak{T})$ *or* $\mathfrak{M}^0(\mathfrak{T})$ *with* $\mathfrak{T} = \boldsymbol{\lambda}, \boldsymbol{\lambda\eta}, \mathfrak{H}, \mathfrak{H}\boldsymbol{\eta}, \mathfrak{B}$ *or* $\mathfrak{B}\boldsymbol{\eta}$. *Then for* $M \in \Lambda$

$$M \text{ has a nf} \Leftrightarrow M \text{ is isolated in } \mathfrak{M}.$$

20.6. Exercises

Chapter 21. Combinatory groups

21.1. Combinatory semigroups

DEFINITION. Let $\mathfrak{M}$ be a λ-algebra. Then

(i) $S(\mathfrak{M})$ is the monoid $(\{\mathbf{1}a | a \in m\}, \circ, \boldsymbol{I})$.

(ii) $G(\mathfrak{M})$ is the subgroup of $S(\mathfrak{M})$ consisting of the invertible elements.

(iii) If $\mathfrak{T}$ is a λ-theory, then $S(\mathfrak{T}) = S(\mathfrak{M}(\mathfrak{T}))$, $G(\mathfrak{T}) = G(\mathfrak{M}(\mathfrak{T}))$.

THEOREM. $S^0(\boldsymbol{\lambda\eta}) = S(\mathfrak{M}^0(\boldsymbol{\lambda\eta}))$ *is a recursively presented semigroup having two generators with an unsolvable word problem.*

21.2. Characterization of invertibility

DEFINITION. $A \in \mathfrak{B}$ is a *hereditary permutation* ($\mathfrak{H}\mathfrak{P}$) if A is of the form

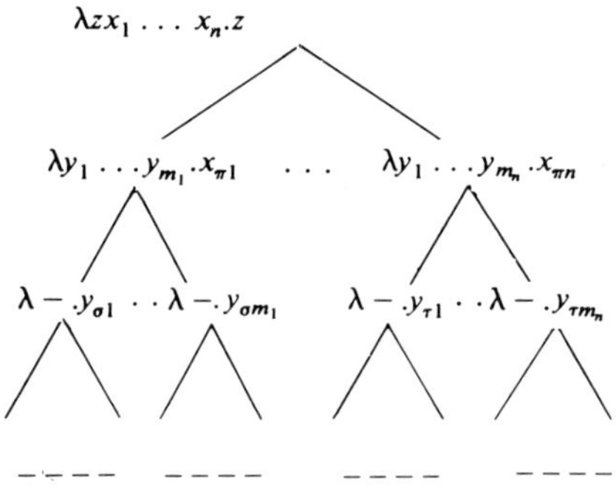

where π, σ, τ are permutations and the numbers $n, m_1, \ldots, m_n, \ldots$ are arbitrary $\geqslant 0$. The tree may be finite or infinite. If the tree is finite, then A is called a *finite* hereditary permutation ($\mathfrak{F}\mathfrak{H}\mathfrak{P}$).

THEOREM. (i) *$M \in S(\lambda\eta)$ is invertible $\Leftrightarrow BT(M)$ is a $\mathcal{FHP}$.*
(ii) *$M \in S(\mathcal{H}^*)$ is invertible $\Leftrightarrow BT(M)$ is a $\mathcal{HP}$.*

COROLLARY. (i) $G(\lambda\eta) = G(\lambda\omega) = G(\mathcal{H}\eta) = G(\mathcal{H}\omega)$.
(ii) $G(\mathcal{H}^*) \supseteq G(\lambda\eta)$.

21.3. The groups $G(\lambda\eta)$ and $G(\mathcal{H}^*)$

DEFINITION. (i) S_ω is the group of permutations on $\mathbb{N}$ with finite support.
(ii) For a group G, let $G^{\underset{\smile}{\omega}}$ be the weak infinite power, i.e. almost all coordinates are the unit element.
(iii) For a group G, let $G^{\underset{\smile}{\omega}} \otimes S_{\underset{\smile}{\omega}}$ be the wreath (semidirect) product of $G^{\underset{\smile}{\omega}}$ and $S_{\underset{\smile}{\omega}}$, where $\pi \subset S_\omega$ acts in the obvious way on elements of $G^{\underset{\smile}{\omega}}$: $\langle x_0, x_1, \ldots \rangle^\pi = \langle x_{\pi 0}, x_{\pi 1}, \ldots \rangle$.

DEFINITION. (i) Let $G_0 = \{e\}$ be the trivial group and define $G_{n+1} = G_n^{\underset{\smile}{\omega}} \otimes S_{\underset{\smile}{\omega}}$. There are obvious maps $f_n : G_n \to G_{n+1}$ and $g_n : G_{n+1} \to G_n$.
(ii) $\vec{G} = \underset{\rightarrow}{\lim}(G_n, f_n)$, $\overleftarrow{G} = \underset{\leftarrow}{\lim}(G_n, g_n)$.
$\overleftarrow{G}^r$ is the *recursive projective limit*, consisting of all recursive (after some coding) sequences $\langle x_0, x_1, \ldots \rangle$ with $g_n(x_{n+1}) = x_n$.

THEOREM. $G(\lambda\eta) \cong \vec{G}, G(\mathcal{H}^*) \cong \overleftarrow{G}^r, G(D_\infty) \supseteq \overleftarrow{G}$.

21.4. Exercises

This completes the survey of part V.

5.8. Exercises

5.8.1. Let $\mathfrak{M}$ be a combinatory algebra. Show that in $\mathfrak{M}$
(i) $\exists a\ \forall xy\ axxy = xyy$,
(ii) $\exists a\ \forall xy\ axxy = xaa$.

5.8.2. (Barendregt and Koymans [1980]). Define the combinatory algebra $\mathfrak{M}(\boldsymbol{CL})$. Show that this structure cannot be made into a λ-algebra.

5.8.3. (Koymans). Let $\mathfrak{M}_1, \mathfrak{M}_2$ be λ-algebras. Construct the categorical product $\mathfrak{M}_1 \times \mathfrak{M}_2$ and show that $\text{Th}(\mathfrak{M}_1 \times \mathfrak{M}_2) = \text{Th}(\mathfrak{M}_1) \cap \text{Th}(\mathfrak{M}_2)$.

5.8.4 (H. Volken). Let $\mathfrak{F} = (X, \cdot)$ be an applicative structure and let $\mathfrak{F} = \cup_n \mathfrak{F}_n$ be a family of functions such that $\forall f \in \mathfrak{F}_n\ f: X^n \to X$. $\mathfrak{F}$ is called a *combinatory family* on $\mathfrak{M}$ if
(1) $\mathfrak{F}$ contains all algebraic functions on $\mathfrak{M}$;
(2) $\forall f \in \mathfrak{F}_{k+1}\ \exists g \in \mathfrak{F}_k\ \forall x, \vec{y}\ g(\vec{y}) \cdot x = f(\vec{y}, x)$.
$\mathfrak{F}$ is called a *λ-family* on $\mathfrak{M}$ if
(1) $\mathfrak{F}$ contains all algebraic functions on $\mathfrak{M}$ and is closed under substitution of constants (e.g. if $f \in \mathfrak{F}_2$ and $a \in X$, then $\lambda\!\!\lambda y.f(a, y) \in \mathfrak{F}_1$);

(2) There is a map $G: \mathfrak{F}_1 \to X$ such that $\forall f \in \mathfrak{F}_1\ \forall x\ G(f).x = f(x)$;

(3) $\forall f \in \mathfrak{F}_{k+1}\ \boldsymbol{\lambda}\vec{y}.G(\boldsymbol{\lambda} x.f(\vec{y}, x)) \in \mathfrak{F}_k$.

(i) Show that there exists a combinatory family on $\mathfrak{M}$ iff $\mathfrak{M}$ can be expanded to a combinatory algebra.

(ii) Show that there exists a λ-family on $\mathfrak{M}$ iff $\mathfrak{M}$ can be expanded to a λ-model.

5.8.5 (F. Honsell). Assume (this is proved in exercise 6.8.15)

(∗) Every finite applicative structure can be embedded into every combinatory algebra. Show that every applicative structure can be embedded into some extensional λ-model. [*Hint*. Use the compactness theorem of first order logic and (∗).] See also exercises 18.4.29 and 18.4.31.

5.8.6 (F. Honsell). Let D be a cpo with $\text{Card}(D) = \aleph_0$. Show that $\text{Card}([D \to D]) = 2^{\aleph_0}$. Therefore there are no countable reflexive cpo's. [*Hint*. Distinguish the following cases:

(1) $\exists x \in D$ x is not compact;

(2) $\forall x \in D$ x is compact;

  (2.1) $\subsetneq$ is not well founded;

  (2.2) $\subsetneq$ is well founded;

    (2.2.1) $\forall x \in D\ \{y | y \sqsubseteq x\}$ is finite;

    (2.2.2) $\exists x \in D\ \{y | y \sqsubseteq x\}$ is not finite.

For e.g. case 1 let $x_0 \subsetneq x_1 \subsetneq x_2 \cdots$ with $\sqcup x_n = x$; use that $D_0 = \{x_0, x_1, \ldots, x\}$ is a continuous lattice, hence injective, see exercise 1.3.17.]

5.8.7 (i) Compute $[\![M]\!]^{D_A}$ for $M = \boldsymbol{I}, \boldsymbol{K}, \boldsymbol{S}, \boldsymbol{\Omega}$. Which of these sets are empty?

(ii) (Longo [1983]). For $f \in [D_A \to D_A]$ define $\lambda^A x.f(x) = (\lambda^G x.f(x)) \cup A$. Show that $\lambda^A x.f(x)$ also represents f.

5.8.8 (Coppo et al. [1983]). A *type structure* is an $S = (D, \leqslant, \wedge, \to, \omega)$ with

(1) $\leqslant$ is a partial order on D with largest element ω;

(2) $a \wedge b = \inf(a, b)$;

(3) $\omega \to \omega = \omega$; $(a \to b) \wedge (a' \to b) = (a \wedge a' \to b)$; $a' \leqslant a,\ b \leqslant b' \ \Rightarrow\ a \to b \leqslant a' \to b'$.

A *filter* in S is a subset $x \subseteq D$ such that $\omega \in x$; $a, b \in x \ \Rightarrow\ a \wedge b \in x$; $a \geqslant b \in x \ \Rightarrow\ a \in x$. Write $|S| = (\{x | x \text{ filter in } S\}, \cdot)$ with

$$x \cdot y = \{b | \exists a \in y\ a \to b \in x\}.$$

Consider the statement

$$(+)\quad \begin{cases} (a_1 \to b_1) \wedge \cdots \wedge (a_n \to b_n) \leqslant c \to d \text{ and } d \neq \omega \quad \Rightarrow \\ c \leqslant a_{i_1} \wedge \cdots \wedge a_{i_k}, b_{i_1} \wedge \cdots \wedge b_{i_k} \leqslant d \text{ for some } \{i_1, \ldots, i_k\} \subseteq \{1, \ldots, n\}. \end{cases}$$

Show that if $S \models (+)$, then $|S|$ is a λ-model. [*Hint*. $|S|$ is an algebraic lattice with principle filters $\uparrow a = \{b | b \geqslant a\}$ as compact elements. It is sufficient to show that a finite sup of step functions ($f_{xy}(z) =$ if $x \subseteq z$ then y else $\emptyset$, for x, y compact) is representable. Now $\sqcup\{f_{\uparrow a_i \uparrow b_i} | i \in I\}$ is represented by $\bigwedge\{a_i \to b_i | i \in I\}$. *Remark*. In Barendregt et al [1983] it is shown that the "free type structure over countably many generators" satisfies (+).]

5.8.9 (Longo, E. Moggi). A category is called *cartesian* if it has a terminal object T and for each two objects a cartesian product. In such a category an arrow $u: U \times U \to U$ is called *Kleene universal* if $\forall f: U \times U \to U\ \exists g: U \to U\ f = u \circ g \times id_U$. Show that combinatory algebras can be described exactly by an object U of a cartesian category such that $T \lhd U$, $U \times U \lhd U$ and there exists a Kleene universal $u: U \times U \to U$. [*Hint*. In one direction, show that there is a universal $u^n: U \times U^n \to U$ for each n. In the other direction, let $\langle X, \cdot \rangle$ be a combinatory algebra. Consider the category with as objects X^n and as arrows $f: X^n \to X^m$ "representable" maps.]

PART II

CONVERSION

Böhm (1967)

Dezani-Ciancaglini (photo by
J. W. Klop, 1978)

CHAPTER 6

CLASSICAL LAMBDA CALCULUS

This chapter is about the set Λ modulo β-convertibility. According to convention 3.2.11 this congruence relation is denoted by $=$. Similarly β-reduction is denoted by $\twoheadrightarrow$.

The main topics that are treated are the fixed point theorems, the introduction of numerals and on these the representation of the recursive functions.

6.1. Fixed point combinators

The fixed point theorem 2.1.5 is one of the basic results in the λ-calculus. The reader may have noticed a peculiarity in the proof of this theorem. In order to show $FX = X$, one starts with X and reduces this to FX, rather than conversely.

6.1.1. THEOREM. $\forall F\ \exists X\ X \twoheadrightarrow FX$.

PROOF. Take $W \equiv \lambda x.F(xx)$ and $X \equiv WW$. Then

$$X \equiv (\lambda x.F(xx))W \rightarrow F(WW) \equiv FX. \quad \square$$

This explains why the related constructions in Gödel's self-referential sentence and the recursion theorem are somewhat puzzling; see §6.7 below.

From the proof of theorem 2.1.5 it follows moreover that fixed points can be found uniformly.

6.1.2. DEFINITION. A *fixed point combinator* is a term M such that

$$\forall F \quad MF = F(MF),$$

i.e. MF is a fixed point of F.

6.1.3. COROLLARY. *Let* $\mathbf{Y} = \lambda f.(\lambda x.f(xx))(\lambda x.f(xx))$. *Then* $\mathbf{Y}$ *is a fixed point combinator.*

PROOF. Let $W = \lambda x.F(xx)$. Then

$$\mathbf{Y}F = WW = F(WW) = F(\mathbf{Y}F). \quad \square$$

The term $\mathbf{Y}$ is called by Curry the *paradoxical combinator*.

Note that one does not have $\mathbf{Y}f \twoheadrightarrow f(\mathbf{Y}f)$. Therefore the following notation is useful.

6.1.4. DEFINITION (Turing [1937a]). Let $A \equiv \lambda xy.y(xxy)$. Define $\boldsymbol{\Theta} \equiv AA$.

6.1.5. COROLLARY. $\boldsymbol{\Theta}F \twoheadrightarrow F(\boldsymbol{\Theta}F)$.

PROOF. $\boldsymbol{\Theta}F \equiv AAF \twoheadrightarrow F(AAF) \equiv F(\boldsymbol{\Theta}F)$. $\square$

The following example shows how the fixed point theorem can be used.

PROBLEM. Construct an F such that

(1) $\qquad Fxy = FyxF$

SOLUTION. (1) follows from

$$F = \lambda xy.FyxF,$$

and this follows from

$$F = (\lambda fxy.fyxf)F.$$

Now define $F \equiv \mathbf{Y}(\lambda fxy.fyxf)$ and we are done. $\square$

In general:

6.1.6. PROPOSITION. *Let* $C \equiv C(f, \vec{x})$ *be a term. Then*

(i) $\exists F\ \forall \vec{N}\ F\vec{N} = C(F, \vec{N})$,

(ii) $\exists F\ \forall \vec{N}\ F\vec{N} \twoheadrightarrow C(F, \vec{N})$.

PROOF. Take $F \equiv \mathbf{Y}(\lambda f\vec{x}.C(f, \vec{x}))$ or, even better, $F \equiv \boldsymbol{\Theta}(\lambda f\vec{x}.C(f, \vec{x}))$. $\square$

For more information about fixed points see §6.5.

6.2. Standard combinators

In §2.1 the combinators $\mathbf{I}$, $\mathbf{K}$ and $\mathbf{S}$ were defined. Other terms or definable operations on terms that play an important role are introduced in this section.

6.2.1. DEFINITION. $\mathbf{\Omega} \equiv \omega\omega$, where $\omega \equiv \lambda x.xx$.

Note that $\mathbf{\Omega}$ is not in nf and only reduces to itself. Therefore by corollary 3.2.9 $\mathbf{\Omega}$ has no nf. In fact $\mathbf{\Omega}$ is the simplest term not having a nf. Also note

$$\mathbf{YI} = \mathbf{\Omega}.$$

6.2.2. DEFINITION (Truth values).

$$\mathbf{T} \equiv \lambda xy.x, \qquad \mathbf{F} \equiv \lambda xy.y.$$

Then $\mathbf{T}MN \twoheadrightarrow M$, $\mathbf{F}MN \twoheadrightarrow N$. Note $\mathbf{T} \equiv \mathbf{K}$ and $\mathbf{F} \twoheadleftarrow \mathbf{KI}$.

6.2.3. DEFINITION (Conditional). Let B (Boolean) be a term. Then

If B then M else N

is the term

$$BMN.$$

If $B = \mathbf{T}$ ($B = \mathbf{F}$), then this equals M (N respectively). If B is neither $\mathbf{T}$ nor $\mathbf{F}$, then BMN may be arbitrary.

As is the case in arithmetic or set theory, ordered pairs can be defined in the λ-calculus. The following definition is due to Church:

6.2.4. DEFINITION (Pairing).

$$[M, N] \equiv \lambda z.zMN,$$

$$(M)_0 \equiv M\mathbf{T}, \qquad (M)_1 \equiv M\mathbf{F}.$$

Then

$$([M_0, M_1])_i \twoheadrightarrow M_i, \quad i = 0, 1.$$

This pairing does not satisfy the conventional restraint of being surjective:

$$[(M)_0, (M)_1] = M$$

does not hold in general. In fact, no such surjective pairing exists, see exercise 15.4.4 and Barendregt [1974].

There are two ways to define ordered n-tuples. Using [,], one can define inductively $[M_0, \ldots, M_n]$.

6.2.5. DEFINITION (finite sequences).

$$[M] \equiv M, \qquad [M_0, \ldots, M_{n+1}] \equiv [M_0, [M_1, \ldots, M_{n+1}]].$$

More direct is $\langle M_0, \ldots, M_n \rangle$.

6.2.6. DEFINITION. $\langle M_0, \ldots, M_n \rangle \equiv \lambda z.zM_0 \cdots M_n$.

Projection functions for these codings are easy to construct.

6.2.7. DEFINITION.

(i) $\pi_i^n \equiv \lambda x.x\mathbf{F}^{\sim i}\mathbf{T}, \quad 0 \leqslant i < n,$
$\pi_n^n \equiv \lambda x.x\mathbf{F}^{\sim n}.$

(ii) $\mathbf{U}_i^n \equiv \lambda x_0 \cdots x_n.x_i, \quad 0 \leqslant i \leqslant n,$
$\mathbf{P}_i^n \equiv \lambda x.x\mathbf{U}_i^n.$

Then it follows by induction on n that for $i \leqslant n$,

$$\pi_i^n[M_0, \ldots, M_n] \twoheadrightarrow M_i;$$

moreover

$$\mathbf{P}_i^n \langle M_0, \ldots, M_n \rangle \twoheadrightarrow M_i.$$

6.2.8. DEFINITION (Composition). $M \circ N \equiv \lambda x.M(Nx)$.

In the λ-calculus various systems of numerals can be defined. A convenient one is the following; see §6.4 for other systems.

6.2.9. DEFINITION (Numerals). For each $n \in \mathbb{N}$ a term $\ulcorner n \urcorner$ is defined as follows

$$\ulcorner 0 \urcorner \equiv \mathbf{I}, \qquad \ulcorner n+1 \urcorner \equiv [\mathbf{F}, \ulcorner n \urcorner].$$

Note that the numerals are distinct normal forms.

6.2.10. LEMMA. (Successor, predecessor, test for zero). *There are terms* $\mathbf{S}^+$, $\mathbf{P}^-$, $\mathbf{Zero}$ *such that*

$$\mathbf{S}^+ \ulcorner n \urcorner = \ulcorner n+1 \urcorner, \qquad \mathbf{P}^- \ulcorner n+1 \urcorner = \ulcorner n \urcorner,$$

$$\mathbf{Zero}\ \ulcorner 0 \urcorner = \mathbf{T}, \qquad \mathbf{Zero}\ \ulcorner n+1 \urcorner = \mathbf{F}.$$

PROOF. Define

$$\mathbf{S}^+ \equiv \lambda x.[\mathbf{F}, x], \qquad \mathbf{P}^- \equiv \lambda x.x\mathbf{F}, \qquad \mathbf{Zero} \equiv \lambda x.x\mathbf{T},$$

then the equations follows easily. □

6.2.11. NOTATION. $M^+ \equiv (\mathbf{S}^+ M)$, $M^- \equiv (\mathbf{P}^- M)$.

Note that $\ulcorner 0 \urcorner^- = \mathbf{F}$.

Note that by combinatory completeness all operations on terms introduced in this section are definable. For example, a P for which

$$\forall M, N \quad PMN = [M, N],$$

is $P \equiv \lambda xy.(\lambda z.zxy) \equiv \lambda xyz.zxy$.

6.3. Lambda definability

The λ-calculus represents a certain class of (partial) functions on the integers. By a classical result of Kleene this is exactly the class of (partial) recursive functions. This section considers total functions. We follow an idea of Turing [1937a] to use the fixed-point combinator to represent primitive recursion and minimalization. Kleene's original proof is a bit more complicated, since the constructions were done in the λI-calculus, see §9.2.

A *numeric function* is a mapping $\varphi : \mathbb{N}^p \to \mathbb{N}$ for some $p \in \mathbb{N}$.

6.3.1. DEFINITION. Let φ be a numeric function with p arguments. φ is called λ-*definable* if for some $F \in \Lambda$

$$(*) \qquad \forall n_1, \ldots, n_p \in \mathbb{N} \quad F \ulcorner n_1 \urcorner \cdots \ulcorner n_p \urcorner = \ulcorner \varphi(n_1, \ldots, n_p) \urcorner .$$

If $(*)$ holds, then φ is said to be λ-*defined by* F. Since numerals are in nf, it follows by the Church-Rosser theorem that if φ is λ-defined by F, then

$$F \ulcorner n_1 \urcorner \cdots \ulcorner n_p \urcorner \twoheadrightarrow \ulcorner \varphi(n_1, \ldots, n_p) \urcorner .$$

NOTATION. If $\vec{n} = n_1, \ldots, n_p$, let

$$\ulcorner \vec{n} \urcorner = \ulcorner n_1 \urcorner, \ldots, \ulcorner n_p \urcorner ;$$

with this notation $(*)$ becomes

$$\forall \vec{n} \in \mathbb{N}^p \quad F \ulcorner \vec{n} \urcorner = \ulcorner \varphi(\vec{n}) \urcorner .$$

It will be proved that for numeric functions

$$\varphi \text{ is } \lambda\text{-definable} \Leftrightarrow \varphi \text{ is recursive.}$$

In §8.4 the notion of λ-definability will be extended to partial numeric functions. Then one can prove that for a partial numeric function φ,

$$\varphi \text{ is } \lambda\text{-definable} \Leftrightarrow \varphi \text{ is partial recursive.}$$

6.3.2. DEFINITION. The *initial functions* are the numeric functions U_i^p, S^+, Z defined as follows.

$$U_i^p(n_0,\ldots,n_p)=n_i,\quad 0\leqslant i\leqslant p,$$

$$S^+(n)=n+1,\qquad Z(n)=0.$$

Let $P(n)$ be a numeric relation. As usual,

$$\mu m[P(m)]$$

denotes the least number m such that $P(m)$ holds if such a number exists; otherwise $\mu m[P(m)]$ is undefined.

6.3.3. DEFINITION. Let $\mathcal{C}$ be a class of numeric functions.

(i) $\mathcal{C}$ is *closed under composition* if for all φ defined by

$$\varphi(\vec{n})=\chi(\psi_1(\vec{n}),\ldots,\psi_m(\vec{n}))$$

with $\chi,\psi_1,\ldots,\psi_m\in\mathcal{C}$, one has $\varphi\in\mathcal{C}$.

(ii) $\mathcal{C}$ is *closed under primitive recursion* if for all φ defined by

$$\varphi(0,\vec{n})=\chi(\vec{n}),$$
$$\varphi(k+1,\vec{n})=\psi(\varphi(k,\vec{n}),k,\vec{n})$$

with $\chi,\psi\in\mathcal{C}$, one has $\varphi\in\mathcal{C}$.

(iii) $\mathcal{C}$ is *closed under minimalization* if for all φ defined by

$$\varphi(\vec{n})=\mu m[\chi(\vec{n},m)=0]$$

with $\chi\in\mathcal{C}$ such that

$$\forall\vec{n}\ \exists m\quad \chi(\vec{n},m)=0,$$

one has $\varphi\in\mathcal{C}$.

6.3.4. DEFINITION. The class $\mathcal{R}$ of *recursive functions* is the least class of numeric functions which contains all initial functions and is closed under composition, primitive recursion and minimalization.

6.3.5. LEMMA. *The initial functions are λ-definable.*

PROOF. Take as defining terms

$$\mathbf{U}_i^p\equiv\lambda x_0\cdots x_p\cdot x_i,$$

$$\mathbf{S}^+\equiv\lambda x\cdot[\mathbf{F},x],$$

$$\mathbf{Z}\equiv\lambda x\cdot\ulcorner 0\urcorner.\quad\square$$

6.3.6. LEMMA. *The λ-definable functions are closed under composition.*

PROOF. Let $\chi, \psi_1, \ldots, \psi_m$ be λ-defined by $G, H_1, \ldots, H_m$ respectively. Then

$$\varphi(\vec{n}) = \chi(\psi_1(\vec{n}), \ldots, \psi_m(\vec{n}))$$

is λ-defined by

$$F \equiv \lambda \vec{x} \cdot G(H_1 \vec{x}) \cdots (H_m \vec{x}). \quad \square$$

6.3.7. LEMMA. *The λ-definable functions are closed under primitive recursion.*

PROOF. Let φ be defined by

$$\varphi(0, \vec{n}) = \chi(\vec{n}),$$

$$\varphi(k+1, \vec{n}) = \psi(\varphi(k, \vec{n}), k, \vec{n}),$$

where χ and ψ are λ-defined by G and H respectively.

The intuitive algorithm to compute $\varphi(k, \vec{n})$ is the following:

Test whether $k = 0$.
If yes, then give output $\chi(\vec{n})$;
if no, then compute $\psi(\varphi(k-1, \vec{n}), k-1, \vec{n})$.

Therefore let F be a term such that

$$Fx\vec{y} = \textit{If } \mathbf{Zero}\ x \textit{ then } G\vec{y} \textit{ else } H(Fx^{-}\vec{y})x^{-}\vec{y}.$$

F exists by proposition 6.1.6 and definition 6.2.3. By induction on k it follows that

$$F \ulcorner k \urcorner \ulcorner \vec{n} \urcorner = \ulcorner \varphi(k, \vec{n}) \urcorner,$$

i.e. φ is λ-defined by F. $\square$

6.3.8. DEFINITION. In order to represent minimalization define for $P \in \Lambda$

$$H_P \equiv \mathbf{\Theta}(\lambda hz.\, \textit{If } Pz \textit{ then } z \textit{ else } hz^{+}),$$

$$\mu P \equiv H_P \ulcorner 0 \urcorner.$$

6.3.9. PROPOSITION. *Let $P \in \Lambda$ be such that for all $n \in \mathbb{N}$*

$$P \ulcorner n \urcorner = \mathbf{T} \quad \text{or} \quad P \ulcorner n \urcorner = \mathbf{F}.$$

Then

(i) $H_P z \twoheadrightarrow$ *If* Pz *then* z *else* $H_P z^{+}$.
(ii) *If* $\exists n P \ulcorner n \urcorner = \mathbf{T}$, *let* $m = \mu n[P \ulcorner n \urcorner = \mathbf{T}]$.
Then $\mu P = \ulcorner m \urcorner$.

PROOF. (i) By corollary 6.1.5.

(ii) By (i)

(1) $P\ulcorner n\urcorner = \mathbf{T} \Rightarrow H_P\ulcorner n\urcorner = \ulcorner n\urcorner$,

(2) $P\ulcorner n\urcorner = \mathbf{F} \Rightarrow H_P\ulcorner n\urcorner = H_P\ulcorner n+1\urcorner$.

If $m = \mu n[P\ulcorner n\urcorner = \mathbf{T}]$, then

$$\forall k < m\ P\ulcorner k\urcorner = \mathbf{F} \quad \text{and} \quad P\ulcorner m\urcorner = \mathbf{T}.$$

Hence by (2)

$$H_P\ulcorner 0\urcorner = H_P\ulcorner 1\urcorner = \cdots = H_P\ulcorner m\urcorner$$

and by (1) $H_P\ulcorner m\urcorner = \ulcorner m\urcorner$. Thus $\mu P \equiv H_P\ulcorner 0\urcorner = \ulcorner m\urcorner$. □

6.3.10. LEMMA. *The λ-definable functions are closed under minimalization.*

PROOF. Let

$$\varphi(\vec{n}) = \mu m[\chi(\vec{n}, m) = 0],$$

where χ is λ-defined by G, say. Now define F by

$$F\vec{x} = \mu[\lambda y.\mathbf{Zero}(G\vec{x}y)].$$

By proposition 6.3.9(ii) F λ-defines φ. □

6.3.11. PROPOSITION. *All recursive functions are λ-definable.*

PROOF. By 6.3.5, 6.3.6, 6.3.7 and 6.3.10. □

6.3.12. LEMMA. *Let φ be λ-defined by F. Then for all $\vec{n}, m \in \mathbb{N}$*

$$\varphi(\vec{n}) = m \Leftrightarrow F\ulcorner \vec{n}\urcorner = \ulcorner m\urcorner.$$

PROOF. (⇒) Trivial by the definition.

(⇐) Suppose $F\ulcorner \vec{n}\urcorner = \ulcorner m\urcorner$. Then $\ulcorner \varphi(\vec{n})\urcorner = \ulcorner m\urcorner$. Since numerals are distinct normal forms it follows from the Church–Rosser theorem that $\varphi(\vec{n}) = m$. □

6.3.13. THEOREM (Kleene). *The λ-definable numeric functions are exactly the recursive functions.*

PROOF. If φ is recursive, then by proposition 6.3.11 φ is λ-definable. If φ is λ-definable, by F say, then by lemma 6.3.12

$$\varphi(\vec{n}) = m \Leftrightarrow \boldsymbol{\lambda} \vdash F\ulcorner \vec{n}\urcorner = \ulcorner m\urcorner.$$

Since λ is recursively axiomated, the RHS is r.e.. It follows that the graph of φ is r.e., hence φ is recursive. □

6.3.14. Corollary. *Let $R \subseteq \mathbb{N}^k$ be a relation. Then R is recursive iff there is a term F such that*

$$(*)\qquad \begin{aligned} F\ulcorner\vec{n}\urcorner &= \mathbf{T} \Leftrightarrow R(\vec{n}),\\ F\ulcorner\vec{n}\urcorner &= \mathbf{F} \Leftrightarrow \neg R(\vec{n}). \end{aligned}$$

Proof. ($\Rightarrow$) Let K_R be the characteristic function of R, i.e.

$$K_R(\vec{n}) = 0 \Leftrightarrow R(\vec{n}),$$

$$K_R(\vec{n}) = 1 \Leftrightarrow \neg R(\vec{n}).$$

Then K_R is recursive and hence can be λ-defined by H, say. Now take $F\vec{x} = \mathbf{Zero}(H\vec{x})$.

($\Leftarrow$) By assumption it follows that R and $\neg R$ are r.e., hence recursive. □

If F is a term such that $(*)$ holds, then F is said to λ-define R.

6.4. Numeral systems

Only a few properties of the numerals are needed to prove theorem 6.3.13

6.4.1. Definition (i) A *numeral system* is a sequence

$$\boldsymbol{d} = \boldsymbol{d}_0, \boldsymbol{d}_1, \ldots$$

consisting of closed terms such that for some λ-terms $S_{\boldsymbol{d}}^+$ and $\mathrm{Zero}_{\boldsymbol{d}}$

$$S_{\boldsymbol{d}}^+ \boldsymbol{d}_n = \boldsymbol{d}_{n+1},$$

$$\mathrm{Zero}_{\boldsymbol{d}} \boldsymbol{d}_0 = \mathbf{T}, \qquad \mathrm{Zero}_{\boldsymbol{d}} \boldsymbol{d}_{n+1} = \mathbf{F}$$

for all $n \in \mathbb{N}$. $S_{\boldsymbol{d}}^+$ and $\mathrm{Zero}_{\boldsymbol{d}}$ are called the *successor* and *test for zero* for $\boldsymbol{d}$.

(ii) $\boldsymbol{d}$ is called a *normal* numeral system if each $\boldsymbol{d}_n$ has a nf.

(iii) $\boldsymbol{s} = \ulcorner 0 \urcorner, \ulcorner 1 \urcorner, \ldots$ with successor $\mathbf{S}^+$ is called the *standard* numeral system.

Notation. Any numeral system $\boldsymbol{d}$ clearly is determined by $\boldsymbol{d}_0$ and $S_{\boldsymbol{d}}^+$. Therefore one writes $\boldsymbol{d} = (\boldsymbol{d}_0, S_{\boldsymbol{d}}^+)$.

6.4.2. DEFINITION. Let $\boldsymbol{d}$ be a numeral system.

(i) A numeric function $\varphi : \mathbb{N}^p \to \mathbb{N}$ is *λ-definable with respect* to $\boldsymbol{d}$ if

$$\exists F \ \forall n_1, \ldots, n_p \in \mathbb{N} \quad F\boldsymbol{d}_{n_1} \cdots \boldsymbol{d}_{n_p} = \boldsymbol{d}_{\varphi(n_1, \ldots, n_p)}.$$

(ii) $\boldsymbol{d}$ is *adequate* iff all recursive functions are λ-definable with respect to $\boldsymbol{d}$.

6.4.3. PROPOSITION. *Let $\boldsymbol{d}$ be a numeral system. Then $\boldsymbol{d}$ is adequate iff*

$$\exists P_{\boldsymbol{d}}^- \ \forall n \subset \mathbb{N} \quad P_{\boldsymbol{d}}^- \boldsymbol{d}_{n+1} = \boldsymbol{d}_n.$$

PROOF. (⇒) By definition. (⇐) As for proposition 6.3.11. □

Such a $P_{\boldsymbol{d}}^-$ is called a predecessor for $\boldsymbol{d}$. Therefore a sequence $\boldsymbol{d} = \boldsymbol{d}_0, \boldsymbol{d}_1, \ldots$ is an adequate numeral system iff $\boldsymbol{d}$ has a successor, test for zero and predecessor.

The standard numerals were chosen the way they were to give an easy representation of the recursive functions. In the following system $\boldsymbol{c}$, due to Church, each numeral $\boldsymbol{c}_n$ has a more direct connection with the number n: $\boldsymbol{c}_n$ is an n-fold iteration operator. Therefore some concrete numeric functions have simple λ-defining terms with respect to $\boldsymbol{c}$, see exercise 6.8.6. In §9.2 the $\boldsymbol{c}_1, \boldsymbol{c}_2, \ldots$ are part of an adequate system for the λI-calculus.

6.4.4. DEFINITION (Church numerals). $\boldsymbol{c} = \boldsymbol{c}_0, \boldsymbol{c}_1, \ldots,$ with

$$\boldsymbol{c}_n \equiv \lambda fx.f^n(x)$$

Let $S_c^+ \equiv \lambda abc.b(abc)$; then clearly S_c^+ is a successor for $\boldsymbol{c}$. Note that $\boldsymbol{c}_1 \equiv \lambda xy.xy \equiv \mathbf{1}$.

6.4.5. LEMMA. *There are $H, H^{-1} \in \Lambda$ such that for all $n \in \mathbb{N}$*

$$H \ulcorner n \urcorner = \boldsymbol{c}_n, \qquad H^{-1}\boldsymbol{c}_n = \ulcorner n \urcorner.$$

PROOF. Define by proposition 6.1.6

$$Hx = \textit{If } \mathbf{Zero}\ x \textit{ then } \boldsymbol{c}_0 \textit{ else } S_c^+(Hx^-);$$

$$H^{-1}x = x\mathbf{S}^+ \ulcorner 0 \urcorner.$$

Then the two equations follow easily. □

6.4.6. COROLLARY. *$\boldsymbol{c}$ is an adequate numeral system.*

PROOF. Define

$$\text{Zero}_c \equiv \textbf{Zero} \circ H^{-1},$$

$$P_c^- \equiv H \circ P^- \circ H^{-1},$$

and use proposition 6.4.3. □

Some other numeral systems are given in the exercises.

6.5. More about fixed points; Gödel numbers

Two proofs will be given for the following theorem. The second one is symmetrical and extends more easily to the n-fold case.

6.5.1. DOUBLE FIXED POINT THEOREM.

$$\forall F, G\ \exists A, B[A = FAB \wedge B = GAB].$$

FIRST PROOF. Define

$$A_b \equiv \boldsymbol{\Theta}(\lambda a.Fab),$$

$$B_0 \equiv \boldsymbol{\Theta}(\lambda b.GA_b b), \qquad A_0 \equiv A_{B_0}.$$

Then

$$A_0 \equiv A_{B_0} \twoheadrightarrow FA_{B_0}B_0 \equiv FA_0B_0,$$

$$B_0 \twoheadrightarrow GA_{B_0}B_0 \equiv GA_0B_0. \quad \square$$

SECOND PROOF. Define

$$X \equiv \boldsymbol{\Theta}(\lambda x.[F(x)_0(x)_1, G(x)_0(x)_1]),$$

$$A \equiv (X)_0, \qquad B \equiv (X)_1.$$

Then

$$X \twoheadrightarrow [F(X)_0(X)_1, G(X)_0(X)_1];$$

so

$$A \equiv (X)_0 \twoheadrightarrow F(X)_0(X)_1 \equiv FAB,$$

and similarly

$$B \twoheadrightarrow GAB. \quad \square$$

6.5.2. MULTIPLE FIXED POINT THEOREM.

$$\forall F_1, \ldots, F_n \quad \exists X_1, \ldots, X_n$$
$$X_1 = F_1 X_1 \cdots X_n,$$
$$\cdots$$
$$X_n = F_n X_1 \cdots X_n.$$

PROOF. As the second proof of theorem 6.5.1, using $\lambda x_1 \cdots x_n.\langle x_1, \ldots, x_n \rangle$. $\square$

In addition to the fixed point combinators $\mathbf{Y}$ and $\mathbf{\Theta}$, many others exist. The following result is independently due to Böhm and van der Mey.

6.5.3. LEMMA. *Let* $G \equiv \lambda yf.f(yf) = \mathbf{SI}$. *Then* $M \in \Lambda$ *is a fixed point combinator iff* $M = GM$, *that is, iff* M *is a fixed point of* G.

PROOF. If $M = GM$, then for all F

$$MF = GMF = F(MF),$$

i.e. M is a fixed point combinator. Conversely, suppose M is one. Then

$$Mf = f(Mf)(f \text{ a variable}).$$

Hence

$$M = \lambda f.Mf = \lambda f.f(Mf) = GM.$$

The reason that $M = \lambda f.Mf$ is as follows: By assumption and the Church–Rosser theorem

$$Mf \twoheadrightarrow f(\cdots) \twoheadleftarrow f(Mf).$$

Since $M \in \Lambda^\circ$, it follows that M must reduce to a term of the form $\lambda f.N$. But then

$$\lambda f.Mf = \lambda f.(\lambda f.N)f = \lambda f.N = M. \quad \square$$

6.5.4. DEFINITION. (i) (Böhm) $\mathbf{Y}^0 \equiv \mathbf{Y}$; $\mathbf{Y}^{n+1} \equiv (\mathbf{Y}^n)(\mathbf{SI})$.
(ii) $\mathbf{Y}_M \equiv \lambda f.WWM$, where $W \equiv \lambda xz.f(xxz)$.

6.5.5. PROPOSITION. (i) *The* $\mathbf{Y}^0, \mathbf{Y}^1, \ldots$ *are fixed point combinators.*
(ii) $\mathbf{Y}_M$ *is a fixed point combinator for each* M.

PROOF. (i) By lemma 6.5.3.

(ii) As ever. □

Note that $\mathbf{Y}^1 \twoheadrightarrow \mathbf{\Theta}$.

6.5.6. DEFINITION (Gödel numbering). (i) It is easy to define, by standard techniques, an effective one-one map $\sharp : \Lambda \to \mathbb{N}$. In the rest of this book $\sharp$ denotes one such map.

(ii) $\sharp M$ is called the Gödel number of M.

The following convention will be used throughout:

6.5.7. CONVENTION. Notions about sets of integers, sequences of integers, etc., are translated to terms via the mapping $\sharp$.

EXAMPLES. (i) A set $\mathcal{A} \subset \Lambda$ is recursive iff $\sharp\mathcal{A} = \{\sharp M \mid M \in \mathcal{A}\}$ is recursive.

(ii) A sequence of terms $M_0, M_1, \ldots$ is recursive iff $\lambda\!\!\!\lambda n.\sharp M_n$ is a recursive sequence.

In fact the convention was already used in the proof of theorem 6.3.13 where it was shown that $\{(M, N) \mid \lambda \vdash M = N\}$ is an r.e. set.

6.5.8. NOTATION. $\ulcorner M \urcorner \equiv \ulcorner \sharp M \urcorner$.

There is little danger of confusion between the $\ulcorner\ \urcorner$ of definitions 6.2.9 and 6.5.8. The first is defined on $\mathbb{N}$, the second on Λ.

6.5.9. SECOND FIXED POINT THEOREM.

$$\forall F\ \exists X \quad F\ulcorner X \urcorner = X.$$

PROOF. By the effectiveness of $\sharp$, there are recursive functions Ap and Num such that Ap $(\sharp M, \sharp N) = \sharp MN$ and $\text{Num}(n) = \sharp\ulcorner n \urcorner$. Let Ap and Num be λ-defined by **Ap** and **Num** $\in \Lambda^0$. Then

$$\mathbf{Ap}\ulcorner M \urcorner \ulcorner N \urcorner = \ulcorner MN \urcorner, \qquad \mathbf{Num}\ulcorner n \urcorner = \ulcorner \ulcorner n \urcorner \urcorner;$$

hence in particular

$$\mathbf{Num}\ulcorner M \urcorner = \ulcorner \ulcorner M \urcorner \urcorner.$$

Now define

$$W \equiv \lambda x.F(\mathbf{Ap}\,x(\mathbf{Num}\,x)), \qquad X \equiv W\ulcorner W \urcorner.$$

Then

$$X \equiv W^{\ulcorner} W^{\urcorner} = F(\mathbf{Ap}^{\ulcorner} W^{\urcorner} (\mathbf{Num}^{\ulcorner} W^{\urcorner}))$$

$$= F^{\ulcorner} W^{\ulcorner} W^{\urcorner\urcorner} \equiv F^{\ulcorner} X^{\urcorner}. \quad \square$$

As for ordinary fixed points one has $X \twoheadrightarrow F^{\ulcorner} X^{\urcorner}$. Moreover the construction is uniform in the following sense.

6.5.10. COROLLARY. $\exists \mathbf{\Theta}_2 \in \Lambda^0\ \forall F \in \Lambda^0\ \mathbf{\Theta}_2^{\ulcorner} F^{\urcorner} \twoheadrightarrow F^{\ulcorner} \mathbf{\Theta}_2^{\ulcorner} F^{\urcorner\urcorner}$.

PROOF. See exercise 8.5.6. $\square$

6.6. Undecidability results

6.6.1. DEFINITION Let $\mathcal{A} \subset \Lambda$.

(i) $\mathcal{A}$ is *non-trivial* if $\mathcal{A} \neq \emptyset$, $\mathcal{A} \neq \Lambda$.

(ii) $\mathcal{A}$ is *closed under equality* if

$$\forall M, N \in \Lambda [\, M \in \mathcal{A} \text{ and } M = N \Rightarrow N \in \mathcal{A}\,].$$

Recall that two sets of integers $\mathcal{A}, \mathcal{B}$ are recursively separable iff there exists a recursive set $\mathcal{C}$ such that $\mathcal{A} \subset \mathcal{C}$ and $\mathcal{B} \cap \mathcal{C} = \emptyset$.

The following theorem is due to Scott [1963]. It is related to Rice's theorem in recursion theory, cf. Rogers [1967], p. 324.

6.6.2. THEOREM. (i) Let $\mathcal{A}, \mathcal{B} \subset \Lambda$ be non empty sets closed under equality. Then $\mathcal{A}$ and $\mathcal{B}$ are not recursively separable.

(ii) Let $\mathcal{A} \subset \Lambda$ be a non-trivial set closed under equality. Then $\mathcal{A}$ is not recursive.

PROOF. (i) Let $M_0 \in \mathcal{A}$, $M_1 \in \mathcal{B}$. Suppose $\mathcal{C}$ is a recursive set such that $\mathcal{A} \subset \mathcal{C}, \mathcal{B} \cap \mathcal{C} = \emptyset$. The characteristic function of $\sharp\mathcal{C}$ is recursive and hence λ-defined by some F. Hence

$$M \in \mathcal{C} \Rightarrow F^{\ulcorner} M^{\urcorner} = {}^{\ulcorner} 0^{\urcorner},$$

$$M \notin \mathcal{C} \Rightarrow F^{\ulcorner} M^{\urcorner} = {}^{\ulcorner} 1^{\urcorner}.$$

Now define

$$G \equiv \lambda x.\, \mathit{If}\ \mathbf{Zero}(Fx)\ \mathit{then}\ M_1\ \mathit{else}\ M_0.$$

Then

$$M \in \mathcal{C} \Rightarrow G\ulcorner M \urcorner = M_1,$$

$$M \notin \mathcal{C} \Rightarrow G\ulcorner M \urcorner = M_0.$$

By the second fixed point theorem, $G\ulcorner X \urcorner = X$ for some X. But then

$$X \in \mathcal{C} \Rightarrow X = G\ulcorner X \urcorner = M_1 \in \mathcal{B} \Rightarrow X \notin \mathcal{C},$$

$$X \notin \mathcal{C} \Rightarrow X = G\ulcorner X \urcorner = M_0 \in \mathcal{A} \Rightarrow X \in \mathcal{C},$$

a contradiction.

(ii) If $\mathcal{A} \subset \Lambda$ is a nontrivial set closed under equality, then (i) applies to $\mathcal{A}$ and its complement. Hence $\mathcal{A}$ cannot be recursive. □

Theorem 6.6.2 is false for the λI-calculus. Take $\mathcal{A} = \{M \in \Lambda_I \mid FV(M) = \{x\}\}$. This set is recursive and in the λI-calculus closed under equality, see lemma 9.1.2(iv). The following relativization of theorem 6.6.2 also holds for the λI-calculus.

6.6.3. Definition. Let $\mathcal{A} \subset \Lambda^0$. $\mathcal{A}$ is *closed under equality of combinators* if

$$\forall M, N \in \Lambda^0[\, M \in \mathcal{A} \text{ and } M = N \Rightarrow N \in \mathcal{A}].$$

6.6.4. Corollary. *Theorem* 6.6.2 *holds for* $\mathcal{A}, \mathcal{B} \subset \Lambda^0$ *which are closed under equality of combinators.*

Proof. Same as for theorem 6.6.2. □

Church [1936] gave one of the first examples of an r.e. set which is not recursive:

6.6.5. Theorem. $\{M \mid M$ *has a* nf$\}$ *is an* r.e. *set which is not recursive.*

Proof. The set is r.e. since

$$M \text{ has } a \text{ nf} \quad \text{iff} \quad \exists N\ N \text{ is in nf and } \lambda \vdash M = N.$$

By theorem 6.6.2 the set is not recursive. □

A theory $\mathcal{T}$ is called *essentially undecidable* iff $\mathcal{T}$ is consistent and has no consistent recursive extension. The following was noticed by Grzegorczyk.

6.6.6. THEOREM. *The λ-calculus (i.e. the theory* $\boldsymbol{\lambda}$*) is essentially undecidable.*

PROOF. Suppose $\mathfrak{T}$ is a consistent extension of $\boldsymbol{\lambda}$. Then $\{M \mid \mathfrak{T} \vdash M = I\}$ is closed under equality and nontrivial. Hence by theorem 6.6.2 not recursive. Therefore $\mathfrak{T}$ is not recursive. □

6.7 Digression: Self-referential sentences and the recursion theorem

To conclude this section it will be shown how the constructions of Gödel's self-referential sentence and the recursion theorem can be interpreted as applications of the fixed point combinator.

Let P be first-order Peano arithmetic. If s is a syntactic object of P, then $\sharp s$ is its Gödel number ("code") and $\ulcorner s \urcorner \equiv \ulcorner \sharp s \urcorner$ the corresponding numeral in P.

I. THEOREM (Gödel). *Let* $A(x)$ *be a formula of* P *with* $\mathrm{FV}(A(x)) = \{x\}$. *Then there exists a sentence* B *of* P *such that*

$$P \vdash B \leftrightarrow A(\ulcorner B \urcorner).$$

(B *says*: "*I have property* A.")

PROOF. Define for $n_1, n_2 \in N$

$$n_1 \sim n_2 \quad \text{iff} \quad \text{for some sentences } A_1, A_2 \text{ of } P \\ n_i = \sharp A_i \text{ and } P \vdash A_1 \leftrightarrow A_2.$$

It is sufficient to show that given $A(x)$ one has

(1) $\qquad \exists n \quad n \sim \sharp A(\ulcorner n \urcorner).$

For then, taking B such that $n = \sharp B$,

$$P \vdash B \leftrightarrow A(\ulcorner n \urcorner) = A(\ulcorner B \urcorner).$$

In order to prove (1) make the following abbreviations.

(i) For a variable x and $n \in \mathbb{N}$

$$\lambda x.n = \langle \sharp x, n \rangle,$$

where $\langle\ ,\ \rangle$ is a primitive recursive pairing function with inverses $(\ )_0$, $(\ )_1$.

(ii) For $n, m \in \mathbb{N}$ write

$$n.m = \text{the code of the result of substituting } \ulcorner m \urcorner \text{ for the free variable with code } (n)_0 \text{ in the formula with code } (n)_1.$$

Then $\cdot$ is primitive recursive and

(2) $$(\lambda x.\sharp A(x)).m = \sharp A(\ulcorner m \urcorner).$$

Since the (primitive) recursive functions are representable in P, it may be assumed that there is a binary function symbol $\circ$ of P such that

(3) $$P \vdash \ulcorner n \urcorner \circ \ulcorner m \urcorner = \ulcorner n.m \urcorner .$$

Now let $v = \lambda x.\sharp A(x \circ x)$ and $n = v.v$. Then

$$n = v.v = (\lambda x.\sharp A(x \circ x)).v$$

$$= \sharp A(\ulcorner v \urcorner \circ \ulcorner v \urcorner) \quad \text{by (2)},$$

$$\sim \sharp A(\ulcorner v.v \urcorner) = \sharp A(\ulcorner n \urcorner).$$

The step $\sim$ is valid, since by (3)

$$P \vdash A(\ulcorner v \urcorner \circ \ulcorner v \urcorner) \leftrightarrow A(\ulcorner v.v \urcorner). \quad \square$$

II. Recursion theorem (Kleene). *Let $\{e\}$ denote the partial recursive function with index e. Suppose f is a total recursive function. Then for some n,*

$$\{f(n)\} \simeq \{n\},$$

i.e. $f(n)$ and n are index of the same partial recursive function.
Proof. Define $x.y \simeq \{x\}(y)$ and

$$x \sim y \Leftrightarrow \forall z \; x.z \simeq y.z.$$

In this notation, one has to prove that for each total recursive f,

$$f(n) \sim n \quad \text{for some } n.$$

Lemma. *Let $\psi(x)$ be partial recursive. Then for some v*
(i) *$v.x \sim \psi(x)$, for all x; (if $\psi(x)\uparrow$, then $v.x$ is index of $\lambda z.\uparrow$).*
(ii) *$\{v\}$ is total.*

PROOF. $\lambda xy.\{\psi(x)\}(y)$ is partial recursive, hence for some e

$$\{e\}(x,y) \simeq \{\psi(x)\}(y).$$

By the s-m-n theorem

$$\{\psi(x)\}(y) \simeq \{s_1(e,x)\}(y).$$

Now v is defined by $\{v\}(x) = s_1(e,x)$. Then

$$v.x.y \simeq s_1(e,x).y \simeq \psi(x).y,$$

so $v.x \sim \psi(x)$. Moreover $\{v\}$ is total since s_1 is primitive recursive. □

NOTATION. The v constructed in the lemma will be denoted by $\lambda x.\psi(x)$. Then

(i) $(\lambda x.\psi(x)).a \sim \psi(a)$,
(ii) $(\lambda x.\psi(x)).a$ is always defined.

Now define $v = \lambda x.f(x.x)$, $n = v.v$. Then by (ii) n is well defined and by (i)

$$n = v.v = (\lambda x.f(x.x)).v \sim f(v.v) = f(n). \quad \square$$

The recursion theorem can be interpreted as the fixed point theorem for an appropriate precomplete numbered set in the sense of Ershov; see exercise 6.8.18.

6.8. Exercises

6.8.1 Prove

$$\langle M_1, \ldots, M_n \rangle = \langle N_1, \ldots, N_n \rangle \Leftrightarrow M_1 = N_1, \ldots, M_n = N_n.$$

6.8.2. Construct $\mathbf{K}^\infty$, $A \in \Lambda^0$ such that
(i) $\mathbf{K}^\infty x = \mathbf{K}^\infty$,
(ii) $Ax = xA$.

6.8.3. Show that for $\mathbf{K}^\infty$ as above one has $\mathbf{K} \# \mathbf{K}^\infty$

6.8.4. Construct $F, \pi \in \Lambda^0$ such that
(i) $\forall n \in \mathbb{N}\ F \ulcorner n \urcorner xy = xy^{\sim n}$
(ii) $\forall n \in \mathbb{N}\ \forall i < n\ \pi \ulcorner n \urcorner \ulcorner i \urcorner = \pi_i^n$.

6.8.5. Construct a sequence $A_0, A_1, \ldots \in \Lambda$ such that

$$A_0 = \mathbf{S} \quad \text{and} \quad A_{n+1} = A_n A_{n+2}.$$

6.8.6. (Rosser). Let $A_+, A_\times, A_{\mathrm{exp}}$ be terms such that

$$A_+ xy = \lambda pq.xp(ypq), \qquad A_\times xy = x \circ y, \qquad A_{\mathrm{exp}} xy = yx.$$

Show that with respect to Church's numerals $c_n \equiv \lambda fx.f^n(x)$ the functions addition, multiplication and exponentiation are λ-defined by A_+, $A_\times$ and $A_{\exp}$ respectively (except $c_0 c_n = \mathbf{I} =_\eta c_1$).

6.8.7. State and prove a general fixed point theorem, combining proposition 6.1.6 and theorems 6.5.2. and 6.5.9.

6.8.8. Show that $\forall M\ \exists M'[M' \text{ in nf} \wedge M'\mathbf{I} = M]$.

6.8.9. Prove (i) $\mathbf{Y}_M = \mathbf{Y}_N \Rightarrow M = N$,

*(ii) $\mathbf{Y}^m = \mathbf{Y}^n \Rightarrow m = n$. [*Hint*. Let $m \neq n$. Introduce a convenient notation to show that $\mathbf{Y}^m$ and $\mathbf{Y}^n$ have no common reduct and apply the CR theorem.]

6.8.10. Show $\exists M\ M = \ulcorner M \urcorner$.

6.8.11. (Church). Show that the set $\{M | M = \mathbf{I}\}$ is not recursive.

6.8.12. Let $\mathcal{A}, \mathcal{B} \subset \Lambda$ be non empty sets closed under equality. Show that $\mathcal{A}$ and $\mathcal{B}$ are effectively inseparable (see e.g. Rogers [1967] for the definition of this concept).

6.8.13. Show that a numeral system $\boldsymbol{d}$ is adequate iff

$$\exists F, F^{-1}\ \forall n \in \mathbb{N}\quad F\ulcorner n \urcorner = \boldsymbol{d}_n \wedge F^{-1}\boldsymbol{d}_n = \ulcorner n \urcorner.$$

Conclude that for all adequate numeral systems $\boldsymbol{d}, \boldsymbol{d}'$

$$\exists G, G^{-1}\ \forall n \in \mathbb{N}\quad G\boldsymbol{d}_n = \boldsymbol{d}'_n \wedge G^{-1}\boldsymbol{d}'_n = \boldsymbol{d}_n.$$

6.8.14. (Klop). Define

$$£ = \lambda abcdefghijklmnopqstuvwxyzr.r(thisisafixedpointcombinator),$$
$$\$ = ££££££££££££££££££££££££££.$$

Show that \$ is a fixed point combinator.

6.8.15. (Barendregt, Dezani and Klop). (i) Let $X = \{x_1, \ldots, x_n\}$ be a finite set and let $\cdot$ be a binary operation on X. Construct terms $X_1, \ldots, X_n \in \Lambda^0$ such that for all $i, j, k < n$

$$X_i X_j = X_k \Leftrightarrow x_i \cdot x_j = x_k.$$

Take e.g. Klein's fourgroup. [*Hint*. First solve (ii).]

(ii) Let $f : \mathbb{N}^2 \to \mathbb{N}$ be recursive. Construct distinct $X_0, X_1, \ldots \in \Lambda^0$ such that for all $n, m \in \mathbb{N}$

$$X_n X_m = X_{f(n,m)}.$$

[*Hint*. Try $X_n \equiv [A, \ulcorner n \urcorner]$.]

(iii) Show that in (ii) the assumption that f is recursive cannot be ommited.

6.8.16. Let $d_0, d_1, \ldots$ be an adequate numeral system. Define $d'_n \equiv \mathbf{YC}d_n$, where $\mathbf{C} \equiv \lambda xyz.x(zy)$. Show that all unary recursive functions can be represented on the $d'_0, d'_1, \ldots$. [*Hint*. Consider $F' \equiv \lambda x.xF$]

6.8.17. (B. Friedman) Let $f_0 \equiv \lambda xyz.y$ and $S_f^+ \equiv \lambda x.\langle x \rangle$. Show that $P_f^- \equiv \langle I \rangle$ and $\text{Zero}_f \equiv \lambda xyz.x(\lambda x'y'z'.z')yz$ make (f_0, S_f^+) into an adequate numeral system.

For the next exercise we need the following concepts from Ershov [1973].

(i) A *numbered set* is a pair $\gamma = (S, \nu)$, where S is a set and $\nu : \mathbb{N} \to S$ is a surjective map.

(ii) $\boldsymbol{P} = \{\psi : \mathbb{N} \to \mathbb{N} | \psi \text{ partial recursive}\}$, $\boldsymbol{F} = \{f : \mathbb{N} \to \mathbb{N} | f \text{ (total) recursive}\}$.

(iii) Let $\gamma = (S, \nu)$ and $\gamma' = (S', \nu')$ be numbered sets. A *morphism* between γ and γ' is a map $\mu : S \to S'$ such that

$$\exists f \in \boldsymbol{F}\quad \nu' \circ f = \mu \circ \nu.$$

In that case it is said that μ is given by f.

(iv) A numbered set $\gamma = (S, \nu)$ is called *precomplete* iff

$$\forall \psi \in \boldsymbol{P}\ \exists f \in \boldsymbol{F}\ \forall x \in \mathrm{Dom}(\psi) \quad \nu(f(x)) = \nu(\psi(x)).$$

6.8.18. (Ershov). Show that if $\gamma = (S, \nu)$ is a precomplete numbered set and $\mu : \gamma \to \gamma$ is a morphism, then $\exists s \in S\ \mu s = s$. [*Hint.* Let μ be given by f. Consider $\psi(x) = f(\{x\}(x))$.]

6.8.19. (i) (van der Poel et al. [1980]) Show that the sequence $\boldsymbol{p}_n = \lambda xy.xy^{\sim n}$ is an adequate numeral system.

(ii) (Böhm, Dezani-Ciancaglini) Show that the following two numeral systems are adequate:

$$\boldsymbol{d} = (\mathbf{Y}, \lambda x.[x, P]), \quad P \text{ arbitrary},$$

$$\boldsymbol{e} = (\mathbf{K}, \lambda x.[x, \mathbf{Y}]).$$

[*Hint.* For $\boldsymbol{d}$ use as a predecessor $\langle \mathbf{K} \rangle$ and as test for zero $[\mathbf{K}^2\mathbf{T}, \mathbf{I}]$.] Hence an adequate numeral system is not necessarily normal.

6.8.20*. A numerical system $\boldsymbol{d}$ is adequate for $\boldsymbol{\lambda\eta}$ iff for all recursive functions $\varphi : \mathbb{N}^k \to \mathbb{N}$ there is a term $F \in \Lambda^0$ such that

$$F\boldsymbol{d}_n =_\eta \boldsymbol{d}_{\varphi(n)}.$$

Show that the following two sequences $\boldsymbol{b}$ and $\boldsymbol{w}$ are numeral systems, adequate for $\boldsymbol{\lambda\eta}$.

(i) (Böhm). If $x_0, \ldots, x_n$, $n \geqslant 1$, is a sequence of variables, then $x_0, \ldots, \tilde{x}_n$ denotes the same sequence with the last two variables interchanged, i.e. $x_0, x_1, \ldots, x_{n-2}, x_n, x_{n-1}$. Define

$$\boldsymbol{b}_n \equiv \lambda x_0 \cdots x_{n+1}.x_0 \cdots \tilde{x}_{n+1}.$$

(ii) (Wadsworth [1980]).

$$\boldsymbol{w}_n \equiv \lambda x_0 \cdots x_n.x_0(x_1(\cdots(x_n(\mathbf{KK})..))x_1 \cdots x_n.$$

6.8.21*. (Barendregt; Wadsworth). Consider the sequence $\boldsymbol{a}_n = \mathbf{K}^n(\mathbf{I})$. Show that $\boldsymbol{a}$ is not a numeral system.

6.8.22*. (i) (C. E. Schaap) Let $\boldsymbol{sch}_n \equiv \lambda x.\mathbf{I}x^{\sim n}$. Show that $\boldsymbol{sch}$ is an adequate numeral system. [*Hint.* Use exercise 2.3.5.]

(ii) (H. den Hoed) Consider the following definitions.

(1) If α is a finite word over $\{0, 1\}$, say $\alpha = 1101$, then $\check{\alpha}$ is the converse, in this case $\check{\alpha} = 1011$.

(2) If α is a finite word over $\{0, 1\}$, say $\alpha = i_0, \ldots, i_k$, then $x\alpha$ is the λ-term $xx_{i_0} \cdots x_{i_k}$, e.g. $x(1101) = xx_1x_1x_0x_1$.

(3) If $n \in N$, then α_n is the word over $\{0, 1\}$ which denotes n in binary notation.

(4) If $n \in N$, then $\boldsymbol{h}_n = \lambda xx_0x_1.x\check{\alpha}_n$.

Show that $\boldsymbol{h}$ is an adequate numeral system. [See van der Poel et al. [1980] for solutions.]

6.8.23. (J. Terlouw). Prove Scott's theorem 6.6.2 without the use of the second fixed point theorem. [*Hint.* Let $\mathcal{A} \subseteq \Lambda$ and $M_0 \in \mathcal{A}$, $M_1 \notin \mathcal{A}$. Define $\mathcal{B} = \{X \mid X \ulcorner X \urcorner \notin \mathcal{A}\}$. If $\mathcal{A}$ were recursive, then there is an $F \in \Lambda$ with

$$X \in \mathcal{B} \Rightarrow F \ulcorner X \urcorner = M_0$$

$$X \notin \mathcal{B} \Rightarrow F \ulcorner X \urcorner = M_1.$$

Derive a contradiction.]

6.8.24. Let $X = \mathbf{\Theta}(f \circ g)$. Show that $g(X)$ is a fixed point of $g \circ f$.

CHAPTER 7

THE THEORY OF COMBINATORS

This chapter studies the formal system combinatory logic, ***CL***, and its relation to $\boldsymbol{\lambda}$. For motivation to introduce this theory see §2.2. Applications to the λ-calculus will be given in chapter 8. The title "Theory of combinators" indicates the informal meta theory over ***CL***.

7.1. Combinatory logic

7.1.1. DEFINITION. ***CL*** is an equational theory formulated in the following language:

Alphabet:	$\boldsymbol{K}, \boldsymbol{S}$	constants,
	$v_0, v_1, \ldots$	variables,
	$=$	equality,
	(,)	improper symbols.

The set of ***CL***-terms, $\mathcal{C}$, is defined inductively as follows:

(i) $x \in \mathcal{C}$;
(ii) $\boldsymbol{K} \in \mathcal{C}$, $\boldsymbol{S} \in \mathcal{C}$;
(iii) $P, Q \in \mathcal{C} \Rightarrow (PQ) \in \mathcal{C}$.

Formulae of ***CL***: $P = Q$, with $P, Q \in \mathcal{C}$.

As for $\boldsymbol{\lambda}$, $x, y, \ldots$ range over arbitrary variables. $P, Q, \ldots$ range over $\mathcal{C}$. Syntactical conventions for ***CL*** are like those for $\boldsymbol{\lambda}$ (e.g. association to the left).

Since there is no variable binding operation in ***CL***, the notions of free variable and of substitution are simpler for ***CL*** than for $\boldsymbol{\lambda}$. FV(P) denotes the set of all variables in P; $P[x:= Q]$ denotes the result of substituting Q for all occurrences x in P.

$$P \text{ is closed} \quad \text{iff} \quad \mathrm{FV}(P) = \emptyset.$$

$$\mathcal{C}^0 = \{P \in \mathcal{C} \mid P \text{ closed}\}.$$

7.1.2. DEFINITION. $\boldsymbol{CL}$ is defined by the following axioms and rules.

(I.1) $\boldsymbol{K}PQ = P$,

(I.2) $\boldsymbol{S}PQR = PR(QR)$.

(II.1) $P = P$,

(II.2) $P = Q \Rightarrow Q = P$,

(II.3) $P = Q, Q = R \Rightarrow P = R$,

(II.4) $P = P' \Rightarrow PR = P'R$,

(II.5) $P = P' \Rightarrow RP = RP'$.

7.1.3. PROPOSITION. *Let $\vec{Q}_1, \vec{Q}_2$ both fit in $\vec{x}$. Then*

$$\boldsymbol{CL} \vdash P_1(\vec{x}) = P_2(\vec{x}),\ \boldsymbol{CL} \vdash \vec{Q}_1 = \vec{Q}_2 \Rightarrow \boldsymbol{CL} \vdash P_1(\vec{Q}_1) = P_2(\vec{Q}_2).$$

PROOF. Like the proof of proposition 2.1.22 but easier since there is no variable binding in $\boldsymbol{CL}$. □

Now it will be shown that λ-abstraction can be simulated by $\boldsymbol{K}$ and $\boldsymbol{S}$. The proof is related to that of the deduction theorem for some Hilbert type formulation of propositional logic, see Howard [1980].

7.1.4. LEMMA. *Define $\boldsymbol{I} \equiv \boldsymbol{SKK}$. Then*

$$\forall P \in \mathcal{C} \quad \boldsymbol{CL} \vdash \boldsymbol{I}P = P.$$

PROOF. $CL \vdash \boldsymbol{I}P \equiv \boldsymbol{SK K}P = \boldsymbol{K}P(\boldsymbol{K}P) = P$. □

7.1.5. DEFINITION. Define $\lambda^* x.P$ by induction on the structure of P as follows:

$$\lambda^* x.x \equiv \boldsymbol{I},$$

$$\lambda^* x.P \equiv \boldsymbol{K}P \quad \text{if } x \notin \mathrm{FV}(P),$$

$$\lambda^* x.PQ \equiv \boldsymbol{S}(\lambda^* x.P)(\lambda^* x.Q).$$

As in notation 2.1.3 set

$$\lambda^* x_1 \cdots x_n.P \equiv \lambda^* x_1.(\cdots(\lambda^* x_n.P)..).$$

EXAMPLE. $\lambda^* xy.yx \equiv \lambda^* x.(\lambda^* y.yx) \equiv \lambda^* x.\boldsymbol{SI}(\boldsymbol{K}x) \equiv \boldsymbol{S}(\boldsymbol{K}(\boldsymbol{SI}))(\boldsymbol{S}(\boldsymbol{KK})\boldsymbol{I})$.

7.1.6. PROPOSITION. (i) $\mathrm{FV}(\lambda^* x.P) = \mathrm{FV}(P) - \{x\}$.

(ii) $\boldsymbol{CL} \vdash (\lambda^* x.P)x = P$.

(iii) $\boldsymbol{CL} \vdash (\lambda^* x.P)Q = P[x := Q]$.

PROOF. (i), (ii) By induction on the structure of P.

Case 1. $P \equiv x$. Then $\lambda^* x.P \equiv \boldsymbol{I}$, hence (i) is trivial and (ii) follows from lemma 7.1.4.

Case 2. $x \notin \mathrm{FV}(P)$. Then $\lambda^* x.P = \boldsymbol{K}P$, hence (i) is immediate and (ii) follows from the axioms for $\boldsymbol{K} : \boldsymbol{K}Px = P$.

Case 3. $P \equiv P_1 P_2, x \in \mathrm{FV}(P_1 P_2)$. Then

$$\lambda^* x.P \equiv \boldsymbol{S}(\lambda^* x.P_1)(\lambda^* x.P_2).$$

Therefore by the induction hypothesis

$$\begin{aligned}\mathrm{FV}(\lambda^* x.P) &= \mathrm{FV}(\lambda^* x.P_1) \cup \mathrm{FV}(\lambda^* x.P_2)\\ &= \mathrm{FV}(P_1 P_2) - \{x\}.\end{aligned}$$

Moreover by the axioms for $\boldsymbol{S}$:

$$\begin{aligned}\boldsymbol{CL} \vdash (\lambda^* x.P)x &\equiv \boldsymbol{S}(\lambda^* x.P_1)(\lambda^* x.P_2)x\\ &= (\lambda^* x.P_1)x((\lambda^* x.P_2)x) = P_1 P_2 = P.\end{aligned}$$

(iii) By (ii) using proposition 7.1.3. □

7.1.7. LEMMA. *Let* $x \notin \mathrm{FV}(Q)$ *and* $x \not\equiv y$, *then*

$$(\lambda^* x.P)[y := Q] \equiv \lambda^* x.P[y := Q].$$

PROOF. By induction on the structure of P. □

7.1.8. COROLLARY. *Let* $P \equiv P(\vec{x})$ *and* $\vec{Q}$ *fit in* $\vec{x}$. *Suppose* $\vec{x} \notin \mathrm{FV}(\vec{Q})$. *Then*

$$\boldsymbol{CL} \vdash (\lambda^* \vec{x}.P)\vec{Q} = P(\vec{Q}).$$

PROOF. By proposition 7.1.6(iii) using lemma 7.1.7. □

The variable condition in lemma 7.1.7 and corollary 7.1.8 are not superfluous. For example,

$$\boldsymbol{CL} \nvdash (\lambda^* xy.x)yQ = x[x := y][y := Q].$$

Therefore it is convenient to assume the variable condition also for $\boldsymbol{CL}$. There is no need however to identify α-congruent terms: they *are* identical.

7.1.9. LEMMA. *Let* $y \notin \mathrm{FV}(P)$. *Then*

$$\lambda^*x.P \equiv \lambda^*y.P[x:=y].$$

PROOF. By induction on the structure of P. □

To conclude this section the rule of extensionality is considered for $\boldsymbol{CL}$.

7.1.10. DEFINITION. $\boldsymbol{CL}+\boldsymbol{ext}$ is $\boldsymbol{CL}$ extended by the following rule of extensionality:

$$\boldsymbol{ext}: \qquad Px = P'x,\ x \notin \mathrm{FV}(PP') \Rightarrow P = P'.$$

7.1.11. LEMMA. (i) $\boldsymbol{CL}+\boldsymbol{ext} \vdash \boldsymbol{K} = \lambda^*xy.x (\equiv \boldsymbol{S}(\boldsymbol{KK})\boldsymbol{I})$, *and* $\boldsymbol{CL}+\boldsymbol{ext} \vdash \boldsymbol{S} = \lambda^*xyz\cdot xz(yz)$.

(ii) $\boldsymbol{CL}+\boldsymbol{ext}$ *is closed under the rule*

$$(\xi) \qquad P = Q \Rightarrow \lambda^*x.P = \lambda^*x.Q.$$

PROOF. (i) $\boldsymbol{CL} \vdash \boldsymbol{K}xy = x = (\lambda^*xy.x)xy$. Hence by applying the rule $\boldsymbol{ext}$ twice

$$\boldsymbol{CL}+\boldsymbol{ext} \vdash \boldsymbol{K} = \lambda^*xy.x.$$

Similarly

$$\boldsymbol{CL}+\boldsymbol{ext} \vdash \boldsymbol{S} = \lambda^*xyz\cdot xz(yz).$$

(ii) Suppose

$$\boldsymbol{CL}+\boldsymbol{ext} \vdash P = Q$$

Then by lemma 7.1.6(ii)

$$\boldsymbol{CL}+\boldsymbol{ext} \vdash (\lambda^*x.P)x = (\lambda^*x.Q)x.$$

Hence by $\boldsymbol{ext}$, using lemma 7.1.6(i),

$$\boldsymbol{CL}+\boldsymbol{ext} \vdash \lambda^*x.P = \lambda^*x.Q. \quad \square$$

7.2. Reduction for *CL*

There is a notion of reduction, $\boldsymbol{w}$, that generates equality provable in $\boldsymbol{CL}$. The corresponding relation $\twoheadrightarrow_w$ is called *weak reduction*.

7.2.1. DEFINITION. $\boldsymbol{w} = \{(\boldsymbol{K}MN, M) | M, N \in \mathcal{C}\} \cup \{(\boldsymbol{S}MNL, ML(NL)) | M, N, L \in \mathcal{C}\}$. As in remark 3.1.7 $\boldsymbol{w}$ induces binary relations $\to_w$, $\twoheadrightarrow_w$ and $=_w$ on $\mathcal{C}$.

$\to_w$ is the smallest relation extending $\boldsymbol{w}$ that is compatible with application and $\twoheadrightarrow_w$ is the reflexive transitive closure of $\to_w$.

$=_w$ is the least equivalence relation extending $\twoheadrightarrow_w$.

$\twoheadrightarrow_w$ is called *weak* reduction because, for example, $\boldsymbol{SK}$ is in w-nf but its corresponding λ-term $(\lambda xyz.xz(yz))(\lambda xy.x)$ does reduce.

7.2.2. PROPOSITION. $M =_w N \Leftrightarrow \boldsymbol{CL} \vdash M = N$

PROOF. Analogous to the proof of proposition 3.2.1. □

7.2.3. THEOREM. $\boldsymbol{w}$ *is* CR.

PROOF. See exercise 7.4.13. □

The following consequences of proposition 7.2.2 and theorem 7.2.3 are summarized as follows.

7.2.4. CHURCH-ROSSER THEOREM FOR CL. (i) *If* $\boldsymbol{CL} \vdash M = N$, *then* $\exists Z \in \mathcal{C}$ $[M \twoheadrightarrow_w Z \wedge N \twoheadrightarrow_w Z]$.

(ii) *If* $\boldsymbol{CL} \vdash M = N$ *and* N *is a* w-nf, *then* $M \twoheadrightarrow_w N$.

(iii) *Let* $M, N \in \mathcal{C}$ *be distinct* w-nfs.
Then $\boldsymbol{CL} \nvdash M = N$. *In particular* $\boldsymbol{CL}$ *is consistent.*

PROOF. By theorem 3.1.12 and corollary 3.1.13. □

Next we mention that equality provable in $\boldsymbol{CL} + \boldsymbol{ext}$ also can be analyzed by a recursive notion of reduction $\boldsymbol{s}$ (strong reduction).

7.2.5. FACT. (i) (Hindley [1967]; Lercher [1967]). There exists a recursive notion of reduction $\boldsymbol{s}$ such that for $M, N \in \mathcal{C}$

$$M =_s N \Leftrightarrow \boldsymbol{CL} + \boldsymbol{ext} \vdash M = N.$$

(ii) (Curry et al. [1958] §6F). Moreover, $\boldsymbol{s}$ is CR.

PROOF. See references. □

That (ii) was proved before (i) is due to the fact that first $\twoheadrightarrow_s$ was defined (Curry's strong reduction $\succ\!\!-$) and only later $\to_s$ and $\boldsymbol{s}$.

Strong reduction will not be considered any further. The reason is that the theory $\boldsymbol{CL}+\boldsymbol{ext}$ is equivalent with $\boldsymbol{\lambda}+\boldsymbol{ext}$ and for the latter theory there is the convenient notion of reduction $\boldsymbol{\beta\eta}$, while strong reduction is rather complicated. In fact, that $\boldsymbol{s}$ is CR is a consequence of $\boldsymbol{\beta\eta}$ being CR, and no direct proof is known. Moreover $\boldsymbol{s}$ is, as a set of pairs, not a function, i.e. an $\boldsymbol{s}$-redex may have several contracta.

In Klop [1980a] some differences between w- and β-reduction are proved. It is shown that if $G_w(P)$ contains a reduction cycle (e.g. $\boldsymbol{SII}(\boldsymbol{SII})$), then it contains infinitely many reduction cycles. This is not so for β-reduction, consider e.g. $G_\beta((\lambda x.xx)(\lambda x.xx))$. In Hindley [1977] the notions w-, s- and β-reduction are compared.

7.3. The relation between CL and λ

Once abstraction is defined in $\boldsymbol{CL}$, there are canonical mappings between $\mathcal{C}$ and Λ.

7.3.1. Definition (standard translations between $\mathcal{C}$ and Λ). The following mappings

$$(\ )_\lambda : \mathcal{C} \to \Lambda, \qquad (\ )_{CL} : \Lambda \to \mathcal{C}$$

are defined inductively as follows:

$$(\ )_\lambda: \quad (x)_\lambda \equiv x,$$
$$(\boldsymbol{K})_\lambda \equiv \mathbf{K},$$
$$(\boldsymbol{S})_\lambda \equiv \mathbf{S},$$
$$(PQ)_\lambda \equiv (P)_\lambda (Q)_\lambda.$$

$$(\ )_{CL}: \quad (x)_{CL} \equiv x,$$
$$(MN)_{CL} \equiv (M)_{CL}(N)_{CL},$$
$$(\lambda x.M)_{CL} \equiv \lambda^* x.(M)_{CL}.$$

Notations. $P_\lambda \equiv (P)_\lambda$, $P_{\lambda,CL} \equiv (P_\lambda)_{CL}$ for $P \in \mathcal{C}$.
$M_{CL} \equiv (M)_{CL}$; $M_{CL,\lambda} \equiv (M_{CL})_\lambda$, for $M \in \Lambda$.

7.3.2. Lemma. (i) $\mathrm{FV}(P) = \mathrm{FV}(P_\lambda)$ *for* $P \in \mathcal{C}$.
(ii) $\mathrm{FV}(M) = \mathrm{FV}(M_{CL})$ *for* $M \in \Lambda$.

Proof. By induction on the structure of M, using lemma 7.1.6 (i). □

7.3.3. Lemma. $\boldsymbol{CL} \vdash P = Q \Rightarrow \lambda \vdash P_\lambda = Q_\lambda$.

PROOF. By induction on the length of proof of $P = Q$. □

The converse is not true however. For example $\lambda \vdash \mathbf{SK} = \mathbf{KI}$, but $\boldsymbol{CL} \nvdash \boldsymbol{SK} = \boldsymbol{KI}$. This is because $\boldsymbol{CL}$ is not closed under the rule ξ, i.e. in general

$$\boldsymbol{CL} \vdash P = Q \not\Rightarrow \boldsymbol{CL} \vdash \lambda^* x.P = \lambda^* x.Q.$$

For example $\boldsymbol{CL} \vdash \boldsymbol{I}x = x$, but $\boldsymbol{CL} \nvdash \boldsymbol{S}(\boldsymbol{KI})\boldsymbol{I} = \boldsymbol{I}$.

Curry extended $\boldsymbol{CL}$ by a finite set $\boldsymbol{A}_\beta$ of closed equations such that $\boldsymbol{CL} + \boldsymbol{A}_\beta$ is equivalent to $\boldsymbol{\lambda}$. We follow his construction.

First an auxiliary abstraction operator is introduced.

7.3.4. DEFINITION. $\lambda_1 x.P$ is defined by induction on the structure of P.

$$\lambda_1 x.x \equiv \boldsymbol{I},$$

$$\lambda_1 x.c \equiv \boldsymbol{K}c \quad \text{if } c \text{ is a variable} \not\equiv x \text{ or } c \in \{\boldsymbol{K}, \boldsymbol{S}\},$$

$$\lambda_1 x.PQ \equiv \boldsymbol{S}(\lambda_1 x.P)(\lambda_1 x.Q).$$

Let $\boldsymbol{A}$ be a set of equations between closed $\boldsymbol{CL}$-terms. $\boldsymbol{CL} + \boldsymbol{A}$ is the theory $\boldsymbol{CL}$ extended by the elements of $\boldsymbol{A}$ as axioms.

7.3.5. LEMMA. *Consider the schemes*

(1) $\boldsymbol{K} = \lambda^* xy.x$,
(2) $\boldsymbol{S} = \lambda^* xyz.xz(yz)$,
(3) $\boldsymbol{S}(\boldsymbol{K}P)(\boldsymbol{K}Q) = \boldsymbol{K}(PQ)$,
(4) $\lambda^* x.\boldsymbol{K}PQ = \lambda^* x.P$,
(5) $\lambda^* x.\boldsymbol{S}PQR = \lambda^* x.PR(QR)$.

(i) If $\boldsymbol{CL} + \boldsymbol{A}$ proves 1, 2 it also proves $P_{\lambda, CL} = P$ for all $P \in \mathcal{C}$.
(ii) If $\boldsymbol{CL} + \boldsymbol{A}$ proves 3, it also proves $\lambda^* x.P = \lambda_1 x.P$ for all $P \in \mathcal{C}$.
(iii) If $\boldsymbol{CL} + \boldsymbol{A}$ proves 3, 4, 5, then $\boldsymbol{CL} + \boldsymbol{A}$ is closed under the rule ξ:

$$\boldsymbol{CL} + \boldsymbol{A} \vdash P = Q \quad \Rightarrow \quad \boldsymbol{CL} + \boldsymbol{A} \vdash \lambda^* x.P = \lambda^* x.Q.$$

PROOF. (i) By induction on the structure of P.

(ii) By induction on the structure of P it follows that

$$\lambda_1 x.P = \boldsymbol{K}P \quad \text{if } x \notin \mathrm{FV}(P),$$

$$\lambda_1 x.P = \lambda^* x.P.$$

(iii) By induction on the length of proof of $P = Q$ in $\boldsymbol{CL} + \boldsymbol{A}$. The axioms of $\boldsymbol{CL}$ follow from 4, 5. The axioms in $\boldsymbol{A}$ are easy to treat. For the rule $P = Q \Rightarrow RP = RQ$, use (ii) and the induction hypothesis. The rest is easy. □

7.3.6. DEFINITION. $\boldsymbol{A}_\beta$ is the following set of axioms.
(A.1) $\boldsymbol{K} = \lambda^* xy.\boldsymbol{K}xy$, (A.1′) $\boldsymbol{K} = \lambda^* xy.x$;
(A.2) $\boldsymbol{S} = \lambda^* xyz.\boldsymbol{S}xyz$, (A.2′) $\boldsymbol{S} = \lambda^* xyz.xz(yz)$;
(A.3) $\lambda^* xy.\boldsymbol{S}(\boldsymbol{K}x)(\boldsymbol{K}y) = \lambda^* xy.\boldsymbol{K}(xy)$;
(A.4) $\lambda^* xy.\boldsymbol{S}(\boldsymbol{S}(\boldsymbol{K}\boldsymbol{K})x)y = \lambda^* xyz.xz$;
(A.5) $\lambda^* xyz.\boldsymbol{S}(\boldsymbol{S}(\boldsymbol{S}(\boldsymbol{K}\boldsymbol{S})x)y)z = \lambda^* xyz.\boldsymbol{S}(\boldsymbol{S}xz)(\boldsymbol{S}yz)$.

7.3.7. LEMMA. *In* $\boldsymbol{CL} + \boldsymbol{A}_\beta$ *one can prove schemes* (1), (2), (3) *and* (5) *of lemma* 7.3.5. *In particular*

$$\lambda^* x.P = \lambda_1 x.P.$$

PROOF. (1) and (2) are given. (3) follows by applying both sides of (A.3) to P and Q. It follows by lemma 7.3.5.(ii) that $\lambda^* x.P = \lambda_1 x.P$. Therefore, to obtain (5), it is sufficient to prove

$$\lambda_1 x.\boldsymbol{S}PQR = \lambda_1 x.PR(QR).$$

This follows by applying both sides of (A.5) to $\lambda_1 x.P$, $\lambda_1 x.Q$ and $\lambda_1 x.R$. □

REMARK. Note that by replacing the RHS of (A.4) by $\lambda^* xy.x$, also scheme (4) will follow this way. However this new version of (A.4) is not a valid equation when translated into λ-terms.

7.3.8. LEMMA. *In* $\boldsymbol{CL} + \boldsymbol{A}_\beta$ *one can prove*
(i) $\lambda^* z.\boldsymbol{S}PQz = \boldsymbol{S}PQ$, *provided* $z \notin \mathrm{FV}(\boldsymbol{S}PQ)$,
(ii) $\lambda^* z.(\lambda^* x.P)z = \lambda^* x.P$, *provided* $z \notin \mathrm{FV}(P)$,
(iii) $\lambda^* z.\boldsymbol{K}PQ = \lambda^* z.P$.

PROOF. (i)

$$\begin{aligned} \boldsymbol{S}PQ &= (\lambda^* xyz.\boldsymbol{S}xyz)PQ && \text{by (A.2),} \\ &= \lambda^* z.\boldsymbol{S}PQz && \text{by lemmas 7.1.7, 7.1.8.} \end{aligned}$$

(ii) *Case* 1. $P \equiv x$. Then $\lambda^* x.P \equiv \boldsymbol{I} \equiv \boldsymbol{S}\boldsymbol{K}\boldsymbol{K}$ and we are done by (i).
Case 2. $x \notin \mathrm{FV}(P)$. Then

$$\begin{aligned} \lambda^* x.P \equiv \boldsymbol{K}P &= (\lambda^* xy.\boldsymbol{K}xy)P && \text{by (A.1),} \\ &= \lambda^* y.\boldsymbol{K}Py && \text{by lemmas 7.1.7, 7.1.8,} \\ &\equiv \lambda^* z.(\lambda^* x.P)z && \text{by lemma 7.1.9.} \end{aligned}$$

Case 3. $P \equiv P_1 P_2$. Then $\lambda^* x.P \equiv \boldsymbol{S}QR$ and we are done by (i).

(iii) $\lambda^* x.\boldsymbol{K}PQ = \lambda_1 x.\boldsymbol{K}PQ$ by lemma 7.3.7,

$$\equiv \boldsymbol{S}(\boldsymbol{S}(\boldsymbol{KK})(\lambda_1 x.P))(\lambda_1 x.Q)$$

$$= (\lambda^* xy.\boldsymbol{S}(\boldsymbol{S}(\boldsymbol{KK})x)y)(\lambda_1 x.P)(\lambda_1 x.Q)$$

$$= (\lambda^* xyz.xz)(\lambda^* x.P)(\lambda^* x.Q) \quad \text{by A.4,}$$

$$= \lambda^* z.(\lambda^* x.P)z$$

$$= \lambda^* x.P \quad \text{by (ii).} \ \square$$

7.3.9. Corollary. *$\boldsymbol{CL} + \boldsymbol{A}_\beta$ proves schemes* (1), . . . , (5) *of lemma* 7.3.5.

7.3.10. Theorem. *$\boldsymbol{\lambda}$ and $\boldsymbol{CL} + \boldsymbol{A}_\beta$ are equivalent in the following sense.*

(i) $\boldsymbol{\lambda} \vdash M_{CL,\lambda} = M$; *in fact* $M_{CL,\lambda} \twoheadrightarrow_\beta M$.

(ii) $\boldsymbol{CL} + \boldsymbol{A}_\beta \vdash P_{\lambda,CL} = P$.

(iii) $\boldsymbol{\lambda} \vdash M = N \Leftrightarrow \boldsymbol{CL} + \boldsymbol{A}_\beta \vdash M_{CL} = N_{CL}$.

(iv) $\boldsymbol{CL} + \boldsymbol{A}_\beta \vdash P = Q \Leftrightarrow \boldsymbol{\lambda} \vdash P_\lambda = Q_\lambda$.

Proof. (i) First show by induction on the structure of $P \in \mathcal{C}$

$$(*) \qquad (\lambda^* x.P)_\lambda \twoheadrightarrow_\beta \lambda x.P_\lambda.$$

Then the statement follows by induction on the structure of $M \in \Lambda$.

(ii) By lemmas 7.3.7 and 7.3.5 (i).

(iii) ($\Rightarrow$) First show by induction on the structure of M that

$$(M[x{:=}\,N])_{CL} \equiv M_{CL}[x{:=}\,N_{CL}].$$

Then the result follows by induction on the length of proof of $M = N$, using that by corollary 7.3.9 and lemma 7.3.5 (iii) $\boldsymbol{CL} + \boldsymbol{A}_\beta$ is closed under the rule ξ.

(iv) ($\Rightarrow$) First show that $\boldsymbol{\lambda}$ proves all translated $\boldsymbol{A}_\beta$ axioms (use ($*$)). Then the result follows by induction on the length of proof of $P = Q$.

(iii) ($\Leftarrow$) Suppose $\boldsymbol{CL} + \boldsymbol{A}_\beta \vdash M_{CL} = N_{CL}$. Then by (iv) ($\Rightarrow$) one has $\boldsymbol{\lambda} \vdash M_{CL,\lambda} = N_{CL,\lambda}$. Hence $\boldsymbol{\lambda} \vdash M = N$, by (i).

(iv) ($\Leftarrow$) Similarly. $\square$

Now it will be examined what happens if extensionality is added.

7.3.11. Lemma. $\boldsymbol{CL} + \boldsymbol{ext} \vdash$ (A.1), (A.1′), (A.2), (A.2′), (A.3), (A.4), (A.5).

PROOF. As a typical example we show (A.3).

$$(\lambda^* xy.\boldsymbol{S}(\boldsymbol{K}x)(\boldsymbol{K}y))xyz = \boldsymbol{S}(\boldsymbol{K}x)(\boldsymbol{K}y)z$$

$$= \boldsymbol{K}xz(\boldsymbol{K}yz) = xy.$$

$$(\lambda^* xy.\boldsymbol{K}(xy))xyz = \boldsymbol{K}(xy)z = xy.$$

Hence the result follows by applying ***ext*** three times. □

7.3.12. THEOREM. ***CL*** + ***ext*** *is equivalent with* $\boldsymbol{\lambda}$ + ***ext*** *in the sense of theorem 7.3.10.*

PROOF. The analogues to (i), (ii) in theorem 7.3.10 follow since $\boldsymbol{\lambda} \subseteq \boldsymbol{\lambda}$ + ***ext*** and ***CL*** + $\boldsymbol{A}_\beta \subseteq$ ***CL*** + ***ext***, by lemma 7.3.11. Analogues to (iii), (iv) follow by induction on the length of proof. Lemma 7.3.2 is needed to show that after translation an application of ***ext*** remains valid. □

By theorem 2.1.29 the theories $\boldsymbol{\lambda}$ + ***ext*** and $\boldsymbol{\lambda\eta}$ are equivalent. Similarly one can axiomatize the rule ***ext*** in ***CL***.

7.3.13. DEFINITION. $\boldsymbol{A}_{\beta\eta}$ is the theory $\boldsymbol{A}_\beta$ extended by the following axiom (A.6) $\lambda^* x.\boldsymbol{S}(\boldsymbol{K}x)\boldsymbol{I} = \boldsymbol{I}$.

7.3.14. THEOREM. ***CL*** + $\boldsymbol{A}_{\beta\eta} \vdash P = Q \Leftrightarrow$ ***CL*** + ***ext*** $\vdash P = Q$. *Hence the four theories*

$$\boldsymbol{\lambda} + \boldsymbol{ext}, \qquad \boldsymbol{\lambda\eta}, \qquad \boldsymbol{CL} + \boldsymbol{ext}, \qquad \boldsymbol{CL} + \boldsymbol{A}_{\beta\eta}$$

are all equivalent.

PROOF. ($\Leftarrow$) Applying both sides of (A.6) to P gives

(6) $\lambda^* x.Px = P$ if $x \notin \mathrm{FV}(P)$.

Then ***CL*** + $\boldsymbol{A}_{\beta\eta}$ is closed under the rule ***ext***: for if $x \notin \mathrm{FV}(PQ)$ and ***CL*** + $\boldsymbol{A}_{\beta\eta} \vdash Px = Qx$, then

$$\boldsymbol{CL} + \boldsymbol{A}_{\beta\eta} \vdash \lambda^* x.Px = \lambda^* x.Qx$$

by corollary 7.3.9 and lemma 7.3.5(iii) and so

$$\boldsymbol{CL} + \boldsymbol{A}_{\beta\eta} \vdash P = Q, \quad \text{by (6)}.$$

The statement now follows by induction on the length of proof in ***CL*** + ***ext*** of $P = Q$.

(⇒) First show that $\boldsymbol{CL}+\boldsymbol{ext}\vdash$(A.6). Then the result follows by induction on the length of proof. □

Now the axioms A_β and $A_{\beta\eta}$ are given explicitly.

7.3.15. COROLLARY. *Consider the following combinatory axioms.*

A_β:

(A.1) $K=S(S(KS)(S(KK)K))(K(SKK))$,

(A.2) $S=S(S(KS)(S(K(S(KS)))(S(K(S(KK)))S)))(K(K(SKK)))$,

$A_{\beta\eta}$:

(A.3) $S(S(KS)(S(KK)(S(KS)K)))(KK)=S(KK)$,

(A.4) $S(KS)(S(KK))=$
$S(KK)(S(S(KS)(S(KK)(SKK)))(K(SKK)))$,

(A.5) $S(K(S(KS)))(S(KS)(S(KS)))=$
$=S(S(KS)(S(KK)(S(KS)(S(K(S(KS)))S))))(KS)$,

(A.6) $S(S(KS)K)(K(SKK))=SKK$.

If we take

$$A_\beta=\{(\text{A.1}),(\text{A.2}),(\text{A.3}),(\text{A.4}),(\text{A.5})\}$$

and

$$A_{\beta\eta}=\{(\text{A.3}),(\text{A.4}),(\text{A.5}),(\text{A.6})\},$$

then (in the sense of the theorem)

(i) $\boldsymbol{CL}+A_\beta$ *and* $\boldsymbol{\lambda}$ *are equivalent,*

(ii) $\boldsymbol{CL}+A_{\beta\eta}$ *and* $\boldsymbol{\lambda\eta}$ *are equivalent.*

PROOF. (i) (A.1′) and (A.2′) of definition 7.3.6 follow from (A.1), . . . , (A.5). The explicit axioms are obtained by working out λ^*x (sometimes using short cuts like λ_2x, see exercise 7.4.3).

(ii) (A.1) and (A.2) follow from (A.3), . . . , (A.6).

Do exercise 7.4.12 for the details. □

It follows that there is a first order description of the concept of λ-algebras. See theorem 5.2.5.

It should be noted that the standard translations do not preserve normal form or reduction.

7.3.16. EXAMPLES. (i) $SK\in\mathcal{C}$ is a w-nf, but $(SK)_\lambda\equiv\mathbf{SK}$ is not a β-nf.

(ii) Let $\omega\equiv SII$ and $P\equiv S(K\omega)(K\omega)$.

Then P is a w-nf, but $P_\lambda=_\beta\lambda x.\Omega$ does not even have a β-nf.

(iii) One has

$$\lambda x.\mathbf{II}\to_\beta\lambda x.\mathbf{I},$$

but for the CL translations

$$S(KI)(KI) \not\twoheadrightarrow_w KI.$$

Also strong reduction is not preserved by the standard translations; see Curry et al. [1958] p. 221.

On the other hand the concept of solvability is invariant under the standard translations. For CL solvability is defined as follows.

7.3.17. DEFINITION. (i) $P \in \mathcal{C}^0$ is *w-solvable* if $\exists \vec{Q}\ P\vec{Q} =_w I$.

(ii) $P \in \mathcal{C}$ is w-solvable if there is a substitution instance $P^* \in \mathcal{C}^0$ that is w-solvable.

In proposition 8.3.22 it will be shown that $M \in \Lambda$ is β-solvable iff M_{CL} is w-solvable.

7.4. Exercises

7.4.1. Show that for $P, Q \in \mathcal{C}$

$$P \twoheadrightarrow_w Q \Rightarrow P_\lambda \twoheadrightarrow_\beta Q_\lambda.$$

7.4.2. Draw $G_w(\Omega_{CL})$ and $G_\beta(\Omega)$.

7.4.3. Apart from λ^* and λ_1 there are other ways to define abstraction in CL.

(i) Show that λ_2 defined inductively as follows is one such possibility.

$$\lambda_2 x.x \equiv SKK,$$

$$\lambda_2 x.P \equiv KP \quad \text{if } x \notin \mathrm{FV}(P),$$

$$\lambda_2 x.Px \equiv P \quad \text{if } x \notin \mathrm{FV}(P),$$

$$\lambda_2 x.PQ \equiv S(\lambda_2 x.P)(\lambda_2 x.Q) \quad \text{if the previous cases do not apply.}$$

Prove $CL \vdash (\lambda_2 x.P)Q = P[x := Q]$.

(ii) Show that if $x \notin \mathrm{FV}(Q)$ and $x \not\equiv y$, then

$$(\lambda_2 x.P)[y := Q] \equiv \lambda_2 x.P[y := Q].$$

Note that the structure of $\lambda_2 x.P$ is in general simpler than that of $\lambda^* x.P$ or $\lambda_1 x.P$. See Curry et al. [1972], §11C for a discussion of the various possible ways of defining abstraction in CL.

7.4.4. Show that

$$\forall P \in \mathcal{C}\ \exists Q \in \mathcal{C}, Q \text{ in } w\text{-nf}, \forall R \in \mathcal{C}\quad QR \twoheadrightarrow_w P.$$

7.4.5. An *S-term* is a CL-term consisting of only S's (and parentheses). Find out which of the following S-terms have a w-nf. See also Barendregt et al. [1976] §7.

(i) $SSSSSSS$.

(ii) (A. Petorossi) $SAA(SAA)$, where $A \equiv SSS$.

*(iii) (M. Baron; M. Duboué). $S(SS)SSSS$.

7.4.6. (Bergstra, Klop [1979]). Show that no S-term P "cycles", i.e. not $P \twoheadrightarrow_{\neq 0\, w} P$.

7.4.7. (Klop). (i) Let P be a term of $\boldsymbol{CL}$ that can be written without parentheses (e.g. $\boldsymbol{SKSSK}$). Show that P has a w-nf (P even strongly normalizes). [*Hint*. Use the previous exercise.]

(ii) Show that (i) becomes false if I is treated as a constant.

7.4.8. Memorize the following definitions; they are frequently used in Curry et al. [1958, 1972].

$$\begin{array}{lll}\text{(i)} & \mathbf{B} \equiv \lambda xyz.x(yz), & \boldsymbol{B} \equiv \mathbf{B}_{CL}, \\ & \mathbf{C} \equiv \lambda xyz.xzy, & \boldsymbol{C} \equiv \mathbf{C}_{CL}, \\ & \mathbf{J} \equiv \lambda xyzw.xy(xwz), & \boldsymbol{J} \equiv \mathbf{J}_{CL}, \\ & \mathbf{W} \equiv \lambda xy.xyy, & \boldsymbol{W} \equiv \mathbf{W}_{CL}, \\ & \mathbf{\Phi} \equiv \lambda xyzw.x(yw)(zw), & \boldsymbol{\Phi} \equiv \mathbf{\Phi}_{CL}, \\ & \mathbf{\Psi} \equiv \lambda xyzw.x(yz)(yw), & \boldsymbol{\Psi} \equiv \mathbf{\Psi}_{CL}.\end{array}$$

(ii) For arbitrary M, $M_* \equiv M\mathbf{I}$. In particular $\mathbf{C}_* = \lambda xy.yx$.

7.4.9. (Hindley). Construct a $P \in \mathcal{C}^0$ in w-nf, such that

$$\forall Q \in \mathcal{C} \quad PQ \twoheadrightarrow_w P.$$

7.4.10. (Böhm, Dezani-Ciancaglini [1972]). Consider the alphabet $\Sigma = \{K, S, (\ ,\ )\}$. Σ^* is the set of all words over Σ (i.e. finite strings $\alpha_1, \ldots, \alpha_n$, with $\alpha_i \in \Sigma$). Note that $\mathcal{C}^0 \subseteq \Sigma^*$. Define

$$\langle P \rangle \equiv \lambda^* x.xP,$$

$$P.Q \equiv \lambda^* x.Q(Px),$$

$$\boldsymbol{B} \equiv \lambda^* xyz.x(yz).$$

Define $\varphi : \Sigma^* \to \mathcal{C}^0$ as follows.

$$\varphi(\boldsymbol{K}) \equiv \langle \boldsymbol{K} \rangle, \qquad \varphi(\boldsymbol{S}) \equiv \langle \boldsymbol{S} \rangle.$$
$$\varphi(\,(\,) \equiv \boldsymbol{B}, \qquad \varphi(\,)\,) \equiv \boldsymbol{I},$$

$$\varphi(\alpha_1\alpha_2 \cdots \alpha_n) \equiv \varphi(\alpha_1) \cdot \varphi(\alpha_2) \cdot \cdots \cdot \varphi(\alpha_n)$$

Show that

$$\forall P \in \mathcal{C} \quad \boldsymbol{CL} + \boldsymbol{ext} \vdash \varphi(P) = \langle P \rangle.$$

[*Hint*. First show that . is associative and that $P.\boldsymbol{I} = \boldsymbol{I}.P = P$.]
Moral. The meaning of P can be found without parsing.

7.4.11. (Church [1936a]). Using results about $\boldsymbol{CL}$, show that the predicate logic with a binary relation and a binary function symbol is undecidable. [*Note*. Kalmàr [1936] showed that the predicate logic with just one binary relation symbol is undecidable. Behmann [1922] showed that the predicate logic with only unary relation symbols is decidable. See also Church [1956].]

7.4.12. Fill in the details needed for the proof of corollary 7.3.15.

7.4.13. Show that the notion of reduction w is CR. [*Hint*. (Rosser [1935]). Define $M \overset{!}{\twoheadrightarrow} N$ iff there are disjoint w-redexes $R_1, \ldots, R_n$ in M and N results by contracting $R_1, \ldots, R_n$. For example $S(KPQ)(SPQR) \overset{!}{\to} SP(PR(QR))$. Show that

(i) $\overset{!}{\to}$ satisfies the diamond property

(ii) $\twoheadrightarrow_w$ is the transitive closure of $\overset{!}{\to}$.]

7.4.14. (Grzegorczyk). (i) Show that if $\mathcal{A} \subseteq \mathcal{C}^0$ is a non trivial set ($\neq \emptyset$, $\neq \mathcal{C}^0$) closed under equality ($M \in \mathcal{A} \wedge M = N \in \mathcal{C}^0 \Rightarrow N \in \mathcal{A}$), then $\mathcal{A}$ is not recursive.

(ii) Prove that the first order theory T_{CL} with axioms

$$\forall xy \quad kxy = x,$$
$$\forall xyz \quad sxyz = xz(yz), \qquad s \neq k$$

is essentially undecidable (that is, T_{CL} has no consistent recursive extensions).

(iii) Show that T_{CL} has no recursive models.

7.4.15. Define $(\ )_{CL2} : \Lambda \to \mathcal{C}$ as follows:

$$(x)_{CL2} = x,$$
$$(MN)_{CL2} = (M)_{CL2}(N)_{CL2},$$
$$(\lambda x.M)_{CL2} = \lambda_2 x.(M)_{CL2}, \quad \text{see exercise 7.4.3.}$$

(i) Show that $\boldsymbol{\lambda} + \boldsymbol{ext}$ and $\boldsymbol{CL} + \boldsymbol{ext}$ are equivalent via the translations $(\ )_\lambda$ and $(\ )_{CL2}$.

(ii) Show that $P_{\lambda, CL2} \equiv P$ and $(P[x:= Q])_{CL2} \equiv P_{CL2}[x:= Q_{CL2}]$ for all $P, Q \in \mathcal{C}$.

CHAPTER 8

CLASSICAL LAMBDA CALCULUS (CONTINUED)

8.1. Bases and enumeration

In this section some applications of the theory of combinators to the λ-calculus are given. The point is that the set Λ^0 can be generated by the λ-terms **K**, **S**. A priori this not obvious since Λ^0 is defined via the set Λ of open terms and not directly by an inductive definition.

8.1.1. DEFINITION. (i) Let $\mathcal{X} \subset \Lambda$. The set of terms *generated by* $\mathcal{X}$, notation $\mathcal{X}^+$, is the least set $\mathcal{Y}$ such that

(1) $\mathcal{X} \subseteq \mathcal{Y}$,

(2) $M, N \in \mathcal{Y} \Rightarrow MN \in \mathcal{Y}$.

(ii) Let $\mathcal{Q} \subset \Lambda$. $\mathcal{X} \subset \Lambda$ is a *basis* for $\mathcal{Q}$ if

$$\forall M \in \mathcal{Q}\ \exists N \in \mathcal{X}^+ \quad N = M.$$

(iii) $\mathcal{X}$ is called a *basis* if $\mathcal{X}$ is a basis for Λ^0.

8.1.2. PROPOSITION. $\{\mathbf{K}, \mathbf{S}\}$ *is a basis. In fact*

$$\forall M \in \Lambda^0\ \exists N \in \{\mathbf{K}, \mathbf{S}\}^+ \quad N \twoheadrightarrow M.$$

PROOF. Clearly if $P \in \mathcal{C}^0$, then $P_\lambda \in \{\mathbf{K}, \mathbf{S}\}^+$. Now let $M \in \Lambda^0$; then $M_{CL} \in \mathcal{C}^0$, hence $M_{CL,\lambda} \in \{\mathbf{K}, \mathbf{S}\}^+$. Moreover $M_{CL,\lambda} \twoheadrightarrow_\beta M$, by theorem 7.3.10(i). □

8.1.3. COROLLARY. *If* $\mathcal{X}$ *is a basis, then*

$$\forall M \in \Lambda^0\ \exists N \in \mathcal{X}^+ \quad N \twoheadrightarrow M.$$

PROOF. By assumption $\exists N_K, N_S \in \mathcal{X}^+ \quad N_K = \mathbf{K} \wedge N_S = \mathbf{S}$. Since **K**, **S** are in nf, it follows by the CR theorem that

$$N_K \twoheadrightarrow \mathbf{K}, \qquad N_S \twoheadrightarrow \mathbf{S}.$$

By the proposition,

$$\forall M \in \Lambda^0 \ \exists L \in \{\mathbf{K}, \mathbf{S}\}^+ \quad L \twoheadrightarrow M.$$

But then

$$\exists L' \in \{N_S, N_K\}^+ \subseteq \mathcal{X}^+ \quad L' \twoheadrightarrow L \twoheadrightarrow M. \quad \square$$

Now it will be proved that there is a basis consisting of one combinator. The given construction is due to Rosser simplifying a construction of the author. Prior to this C. A. Meredith (see Meredith and Prior [1963]) had found one point bases by considering a single formula axiomatizing positive implicational logic. See also exercise 8.5.16.

8.1.4. PROPOSITION. *There exists a basis consisting of one element* **X**.

PROOF. Define $\mathbf{X} \equiv \langle \mathbf{K}, \mathbf{S}, \mathbf{K} \rangle$. It can be readily verified that

$$\mathbf{XXX} = \mathbf{K} \quad \text{and} \quad \mathbf{X}(\mathbf{XX}) = \mathbf{S}.$$

The result now follows from proposition 8.1.2. $\square$

8.1.5. DEFINITION. A term $M \in \Lambda$ *enumerates* a set $\mathcal{A} \subset \Lambda$ if

$$\forall N \in \mathcal{A} \ \exists n \in \mathbb{N} \quad M \ulcorner n \urcorner = N.$$

If one wants to enumerate the set Λ^0, then it seems that one has to enumerate also all subterms of terms in Λ^0. This is impossible, since no (finite) term can produce all free variables. This difficulty will be avoided, essentially by constructing the enumeration via a base. Following Kleene [1936] a term $\mathbf{E} \in \Lambda^0$ will be constructed enumerating Λ^0.

8.1.6. THEOREM. *There is a term* $\mathbf{E} \in \Lambda^0$ *such that*

$$\forall M \in \Lambda^0 \quad \mathbf{E} \ulcorner M \urcorner \twoheadrightarrow M.$$

PROOF. The proof is given in several steps.

(1) *Lemma. Let* $\{\mathbf{X}\}$ *be the one point base for* Λ^0 *constructed in proposition* 8.1.4. *Then*

$$\forall M \in \Lambda^0 \ \exists M' \in \{\mathbf{X}\}^+ \quad M' \twoheadrightarrow M.$$

Moreover, M′ can be found effectively from M.

Proof. By corollary 8.1.3 and its proof. $\square_1$

(2) *Definition*. For $M \in \{\mathbf{X}\}^+$ define $\natural M \in \mathbb{N}$ inductively as follows:

$$\natural \mathbf{X} = 0, \qquad \natural AB = \langle \natural A, \natural B \rangle,$$

where $\langle\ ,\ \rangle$ is some recursive pair function such that 0 is not a pair and having recursive projections p_0, p_1.

(3) *Lemma*. $\exists F \in \Lambda^0 \ \ \forall M \in \{\mathbf{X}\}^+ \ \ F \ulcorner \natural M \urcorner \twoheadrightarrow M$.
Proof. Let p_0, p_1 be λ-defined by respectively $P_0, P_1 \in \Lambda^0$. Define F by

$$Fx \twoheadrightarrow \textit{If } \mathbf{Zero}\ x \textit{ then } \mathbf{X} \textit{ else } F(P_0 x)(F(P_1 x)).$$

By induction on the structure of $M \in \{\mathbf{X}\}^+$ it follows that $F \ulcorner \natural M \urcorner \twoheadrightarrow M$. $\square_3$

(4) *Lemma*. $\exists G \in \Lambda^0 \ \ \forall M \in \Lambda^0 \ \ G \ulcorner M \urcorner \twoheadrightarrow \ulcorner \natural(M') \urcorner$, *with* M' *as in* (1).
Proof. By (1) and (2), $\natural M'$ can be found effectively from M and hence from $\# M$. Therefore by Church's thesis there exists a recursive function g such that

$$g(\# M) = \natural(M').$$

Let G be a λ-defining term for g. Then by definition 6.3.1

$$G \ulcorner M \urcorner \twoheadrightarrow \ulcorner \natural(M') \urcorner . \quad \square_4$$

(5) *End of the proof*. Finally define $\mathbf{E} \equiv \lambda x.F(Gx)$ with F and G as above. Then for all $M \in \Lambda^0$

$$\mathbf{E} \ulcorner M \urcorner \twoheadrightarrow F(G \ulcorner M \urcorner) \twoheadrightarrow F \ulcorner \natural(M') \urcorner \twoheadrightarrow M' \twoheadrightarrow M. \quad \square_5 \quad \square$$

From now on $\mathbf{E}$ denotes the term constructed above.
Terms containing at most a fixed finite set of variables can also be enumerated.

8.1.7. COROLLARY. *For each* $\vec{x}$ *there is a term* $\mathbf{E}_{\vec{x}} \in \Lambda^0(\vec{x})$ *such that*

$$\forall M \in \Lambda^0(\vec{x}) \quad \mathbf{E}_{\vec{x}} \ulcorner M \urcorner \twoheadrightarrow M.$$

PROOF. Let $\vec{x}$ be given. By the effectiveness of the Gödel-numbering there exists a recursive function f such that for all $M \in \Lambda$

$$f(\# M) = \#(\lambda \vec{x}.M).$$

Let F λ-define f; then

$$\forall M \in \Lambda \quad F\ulcorner M\urcorner \twoheadrightarrow \ulcorner\lambda\vec{x}.M\urcorner .$$

Now define

$$\mathbf{E}_{\vec{x}} \equiv \lambda a.\mathbf{E}(Fa)\vec{x}.$$

Then for $M \in \Lambda^0(\vec{x})$

$$\begin{aligned}\mathbf{E}_{\vec{x}}\ulcorner M\urcorner &\twoheadrightarrow \mathbf{E}(F\ulcorner M\urcorner)\vec{x}\\ &\twoheadrightarrow \mathbf{E}\ulcorner\lambda\vec{x}.M\urcorner\,\vec{x}\\ &\twoheadrightarrow (\lambda\vec{x}.M)\vec{x} \quad \text{since } \lambda\vec{x}.M \text{ is closed,}\\ &\twoheadrightarrow M. \quad \Box\end{aligned}$$

8.2. Uniformity; infinite sequences

Infinite sequences of terms that are 'uniform' can be coded as a single term.

8.2.1. DEFINITION. Let $M_n \in \Lambda$ be defined for each $n \in \mathbb{N}$. M_n is *uniform in n* if for some F

$$(*) \qquad \forall n \in \mathbb{N} \quad F\ulcorner n\urcorner = M_n.$$

If $(*)$ holds, then F is said to λ-define the sequence $\lambda\!\!\lambda n.M_n$.

8.2.2. PROPOSITION. *Let M_n be a sequence of terms such that*
(i) $\exists\vec{x}\forall n \in \mathbb{N}\ \ M_n \in \Lambda^0(\vec{x})$,
(ii) $\lambda\!\!\lambda n.\#M_n$ *is recursive.*
Then M_n is uniform in n.

PROOF. Let G λ-define $\lambda\!\!\lambda n.\#M_n$. Then by corollary 8.1.7

$$(\mathbf{E}_{\vec{x}} \circ G)\ulcorner n\urcorner = \mathbf{E}_{\vec{x}}\ulcorner M_n\urcorner = M_n.$$

Hence M_n is uniform in n. $\Box$

Note that condition (i) above is also necessary. If $F\ulcorner n\urcorner = M_n$ for all n, then $M_n \in \Lambda^0(\vec{x})$, where $\vec{x} = \mathrm{FV}(F)$.

Condition (ii), however, is not necessary. Let $M_n \equiv \mathbf{I}^{\sim f(n)}$, where f is some nonrecursive function. Then (ii) is not satisfied, although for each n, $M_n = \mathbf{I}$ and hence M_n is uniform in n.

Let M_n be uniform in n. We want to code the infinite sequence $M_0, M_1, \ldots$ as a single term $[M_n]_{n\in\mathbb{N}}$.

8.2.3. DEFINITION. Let M_n be sequence uniform in n, say

$$F\ulcorner n\urcorner = M_n \quad \text{for all } n \in \mathbb{N}.$$

Define

$$A \equiv \mathbf{\Theta}(\lambda ax.[Fx, a(\mathbf{S}^{+}x)]),$$

$$[M_n]_{n\in\mathbb{N}} \equiv A\ulcorner 0\urcorner,$$

$$\boldsymbol{\pi}_i \equiv \boldsymbol{\pi}_i^{i+1} \equiv \lambda x.x\mathbf{F}^{\sim i}\mathbf{T} \quad \text{(cf. definition 6.2.7)}.$$

A is called the *generator* of $[M_n]_{n\in\mathbb{N}}$. Note that A and $[M_n]_{n\in\mathbb{N}}$ depend on the choice of F λ-defining $\lambda\!\!\lambda n.M_n$. Whenever necessary we say that A and $[M_n]_{n\in\mathbb{N}}$ are defined via F. If there is little danger of confusion we abbreviate $[M_n]_{n\in\mathbb{N}}$ as $[M_n]$ or write $[M_0, M_1, \ldots]$ instead.

8.2.4. LEMMA. *If* $[M_n]$ *is defined via* F, *then* $\mathrm{FV}([M_n]) = \mathrm{FV}(F)$.

PROOF. $[M_n] \equiv \mathbf{\Theta}(\lambda ax.[Fx, a(\mathbf{S}^{+}x)])\ulcorner 0\urcorner$. □

8.2.5. PROPOSITION. (i) *Let* A *be the generator of* $[M_n]_{n\in\mathbb{N}}$. *Then for all* $i \in \mathbb{N}$

$$[M_n]_{n\in\mathbb{N}} = [M_0, \ldots, M_i, A\ulcorner i+1\urcorner]$$

(ii) For all $i \in \mathbb{N}$

$$\boldsymbol{\pi}_i[M_n]_{n\in\mathbb{N}} = M_i.$$

PROOF. Let A,$[M_n]$ be defined via F. Note that for all $i \in \mathbb{N}$

$$A\ulcorner i\urcorner = [F\ulcorner i\urcorner, A\ulcorner i+1\urcorner] = [M_i, A\ulcorner i+1\urcorner].$$

Therefore

$$\begin{aligned}
[M_n] &\equiv A\ulcorner 0\urcorner \\
&= [M_0, A\ulcorner 1\urcorner] \\
&= [M_0, [M_1, A\ulcorner 2\urcorner]] \equiv [M_0, M_1, A\ulcorner 2\urcorner] \\
&= \cdots \\
&= [M_0, \ldots, M_i, A\ulcorner i+1\urcorner].
\end{aligned}$$

(ii) $\boldsymbol{\pi}_i[M_n] = \boldsymbol{\pi}_i^{i+1}[M_0, \ldots, M_i, A\ulcorner i+1\urcorner] = M_i$. □

8.2.6. COROLLARY. *Let the sequence* $\lambda\!\!\lambda n.M_n$ *be* λ*-defined by* F *and suppose that for all* $n \in \mathbb{N}$ $F\ulcorner n \urcorner \twoheadrightarrow M_n$. *Let* $[M_n]$ *with generator* A *be defined via* F. *Then for all* $i \in \mathbb{N}$

(i) $[M_n] \twoheadrightarrow [M_0, \ldots, M_i, A\ulcorner i+1 \urcorner]$;

(ii) $\pi_i[M_n] \twoheadrightarrow M_i$.

PROOF. In this case for all $i \in \mathbb{N}$

$$A\ulcorner i \urcorner \twoheadrightarrow \left[M_i, A\ulcorner i+1 \urcorner \right].$$

Then (i) and (ii) follow as above. □

REMARK. If the sequence $\lambda\!\!\lambda n.M_n$ is λ-defined by F, one could have defined

$$\left[M_n \right]'_{n \in \mathbb{N}} \equiv F, \qquad \pi'_i \equiv \lambda x.x\ulcorner i \urcorner .$$

Then one has also

$$\pi'_i[M_n]' = M_i.$$

But $[M_n]$ codes the sequence in a more intrinsic way: no numerals are needed to produce the term of the sequence – the numerals are to say built in. This will be useful e.g., see proposition 8.2.8. Moreover the Böhm tree of $[M_n]$ (see §10.1) is built up directly from the Böhm trees of the M_n, $n \in \mathbb{N}$.

As an application of the coding of infinite sequences a so-called universal generator will be constructed. This is a term whose reducts become arbitrarily complex.

8.2.7. DEFINITION. (i) Let R be a notion of reduction. The *R-family* of a term M is the set

$$\mathcal{F}_R(M) = \{ N \mid \exists M' \ M \twoheadrightarrow_R M' \text{ and } N \subset M' \}.$$

(ii) M is an *R-universal generator* (R-UG) if $\mathcal{F}_R(M) = \Lambda$.

8.2.8. PROPOSITION. *There exists a closed* UG (*i.e.* β-UG).

PROOF. Consider $M \equiv [\mathbf{E}\ulcorner 0 \urcorner, \mathbf{E}\ulcorner 1 \urcorner, \ldots]$ defined via $\mathbf{E}$. For $N \in \Lambda^0$ there exists an $i \in \mathbb{N}$ such that $\mathbf{E}\ulcorner i \urcorner \twoheadrightarrow N$. Hence

$$M \twoheadrightarrow [\ldots, \mathbf{E}\ulcorner i \urcorner, \ldots] \twoheadrightarrow [\ldots, N, \ldots].$$

Therefore $\Lambda^0 \subset \mathcal{F}(M)$. Since each term is subterm of its closure, also $\Lambda \subset \mathcal{F}(M)$, and so $\mathcal{F}(M) = \Lambda$. Hence M is a UG. By lemma 8.2.4 M is closed. □

Note that if M is an R-UG, then $G_R(M)$ is universal in the sense that for each $N \in \Lambda$, $G_R(N)$ is a subgraph of $G_R(M)$. Thus the term constructed in proposition 8.2.8 has a universal β-graph.

Universal generators will play a role in connection with the ω-rule; see §17.3.

The concept of uniformity can be extended as follows.

8.2.9. DEFINITION. Let for each $A \in \Lambda$, $M_A \in \Lambda$ be defined. M_A is *uniform in A* if for some F

$$(*) \qquad \forall A \quad FA = M_A.$$

As before, if $(*)$ holds, F is said to λ-define the map $\lambda\!\!\!\lambda A.M_A$.

8.2.10. PROPOSITION. *M_A is uniform in A iff for some variable x and all A*

$$M_A = M_x[x:=A].$$

PROOF. ($\Rightarrow$) Suppose $\forall A \; FA = M_A$. Let $x \notin F$. Then

$$M_A = FA = Fx[x:=A] = M_x[x:=A].$$

($\Leftarrow$) Suppose $\forall A \; M_A = M_x[x:=A]$. Then $\lambda x.M_x$ λ-defines $\lambda\!\!\!\lambda A.M_A$.

8.3. Solvability; head normal forms

Remember the definition of the notion of solvability.

8.3.1. DEFINITION. (i) Let $M \in \Lambda^0$. M is *solvable* if

$$\exists n \; \exists N_1, \ldots, N_n \in \Lambda \quad MN_1 \cdots N_n = \mathbf{I}$$

(ii) An arbitrary $M \in \Lambda$ is *solvable* if a closure $\lambda\vec{x}.M$ of M is solvable (this is independent of the choice of $\vec{x}$).

(iii) $M \in \Lambda$ is *unsolvable* iff M is not solvable.

8.3.2. EXAMPLES. $\mathbf{K}$ is solvable: $\mathbf{KII} = \mathbf{I}$. Similarly $\mathbf{S}$ is solvable. $x\mathbf{I}\Omega$ is solvable: $(\lambda x.x\mathbf{I}\Omega)\mathbf{K} = \mathbf{I}$. $\mathbf{Y}$ is solvable: $\mathbf{Y}(\mathbf{KI}) = \mathbf{KI}(\mathbf{Y}(\mathbf{KI})) = \mathbf{I}$. On the other hand Ω is unsolvable: $\forall \vec{N} \; \Omega\vec{N} = \mathbf{I}$ cannot hold since $\Omega\vec{N} \twoheadrightarrow M \Rightarrow M \equiv \Omega\vec{N}'$ with $\vec{N} \twoheadrightarrow \vec{N}'$.

To see the particular role of $\mathbf{I}$ in definition 8.3.1(i), note that a closed M is solvable iff $\forall P \; \exists \vec{N} \; M\vec{N} = P$.

The following lemma explains the use of the closure operation in definition 8.3.1(ii).

8.3.3. LEMMA. *Let* $M \in \Lambda$. (*i*) *M is solvable iff there exists a* (*closed*) *substitution instance* M^* *of M and terms* $\vec{N} \in \Lambda^0$ *such that* $M^*\vec{N} = \mathbf{I}$.
(ii) *M is solvable iff* $\lambda x.M$ *is solvable.*

PROOF. (i) Let $\lambda x_1 \cdots x_n.M$ be the closure of M.
($\Rightarrow$) Suppose M is solvable. Then for some terms $N_1, \ldots, N_m$

$$(*) \qquad (\lambda x_1 \cdots x_n.M)N_1 \cdots N_m = \mathbf{I}.$$

By making closed substitutions in the LHS it may be assumed that the $\vec{N}$ are closed. Moreover by adding $\mathbf{I}$'s to the sequence $N_1, \ldots, N_m$ it may be assumed that $m > n$. It follows that

$$(**) \quad M[x_1 := N_1] \cdots [x_n := N_n] N_{n+1} \cdots N_m = \mathbf{I},$$

and since $M^* \equiv M[x_1 := N_1] \cdots [x_n := N_n]$ is a closed substitution instance of M, the result follows.
($\Leftarrow$) If $(**)$ holds, then $(*)$ holds and M is solvable.
(ii) Let $x_1 \equiv x$. Then by (i)
M is solvable $\Leftrightarrow$
$\Leftrightarrow \exists \vec{N}, \vec{P} \in \Lambda^0 \quad M[x_1 := N_1] \cdots [x_n := N_n]\vec{P} = \mathbf{I}$
$\Leftrightarrow \exists \vec{N}, \vec{P} \in \Lambda^0 \quad (\lambda x.M)N_1[x_2 := N_2] \cdots [x_n := N_n]\vec{P} = \mathbf{I}$
$\Leftrightarrow \exists \vec{N}, \vec{P} \in \Lambda^0 \quad (\lambda x.M)[x_2 := N_2] \cdots [x_n := N_n]N_1\vec{P} = \mathbf{I}$
$\Leftrightarrow \lambda x.M$ is solvable. □

8.3.4. COROLLARY. *If M is unsolvable, then so are* $MN, M[x := N]$ *and* $\lambda x.M$, *for all N.*

PROOF. By lemma 8.3.3. □

8.3.5. COROLLARY. *The definition of solvability of open terms* $M \in \Lambda$ *is independent of the order of the variables* $\vec{x}$ *in the closure* $\lambda \vec{x}.M$.

PROOF. By lemma 8.3.3(i). □

Now a syntactic characterization of solvability will be given in terms of the so-called head normal forms and head reduction. These notions are due to Wadsworth [1971].

8.3.6. DEFINITION. (i) M is an *application term* if M is of the form NL.
(ii) M is an *abstraction term* if M is of the form $\lambda x.N$.

8.3.7. LEMMA. (i) *Each term M is either a variable, an application term or an abstraction term.*
(ii) *Each application term M is of the form*

$$M \equiv N_1 N_2 \cdots N_n; \quad n \geqslant 2,$$

with N_1 *not an application term.*

(iii) *Each abstraction term M is of the form*

$$M \equiv \lambda x_1 \cdots x_n . N, \quad n \geqslant 1,$$

with N not an abstraction term.

PROOF. By induction on the length of M. □

8.3.8. COROLLARY. *Each M is of one of the following two forms:*
(a) $M \equiv \lambda x_1 \cdots x_n . x M_1 \cdots M_m$, $n, m \geqslant 0$,
(b) $M \equiv \lambda x_1 \cdots x_n . (\lambda x M_0) M_1 \cdots M_m$, $n \geqslant 0, m \geqslant 1$.

PROOF. If M is a variable, then M is of form (*a*) with $n = m = 0$. If M is an application term, then $M \equiv N_1 N_2 \cdots N_n$ with N_1 not an application term. Hence M is of the form (a) or (b) with $n = 0$, depending whether N_1 is a variable or an abstraction term. Similarly M is of the right form if M is an abstraction term. □

8.3.9. DEFINITION. (i) A term M *is* a *head normal form* (hnf) if M is of the form $M \equiv \lambda x_1 \cdots x_n . x M_1 \cdots M_m$, $n, m \geqslant 0$. The *head variable* of this M is x. HNF is the set of hnf's.

(ii) M *has* a head normal form if $M = M'$ for some $M' \in$ HNF.

(iii) If M is of the form

$$M \equiv \lambda x_1 \cdots x_n . (\lambda x . M_0) M_1 \cdots M_m, \quad n \geqslant 0, m \geqslant 1,$$

then $(\lambda x . M_0) M_1$ is called the *head redex* of M.

Note that the head redex of a term is also the leftmost redex, but not conversely (e.g. $\lambda x . x((\lambda a . a) b)$).

8.3.10. DEFINITION. (i) Suppose M has Δ as head redex. Write

$$M \underset{\mathrm{h}}{\rightarrow} N$$

if $M \xrightarrow{\Delta} N$, i.e. N results from M by contracting Δ. $\underset{\mathrm{h}}{\rightarrow}$ is called a *one step head reduction*.

(ii) $\underset{\mathrm{h}}{\twoheadrightarrow}$ is the transitive, reflexive closure of $\underset{\mathrm{h}}{\rightarrow}$.

(iii) The *head reduction* (*path*) of M is the uniquely determined sequence $M_0, M_1, \ldots$ such that

$$M \equiv M_0 \underset{\mathrm{h}}{\rightarrow} M_1 \underset{\mathrm{h}}{\rightarrow} \cdots .$$

If say M_n is a hnf, then the head reduction of M is said to *terminate* at M_n. Otherwise M has an *infinite* head reduction.

The following result of Wadsworth is an immediate consequence of Curry's standardization theorem 11.4.7.

8.3.11. THEOREM. *M has a* hnf *iff the head reduction path of M terminates.*

PROOF. See corollary 11.4.8. □

8.3.12. LEMMA. *If $M \underset{h}{\rightarrow} M'$, then $M[z:=N] \underset{h}{\rightarrow} M'[z:=N]$.*

PROOF. By assumption

$$M \equiv \lambda\vec{x}.(\lambda y.N_0)N_1N_2\cdots N_m$$

and

$$M' \equiv \lambda\vec{x}.N_0[y:=N_1]N_2\cdots N_m.$$

Hence

$$M[z:=N] \equiv \lambda\vec{x}.(\lambda y.N_0[z:=N])N_1[z:=N]N_2^*\cdots N_m^*$$

and

$$M'[z:=N] \equiv \lambda\vec{x}.N_0[y:=N_1][z:=N]N_2^*\cdots N_m^*,$$

where $N_i^* \equiv N_i[z:=N]$ for $2 \leqslant i \leqslant m$.
Now by the substitution lemma 2.1.16 and the variable convention 2.1.13 it follows that

$$M[z:=N] \underset{h}{\rightarrow} M'[z:=N]. \quad \square$$

8.3.13. PROPOSITION. (i) $\lambda x.M$ *has a* hnf $\Leftrightarrow M$ *has a* hnf.
(ii) $M[z:=N]$ *has a* hnf $\Rightarrow M$ *has a* hnf.
(iii) MN *has a* hnf $\Rightarrow M$ *has a* hnf.

PROOF. (i) By the fact that if $\lambda x.M \twoheadrightarrow N$, then $N \equiv \lambda x.N'$ and $M \twoheadrightarrow N'$.
(ii) Suppose M has no hnf. Then by theorem 8.3.11 its head reduction

$$M \equiv M_0 \underset{h}{\rightarrow} M_1 \underset{h}{\rightarrow} \cdots$$

is infinite. Hence by lemma 8.3.12 the head reduction of $M[z:=N]$ would be infinite, contradicting that $M[z:=N]$ has a hnf.
(iii) Let

$$(*) \qquad M \equiv M_0 \underset{h}{\rightarrow} M_1 \underset{h}{\rightarrow} \cdots$$

be the head reduction of M.

Case 1. M_k is not an abstraction term for any k. Then

$$MN \equiv M_0 N \underset{h}{\rightarrow} M_1 N \underset{h}{\rightarrow} \cdots$$

is the head reduction of MN. Since the latter reduction is finite, (∗) must also be finite. Hence M has a hnf.

Case 2. For some k, M_k is an abstraction term, say $M_k \equiv \lambda x.M'$. Choose k minimal. The head reduction of MN begins by

$$MN \equiv M_0 N \underset{h}{\rightarrow} \cdots \underset{h}{\rightarrow} M_k N \equiv (\lambda x.M')N \underset{h}{\rightarrow} M'[x:=N] \underset{h}{\rightarrow} \cdots .$$

Now

$$\begin{aligned} MN \text{ has a hnf} &\Rightarrow M'[x:=N] \text{ has a hnf} \\ &\Rightarrow M' \text{ has a hnf}, \quad \text{by (ii)}, \\ &\Rightarrow M_k \equiv \lambda x.M' \text{ has a hnf}, \quad \text{by (i)}, \\ &\Rightarrow M \text{ has a hnf}. \quad \square \end{aligned}$$

Now we can give a characterization of solvability in terms of hnf's.

8.3.14. THEOREM (Wadsworth). *M is solvable $\Leftrightarrow$ M has a* hnf.

PROOF. By lemma 8.3.3(ii) and proposition 8.3.13(i) it may be assumed that M is closed.

($\Rightarrow$) If $M\vec{N} = \mathbf{I}$, then $M\vec{N}$ has a hnf. Hence by proposition 8.3.13(iii) M has a hnf.

($\Leftarrow$) If $M = \lambda x_1 \cdots x_n.x_i M_1 \cdots M_m$, then $M(\mathbf{K}^m\mathbf{I})^{\sim n} = \mathbf{K}^m\mathbf{I}M_1^* \cdots M_m^* = \mathbf{I}$. Hence M is solvable. $\square$

In particular normal forms are solvable, or, conversely, unsolvable terms have no nf.

8.3.15. COROLLARY. *M is unsolvable $\Leftrightarrow$ M is hereditarily without a* nf, *i.e. for all substitution instances M^* and all sequences $\vec{N}$, $M^*\vec{N}$ has no* nf.

PROOF. ($\Rightarrow$) If $M^*\vec{N}$ had a nf, then by theorem 8.3.14 and lemma 8.3.3(i) for some $\vec{P}$

$$(M^*\vec{N})^*\vec{P} = \mathbf{I},$$

where $(M^*\vec{N})^*$ is a closed instance of $M^*\vec{N}$.

Thus

$$M^{**}\vec{N}^*\vec{P} = \mathbf{I}$$

and M would be solvable by lemma 8.3.3(i).

($\Leftarrow$) If M is solvable, then by lemma 8.3.3(i) $M^*\vec{N} = \mathbf{I}$ for some $\vec{N}$. $\square$

Now some results are proved that will be needed in chapter 10.

8.3.16. LEMMA. *Let* $M \equiv \lambda x_1 \cdots x_n.xM_1 \cdots M_m$. *If* $M \twoheadrightarrow N$, *then* $N \equiv \lambda x_1 \cdots x_n.xN_1 \cdots N_m$ *for some* $\vec{N}$ *with* $M_i \twoheadrightarrow N_i$.

PROOF. The only possible redexes in M are in the $M_1, \ldots, M_m$. Hence if $M \to N$ or $M \twoheadrightarrow N$, then $N \equiv \lambda x_1 \cdots x_n.xN_1 \cdots N_m$, with $M_i \to N_i$ or $M_i \twoheadrightarrow N_i$. □

8.3.17. COROLLARY. (i) *Let* $M \in \mathrm{HNF}$ *and* $M \twoheadrightarrow N$. *Then* $N \in \mathrm{HNF}$.

(ii) *Let M have the* hnfs

$$N \equiv \lambda x_1 \cdots x_n.xN_1 \cdots N_m$$

and

$$N' \equiv \lambda x_1 \cdots x_{n'}.x'N_1' \cdots N_{m'}'$$

Then $n = n'$, $x \equiv x'$, $m = m'$ *and* $N_i = N_i'$ *for* $1 \leqslant i \leqslant m$.

PROOF. (i) Immediate by lemma 8.3.16.

(ii) By assumption $N = M = N'$. Hence by the CR theorem $\exists Z$ $N \twoheadrightarrow Z \twoheadleftarrow N'$. By lemma 8.3.16 Z is of the form $\lambda x_1 \cdots x_n.xZ_1 \cdots Z_m$, $n = n'$, $x \equiv x'$, $m = m'$ and $N_i \twoheadrightarrow Z_i \twoheadleftarrow N_i'$ for $1 \leqslant i \leqslant m$. □

8.3.18. LEMMA. *The set of normal forms*, NF, *can be defined in either of the following two ways*:

(i)
$$x \in \mathrm{NF};$$

$$M_1, \ldots, M_m \in \mathrm{NF} \Rightarrow \lambda x_1 \cdots x_n.xM_1 \cdots M_m \in \mathrm{NF}, \quad n, m \geqslant 0.$$

(ii)
$$x \in \mathrm{NF};$$

$$M_1, \ldots, M_m \in \mathrm{NF} \Rightarrow xM_1 \cdots M_m \in \mathrm{NF}, \quad \textit{with } m \geqslant 0;$$

$$M \in \mathrm{NF} \Rightarrow \lambda x.M \in \mathrm{NF}.$$

PROOF. (i) Let $\mathfrak{X}$ be the set determined by the inductive definition. Clearly $\mathfrak{X} \subset \mathrm{NF}$. Now let M be a nf. Then by corollary 8.3.8 M is of the form $\lambda x_1 \cdots x_n.xM_1 \cdots M_m$. Moreover the $M_1, \ldots, M_m$ are again in nf. By induction on the length of M it follows that $M \in \mathfrak{X}$.

(ii) The set defined by this inductive definition is the same as that defined in (i). □

8.3.19. COROLLARY. *M has a* nf $\Leftrightarrow \lambda \vec{x}.M$ *has a* nf.

PROOF. (⇒) Suppose $M = \lambda\vec{z}.y\vec{N}$. Then $\lambda\vec{x}.M = \lambda\vec{x}\vec{z}.y\vec{N} \in \mathrm{NF}$.
(⇐) Suppose $\lambda\vec{x}.M \twoheadrightarrow \lambda\vec{z}.y\vec{N}$. Then $\vec{z} = \vec{x}, \vec{w}$ and $M \twoheadrightarrow \lambda\vec{w}.y\vec{N} \in \mathrm{NF}$. □

A term M may have several hnf's. For example $M = \lambda x.\mathbf{I}x(\mathbf{II})$ has the hnf's $\lambda x.x(\mathbf{II})$ and $\lambda x.x\mathbf{I}$. Theorem 8.3.11 provides a canonical choice.

8.3.20. DEFINITION. If M has a hnf, then the last term of the terminating head reduction of M is called *the (principal) head normal form* of M.

For example, let $M = (\lambda x.xx)\mathbf{I}y(\mathbf{I}a)$. Then ya is a hnf of M and the principal hnf of M is $y(\mathbf{I}a)$.

Next lemma is used to compare solvability in $\boldsymbol{\lambda}$ and in $\boldsymbol{CL}$.

8.3.21. LEMMA (Hindley [1977]). (i) *If* $M \underset{\mathrm{h}}{\rightarrow} N$ *and* M *is not of the form* $\lambda z.M_1$, *then* $M_{CL} \twoheadrightarrow_w N_{CL}$.
(ii) *Let* $M \underset{\mathrm{h}}{\twoheadrightarrow} x$. *Then* $M_{CL} \twoheadrightarrow_w x$ *(and similarly* $M_{CL2} \twoheadrightarrow_w x$, *where* $(\ )_{CL2}$ *is defined in exercise* 7.4.15).

PROOF. (i) By assumption $M \underset{\mathrm{h}}{\rightarrow} N$ is $(\lambda x.R)T\vec{U} \underset{\mathrm{h}}{\rightarrow} R[x:=T]\vec{U}$. Hence

$$\begin{aligned} M_{CL} &\equiv (\lambda^* x.R_{CL})T_{CL}\vec{U}_{CL} \\ &\twoheadrightarrow_w R_{CL}[x:=T_{CL}]\vec{U}_{CL} \\ &\equiv \left(R[x:=T]\vec{U}\right)_{CL} \equiv N_{CL}. \end{aligned}$$

(ii) By assumption one has the head reduction

$$\sigma : M \equiv M_1 \underset{\mathrm{h}}{\rightarrow} M_2 \underset{\mathrm{h}}{\rightarrow} \cdots \underset{\mathrm{h}}{\rightarrow} M_n \equiv x.$$

Since the last term is a variable, none of the M_i is of the form $\lambda y.Z$. Therefore the result follows by (i). (Similarly for $(\ )_{CL2}$ using exercise 7.4.15.) □

The following result is taken from Barendregt [1971]. The present proof is due to Hindley [1977].

8.3.22. PROPOSITION. (i) *Let* $M \in \Lambda$. *Then*

$$M \text{ is } \beta\text{-solvable} \Leftrightarrow M_{CL} \text{ is w-solvable}.$$

(ii) *Let* $P \in \mathcal{C}$. *Then*

$$P \text{ is w-solvable} \Leftrightarrow P_\lambda \text{ is } \beta\text{-solvable}.$$

PROOF. (i) Without loss of generality we may assume that M is closed.

($\Leftarrow$) Suppose M_{CL} is w-solvable. Then $M_{CL}\vec{Q} =_w \boldsymbol{I}$, for some $\vec{Q}$. Hence

$$M\vec{Q}_\lambda = M_{CL,\lambda}\vec{Q}_\lambda = \boldsymbol{I}_\lambda = \mathbf{I}$$

and therefore M is β-solvable.

($\Rightarrow$) If M is β-solvable, then $M\vec{N} = \mathbf{I}$, hence $M\vec{N}x = x$. By theorem 8.3.11 it follows that $M\vec{N}x \twoheadrightarrow_{\mathrm{h}} x$. Then $M_{CL}\vec{N}_{CL}x \twoheadrightarrow_w x$, by lemma 8.3.21 (ii). Therefore $M_{CL}N_{CL}\boldsymbol{I} \twoheadrightarrow_w \boldsymbol{I}$, i.e. M_{CL} is w-solvable.

(ii) Similarly, using also exercise 7.4.15. □

8.4. Lambda definability of partial functions

In this section the notion of λ-definability will be extended to partial functions. It will be proved that of the partial numeric functions exactly the partial recursive functions are λ-definable.

A *partial numeric function* is a partial mapping $\varphi : \mathbb{N}^p \hookrightarrow \mathbb{N}$ for some $p \in \mathbb{N}$. Let φ, ψ be two partial functions. Say $\varphi(\vec{n}) \simeq \psi(\vec{m})$ holds iff $\varphi(\vec{n}) = a \Leftrightarrow \psi(\vec{m}) = a$. That is if the LHS is defined, so is the RHS and has the same value and conversely.

Let $\chi, \psi_1, \ldots, \psi_m$ be partial numeric functions, χ with m arguments and $\psi_1, \ldots, \psi_m$ all with the same number of arguments. Then

$$\chi(\psi_1(\vec{n}), \ldots, \psi_m(\vec{n}))$$

denotes the partial numeric function φ such that

$$\varphi(\vec{n}) = a \quad \text{iff} \quad \exists a_1 \cdots a_m[\,\psi_i(\vec{n}) = a_i \text{ for } 1 \leqslant i \leqslant m,$$

$$\text{and } \chi(a_1, \ldots, a_m) = a\,].$$

That is, in order that $\varphi(\vec{n})$ be defined, all the $\psi_i(\vec{n})$ have to be defined. Remember that if φ is partial, $\varphi(\vec{n})\downarrow$ means that φ is defined at $\vec{n}$ (i.e. $\exists a \varphi(\vec{n}) = a$) and $\varphi(\vec{n})\uparrow$ means that φ is undefined at $\vec{n}$.

As mentioned before, the original notion of λ-definability was as follows.

A partial numeric function φ with p arguments is λ-definable iff there exists an $F \in \Lambda$ such that for all $\vec{n} \in \mathbb{N}^p$

$$F\ulcorner\vec{n}\urcorner = \ulcorner\varphi(\vec{n})\urcorner \quad \text{if } \varphi(\vec{n})\downarrow,$$

$$F\ulcorner\vec{n}\urcorner \text{ has no nf} \qquad \text{else.}$$

In the spirit of proposal 2.2.14 this definition is changed into the following.

8.4.1. DEFINITION. A partial numeric function φ with p arguments is λ-*definable* if for some $F \in \Lambda$

$$(*) \qquad \forall \vec{n} \in \mathbb{N}^p \quad F\ulcorner \vec{n} \urcorner = \ulcorner \varphi(\vec{n}) \urcorner \quad \text{if } \varphi(\vec{n})\downarrow, \qquad F\ulcorner \vec{n} \urcorner \text{ is unsolvable} \quad \text{else.}$$

If $(*)$ holds, then φ is said to be λ-*defined by* F.

For total functions this definition coincides with definition 6.3.1. Therefore the following is immediate.

8.4.2. LEMMA. *The total recursive functions are* λ-*definable as partial functions.*

8.4.3. DEFINITION. Let $\mathcal{C}$ be a class of partial numeric functions.

(i) $\mathcal{C}$ is *closed under composition* if for all φ defined by

$$\varphi(\vec{n}) \simeq \chi(\psi_1(\vec{n}), \ldots, \psi_m(\vec{n}))$$

with $\chi, \psi_1, \ldots, \psi_m \in \mathcal{C}$ one has $\psi \in \mathcal{C}$.

(ii) $\mathcal{C}$ is *closed under minimalisation* if for all φ defined by

$$\varphi(\vec{n}) = \mu m[\chi(\vec{n}, m) = 0],$$

where $\chi \in \mathcal{C}$ and is total*, one has $\varphi \in \mathcal{C}$.

8.4.4. DEFINITION. The class $\mathcal{PR}$ of *partial recursive functions* is the least class of partial numeric functions which contains the total recursive functions and is closed under composition and minimalization.

Providing λ-defining terms for partial functions presents the following difficulty. The representation of a composition is not necessarily the composition of the representations, as was the case for total functions, see example 2.2.9.

This problem will be resolved in lemma 8.4.6.

8.4.5. LEMMA. (i) $\forall m \in \mathbb{N}\ \ulcorner m \urcorner\, \mathbf{KII} = \mathbf{I}$, *that is the numerals are uniformly solvable.*

(ii) *Let* $F \in \Lambda$ λ-*define a partial numeric function* φ. *Then for all* $\vec{n}$

$$F\ulcorner \vec{n} \urcorner\, \mathbf{KII} = \mathbf{I} \qquad \text{if } \varphi(\vec{n})\downarrow,$$

$$F\ulcorner \vec{n} \urcorner\, \mathbf{KII} \text{ is unsolvable} \qquad \text{else.}$$

* The requirement that χ be total may be dropped at the expense of having to modify the proof of lemma 8.4.11 by employing the jamming factors used in the proof of lemma 8.4.6.

PROOF. (i) One has

$$\ulcorner 0 \urcorner\, \mathbf{KII} = \mathbf{IKII} = \mathbf{I}.$$

$$\ulcorner n+1 \urcorner\, \mathbf{KII} = [\mathbf{F}, \ulcorner n \urcorner]\mathbf{KII} = \mathbf{FII} = \mathbf{I}.$$

(ii) If $\varphi(\vec{n})\uparrow$, then $F\ulcorner n \urcorner$ is unsolvable and so is $F\ulcorner \vec{n} \urcorner\, \mathbf{KII}$ by corollary 8.3.4. □

The following lemma uses a trick first employed in Lercher [1963].

8.4.6. LEMMA. *The λ-definable partial numeric functions are closed under composition.*

PROOF. Let $\varphi(\vec{n}) \simeq \chi(\psi_1(\vec{n}), \ldots, \psi_m(\vec{n}))$, where $\chi, \psi_1, \ldots, \psi_m$ are λ-defined by $G, H_1, \ldots, H_m$ say. Define

$$F \equiv \lambda\vec{x}.(H_1\vec{x}\mathbf{KII}) \cdots (H_m\vec{x}\mathbf{KII})(G(H_1\vec{x}) \cdots (H_m\vec{x})).$$

We claim F λ-defines φ. Indeed, if one of the $\psi_i(\vec{n})$ is undefined, then $F\ulcorner \vec{n} \urcorner$ is unsolvable since the ith "jamming factor" $H_i\ulcorner \vec{n} \urcorner\, \mathbf{KII}$ is in that case unsolvable by lemma 8.4.5(ii). If all the $\psi_i(\vec{n})$ are defined, then the jamming factors are all $\mathbf{I}$ and hence $F\ulcorner \vec{n} \urcorner = G(H_1\ulcorner \vec{n} \urcorner) \cdots (H_m\ulcorner \vec{n} \urcorner)$ as it should be. □

In order to define partial functions that are defined by minimalization a result of part III is needed. First some definitions.

8.4.7. DEFINITION. (i) Let $\Delta \subset M$ be an occurrence of a redex, $\Delta \equiv (\lambda x.A)B$. Then the first occurrence of λ in Δ is called *the* λ *of* Δ.

(ii) Let $\Delta_1, \Delta_2 \subset M$ be occurrences if redexes in M. Δ_1 is *to the left of* Δ_2 if the λ of Δ_1 is to the left of the λ of Δ_2. Write $\Delta_1 < \Delta_2$ if Δ_1 is to the left of Δ_2 and $\Delta_1 \leqslant \Delta_2$ if $\Delta_1 < \Delta_2$ or $\Delta_1 \equiv \Delta_2$.

(iii) A redex occurrence $\Delta \subset M$ is called the *leftmost redex* of M if Δ is to the left of all other redexes in M.

EXAMPLE. Consider

$$M \equiv \lambda a.\underline{(\lambda b.\ \underline{(\lambda c.c)b}\ b)d}\ \underline{((\lambda e.I)a)}\,.$$

The redexes of this term are underlined. The leftmost redex of M is $(\lambda b.(\lambda c.c)bb)d$.

Note that the head redex of M is always leftmost, but not conversely; take e.g. $M \equiv \lambda x.x((\lambda y.y)x)$.

8.4.8. DEFINITION. Let σ be a (finite or infinite) reduction path of M

$$\sigma : M = M_0 \xrightarrow{\Delta_0} M_1 \xrightarrow{\Delta_1} \cdots$$

Then σ is called a *quasi leftmost reduction* if

$$\forall n\ \exists m \geqslant n \quad \Delta_m \text{ is leftmost in } M_m,$$

i.e. the leftmost steps in σ are cofinal.

8.4.9. THEOREM. *If M has an infinite quasi leftmost reduction, then M has no* nf.

PROOF. See theorem 13.2.6. □

Now we can prove the following application.

8.4.10. PROPOSITION. *Let P be such that for all $n \in N$ one has $P\ulcorner n \urcorner = \mathbf{F}$. Then*

(i) *μP has no* nf.
(ii) *μP is unsolvable.*

PROOF. (i) By definition 6.3.8 one has $\mu P = H_P \ulcorner 0 \urcorner$, with

$$H_P = \mathbf{\Theta}(\lambda hx.\ \textit{If } Px \textit{ then } x \textit{ else } hx^+).$$

Then

$$H_P \ulcorner n \urcorner \twoheadrightarrow \textit{If } P\ulcorner n \urcorner \textit{ then } \ulcorner n \urcorner \textit{ else } H_P \ulcorner n+1 \urcorner .$$

Therefore μP has the following reduction path.

$$\begin{aligned} \mu P &= H_P \ulcorner 0 \urcorner \\ &\twoheadrightarrow \textit{If } P\ulcorner 0 \urcorner \textit{ then } \ulcorner 0 \urcorner \textit{ else } H_P \ulcorner 1 \urcorner \\ &\underset{\neq i}{\twoheadrightarrow} H_P \ulcorner 1 \urcorner \\ &\twoheadrightarrow \textit{If } P\ulcorner 1 \urcorner \textit{ then } \ulcorner 1 \urcorner \textit{ else } H_P \ulcorner 2 \urcorner \\ &\underset{\neq i}{\twoheadrightarrow} H_P \ulcorner 2 \urcorner \\ &\twoheadrightarrow \cdots \end{aligned}$$

Here $M \underset{\neq i}{\twoheadrightarrow} N$ indicates that in the given reduction at least one leftmost redex is contracted. It follows that μP has an infinite quasi leftmost reduction and therefore by theorem 8.4.9 has no nf.

(ii) Take a closed substitution instance of μP. By definition 6.3.8 this is of the form $\mu(P^*)$, where P^* is a closed substitution instance of P.
Similarly to (i) one proves that for all $\vec{Z}$

$$\mu P^* \vec{Z} \text{ has no nf.}$$

Hence by corollary 8.3.15 μP is unsolvable. (Alternatively, exercise 13.6.13 may be used to show that μP is unsolvable). □

8.4.11. LEMMA*. *The λ-definable partial numeric functions are closed under minimalization.*

PROOF. Let $\varphi(\vec{n}) \simeq \mu m[\chi(\vec{n}, m) = 0]$, where χ is total and λ-defined by, say, G. Define

$$F \equiv \lambda \vec{x}.\mu[\lambda y.\,\mathbf{Zero}(G\vec{x}y)].$$

If $\varphi(\vec{n})\downarrow$, then $\exists m \chi(\vec{n}, m) = 0$. Hence by proposition 6.3.9(ii)

$$F \ulcorner \vec{n} \urcorner = \varphi(\vec{n}).$$

If $\varphi(\vec{n})\uparrow$, then $\forall m \chi(\vec{n}, m) \neq 0$ and so $\forall m$ $\mathbf{Zero}(G \ulcorner \vec{n} \urcorner \ulcorner m \urcorner) = \mathbf{F}$. Hence by proposition 8.4.10

$$F \ulcorner \vec{n} \urcorner = \mu[\lambda y.\,\mathbf{Zero}(G \ulcorner \vec{n} \urcorner y)]$$

is unsolvable. Thus F λ-defines φ. □

8.4.12. LEMMA. *If F λ-defines a partial φ, then*

$$\varphi(\vec{n}) = m \Leftrightarrow F \ulcorner \vec{n} \urcorner = \ulcorner m \urcorner .$$

PROOF. ($\Rightarrow$) By definition.
($\Leftarrow$) If $F \ulcorner \vec{n} \urcorner = \ulcorner m \urcorner$, then as m is solvable, $\varphi(\vec{n})\downarrow$ and $\varphi(\vec{n}) = m'$. But then $\ulcorner m \urcorner = \ulcorner m' \urcorner$ and hence $m = m'$. □

8.4.13. THEOREM (Kleene). *A partial numeric function is partial recursive iff it is λ-definable.*

PROOF. By definition 8.4.4, lemmas 8.4.2, 8.4.6 and 8.4.11 it follows that the partial recursive functions are all λ-definable. Conversely, let φ be λ-definable by F. Then by lemma 8.4.12

$$\varphi(\vec{n}) = m \Leftrightarrow \lambda \vdash F \ulcorner \vec{n} \urcorner = \ulcorner m \urcorner$$

* See footnote on p. 175.

Since the RHS is r.e., so is the LHS and hence the graph of φ. Thus φ is partial recursive. □

8.5. Exercises

8.5.1 (Rosser). Show that the following terms each form a one point base.

(i) $X_0 = \langle \mathbf{K}^4\mathbf{I}, \mathbf{S}, \mathbf{K}\rangle$.

(ii) $X_1 = \langle \mathbf{K}^2\mathbf{K}, \mathbf{K}, \mathbf{KS}\rangle$.

8.5.2. Construct a one point base for $\Lambda^0(x_1, \ldots, x_n)$.

8.5.3. Show that Λ cannot be enumerated by a single term.

8.5.4. (i) Derive the fixed point theorem 2.1.5 from the second fixed point theorem 6.5.9, using $\mathbf{E}$.

(ii) Let $F \in \Lambda^0$. Define $W \equiv \lambda x.F(\mathbf{E}xx)$. Show that $W\ulcorner W\urcorner$ is a fixed point of F.

(iii) Show $\forall F \in \Lambda^0\ \exists n \in \mathbb{N}\ F\ulcorner n\urcorner = \mathbf{E}\ulcorner n\urcorner$.

(iv) Let $\omega \equiv \lambda xy.\mathbf{E}y(xxy)$ and $G \equiv \omega\omega$. Show that G enumerates a set of fixed points of closed terms.

8.5.5. Show that for some $\mathbf{E} \in \mathcal{C}^0$

$$\forall M \in \mathcal{C}^0\ \exists n \in \mathbb{N}\quad \mathbf{E}(\ulcorner n_{CL}\urcorner) \twoheadrightarrow_w M.$$

8.5.6. (i) Prove corollary 6.5.10.

(ii) Show that $\neg\exists Y \in \Lambda\ \forall F \in \Lambda^0\ YF \twoheadrightarrow F\ulcorner YF\urcorner$.

8.5.7. (i) Show that $\ulcorner M\urcorner$ is not uniform in M.

(ii) Show that μP is uniform in P.

8.5.8. Let $\mathbf{K}^\infty \equiv \mathbf{YK}$. Show that

$$M \text{ is solvable} \Rightarrow M \# \mathbf{K}^\infty.$$

The converse is also true.

8.5.9. Let $C \equiv \mathbf{Y}(\lambda cab.b(cb(ca)))$.
Show that Cab has no nf but is solvable.

8.5.10. Construct a term M such that

$$M \text{ has a nf} \Leftrightarrow \text{Fermat's last theorem is false.}$$

8.5.11. Define the μ operator

$$\mu m[\varphi(\vec{n}, m) = 0]$$

also for partial φ. Show that the λ-definable partial functions are also closed under this kind of minimalization.

8.5.12. Show that the notions "M has a nf" and "M is solvable" are Σ^0_1-complete.

8.5.13. Construct a term $F \in \Lambda^0$ such that

$$F\ulcorner n\urcorner = \lambda xy.x^n yx^{\sim n}.$$

8.5.14. (i) Let $S = \mathfrak{M}^0(\boldsymbol{\lambda})$ be the term model consisting of closed λ-terms modulo β-convertibility. Define a surjection $\nu : \mathbb{N} \to S$ by $\nu(n) = \mathbf{E}\ulcorner n\urcorner$. Show that $\gamma(\boldsymbol{\lambda}) = (S, \nu)$ is a precomplete numbered set (the definition is just before exercise 6.8.18). Show that $\mu : S \to S$ defined by $\mu(M) = FM$, with $F \in \Lambda^0$, is a morphism.

(ii) Show that for all total recursive functions f

$$(*)\qquad \exists n \in \mathbb{N}\quad \mathbf{E}\ulcorner n\urcorner = \mathbf{E}\ulcorner f(n)\urcorner.$$

[*Hint*. This follows directly from (i) and exercise 6.8.18, or alternatively, use exercise 8.5.4(iii).]
(iii) Show that (∗) and the second fixed point theorem 6.5.9 are directly equivalent.
(iv) Show that for all recursive f such that $\forall M\, \exists n\; M = E^{\ulcorner} f(n)^{\urcorner}$ one has
$\mathbf{E}\,{}^{\ulcorner}f(n)^{\urcorner} = \mathbf{E}\,{}^{\ulcorner}f(m)^{\urcorner}$ for some $n \neq m$.

8.5.15* (Craig, in Curry et al. [1958], p. 183). A *proper combinator* is a closed λ-term M of the form $\lambda\vec{x}.P(\vec{x})$, with $P(\vec{x}) \in \{\vec{x}\}^+$. Show that a basis consisting of proper combinators contains at least two elements. [*Hint*. (P. Bellot). Show that if $\{P\}$ is a basis with P proper, then P is a projection $(=\lambda x_1 \cdots x_n.x_i)$. This is impossible. (First assume that P is a new constant with its own contraction rule; then apply theorem 13.2.2.).]

8.5.16 (i) (C. A. Meredith). Let $H \equiv \lambda abcd.cd(a(\lambda x.d))$. Show that $\{H\}$ is a basis. [*Hint*. Let $H_1 \equiv H$, $H_{n+1} \equiv H_n H$, $U \equiv H_3 H_2$, $X \equiv H_4(\mathbf{K}H_4)$, $Y \equiv XX$ and $Z \equiv H_4(H_4 Y)(KH_4)$. Then $H_4(H_4 U H_2)H_2 = \mathbf{K}$ and $X(UZ) = \mathbf{S}$.]
(ii) (Barendregt). Let $X \equiv \lambda x.x(x\mathbf{S}(\mathbf{KK}))\mathbf{K}$. Show that $\{X\}$ is a basis. [*Hint*. $XXX = \mathbf{K}$, $X\mathbf{K} = \mathbf{S}$.]
(iii) (Böhm). Let $X \equiv \lambda x.x(x\mathbf{S}(\mathbf{K}^3\mathbf{I}))\mathbf{K}$. Show that $\{X\}$ is a basis. [*Hint*. $XX = \mathbf{K}$, $X\mathbf{K} = \mathbf{S}$.]
(iv) (Rosser). Find a $J \in \Lambda^0$ such that $JJ = \mathbf{S}$ and $J\mathbf{S} = \mathbf{K}$.

8.5.17. Infinite fixed point theorem (Klop).
(i) Let f be a unary recursive function and let $M_n \in \Lambda^0$ be a recursive sequence. For $n \in \mathrm{Seq} - \mathbf{N}$ write $n = \langle n_0, \ldots, n_{\mathrm{lh}(n)} \rangle$. Construct a sequence $X_0, X_1, \ldots \in \Lambda^0$ such that one has for all n

$$X_n = M_n X_{m_0} \cdots X_{m_k},$$

where $m = f(n)$ and $k = \mathrm{lh}(m)$.
(ii) Deduce the multiple fixed point theorem 6.5.2 from (i).

8.5.18. Show that on ${}^{\ulcorner}0^{\urcorner}_{CL}, {}^{\ulcorner}1^{\urcorner}_{CL}, \ldots$ all partial recursive functions can be represented in *CL*. [*Hint*. Use proposition 8.3.22.]

8.5.19. Show that one may assume that $\mathbf{E}_{\vec{x}}$ is in nf. [*Hint*. A solution is in the proof of lemma 16.3.15.]

8.5.20 (D. Turner). Remember $\mathbf{\Phi} \equiv \lambda fabc.f(ac)(bc)$. Show that

$$\lambda^* x_1 \cdots x_n.PQ = \mathbf{\Phi}^{n-1}S(\lambda^* x_1 \cdots x_n.P)(\lambda^* x_1 \cdots x_n.Q).$$

Therefore $\{\mathbf{I}, \mathbf{K}, \mathbf{S}, \mathbf{\Phi}\} \cup \{\mathbf{U}_i^n \mid n \geqslant 2,\ 1 \leqslant i \leqslant n\}$ is an efficient base for multiple abstraction.

CHAPTER 9

THE λI-CALCULUS

Remember the definition of the restricted class Λ_I:

$$x \in \Lambda_I,$$

$$M \in \Lambda_I,\ x \in \mathrm{FV}(M) \Rightarrow (\lambda x.M) \in \Lambda_I,$$

$$M, N \in \Lambda_I \Rightarrow (MN) \in \Lambda_I.$$

The elements of Λ_I are called λI-terms. $\boldsymbol{\lambda I}$ is the formal theory consisting of equations between λI-terms provable from the axioms and rules of $\boldsymbol{\lambda}$ restricted to Λ_I. See §2.2 for a discussion about the full and the restricted theory.

The development parallels that of the full λ-calculus. The partial recursive functions will be represented by λI-terms. A combinatory equivalent of the theory will be given along the lines of §7.1. By analyzing the concept of solvability for the λI-calculus, it turns out that there are several approximations of $\mathbf{K}$ by λI-terms.

9.1. Generalities

It will be proved that the full λ-calculus is a conservative extension of the λI-calculus. Several concepts for the full λ-calculus can be relativized to the λI-calculus. A result of chapter 11 is borrowed, which states that if $M \in \Lambda_I$ has a nf, then M strongly normalizes.

9.1.1. NOTATION. (i) The same syntactic conventions as for $\boldsymbol{\lambda}$ are used for $\boldsymbol{\lambda I}$.

(ii) If necessary to distinguish, the full λ-calculus is called the λK-calculus. Similarly one distinguishes between $\boldsymbol{\lambda I}$ and $\boldsymbol{\lambda K}$, and between Λ_I^0 and Λ_K^0.

(iii) $\Lambda_I^0(\vec{x})$ is defined a bit differently from the K-case:

$$\Lambda_I^0(\vec{x}) = \{M \in \Lambda_I | \mathrm{FV}(M) = \{\vec{x}\}\}.$$

The reason for the modified definition of $\Lambda_I^0(\vec{x})$ is that only classes of terms with a fixed set of variables can be enumerated by a λI-term, see lemma 9.1.2(iv).

The theory $\boldsymbol{\lambda I}$ has the same axioms and rules as $\boldsymbol{\lambda K}$, but relativized to Λ_I. For example,

$$(\lambda x.M)N = M[x:=N]$$

is an axiom of $\boldsymbol{\lambda I}$ for all $M, N \in \Lambda_I$.

The following shows that this relativization makes sense.

9.1.2. Lemma. (i) $M, N \in \Lambda_I \Rightarrow M[x:=N] \in \Lambda_I$.

(ii) $\lambda x.M \in \Lambda_I \Rightarrow \mathrm{FV}((\lambda x.M)N) = \mathrm{FV}(M[x:=N])$.

(iii) $M \in \Lambda_I$, $M \twoheadrightarrow_{\beta\eta} N \Rightarrow N \in \Lambda_I$.

(iv) $M \in \Lambda_I$, $M \twoheadrightarrow_{\beta\eta} N \Rightarrow \mathrm{FV}(M) = \mathrm{FV}(N)$.

Proof. (i) By induction on the structure of M.

(ii) The assumption $M \in \Lambda_I$ is necessary: $\mathrm{FV}((\lambda x.I)y) \neq \mathrm{FV}(I)$. Once this is noticed, the result is obvious.

(iii) By induction on the generation of $M \twoheadrightarrow_{\beta\eta} N$, using (i) for the base and (ii) for the clause

$$P \to Q \Rightarrow \lambda x.P \to \lambda x.Q.$$

(iv) Similarly. □

9.1.3. Corollary. (i) $\boldsymbol{\lambda K}$ *is conservative over* $\boldsymbol{\lambda I}$.

(ii) $\boldsymbol{\lambda K \eta}$ *is conservative over* $\boldsymbol{\lambda I \eta}$.

Proof. (i) Suppose $M, N \in \Lambda_I$ and $\lambda K \vdash M = N$. Then $M =_\beta N$, hence by the Church–Rosser theorem

$$\exists Z \quad M \twoheadrightarrow Z, \quad N \twoheadrightarrow Z.$$

By lemma 9.1.2 (iii) it follows that $Z \in \Lambda_I$. But then

$$\boldsymbol{\lambda I} \vdash M = Z = N.$$

(ii) Similarly, using the CR theorem for $\beta\eta$. □

Relativized to the λI-calculus, the notion of solvability becomes different. In fact, for λK-terms one can also distinguish two kinds of solvability.

9.1.4. Definition. (i) Let $M \in \Lambda_K^0$. M is *K-solvable* iff $\exists \vec{N} \in \Lambda_K$ $M\vec{N} = I$. M is *I-solvable* if $\exists \vec{N} \in \Lambda_I$ $M\vec{N} = I$.

(ii) A general $M \in \Lambda_K$ is K- or I-solvable iff its closure $\lambda \vec{x}.M$ is.

Many other concepts defined for the full λK-calculus can be relativized to the λI-calculus.

Now (for the last time) a result about reduction has to be borrowed from part III. As was noted before, the λK-term $\mathbf{K I \Omega}$ has a nf, but nevertheless an infinite reduction path. For λI-terms this is impossible.

9.1.5. THEOREM (Church, Rosser [1936]). *If* $M \in \Lambda_I$ *and* M *has a* nf, *then* SN(M), *i.e. all reduction paths starting with* M *terminate. In particular the reduction graph* $G(M)$ *is finite.*

PROOF. See corollary 11.3.5. □

9.1.6. COROLLARY. *Let* $M \in \Lambda_I$ *have a* nf. *Then for all* $N \subset M$, N *has a* nf.

PROOF. Suppose $M \equiv C[N]$ and N has no nf. Then N has an infinite reduction path, and hence so has M, contradicting theorem 9.1.5. □

It should be noted that corollary 9.1.6. is somewhat weaker than theorem 9.1.5: in the λK-calculus there are terms such that each subterm has a nf, but the term itself has an infinite reduction path.

9.1.7. EXAMPLE. Consider $M \equiv (\lambda x.\mathbf{F}(xx))(\lambda x.\mathbf{F}(xx))$. Then $M \in \Lambda_K$ and all subterms of M have a nf but $\infty(M)$.

PROOF. Let $W \equiv \lambda a.\mathbf{F}(aa)$. Then $M \equiv WW$. Since $\mathbf{F} \equiv \lambda xy.y$ every subterm of M (including M itself) has a nf. An infinite reduction path of M is the following

$$WW \to \mathbf{F}(WW) \to \mathbf{F}(\mathbf{F}(WW)) \cdots . \quad \square$$

9.2. Definability

In this subsection it will be proved that for some system of numerals the partial recursive functions can be defined by λI-terms.

The numerals $\ulcorner n \urcorner$ defined in §2.1 are λK-terms. However, Church's numerals c_n, except c_0, are λI-terms. After modifying c_0 these latter numerals will be used as an adequate numeral system in the λI-calculus. There is a modification of the standard numerals which also gives an adequate λI-system; see exercise 9.5.11.

9.2.1. DEFINITION. $\mathbf{c}_0^I = \lambda xy.x\mathbf{II}y$, $\mathbf{c}_{n+1}^I = \mathbf{c}_{n+1}$.

Then for each n, $\mathbf{c}_n^I$ is a nf $\in \Lambda_I^0$ and $\mathbf{c}_n^I\mathbf{II} = \mathbf{I}$. Also note that

$$\mathbf{c}_0^I \mathbf{c}_n^I \mathbf{c}_m^I = \mathbf{c}_m^I .$$

This motivates the choice of $\mathbf{c}_0^I$ as approximating $\mathbf{c}_0 \equiv \lambda xy.y$.

In this subsection λ-definability of a partial numeric function will always refer to the sequence $c_0^I, c_1^I, \ldots$.

9.2.2. NOTATION. (i) $\llcorner n \lrcorner = c_n^I$.
(ii) $\llcorner M \lrcorner = \llcorner \sharp M \lrcorner$.
(iii) If $\vec{n} = n_0, \ldots, n_k$, then $F \llcorner \vec{n} \lrcorner = F \llcorner n_0 \lrcorner \cdots \llcorner n_k \lrcorner$.

9.2.3. DEFINITION. A partial numeric function φ is *λI-definable* if for some $F \in \Lambda_I^0$

$$(*) \qquad \begin{array}{ll} F \llcorner \vec{n} \lrcorner = \llcorner m \lrcorner & \text{if } \varphi(\vec{n}) = m, \\ F \llcorner \vec{n} \lrcorner \text{ has no nf} & \text{if } \varphi(\vec{n})\uparrow. \end{array}$$

If (*) holds, then φ is λI-defined by F.

From corollary 9.4.21 it will follow that this is the proper relativization of definition 8.4.1 to the λI-calculus.

The truth values and the conditional can be partially imitated in the λI-calculus.

9.2.4. DEFINITION. $\mathbf{T}_I \equiv \lambda xy.y\mathbf{II}x, \mathbf{F}_I \equiv \lambda x.x\mathbf{III}(=\mathbf{T}_I\mathbf{I})$.

9.2.5. LEMMA. *Let B take values $\mathbf{T}_I$ and $\mathbf{F}_I$. Let P, Q be such that $P\mathbf{II} = \mathbf{I}$ and $Q\mathbf{II} = \mathbf{I}$. Then*

If B then P else Q

can be represented by

$$BPQ.$$

In particular this is the case for

$$P, Q \in \{\mathbf{I}, \mathbf{T}_I, \mathbf{F}_I, \llcorner 0 \lrcorner, \llcorner 1 \lrcorner, \ldots\}.$$

PROOF. Trivial. □

9.2.6. DEFINITION. (i) $\mathbf{Zero}_I \equiv \lambda x.x(\mathbf{T}_I\mathbf{F}_I)\mathbf{T}_I\mathbf{T}_I\mathbf{F}_I$.
(ii) $\mathbf{U}_{Ii}^k = \lambda x_0 \cdots x_k.(x_0\mathbf{II}) \cdots (x_k\mathbf{II})x_i$.

9.2.7. LEMMA. (i) $\mathbf{Zero}_I \llcorner 0 \lrcorner = \mathbf{T}_I$, $\mathbf{Zero}_I \llcorner n+1 \lrcorner = \mathbf{F}_I$.
(ii) $\mathbf{U}_{Ii}^k \llcorner \vec{n} \lrcorner = \llcorner n_i \lrcorner$ *for* $\vec{n} = n_0, \ldots, n_k$, *and* $0 \leqslant i \leqslant k$. □

9.2.8. PROPOSITION. *The initial functions (see definition 6.3.2) are λI-definable.*

PROOF. Take as defining λI-terms

$$\mathbf{U}^k_{Ii},$$
$$\mathbf{S}^+_I \equiv \lambda x.\ \textit{If}\ \mathbf{Zero}_I x\ \textit{then}\ \llcorner 1 \lrcorner\ \textit{else}\ (S^+_c\ x),$$

where $S_c^+ \equiv \lambda abc.b(abc)$ was defined in definition 6.4.4. Note that $S_c^+ \llcorner 0 \lrcorner \mathbf{II} = \mathbf{I}$, hence lemma 9.2.5 applies.

$$\mathbf{Z} \equiv \lambda x.x\mathbf{II}\llcorner 0 \lrcorner. \quad \square$$

From now on $\mathbf{S}^+_I$ will denote the representation of the successor defined in this proof.

9.2.9. PROPOSITION. *The partial λI-definable functions are closed under composition.*

PROOF. Let $\chi, \psi_1, \ldots, \psi_m$ be λI-defined by $G, H_1, \ldots, H_m$ respectively. Then

$$\varphi(\vec{n}) = \chi(\psi_1(\vec{n}), \ldots, \psi_m(\vec{n}))$$

is λI-defined by

$$F \equiv \lambda \vec{x}.G(H_1\vec{x}) \cdots (H_m\vec{x}).$$

In contrast to the situation for λK-definability (see §8.4), this is also true for partial functions. Namely if one of the $\psi_i(\vec{n})$ is undefined, then $H_i \llcorner \vec{n} \lrcorner$, has no nf and hence by corollary 9.1.6, $F \llcorner \vec{n} \lrcorner$ also has no nf. $\square$

9.2.10. DEFINITION. Let $\mathbf{P}^k_{Ii} \equiv \lambda x.x\mathbf{U}^k_{Ii}$. Then $\mathbf{P}^k_{Ii}\langle M_0, \ldots, M_k \rangle = M_i$, for $0 \leqslant i \leqslant k$, if $\forall i \leqslant k\ M_i\mathbf{II} = \mathbf{I}$.

9.2.11. PROPOSITION. *The λI-definable total functions are closed under primitive recursion.*

PROOF. Let φ be defined by

$$\varphi(0, \vec{n}) = \chi(\vec{n}),$$
$$\varphi(k+1, \vec{n}) = \psi(\vec{n}, k, \varphi(k, \vec{n})),$$

where χ and ψ are λI-defined by G and H respectively. Let

$$M_{k,\vec{n}} = \langle \llcorner k+1 \lrcorner, \llcorner \varphi(k+1, \vec{n}) \lrcorner, \llcorner \varphi(k, \vec{n}) \lrcorner \rangle.$$

If $M_{k,\vec{n}}$ can be defined uniformly in k,n by a λI-term, say for some $M' \in \Lambda_I^0$ $M' \llcorner k \lrcorner \llcorner \vec{n} \lrcorner = M_{k,\vec{n}}$, then φ can be λI-defined by

$$F \equiv \lambda x\vec{y}.\mathbf{P}^2_{I2}(M'x\vec{y}).$$

In order to find M', define

$$X \equiv \lambda \vec{a} x.\langle \mathbf{S}_I^+(\mathbf{P}^2_{I0}x),\ H\vec{a}(\mathbf{P}^2_{I0}x)(\mathbf{P}^2_{I1}x),\ \mathbf{P}^2_{I1}x\rangle.$$

Then

$$X \llcorner \vec{n} \lrcorner M_{k,\vec{n}} = M_{k+1,\vec{n}}$$

and

$$X \llcorner \vec{n} \lrcorner \langle \llcorner 0 \lrcorner, G \llcorner \vec{n} \lrcorner, \llcorner 0 \lrcorner \rangle = M_{0,\vec{n}}.$$

Hence

$$\begin{aligned} M_{k,\vec{n}} &= (X \llcorner \vec{n} \lrcorner)^{k+1} \langle \llcorner 0 \lrcorner, G \llcorner \vec{n} \lrcorner, \llcorner 0 \lrcorner \rangle \\ &= \llcorner k+1 \lrcorner (X \llcorner \vec{n} \lrcorner) \langle \llcorner 0 \lrcorner, G \llcorner \vec{n} \lrcorner, \llcorner 0 \lrcorner \rangle . \end{aligned}$$

It follows that $M_{k,\vec{n}}$ is uniform in $k, \vec{n}$ and we are done. □

9.2.12. LEMMA. *Let $A_0, A_1 \in \Lambda_I^0$ be such that for some $k \in \mathbb{N}$*

$$A_i \mathbf{I}^{\sim k} = \mathbf{I}, \quad i = 0, 1.$$

Then for some $M \in \Lambda_I^0$

$$M\mathbf{T}_I = A_0, \qquad M\mathbf{F}_I = A_1.$$

PROOF. Let $\mathbf{T}_k \equiv \lambda xy.y\mathbf{I}^{\sim k}x$, $\mathbf{F}_k \equiv \lambda xy.x\mathbf{I}^{\sim k}y$. Note that

$$\mathbf{T}_k\mathbf{II} = \mathbf{F}_k\mathbf{II} = \mathbf{I}.$$

Define

$$M \equiv \lambda x.x\mathbf{T}_k\mathbf{F}_k A_0 A_1.$$

Then

$$M\mathbf{T}_I = \mathbf{T}_I\mathbf{T}_k\mathbf{F}_k A_0 A_1 = \mathbf{T}_k A_0 A_1 = A_0,$$

and similarly $M\mathbf{F}_I = A_1$. □

The following construction is due to Kleene.

9.2.13. Definition. Let $P \in \Lambda_I^0$ be such that for all $n \in \mathbb{N}$

$$P\llcorner n \lrcorner = \mathbf{T}_I \quad \text{or} \quad P\llcorner n \lrcorner = \mathbf{F}_I.$$

In order to represent minimalization define

$$A_0 \equiv \lambda xwt.w\mathbf{T}_I\mathbf{I}^{\sim 3}(tx)\mathbf{I}^{\sim 2}x,$$

$$A_1 \equiv \lambda xwt.w(t(\mathbf{S}_I^+x))(\mathbf{S}_I^+x)wt.$$

Then

$$A_i\mathbf{I}^{\sim 3} = \mathbf{I} \quad \text{for } i = 0, 1,$$

(note that $\mathbf{S}_I^+\mathbf{I} = \llcorner 2 \lrcorner$). Hence by lemma 9.2.12 there is a $W \in \Lambda_I^0$ such that

$$W\mathbf{T}_I = A_0, \qquad W\mathbf{F}_I = A_1.$$

Finally define

$$H_P \equiv \lambda x.W(Px)xWP, \qquad \boldsymbol{\mu}_I P \equiv H_P\llcorner 0 \lrcorner.$$

9.2.14. Lemma. *Let P, H_P and $\boldsymbol{\mu}_I P$ be as above.*
(i) $H_P\llcorner n \lrcorner = \llcorner n \lrcorner$, *if* $P\llcorner n \lrcorner = \mathbf{T}_I$;
$= H_P\llcorner n+1 \lrcorner$, *if* $P\llcorner n \lrcorner = \mathbf{F}_I$.
(ii) *If* $\exists n\ P\llcorner n \lrcorner = \mathbf{T}_I$, *let* $m = \mu n[P\llcorner n \lrcorner = \mathbf{T}_I]$. *Then* $\boldsymbol{\mu}_I P = \llcorner m \lrcorner$.
(iii) *If* $\forall n\ P\llcorner n \lrcorner = \mathbf{F}_I$, *then* $\mu_I P$ *has no* nf.

Proof. (i) If $P\llcorner n \lrcorner = \mathbf{T}_I$, then

$$H_P\llcorner n \lrcorner = W\mathbf{T}_I\llcorner n \lrcorner WP = A_0\llcorner n \lrcorner WP$$

$$= W\mathbf{T}_I\mathbf{I}^{\sim 3}(P\llcorner n \lrcorner)\mathbf{I}^{\sim 2}\llcorner n \lrcorner$$

$$= A_0\mathbf{I}^{\sim 3}\mathbf{T}_I\mathbf{I}^{\sim 2}\llcorner n \lrcorner = \llcorner n \lrcorner.$$

If $P\llcorner n \lrcorner = \mathbf{F}_I$, then

$$H_P\llcorner n \lrcorner = W\mathbf{F}_I\llcorner n \lrcorner WP = A_1\llcorner n \lrcorner WP$$

$$= W(P\llcorner n+1 \lrcorner)\llcorner n+1 \lrcorner WP = H_P\llcorner n+1 \lrcorner.$$

(ii) As for proposition 6.3.9(ii).

(iii) In this case

$$\begin{aligned}\mu_I P \equiv H_P \ulcorner 0 \urcorner \quad &\to \quad W(P\ulcorner 0\urcorner)\ulcorner 0\urcorner WP\\ &\underset{\neq 0}{\twoheadrightarrow} \quad W(P\ulcorner 1\urcorner)\ulcorner 1\urcorner WP\\ &\cdots\\ &\underset{\neq 0}{\twoheadrightarrow} \quad W(P\ulcorner n\urcorner)\ulcorner n\urcorner WP\\ &\cdots\end{aligned}$$

Thus $\mu_I P$ has an infinite reduction path and therefore by theorem 9.1.5 $\mu_I P$ has no nf. □

9.2.15. PROPOSITION. *The partial λI-definable functions are closed under minimalization.*

PROOF. As for lemma 8.4.11 using lemma 9.2.14. □

9.2.16. THEOREM (Kleene). *A partial numeric function is λI-definable iff it is partial recursive.*

PROOF. Analogous to the proof of theorem 8.4.13, using the results of this subsection. □

9.3. Combinators

In this section a theory $\boldsymbol{CL}_I$ is developed, the so-called combinatory version of $\boldsymbol{\lambda I}$. The starting point, due to Rosser [1935], is that, as in the unrestricted case, combinatory completeness follows from a finite number of instances. $\boldsymbol{CL}_I$ is a theory without bound variables and is like $\boldsymbol{CL}$, but with a different set of constants. Again an important application of the combinatory theory is that it provides a basis for the closed terms.

To stress the difference between the two combinatory theories, $\boldsymbol{CL}$ and $\boldsymbol{CL}_I$, the full theory $\boldsymbol{CL}$ is called sometimes $\boldsymbol{CL}_K$.

9.3.1. DEFINITION. $\boldsymbol{CL}_I$ is an equational theory like $\boldsymbol{CL}_K$. The constants of $\boldsymbol{CL}_I$ are

$$\boldsymbol{I},\quad \boldsymbol{B},\quad \boldsymbol{C},\quad \text{and}\quad \boldsymbol{S}$$

instead of $\boldsymbol{K}$ and $\boldsymbol{S}$ for $\boldsymbol{CL}_K$. Terms of $\boldsymbol{CL}_I$ are built up from these constants and variables as in $\boldsymbol{CL}_K$. $\mathcal{C}_I$ is the set of $\boldsymbol{CL}_I$-terms. Formulas of $\boldsymbol{CL}_I$ are equations between $\boldsymbol{CL}_I$-terms.

Instead of the axioms of group I for $\boldsymbol{CL}_K$ (see definition 7.1.2) $\boldsymbol{CL}_I$ has the following axioms:

$$\begin{aligned} \boldsymbol{I}M &= M, \\ \boldsymbol{B}MNL &= M(NL), \\ \boldsymbol{C}MNL &= MLN, \\ \boldsymbol{S}MNL &= ML(NL), \end{aligned}$$

where M, N, L are arbitrary $\boldsymbol{CL}_I$-terms. The axioms and rules in group (II) of $\boldsymbol{CL}_K$, stating that $=$ is an equality relation (see definition 7.1.2), remain valid for $\boldsymbol{CL}_I$.

The same conventions will be used for $\boldsymbol{CL}_I$ as for $\boldsymbol{CL}_K$.

Now it will be shown that λI-abstraction can be simulated by the constants of $\boldsymbol{CL}_I$.

9.3.2. DEFINITION. For $M \in \boldsymbol{CL}_I$ with $x \in \mathrm{FV}(M)$, define $\lambda^* x.M$ by induction on the structure of M as follows.

$$\lambda^* x.x \equiv \boldsymbol{I},$$

$$\lambda^* x.PQ \equiv \begin{cases} \boldsymbol{B}P(\lambda^* x.Q) & \text{if } x \notin \mathrm{FV}(P) \text{ and } x \in \mathrm{FV}(Q), \\ \boldsymbol{C}(\lambda^* x.P)Q & \text{if } x \in \mathrm{FV}(P) \text{ and } x \notin \mathrm{FV}(Q), \\ \boldsymbol{S}(\lambda^* x.P)(\lambda^* x.Q) & \text{if } x \in \mathrm{FV}(P) \text{ and } x \in \mathrm{FV}(Q). \end{cases}$$

As in the case for $\boldsymbol{CL}_K$, one now can prove combinatory completeness.

9.3.3. THEOREM. (i) $\mathrm{FV}(\lambda^* x.M) = \mathrm{FV}(M) - \{x\}$;

(ii) $(\lambda^* x_1 \cdots x_n.M)N_1 \cdots N_m = M[x_1 := N_1] \cdots [x_n := N_n]$;

provided that the notation makes sense, i.e. $x \in \mathrm{FV}(M)$ *in* (i) *and similarly for* (ii). □

As in the case for $\boldsymbol{CL}_K$, equality provable in $\boldsymbol{CL}_I$ can be generated by a notion of reduction, which is defined by

$$\boldsymbol{w}_I = \{\langle \boldsymbol{I}M, M\rangle \mid M \in \mathcal{C}_I\} \cup \cdots \cup$$
$$\cup \{\langle \boldsymbol{S}MNL, ML(NL)\rangle \mid M, N, L \in \mathcal{C}_I\}$$

Moreover this $\boldsymbol{w}_I$ is CR; see exercise 9.5.15.

It is clear how standard translations

$$(\ )_{\lambda I}:\mathcal{C}_I\to\Lambda_I,$$

$$(\ )_{CL_I}:\Lambda_I\to\mathcal{C}_I$$

can be defined. In particular one has

$$(\boldsymbol{I})_{\lambda I}=\mathbf{I},$$

$$(\boldsymbol{B})_{\lambda I}=\mathbf{B}\equiv\lambda xyz.x(yz),$$

$$(\boldsymbol{C})_{\lambda I}=\mathbf{C}\equiv\lambda xyz.xzy,$$

$$(\boldsymbol{S})_{\lambda I}=\mathbf{S}.$$

In the same way as for the K-case one can construct axioms $\boldsymbol{A}_{I\beta(\eta)}$ such that $\boldsymbol{\lambda I}$ and $\boldsymbol{CL}_I+\boldsymbol{A}_{I\beta}$ are equivalent and $\boldsymbol{\lambda I}$, $\boldsymbol{\lambda I}+\boldsymbol{ext}$, $\boldsymbol{CL}_I+\boldsymbol{A}_{I\beta\eta}$ and $\boldsymbol{CL}_I+\boldsymbol{ext}$ are all equivalent. See exercise 9.5.12.

Now some applications of $\boldsymbol{CL}_I$ to the λI-calculus are given.

9.3.4. Definition. $\mathcal{X}\subseteq\Lambda_I^0$ is an *I-basis* if

$$\forall M\in\Lambda_I^0\ \exists N\in\mathcal{X}^+\quad N=M.$$

9.3.5. Proposition. *The set* $\mathcal{X}=\{\mathbf{I},\mathbf{B},\mathbf{C},\mathbf{S}\}$ *is an I-basis. In fact*

$$\forall M\in\Lambda_I^0\ \exists N\in\mathcal{X}^+\quad N\twoheadrightarrow M.$$

Proof. As for the K-case, proposition 8.1.2. □

9.3.6. Corollary. *If* $\mathcal{X}$ *is an I-basis, then*

$$\forall M\in\Lambda_I^0\ \exists N\in\mathcal{X}^+\quad N\twoheadrightarrow M.$$

Proof. As for corollary 8.1.3. □

9.3.7. Proposition. (Rosser [1935]). *Let*

$$\mathbf{J}\equiv\lambda abcd.ab(adc).$$

Then $\{\mathbf{I},\mathbf{J}\}$ *is an I-basis.*

PROOF. Note that

$$\mathbf{JII} \to \mathbf{C}_*(\equiv \lambda ab.ba),$$

$$\mathbf{JC}_*(\mathbf{JC}_*)(\mathbf{JC}_*) \twoheadrightarrow \mathbf{C},$$

$$\mathbf{C}(\mathbf{JIC})(\mathbf{JI}) \twoheadrightarrow \mathbf{B},$$

$$\mathbf{C}(\mathbf{C}(\mathbf{BC}(\mathbf{C}(\mathbf{BJC}_*)\mathbf{C}_*))\mathbf{C}_*) \twoheadrightarrow \mathbf{W}(\equiv \lambda ab.abb),$$

$$\mathbf{B}(\mathbf{B}(\mathbf{BW})\mathbf{C})(\mathbf{BB}) \twoheadrightarrow \mathbf{S}.$$

Hence $\{\mathbf{I}, \mathbf{J}\}$ is a basis for $\{\mathbf{I}, \mathbf{B}, \mathbf{C}, \mathbf{S}\}$ and therefore also for Λ_I^0. □

From now on $\mathbf{J} \equiv \lambda abcd.ab(adc)$.

Note that 266 symbols (not counting brackets) are needed to express $\mathbf{S}$ in terms of $\mathbf{I}$ and $\mathbf{J}$.

The following proposition was first proved in Klop [1975] by a different construction.

9.3.8. PROPOSITION. *There exists an I-basis consisting of one element.*

PROOF. Define

$$\mathbf{K}^* \equiv \lambda xy.y\mathbf{I}^{\sim 4}x, \qquad \mathbf{X}_I \equiv \langle \mathbf{K}^*, \mathbf{J}, \mathbf{I} \rangle.$$

Note that $\mathbf{K}^*xN = x$ for $N \in \{\mathbf{I}, \mathbf{J}\}$, ("$\mathbf{K}^*$ is a local K").

Then $\{\mathbf{X}_I\}$ is a basis for $\{\mathbf{I}, \mathbf{J}\}$ and hence for Λ_I^0:

$$\mathbf{X}_I\mathbf{X}_I \twoheadrightarrow \mathbf{X}_I\mathbf{K}^*\mathbf{JI} \twoheadrightarrow \mathbf{K}^*\mathbf{K}^*\mathbf{JIJI}$$

$$\twoheadrightarrow \mathbf{K}^*\mathbf{IJI} \twoheadrightarrow \mathbf{II} \twoheadrightarrow \mathbf{I},$$

$$\mathbf{X}_I\mathbf{I} \twoheadrightarrow \mathbf{IK}^*\mathbf{JI} \twoheadrightarrow \mathbf{K}^*\mathbf{JI} \twoheadrightarrow \mathbf{J}. \quad \square$$

From now on $\mathbf{X}_I$ denotes the term constructed in this proof.

9.3.9. LEMMA. *For each $M \in \Lambda_I^0$, there exists a normal $M' \in \Lambda_I^0$ such that*

$$M'\mathbf{I} \twoheadrightarrow \mathbf{I}, \qquad M'\mathbf{X}_I \twoheadrightarrow M.$$

PROOF. Let $M_1 \in \{\mathbf{X}_I\}^+$ be such that $M_1 \twoheadrightarrow M$. Let M_2 be obtained from M_1 by replacing each occurrence $\mathbf{X}_I$ by the variable x. Set $M' \equiv \lambda x.M_2$. Clearly $M' \in \Lambda_I^0$ and is in nf. Moreover

$$M'\mathbf{I} \twoheadrightarrow \mathbf{I} \quad \text{and} \quad M'\mathbf{X}_I \to M_1 \twoheadrightarrow M. \quad \square$$

9.3.10. LEMMA. $\forall A_0, A_1 \in \Lambda_I^0\ \exists F \in \Lambda_I^0$

$$F\llcorner i \lrcorner \twoheadrightarrow A_i, \quad i = 0, 1.$$

PROOF. Let A_i' be such that

$$A_i'\mathbf{I} \twoheadrightarrow \mathbf{I} \quad \text{and} \quad A_i'\mathbf{X}_I \twoheadrightarrow A_i \quad \text{for } i = 0, 1.$$

Define $F \equiv \lambda x.\ \mathbf{Zero}_I x A_0' A_1' \mathbf{X}_I$. Then

$$F\llcorner 0 \lrcorner \twoheadrightarrow \mathbf{T}_I A_0' A_1' \mathbf{X}_I \twoheadrightarrow A_0' \mathbf{X}_I \twoheadrightarrow A_0$$

and similarly

$$F\llcorner 1 \lrcorner \twoheadrightarrow A_1. \quad \square$$

Theorem 10.5.2 gives a considerable strengthening of lemma 9.3.10. See also exercise 9.5.2.

9.3.11. PROPOSITION (Kleene [1936]). *Let $G, H \in \Lambda_I^0$. Then there exists an $F \in \Lambda_I^0$ such that*

$$F\llcorner 0 \lrcorner \twoheadrightarrow G, \qquad F\llcorner n+1 \lrcorner \twoheadrightarrow HF\llcorner n+1 \lrcorner.$$

PROOF. Let the function sg be λI-defined by $M \in \Lambda_I^0$, i.e.

$$M\llcorner 0 \lrcorner = \llcorner 0 \lrcorner \quad \text{and} \quad M\llcorner n+1 \lrcorner = \llcorner 1 \lrcorner \quad \text{for all } n \in \mathbb{N}.$$

Define

$$P \equiv \lambda xy.H(\lambda z.y(Mz)zy)x.$$

By lemma 9.3.10 there exist $Q, R \in \Lambda_I^0$ such that

$$Q\llcorner 0 \lrcorner \twoheadrightarrow \lambda x.x\llcorner 0 \lrcorner \llcorner 1 \lrcorner, \qquad Q\llcorner 1 \lrcorner \twoheadrightarrow G$$

and

$$R\llcorner 0 \lrcorner \twoheadrightarrow Q, \qquad R\llcorner 1 \lrcorner \twoheadrightarrow P.$$

Now define

$$F \equiv \lambda z.R(Mz)zR.$$

Then

$$F\llcorner 0 \lrcorner \twoheadrightarrow R\llcorner 0 \lrcorner \llcorner 0 \lrcorner R \twoheadrightarrow Q\llcorner 0 \lrcorner R \twoheadrightarrow R\llcorner 0 \lrcorner \llcorner 1 \lrcorner \twoheadrightarrow Q\llcorner 1 \lrcorner \twoheadrightarrow G$$

and

$$F\ulcorner n+1\urcorner \twoheadrightarrow R\ulcorner 1\urcorner\ulcorner n+1\urcorner R \twoheadrightarrow P\ulcorner n+1\urcorner R$$

$$\twoheadrightarrow H(\lambda z.R(Mz)zR)\ulcorner n+1\urcorner \twoheadrightarrow HF\ulcorner n+1\urcorner. \quad \square$$

9.3.12. THEOREM (Kleene [1936]). *There exists a term* $\mathbf{E}_I \in \Lambda_I^0$ *such that for all* $M \in \Lambda_I^0$

$$\mathbf{E}_I\ulcorner M\urcorner \twoheadrightarrow M.$$

PROOF. The proof is in two steps.

(1) *Lemma.* $\exists F \in \Lambda_I^0\ \forall M \in \Lambda_I^0\ \exists n \in \mathbb{N}\ F\ulcorner n\urcorner \twoheadrightarrow M.$

Proof. As in the proof of theorem 8.1.6 step 3 let $P_0, P_1 \in \Lambda_I^0$ be terms λI-defining the recursive projections p_0, p_1. By proposition 9.3.11 there exists an $F \in \Lambda_I^0$ such that

$$\begin{aligned} F\ulcorner n\urcorner &\twoheadrightarrow \mathbf{X}_I && \text{if } n=0,\\ &\twoheadrightarrow F(P_0\ulcorner n\urcorner)(F(P_1\ulcorner n\urcorner)) && \text{else.} \end{aligned}$$

Then as in the proof of 8.1.6 step 3 it follows that F has the required properties. $\square_1$

(2) *End of the proof.* As in the proof of theorem 8.1.6 steps 4 and 5 the F constructed in (1) can be modified to obtain $\mathbf{E}_I$. $\square_2$ $\square$

From now on $\mathbf{E}_I$ denotes the term constructed in theorem 9.3.12.

9.3.13. REMARK. As for the K-case there is also an enumerator $\mathbf{E}_{I,\vec{x}}$ for $\Lambda_I^0(\vec{x})$, i.e. a λI-term such that

$$\forall M \in \Lambda_I^0(\vec{x}) \quad \mathbf{E}_{I,\vec{x}}\ulcorner M\urcorner \twoheadrightarrow M.$$

Note however the difference between

$$\Lambda_I^0(\vec{x}) = \{M \in \Lambda_I \mid \mathrm{FV}(M) = \{\vec{x}\}\}$$

and

$$\Lambda_K^0(\vec{x}) = \{M \in \Lambda_K \mid \mathrm{FV}(M) \subset \{\vec{x}\}\}.$$

9.3.14. DEFINITION. A sequence $\{M_n\}$ of terms is *I-uniform* if for some $F \in \Lambda_I$

$$(*) \qquad F\ulcorner n\urcorner = M_n.$$

When $(*)$ holds, then M_n is said to be I-uniform *via* F.

The sequence $x_0, x_0x_0, x_0x_0x_0, \ldots$ is I-uniform.

The sequence $x_0, x_1, x_0, x_1, \ldots$ for different variables x_0, x_1 is K- but not I-uniform.

Using $\mathbf{E}_{I,\vec{x}}$ one can prove that a sequence M_n is I-uniform in n if

(i) $\forall n\ M_n \in \Lambda_I^0(\vec{x})$ for some $\vec{x}$

(ii) $\lambda\!\!\!\lambda n.\sharp M_n$ is recursive.

If M_n is I-uniform via $F \in \Lambda_I$, then $[M_n]_{n\in\mathbb{N}}$ can be defined as for the K-case via F.

The term

$$[\mathbf{E}_I \ulcorner n \urcorner]_{n\in\mathbb{N}}$$

is a universal generator for the λI-calculus.

Together with the second fixed point theorem the term $\mathbf{E}_{I,\vec{x}}$ can be used to provide many generalizations of lemma 9.3.11.

9.3.15. Fixed point theorems (i) $\forall F \in \Lambda_I\ \exists X \in \Lambda_I\ X = FX$.

(ii) $\forall F \in \Lambda_I\ \exists X \in \Lambda_I\ X = F\ulcorner X \urcorner$.

(iii) *Moreover in* (i), (ii) $\mathrm{FV}(X) = \mathrm{FV}(F)$ *and* $X \twoheadrightarrow FX$ (*resp.* $X \twoheadrightarrow F\ulcorner X \urcorner$).

Proof. As for the K-case. Note that $\mathbf{Y}, \mathbf{\Theta} \in \Lambda_I^0$. □

The following construction is a typical example of the use of the second fixed point theorem in conjunction with $\mathbf{E}_I$.

9.3.16. Application. There exists an $F \in \Lambda_I^0$ such that

$$\begin{aligned} F\ulcorner k \urcorner &= G\ulcorner k \urcorner \quad \text{if } k \text{ is even,} \\ &= HF\ulcorner k \urcorner \quad \text{if } k \text{ is odd.} \end{aligned}$$

Proof. As in the proof of theorem 6.5.9 let Ap and Num be recursive functions such that

$$\mathrm{Ap}(\sharp P, \sharp Q) = \sharp(PQ), \qquad \mathrm{Num}(n) = \sharp(\ulcorner n \urcorner).$$

Define

$$\begin{aligned} p(f, k) &= \mathrm{Ap}(\sharp G, \mathrm{Num}(k)) &&\text{if } k \text{ is even,} \\ &= \mathrm{Ap}(\mathrm{Ap}(\sharp H, f), \mathrm{Num}(k)) &&\text{if } k \text{ is odd.} \end{aligned}$$

Then p is recursive, and hence λI-definable by say $P \in \Lambda_I^0$. Then for any term M

$$\begin{aligned} P\ulcorner M \urcorner\ulcorner k \urcorner &= \ulcorner \mathrm{Ap}(\sharp G, \sharp\ulcorner k \urcorner) \urcorner = \ulcorner G\ulcorner k \urcorner\urcorner &&\text{if } k \text{ is even,} \\ &= \ulcorner \mathrm{Ap}(\mathrm{Ap}(\sharp H, \sharp M), \mathrm{Num}(k)) \urcorner = \ulcorner HM\ulcorner k \urcorner\urcorner &&\text{if } k \text{ is odd.} \end{aligned}$$

By the second fixed point theorem 9.3.15(ii) there is an $F \in \Lambda_I^0$ such that

$$F = \lambda x.\mathbf{E}_I(P\ulcorner F\urcorner x).$$

Hence

$$F\ulcorner k\urcorner = \mathbf{E}_I(P\ulcorner F\urcorner\ulcorner k\urcorner) = \mathbf{E}_I\ulcorner G\ulcorner k\urcorner\urcorner = \mathbf{G}\ulcorner k\urcorner \quad \text{if } k \text{ is even}$$

$$= \mathbf{E}_I\ulcorner HF\ulcorner k\urcorner\urcorner = HF\ulcorner k\urcorner \quad \text{if } k \text{ is odd.} \quad \square$$

Of course a construction in the style of the proof of proposition 9.3.11 could have been given too (see exercise 9.5.9). But the advantage of the method followed is that one can rely on Church's thesis for recursive functions: it is relatively simple to prove that an effectively given numeric function is recursive. A direct construction of the term above is more involved.

9.4. Solvability

In this section it will be shown that in the λI-calculus, M is solvable iff M has a nf. From the method of proof it follows that a finite set $\mathcal{X}$ of closed nf's can be solved in a uniform way. This makes it possible to define a local K for $\mathcal{X}$: there is a $\mathbf{K}^* \in \Lambda_I^0$ such that

$$(*) \qquad \mathbf{K}^* xN = x \quad \text{for } N \in \mathcal{X}.$$

These results were proved in Barendregt [1973a]. The method of proof was simplified by Klop [1975]. By the method of his proof, the local K can be made impredicative, that is $(*)$ even holds if $N \in \{C_1[\mathbf{K}^*], \ldots, C_n[\mathbf{K}^*]\}$, where $C_1[\ ], \ldots, C_n[\ ]$ are previously given contexts such that all occurrences of x in $C_i[x]$ are passive, i.e. do not occur in a subterm $(xM) \subset C_i[x]$.

In order to prove that the nf's are I-solvable, the following class SO of λI-terms is introduced.

9.4.1. NOTATION. Let

$$\vec{P}_0 \equiv P_{00}, \ldots, P_{0n_0},$$

$$\ldots$$

$$\vec{P}_m \equiv P_{m0}, \ldots, P_{mn_m}$$

be some (non empty) sequences of terms. Then

$$\{\vec{P}_0, \ldots, \vec{P}_m\} \equiv \lambda x_0 \cdots x_m \cdot (x_0\vec{P}_0) \cdots (x_m\vec{P}_m).$$

Sometimes the matrix notation

$$\begin{bmatrix} P_{00} & \cdots & P_{0n_0} \\ \cdots & & \cdots \\ P_{m0} & \cdots & P_{mn_m} \end{bmatrix}$$

is used to indicate $\{\vec{P}_0, \ldots, \vec{P}_m\}$.

9.4.2. DEFINITION. The class $\mathrm{SO} \subset \Lambda_I^0$ is defined inductively as follows:

$$\mathbf{I} \in \mathrm{SO},$$

$$\vec{P}_0 \in \mathrm{SO}, \ldots, \vec{P}_m \in \mathrm{SO} \Rightarrow \{\vec{P}_0, \ldots, \vec{P}_m\} \in \mathrm{SO}.$$

It is useful to assign to each $M \in \mathrm{SO}$ a certain tree $T(M)$ (different from $\mathrm{BT}(M)$ defined in the next chapter).

Remember that $\mathrm{Seq} \subset \mathbb{N}$ is the set of sequence numbers. On Seq one has the relations and functions $<$, $\leqslant$, lh and $*$; see p. xiii.

9.4.3. DEFINITION. (i) A *tree* is a set A of sequence numbers such that

(1) $\alpha \in A, \beta \leqslant \alpha \Rightarrow \beta \in A$,

(2) $\alpha * \langle n+1 \rangle \in A \Rightarrow \alpha * \langle n \rangle \in A$.

The elements of A are called the *nodes* of the tree.

(ii) The *subtree* of A at node α (notation A_α) is the tree $\{\beta \mid \alpha * \beta \in A\}$.

9.4.4. EXAMPLE.

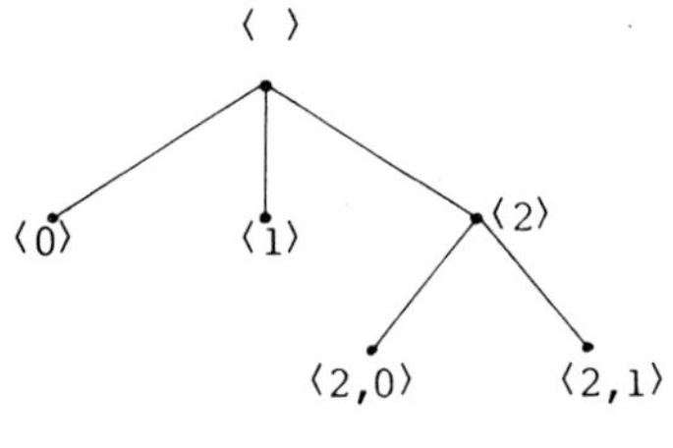

is a tree. But what really matters is the structure

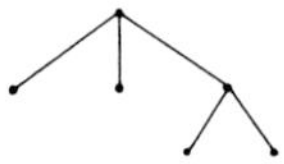

The subtree at node $\langle 2 \rangle$ is

9.4.5. DEFINITION. Let $\overrightarrow{\mathrm{SO}}$ be the set of finite sequences of elements of SO.

For each $P \in \mathrm{SO}$ and each $\vec{P} \in \overrightarrow{\mathrm{SO}}$ certain trees $T(P)$ and $T(\vec{P})$ are inductively defined as follows.

(1) $T(\mathbf{I}) = \{\langle\ \rangle\}$;

(2) $T(P_0, \ldots, P_n) = \{\langle\ \rangle\} \cup \{\langle i \rangle * \alpha | \alpha \in T(P_i), 0 \leqslant i \leqslant n\}$;

(3) $T(\{\vec{P}_0, \ldots, \vec{P}_n\}) = \{\langle\ \rangle\} \cup \{\langle i \rangle * \alpha | \alpha \in T(\vec{P}_i), 0 \leqslant i \leqslant n\}$.

Informally this can be written as

(1) $T(\mathbf{I}) = \cdot$,

(2) $T(P_0, \ldots, P_n) =$ 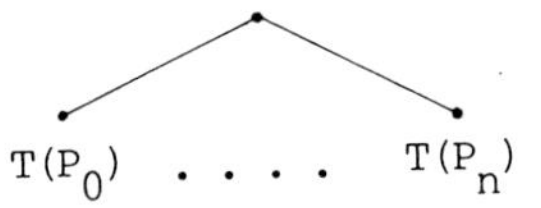

,

(3) $T(\{\vec{P}_0, \ldots, \vec{P}_n\}) =$ 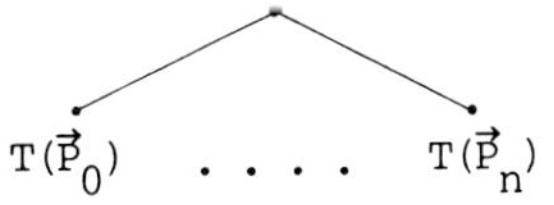

.

EXAMPLE. Let

$$P \equiv \lambda x_0 x_1 x_2.(x_0 \mathbf{II})(x_1(\lambda y_0 y_1.(y_0 \mathbf{I})(y_1 \mathbf{II}))\mathbf{I})(x_2 \mathbf{III}).$$

Then $T(P)$ is

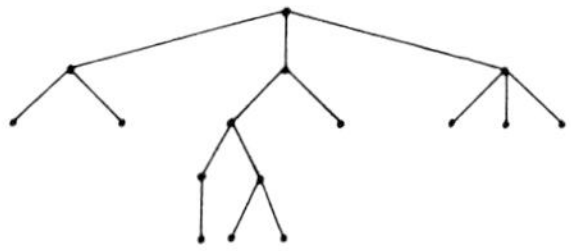

Note that subtrees at sequence numbers with an even (odd) length correspond to objects $\in \mathrm{SO}$ ($\in \overrightarrow{\mathrm{SO}}$ respectively).

9.4.6. DEFINITION. The following subclasses $\mathrm{SO}_{n,m} \subset \mathrm{SO}$ are defined by induction on n. If $\vec{P} = P_1, \ldots, P_k$, write $\vec{P} \in \overrightarrow{\mathrm{SO}}_{n,m}$ for $P_1, \ldots, P_k \in \mathrm{SO}_{n,m}$.

$$\mathrm{SO}_{0,m} = \{\mathbf{I}\},$$

$$\mathrm{SO}_{n+1,m} = \mathrm{SO}_{n,m} \cup \{\{\vec{P}_0, \ldots, \vec{P}_k\} | k \leqslant m \text{ and } \vec{P}_0, \ldots, \vec{P}_k \in \overrightarrow{\mathrm{SO}}_{n,m}\}$$

Clearly $\mathrm{SO} = \cup_{n,m} \mathrm{SO}_{n,m}$. Note, however, that for $n \neq 0$ the set $\mathrm{SO}_{n,m}$ is infinite. In terms of trees $\mathrm{SO}_{n,m}$ can be defined as follows. Define

$$\mathrm{Seq}_{n,m} = \{\alpha \in \mathrm{Seq} | \mathrm{lh}(\alpha) \leqslant 2n \wedge \forall k \leqslant \mathrm{lh}(\alpha)\ \alpha(2k) \leqslant m\}$$

Then $\mathrm{SO}_{n,m} = \{P \in \mathrm{SO} | T(P) \subset \mathrm{Seq}_{n,m}\}$.

9.4.7. DEFINITION. Let $\mathcal{X} \subset \Lambda$. $\mathcal{X}$ is *closed under application* (*modulo* β) if $\forall M, N \in \mathcal{X} \quad MN \in_\beta \mathcal{X}$.

9.4.8. PROPOSITION. (i) $\mathrm{SO}_{n,m}$ *is closed under application*
(ii) SO *is closed under application*.

PROOF. The proof is in several steps.
(1) *Lemma. If* $M \in \mathrm{SO}_{n+1,m}$, *then either* $M \equiv \mathsf{I}$ *or*

$$M \equiv \{\vec{P}_0, \ldots, \vec{P}_k\} \text{ with } k \leqslant m \text{ and } \vec{P}_i \in \overrightarrow{\mathrm{SO}}_{n,m} \text{ for } 0 \leqslant i \leqslant k.$$

Proof. By induction on n. $\Box_1$

(2) *Lemma. Let* $M, N \in \mathrm{SO}_{n+1,m}$ *with* $M \equiv \{\vec{P}_0, \ldots, \vec{P}_p\}$, *where* $p \leqslant m$ *and* $\vec{P}_i \in \mathrm{SO}_{n,m}$ *for* $0 \leqslant i \leqslant p$. *Let*

$$L \equiv \lambda x_0 \cdots x_p . N(x_0 \vec{P}_0) \cdots (x_p \vec{P}_p).$$

then $L \in_\beta \mathrm{SO}_{n+1,m}$.

Proof. If $N \equiv \mathsf{I}$, then $L = M$ and we are done. Otherwise, by (1)

$$N \equiv \{\vec{Q}_0, \ldots, \vec{Q}_q\} \text{ with } \vec{Q}_i \in \overrightarrow{\mathrm{SO}}_{n,m} \text{ for } 0 \leqslant i \leqslant q,\ q \leqslant m.$$

Case 1. $p \geqslant q$. Then

$$\begin{aligned} L &\equiv \lambda x_0 \cdots x_p . (\lambda y_0 \cdots y_q . (y_0 \vec{Q}_0) \cdots (y_q \vec{Q}_q))(x_0 \vec{P}_0) \cdots (x_p \vec{P}_p) \\ &= \lambda x_0 \cdots x_p . (x_0 \vec{P}_0 \vec{Q}_0) \cdots (x_q \vec{P}_q \vec{Q}_q)(x_{q+1} \vec{P}_{q+1}) \cdots (x_p \vec{P}_p) \\ &\equiv \{\vec{P}_0 \vec{Q}_0, \ldots, \vec{P}_q \vec{Q}_q, \vec{P}_{q+1}, \ldots, \vec{P}_p\} \in \mathrm{SO}_{n+1,m}. \end{aligned}$$

Case 2. $q > p$. Then similarly

$$L = \{\vec{P}_0 \vec{Q}_0, \ldots, \vec{P}_p \vec{Q}_p, \vec{Q}_{p+1}, \ldots, \vec{Q}_q\} \in \mathrm{SO}_{n+1,m}. \quad \Box_2$$

(3) *Lemma. Suppose* $\mathrm{SO}_{n,m}$ *is closed under application. Then*

$$M \in \mathrm{SO}_{n+1,m},\ N \in \mathrm{SO}_{n,m} \Rightarrow MN \in_\beta \mathrm{SO}_{n+1,m}.$$

Proof. If $M \equiv \mathsf{I}$ we are done. Otherwise

$$M \equiv \{\vec{P}_0, \ldots, \vec{P}_p\}, \quad \text{with } \vec{P}_i \in \overrightarrow{\mathrm{SO}}_{n,m},\ 0 \leqslant i \leqslant p.$$

Now

$$MN = \lambda x_1 \cdots x_p . N\vec{P}_0 (x_1 \vec{P}_1) \cdots (x_p \vec{P}_p).$$

By assumption

$$N\vec{P}_0 \in_\beta \mathrm{SO}_{n,m} \subset \mathrm{SO}_{n+1,m}.$$

Hence by lemma 2 $MN \in_\beta \mathrm{SO}_{n+1,m}$. $\square_3$

(4) *Proof of* 9.4.8. (i) By induction on n. The case $n = 0$ is trivial, so consider the case $n+1$.

Let $M, N \in \mathrm{SO}_{n+1,m}$. If $M \equiv \mathbf{I}$, then trivially $MN \in_\beta \mathrm{SO}_{n+1,m}$. Otherwise

$$M \equiv \{\vec{P}_0, \ldots, \vec{P}_p\}, \quad \text{with } \vec{P}_i \in \overrightarrow{\mathrm{SO}}_{n,m}, \ 0 \leqslant i \leqslant p.$$

Hence $MN = \lambda x_1 \cdots x_p . N\vec{P}_0(x_1\vec{P}_1) \cdots (x_p\vec{P}_p)$.
By lemma 3 and the induction hypothesis

$$N\vec{P}_0 \in_\beta \mathrm{SO}_{n+1,m}.$$

Hence by lemma 2 one has $MN \in_\beta \mathrm{SO}_{n+1,m}$.

(ii) Immediate since $\mathrm{SO} = \cup_{n,m}\mathrm{SO}_{n,m}$. $\square_4$ $\square$

9.4.9. LEMMA. (i) $\forall n, m \in \mathbb{N}\ \exists k \in \mathbb{N}\ \forall M \in \mathrm{SO}_{n,m}\ M\mathbf{I}^{\sim k} = \mathbf{I}$.

(ii) $\forall M \in \mathrm{SO}\ \exists k \in \mathbb{N}\ M\mathbf{I}^{\sim k} = \mathbf{I}$.

PROOF. (i) By induction on n. For $n = 0$, take $k = 0$. For $n+1$, suppose that for some k_0

$$(*) \qquad P \in \mathrm{SO}_{n,m} \Rightarrow P\mathbf{I}^{\sim k_0} = \mathbf{I}.$$

Take $k = m + k_0$. Then

$$M \in \mathrm{SO}_{n+1,m} \Rightarrow M\mathbf{I}^{\sim k} = \mathbf{I}.$$

Indeed, if $M \equiv \mathbf{I}$, this is trivial. Otherwise

$$M \equiv \{\vec{P}_0, \ldots, \vec{P}_p\} \quad \text{with } p \leqslant m \text{ and } \vec{P}_i \in \overrightarrow{\mathrm{SO}}_{n,m}$$

for $0 \leqslant i \leqslant p$. Hence $M\mathbf{I}^{\sim p} = \vec{P}_0(\vec{P}_1) \cdots (\vec{P}_p) \in \mathrm{SO}_{n,m}$, by proposition 9.4.8(i). Therefore $M\mathbf{I}^{\sim p + k_0} = \mathbf{I}$ by $(*)$. A fortiori $M\mathbf{I}^{\sim k} = \mathbf{I}$.

(ii) Immediate by (i). $\square$

9.4.10. DEFINITION. (i) $\subset$ and $\vec{\subset}$ are binary relations on SO and $\overrightarrow{\mathrm{SO}}$ respectively defined by simultaneous induction as follows.

(1) $\mathbf{I} \subset P$,

(2) $\{\vec{P}_0, \ldots, \vec{P}_p\} \subset \{\vec{Q}_0, \ldots, \vec{Q}_q\} \Leftrightarrow p \leqslant q$ and $\forall i \leqslant p\ \vec{P}_i \,\vec{\subset}\, \vec{Q}_i$,

(3) $P_0, \ldots, P_p \,\vec{\subset}\, Q_0, \ldots, Q_q \Leftrightarrow p \leqslant q$ and $\forall i \leqslant p\ P_i \subset Q_i$.

(ii) $\cup$ and $\vec{\cup}$ are binary operations on SO and $\overrightarrow{\text{SO}}$ respectively defined by simultaneous induction as follows

(1) $\mathbf{I} \cup P = P \cup \mathbf{I} = P$.

(2) $\{\vec{P}_0, \ldots, \vec{P}_p\} \cup \{\vec{Q}_0, \ldots, \vec{Q}_q\} = \{\vec{P}_0 \vec{\cup} \vec{Q}_0, \ldots, \vec{P}_p \vec{\cup} \vec{Q}_p, \vec{Q}_{p+1}, \ldots, \vec{Q}_q\}$ if $q \geqslant p$. Similarly if $p \geqslant q$

$$\{\vec{P}_0, \ldots\} \cup \{\vec{Q}_0, \ldots\} = \{\vec{P}_0 \vec{\cup} \vec{Q}_0, \ldots, \vec{P}_q \vec{\cup} \vec{Q}_q, \vec{P}_{q+1}, \ldots, \vec{P}_p\}.$$

(3) $P_0, \ldots, P_p \vec{\cup} Q_0, \ldots, Q_q = P_0 \cup Q_0, \ldots, P_p \cup Q_p, Q_{p+1}, \ldots, Q_q$, if $q \geqslant p$. Similarly if $p \geqslant q$.

9.4.11. Lemma. (i) *For* $P, Q \in \text{SO}$

$$P \subset Q \Leftrightarrow T(P) \subset T(Q) \quad (\textit{as sets of sequence numbers})$$

and

$$T(P \cup Q) = T(P) \cup T(Q).$$

(ii) *For* $\vec{P}, \vec{Q} \in \overrightarrow{\text{SO}}$

$$\vec{P} \vec{\subset} \vec{Q} \Leftrightarrow T(\vec{P}) \subset T(\vec{Q})$$

and

$$T(\vec{P} \vec{\cup} \vec{Q}) = T(\vec{P}) \cup T(\vec{Q}).$$

Proof. By induction on the definition of the relations and operations. □

Examples.

(i) $\lambda xy.(x\mathbf{II})(y\mathbf{III}) \subset \lambda xyz.(x\mathbf{I}(\lambda p.p\mathbf{I}))(y\mathbf{I}(\lambda pq.(p\mathbf{I})(q\mathbf{I}))\mathbf{II})(z\mathbf{I})$,
Tree picture:

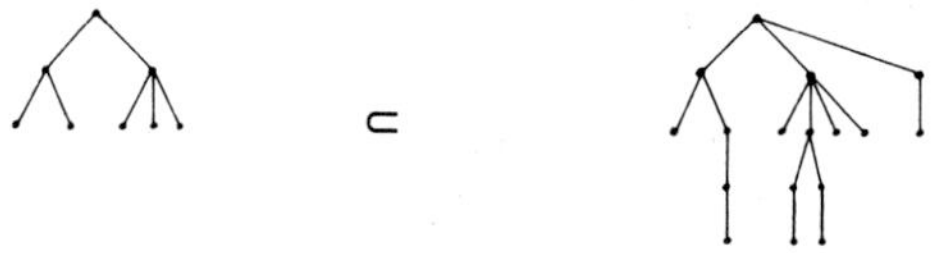

(ii) $\lambda xy.(x\mathbf{I}(\lambda p.p\mathbf{I}))(y(\lambda p.p\mathbf{III}))$

$$\cup\, \lambda xyz.(x(\lambda p.p\mathbf{II})\mathbf{I})(y(\lambda pq.(p\mathbf{I})(q\mathbf{I})))(z\mathbf{I})$$

$$= \lambda xyz.(x(\lambda p.(p\mathbf{II}))(\lambda p.p\mathbf{I}))(y(\lambda pq.(p\mathbf{III})(q\mathbf{I})))(z\mathbf{I}).$$

Tree picture:

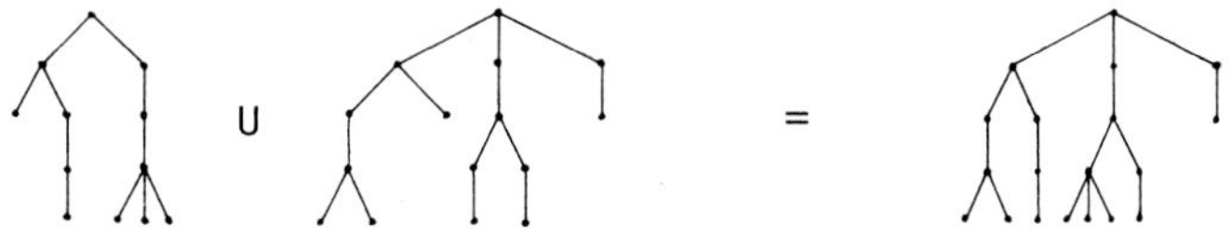

9.4.12. Corollary. $\subset$ *and* $\cup$ *(respectively* $\vec{\subset}$ *and* $\vec{\cup}$*) enjoy the usual Boolean properties of inclusions and union (e.g.* $\subset$ *is transitive,* $P \subset (P \cup Q)$ *etcetera).*

Proof. Immediate using T. □

9.4.13. Definition. Let $M \in \Lambda_K$, with $\mathrm{FV}(M) \subseteq \{x_0, \ldots, x_n\}$ (the $\vec{x}$ in their standard order); let $\vec{P} \equiv P_0, \ldots, P_p$ be a sequence of closed terms with $p \geqslant n$. Then

$$M \between \vec{P} \between \equiv M[x_0, \ldots, x_n := P_0, \ldots, P_n] P_{n+1}, \ldots P_p.$$

9.4.14. Definition. Let $M \in \Lambda_K$. $\vec{P} \in \overrightarrow{\mathrm{SO}}$ is a *critical sequence* for M if

$$\forall \vec{Q} \vec{\supset} \vec{P} \quad M \between \vec{Q} \between \in_\beta \mathrm{SO}.$$

9.4.15. Main lemma. *For each normal* $M \in \Lambda_K$ *there is a critical sequence* $\vec{P} \in \overrightarrow{\mathrm{SO}}$.

Proof. By induction on the generation of nf's in lemma 8.3.18 (ii).

If $M \equiv x$, take for $\vec{P}$ the singleton sequence $\mathbf{I}$.

Suppose $M \equiv \lambda x.N$, with say

$$M \equiv M(x_0, \ldots, x_n) \equiv \lambda x_{n+1}.N(x_0, \ldots, x_n, x_{n+1}).$$

Then also N is in nf, hence by the induction hypothesis N has a critical sequence $\vec{P}$, i.e.

$$\vec{Q} \vec{\supset} \vec{P} \Rightarrow N \between \vec{Q} \between \in_\beta \mathrm{SO}.$$

Then also $\vec{P}$ is a critical sequence for M:

$$\vec{Q} \vec{\supset} \vec{P} \Rightarrow M \between \vec{Q} \between \equiv M(Q_0, \ldots, Q_n) Q_{n+1} \cdots Q_q$$

$$=_\beta N(Q_0, \ldots, Q_n, Q_{n+1}) Q_{n+2} \cdots Q_q$$

$$\equiv N \between \vec{Q} \between \in_\beta \mathrm{SO}.$$

Suppose $M \equiv xM_0 \cdots M_k$, with say $x = x_0$ and $M_i \equiv M_i(x_0, \ldots, x_n)$ for $0 \leqslant i \leqslant k$. By the induction hypothesis there exist critical sequences $\vec{P}_i$ for each M_i.

In order to find a critical sequence for M, let us evaluate $M\between\vec{Q}\between$ where

(1) $\vec{Q} \equiv Q_0, \ldots, Q_q \in \overrightarrow{\mathrm{SO}}$, with $q \geqslant n$.

$$M\between\vec{Q}\between = Q_0 M_0(Q_0, \ldots, Q_n) \\ \cdots \\ M_k(Q_0, \ldots, Q_n)Q_{n+1} \cdots Q_q.$$

Now suppose moreover

(2) $Q_0 = \{\vec{R}_0, \ldots, \vec{R}_r\}$ with $r \geqslant k$. Then

$$M\between\vec{Q}\between = [\lambda x_{k+1} \cdots x_r.(M_0(Q_0, \ldots, Q_n)\vec{R}_0) \\ \cdots \\ (M_k(Q_0, \ldots, Q_n)\vec{R}_k) \\ (x_{k+1}\vec{R}_{k+1}) \\ \cdots \\ (x_r\vec{R}_r)]Q_{n+1} \cdots Q_q.$$

By sublemma 2 in the proof of lemma 9.4.8 and lemma 9.4.8 (ii) itself, it follows that $M\between\vec{Q}\between \in_\beta \mathrm{SO}$ provided that

$$M_i(Q_0, \ldots, Q_n)\vec{R}_i \in_\beta \mathrm{SO} \quad \text{for } 0 \leqslant i \leqslant k.$$

Now by the induction hypothesis this is the case if

(3) $Q_0, \ldots, Q_n, \vec{R}_i \mathrel{\vec{\supset}} \vec{P}_i$ for $0 \leqslant i \leqslant k$.

Hence $\vec{P}^M$ is a critical sequence for M if

$$\vec{Q} \mathrel{\vec{\supset}} \vec{P}^M \Rightarrow (1) \wedge (2) \wedge (3).$$

Such a $\vec{P}^M$ is constructed in the following sublemma and hence we are done.

Sublemma. Let $n, k \in \mathbb{N}$ and let $\vec{P}_i \in \overrightarrow{\mathrm{SO}}$, $i \leqslant k$. Then there exists a $\vec{P}^* \in \overrightarrow{\mathrm{SO}}$ such that if $\vec{Q} \mathrel{\vec{\supset}} \vec{P}^*$, then

(1) $\vec{Q} \equiv Q_0, \ldots, Q_q$ with $q \geqslant n$,

(2) $Q_0 \equiv \{\vec{R}_0, \ldots, \vec{R}_r\}$ with $r \geqslant k$,

(3) $Q_0, \ldots, Q_n, \vec{R}_i \mathrel{\vec{\supset}} \vec{P}_i$ for $0 \leqslant i \leqslant k$.

Proof. Suppose

$$\vec{P}_0 = P_{00}, \ldots, P_{0m_0},$$

$$\ldots$$

$$\vec{P}_k = P_{k0}, \ldots, P_{km_k}$$

and define

$$P^+ = \cup \{ P_{ij} | 0 \leqslant i \leqslant k, 0 \leqslant j \leqslant m_i \},$$

$$m = \max\{ m_i | 0 \leqslant i \leqslant k \}.$$

Finally set

$$\vec{P}^* = P_0^+ \cup \begin{bmatrix} P_{00}^+ & \cdots & P_{0m}^+ \\ \cdots & & \\ P_{k0}^+ & \cdots & P_{km}^+ \end{bmatrix}, P_1^+, \ldots, P_n^+$$

where

$$P_i^+ \equiv P^+ \quad \text{for } 0 \leqslant i \leqslant n$$

and

$$P_{ij}^+ \equiv P^+ \quad \text{for } 0 \leqslant i \leqslant k, 0 \leqslant j \leqslant m.$$

Now suppose $\vec{Q} \vec{\supset} \vec{P}^*$. It will be shown that (1), (2) and (3) hold.

(1) Trivial.

(2) Since $Q_0 \supset [P_{ij}^+] \equiv \{ \vec{P}_0^+, \ldots, \vec{P}_k^+ \}$ it follows that

$$Q_0 \equiv \{ \vec{R}_0, \ldots, \vec{R}_r \} \quad \text{with } r \geqslant k.$$

(3) Since P^+ is the supremum of the P_{ij}, it suffices to show that

(a) $Q_i \supset P^+$ for $0 \leqslant i \leqslant n$;

(b) $\forall i \leqslant k \; \vec{R}_i \equiv R_{i0}, \ldots, R_{is_i}$ and $s_i \geqslant m$;

(c) $R_{ij} \supset P^+$ for $0 \leqslant i \leqslant k$ and $0 \leqslant j \leqslant m$.

As to (a), since $\vec{Q} \vec{\supset} \vec{P}^*$, one has $Q_i \supset P_i^+ \equiv P^+$.

As to (b), (c), since

$$\{ \vec{R}_0, \ldots, \vec{R}_r \} \equiv Q_0 \supset \begin{pmatrix} P_{00}^+ & \cdots & P_{0m}^+ \\ P_{k0}^+ & \cdots & P_{km}^+ \end{pmatrix}$$

one has

$$R_{i0}, \ldots, R_{is_i} \equiv \vec{R}_i \supset P_{i0}^+, \ldots, P_{im}^+$$

which means

$$s_i \geqslant m \quad \text{for } 0 \leqslant i \leqslant k$$

and

$$R_{ij} \supset P_{ij}^+ = P^+ \quad \text{for } 0 \leqslant i \leqslant k, 0 \leqslant j \leqslant m. \quad \Box_{\text{sublemma}} \quad \Box$$

9.4.16. COROLLARY. *Let* $M \in \Lambda_K$ *be a* nf. *Then*
$\exists \vec{P} \in \text{SO}\ \forall n, m \in \mathbb{N}\ \ \forall \vec{Q} \in \text{SO}_{n,m}$
$[\vec{Q} \mathrel{\ddot{\supset}} \vec{P} \Rightarrow M \between \vec{Q} \between \in_\beta \text{SO}_{n,m}]$.

PROOF. Analogous to the previous proof. (Choose $\vec{P}$ such that if $\vec{Q} \mathrel{\ddot{\supset}} \vec{P}$, then $\vec{Q} \notin \text{SO}_{0,m}$). $\Box$

For the construction of an impredicative local K a bound on the SO class of P_0 is needed.

9.4.17. DEFINITION. Let $M \in \Lambda_K$ be a nf and x be a variable. Define numbers

$$n_x(M) \quad \text{and} \quad m_x(M)$$

by induction on the generation of nf's in lemma 8.3.18 (ii).

$$n_x(z) = m_x(z) = 0,$$

$$n_x(\lambda z.M) = n_x(M),$$

$$m_x(\lambda z.M) = m_x(M),$$

$$n_x(zM_0 \cdots M_k) = \begin{cases} \max\{n_x(M_i) \mid 0 \leqslant i \leqslant k\} & \text{if } z \not\equiv x, \\ \max_i \{n_x(M_i)\} + 1 & \text{if } z \equiv x \text{ and some } M_i \\ & \text{contains a } \lambda, \\ 0 & \text{else}; \end{cases}$$

$$m_x(zM_0 \cdots M_k) = \begin{cases} \max_i \{m_x(M_i)\} & \text{if } z \not\equiv x, \\ \max_i \{k, m_x(M_i)\} & \text{if } x \equiv z \text{ and some } M_i \text{ contains} \\ & \text{a } \lambda, \\ 0 & \text{else.} \end{cases}$$

9.4.18. COROLLARY. *For all* $M \equiv M(x_0, \ldots, x_n) \in \Lambda_K$ *in* nf

$$\exists \vec{P} \equiv P_0, \ldots, P_p\Big[P_0 \in \mathrm{SO}_{n_{x_0}(M),\, m_{x_0}(M)} \wedge$$

$$\wedge \forall n, m\, \forall \vec{Q} \in \mathrm{SO}_{n,m}\big[\vec{Q} \sqsupset \vec{P} \Rightarrow M\between\vec{Q}\between \in_{\beta} \mathrm{SO}_{n,m}\big]\Big].$$

PROOF. Repeat the proof of the main lemma 9.4.15 and note that if $M \equiv x_0 M_0 \cdots M_k$ and none of the $M_0, \ldots, M_k$ contains a lambda, then in the critical sequence $\vec{P} \equiv P_0, \ldots, P_p$ one can take $P_0 \equiv \mathbf{I}$. In the other case the bounds follow by the definition of the critical sequence $\vec{P}$ for M. □

Now we can collect the results.

9.4.19. COROLLARY. *Let* $M \in \Lambda_K$ *have a* nf. *Then* M *is* I*-solvable.*

PROOF. Let $M \equiv M(\vec{x})$. By the main lemma 9.4.15 for some $\vec{Q} \in \Lambda_I^0$

$$M\between\vec{Q}\between \equiv M(Q_0, \ldots, Q_n)Q_{n+1} \cdots Q_q \in_{\beta} \mathrm{SO}.$$

Hence by lemma 9.4.9 for some k

$$(\lambda\vec{x}.M(\vec{x}))Q_0 \cdots Q_q \mathbf{I}^{\sim k} = \mathbf{I},$$

i.e. M is I-solvable. □

9.4.20. THEOREM. *For a closed* $M \in \Lambda_I$ *the following statements are equivalent.*

(a) M *has a* nf,
(b) $\exists \vec{N} \in \Lambda_I^0\ M\vec{N} = \mathbf{I}$,
(c) $\exists F \in \Lambda_I^0\ FM = \mathbf{I}$.

PROOF. (a)⇒(b). By corollary 9.4.19.
(b)⇒(c). If $M\vec{N} = \mathbf{I}$, then for $F \equiv \lambda x.x\vec{N}$ one has $FM = \mathbf{I}$.
(c)⇒(a). If $FM = \mathbf{I}$, then FM has a nf. Hence by corollary 9.1.7 M has a nf. □

9.4.21. COROLLARY. *In the* λI*-calculus*:

M *has a* nf *iff* M *is solvable*.

PROOF. By lemma 8.3.3(ii) and corollary 8.3.19 it may be assumed that M is closed. But then the result follows. □

By the proof of corollary 9.4.19, via the main lemma 9.4.15 it follows that a finite set of normal terms can be solved uniformly by λI-terms.

9.4.22. THEOREM. Let $M_0, \ldots, M_n \in \Lambda_K$ have nfs. Then

$$\exists \vec{Q} \in \Lambda_I^0 \ \forall i \leqslant n \quad M_i \between \vec{Q} \between = \mathbf{I}.$$

PROOF. By the main lemma 9.4.15 each M_i has a critical sequence $\vec{P}_i$. Take

$$\vec{P} = \vec{P}_0 \vec{\cup} \cdots \vec{\cup} \vec{P}_n.$$

Then

$$M_i \between \vec{P} \between \in_\beta \mathrm{SO} \quad \text{for } 0 \leqslant i \leqslant n.$$

Hence by lemma 9.4.9 (ii) for some k

$$\forall i \leqslant n \quad M_i \between \vec{P} \between \mathbf{I}^{\sim k} = \mathbf{I}.$$

Thus we can take $\vec{Q} = \vec{P}, \mathbf{I}^{\sim k}$. □

See exercise 10.6.11 for an alternative proof of theorem 9.4.22.

9.4.23. DEFINITION. Let $\mathcal{X} \subset \Lambda_K$. $K^* \in \Lambda_I^0$ is a *local* K for $\mathcal{X}$ if

$$\forall M \in \Lambda_K \ \forall N \in \mathcal{X} \quad K^* MN = M.$$

9.4.24. COROLLARY. *Let* $\mathcal{X} \subset \Lambda_K^0$ *be a finite set of terms having a* nf. *Then there is a local* K *for* $\mathcal{X}$.

PROOF. By theorem 9.4.22 there exist $\vec{Q} \in \Lambda_I^0$ such that

$$\forall N \in \mathcal{X} \quad N\vec{Q} = \mathbf{I}.$$

Define $\mathbf{K}^* \equiv \lambda ab.b\vec{Q}a$. Then

$$\forall M \in \Lambda_K \ \forall N \in \mathcal{X} \quad \mathbf{K}^* MN = N\vec{Q}M = M. \quad \square$$

Next will be constructed an impredicative local K. That is, a term $K^* \in \Lambda_I^0$ which is a local K for a given set together with some given contexts of K^* itself.

9.4.25. THEOREM. *Let* $\mathcal{X} \subset \Lambda_I^0$ *be a finite set of terms having a* nf. *Let* $C_0[\ ], \ldots, C_k[\ ]$ *be some contexts such that for* $0 \leqslant i \leqslant k$

(a) $C_i[x] \in \Lambda_K^0(x)$ *and is in* nf, *and*

(b) x *occurs only passively in* $C_i[x]$.

Then some $\mathbf{K}^*$ *is a local K for*

$$\mathcal{X} \cup \{C_0[\mathbf{K}^*], \ldots, C_k[\mathbf{K}^*]\}.$$

Moreover for this $\mathbf{K}^*$

$$\mathbf{K}^*\mathbf{II} = \mathbf{I}.$$

PROOF. Define for $0 \leqslant i \leqslant k$

$$N_i(x) \equiv C_i[\lambda ab.xba].$$

Since the x in $C_i[x]$ are all passive, the $N_i(x)$ are again in nf. Moreover

$$\forall i \leqslant k \quad n_x(N_i(x)) = m_x(N_i(x)) = 0.$$

By taking the union of the critical sequences of the members of $\mathcal{X}$ one obtains using corollary 9.4.16

(1) $$\exists \vec{P} \in \mathrm{SO} \ \forall n,m \ \forall \vec{Q} \in \mathrm{SO}_{n,m} \ \forall N \in \mathcal{X}$$
$$[\vec{Q} \mathrel{\vec{\supset}} \vec{P} \Rightarrow N\vec{Q} \in_\beta \mathrm{SO}_{n,m}].$$

And similarly by using corollary 9.4.18

(2) $$\exists \vec{P}' \equiv P_0', \ldots, P_p' \in \mathrm{SO}[P_0' \in \mathrm{SO}_{0,0} \wedge \forall n, m \ \forall \vec{Q}' \in \mathrm{SO}_{n,m}$$
$$[\vec{Q}' \mathrel{\vec{\supset}} \vec{P}' \Rightarrow \forall i \leqslant k \ N_i(Q_0')Q_1' \cdots Q_q' \in_\beta \mathrm{SO}_{n,m}]].$$

Let $\vec{P} = P_0, \ldots, P_p$. Since $\mathrm{SO}_{0,0} = \{\mathbf{I}\}$, we have $\vec{P}' = \mathbf{I}, P_1', \ldots, P_{p'}'$. Define $R = P_0 \cup \cdots \cup P_p \cup P_1' \cup \cdots \cup P_{p'}'$, and $\vec{R} = R_0, \ldots, R_r$ where

$$r = \max(p, p') \text{ and } \forall i \leqslant r \ R_i \equiv R.$$

Since $R \in \mathrm{SO}$, one has $R \in \mathrm{SO}_{n,m}$, for some n, m.

By (1) and (2) it follows that

(3) $$\forall N \in \mathcal{X} \quad N\vec{R} \in_\beta \mathrm{SO}_{n,m} \subset \mathrm{SO}_{n+1,m},$$

and (since $P_0' \equiv \mathbf{I}$)

(4) $$\forall i \leqslant k \quad Q_0 \in \mathrm{SO}_{n+1,m} \Rightarrow N_i(Q_0)\vec{R} \in_\beta \mathrm{SO}_{n+1,m}.$$

Now by lemma 9.4.9(i) for some $k' \in \mathbb{N}$

(5) $$M \in \mathrm{SO}_{n+1,m} \Rightarrow M\mathbf{I}^{\sim k'} = \mathbf{I}.$$

Therefore by (3) and (4)

(6) $\forall N \in \mathcal{X} \quad N\vec{R}\mathbf{I}^{\sim k'} = \mathbf{I}$

(7) $Q_0 \in \mathrm{SO}_{n+1,m} \Rightarrow \forall i \leqslant k \;\; N_i(Q_0)\vec{R}\mathbf{I}^{\sim k'} = \mathbf{I}.$

Now take $Q_0 \equiv \lambda x.x\vec{R}\mathbf{I}^{\sim k'}$. Then $Q_0 \in \mathrm{SO}_{n+1,m}$ and hence by (7)

(8) $\forall i \leqslant k \quad N_i(Q_0)\vec{R}\mathbf{I}^{\sim k'} = \mathbf{I}.$

Finally define $\mathbf{K}^* \equiv \lambda ab.b\vec{R}\mathbf{I}^{\sim k'}a$. Then by (5) (note that $\mathbf{I}\vec{R} \in_\beta \mathrm{SO}_{n,m}$)

(9) $K^*\mathbf{II} = \mathbf{I}.$

Moreover by (6) and (8)

(10) $\forall M \in \Lambda_K \; \forall N \in \mathcal{X} \quad \mathbf{K}^*MN = M$

(11) $\forall M \in \Lambda_K \; \forall i \leqslant k \quad \mathbf{K}^*M(N_i(Q_0)) = M$

But

$$N_i(Q_0) = C_i[\lambda ab.Q_0 ba] = C_i[\mathbf{K}^*].$$

Hence by (11)

(12) $\forall M \in \Lambda_K \; \forall i \leqslant k \quad \mathbf{K}^*M(C_i[\mathbf{K}^*]) = M.$

By (9), (10) and (12) we are done. □

9.4.26. Corollary. *In the statement of theorem* 9.4.25 *it may be required that* $\mathbf{K}^*$ *is a local K for*

$$\mathcal{X} \cup \{C_0[\mathbf{K}^*], \ldots, C_k[\mathbf{K}^*]\} \cup \{\llcorner n \lrcorner \mid n \in \mathbb{N}\}.$$

Proof. Observe

$$P, Q \in \mathrm{SO}_{n,m} \Rightarrow \llcorner k \lrcorner PQ \in_\beta \mathrm{SO}_{n,m}. \quad \square$$

Note that theorem 9.4.25 becomes false if the condition that x occurs only passively in $C_i[x]$ is dropped.

Example. Let $\mathcal{X} = \{\mathbf{I}\}$ and let $C_0[x] = x\mathbf{II}(\lambda z.zz)(\lambda z.zz)$. In spite of the fact that $\mathbf{I}$ and $C_0[x]$ are in nf, there is no $\mathbf{K}^*$ local K for $\{\mathbf{I}, C_0[\mathbf{K}^*]\}$:

$$C_0[\mathbf{K}^*] = \mathbf{K}^*\mathbf{II}(\lambda z.zz)(\lambda z.zz) = \mathbf{\Omega}.$$

and hence

$$\mathbf{K}^*\mathbf{I}(C_0[\mathbf{K}^*]) = \mathbf{I}$$

is impossible by corollary 9.1.6.

See exercises 9.5.8 and 9.5.10 for applications of theorem 9.4.25.

9.5. Exercises

9.5.1. (i) Construct an $M \in \Lambda_I$ such that for all n

$$M\lfloor 0\rfloor = \mathbf{I}, \qquad M\lfloor n+1\rfloor = \mathbf{S}.$$

(ii) Construct an $M \in \Lambda_I$ such that for all n

$$M\lfloor 0\rfloor = \mathbf{\Omega}, \qquad M\lfloor n+1\rfloor = M.$$

9.5.2.(i) Let $M_0, \ldots, M_n \in \Lambda_I^0$. Construct an $F \in \Lambda_I^0$ such that

$$\forall i < n \quad F\lfloor i\rfloor = M_i.$$

(ii) *Idem* without the use of $\mathbf{E}_I$.

9.5.3. Construct a $P \in \mathcal{C}_I$ such that P is in w-nf, but P_λ has no nf.

9.5.4. Construct a $\mathbf{K}^* \in \Lambda_I^0$ which is a local K for:

(i) $\{\mathbf{I}, \mathbf{B}, \mathbf{C}, \mathbf{S}\}$,

(ii) $\{\mathbf{S}, \lambda x.x(\lambda y.yy)(\lambda y.yy), \mathbf{K}^*\}$.

9.5.5. Where does the proof of theorem 6.6.2 break down for the λI-calculus? Give an adequate modification for the λI-calculus and prove it.

9.5.6. Draw in a Venn diagram the sets

$$\Lambda_K^0,\ \Lambda_I^0, \{M \in \Lambda_K^0 | M \text{ has a nf}\},$$

$$\{M \in \Lambda_K^0 | M \text{ is } I\text{-unsolvable}\} \quad \text{and} \quad \{M \in \Lambda_K^0 | M \text{ is } K\text{-unsolvable}\}.$$

Construct seven terms to show that the sets have no more relations than indicated in the diagram.

*9.5.7 (Klop). If $M \equiv \lambda x_1 \cdots x_n.x_i M_1 \cdots M_m$ is a hnf, then n is the *arity* of M. Show that the SO terms have maximal solving power, that is, for each normal $M \in \Lambda_K^0$ of arity n

$$\exists P_1, \ldots, P_n \in \mathrm{SO} \quad MP_1 \cdots P_n = \mathbf{I}.$$

*9.5.8. Prove the result in application 9.3.16 using an impredicative local K.

*9.5.9. Prove the result in application 9.3.16 directly, without the use of the second fixed point theorem or an impredicative local K.

*9.5.10. Construct a λI-defining term for every partial recursive function using an impredicative local K.

*9.5.11. Let $\ulcorner 0\urcorner = \mathbf{I}$, $\ulcorner n+1\urcorner = [\mathbf{F}_I, \ulcorner n\urcorner]$. Show that $\{\ulcorner n\urcorner | n \in \mathbb{N}\}$ is an adequate set of numerals for $\boldsymbol{\lambda I}$. [*Hint*. Use an impredicative local K to represent primitive recursion and minimalization.]

9.5.12. Construct finite sets $A_{I\beta}$ and $A_{I\beta\eta}$ consisting of equations between closed CL_I-terms such that the theories $CL_I + A_{I\beta}$ and $CL_I + A_{I\beta\eta}$ become equivalent with $\boldsymbol{\lambda I}$ and $\boldsymbol{\lambda I\eta}$ respectively.

9.5.13. (i) Let $\mathbb{N}^* = \mathbb{N} \cup \{*\}$, where $* \notin \mathbb{N}$. Define for $n, m \in \mathbb{N}$

$$n \cdot m = \begin{cases} \{n\}(m) & \text{if defined,} \\ * & \text{else.} \end{cases}$$

Moreover define

$$n \cdot * = * \cdot n = * \cdot * = *.$$

Show that there are elements $i, b, c, s \in \mathbb{N}$ such that the structure $\mathcal{K}_1 = (\mathbb{N}^*, \cdot, i, b, c, s)$ is a model of $\boldsymbol{CL}_I$. [*Hint*. Use the s-m-n theorem of recursion theory.] This model is called the *first Kleene model* of $\boldsymbol{CL}_I$.

(ii) Show that for some $k \in \mathbb{N}$

$$k \cdot m \cdot n = m \quad \text{for all } m, n \in \mathbb{N}.$$

Why is the structure $(\mathbb{N}^*, \cdot, k, s)$ not a model for $\boldsymbol{CL}_K$? *Note*. In Barendregt [1975] it is essentially shown that

$$M \text{ has no } w\text{-nf} \Leftrightarrow \mathcal{K}_1 \models M = *.$$

Hence Con($\{M = N \mid M, N \in \mathcal{C}_I$ have no w-nf$\}$).

*9.5.14 (Kleene). Let $\mathbb{B} = \mathbb{N}^{\mathbb{N}}$ equipped with the product topology. For $\alpha \in \mathbb{B}$ and $n \in \mathbb{N}$, let $\bar{\alpha}(n) = \langle \alpha(0), \ldots, \alpha(n-1) \rangle$, $\bar{\alpha}(0) = \langle\ \rangle$.
Let $\mathbb{B}^* = \mathbb{B} \cup \{*\}$ with $* \notin \mathbb{B}$. For $\alpha, \beta \in \mathbb{B}$ define

$$\alpha \mid \beta = \gamma \quad \text{iff} \quad \begin{array}{l} \forall n\, \exists m\, \alpha(\langle n \rangle * \bar{\beta}(m)) \neq 0 \text{ and} \\ \forall n\, \gamma(n) = \alpha(\mu m[\alpha(\langle n \rangle * \bar{\beta}(m)] \neq 0) - 1, \end{array}$$

$$= * \quad \text{else.}$$

Moreover define $\alpha \cdot * = * \cdot \alpha = * \cdot * = *$.
Construct $\iota, \beta, \gamma, \sigma \in \mathbb{B}$ such that $\mathcal{K}_2 = (\mathbb{B}^*, |, \iota, \beta, \gamma, \sigma)$ is a model of $\boldsymbol{CL}_I$. This structure is called the *second Kleene model* of $\boldsymbol{CL}_I$. [*Hint*. Show that for each continuous $F : \mathbb{B} \to \mathbb{B}$ there exists an $\alpha \in \mathbb{B}$ such that $\forall \beta \in \mathbb{B}\ \alpha \mid \beta = F(\beta)$.]

9.5.15. Show that the notion of reduction $\boldsymbol{w}_I$ is CR. [*Hint*. Use the method of exercise 7.4.13.]

9.5.16. (Böhm, Dezani-Ciancaglini). Let $\boldsymbol{c} = c_0, c_1, \ldots \in \Lambda_K$ be the Church numerals with successor S_c^+. Let $A_\times = \mathbf{B}$ and $A_{\exp} = \mathbf{C}_*$ represent multiplication and exponentiation on $\boldsymbol{c}$ (see exercises 6.8.6 and 7.4.8).

(i) Show that $\{c_1, S_c^+, A_\times, A_{\exp}\}$ is an I-base (in $\lambda \boldsymbol{I}\eta$).

(ii) Show that $\{c_0, S_c^+, A_\times, A_{\exp}\}$ is a K-base (in $\lambda \boldsymbol{K}$).

[*Hint*. (Church, Curry). For (i) note that

$$\mathbf{C} = \mathbf{B(C_*(BBC_*))(BBC_*)},$$

$$\mathbf{I} = \mathbf{BCC},$$

$$\mathbf{W_*} = \mathbf{B(C}c_2\mathbf{I)C_*},$$

$$\mathbf{W} = \mathbf{B(B(C_*(BW_*(B(C_*C_*)(B(BBB)C_*))))(BBC_*))(B(C_*(B(C_*I)((C_*I))))B)},$$

$$\mathbf{S} = \mathbf{C(CB(CB(CB)(CB(CB)))(CB))W} = \mathbf{B(B(BW)C)(BB)},$$

$$\mathbf{J} = \mathbf{B(BC(BC))(B(W(BBB))C)}.$$

Hence $\{c_2, A_\times, A_{\exp}\}$ is an I-base. For (ii) note that $\mathbf{K} = \mathbf{C}c_0$.]

Moral. "Combinators are generalized numerals."

9.5.17. Show that $\{M \in \Lambda \mid \infty(M)\}$ is a Π_1^0-complete set.

9.5.18. Show that if $M \in \Lambda_K$ is I-solvable, then M does not necessarily have a nf.

CHAPTER 10

BÖHM TREES

10.1. Basics

For each $M \in \Lambda$ we will define a certain tree $\mathrm{BT}(M)$, the so-called Böhm tree of M. The notion is suggested by the original proof of Böhm's theorem 10.4.2, the notion of hnf and proposal 2.2.14 (unsolvable $\Leftrightarrow$ undefined). Böhm trees will play an important role in the analysis of the models $P\omega$ and D_∞.

Terms and their BT's roughly relate to each other as a real number relates to its continued fraction expansion. If M has an nf, then $\mathrm{BT}(M)$ is finite. In this respect nf's correspond to rational numbers. For example in §10.2 it is shown that with respect to an appropriate topology on Λ the normal forms are a dense subset.

First $\mathrm{BT}(M)$ will be introduced informally. Remember that $\mathrm{Seq} \subset \mathbb{N}$ is the set of sequence numbers. On Seq one has the relations and functions $<$, $\leqslant$, lh and $*$; see p. xiii. A *partial map* $\varphi : X \rightharpoonup Y$ is a map φ with $\mathrm{Dom}(\varphi) \subseteq X$. For $x \in X$ the notation $\varphi(x)\downarrow$ means that $\varphi(x)$ is defined, i.e. $x \in \mathrm{Dom}(\varphi)$; $\varphi(x)\uparrow$ means that $\varphi(x)$ is undefined, i.e. $x \notin \mathrm{Dom}(\varphi)$.

10.1.1. Definition. Let Σ be a set of symbols.

(i) A Σ-*labelled tree* is a tree where at each node an element of Σ is written.

(ii) More formally, a Σ-labelled tree is a partial map $\varphi : \mathrm{Seq} \rightharpoonup \Sigma$ such that the set $T_\varphi = \{\alpha \in \mathrm{Seq} \mid \varphi(\alpha)\downarrow\}$ is a tree. T_φ is called the *underlying naked tree*. The *label* at node $\alpha \in T_\varphi$ is $\varphi(\alpha)$.

Example. Let $\Sigma = \{a, b, c\}$. A Σ-labelled tree is e.g.

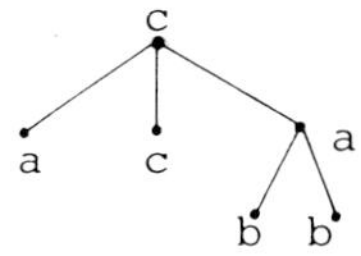

Another notation for this tree is

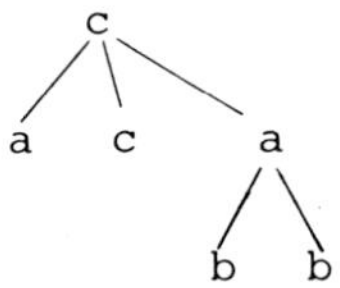

10.1.2. Notation. (i) The letters $A, B, \ldots$ will be used for labelled trees. Thus A *is* some partial map φ.

(ii) $|A|$ is the underlying tree T_A. We write $\alpha \in A$ for $\alpha \in T_A$.

10.1.3. Informal definition. Let

$$\Sigma = \{\bot\} \cup \{\lambda x_1 \cdots x_n.y \mid n \in \mathbb{N}, x_1, \ldots, x_n, y \text{ variables}\}.$$

Then BT(M) is a Σ-labelled tree defined as follows.

$\text{BT}(M) = \bot$ if M is unsolvable (i.e. one single node with label $\bot$),

$\text{BT}(M) = \lambda\vec{x}.y$ with subtrees $\text{BT}(M_1) \cdots \text{BT}(M_m)$ if M is solvable and has as principal hnf $\lambda\vec{x}.yM_1 \cdots M_m$.

Remarks. (i) Remember that by theorem 8.3.14 a λ-term M is solvable iff M has a hnf.

(ii) If M has $\lambda\vec{x}.yM_1 \cdots M_m$ as principal hnf, then the M_i may be more complex than M itself. Therefore 10.1.3 is not an inductive definition. Rather it describes a process that yields a possibly infinite tree.

(iii) Note that in accordance with proposal 2.2.14 unsolvable terms all have the same Böhm tree.

(iv) Böhm trees were introduced in Barendregt [1977], with instead of "$\bot$" the symbol "Ω".

The formal definition of Böhm trees can be given as follows:

10.1.4. Definition. Let Σ be the set as in definition 10.1.3. The Böhm tree of a λ-term M (notation BT(M)) is the Σ-labelled tree defined as follows:

if M is unsolvable, then

$$\text{BT}(M)(\langle\ \rangle) = \bot,$$
$$\text{BT}(M)(\langle k \rangle * \alpha)\uparrow \qquad \text{for all } k, \alpha;$$

if M is solvable, say M has the principal hnf $\lambda x_1 \cdots x_n.yM_0 \cdots M_{m-1}$,

then

$$\mathrm{BT}(M)(\langle\ \rangle) = \lambda x_1 \cdots x_n . y,$$

$$\begin{aligned} \mathrm{BT}(M)(\langle k \rangle * \alpha) &= \mathrm{BT}(M_k)(\alpha) && \text{for all } \alpha \text{ and } k < m, \\ &= \uparrow && \text{for all } \alpha \text{ and } k \geqslant m. \end{aligned}$$

Free and bound variables in a Böhm tree are defined as for terms. Trees differing only in the names of bound variables are identified. The best way to do this is to use the notation of de Bruijn explained in appendix C. To keep matters readable we will write (labels in) Böhm trees in the naive way (i.e. with names for bound variables) and assume the variable convention, for example by using at node α the bound variables $x_0^\alpha, x_1^\alpha, \ldots$.

10.1.5. EXAMPLES.

(i) $\mathrm{BT}(\mathbf{S}) = \lambda abc.$

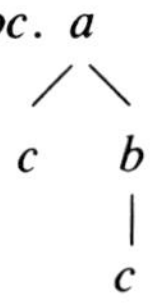

(ii) $\mathrm{BT}(\mathbf{S}a\Omega) = \lambda c.$

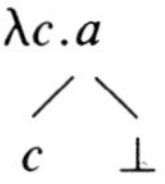

(iii) $\mathrm{BT}(\mathbf{Y}) = \lambda f.$

Indeed, note that $\mathbf{Y} \equiv \lambda f.\omega_f\omega_f$, with $\omega_f \equiv \lambda x.f(xx)$ and $\omega_f\omega_f = f(\omega_f\omega_f)$. Hence

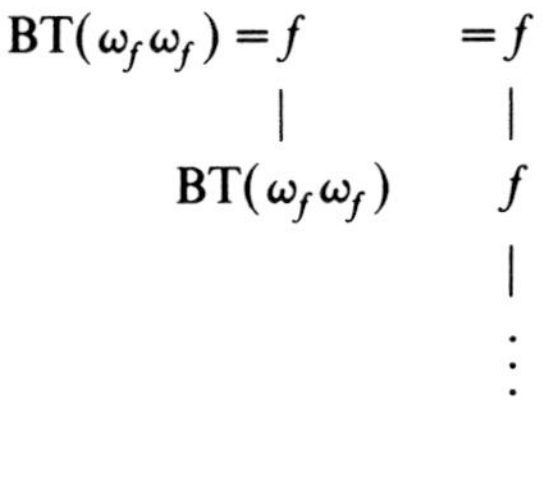

(iv) Let $A \equiv \mathbf{\Theta}(\lambda ax.\langle ax \rangle)$. Then $Ax \twoheadrightarrow \langle Ax \rangle \equiv \lambda z.z(Ax)$ and

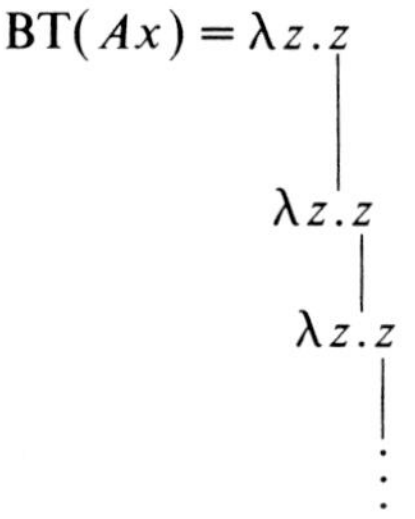

(v) Let M_n be uniform in n. Then

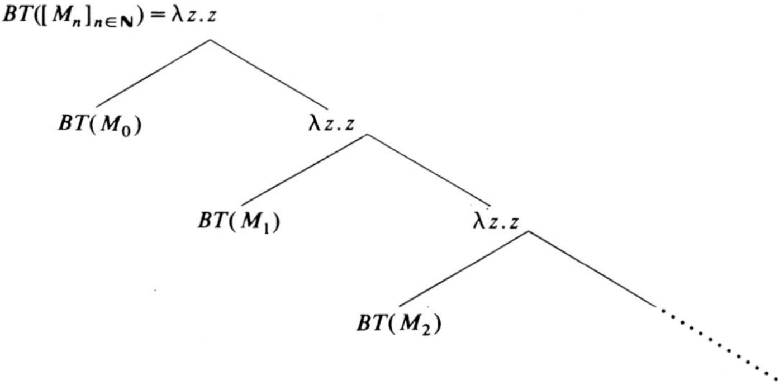

Note that $\mathrm{BT}([M_n])$ is independent of the generator of $[M_n]$ and its defining term. Moreover

$$\forall i \quad \mathrm{BT}(M_i) = \mathrm{BT}(N_i) \Leftrightarrow \mathrm{BT}([M_n]) = \mathrm{BT}([N_n])$$

for uniform M_n, N_n.

(vi) Let $M \equiv \mathbf{\Theta}(\lambda mab.a(mm))$. Then $M \to \lambda ab.a(MM)$ and

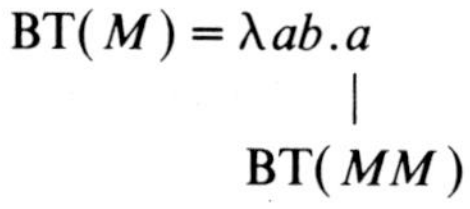

Now

$$\begin{aligned} MM &\to (\lambda ab.a(MM))M \\ &\to \lambda b.M(MM) \\ &\to \lambda b.(\lambda a'b'.a'(MM))(MM) \\ &\to \lambda bb'.(MM)(MM). \end{aligned}$$

Hence MM has an infinite head reduction and is therefore by theorem 8.3.11 unsolvable. It follows that

$$\mathrm{BT}(M) = \lambda ab.a \atop \quad\quad\quad \begin{array}{c} | \\ \bot \end{array}$$

10.1.6. PROPOSITION. *If* $M = N$, *then* $\mathrm{BT}(M) = \mathrm{BT}(N)$.

PROOF. Suppose $M = N$. By induction on $\mathrm{lh}(\alpha)$ it will be shown that $\mathrm{BT}(M)(\alpha) = \mathrm{BT}(N)(\alpha)$.

Suppose $\mathrm{lh}(\alpha) = 0$. Then $\alpha = \langle\ \rangle$. If M is unsolvable, so is N and $\mathrm{BT}(M)(\langle\ \rangle) = \bot = \mathrm{BT}(N)(\langle\ \rangle)$. If both M, N are solvable, then they have hnf's which by corollary 8.3.17(ii) have the form

$$M = \lambda x_1 \cdots x_n.xM_0 \cdots M_{m-1},$$

$$(*) \qquad N = \lambda x_1 \cdots x_n.xN_0 \cdots N_{m-1}$$

$$\text{with} \quad M_k = N_k \quad \text{for } k < m.$$

Now $\mathrm{BT}(M)(\langle\ \rangle) = \lambda x_1 \cdots x_n.x = \mathrm{BT}(N)(\langle\ \rangle)$.

Suppose $\mathrm{lh}(\alpha) > 0$. Then for some k, α' one has $\alpha = \langle k \rangle * \alpha'$. If M, N are unsolvable, then $\mathrm{BT}(M)(\alpha) = \uparrow = \mathrm{BT}(N)(\alpha)$. If M, N are solvable, then they have hnfs satisfying ($*$). Hence if $k \geqslant m$, then

$$\mathrm{BT}(M)(\langle k \rangle * \alpha') = \uparrow = \mathrm{BT}(N)(\langle k \rangle * \alpha');$$

if $k < m$, then

$$\mathrm{BT}(M)(\langle k \rangle * \alpha') = \mathrm{BT}(M_k)(\alpha') = \mathrm{BT}(N_k)(\alpha')$$

$$= \mathrm{BT}(N)(\langle k \rangle * \alpha')$$

by the induction hypothesis. □

The Böhm trees as introduced above are not effective: an oracle is needed since the notion of (un)solvability is not recursive. Therefore the following variant of labelled trees is introduced.

10.1.7. DEFINITION. Let Σ be a set (of symbols).

(i) A *partially* Σ-*labelled tree* is a partial map

$$\varphi : \mathrm{Seq} \rightharpoonup \Sigma \times \mathbb{N}$$

such that

(1) $\varphi(\sigma)\downarrow \wedge\ \tau < \sigma \Rightarrow \varphi(\tau)\downarrow$.

(2) $\varphi(\sigma) = \langle a, n \rangle \Rightarrow \forall k \geqslant n \varphi(\sigma * \langle k \rangle)\uparrow$.

(ii) The *underlying* (*naked*) *tree* of a partially Σ-labelled tree φ is

$$T_\varphi = \{\langle\ \rangle\} \cup \{\sigma \in \text{Seq} | \sigma = \sigma' * \langle k \rangle \wedge \varphi(\sigma') = \langle a, n \rangle \wedge k < n\}$$

(iii) Let $\sigma \in T_\varphi$. If $\varphi(\sigma) = \langle a, n \rangle$, the a is the *label at node* σ. If $\varphi(\sigma)\uparrow$, then the node σ is not labelled.

REMARKS. (i) The intuitive meaning of $\varphi(\sigma) = \langle a, n \rangle$ is: node σ has as label the word a and n successors in the tree. If $\sigma \in T_\varphi$, then σ does not necessarily have a label.

(ii) Clearly T_φ is a tree: if $\sigma \in T_\varphi$ and $\varphi(\sigma)\downarrow$, then by 10.1.7(1) for all $\sigma' < \sigma$, $\varphi(\sigma')\downarrow$ and hence $\sigma' \in T_\varphi$. If $\langle\ \rangle \neq \sigma \in T_\varphi$ and $\varphi(\sigma)\uparrow$, then $\sigma = \sigma' * \langle k \rangle$ and $\varphi(\sigma')\downarrow$; therefore for all $\sigma'' \leqslant \sigma'$, $\sigma'' \in T_\varphi$ and thus $\sigma'' \in T_\varphi$ for all $\sigma'' < \sigma$. Also $\sigma * \langle k+1 \rangle \in T_\varphi \Rightarrow \sigma * \langle k \rangle \in T_\varphi$.

(iii) If $\sigma \in T_\varphi$, then σ has only finitely many successors: if $\varphi(\sigma)\uparrow$, then σ has no successors; if $\varphi(\sigma)\downarrow$, then this follows from 10.1.7(i)(2).

10.1.8. NOTATIONS. (i) Partially labelled trees will be denoted by $A, B, \ldots$. $|A|$ is the underlying tree T_A corresponding to A. Write $\alpha \in A$ for $\alpha \in |A|$.

(ii) Write

$$A(\alpha) = \bot \quad \text{if } A(\alpha)\uparrow \text{ and yet } \alpha \in A,$$
$$A(\alpha) \quad \uparrow\uparrow \quad \text{if } A(\alpha)\uparrow \text{ and } \alpha \notin A.$$

Then there are three cases

(1) $A(\alpha)\downarrow$,

(2) $A(\alpha) = \bot$,

(3) $A(\alpha)\uparrow\uparrow$.

Note that $\alpha \in A$ in cases (1), (2); $A(\alpha)\uparrow$ in cases (2), (3).

EXAMPLE. Let $\Sigma = \{a, b, c\}$ and define A by

$$A(\langle\ \rangle) = \langle a, 3 \rangle,$$
$$A(\langle 0 \rangle) = \langle b, 0 \rangle, A(\langle 1 \rangle)\uparrow, A(\langle 2 \rangle) = \langle c, 2 \rangle,$$
$$A(\langle 2, 0 \rangle) = \langle a, 0 \rangle, A(\langle 2, 1 \rangle)\uparrow.$$

Then A is the partially Σ-labelled tree

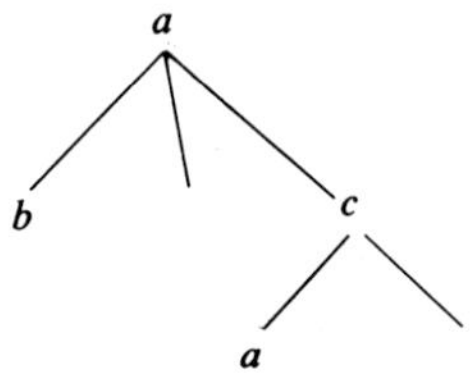

and one has $A(\langle 0 \rangle)\downarrow$, $A(\langle 1 \rangle)\uparrow$, $A(\langle 2 \rangle)\downarrow$ and $A(\langle 3 \rangle)\uparrow\uparrow$.

10.1.9. DEFINITION. Let Σ_1 be the set

$$\{\lambda x_1 \cdots x_n.y \mid n \geqslant 0, x_1, \ldots, x_n, y \text{ variables}\}.$$

The *effective Böhm tree* of M (notation $\mathrm{BT}^{\mathrm{e}}(M)$) is the partially Σ_1 labelled tree defined as follows:

if M is unsolvable, then for all σ

$$\mathrm{BT}^{\mathrm{e}}(M)(\sigma)\uparrow;$$

if M is solvable, and has the principal hnf $\lambda x_1 \cdots x_n.yM_0 \cdots M_{m-1}$,

$$\mathrm{BT}^{\mathrm{e}}(M)(\langle\ \ \rangle) = \langle \lambda x_1 \cdots x_n.y, m\rangle$$

and for all σ

$$\begin{aligned} \mathrm{BT}^{\mathrm{e}}(M)(\langle k\rangle * \sigma) &= \mathrm{BT}^{\mathrm{e}}(M_k)(\sigma) \quad \text{if } k < m,\\ &= \uparrow \qquad\qquad\qquad \text{if } k \geqslant m. \end{aligned}$$

10.1.10. REMARKS. (i) It is easy to show that $\mathrm{BT}^{\mathrm{e}}(M)$ is indeed a partially labelled tree; see exercise 10.6.1(i).

(ii) Let $M \equiv \lambda xy.yx(\Omega\Omega)$. Then $\mathrm{BT}(M)$ and $\mathrm{BT}^{\mathrm{e}}(M)$ are

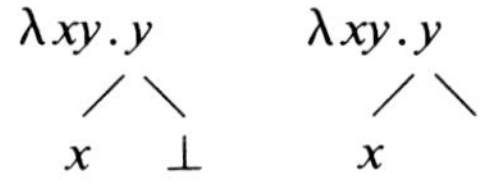

respectively.

(iii) Note that in general the underlying trees of $\mathrm{BT}(M)$ and $\mathrm{BT}^{\mathrm{e}}(M)$ are identical, see exercise 10.6.1(ii). Therefore the only difference between the two objects is as in (ii): the labels $\perp$ in $\mathrm{BT}(M)$ are removed in $\mathrm{BT}^{\mathrm{e}}(M)$.

So the objects $\mathrm{BT}(M)$ and $\mathrm{BT}^{\mathrm{e}}(M)$ are isomorphic. The only difference is intensional, i.e. in the way the objects are given to us (cf. Troelstra [1975]). It will turn out that the effective Böhm trees have several technical advantages.

10.1.11. CONVENTION. (i) From now on only the effective Böhm trees will be considered and will nevertheless be denoted by $\mathrm{BT}(M)$.

(ii) The informal notation of the examples 10.1.5 will still be used for making pictures of Böhm trees. Labels $\perp$ are drawn or omitted as we please.

10.1.12. DEFINITION. (i) A *Böhm-like tree* is a partially Σ_1-labelled tree with Σ_1 as in definition 10.1.9: $\mathfrak{B}$ is the set of all Böhm-like trees.

(ii) $\Lambda\mathfrak{B} = \{A \in \mathfrak{B} \mid \exists M \in \Lambda\, \mathrm{BT}(M) = A\}$. Note that $\Lambda\mathfrak{B}$ relativizes to $\Lambda_K\mathfrak{B}$ and $\Lambda_I\mathfrak{B}$.

(iii) $A \in \mathfrak{B}$ is *r.e.* iff the partial function A is partial recursive (after some coding of Σ_1).

(iv) $A \in \mathfrak{B}$ is $\perp$*-free* iff $\forall \alpha \in A\ A(\alpha)\downarrow$.

(v) If $A \in \mathfrak{B}$, then $d(A) = \sup\{\mathrm{lh}(\alpha) \mid \alpha \in A\}$. Note that $d(A) < \infty$ iff A is finite.

Given a tree A and a node $\alpha \in A$, then the subtree of A at α consists of all $\beta \in A$ extending α. More precisely:

10.1.13. DEFINITION. (i) Let $A \in \mathfrak{B}$ and $\alpha \in \mathrm{Seq}$. If $\alpha \in A$, then the *subtree of A at node* α (notation A_α) is

$$A_\alpha = \lambda\!\!\!\lambda \beta.A(\alpha * \beta).$$

Clearly $\forall A \in \mathfrak{B}\ \forall \alpha\ A_\alpha \in \mathfrak{B}$.

(ii) $\mathrm{BT}_\alpha(M) = (\mathrm{BT}(M))_\alpha$.

(iii) Let $M \in \Lambda$ and $\alpha \in \mathrm{BT}(M)$. Define $M_\alpha \in \Lambda$ by induction on $\mathrm{lh}(\alpha)$:

$$M_{\langle\ \rangle} \equiv M,$$

$$M_{\langle i \rangle * \alpha} \equiv (M_i)_\alpha \quad \text{if } \lambda\vec{x}.yM_0 \cdots M_{m-1} \text{ is the principal hnf of } M.$$

Note that if M has no hnf or $i > m$, then $\langle i \rangle * \alpha \notin \mathrm{BT}(M)$.

10.1.14. EXAMPLES. (i) Let A be

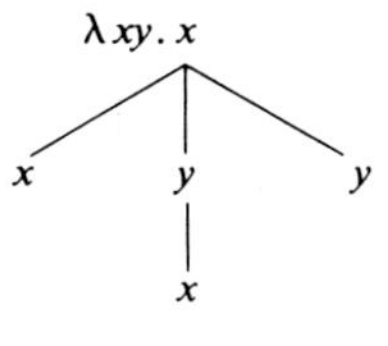

Then

$$A_{\langle\ \rangle} = A, \qquad A_{\langle 1 \rangle} = \begin{array}{c} y \\ | \\ x \end{array},$$

$$A_{\langle 0 \rangle} = A_{\langle 1,0 \rangle} = x, \quad \text{and} \quad A_{\langle 2 \rangle} = y.$$

(ii) Let $M = \lambda x.\mathbf{I}x\Omega(\mathbf{I}x)$. Then $M_{\langle 0 \rangle} = \Omega$ and $M_{\langle 1 \rangle} \equiv \mathbf{I}x$.

10.1.15. LEMMA. *For $M \in \Lambda$ and $\alpha \in \mathrm{BT}(M)$*

$$\mathrm{BT}(M_\alpha) = \mathrm{BT}_\alpha(M).$$

Proof. By induction on $\text{lh}(\alpha)$. The case $\alpha = \langle\ \rangle$ is trivial, and if $\alpha = \langle i \rangle * \beta$ and M has a principal hnf, say $\lambda\vec{x}.yM_0 \cdots M_{m-1}$, then

$$\begin{aligned} \text{BT}(M_\alpha) &= \text{BT}((M_i)_\beta) \\ &= \text{BT}_\beta(M_i) \quad \text{by the induction hypothesis,} \\ &= \text{BT}_{\langle i \rangle * \beta}(M). \end{aligned}$$

The last equality holds since for all γ

$$\begin{aligned} \text{BT}_\beta(M_i)(\gamma) &= \text{BT}(M_i)(\beta * \gamma) \\ &= \text{BT}(M)(\langle i \rangle * \beta * \gamma) = \text{BT}_{\langle i \rangle * \beta}(M)(\gamma). \quad \square \end{aligned}$$

Each finite Böhm-like tree is the Böhm tree of a λ-term.

10.1.16. Definition. Let $A \in \mathfrak{B}$ be finite. By induction on the $d(A)$, a λ-term $M(A)$ (sometimes denoted as M_A), will be defined having A as Böhm tree.

Case 1. $A = \bot$. Take $M(A) \equiv \Omega$.

Case 2. $A = \lambda\vec{x}.y$. Take $M(A) \equiv \lambda\vec{x}.y$.

Case 3. $A = \begin{array}{c}\lambda\vec{x}.y \\ / \quad \backslash \\ A_1 \cdots A_n\end{array}$. Take $M(A) \equiv \lambda\vec{x}.yM(A_1) \cdots M(A_n)$.

10.1.17. Corollary. *For finite* $A \in \mathfrak{B}$, $\text{BT}(M(A)) = A$. $\square$

Example. Let A be

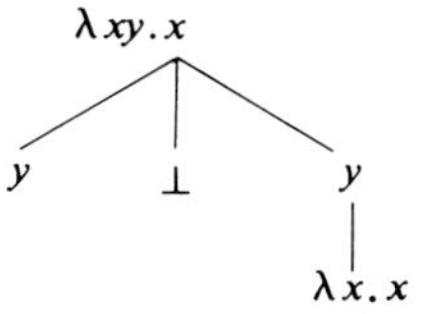

Then $M(A) \equiv \lambda xy.xy\Omega(y\mathbf{I})$.

Note that $M \in \Lambda$ has a nf iff $\text{BT}(M)$ is finite and $\bot$-free.

10.1.18. Definition. (i) Let $A \in \mathfrak{B}$. For $k \in \mathbb{N}$ define

$$A^k(\alpha) = \begin{cases} A(\alpha) & \text{if } \text{lh}(\alpha) < k, \\ \uparrow & \text{else.} \end{cases}$$

(ii) $\text{BT}^k(M) = (\text{BT}(M))^k$.

(iii) $M^{(k)} \equiv M(\text{BT}^k(M))$.

(iv) For $A, B \in \mathfrak{B}$ write $A =_k B$ iff $A^k = B^k$.

Note that A^k is a finite Böhm tree resulting from A by cutting off all subtrees at depth k. For example, if A is

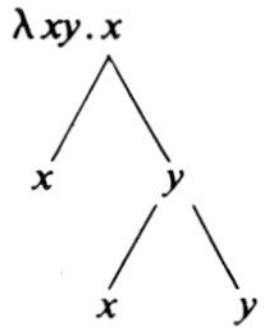

then

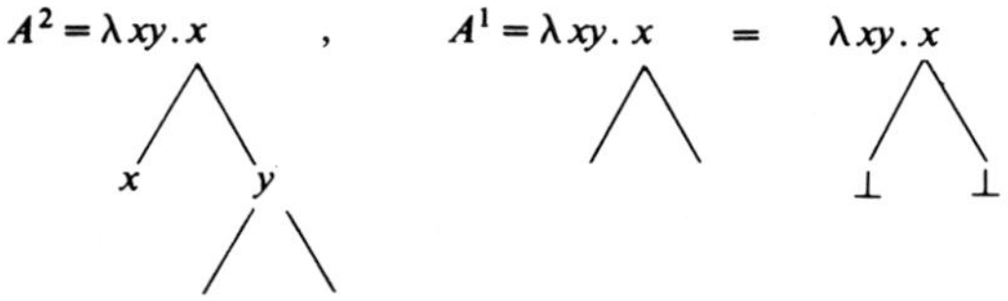

and $A^0 = \perp$.

10.1.19. LEMMA. *For* $M \in \Lambda$ $\mathrm{BT}(M^{(k)}) = \mathrm{BT}^k(M)$.

PROOF. $\mathrm{BT}(M^{(k)}) = \mathrm{BT}(M(\mathrm{BT}^k(M))) = \mathrm{BT}^k(M)$ by corollary 10.1.17. □

Now a characterization will be given of $\Lambda\mathfrak{B}$, i.e. of those trees that are the tree of a term.

Intuitively it should be obvious what the set of free variables of an $A \in \mathfrak{B}$ is. The following definition makes this notion more explicit.

10.1.20. DEFINITION. Let $A \in \mathfrak{B}$.

(i) Let $\sigma \in A$. If $A(\sigma) = \langle \lambda x_1 \cdots x_n . y, m \rangle$, define

$$\vec{x}_\sigma = x_1, \ldots, x_n, \qquad y_\sigma = y, \qquad m_\sigma = m.$$

If $A(\sigma) = \uparrow$, then $\vec{x}_\sigma = y_\sigma = m_\sigma = \uparrow$.

(ii) If $\sigma \in A$, then $\vec{x}_{\bar{\sigma}}$ (the set of binding variables up to σ) is defined inductively as follows (see also the remark before 10.1.5):

$$\vec{x}_{\overline{\langle\,\rangle}} = \vec{x}_{\langle\,\rangle}, \qquad \vec{x}_{\overline{\sigma * \langle k \rangle}} = \vec{x}_{\bar{\sigma}}, \vec{x}_{\sigma * \langle k \rangle}.$$

Example. $\vec{x}_{\overline{\langle 1,0 \rangle}} = \vec{x}_{\langle\,\rangle}, \vec{x}_{\langle 1 \rangle}, \vec{x}_{\langle 1,0 \rangle}$.

(iii) $\mathrm{FV}_A(\sigma) = \begin{cases} \{y_\sigma\} - \{\vec{x}_{\bar{\sigma}}\} & \text{if } A(\sigma)\downarrow, \\ \emptyset & \text{else.} \end{cases}$

(iv) $\mathrm{FV}(A) = \bigcup \{\mathrm{FV}_A(\sigma) \mid \sigma \in A\}$.

(v) A is *closed* if $\mathrm{FV}(A) = \emptyset$.

EXAMPLE. Let A be

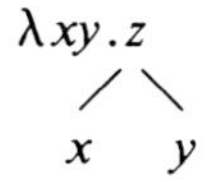

Then $\vec{x}_{\langle\ \rangle} = x, y$; $y_{\langle\ \rangle} = z$, $m_{\langle\ \rangle} = 2$ etc. $\mathrm{FV}(A) = \{z\}$.

10.1.21. PROPOSITION. *Let $A = \mathrm{BT}(M)$ and let $\vec{x}_\alpha, y_\alpha, m_\alpha$ be as in definition* 10.1.20. *If $A(\alpha) = \downarrow$, then M_α has the principal* hnf

$$\lambda\vec{x}_\alpha . y_\alpha M_{\alpha * \langle 0\rangle} \cdots M_{\alpha * \langle m_\alpha - 1\rangle}.$$

PROOF. This is so by definition. Do exercise 10.6.2. □

10.1.22. REMARK. Note that $\mathrm{FV}(\mathrm{BT}(M)) \subseteq \mathrm{FV}(M)$; see exercise 10.6.3. The inclusion may be proper. Let e.g.

$$M \rightarrow \lambda zx.x(Mz),$$

then $\mathrm{BT}(Mz)$ looks like

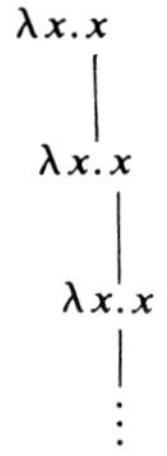

and hence is closed, but Mz is not closed (and not even convertible to a closed term). We say that in $\mathrm{BT}(Mz)$, "*z is pushed into infinity*".

10.1.23. THEOREM. *Let $A \in \mathfrak{B}$. Then*

$$A \in \Lambda_K\mathfrak{B} \Leftrightarrow \mathrm{FV}(A) \textit{ is finite and } A \textit{ is } \text{r.e.}$$

PROOF. ($\Rightarrow$) If $A = \mathrm{BT}(M)$, then by remark 10.1.22 $\mathrm{FV}(A) \subseteq \mathrm{FV}(M)$ is finite. Moreover, as $\mathrm{BT}(M)$ is given by an effective procedure, A is r.e. by Church's thesis.

($\Leftarrow$) Let A be partial recursive and let $\mathrm{FV}(A) = \vec{a}$. Define inductively $\vec{z}_\alpha$:

$$\begin{aligned} \vec{z}_{\langle\ \rangle} &= \vec{a} \quad \text{if } A(\langle\ \rangle)\downarrow, \\ &= \uparrow \quad \text{else.} \end{aligned}$$

$$\begin{aligned} \vec{z}_{\alpha * \langle k\rangle} &= \vec{z}_\alpha, \vec{x}_\alpha \quad \text{if } A(\alpha)\downarrow, \\ &= \uparrow \quad \text{else} \end{aligned}$$

(where $\vec{x}_\alpha$ is defined in definition 10.1.20(i)). Note that for all α such that $A(\alpha)\downarrow$

(1) $$\vec{z}_\alpha, \vec{x}_\alpha = \vec{a}, \vec{x}_{\bar{\alpha}} = \vec{z}_{\alpha * \langle k \rangle} \quad \text{for all } k < m_\alpha.$$

By theorem 8.1.6 there is an $\mathbf{E} \in \Lambda^0$ such that $\mathbf{E}\ulcorner M \urcorner \twoheadrightarrow M$. It may be assumed that if M is unsolvable then $\mathbf{E}M$ is unsolvable. (This is in fact true for the $\mathbf{E}$ constructed in theorem 8.1.6, but if you do not wish to check this, take

$$\mathbf{E}' \equiv \lambda x.x\mathbf{T}\mathbf{I}\mathbf{I}\mathbf{E}x).$$

If $A(\alpha)\downarrow$, define

$$B_\alpha \equiv \lambda m \lambda \vec{z}_\alpha \lambda \vec{x}_\alpha . y_\alpha \Big(\mathbf{E} m \ulcorner \alpha * \langle 0 \rangle \urcorner \vec{z}_{\alpha * \langle 0 \rangle} \Big) \cdots$$

$$\cdots \Big(\mathbf{E} m \ulcorner \alpha * \langle m_\alpha - 1 \rangle \urcorner \vec{z}_{\alpha * \langle m_\alpha - 1 \rangle} \Big).$$

Note that by (1), one has $B_\alpha \in \Lambda^0$ for all α such that $A(\alpha)\downarrow$.

Since A is partial recursive, there is a partial recursive function ψ such that

$$\psi(\alpha) = \begin{cases} \# B_\alpha & \text{if } A(\alpha)\downarrow, \\ \uparrow & \text{else.} \end{cases}$$

Let F λ-define ψ. By the second fixed point theorem 6.5.9, there exists a term $M \in \Lambda^0$ such that

$$M \twoheadrightarrow \lambda s.\mathbf{E}(Fs) \ulcorner M \urcorner .$$

If $\psi(\alpha) = \downarrow$,

$$\begin{aligned} M \ulcorner \alpha \urcorner \vec{z}_\alpha &\twoheadrightarrow \mathbf{E}(F \ulcorner \alpha \urcorner) \ulcorner M \urcorner \vec{z}_\alpha \\ &\twoheadrightarrow \mathbf{E} \ulcorner B_\alpha \urcorner \ulcorner M \urcorner \vec{z}_\alpha \\ &\twoheadrightarrow B_\alpha \ulcorner M \urcorner \vec{z}_\alpha \\ &\twoheadrightarrow \lambda \vec{x}_\alpha . y_\alpha \Big(\mathbf{E} \ulcorner M \urcorner \ulcorner \alpha * \langle 0 \rangle \urcorner \vec{z}_{\alpha * \langle 0 \rangle} \Big) \cdots \end{aligned}$$

(2) $$\twoheadrightarrow \lambda \vec{x}_\alpha . y_\alpha \Big(M \ulcorner \alpha * \langle 0 \rangle \urcorner \vec{z}_{\alpha * \langle 0 \rangle} \Big) \cdots$$

Similarly, if $A(\alpha)\uparrow$, then $M \ulcorner \alpha \urcorner \vec{z}_\alpha$ is unsolvable.

Claim. For all α one has $\mathrm{BT}(M\ulcorner\alpha\urcorner\vec{z}_\alpha)=A_\alpha$. Indeed, if $A(\alpha)\uparrow$, then A_α and $\mathrm{BT}(M\ulcorner\alpha\urcorner\vec{z}_\alpha)$ are both the empty tree, since then $M\ulcorner\alpha\urcorner\vec{z}_\alpha$ is unsolvable. If $A(\alpha)\downarrow$, then we will show by induction on $\mathrm{lh}(\beta)$ that

$$\mathrm{BT}(M\ulcorner\alpha\urcorner\vec{z}_\alpha)(\beta)=A(\alpha*\beta)\quad(=A_\alpha(\beta)).$$

If $\beta=\langle\ \rangle$, by (2),

$$\mathrm{BT}(M\ulcorner\alpha\urcorner z_\alpha)(\langle\ \rangle)=\langle\lambda\vec{x}_\alpha.y_\alpha,m_\alpha\rangle=A(\alpha).$$

Suppose $\beta=\langle k\rangle*\beta'$. If $k<m_\alpha$, then

$$\begin{aligned}&\mathrm{BT}(M\ulcorner\alpha\urcorner\vec{z}_\alpha)(\beta)=\\&=\mathrm{BT}(M\ulcorner\alpha*\langle k\rangle\urcorner\vec{z}_{\alpha*\langle k\rangle})(\beta')\quad\text{by the definition of BT and (2),}\\&=A(\alpha*\langle k\rangle*\beta')\quad\text{by the induction hypothesis,}\\&=A(\alpha*\beta).\end{aligned}$$

If $k\geqslant m_\alpha$, then

$$\mathrm{BT}(M\ulcorner\alpha\urcorner\vec{z}_\alpha)(\langle k\rangle*\beta')=\uparrow$$

and by condition 2 in definition 10.1.7(i) also

$$A(\alpha*\langle k\rangle*\beta')=\uparrow.$$

This proves the claim. It follows that

$$\mathrm{BT}(M\ulcorner\langle\ \rangle\urcorner\vec{z}_{\langle\ \rangle})=A_{\langle\ \rangle}=A,$$

hence $A\in\Lambda_K\mathfrak{B}$. □

Now an analogous characterization of $\Lambda_I\mathfrak{B}$ will be given.

10.1.24. Definition. Let $A\in\mathfrak{B}$ and let $\vec{x}_\alpha, y_\alpha$ be defined as in definition 10.1.20(i). A *variable indicator* for A is a partial map

$$\chi:\mathrm{Seq}\rightharpoonup\{\text{sequences of variables}\}$$

such that:

(1) $\alpha\in A\Leftrightarrow\chi(\alpha)\downarrow$,
(2) $\{\vec{x}_\alpha\}\cup\{\chi(\alpha)\}=\{y_\alpha\}\cup\bigcup\{\chi(\alpha*\langle i\rangle)\mid i<m_\alpha\}$,
(3) $\{\vec{x}_\alpha\}\cap\{\chi(\alpha)\}=\emptyset$.

In the proof of the following theorem it will be seen that if $M\in\Lambda_I$, then $\chi(\alpha)=\mathrm{FV}(M_\alpha)$ is a variable indicator for $\mathrm{BT}(M)$.

10.1.25. THEOREM. *Let* $A \in \mathfrak{B}$. *Then*

$$A \in \Lambda_I \mathfrak{B} \Leftrightarrow \mathrm{FV}(A) \text{ is finite, } A \text{ is r.e.}$$

and has a partial recursive variable indicator.

PROOF. ($\Rightarrow$) Since $A \in \Lambda_I \mathfrak{B} \subseteq \Lambda_K \mathfrak{B}$ it follows from theorem 10.1.25 that $\mathrm{FV}(A)$ is finite and A is r.e. Let $A = \mathrm{BT}(M)$, with $M \in \Lambda_I$. Define

$$\chi(\alpha) = \begin{cases} \mathrm{FV}(M_\alpha) & \text{if } \alpha \in A\downarrow, \\ \uparrow & \text{else.} \end{cases}$$

Then χ is partial recursive. Moreover χ is a variable indicator. Condition 1 in definition 10.1.24 is trivially satisfied. If $A(\alpha)\downarrow$ then by proposition 10.1.21 M_α has the principal hnf

$$\lambda \vec{x}_\alpha . y_\alpha M_{\alpha * \langle 0 \rangle} \cdots M_{\alpha * \langle m_\alpha - 1 \rangle} \in \Lambda_I .$$

Hence by lemma 9.1.2(iv) it is clear that conditions 2 and 3 are satisfied as well.

($\Leftarrow$) Let

$$\vec{z}_\alpha = \chi(\alpha),$$
$$\vec{x}_\alpha, y_\alpha, m_\alpha \quad \text{as in definition 10.1.20.}$$

Define

$$B_\alpha \equiv \lambda m \vec{z}_\alpha \vec{x}_\alpha . y_\alpha \big(\mathbf{E}_I m \ulcorner \alpha * \langle 0 \rangle \urcorner \vec{z}_{\alpha * \langle 0 \rangle} \big) \cdots ,$$

$$\psi(\alpha) = \# B_\alpha .$$

Since χ is a variable indicator it follows that $B_\alpha \in \Lambda_I^0$ if $A(\alpha)\downarrow$. Moreover since A and χ are partial recursive, so is ψ. The rest of the proof proceeds analogously to the proof of theorem 10.1.23. □

One might wonder why the characterization of $\Lambda_I \mathfrak{B}$ cannot be given in a simpler way.

10.1.26. DEFINITION. $A \in \mathfrak{B}$ *looks like a* λI*-tree* iff $\mathrm{FV}(A)$ is finite, A is r.e. and

$$\forall \alpha \in A \quad \{\vec{x}_\alpha\} \subseteq \bigcup \{\mathrm{FV}_A(\beta) \mid \beta > \alpha\}.$$

In exercise 10.6.4 it will be shown that for some $A \in \Lambda_K \mathfrak{B}$, A looks like a λI-tree but has no variable indicator; hence $A \notin \Lambda_I \mathfrak{B}$.

10.2. Comparing Böhm trees; the tree topology on Λ

Böhm like trees are in fact partial functions: $\mathfrak{B} \subseteq \mathrm{Seq} \rightarrowtail \Sigma_1$. Since partial functions with inclusion form a cpo, see example 1.2.30, the relation $\subseteq$ is also a partial order on $\mathfrak{B}$.
Note that for $A, B \in \mathfrak{B}$

$A \subseteq B \Leftrightarrow$ A results from B (both drawn as effective trees) by cutting off some subtrees.

10.2.1. EXAMPLES.

(1) 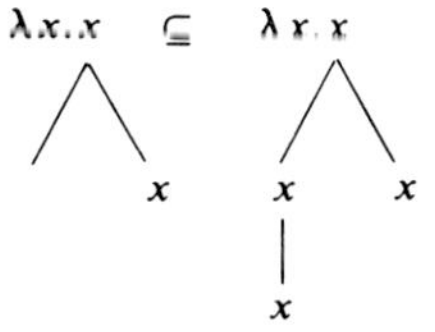

(2) 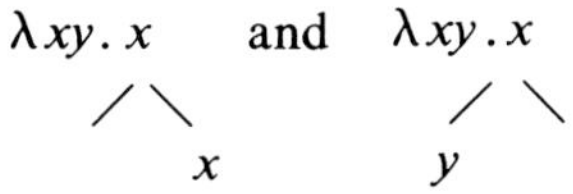

are consistent (see definition 1.2.28).

(3) 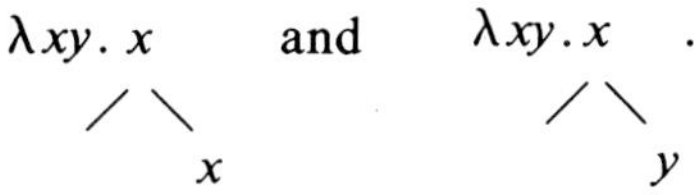

are not consistent. Also

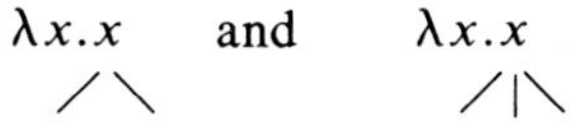

are not consistent, since for the first tree $A(\langle\ \rangle) = \langle \lambda x.x, 2\rangle$ and for the second one $A(\langle\ \rangle) = \langle \lambda x.x, 3\rangle$.

In proposition 1.2.31(ii) it is proved that $\mathrm{Seq} \rightarrowtail \Sigma_1$ is a coherent algebraic cpo. The same is true for the subset $\mathfrak{B}$.

10.2.2. PROPOSITION. (i) $(\mathfrak{B}, \subseteq)$ *is a coherent algebraic* cpo, *with A compact iff A finite.*

(ii) *If* $\Phi \subseteq \mathfrak{B}$ *is non empty, then* $\cap \Phi \in \mathfrak{B}$ *and is the infimum of* Φ.

PROOF. Let $\Phi \subseteq \mathfrak{B}$ be consistent. Then $\cup \Phi$ is a partial function. It is not hard to show that $\cup \Phi \in \mathfrak{B}$. Therefore $\mathfrak{B}$ is a coherent cpo. Each Böhm like tree is the union of finite ones ($A = \cup_k A^{(k)}$). Clearly finite trees are compact. Hence $\mathfrak{B}$ is algebraic.

(ii) Also easy. □

10.2.3. NOTATION. Let $M, N \in \Lambda$.
 (i) $M \approx N$ iff $\mathrm{BT}(M) = \mathrm{BT}(N)$.
 (ii) $M \sqsubseteq\!\!\!\sim N$ iff $\mathrm{BT}(M) \subseteq \mathrm{BT}(N)$.

The tree topology on Λ.

10.2.4. DEFINITION. Consider the cpo $\mathfrak{B} = (\mathfrak{B}, \subseteq)$ with the Scott topology. The *tree* topology on the set Λ is the smallest one that makes the map

$$BT: \Lambda \to \mathfrak{B}$$

continuous; i.e. the open sets of Λ are of the form $\mathrm{BT}^{-1}(O)$ with O Scott open in $\mathfrak{B}$.

Using the tree topology, familiar λ-calculus concepts can be expressed topologically, e.g. nf's are isolated points and unsolvable terms are compactification points, see § 20.5.

In §14.3 it will be proved that application and abstraction are continuous with respect to the tree topology on Λ. For application this is a non trivial result which has several interesting consequences.

In § 20.5 the tree topology for term models will be defined as the quotient topology.

Note that the tree topology on Λ itself is not yet T_0, for if $\mathrm{BT}(M) = \mathrm{BT}(N)$, then M, N cannot be separated.

Topological notions used for Λ without specifications always refer to the tree topology.

10.2.5. EXAMPLE. Let $\mathrm{SOL} \subseteq \Lambda$ be the set of solvable terms. Then SOL is open.

PROOF. In a cpo the set $\{x \mid x \neq \bot\}$ is always Scott open. Hence $\mathrm{SOL} = \mathrm{BT}^{-1}\{A \mid A \neq \bot\}$ is open in Λ. $\square$

10.2.6. LEMMA. *$O \subseteq \Lambda$ is open iff*
 (1) $M \in O,\ M \sqsubseteq\!\!\!\sim N \Rightarrow N \in O$,
 (2) *if* $M \in O$ *and* $BT(M) = \bigcup_i BT(M_i)$, *with* $\{BT(M_i)\}_i \subseteq \mathfrak{B}$ *directed, then* $\exists i\ M_i \in O$.

PROOF. ($\Rightarrow$) By assumption $O = \mathrm{BT}^{-1}(X)$ with $X \subseteq \mathfrak{B}$ open. Then (1), (2) follow from the definition of Scott topology.

($\Leftarrow$) Let $O \subseteq \Lambda$ and assume (1), (2). Define

$$X = \mathrm{BT}(O) = \{\mathrm{BT}(M) \mid M \in O\},$$

$$X^{\vee} = \{B \in \mathfrak{B} \mid \exists A \in X\ A \subseteq B\}.$$

Then $\mathrm{BT}^{-1}(X^{\vee}) = O$. Claim: $X^{\vee}$ is Scott open. The first condition is trivial.

As to the second condition, let $\bigcup A_i \in X^{\vee}$ with $\{A_i\}_i$ directed. Then for some B

$$\bigcup A_i \supseteq B \in X$$

i.e. $\bigcup A_i \supseteq \mathrm{BT}(M)$ with $M \in O$, hence

$$\bigcup_{i,n}(A_i^{(n)} \cap \mathrm{BT}(M)) = \mathrm{BT}(M).$$

Set

$$\mathrm{BT}(M_i^{(n)}) = A_i^{(n)} \cap \mathrm{BT}(M),$$

then $\{\mathrm{BT}(M_i^{(n)})\}_{i,n}$ is directed and

$$\bigcup_{i,n} \mathrm{BT}(M_i^{(n)}) = \mathrm{BT}(M).$$

By condition (2) for some i, n

$$M_i^{(n)} \in O.$$

But then $A_i \supseteq \mathrm{BT}(M_i^{(n)}) \in X$, hence $A_i \in X^{\vee}$. □

10.2.7. COROLLARY. (i) *The sets*

$$O_{M,k} = \{N \in \Lambda \mid M^{(k)} \sqsubseteq\!\!\!\sim N\}$$

form a base for the tree topology on Λ.

(ii) *The set* NF *of* β*-normal forms is dense in* Λ.

PROOF. (i) By the lemma these sets are open. Now let $N \in O$, with $O \subseteq \Lambda$ open. Since

$$\mathrm{BT}(N) = \bigcup_i \mathrm{BT}(N^{(i)})$$

it follows by the lemma that for some k

$$N^{(k)} \in O.$$

But then $N \in O_{N,k} \subseteq O$.

(ii) Let $O_{M,k}$ be a basis open set and let $A = \mathrm{BT}(M^{(k)})$. Define A_1 to be A with all $\perp$'s replaced by $\lambda x.x$ and $M_1 \equiv M(A_1)$. Then $A \subseteq A_1$, hence $M^{(k)} \sqsubseteq\!\!\!\sim M_1$, i.e. $M_1 \in O_{M,k}$. Since M_1 is a nf, the result follows by (i). □

Infinite η *reduction for trees.*

Note that although $\lambda x.x =_\eta \lambda xy.xy$, the Böhm trees of these terms differ. Therefore some kind of "η-conversion" will be considered for Böhm like trees. Since these are infinite objects, the conversion will have an infinitary character.

The notion will be used in the rest of this chapter and in the analysis of the models D_∞ and $P\omega$ in §§19.1 and 19.2.

10.2.8. DEFINITION. (i) Let $A \in \mathfrak{B}$ and let $\alpha \in A$ have the label $\langle \lambda \vec{x}.y, n \rangle$. An η-expansion of A at α is the result A' of replacing in A the subtree A_α, which has the form

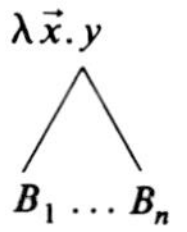

by

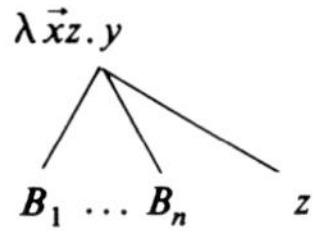

(ii) *Notation.* $A' \to_\eta A$ if A' is an η-expansion of A at some node $\alpha \in A$ with $A(\alpha) \neq \bot$. The transitive reflexive closure of $\to_\eta$ is denoted by $\twoheadrightarrow_\eta$.

Wadsworth [1971] remarked that one can have also infinite η-expansions as shown by the following.

10.2.9. EXAMPLE. Let $J \equiv \boldsymbol{\Theta}(\lambda jxy.x(jy))$. Then $Jx \twoheadrightarrow \lambda z.x(Jz)$, hence

$B = BT(Jx) =$

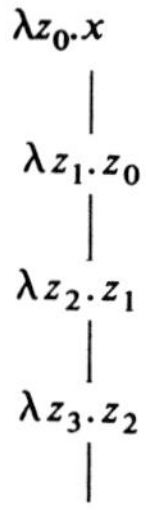

One can consider B as the limit of the following series of η-expansions:

$$A = x\ {}_\eta\!\leftarrow \mathrm{BT}(\lambda z_0.xz_0)\,{}_\eta\!\leftarrow \mathrm{BT}(\lambda z_0.x(\lambda z_1.z_0 z_1))\,{}_\eta\!\leftarrow \ldots .$$

Therefore B is called an *infinite η-expansion* of A (and A an *infinite η-reduct* of B). The following will define this notion in general.

10.2.10. DEFINITION. Let $A \in \mathfrak{B}$ and $X \subseteq \mathrm{Seq}$.

(i) X *extends* A iff

(1) X is a tree and $|A| \subseteq X$; moreover X is finitely branching.

(2) $A(\alpha) = \bot \Rightarrow \alpha$ is an endpoint (i.e. terminal node) in X.

(ii) If X extends A, then $(A:X)$ is the Böhm like tree (with underlying tree X) defined as follows.

(1) $$(A;X)(\alpha)=A(\alpha)$$
if $\alpha \in A$ and has the same number of successors in A as in X.

(2) $$(A;X)(\alpha)=\langle \lambda \vec{x} z_0^\alpha \cdots z_{k-1}^\alpha . y,\ m+k\rangle$$
if $A(\alpha)=\langle \lambda \vec{x}.y, m\rangle$ and α has $m+k$ successors in X.

$$(A;X)(\alpha)=\langle \lambda z_0^\alpha \cdots z_{n-1}^\alpha . z_i^\beta,\ n\rangle$$

(3) if $\alpha=\beta * \langle k+i\rangle \in X-|A|$, $\beta \in A$ and β has k successors in A and α has n successors in X;

or

(4) if $\alpha=\beta * \langle i\rangle \in X-|A|$, $\beta \notin A$ and α has n successors in X.

$$(A;X)(\alpha)=\uparrow \quad \text{if } \alpha \notin X.$$

(The numbers (1), ..., (4) refer to the next example.)

(iii) B is a *(possibly) infinite η-expansion* of A (notation $B \geqslant_\eta A$ or $A \leqslant_\eta B$) if for some $X \subseteq$ Seq extending A one has $B=(A;X)$.

The tree $(A;X)$ is simpler than it seems.

10.2.11. Examples. (i) Let

$A=\lambda x.x$

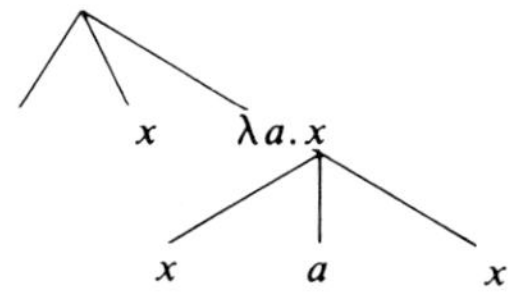

$,|A| =$

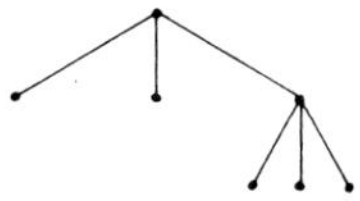

$X =$

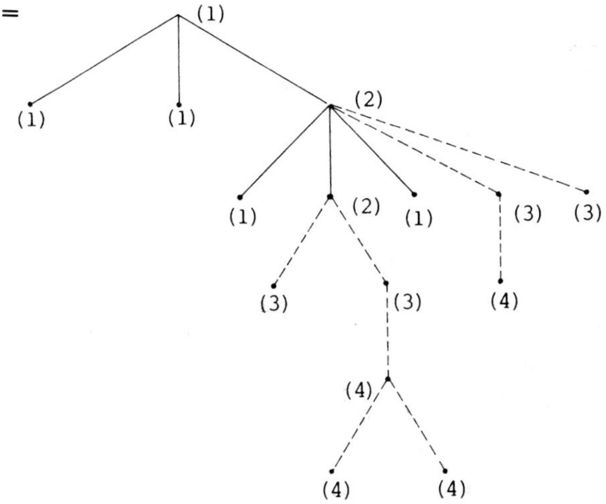

Then

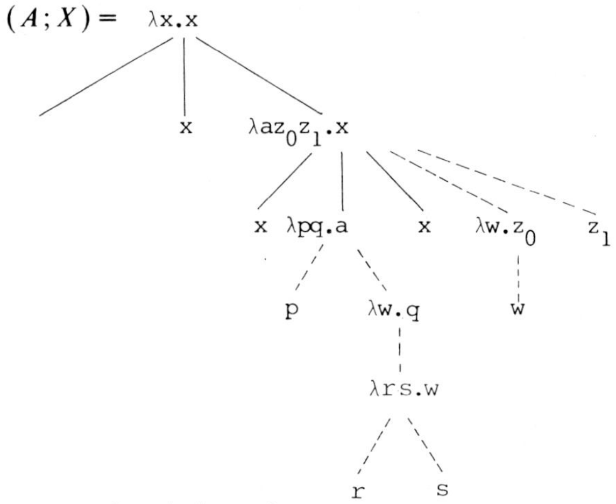

(ii) Let $A = x$; then $|A| = \cdot$. Let

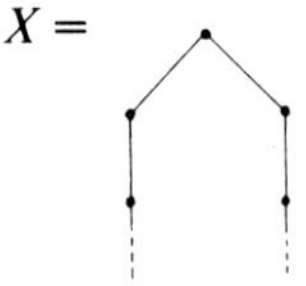

Then

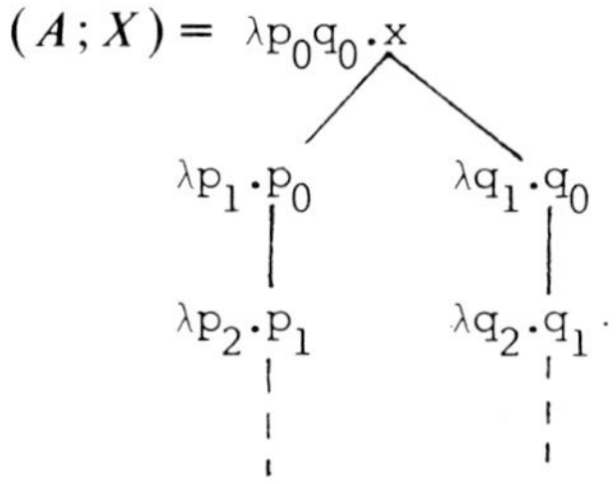

Thus for X extending A, the tree $(A;X)$ is the obvious (infinite) η-expansion of A with underlying tree X.

10.2.12. LEMMA. (i) *$(\mathfrak{B}, \leqslant_\eta)$ is a partially ordered set.*
(ii) *If $A \leqslant_\eta B$ and $|B| - |A|$ is finite, then $B \twoheadrightarrow_\eta A$.*

PROOF. (i) Obviously $\leqslant_\eta$ is reflexive and transitive. Note that if $X = |A|$, then $(A;X) = A$. Hence

$$A \leqslant_\eta B \leqslant_\eta A \Rightarrow B = (A;|B|) \wedge |A| = |B|$$
$$\Rightarrow A = B.$$

(ii) Obvious. □

10.2.13. LEMMA. *Suppose* $A \leqslant_\eta A_1$ *and* $A \leqslant_\eta A_2$. *Then*

(i) $\exists B\ A_1 \leqslant_\eta B \wedge A_2 \leqslant_\eta B$. (*Upside down Church–Rosser property. The usual form also holds, see proposition* 10.2.15.)

(ii) $A_1 \subseteq A_2 \Rightarrow A_1 = A_2$.

PROOF. Let $A_i = (A; X_i)$ for $i = 1, 2$.

(i) Take $B = (A; X_1 \cup X_2)$.

(ii) Since $A_1 \subseteq A_2$ one has $X_1 \subseteq X_2$. Suppose $\alpha \in X_2 - X_1$, then $\beta \in A_1$ and $A_1(\beta)\uparrow$ for some $\beta < \alpha$. But then already $\beta \in A$ and $A(\beta)\uparrow$. By definition 10.2.10(i)(2) it follows that β is a terminal node in X_2, contradicting $\beta < \alpha \in X_2$. Therefore $X_1 = X_2$ and the result follows. □

10.2.14. LEMMA. *Let* $A \subseteq B$. *Then*

(i) $B \leqslant_\eta B' \Rightarrow \exists A'\ A \leqslant_\eta A' \subseteq B'$,

(ii) $A \leqslant_\eta A' \Rightarrow \exists B'\ A' \subseteq B' \geqslant_\eta B$,

(iii) $A \geqslant_\eta A' \Rightarrow \exists B'\ A' \subseteq B' \leqslant_\eta B$.

Diagrammatically:

(i)

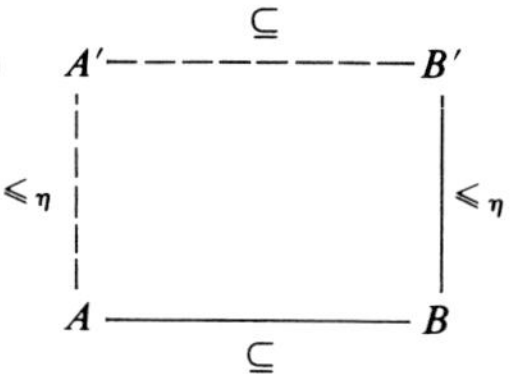

(ii)

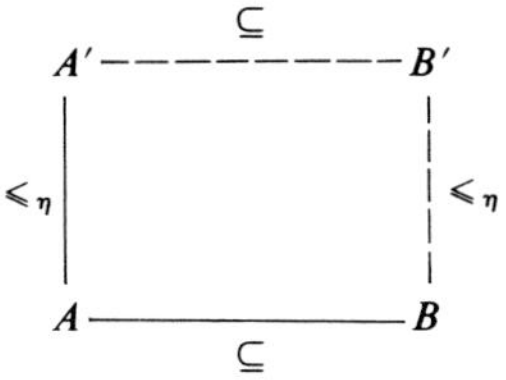

(iii)

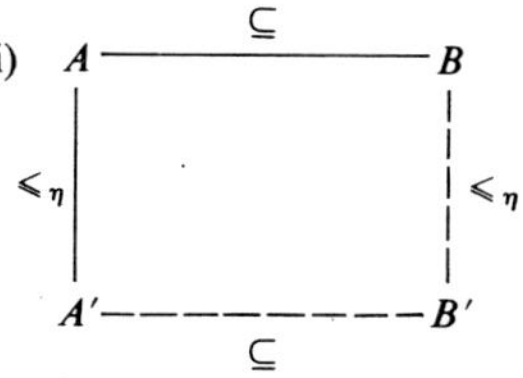

PROOF. (i) Let $B' = (B; X)$. Then take $A' = (A; X')$, where

$$X' = \{\alpha \in X \mid \neg \exists \beta < \alpha A(\beta) = \bot\}.$$

(ii) Let $A' = (A; X)$. Then take $B' = (B; X \cup |B|)$.

(iii) Let $A = (A'; X)$. Define

$$B'(\alpha) = \begin{cases} A'(\alpha) & \text{if } A'(\alpha)\downarrow, \\ B(\alpha) & \text{if } \exists \beta \leqslant \alpha A'(\beta) = \bot, \\ \uparrow & \text{else.} \end{cases}$$

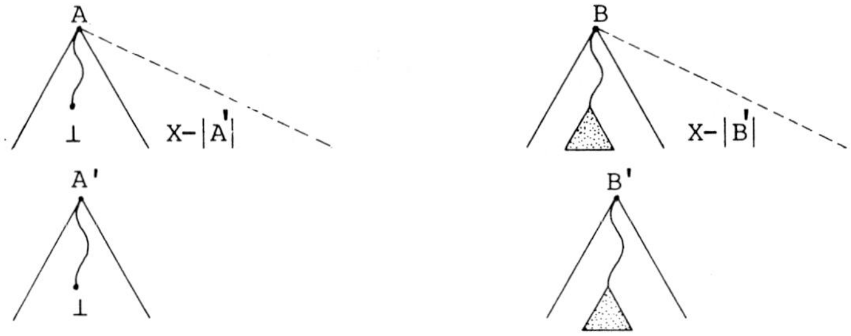

Then one has $B = (B'; X \cup |B'|) \geqslant_\eta B'$ and $A' \subseteq B'$. □

Note that in general

$$A \subseteq B \geqslant_\eta B' \not\Rightarrow \exists A' A \geqslant_\eta A' \subseteq B.$$

Take e.g.

$$A = \begin{array}{c} \lambda z.x, \\ | \\ \end{array} \qquad B = \begin{array}{c} \lambda z.x, \\ | \\ z \end{array} \qquad B' = x.$$

10.2.15. Proposition. (i) *Each* $A \in \mathfrak{B}$ *has an* infinite η-nf, *notation* $\infty\eta(A)$, *which has the following properties.*

(1) $\infty\eta(A) \leqslant_\eta A$,

(2) $\forall B[B \leqslant_\eta A \Rightarrow \infty\eta(A) \leqslant_\eta B]$.

(ii) *Moreover* $\infty\eta(A)$ *satisfying* (1) *and* (2) *is unique.*

Proof. (i) Define $\infty\eta$ on $\mathfrak{B}$ as follows.

$$\infty\eta(\bot) = \bot$$

$$\infty\eta\left(\begin{array}{c}\lambda x_1 \cdots x_n . y \\ \diagup \quad \diagdown \\ A_1 \cdots A_m\end{array}\right) =$$

$$= \begin{cases} \infty\eta\left(\begin{array}{c}\lambda x_1 \cdots x_{n-1} . y \\ \diagup \quad \diagdown \\ A_1 \cdots A_{m-1}\end{array}\right) & \text{if } x_n \leqslant_\eta A_m \text{ and } x_n \notin \mathrm{FV}(A_i),\ 1 \leqslant i \leqslant m-1; \\[2ex] \begin{array}{c}\lambda x_1 \cdots x_n . y \\ \diagup \quad \diagdown \\ \infty\eta(A_1) \cdots \infty\eta(A_m)\end{array} & \text{else.} \end{cases}$$

Working our way through the tree, we see that $\infty\eta(A)$ is well-defined and that (1) holds. Also condition (2) holds, since in $\infty\eta(A)$ all possible η-contractions are made.

(ii) If $\infty\eta'(A)$ satisfies conditions (1) and (2), then

$$\infty\eta'(A) \leqslant_\eta \infty\eta(A) \leqslant_\eta \infty\eta'(A).$$

Hence by lemma 10.2.12(i) $\infty\eta'(A) = \infty\eta(A)$. □

10.2.16. Remark. In exercise 10.6.6 it will be shown that $\Lambda\mathfrak{B}$ is not closed under $\infty\eta$, i.e. for some $M \in \Lambda$ the tree $\infty\eta(\mathrm{BT}(M))$ is not the Böhm tree of a term.

10.2.17. Corollary. $A \geqslant_\eta B \Rightarrow \infty\eta(A) = \infty\eta(B)$.

Proof. By the uniqueness of the infinite η-nf. □

A sequence number α belongs *virtually* to a Böhm like tree A iff α belongs to some η-expansion of A. Clearly α belongs virtually to A iff $\neg\exists\beta < \alpha A(\beta) = \perp$.

The following definition gives the virtual label of a Böhm like tree at virtual nodes.

10.2.18. Definition. For $A \in \mathfrak{B}$ and $\alpha \in \mathrm{Seq}$ let $X_\alpha \subseteq \mathrm{Seq}$ be the least set (if it exists) such that $\alpha \in X_\alpha$ and X_α extends A. Clearly X_α exists iff $\neg\exists\beta < \alpha A(\beta) = \perp$. Define

$$\text{(i)} \qquad A|\alpha = \begin{cases} (A;\, X_\alpha)(\alpha) & \text{if } \neg\exists\beta < \alpha A(\beta) = \perp, \\ \perp & \text{if } A(\alpha) = \perp, \\ \uparrow\uparrow & \text{else.} \end{cases}$$

As in 10.1.8 one can have $A|\alpha = \langle\lambda\vec{x}.y,\, m\rangle$, $= \perp$ or $= \uparrow\uparrow$.

(ii) $M|\alpha = \mathrm{BT}(M)|\alpha$.

(iii) $M_\alpha = (M;\, X_\alpha)_\alpha$, where α is a virtual node of $\mathrm{BT}(M)$.

Example. Let

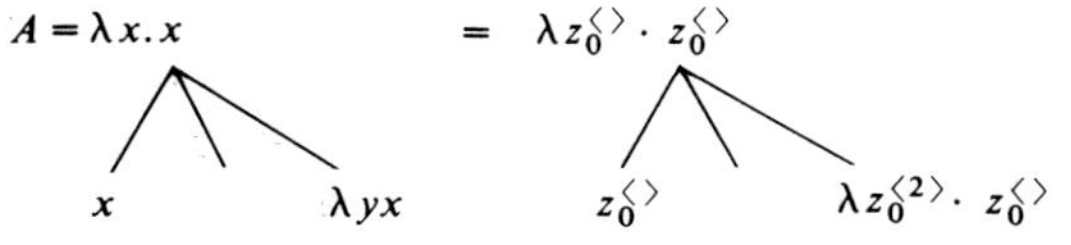

and $\alpha_1 = \langle 0, 1\rangle, \alpha_2 = \langle 1\rangle, \alpha_3 = \langle 1, 0\rangle, \alpha_4 = \langle 2, 2\rangle$. Then $A|\alpha_1 = z_1^{\langle 0\rangle}$; $A|\alpha_2 = \perp$; $A|\alpha_3 = \uparrow\uparrow$ and $A|\alpha_4 = z_3^{\langle 2\rangle}$ (see figure 10.1).

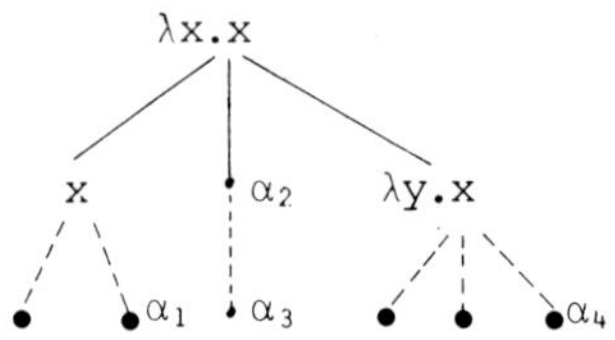

FIG. 10.1.

Equivalent hnf's and locally equivalent Böhm trees.

The following equivalence relation on hnf's was introduced in Böhm [1968].

10.2.19. DEFINITION. (i) Let $M \equiv \lambda x_1 \cdots x_n.yM_1 \cdots M_m$ and $N \equiv \lambda x_1 \cdots x_{n'}.y'N_1 \cdots N_{m'}$ be two hnf's. Then M is *equivalent* with N, written

$$M \sim N$$

iff $y \equiv y'$ and $n - m = n' - m'$ (these are possibly negative integers).

(ii) For arbitrary $M, N \in \Lambda$ say $M \sim N$ iff either both M, N are unsolvable or both M, N are solvable and have equivalent hnf's.

10.2.20. REMARKS. (i) By the variable convention it follows that in definition 10.2.19(i) the condition $y \equiv y'$ holds only if both variables are free or both variables are bound. E.g. $\lambda x.yM \not\sim \lambda y.yM$ and $\lambda x.xM \sim \lambda yz.yMN$.

(ii) Let M, N be hnf's. Let $\vec{x}$ be a string of variables such that $M\vec{x} = yM_1 \cdots M_m$, $N\vec{x} = y'N_1 \cdots N_{m'}$. Then $M \sim N$ iff $y \equiv y'$ and $m = m'$.

(iii) By corollary 8.3.17(ii) it follows that for M, N not in hnf the notion $M \sim N$ is well-defined.

10.2.21. DEFINITION. (i) Define for elements of Σ_1 (the label set for Böhm like trees)

$$\langle \lambda x_1 \cdots x_n.y, m \rangle \sim \langle \lambda x_1 \cdots x_{n'}.y', m' \rangle$$

$$\text{iff } y \equiv y' \text{ and } n - m = n' - m'.$$

(ii) Let $A, B \in \mathfrak{B}$ and $\alpha \in \text{Seq}$. Then $A \sim_\alpha B$ iff $A|\alpha \sim B|\alpha$ (both $A|\alpha$ and $B|\alpha$ are defined and are equivalent or both are undefined (i.e. $\perp$ or $\uparrow\uparrow$)).

10.2.22. LEMMA. *If $A \leqslant_\eta B$, then $\forall \alpha A \sim_\alpha B$.*

PROOF. Note that if $B \to_\eta A$, then $\forall \alpha A \sim_\alpha B$, see figure 10.2.
Since the relation $\geqslant_\eta$ is the transfinite transitive closure of $\to_\eta$, the conclusion holds. $\square$

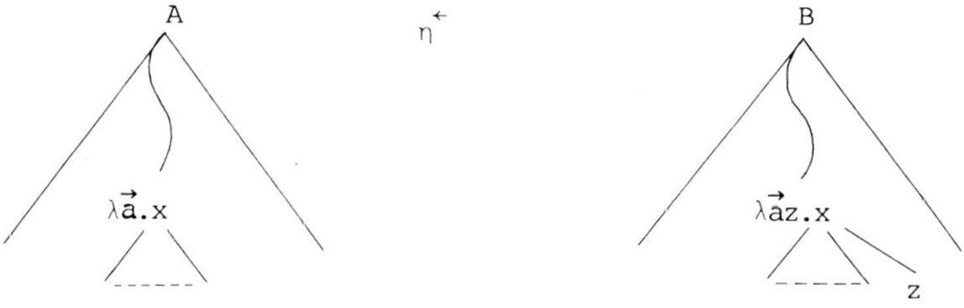

FIG. 10.2.

Special Böhm tree inclusions.

The following two relations on trees are important for the analysis of the models $P\omega$ and D_∞ in chapter 19.

10.2.23. DEFINITION. Let $A, B \in \mathfrak{B}$. Then
(i) $A \,{}^{\eta}\!\subseteq B \Leftrightarrow \exists A'\ A \leqslant_\eta A' \subseteq B$,
(ii) $A \,{}^{\eta}\!\subseteq^{\eta} B \Leftrightarrow \exists A', B'\ A \leqslant_\eta A' \subseteq B' \geqslant_\eta B$.

EXAMPLES.

(i)

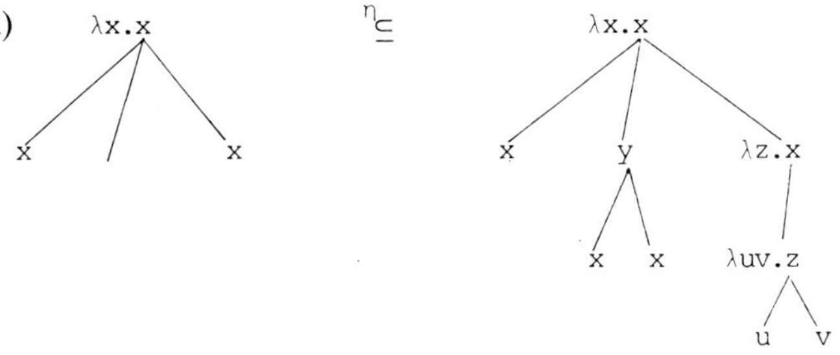

(ii)

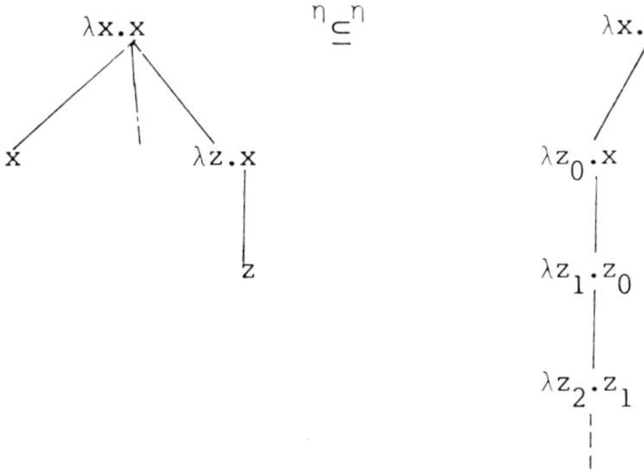

10.2.24. LEMMA. (i) ${}^{\eta}\!\subseteq$ *is a partial order on* $\mathfrak{B}$.
(ii) ${}^{\eta}\!\subseteq^{\eta}$ *is reflexive and transitive.*

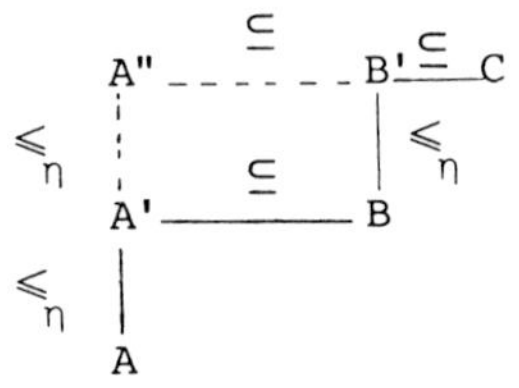

FIG. 10.3.

PROOF. (i) Reflexivity is clear. As to transitivity, suppose $A\ {}^{\eta}\!\subseteq B\ {}^{\eta}\!\subseteq C$. Then

$$\exists A', B' \quad A \leqslant_\eta A' \subseteq B \leqslant_\eta B' \subseteq C.$$

By lemma 10.2.14(i) $\exists A''\ A' \leqslant_\eta A'' \subseteq B'$. Hence $A \leqslant_\eta A'' \subseteq C$, i.e. $A\ {}^{\eta}\!\subseteq C$ (see figure 10.3).

Now suppose $A\ {}^{\eta}\!\subseteq B\ {}^{\eta}\!\subseteq A$ in order to show $A = B$. Then $\exists A', B' A \leqslant_\eta A' \subseteq B \leqslant_\eta B' \subseteq A$. Let $A' = (A; X)$ and $B' = (B; Y)$. Then

$$|A| \subseteq X \subseteq |B| \subseteq Y \subseteq |A|.$$

Hence $|A| = X = |B| = Y$. Therefore $A = (A; X) \subseteq B$ and similarly $B \subseteq A$, i.e. $A = B$.

(ii) Similarly, using also lemmas 10.2.13 and 10.2.14(ii). □

10.2.25. DEFINITION. Write

$$A =_\eta B \quad \text{if} \quad A\ {}^{\eta}\!\subseteq{}^{\eta} B\ {}^{\eta}\!\subseteq{}^{\eta} A.$$

By lemma 10.2.24(ii) $=_\eta$ is an equivalence relation on $\mathfrak{B}$. Note that

$$A \leqslant_\eta B \Rightarrow A =_\eta B.$$

Remember that for $A, B \in \mathfrak{B}$ one has $A =_k B$ iff $A^k = B^k$. Similarly one defines

$$A \subseteq_k B \Leftrightarrow A^k \subseteq B^k.$$

10.2.26. LEMMA. *For* $A, B \in \mathfrak{B}$

$$A \leqslant_\eta B \Leftrightarrow \forall k\ \exists A_k \left[A_k \twoheadrightarrow_\eta A \wedge A_k =_k B \right].$$

PROOF. ($\Rightarrow$) One has $B = (A; X)$ for some X extending A. Define

$$X_k = |A| \cup \{\alpha \in X \,|\, \mathrm{lh}(\alpha) \leqslant k\}.$$

Then X_k extends A and, because $X_k - |A|$ is finite

$$(A;\, X_k) \twoheadrightarrow_\eta A$$

for all k. Moreover

$$(A,\, X_k) =_k (A;\, X) = B.$$

Therefore one can take $A_k = (A;\, X_k)$.

($\Leftarrow$) Let the A_k be given. Define $X_k = |A_k^k|$ and $X = \bigcup_k X_k$. Then X extends A and $(A;\, X) = B$. Hence $A \leqslant_\eta B$. □

10.2.27. Corollary. (i) $A\ {}^\eta\!\subseteq B \Leftrightarrow \forall k\ \exists A_k\ [A_k \twoheadrightarrow_\eta A \wedge A_k \subseteq_k B]$.

(ii) $A^\eta \subseteq^\eta B \Leftrightarrow \forall k\ \exists A_k, B_k\ [A_k \twoheadrightarrow_\eta A \wedge B_k \twoheadrightarrow_\eta B \wedge A_k \subseteq_k B_k]$.

Proof. (i) ($\Rightarrow$) By assumption $A \leqslant_\eta A' \subseteq B$ for some A'. Hence by the lemma

$$\forall k \quad \exists A_k \left[A_k \twoheadrightarrow_\eta A \wedge A_k =_k A' \right]$$

and since $A' \subseteq B$

$$\forall k \quad \exists A_k \left[A_k \twoheadrightarrow_\eta A \wedge A_k \subseteq_k B \right].$$

($\Leftarrow$) Let the A_k be given. Define $X_k = |A_k^k|$, $X = \bigcup_k X_k$. Then X extends A and for $A' = (A;\, X)$ one has $A \leqslant_\eta A' \subseteq B$, i.e. $A\ {}^\eta\!\subseteq B$.

(ii) Similarly. □

The following notions are introduced in order to analyse when it is the case that $A\ {}^\eta\!\not\subseteq B$.

10.2.28. Definition. Let $A, B \in \mathfrak{B}$.

(i) A *fits in* B iff $\exists A' \twoheadrightarrow_\eta A A' \subseteq_1 B$.

(ii) A *supersedes* B (notation A sup B) iff A does not fit in B. Say $A\ \mathrm{sup}_\alpha B \Leftrightarrow A_\alpha$ sup B_α for $\alpha \in$ Seq.

Let Σ_1 be the set of labels of Böhm-like trees and let $a, b \in \Sigma_1 \cup \{\uparrow\}$ where $\uparrow$ stands for undefined.

(iii) a *fits in* b iff either $a = \uparrow$ or $a = \langle \lambda x_1 \cdots x_n.y,\, m \rangle$ and $b = \langle \lambda x_1 \cdots x_{n+k}.y,\, m + k \rangle$.

(iv) a *sup* b iff a does not fit in b.

Examples. (i) $\perp$ fits in every tree.

```
(ii) λx.x fits in λxy.x  fits in λxyz.x.
      |             / \              /|\
      x            x   x            x x  z
(iii) λx.x sup λxy. y    ;λx.x sup λx.x.
      |          / \         |       / \
      x         x   x        x      x   x
```

(iv) A fits in $B \Leftrightarrow A(\langle\ \rangle)$ fits in $B(\langle\ \rangle)$.

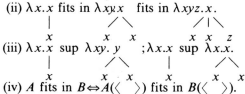

10.2.29. LEMMA. *Let $A, B \in \mathfrak{B}$ such that $A \subseteq_k B$.*

(i) *Suppose that $A(\alpha)$ fits in $B(\alpha)$ for every $\alpha \in A \cap B$ with $\mathrm{lh}(\alpha) = k$. Then*

$$\exists A' \twoheadrightarrow_\eta A \quad A' \subseteq_{k+1} B.$$

(ii) *Suppose that $A(\alpha) \sim B(\alpha)$ for every $\alpha \in A \cap B$ such that $A(\alpha)\downarrow$ and $lh(\alpha) = k$. Then*

$$\exists A' \twoheadrightarrow_\eta A \;\; \exists B' \twoheadrightarrow_\eta B \quad A' \subseteq_{k+1} B'.$$

PROOF. (i) Make at each node $\alpha \in A$ with $\mathrm{lh}(\alpha) = k$ and $A(\alpha)\downarrow$ the appropriate η-expansion of A that makes $A(\alpha)$ fit into $B(\alpha)$. Then one obtains $A' \subseteq_{k+1} B$. For example:

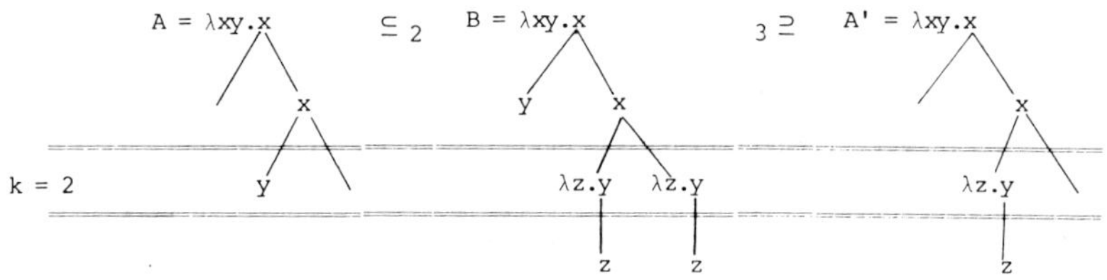

(ii) Similarly make η-expansions both in A and in B. For example:

Take

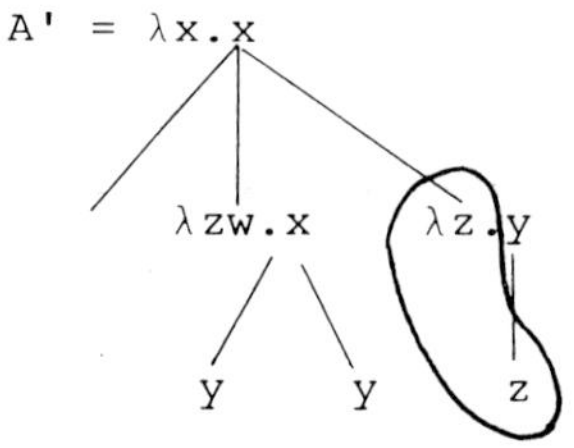

and

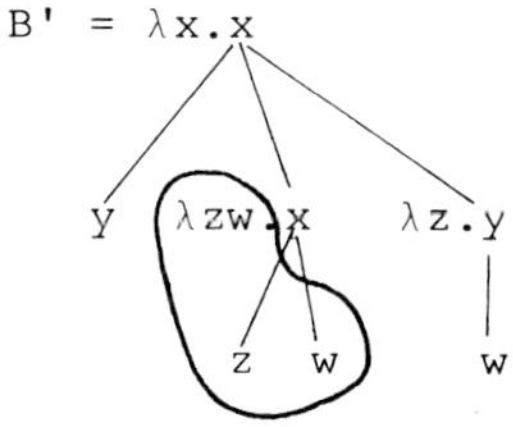

Then $A' \subseteq_2 B'$. □

Remember that

$$\alpha \in \mathrm{Dom}(A) \Leftrightarrow A(\alpha)\downarrow,$$

$$\alpha \in A \Leftrightarrow A(\alpha)\downarrow \vee A(\alpha) = \bot.$$

10.2.30. Lemma. (i) $A\ {}^{\eta}\!\not\subseteq B \Rightarrow \exists \alpha \in B\ [A \ \mathrm{sup}_\alpha\ B]$.
(ii) $A\ {}^{\eta}\!\not\subseteq^{\eta} B \Rightarrow \exists \alpha \in \mathrm{Dom}(A)\ [A \not\sim_\alpha B]$.

Proof. (i) Suppose $A\ {}^{\eta}\!\not\subseteq B$. By corollary 10.2.27(i), choose the least k for which

(1) $\forall A' \to_\eta A\ A' \not\subseteq_k B$.

Then $k > 0$ and for some $A_0 \twoheadrightarrow_\eta A$ one has $A_0 \subseteq_{k-1} B$. It may be assumed that A_0 is a minimal η-expansion of A such that $A_0 \subseteq_{k-1} B$. In particular it then follows that

(2) $\neg \exists \alpha[\mathrm{lh}(\alpha) \geqslant k-1 \wedge A_0$ is an η-expansion of A at $\alpha]$.

By (1) it follows that

$$\neg \exists A' \twoheadrightarrow_\eta A_0 \twoheadrightarrow_\eta A \quad A' \subseteq_k B$$

Therefore by the contrapositive of lemma 10.2.29(i)

$$\exists \alpha \in A_0 \cap B\ \left[\mathrm{lh}(\alpha) = k-1 \wedge A_0 \,\mathrm{sup}_\alpha\, B\right].$$

It now follows by (2) that $A_0(\alpha) = A(\alpha)$, hence (since $A\ \mathrm{sup}_\alpha\ B$ iff $A(\alpha)$ sup $B(\alpha)$)

$$\exists \alpha \in B\ \left[A\ \mathrm{sup}_\alpha\ B\right].$$

(ii) Similarly, using lemma 10.2.29(ii). □

10.2.31. Theorem. *The following statements are equivalent.*

(i) $A =_\eta B$.

(ii) $\infty\eta(A) = \infty\eta(B)$.

(iii) $\forall k\ \exists A' \twoheadrightarrow_\eta A\ \exists B' \twoheadrightarrow_\eta B\ A' =_k B'$.

(iv) $\forall \alpha\ A \sim_\alpha B$.

Proof. (i)⇒(ii). By assumption

$$\exists A', B'', B'', A'' \quad A \leqslant_\eta A' \subseteq B' \geqslant_\eta B \leqslant_\eta B'' \subseteq A'' \geqslant_\eta A.$$

Using lemmas 10.2.13(i) and 10.2.14(i), (ii) one can draw the following diagram:

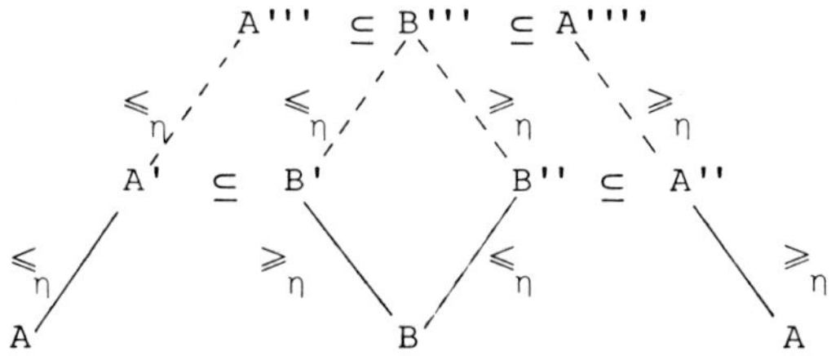

By lemma 10.2.13 (ii) one has $A''' = A''''$, hence $A''' = B'''$. Therefore by corollary 10.2.17

$$\infty\eta(A) = \infty\eta(A''') = \infty\eta(B''') = \infty\eta(B).$$

(ii)⇒(iii). By assumption $A \geqslant_\eta \infty\eta(A) \leqslant_\eta B$. Hence by lemma 10.2.13 (i) for some C one has $C \geqslant_\eta A, B$. Therefore by lemma 10.2.26

$$\forall k\ \exists A' \twoheadrightarrow_\eta A, B' \twoheadrightarrow_\eta B \quad A' =_k C =_k B'.$$

(iii)⇒(iv). Let $\alpha \in \text{Seq}$ be given and let $k = \text{lh}(\alpha) + 1$. By assumption

(1) $$\exists A' \twoheadrightarrow_\eta A, B' \twoheadrightarrow_\eta B \quad A' =_k B'.$$

Then

$$\begin{aligned} A|\alpha &\sim A'|\alpha && \text{by lemma 10.2.22,} \\ &= B'|\alpha && \text{by (1),} \\ &\sim B|\alpha && \text{by lemma 10.2.22.} \end{aligned}$$

(iv)⇒(i). By the contrapositive of lemma 10.2.30 (ii) one has

$$\forall \alpha (A \sim_\alpha B) \Rightarrow A\ {}^{\eta}{\subseteq}^{\eta} B$$

and the statement follows. □

The relations on trees define relations on terms.

10.2.32. DEFINITION. Let $M, N \in \Lambda, \alpha \in \mathrm{Seq}$.

(i) $M\ {}^{\eta}\underset{\sim}{\sqsubseteq}\ N \Leftrightarrow \mathrm{BT}(M)\ {}^{\eta}\subseteq \mathrm{BT}(N)$.

(ii) $M\ {}^{\eta}\underset{\sim}{\sqsubseteq}{}^{\eta} N \Leftrightarrow \mathrm{BT}(M)\ {}^{\eta}\subseteq^{\eta} \mathrm{BT}(N)$.

(iii) $M \lesssim_{\eta} N \Leftrightarrow \mathrm{BT}(M) \leqslant_{\eta} \mathrm{BT}(N)$.

(iv) $M \eqsim_{\eta} N \Leftrightarrow \mathrm{BT}(M) =_{\eta} \mathrm{BT}(N)$.

(v) $M \sim_{\alpha} N \Leftrightarrow \mathrm{BT}(M) \sim_{\alpha} \mathrm{BT}(N)$.

In exercise 10.6.7 it will be shown that

$$M\ {}^{\eta}\underset{\sim}{\sqsubseteq}\ N \Leftrightarrow \exists M'\ M \lesssim_{\eta} M' \underset{\sim}{\sqsubseteq} N,$$

$$M\ {}^{\eta}\underset{\sim}{\sqsubseteq}{}^{\eta} N \Leftrightarrow \exists M', N'\ M \lesssim_{\eta} M' \underset{\sim}{\sqsubseteq} N' \gtrsim_{\eta} N$$

(this is not immediate; the required intermediate tree may not be the BT of a term).

10.3. The Böhm out technique

Let $A = \mathrm{BT}(M)$ and let A_{α} be a subtree. The Böhm out technique consists in finding a context $C[\ \ ]$ such that roughly $\mathrm{BT}(C[M]) = A_{\alpha}$. (The subtree A_{α} is "Böhmed out".) The method was first used in Böhm [1968] for separating different $\beta\eta$-nf's M and N, i.e. constructing a context $C[\ \ ]$ such that say $C[M] = \ulcorner 0 \urcorner$, $C[N] = \ulcorner 1 \urcorner$.

10.3.1. EXAMPLES. (i) Let

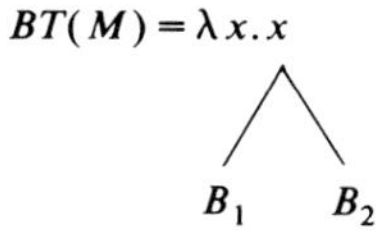

and suppose we are interested in B_2. Define $C[\ \ ] \equiv [\ \ ]\mathbf{F}$. Then $\mathrm{BT}(C[M]) = B_2$ (provided x does not occur in B_2).

(ii) Let

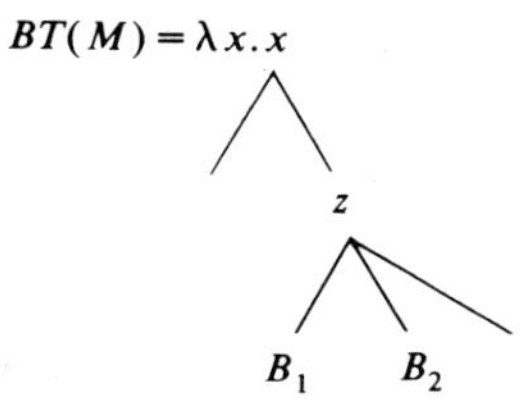

and suppose we want B_2.

Define $C[\ \ ]\equiv(\lambda z.[\ \ ]\mathbf{F})\mathbf{U}_1^2$. Then $\mathrm{BT}(C[M])=B_2$.

(iii) Less obvious is the following. Let

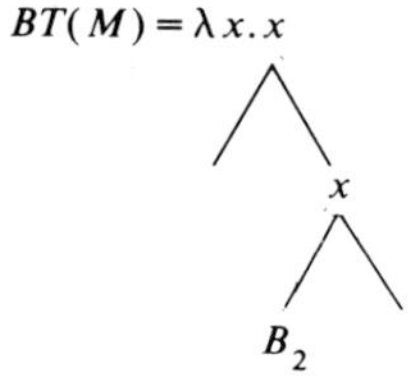

and suppose we want B_2. If we take $C_0[\ \ ]\equiv[\ \ ]\mathbf{F}$, then $C_0[M]=\Omega$. However now take $C[\ \ ]\equiv[\ \ ]\mathbf{P}_2\mathbf{FT}$, where $\mathbf{P}_2=\lambda ab.\langle a,b\rangle$. Then $C[M]=\langle\Omega,\langle B_2,\Omega\rangle\rangle\mathbf{FT}=B_2$.

Notice that one has, in general, not $C[M]=B_2$ but rather $C[M]=B_2^*$, a substitution instance of B_2. One cannot do better.

10.3.2. Definition. (i) For $M\in\Lambda$ an *instance* M^* is the result of substituting some terms for some free variables in M.

(ii) *Notation.* $\exists *\ \cdots M^*\cdots$ means that for some instance M^* of M one has $\cdots M^*\cdots$. Similarly for $\forall *\ \cdots$.

10.3.3. Definition. (i) A *transformation* f is a map $f:\Lambda\to\Lambda$.

(ii) A *solving transformation* f is defined either by

$$f(P)=Px \quad \text{for some } x$$

or

$$f(P)=P[x:=N] \quad \text{for some } x, N.$$

(iii) A *Böhm transformation* is a finite composition of solving transformations (including the identity as a composition of zero transformations).

(iv) *Notations.* π ranges over Böhm transformations; M^π stands for $\pi(M)$.

10.3.4. Lemma. (i) $\forall\pi\ \exists C_\pi[\ \ ]\ \forall M\ \ M^\pi=C_\pi[M]$.

(ii) *In fact* $C_\pi[\ \ ]$ *in* (i) *can be chosen such that*

$$\forall\vec{x}\ \exists\vec{N}\ \forall M\in\Lambda^0(\vec{x})\quad C_\pi[M]=(\lambda\vec{x}.M)\vec{N}.$$

Proof. (i) If $M^\pi=Mx$, take $C_\pi[\ \ ]=[\ \ ]x$; if $M^\pi=M[x:=N]$, take $C_\pi[\ \ ]=(\lambda x.[\ \ ])N$; and if $\pi=\pi_1\circ\pi_2$, let $C_\pi[\ \ ]=C_{\pi_1}[C_{\pi_2}[\ \ ]]$.

(ii) Again this is clear if π is a solving transformation. Now let $\pi = \pi_1 \circ \pi_2$ where π_1 is a solving transformation and $C_{\pi_2}[M] = (\lambda\vec{x}.M)\vec{N}$ for $M \in \Lambda^0(\vec{x})$.

Case 1. $(\ )^{\pi_1} = (\ )y$. Then $C_\pi[M] = (\lambda\vec{x}.M)\vec{N}y$ for $M \in \Lambda^0(\vec{x})$.

Case 2. $(\ )^{\pi_1} = (\ )[y := P]$. Then $C_\pi[M] = (\lambda\vec{x}.M)\vec{N}^*$ for $M \in \Lambda^0(\vec{x})$. where $* = [y := P]$. □

10.3.5. DEFINITION. (i) A hnf $M \equiv \lambda x_1 \cdots x_n.yM_1 \cdots M_m$ is called *λ-free* if $n = 0$, i.e. if $M \equiv yM_1 \cdots M_m$.

(ii) A hnf $M \equiv \lambda\vec{x}.y\vec{M}$ is called *head original* if $y \notin FV(\vec{M})$.

(iii) A λ-term M is *ready* if M is unsolvable or has a λ-free and head original hnf.

Now it will be shown that a λ-term can always be made ready. Remember that $\mathbf{U}_i^n \equiv \lambda x_0 \cdots x_n.x_i$; these terms are called *selectors*. A *permutator* is a term of the form $\lambda x_1 \cdots x_n.x_{\sigma_1} \cdots x_{\sigma_n}$, where σ is a permutation. A particular group of permutators is defined by

$$\mathbf{P}_n \equiv \lambda x_1 \cdots x_n.\langle x_1, \ldots, x_n\rangle \equiv \lambda x_1 \cdots x_{n+1}.x_{n+1}x_1 \cdots x_n.$$

10.3.6. LEMMA. (i) $\forall M\ \exists\pi\ M^\pi$ *is ready.*

(ii) $\forall M\ \forall\alpha \in BT(M)\ \exists\pi\ [M^\pi$ *is ready and* $\exists *\ (M^\pi)_\alpha = (M_\alpha)^*]$.

(iii) *The substitution needed in* (*ii*) *is done only in the head variable of M* (*if M has a hnf*).

PROOF. (i) If M is unsolvable, then take $M^\pi = M$. If M is solvable, let $\lambda x_1 \cdots x_n.yM_1 \cdots M_m$ be its (principal) hnf. Define

$$N^\pi \equiv Nx_1 \cdots x_n[y := \mathbf{P}_m]a,$$

where a is fresh. Then

$$M^\pi \equiv \mathbf{P}_m M_1^* \cdots M_m^* a = aM_1^* \cdots M_m^*$$

and this is ready.

(ii) [The construction in (i) is not sufficient now; it may mix up the structure of subtrees of M. E.g. let

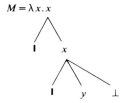

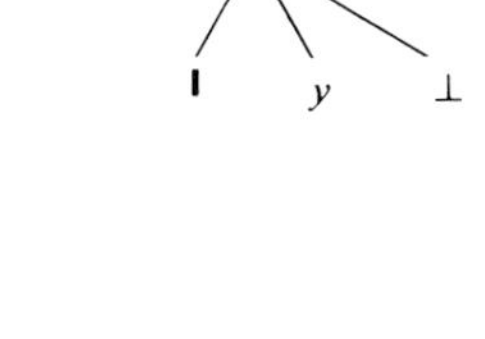

Then

$$M^{\pi} = Mx[x := \mathbf{P}_2]a = \mathbf{P}_2\mathbf{I}(\mathbf{P}_2\mathbf{I}y\Omega)a$$

$$= \mathbf{P}_2\mathbf{I}(\mathbf{P}_2\mathbf{I}y\Omega)a = a\mathbf{I}(\Omega\mathbf{I}y) =$$ 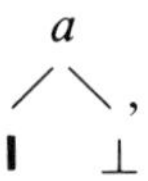,

and hence $(M^{\pi})_{\langle 1,0\rangle} \neq (M_{\langle 1,0\rangle})^*$.] Again the situation is trivial if M is unsolvable. Otherwise M has a hnf, say $M = \lambda x_1 \cdots x_n.yM_1 \cdots M_m$. Let $\mathrm{lh}(\alpha) = k$ and let the nodes of $\mathrm{BT}(M)$ of length $\leqslant k$ have at most q successors in the tree. Define

$$N^{\pi} = Nx_1 \cdots x_n[y := \mathbf{P}_q]a_{m+1} \cdots a_q b.$$

Then since

$$M^{\pi} = \mathbf{P}_q M_1^* \cdots M_m^* a_{m+1} \cdots a_q b = bM_1^* \cdots M_m^* a_{m+1} \cdots a_q,$$

where $* = [y := \mathbf{P}_q]$, it follows that $\mathrm{BT}^{k+1}(M^{\pi})$ results from $\mathrm{BT}^{k+1}(M)$ by replacing the top

(1) 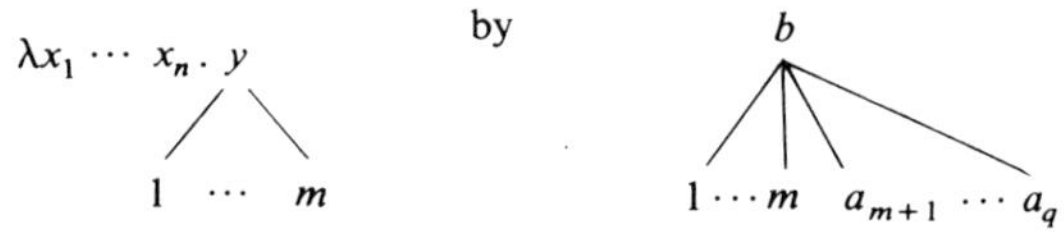

and the internal nodes (of length $\leqslant k$)

(2) 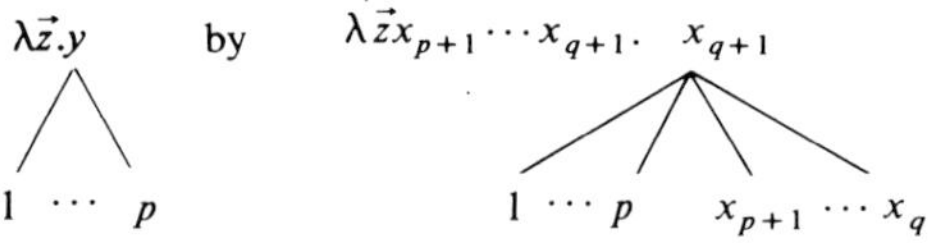

Clearly M^{π} is ready and $(M^{\pi})_{\alpha}$ is an $[y := \mathbf{P}_q]$ instance of M_{α}.

(iii) Immediate. □

10.3.7. Proposition (Böhm out lemma).

(i) $\forall M\ \forall \alpha \in \mathrm{BT}(M) \exists \pi\ \exists *\ \ M^{\pi} = (M_{\alpha})^*$.

(ii) *The substitution* $*$ *in* (i) *is done only in the variables in* M_{α} *that occur as head variable at a node* $\beta < \alpha$.

(iii) *The transformation* π *in* (i) *is such that*

$$M^{\pi} \equiv M[x_1 := N_1] \cdots [x_n := N_n]\vec{P},$$

for some $\vec{N}, \vec{P}$ *which are either variables, permutators, or selectors, and where* $\{\vec{x}\}$ *consists of those free variables of M that are the head variable of a node* $\beta < \alpha$ *in* BT(M).

Proof. (i) By induction on lh(α) it will be shown that

$$\forall M \quad [\alpha \in \mathrm{BT}(M) \Rightarrow \exists \pi, * \;\; M^{\pi} = (M_{\alpha})^{*}].$$

If $\alpha = \langle\;\rangle$, hence $M_{\langle\;\rangle} \equiv M$ and we can take $\pi = \mathrm{id}$. Suppose $\alpha = \langle j \rangle * \beta$. Using lemma 10.3.6 let π_0 be such that

(1) $\qquad M^{\pi_0} = xM_0 \cdots M_m$ is ready

and moreover for some $*_0$

(2) $\qquad (M_{\alpha})^{*_0} = (M^{\pi_0})_{\alpha} = (M_j)_{\beta}.$

Define

$$(\;)^{\pi_1} = (\;)[x := \mathbf{U}_j^n], \qquad \pi_{10} = \pi_1 \circ \pi_0.$$

Then by (1)

$$M^{\pi_{10}} = (xM_1 \cdots M_m)^{\pi_1} = M_j.$$

By the induction hypothesis applied to β

$$\exists \pi_2 \; \exists *_2 \quad M_j^{\pi_2} = ((M_j)_{\beta})^{*_2}.$$

Hence by (2)

$$(M_j)^{\pi_2} = M_{\alpha}{}^{*_0 *_2}$$

Define $\pi = \pi_2 \circ \pi_1 \circ \pi_0$ and we are done.
(ii), (iii) Immediate. □

Without extra work one can also Böhm out at a virtual node of a tree.

10.3.8. Corollary. $\forall M \; \forall \alpha$ *virtual in* BT(M) $\exists \pi \; \exists * \quad M^{\pi} = (M_{\alpha})^{*}$. *Moreover* π *and* $*$ *can be chosen as described in proposition* 10.3.7 (ii), (iii).

Proof. By two examples.
(1) Let

$$M = \lambda x.x \quad \text{with sons } x \;\; x \qquad \text{and} \quad \alpha = \langle 2 \rangle.$$

Then M_α can be determined by drawing the η-expansion

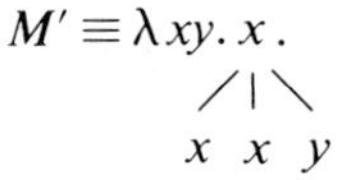

To Böhm out at α in M' one uses π defined by

$$(\ \ )^\pi = (\ \ )xy\big[x := \mathbf{U}_2^2\big].$$

This π also works for M:

$$M^\pi = \mathbf{U}_2^2\mathbf{U}_2^2\mathbf{U}_2^2 y = y.$$

(2) Let M be as in (1) and let $\alpha = \langle 2, 1\rangle$. Take

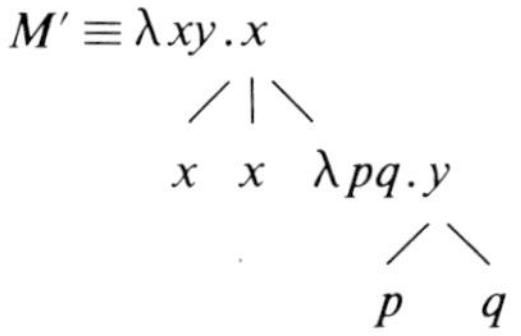

Define $(\ \ )^\pi = (\ \ )xy[x := \mathbf{U}_2^2]pq[y := \mathbf{U}_1^1]$. Then $M^\pi = q$. □

Note that by the preceding proof no substitutions are needed in the term M itself, if α is virtually in $\mathrm{BT}(M)$.

The following result is taken from Barendregt et al. [1976a]; for an application see theorem 20.2.6.

10.3.9. Corollary. *Let* $M \in \Lambda^0(x)$, $x \in \mathrm{FV}(\mathrm{BT}(M))$. *Then for some* $\vec{P}, \vec{Q} \in \Lambda$ *such that* $x \notin \mathrm{FV}(\vec{P})$ *one has*

(i) $M\vec{P} = x\vec{Q}$.

(ii) *In* (*i*) *one may require that the* $\vec{P}$ *are closed and each of them is either of the form* $\mathbf{U}_i^n$ *or* $\mathbf{P}_m$.

Proof. (i) Let α be a node of minimal length such that x occurs as the free head variable at node α (i.e. is not bound at a node $\beta < \alpha$) in $\mathrm{BT}(M)$. Then $M_\alpha \equiv \lambda\vec{y}.x\vec{N}$. By proposition 10.3.7 (i), (ii), (iii) for some π, $*$

$$M^\pi \equiv M\vec{P} = (\lambda\vec{y}.x\vec{N})^* = \lambda\vec{y}.x\vec{N}^*.$$

Therefore $M\vec{P}\vec{y} = x\vec{N}^*$ as required.

(ii) By proposition 10.3.7 (iii) the members of $\vec{P}\vec{y}$ are variables $\not\equiv x$ or of the form $\mathbf{U}_i^n$ or $\mathbf{P}_m$. By substituting in (1) some terms $\mathbf{I} \equiv \mathbf{U}_0^0$ for variables $\not\equiv x$, one may assume that the $\vec{P} \in \Lambda^0$. □

In the next section the Böhm out technique will have to be applied to several terms at once. From now on $\mathscr{F}$ will stand for finite sequences of terms (possibly with repetitions). Notation $\mathscr{F}=\{M_1,\ldots,M_n\}$.

10.3.10. DEFINITION. Let $\mathscr{Q}\subset\Lambda$ and $\alpha\in\text{Seq}$.

(i) $\mathscr{Q}$ is *ready* (λ-*free*) if $\forall M\in\mathscr{Q}\ M$ is ready (λ-free, respectively).

(ii) π is α-$\mathscr{Q}$-*faithful* if

$$\forall M, N\in\mathscr{Q}\ \ [M\sim_\alpha N\Leftrightarrow M^\pi\sim N^\pi]\wedge[M|\alpha\downarrow\Leftrightarrow M^\pi \text{ solvable}].$$

π is $\mathscr{Q}$-*faithful* if π is $\langle\ \ \rangle$-$\mathscr{Q}$-faithful.

(iii) Let $M,N\in\Lambda$. Then M,N *agree up to* α if $\forall\beta<\alpha M|\beta=N|\beta$.

(iv) $\mathscr{Q}$ *agrees up to* α if $\forall M,N\in\mathscr{Q}\ M,N$ agree up to α.

10.3.11. LEMMA. *Suppose $\mathscr{F}$ agrees up to α. Then for some π*

(1) *$\mathscr{F}^\pi$ is ready.*

(2) *$\mathscr{F}^\pi$ agrees up to α.*

(3) $\forall M,N\in\mathscr{F}[M\sim_\alpha N\Leftrightarrow M^\pi\sim_\alpha N^\pi]$.

PROOF. This is a corollary to the proof of lemma 10.3.6 (ii). Suppose that $\alpha\neq\langle\ \ \rangle$ and that the elements of $\mathscr{F}$ are solvable (the other cases are simpler). Then for $M_i\in\mathscr{F}$ one has

$$M_i=\lambda\vec{x}.yN_{i1}\cdots N_{im}.$$

Define π by

$$(\ \ )^\pi=(\ \ )\vec{x}[y:=\mathbf{P}_q]a_1\cdots a_r,$$

where q, r are large (the attentive reader will easily see just how large these need be). Then

$$M_i^\pi=\mathbf{P}_q\vec{M}_i\vec{a}=a_j\cdots$$

which is ready. This establishes (1).

As for (2), let $\beta<\alpha$. For $M\in\mathscr{F}$ one has that $\text{BT}(M^\pi)$ is obtained from $\text{BT}(M)$ by the changes (1), (2) in the proof of lemma 10.3.6 (ii). Let $M,N\in\mathscr{F}$. There are three cases.

Case 1. $M|\beta=N|\beta=\langle\lambda\vec{z}.y',m\rangle, y'\not\equiv y$. Then

$$M^\pi|\beta=N^\pi|\beta=\langle\lambda\vec{z}.y',m\rangle.$$

Case 2. $M|\beta=N|\beta=\langle\lambda\vec{z}.y,m\rangle$. Then

$$M^\pi|\beta=N^\pi|\beta=\langle\lambda\vec{z}x_{m+1}\cdots x_{q+1}.x_{q+1},q\rangle.$$

Case 3. $M|\beta = N|\beta = \uparrow$. Then $M^\pi|\beta = N^\pi|\beta = \uparrow$.

As for (3), let $M, N \in \mathcal{F}$ and suppose $M|\alpha, N|\alpha$ are both defined (the other cases are simpler). If $M|\alpha \sim N|\alpha$, then as above $M^\pi|\alpha \sim N^\pi|\alpha$. Suppose $M \not\sim_\alpha N$ in order to show $M^\pi \not\sim_\alpha N^\pi$. Let

$$M|\alpha = \langle \lambda z_1 \cdots z_{n_1}.y_1, m_1\rangle, \qquad N|\alpha = \langle \lambda z_1 \cdots z_{n_2}.y_2, m_2\rangle.$$

Case 1. $y_1 \not\equiv y_2$. Then also $M^\pi \not\sim_\alpha N^\pi$. (Distinguish $y_1 \not\equiv y$, $y_2 \not\equiv y$ and $y_1 \equiv y, y_2 \not\equiv y$.)

Case 2. $y_1 \equiv y_2, n_1 - m_1 \neq n_2 - m_2$. Subcase 2.1. $y_1 \equiv y_2 \not\equiv y$. Then $M^\pi|\alpha = M|\alpha$ and similarly for N, so $M^\pi \not\sim_\alpha N^\pi$. Subcase 2.2. $y_1 \equiv y_2 \equiv y$. Then

$$M^\pi|\alpha = \langle \lambda z_1 \cdots z_{n_1} x_{m_1+1} \cdots x_{q+1}.x_{q+1}, q\rangle,$$

$$N^\pi|\alpha = \langle \lambda z_1 \cdots z_{n_2} x_{m_2+1} \cdots x_{q+1}.x_{q+1}, q\rangle$$

and hence $M^\pi \not\sim_\alpha N^\pi$, since

$$n_1 + (q+1) - m_1 - q \neq n_2 + (q+1) - m_2 - q. \quad \square$$

For later use we need the following result.

10.3.12. LEMMA. (i) *Let* $\mathcal{A} \subseteq \Lambda$. *Define* $(\ )^\pi = (\ )x$. *Then if* $x \notin \mathrm{FV}(\mathcal{A})$, π *is* $\mathcal{A}$*-faithful.*

(ii) *Let* $\mathcal{A}_k = \{M \in \Lambda |\ \|M\| < k,\ M$ in $\beta\eta$-nf$\}$. *Define* $(\ )^\pi = (\ )[x := \mathbf{P}_k]$. *Then*

(1) π *is* $\mathcal{A}_k$*-faithful.*

(2) $\mathcal{A}_k^\pi \subset \mathrm{NF}$.

(3) π *is injective on* $\mathcal{A}_k (M^\pi = N^\pi \Rightarrow M \equiv N$, *for* $M, N \in \mathcal{A}_k)$.

PROOF. (i) Easy.

(ii) By the same method as lemma 10.3.11 one shows (1). As for (2), by induction on the depth d of BT(M) one shows

$$M \in \mathcal{A}_k \Rightarrow M^\pi \text{ has a } \beta\eta\text{-nf}.$$

Suppose $d = 0$. Then $M = \lambda\vec{y}.z$ and hence $M[x := \mathbf{P}_k]$ has a $\beta\eta$-nf, both if

$$z \not\equiv x \text{ and if } z \equiv x.$$

Suppose $d > 0$. Then

$$\mathrm{BT}(M) = \lambda\vec{y}.z$$

$$\diagup \quad \diagdown$$

$$\Delta_1 \qquad \Delta_p$$

If $z \not\equiv x$, then

$$\begin{array}{l} \mathrm{BT}(M^{\pi}) = \lambda\vec{y}.z \\ \qquad\qquad\quad / \quad \backslash \\ \qquad\qquad\; \Delta_1^{\pi} \quad \Delta_p^{\pi} \end{array}$$

and the result follows from the induction hypothesis.
If z is the free variable x, then

$$\begin{array}{l} \mathrm{BT}(M^{\pi}) = \text{“}\lambda\vec{y}.\mathbf{P}_k\text{”} = \lambda\vec{y}z_{p+1}\cdots z_{k+1}.z_{k+1} \\ \qquad\qquad\quad /\backslash \qquad\qquad\qquad / \;\; | \;\; \backslash \quad \backslash \\ \qquad\quad\;\; \Delta_1^{\pi} \;\; \Delta_r^{\pi} \qquad\quad \Delta_1^{\pi} \cdots \Delta_p^{\pi} \; z_{p+1} \cdots z_k \end{array}$$

since $k > \|M\| > p$, and the result follows again from the induction hypothesis.

As for (3), also by induction on d it is clear that from $\mathrm{BT}(M^{\pi})$ one can reconstruct $\mathrm{BT}(M)$, for $M \in \mathcal{Q}_k$. [Note that since M is a $\beta\eta$-nf, in $\mathrm{BT}(M^{\pi})$ the subtree Δ_p^{π} is not equal to the last variable in $\vec{y}$ and therefore can be retraced.] Hence π is injective on $\mathcal{Q}_k$. □

10.3.13. Proposition. *Suppose $\mathcal{F}$ agrees along α. Then there exists a π which is α-$\mathcal{F}$-faithful.*

Proof. Induction on $\mathrm{lh}(\alpha)$. If $\alpha = \langle\;\rangle$, take $\pi = \mathrm{id}$. Otherwise, suppose $\alpha = \langle j \rangle * \beta$. By assumption

(1) $\qquad \forall M, N \in \mathcal{F} \quad M|\langle\;\rangle = N|\langle\;\rangle.$

For notational simplicity assume $\mathcal{F} = \{M, N\}$.

Case 1. M, N, are unsolvable. Then take $\pi = \mathrm{id}$.

Case 2. M, N are solvable. By (1) one has, say,

$$M = \lambda\vec{x}.yM_1\cdots M_p, \qquad N = \lambda\vec{x}.yN_1\cdots N_p.$$

By lemma 10.3.11 there is a π_0 such that

(2) $\qquad \mathcal{F}^{\pi_0}$ is ready,

(3) $\qquad M \sim_{\alpha} N \Leftrightarrow M^{\pi_0} \sim_{\alpha} N^{\pi_0},$

(4) $\qquad \mathcal{F}^{\pi_0}$ agrees up to α.

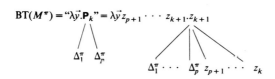

By (1), (2) one has, say,

$$\mathfrak{F}^{\pi_0} = \{aP_0 \cdots P_q, aQ_0 \cdots Q_q\}.$$

Define $(\ )^{\pi_1} = (\ )[a := \mathbf{U}_j^q]$. Then

$$\mathfrak{F}^{\pi_1 \circ \pi_0} = \{P_j, Q_j\}.$$

Moreover, by (4), $\mathfrak{F}^{\pi_1 \circ \pi_0}$ agrees along β. Hence by the induction hypothesis there is a π_2 which is β-$\mathfrak{F}^{\pi_1 \circ \pi_0}$-faithful. Then

$$\begin{aligned} M \sim_\alpha N &\Leftrightarrow a\vec{P} \sim_\alpha a\vec{Q} \quad \text{by (3)} \\ &\Leftrightarrow P_j \sim_\beta Q_j \\ &\Leftrightarrow P_j^{\pi_2} \sim Q_j^{\pi_2} \\ &\Leftrightarrow M^\pi \sim N^\pi \end{aligned}$$

where $\pi = \pi_2 \circ \pi_1 \circ \pi_0$. Therefore this π is α-$\mathfrak{F}$-faithful. □

10.4. Separability of terms

A set $\mathfrak{F} = \{M_1, \ldots, M_n\}$ of λ-terms is called *separable* if the elements can be mapped on arbitrary terms by a "definable" function.

Before examining the concept of separability in general, the case $n = 2$ is treated. The result is due to Böhm [1968].

10.4.1. Lemma. (i) *Let $M, N \in \Lambda$ be solvable. Then*

$$M \not\sim N \Rightarrow \forall P, Q \in \Lambda\ \exists \pi\ [M^\pi = P \wedge N^\pi = Q].$$

(ii) *Let M be solvable. Then*

$$M \not\sim N \Rightarrow \forall P \in \Lambda\ \exists \pi\ [M^\pi = P \wedge N^\pi \textit{ is unsolvable}].$$

Proof. (i) By theorem 8.3.14 M, N have hnf's, say

$$M = \lambda x_1 \cdots x_n . y M_1 \cdots M_m, \qquad N = \lambda x_1 \cdots x_{n'} . y' N_1 \cdots N_{m'}.$$

Suppose $M \not\sim N$. Then $y \not\equiv y'$ or $n - m \neq n' - m'$.

Case 1. $y \not\equiv y'$. Assume $n' \geqslant n$, say $n' = n + k$. Define

$$(\ )^{\pi_0} = (\ )x_1 \cdots x_{n+k},$$

$$(\ )^{\pi_1} = (\ )[y := \lambda a_1 \cdots a_{m+k} . P][y' := \lambda a_1 \cdots a_{m'} . Q]$$

and $\pi=\pi_1\circ\pi_0$. Then

$$M^\pi=(yM_1\cdots M_m x_{n+1}\cdots x_{n+k})^{\pi_1}=P,$$

$$N^\pi=(y'N_1\cdots N_{m'})^{\pi_1}=Q.$$

Case 2. $y\equiv y'$ and $n-m\neq n'-m'$. Let $n'\geqslant n$. Define

$$(\ )^{\pi_0}=(\ )x_1\cdots x_{n'}.$$

Then one has (using the self-explanatory notation $\overset{\pi}{\to}$), say,

$$M\overset{\pi_0}{\to}yM_1\cdots M_m x_{n+1}\cdots x_{n'}\equiv yL_1\cdots L_p,$$

$$N\overset{\pi_0}{\to}yN_1\cdots N_{m'}\equiv yL'_1\cdots L'_{p'}$$

where $p=m+n'-n$ and $p'=m'$. Since $p\neq p'$, let $p=p'+k$, say. Define

$$(\ )^{\pi_1}=(\ )ab_1\cdots b_k,$$

$$(\ )^{\pi_2}=(\ )[y:=\lambda z_1\cdots z_{p+1}.z_{p+1}].$$

Then

$$yL_1\cdots L_p\overset{\pi_1}{\to}yL_1\cdots L_p ab_1\cdots b_k\overset{\pi_2}{\to}ab_1\cdots b_k,$$

$$yL'_1\cdots L'_{p'}\overset{\pi_1}{\to}yL'_1\cdots L'_{p'}ab_1\cdots b_k\overset{\pi_2}{\to}b_k.$$

Finally let

$$(\ )^{\pi_3}=(\ )[a:=\lambda b_1\cdots b_k.P][b_k:=Q],$$

$$\pi=\pi_3\circ\pi_2\circ\pi_1\circ\pi_0.$$

Then $M^\pi=P,N^\pi=Q.$

(ii) Again $M=\lambda x_1\cdots x_n.yM_1\cdots M_m$ and assume N unsolvable. Define

$$(\ )^\pi=(\ )x_1\cdots x_n[y:=\lambda a_1\cdots a_m.P].$$

Then $M^\pi=P$ and N^π is still unsolvable. □

10.4.2. THEOREM (Böhm [1968]). *Let M, N be distinct $\beta\eta$-nf's. Then*
(i) $\forall P, Q \exists \pi [M^{\pi} = P \wedge N^{\pi} = Q]$
(ii) *If moreover* $M, N \in \Lambda^0$, *then* $\forall P, Q \exists \vec{L} [M\vec{L} = P \wedge N\vec{L} = Q]$.

PROOF. (i) By assumption $M \not\simeq_{\eta} N$. Hence by theorem 10.2.31

$$M \not\sim_{\alpha} N, \quad \text{(see also exercise 10.6.9)},$$

for some α. Let α be such with minimal length. Then the set $\{M, N\}$ agrees along α. Hence by proposition 10.3.13 for some π_0

$$M^{\pi_0} \not\sim N^{\pi_0}.$$

Now apply the preceding lemma.
(ii) By (i), since for all π and closed M one can write $M^{\pi} = M\vec{L}$. □

It follows that for terms having a nf, the $\lambda\beta\eta$-calculus is Hilbert–Post complete. For terms not having a nf this is not true. See chapters 16 and 17.

10.4.3. COROLLARY. (i) *Let M, N be distinct $\beta\eta$-nf's. Then $M = N$ is inconsistent with* $\boldsymbol{\lambda}$.
(ii) *For M, N having a* nf *one has in* $\boldsymbol{\lambda\eta}$ $M = N$ *is provable or inconsistent.*

PROOF. (i) Given P, Q there exists by the theorem a π such that $M^{\pi} = P$, $N^{\pi} = Q$. Hence

$$\boldsymbol{\lambda} + M = N \vdash P = M^{\pi} = N^{\pi} = Q,$$

therefore

$$\boldsymbol{\lambda} + M = N \quad \text{proves every equation.}$$

(ii) If M, N have β-nf's, then by reducing all η-redexes also β-η-nf's, say, M', N'. If $M' \equiv N'$, then $\boldsymbol{\lambda\eta} \vdash M = N$. If $M' \not\equiv N'$, then by (i)

$$\neg \mathrm{Con}(\boldsymbol{\lambda\eta} + M = N). \quad \square$$

Now general separability for the λK-calculus will be considered. The formulation and proof of the final result is due to Coppo, Dezani–Ciancaglini and Ronchi della Rocca [1978].

10.4.4. DEFINITION. Let $\mathcal{F} = \{M_1, \ldots, M_p\}$ be a set of λ-terms.
(i) If $\mathcal{F} \subseteq \Lambda^0$, then $\mathcal{F}$ is called *separable* if

$$(+) \qquad \forall N_1 \cdots N_p \in \Lambda \; \exists F \in \Lambda \quad FM_1 = N_1 \wedge \cdots \wedge FM_p = N_p.$$

(ii) If $\mathcal{F} \subseteq \Lambda$ is arbitrary, then $\mathcal{F}$ is *separable* if its closure $\lambda\vec{x}.\mathcal{F} = \{\lambda\vec{x}.M_1, \ldots, \lambda\vec{x}.M_p\}$ is separable in the sense (i).

One can define η-separability by changing $=$ in $(+)$ by $=_\eta$. In chapter 17 it will be seen that

$$\mathcal{F} \text{ if } \eta\text{-separable} \Leftrightarrow \mathcal{F} \text{ is separable.}$$

In fact this holds much more generally.

10.4.5. Lemma. *$\{M_1, \ldots, M_p\} \subseteq \Lambda$ is separable* $\Leftrightarrow$

$$\forall N_1, \ldots, N_p \; \exists C[\;\;] \quad C[M_1] = N_1 \wedge \cdots \wedge C[M_p] = N_p.$$

Proof. ($\Rightarrow$) Suppose $F(\lambda\vec{x}.M_i) = N_i$. Take $C[\;\;] = F(\lambda\vec{x}.[\;\;])$.

($\Leftarrow$) By lemma 2.1.20. □

For the remainder of this section, let $\mathcal{F}$ denote a finite set of terms.

10.4.6. Definition. A sequence number α is *useful* for $\mathcal{F}$ if
(1) $\forall M \in \mathcal{F} M|\alpha\downarrow$,
(2) $\exists M, N \in \mathcal{F} M \not\sim_\alpha N$.

The following definition is by induction on the number of elements of $\mathcal{F}$.

10.4.7. Definition. $\mathcal{F}$ is *distinct* if $\mathcal{F}$ consists of one element or some $\alpha \in \text{Seq}$ is useful for $\mathcal{F}$ and the $\sim_\alpha$ equivalence classes of elements of $\mathcal{F}$ are all distinct.

Important examples of distinct sets are given by the following lemma.

10.4.8. Lemma. *Let $\mathcal{F}$ consist of terms having different $\beta\eta$-nf's. Then $\mathcal{F}$ is distinct.*

Proof. By induction on the number p of elements of $\mathcal{F}$.
The case $p = 1$ is trivial, so suppose
$p > 1$. Let $M, N \in \mathcal{F}$ have different $\beta\eta$-nf's. Then $M \not\approx_\eta N$, hence by theorem 10.2.31 for some α one has $M \not\sim_\alpha N$. Since the elements of $\mathcal{F}$ have nf's it follows that

$$\forall L \in \mathcal{F} \quad L|\alpha\downarrow.$$

Hence α is useful for $\mathcal{F}$. By the induction hypothesis it follows that the $\sim_\alpha$ equivalence classes are all distinct. Therefore $\mathcal{F}$ is distinct. □

The main result of Coppo et al. [1978] is that in the λK-calculus

$$\mathcal{F} \text{ is separable} \Leftrightarrow \mathcal{F} \text{ is distinct.}$$

In this section only $\Leftarrow$ will be proved. The implication $\Rightarrow$ is postponed until §14.

10.4.9. DEFINITION. $\mathfrak{F}$ is *original* if $\mathfrak{F}$ consists of λ-free hnf's and $\forall M, N \in \mathfrak{F}$ $[M \not\sim N \Rightarrow M, N$ have different head variables].

10.4.10. LEMMA. *Let $\mathfrak{F}$ consist of solvable terms.*
 (i) $\exists \pi$ *π is $\mathfrak{F}$-faithful and $\mathfrak{F}^\pi$ is λ-free.*
 (ii) $\exists \pi$ *π is $\mathfrak{F}$-faithful and $\mathfrak{F}^\pi$ is original.*

PROOF. Define $(\ )^\pi = (\ )x_1 \cdots x_n$, with the $\vec{x}$ fresh and n sufficiently large. Then by corollary 10.3.12(i) the transformation π is $\mathfrak{F}$-faithful.
 (ii) By (i) it may be assumed that $\mathfrak{F}$ is λ-free. Let

$$\mathfrak{F}_y = \{M \in \mathfrak{F} \mid y \text{ is the head variable of (the hnf of) } M\}.$$

If $M, N \in \mathfrak{F}_y$, say $M = yM_1 \cdots M_p, N = yN_1 \cdots N_q$, then $M \sim N \Leftrightarrow p = q$. Let

$$X(\mathfrak{F}) = \{p \mid \exists M \in \mathfrak{F}\, M = yM_1 \cdots M_p\}$$

and $p = \max X(\mathfrak{F})$. Now define π_y as follows

$$(\ )^{\pi_y} = (\ )a_1 \cdots a_{p+1}[y := \mathbf{P}_p],$$

where the $\vec{a}$ are fresh. Then $\mathfrak{F}_y^{\pi_y}$ is original and π_y is $\mathfrak{F}_y$- and even $\mathfrak{F}$-faithful. [*Example*. Let $\mathfrak{F}_y$ be

$$yPP$$
$$yPQ$$
$$yPPP$$
$$yPPPP.$$

Then $\mathfrak{F}_y^{\pi_y}$ is

$$\begin{aligned}
&yPPa_1a_2a_3a_4a_5 && [y := P_4] = a_3P^*P^*a_1a_2a_4a_5\\
&yPQa_1a_2a_3a_4a_5 && [y := P_4] = a_3P^*Q^*a_1a_2a_4a_5\\
&yPPPa_1a_2a_3a_4a_5 && [y := P_4] = a_2P^*P^*P^*a_1a_3a_4a_5\\
&yPPPPa_1a_2a_3a_4a_5 && [y := P_4] = a_1P^*P^*P^*P^*a_2a_3a_4a_5.]
\end{aligned}$$

Performing consecutively for each head variable z in $\mathfrak{F}$ such Böhm transformation π_z yields the required π. □

10.4.11. COROLLARY. *Let $\mathfrak{F}$ consist of solvable terms. Let $\mathfrak{F} = \mathfrak{F}_1 \cup \cdots \cup \mathfrak{F}_q$ be the partition of $\mathfrak{F}$ into $\sim$-equivalence classes. Then*

$$\forall N_1 \cdots N_q\ \exists \pi\ \forall M \in \mathfrak{F}_k\quad M^\pi = N_k, \quad 1 \leqslant k \leqslant q.$$

PROOF. Let $\mathscr{F} = \{M_1, \ldots, M_p\}$ be given. By the lemma it may be assumed that $\mathscr{F}$ is original. This means that for $1 \leqslant i, j \leqslant p$

$$M_i = y_i M_{i1} \cdots M_{im_i} \text{ and } M_i \sim M_j \Leftrightarrow y_i = y_j.$$

Let $N_1, \ldots, N_q$ be given. Define π as follows:

$$[\quad]^\pi = [\quad][y_{i_1} := \lambda x_1 \cdots x_{m_{i_1}}.N_1] \cdots [y_{i_q} := \lambda x_1 \cdots x_{m_{i_q}}.N_q],$$

where $\{y_{i_1}, \ldots, y_{i_q}\}$ are the different head variables of $\mathscr{F}$. Then π clearly works. [*Example*. $\mathscr{F} = \{xPP, xPQ, yPP, zPQR\}$,

$$[\quad]^\pi = [\quad][x := \lambda x_1 x_2.N_1][y := \lambda x_1 x_2.N_2][z := \lambda x_1 x_2 x_3.N_3].$$

Then $\mathscr{F}^\pi = \{N_1, N_1, N_2, N_3\}$.]. $\square$

10.4.12. PROPOSITION. *$\mathscr{F}$ distinct $\Rightarrow \mathscr{F}$ separable.*

PROOF. By induction on Card($\mathscr{F}$). Suppose Card($\mathscr{F}$) > 1, for otherwise it is trivial.

By assumption some α is useful for $\mathscr{F}$. Let α be such with minimal length. Then

(1) $\exists M, N \in \mathscr{F} \quad M \not\sim_\alpha N$,

(2) $\forall M \in \mathscr{F} \quad M | \alpha \downarrow$,

(3) $\forall \beta < \alpha \quad \forall M, N \in \mathscr{F} \quad M \sim_\beta N$.

Let $\mathscr{F} = \mathscr{F}_1 \cup \cdots \cup \mathscr{F}_k$ be the partition of $\mathscr{F}$ into $\sim_\alpha$ equivalence classes. By (1) Card($\mathscr{F}_i$) < Card($\mathscr{F}$), hence, by the induction hypothesis $\mathscr{F}_i$ is separable for $1 \leqslant i \leqslant k$.

By proposition 10.3.13 and (2), (3) for some π_1

$$\forall M, N \in \mathscr{F} \quad [M^{\pi_1} \sim N^{\pi_1} \Leftrightarrow M \sim_\alpha N] \wedge M^{\pi_1} \text{ solvable.}$$

Claim. For all $F_1, \ldots, F_k$ there exists a π such that

(4) $\qquad \forall M \in \mathscr{F}_i \quad M^\pi = F_i, \quad 1 \leqslant i \leqslant k.$

Indeed, observe that $\mathscr{F}^{\pi_1} = \mathscr{F}_1^{\pi_1} \cup \cdots \cup \mathscr{F}_k^{\pi_1}$ is a partition of $\mathscr{F}^{\pi_1}$ into $\sim$ equivalence classes. Hence, by corollary 10.4.11, given $F_1, \ldots, F_k$ there exists a π_2 such that

(5) $\qquad \forall M \in \mathscr{F}_i^{\pi_1} \quad M^{\pi_2} = F_i, \quad 1 \leqslant i \leqslant k.$

Now define $\pi = \pi_2 \circ \pi_1$. Then by (5)

$$\forall M \in \mathscr{F}_i \quad M^\pi = (M^{\pi_1})^{\pi_2} = F_i,$$

proving the claim.

Let $\mathrm{FV}(\mathcal{F}) \subseteq \{\vec{x}\}$. Given $F_1, \ldots, F_k$, find a π such that (4) holds. Define

$$C[\ \ ] = C_\pi[\ \ ](\lambda \vec{x}.[\ \ ]),$$

where $C_\pi[\ \ ]$ is such that $\forall M\ C_\pi[M] = M^\pi$ (by lemma 10.3.4 this exists). Then

$$\forall M \in \mathcal{F}_i C[M] = C_\pi[M](\lambda \vec{x}.M)$$

$$= F_i(\lambda \vec{x}.M) \quad \text{by (4).}$$

Since the $\mathcal{F}_i$ are separable we may choose F_i such that for all $M \in \mathcal{F}_i$ the term $F_i(\lambda \vec{x}.M)$ equals a prescribed value. Therefore $\mathcal{F}$ is separable. □

In chapter 14 the converse implication will be proved.

10.4.13. THEOREM (Coppo et al. [1978]). *For the* λK*-calculus one has*

$\mathcal{F}$ *is separable* $\Leftrightarrow$ $\mathcal{F}$ *is distinct*.

PROOF. By propositions 10.4.12 and 14.4.14. □

10.4.14. COROLLARY. *Let* $\mathcal{F} = \{M_1, \ldots, M_n\}$ *be a set of distinct* $\beta\eta$-nf's. *Then* $\mathcal{F}$ *is separable.*

PROOF. Immediate by lemma 10.4.8. □

10.5. Separability in the λI-calculus

The notion of separability relativizes in the obvious way.

10.5.1. DEFINITION. Let $\mathcal{F} = \{M_1, \ldots, M_p\} \subseteq \Lambda_K$. Then $\mathcal{F}$ is I-separable $\Leftrightarrow$

$$\forall L_1 \cdots L_p \in \Lambda_I^0 \quad \exists F \in \Lambda_I \left[FM_1 = L_1 \wedge \cdots \wedge FM_p = L_p\right].$$

It is clear that if $\mathcal{F} \subseteq \Lambda_I$ is I-separable, then $\mathcal{F} \subseteq \Lambda_I^0$: free variables cannot be thrown away. For $\mathcal{F} \subseteq \Lambda_I^0$ one can completely characterize separability.

10.5.2. THEOREM. *Let* $\mathcal{F} = \{M_1, \ldots, M_p\} \subseteq \Lambda_I^0$. *Then* $\mathcal{F}$ *is* I*-separable* $\Leftrightarrow$ $\mathcal{F}$ *consists of terms having distinct* $\beta\eta$-nf's.

PROOF. ($\Rightarrow$) By assumption $\exists F \in \Lambda_I[FM_1 = \ulcorner 1 \urcorner \wedge \cdots \wedge FM_p = \ulcorner p \urcorner]$ (Church's numerals). Hence by corollary 9.1.6 all the M_i have a β-nf. By reducing all η-redexes it follows that the M_i have a $\beta\eta$-nf. If M_i, M_j have the same $\beta\eta$-nf, then $\lambda\eta \vdash \ulcorner i \urcorner = \ulcorner j \urcorner$, hence $i = j$.

($\Leftarrow$) By the next theorem. □

In fact something stronger can be proved.

10.5.3. THEOREM. *Let* $\mathcal{F} = \{M_1, \ldots, M_p\} \subseteq \Lambda_K^0$ *be a set of distinct* $\beta\eta$-nf's. *Then* $\mathcal{F}$ *is I-separable.*

PROOF. This occupies the rest of this section. □

10.5.4. DEFINITION. (i) An *I-solving* transformation π is one defined by either

$$M^\pi = Mx \quad \text{for some } x,$$

or

$$M^\pi = M[x := N] \quad \text{for some } x \text{ and } N \in \Lambda_I.$$

(ii) An *I-Böhm* transformation is the finite composition of I-solving transformations.

(iii) $\pi \in I$ denotes that π is an I-Böhm transformation.

10.5.5. DEFINITION. (i) A *distinct normal set* (dns) is a finite set $\mathcal{F} = M_1, \ldots, M_p$ of terms having distinct $\beta\eta$-nf's.

(ii) $\mathcal{F}$ ranges over dns's.

10.5.6. DEFINITION. If $M = \lambda x_1 \cdots x_n . y M_1 \cdots M_m$, then the argument number of M (notation $\natural(M)$) is the integer $m - n$. Note that for hnf's one has

$M \sim N \Leftrightarrow M$ and N have the same head variable and $\natural(M) = \natural(N)$. Moreover

$$\natural(xM_1 \cdots M_n) = n, \qquad \natural(My) = \natural(M) + 1,$$

$$\natural(\lambda x.M) = \natural(M) - 1.$$

10.5.7. DEFINITION. (i) $\mathcal{F}_I^* = \{\pi \in I \mid \pi \text{ is } \mathcal{F}\text{-faithful and } \mathcal{F}^\pi \text{ is a dns}\}$.

10.5.8. LEMMA. (i) *If* $\pi \in \mathcal{F}_I^*$ *and* $\pi' \in (\mathcal{F}^\pi)_I^*$, *then* $\pi' \circ \pi \in \mathcal{F}_I^*$.

(ii) *Let x be fresh. Define* $(\ )^\pi = (\ )x$. *Then* $\pi \in \mathcal{F}_I^*$.

PROOF. (i) $\mathcal{F}$ is a dns$\Rightarrow\pi(\mathcal{F})$ is a dns$\Rightarrow\pi'\circ\pi(\mathcal{F})$ is a dns. Moreover for $M,N\in\mathcal{F}$

$$\pi'\circ\pi(M)\sim\pi'\circ\pi(N)\Rightarrow\pi(M)\sim\pi(N)\Rightarrow M\sim N.$$

(ii) Clearly $\pi\in I$. Moreover

(1) π is $\mathcal{F}$-faithful. This is so by lemma 10.3.12(i).

(2) $\mathcal{F}^{\pi}$ is a dns. Clearly $\mathcal{F}^{\pi}$ consists of $\beta\eta$-nf's. Moreover these are different: suppose Mx, $M'x$ (with $M, M'\in\mathcal{F}$, $M\not\equiv M'$) have the same $\beta\eta$-nf. Then also $\lambda x.Mx=_{\beta\eta}\lambda x.M'x$ and hence (x is fresh) $M=_{\beta\eta}M'$ contradicting that $\mathcal{F}$ is a dns. [At this place is needed that terms in a dns have distinct η-nf's. Otherwise e.g. the sequence $\lambda x.zx$, z would become zx, zx.] □

10.5.9. COROLLARY. $\forall\mathcal{F}\ \exists\pi\in\mathcal{F}_I^*\ \mathcal{F}^{\pi}$ *is* λ*-free*

PROOF. Take $(\ )=(\ )x_1\cdots x_p$, with p large enough. □

10.5.10. DEFINITION. (i) A *block* in $\mathcal{F}$ is a $\sim$-equivalence class within $\mathcal{F}$.

(ii) The *head variable* of a block is the head variable of any of its elements.

Remember that $\mathcal{F}$ is *original* iff $\mathcal{F}$ is λ-free and different blocks in $\mathcal{F}$ have different head variables.

10.5.11. DEFINITION. Let $\mathfrak{B}$ be a λ-free block (in some $\mathcal{F}$), say $\mathfrak{B}$ is

$$M_1=yM_{11}\cdots M_{1m},$$
$$\cdots$$
$$M_q=yM_{q1}\cdots M_{qm}.$$

Then $\mathfrak{B}$ is *x-straight* iff
if $x\in\mathrm{FV}(M_{i_0j_0})$ for some $M_{i_0j_0}$ in the block, then
$x\not\equiv y$ and for all $1\leqslant i\leqslant q$ one has $M_{ij_0}=x$.

10.5.12. EXAMPLES. (i) $y\mathbf{I}xx$ and $x\mathbf{I}$ are x-straight.
$y\mathbf{S}xx$ $\quad x\mathbf{S}$

(ii) $y\mathbf{I}x$, $x\mathbf{I}x$ and $y\mathbf{I}(xy)x$ are not x-straight.
yxx $\quad x\mathbf{S}x$ $\quad y\mathbf{S}(xy)x$

10.5.13. DEFINITION. $\mathcal{F}$ is *special* iff

(1) $\mathcal{F}$ is original,

(2) If x is the head variable of some block in $\mathcal{F}$, then all blocks in $\mathcal{F}$ are x-straight.

Now we want to show that every dns can be transformed by a π into a special one.

10.5.14. NOTATIONS. (i) Remember that $\mathbf{P}_k \equiv \lambda x_1 \cdots x_{k+1}.x_{k+1}x_1 \cdots x_k$.
(ii) If $M_1, \ldots, M_p$ is a sequence of terms, then

$$M_1, \ldots, \hat{M}_i, \ldots, M_p$$

is the sequence $M_1, \ldots, M_{i-1}, M_{i+1}, \ldots, M_p$ for some i with $1 \leqslant i \leqslant p$.
(iii) $\mathcal{A}_k = \{M \mid M \text{ is a } \beta\eta\text{-nf} \wedge \|M\| < k\}$.

10.5.15. DEFINITION. Let $\mathcal{F}$ be a λ-free dns. In $\mathcal{F}$ the *multiblock with head variable* x is the set

$$\mathcal{F}_x = \{M \in \mathcal{F} \mid x \text{ is the head variable of } M\}.$$

10.5.16. LEMMA. *Let $\mathcal{B}$ be a multiblock in some λ-free $\mathcal{F}$. Then $\exists \pi \in \mathcal{F}_I^*$ $\mathcal{B}^\pi$ is special.*

PROOF. Let $\mathcal{B}$ be

$$\boxed{\begin{array}{l} xM^1_{11} \cdots M^1_{1m_1} \\ \cdots \\ xM^1_{n_11} \cdots M^1_{n_1m_1} \end{array}}$$

$$\boxed{\begin{array}{l} xM^2_{11} \cdots\cdots M^2_{1m_2} \\ \cdots \end{array}}$$

$$\cdots$$

$$\cdots$$

$$\boxed{\begin{array}{l} xM^k_{11} \cdots\cdots\cdots M^k_{1m_q} \\ \cdots \end{array}}$$

where $m_1 < m_2 < \cdots < m_q$. Define

$$(\ )^\pi = (\ )[x := \mathbf{P}_k] z_1 \cdots z_{k+1}$$

where $k > \|M\|$ for all $M \in \mathcal{F}$ and the $\vec{z}$ are fresh.

First it will be shown that $\mathcal{B}^\pi$ is special. Let $M \in \mathcal{B}$, $M = xM_1 \cdots M_m$. Then

$$M^\pi = z_{k+1-m} M_1^* \cdots M_m^* z_1 \cdots \hat{z}_{k+1-m} \cdots z_{k+1},$$

where $M_i^* = M_i[x:= \mathbf{P}_k]$. Hence $\mathcal{B}^\pi$ is

$$\boxed{\begin{array}{l} z_{k+1-m_1} M_{11}^{1*} \cdots M_{1m_1}^{1*} z_1 \cdots \hat{z}_{k+1-m_1} \cdots z_{k+1} \\ \cdots \\ z_{k+1-m_1} M_{n_1 1}^{1} \cdots M_{n_1 m_1}^{1} z_1 \cdots \hat{z}_{k+1-m_1} \cdots z_{k+1} \end{array}}$$

$$\cdots$$

$$\cdots$$

$$\boxed{\begin{array}{l} z_{k+1-m_q} M_{11}^{q*} \cdots M_{1m_q}^{q*} z_1 \cdots \hat{z}_{k+1-m_q} \cdots z_{k+1} \\ \cdots \end{array}}$$

Therefore it is clear that $\mathcal{B}^\pi$ is original. Since the $\vec{z}$ are fresh, $\mathcal{B}^\pi$ is also special.

It will now be shown that $\pi \in \mathcal{F}_I^*$.

(1) Since $\mathbf{P}_k \in \Lambda_I^0$ one has $\pi \in I$.

(2) By lemmas 10.3.12 and 10.5.8 $\mathcal{F}^\pi$ is a dns.

(3) Since $k > \|M\|$ for $M \in \mathcal{F}$ one has $\mathcal{F} \subseteq \mathcal{Q}_k$ and hence by lemmas 10.3.12 and 10.5.8 π is $\mathcal{F}$-faithful. □

10.5.17. Corollary. $\forall \mathcal{F}\ \exists \pi \in \mathcal{F}_I^*$ *$\mathcal{F}^\pi$ is special.*

Proof. By corollary 10.5.9 one may assume that $\mathcal{F}$ is λ-free. Successive applications of lemma 10.5.16 to the different multiblocks $\mathcal{F}_x$ yields a dns $\mathcal{F}^\pi$, with $\pi \in \mathcal{F}_I^*$, that is original. Let z be one of the head variables of $\mathcal{F}^\pi$ that is substituted in the head variable x of $\mathcal{F}_x$. Then not only blocks in $\mathcal{F}_x^\pi$ become z-straight, but also those in $(\mathcal{F} - \mathcal{F}_x)^\pi$ since z is fresh. Therefore $\mathcal{F}^\pi$ is special. □

10.5.18. Definition. $\mathcal{F}$ is *discrete* iff the terms of $\mathcal{F}$ are not all $\sim$-equivalent.

It will be shown that each $\mathcal{F}$ can be I-transformed into a discrete dns. To this purpose an algorithm is constructed, intended to split blocks. In order to show that this algorithm terminates, a natural number $d(M,N)$ is defined, indicating the depth of the essential difference in $\mathrm{BT}(M)$ and $\mathrm{BT}(N)$.

10.5.19. Definition. Let M, N have different $\beta\eta$-nf's. Then $M \not\sim_\eta N$. Hence by theorem 10.2.31 (see also exercise 10.6.9) $M \not\sim_\alpha N$ for some α. Define

$$d(M,N) = \min\{\mathrm{lh}(\alpha) \mid M \not\sim_\alpha N\}.$$

10.5.20. LEMMA. *$\forall \mathfrak{F}\, \forall M \not\equiv N \in \mathfrak{F}\, \exists \pi \in \mathfrak{F}_I^*$ [$\mathfrak{F}^\pi$ is special and $d(M^\pi, N^\pi) = d(M, N)$].*

PROOF. Let $\mathcal{C}$ consist of terms having different $\beta\eta$-nf's. A Böhm transformation π is called *$\mathcal{C}$-conservative* iff $\forall M \not\equiv N \in \mathcal{C}\; d(M^\pi, N^\pi) = d(M, N)$. It will be shown that the components of the π making $\mathfrak{F}$ special are all conservative on their appropriate domains so that π itself is $\mathfrak{F}$-conservative.

(1) The transformation $(\ \ )^{\pi_0} = (\ \ )x$ is clearly $\mathcal{C}$-conservative for $x \notin \mathrm{FV}(\mathcal{C})$. Hence the transformation that makes a dns $\mathfrak{F}$ λ-free is $\mathfrak{F}$-conservative.

(2) Now it will be shown that the transformation $(\ \ )^\pi = (\ \ )[x := \mathbf{P}_k]$ is $\mathcal{C}_k$ conservative. Let $M, N \in \mathcal{C}_k$, $M \not\equiv N$. By induction on $k = d(\mathrm{BT}(M)) + d(\mathrm{BT}(N))$ it will be shown that $d(M_1^\pi, M_2^\pi) = d(M_1, M_2)$.

$k = 0$. Then $M = \lambda\vec{y}_i.z_1$, $N = \lambda\vec{y}_2.z_2$. If $d(M, N) = 0$, then $M \not\sim N$ and hence by lemma 10.3.12(ii) $M^\pi \not\sim N^\pi$, i.e. $d(M^\pi, N^\pi) = 0$. If $d(M, N) \neq 0$, then $M \sim N$ which in this case implies $M \equiv N$ contrary to the assumption.

$k > 0$. If $d(M, N) = 0$, then again $d(M^\pi, N^\pi) = 0$. If $d(M, N) \neq 0$, then $M \sim N$. We may assume that M, N are λ-free: $M = yM_1 \cdots M_m$, $N = yN_1 \cdots N_m$.

Case 1. $y \equiv x$. Then the λ-free forms of M^π, N^π are $z_{k+1}M_1^\pi \cdots M_m^\pi z_{m+1} \cdots z_k$, $z_{k+1}N_1^\pi \cdots N_m^\pi z_{m+1} \cdots z_k$ respectively. Now

$$d(M^\pi, N^\pi) = \mathrm{Max}\{1 + d(M_i^\pi, N_i^\pi) | 1 \leqslant i \leqslant m\}$$

$$= \mathrm{Max}\{1 + d(M_i, N_i) | 1 \leqslant i \leqslant m\}, \text{ by the induction hypothesis,}$$

$$= d(M, N).$$

Case 2. $y \not\equiv x$. Then the result follows similarly. □

10.5.21. LEMMA. *$\forall M_1 \neq M_2 \in \mathfrak{F}[M_1 \sim M_2 \Rightarrow \exists \pi \in \mathfrak{F}_I^*\, d(M_1^\pi, M_2^\pi) < d(M_1, M_2)]$*

PROOF. By lemma 10.5.20 it may be assumed that $\mathfrak{F}$ is special. Assume $M_1 \neq M_2$, $M_1 \sim M_2$. Then M_1, M_2 occur in the same block in $\mathfrak{F}$. Let this block be

$$M_1 = x_1 M_{11} \cdots M_{1m}$$
$$M_2 = x_1 M_{21} \cdots M_{2m}$$
$$\cdots$$
$$M_n = x_1 M_{n1} \cdots M_{nm}$$

Since $M_1 \sim M_2$ one has $d(M_1, M_2) > 0$ and therefore for some i_0

(1) $$d(M_1, M_2) = d(M_{1i_0}, M_{2i_0}) + 1$$

and $M_{1i_0} \neq M_{2i_0}$. For $1 \leqslant j \leqslant n$ let $M_{ji_0} = \lambda b_1 \cdots b_{q_j}.y_j L_{j1} \cdots L_{jr_j}$ and set $q = \max\{q_1, \ldots, q_n\}$. By the variable convention it may be assumed that the $b_1, \ldots, b_q$ are not free in $\mathcal{F}$. Define

$$F \equiv \lambda a_1 \cdots a_m b_1 \cdots b_q . a_{i_0} b_1 \cdots b_p a_1 \cdots \hat{a}_{i_0} \cdots a_m,$$

$$(\quad)^{\pi} = (\quad) b_1 \cdots b_q [x_1 := F].$$

First it will be shown that $\pi \in \mathcal{F}_I^*$. It is clear that $\pi \in I$. Now let $\mathcal{F}$ be

$$\boxed{\begin{array}{ll} x_1 M_{11} \cdots M_{1i_0} \cdots M_{1m} & M_{1i_0} = \lambda b_1 \cdots b_{q_1} . y_1 L_{11} \cdots L_{1r_1} \\ \cdots & \\ x_1 M_{n1} \cdots M_{ni_0} \cdots M_{nm} & M_{ni_0} = \lambda b_1 \cdots b_{q_n} . y_n L_{n1} \cdots L_{nr_n} \end{array}}$$

$$\boxed{\begin{array}{l} x_2 \cdots x_1 \text{ (possibly)} \cdots \\ \cdots \\ x_2 \cdots x_1 \text{ (possibly)} \cdots \end{array}}$$

$\cdots$

$\cdots$

$$\boxed{\begin{array}{l} x_k \cdots \\ \cdots \\ x_k \cdots \end{array}}$$

Since $\mathcal{F}$ is special, x_1 occurs actively only in the first block. Therefore $\mathcal{F}^{\pi}$ is

$$\begin{array}{r} M_1^{\pi} = \\ M_2^{\pi} = \\ \\ \\ \end{array} \boxed{\begin{array}{l} y_1 L_{11} \cdots L_{1r_1} b_{q_1+1} \cdots b_p M_{11} \cdots \hat{M}_{1i_0} \cdots M_{1m} \\ y_2 L_{21} \cdots L_{2r_2} b_{q_2+1} \cdots b_p M_{21} \cdots \hat{M}_{2i_0} \cdots M_{2m} \\ \cdots \\ y_n L_{n1} \cdots L_{nr_n} b_{q_n+1} \cdots b_p M_{n1} \cdots \hat{M}_{ni_0} \cdots M_{nm} \end{array}}$$

$$\boxed{\begin{array}{l} x_2 \cdots F \text{ (possibly)} \cdots \vec{b} \\ \cdots \\ x_2 \cdots F \text{ (possibly)} \cdots \vec{b} \end{array}}$$

$\cdots$

$\cdots$

$$\boxed{\begin{array}{l} x_k \cdots \vec{b} \\ \cdots \\ x_k \cdots \vec{b} \end{array}}$$

Clearly $\mathfrak{F}^\pi$ consists of terms having a $\beta\eta$-nf. Moreover the $\vec{y}$ are distinct from all the $\vec{x}$: if, say, $y_2 \equiv x_2$, then since $\mathfrak{F}$ is special, it would follow that $y_2 = M_{1i_0} = M_{2i_0}$, contradicting the choice of i_0. It follows that π is $\mathfrak{F}$-faithful. In order to prove that $\mathfrak{F}^\pi$ is a dns, we have only to show that the π-image of each separate block in $\mathfrak{F}$ consists of terms having distinct $\beta\eta$-nf's. For the first block this is true, since each term can be reconstructed from its image. Also the other blocks remain a dns, since the possible substitution $[x_1 := F]$ is innocent (the blocks are x_1-straight). Thus indeed $\pi \in \mathfrak{F}_I^*$.

Finally we show that $d(M_1^\pi, M_2^\pi) < d(M_1, M_2)$. One has

$$\begin{aligned} d(M_1^\pi, M_2^\pi) &= 1 + d(L_{1j_0}, L_{2j_0}) \quad \text{for some } j_0,\\ &= d(M_{1i_0}, M_{2i_0})\\ &< d(M_1, M_2) \quad \text{by (1).} \quad \square \end{aligned}$$

10.5.22. COROLLARY.

$$\forall \mathfrak{F}\ \forall M_1 \neq M_2 \in \mathfrak{F}\ \exists \pi \in \mathfrak{F}_I^* \quad M_1^\pi \not\sim M_2^\pi.$$

PROOF. If $M_1 \sim M_2$, the lemma yields a $\pi_1 \in \mathfrak{F}_I^*$ such that $d(M_1^{\pi_1}, M_2^{\pi_1}) < d(M_1, M_2)$. If $M_1^{\pi_1} \not\sim M_2^{\pi_1}$ we are done. Otherwise the lemma applies again. Since the $d(\text{-},\text{-})$ cannot decrease forever, eventually one has $M_1^\pi \not\sim M_2^\pi$. □

10.5.23. PROPOSITION. $\forall \mathfrak{F}\ \exists \pi \in \mathfrak{F}_I^*\ \mathfrak{F}^\pi$ *is discrete.*

PROOF. Let $\mathfrak{F}$ be $M_1, \ldots, M_p$. By applying the preceding result at most p times, the appropriate π can be found (use the faithfulness of the transformations involved). □

10.5.24. DEFINITION. A dns $\mathfrak{F}$ is *regular* if $\mathfrak{F}$ is discrete, special and the only free variables in $\mathfrak{F}$ are its head variables (that may occur in different places however).

Examples. (i) $\{x_1\mathbf{I}x_2\mathbf{S},\ x_2x_1\mathbf{SS},\ x_3x_1x_1x_2\mathbf{K}\}$ is regular.

(ii) $\{x_1\mathbf{IS},\ x_2\mathbf{S}(x_1\mathbf{I})\}$ is not regular.

10.5.25. LEMMA. $\forall \mathfrak{F}\ \exists \pi \in \mathfrak{F}_I^*\ \mathfrak{F}^\pi$ *is regular.*

PROOF. By proposition 10.5.23 and corollary 10.5.17 it may be assumed that $\mathfrak{F}$ is discrete and special. Let $\{x_1, \ldots, x_p\}$ be the head variables of the terms in $\mathfrak{F}$ and let $\{y_1, \ldots, y_m\} = \mathrm{FV}(\mathfrak{F}) - \{x_1, \ldots, x_p\}$. Define

$$(\ )^{\pi_1} = (\ )[y_1 := \mathbf{P}_{k_1}]$$

where k_1 is so large that $\mathfrak{F} \subseteq \mathfrak{A}_{k_1}$. Then by lemma 10.3.12 one has $\pi_1 \in \mathfrak{F}_I^*$

and $\mathcal{F}^{\pi_1}$ has less free non-head variables than $\mathcal{F}$. Continuing this way finally a $\pi \in \mathcal{F}_I^*$ is obtained such that $\mathcal{F}^{\pi}$ is regular. □

10.5.26. LEMMA. *Let $\mathcal{F}$ be $M_1, \ldots, M_p$ and let $k_1, \ldots, k_p \in \mathbb{N}$. Then for some $\pi \in I$ one has $\mathcal{F}^{\pi} = \{\llcorner k_1 \lrcorner \cdots \llcorner k_p \lrcorner\}$.*

PROOF. By lemma 10.5.25 it may be assumed that $\mathcal{F}$ is regular. Say $\mathcal{F}$ is

$$x_1 M_{11} \cdots M_{1m_1}$$
$$\cdots$$
$$x_p M_{p1} \cdots M_{pm_p}$$

and either $M_{ij} \in \Lambda^0$ or $M_{ij} \in \{x_1, \ldots, x_p\}$ for all i,j with $1 \leqslant i \leqslant p$, $1 \leqslant j \leqslant m_i$.
By theorem 9.4.22 there exists a uniform λI-solution $\vec{O} \in \mathrm{SO}$ for the closed terms among the M_{ij}, i.e.

$$(1) \qquad M_{ij} \in \Lambda^0 \Rightarrow M_{ij}\vec{O} = \mathbf{I}.$$

By adding some $\mathbf{I}$'s it may be assumed that $\vec{O} = O_1, \ldots, O_r$ with $r > m_i + 1$ for all i, $1 \leqslant i \leqslant p$.
Now define, for $1 \leqslant i \leqslant p$,

$$L_i = \lambda y_1 \cdots y_{m_i}.(y_1 \vec{O}\mathbf{I}^{\sim q}) \cdots (y_{m_i}\vec{O}\mathbf{I}^{\sim q})\llcorner k_i \lrcorner$$

where q has to be determined yet. Note that

$$L_i\vec{O}\mathbf{I}^{\sim q} = (O\vec{O}\mathbf{I}^{\sim q}) \cdots (O_{m_i}\vec{O}\mathbf{I}^{\sim q})\llcorner k_i \lrcorner O_{m_i+1} \cdots O_r\mathbf{I}^{\sim q}.$$

By lemma 9.4.9(ii) there is a q_1 such that for $q \geqslant q_1$ the SO terms $O_j\vec{O}$ are solved by $\mathbf{I}^{\sim q}$, i.e.

$$O_j\vec{O}\mathbf{I}^{\sim q} = \mathbf{I}.$$

Then, for $1 \leqslant i \leqslant p$, one has

$$\begin{aligned} L_i\vec{O}\mathbf{I}^{\sim q} &= \llcorner k_i \lrcorner O_{m_i+1} O_{m_i+2} \cdots O_r\mathbf{I}^{\sim q} \\ &= \begin{cases} O_{m_i+1}^{k_i}(O_{m_i+2}) \cdots O_r\mathbf{I}^{\sim q} & \text{if } k_i \neq 0, \\ O_{m_i+1}\mathbf{I}\mathbf{I}O_{m_i+2} \cdots O_r\mathbf{I}^{\sim q} & \text{else.} \end{cases} \\ &= H_i\mathbf{I}^{\sim q} \end{aligned}$$

for a certain SO term H_i which is independent of q. Again by lemma 9.4.9(ii) there is a q_2 such that if $q \geqslant q_2$, then $H_i \mathbf{I}^{\sim q} = \mathbf{I}$ for all $1 \leqslant i \leqslant p$. It follows that if $q = \max\{q_1, q_2\}$, then

(2) $$L_i \vec{O} \mathbf{I}^{\sim q} = \mathbf{I},$$

(3) $$M_{ij} \vec{O} \mathbf{I}^{\sim q} = \mathbf{I} \quad \text{for } M_{ij} \in \Lambda^0, \quad \text{by (1)}.$$

Define

$$(\ )^{\pi} = (\ )[x_1 := L_1] \cdots [x_p := L_p]$$

(where the q in the definition of the L_i is $\max\{q_1, q_2\}$). Then $\pi \in I$ and $\mathcal{F}^{\pi}$ is

$$L_1 M_{11}^* \cdots M_{1m_1}^*$$
$$\cdots$$
$$L_p M_{p1}^* \cdots M_{pm_p}^*$$

where

(4) $$\text{either } M_{ij}^* \equiv M_{ij} \in \Lambda^0 \quad \text{or} \quad M_{ij}^* \in \{L_1, \ldots, L_p\}.$$

Therefore

$$\begin{aligned} M_i^{\pi} &= L_i M_{i1}^* \cdots M_{im_i}^* \\ &= (M_{i1}^* \vec{O} \mathbf{I}^{\sim q}) \cdots (M_{im_i}^* \vec{O} \mathbf{I}^{\sim q}) \llcorner k_i \lrcorner \\ &= \llcorner k_i \lrcorner, \text{ by (4), (2) and (3).} \quad \square \end{aligned}$$

10.5.27. LEMMA. *There are $P, Q, E \in \Lambda_I^0(\vec{x})$ such that*

$$\forall N_1 \cdots N_p \in \Lambda_I^0(\vec{x}) \ \exists k_1, \ldots, k_p \quad \llcorner k_i \lrcorner PQE = N_i, \quad 1 \leqslant i \leqslant p.$$

PROOF. Let $P = \lambda z.\langle zS^+ \rangle$, $Q = \langle \llcorner 0 \lrcorner \rangle$ and $E = \mathbf{E}_{I,\vec{x}}$, where S^+ is the successor for Church's numerals and $\mathbf{E}_{I,\vec{x}} \in \Lambda_I^0(\vec{x})$ is constructed in remark 9.3.13 with

$$\forall N \in \Lambda_I^0(\vec{x}) \ \exists k \in \mathbb{N} \quad \mathbf{E}_{I,\vec{x}} \llcorner k+1 \lrcorner = N.$$

Now let $N_1, \ldots, N_p \in \Lambda_I^0(\vec{x})$ be given. Find $k_1, \ldots, k_p \in \mathbb{N}$ such that $E\llcorner k_i + 1\lrcorner = N_i$. First note that $P^n(Q) = \langle\llcorner n\lrcorner\rangle$. Then, for $1 \leqslant i \leqslant p$,

$$\llcorner k_i + 1\lrcorner PQE = P^{k_i+1}(Q)E = \langle\llcorner k_i + 1\lrcorner\rangle E = E\llcorner k_i + 1\lrcorner = N_i. \quad \square$$

Finally the promised result.

10.5.28. THEOREM. *Let* $\mathfrak{F} = \{M_1, \ldots, M_p\} \subseteq \Lambda_K^0$ *be a* dns. *Then*

$$\forall N_1, \ldots, N_p \in \Lambda_I^0(\vec{x})\ \exists \pi \in I \quad \mathfrak{F}^\pi = \{N_1, \ldots, N_p\}.$$

PROOF. By lemmas 10.5.26 and 10.5.27. □

10.5.29. COROLLARY. *Let* $M_1, \ldots, M_p \in \Lambda_K^0$ *be distinct* $\beta\eta$-nf's. *Then*

$$\forall N_1, \ldots, N_p \in \Lambda_I^0(\vec{x})\ \exists \vec{L} \in \Lambda_I^0(\vec{x})$$
$$[M_1\vec{L} = N_1 \wedge \cdots \wedge M_p\vec{L} = N_p].$$

PROOF. By the theorem and lemma 10.3.4 (ii). □

Now theorem 10.5.3 and Böhm's theorem for $\boldsymbol{\lambda I}$ follow.

10.5.30. COROLLARY. *Let* $\mathfrak{F} = \{M_1, \ldots, M_n\} \subseteq \Lambda_K^0$ *consist of distinct* $\beta\eta$-*normal forms. Then* $\mathfrak{F}$ *is I-separable.*

PROOF. Immediate, taking $\vec{x}$ empty. □

10.5.31. THEOREM. *If* $M, N \in \Lambda_I$ *have different* $\beta\eta$-nf's, *then* $M \#_I N$.

PROOF. Immediate. □

10.6. Exercises

10.6.1. (i) Show that $\mathrm{BT}^e(M)$ as defined in 10.1.9 is indeed a partially labelled tree.
(ii) Show that $|\mathrm{BT}(M)| = |\mathrm{BT}^e(M)|$.

10.6.2. Prove proposition 10.1.21.

10.6.3. Prove that for $A = \mathrm{BT}(M)$ one has $\mathrm{FV}(A) \subseteq \mathrm{FV}(M)$.

10.6.4. Show that some $A \in \Lambda_K\mathfrak{B}$ looks like a λI-tree but nevertheless $A \notin \Lambda_I\mathfrak{B}$. [*Hint*. Use the fact that $\{n|\{n\}(n) = 0\}$ and $\{n|\{n\}(n) \neq 0\}$ are recursively inseparable r.e. sets. Let $\{e\}(n) = m \Leftrightarrow \exists z[T(e, n, z) \wedge U(z) = m]$, the Kleene normal form for partial recursive functions. Let $A_n \in \mathfrak{B}$ be such that

$$A_n = \begin{cases} \mathrm{BT}(z^m x) & \text{if } T(n, n, m) \wedge U(m) = 0, \\ \mathrm{BT}(z^m y) & \text{if } T(n, n, m) \wedge U(m) \neq 0, \\ \mathrm{BT}(\boldsymbol{\Theta} z) & \text{if } \forall m \neg T(n, n, m). \end{cases}$$

Finally for A take the tree

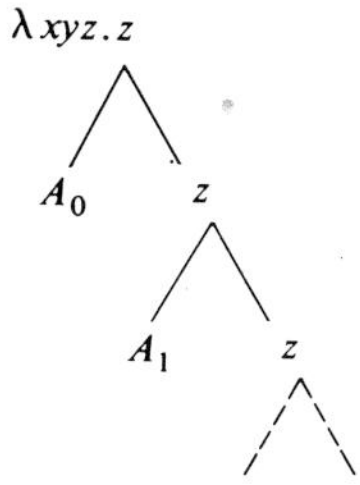

10.6.5. Find terms having as Böhm trees the following trees. [*Hint*. Do not use theorem 10.1.23.]

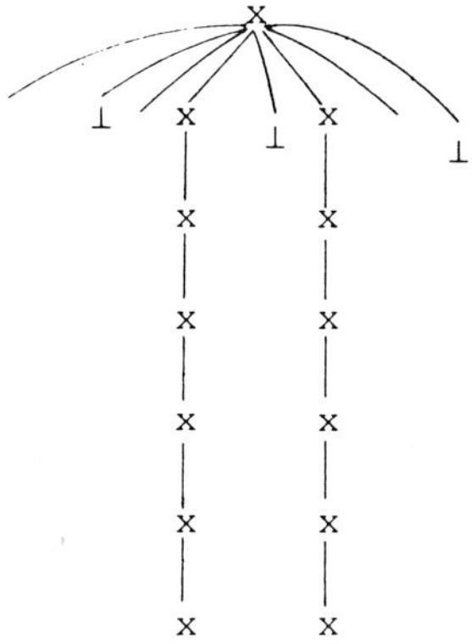

Palma.

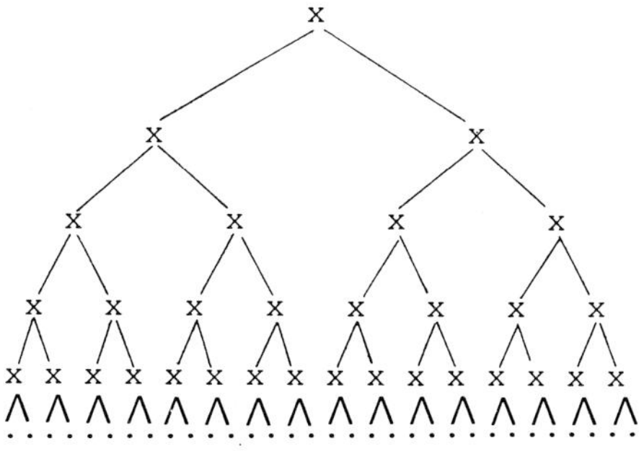

Taxus.

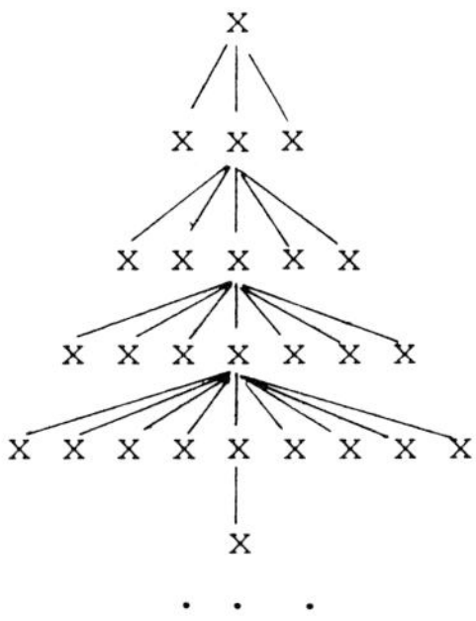

Pinus.

10.6.6. Construct a tree $A \in \Lambda\mathfrak{B}$ such that $\infty\eta(A) \notin \Lambda\mathfrak{B}$. [*Hint*. Make a construction analogous to that for exercise 10.6.4.]

10.6.7. Prove

(i) $M \,{}^{\eta}\!\underset{\sim}{\sqsubseteq}\, N \Leftrightarrow \exists M' M \lesssim_{\eta} M' \underset{\sim}{\sqsubseteq} N$.

(ii) $M \,{}^{\eta}\!\underset{\sim}{\sqsubseteq}{}^{\eta} N \Leftrightarrow \exists M', N' M \lesssim_{\eta} M' \underset{\sim}{\sqsubseteq} N' \gtrsim_{\eta} N$. [*Hint*. Use theorem 10.1.23.]

10.6.8. Let $M \in \Lambda$ be such that for all $s \in \mathrm{Seq}$ one has

$$M\,\ulcorner s \urcorner \twoheadrightarrow [M\,\ulcorner s * \langle n\rangle \urcorner]_{n\in\mathbf{N}}. \text{ Construct } \mathrm{BT}(M\,\ulcorner\langle\ \rangle\urcorner).$$

10.6.9. Show directly that if M, N are terms with different $\beta\eta$-nf, then $\exists\alpha\ M \not\sim_{\alpha} N$.

10.6.10. Let $\mathfrak{F} = \{\mathbf{S}, \mathbf{I}, \mathbf{C}, \mathbf{K}\}$. Construct a Böhm-transformation π such that $\mathfrak{F}^{\pi} = \{\mathbf{K}, \mathbf{I}, \mathbf{S}, \mathbf{S}\}$.

10.6.11. Use the Böhm-out technique to prove corollary 9.4.21.

10.6.12. (i) Show that if $M, N \in \Lambda$ have equal finite $\perp$-free Böhm trees then $\boldsymbol{\lambda} \vdash M = N$.

(ii) Show that $\mathrm{BT}(M)$ is finite and $\perp$-free iff M has a nf.

10.6.13. Let $F \in \Lambda^0$ define in $\mathfrak{M}(\lambda)$ a non constant map with a nf M_0 in its range. Show that then $x \in \mathrm{BT}(Fx)$ for all x. [*Hint*. Otherwise $\mathrm{BT}(FM) = \mathrm{BT}(FN)$ for all $M, N \in \Lambda$; in particular $\mathrm{BT}(Fx) = \mathrm{BT}(M_0)$. But then by the previous exercise $\lambda \vdash Fx = M_0$. Therefore F is constant on $\mathfrak{M}(\lambda)$.]

10.6.14. Let $\{n\}(m)$ be the value of the nth partial recursive function applied to m. Define

$$v_n = \begin{cases} x & \text{if } \{n\}(n) = 0, \\ y & \text{if } \{n\}(n) = 1, \\ \perp & \text{else.} \end{cases}$$

Show that

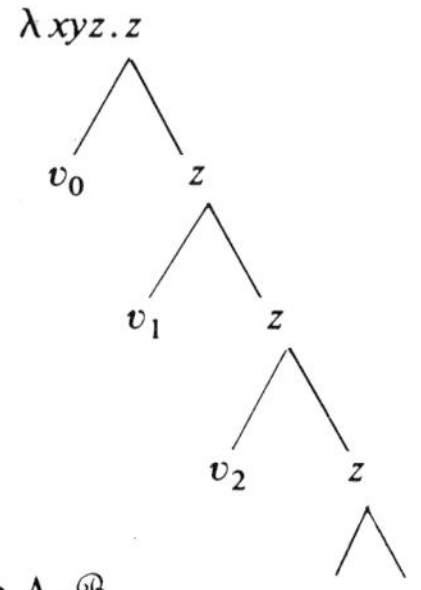

is not in $\Lambda_I\mathfrak{B}$.

10.6.15. (Coppo et al. [1978]). Construct an $\mathfrak{F} = \{M_1, M_2, M_3\}$ that is not separable, but such that nevertheless $\{M_1, M_2\}$, $\{M_2, M_3\}$ and $\{M_3, M_1\}$ are separable.

10.6.16.* Given $M \in \Lambda$ find the place of the following sets in the arithmetical hierarchy:

(i) $\{\alpha | \mathrm{BT}(M)(\alpha)\downarrow\}$,

(ii) $\{\alpha | \mathrm{BT}(M)(\alpha) = \perp\}$,

(iii) $\{\alpha | \mathrm{BT}(M)(\alpha)\uparrow\uparrow\}$,

(iv) $\{\alpha | \alpha \in \mathrm{BT}(M)\}$.

10.6.17.* (i) Write a program such that $\mathrm{BT}(M)$ appears on a screen, when M is given as input to a computer.

(ii) Include zoom facilities.

10.6.18. Construct an $M \in \Lambda_K$ (respectively $\in \Lambda_I$) such that $M(\lambda x.x) = \llcorner 1 \lrcorner$ and $M(\lambda x.xxx) = \llcorner 2 \lrcorner$.

10.6.19. Show that the following problem is not recursively solvable. Given $M \in \Lambda_K$, is there an $M' \in \Lambda_I$ such that $\mathrm{BT}(M') = \mathrm{BT}(M)$?

PART III

REDUCTION

Berry (photo by
the author, 1978)

Hindley (1978)

Klop (photo by
B. Holtkamp, 1976)

Lévy (photo by
the author, 1976)

Mitschke (1972)

As we have seen, reduction is useful to analyze convertibility. For various extensions $\mathfrak{T}$ of $\boldsymbol{\lambda}$ there is a corresponding notion of reduction $\boldsymbol{R}$ such that $\mathfrak{T} \vdash M = N \Leftrightarrow M =_R N$ and $\boldsymbol{R}$ is Church–Rosser. This gives a proof-theoretic analysis of $\mathfrak{T}$: if M, N do not have a common R-reduct, then $\mathfrak{T} \nvdash M = N$. Chapters 11 and 15 prove these CR properties, once more for $\boldsymbol{\beta}$ and also for other notions of reduction. Moreover in chapter 11 other important theorems on β-reduction are proved (finiteness of developments, conservation theorem for the λI-calculus, standardization).

In chapter 13 the notion of reduction strategies is introduced. These are often useful to show that two terms have no common reduct: if $x \notin \mathrm{FV}(M)$ and

$$(1) \qquad \forall N' \quad [N \twoheadrightarrow_R N' \Rightarrow x \in \mathrm{FV}(N')],$$

then M, N do not have a common R-reduct (since variables usually cannot be created in a reduction). In order to show (1) the reduction graph of M must be inspected and this is often rather complicated. But (1) is true if it is on a "cofinal" reduction path in $G_R(M)$. Such a path is constructed by several reduction strategies.

In chapter 12 equivalence of reductions is studied. This notion was introduced in Lévy [1978] in connection with the search for optimal reduction strategies.

Chapter 14 shows that the λ-calculus is "locally strongly normalizable". This result has various applications.

More information on reduction can be found in Klop [1980].

CHAPTER 11

FUNDAMENTAL THEOREMS

Reduction was introduced in order to analyze β-conversion. In part II we have seen already several applications of the Church–Rosser theorem and the standardization theorem. These and other important results on β-reduction will be proved in this chapter.

11.1. The Church–Rosser theorem

There are many ways to prove the Church–Rosser theorem. In §3.2 a short proof due to Tait and Martin-Löf was given. In this section a bit longer but more perspicuous proof is presented. These two proofs will be compared in §11.2.

In order to prove that $\twoheadrightarrow$ (i.e. $\twoheadrightarrow_\beta$) satisfies the diamond property, it suffices by lemma 3.2.2 to show that this is so for $\underset{=}{\rightarrow}$. However that is not true. The following lemma throws some light on the situation.

11.1.1. LEMMA. (i) *The relations* $\rightarrow$ *and* $\underset{=}{\rightarrow}$ *do not satisfy the diamond property.*

(ii) *The relation* $\rightarrow$ *satisfies the weak diamond property.*

PROOF. (i) Let $R \rightarrow R'$ be, say $\mathbf{II} \rightarrow \mathbf{I}$ and consider

$$(\lambda x.xx)R \rightarrow RR$$

$$(\lambda x.xx)R \rightarrow (\lambda x.xx)R'.$$

A common reduct would be $R'R'$, but this cannot be reached in one step from RR. Hence $\rightarrow$ does not satisfy the full diamond property (nor does its reflexive closure).

(ii) Suppose

$$M \rightarrow M_1, \qquad M \rightarrow M_2$$

in order to construct an M_3 such that

$$M_1 \twoheadrightarrow M_3, \qquad M_2 \twoheadrightarrow M_3.$$

Let $(\Delta_i): M \to M_i$, $i = 1, 2$, with $\Delta_i \equiv (\lambda x_i . P_i) Q_i$. The possible relative positions of Δ_1 and Δ_2 in M are given in the following table.

(1) $\Delta_1 \cap \Delta_2 = \emptyset$ (i.e. Δ_1, Δ_2 disjoint)	
(2) $\Delta_1 = \Delta_2$	
(3) $\Delta_1 \subset \Delta_2$	(3.1) $\Delta_1 \subset P_2$
	(3.2) $\Delta_1 \subset Q_2$
(4) $\Delta_2 \subset \Delta_1$	(4.1) $\Delta_2 \subset P_1$
	(4.2) $\Delta_2 \subset Q_1$

Let $\Delta_i' \equiv P_i[x_i := Q_i]$.

Case 1. Then

$$M \equiv \cdots \Delta_1 \cdots \Delta_2 \cdots$$

$$M_1 \equiv \cdots \Delta_1' \cdots \Delta_2 \cdots$$

$$M_2 \equiv \cdots \Delta_1 \cdots \Delta_2' \cdots$$

Then take

$$M_3 \equiv \cdots \Delta_1' \cdots \Delta_2' \cdots.$$

Case 2. Then $M_1 \equiv M_2$ and we can take $M_3 \equiv M_1$.

Case (3.1). Then $M \equiv \cdots ((\lambda x_2 . \cdots \Delta_1 \cdots) Q_2) \cdots$, where $\cdots \Delta_1 \cdots \equiv P_2$,

$$M_1 \equiv \cdots ((\lambda x_2 . \cdots \Delta_1' \cdots) Q_2) \cdots$$

$$M_2 \equiv \cdots (\cdots \Delta_1 \cdots)[x_2 := Q_2] \cdots.$$

Take

$$M_3 \equiv \cdots (\cdots \Delta_1' \cdots)[x_2 := Q_2] \cdots.$$

Then clearly $M_1 \to M_3$ and $M_2 \to M_3$ by the substitutivity of $\boldsymbol{\beta}$.

Case (3.2). Then $M \equiv \cdots ((\lambda x_2 . P_2)(\cdots \Delta_1 \cdots)) \cdots$, where $\cdots \Delta_1 \cdots \equiv Q_2$,

$$M_1 \equiv \cdots ((\lambda x_2 . P_2)(\cdots \Delta_1' \cdots)) \cdots$$

$$M_2 \equiv \cdots (P_2[x_2 := (\cdots \Delta_1 \cdots)]) \cdots.$$

Take

$$M_3 \equiv \cdots (P_2[x_2 := (\cdots \Delta_1' \cdots)]),$$

then clearly $M_1 \to M_3$ and $M_2 \twoheadrightarrow M_3$ by remark 3.1.7 (i).

Cases (4.1) and (4.2) can be treated analogously to cases (3.1) and (3.2). □

Due to the existence of infinite reduction paths it does not automatically follow from lemma 11.1.1 that $\boldsymbol{\beta}$ is CR, i.e. that $\twoheadrightarrow$ satisfies the diamond lemma (see exercise 3.5.10). The diamond property for $\twoheadrightarrow$ does follow, however, from the following "strip lemma", which is a strengthening of lemma 11.1.1:

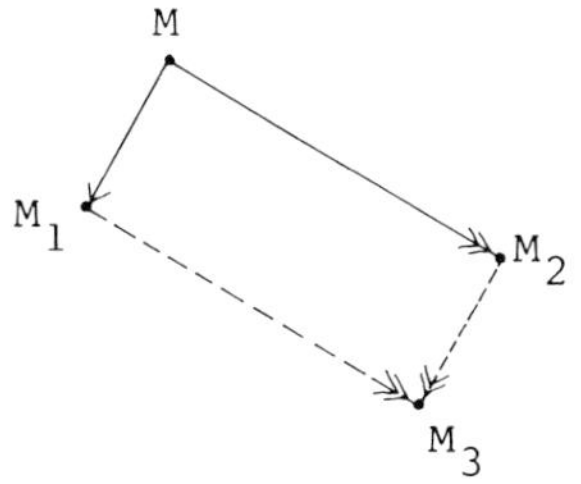

The idea of the proof of this lemma is as follows. Suppose $M \xrightarrow{\Delta} M_1$. If one keeps track of what happens with Δ during the reduction $M \twoheadrightarrow M_2$, then by reducing all "residuals" of Δ in M_2 one obtains M_3. In order to do the necessary bookkeeping, it is convenient to mark some redexes. For this it is sufficient to give an index to the first lambda of a redex. (For applications later on several indices will be allowed.) For these reasons the following auxiliary extension of Λ is introduced.

11.1.2. DEFINITION. (i) Λ' is a set of words over the following alphabet

$v_0, v_1, \ldots$	variables,
$\lambda, \lambda_0, \lambda_1, \ldots$	lambdas,
(,)	parentheses.

(ii) Λ' is inductively defined as follows.

$$x \in \Lambda',$$
$$M \in \Lambda' \Rightarrow (\lambda x.M) \in \Lambda',$$
$$M, N \in \Lambda' \Rightarrow (MN) \in \Lambda',$$
$$M, N \in \Lambda' \Rightarrow ((\lambda_i x.M)N) \in \Lambda' \quad \text{for all } i \in \mathbb{N}$$

(x denotes an arbitrary variable).

(iii) If $M \in \Lambda'$, then $|M| \in \Lambda$ is obtained from M by leaving out all indices. For example, $|(\lambda_1 x.x)((\lambda_2 x.x)(\lambda x.x))| \equiv \mathbf{I}(\mathbf{II})$.

The elements of Λ' are called λ'-terms. The same conventions are adopted as for λ-terms. The notion of reduction $\boldsymbol{\beta}$ is extended to $\boldsymbol{\beta}'$ on Λ' as follows.

11.1.3. Definition. (i) Substitution on Λ' is defined in the obvious way. In particular

$$((\lambda_i x.M)N)[z:=L] \equiv (\lambda_i x.M[z:=L])(N[z:=L]).$$

(ii) The notion of reduction $\boldsymbol{\beta}'$ on Λ' is defined by $\boldsymbol{\beta}' = \boldsymbol{\beta}_0 \cup \boldsymbol{\beta}_1$ where $\boldsymbol{\beta}_0$ and $\boldsymbol{\beta}_1$ are defined by the following contraction rules:

$$\boldsymbol{\beta}_0 : (\lambda_i x.M)N \to M[x:=N],$$

$$\boldsymbol{\beta}_1 : (\lambda x.M)N \to M[x:=N],$$

where $i \in \mathbb{N}$ and $M, N \in \Lambda'$.

(iii) By remark 3.1.7(ii) the notion $\boldsymbol{\beta}'$ generates relations $\to_{\beta'}$ and $\twoheadrightarrow_{\beta'}$ on Λ': $M \to_{\beta'} N$ iff for some (indexed) context $C[\ ]$ with one hole and some $(P, Q) \in \boldsymbol{\beta}'$

$$M \equiv C[P] \quad \text{and} \quad N \equiv C[Q],$$

$\twoheadrightarrow_{\beta'}$ is the reflexive transitive closure of $\to_{\beta'}$.

In the next section the notion of reduction $\boldsymbol{\beta}_0$ will play an important role. For the purpose of this section the set Λ' and the notion $\boldsymbol{\beta}'$ could have been given simpler (using just one index).

11.1.4. Definition. Let $M \in \Lambda'$. Define $\varphi(M) \in \Lambda$ by induction on the structure of M as follows:

$$\varphi(x) \equiv x,$$

$$\varphi(PQ) \equiv \varphi(P)\varphi(Q) \quad \text{if } P \not\equiv \lambda_i x.P',$$

$$\varphi(\lambda x.P) \equiv \lambda x.\varphi(P),$$

$$\varphi((\lambda_i x.P)Q) \equiv \varphi(P)[x:=\varphi(Q)].$$

In other words, φ contracts all the redexes with an index (from the inside to the outside; in section 11.2 it will be shown that other ways of contracting all the indexed redexes always lead to the same result).

11.1.5. Notation. If $|M| \equiv N$ or $\varphi(M) \equiv N$, then this will be denoted by

$$M \underset{|\,|}{\to} N \quad \text{or} \quad M \underset{\varphi}{\to} N$$

respectively. This is convenient for a schematical formulation of statements.

11.1.6. LEMMA.

(i)

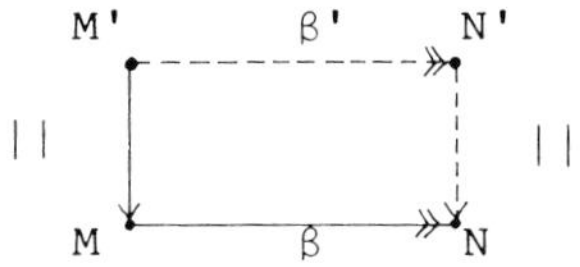

$M', N' \in \Lambda'$,

$M, N \in \Lambda$.

(ii)

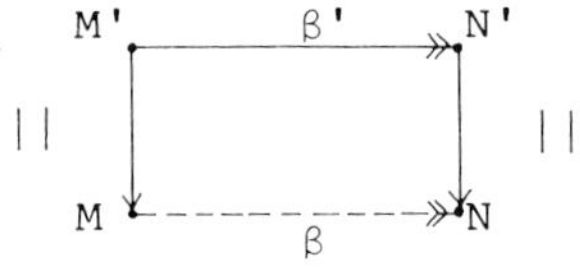

$M', N' \in \Lambda'$,

$M, N \in \Lambda$.

PROOF. (i) First suppose $M \twoheadrightarrow_\beta N$ is a one step reduction. Then N is obtained by contracting a redex in M and N' can be obtained by contracting the corresponding redex in M'. The general statement follows by transitivity.

(ii) Similar but easier: just leave out all indices from a reduction path from M' to N'. □

11.1.7. LEMMA. (i) *Let* $M, N \in \Lambda'$. *Then*

$$\varphi(M[x:=N]) \equiv \varphi(M)[x:=\varphi(N)].$$

(ii)

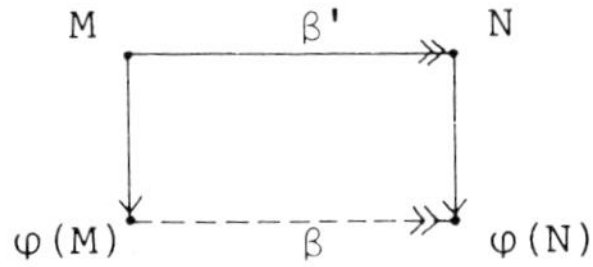

$M, N \in \Lambda'$.

PROOF. (i) By induction on the structure of M, using the substitution lemma in case $M \equiv (\lambda_i y.P)Q$. The conditions for the substitution lemma may be assumed to hold by the variable convention 2.1.13.

(ii) By induction on the generation of $\twoheadrightarrow_{\beta'}$, using (i). □

11.1.8. LEMMA.

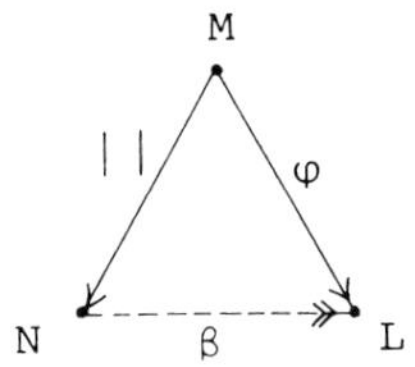

$M \in \Lambda'$,

$(N, L \in \Lambda)$.

PROOF. By induction on the structure of M. □

11.1.9. STRIP LEMMA.

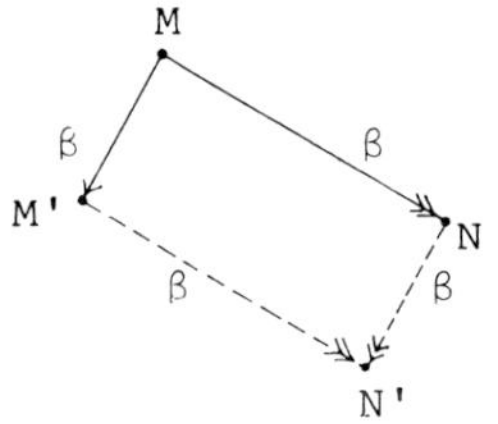

$M, M', N, N' \in \Lambda$.

PROOF. Let M' be the result of contracting the redex occurrence Δ in M. Let $\tilde{M} \in \Lambda'$ be obtained from M by indexing Δ. Then $|\tilde{M}| \equiv M$ and $\varphi(\tilde{M}) \equiv M'$. By lemmas 11.1.6 (i), 11.1.7 (ii) and 11.1.8 we can erect the following diagram

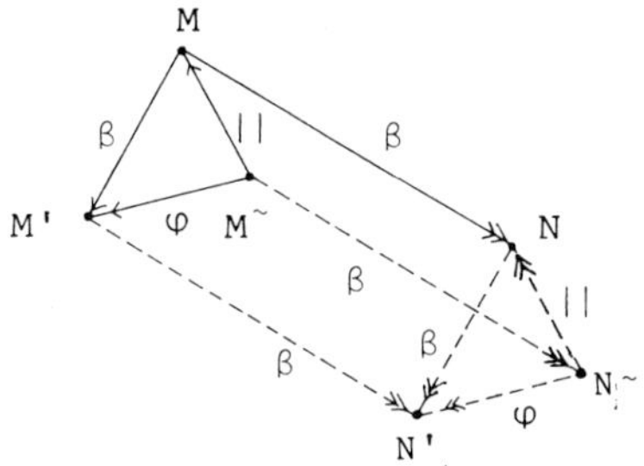

which proves the strip lemma. □

11.1.10. CHURCH–ROSSER THEOREM. *β is* CR. *That is*,

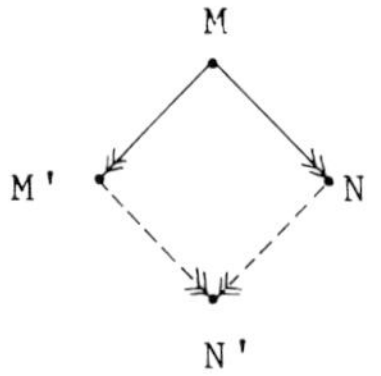

$M, M', N, N' \in \Lambda$.

PROOF. If $M \twoheadrightarrow M'$, then

$$M \equiv M_0 \to M_1 \to \cdots \to M_n \equiv M'.$$

Hence the diamond property follows from the strip lemma and a simple diagram chase:

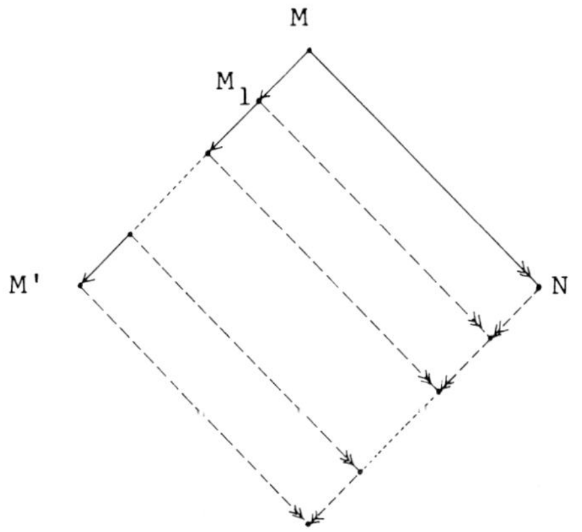

□

In chapter 3 we have proved that $\boldsymbol{\beta\eta}$ is CR. It is instructive to notice that the proof given for $\boldsymbol{\beta}$ does not generalize immediately to $\boldsymbol{\beta\eta}$ (see exercise 11.5.4).

11.2. The finiteness of developments

The main theorem in this section states that for each $M \in \Lambda$ the so called developments (a special kind of reduction starting with M) are always finite. This theorem (denoted by FD) has important consequences, among them being the CR theorem, the conservation theorem for the restricted theory and the standardization theorem.

FD was first proved by Church and Rosser [1936] for the λI-calculus in order to prove the CR theorem for that theory. For the full λ-calculus FD was proved by Schroer [1965] and independently by Hyland [1973] and Hindley [1978]. The proof given below is taken from Barendregt et al. [1976] and is a simplification of that of Hyland.

One formulation of FD is simply

$$\mathrm{SN}(\boldsymbol{\beta}_0),$$

that is, reductions on Λ' contracting only indexed redexes are always finite. Often this theorem is formulated in terms of "residuals". It is convenient to introduce this terminology.

11.2.1. LEMMA (Projecting). *Let σ' be a $\boldsymbol{\beta}'$-reduction starting with $M' \in \Lambda'$, say*

$$\sigma' : M' \equiv M'_0 \overset{\Delta'_0}{\underset{\beta'}{\to}} M'_1 \overset{\Delta'_1}{\underset{\beta'}{\to}} \cdots .$$

Then $|\sigma'|$ *defined by*

$$|\sigma'| : |M'| \equiv |M_0'| \stackrel{|\Delta_0'|}{\rightarrow} |M_1'| \stackrel{|\Delta_1'|}{\rightarrow} \cdots$$

is a β*-reduction starting with* $|M'|$.

PROOF. Obvious, just erase all indices. □

The following result is a strengthening of lemma 11.1.6 (i).

11.2.2. LEMMA (Lifting). *Let* σ *be a* β*-reduction starting with* $M \in \Lambda$. *Then for each* $M' \in \Lambda'$ *with* $|M'| \equiv M$ *there is a* β'*-reduction* σ' *starting with* M' *such that* $|\sigma'| = \sigma$.

PROOF. Obvious; just give the right indices to the terms in the reduction σ. □

Let $\mathcal{F}$ be a set of redex occurrences in a λ-term M. If we are interested in what happens with the elements of $\mathcal{F}$ during a reduction, then we can lift M to Λ' by indexing the elements of $\mathcal{F}$.

11.2.3. DEFINITION. (i) Let $M \in \Lambda$; then $\Delta \in M$ denotes that Δ is a redex occurrence in M.

(ii) Let $\mathcal{F}$ be a set of redex occurrences. Then $\mathcal{F} \subseteq M$ denotes that $\forall \Delta \in \mathcal{F}\ \Delta \in M$.

(iii) Let $\mathcal{F} \subseteq M \in \Lambda$. Then $(M, \mathcal{F}) \in \Lambda'$ is the indexed term obtained from M by indexing the redex occurrences of M that are in $\mathcal{F}$ by 0. In this notation $M \in \Lambda$ is identified with $(M, \emptyset) \in \Lambda'$.

EXAMPLE. Let $M \equiv (\mathbf{I}y)(\mathbf{I}y)(\mathbf{I}z)$. Then M has three redex occurrences (the first and second $(\mathbf{I}y)$ and $(\mathbf{I}z)$). Let $\mathcal{F} = \{$the second $\mathbf{I}y$, $\mathbf{I}z\}$. Then $\mathcal{F} \subseteq M$ and $(M, \mathcal{F}) = (\lambda x.x)y((\lambda_0 x.x)y)((\lambda_0 x.x)z)$.

11.2.4. DEFINITION. Let $M, N \in \Lambda$ and let $\sigma : M \twoheadrightarrow N$.

(i) Let $\mathcal{F} \subseteq M$. The set of *residuals* of $\mathcal{F}$ in N relative to σ (notation $\mathcal{F}/\sigma$) is defined as follows.

Let $M' \equiv (M, \mathcal{F})$ and lift σ to $\sigma' : M' \twoheadrightarrow N'$. Then $|N'| \equiv N$. See figure 11.1. It is clear that β'-reductions do not create new indices, therefore N' has only 0 indices and hence $N' \equiv (N, \mathcal{F}')$ for some $\mathcal{F}'$.

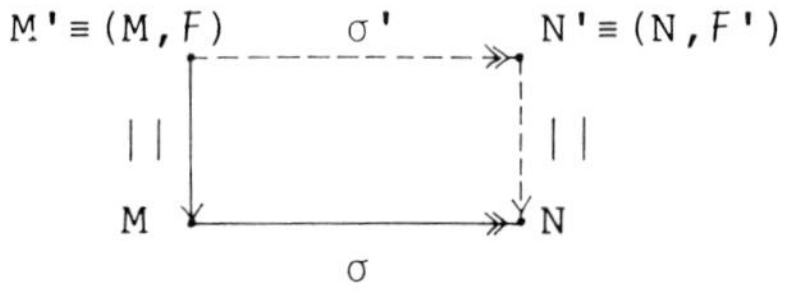

FIG. 11.1

Now $\mathcal{F}/\sigma = \mathcal{F}'$.

(ii) If $\Delta \in M$, then the residuals of Δ in N relative to σ, notation Δ/σ, is the set $\{\Delta\}/\sigma$.

Also for β'-reductions one can define residuals. Let $\mathcal{F}' \subseteq M' \stackrel{\sigma'}{\twoheadrightarrow}_{\beta'} N'$. Then

$$\mathcal{F}'/\sigma' = \{\Delta' \in N' \mid |\Delta'| \in |\mathcal{F}'|/|\sigma'|\}.$$

The intuition behind residuals is this. Given a reduction σ, mark a set of redexes in the begin term of σ and follow this set throughout the reduction path. Since the marking does not affect the reduction itself, lemmas 11.2.5, 11.2.6 and 11.2.8 are obvious.

11.2.5. LEMMA. *Let $M, N \in \Lambda$, $\sigma : M \twoheadrightarrow N$ and $\mathcal{F} = \{\Delta_1, \ldots, \Delta_n\} \subseteq M$. Then $\mathcal{F}/\sigma = \Delta_1/\sigma \cup \cdots \cup \Delta_n/\sigma$.* □

11.2.6. LEMMA. *Let $\sigma : M \twoheadrightarrow N$, $\tau : N \twoheadrightarrow L$, and $\mathcal{F} \subseteq M$. Then $\mathcal{F}/\sigma + \tau = (\mathcal{F}/\sigma)/\tau$.* □

By lemmas 11.2.5 and 11.2.6 residuals in general are determined by residuals of a single redex relative to a one step reduction.

11.2.7. EXAMPLES. Let $\Delta \equiv (\lambda a.a(\mathbf{I}x))(xb)$. Consider the following (one step) reductions.

(i) $(\lambda x.xx)a\Delta \to aa\Delta$,
(ii) $(\lambda x.xx)\Delta \to \Delta\Delta$,
(iii) $(\lambda x.y)\Delta \to y$,
(iv) $(\lambda x.x)\Delta \to (\lambda x.x)(xb(\mathbf{I}x))$,
(v) $(\lambda x.\Delta)P \to (\lambda a.a(\mathbf{I}P))(Pb)$,
(vi) $\Delta \to (\lambda a.ax)(xb)$.

In (i) the residual of Δ (relative to the given reduction) is as a term unchanged. In (ii) Δ has two residuals. In (iii) and (iv) Δ has no residuals. In (v) the residual of Δ is $\Delta[x:=P]$. In (vi) the residual of Δ is $(\lambda a.ax)(xb)$.

The following lemma shows that one can find out simultaneously the residuals of several redexes by giving them different indices and following these indexed redexes.

11.2.8. LEMMA. *Let $\sigma' : M' \twoheadrightarrow_{\beta'} N'$, $M', N' \in \Lambda'$ and let $\sigma = |\sigma'|$. Define for $P \in \Lambda'$, $|P|_i = \{\Delta \mid \Delta \in P$ is an i-redex$\}$. Then $|M'|_i/\sigma = |N'|_i$.*

11.2.9. COROLLARY. *Let $\sigma : M \twoheadrightarrow N$, $M, N \in \Lambda$ and let $\Delta_0, \Delta_1 \in M$ be different redex occurrences. Then $(\Delta_0/\sigma) \cap (\Delta_1/\sigma) = \emptyset$.*

PROOF. Let M' be obtained from M by indexing Δ_i with i. Then the result follows by lifting σ. □

It is important to note that Δ/σ depends on σ and not just on the first and last terms of σ.

11.2.10. EXAMPLE (Lévy). Consider

$$\mathbf{I}(\mathbf{I}x) \to \mathbf{I}x.$$

This one step reduction can be obtained in two ways:

$$\sigma_1 : \mathbf{I}(\mathbf{I}x) \overset{\mathbf{I}x}{\to} \mathbf{I}x,$$

$$\sigma_2 : \mathbf{I}(\mathbf{I}x) \overset{\mathbf{I}(\mathbf{I}x)}{\to} \mathbf{I}x.$$

Now $\mathbf{I}x/\sigma_1 = \emptyset$ but $\mathbf{I}x/\sigma_2 = \{\mathbf{I}x\}$. This situation is studied in chapter 12.

If $\mathcal{F} \subseteq M$ and one has in mind a certain reduction starting from M, then one may speak about "the residuals of $\mathcal{F}$" without specifying that reduction path.

11.2.11. DEFINITION. (i) Let $M \in \Lambda$ and $\mathcal{F} \subseteq M$. A *development* of $(M, \mathcal{F})$ is a reduction path

$$\sigma : M \equiv M_0 \overset{\Delta_0}{\to} M_1 \overset{\Delta_1}{\to} \cdots$$

such that each redex $\Delta_i \in M_i$ is a residual of a redex in $\mathcal{F}$ (relative to $(\Delta_0) + \cdots + (\Delta_{i-1})$).

(ii) $\sigma : M \twoheadrightarrow N$ is a *complete development* of $(M, \mathcal{F})$, notation $\sigma : (M, \mathcal{F}) \underset{\text{cpl}}{\twoheadrightarrow} N$, if σ is a development of $(M, \mathcal{F})$ and moreover $\mathcal{F}/\sigma = \emptyset$.

(iii) A *development* of M is a development of $(M, \mathcal{F}_M)$ where $\mathcal{F}_M$ is the set of all redex occurrences in M.

(iv) $M \underset{\text{dev}}{\twoheadrightarrow} N$ iff N occurs in some development of M.

Developments and $\boldsymbol{\beta}_0$-reductions correspond to each other in the following way.

11.2.12. LEMMA. *σ is a development of $(M, \mathcal{F})$ iff σ lifted to σ' starting with $(M, \mathcal{F})$ is a β_0-reduction.*

PROOF. Note that σ contracts only residuals of redexes in $\mathcal{F}$ iff σ' contracts only indexed redexes. □

Now it will be proved that all developments are finite. By lemma 11.2.12 it suffices to show that $\boldsymbol{\beta}_0$ strongly normalizes.

To get some intuition, consider

$$(\lambda_0 x.xx)(\lambda x.xx) \to_{\beta_0} (\lambda x.xx)(\lambda x.xx) \in \beta_0\text{-NF}.$$

The second $(\lambda x.xx)$ cannot have an index because it is not the first part of a redex. That on the other hand β-reductions can be infinite is caused by the "creation" of new redexes. If only (residuals of) old redexes are contracted, then a reduction always terminates. That is what will be shown now.

The idea of proof is to assign to each $M \in \Lambda'$ a set of special norms (positive integers) such that

$$M \to_{\beta_0} N \Rightarrow \begin{array}{l}\text{for each special norm for } M \text{ there is a}\\ \text{strictly smaller one for } N.\end{array}$$

These special norms are introduced via an auxiliary system Λ'^*. The proof occupies 11.2.13–11.2.21.

11.2.13. Definition. Λ'^* is the set of weighted λ'-terms defined as follows.

$$\begin{array}{ll}x^n \in \Lambda'^* & \text{for every variable and every } n \in \mathbb{N},\ n > 0,\\ M \in \Lambda'^* \Rightarrow (\lambda x.M) \in \Lambda'^*, & \\ M, N \in \Lambda'^* \Rightarrow (MN) \in \Lambda'^*, & \\ M, N \in \Lambda'^* \Rightarrow ((\lambda_i x.M)N) \in \Lambda'^* & \text{for all } i \in \mathbb{N}.\end{array}$$

The positive integers attached to variables are called *weights*. Note that only variables not immediately preceded by a lambda are weighted.

Each $M \in \Lambda'^*$ can be considered as a pair $M \equiv (M_0, I)$ where $M_0 \in \Lambda'$ is obtained from M by leaving out all weights and I is an *weighting*, i.e. a map which assigns to each variable occurrence (not immediately preceded by a λ) a positive integer.

11.2.14. Definition. The notion of reduction $\boldsymbol{\beta}_0$ is extended to Λ'^* as follows. First define substitution for Λ'^* by

$$x^n[x := N] \equiv N$$

and the usual other rules. Then define $\boldsymbol{\beta}_0^*$ by the contraction rule

$$\boldsymbol{\beta}_0^* : (\lambda_i x.M)N \to M[x := N] \quad \text{for } M, N \in \Lambda'^*.$$

As usual, $\boldsymbol{\beta}_0^*$ generates relations $\to_{\beta_0^*}$ and $\twoheadrightarrow_{\beta_0^*}$.

Note that as for $\boldsymbol{\beta}_0$, only indexed redexes are allowed to be contracted in a β_0^*-reduction.

11.2.15. Definition. Let $M \in \Lambda'^*$. For $N \subset M$ define

$$\|N\|' = \text{sum of the weights occurring in } N.$$

Note that $\|N\|' > 0$.

11.2.16. Definition. Let $M \equiv (M_0, I) \in \Lambda'^*$. The weighting I is called *decreasing* if for every β_0^*-redex $(\lambda_i x.P)Q$ in M one has

$$\|x\|' > \|Q\|' \quad \text{for all occurrences of } x \text{ in } P.$$

Example. $(\lambda_i x.x^6x^7)(\lambda x.x^2x^3)$ has a decreasing weighting, but not $(\lambda_i x.x^4x^7)(\lambda x.x^2x^3)$.

11.2.17. Lemma. *Let $M \in \Lambda'$. Then there is a decreasing weighting for M.*

Proof. Number the occurrences of variables in M from the right to the left, starting with the number 0. Give the nth occurrence the index 2^n. Example: if $M \equiv xy((\lambda_i z.z)(xx))$ the result is

$$x^{16}y^8((\lambda_i z.z^4)(x^2x^1)).$$

Since $2^n > 2^{n-1} + \cdots + 2 + 1$, this is a decreasing weighting. □

The notion of residuals makes sense also for reductions in Λ'^*. This notion will be used informally in the next proof.

11.2.18. Lemma. *Let $M^* \equiv (M, I) \in \Lambda'^*$, with I decreasing and let*

$$M^* \to_{\beta_0^*} N^* \equiv (N, I').$$

Then (i) $\|M^*\|' > \|N^*\|'$.

(ii) *I' is a decreasing weighting.*

Proof. Let $\Delta_1 \equiv (\lambda_i x_1.P_1)Q_1$ be the β_0^*-redex contracted in $M^* \to_{\beta_0^*} N^*$.

(i) Each x_1 in P_1 is replaced by Q_1. Since $\|x_1\|' > \|Q_1\|'$ this means that the sum of the weights in the contractum is decreased. Also if P_1 contains no x_1 this holds, since then Q_1 vanishes and $\|Q_1\|' > 0$.

(ii) In order to verify that I' is decreasing, let $\Delta_0 \equiv (\lambda_j x_0.P_0)Q_0$ be a β_0^*-redex in N^*. Since Δ_0 is indexed, it is the residual of a redex in M^*, say $\Delta_2 \equiv (\lambda_j x_2.P_2)Q_2$.

The possibilities for the relative positions of the redexes Δ_1 and Δ_2 are given in the table on p. 274.

In only two cases it is nontrivial to verify that for x_0 in P_0 one has $\|x_0\|' > \|Q_0\|'$. *Case* (3.2). $\Delta_1 \subset Q_2$. Then

$$M^* \equiv \cdots (\lambda_j x_2.P_2)\boxed{\cdots ((\lambda_i x_1.P_1)Q_1)\cdots}_2 \cdots$$

$$\beta_0^* \downarrow$$

$$N^* \equiv \cdots (\lambda_j x_2.P_2)\boxed{\cdots P_1[x_1 := Q_1]\cdots}_0 \cdots,$$

where $\boxed{}_2 \equiv Q_2$ and $(\lambda_j x_2.P_2)\boxed{}_0 \equiv (\lambda_j x_0.P_0)Q_0$.

Since M^* has a decreasing weighting one has

(1) $\quad \|(\lambda_i x_1.P_1)Q_1\|' > \|P_1[x_1 := Q_1]\|'$

and for all $x_2(\equiv x_0)$ in $P_2(\equiv P_0)$

(2) $\quad \|x_2\|' > \|Q_2\|'$.

From (1) it follows that $\|Q_2\|' > \|Q_0\|'$, hence by (2)

$$\|x_0\|' > \|Q_0\|'.$$

Case (4.1). $\Delta_2 \subset P_1$. Then

$$M^* \equiv \cdots \left(\lambda_i x_1.\boxed{\cdots x_1 \cdots ((\lambda_j x_2.P_2)Q_2)\cdots}_1\right)Q_1 \cdots$$

$$\beta_0^* \downarrow$$

$$N^* \equiv \cdots$$

$$\boxed{\cdots Q_1 \cdots ((\lambda_j x_2.P_2[x_1 := Q_1])(Q_2[x_1 := Q_1]))\cdots}\cdots,$$

where $\boxed{}_1 \equiv P_1$ and $(\lambda_i x_0.P_0)Q_0 \equiv (\lambda_j x_2.P_2[x_1 := Q_1])(Q_2[x_1 := Q_1])$.

Since M^* has a decreasing weighting one has

(1) $\quad \|x_1\|' > \|Q_1\|' \quad$ for all x_1 in P_1

and

(2) $\quad \|x_2\|' > \|Q_2\|' \quad$ for all x_2 in P_2.

By (1) it follows that

$$\|Q_2\|' \geqslant \|Q_2[x_1 := Q_1]\|' \quad (= \text{holds if } x_1 \notin \mathrm{FV}(Q_2))$$

and hence by (2)

$$\|x_2\|' > \|Q_2[x_1 := Q_1]\|' \quad \text{for all } x_2 \text{ in } P_2[x_1 := Q_1],$$

since by the variable convention it may be assumed that x_2 does not occur in Q_1. □

11.2.19. Lemma. *Let $M, N \in \Lambda'$ and let $M^* \equiv (M, I) \in \Lambda'^*$. If $M \twoheadrightarrow_{\beta_0} N$, then for some weighting I'*

$$M^* \twoheadrightarrow_{\beta_0^*} N^* \equiv (N, I'):$$

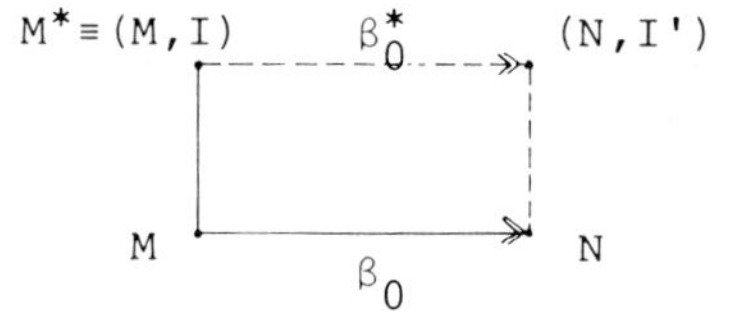

Proof. As in the proof of 11.1.6 (i), copy the reduction $M \twoheadrightarrow_{\beta_0} N$ with the weighted terms. □

11.2.20. Proposition. *On Λ' the notion of reduction $\boldsymbol{\beta}_0$ is strongly normalizing.*

Proof. Suppose

$$\sigma : M \equiv M_0 \to_{\beta_0} M_1 \to_{\beta_0} \cdots$$

is a β_0-reduction starting with $M \in \Lambda'$. By lemma 11.2.17 there is a decreasing weighting I for M. But then by lemma 11.2.19 σ induces a reduction

$$\sigma^* : M^* \equiv (M_0, I) \to_{\beta_0^*} (M_1, I_1) \to_{\beta_0^*} \cdots .$$

By lemma 11.2.18 each weighting I_i is decreasing. Hence again by that lemma

$$\|(M_0, I)\| > \|(M_1, I_1)\| > \cdots .$$

Thus σ^* and therefore σ must be finite. □

11.2.21. Theorem (FD: Finiteness of developments). *Let $M \in \Lambda$. Then all developments of M are finite.*

Proof. By proposition 11.2.20 and lemma 11.2.12. □

11.2.22. Corollary. *Let $M \in \Lambda$.*

(i) *For $\mathcal{F} \subseteq M$ each development of $(M, \mathcal{F})$ can be extended to a complete one.*

(ii) *The set $\{M \mid M \twoheadrightarrow_{\text{dev}} N\}$ is finite.*

Proof. (i) By the theorem there is a development of $(M, \mathcal{F})$ of maximal length. This is a complete one.

(ii) Each term has only finitely many one step reducts. Hence the result follows by the theorem and König's lemma. (By the proof of the theorem one can compute a bound on the maximal length of a development of M (see exercise 11.5.8), hence the argument is constructive). □

Now it will be proved that all complete developments of an $(M, \mathcal{F})$ terminate with the same result. In terms of $\boldsymbol{\beta}_0$ this just means that β_0-nf's are unique.

11.2.23. Lemma. (i) *$\boldsymbol{\beta}_0$ is weakly Church–Rosser.*

(ii) *In fact, let $M, M_1, M_2 \in \Lambda'$ and*

$$\sigma : M \overset{\Delta_1}{\rightarrow}_{\beta_0} M_1, \qquad \tau : M \overset{\Delta_2}{\rightarrow}_{\beta_0} M_2.$$

Then there are reductions

$$\sigma' : M_2 \twoheadrightarrow_{\beta_0} M_3, \qquad \tau' : M_1 \twoheadrightarrow_{\beta_0} M_3$$

where σ' (τ' respectively) is a β_0-reduction obtained by contracting the residuals Δ_1/τ (Δ_2/σ respectively) one after the other from the left to the right.

(iii) *Similarly for $\boldsymbol{\beta}'$.*

Proof. (i) Analogous to lemma 11.1.1(ii) (checking that the indices match).

(ii) This is just the information obtained while proving (i).

(iii) Equally simple. □

11.2.24. Corollary. (i) *The notion of reduction $\boldsymbol{\beta}_0$ on Λ' is Church–Rosser.*

(ii) *Each $M' \in \Lambda'$ has a unique β_0-nf.*

Proof. (i) By the lemma and propositions 11.2.20 and 3.1.25.

(ii) By (i), proposition 11.2.20 and corollary 3.1.13. □

11.2.25. Theorem (FD!). *Let $M \in \Lambda$ and $\mathcal{F} \subseteq M$.*

(i) *All developments of M are finite.*

(ii) *All developments of $(M, \mathcal{F})$ can be extended to a complete development of $(M, \mathcal{F})$.*

(iii) *All complete developments of $(M, \mathcal{F})$ end with the same term.*

PROOF. (i), (ii) By FD and its corollary.
(iii) By corollary 11.2.24 and lemma 11.2.12. □

Corollary 11.2.24 (ii) enables us to define the following.

11.2.26. DEFINITION. Let $M' \in \Lambda'$. Then $\mathrm{Cpl}(M')$ is the unique β_0-nf of M'. Often this notion will be applied to $M' \equiv (M, \mathcal{F})$ with $\mathcal{F} \subseteq M$.

EXAMPLES. Let $M \equiv (\lambda x.x)((\lambda x.x\mathbf{I})\mathbf{I})$ and let $\Delta_1 \equiv M$, $\Delta_2 \equiv (\lambda x.x\mathbf{I})\mathbf{I}$ be the first and second redexes in M. Then

$$\mathrm{Cpl}(M, \{\Delta_1, \Delta_2\}) = \mathbf{II},$$
$$\mathrm{Cpl}(M, \{\Delta_1\}) = (\lambda x.x\mathbf{I})\mathbf{I},$$
$$\mathrm{Cpl}(M, \{\Delta_2\}) = (\lambda x.x)(\mathbf{II}).$$

Now an alternative proof of the Church–Rosser theorem for $\boldsymbol{\beta}$ will be given using FD!. The method is implicit in Curry and Feys [1958].

11.2.27. DEFINITION. For $M, N \in \Lambda$ define

$$M \underset{1}{\twoheadrightarrow} N$$

if $\mathrm{Cpl}(M, \mathcal{F}) = N$, for some $\mathcal{F}$.

There is no ambiguity with the notion $\underset{1}{\twoheadrightarrow}$ of definition 3.2.3: the two relations are the same; see exercise 11.5.3.

EXAMPLE. Let $\omega = \lambda x.xx$ and let R be a redex with contractum R'. Then

$$\omega R \underset{1}{\twoheadrightarrow} RR, \qquad \omega R \underset{1}{\twoheadrightarrow} R'R', \qquad \omega R \underset{1}{\twoheadrightarrow} \omega R',$$

but not

$$\omega R \underset{1}{\twoheadrightarrow} RR'.$$

11.2.28. LEMMA. (i) *$\twoheadrightarrow_\beta$ is the transitive closure of $\underset{1}{\twoheadrightarrow}$.*
(ii) *$\underset{1}{\twoheadrightarrow}$ satisfies the diamond lemma.*

PROOF. (i) Same as for lemma 3.2.7.
(ii) Define $M_3 = \mathrm{Cpl}(M, \mathcal{F}_1 \cup \mathcal{F}_2)$. Then $M \underset{1}{\to} M_3$.
Now $M \underset{1}{\twoheadrightarrow} M_1$ results from a (partial) development of $(M, \mathcal{F}_1 \cup \mathcal{F}_2)$. Hence by completely developing the residuals of $\mathcal{F}_1 \cup \mathcal{F}_2$ in M_1 (relative to the given reduction $M \underset{1}{\twoheadrightarrow} M_1$) one obtains by FD!

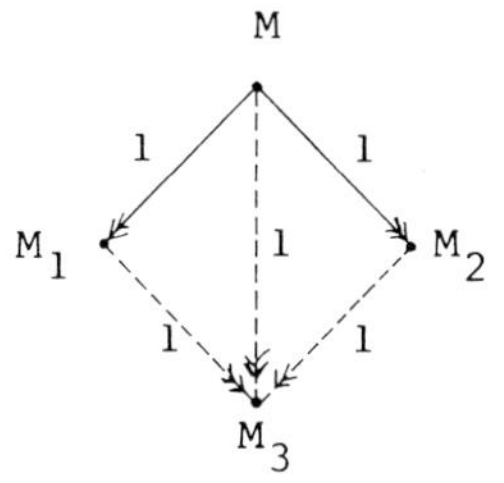

FIG. 11.2.

$M_1 \underset{1}{\twoheadrightarrow} M_3$. Similarly $M_2 \underset{1}{\twoheadrightarrow} M_3$ and one has a diamond; see figure 11.2. □

11.2.29. COROLLARY. *$\boldsymbol{\beta}$ is Church–Rosser.*

PROOF. By the lemmas 11.2.28 and 3.2.2. □

The proofs of the CR theorem in §3.2 and §11.1 are both related to the proof just given.

In §3.2 the relation $\underset{1}{\twoheadrightarrow}$ is the same as the one defined in this section (see exercise 11.5.3). However one did not need to know FD!; a direct inductive definition was possible.

In §11.1 the map $\varphi : \Lambda' \to \Lambda$ is such that $\varphi(M, \mathcal{F}) = \mathrm{Cpl}(M, \mathcal{F})$; see exercise 11.5.1. Therefore also that proof is essentially the same as the one in this section.

11.3. The conservation theorem for λI

In this section theorem 9.1.5 will be proved, which stated that for $M \in \Lambda_I$ one has

$$M \text{ has a nf} \Rightarrow M \text{ is strongly normalizable}.$$

For $M \in \Lambda_K$ this is wrong: $\mathbf{KI}\Omega$ has a nf, but nevertheless $\infty(\mathbf{KI}\Omega)$. See also example 9.1.7.

The conservation theorem is taken from Church [1941]. The proof below is due to Barendregt et al. [1976].

Let $\Lambda'_I = \{M \in \Lambda' \mid |M| \in \Lambda_I\}$.

11.3.1. LEMMA. *Let $M \in \Lambda'_I$ contain the redex occurrences Δ_1, Δ_2 of which only Δ_1 is indexed. Consider the reduction*

$$M \overset{\Delta_1}{\to}_{\beta_0} N.$$

Then Δ_2 has at least one residual in N (which is not indexed).

PROOF. Since $M \in \Lambda'_I$, Δ_1 is an I-redex. Hence in $M \overset{\Delta_1}{\underset{\beta_0}{\rightarrow}} N$ the only redex that disappears (i.e. has no residual) is Δ_1. □

Lemma 11.3.1 is of course false if $M \in \Lambda'_K$. Consider $(\lambda_0 x.\mathbf{I})\Delta_2 \rightarrow \mathbf{I}$.

11.3.2. COROLLARY. *Let* $M' \equiv (M, \mathcal{F}) \in \Lambda'_I$ *and let*

$$\sigma : M' \twoheadrightarrow_{\beta_0} N' \equiv (N, \mathcal{F}').$$

Let Δ *be a redex occurrence in* M', *with* $\Delta \notin \mathcal{F}$. *Then* $\Delta/\sigma \neq \emptyset$.

PROOF. Let σ be

$$M' \rightarrow_{\beta_0} M'_1 \rightarrow_{\beta_0} \cdots \rightarrow_{\beta_0} N'.$$

By lemma 11.3.1 Δ has a residual Δ_1 in M'_1 (which is not indexed); Δ_1 one in M'_2, and so on. Hence by lemma 11.2.6 we are done. □

11.3.3. LEMMA. *Let* $M' \equiv (M_0, \mathcal{F}) \in \Lambda'_I$ *and let* $M' \overset{\Delta}{\rightarrow}_{\beta'} N'$.

(i) *If* Δ *is a* β_0*-redex, i.e.* Δ *is indexed, then*

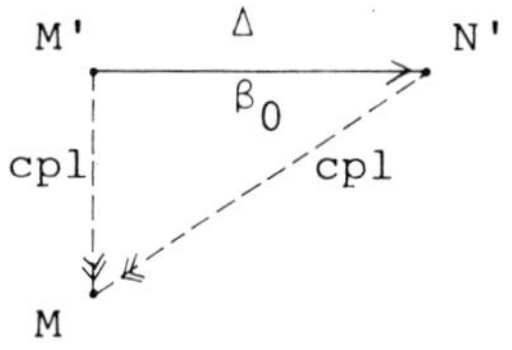

(ii) *If* Δ *is a* β_1*-redex, i.e.* Δ *is not indexed, then*

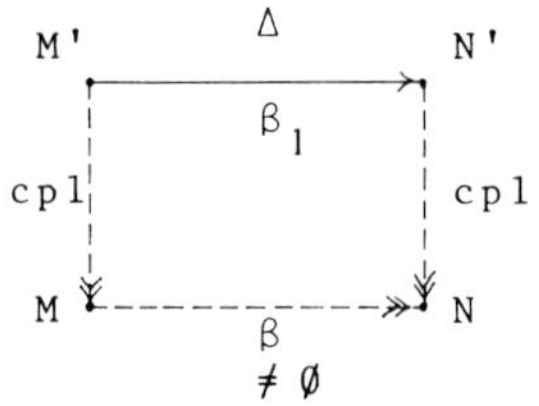

PROOF. (i) Let $M \equiv \text{Cpl}(M')$. Since Δ is indexed, one has $\Delta \in \mathcal{F}$ and therefore $M' \overset{\Delta}{\rightarrow}_{\beta_0} N'$ is an (uncompleted) development of M'. Hence it follows by FD! (theorem 11.2.25) that also $M \equiv \text{Cpl}(N')$.

(ii) Since Δ is not indexed, $\Delta \notin \mathcal{F}$. Note that

$$M' \overset{\Delta}{\rightarrow}_{\beta_1} N' \underset{\text{cpl}}{\twoheadrightarrow} N$$

is a complete development of $M'' = (M_0, \mathcal{F} \cup \{\Delta\})$. Hence by FD!

$$M' \underset{\text{cpl}}{\twoheadrightarrow} M$$

can be extended to a complete development of M'' to N. Therefore

$$\sigma : M \twoheadrightarrow_\beta N,$$

where σ is a complete development of the residuals of Δ in M (relative to some reduction $M' \twoheadrightarrow M$). Since by corollary 11.3.2 Δ had at least one such residual, one has

$$M \underset{\neq \emptyset\ \beta}{\twoheadrightarrow} N. \quad \square$$

11.3.4. Conservation theorem (for λI). *Let $M \in \Lambda_I$ and $M \to N$. Then $\infty(M) \Rightarrow \infty(N)$.*

Proof. Suppose $M \to N$ by contracting Δ. Let

$$\sigma : M \equiv M_0 \to M_1 \to \cdots$$

be an infinite reduction starting with M. Let $\mathcal{F} = \{\Delta\}$. By lemmas 11.2.2 and 11.3.3 one can erect the diagram in figure 11.3.
It remains to be shown that

$$\zeta : N_0 \underset{=}{\to} N_1 \underset{=}{\to} N_2 \underset{=}{\to} \cdots$$

is an infinite reduction. By lemma 11.3.3, $N_i \equiv N_{i+1}$ only if the reduction

$$(M_i, \mathcal{F}_i) \to_{\beta'} (M_{i+1}, \mathcal{F}_{i+1})$$

is a β_0-reduction.

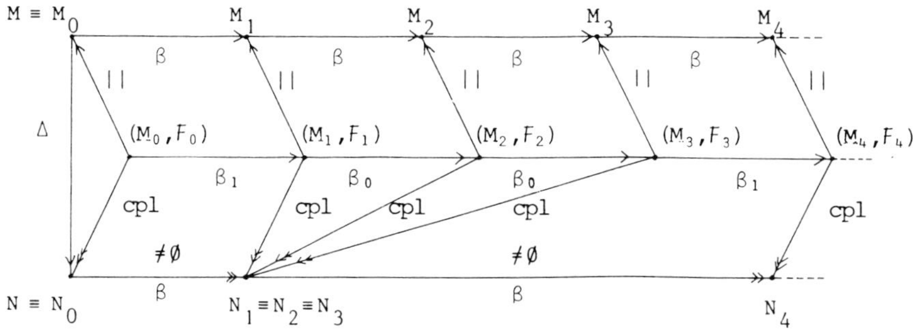

Fig. 11.3.

But by proposition 11.2.20 this happens consecutively only a finite number of times. Therefore ζ is an infinite reduction path. □

11.3.5. COROLLARY. *If* $M \in \Lambda_I$ *has a* nf, *then* M *strongly normalizes and hence* $G(M)$ *is finite.*

PROOF. Let $M \to M_1 \to \cdots \to N$ be a reduction of M to nf. Since $\neg\infty(N)$, it follows by the contrapositive of theorem 11.3.4 that $\neg\infty(M)$, i.e. SN(M). By König's lemma it follows that $G(M)$ is finite. □

Theorem 11.3.4 can be formulated in a way which is also valid for $\boldsymbol{\lambda K}$.

11.3.6. DEFINITION. Let $\Delta \equiv (\lambda x.P)Q \in \Lambda_K$. Then Δ is an *I-redex* if $x \in \mathrm{FV}(P)$, otherwise it is a *K-redex*.

11.3.7. CONSERVATION THEOREM. *Let* $M, N \in \Lambda_K$ *and* $M \overset{\Delta}{\to} N$, *where* Δ *is an I-redex. Then* $\infty(M) \Rightarrow \infty(N)$.

PROOF. See theorem 13.4.12. □

In §13.4 it will be shown that the proof of theorem 11.3.4 cannot be generalized immediately to yield 11.3.7.

11.4. Standardization

The standardization theorem of Curry and Feys [1958] is a useful result stating that if $M \twoheadrightarrow N$, then there is a 'standard' reduction from M to N.

In terms of residuals the notion of standard reduction can be formulated as follows. Remember that if $\Delta, \Delta' \in M$, then Δ is to the left of Δ' if the main λ in Δ is to the left of the main λ in Δ'.

11.4.1. DEFINITION. (i) Let

$$\sigma : M_0 \overset{\Delta_0}{\to} M_1 \overset{\Delta_1}{\to} M_2 \overset{\Delta_2}{\to} \cdots$$

be a reduction. σ is called a *standard reduction* if $\forall i\ \forall j < i$ [Δ_i is not a residual of a redex to the left of Δ_j (relative to the given reduction from M_j to M_i)].

(ii) Write $M \underset{s}{\twoheadrightarrow} N$ If there is a standard reduction $\sigma : M \to N$.

Standard reductions make contractions from the left to the right possibly with some jumps. They also can be described as follows.

"After each contraction of a redex R, index the lambdas of redexes to the left of R. Redexes with indexed lambdas are not allowed to be contracted anymore. Indexed lambdas remain indexed after contractions of other redexes."

EXAMPLE. Consider the following reductions (the contracted redexes are underlined).

(i) $\lambda a.(\lambda b.\underline{(\lambda c.c)b}\,b)d \to$
$\lambda a.\underline{(\lambda b.bb)d} \to$
$\lambda a.dd.$

(ii) $\lambda a.\underline{(\lambda b.(\lambda c.c)bb)d} \to$
$\lambda a.\underline{(\lambda c.c)d}\,d \to$
$\lambda a.dd.$

Both reductions have the same start and terminal. The first one is not standard, the second one is.

Note that if $\sigma = \tau + \rho$ is standard, then so are τ and ρ, but not conversely.

Now we will present a proof of the standardization theorem due to Mitschke [1979].

11.4.2. DEFINITION. (i) Let $M \in \Lambda$ and $\Delta \in M$ be a redex. Then Δ is called *internal* in M if Δ is not the head redex in M.

(ii) $M \underset{\mathrm{i}}{\twoheadrightarrow} N$ if there is a reduction (a so called *internal reduction*)

$$\sigma : M \equiv M_0 \overset{\Delta_0}{\to} M_1 \overset{\Delta_1}{\to} \cdots \to M_n \equiv N$$

such that Δ_i is internal in M_i for $0 \leqslant i < n$.

(iii) $M \underset{1,\mathrm{i}}{\twoheadrightarrow} N$ if there is a reduction $\sigma : M \underset{\mathrm{i}}{\twoheadrightarrow} N$ which is at the same time a complete reduction of some $(M, \mathcal{F})$, i.e. $\sigma : M \underset{1}{\twoheadrightarrow} N$.

Remember that $\underset{\mathrm{h}}{\twoheadrightarrow}$ denotes head reduction.

EXAMPLES. Let $M \equiv \lambda x.(\lambda z.zz)(\mathbf{I}(\mathbf{I}x))$. Then $\mathbf{I}x$ and $\mathbf{I}(\mathbf{I}x)$ are internal redexes and $(\lambda z.zz)(\mathbf{I}(\mathbf{I}x))$ is the head redex. One has

$$M \underset{\mathrm{i}}{\to} \lambda x.(\lambda z.zz)(\mathbf{I}x),$$

$$M \underset{1,\mathrm{i}}{\twoheadrightarrow} \lambda x.(\lambda z.zz)x,$$

$$M \underset{\mathrm{h}}{\to} \lambda x.(\mathbf{I}(\mathbf{I}x))(\mathbf{I}(\mathbf{I}x)),$$

$$M \underset{\mathrm{h}}{\twoheadrightarrow} \lambda x.x(\mathbf{I}(\mathbf{I}x)),$$

$$M \underset{1}{\twoheadrightarrow} \lambda x.xx.$$

11.4.3. LEMMA. *Let* $\sigma : M \xrightarrow{\Delta} N$, *where* Δ *is an internal redex of* M.

(i) *If* N *has a head redex, then so has* M.

(ii) *If* Δ_h *is the head redex of* M, *then* Δ_h/σ *consists of exactly one element which is the head redex of* N.

(iii) *If* Δ_i *is an internal redex of* M, *then all elements of* Δ_i/σ *are internal redexes of* N.

PROOF. (i) If M has no head redex, then M is in hnf, but then also N is in hnf, contradiction.

(ii) Give the head redex Δ_h in M an index, say 0. Then by contracting internal redexes this redex will neither be cancelled nor be duplicated. Clearly the 0-redex remains the head redex all the time.

(iii) Equally simple. □

11.4.4. LEMMA.

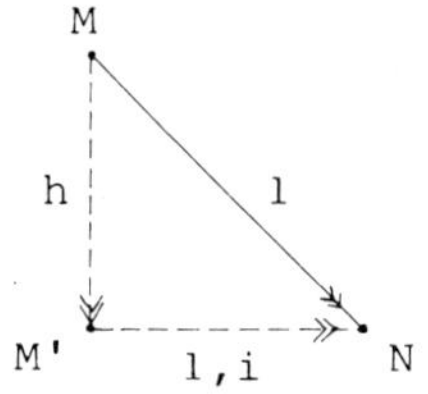

$M, M', N \in \Lambda$.

PROOF. Let N be the complete reduct of $(M, \mathcal{F})$. Now develop $(M, \mathcal{F})$ as follows. First contract consecutively the indexed redexes that are head redexes. By FD this process stops say at M'. Then complete the development by contracting the left-over internal indexed redexes (i.e. the residuals of $\mathcal{F}$ in M'). By FD! this leads again to N. Clearly $M \underset{h}{\twoheadrightarrow} M'$ and $M' \underset{l}{\twoheadrightarrow} N$. By lemma 11.4.3 (iii) $M' \underset{l,i}{\twoheadrightarrow} M$ even. □

11.4.5. LEMMA.

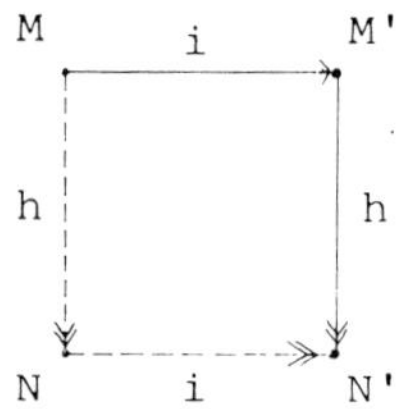

$M, M', N, N' \in \Lambda$.

PROOF. First it will be shown that

(∗)

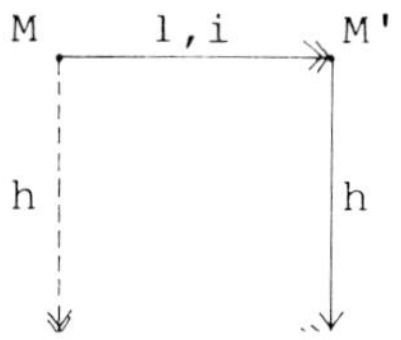

Let M' be the complete reduct of say $(M, \mathcal{F})$, where all the elements of $\mathcal{F}$ are internal redexes. By lemma 11.4.3(i) M has a head redex, say Δ. By 11.4.3(ii) Δ has exactly one residual Δ' in M' and $M' \overset{\Delta'}{\underset{h}{\to}} N'$. Hence

$$M \underset{l,i}{\twoheadrightarrow} M' \underset{h}{\to} N'$$

is a complete development of $(M, \mathcal{F} \cup \{\Delta\})$. Let M_1 be obtained from M by contracting Δ. By FD! one has $M_1 \underset{l}{\twoheadrightarrow} N'$ by a complete development of all residuals of $\mathcal{F}$ in M_1. Hence by lemma 11.4.4 $\exists N\ M_1 \underset{h}{\twoheadrightarrow} N \underset{l,i}{\twoheadrightarrow} N'$. This shows ($*$); see figure 11.4.

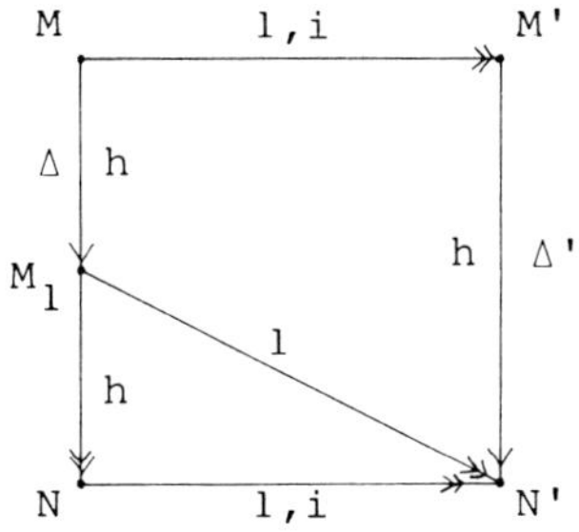

FIG. 11.4.

Now, since $M \underset{i}{\to} M' \Rightarrow M \underset{l,i}{\twoheadrightarrow} M'$, the statement of the lemma follows by ($*$) and a diagram chase suggested in figure 11.5.

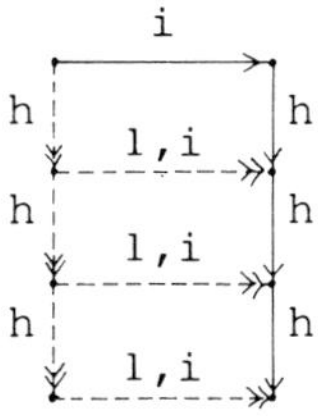

FIG. 11.5.

□

11.4.6. MAIN LEMMA.

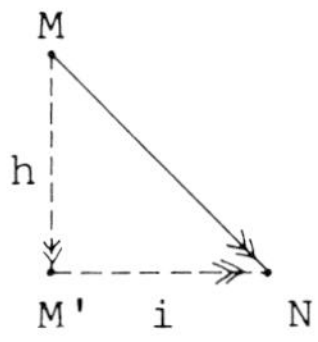

$M, N, M' \in \Lambda$.

PROOF. Any reduction $M \twoheadrightarrow N$ is of the form

$$M \underset{h}{\twoheadrightarrow} M_1 \underset{i}{\twoheadrightarrow} M_2 \underset{h}{\twoheadrightarrow} M_3 \underset{i}{\twoheadrightarrow} \cdots \underset{i}{\twoheadrightarrow} N.$$

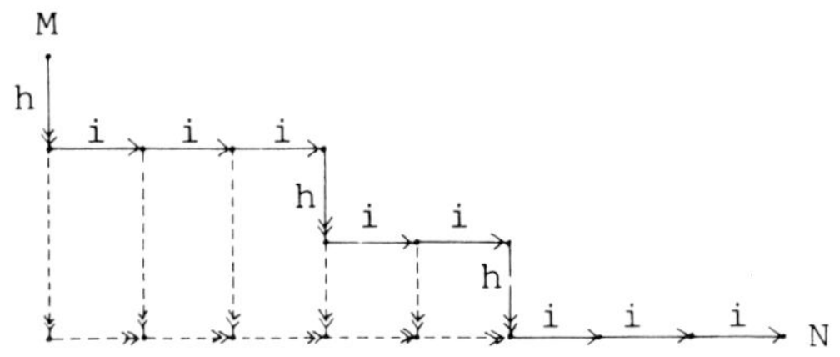

FIG. 11.6.

This can be changed into the required reduction by lemma 11.4.5 and a diagram chase suggested in figure 11.6. □

Now we can prove the standardization theorem of Curry and Feys [1958].

11.4.7. STANDARDIZATION THEOREM. *If* $M \twoheadrightarrow N$, *then* $M \underset{s}{\twoheadrightarrow} N$.

PROOF. By induction on the length of N. By lemma 11.4.6

$$\exists Z \quad M \underset{h}{\twoheadrightarrow} Z \underset{i}{\twoheadrightarrow} N.$$

If N is a variable x, then $Z \equiv x$ and we are done (a head reduction is clearly a standard one).

If $N \equiv \lambda x_1 \cdots x_n.N_0 N_1 \cdots N_m$, with $n+m>0$, then Z must be of the form

$$Z \equiv \lambda x_1 \cdots x_n.Z_0 Z_1 \cdots Z_m$$

and

$$Z_i \twoheadrightarrow N_i, \quad 0 \leqslant i \leqslant m.$$

By the induction hypothesis

$$\exists \sigma_i \quad \sigma_i : Z_i \underset{s}{\twoheadrightarrow} N_i, \quad 0 \leqslant i \leqslant m.$$

Let $\sigma : M \underset{h}{\twoheadrightarrow} Z$. Then

$$\sigma + \sigma_0 + \cdots + \sigma_m : M \underset{s}{\twoheadrightarrow} N. \quad \square$$

11.4.8. COROLLARY. *M has a* hnf *iff the head reduction path of M terminates.*

PROOF. (⇒) Let $M = \lambda \vec{x}.y\vec{M}$. By the CR theorem $M \twoheadrightarrow Z$, $\lambda \vec{x}.y\vec{M} \twoheadrightarrow Z$, for some Z. But then $Z \equiv \lambda \vec{x}.y\vec{N}$, with $M_i \twoheadrightarrow N_i$. Therefore by the standardization theorem

(1) $$M \underset{s}{\twoheadrightarrow} \lambda\vec{x}.y\vec{N}.$$

Let this reduction be

$$M \equiv M_0 \overset{\Delta_0}{\to} M_1 \overset{\Delta_1}{\to} \cdots \to \lambda\vec{x}.y\vec{N}.$$

If all the Δ_i are head redexes, then (1) is a terminating head reduction. Otherwise let Δ_i be the first internal redex. Then M_i must be in hnf, for otherwise its head redex would remain ($M_i \twoheadrightarrow \lambda\vec{x}.y\vec{N}$ is standard). Therefore $M \twoheadrightarrow M_i$ is a terminating head reduction.

(⇐) Trivial. □

11.5. Exercises

11.5.1. Let $(M, \mathcal{F}) \in \Lambda'$. Show that $\mathrm{Cpl}(M, \mathcal{F}) = \varphi(M, \mathcal{F})$, where φ is introduced in definition 11.1.4.

11.5.2. Construct a reduction $\sigma : M \twoheadrightarrow N$ such that for some redex $\Delta \in M$ not all elements of Δ/σ are disjoint. Conclude that the method of exercise 7.4.13 for proving the Church–Rosser property for $\boldsymbol{w}$ does not extend to $\boldsymbol{\beta}$.

11.5.3. Prove that the relations $\underset{1}{\twoheadrightarrow}$ as defined in 3.2.3 and 11.2.27 are the same.

11.5.4. Show that the proof given in §11.1 that $\boldsymbol{\beta}$ is CR does not generalize immediately to $\boldsymbol{\beta\eta}$. [*Hint*. Consider $\lambda x(\lambda y.P)x$. This term contains a $\boldsymbol{\beta}$-redex and is an $\boldsymbol{\eta}$-redex. If one of them is contracted, the other disappears. Similarly for $(\lambda x.Mx)N$.]

11.5.5. State and prove for CL the standardization theorem and FD!, and also for CL_I the conservation theorem.

11.5.6 (Schroer). Let $\omega \equiv \lambda x.xx$ and $M \equiv (\lambda y.\omega y)(\lambda y.\omega y)$. Draw $G(M)$. For what N does one have $M \underset{1}{\twoheadrightarrow} N$?

11.5.7. Let $\omega \equiv \lambda axz.z(aax)$. Show that if $\omega\omega x \twoheadrightarrow M$, then $x \in \mathrm{FV}(M)$. [*Hint*. Consider a standard reduction of minimal length.]

11.5.8. (i) Show that a development of M has length $< 2^{\|M\|}$.

(ii) Show that there is a real $\alpha > 0$ and terms $M_0, M_1, \ldots$ such that

$$\lim_{n\to\infty} \|M_n\| = \infty,$$

$$2^{\alpha\|M_n\|} < \text{maximal length of a development of } M_n.$$

11.5.9 (S. Micali). Show that if $\Delta \in M$ and $\sigma : M \twoheadrightarrow N$ is a development, then the residuals of Δ w.r.t. σ are disjoint subterms of N. (cf. exercise 11.5.2.)

CHAPTER 12

STRONGLY EQUIVALENT REDUCTIONS

In this chapter a relation $\cong$, strong equivalence, will be defined for reductions. Using this notion, the standardization theorem can be improved as follows.

For a given reduction $\sigma : M \twoheadrightarrow N$, there is a unique standard reduction

$$\sigma_s : M \twoheadrightarrow N \quad \text{such that } \sigma \cong \sigma_s.$$

Also FD! and CR can be strengthened:

(FD!$^+$) All complete developments of an $(M, \mathcal{F})$ end in the same term and are strongly equivalent.

(CR$^+$) 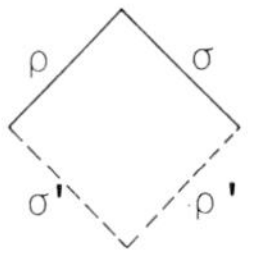

$\sigma + \rho' \cong \rho + \sigma'$.

The plan of this chapter is as follows. First in §12.1 the diagram of two coinitial reductions is introduced. Using these diagrams in §12.2 the equivalence $\cong$ is introduced and CR$^+$ and FD!$^+$ are proved. Finally in §12.3 the strengthening of the standardization theorem is given.

12.1. Reduction diagrams

Let $\sigma : M \twoheadrightarrow N$ be a reduction and $\Delta \in M$ a redex occurrence. As was noted in 11.2.10 the set of residuals Δ/σ may depend on σ and not just on M, N, Δ.

12.1.1. Definition (Hindley). Let $\sigma_i : M_i \twoheadrightarrow N_i$, $i = 1, 2$, be two reductions.

(i) σ_1, σ_2 are (*weakly*) *equivalent* (notation $\sigma_1 \simeq \sigma_2$) if $M_1 \equiv M_2$ and $N_1 \equiv N_2$.

(ii) σ_1, σ_2 are *H-equivalent* (notation $\sigma_1 \cong_H \sigma_2$) if $\sigma_1 \simeq \sigma_2$ and $\forall \Delta \in M_1$ $\Delta/\sigma_1 = \Delta/\sigma_2$.

Below an equivalence $\cong$ on reductions will be defined that is stronger than $\cong_H$. This concept is due to Berry and Lévy; see Lévy [1978], where also the improvements of CR, FD! and the standardization theorem are given.

We will define $\cong$ via diagrams as introduced in Klop [1980] for this purpose. The diagram of $\sigma : M \twoheadrightarrow N_1$ and $\rho : M \twoheadrightarrow N_2$ results from trying to find a common reduct of N_1, N_2 by continuously applying the weak diamond property.

12.1.1. DEFINITION. Let $\boldsymbol{R}$ be a notion of reduction.

(i) Remember that $M \overset{\Delta}{\to}_R N$ denotes that N results from M by contracting the R-redex $\Delta \in M$. This notion is extended to

$$M \underset{=}{\overset{\Delta}{\to}}_R N$$

where now Δ also may be the *empty redex* $\emptyset$. In that case

$$M \underset{=}{\overset{\emptyset}{\to}}_R N$$

is the empty reduction, i.e. nothing happens to M and $N \equiv M$.

(ii) An $\boldsymbol{R}$-$=$ *-reduction* is a sequence

$$\sigma : M_0 \underset{=}{\overset{\Delta_0}{\to}}_R M_1 \underset{=}{\overset{\Delta_1}{\to}}_R \cdots$$

where each Δ_i is either an R-redex or empty. If the Δ_i are all $\emptyset$, then σ is denoted also by $\emptyset$.

$\sigma : M \underset{=}{\overset{\Delta}{\to}}_R N$ is called a one step R-$=$-reduction.

$\sigma : M \underset{=}{\twoheadrightarrow}_R N$ expresses that σ is an R-$=$-reduction from M to N.

As usual, no mention of $\boldsymbol{R}$ is made when $\boldsymbol{R} = \boldsymbol{\beta}$. In the rest of this section $\boldsymbol{R}$ will denote $\boldsymbol{\beta}$ or $\boldsymbol{\beta}'$, and terms will range over Λ or Λ' accordingly.

12.1.2. DEFINITION. Let $\sigma : M \underset{=}{\overset{\Delta_1}{\to}}_R M_1$, $\rho : M \underset{=}{\overset{\Delta_2}{\to}}_R M_2$. Consider $\Delta_1/\rho \subset M_2$. This is a set of disjoint redexes. Define σ/ρ as the reduction starting with M_2 obtained by contracting consecutively (from the left to the right) the elements of Δ_1/ρ. Similarly ρ/σ is defined; see figure 12.1.

If $\Delta_1 = \emptyset$, then $\Delta_1/\rho = \emptyset$ and hence $\sigma/\rho = \emptyset$. But $\sigma/\rho = \emptyset$ is also possible in other cases; see example 12.1.5.

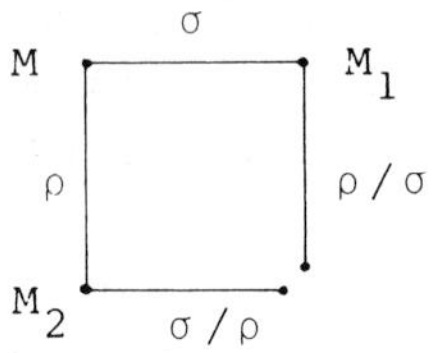

FIG. 12.1.

12.1.3. LEMMA. *Let σ, ρ be one step R-=-reductions. Then σ/ρ and ρ/σ end in the same term. Moreover, $\sigma+\rho/\sigma \cong_H \rho+\sigma/\rho$.*

PROOF. By the proof of lemma 11.1.1(ii) (for $\boldsymbol{R}=\boldsymbol{\beta}'$ seeing that the indices match). The rest follows from lemma 11.2.8. (If this is not clear, see the proof of proposition 12.2.3(i).) □

12.1.4. DEFINITION. Let σ, ρ be two coinitial one step R-=-reductions. Then the *elementary R-diagram* of σ, ρ is

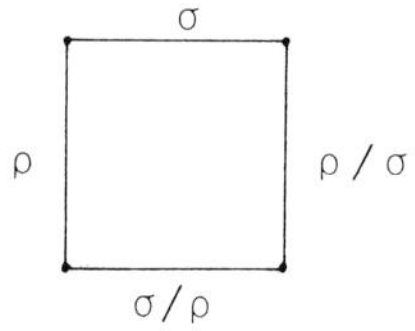

12.1.5. EXAMPLES. Let $M \to M'$ be a one step reduction. Then the following are elementary diagrams.

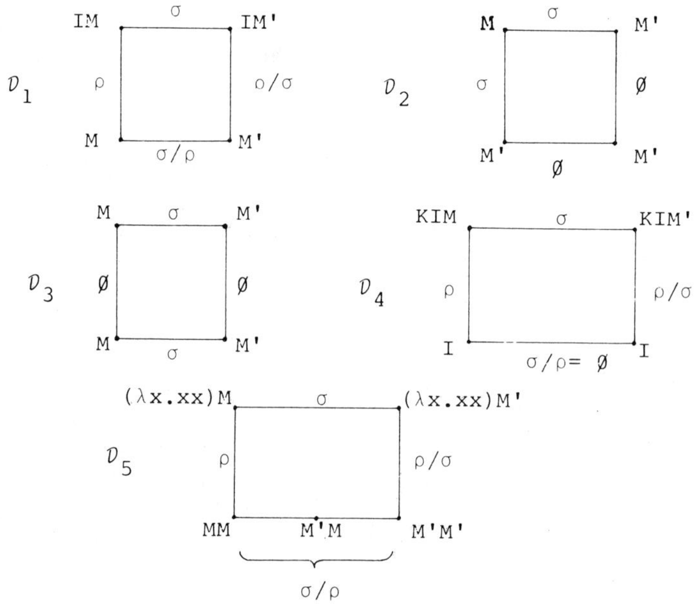

Example $\mathfrak{D}_5$ shows that σ/ρ may be a reduction of arbitrary length. $=$-reductions are introduced because of examples like $\mathfrak{D}_2$ and $\mathfrak{D}_4$.

12.1.6. Lemma. *Let σ be a one step R-$=$-reduction.*

(i) $\sigma/\sigma = \emptyset$.

(ii) $\sigma/\emptyset = \sigma$.

(iii) $\emptyset/\sigma = \emptyset$.

Proof. See examples $\mathfrak{D}_2$ and $\mathfrak{D}_4$. □

12.1.7. Definition. Let σ/ρ be a side of an elementary diagram. σ/ρ *splits* if it consists of more than one reduction step. An elementary diagram *splits* if one of its sides does.

Example 12.1.5 $\mathfrak{D}_5$ splits. An elementary diagram can split on at most one side; see exercise 12.4.1.

Convention. If the elementary diagram of σ, ρ splits, it will be drawn as either

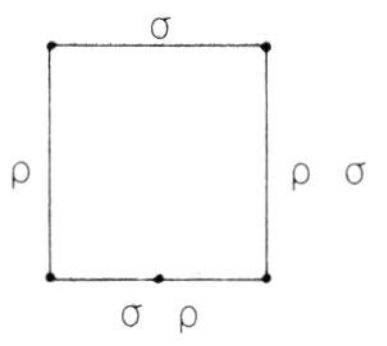

or

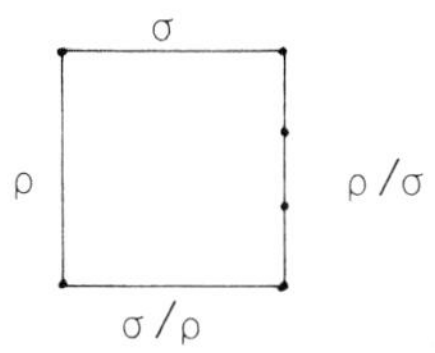

depending on which side splits and on the number of one step reductions into which it splits.

12.1.8. Definition. Given two coinitial R-$=$-reductions $\sigma : M \underset{=}{\twoheadrightarrow}_R M_1, \rho : M \underset{=}{\twoheadrightarrow}_R M_2$. Split σ, ρ into one step R-$=$-reductions: $\sigma = \sigma_1 + \cdots + \sigma_n$ and $\rho = \rho_1 + \cdots + \rho_m$. One can try to find a common reduct of M_1, M_2 by drawing elementary diagrams as follows. Start with the situation

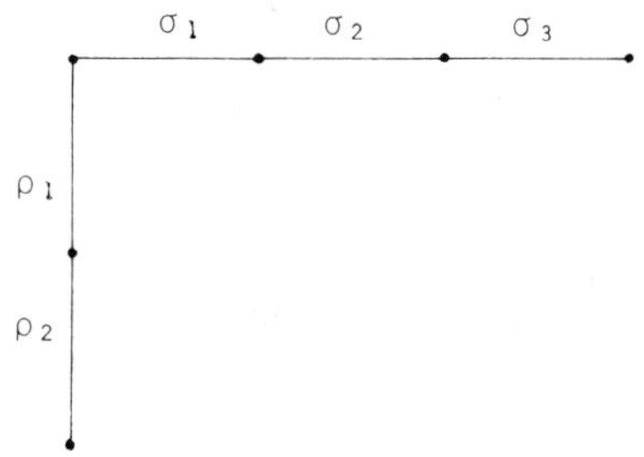

draw the elementary diagram of σ_1, ρ_1

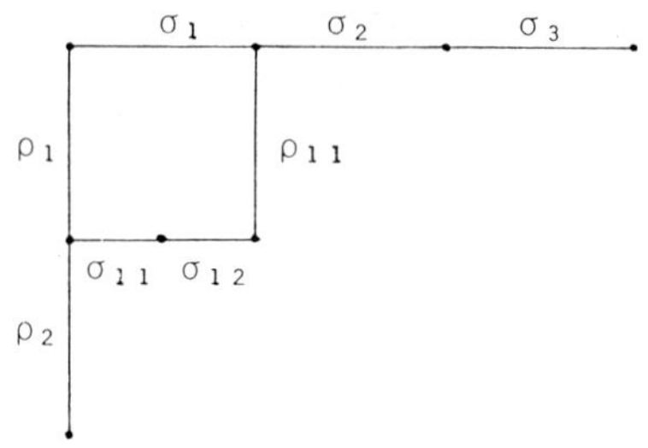

then that of ρ_2, σ_{11} and ρ_{11}, σ_2

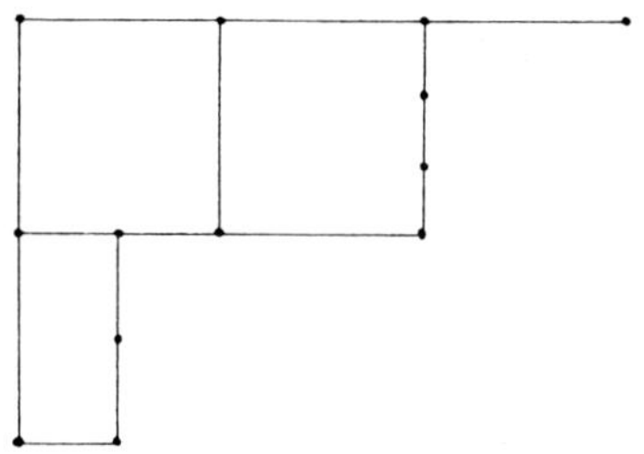

etcetera, until one obtains after some steps

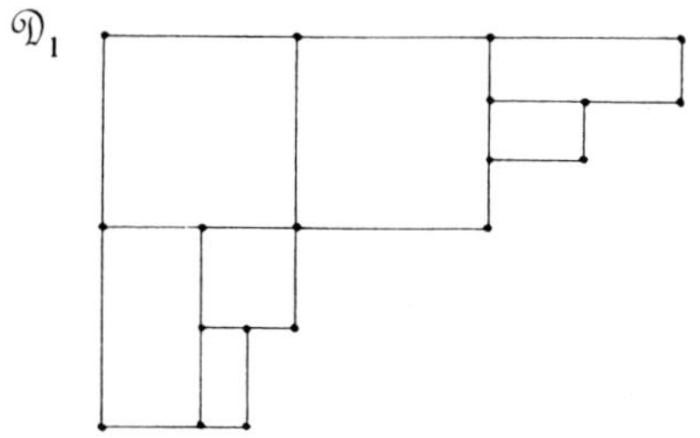

etcetera and finally, say,

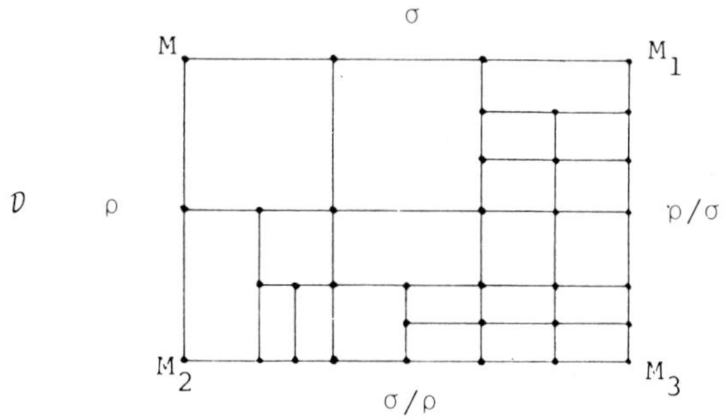

Figure $\mathfrak{D}$, if it exists, is called the *R-diagram* of σ and ρ, $\mathfrak{D}_R(\sigma, \rho)$. The obtained R-$\overset{=}{}$-reductions $M_1 \underset{=}{\rightarrow}_R M_3$, $M_2 \underset{=}{\rightarrow}_R M_3$ are denoted by ρ/σ, σ/ρ respectively. A figure like $\mathfrak{D}_1$ is called a *prediagram* of σ, ρ. $\mathfrak{D}_\beta$ is denoted as $\mathfrak{D}$, $\mathfrak{D}_{\beta'}$ as $\mathfrak{D}'$.

It is not immediate that $\mathfrak{D}_R(\sigma, \rho)$ always exists. In principle one could imagine that Escher-like pictures appear, e.g.

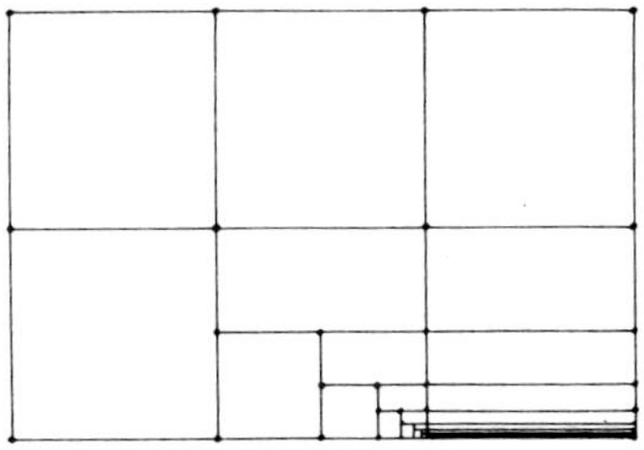

or

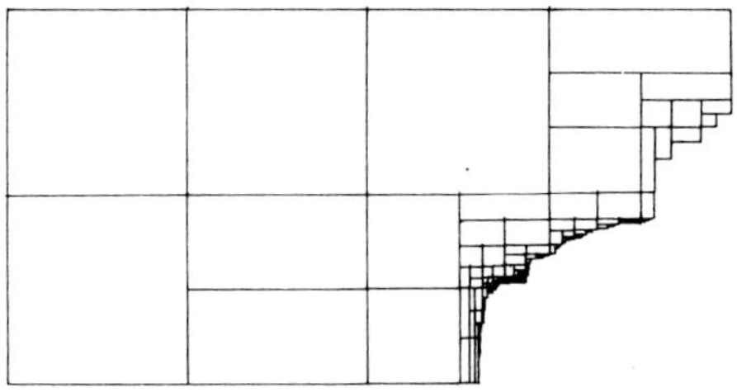

But in 12.1.14 it will be proved that R-diagrams always do exist for $\boldsymbol{R} = \boldsymbol{\beta}$ or $\boldsymbol{R} = \boldsymbol{\beta}'$. For δ-reduction, see §15.3, Escher pictures do appear.

12.1.9. PROPOSITION. (i) (*Projecting*). *Let $\mathfrak{D}' = \mathfrak{D}'(\sigma', \rho')$ be a β'-diagram and let $|\mathfrak{D}'|$ be obtained by erasing all indices in $\mathfrak{D}'$. Then $\mathfrak{D} = \mathfrak{D}(\sigma, \rho)$ exists with $\sigma = |\sigma'|$, $\rho = |\rho'|$ and $|\mathfrak{D}'| = \mathfrak{D}$.*

(ii) (*Lifting*). *Let $\sigma : M \twoheadrightarrow M_1$, $\rho : M \twoheadrightarrow M_2$ and let $M = |M'|$ with $M' \in \Lambda'$. Lift σ, ρ to σ', ρ' starting with M'. Then $\mathfrak{D}' = \mathfrak{D}'(\sigma', \rho')$ exists and $|\mathfrak{D}'| = \mathfrak{D}$.*

PROOF. (i) For elementary β'-diagrams this is obvious. The general case follows by a diagram chase.

(ii) Similarly. □

12.1.10. LEMMA. (i) *Let*

$$\rho' : M' \overset{\Delta}{\underset{=}{\rightarrow}}_{\beta_0} M_1', \qquad \sigma' : M' \underset{=}{\rightarrow}_{\beta'} M_2'.$$

Then ρ'/σ' is a β_0-$=$-reduction.

(ii) *Let*

$$\rho' : M' \twoheadrightarrow_{\beta_0} M_1', \qquad \sigma' : M' \twoheadrightarrow_{\beta'} M_2'$$

and suppose $\mathfrak{D}'(\rho', \sigma')$ *exists. Then* ρ'/σ' *is a* β_0*-=-reduction.*

PROOF. (i) By assumption Δ is an indexed redex. Hence Δ/σ consists of indexed redexes (or is empty). Hence ρ'/σ' is by definition a β_0-=-reduction.

(ii) By (i) and a diagram chase. □

12.1.11. DEFINITION. An =-reduction ρ starting with M is an =-*development* of M if ρ^-, obtained from ρ by leaving out all empty steps, is a development of M.

12.1.12. PROPOSITION. *Let* $\rho : (M, \mathfrak{F}) \underset{\text{dev}}{\twoheadrightarrow} M_1$ *and* $\sigma : M \to M_2$. *Suppose* $\mathfrak{D} = \mathfrak{D}(\rho, \sigma)$ *exists. Then*

(i) ρ/σ *is an* =*-development of* $(M_2, \mathfrak{F}/\sigma)$.

(ii) *If moreover* ρ *is a complete development of* $(M, \mathfrak{F})$, *then* ρ/σ *is a complete* =*-development of* $(M_2, \mathfrak{F}/\sigma)$.

PROOF. (i) Let $M' \equiv (M, \mathfrak{F}) \in \Lambda'$. Lift $\mathfrak{D}$ to M', obtaining $\mathfrak{D}'$, say,

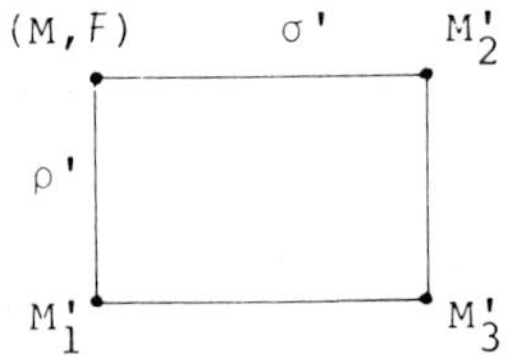

ρ' is by lemma 11.2.12 a β_0-reduction. Hence by lemma 12.1.10(ii) ρ'/σ' is a β_0-reduction. Clearly $\rho/\sigma = |\rho'/\sigma'|$ is a development of $(M_2, \mathfrak{F}/\sigma)$, since $\mathfrak{F}/\sigma = \{|\Delta'| \in M_2 | \Delta' \in M_2'$ and Δ' is indexed$\}$.

(ii) Now suppose $\rho : (M, \mathfrak{F}) \underset{\text{cpl}}{\twoheadrightarrow} M_1$, then it follows that $M_1' \in \Lambda$. Hence $M_3' \in \Lambda$ and thus ρ/σ is a complete =-development of $(M_2, \mathfrak{F}/\sigma)$. □

The following lemma follows from FD, but not quite immediately.

12.1.13. LEMMA. *Let* σ, ρ *be two* =*-developments of* M. *Then* $\mathfrak{D}(\sigma, \rho)$ *exists and* σ/ρ *and* ρ/σ *are also* =*-developments.*

PROOF. The proof is done in several steps.

(1) DEFINITION. *Multisets* $\subseteq \mathbb{N}$ are sets in which each element k may occur more than once, i.e. with multiplicity $m_k \in \mathbb{N}$. More formally, a multiset $X \subseteq \mathbb{N}$ is a pair (X, m) where $m: X \to \mathbb{N}$.

Example. $\{0,3,0,0,4,3\}$ is the multiset with $m_0 = 3, m_3 = 2, m_4 = 1$.

For each multiset $X = (X, m) \subseteq \mathbb{N}$, define the ordinal

$$\mathrm{Ord}(X) = \omega^{k_1} \cdot m_{k_1} + \cdots + \omega^{k_p} \cdot m_{k_p},$$

where

$$X = \{k_1, \ldots, k_p\} \quad \text{with } k_1 > \cdots > k_p.$$

(2) DEFINITION. Let a particular way in which the diagram construction proceeds be given. If the process is not finished at stage n, one has a pre-diagram like

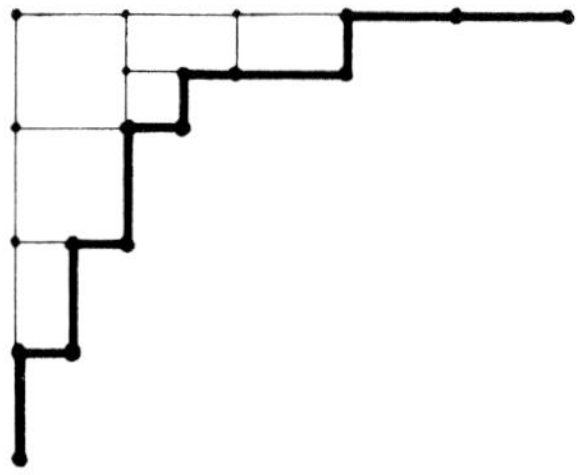

stage n

Now let D_n be the finite multiset of terms on the south east edge of this pre-diagram (bold face line).

(3) LEMMA. *Each redex that is contracted in a pre-diagram of σ, ρ is a residual (with respect to all possible reduction paths) of a redex in M.*

PROOF. This is true for the initial pre-diagram (consisting of σ, ρ) since by assumption σ, ρ are developments. After adding a new elementary diagram, say for σ_1, ρ_1, the statement remains true since the redexes contracted in σ_1/ρ_1 and ρ_1/σ_1 are residuals of redexes contracted in σ_1, ρ_1 and hence also redexes in M. (The statement in parentheses follows from lemma 12.1.3.) $\square_3$

(4) DEFINITION. Let $\mathscr{Q} = \{N \mid M \underset{\text{dev}}{\twoheadrightarrow} N\}$. By FD, $\mathscr{Q}$ is a finite set. Moreover by lemma 3 all terms in a pre-diagram are in $\mathscr{Q}$. (We are not done yet since there may be infinitely many duplications caused by empty reductions).

For $N, N' \in \mathscr{Q}$, write $N \underset{M}{\twoheadrightarrow} N'$ if there exists a development

$$\sigma_0 + \sigma : M \twoheadrightarrow N \twoheadrightarrow N',$$

with $\sigma : N \twoheadrightarrow N'$ non empty.

For $N \in \mathcal{Q}$ define

$$|||N||| = \text{card}\{N' \in \mathcal{Q} \mid N \twoheadrightarrow_M N'\}.$$

Since, by FD, there are no loops in $\twoheadrightarrow_M$ reductions, it follows that if $N \twoheadrightarrow_M N'$, then $|||N||| > |||N'|||$.

Finally define for each n the ordinal $\alpha_n < \omega^\omega$ as follows. $\alpha_n = \text{Ord}(|||D_n|||)$, where $|||D_n|||$ is the multiset $\{|||M_1|||, \ldots, |||M_p|||\}$, if $D_n = \{M_1, \ldots, M_p\}$.

(5) LEMMA. *Let $X \subseteq \mathbb{N}$ be a multiset. If X' is obtained from X by replacing one element k by new elements $k_1, \ldots, k_q < k$, then* $\text{Ord}(X) > \text{Ord}(X')$.
PROOF. By example. Let $X = \{3,5,7,5\}$ and $X' = \{3,4,4,3,7,5\}$. Then

$$\text{Ord}(X) = \omega^7 + \omega^5.2 + \omega^3,$$

$$\text{Ord}(X') = \omega^7 + \omega^5 + \omega^4.2 + \omega^3.2.$$

Now

$$\omega^5 + \text{---} > \omega^4.2 + \omega^3 + \text{---} \quad (\text{for --- } < \omega^5).$$

Hence

$$\text{Ord}(X) > \text{Ord}(X'). \quad \square_5$$

(6) LEMMA. *If at stage $n+1$ in the diagram construction the newly drawn elementary diagram is splitting, then $\alpha_n > \alpha_{n+1}$.*
PROOF. Let the elementary diagram that is added at stage $n+1$ be, say,

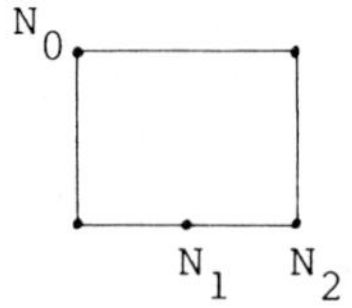

Then $D_{n+1} = D_n - \{N_0\} \cup \{N_1, N_2\}$. Since by (2) $N_0 \twoheadrightarrow_M N_1, N_2$ one has by (4) $|||N_0||| > |||N_1|||, |||N_2|||$. Hence (5) applies and thus $\alpha_n = \text{Ord}(|||D_n|||) > \text{Ord}(|||D_{n+1}|||) = \alpha_{n+1}$. $\square_6$

(7) CLAIM. $\mathfrak{D}(\sigma, \rho)$ exists.
PROOF. It follows from (6) that after finitely many steps in the construction of $\mathfrak{D}(\sigma, \rho)$ no new splitting elementary diagrams are added. After that stage, say stage n_0, only non-splitting elementary diagrams are added and

hence the pre-diagrams cannot explode (or rather implode) to an Escher figure. E.g.

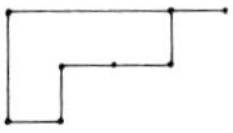

yields

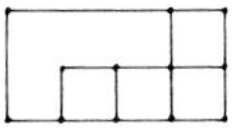

stage n_0 final stage. $\square_7$

(8) CLAIM. σ/ρ and ρ/σ are $=$-developments.
PROOF. By 12.1.12(i). $\square_8$ $\square$

12.1.14. THEOREM. *For each coinitial pair of finite β-reductions σ, ρ the diagram $\mathcal{D}(\sigma, \rho)$ exists. Hence σ/ρ and ρ/σ are well-defined.*

PROOF. Given, say,

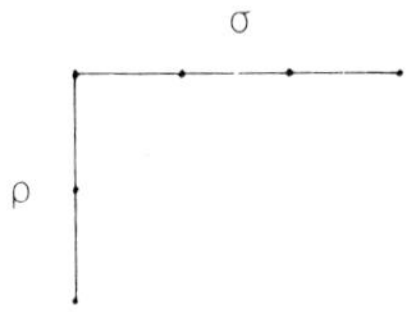

(where it is assumed that $\sigma = \sigma_1 + \sigma_2 + \sigma_3$, with σ_i one step reductions and similarly for $\rho = \rho_1 + \rho_2$), draw the lines

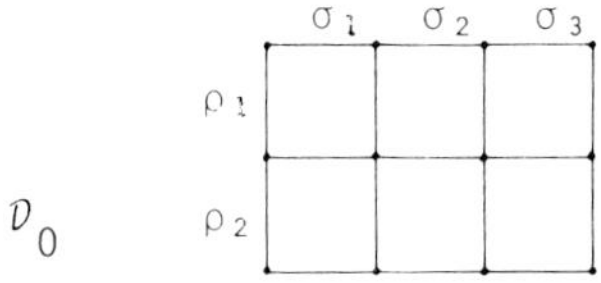

Since σ_1, ρ_1 are developments, it follows from lemma 12.1.13 that $\mathcal{D}(\sigma_1, \rho_1)$ exists and that ρ_1/σ_1 and σ_1/ρ_1 are $=$-developments. Another application of lemma 12.1.13 shows that $\mathcal{D}(\sigma_2, \rho_1/\sigma_1)$ exists. This way proceeding it follows that all the rectangles in $\mathcal{D}_0$ can be filled, obtaining $\mathcal{D}(\sigma, \rho)$. $\square$

12.2. Strong versions of CR and FD!

Now the promised strengthening of $\cong_H$ can be defined. In the rest of this chapter the results are all about ordinary β-reduction.

12.2.1. DEFINITION (Lévy). Let σ, ρ be two coinitial reductions. Then σ is *strongly equivalent* with ρ (notation $\sigma \cong \rho$) if $\sigma/\rho = \rho/\sigma = \emptyset$.

It is not immediate that $\cong$ is an equivalence relation. This, and the compatibility of $\cong$ with respect to the operations + and /, will be shown in 12.2.2 and 12.2.7.

12.2.2. PROPOSITION. *The following equations hold, provided that the terms make sense.*

(i) $\rho + \emptyset = \emptyset + \rho = \rho$.
(ii) $\rho + (\sigma + \tau) = (\rho + \sigma) + \tau$.
(iii) $(\rho_1 + \rho_2)/\sigma = \rho_1/\sigma + \rho_2/(\sigma/\rho_1)$.
(iv) $\sigma/(\rho_1 + \rho_2) = (\sigma/\rho_1)/\rho_2$.
(v) $\sigma/\emptyset = \sigma$.
(vi) $\emptyset/\sigma = \emptyset$.
(vii) $\sigma/\sigma = \emptyset$.
(viii) $\rho \cong \rho', \sigma \cong \sigma' \Rightarrow \rho + \sigma \cong \rho' + \sigma'$.
(ix) $\rho + \sigma \cong \rho + \sigma' \Rightarrow \sigma \cong \sigma'$.
(x) $\rho \cong \emptyset \Rightarrow \rho = \emptyset$.
(xi) $\rho + (\sigma/\rho) \cong \sigma + (\rho/\sigma)$.

PROOF. (i), (ii). Trivial.
(iii), (iv).

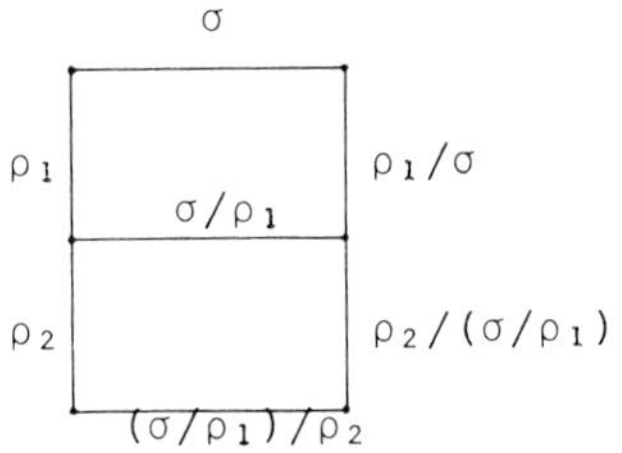

(v), (vi), (vii). If σ is a one step =-reduction, this is lemma 12.1.6. For more steps, use (iii) and (iv) or draw a diagram.

(viii). Suppose $\rho \cong \rho', \sigma \cong \sigma'$, i.e. $\rho/\rho' = \rho'/\rho = \emptyset, \sigma/\sigma' = \sigma'/\sigma = \emptyset$. Then

$$\begin{aligned}(\rho + \sigma)/(\rho' + \sigma') &= ((\rho + \sigma)/\rho')/\sigma' \\ &= (\rho/\rho' + \sigma/(\rho'/\rho))/\sigma' \\ &= (\emptyset + \sigma/\emptyset)/\sigma' \\ &= \sigma/\sigma' = \emptyset.\end{aligned}$$

Similarly $(\rho' + \sigma')/(\rho + \sigma) = \emptyset$. Hence $\rho + \sigma \cong \rho' + \sigma'$. Alternatively, look at figure 12.2.

(ix) Draw $\mathcal{D}(\rho + \sigma, \rho + \sigma')$.
(x) If $\rho \cong \emptyset$, then $\rho = \rho/\emptyset = \emptyset$.
(xi) Compute or draw a picture. □

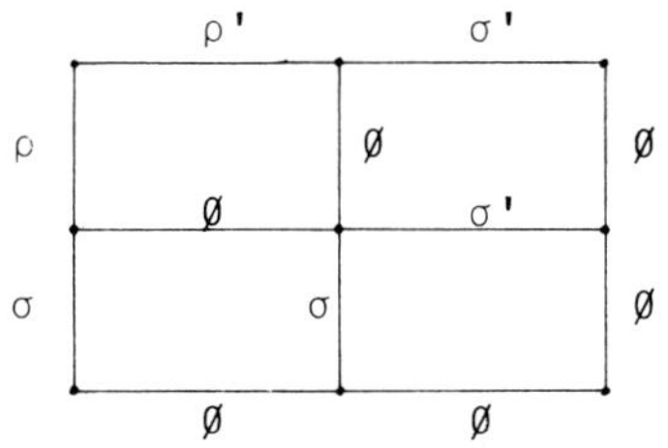

FIG. 12.2.

12.2.3. PROPOSITION. (i) $\rho \cong \sigma \Rightarrow \rho \cong_H \sigma$
(ii) *But the converse is false.*

PROOF. (i) Suppose $\rho \cong \sigma$. Let $\mathfrak{D} = \mathfrak{D}(\rho, \sigma)$ be, say,

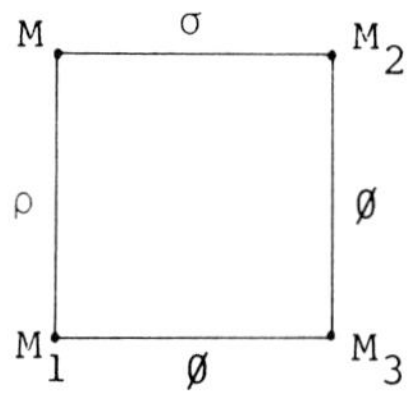

Then $M_1 \equiv M_3 \equiv M_2$. Hence $\rho \simeq \sigma$.

Now consider $M' \in \Lambda'$ obtained from M by indexing all redexes in M with different numbers. Lift $\mathfrak{D}$ to M', obtaining, say,

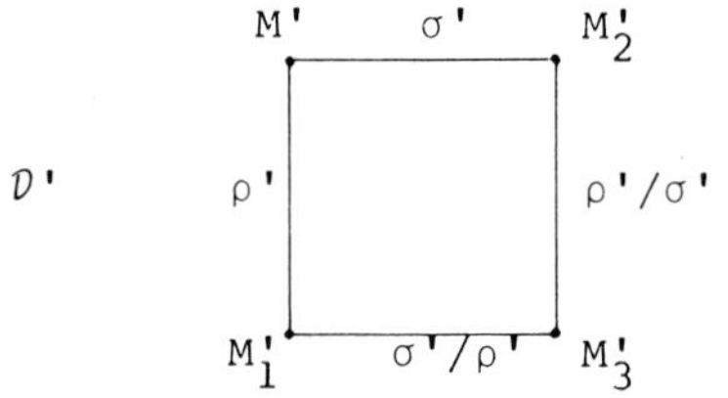

with $|\mathfrak{D}'| = \mathfrak{D}$. Hence $\sigma'/\rho' = \rho'/\sigma' = \emptyset$ and therefore $M_1' \equiv M_3' \equiv M_2'$.

Let $\Delta \in M$. We have to show that $\Delta/\rho = \Delta/\sigma$. Let the $\Delta' \in M'$ corresponding to Δ have the index i. Now by lemma 11.2.8

$$\Delta/\rho = \{|\Delta''| \mid \Delta'' \in M_1' \text{ has index } i\}$$

$$= \{|\Delta''| \mid \Delta'' \in M_2' \text{ has index } i\} = \Delta/\sigma$$

since $M_1' \equiv M_2'$. Thus indeed $\rho \cong_H \sigma$.

(ii) Consider $M \equiv (\lambda z.z(zx))\mathbf{I}$, and

$$\rho : M \xrightarrow{M} \mathbf{I}(\mathbf{I}x) \xrightarrow{\mathbf{I}x} \mathbf{I}x,$$

$$\sigma : M \xrightarrow{M} \mathbf{I}(\mathbf{I}x) \xrightarrow{\mathbf{I}(\mathbf{I}x)} \mathbf{I}x.$$

Then $\mathcal{D}(\rho,\sigma)$ is

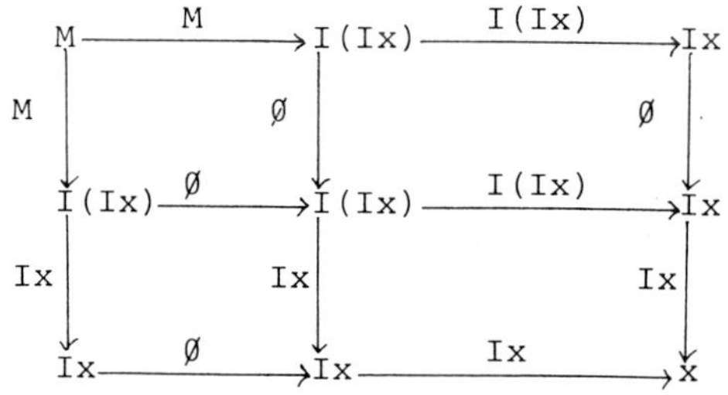

Thus $\rho \not\cong \sigma$. But $\rho \cong_H \sigma$, since M is the only redex occurrence in M and $M/\rho = M/\sigma = \emptyset$. □

Now the improved versions of CR and FD! can be given.

12.2.4. THEOREM (CR$^+$).

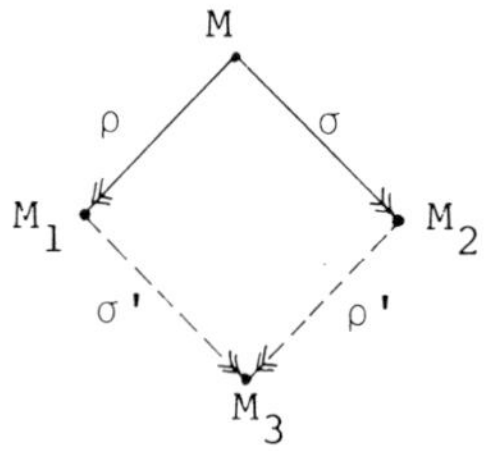

$\rho+\sigma' \cong \sigma+\rho'$

PROOF. Let $\rho' = \rho/\sigma$, $\sigma' = \sigma/\rho$. The strong equivalence follows from proposition 12.2.2(xi). □

12.2.5. THEOREM (FD!$^+$). *All developments of an $(M, \mathcal{F})$ are finite and hence can be extended to a complete one. Moreover all complete developments of an $(M, \mathcal{F})$ end in the same term and are strongly equivalent.*

PROOF. By FD! it suffices to show that for

$$\rho : (M, \mathcal{F}) \underset{\text{cpl}}{\twoheadrightarrow} M_1, \qquad \sigma : (M, \mathcal{F}) \underset{\text{cpl}}{\twoheadrightarrow} M_1$$

one has $\rho \cong \sigma$.

Consider $\mathcal{D} = \mathcal{D}(\rho, \sigma)$ and $\mathcal{D}'$ which is $\mathcal{D}$ lifted to $M' \equiv (M, \mathcal{F}) \in \Lambda'$. Then $|\mathcal{D}'| = \mathcal{D}$. Since ρ, σ are complete developments of $(M, \mathcal{F})$ it follows by lemma 11.2.12 that ρ', σ' are β_0-reductions ending in $M_1' \in \Lambda$. But then by lemma 12.1.10(ii) both ρ'/σ' and σ'/ρ' are also β_0-$=$-reductions and since $M_1' \in \Lambda$, one has $\rho'/\sigma' = \sigma'/\rho' = \emptyset$.

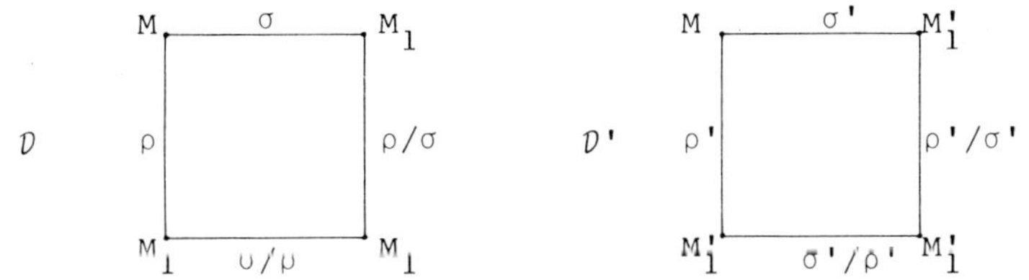

Therefore $\rho/\sigma = |\rho'/\sigma'| = \emptyset$ and similarly $\sigma/\rho = \emptyset$. Thus $\rho \cong \sigma$. $\square$

The following lemma, due to Lévy, is used in order to show that $\cong$ is an equivalence relation, compatible with the operation $/$.

12.2.6. CUBE LEMMA. *Let*

$$\sigma_1 : M \twoheadrightarrow M_1, \qquad \sigma_2 : M \twoheadrightarrow M_2, \qquad \sigma_3 : M \twoheadrightarrow M_3.$$

Then

$$(\sigma_1/\sigma_2)/(\sigma_3/\sigma_2) \cong (\sigma_1/\sigma_3)/(\sigma_2/\sigma_3),$$

$$(\sigma_2/\sigma_3)/(\sigma_1/\sigma_3) \cong (\sigma_2/\sigma_1)/(\sigma_3/\sigma_1),$$

$$(\sigma_3/\sigma_1)/(\sigma_2/\sigma_1) \cong (\sigma_3/\sigma_2)/(\sigma_1/\sigma_2),$$

see figure 12.3.

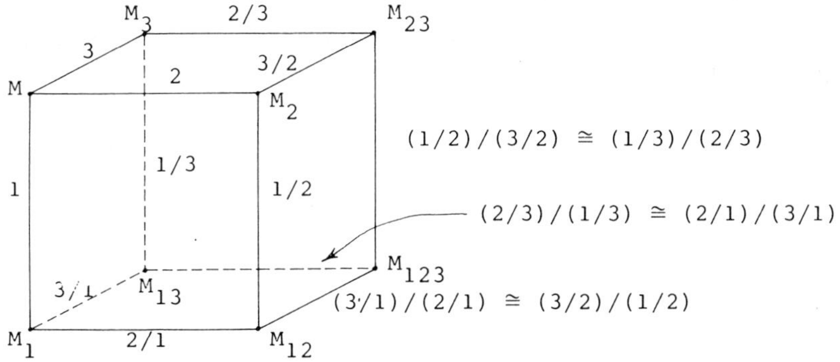

FIG. 12.3.

PROOF. First suppose that $\sigma_1, \sigma_2, \sigma_3$ are complete developments, say $\sigma_i : (M, \mathcal{F}_i) \twoheadrightarrow_{\text{cpl}} M_i$. By lemma 12.1.12(ii)

$$(\sigma_1/\sigma_2) : (M_2, \mathcal{F}_1/\sigma_2) \twoheadrightarrow_{\text{cpl}} M_{12}$$

and therefore by the same lemma

$$(\sigma_1/\sigma_2)/(\sigma_3/\sigma_2) : (M_{23}, (\mathcal{F}_1/\sigma_2)/(\sigma_3/\sigma_2)) \twoheadrightarrow_{\text{cpl}} M_{123}.$$

Similarly

$$(\sigma_1/\sigma_3)/(\sigma_2/\sigma_3) : (M_{23}, (\mathcal{F}_1/\sigma_3)/(\sigma_2/\sigma_3)) \twoheadrightarrow_{\text{cpl}} M_{123}.$$

Now by lemma 11.2.6

$$\begin{aligned}(\mathcal{F}_1/\sigma_2)/(\sigma_3/\sigma_2) &= \mathcal{F}_1/(\sigma_2 + (\sigma_3/\sigma_2)) \\ &= \mathcal{F}_1/(\sigma_3 + (\sigma_2/\sigma_3)) \\ &= (\mathcal{F}_1/\sigma_3)/(\sigma_2/\sigma_3),\end{aligned}$$

with the middle equation holding by lemma 12.2.2(xi) and proposition 12.2.3(i):

$$\sigma_2 + (\sigma_3/\sigma_2) \cong_{\text{H}} \sigma_3 + (\sigma_2/\sigma_3).$$

Hence by FD!$^+$

$$(\sigma_1/\sigma_2)/(\sigma_3/\sigma_2) \cong (\sigma_1/\sigma_3)/(\sigma_2/\sigma_3).$$

Similarly the other equations hold.

The general case follows by writing $\sigma_i = \sigma_{i1} + \cdots + \sigma_{in_i}$, $i = 1,2,3$, drawing an $n_1 \times n_2 \times n_3$ block and repeating the argument for $n_1 \times n_2 \times 1$ layers, using lemma 12.2.2(viii). [Because one does not know yet that $\cong$ is transitive, one has to repeat the argument for the simple case, rather than to apply it several times.] $\square$

See exercise 12.4.4 for a categorical proof of the cube lemma.

12.2.7. COROLLARY. (i) $\cong$ *an equivalence relation.*

(ii) $\rho \cong \rho', \sigma \cong \sigma' \Rightarrow \rho/\sigma \cong \rho'/\sigma'$.

PROOF. (i) The reflexivity follows from proposition 12.2.2(vii). The symmetry is trivial. For the transitivity suppose $\rho \cong \sigma, \sigma \cong \tau$. Then $\rho/\sigma = \sigma/\rho =$

$\sigma/\tau = \tau/\sigma = \emptyset$. Hence by the cube lemma and proposition 12.2.2(v, vi)

$$\rho/\tau = (\rho/\tau)/(\sigma/\tau) \cong (\rho/\sigma)/(\tau/\sigma) = \emptyset.$$

Hence $\rho/\tau = \emptyset$ and similarly $\tau/\rho = \emptyset$.

(ii) It will be shown that

(a) $\rho \cong \rho' \Rightarrow \rho/\sigma \cong \rho'/\sigma$,

(b) $\sigma \cong \sigma' \Rightarrow \rho/\sigma \cong \rho/\sigma'$.

Then the result follows by the transitivity of $\cong$. As to (a), suppose $\rho \cong \rho'$. Then $\rho/\rho' = \rho'/\rho = \emptyset$. Then by the cube lemma and proposition 12.2.2(vi)

$$(\rho/\sigma)/(\rho'/\sigma) \cong (\rho/\rho')/(\sigma/\rho') = \emptyset$$

and similarly $(\rho'/\sigma)/(\rho/\sigma) \cong \emptyset$. Then one has $\rho/\sigma \cong \rho'/\sigma$.

As to (b), suppose $\sigma \cong \sigma'$. Then $\sigma/\sigma' = \sigma'/\sigma = \emptyset$. Hence

$$(\rho/\sigma) = (\rho/\sigma)/(\sigma'/\sigma) \cong (\rho/\sigma')/(\sigma/\sigma') = (\rho/\sigma'),$$

by the cube lemma. □

12.3. Strong version of standardization

Now we shall treat the improvement of the standardization theorem, mentioned in the beginning of this chapter. The proof given below is due to Klop and has the advantage of giving an explicit algorithm for finding a standard reduction equivalent to a given one. Moreover it also generalizes to $\beta\eta$-reduction; see Klop [1980], Ch. 4.

12.3.1. DEFINITION. Let $\sigma : M \twoheadrightarrow N$, say $\sigma = (\Delta_0) + \cdots + (\Delta_n)$. Let $\Delta \in M$.

(i) Δ is *contracted* in σ if for some $k \leqslant n$, Δ_k is a residual of Δ (relative to the given reduction $(\Delta_0) + \cdots + (\Delta_{k-1})$).

(ii) Δ is *secured* in σ if Δ is contracted in σ and moreover $(\Delta)/\sigma = \emptyset$.

(iii) $\text{lmc}(\sigma) \in M$ is the leftmost redex occurrence which is contracted in σ.

Remember that for $\Delta, \Delta' \in M$ we write $\Delta < \Delta'$ iff Δ is to the left of Δ'. Similarly $\Delta \leqslant \Delta'$ iff $\Delta < \Delta'$ or $\Delta = \Delta'$.

12.3.2. LEMMA. *Let* $\sigma : M \twoheadrightarrow N$ *and let* $\Delta \equiv \text{lmc}(\sigma) \in M$.

(i) *Suppose* $\sigma = \sigma' + \sigma''$, *where* σ' *is a one step reduction. Then either* $(\Delta)/\sigma' = \emptyset$, *in which case* Δ *is contracted in* σ', *or* $(\Delta)/\sigma' = (\text{lmc}(\sigma''))$.

(ii) *Same as* (i), *without the requirement that* σ' *be a one step reduction.*

(iii) Δ *is secured in* σ.

PROOF. (i) Let $\sigma' = (\Delta_0) : M \to M_1$. Since $\Delta \equiv \mathrm{lmc}(\sigma)$ one has $\Delta \leqslant \Delta_0$. Therefore, if $(\Delta)/\sigma' = \emptyset$, then $\Delta = \Delta_0$, hence Δ is contracted in σ'. (If $\Delta_0 \leqslant \Delta$, then $(\Delta)/(\Delta_0) = \emptyset$ and $\Delta \neq \Delta_0$ is possible: $(\lambda x.\mathbf{I})\Delta \xrightarrow{\Delta_0} \mathbf{I}$.) If $(\Delta)/\sigma' \neq \emptyset$, then $\Delta \not\equiv \Delta_0$ and hence $\Delta < \Delta_0$. Thus $M \equiv \cdots \lambda_\Delta \cdots \Delta_0 \cdots$, where λ_Δ is the first λ of Δ. Then clearly Δ/σ' consists of one element, say Δ'. Since Δ is contracted in σ, but not in σ', Δ' must be contracted in σ''. If Δ' were not $\mathrm{lmc}(\sigma'')$, then Δ would not be $\mathrm{lmc}(\sigma)$. Thus $\Delta' \equiv \mathrm{lmc}(\sigma'')$, hence $(\Delta)/\sigma' = (\mathrm{lmc}(\sigma''))$.

(ii) By transitivity.

(iii) Since Δ is contracted in $\sigma, \sigma = \sigma' + \sigma_0 + \sigma''$, where σ_0 contracts the residual Δ_0 of Δ with respect to σ' (Δ_0 is unique by (ii)). Then $\Delta/\sigma = \Delta/\sigma'/\sigma_0/\sigma'' = \Delta_0/\sigma_0/\sigma'' = \emptyset/\sigma'' = \emptyset$ (association to the left). □

12.3.3. DEFINITION. Let σ: $M \twoheadrightarrow N$ be a given reduction. Then the *standardization* of σ (notation σ_S) is defined by the following algorithm.

$$\sigma_0 = \sigma$$

$$\Delta_0 = \mathrm{lmc}(\sigma_0)$$

$$\sigma_{k+1} = \sigma_k/(\Delta_k)$$

$$\Delta_{k+1} = \mathrm{lmc}(\sigma_{k+1})$$

$$\sigma_S = (\Delta_0) + (\Delta_1) + \cdots$$

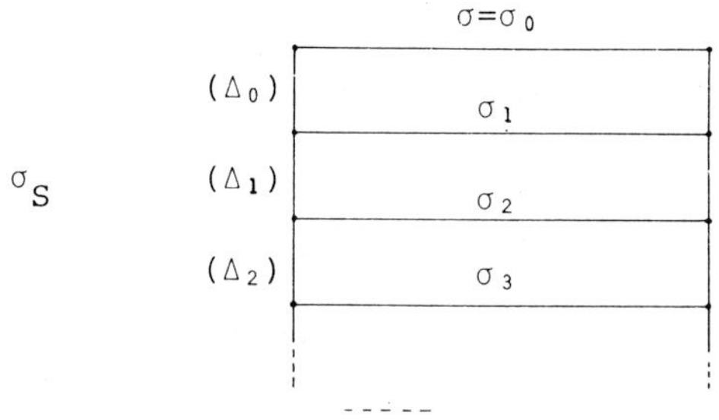

The algorithm for σ_S stops if $\sigma_n = \emptyset$ for some n. In that case $\sigma_S = (\Delta_0) + \cdots + (\Delta_{n-1})$.

First we want to show that if σ is finite, so is σ_S.

12.3.4. LEMMA. *Let σ be a development of M. Then σ_S is a development of M and hence finite.*

PROOF. Let σ be a development of $(M, \mathscr{F})$ and let $\sigma_S = (\Delta_0) + (\Delta_1) + \cdots$.

Claim. Each Δ_i is a residual of a redex in $\mathscr{F}$ relative to $(\Delta_0) + \cdots + (\Delta_{i-1})$.

Indeed, since $\Delta_i = \mathrm{lmc}(\sigma_i)$ with $\sigma_i = \sigma/((\Delta_0) + \cdots + (\Delta_{i-1}))$. There is a step in σ_i, say (Δ_i'), with Δ_i' a residual of Δ_i. Since σ is a development of $\mathscr{F}$, it follows by proposition 12.1.12 (i) that σ_i is a development of $\mathscr{F}_i = \mathscr{F}/(\Delta_0) + \cdots + (\Delta_{i-1})$. Hence Δ_i' is also a residual of a redex $\Delta \in \mathscr{F}_i$. But since different redexes have disjoint sets of residuals, it follows that $\Delta_i \equiv \Delta$. Therefore $\Delta_i \in \mathscr{F}_i$.

By the claim σ_S is a development of $(M, \mathscr{F})$ and hence by FD finite. □

12.3.5. DEFINITION. Let σ, σ' be $=$-reductions. σ' is a *refinement* of σ if σ can be obtained from σ' by leaving out some empty steps.

EXAMPLE. $\mathbf{II} \underset{=}{\to} \mathbf{II} \underset{=}{\to} \mathbf{I} \underset{=}{\to} \mathbf{I}$ is a refinement of $\mathbf{II} \underset{=}{\to} \mathbf{I}$.

12.3.6. LEMMA. *Let $\sigma = \sigma' + \sigma''$, where σ' is a one step reduction. Then σ_S/σ' is a refinement of $(\sigma'')_S$.*

PROOF. Let $\sigma_S = (\Delta_0) + (\Delta_1) + \cdots$. Define (see figure 12.4)

$$\sigma_0' = \sigma', \qquad \sigma_{k+1}' = \sigma_k'/(\Delta_k).$$

$$\rho_k = (\Delta_k)/\sigma_k',$$

$$\sigma_0'' = \sigma'', \qquad \sigma_{k+1}'' = \sigma_k''/\rho_k.$$

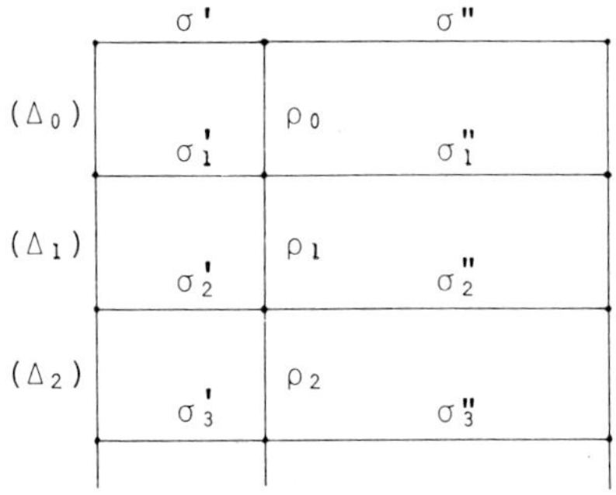

FIG. 12.4.

Since for all k $\Delta_k = \mathrm{lmc}(\sigma_k' + \sigma_k'')$ it follows from lemma 12.3.2 (i) that either $\rho_k = \emptyset$ and then $\sigma_{k+1}'' = \sigma_k''$ or $\rho_k = (\mathrm{lmc}(\sigma_k''))$. Hence $\sigma_S/\sigma' = \rho_0 + \rho_1 + \cdots$ is indeed a refinement of $(\sigma'')_S$. $\square$

12.3.7. COROLLARY. *Suppose $\sigma = \sigma' + \sigma''$, where σ' is a one step reduction. Then*

$$\sigma_S''\text{-}\textit{is finite} \quad \Rightarrow \quad \sigma_S \textit{ is finite}.$$

PROOF. Suppose σ_S'' is finite. Now σ_S/σ' is a refinement of σ_S'' and hence for some n $\emptyset = \rho_n = \rho_{n+1} = \cdots$, assuming the notation of the proof of the lemma.

Claim. $\forall k \geqslant n$ $\Delta_k = \mathrm{lmc}(\sigma_k')$. Indeed, by definition $\Delta_k = \mathrm{lmc}(\sigma_k' + \sigma_k'')$. Hence $\Delta_k \leqslant \mathrm{lmc}(\sigma_k')$. But by lemma 12.3.2 (ii) applied to Δ_k and $\sigma_k' + \sigma_k''$, $\rho_k = \emptyset$ is only possible if Δ_k is contracted in σ_k'. Thus also $\mathrm{lmc}(\sigma_k') \leqslant \Delta_k$, i.e. $\Delta_k \equiv \mathrm{lmc}(\sigma_k')$.

By the claim and the definition of the standardization it follows that $(\sigma_n')_S = (\Delta_n) + (\Delta_{n-1}) + \cdots$.

By lemma 12.1.12 (i) $\sigma_n' = \sigma'/((\Delta_0) + \cdots + (\Delta_{n-1}))$ is a development. Hence lemma 12.3.4 applies showing that $(\Delta_n) + (\Delta_{n+1}) + \cdots$ is finite. Thus σ_S is finite. □

12.3.8. PROPOSITION. *Let σ be finite. Then σ_S is finite.*

PROOF. Write $\sigma = \sigma_n + \sigma_{n-1} + \cdots + \sigma_1 + \emptyset$. By induction on k it follows from the previous corollary that $(\sigma_k + \cdots + \sigma_1 + \emptyset)_S$ is finite, in particular σ_S is finite. □

12.3.9. COROLLARY. *Let σ be finite. Then $\sigma \cong \sigma_S$.*

PROOF. Define, see figure 12.5,

$$\sigma_S = (\Delta_0) + \cdots + (\Delta_n),$$

$$\sigma_0 = \sigma, \qquad \sigma_{k+1} = \sigma_k / (\Delta_k),$$

$$\rho_k = (\Delta_k)/\sigma_k, \quad 0 \leqslant k \leqslant n.$$

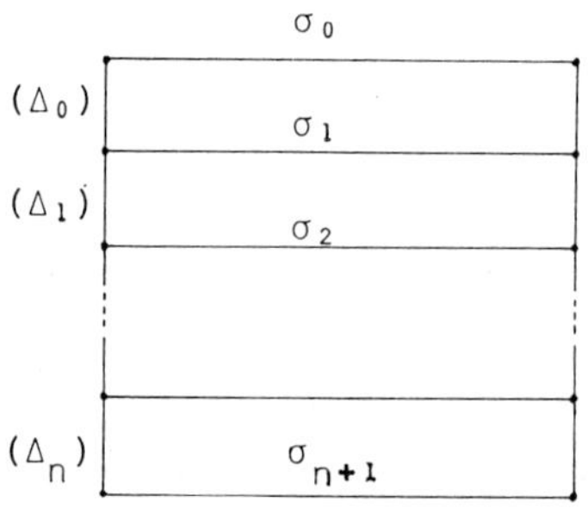

FIG. 12.5.

By definition $\Delta_k = \mathrm{lmc}(\sigma_k)$, hence by lemma 12.3.2 (iii) $\rho_k = (\Delta_k)/\sigma_k = \emptyset$. Thus $\sigma_S/\sigma = \rho_0 + \cdots + \rho_n = \emptyset$.

Conversely, $\sigma/\sigma_S = \sigma_{n+1}$. If this were not $\emptyset$, then the algorithm for σ_S would not have stopped. □

Now we will show that σ_S is a standard reduction.

12.3.10. LEMMA. *Define for a β'-reduction σ:*

Index$(\sigma) = \{i \mid$ *there is an i-redex contracted in* $\sigma\}$. *Let ρ, σ be β'-reductions. Then*

$$\mathit{Index}(\sigma/\rho) \subseteq \mathit{Index}(\sigma).$$

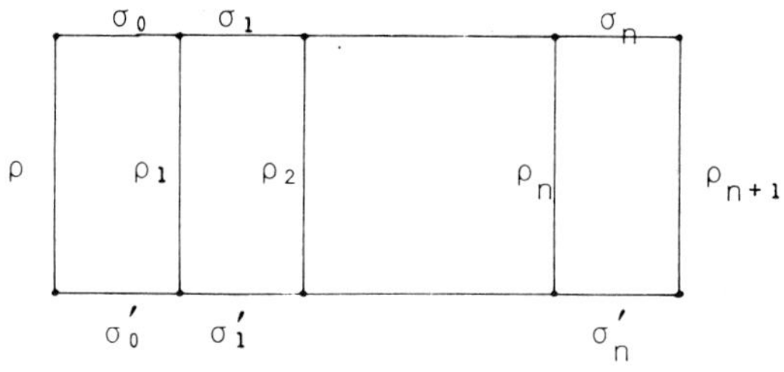

FIG. 12.6.

PROOF. Let $\sigma = \sigma_0 + \cdots + \sigma_n$;

$$\rho_0 = \rho, \qquad \rho_{k+1} = \rho_k/\sigma_k,$$

$$\sigma_k' = \sigma_k/\rho_k \quad \text{for } 0 \leqslant k \leqslant n.$$

Then $\sigma/\rho = \sigma_0' + \cdots + \sigma_n'$; see figure 12.6.

Let $\sigma_k : M_k \overset{\Delta_k}{\to}_{\beta'} M_{k+1}$, $\sigma_k' : M_k' \twoheadrightarrow_{\beta'} M_{k+1}'$. By lemma 12.1.12 (i) σ_k' is a development of $(M_k', \Delta_k/\rho_k)$. Moreover all elements of Δ_k/ρ_k have the same index as Δ_k. Hence

$$\text{Index}(\sigma_k') \subseteq \text{Index}(\sigma_k)$$

($\subseteq$ because Δ_k/ρ_k may be empty). Therefore

$$\text{Index}(\sigma) = \bigcup_i \text{Index}(\sigma_i) \supseteq \bigcup_i \text{Index}(\sigma_i') = \text{Index}(\sigma/\rho). \quad \square$$

12.3.11. PROPOSITION. *For each reduction path σ, finite or infinite, σ_S is a standard reduction.*

PROOF. Let $\sigma_S = (\Delta_0) + \cdots + (\Delta_i) + \cdots$ with $\Delta_i \in M_i$. We must show that for all k, k' with $k < k'$ and all $\Delta \in M_k$

$$(*) \qquad \Delta < \Delta_k \quad \Rightarrow \quad \begin{array}{l}\Delta_{k'} \text{ is not a residual of } \Delta \text{ with respect to} \\ (\Delta_k) + (\Delta_{k+1}) + \cdots + (\Delta_{k'-1}).\end{array}$$

Let $\sigma_0 = \sigma$, $\sigma_{i+1} = \sigma_i/(\Delta_i)$; see figure 12.5.

Consider $\mathfrak{D} = \mathfrak{D}((\Delta_k) + \cdots + (\Delta_{k'}), \sigma_k)$. Let $M_k' \in \Lambda'$ be M_k where Δ is indexed by 0 and all other redexes by 1. Lift $\mathfrak{D}$ to M_k' obtaining say $\mathfrak{D}'$; identify the (sub)term occurrences in $\mathfrak{D}'$ with their corresponding ones in $\mathfrak{D}$. In order to prove ($*$), by lemma 11.2.8 it is sufficient to show that the redex $\Delta_{k'}$ in $\mathfrak{D}'$ is not indexed by 0. Since $\Delta < \Delta_k = \text{lmc}(\sigma_k)$, Δ is not contracted in σ_k; hence $0 \notin \text{Index}(\sigma)$. By lemma 12.3.10 it follows that $0 \notin \text{Index}(\sigma_{k'})$. But then $\Delta_{k'} = \text{lmc}(\sigma_{k'})$ cannot have index 0. □

The final point is that for each finite σ there is at most one standard reduction σ' with $\sigma' \cong \sigma$.

12.3.12. Lemma. *Let $\sigma \equiv (\Delta_1) + \cdots + (\Delta_n)$ be a finite standard reduction. Let $\Gamma < \Delta_1$. Then Γ/σ consists of exactly one element.*

Proof. Let $\sigma_k = (\Delta_1) + \cdots + (\Delta_k)$. By induction on $k \leqslant n$ the following stronger statement will be shown: Γ/σ_k consists of one element, say Γ_k, and unless $k = n$, $\Gamma_k < \Delta_{k+1}$. The case $k = 0$ is trivial. So suppose $\Gamma/\sigma_k = \{\Gamma_k\}$ with $\Gamma_k < \Delta_{k+1}$. Now let $(\Delta_{k+1}) : M_{k+1} \to M_{k+2}$. Then

$$M_{k+1} \equiv \cdots \lambda \cdots \Delta_{k+1} \cdots$$

where the λ displayed is the λ of Γ_k, and

$$M_{k+2} \equiv \cdots \lambda \cdots \square \cdots,$$

where $\square$ is the contractum of Δ_{k+1}. Hence it follows that $\Gamma/\sigma_{k+1} = \Gamma/\sigma_k/(\Delta_{k+1}) = \Gamma_k/(\Delta_{k+1})$ consists of one element, say Γ_{k+1}. Moreover if $k+1 \neq n$, then since $(\Delta_{k+1}) + (\Delta_{k+2})$ is a standard reduction, it follows that $\Gamma_{k+1} < \Delta_{k+2}$. □

12.3.13. Proposition. *Let ρ, σ be finite standard reductions such that $\rho \cong \sigma$. Then $\rho = \sigma$.*

Proof. Let

$$\rho = (\Gamma_0) + \cdots + (\Gamma_n), \qquad \sigma = (\Delta_0) + \cdots + (\Delta_m).$$

Claim. $\Gamma_0 \equiv \Delta_0$. Suppose $\Gamma_0 < \Delta_0$. Then by lemma 12.3.12 $\Gamma_0/\sigma \neq \emptyset$ and hence by proposition 12.1.12 (ii), $(\Gamma_0)/\sigma \neq \emptyset$. But then $\rho \not\cong \sigma$. Similarly $\Delta_0 < \Gamma_0$ is not possible.

By the claim and proposition 12.2.2 (ix) it follows that

$$(\Gamma_1) + \cdots + (\Gamma_n) \cong (\Delta_1) + \cdots + (\Delta_m).$$

Continuing in this way, it follows that $\Gamma_0 \equiv \Delta_0, \Gamma_1 \equiv \Delta_1, \cdots$. If $n < m$, then

$$(\Delta_{n+1}) + \cdots + (\Delta_m) \cong \emptyset.$$

But since the Δ_i are real redexes (i.e. not empty) it follows by proposition 12.2.2 (x) that this is not possible, hence $n = m$. □

12.3.14. THEOREM. *For each finite* σ, *its standardization* σ_S *is the unique standard reduction such that* $\sigma_S \cong \sigma$.

PROOF. By corollary 12.3.9 and propositions 12.3.11 and 12.3.13. □

In §14.2 another proof of this theorem will be given.

12.4. Exercises

12.4.1. Let σ, ρ be coinitial one step reductions. Show that the elementary diagram of σ, ρ splits at most on one side.

12.4.2. (Lévy; Berry). Let σ, τ be coinitial finite reductions. Define $\sigma \leqslant \tau \Leftrightarrow \sigma/\tau = \emptyset$. Let $\mathfrak{R}_\omega(M) = \{\sigma \mid \sigma \text{ is a finite reduction starting with } M\}$

(i) Show that $\leqslant$ induces a partial ordering on $\mathfrak{R}_\omega(M)/\cong$.

(ii) Show that $\mathfrak{R}_\omega(M)/\cong$ with $\leqslant$ is an upper semi lattice which is not a lattice.

(iii) Show that $\sigma \leqslant \tau \Leftrightarrow \exists \rho\ \sigma + \rho \cong \tau$.

(iv) Show that $\sigma + \rho \leqslant \sigma + \rho' \Leftrightarrow \rho \leqslant \rho'$.

12.4.3. (i) Show that $\rho + \sigma \cong \rho' + \sigma \Rightarrow \rho \cong \rho'$ in general does not hold.

(ii) Show that $\rho \cong \rho' \Leftrightarrow \forall \sigma\ \sigma/\rho \cong \sigma/\rho'$.

12.4.4. Define the following category $\mathbb{C}$. The set of objects of $\mathbb{C}$ is Λ. The set of morphisms between $M, N \in \Lambda$ is $\text{Hom}(M,N) = \{\sigma \mid \sigma : M \twoheadrightarrow N\} / \cong$, i.e. reductions from M to N modulo $\cong$.

(i) Show that in $\mathbb{C}$

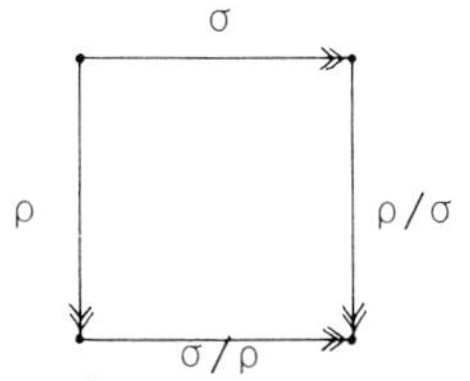

is a pushout.

(ii) Show that in any category with pushouts the cube lemma 12.2.6 holds for pushouts.

12.4.5. Let $\sigma_1, \sigma_2, \sigma_3$ be coinitial reductions. Show that there is no canonical way to define a three dimensional diagram $\mathfrak{D}_3(\sigma_1, \sigma_2, \sigma_3)$-analogous to $\mathfrak{D}(\sigma_1, \sigma_2)$. [*Hint*. Consider $M = (\lambda x.xxx)((\lambda y.yy)(\mathbf{II}))$.]

12.4.6. Show that if σ is an infinite reduction path, then σ_S is also infinite.

12.4.7. Show that if $\Delta \in M$ and $\sigma : M \twoheadrightarrow N$, then $(\Delta)/\sigma$ is a complete development of $(N, \{\Delta\}/\sigma)$.

CHAPTER 13

REDUCTION STRATEGIES

A term may be reduced in several ways. Therefore its reduction graph can become quite complicated. A reduction strategy provides a choice of how to reduce a term.

Reduction strategies can be quite useful for proving negative results such as showing that a certain term has no nf or that two terms have no common reduct (see applications 13.2.3 and 13.2.13).

13.1. Classification of strategies

13.1.1. DEFINITION. Let $\boldsymbol{R}$ be a notion of reduction.

(i) An *R-(reduction) strategy* is a map $F : \Lambda \to \Lambda$ such that for all $M \in \Lambda$

$$M \twoheadrightarrow_R F(M).$$

(ii) An R-strategy F is a *one step* R-strategy (or R-1-strategy) if for all M not in R-nf

$$M \to_R F(M).$$

(iii) An R-strategy is *recursive* if it is so after coding of the terms. A strategy is *effective* if it is not just general recursive, but can be computed in a relatively simple way.

(To explain the difference between recursive and effective define

$$\begin{aligned} f(n) &= 0 \quad \text{if the } n\text{th partial recursive function} \\ &\qquad\quad \text{with input } n \text{ converges in less than } n \text{ steps,} \\ &= 1 \quad \text{else.} \end{aligned}$$

Then f is recursive, but not effective in our sense.)

13.1.2. DEFINITION. Let F be an R-strategy. The F *(reduction) path* of a term M is the sequence of terms

$$M, F(M), F^2(M), \ldots$$

The following notions are taken from Barendregt et al. [1976]

13.1.3. DEFINITION. Let F be an R-strategy.

(i) F is *normalizing* if for each $M \in \Lambda$
M has an R-nf $\Rightarrow F^n(M)$ is in R-nf, for some $n \in \mathbb{N}$.

(ii) F is *cofinal* if for each $M \in \Lambda$ the F path of M is cofinal in $G_R(M)$, i.e. $\forall N \in G_R(M)\ \exists n\ N \twoheadrightarrow_R F^n(M)$.

(iii) F is *Church–Rosser* (CR) if for each $M, N \in \Lambda$

$$M =_R N \Rightarrow \text{the } F \text{ paths of } M, N \text{ intersect},$$

i.e. $\exists m, n\ F^m(M) \equiv F^n(N)$.

13.1.4. LEMMA. *Let F be an R-strategy and suppose* **R** *is Church–Rosser. Then*

(i) *F is* CR $\Rightarrow$ *F is cofinal,*

(ii) *F is cofinal $\Rightarrow$ F is normalizing.*

PROOF. (i) Let $N \in G_R(M)$. Then $M =_R N$. Hence by assumption

$$N \twoheadrightarrow_R F^n(N) \equiv F^m(M),$$

for some n, m. Thus the F path of M is cofinal in $G_R(M)$.

(ii) Let N be an R-nf of M. Then $N \in G_R(M)$. Hence by assumption for some k

$$N \twoheadrightarrow_R F^k(M).$$

But then, since N is in R-nf, $F^k(M) \equiv N$. $\square$

It follows that in order to obtain (recursive) normalizing, cofinal and CR strategies, it suffices to construct a CR one. However, in §§13.2, 13.3 separate constructions will be given for the three kinds of strategies (all for the notion of reduction β). The reason is that although there is a recursive CR strategy, it is not very effective. There is an effective cofinal strategy, but it is not a 1-strategy. And also there exists an effective 1-strategy which is normalizing.

13.1.5. DEFINITION. An R-strategy F is *perpetual* if for all $M \in \Lambda$
$\infty_R(M) \Rightarrow$ the F path of M is infinite (and does not contain empty reduction steps).

In §13.4 an effective perpetual β-strategy will be constructed.

13.1.6. DEFINITION. Let F be an R-strategy.

(i) The *length* of the F path of M (notation $L_F(M)$) is

$$\mu n[\, F^n(M) \text{ is in } R\text{-nf}\,].$$

If the F-path of M does not find an R-nf, then $L_F(M) = \infty$.

(ii) The *breadth* of the F path of M (notation $B_F(M)$) is

$$\sup\{\| F^n(M)\| \mid n \in \mathbb{N}\}.$$

Also $B_F(M)$ may be ∞.

13.1.7. DEFINITION. Let F, G be R-strategies.

(i) $F \leqslant_L G$ if $\forall M\ L_F(M) \leqslant L_G(M)$.

(ii) F is *L-better* than G if $F \leqslant_L G$ and not $G \leqslant_L F$.

(iii) F is *L-optimal* if F is normalizing and no R-strategy is L-better than F.

(iv) F is *L-1-optimal* if F is normalizing and F is an R-1-strategy and no R-1-strategy is L-better than F.

Similarly one defines $F \leqslant_B G$, F is B-better than G, F is B-optimal and F is B-1-optimal. In definition 13.1.7 (iii) and (iv) it is not necessary to require that F be normalizing (it follows from the context). However, for the corresponding definitions of B(-1)-optimal it is necessary to do so.

It is trivial that there are (1-)optimal strategies. But in §13.5 it will be shown that there are no recursive L(-1)-optimal strategies.

In the rest of this chapter, only β-strategies are considered.

13.2. Effective normalizing and cofinal strategies

13.2.1. DEFINITION. (i) *The leftmost reduction strategy*, F_ℓ, is defined as follows:

$$F_\ell(M) = M \quad \text{if } M \text{ is in nf,}$$
$$= M' \quad \text{if } M \xrightarrow{\Delta} M' \text{ and } \Delta \text{ is the leftmost redex in } M.$$

(ii) An initial segment of an F_ℓ-path is called a *leftmost reduction*.

The following is proved in Curry et al. [1958], p. 142.

13.2.2. NORMALIZATION THEOREM. *F_ℓ is an effective normalizing 1-strategy.*

PROOF. F_ℓ is clearly an effective 1-strategy. In order to show that F_ℓ is normalizing, suppose that M has the nf N. Then by the Church–Rosser theorem $M \twoheadrightarrow N$. Hence there is a standard reduction

$$\sigma : M \equiv M_0 \xrightarrow{\Delta_0} M_1 \xrightarrow{\Delta_1} \cdots \xrightarrow{\Delta_{n-1}} M_n \equiv N.$$

We claim that σ is the F_ℓ reduction path of M. Otherwise for some i, Δ_i is not the leftmost redex R_i in M_i. Then R_i is frozen and hence remains a redex (maybe somewhat changed internally) in the following terms. But then N is not a nf. □

13.2.3. Application. Let $\omega \equiv (\lambda bxz.z(bbx))$ and $A \equiv \omega\omega x$. Then the leftmost reduction path of A is

$$\begin{aligned} A &\to (\lambda xz.z(\omega\omega x))x \\ &\to \lambda z.z(\omega\omega x) \equiv \langle A \rangle \\ &\to \cdots \\ &\to \langle\langle A \rangle\rangle \\ &\to \cdots \\ &\quad \cdots \end{aligned}$$

Thus by the normalization theorem A has no nf. As the full reduction graph of A is complicated, see exercise 3.5.4, we see that the normalization theorem is quite useful to prove that certain terms have no nf.

For the λ-definability of the partial recursive functions, treated in §8.4, a sharpening of theorem 13.2.2 is needed.

13.2.4. Definition. (i) $M \underset{\ell}{\to} N$ if $M \xrightarrow{\Delta} N$ and Δ is the left-most redex in M.

(ii) $M \underset{\neq \ell}{\to} N$ if $M \xrightarrow{\Delta} N$ and Δ is not the leftmost redex in M.

(iii) $\underset{\ell}{\twoheadrightarrow}$ and $\underset{\neq \ell}{\twoheadrightarrow}$ are the transitive reflexive closure of $\underset{\ell}{\to}$, $\underset{\neq \ell}{\to}$ respectively. $\underset{\ell \neq \emptyset}{\twoheadrightarrow}$ is the transitive closure of $\underset{\ell}{\to}$.

Remember that a quasi leftmost reduction of M is of the following form:

$$\sigma : M = M_0 \xrightarrow{\Delta_0} M_1 \xrightarrow{\Delta_1} \cdots$$

such that

$$\forall i \ \exists j \geqslant i \ [\Delta_j \text{ is the leftmost redex in } M_j].$$

Now we want to show that if M has an infinite quasi leftmost reduction, then M has no nf.

13.2.5. LEMMA. (i)

$$\begin{array}{ccc} M & \xrightarrow[\neq \ell]{} \!\!\!\!\to & M' \\ {\scriptstyle \ell}\downarrow & & \downarrow{\scriptstyle \ell} \\ N & \underset{\beta}{\dashrightarrow}\!\!\!\!\to & N' \end{array} \qquad M, M', N, N' \in \Lambda.$$

(ii)

$$\begin{array}{ccc} M & \xrightarrow[\neq \ell]{} \!\!\!\!\to & M' \\ {\scriptstyle \ell \neq \emptyset}\downarrow\!\!\!\downarrow & & \downarrow\!\!\!\downarrow{\scriptstyle \ell \neq \emptyset} \\ N & \underset{\neq \ell}{\dashrightarrow}\!\!\!\!\to & N' \end{array} \qquad M, M', N, N' \in \Lambda.$$

PROOF. (i) Let $M \underset{\ell}{\rightarrow} N$ and $M \underset{\neq \ell}{\twoheadrightarrow} M'$ be

$$\cdots (\lambda x.P)Q \cdots \underset{\ell}{\rightarrow} \cdots P[x:= Q] \cdots$$

and

$$\cdots (\lambda x.P)Q \cdots \underset{\neq \ell}{\twoheadrightarrow} \cdots (\lambda x.P')Q' \cdots '$$

respectively, where $P \twoheadrightarrow_\beta P'$, $Q \twoheadrightarrow_\beta Q'$ and $\cdots \twoheadrightarrow_\beta \cdots '$.

By the substitutivity of β

$$\cdots P[x:= Q] \cdots \twoheadrightarrow_\beta \cdots P'[x:= Q'] \cdots ';$$

but since $M' \underset{\ell}{\rightarrow} N'$

$$N' \equiv \cdots P'[x:= Q'] \cdots '$$

and therefore $N \twoheadrightarrow_\beta N'$; see figure 13.1.

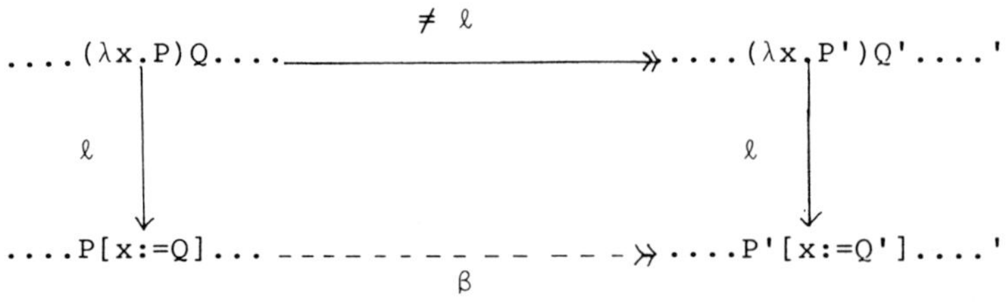

FIG. 13.1.

(ii) Notice that if $M \underset{s}{\twoheadrightarrow} N$, then this reduction consists of some (possibly zero) leftmost reductions, followed by some (possibly zero) $\neq \ell$ reductions; see figure 13.2.

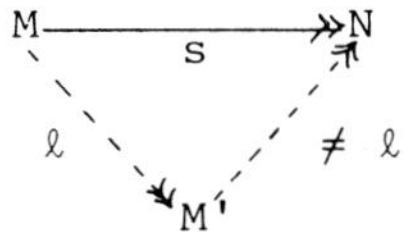

FIG. 13.2.

Now by (i), the standardization theorem 11.4.7 and the remark just made, the diagram in figure 13.3 shows that we are done. □

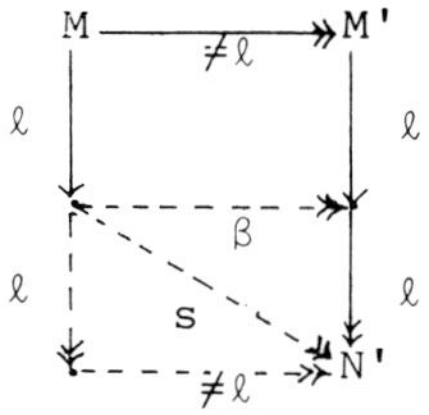

FIG. 13.3.

13.2.6. THEOREM. *If M has an infinite quasi-leftmost reduction, then M has no* nf.

PROOF. Using lemma 13.2.5 an infinite quasi-leftmost reduction can be changed into an infinite leftmost reduction, see figure 13.4.

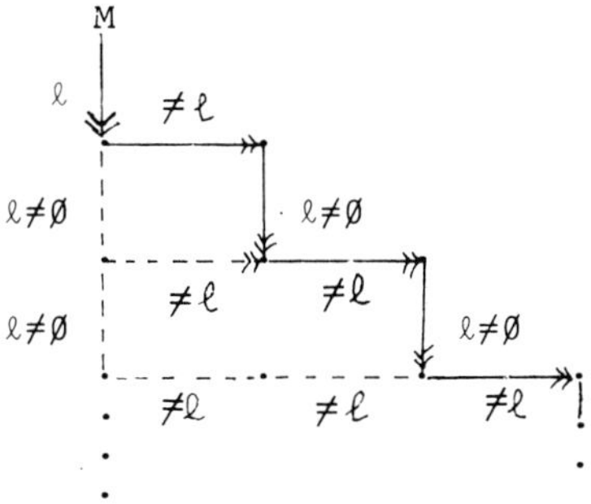

FIG. 13.4.

Hence by the normalization theorem 13.2.2. we are done. □

Now an effective cofinal strategy will be defined which, however, will not be a one step strategy. The construction is independently due to W. Gross and Knuth [1970].

13.2.7. DEFINITION. The reduction strategy F_{gk} is defined by

$$F_{gk}(M) = \mathrm{Cpl}(M, \mathcal{F}_M),$$

where $\mathcal{F}_M$ is the set of all redexes in M. Write $M \underset{gk}{\twoheadrightarrow} N$ if $F_{gk}(M) = N$.

F_{gk} is called the Gross–Knuth strategy. Note that

$$M \underset{gk}{\twoheadrightarrow} N \Rightarrow M \underset{1}{\twoheadrightarrow} N.$$

13.2.8. LEMMA.

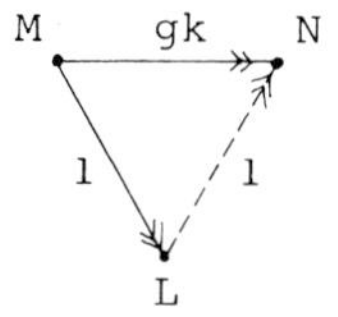

PROOF. By assumption $(M, \mathcal{F}_M) \underset{cpl}{\twoheadrightarrow} N$ and $(M, \mathcal{F}) \underset{cpl}{\twoheadrightarrow} L$ for some $\mathcal{F} \subset \mathcal{F}_M$.

By completely developing the residuals of $\mathcal{F}_M - \mathcal{F}$ in L, one obtains by FD! (theorem 11.2.25) $L \underset{1}{\twoheadrightarrow} N$. □

13.2.9. THEOREM. *F_{gk} is an effective cofinal strategy.*

PROOF. Let $\underset{gk}{\twoheadrightarrow}{}^*$ be the transitive closure of $\underset{gk}{\twoheadrightarrow}$. It has to be shown that

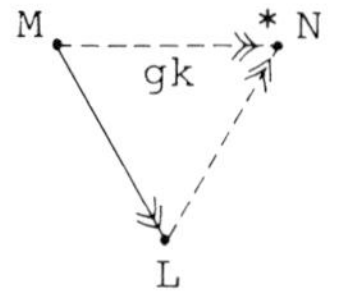

Since $\twoheadrightarrow$ is the transitive closure of $\underset{1}{\twoheadrightarrow}$ (lemma 11.2.28 (i)) this follows by a simple diagram drawing suggested by figure 13.5. using lemmas 13.2.8 (triangles) and 11.2.28 (ii) (parallelograms). □

It is open whether there exists a recursive cofinal 1-strategy. Probably this is not the case.

Now theorem 13.2.9 will be strengthened.

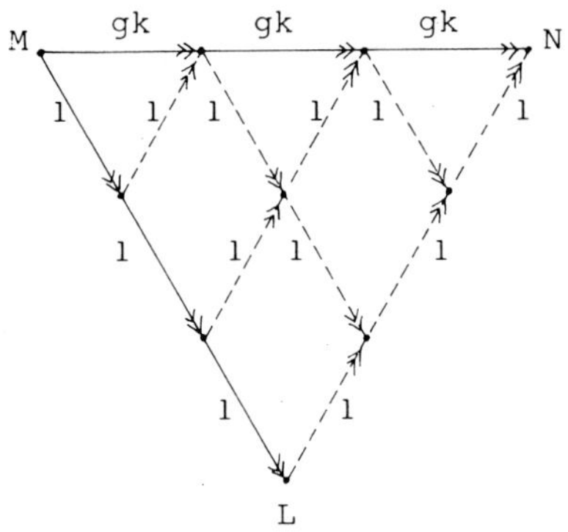

FIG. 13.5.

13.2.10. DEFINITION. Let $M \in \Lambda$. A *quasi-Gross–Knuth* reduction of M is a path

$$M \equiv M_0 \twoheadrightarrow M_1 \twoheadrightarrow M_2 \twoheadrightarrow \cdots$$

such that

$$\forall i \ \exists j \geqslant i \quad M_j \underset{\mathrm{gk}}{\twoheadrightarrow} M_{j+1}.$$

13.2.11. THEOREM. *Any quasi-Gross–Knuth reduction path of M is cofinal in $G(M)$.*

PROOF. A quasi-Gross–Knuth reduction of M is of the form, say,

$$M_1 \underset{1}{\twoheadrightarrow} M_1 \underset{\mathrm{gk}}{\twoheadrightarrow} M_2 \underset{1}{\twoheadrightarrow} M_3 \underset{1}{\twoheadrightarrow} M_4 \underset{\mathrm{gk}}{\twoheadrightarrow} M_5 \underset{1}{\twoheadrightarrow} \cdots .$$

Using a diagram chase suggested by figure 13.6, the result follows from theorem 13.2.9 (large triangle), lemma 13.2.8 (small triangles) and 11.2.28 (ii) (parallelograms). □

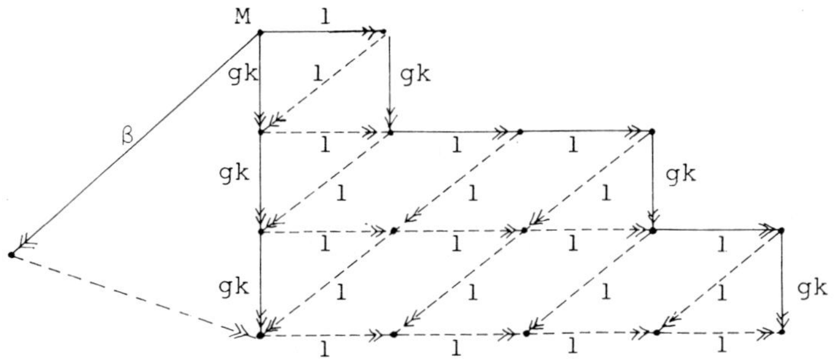

FIG. 13.6.

Theorem 13.2.11 can be used to show the non-convertibility of two terms. Remember that $x \in_\beta M$ iff $\forall N =_\beta M\ x \in \mathrm{FV}(N)$.

13.2.12. COROLLARY. *Let* $M \equiv M_0 \twoheadrightarrow M_1 \twoheadrightarrow \cdots$ *be a quasi-Gross–Knuth reduction. Suppose* $\forall i\ x \in \mathrm{FV}(M_i)$. *Then*

(i) $x \in_\beta M$,

(ii) $x \notin \mathrm{FV}(N) \Rightarrow M \neq_\beta N$.

PROOF. Suppose $M = N$. Then by the Church–Rosser theorem for some Z

$$M \twoheadrightarrow Z, \qquad N \twoheadrightarrow Z.$$

Claim. $x \in \mathrm{FV}(Z)$. Indeed, by theorem 13.2.11 for some i

$$Z \twoheadrightarrow M_i.$$

Since $x \in \mathrm{FV}(M_i)$ it follows by proposition 3.3.12 that $x \in \mathrm{FV}(Z)$.

But then since $N \twoheadrightarrow Z$, also $x \in \mathrm{FV}(N)$. Therefore $x \in_\beta M$.

(ii) Immediate by (i). □

13.2.13. APPLICATION. Let $A \equiv \mathbf{\Theta}(\lambda ax.\langle ax \rangle)$. Note that $Ax \twoheadrightarrow \langle Ax \rangle$. Hence

$$\begin{array}{rl} \mathrm{BT}(Ax) = & \lambda z.z \\ & \quad | \\ & \lambda z.z \\ & \quad | \\ & \lambda z.z \\ & \quad | \\ & \quad \vdots \end{array}$$

and therefore $\mathrm{BT}(Ax) = \mathrm{BT}(Ay)$ for all x,y. Nevertheless $Ax \neq Ay$ if $x \not\equiv y$.

PROOF. Let $B \equiv \lambda pq.q(ppq)$, $C \equiv \lambda ax.\langle ax \rangle$. Note that Ax has the following quasi-Gross–Knuth reduction path

$$Ax \equiv BBCx \underset{\mathrm{gk}}{\twoheadrightarrow} (\lambda y.y(BBy))Cx \twoheadrightarrow$$

$$\twoheadrightarrow \langle BBCx \rangle \underset{\mathrm{gk}}{\twoheadrightarrow} (\lambda y.y(BBCy))Cx \twoheadrightarrow$$

$$\twoheadrightarrow \langle\langle BBCx \rangle\rangle \underset{\mathrm{gk}}{\twoheadrightarrow} \cdots$$

Hence, since $x \notin \mathrm{FV}(Ay)$, the result follows by corollary 13.2.12. □

13.3. A recursive CR strategy

In this section it will be proved that there is a recursive CR strategy. The construction is taken from Bergstra and Klop [1979].

13.3.1. DEFINITION. $M \in \Lambda$ is called *minimal* if

$$\forall N \quad [N = M \Rightarrow N \twoheadrightarrow M].$$

EXAMPLES. (1) Each nf is minimal.
(2) $\mathbf{\Omega}$ is minimal.
(3) **WWW**, with $\mathbf{W} \equiv \lambda xy.xyy$, is minimal.

13.3.2. LEMMA. *If M is minimal, then either M is an* nf *or M has no* nf.

PROOF. Suppose M has the nf N. By the minimality of M it follows that $N \twoheadrightarrow M$. But then $N \equiv M$ by corollary 3.2.9 (i). Hence M is in nf. □

13.3.3. DEFINITION. Let $H \in \Lambda_{\sigma}\!\!\rightarrow\Lambda$ be a partial mapping.
(i) H is *finite* if $\mathrm{Dom}(H)$ is finite.
(ii) H is a *partial reduction strategy* if for all $M \in \mathrm{Dom}(H) M \twoheadrightarrow H(M)$.
(iii) A partial reduction strategy H is CR if for all $M, N \in \mathrm{Dom}(H)$

$$M =_{\beta} N \Rightarrow \exists p, q \in \mathbb{N} \ \forall p' \leqslant p, q' \leqslant q$$

$$[H^{p'}(M), H^{q'}(N) \in \mathrm{Dom}(H) \text{ and } H^{p}(M) \equiv H^{q}(N)].$$

(iv) An *H-cycle* is a finite sequence $\langle M_0, \ldots, M_n \rangle$ such that

$$H(M_0) \equiv M_1, H(M_1) \equiv M_2, \ldots, H(M_n) \equiv M_0.$$

This cycle is *linked* to a term M if $M =_{\beta} M_i$, for some $i \leqslant n$.
(v) Let $\mathcal{C} = \langle M_0, \ldots, M_n \rangle$ and $\mathcal{C}' = \langle M_0', \ldots, M_{n'}' \rangle$ be two H-cycles. $\mathcal{C}$ and $\mathcal{C}'$ are *linked* if $M_i =_{\beta} M_j'$ for some $i \leqslant n, j \leqslant n'$. $\mathcal{C}$ and $\mathcal{C}'$ are *identical* if $n = n'$ and $M_0' \equiv M_i$ for some $i \leqslant n$.
(vi) Let $\mathcal{X} \subset \Lambda$. The *closure* of $\mathcal{X}$ *under* H (notation $\mathrm{Cl}_H(\mathcal{X})$) is the least set $\mathcal{X}'$ such that

$$\mathcal{X} \subset \mathcal{X}' \quad \text{and} \quad \forall M \in \mathcal{X}' \cap \mathrm{Dom}(H) \quad H(M) \in \mathcal{X}'.$$

(vii) An H-cycle $\mathcal{C}$ is *minimal* if each $M \in \mathcal{C}$ is minimal. Clearly this is the case iff some $M \in \mathcal{C}$ is minimal.

The following shows what requirements must be met by a CR-strategy.

13.3.4. LEMMA. *Suppose F is a* CR-*strategy and* $\mathcal{C}_1, \mathcal{C}_2$ *are F-cycles. Then*
(i) $\mathcal{C}_1$ *is minimal,*
(ii) *If* $\mathcal{C}_1, \mathcal{C}_2$ *are linked, then they are identical.*

PROOF. (i) Let $M \in \mathcal{C}$ and $M \twoheadrightarrow N$. Then

$$\exists n, m \quad F^n(N) \equiv F^m(M) \in \mathcal{C}$$

and hence $N \twoheadrightarrow F^m(M) \twoheadrightarrow M$. Therefore M is minimal.
(ii) Let $M_i \in \mathcal{C}_i$ and $M_1 = M_2$. Then

$$\exists n, m \quad F^n(M_1) \equiv F^m(M_2).$$

It follows that the two cycles are identical. □

13.3.5. LEMMA. *There is a sequence of sets* $\mathcal{S}_n \subset \Lambda$ *such that*
(i) $\mathcal{S}_n$ *is finite and computable from n,*
(ii) $M, N \in \mathcal{S}_n \Rightarrow M =_\beta N$,
(iii) $M =_\beta N \Rightarrow$ *for some n (computable from* M, N*)* $M, N \in \mathcal{S}_n$.

PROOF. Let $M_0, M_1, M_2, \ldots$ be an effective listing of Λ. Define $\mathrm{CR}_n(M, N)$ iff both M, N reduce to some Z in less than n steps. Let

$$\|M\|_1 = \|M\| + \Sigma\{i \mid v_i \in \mathrm{FV}(M)\},$$

where $\{v_0, v_1, \ldots\}$ is the set of variables of the λ-calculus. Then $\{M \mid \|M\|_1 < n\}$ is always finite. Let $\langle n, m, l\rangle$ be a recursive bijection of $\mathbb{N}^3$ onto $\mathbb{N}$ with recursive projections

$$(\langle n_0, n_1, n_2\rangle)_i = n_i, \quad i = 0, 1, 2.$$

Now define

$$\mathcal{S}_n = \{N \mid \|N\|_1 \leqslant (n)_0 \text{ and } \mathrm{CR}_{(n)_1}(M_{(n)_2}, N)\}.$$

Then (i) clearly holds by Church's Thesis. As for (ii), if $M, N \in \mathcal{S}_n$, then $M =_\beta M_{(n)_2} =_\beta N$. As for (iii), if $M =_\beta N$, then by the Church–Rosser theorem $\mathrm{CR}_{n_1}(M, N)$ for some n_1. Let $M \equiv M_{n_2}$ and let $n_0 = \max(\|M\|_1, \|N\|_1)$. Then $M, N \in \mathcal{S}_{\langle n_0, n_1, n_2\rangle}$. □

13.3.6. LEMMA. *Let* $\mathcal{S} \subset \Lambda$ *be finite.*
(i) *The following predicate of M is recursive*

$$(*) \qquad \exists N \notin \mathcal{S} \quad M \twoheadrightarrow N.$$

(ii) *If* $(*)$ *does not hold, then* $G(M) \subseteq \mathcal{S}$ *and hence is finite.*

(iii) *Let H be a finite partial strategy. If $(*)$ does not hold then the following predicate of M is recursive*

there is an H-cycle in $\mathfrak{S}$ linked to M.

PROOF. (i) Let M be given and set

$$\mathfrak{M}_n = \{N \mid M \twoheadrightarrow N \text{ in less than } n \text{ steps}\}.$$

Note that the $\mathfrak{M}_n$ are finite and recursive in n. Clearly $\mathfrak{M}_n \subseteq \mathfrak{M}_{n+1}$ and if $\mathfrak{M}_{n+1} = \mathfrak{M}_n$, then for all k, $\mathfrak{M}_{n+k} = \mathfrak{M}_n$.

Now compute the least $n (\leqslant \text{Card } \mathfrak{S})$ such that

(1) $\quad \mathfrak{M}_n \not\subseteq \mathfrak{S}$ or (2) $\mathfrak{M}_n = \mathfrak{M}_{n+1} \subseteq \mathfrak{S}$.

Then $(*)$ holds iff (1) does.

(ii) If $(*)$ does not hold, then (2) and $G(M) = \mathfrak{M}_n$ for that n.

(iii) Let $\mathcal{C} = \langle M_0, \ldots, M_n \rangle$ be an H-cycle in $\mathfrak{S}$. Compute $G(M)$. Then $\mathcal{C}$ is linked to M iff $M_0 \in G(M)$. Repeat this for all H-cycles in $\mathfrak{S}$. □

13.3.7. MAIN CONSTRUCTION. There is a recursive sequence $F_0 \subseteq F_1 \subseteq \ldots$ of finite partial reduction strategies such that the following holds. Let $\mathfrak{S}_k$ be as in lemma 13.3.5 and set

$$\mathcal{G}_0 = \emptyset, \qquad \mathcal{G}_{k+1} = \mathrm{Cl}_{F_k}(\mathfrak{S}_k).$$

Then for all k

(i) $\mathrm{Dom}(F_k) \supseteq \mathcal{G}_k$,

(ii) $F_k \restriction \mathcal{G}_k$ is a partial CR strategy,

(iii) If $\mathrm{Dom}(F_k)$ contains an F_k-cycle $\mathcal{C} = \langle M_0, \ldots, M_n \rangle$, then M_0 is minimal,

(iv) If $\mathrm{Dom}(F_k)$ contains two linked F_k-cycles, they are identical.

PROOF. F_k will be constructed by induction on k such that (i), ..., (iv) hold. Moreover F_k will be computable from k.

Take $F_0 = \emptyset$. Then (i), ..., (iv) are satisfied.

Suppose now that F_k has been constructed satisfying (i), ..., (iv). Let

$(*) \qquad \mathrm{Dom}(F_{k+1}) = \mathcal{G}_{k+1} \cup \mathrm{Dom}(F_k),$

$$\mathcal{A}_{k+1} = \mathrm{Dom}(F_{k+1}) - \mathrm{Dom}(F_k)$$

and set

$$F_{k+1}(M) = F_k(M) \quad \text{if } M \in \mathrm{Dom}(F_k),$$

$$= M_{k+1} \quad \text{if } M \in \mathcal{A}_{k+1},$$

where M_{k+1} is defined as follows (see also figure 13.7).

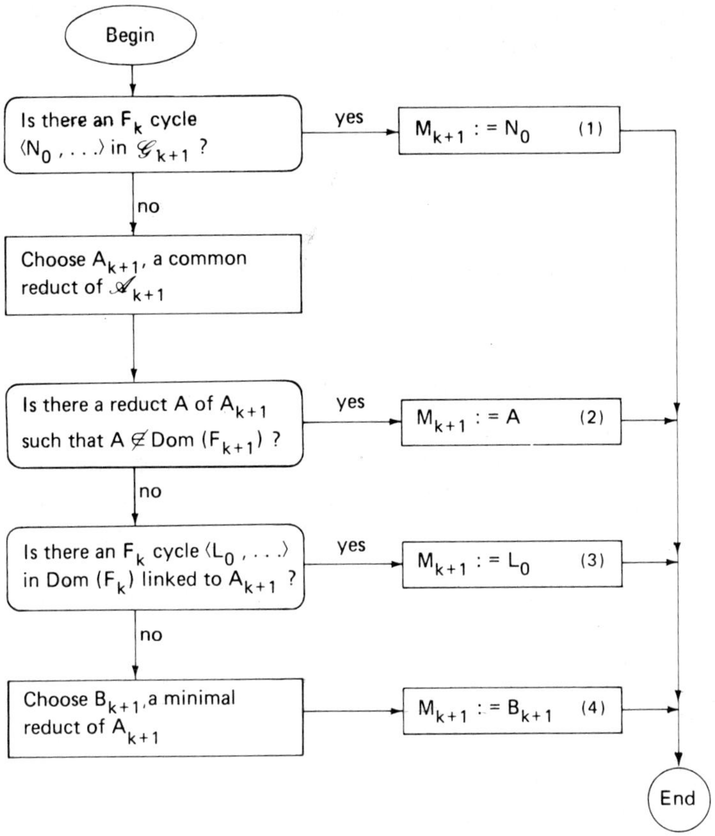

FIG. 13.7. Computation of M_{k+1}.

Decide whether there is an F_k-cycle $\mathcal{C} = \langle N_0, \ldots, N_m \rangle$ in $\mathcal{G}_{k+1}$. If so, then by (iii) N_0 is minimal, hence $M \twoheadrightarrow N_0$ ($M =_\beta N_0$, since $M, N_0 \in \mathcal{G}_{k+1}$). Set

(1) $\qquad M_{k+1} \equiv N_0,$

(where N_0 is chosen in some canonical way).

If not, compute a common reduct, say A_{k+1} (not necessarily in $\mathcal{G}_{k+1}$), of all members of $\mathcal{A}_{k+1}$. Decide (and this is possible by lemma 13.3.6 (i)) whether there exists a reduct of A_{k+1} not in Dom(F_{k+1}). If so, then choose one such reduct, say A, and set

(2) $\qquad M_{k+1} \equiv A.$

If not, decide whether there exists in Dom(F_k) an F_k-cycle $\langle L_0, \ldots, L_p \rangle$ linked to A_{k+1} (possible by lemma 13.3.6 (iii) in this case). If so, then set

(3) $\qquad M_{k+1} \equiv L_0.$

If not, choose a $B_{k+1} \in \text{Dom}(F_{k+1})$ which is a reduct of A_{k+1} and is minimal (B_{k+1} exists since in this case $G(A_{k+1})$ is finite by lemma 13.3.6 (ii)). Finally set

$$(4) \qquad M_{k+1} \equiv B_{k+1}.$$

The computation for M_{k+1} can be drawn as a flowchart given in figure 13.7.

This ends the construction of M_{k+1} and the definition of F_{k+1}. By the construction F_{k+1} is computable from F_k and $\mathcal{E}_k$. Hence $\lambda k.F_k$ is recursive. Clearly $F_0 \subseteq F_1 \subseteq \cdots$.

Now (i), ..., (iv) will be verified for F_{k+1}.

(i) Immediate from (*).

(ii) *Case* 1. M_{k+1} is defined by (1). All members of $\mathcal{A}_{k+1}$ go via F_{k+1} to N_0. Members of $\mathcal{G}_{k+1} \cap \text{Dom}(F_k)$ either go via F_{k+1} to $\mathcal{A}_{k+1}$ and hence to N_0 or cycle in $\mathcal{G}_{k+1} \cap \text{Dom}(F_k)$. But then by the induction hypothesis (iv) they also go to N_0.

Case 2. M_{k+1} is defined by (2), (3) or (4). Then there is no F_k-cycle in $\mathcal{G}_{k+1}$. Hence all members of $\mathcal{G}_{k+1} \cap \text{Dom}(F_k)$ go via F_{k+1} to $\mathcal{A}_{k+1}$ and hence to M_{k+1} and so do the members of $\mathcal{A}_{k+1}$.

(iii), (iv). If M_{k+1} is defined by (1), (2), or (3), no new cycles are created. Hence (iii) and (iv) follow from the induction hypothesis.

If M_{k+1} is defined by (4) and a new cycle $\mathcal{C}$ is created, then (iii) is satisfied because B_{k+1} is minimal and (iv) is satisfied because no other F_{k+1}-cycles are linked to $\mathcal{C}$. □

13.3.8. COROLLARY. *There exists a recursive strategy F_{CR} which is* CR.

PROOF. Let $F_0, F_1, \ldots$ be as in construction 13.3.7 and define $F_{\text{CR}} = \bigcup_n F_n$. Then F_{CR} is a total strategy since each $M \in \Lambda$ belongs to some $\mathcal{E}_k \subseteq \mathcal{G}_{k+1}$, by lemma 13.3.5 (iii). Moreover, since this k can be found effectively, F_{CR} is recursive.

If $M = N$, then by lemma 13.3.5.(iii) for some n one has $M, N \in \mathcal{E}_n \subseteq \mathcal{G}_{n+1}$. Hence since $F_{\text{CR}} \restriction \mathcal{G}_{n+1} = F_{n+1} \restriction \mathcal{G}_{n+1}$ is CR, for some p, q

$$F_{\text{CR}}^p(M) \equiv F_{\text{CR}}^q(N).$$

Thus F_{CR} is CR. □

By definition F_{CR} is not a 1-strategy. In exercise 13.6.6 a (non recursive) 1-strategy will be constructed which is CR. See also Bergstra–Klop [1979] for a recursive 1-strategy which is CR on S-terms.

13.4. An effective perpetual strategy

In this section an effective perpetual strategy will be constructed. As an application the general conservation theorem 11.3.7 will be proved. The results are taken from Barendregt et al. [1976].

13.4.1. DEFINITION. Let the reduction strategy F_∞ be defined by induction on the length of the terms as follows:

$$F_\infty(M) = \begin{cases} M \text{ if } M \text{ is in nf.} \\ \text{Otherwise, let } M \equiv C[(\lambda x.P)Q] \text{ where } R \equiv (\lambda x.P)Q \\ \text{is the left-most redex of } M. \text{ Then:} \\ \begin{cases} C[P[x:=Q]] \text{ if } R \text{ is an } I\text{-redex.} \\ \text{Otherwise (if } R \text{ is a } K\text{-redex):} \\ \begin{cases} C[P] \text{ if } Q \text{ is in nf.} \\ C[(\lambda x.P)(F_\infty(Q))] \text{ if } Q \text{ is not in nf.} \end{cases} \end{cases} \end{cases}$$

The explicit action of F_∞ can be described by introducing the following concepts.

13.4.2. DEFINITION. (i) Let R be the redex $(\lambda x.P)Q$. The *re* of R is $(\lambda x.P)$ and the *dex* of R is Q.

(ii) Let M be a term not in nf. The *derived term* of M (notation M^+) is the dex of the left-most redex in M.

(iii) Let M be a term. Its *derived sequence* $M^0, M^1, \ldots, M^n$ is defined by $M^0 \equiv M$, $M^{k+1} \equiv (M^k)^+$, as long as M^k is not in nf, otherwise M^{k+1} is not defined. Clearly each derived sequence is finite.

(iv) R^i, the left-most redex of M^i, is called the *special redex of order i* of M $(0 \leqslant i \leqslant n)$. See figure 13.8.

$$M \equiv M^0$$
$$\cup$$
$$R^0 \equiv (\lambda x_0.P_0)M^1$$
$$\cup$$
$$R^1 \equiv (\lambda x_1.P_1)M^2$$
$$\cup \quad \ddots$$
$$R^{n-1} \equiv (\lambda x_{n-1}.P_{n-1})M^n \quad \text{where } M^n \text{ is in nf.}$$

FIG. 13.8.

13.4.3. REMARK. As can be seen from definitions 13.4.1 and 13.4.2 F_∞ contracts the first I-redex in the sequence $R^0, R^1, \ldots, R^{n-1}$ if there is such a redex, otherwise F_∞ contracts R^{n-1}.

13.4.4. LEMMA. *Let* $M \equiv C[(\lambda x.P)Q]$, *where* $R \equiv (\lambda x.P)Q$ *is the leftmost redex in* M. *If* $M \underset{\neq \ell}{\twoheadrightarrow} M'$, *then* $M' \equiv C'[(\lambda x.P')Q']$, *where* $P \twoheadrightarrow P'$, $Q \twoheadrightarrow Q'$ *and* $C[z] \twoheadrightarrow C'[z]$ *for all variables* z.

PROOF. If $M \underset{\neq \ell}{\rightarrow} M'$ then this is evident: as R is leftmost, nothing is substituted in R nor is R substituted in some variable. The general statement follows by transitivity. □

13.4.5. LEMMA. *Let* $M \equiv C[(\lambda x.P)Q]$ *where* $R \equiv (\lambda x.P)Q$ *is the left-most redex. Suppose that*

(i) R *is a K-redex,*
(ii) $\infty(M)$ *and*
(iii) *Not* $\infty(Q)$.

Then $\infty(C[P])$.

PROOF. Let

$$\sigma : M \equiv M_0 \rightarrow M_1 \rightarrow M_2 \rightarrow \cdots$$

be an infinite reduction path. There are two cases.

(1) For all k one has $M \underset{\neq \ell}{\twoheadrightarrow} M_k$. Then by lemma 13.4.4 σ is

$$C_0[(\lambda x.P_0)Q_0] \rightarrow C_1[(\lambda x.P_1)Q_1] \rightarrow C_2[(\lambda x.P_2)Q_2] \cdots$$

with $C_n[z] \twoheadrightarrow C_{n+1}[z]$, $P_n \twoheadrightarrow P_{n+1}$, $Q_n \twoheadrightarrow Q_{n+1}$. Now because not $\infty(Q)$, there is an m such that $Q_m \equiv Q_{m'}$ for all $m' \geqslant m$. That is, in the one step reduction

$$C_{m'}[(\lambda x.P_{m'})Q_{m'}] \rightarrow C_{m'+1}[(\lambda x.P_{m'+1})Q_{m'+1}]$$

a redex outside $Q_{m'+1}$ is contracted.

Therefore also

$$C_{m'}[P_{m'}] \rightarrow C_{m'+1}[P_{m'+1}].$$

Hence

$$C[P] \twoheadrightarrow C_m[P_m] \rightarrow C_{m+1}[P_{m+1}] \cdots$$

is an infinite reduction starting with $C[P]$ and thus $\infty(C[P])$.

(2) For some k $M \underset{\neq \ell}{\twoheadrightarrow} M_k \underset{\ell}{\rightarrow} M_{k+1}$. Then by lemma 13.4.4 σ is

$$C_0[(\lambda x.P_0)Q_0] \underset{\neq \ell}{\twoheadrightarrow} C_k[(\lambda x.P_k)Q_k] \underset{\ell}{\rightarrow} C_k[P_k] \rightarrow \cdots.$$

Hence

$$C[P] \twoheadrightarrow C_k[P_k] \rightarrow \cdots$$

which shows that $\infty(C[P])$. $\square$

Lemma 13.4.5 is false if R is not the left-most redex, see exercise 13.6.7.

13.4.6. THEOREM. *F_∞ is an effective perpetual one step strategy.*

PROOF. By remark 13.4.3 it is clear that F_∞ is an effective one step strategy. In order to prove that F_∞ is perpetual, let $M \equiv C[(\lambda x.P)Q]$, where $R \equiv (\lambda x.P)Q$ is the left-most redex in M. Suppose that $\infty(M)$ and let

$$\sigma : M \equiv M_0 \rightarrow M_1 \rightarrow M_2 \rightarrow \cdots$$

be an infinite reduction path.

That $\infty(F_\infty(M))$ will be proved by induction on the length of M (the induction hypothesis being needed only in case 2.2.2).

Case 1. R is an I-redex. Then $F_\infty(M) \equiv C[P[x:=Q]]$.

Case 1.1. For all k one has $M \underset{\neq \ell}{\twoheadrightarrow} M_k$. Hence by lemma 13.4.4 σ is

$$C_0[(\lambda x.P_0)Q_0] \rightarrow C_1[(\lambda x.P_1)Q_1] \rightarrow \cdots$$

with $P_k \rightarrow P_{k+1}$, $Q_k \rightarrow Q_{k+1}$, $C_k[z] \rightarrow C_{k+1}[z]$. Now we show that $\infty(C[P[x:=Q]])$. If $\infty(Q)$ this is so, since $x \in \mathrm{FV}(P)$. If $\infty(P)$ this is so by substitutivity. If neither $\infty(Q)$ nor $\infty(P)$, then $\infty(C[z])$ and the result follows again by substitutivity.

Case 1.2. For some k one has $M \underset{\neq \ell}{\twoheadrightarrow} M_k$ and $M_k \underset{\ell}{\rightarrow} M_{k+1}$. Hence σ is

$$C[(\lambda x.P)Q] \twoheadrightarrow C_k[(\lambda x.P_k)Q_k] \rightarrow C_k[P_k[x:=Q_k]] \equiv M_{k+1} \rightarrow \cdots$$

Then also $\infty(F_\infty(M))$, since

$$F_\infty(M) \equiv C_0[P_0[x:=Q_0]] \twoheadrightarrow C_k[P_k[x:=Q_k]].$$

Case 2. R is a K-redex.

Case 2.1. Q is in nf. Then $F_\infty(M) = C[P]$ and because not $\infty(Q)$ we have by lemma 13.4.5 $\infty(C[P])$.

Case 2.2. Q is not in nf. Then $F_\infty(M) = C[(\lambda x.P)(F_\infty(Q))]$.

Case 2.2.1. not $\infty(Q)$. By lemma 13.4.5 $\infty(C[P])$, hence $\infty(F_\infty(M))$ because $F_\infty(M) = C[(\lambda x.P)(F_\infty(Q))] \to C[P]$.

Case 2.2.2. $\infty(Q)$. By induction hypothesis $\infty(F_\infty(Q))$, and hence $\infty(F_\infty(M))$. □

REMARK. The proof of theorem 13.4.6 is non-constructive; however realizing the explicit action of F_∞ (see remark 13.4.3) the argument can be made constructive.

As an application of the perpetuity of F_∞ the general conservation theorem 11.3.7 will be proved.

First let us note that the proof of the conservation theorem for the λI-calculus does not generalize to the λK-calculus. Recall that the former proof was as follows.

Suppose $M \overset{\Delta}{\to} M'$, where Δ is an I-redex and $\infty(M)$. Let

$$\sigma : M \equiv M_0 \to M_1 \to \cdots$$

be an infinite reduction path. Then an infinite reduction starting with M' is

$$\sigma' : M' \equiv M'_0 \twoheadrightarrow M'_1 \twoheadrightarrow M'_2 \twoheadrightarrow \cdots$$

where each M'_k is the complete reduct of all residuals of Δ in M_k. Hence $\infty(M')$.

The following example shows that this method of proof is false for λK:

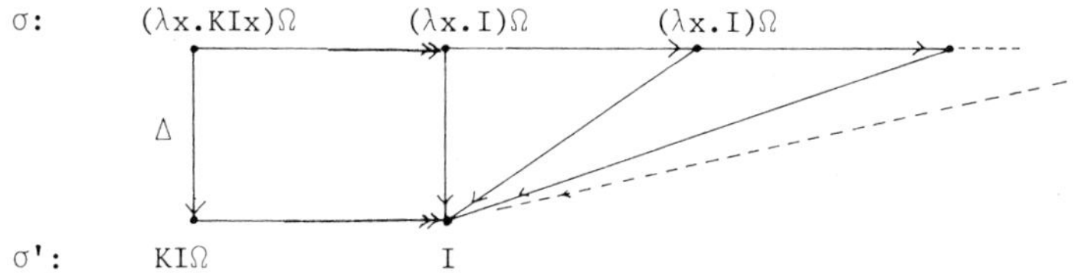

Therefore the sequence σ is said to be *non-projectible*. The general conservation theorem will be proved by observing that if $\infty(M)$, then the F_∞ path of M is an infinite reduction of M which is projectible and hence $\infty(M')$. The proof occupies 13.4.7–13.4.12.

13.4.7. DEFINITION. (i) $M \in \Lambda'^I$ if $M \equiv (M_0, \mathcal{F}) \in \Lambda'$ and $\Delta \in \mathcal{F} \Rightarrow \Delta$ is an I-redex (only I-redexes are indexed).

(ii) Let $M \in \Lambda'$. The *special redexes* of M are defined as for λ-terms (definition 13.4.2(iv)).

13.4.8. LEMMA. *A special redex R of $M \in \Lambda'$ is not part of the* re *of any redex in M.*

PROOF. By induction on the order i of R.

If $i = 0$, then R is the left-most redex of M. If R were in the re of some redex of M, then R would not be the left-most redex of M.

If $i > 0$, then R is the special redex of order i of M^+. By the induction hypothesis, R is not part of the re in a redex in M^+. Hence if R were part of some re in M, then also M^+ is part of this re. But then R^0 (see definition 13.4.2) would not be the left-most redex in M. □

13.4.9. LEMMA. *Let $M, N \in \Lambda'$. If $M \to_{\beta'} N$ by contracting a special redex Δ in M, then*

$$M \in \Lambda'^I \Rightarrow N \in \Lambda'^I.$$

PROOF. An indexed I-redex $(\lambda_i x.P)Q$ can degenerate to a K-redex only if inside P all free occurrences of x are erased. Since Δ is a special redex, $\Delta \not\subset P$ by lemma 13.4.8, and so this cannot happen. □

13.4.10. COROLLARY.

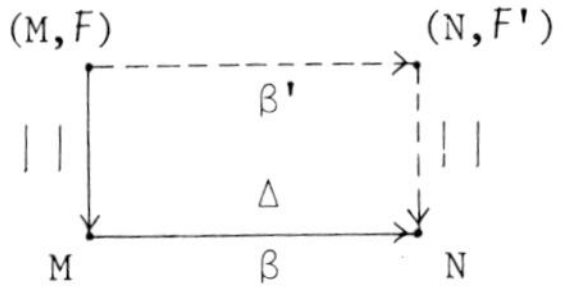

Δ special redex

$(M,F) \in \Lambda'^I$

$(N,F') \in \Lambda'^I.$

PROOF. By lemmas 11.2.2 and 13.4.9. □

13.4.11. LEMMA. *Let $M', N' \in \Lambda'$*

(i)

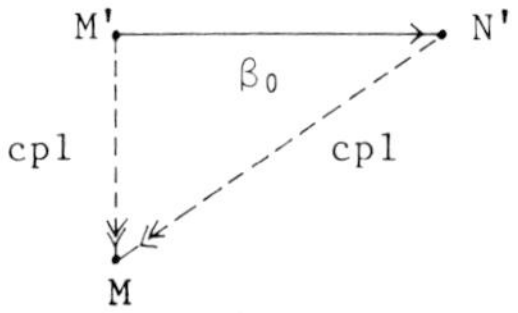

(ii)

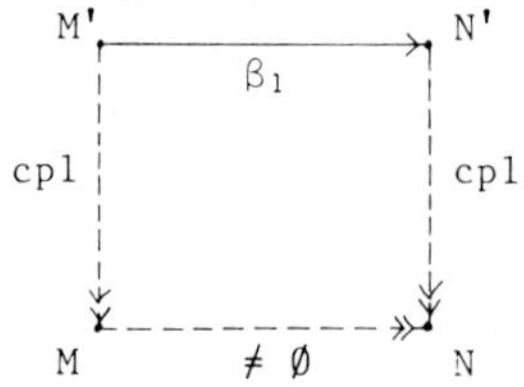

$M' \in \Lambda'^I.$

PROOF. Analogous to the proof of lemma 11.3.3, using that in (ii) $M' \in \Lambda'^I$. □

13.4.12. CONSERVATION THEOREM. *Let* $M \xrightarrow{\Delta} M'$ *where* Δ *is an I-redex. Then* $\infty(M) \Rightarrow \infty(M')$.

PROOF. Let $M_n \equiv F_\infty^n(M)$. Assume $\infty(M)$. By the perpetuity of F_∞

$$\sigma : M \equiv M_0 \xrightarrow{\Delta_0} M_1 \xrightarrow{\Delta_1} M_2 \xrightarrow{\Delta_2} \cdots$$

is an infinite path. By remark 13.4.3 each Δ_k is a special redex.

Let $\mathcal{F}_0 = \{\Delta\}$. Then $(M_0, \mathcal{F}_0) \in \Lambda'^I$. By corollary 13.4.10 there are $\mathcal{F}_k$ such that for all k

$$(M_k, \mathcal{F}_k) \sqsubseteq \Lambda'^I \quad \text{and} \quad (M_k, \mathcal{F}_k) \to_{\beta'} (M_{k+1}, \mathcal{F}_{k+1}).$$

Let M'_k be the complete development of $(M_k, \mathcal{F}_k)$. Then $M' \equiv M'_0$. If

$$(M_k, \mathcal{F}_k) \to_{\beta_1} (M_{k+1}, \mathcal{F}_{k+1})$$

then by lemma 13.4.11 (i)

$$M'_k \underset{\neq \emptyset}{\twoheadrightarrow} M'_{k+1}.$$

If, on the other hand,

$$(M_k, \mathcal{F}_k) \to_{\beta_0} (M_{k+1}, \mathcal{F}_{k+1})$$

then by lemma 13.4.11 (ii)

$$M'_k \equiv M'_{k+1}.$$

Hence we have the situation in figure 13.9.

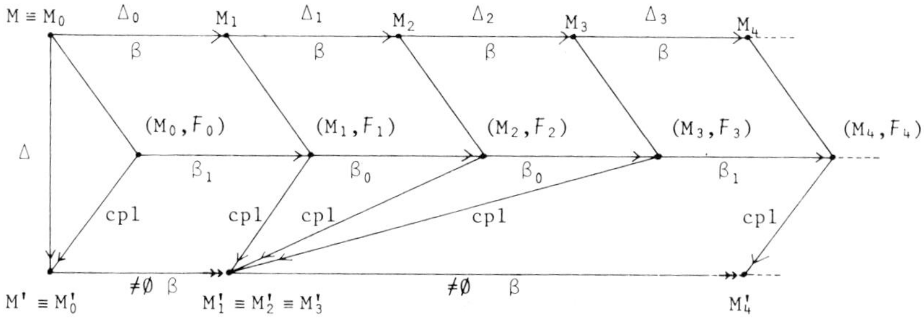

FIG. 13.9.

By theorem 11.2.20 a sequence of consecutive $\rightarrow_{\beta_0}$ is always finite. Therefore a subsequence of the M_i' is an infinite reduction path for M', i.e. $\infty(M')$. □

Note that in contrast to F_ℓ, the strategy F_∞ considers the "infra structure" of redexes (i.e. whether Δ is an I- or a K-redex) and not merely their positions. In exercise 13.6.8 it will be shown that this is essential for a perpetual strategy.

13.4.13 DEFINITION. Let R be a redex with contractum R'. R is *perpetual* if $\forall C[\ \ ][\infty C[R] \Rightarrow \infty C[R']]$.

Theorem 13.4.12 states that I-redexes are perpetual. In Bergstra–Klop [198+] the following characterization is given for the perpetuity of K-redexes.

13.4.14. DEFINITION. Let $M, N \in \Lambda$. Then

$$M \geqslant_\infty N \quad \text{if} \quad \forall *\ \left[\infty(N^*) \Rightarrow \infty(M^*)\right],$$

where $*$ ranges over substitution instances.

13.4.15. THEOREM. *A K-redex $(\lambda x.M)N$ is perpetual iff $M \geqslant_\infty N$.*

PROOF. See Bergstra–Klop [198+]. □

13.4.16. COROLLARY. *A redex $(\lambda x.M)N$ is perpetual iff $x \in \mathrm{FV}(M)$ or $M \geqslant_\infty N$.*

PROOF. By theorems 13.4.12 and 13.4.15. □

13.5. Optimal strategies

In this section it will be proved that there are no recursive L-optimal, L-1-optimal and B-optimal strategies. It is open whether there exists a recursive B-1-optimal strategy; however, this seems impossible. Moreover it will be shown that there is no strategy which is both L-1- and B-1-optimal. The terminology and results are taken from Barendregt et al. [1976]. For another approach to optimal reduction, see Lévy [1980].

It is trivial that there are non-recursive optimal strategies.

13.5.1. PROPOSITION. (i) *There exists an L-optimal strategy.*

(ii) *There exists an L-1-optimal strategy.*

(iii) *Similarly for B-optimal and B-1-optimal.*

PROOF. (i) Define

$$F(M)=\begin{cases} M & \text{if } M \text{ is in nf,}\\ N & \text{if } M \underset{\neq\emptyset}{\twoheadrightarrow} N,\ N \text{ in nf,}\\ F_\ell(M) & \text{if } M \text{ has no nf.}\end{cases}$$

Then

$$L_F(M)=\begin{cases} 0 & \text{if } M \text{ is in nf,}\\ 1 & \text{if } M \text{ has a nf,}\\ \infty & \text{if } M \text{ has no nf.}\end{cases}$$

Hence F is L-optimal.

(ii) If M has a nf, let σ_M be the shortest reduction of M to nf. Define

$$F(M)=\begin{cases} M & \text{if } M \text{ is in nf,}\\ M_1 & \text{if } M \text{ has a nf and } \sigma_M : M\to M_1\to \dots,\\ F_\ell(M) & \text{else.}\end{cases}$$

Then F is L-1-optimal.

(iii) Similarly. □

13.5.2. PROPOSITION. (i) *There exists no recursive L-optimal strategy.*

(ii) *There exists no recursive B-optimal strategy.*

PROOF. (i) If F is an L-optimal strategy, then for all M having a nf $F(M)$ is a nf. Hence

$$M \text{ has a nf} \Leftrightarrow F(M) \text{ is a nf.}$$

So if F were recursive, $\{M|M \text{ has a nf}\}$ would be recursive, contrary to theorem 6.6.5.

(ii) Consider $\mathscr{Q}=\{M|M \text{ has a nf } N \text{ and } \|N\|\leqslant\|M\|\}$. Clearly $\mathscr{Q}$ is a Σ_1^0-complete set (do exercise 13.6.15) and hence $\mathscr{Q}$ is not recursive. Define

$$\Lambda_n=\{M\in\Lambda \mid \|M\|\leqslant n\}.$$

Note that each Λ_n is finite. Suppose that F is a B-optimal strategy. *Claim*:

$$M\in\mathscr{Q}\Leftrightarrow \text{the } F \text{ path of } M \text{ lies entirely in } \Lambda_{\|M\|}.$$

Indeed, ($\Leftarrow$) is trivial since F is normalizing. ($\Rightarrow$) follows, because otherwise F could be improved by setting $F(M) \equiv N$ where N is the nf of M. Thus if F were recursive, then $\mathscr{Q}$ would be too, contradiction. $\square$

Now we show that also there exists no recursive optimal L-1-strategy.

13.5.3. DEFINITION. If M has a nf, then $n(M)$ is the length of the shortest possible (one step) reduction path of M to nf. Otherwise $n(M) = \infty$.

13.5.4. LEMMA. (i) *If* $A =_\beta \lambda xy.\mathbf{I}$, *then for all* B, C

$$n(ABC) = n(A) + 2.$$

(ii) *If* $A =_\beta a$, *then for all* B, C

$$n(ABC) = n(A) + n(B) + n(C).$$

PROOF. Do exercise 13.6.12. $\square$

13.5.5. LEMMA. *Let F be an L-1-optimal strategy. Let*

$$M \equiv (\lambda x.xAx)(\lambda y.yB(\mathbf{II})),$$

where A, B are in nf. *Then*

(i) $AB = \lambda xy.\mathbf{I} \Rightarrow F(M) \equiv (\lambda y.yB(\mathbf{II}))A(\lambda y.yB(\mathbf{II}))$,

(ii) $AB = a \Rightarrow F(M) \equiv (\lambda x.xAx)(\lambda y.yB\mathbf{I})$.

PROOF. (i) By assumption and the Church–Rosser theorem AB $\twoheadrightarrow \lambda xy.\mathbf{I}$. If in M the redex $\mathbf{II}$ is contracted first, then after that the shortest reduction to nf is

$$\begin{aligned}\sigma : M &\equiv (\lambda x.xAx)(\lambda y.yB(\mathbf{II}))\\ &\to (\lambda x.xAx)(\lambda y.yB\mathbf{I})\\ &\to (\lambda y.yB\mathbf{I})A(\lambda y.yB\mathbf{I})\\ &\to AB\mathbf{I}(\lambda y.yB\mathbf{I}) \underset{\sigma_1}{\twoheadrightarrow} \mathbf{I},\end{aligned}$$

where σ_1 is a reduction of shortest possible length. By lemma 13.5.4 (i)

$$\|\sigma\| = 3 + \|\sigma_1\| = 3 + n(AB) + 2 = n(AB) + 5.$$

If in M the left-most redex is contracted first, then after that the shortest reduction to nf is

$$\sigma' : M \equiv (\lambda x.xAx)(\lambda y.yB(\mathbf{II})) \to$$

$$M_2 \equiv (\lambda y.yB(\mathbf{II}))A(\lambda y.yB(\mathbf{II}))$$

$$\to AB(\mathbf{II})(\lambda y.yB(\mathbf{II})) \overset{\sigma_1'}{\twoheadrightarrow} I,$$

where again σ_1' is a reduction of shortest possible length. Again by lemma 13.5.4 (i)

$$\|\sigma'\| = 2 + \|\sigma_1'\| = 2 + n(AB) + 2 = n(AB) + 4.$$

Thus if F is l-1-optimal, then $F(M) \equiv M_2$.

(ii) Now $AB \to a$. Again if $\mathbf{II}$ in M is contracted first, then after that the shortest possible reduction to nf is

$$\sigma : M \equiv (\lambda x.xAx)(\lambda y.yB(\mathbf{II})) \to$$

$$M_1 \equiv (\lambda x.xAx)(\lambda y.yB\mathbf{I})$$

$$\to (\lambda y.yB\mathbf{I})A(\lambda y.yB\mathbf{I})$$

$$\to AB\mathbf{I}(\lambda y.yB\mathbf{I}) \overset{\sigma_1}{\twoheadrightarrow} a\mathbf{I}(\lambda y.yB\mathbf{I}),$$

where σ_1 is shortest possible. By lemma 13.5.4 (ii)

$$\|\sigma\| = 3 + \|\sigma_1\| = 3 + n(AB) + 0 + 0 = n(AB) + 3.$$

If in M the left-most redex is contracted first, then a shortest possible reduction to nf proceeds as follows:

$$\sigma' : M \equiv (\lambda x.xAx)(\lambda y.yB(\mathbf{II}))$$

$$\to (\lambda y.yB(\mathbf{II}))A(\lambda y.yB(\mathbf{II}))$$

$$\to AB(\mathbf{II})(\lambda y.yB(\mathbf{II})) \overset{\sigma_1'}{\twoheadrightarrow} a\mathbf{I}(\lambda y.yB\mathbf{I}),$$

where σ_1' is shortest possible. By lemma 13.5.4 (ii)

$$\|\sigma'\| = 2 + n(AB(\mathbf{II})(\lambda y.yB(\mathbf{II})) =$$

$$= 2 + n(AB) + 1 + 1 = n(AB) + 4.$$

Thus now $F(M) \equiv M_1$, since F is L-1-optimal. □

13.5.6. THEOREM. *There exists no recursive L-1-optimal strategy.*

PROOF. By Scott's theorem 6.6.2 (i) the disjoint r.e. sets

$$\mathcal{A} = \{N \mid N = \lambda xy.\mathbf{I}\}, \qquad \mathcal{B} = \{N \mid N = a\}$$

are recursively inseparable. Hence so are the disjoint r.e. sets

$$\#\mathcal{A} = \{n \mid \mathbf{E}_a \ulcorner n \urcorner = \lambda xy.\mathbf{I}\}, \qquad \#\mathcal{B} = \{n \mid \mathbf{E}_a \ulcorner n \urcorner = a\}.$$

By exercise 8.5.19 it may be assumed that $\mathbf{E}_a$ is in nf.

Now consider

$$M_n \equiv (\lambda x.x\mathbf{E}_a x)(\lambda y.y \ulcorner n \urcorner (\mathbf{II})).$$

Suppose F were a recursive L-1-optimal strategy. Then the set

$$\mathcal{C} = \{n \mid M_n \underset{\ell}{\rightarrow} F(M_n)\}$$

is recursive. By lemma 13.5.5 $\mathcal{C}$ separates $\#\mathcal{A}$ and $\#\mathcal{B}$, which is impossible. □

13.5.7. THEOREM. *There is no one step strategy F which is both L-1- and B-1-optimal.*

PROOF. Consider the term

$$M \equiv (\lambda xy.pxx(y\mathbf{I}))((\lambda x.pxx)A)\mathbf{I},$$

where A is in nf and very long. Let Δ_ℓ be the left-most redex of M and Δ_i the internal one. Claim:

(i) In order to minimalize $L_F(M)$, F must contract Δ_i.

(ii) In order to minimalize $B_F(M)$, F must contract Δ_ℓ.

(i) is clear, since contracting Δ_ℓ duplicates Δ_i. As to (ii), compare the reductions starting with contracting Δ_ℓ and Δ_i:

$$\sigma: \quad M \overset{\Delta_\ell}{\rightarrow}$$

$$(\lambda y.p((\lambda x.pxx)A)((\lambda x.pxx)A)(y\mathbf{I}))\mathbf{I} \rightarrow$$

$$p((\lambda x.pxx)A))(\lambda x.pxx)A)(\mathbf{II}) \rightarrow$$

$$p((\lambda x.pxx)A)((\lambda x.pxx)A)\mathbf{I} \rightarrow$$

$$p(pAA)((\lambda x.pxx)A)\mathbf{I} \rightarrow$$

$$p(pAA)(pAA)\mathbf{I};$$

(since A is very long one could not have done better).

$$\sigma' : M \overset{\Delta_i}{\to}$$

$$(\lambda xy.\, pxx(y\mathbf{I}))(pAA)\mathbf{I} \to$$

$$M^* \equiv (\lambda y.\, p(pAA)(pAA)(y\mathbf{I}))\mathbf{I} \to$$

$$p(pAA)(pAA)(\mathbf{II}) \to$$

$$p(pAA)(pAA)\mathbf{I}.$$

Now M^* is longer than any of the terms in the previous reduction σ. Thus F must contract Δ_ℓ. This proves the claim.

Since a 1-strategy cannot contract Δ_ℓ and Δ_i at once, F does not exist.

□

13.6. Exercises

13.6.1. Show that F_ℓ is not cofinal.

13.6.2. Show that F_{gk} is not CR.

13.6.3. Let $C[a]$ be a context such that a occurs only passively in $C[a]$. Let $F \equiv \mathbf{\Theta}(\lambda f\vec{x}.C[f\vec{x}])$. Then $F\vec{x} \twoheadrightarrow C[F\vec{x}]$.
The *natural reduction path* of $F\vec{x}$ is

$$\sigma : F\vec{x} \twoheadrightarrow C[F\vec{x}] \twoheadrightarrow C[C[F\vec{x}]] \twoheadrightarrow \cdots.$$

Prove that σ is cofinal in $G(M)$.

13.6.4. Let $H \equiv \mathbf{\Theta}(\lambda hx.[hx, hx])$. Show that $H\mathbf{K} \neq H\mathbf{I}$.

13.6.5 (Klop). $\sigma : M_0 \to M_1 \to \cdots$ is a *maximal* reduction path if σ is either infinite or ends in a nf. Define

$$\mathcal{R}^m(M) = \{\sigma | \sigma \text{ is a maximal reduction path starting with } M\}.$$

Let $\sigma, \sigma' \in \mathcal{R}^m(M)$, such that

$$\sigma : M_0 \to M_1 \to \ldots,$$

$$\sigma' : M_0' \to M_1' \ldots .$$

Define $\sigma \leqslant \sigma'$ iff $\forall n\, \exists m\; M_n \twoheadrightarrow M_m'$.

$$\sigma \sim \sigma' \quad \text{iff} \quad \sigma \leqslant \sigma' \text{ and } \sigma' \leqslant \sigma.$$

Then $\sim$ is an equivalence relation on $\mathcal{R}^m(M)$. Let $[\sigma]$ be the $\sim$ equivalence class of σ. Define

$$[\sigma] \leqslant [\sigma'] \Leftrightarrow \sigma \leqslant \sigma'$$

(this definition is independent of the choice of the representatives of the equivalence classes).

Finally the *spectrum* of M is the structure

$$\text{Spec}(M) = (\mathcal{R}^m(M)/\sim, \lessdot).$$

(i) If M is minimal, show that then Spec(M) is a singleton.
(ii) Show that Spec(M) always has a largest element.
(ii) Consider the following terms

$$M_0 \equiv \mathbf{K}\mathbf{I}\Omega,$$

$$M_1 \equiv (\lambda x.\mathbf{I}(xx))(\lambda x.\mathbf{I}(xx)) = \mathbf{\Theta}(\mathbf{I}),$$

$$M_2 \equiv [\Omega_3, \Omega_3], \qquad \Omega_3 \equiv (\lambda x.xxx)(\lambda x.xxx),$$

$$M_3 \equiv (\lambda y.\omega y)(\lambda y.\omega y),\ \omega \equiv (\lambda x.xx).$$

Each of these terms has as spectrum one of the structures given in figure 13.10. Find out which term corresponds to which structure

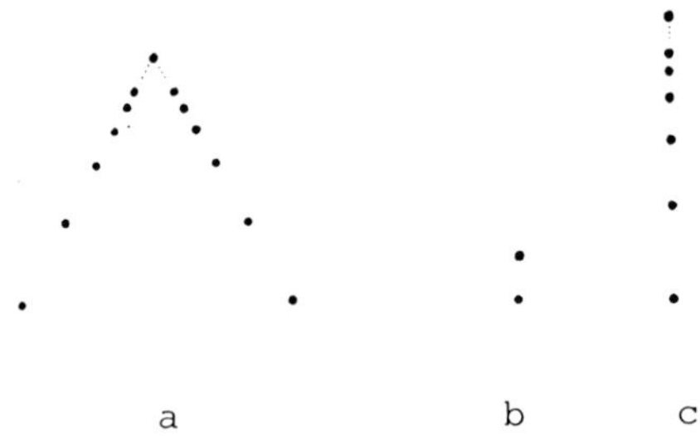

FIG. 13.10.

13.6.6. (Bergstra, Klop). Show that there exists a (non-recursive) one step CR strategy. (As was mentioned it is open whether there exists a recursive 1-strategy which is cofinal or CR.)

13.6.7. Show that lemma 13.4.5. does not hold if R is not left-most.

13.6.8. The *skeleton* of a term M is the result of replacing each variable (free or bound) by $\square$. Thus the skeleton of $y(\lambda x.xx)$ is $\square(\lambda\square.\square\square)$.

A 1-strategy is a *skeleton strategy* if it can be determined from the skeleton of a term which redex is going to be contracted. E.g. F_ℓ is a skeleton strategy.

(i) Show that a perpetual 1-strategy is never a skeleton strategy.
(ii) Show that a B-1-optimal strategy is never a skeleton strategy.

13.6.9 (Böhm). Let

$$M_0 \equiv H\mathbf{I}H, \qquad H \equiv \lambda xy.x(\lambda z.yzy)x,$$

$$M_1 \equiv LL\mathbf{I}, \qquad L \equiv \lambda xy.x(yy)x,$$

$$M_2 \equiv PQ, \qquad P \equiv \lambda x.x\mathbf{I}x, \qquad Q \equiv \lambda xy.xy\mathbf{I}(xy).$$

Draw $G(M_0)$, $G(M_1)$, $G(M_2)$.

13.6.10. Show that for $F = F_{gk}$ as defined in 13.2.7 one has

(i) $F(\lambda\vec{x}.yM_1 \cdots M_n) = \lambda\vec{x}.yF(M_1) \cdots F(M_n)$.
(ii) $F(\lambda\vec{x}.(\lambda y.M_0)M_1 \cdots M_n) = \lambda\vec{x}.F(M_0)[y:= F(M_1)]F(M_2) \cdots F(M_n)$.

13.6.11 (Bergstra–Klop). Write $M >_{\infty} N$ iff $M \geqslant_{\infty} N$ and $N \not\geqslant_{\infty} M$. Show that

(i) $xxx >_{\infty} xx$; $xx\mathbf{I} >_{\infty} xx$.

(ii) xIx and xx are incomparable with respect to $\geqslant_{\infty}$.

(iii) $M \supset N \Rightarrow M \geqslant_{\infty} N$.

13.6.12. Prove lemma 13.5.4.

13.6.13. Define the concept "quasi head reduction". Show that if there is an infinite quasi head reduction starting with M, then M is unsolvable.

13.6.14 (Klop). Let $\sigma : M_0 \to M_1 \to \cdots$ be a reduction. A redex $\Delta \in M_i$ is called *secured* if for some $j > i$ there is no residual of Δ in M_j with respect to the given reduction; σ is *secured* if Δ is secured for all i and all $\Delta \in M_i$.

Show that if σ is secured, than σ is cofinal in $G(M)$.

13.6.15. Prove that the set $\{M \mid M \text{ has a nf } N \text{ and } \|N\| < \|M\|\}$ is not recursive.

CHAPTER 14

LABELLED REDUCTION

In § 14.1 an extension of the λ-terms is considered, together with a notion of reduction. The resulting system is called the labelled λ⊥-calculus. The main theorem in § 14.1 is that this system is strongly normalizing. In chapter 19 labelled reduction is used for the local analysis of the λ-models D_∞, $P\omega$.

Given a finite set of finite β-reduction paths in the ordinary λ-calculus, one can embed them isomorphically in the labelled λ-calculus. Therefore the λ-terms with β-reduction are "locally strongly normalizable". In § 14.2 several applications of this fact are given, including nice proofs of the CR- and the (strong version of the) standardization theorem. Another such application is given in § 14.3: the continuity of the λ-calculus operations on Λ with respect to the tree topology. Finally in § 14.4 it is proved that λ-calculus computations are essentially sequential.

14.1. Strong normalization

The labelled λ-calculus studied in this section was introduced by Hyland [1976] and Wadsworth [1976] as a tool for examining the λ-models D_∞ and $P\omega$.

In Lévy [1975], [1978] a more general labelled λ-calculus is considered. That system is related to the notion of strongly equivalent reductions, see exercise 14.5.5.

14.1.1. Definition. The set of labelled λ-terms, notation $\Lambda\bot^{\mathbb{N}}$, is defined as follows.

Alphabet

$v_0, v_1, \ldots,$	variables,
$(\,,), \lambda,$	improper symbols,
$\bot,$	constant,
$0, 1, \ldots, n, \ldots,$	labels (for each $n \in \mathbb{N}$).

Terms

(i) $\Lambda\bot^{\mathbb{N}}$ is the smallest class X such that

$$\begin{aligned}
&x \in X, && \text{for variables } x,\\
&\bot \in X, &&\\
&M, N \in X \Rightarrow (MN) \in X, &&\\
&M \in X \Rightarrow (\lambda x.M) \in X, &&\\
&M \in X \Rightarrow (M^n) \in X && \text{for all } n \in \mathbb{N}.
\end{aligned}$$

(ii) $\Lambda\bot$ is the subclass of $\Lambda\bot^{\mathbb{N}}$ consisting of those terms that do not have any labels.

(iii) $|\ \ |: \Lambda\bot^{\mathbb{N}} \to \Lambda\bot$ is the map that erases all labels.

Substitution

For $M, N \in \Lambda\bot^{\mathbb{N}}$ the substitution $M[x:=N]$ is defined inductively as follows.

$$x[x:=N] \equiv N,$$

$$y[x:=N] \equiv y,$$

$$\bot[x:=N] \equiv \bot,$$

$$(M_1M_2)[x:=N] \equiv M_1[x:=N]M_2[x:=N],$$

$$(\lambda y.M)[x:=N] \equiv \lambda y.M[x:=N],$$

$$(M^n)[x:=N] \equiv (M[x:=N])^n.$$

Before introducing the notions of reduction on $\Lambda\bot^{\mathbb{N}}$ that are important, an auxiliary such notion is needed.

14.1.2. DEFINITION. Define on $\Lambda\bot^{\mathbb{N}}$ the following notion of reduction

$$\textbf{\textit{label}}: (M^n)^m \to M^{min(n,m)}.$$

14.1.3. LEMMA. *Each labelled λ-term M has a unique label-*nf*, say $M!$.*

PROOF. Each term does have a label-nf, since contraction decreases the length of a term. As the function min(n, m) is associative, $\underset{=}{\to}_{label} \models \diamond$; hence by lemma 3.2.2 ***label*** is Church-Rosser. Therefore the *label*-nf is unique. □

EXAMPLE. $((\lambda x.((x^2)^3(x^7)^4)^8)^7)^6! \equiv (\lambda x.(x^2x^4)^8)^6$.

14.1.4. DEFINITION. On the set of labelled λ-terms the following notions of reduction are introduced.

(i) (1) $\boldsymbol{\beta}_+ : (\lambda x.M)^{n+1}N \to (M[x:=N^n])^n$.

(2) $\boldsymbol{\beta}_\perp : (\lambda x.M)^0 N \to (M[x:=\perp])^0$.

$$\perp : \begin{cases} \perp^n \to \perp, \\ \lambda x.\perp \to \perp, \\ \perp M \to \perp. \end{cases}$$

In the above $M, N \in \Lambda\perp^{\mathbb{N}}$ and $n \in \mathbb{N}$ is arbitrary.

(ii)

$$\boldsymbol{lab.\beta} = \boldsymbol{\beta}_+ \cup \boldsymbol{\beta}_\perp \cup \perp \cup \boldsymbol{label}.$$

$$\boldsymbol{+} = \boldsymbol{\beta}_+ \cup \perp \cup \boldsymbol{label}.$$

A notion of reduction R on $\Lambda\perp^{\mathbb{N}}$ induces relations $\to_R$, $\twoheadrightarrow_R$ and $=_R$ compatible with the operations. In particular

$$M \to_R N \Rightarrow M^n \to_R N^n.$$

14.1.5. EXAMPLE. Using the notation $M^{n,m} \equiv (M^n)^m$ one has

$$L \equiv (\lambda x.x^1x)^3(\lambda x.xx) \to_{\beta_+}$$

$$((\lambda x.xx)^{2,1}(\lambda x.xx)^2)^2 \twoheadrightarrow_{label}$$

$$((\lambda x.xx)^1(\lambda x.xx)^2)^2 \to_{\beta_+}$$

$$((\lambda x.xx)^{2,0}(\lambda x.xx)^{2,0})^{0,2} \twoheadrightarrow_{label}$$

$$((\lambda x.xx)^0(\lambda x.xx)^0)^0 \to_{\beta_\perp}$$

$$(\perp\perp)^{0,0} \to_{label} (\perp\perp)^0 \twoheadrightarrow_\perp \perp.$$

Therefore $L \twoheadrightarrow_{lab.\beta} \perp$, i.e., L has a $lab.\beta$-nf. L also has a $+$-nf, namely $(\omega^0\omega^0)^0$ with $\omega \equiv \lambda x.xx$. Note that it is hygienic to reduce M to $M!$.

14.1.6. LEMMA. (i) ***lab*.β** *is substitutive*.

(ii) ***lab*.β** *is weakly Church-Rosser*.

(iii) (i) *and* (ii) *hold for* **+**.

PROOF. (i) This is a trivial extension of the proof that $\boldsymbol{\beta}$ is substitutive (proposition 3.1.16).

(ii) This is an easy extension of the proof that $\boldsymbol{\beta}$ is weakly Church-Rosser (lemma 11.1.1). Some examples

$$\begin{array}{ccc}
(\lambda x.(\lambda y.yx)^8 b)^3 a & \to & (\lambda x.(b^7 x)^7)^3 a \\
\downarrow & & \downarrow \\
((\lambda y.ya^2)^8 b)^2 & \to & (b^7 a^2)^{7,2}
\end{array}$$

$$\begin{array}{ccccc}
(\lambda x.\bot)^3 a & \to & \bot^2 & & \\
\downarrow & & \downarrow & & \\
\bot^3 a & \to \bot a \to & \bot & &
\end{array}$$

(iii) Similarly. □

Now it will be proved that every labelled λ-term is strongly lab.β-normalizable. The proof is due to van Daalen [1980] and occupies 14.1.8–14.1.12. The main step is to show that if M, N are strongly normalizing, then so is $M[x:= N]$.

Other proofs are due to R. de Vrijer (using a computability argument familiar from the typed λ-calculus) and Klop [1980] (using an interpretation into the labelled λI-calculus and the conservation theorem).

In the rest of this section $\to$ and $\twoheadrightarrow$ denote $\to_{lab.\beta}$ and $\twoheadrightarrow_{\text{lab.}\beta}$.

14.1.7. DEFINITION. (i) $\mathcal{SN} = \{M \in \Lambda\bot^{\mathbb{N}} | M$ is strongly *lab.*β-normalizable$\}$

(ii) If $M \in \mathcal{SN}$, then $d(M)$ is the length of the longest *lab.*β-reduction path starting with M.

14.1.8. LEMMA. *Let $M, N \in \Lambda\bot^{\mathbb{N}}$ with $M \in \mathcal{SN}$. For $L \in \Lambda\bot^{\mathbb{N}}$ write $L^* = L[x:= N]$. Suppose $M^* \twoheadrightarrow (\lambda y.P)^n$. Then one has one of the following two possibilities*:

(1) $M \twoheadrightarrow (\lambda y.P_1)^n$, *and* $P_1^* \twoheadrightarrow P$,

(2) $M \twoheadrightarrow L \equiv xU_1 \cdots U_m$ (*possibly some labels are left out*)

with $m \geqslant 0$ *and* $L^* \twoheadrightarrow (\lambda y.P)^n$.

PROOF. As the result has nothing to do with labels, we will not mention them. More interesting is that one even does not need that M is SN; see exercise 15.4.8. The present proof does use that $M \in \mathcal{SN}$, however, and is by induction on $(d(M), \| M \|)$ ordered lexicographically, i.e. $(n,m) < (n',m')$ iff $n < n'$ or ($n = n'$ and $m < m'$). (Equivalently: by induction on the ordinal $\omega.d(M)+\|M\|$.) For each M the statement will either be proved directly or be deduced from the induction hypothesis, i.e. the statement for M' with smaller $(d(M'), \|M'\|)$. We distinguish cases according to the shape of M.

Case 1. M is a variable. If $M \equiv x$, then we have (2). If $M \not\equiv x$, then not $M^* \twoheadrightarrow (\lambda y.P)$.

Case 2. $M \equiv \lambda y.M_1$. Then we have (1).

Case 3. $M \equiv M_1 M_2$. Then $M^* \equiv M_1^* M_2^* \twoheadrightarrow \lambda y.P$. This is only possible if

(3) $\qquad M_1^* \twoheadrightarrow \lambda z.Q,$

(4) $\qquad Q[z:=M_2^*] \twoheadrightarrow \lambda y.P.$

By (3) and the induction hypothesis ($d(M_1) \leqslant d(M)$, $\|M_1\| < \|M\|$) there are two cases:

(5) $\qquad M_1 \twoheadrightarrow \lambda z.Q_1$ and $Q_1^* \twoheadrightarrow Q$;

or

(6) $\qquad M_1 \twoheadrightarrow L_1 = xV_1 \cdots V_m$, and $L_1^* \twoheadrightarrow \lambda z.Q$.

Assume (5). Then

(7) $\qquad M_1 M_2 \twoheadrightarrow (\lambda z.Q_1)M_2 \to Q_1[z:=M_2];$

(8) $$M_1^* M_2^* \twoheadrightarrow (\lambda z.Q_1^*)M_2^* \to Q_1^*[z:=M_2^*] \equiv (Q_1[z:=M_2])^*$$
$$\twoheadrightarrow Q[z:=M_2^*] \twoheadrightarrow \lambda y.P,$$

by (5), (4). Since $d(Q_1[z:=M_2]) < d(M)$ (by (7)) it follows from the last part of the reduction in (8) and the induction hypothesis that there are again two cases:

(9.1) $\qquad Q_1[z:=M_2] \twoheadrightarrow (\lambda y.P_2)$ and $P_2^* \twoheadrightarrow P$;

or

(9.2) $\qquad Q_1[z:=M_2] \twoheadrightarrow x\vec{W}$ and $(x\vec{W})^* \twoheadrightarrow \lambda y.P$.

Now $M = M_1 M_2 \twoheadrightarrow Q_1[z:=M_2]$, by (5); hence in both cases we are done ((9.1)$\Rightarrow$(1), (9.2)$\Rightarrow$(2)).

Assume (6). Then

$$M_1 M_2 \twoheadrightarrow xV_1 \cdots V_m M_2 \quad \text{and} \quad (x\vec{V}M_2)^* \twoheadrightarrow (\lambda z.Q)M_2^* \twoheadrightarrow \lambda y.P,$$

by (4), and we have (2). □

14.1.9. LEMMA. *Let* $(..(M^p M_1)^{p_1} \cdots M_m)^{p_m} \twoheadrightarrow (\lambda y.N)^q$, $m \geqslant 0$. *Then* $q \leqslant p$.

PROOF. By induction on m. Note that

$$(1) \qquad Q_1^{q_1} \twoheadrightarrow Q_2^{q_2} \Rightarrow q_2 \leqslant q_1,$$

since an outer label can only be decreased (by label-contractions). If $m = 0$, then $M^p \twoheadrightarrow (\lambda y.N)^q$ and hence $q \leqslant p$ by (1). If $m > 0$, then, leaving out some labels, one must have

$$M^p M_1 \cdots M_{m-1} \twoheadrightarrow (\lambda z.N_1)^{q_1}, \qquad M_m \twoheadrightarrow M'_m$$

and (if $q_1 \neq 0$)

$$(\lambda z.N_1)^{q_1} M'_m \to \left(N_1\left[z := M_m'^{q_1 - 1}\right]\right)^{q_1 - 1}$$
$$\twoheadrightarrow (\lambda y.N)^q.$$

Hence $q \leqslant q_1 - 1 \leqslant q_1 \leqslant p$ by (1) and the induction hypothesis. □

The first of the following two lemmas is a special case of the second. Nevertheless it needs to be proved separately.

14.1.10. LEMMA. $M \in \mathcal{SN} \Rightarrow M[x := \bot] \in \mathcal{SN}$.

PROOF. By induction on $(d(M), \|M\|)$ ordered lexicographically. Write P^* for $P[x := \bot]$.

Case 1. M is a variable. Then the statement is obvious.

Case 2. $M \equiv \lambda y.M_1$. Then $M^* \equiv \lambda y.M_1^*$ and the statement follows from the induction hypothesis $M_1^* \in \mathcal{SN}$.

Case 3. $M \equiv M_1^n$. Then $M^* \equiv (M_1^*)^n$ and the statement follows from the induction hypothesis.

Case 4. $M \equiv M_1 M_2$. Then $M^* \equiv M_1^* M_2^*$. By the induction hypothesis $M_1^*, M_2^* \in \mathcal{SN}$. Suppose that there is an infinite reduction σ starting from M^*. Then one must have $M_1^* \twoheadrightarrow (\lambda z.P)^n$, otherwise the reductions of M_1^* and M_2^* remain separate and σ cannot be infinite. By lemma 14.1.8 one can distinguish two subcases.

Subcase 4.1. $M_1 \twoheadrightarrow (\lambda z.P_1)^n$ and $P_1^* \twoheadrightarrow P$. Then if $n > 0$ one has

$$(1) \qquad \sigma: M^* \equiv M_1^* M_2^* \twoheadrightarrow (\lambda z.P)^n N_2^* \to \left(P\left[z := (N_2^*)^{n-1}\right]\right)^{n-1} \twoheadrightarrow \cdots$$

ad infinitum with $M_2^* \twoheadrightarrow N_2^*$. On the other hand

$$M \equiv M_1 M_2 \twoheadrightarrow (\lambda z.P_1)^n M_2$$
$$\to \left(P_1\left[z := M_2^{n-1}\right]\right)^{n-1} \equiv Q, \text{ say}.$$

Hence $d(M) > d(Q)$. Therefore by the induction hypothesis $Q^* \in \mathcal{SN}$. But

$$Q^* \equiv \big(P_1^*\big[z := (M_2^*)^{n-1}\big]\big)^{n-1}$$

$$\twoheadrightarrow \big(P\big[z := (N_2^*)^{n-1}\big]\big)^{n-1};$$

therefore $P[z := (N_2^*)^{n-1}]^{n-1} \in \mathcal{SN}$, contradicting (1). If $n = 0$, then the contradiction can be obtained similarly.

Subcase 4.2. $M_1 \twoheadrightarrow x\vec{N}$ and $(x\vec{N})^* \equiv \bot\vec{N} \twoheadrightarrow (\lambda z.P)^n$. This is impossible. □

14.1.11. Corollary (main lemma). $M, N \in \mathcal{SN} \Rightarrow M[x := N] \in \mathcal{SN}$.

Proof. Let $l(N)$ be the outer label of N, i.e.

$$l(\bot) = l(x) = l(PQ) = l(\lambda x.P) = 0, \qquad l(P^n) = n.$$

The statement will be proved by induction on the triple $(l(N), d(M), \|M\|)$ ordered lexicographically. Write P^* for $P[x := N]$.

Cases 1, 2, 3. $M \equiv z$, $M \equiv \lambda y.M_1$ or $M \equiv (M_1)^n$. As in the proof of lemma 14.1.10.

Case 4. $M \equiv M_1M_2$. Suppose there is an infinite reduction σ starting with M^*. As in the proof of lemma 14.1.10 one must have $M_1^* \twoheadrightarrow (\lambda y.P)^n$, $M_2^* \twoheadrightarrow N_2^*$ and

(1) $$\sigma : M_1^*M_2^* \twoheadrightarrow (\lambda y.P)^n N_2^*$$

$$\rightarrow \begin{cases} \big(P\big[y := (N_2^*)^{n-1}\big]\big)^{n-1} & \text{if } n \neq 0, \\ \big(P[y := \bot]\big)^0 & \text{if } n = 0, \end{cases}$$

$$\twoheadrightarrow \cdots$$

ad infinitum. If $n = 0$, then the contradiction follows from lemma 14.1.10. Suppose $n \neq 0$. One can again distinguish two subcases.

Subcase 4.1. $M_1 \twoheadrightarrow \lambda y.P_1$ and $P_1^* \twoheadrightarrow P$. This case is treated as in the proof of lemma 14.1.10.

Subcase 4.2. $M_1 \twoheadrightarrow x\vec{Q}$ and $(x\vec{Q})^* \equiv N\vec{Q}^* \twoheadrightarrow (\lambda y.P)^n$. Then by lemma 14.1.9 one has $n \leqslant l(N)$. Therefore the induction hypothesis applies to P and $(N_2^*)^{n-1}$, i.e. $P[y := (N_2^*)^{n-1}] \in \mathcal{SN}$. This contradicts (1). □

14.1.12. Theorem (Strong normalization theorem). *Let* $M \in \Lambda\bot^{\mathbb{N}}$. *Then every lab.β-reduction starting with M terminates.*

PROOF. By induction on the structure of M. If M is a variable, this is trivial, and if $M \equiv \lambda y.M_1$ or $M \equiv (M_1)^n$, the result follows from the induction hypothesis. So suppose $M \equiv M_1 M_2$ and that σ is an infinite reduction starting with M. Since by the induction hypothesis $M_1, M_2 \in \mathbb{SN}$, one must have $M_1 \twoheadrightarrow (\lambda y.P)^n$, $M_2 \twoheadrightarrow Q$ and

$$\begin{aligned}\sigma : M_1 M_2 &\twoheadrightarrow (\lambda y.P)^n Q \\ &\rightarrow \begin{cases}(P[y:= Q^{n-1}])^{n-1} & \text{if } n \neq 0, \\ (P[y:= \perp])^0 & \text{if } n = 0,\end{cases} \\ &\twoheadrightarrow \cdots\end{aligned}$$

ad infinitum. Since M_1, $M_2 \in \mathbb{SN}$, also P, $Q^{n-1} \in \mathbb{SN}$. Therefore by the main lemma $(P[y:= Q^{n-1}])^{n-1} \in \mathbb{SN}$ or $(P[y:= \perp])^0 \in \mathbb{SN}$; a contradiction. □

14.2. Applications

Applications of the strong normalization theorem for the labelled λ-calculus start with the simple observation that ordinary β-reductions can be lifted to labelled reductions and thus become strongly normalizable. Therefore one may say that β-reductions are "locally strongly normalizing". This idea is due to Lévy [1975], [1978].

14.2.1. LEMMA (Lifting). (i) *Let $M, N \in \Lambda$ and $M \twoheadrightarrow_\beta N$. Then for some $M', N' \in \Lambda\perp^{\mathbb{N}}$ with $|M'| \equiv M$, $|N'| \equiv N$ one has $M' \twoheadrightarrow_+ N'$.*

(ii) *Similarly for $M, N_1, \ldots, N_n \in \Lambda$ with $M \twoheadrightarrow_\beta N_i$, $1 \leqslant i \leqslant n$.*

PROOF. (i) Simply give all subterms of M (of the form $\lambda x.P$) high enough labels, e.g. always k where k is the length of the reduction $M \twoheadrightarrow_\beta N$.

EXAMPLE. $(\lambda x.xx)\mathbf{I}a \rightarrow \mathbf{I}\mathbf{I}a \rightarrow \mathbf{I}a \rightarrow a$ becomes

$$(\lambda x.xx)^3 \mathbf{I}^3 a \twoheadrightarrow_+ (\mathbf{I}^2\mathbf{I}^2)^2 a \twoheadrightarrow_+ \mathbf{I}^1 a \rightarrow_+ a^0.$$

(ii) Similar to (i). □

14.2.2. LEMMA (Projecting). *Let $\sigma' : M'_0 \rightarrow_+ M'_1 \rightarrow_+ \cdots$ be a +-reduction path. Suppose $|M'_0| \in \Lambda$. Define*

$$|\sigma'| : |M'_0| \underset{=}{\rightarrow} |M'_1| \underset{=}{\rightarrow} \cdots$$

Then $|\sigma'|$ is a β-reduction path.

PROOF. Since $|M_0'| \in \Lambda$, the term M_0' does not contain any $\perp$'s and therefore the same is true for the M_i' (there are no $\beta_\perp$-redexes). Hence $|M_i'| \in \Lambda$ for all i. The rest is obvious. □

The first application is an alternative proof of the Church–Rosser theorem for the labelled λ-calculus. As a corollary one obtains the ordinary Church–Rosser theorem.

14.2.3. THEOREM (Church–Rosser theorem for the labelled λ-calculus).
(i) *The notion of reduction* $\textbf{\textit{lab.}}\boldsymbol{\beta}$ *on* $\Lambda\perp^{\mathbb{N}}$ *is Church–Rosser.*
(ii) *The same is true for* $+$.

PROOF. (i) By proposition 3.1.25, since $\textbf{\textit{lab.}}\boldsymbol{\beta}$ is strongly normalizing and weakly Church–Rosser (lemma 14.1.6 (ii)).
(ii) Clearly the notion of reduction $+$ is strongly normalizing. By lemma 14.1.6 (iii) it is also weakly Church–Rosser. □

14.2.4. COROLLARY (Church–Rosser theorem for β-reduction). *The notion of reduction* $\boldsymbol{\beta}$ *is Church–Rosser.*

PROOF. Given $M \twoheadrightarrow M_1, M \twoheadrightarrow M_2$, lift these reductions to $\Lambda\perp^{\mathbb{N}}$. Find a common reduct there and project. □

Also the finite development theorem (in fact FD!) follows easily.

14.2.5. COROLLARY (FD!) *Let* $M \in \Lambda$ *and* $\mathcal{F}$ *be a set of redexes* $\subseteq M$. *Then all developments of* $(M, \mathcal{F})$ *are finite. Complete developments terminate in the same term.*

PROOF. Let $(M, \mathcal{F})$ be given. Define $M' \in \Lambda\perp^{\mathbb{N}}$ to be M with all redexes $(\lambda x.P)Q$ in $\mathcal{F}$ replaced by $(\lambda x.P)^1 Q$. Clearly a development of $(M, \mathcal{F})$ corresponds to a $+$-reduction of M' (via projecting). By the strong normalization theorem 14.1.12 all $+$-reductions are finite; by theorem 14.2.3 (ii) complete $+$-reductions all end with the same term. □

Before considering applications of strong normalization giving new results, still another proof of the standardization theorem (in fact of the strong version, theorem 12.3.14) will be given. The method is due to Klop [1980] and has the virtue that it illuminates the process of standardization. The proof occupies 14.2.6–14.2.10.

14.2.6. DEFINITION. (i) RED $= \{\sigma \mid \sigma$ is some finite β-reduction path$\}$. On RED one has the partial operation $+$ ($\sigma + \tau$ is defined only when the endpoint of σ is the beginning point of τ).

(ii) Let $M \in \Lambda$ and $\Delta_1, \Delta_2 \subset M$ be two redexes with $\Delta_2 < \Delta_1$ (i.e. Δ_2 to the left of Δ_1). Consider $\sigma : M \overset{\Delta_1}{\to} M_1 \overset{\Delta_2'}{\to} M_2$ obtained by contracting first Δ_1 and then the unique residual Δ_2' of Δ_2. Such a σ is the smallest reduction that is not standard and is called a *Klop-reduction-redex* or simply K-redex.

(iii) If σ is a K-redex as in (ii), then its *contractum* is

$$\tau : M \overset{\Delta_2}{\to} M_3 \overset{\Delta_1'}{\to} \cdots \overset{\Delta_1'}{\to} M_2$$

where

$$\begin{array}{ccc} M & \xrightarrow{\Delta_1} & M_1 \\ {\scriptstyle \Delta_2}\downarrow & & \downarrow{\scriptstyle \Delta_2'} \\ M_3 & \xrightarrow{\Delta_1'} \cdots \xrightarrow{\Delta_1'} & M_2 \end{array}$$

is an elementary diagram (there may be $n \geqslant 0$ residuals Δ_1' of Δ_1).

(iv) On RED the following notion of reduction is introduced:

$$\boldsymbol{K} = \{(\sigma, \tau) | \sigma \text{ is a } K\text{-redex and } \tau \text{ its contractum}\}.$$

(v) As usual, K induces the following binary relations on RED:

$\to_K$ (which is compatible with $+$),

$\twoheadrightarrow_K$ (reflexive, transitive),

$=_K$ (equivalence relation).

14.2.7. LEMMA. $\to_K$ *is acyclic, that is, there does not exist*

(1) $$\sigma_0 \to_K \sigma_1 \to_K \cdots \to_K \sigma_n \equiv \sigma_0,\ n > 0.$$

PROOF. By induction on k, the number of β-reduction steps in σ_0 a contradiction will be derived by assuming (1).

If $k = 0$, then σ_0 does not contain a K-redex. So let $k > 0$. Suppose for some $i < n$ the K-redex in σ_i is at the beginning of that reduction. Let i be the smallest such number. Then one has the situation in figure 14.1, where $\Delta_1 < \Delta_0$. Moreover σ_n must start with a contraction of $\Delta_2 \leqslant \Delta_1 < \Delta_0$ (if $\Delta_1 < \Delta_2$, then Δ_1 remains the first contracted redex). But then $\sigma_n \not\equiv \sigma_0$, a contradiction.

If for no σ_i the K-redex is at the beginning, then erasing the first step in $\sigma_0, \ldots, \sigma_n$ yields again a $\to_K$ cycle $\sigma_0', \ldots, \sigma_n'$ with shorter σ_0'. By the induction hypothesis this gives a contradiction. □

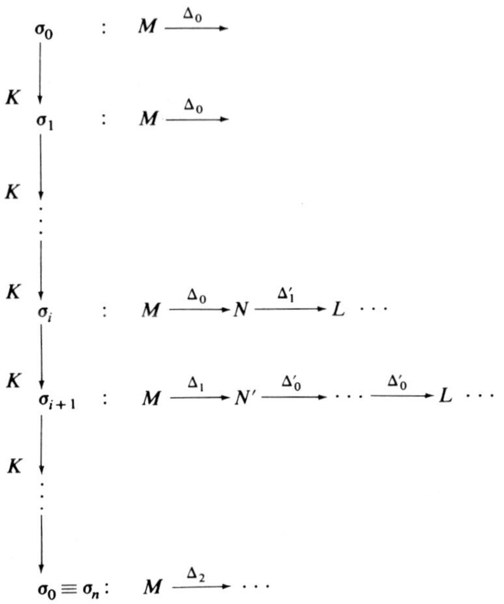

FIG. 14.1

14.2.8. PROPOSITION. (i) *The notion of reduction* K *on* RED *is strongly normalizing.*

(ii) *If* σ *is in* K-nf, *then* σ *is standard.*

PROOF. (i) Suppose $\sigma \rightarrow_K \tau$ and let σ start with M. By lemma 14.2.1 (i) one can lift σ to a $+$-reduction σ' starting with $M' \in \Lambda \perp^{\mathbb{N}}$.

Contracting a K-redex can be done also in the presence of labels. Hence τ can be lifted to a $+$-reduction τ' starting with the same M'.

Now suppose there is an infinite K-reduction

$$\sigma_0 \rightarrow_K \sigma_1 \rightarrow_K \cdots$$

By the argument just given there are $+$-reductions $\sigma_0', \sigma_1', \ldots$ with $|\sigma_i'| \equiv \sigma_i$ all starting with the same M'. From the strong normalization theorem for $+$-reductions and König's lemma it easily follows that there are only finitely many $+$-reductions starting from a fixed term (see exercise 3.5.9). So $\sigma_i' \equiv \sigma_j'$ for some $i \neq j$ and hence $\sigma_i \equiv \sigma_j$. This contradicts lemma 14.2.8.

(ii) If $\sigma : M_0 \rightarrow M_1 \rightarrow \cdots \rightarrow M_n$ is not a standard reduction, let $k < n$ be the smallest number such that $M_0 \rightarrow \cdots \rightarrow M_{k+1}$ is not standard. But then $M_{k-1} \rightarrow M_k \rightarrow M_{k+1}$ is a K-redex and hence σ is not a K-nf. $\square$

The converse of the following proposition is also true, see exercise 14.5.9.

14.2.9. PROPOSITION. *If* $\sigma =_K \tau$, *then* $\sigma \cong \tau$.

PROOF. Since $\cong$ is an equality relation on (RED, +) by theorem 12.2.2(viii), it is sufficient to show

$$(\sigma, \tau) \in K \Rightarrow \sigma \cong \tau.$$

But if $(\sigma, \tau) \in K$, then σ and τ are the sides of an elementary and diagram, hence $\sigma \cong \tau$ by proposition 12.2.2 (xi). □

14.2.10. THEOREM. *Every* $\sigma \in$ RED *has a unique* K-nf σ_S. *Moreover* σ_S *is the unique standard reduction with* $\sigma \cong \sigma_S$.

PROOF. By proposition 14.2.8 each σ has a K-nf which is standard. Suppose τ, τ' are K-nf's of σ. Then by lemma 14.2.9 one has $\tau \cong \tau'$ and since τ, τ' are standard it follows by proposition 12.3.13 that $\tau \equiv \tau'$. Therefore the K-nf of σ is unique. The rest is clear. □

Next as an application a new result. Welch [1975] introduced the following notion of inside out reduction and conjectured theorem 14.2.12.

14.2.11. DEFINITION. (i) Let $M \in \Lambda$ and

$$\sigma : M \equiv M_0 \xrightarrow{\Delta_0} M_1 \xrightarrow{\Delta_1} \cdots$$

be a reduction. Then σ is *inside out* (i.o.) if Δ_i is not a residual of a redex $\Delta'_j \subset \Delta_j$ for all $j < i$.

(ii) Write $M \underset{\text{i.o.}}{\twoheadrightarrow} N$ if there is an i.o. reduction $\sigma : M \twoheadrightarrow N$.

EXAMPLES. (i) $\mathbf{I}((\lambda x.xx)a) \rightarrow \mathbf{I}(aa) \rightarrow aa$ is i.o.

(ii) $\mathbf{I}((\lambda x.xx)a) \rightarrow (\lambda x.xx)a \rightarrow aa$ is not i.o.

One sees that i.o. reductions are dual to standard reductions, where outer redexes have to be contracted first.

The following result, due to Lévy [1975], shows that the set $\{N \mid M \underset{\text{i.o.}}{\twoheadrightarrow} N\}$ is cofinal in $G(M)$.

14.2.12. THEOREM (Completeness of inside out reductions). *If* $M \twoheadrightarrow N$, *then* $M \underset{\text{i.o.}}{\twoheadrightarrow} N_1$ *and* $N \twoheadrightarrow N_1$ *for some* N_1; *see figure* 14.2.

PROOF. Lift $M \twoheadrightarrow N$ to $M' \twoheadrightarrow_+ N'$. Perform a +-reduction on M' by each time contracting an internal +-redex (i.e. without proper subredexes).

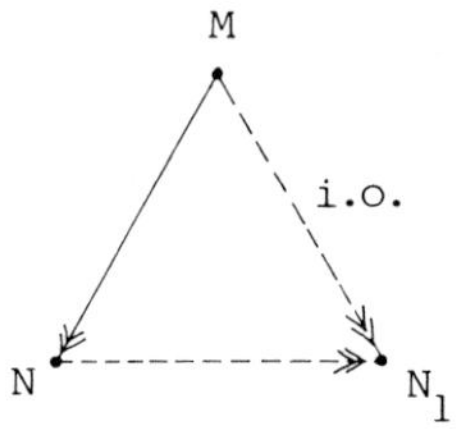

FIG. 14.2.

Since $+$-reductions strongly normalize this process stops, say at N_1'. Then N_1' is the $+$-nf of M'. Hence $N' \twoheadrightarrow_+ N_1'$ by the CR property for $+$. Projecting down one obtains $M \twoheadrightarrow_\beta N_1$, $N \twoheadrightarrow_\beta N_1$ and clearly the first reduction is inside out. □

14.3. Continuity

In this section it will be proved that the operations application and abstraction on Λ are continuous w.r.t. the tree topology. This fact turns out to be quite useful. It replaces several arguments which would otherwise require some analysis of reduction. The essential lemma for the continuity theorem is proposition 14.3.19 and was proved in Wadsworth [1971], in Lévy [1975] and in Welch [1975], using different methods. We follow Lévy's proof (which makes use of some ideas of Wadsworth and Welch).

14.3.1. DEFINITION. (i) The set $\Lambda\bot$ of $\lambda\bot$-terms is obtained by adding a constant $\bot$ to the formation rules of terms (so $\Lambda\bot = |\Lambda\bot^{\mathbf{N}}|$).

(ii) On $\Lambda\bot$ the following notions of reduction are introduced

$$\boldsymbol{\beta}: (\lambda x.P)Q \to P[x := Q],$$

$$\bot_1 : \bot P \to \bot, \qquad \bot_2 : \lambda x.\bot \to \bot,$$

$$\bot = \bot_1 \cup \bot_2, \qquad \boldsymbol{\beta}\bot = \boldsymbol{\beta} \cup \bot.$$

14.3.2. PROPOSITION. (i) $\boldsymbol{\beta}(\bot)$ *is* CR.

(ii) *Each* $P \in \Lambda\bot$ *has a unique* $\bot$-nf.

PROOF. (i) By lifting (lemma 14.2.1), the CR property for ***lab.β*** (theorem 14.2.3) and projecting (lemma 14.2.2).

(ii) $\bot$-reduction decreases the length of a term, hence is strongly normalizing. Moreover, one has $\underset{=}{\to}_\bot \models \Diamond$; by proposition 3.2.2 it follows that $\bot$ is CR and therefore $\bot$-nf's are unique. □

14.3.3. LEMMA. *Let $P \in \Lambda \perp$. Then*

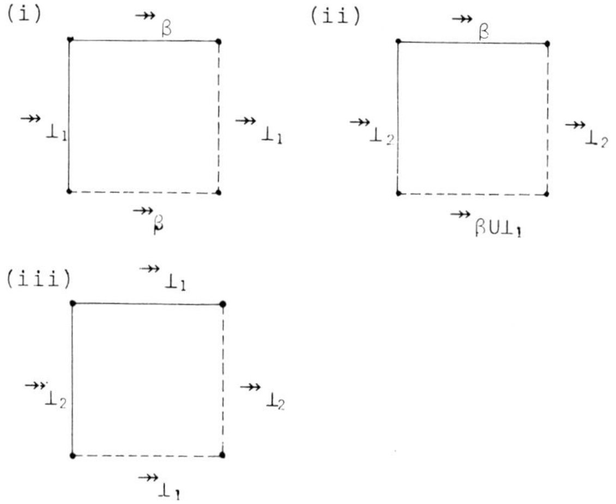

PROOF. By a simple case distinction one first shows

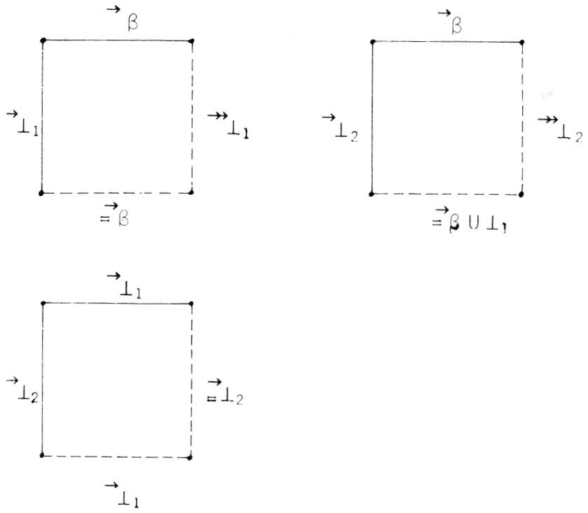

The rest follows by some simple diagram chases. □

The notion of Böhm tree is extended to $\Lambda \perp^{(\mathbb{N})}$ by treating $\perp$ as $\boldsymbol{\Omega}$ (and ignoring labels).

14.3.4. DEFINITION. (i) For $P \in \Lambda\perp$, let $P[\perp := Q]$ be the result of replacing all $\perp$'s by Q, and let $\mathrm{BT}(P) = \mathrm{BT}(P[\perp := \boldsymbol{\Omega}])$.

(ii) For $P \in \Lambda\perp^{\mathbb{N}}$, let $\mathrm{BT}(P) = \mathrm{BT}(|P|)$.

(iii) Let A be a finite Böhm tree. Then $M[A] \in \Lambda\bot$ is obtained from $M(A)$ (see definition 10.1.16) by replacing all Ω's by $\bot$.

(iv) Let $M \in \Lambda$. Then $M^{[n]} \equiv M[\mathrm{BT}^n(M)]$.

Note that $\mathrm{BT}(M^{[n]}) \equiv \mathrm{BT}^n(M)$, by lemma 10.1.19; also $M^{[n]} \gtrsim M^{(n)}$.

EXAMPLES. (i) $\mathrm{BT}(\lambda x.x(\lambda z.\bot)) = \begin{array}[t]{c}\lambda x.x\\ |\\ \bot\end{array}$

(ii) If Y is a fixed point combinator, then $Y^{[2]} \equiv \lambda f.f(f(\bot))$.

The following terminology (in a modified form) comes from Wadsworth [1971].

14.3.5. DEFINITION. Let $M \in \Lambda\bot$.

(i) $P \in \Lambda\bot$ *approximates* M (notation $P \underset{\sim}{\sqsubseteq} M$) if $\mathrm{BT}(P) \subseteq \mathrm{BT}(M)$.

(ii) $P \in \Lambda\bot$ is an *approximate normal form* (anf) of M if $P \underset{\sim}{\sqsubseteq} M$ and P is a $\beta\bot$-nf.

(iii) $\mathcal{A}(M) = \{P \in \Lambda\bot \mid P \text{ is an anf of } M\}$.

EXAMPLES. (i) $\lambda z.xz\bot \underset{\sim}{\sqsubseteq} \lambda z.xz\mathbf{K}$; $\mathbf{S}x\Omega \underset{\sim}{\sqsubseteq} \lambda z.xz\mathbf{K}$; $\lambda x.x\bot \in \mathcal{A}(\lambda x.\mathbf{I}x\mathbf{S})$.

(ii) $M^{[n]} \in \mathcal{A}(M)$.

In order to prove something about approximation it is useful to go back to Wadsworth's original definition.

14.3.6. DEFINITION. (i) Let $M \in \Lambda\bot$. Then $\alpha(M) \in \Lambda\bot$ is obtained from M by replacing the outermost (i.e. $\subset$-maximal) redexes by $\bot$. One can define α inductively as follows:

$$\alpha(\lambda\vec{x}.yM_1\cdots M_n) \equiv \lambda\vec{x}.y\alpha(M_1)\cdots\alpha(M_n),$$

$$\begin{aligned}\alpha(\lambda\vec{x}.(\lambda y.P)QM_1\cdots M_n) &\equiv \alpha(\lambda\vec{x}.\bot M_1\cdots M_n)\\ &\equiv \lambda\vec{x}.\bot\,\alpha(M_1)\cdots\alpha(M_n).\end{aligned}$$

(ii) $\omega(M)$ is the $\bot$-nf of $\alpha(M)$. ω can be defined inductively by

$$\omega(\lambda\vec{x}.yM_1\cdots M_n) \equiv \lambda\vec{x}.y\omega(M_1)\cdots\omega(M_n),$$

$$\omega(\lambda\vec{x}.(\lambda y.P)Q\vec{M}) \equiv \omega(\lambda\vec{x}.\bot\vec{M}) \equiv \bot.$$

(iii) $\mathcal{A}'(M) = \{\omega(N) \mid M \twoheadrightarrow_\beta N\}$.

EXAMPLE. (i) $\alpha(z(\lambda x.(\lambda y.y)xz)) \equiv z(\lambda x.\bot z)$.
(ii) $\omega(z(\lambda x.(\lambda y.y)xz)) \equiv z\bot$.

14.3.7. LEMMA. *Let* $M \in \Lambda\bot$. *Then*
(i) $\omega(M) \sqsubseteq M$,
(ii) $M \twoheadrightarrow_\beta N \Rightarrow \omega(M) \sqsubseteq \omega(N)$.

PROOF. (i) By induction on the length of M. If $M \equiv \lambda\vec{x}.(\lambda y.P)Q\vec{N}$, then $\omega(M) \equiv \bot \sqsubseteq M$. If $M \equiv \lambda\vec{x}.yN_1 \cdots N_n$, then

$$\omega(M) \equiv \lambda\vec{x}.y\omega(N_1) \cdots \omega(N_n) \sqsubseteq M$$

by the induction hypothesis.

(ii) Similarly one shows first by induction $M \to_\beta N \Rightarrow \omega(M) \sqsubseteq \omega(N)$. (Typical case: $\lambda\vec{x}.\mathbf{I}y\vec{M} \to \lambda\vec{x}.y\vec{M}$). The rest follows by transitivity. □

14.3.8. DEFINITION. Let $M \in \Lambda$ and $\mathcal{X} \subseteq \Lambda\bot$. Then
(i) $\bigsqcup\mathcal{X} = M$ if $\bigcup\{\mathrm{BT}(P) | P \in \mathcal{X}\} = \mathrm{BT}(M)$
(ii) $\mathcal{X}$ is *directed* if $\{\mathrm{BT}(P) | P \in \mathcal{X}\}$ is directed in $(\mathfrak{B}, \subseteq)$.

14.3.9. LEMMA. (i) $\mathcal{Q}(M)$ *is directed.*
(ii) $\mathcal{Q}'(M)$ *is directed.*

PROOF. (i) Let $P, P' \in \mathcal{Q}(M)$. Then $P \sqcup P' = M[\mathrm{BT}(P) \cup \mathrm{BT}(P')] \in \mathcal{Q}(M)$.
(ii) By the Church–Rosser theorem and lemma 14.3.7 (ii). □

14.3.10. PROPOSITION. (i) $\mathcal{Q}'(M) \subseteq \mathcal{Q}(M)$.
(ii) $M = \bigsqcup\mathcal{Q}(M) = \bigsqcup\mathcal{Q}'(M)$.

PROOF. (i) Let $\omega(N) \in \mathcal{Q}'(M)$ with $M \twoheadrightarrow_\beta N$. Then $\mathrm{BT}(M) = \mathrm{BT}(N)$, hence $\omega(N) \sqsubseteq M$, by lemma 14.3.7. Clearly $\omega(N)$ is a $\beta\bot$-nf, so $\omega(N) \in \mathcal{Q}(M)$.
(ii) Clearly $M = \bigsqcup\mathcal{Q}(M) \sqsupseteq \bigsqcup\mathcal{Q}'(M)$, in the obvious BT sense.
Claim:

$$\forall P \in \mathcal{Q}(M)\ \exists P' \in \mathcal{Q}'(M) \quad P \sqsubseteq P'.$$

Intuitively this should be clear if one realizes how a Böhm tree "grows". [If not, define $g(M, n)$, the "growth of $\mathrm{BT}(M)$ by the nth day", by induction on n:

$$g(M,0)=M,$$

$$g(M,n+1)=\lambda\vec{x}.yg(M_1,n)\cdots g(M_m,n)$$

if M has the principal hnf $\lambda\vec{x}.y\vec{M}$;

$$=M \qquad \text{if } M \text{ is unsolvable.}$$

Then by induction on n one shows

$$M \twoheadrightarrow_\beta g(M,n) \quad \text{and} \quad M^{[n]} \sqsubseteq \omega(g(M,n)).$$

Now let $P \in \mathcal{A}(M)$. Then for some n one has $P \sqsubseteq M^{[n]}$ and therefore $P \sqsubseteq \omega(g(M,n)) \in \mathcal{A}'(M)$.]

Using the claim it follows that

$$M \sqsupseteq \bigsqcup \mathcal{A}'(M) \sqsupseteq \bigsqcup \mathcal{A}(M) = M. \quad \square$$

The following corollary expresses $\sqsubseteq$ in terms of its restriction to terms with finite trees.

14.3.11. COROLLARY. *Let* $M, N \in \Lambda(\perp)$. *Then*

$$M \sqsubseteq N \quad \text{iff} \quad \forall M'_\beta \twoheadleftarrow M \ \exists N'_\beta \twoheadleftarrow N \ \omega(M') \sqsubseteq \omega(N').$$

PROOF. ($\Leftarrow$) Since $M = \bigsqcup\{\omega(M') | M \twoheadrightarrow_\beta M'\}$ by the proposition.

($\Rightarrow$) Let $M \twoheadrightarrow_\beta M'$. Then (by propositions 10.1.6 and 14.3.10 and lemma 14.3.7)

$$\omega(M') \sqsubseteq M' \approx M = \bigsqcup\{\omega(N') | N \twoheadrightarrow_\beta N'\},$$

i.e.

$$\mathrm{BT}(\omega(M')) \subseteq \cup \{\mathrm{BT}(\omega(N')) | N \twoheadrightarrow_\beta N'\}.$$

Since $\mathrm{BT}(\omega(M'))$ is a compact element of $(\mathfrak{B}, \subseteq)$ and the RHS is directed, one has for some $N'_\beta \twoheadleftarrow N$

$$\mathrm{BT}(\omega(M')) \subseteq \mathrm{BT}(\omega(N')),$$

i.e. $\omega(M') \sqsubseteq \omega(N')$. $\square$

14.3.12. LEMMA. *Let* $M \in \Lambda\perp$ *and* $C[\ ]$ *be a context over* $\Lambda\perp$. *Then* $C[\perp] \precsim C[M]$.

PROOF. Let $C[\perp] \twoheadrightarrow_\beta L$. Then $C[M] \twoheadrightarrow_\beta L[\perp := M]$. Moreover $\omega(L) \precsim \omega(L[\perp := M])$, as one can show easily by induction on the length of the term L (three cases: $L \equiv \lambda\vec{x}.y\vec{L}$; $\equiv \lambda\vec{x}.\perp\vec{L}$; $\equiv \lambda\vec{x}.(\lambda y.P)Q\vec{L}$). Hence corollary 14.3.11 applies. □

14.3.13. COROLLARY. $P \in \mathscr{A}(M) \Rightarrow C[P] \precsim C[M]$.

PROOF. By assumption P is a $\beta\perp$-nf $\precsim M$. Hence $P = D[\perp, \ldots, \perp]$, $M = D[M_1, \ldots, M_n]$. Therefore

$$C[P] \equiv C[D[\vec{\perp}]] \precsim C[D[\vec{M}]] \equiv C[M].$$

by repeated application of the lemma. □

14.3.14. LEMMA. (i) $P \twoheadrightarrow_\perp Q \Rightarrow \omega(P) \equiv \omega(Q)$.
(ii) $P \rightarrow_\perp Q \Rightarrow P \approx Q$.

PROOF. (i) It is sufficient to show that $P \rightarrow_\perp Q \Rightarrow \omega(P) \equiv \omega(Q)$. This follows by induction on the length of P.

(ii) First assume $P \rightarrow_{\perp_1} Q$. Then $P \equiv C[\perp M], Q \equiv C[\perp]$. By lemma 14.3.12 one has $Q \precsim P$. To show the converse, let $P \twoheadrightarrow_\beta P'$. Then by lemma 14.3.3 (i) $Q \twoheadrightarrow_\beta Q'$ and $P' \twoheadrightarrow_{\perp_1} Q'$. By (i) it follows that $\omega(P') \approx \omega(Q')$ and hence by corollary 14.3.11 we are done.

Now assume $P \rightarrow_{\perp_2} Q$. Then, using the result for $\rightarrow_{\perp_1}$, a similar argument shows $P \approx Q$. □

14.3.15. COROLLARY. *Let* $P, Q \in \Lambda\perp$. *Then*

$$P =_{\beta\perp} Q \Rightarrow P \approx Q$$

PROOF. By proposition 10.1.6 (generalized to $\Lambda\perp$) one has $P =_\beta Q \Rightarrow P \approx Q$. By the lemma the same is true for $\rightarrow_\perp$. Since $=_{\beta\perp}$ is generated by $=_\beta$ and $\rightarrow_\perp$, the result follows. □

The following notion is due to Welch.

14.3.16. DEFINITION. (i) Let $M \in \Lambda$ and $\mathscr{F} \subset M$. Then M reduces to N *without touching* $\mathscr{F}$ (notation $M \underset{\text{non } \mathscr{F}}{\twoheadrightarrow} N$) if there is a reduction $\sigma : M \twoheadrightarrow N$ such that a residual of an element of $\mathscr{F}$ is never contracted.

(ii) If $P \subset M$, write $M \underset{\text{non } P}{\twoheadrightarrow} N$ if $M \underset{\text{non } \mathscr{F}_P}{\twoheadrightarrow} N$, where $\mathscr{F}_P$ is the set of all redexes $\subset P$.

14.3.17. LEMMA. *Let $M \underset{\text{non } \mathscr{F}}{\twoheadrightarrow} N$ by a reduction σ. Then*

$$M[\mathscr{F} := \bot] \twoheadrightarrow N[\mathscr{F}' := \bot],$$

where $[\mathscr{F} := \bot]$ denotes the replacement of the ($\subset$-maximal) redexes in $\mathscr{F}$ by $\bot$ and $\mathscr{F}'$ is the set of residuals of $\mathscr{F}$ with respect to σ.

PROOF. By transitivity one may assume $M \overset{\Delta}{\underset{\text{non } \mathscr{F}}{\to}} N$. The conclusion is proved by an easy distinction of cases ((1) Δ disjoint from $\mathscr{F}$; (2) $\Delta \subset \Delta_1 \in \mathscr{F}$; (3) some maximal element of $\mathscr{F}$ is sub Δ). □

The following theorem was first proved by Welch, under the assumption that theorem 14.2.12 was true, namely, that inside out reductions are complete.

14.3.18. PROPOSITION. *Let $C[M], N \in \Lambda$. Suppose $C[M] \twoheadrightarrow N$. Then*

$$\exists M_1 {}_{\beta}\!\twoheadleftarrow M \;\; \exists N_1 {}_{\beta}\!\twoheadleftarrow N \quad C[M_1] \underset{\text{non } M_1}{\twoheadrightarrow} N_1.$$

PROOF. Lift $C[M] \twoheadrightarrow N$ to the +-reduction $C'[M'] \twoheadrightarrow N'$ in $\Lambda \bot^{\mathbb{N}}$. Let M_1' be the +-nf of M'. Then by the CR property for +

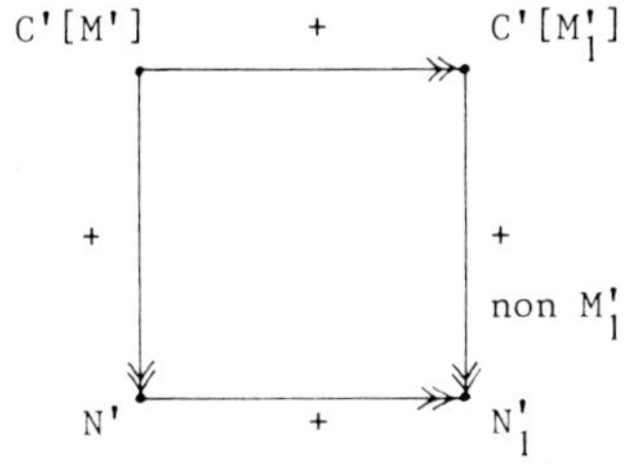

By projecting down one obtains the result. □

The next result was first proved in Wadsworth [1971]. The present proof is due to Lévy [1975].

14.3.19. PROPOSITION. *Let $C[M] \in \Lambda$. Then*

$$\forall P \in \mathscr{A}'(C[M]) \; \exists Q \in \mathscr{A}'(M) \quad P \underset{\sim}{\sqsubseteq} C[Q].$$

PROOF. Let $P \in \mathcal{A}'(C[M])$. Then $P \equiv \omega(N)$ with $C[M] \twoheadrightarrow N$. By proposition 14.3.18 for some $M_1, N_1 \in \Lambda$

(1) $$M \twoheadrightarrow M_1, \qquad N \twoheadrightarrow N_1,$$

(2) $$C[M_1] \underset{\text{non } M_1}{\twoheadrightarrow} N_1.$$

Take $Q \equiv \omega(M_1)$. Then $Q \in \mathcal{A}'(M)$. It remains to show $P \underset{\sim}{\sqsubset} C[Q]$. By (2) and lemma 14.3.17

(3) $$C[M_1][\mathcal{F} := \bot] \twoheadrightarrow_\beta N_1[\mathcal{F}' := \bot],$$

where $\mathcal{F}$ is the set of redex occurrences in M_1. Now

$$\begin{aligned}
P \equiv \omega(N) &\underset{\sim}{\sqsubset} \omega(N_1) && \text{by (1) and lemma 14.3.7 (ii),}\\
&\equiv \omega(N_1[\mathcal{F}' := \bot]) && \text{since all redexes have to be}\\
& && \text{replaced by } \bot \text{ anyway,}\\
&\underset{\sim}{\sqsubset} N_1[\mathcal{F}' := \bot] && \text{by lemma 14.3.7 (i),}\\
&\approx C[M_1][\mathcal{F} := \bot] && \text{by (3) and lemma 14.3.15,}\\
&\equiv C[\alpha(M_1)]\\
&\approx C[\omega(M_1)] && \text{by lemma 14.3.15,}\\
&\equiv C[Q]. \ \square
\end{aligned}$$

14.3.20. COROLLARY. *Let* $C[\ ] \in \Lambda[\ ]$ *and* $M, N \in \Lambda$. *Then*

(i) $C[M] = \bigsqcup\{C[Q] \| Q \in \mathcal{A}'(M)\} = \bigsqcup\{C[Q] \| Q \in \mathcal{A}(M)\}$

(ii) $C[M] = \bigsqcup_n C[M^{[n]}]$.

(iii) $M \underset{\sim}{\sqsubset} N \Rightarrow C[M] \underset{\sim}{\sqsubset} C[N]$.

PROOF. (i) By corollary 14.3.13 one has $C[Q] \underset{\sim}{\sqsubset} C[M]$ for all $Q \in \mathcal{A}(M)$. Therefore

$$\bigsqcup\{C[Q] | Q \in \mathcal{A}'(M)\} \underset{\sim}{\sqsubset} \bigsqcup\{C[Q] | Q \in \mathcal{A}(M)\} \underset{\sim}{\sqsubset} C[M].$$

Since $C[M] = \bigsqcup\{P | P \in \mathcal{A}'(C[M])\}$, by proposition 14.3.10 (ii), the rest follows from the proposition.

(ii) Note that $M^{[n]} \in \mathcal{A}(M)$ and that if $P \in \mathcal{A}(M)$, then $P \underset{\sim}{\sqsubset} M^{[p]}$, for some p; now use (i).

(iii) Assume $M \underset{\sim}{\sqsubseteq} N$. Then

$$C[M] = \bigsqcup\{C[P] | P \in \mathfrak{A}(M)\}, \quad \text{by (i)},$$

$$\underset{\sim}{\sqsubseteq} C[N], \quad \text{by corollary 14.3.13},$$

since $P \underset{\sim}{\sqsubseteq} M \Rightarrow P \underset{\sim}{\sqsubseteq} N$. □

14.3.21. Corollary. *The map* $\lambda\!\!\!\lambda M.C[M] : \Lambda \to \Lambda$ *is continuous with respect to the tree topology.*

Proof. Remember that the sets $O_{M,k} = \{N | M^{[k]} \underset{\sim}{\sqsubseteq} N\}$ form a basis for the tree topology. Therefore we must show that if $C[M] = N$, then

$$\forall k\ \exists m\ \forall M' \quad [M' \in O_{M,m} \Rightarrow C[M'] \in O_{N,k}].$$

Assume $C[M] = N$ and let k be given. Define $P \equiv N^{[k]} \in \mathfrak{A}(C[M])$. By proposition 14.3.19 for some $Q \in \mathfrak{A}'(M)$ one has

(1) $\qquad P \underset{\sim}{\sqsubseteq} C[Q]$

Now $Q \underset{\sim}{\sqsubseteq} M = \bigsqcup\{M^{[m]} | m \in \mathbb{N}\}$, which is (after taking Böhm trees) a directed supremum. Since $\mathrm{BT}(Q)$ is finite, it is compact in $(\mathfrak{B}, \subseteq)$ and hence $Q \underset{\sim}{\sqsubseteq} M^{[m]}$ for some m. It follows that

$$\begin{aligned} M' \in O_{M,m} &\Rightarrow M^{[m]} \underset{\sim}{\sqsubseteq} M' \\ &\Rightarrow Q \underset{\sim}{\sqsubseteq} M' \\ &\Rightarrow C[Q] \underset{\sim}{\sqsubseteq} C[M'] \\ &\Rightarrow P \underset{\sim}{\sqsubseteq} C[M'] \quad \text{by (1)}, \\ &\Rightarrow C[M'] \in O_{N,k} \quad \text{since } P \equiv N^{[k]}. \ \square \end{aligned}$$

14.3.22. Continuity theorem. *On* Λ *the operations abstraction and application are continuous with respect to the tree topology. That is*

(i) *Define* $\mathrm{Abs}_x(M) = \lambda x.M$. *Then* $\mathrm{Abs}_x : \Lambda \to \Lambda$ *is continuous.*

(ii) *Define* $\mathrm{Ap}(M, N) = MN$. *Then* $\mathrm{Ap} : \Lambda^2 \to \Lambda$ *is continuous.*

PROOF. (i) Trivial: $M' \in O_{M,k} \Rightarrow \lambda x.M' \in O_{\lambda x.M,k}$.

(ii) We must show that if $MN = L$, then

$$\forall k\ \exists m,n\ \forall M' \in O_{M,m}\ \forall N' \in O_{N,n}\quad M'N' \in O_{L,k}.$$

So assume $MN = L$ and let k be given. By corollary 14.3.21 Ap is continuous in each of its arguments separately. Therefore there is an n such that

$$N' \in O_{N,n} \Rightarrow MN' \in O_{L,k}.$$

In particular $MN^{(n)} \in O_{L,k}$. Now be continuity in the first argument there is an m such that

$$M' \in O_{M,m} \Rightarrow M'N^{(n)} \in O_{L,k};$$

in particular $M^{(m)}N^{(n)} \in O_{L,k}$. But then

$$M' \in O_{M,m}, N' \in O_{N,n} \Rightarrow$$

$$\Rightarrow M'N' \sqsupseteq\!\!\!\sim M^{(m)}N' \sqsupseteq\!\!\!\sim M^{(m)}N^{(n)} \sqsupseteq\!\!\!\sim L^{(k)}$$

by corollary 14.3.20 (iii),

$$\Rightarrow M'N' \in O_{L,k}. \quad \square$$

The continuity theorem is a memorable result ready for applications. It replaces arguments usually proved by an analysis of reductions. As an example we show the "genericity lemma" (so called because it states that if an unsolvable is mapped on a nf, then every term has that property; in other words unsolvables are generic).

A point x in a topological space X is a *compactification point* if X is the only neighborhood of x.

14.3.23. LEMMA. *Let* $M \in \Lambda$. *Then*:

(i) M *is isolated* $\Leftrightarrow M$ *has a* nf,

(ii) M *is a compactification point* $\Leftrightarrow M$ *is unsolvable.*

PROOF. (i) ($\Rightarrow$) If M is isolated, then $\{M\} = O_{M,n}$ for some n. Therefore

$$\forall P\quad \left[M^{(n)} \sqsubseteq\!\!\!\sim P \Rightarrow P \approx M\right].$$

By taking $P \equiv M^{(n)}$ it follows that $\mathrm{BT}(M) = \mathrm{BT}^n(M)$. Moreover $\mathrm{BT}(M)$ is $\perp$-free. Therefore M has a nf.

($\Leftarrow$) If M has a nf, then BT(M) is finite and $\bot$-free. Therefore $\{M\} = O_{M,k}$, where $k = d(\mathrm{BT}(M))$.

(ii) ($\Rightarrow$) If M is not unsolvable, then $M = \lambda\vec{x}.y\vec{M}$, hence $M^{[1]} \equiv \lambda\vec{x}.y\vec{\bot}$. Therefore $O_{M,1} \neq \Lambda$, so M is not a compactification point.

($\Leftarrow$) If M is unsolvable, then $O_{M,n} = \{P \mid \bot \sqsubseteq P\} = \Lambda$ for all n. Then M is a compactification point. □

14.3.24. PROPOSITION (Genericity lemma). *Let $M, N \in \Lambda$ with M unsolvable and N having a* nf. *Then for all $C[\ \ ] \in \Lambda$*

$$C[M] = N \Rightarrow \forall L \in \Lambda \ \ C[L] = N.$$

PROOF. The set $\{N\}$ is open by lemma 14.3.23. By continuity (corollary 14.3.21) there is a neighborhood O of M such that

$$\forall L \in O \quad C[L] = N.$$

But $O = \Lambda$ by lemma 14.3.23. □

Similarly one obtains the following

14.3.25. COROLLARY. *Let $M, N \in \Lambda$ with M unsolvable and N $\bot$-free. Then for all $C[\ \ ]$ one has*

$$C[M] \precsim N \Rightarrow \forall L \ C[L] \precsim N.$$

PROOF. By continuity one has

$$\forall n \ \exists m \quad C[O_{M,m}] \subseteq O_{N,n}.$$

Since M is unsolvable, $O_{M,m} = \Lambda$ for all m. Hence

$$\forall n \ \forall L \quad C[L] \sqsupseteq N^{(n)}.$$

But then $C[L] \sqsupseteq \bigsqcup_n N^{(n)} = N$. Since N is $\bot$-free one has $C[L] \precsim N$ for all L. □

In exercise 14.5.7 it is shown that this corollary does not hold if $\precsim$ is replaced by $=_\beta$.

14.4. Sequentiality and stability

Berry [1978] showed that the computation of a definable λ-calculus function is sequential rather than parallel. As a consequence it follows that there is no "parallel or" (cf. Plotkin [1977]), i.e. no $F \in \Lambda$ such that

$$
\begin{aligned}
FMN &= \mathbf{I} && \text{if } M \text{ or } N \text{ is solvable,}\\
&= \text{unsolvable} && \text{else.}
\end{aligned}
$$

Such an F is clearly parallel computable (simultaneously try to find the hnf of M and N; if you find one, then give output **I**, else give no output).

Now Berry's results, theorems 14.4.8 and 14.4.10, and some consequences will be presented.

It is convenient to work with contexts with numbered holes.

14.4.1. DEFINITION. (i) The set of *multiple numbered contexts*, notation $\Lambda[\ ]_{\mathbb{N}}$, is defined as follows:

$$
\begin{aligned}
&x, [\ ]_i \in \Lambda[\ ]_{\mathbb{N}},\\
&M, N \in \Lambda[\ ]_{\mathbb{N}} \Rightarrow (MN), (\lambda x.N) \in \Lambda[\ ]_{\mathbb{N}}.
\end{aligned}
$$

Example. $(\lambda x.[\ ]_{13}y)[\ ]_2 \in \Lambda[\ ]_{\mathbb{N}}$.

(ii) Let $C \in \Lambda[\ ]_{\mathbb{N}}$ be such that the "holes" in C are among $[\ ]_{i_1}, \ldots, [\ ]_{i_n}$ with $i_1 < i_2 < \cdots < i_n$. Let $\vec{M} \equiv M_1, \ldots, M_n \in \Lambda$. Then

$$
C[M_1, \ldots, M_n] \equiv C[\vec{M}]
$$

is the result of placing M_j in the hole $[\ ]_{i_j}$ for $1 \leqslant j \leqslant n$ (some free variables in M_j may become bound).

Let $\vec{M} \equiv M_1, \ldots, M_n$. Then $\vec{M} \sqsubseteq \vec{M}'$ means that $\vec{M}' \equiv M_1', \ldots, M_n'$ and $M_i \sqsubseteq M_i'$ for $1 \leqslant i \leqslant n$.

14.4.2. DEFINITION. Let $C \in \Lambda[\ ]_{\mathbb{N}}$, $\vec{M} \in \Lambda$, $C[\vec{M}] = N$ and $N|\alpha = \perp$ (i.e. at node α in $\mathrm{BT}(N)$ one has a $\perp$).

(i) $C[\vec{M}]$ is *α-constant* if $\forall \vec{M}' \sqsupseteq \vec{M}\ C[\vec{M}']|\alpha = \perp$.

(ii) Let $1 \leqslant i \leqslant n$ and $\beta \in \mathrm{Seq}$. Then $N|\alpha (= \perp)$ *is caused by* $M_i|\beta$ (in $C[\vec{M}]$) if

(1) $M_i|\beta = \perp$,

(2) $[M_i'|\beta = \perp \Rightarrow C[\vec{M}']|\alpha = \perp]$ and $[M_i'|\beta = z \Rightarrow C[\vec{M}']|\alpha \neq \perp]$,

for all $\vec{M}' \sqsupseteq \vec{M}$ and fresh variables z.

EXAMPLE. Let $C \equiv \lambda x.x[\ ]_1(\Omega[\ ]_2)$. Then $N \equiv C[\Omega_1, \Omega_2]$ with $\Omega_1 \equiv \Omega_2 \equiv \Omega$, has Böhm tree

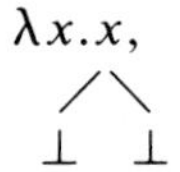

so $N|\langle 0\rangle = N|\langle 1\rangle = \perp$. Now $C[\Omega, \Omega]$ is $\langle 1\rangle$-constant, but not $\langle 0\rangle$-constant. Moreover $N|\langle 0\rangle$ is caused by $\Omega_1|\langle\ \rangle$.

14.4.3. LEMMA. *Let* $C[\vec{\Omega}] = N$ *with* $\vec{\Omega} \equiv \Omega_1, \ldots, \Omega_n$, $\Omega_1 \equiv \cdots \equiv \Omega_n \equiv \Omega$ *and* $N|\alpha = \perp$. *Then either*

(1) $C[\vec{\Omega}]$ *is* α*-constant, or*

(2) $N|\alpha$ *is caused by* $\Omega_i|\langle\ \rangle$ *for some* $1 \leqslant i \leqslant n$.

PROOF. Suppose $C[\vec{\Omega}]$ is not α-constant. Then $C[\vec{M}]\|\alpha \neq \perp$ for some $\vec{M}$. In particular $C[\vec{M}]$ has a hnf, hence its head reduction terminates in, say, k steps. By induction on $(\mathrm{lh}(\alpha), k)$ we will show (2).

By a little thought one sees that C must have one of the following three forms, cf. corollary 8.3.8.

Case 1. $C[\ ] \equiv \lambda\vec{x}.[\ ]_i C_1 \cdots C_m$. Then $\alpha = \langle\ \rangle$ and $N|\langle\ \rangle$ is caused by $\Omega_i|\langle\ \rangle$.

Case 2. $C[\ ] \equiv \lambda\vec{x}.yC_1 \cdots C_m$. Then $\alpha = \langle j\rangle * \alpha'$ with $\alpha' \in \mathrm{Seq}$, $1 \leqslant j \leqslant m$ and $C_j[\vec{\Omega}]\|\alpha' = \perp$. Moreover $C_j[\vec{M}]\|\alpha' \neq \perp$. Hence by the induction hypothesis $C[\vec{\Omega}]\|\alpha = C_j[\vec{\Omega}]\|\alpha'$ is caused by some $\Omega_i|\langle\ \rangle$.

Case 3. $C[\ ] \equiv \lambda\vec{x}.(\lambda y.P)QC_1 \cdots C_m$. Then

$$C[\vec{M}] \to_h \lambda\vec{x}.P[\vec{M}][y := Q[\vec{M}]]C_1[\vec{M}] \cdots$$

$$\equiv C_*[\vec{M}, \vec{M}[y := Q[\vec{M}]]]$$

$$\equiv C_*[\vec{M}, \vec{M}^*].$$

Also $C[\vec{\Omega}] = C_*[\vec{\Omega}, \vec{\Omega}]$. Hence

$$C_*[\vec{\Omega}, \vec{\Omega}]\|\alpha = \perp \quad \text{and} \quad C_*[\vec{M}, \vec{M}^*]\|\alpha \neq \perp.$$

Note that the head reduction of $C_*[\vec{M}, \vec{M}^*]$ to hnf is $< k$. Therefore by the induction hypothesis $N|\alpha$ is caused by some $\Omega_j|\langle\ \rangle$ (in $C_*[\vec{\Omega}, \vec{\Omega}]$). But then it is also caused by the $\Omega_i|\langle\ \rangle$ in $C[\vec{\Omega}]$ which has Ω_j as residual. □

14.4.4. COROLLARY. *Let* $\vec{P} = P_1, \ldots, P_n \in \Lambda\perp$ *all be in* $\beta\perp$-nf *and let* $C[\vec{P}]\|\alpha = \perp$. *Then either*

(1) $C[\vec{P}]$ *is* α*-constant, or*

(2) $C[\vec{P}]\|\alpha$ *is caused by some* $P_i|\beta$ *(with* $1 \leqslant i \leqslant n$ *and* $\beta \in \mathrm{Seq}$*).*

PROOF. Let $C_1 \in \Lambda[\ ]_{\mathbb{N}}$ be obtained from $C[\vec{P}]$ by replacing the different $\perp$'s in the $\vec{P}$ in $C[\vec{P}]$ by $[\ ]_1, [\ ]_2, \ldots$. Then one has $C[\vec{P}] \equiv C_1[\vec{\perp}] \approx C_1[\vec{\Omega}]$ and

$$\forall \vec{P}' \sqsupseteq \vec{P}\ \exists \vec{M}\quad C[\vec{P}'] = C_1[\vec{M}].$$

Now the result follows from lemma 14.4.3. □

14.4.5. DEFINITION. Let $M, N, L \in \Lambda(\perp)$. Then

(i) $M \sqcap N \approx L$ if $\mathrm{BT}(M) \cap \mathrm{BT}(N) = \mathrm{BT}(L)$.

(ii) $M \uparrow N$ if $\exists P\ M, N \sqsubseteq P$.

(iii) For sequences of the same length, one uses the self-explanatory notation $\vec{M} \sqcap \vec{N} \approx \vec{L}$ and $\vec{M} \uparrow \vec{N}$.

EXAMPLE. $\lambda x.xba \sqcap \lambda x.xab \approx \lambda x.x\perp\perp$, $\lambda x.xaa \sqcap \lambda x.xab \approx \lambda x.xa\perp$.

14.4.6. LEMMA. $\forall M, N \in \Lambda(\perp)\ \exists L \in \Lambda\ M \sqcap N \approx L$.

PROOF. Let $A = \mathrm{BT}(M) \cap \mathrm{BT}(N)$. Then A is r.e. and has finitely many free variables. Hence theorem 10.1.23 applies. □

We will work with $M \sqcap N$ as if it is a term. However it is determined only up to $\approx$.

14.4.7. LEMMA. *Let* $C \in \Lambda[\ ]_{\mathbb{N}}$, $\vec{M} \in \Lambda$, $\vec{P} \in \Lambda\perp$ *with* $\vec{M} \uparrow \vec{P}$ *and* $\vec{P} \equiv P_1, \ldots, P_n$ *all in* $\beta\perp$-nf. *Then*

$$C[\vec{M} \sqcap \vec{P}] \approx C[\vec{M}] \sqcap C[\vec{P}].$$

PROOF. Clearly $\vec{M} \sqcap \vec{P} \sqsubseteq \vec{M}, \vec{P}$. Hence by monotonicity $C[\vec{M} \sqcap \vec{P}] \sqsubseteq C[\vec{M}] \sqcap C[\vec{P}]$. Suppose the inequality is strict. Then for some $\alpha \in \mathrm{Seq}$

$$C[\vec{M} \sqcap \vec{P}] | \alpha = \perp, \qquad (C[\vec{M}] \sqcap C[\vec{P}]) | \alpha \neq \perp,$$

Hence $C[\vec{M}] \| \alpha \neq \perp$ and $C[\vec{P}] \| \alpha \neq \perp$. Therefore $C[\vec{M} \sqcap \vec{P}]$ is not α-constant and it follows by corollary 14.4.4 that $C[\vec{M} \sqcap \vec{P}] \| \alpha$ is caused by some $(M_i \sqcap P_i) \| \beta$. Then $(M_i \sqcap P_i) | \beta = \perp$, $M_i | \beta \neq \perp$ (otherwise $C[\vec{M}] \| \alpha = \perp$) and $P_i | \beta \neq \perp$ (similarly). This contradicts $M_i \uparrow P_i$. □

Now we are able to state and prove the sequentiality theorem. This result is about contexts $C[\ ]$ considered as a function with the arguments to be put in the holes. It states that if in (the Böhm tree of) the output

$C[\vec{M}]$ there is a $\perp$, then either this $\perp$ is independent of the arguments $\vec{M}$, or $\perp$ is caused by a specific $\perp$ in (the Böhm tree of) one of the arguments. This is not the case with functions like the parallel or:

$$\perp \text{“or”} \perp = \perp,$$

$$\perp \text{“or”} \mathbf{T} = \mathbf{T},$$

$$\mathbf{T} \text{“or”} \perp = \mathbf{T}.$$

14.4.8. Sequentiality Theorem. *Let* $\vec{M} = M_1, \ldots, M_n$ *and* $C[\vec{M}]\|\alpha = \perp$. *Then either*

(1) $C[\vec{M}]$ *is* α*-constant, or*

(2) $C[\vec{M}]\|\alpha$ *is caused by some* $M_i|\beta$ *with* $1 \leqslant i \leqslant n$ *and* $\beta \in \text{Seq}$.

Proof. Suppose $C[\vec{M}]$ is not α-constant. Then

(3) $C[\vec{M}']\|\alpha \neq \perp$

for some $\vec{M}' \underset{\sim}{\sqsupset} \vec{M}$. By continuity it follows that

(4) $C[\vec{P}]\|\alpha \neq \perp$ for some $P_i \in \mathscr{A}(M_i')$, $1 \leqslant i \leqslant n$.

Since $\vec{P} \uparrow \vec{M}$ (namely both $\underset{\sim}{\sqsubseteq} \vec{M}'$) it follows by lemma 14.4.7 that

$$C[\vec{P} \sqcap \vec{M}]|\alpha = (C[\vec{P}] \sqcap C[\vec{M}])|\alpha = \perp,$$

as $C[\vec{M}]\|\alpha = \perp$. By (3) it follows that $C[\vec{P} \sqcap \vec{M}]$ is not α-constant. Since the $\vec{P} \sqcap \vec{M}$ have finite Böhm trees it follows by corollary 14.4.4 that

(5) $C[\vec{P} \sqcap \vec{M}]\|\alpha$ is caused by some $P_i \sqcap M_i|\beta$.

Claim: $C[\vec{M}]\|\alpha$ is caused by $M_i|\beta$. Indeed, note that $P_i|\beta \neq \perp$ (since otherwise $C[\vec{P}]\|\alpha = \perp$ by (5), contradicting (4)) and by (5) one has $P_i \sqcap M_i|\beta = \perp$; therefore $M_i|\beta = \perp$.

Moreover assume $\vec{M} \underset{\sim}{\sqsubseteq} \vec{N}$. Then $\vec{P} \sqcap \vec{M} \underset{\sim}{\sqsubseteq} \vec{N}$, hence

$$N_i|\beta = \perp \Rightarrow C[\vec{N}]|\alpha = \perp$$

and

$$N_i|\beta = z(\text{fresh}) \Rightarrow C[\vec{N}]|\alpha \neq \perp. \quad \square$$

As a consequence of the sequentiality theorem we will now show that λ-definable functions are “stable”, i.e. preserve (Böhm tree) intersections of bounded sets.

14.4.9. Definition. Let $\mathscr{X} \subseteq \Lambda$. Then

(i) $\sqcap \mathscr{X} \approx M$ if $\text{BT}(M) = \bigcap \{\text{BT}(N) | N \in \mathscr{X}\}$.

(ii) $\uparrow \mathscr{X}$ if $\exists M \in \Lambda\ \forall N \in \mathscr{X}\ N \underset{\sim}{\sqsubseteq} M$.

It is not the case that for all $\mathcal{X} \subseteq \Lambda$ there is an $M \in \Lambda$ such that $\sqcap \mathcal{X} \approx M$. However, $\cap \{\mathrm{BT}(N) | N \in \mathcal{X}\}$ is always a Böhm-like tree.

14.4.10. STABILITY THEOREM. *Let* $\vec{\mathcal{X}} = \mathcal{X}_1 \ldots, \mathcal{X}_n \subseteq \Lambda$ *and assume* $\uparrow \mathcal{X}_1, \ldots, \uparrow \mathcal{X}_n$. *Then*

$$C[\sqcap \mathcal{X}_1, \ldots, \sqcap \mathcal{X}_n] \approx \sqcap C[\mathcal{X}_1, \ldots, \mathcal{X}_n];$$

more precisely, if $\sqcap \mathcal{X}_i \approx M_i$ *for* $1 \leqslant i \leqslant n$, *then*

$$C[M_1, \ldots, M_n] \approx \sqcap \{C[N_1, \ldots, N_n] | N_i \in \mathcal{X}_i, 1 \leqslant i \leqslant n\}.$$

PROOF. Clearly $M_i \underset{\sim}{\sqsubseteq} N_i$ for all $N_i \in \mathcal{X}_i$. Therefore by monotonicity

$$\mathrm{BT}(C[\vec{M}]) \subseteq \cap \{\mathrm{BT}(C[\vec{N}]) | \vec{N} \in \vec{\mathcal{X}}\}.$$

Arguing towards a contradiction, suppose that the inequality is strict. Then for some $\alpha \in \mathrm{Seq}$ one has

(1) $C[\vec{M}] | \alpha = \perp$, and

(2) $\forall \vec{N} \in \vec{\mathcal{X}}\ C[\vec{N}] | \alpha \neq \perp$.

It follows that $C[\vec{M}]$ is not α-constant. Hence by the sequentiality theorem, $C[\vec{M}] | \alpha$ is caused by some $M_i | \beta$. Then for all $\vec{N} \in \vec{\mathcal{X}}$ one has $\vec{M} \underset{\sim}{\sqsubseteq} \vec{N}$ and

$$N_i | \beta = \perp \Rightarrow C[\vec{N}] | \alpha = \perp .$$

Therefore by (2) one has $\forall N_i \in \mathcal{X}_i\ N_i | \beta \neq \perp$. Since $\uparrow \mathcal{X}_i$, for all $N, N' \in \mathcal{X}_i$ one has $N | \beta = N' | \beta \neq \perp$. Therefore $M_i | \beta = \sqcap \mathcal{X}_i | \beta \neq \perp$, contradicting that $M_i | \beta$ causes $C[\vec{M}] | \alpha$. □

14.4.11. COROLLARY. *If* $\vec{M} \uparrow \vec{N}$, *then* $C[\vec{M} \sqcap \vec{N}] \approx C[\vec{M}] \sqcap C[\vec{N}]$.

PROOF. Immediate by the theorem since by lemma 14.4.6 $\vec{M} \sqcap \vec{N}$ always exists as a term. □

The following consequence of the sequentiality theorem shows that if λ-definable function C of n-arguments is constant (modulo $\approx$) on n "perpendicular lines", then C is constant (mod $\approx$) on all of Λ^n.

14.4.12. THEOREM. *Let* $n \in \mathbb{N}$ *and* $M_{ij}, N_i \in \Lambda$ *for* $1 \leqslant i \leqslant n$ *and* $1 \leqslant j \leqslant n$. *Suppose that for all* $Z \in \Lambda$

$$\begin{array}{ll} C[M_{11}, M_{12}, \cdots, M_{1n-1}, Z] & \approx N_1, \\ C[M_{21}, M_{22}, \cdots, Z, \quad M_{2n}] & \approx N_2, \\ \cdots & \\ C[Z, \quad M_{n2}, \cdots, M_{n\,n-1}, M_{nn}] & \approx N_n. \end{array}$$

Then for all $\vec{Z} = Z_1, \ldots, Z_n \in \Lambda$ *one has*

$$C[\vec{Z}] \approx N \approx N_1 \approx \cdots \approx N_n.$$

PROOF. For simplicity suppose $n = 3$. Then for all Z

$$(1) \qquad \begin{cases} C[M_{11}, M_{12}, Z \quad] \approx N_1, \\ C[M_{21}, Z, \quad M_{23}] \approx N_2, \\ C[Z, \quad M_{32}, M_{33}] \approx N_3. \end{cases}$$

Let $N = C[\Omega, \Omega, \Omega]$. Then $N \underset{\sim}{\sqsubset} N_i$, $1 \leqslant i \leqslant 3$. Suppose one inequality is strict. Then for some $\alpha \in \text{Seq}$ one has $N|\alpha = \bot$ and $N_i|\alpha \neq \bot$. It follows that $C[\vec{\Omega}]$ is not α-constant, hence by the sequentiality theorem $N|\alpha$ is caused by say $\Omega_3|\langle\ \rangle$. But then

$$C[M_{11}, M_{12}, \Omega]|\alpha = \bot, \qquad C[M_{11}, M_{12}, z]|\alpha \neq \bot,$$

contradicting (1). So we have proved $N \approx N_1 \approx N_2 \approx N_3$.

Suppose $\exists M_1, M_2, M_3\ N' \equiv C[M_1, M_2, M_3] \underset{\sim}{\sqsupset} N$, say $N|\alpha = \bot$ and $N'|\alpha \neq \bot$. Then $C[\vec{\Omega}]$ is not α-constant, hence $N|\alpha$ is caused by, say, $\Omega_2|\langle\ \rangle$. But then

$$C[M_{21}, z, M_{23}] \approx N_2 \approx N$$

by (1) and $C[M_{21}, z, M_{23}]|\alpha \neq \bot$. Contradiction. □

The theorem probably also holds with $\approx$ replaced by $=_\beta$.

The following application shows that there is no "parallel or" in the λ-calculus.

APPLICATION. For no $F \in \Lambda$ one has

$$\begin{array}{ll} FMN = \mathbf{I} & \text{if } M \text{ or } N \text{ solvable,} \\ \quad = \text{unsolvable} & \text{else.} \end{array}$$

Indeed, otherwise $\forall Z$, $F\mathbf{I}Z \approx FZ\mathbf{I} \approx \mathbf{I}$ but $F\Omega\Omega \approx \Omega$, contradicting the theorem.

The following results, taken from Coppo et al. [1978], were needed in § 10.4.

14.4.13. LEMMA. *If* $\mathscr{F} = \{M_1, \ldots, M_n\} \subseteq \Lambda$ *with* $n > 1$ *is separable, then there is an* $\alpha \in \mathrm{Seq}$ *useful for* $\mathscr{F}$.

PROOF. Let $C[M_i] = x_i$, $1 \leqslant i \leqslant n$, and suppose towards a contradiction that

(1) $\qquad \neg\exists\alpha \in \mathrm{Seq} \quad \alpha$ is useful for $\mathscr{F}$.

By continuity, corollary 14.3.21, one has for some $k \in \mathbb{N}$

(2) $\qquad C[M_i^{[k]}] = x_i, \quad 1 \leqslant i \leqslant n.$

By making some η-expansions in the $M_i^{[k]}$ one may assume that for $1 \leqslant i,j \leqslant n$

(3) $\qquad M_i^{[k]} \sim_\alpha M_j^{[k]} \Rightarrow \mathrm{BT}(M_i^{[k]})(\alpha) = \mathrm{BT}(M_j^{[k]})(\alpha).$

[Use that the $M_i^{[k]}$ have finite Böhm trees. In (2) one will get on the RHS some η-expansions of x_i; this does not affect the separability.]

By (1) no $\alpha \in \mathrm{Seq}$ is useful for $\mathscr{F}^{[k]} = \{M_1^{[k]}, \ldots\}$; hence

(4) $\qquad M_i^{[k]} \not\sim_\alpha M_j^{[k]} \Rightarrow \exists h \;\; M_h^{[k]}|\alpha = \bot.$

Replace in $\mathrm{BT}(M_i^{[k]})$ all labels at nodes α with $\exists h \;\; M_h^{[k]}|\alpha = \bot$ by $\bot$. By (3) and (4) the result, say A, is independent of i. Let

$$D[\;\vec{}\;] \equiv D[\;\;]_1 \cdots [\;\;]_m \equiv M[A][\bot := [\;\;]].$$

Then there are $\vec{N}_i = N_{i1}, \ldots, N_{im}$ such that for $1 \leqslant i \leqslant n$

(5) $\qquad M_i^{[k]} \approx D[\vec{N}_i],$

(6) $\qquad \forall j \; \exists i \quad N_{ij} = \Omega.$

Consider $B = \mathrm{BT}(C[D[\vec{\Omega}]])$, with $\Omega_j = \Omega$, $1 \leqslant j \leqslant m$.

Case 1. B is $\bot$-free. Then by monotonicity (corollary 14.3.20(iii))

$$\mathrm{BT}(C[M_i^{[k]}]) = \mathrm{BT}(C[D[\vec{N}_i]]) = B$$

independently of i; this contradicts (2).

Case 2. $B|\beta = \perp$, for some β. By the sequentiality theorem 14.4.8 and (2) this must be caused by say Ω_j. By (6) one has $N_{ij} = \Omega$ for some i. Then

$$\begin{aligned}\perp &= \mathrm{BT}(C[D[\vec{N}_i]])|\beta\\ &= \mathrm{BT}(x_i)|\beta, \quad \text{by (2), (5);}\end{aligned}$$

again a contradiction. □

14.4.14. PROPOSITION. *If* $\mathcal{F} = \{M_1, \ldots, M_n\}$ *is separable, then* $\mathcal{F}$ *is distinct.*

PROOF. By induction on n. If $n = 1$, then $\mathcal{F}$ is distinct by definition. If $n > 1$, then by the previous lemma there is a useful α for $\mathcal{F}$. The $\sim_\alpha$ classes in $\mathcal{F}$ are still separable and of smaller cardinality. By the induction hypothesis they are distinct. Therefore $\mathcal{F}$ is distinct. □

14.5. Exercises

14.5.1. (i) Show that

$$M \twoheadrightarrow N \Rightarrow \exists N'\left[M \underset{\text{i.o.}}{\twoheadrightarrow} N' \wedge N \underset{\text{i.o.}}{\twoheadrightarrow} N'\right].$$

(ii) Show that

$$M \twoheadrightarrow N \not\Rightarrow M \underset{\text{i.o.}}{\twoheadrightarrow} N$$

14.5.2. (i) Suppose $M \overset{\Delta}{\rightarrow} N \equiv (\lambda y.R)S$ and M is not a redex. Show that either

$$M \equiv \mathbf{I}(\lambda y.R)S \quad \text{and} \quad \Delta \equiv \mathbf{I}(\lambda y.R)$$

or

$$M \equiv (\lambda xy.R_1)QS, \qquad \Delta \equiv (\lambda xy.R_1)Q \quad \text{and} \quad R_1[x:=Q] \equiv R.$$

(ii) Suppose $M[x:= N]$ is a β-redex and $M \not\equiv x$. Show that $M \equiv xQ$ and $N \equiv (\lambda y.P)$.

14.5.3. (Creation of redexes, Lévy [1978].) Let $M \overset{\Delta}{\rightarrow}_\beta N$ and suppose $(\lambda y.R)S \subseteq N$ is created in this one step reduction (i.e. not residual of a redex in M). Show that $M \rightarrow N$ must be one of the following cases:

(1) $C[\mathbf{I}(\lambda y.R)S] \rightarrow C[(\lambda y.R)S]$
(2) $C[(\lambda xy.R_1)QS] \rightarrow C[(\lambda y.R_1[x:= Q])S] \equiv C[(\lambda y.R)S]$
(3) $C[(\lambda x.D[xS])(\lambda y.R)] \rightarrow C[D[(\lambda y.R)S]]$.

14.5.4. Show that there is essentially one $M \in \Lambda$ such that $M \rightarrow M$. (i.e. $M \rightarrow M$ but not so for a proper subterm of M.) [*Hint*: Use exercise 14.5.2 (ii).]

14.5.5. (Lévy's labelled λ-calculus (as formulated in Klop [1980]).) Let $L_0 = \{a, b, c, \ldots\}$ be an infinite set of symbols. Define inductively the set L of Lévy labels

$$\begin{aligned}&\alpha \in L_0 \Rightarrow \alpha \in L,\\ &\alpha, \beta \in L \Rightarrow \alpha\beta \in L,\\ &\alpha \in L \Rightarrow \underline{\alpha} \in L.\end{aligned}$$

Here $\alpha\beta$ is the concatenation of α and β without brackets.

Λ^L is defined by adding to the formation rules of λ-terms

$$M \in \Lambda^L, \alpha \in L \Rightarrow (M^\alpha) \in \Lambda^L.$$

Substitution on Λ^L is defined by adding the clause

$$(M)^\alpha[x:=L] \equiv (M[x:=L])^\alpha$$

Let $P \subseteq L$ be given. The following notions of reduction are defined on Λ^L:

$$\boldsymbol{\beta}^P: (\lambda x.M)^\alpha N \to M^\alpha[x:=N^\alpha] \quad \text{provided that } \alpha \in P,$$
$$\boldsymbol{lab}: (M^\alpha)^\beta \to M^{\alpha\beta},$$
$$\boldsymbol{\beta}_L^P = \boldsymbol{\beta}^P \cup \boldsymbol{lab}.$$

Write β^P for β_l^P. Define for $\alpha \in L$ the height $h(\alpha)$:

$$h(\alpha) = 0 \quad \textit{if } \alpha \in L_0,$$

$$h(\alpha\beta) = \max\{h(\alpha), h(\beta)\},$$

$$h(\underline{\alpha}) = h(\alpha) + 1.$$

$P \subseteq L$ is bounded if $\exists n \forall \alpha[\alpha \in P \Rightarrow h(\alpha) \leqslant n]$.

(i) Show that if P is bounded, then β^P is strongly normalizing. [*Hint.* Use SN for +-reduction.]

(ii) Let $M, N \in \Lambda$ and $\sigma: M \twoheadrightarrow N$, $\tau: M \twoheadrightarrow N$. Let $M' \in \Lambda^L$ be M with all subterms labelled by different symbols in L_0. Show that σ, τ can be lifted to $\sigma', \tau': M' \to_{\beta^P} N'$. Moreover

$$\sigma \simeq \tau \quad \text{iff} \quad \sigma' \equiv \tau'.$$

14.5.6. Show that (i) $\neg \exists F \in \Lambda\ F\mathbf{I}\Omega = \mathbf{K} \wedge F\Omega\mathbf{I} = \mathbf{S}$,

(ii) $\neg \exists F, G \in \Lambda^0\ FGx = FxG = x$.

14.5.7. Show that

$$C[M] = N, M \text{ unsolvable and } N \perp\text{-free} \not\Rightarrow \forall P\ C[P] = N.$$

[*Hint.* Let $C[x]$ push x into infinity" in BT($C[x]$).]

14.5.8. (i) Show that application Ap : $\Lambda \times \Lambda \to \Lambda$ is not an open map.

(ii) Show that the λ-calculus operations are in general not uniformly continuous in the following sense: there is an $F \in \Lambda^0$ such that not

$$\forall k\ \exists k'\ \forall M, N\ [N \in O_{M,k'} \Rightarrow FN \in O_{FM,k}].$$

(iii) Let $f: \Lambda \to \Lambda$ be a continuous map. Show that in general there is no $F \in \Lambda$ such that $\forall M\ FM = f(M)$.

14.5.9. Let σ, τ be two β-reductions. Show that

$$\sigma \simeq \tau \Rightarrow \sigma \simeq_K \tau$$

14.5.10. Construct a set $\mathcal{X} \subseteq \Lambda^0$ such that $\cap\{\text{BT}(M) | M \in \mathcal{X}\}$ is not the Böhm tree of a term.

14.5.11. Show that $\mathcal{Q}(M) = \{\omega(N) | N =_\beta M\}$.

CHAPTER 15

OTHER NOTIONS OF REDUCTION

15.1. BH-reduction

Because $\beta\eta$-reduction analyzes the equality of the extensional λ-calculus $\boldsymbol{\lambda\eta}$, it is useful to have a closer look at this notion. The first aim is to prove that

$$M \text{ has a } \beta\text{-nf} \Leftrightarrow M \text{ has a } \beta\eta\text{-nf}.$$

Originally this was proved in Curry et al. [1972]. The proof below is a simplification of that in Barendregt et al. [1976] and occupies 15.1.1–15.1.5.

We extend the set Λ with markers "η" to trace η-redexes.

15.1.1. DEFINITION. (i) Λ^η is the set of terms defined as follows.

$$x \in \Lambda^\eta \quad \text{for variables } x,$$
$$P, Q \in \Lambda^\eta \Rightarrow (PQ) \in \Lambda^\eta,$$
$$P \in \Lambda^\eta \Rightarrow (\lambda x.P) \in \Lambda^\eta,$$
$$P \in \Lambda^\eta \Rightarrow P^\eta \in \Lambda^\eta.$$

(ii) On Λ^η we define the notion of reduction $\boldsymbol{\beta}^\eta$ by the following contraction rules

$$\boldsymbol{\beta}^\eta \begin{cases} (\lambda x.P)Q \to P[x := Q] \\ P^\eta Q \to PQ \end{cases}$$

where $P^\eta[x := Q] \equiv (P[x := Q])^\eta$.

(iii) If $P \in \Lambda^\eta$, then $|P|$ is P without η's.

(iv) $\varphi : \Lambda^\eta \to \Lambda$ is defined by

$$\varphi(x) = x,$$

$$\varphi(PQ) = \varphi(P)\varphi(Q),$$

$$\varphi(\lambda x.P) = \lambda x.\varphi(P),$$

$$\varphi(P^\eta) = \lambda z.\varphi(P)z.$$

NOTATION. $P \overset{||}{\rightarrow} M$ means $|P| \equiv M$; similarly for φ.

15.1.2. LEMMA. *Let* $P, Q \in \Lambda^\eta$ *and* $M, M' \in \Lambda$. *Then*

(i) $P \twoheadrightarrow_{\beta\eta} Q \Rightarrow \varphi(P) \twoheadrightarrow_\beta \varphi(Q)$.

(ii) $\varphi(P) \twoheadrightarrow_\eta |P|$.

(iii)

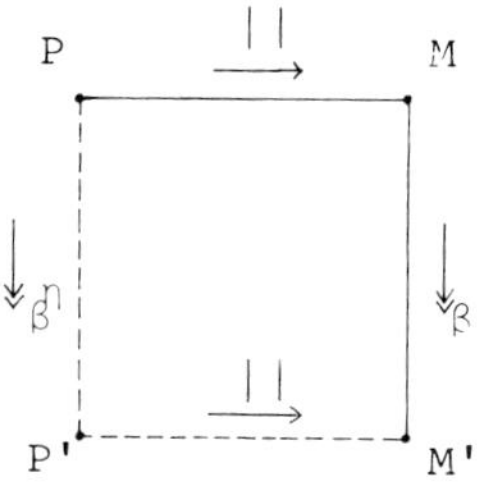

$P, P' \in \Lambda^\eta$;

$M, M' \in \Lambda$.

PROOF. (i) By induction on the generation of $\twoheadrightarrow_{\beta\eta}$. using $\varphi(P[x:=Q]) \equiv \varphi(P)[x:=\varphi(Q)]$.

(ii) By induction on the structure of P.

(iii) The $\twoheadrightarrow_\beta$ reduction can be imitated by $\twoheadrightarrow_{\beta\eta}$ since the η's are not in the way (i.e. $P_1^\eta P_2 \rightarrow_{\beta\eta} P_1 P_2$). □

15.1.3. LEMMA. *Let* $P \in \Lambda^\eta$. *Then*

$$|P| \text{ is a } \beta\text{-nf} \Rightarrow \varphi(P) \text{ has a } \beta\text{-nf}.$$

PROOF. Induction on the structure of $|P|$. First note that

(1) $\varphi(P^{\eta\eta}) =_\beta \varphi(P^\eta)$,

(2) $\varphi((\lambda x.P)^\eta) =_\beta \varphi(\lambda x.P)$,

(3) $\varphi(P^\eta Q) =_\beta \varphi(PQ)$.

Case 1. $|P| \equiv x$. Then $P \equiv x^{\cdots}$, where $\cdots$ indicate zero or more η's. Hence by (1) it follows that $\varphi(P) \equiv x$ or $\equiv \lambda z.xz$ and we are done.

Case 2. $|P| \equiv \lambda x.M$. Then $P \equiv (\lambda x.Q)^{\cdots}$. By (2)

$$\varphi(P) =_\beta \varphi(\lambda x.Q) \equiv \lambda x.\varphi(Q)$$

and the result follows by the induction hypothesis.

Case 3. $|P| \equiv xM_1 \cdots M_n$. Then $P \equiv (\cdots(x^{\cdots}P_1)^{\cdots} \cdots P_n)^{\cdots}$. Now by (3) and (1) one has either

$$\varphi(P) =_\beta \varphi(xP_1 \cdots P_n) = x\varphi(P_1) \cdots \varphi(P_n)$$

or

$$\varphi(P) =_\beta \varphi((xP_1 \cdots P_n)^\eta) = \lambda z.x\varphi(P_1) \cdots \varphi(P_n)z.$$

In both cases the result follows from the induction hypothesis. □

15.1.4. LEMMA. *If* $M \rightarrow_\eta M'$ *and* M' *has a* β-nf, *then* M *has one too.*

PROOF. Let $M \equiv C[\lambda x.Lx]$, $M' \equiv C[L]$ and N' be the nf of M'. Take $P \equiv C[L^\eta]$. Then $\varphi(P) \equiv M$ and $|P| \equiv M'$ and we have, using lemma 15.1.2,

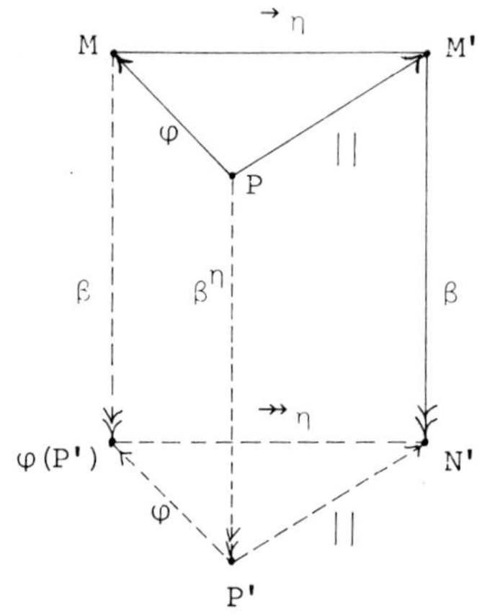

FIG. 15.1.

By lemma 15.1.3 it follows that $\varphi(P')$ and therefore M has a β-nf. □

15.1.5. COROLLARY. *M has a* β-nf $\Leftrightarrow$ *M has a* $\beta\eta$-nf.

PROOF. (⇒) Trivial, since η contractions decrease the length of a term and do not create new redexes.

(⇐) By induction on the number of steps in a $\beta\eta$-reduction of M to $\beta\eta$-nf. □

15.1.6. COROLLARY (Postponement of η-reductions).

$$M \twoheadrightarrow_{\beta\eta} N \Rightarrow \exists L \ \ M \twoheadrightarrow_\beta L \twoheadrightarrow_\eta N.$$

PROOF. Figure 15.1 shows

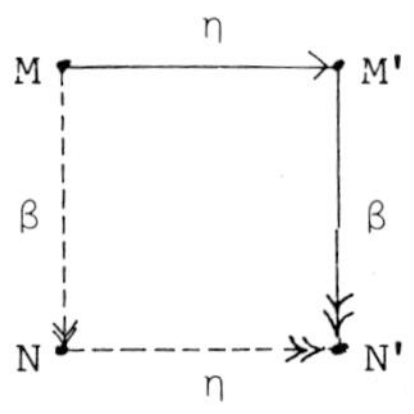

hence

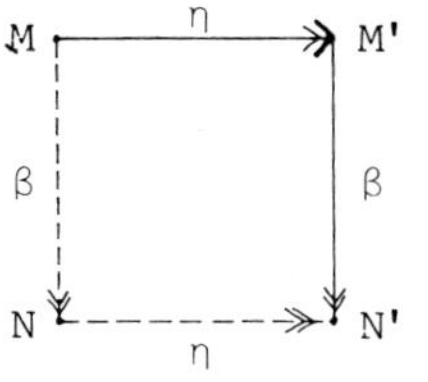

Therefore

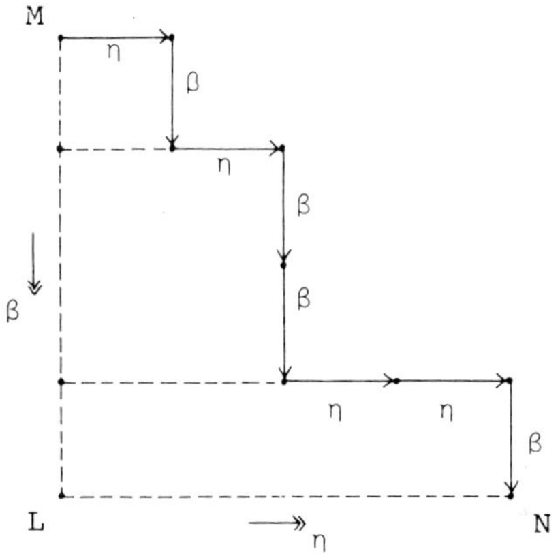

FIG. 15.2.

□

Remember that $M \in \Lambda$ is $\beta\eta$-solvable iff $\exists \vec{P}\ M^* \vec{P} =_{\beta\eta} \mathbf{I}$, where M^* is the closure of M.

15.1.7. PROPOSITION. *M is $\beta\eta$-solvable$\Leftrightarrow$$M$ is solvable.*

PROOF. ($\Leftarrow$) Trivial.

($\Rightarrow$) Let $M^*\vec{P} =_{\beta\eta} \mathbf{I}$. By corollary 15.1.5 it follows that $M^*\vec{P}$ has a β-nf, say $M^*\vec{P} =_{\beta} N$. Then $N =_{\beta\eta} \mathbf{I}$, hence $N \twoheadrightarrow_{\beta\eta} \mathbf{I}$ by corollary 3.3.10 (i). Since N is a β-nf, it follows that $N \twoheadrightarrow_{\eta} \mathbf{I}$ (contraction of η-redexes does not create β-redexes). Let k be the number of steps in a reduction $\sigma : N \twoheadrightarrow_{\eta} \mathbf{I}$. By induction on k it follows that

(1) $\qquad N \equiv \lambda x_1 \cdots x_n . x_1 N_2 \cdots N_n,$

with $n \geqslant 1$, $\mathrm{FV}(N_i) = \{x_i\}$ and

(2) $\qquad N_i \twoheadrightarrow_{\eta} x_i$ in less than k steps.

Again by induction on k we show that N is solvable.

If $k=0$, then $N \equiv \mathbf{I}$ and we are done. So let
$k>0$. Then $n \geqslant 2$. By (2) and the substitutivity of η it follows that $N_i[x_i := \mathbf{I}] \twoheadrightarrow_\eta \mathbf{I}$ in less than k steps. Hence by the induction hypothesis

$$\exists P_{i1} \cdots P_{ik_i} \quad N_i[x_i := \mathbf{I}] P_{i1} \cdots P_{ik_i} = \mathbf{I}, \quad 2 \leqslant i \leqslant n.$$

Then

$$N L_1 \cdots L_n = \mathbf{I}$$

where $L_1 \equiv \lambda y_2 \cdots y_n.(y_2 P_{11} \cdots P_{1k_1}) \cdots (y_n P_{n1} \cdots P_{nk_n})$ and $L_2 \equiv \cdots \equiv L_n \equiv \mathbf{I}$. So indeed N is solvable.

It follows that $M^* \vec{P} \vec{L} = \mathbf{I}$ and we are done. □

Finally we mention that in Klop [1980] a natural form of the standardization theorem is proved for $\beta\eta$-reduction and that contracting always the leftmost $\beta\eta$-redex is a normalizing strategy. Because these results are much more complicated than for β-reduction (for example the first statement does not immediately imply the second one) time does not permit us to include them.

15.2. BHΩ-reduction

The notion of reduction $\mathbf{\Omega}$ is introduced because $\boldsymbol{\beta} \cup \mathbf{\Omega}$ analyzes provability in the theory $\mathcal{H}$. This section proves several results about this notion in connection with $\beta\eta$-reduction.

15.2.1. Definition. (i) The notion of reduction $\mathbf{\Omega}$ is defined by the following contraction rule

$$\mathbf{\Omega} : M \to \Omega \quad \text{if } M \text{ is unsolvable and } M \not\equiv \Omega.$$

(ii) $\boldsymbol{\beta\Omega} = \boldsymbol{\beta} \cup \mathbf{\Omega}$; $\boldsymbol{\beta\eta\Omega} = \boldsymbol{\beta\eta} \cup \mathbf{\Omega}$.

15.2.2. Lemma. *$\mathbf{\Omega}$ is substitutive and hence so are $\boldsymbol{\beta\Omega}$ and $\boldsymbol{\beta\eta\Omega}$.*

Proof. Let $(M, \Omega) \in \mathbf{\Omega}$. Then M is unsolvable, and so $M[x:=N]$ is unsolvable for all N by corollary 8.3.4. Therefore

$$\big(M[x:=N], \Omega(\equiv \Omega[x:=N])\big) \in \mathbf{\Omega}. \quad \square$$

In order to show that $\boldsymbol{\beta\eta\Omega}$ is CR we need that if M is an $\mathbf{\Omega}$-redex and within M a $\boldsymbol{\beta}$-, $\boldsymbol{\eta}$- or $\mathbf{\Omega}$-contraction takes place, then the resulting M' is still an $\mathbf{\Omega}$-redex. The following notion is due to Wadsworth.

15.2.3. DEFINITION. M is *solvably equivalent* with M' (notation $M \sim_s M'$) if

$$\forall C[\ \ ]\ \ [C[M] \text{ solvable} \Leftrightarrow C[M'] \text{ solvable}].$$

Clearly $\sim_s$ is an equality relation on Λ.

15.2.4. LEMMA. (i) $M =_\beta N \Rightarrow M \sim_s N$.
(ii) $M =_\eta N \Rightarrow M \sim_s N$.
(iii) $M =_\Omega N \Rightarrow M \sim_s N$.

PROOF. (i) Let $M =_\beta N$ and $C[M]$ be solvable. Then $C^*[M]\vec{P} = \mathsf{I}$ and hence $C^*[N]\vec{P} = \mathsf{I}$, where $C^*[\ \ ] \equiv \lambda\vec{x}.C[\ \ ]$. So $C[N]$ is solvable.

(ii) Let $M =_\eta N$ and $C[M]$ be solvable. Then $C^*[N]\vec{P} =_\eta C^*[M]\vec{P} = \mathsf{I}$ for some $\vec{P}$. Hence $C[N]$ is $\beta\eta$-solvable and so it is solvable by proposition 15.1.7.

(iii) Since $\sim_s$ is an equality relation it is sufficient to show for $(M, \Omega) \in \mathbf{\Omega}$ that $M \sim_s \Omega$. So let M be unsolvable and suppose $C[M]$ is solvable. Then for some $\vec{P}$, $\vec{x}$ one has

$$(\lambda\vec{x}.C[M])\vec{P} = \mathsf{I}.$$

By the genericity lemma, proposition 14.3.24, it follows that

$$(\lambda\vec{x}.C[\Omega])\vec{P} = \mathsf{I}.$$

Therefore $C[\Omega]$ is solvable. Similarly, one shows

$$C[\Omega] \text{ solvable} \Rightarrow C[M] \text{ solvable}. \quad \square$$

15.2.5. LEMMA. *The notion of reduction* $\mathbf{\Omega}$ *is* CR.

PROOF. By lemma 3.2.2 it is sufficient to show that $\underline{\rightarrow}_\Omega \models \diamond$. Assume $M \overset{\Delta_1}{\underline{\rightarrow}}_\Omega M_1$, $M \overset{\Delta_2}{\underline{\rightarrow}}_\Omega M_2$ (if $M \equiv M_1$ or $M \equiv M_2$, then the situation is trivial).

Case 1. Δ_1, Δ_2 are disjoint subterms of M. Then one can find a common reduct M_3 by replacing both Δ_1, Δ in M by $\mathbf{\Omega}$.

Case 2. Δ_1 and Δ_2 overlap, say $\Delta_1 \subset \Delta_2$. Then take $M_3 \equiv M_2$. This works,

$$\begin{array}{lcl} M \equiv C[\Delta_2] \equiv C[D[\Delta_1]] & \overset{\Delta_2}{\rightarrow} & M_2 \equiv C[\mathbf{\Omega}] \\ \Delta_1 \downarrow & & \downarrow \emptyset \\ M_1 \equiv C[D[\mathbf{\Omega}]] & \overset{D[\Omega]}{\rightarrow} & M_3 \equiv C[\mathbf{\Omega}] \end{array}$$

FIG. 15.3.

for $\Delta_1 \sim_s \mathbf{\Omega}$ by lemma 15.2.4 (iii), and so Δ_2 with Δ_1 replaced by $\mathbf{\Omega}$ is still unsolvable; see figure 15.3. □

In order to show that $\boldsymbol{\beta}\mathbf{\Omega}$ and $\boldsymbol{\beta\eta}\mathbf{\Omega}$ are CR the lemma of Hindley-Rosen does not apply, since $\twoheadrightarrow_\beta$ and $\twoheadrightarrow_\Omega$ do not commute:

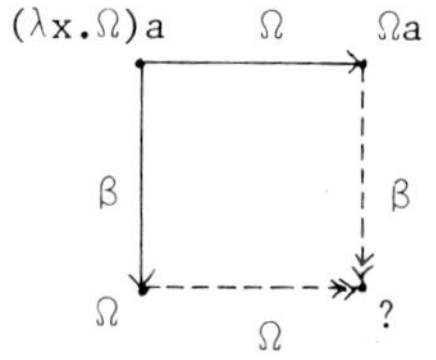

Therefore a different proof strategy is used, one that was originally employed for the $\boldsymbol{\beta\eta}$ case by Curry and Feys [1958].

First some more postponement properties (for $\boldsymbol{\beta\eta}\mathbf{\Omega}$-reduction) are proved.

15.2.6. LEMMA.

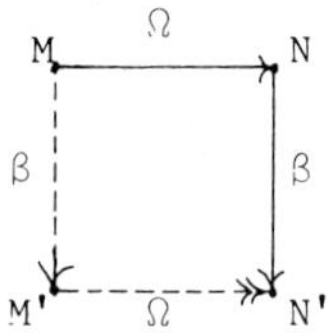

PROOF. Let $\Delta \equiv (\lambda x.P)Q$ be the β-redex contracted in N with contractum Δ'. Then $N \equiv C[\Delta]$, $N' \equiv C[\Delta']$. Moreover N is the result of replacing an unsolvable $H \subset M$ by $\mathbf{\Omega}$.

Case 1. In N the subterms Δ and $\mathbf{\Omega}$ are disjoint. Then the diagram is completed as follows:

$$\begin{array}{lcl} M \equiv \cdot\cdot H \cdots \Delta \cdots \rightarrow_\Omega & & N \equiv \cdot\cdot \mathbf{\Omega} \cdots \Delta \cdots \\ {\scriptstyle\beta}\downarrow & & \downarrow \beta \\ M' \equiv \cdot\cdot H \cdots \Delta' \cdots \rightarrow_\Omega & & N' \equiv \cdot\cdot \mathbf{\Omega} \cdots \Delta' \cdots \end{array}$$

Case 2. $\mathbf{\Omega} \subset \Delta$.

Subcase 2.1. $\mathbf{\Omega} \subset P$. Then $P \equiv D[\mathbf{\Omega}]$ and one has

$$\begin{array}{lcl} M \equiv C[(\lambda x.D[H])Q] \rightarrow_\Omega & & N \equiv C[(\lambda x.D[\mathbf{\Omega}])Q] \\ {\scriptstyle\beta}\downarrow & & \downarrow{\scriptstyle\beta} \\ M' \equiv C[D[H][x:=Q]] \rightarrow_\Omega & & N' \equiv C[D[\mathbf{\Omega}][x:=Q]], \end{array}$$

by the substitutivity of $\mathbf{\Omega}$.

Subcase 2.2. $\Omega \subset Q$. Similar, but now one has $M' \twoheadrightarrow_\Omega N'$.

Subcase 2.3. $\Omega \equiv \Delta$. Then one has $M \equiv C[H]$ and one can take $M' \equiv C[H']$, where H' is any one step reduct of the unsolvable H.

Case 3. $\Delta \subset \Omega$. Then $\Delta \equiv \Omega$ and this is subcase 2.3. □

15.2.7. PROPOSITION (Postponement of Ω-reduction).

$$M \twoheadrightarrow_{\beta\Omega} N \Rightarrow \exists L \;\; M \twoheadrightarrow_\beta L \twoheadrightarrow_\Omega N.$$

PROOF. By lemma 15.2.6 one obtains by a diagram chase

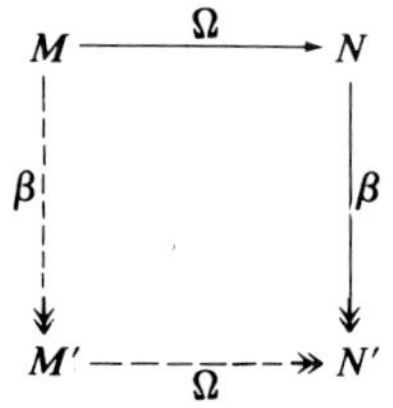

hence by another diagram chase the same holds with $\to_\Omega$ replaced by $\twoheadrightarrow_\Omega$. But then the result follows using a final diagram chase as in figure 15.2. □

REMARK. When combined the diagram chase in the above proof looks like

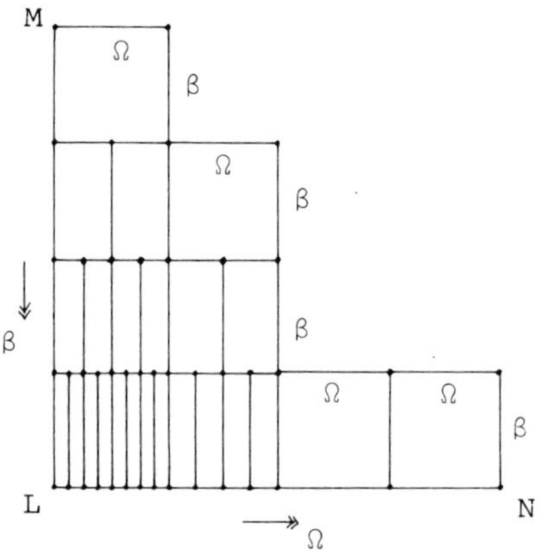

15.2.8. LEMMA.

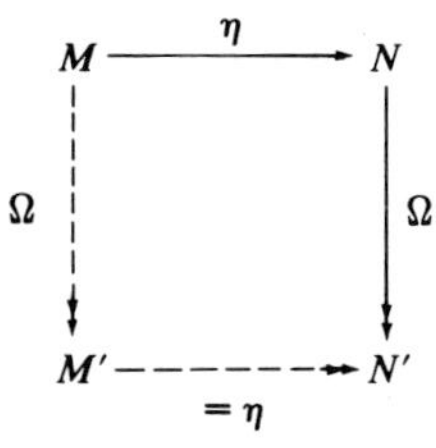

PROOF. Let $M \to_\eta N$ by contracting $\lambda x.Px$ to P and $N \to_\Omega N'$ by contracting H to $\mathbf{\Omega}$.

Case 1. In N the subterms P and H are disjoint. Easy.

Case 2. $H \subset P$. Then $P \equiv P_0[H]$ and one has

$$\begin{array}{ccc} M \equiv C[\lambda x.P_0[H]x] & \to_\eta & N \equiv C[P_0[H]] \\ \Omega\downarrow & & \downarrow\Omega \\ M' \equiv C[\lambda x.P_0[\mathbf{\Omega}]x] & \to_\eta & N' \equiv C[P_0[\mathbf{\Omega}]]. \end{array}$$

Case 3. $P \subset H$. Then $H \equiv H_0[P]$ and one has

$$\begin{array}{ccc} M \equiv C[H_0[\lambda x.Px]] & \to_\eta & N \equiv C[H_0[P]] \\ \Omega\downarrow & & \downarrow\Omega \\ M' \equiv C[\mathbf{\Omega}] & \underset{\equiv}{\rule{4em}{0.4pt}} & N' \equiv C[\mathbf{\Omega}]. \end{array} \quad \square$$

15.2.9. PROPOSITION (Postponement of Ω- and η-reduction). *If* $M \twoheadrightarrow_{\beta\eta\Omega} N$, *then*

$$\exists L_1, L_2 \quad M \twoheadrightarrow_\beta L_1 \twoheadrightarrow_\Omega L_2 \twoheadrightarrow_\eta N.$$

PROOF. First one shows, using lemma 15.2.8, that

$$\begin{array}{ccc} M & \overset{\eta}{\twoheadrightarrow} & N \\ \Omega \downarrow & & \downarrow \Omega \\ M' & \underset{\eta}{\twoheadrightarrow} & N' \end{array} \; ;\text{moreover} \; \begin{array}{ccc} M & \overset{\eta}{\twoheadrightarrow} & N \\ \beta \downarrow & & \downarrow \beta \\ M' & \underset{\eta}{\twoheadrightarrow} & N' \end{array}$$

by corollary 15.1.8. Now assume $M \twoheadrightarrow_{\beta\eta\Omega} N$. By the staircase diagram chase one postpones the η-reduction obtaining $M \twoheadrightarrow_{\beta\Omega} L_2 \twoheadrightarrow_\eta N$. Then the result follows from proposition 15.2.7. $\square$

The notions of reduction $\boldsymbol{\eta}$ and $\mathbf{\Omega}$ are so simple that nf's always exist.

15.2.10. LEMMA. (i) *Each term has a unique* η-nf.

(ii) *Each term has a unique* Ω-nf.

PROOF. (i) η-contractions shorten the length of a term, hence after finitely many steps one reaches an η-nf. Since $\boldsymbol{\eta}$ is CR, one has uniqueness.

(ii) Call an Ω-redex *maximal* if it is not properly contained in another Ω-redex. The maximal Ω-redexes are mutually disjoint. By replacing them all by $\mathbf{\Omega}$ no new Ω-redexes are created (since $H \sim_s \Omega$ for unsolvable H). Therefore M has an Ω-nf, which is unique since $\mathbf{\Omega}$ is CR. $\square$

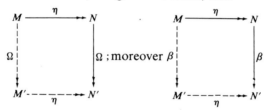

15.2.11. DEFINITION. Let $M \in \Lambda$. Then
(i) $\boldsymbol{\eta}(M)$ is the η-nf of M,
(ii) $\boldsymbol{\Omega}(M)$ is the Ω-nf of M.

EXAMPLES. (i) $\boldsymbol{\eta}(a(\lambda x.y(\lambda z.xz))) = ay$.
(ii) $\boldsymbol{\Omega}(a((\lambda x.x)\omega_3\omega_3)((\lambda x.z(xx))\omega_3) = a\boldsymbol{\Omega}((\lambda x.z(xx))\omega_3)$.

15.2.12. LEMMA. (i) $\boldsymbol{\eta}(P)[x:=\boldsymbol{\eta}(Q)] \twoheadrightarrow_\eta \boldsymbol{\eta}(P[x:=Q])$.
(ii) $\boldsymbol{\Omega}(P)[x:=\boldsymbol{\Omega}(Q)] \twoheadrightarrow_\Omega \boldsymbol{\Omega}(P[x:=Q])$.

PROOF. (i) By the substitutivity of $\boldsymbol{\eta}$ one has

$$\boldsymbol{\eta}(P)[x:=\boldsymbol{\eta}(Q)] =_\eta P[x:=\boldsymbol{\eta}(Q)] =_\eta P[x:=Q] =_\eta \boldsymbol{\eta}(P[x:=Q]),$$

and the last term is in η-nf. Hence by corollary 3.1.13 and the fact that $\boldsymbol{\eta}$ is CR (lemma 3.3.7), the result follows.
(ii) Similarly. □

15.2.13. LEMMA. (i) $M \to_\beta N \Rightarrow \boldsymbol{\Omega}(M) \twoheadrightarrow_{\beta\Omega} \boldsymbol{\Omega}(N)$.
(ii) $M \to_\eta N \Rightarrow \boldsymbol{\Omega}(M) \twoheadrightarrow_{\eta\Omega} \boldsymbol{\Omega}(N)$.
(iii) $M \to_\beta N \Rightarrow \boldsymbol{\eta}(M) \twoheadrightarrow_{\beta\eta} \boldsymbol{\eta}(N)$.
(iv) $M \to_\Omega N \Rightarrow \boldsymbol{\eta}(M) \twoheadrightarrow_{\eta\Omega} \boldsymbol{\eta}(N)$.

PROOF. (i) Note that $\boldsymbol{\Omega}$ can be defined as follows

$$\begin{aligned}
\boldsymbol{\Omega}(x) &= x, \\
\boldsymbol{\Omega}(MN) &= \boldsymbol{\Omega}(M)\boldsymbol{\Omega}(N) && \text{if } MN \text{ is solvable,} \\
&= \Omega && \text{else,} \\
\boldsymbol{\Omega}(\lambda x.M) &= \lambda x.\boldsymbol{\Omega}(M) && \text{if } \lambda x.M \text{ is solvable,} \\
&= \Omega && \text{else.}
\end{aligned}$$

The statement is proved by induction on the generation of $M \to_\beta N$.
Case 1. $M \to_\beta N$ is $(\lambda x.P)Q \to_\beta P[x:=Q]$. Then

$$\begin{aligned}
\boldsymbol{\Omega}(M) &= (\lambda x.\boldsymbol{\Omega}(P))\boldsymbol{\Omega}(Q) && \text{if } M \text{ is solvable,} \\
&= \Omega && \text{else.}
\end{aligned}$$

In the first case $\boldsymbol{\Omega}(M) \twoheadrightarrow_\Omega \boldsymbol{\Omega}(N)$ by lemma 15.2.12 (ii). In the second case $\boldsymbol{\Omega}(M) \equiv \boldsymbol{\Omega}(N) \equiv \Omega$.
Case 2. $M \to_\beta N$ is $ZP \to_\beta ZP'$ and is a direct consequence of $P \to_\beta P'$.

Then

$$\Omega(M) = \Omega(Z)\Omega(P) \quad \text{if } M \text{ is solvable,}$$
$$= \Omega \qquad\qquad \text{else.}$$

In the first case $\Omega(M) \twoheadrightarrow_{\beta\Omega} \Omega(Z)\Omega(P')$ by the induction hypothesis. In the second, $\Omega(M) \equiv \Omega(N) \equiv \Omega$.

Case 3. $M \to_\beta N$ is $PZ \to_\beta P'Z$ or $\lambda x.P \to_\beta \lambda x.P'$ and is a direct consequence of $P \to_\beta P'$. Proof is similar.

(ii) Similarly, using lemma 15.2.4 (ii).

(iii) Note that $\boldsymbol{\eta}(M)$ can be defined by

$$\boldsymbol{\eta}(x) = x,$$
$$\boldsymbol{\eta}(MN) = \boldsymbol{\eta}(M)\boldsymbol{\eta}(N),$$
$$\boldsymbol{\eta}(\lambda x.M) = \boldsymbol{\eta}(M_1) \qquad \text{if } M \equiv M_1 x \text{ with } x \notin \mathrm{FV}(M_1),$$
$$= \lambda x.\boldsymbol{\eta}(M) \quad \text{else.}$$

Again we use induction.

Case 1. $M \to_\beta N$ is $(\lambda x.P)Q \to_\beta P[x := Q]$. Then

$$\boldsymbol{\eta}(M) = \boldsymbol{\eta}(P_1)\boldsymbol{\eta}(Q) \qquad \text{if } P \equiv P_1 x \text{ with } x \notin \mathrm{FV}(P_1),$$
$$= (\lambda x.\boldsymbol{\eta}(P))\boldsymbol{\eta}(Q) \quad \text{else.}$$

In the first case

$$\boldsymbol{\eta}(M) \equiv \boldsymbol{\eta}(P_1 x)[x := \boldsymbol{\eta}(Q)]$$
$$\twoheadrightarrow_\eta \boldsymbol{\eta}((P_1 x)[x := Q]) \quad \text{by lemma 15.2.12 (i),}$$
$$\equiv \boldsymbol{\eta}(N).$$

In the second case

$$\boldsymbol{\eta}(M) \twoheadrightarrow_\beta \boldsymbol{\eta}(P)[x := \boldsymbol{\eta}(Q)]$$
$$\twoheadrightarrow_\eta \boldsymbol{\eta}(P[x := Q]) \equiv \boldsymbol{\eta}(N).$$

Case 2. $M \to_\beta N$ is $ZP \to_\beta ZP'$ or $PZ \to_\beta P'Z$ and follows from $P \to_\beta P'$. Then the result follows from the induction hypothesis.

Case 3. $M \to_\beta N$ is $\lambda x.P \to_\beta \lambda x.P'$ and follows from $P \to_\beta P'$.

Subcase 3.1. $\boldsymbol{\eta}(M) \equiv \boldsymbol{\eta}(P_1)$ because $P \equiv P_1 x$ with $x \notin \mathrm{FV}(P_1)$.

Subcase 3.1.1. $P' \equiv P_1'x$ with $P_1 \to_\beta P_1'$. Then

$$\boldsymbol{\eta}(M) \equiv \boldsymbol{\eta}(P_1)$$

$$\twoheadrightarrow_{\beta\eta} \boldsymbol{\eta}(P_1') \quad \text{by the induction hypothesis,}$$

$$\equiv \boldsymbol{\eta}(N).$$

Subcase 3.1.2. $P \equiv P_1 x \equiv (\lambda z.P_2)x$ and $P' \equiv P_2[z:=x]$. Then

$$\boldsymbol{\eta}(M) \equiv \boldsymbol{\eta}(P_1) \equiv \boldsymbol{\eta}(\lambda z.P_2)$$

$$\equiv \boldsymbol{\eta}(\lambda x.P_2[z:=x]) \equiv \boldsymbol{\eta}(N).$$

Subcase 3.2. $\boldsymbol{\eta}(M) \equiv \lambda x.\boldsymbol{\eta}(P)$.

Subcase 3.2.1. $\boldsymbol{\eta}(N) \equiv \boldsymbol{\eta}(P_1')$ because $P' \equiv P_1'x$ and $x \notin \mathrm{FV}(P_1')$. Then

$$\boldsymbol{\eta}(M) \equiv \lambda x.\boldsymbol{\eta}(P)$$

$$\twoheadrightarrow_{\beta\eta} \lambda x.\boldsymbol{\eta}(P') \quad \text{by the induction hypothesis,}$$

$$\equiv \lambda x.\boldsymbol{\eta}(P_1')x \twoheadrightarrow_\eta \boldsymbol{\eta}(P_1') \equiv \boldsymbol{\eta}(N).$$

Subcase 3.2.2. $\boldsymbol{\eta}(N) \equiv \lambda x.\boldsymbol{\eta}(P')$. Then

$$\boldsymbol{\eta}(M) \equiv \lambda x.\boldsymbol{\eta}(P)$$

$$\twoheadrightarrow_{\beta\eta} \lambda x.\boldsymbol{\eta}(P') \equiv \boldsymbol{\eta}(N) \quad \text{by the induction hypothesis.}$$

(iv) Similarly, making again sub- and subsubcases in case $M \to_\Omega N$ is $\lambda x.P \to_\Omega \lambda x.P'$. The base of the induction argument uses lemma 15.2.4 (ii). □

15.2.14. COROLLARY. (i) $M \twoheadrightarrow_{\beta\Omega} N \Rightarrow \boldsymbol{\Omega}(M) \twoheadrightarrow_{\beta\Omega} \boldsymbol{\Omega}(N)$; $M \twoheadrightarrow_{\beta\eta\Omega} N \Rightarrow \boldsymbol{\Omega}(M) \twoheadrightarrow_{\beta\eta\Omega} \boldsymbol{\Omega}(N)$.

(ii) $M \twoheadrightarrow_{\beta\eta} N \Rightarrow \boldsymbol{\eta}(M) \twoheadrightarrow_{\beta\eta} \boldsymbol{\eta}(N)$; $M \twoheadrightarrow_{\beta\eta\Omega} N \Rightarrow \boldsymbol{\eta}(M) \twoheadrightarrow_{\beta\eta\Omega} \boldsymbol{\eta}(N)$.

PROOF. (i) Immediate by (i) and (ii) of the lemma. ($M \to_\Omega N \Rightarrow \boldsymbol{\Omega}(M) \equiv \boldsymbol{\Omega}(N)$.)

(ii) Immediate by (iii) and (iv) of the lemma. □

15.2.15. THEOREM. (i) $\boldsymbol{\beta\Omega}$ *is* CR.

(ii) $\boldsymbol{\beta\eta\Omega}$ *is* CR.

PROOF. (i)

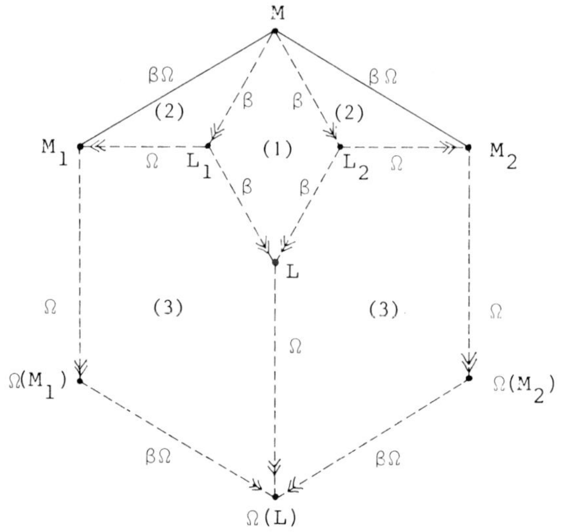

FIG. 15.4.

Comments. (1) By the postponement of Ω-reduction.

(2) By the CR property for $\boldsymbol{\beta}$.

(3) Note that $\boldsymbol{\Omega}(L_i) \equiv \boldsymbol{\Omega}(M_i)$ and use corollary 15.2.14 (i).

(ii) Replace in figure 15.4 first all Ω's by η's and then all β's by $\beta\Omega$'s. □

In order to show that a reduction path in $G_{\beta\eta(\Omega)}(M)$ is cofinal, the following theorem together with theorem 13.2.11 is often useful.

15.2.16. THEOREM. (i) *Let σ be a cofinal reduction path in $G_\beta(M)$ such that infinitely many terms on σ are in* $\eta\Omega$-nf. *Then σ is cofinal in $G_{\beta\eta\Omega}(M)$.*

(ii) *Same result as in* (i), *but without the two* Ω's.

PROOF. (i) If $M \twoheadrightarrow_{\beta\eta\Omega} N$, then N has a $\beta\eta\Omega$-reduct N' on σ, as shown by figure 15.5.

Comments. (1) Proposition 15.2.9.

(2) σ cofinal in $G_\beta(M)$.

(3) By corollary 15.2.14 (i), noting that $\boldsymbol{\Omega}(L_2) \equiv \boldsymbol{\Omega}(L_1)$, $\Omega(N') \equiv N'$.

(4) By corollary 15.2.14 (ii), noting that $\boldsymbol{\eta}(N) \equiv \boldsymbol{\eta}(L)$.

(5) Corollary 15.2.14 (ii).

(ii) Similarly. □

By the same method one obtains a stronger but a little less memorable result.

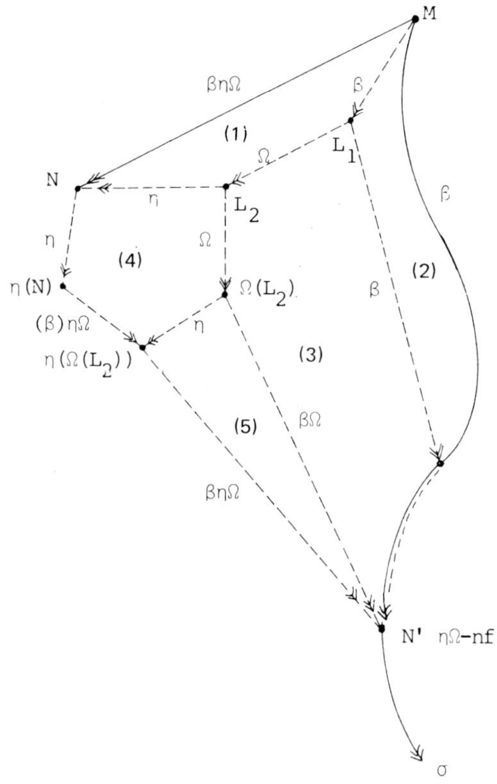

FIG. 15.5.

15.2.17. COROLLARY. (i) *Let*

$$\sigma : M \to M_1 \to M_2 \to \cdots$$

be a $\beta\eta\Omega$-*reduction path such that*

(1) $M \twoheadrightarrow_\beta M' \Rightarrow \exists i\ M' \twoheadrightarrow_{\beta\eta\Omega} M_i$.

(2) *Infinitely many terms on* σ *are in* $\eta\Omega$-*nf*.

Then σ *is cofinal in* $G_{\beta\eta\Omega}(M)$.

(ii) *Similar to* (*i*), *but without the* Ω'*s*. $\square$

Now we will construct a cofinal $\beta\eta(\Omega)$-strategy. Remember that $F_{gk}(M)$ is the result of completely developing all redexes in M, see p. 326.

15.2.18. LEMMA. (i) $M \to_\Omega N \Rightarrow F_{gk}(M) \twoheadrightarrow_\Omega F_{gk}(N)$.

(ii) $M \to_\eta N \Rightarrow F_{gk}(M) \twoheadrightarrow_\eta F_{gk}(N)$.

PROOF. Corollary 8.3.8 states that a λ-term M is always of one of the following two forms:

(1) $M \equiv \lambda\vec{x}.yM_1 \cdots M_n$, $n \geqslant 0$, $\vec{x}$ possibly empty;

(2) $M \equiv \lambda\vec{x}.(\lambda y, M_0)M_1 \cdots M_n$, $n \geqslant 1$, $\vec{x}$ possibly empty.
The statements are proved by induction on the length of M.

(i) Let $M \overset{H}{\rightarrow}_{\Omega} N$.

Case 1. M is of form (1). Then $H \subseteq M_i$ for some i and the result follows from the induction hypothesis, using exercise 13.6.10.

Case 2. M is of form (2).

Subcase 2.1. $H \subset M_i$. Then the result follows again from the induction hypothesis.

Subcase 2.2. $H \equiv (\lambda y.M_0)M_1 \cdots M_j$ with $0 \leqslant j \leqslant n$. Then

$$F_{\mathrm{gk}}(M) \equiv \lambda\vec{x}.F_{\mathrm{gk}}(H)F_{\mathrm{gk}}(M_{j+1}) \cdots F_{\mathrm{gk}}(M_n),$$

$$F_{\mathrm{gk}}(N) \equiv \lambda\vec{x}.\Omega F_{\mathrm{gk}}(M_{j+1}) \cdots F_{\mathrm{gk}}(M_n)$$

by exercise 13.6.10. Since $F_{\mathrm{gk}}(H) =_{\beta} H$ is unsolvable one has $F_{\mathrm{gk}}(M) \twoheadrightarrow_{\Omega} F_{\mathrm{gk}}(N)$.

Subcase 2.3. $H \equiv M$. Then $N \equiv \boldsymbol{\Omega}$ and $F_{\mathrm{gk}}(M) \twoheadrightarrow_{\Omega} F_{\mathrm{gk}}(\boldsymbol{\Omega}) \equiv \boldsymbol{\Omega}$.

(ii) Let $M \overset{\Delta}{\rightarrow}_{\eta} N$ with $\Delta \equiv \lambda x.Px$.

Case 1. M is of shape (1).

Subcase 1.1. $\Delta \subset M_i$ for some i. Then we are done by the induction hypothesis and exercise 13.6.10.

Subcase 1.2. $M \equiv \lambda x_1 \cdots x_m.yM_1 \cdots M_{n-1}x_m$ and $\Delta \equiv \lambda x_m \cdot yM_1 \cdots M_{n-1}x_m$. Then $N \equiv \lambda x_1 \cdots x_{m-1}.yM_1 \cdots M_{n-1}$ and the result follows easily.

Case 2. M is of form (2).

Subcase 2.1. $\Delta \subset M_i$ for some i. As before.

Subcase 2.2. $\Delta \equiv \lambda y.M_0 \equiv \lambda y.Py$. Then $M \equiv \lambda\vec{x}.(\lambda y.Py)M_1 \cdots M_n$, $N \equiv \lambda\vec{x}.PM_1 \cdots M_n$. Then (by accident) also $M \rightarrow_{\beta} N$ without creating new β-redexes. Therefore $F_{\mathrm{gk}}(M) \equiv F_{\mathrm{gk}}(N)$ and we are done.

Subcase 2.3. $M \equiv \lambda x_1 \cdots x_m.(\lambda y.M_0)M_1 \cdots M_{n-1}x_m$ and $\Delta \equiv \lambda x_m.(\lambda y.M_0)M_1 \cdots M_{n-1}x_m$. As before. □

The following definition and theorem apply both to $\beta\eta$- and $\beta\eta\Omega$-reduction.

15.2.19. Definition. Let σ be the $\beta\eta(\Omega)$-reduction

$$\sigma : M \equiv M_0 \twoheadrightarrow_R M_1 \twoheadrightarrow_R M_2 \twoheadrightarrow_R \cdots$$

where $\boldsymbol{R} = \boldsymbol{\beta\eta}(\boldsymbol{\Omega})$. Then σ is called a *quasi-Gross-Knuth* reduction path of M if

(1) $F_{\mathrm{gk}}(M_i) = M_{i+1}$ for infinitely many i,

(2) M_j is an $\eta(\Omega)$-nf for infinitely many j.

15.2.20. THEOREM. *Any quasi-Gross-Knuth $\beta\eta(\Omega)$-reduction path of M is cofinal in $G_{\beta\eta(\Omega)}(M)$.*

PROOF. By lemma 15.2.18 one has

(1) $$P \twoheadrightarrow_{\eta(\Omega)} Q \Rightarrow F_{gk}(P) \twoheadrightarrow_{\eta(\Omega)} F_{gk}(Q).$$

Claim

(2) $$P \twoheadrightarrow_{\beta} Q \Rightarrow F_{gk}(P) \twoheadrightarrow_{\beta} F_{gk}(Q).$$

It is clearly sufficient to show (2) for $P \rightarrow_{\beta} Q$. This follows from lemma 13.2.8 and the following diagram:

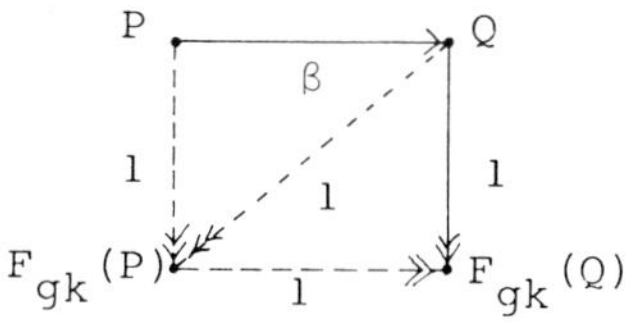

By (1) and (2) one obtains

(3) $$P \twoheadrightarrow_{\beta\eta(\Omega)} Q \Rightarrow F_{gk}(P) \twoheadrightarrow_{\beta\eta(\Omega)} F_{gk}(Q).$$

The statement will be proved now using corollary 15.2.17. The second condition in that result is fulfilled by definition 15.2.19 (2). As to the first one, let $M \twoheadrightarrow_{\beta} M'$. Then the following diagram shows that M' $\beta\eta(\Omega)$-reduces to a term on σ.

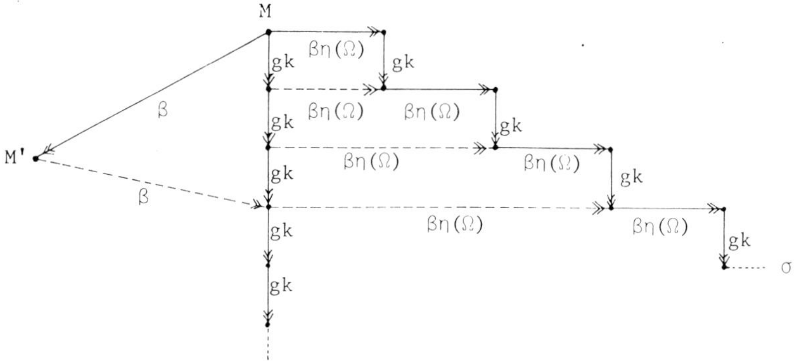

the triangle follows by theorem 13.2.9 and the rectangles by (3) above. □

EXAMPLE. Let

$$\sigma : M \underset{F_{gk}}{\twoheadrightarrow} M_1 \twoheadrightarrow_{\eta\Omega} M_1' \underset{F_{gk}}{\twoheadrightarrow} M_2 \twoheadrightarrow_{\eta\Omega} M_2' \underset{F_{gk}}{\twoheadrightarrow} \cdots$$

where M_i' is the $\eta(\Omega)$-nf of M_i. Then σ is a quasi-Gross-Knuth $\beta\eta\Omega$-reduction and hence cofinal in $G_{\beta\eta(\Omega)}(M)$.

See exercise 15.4.2 for applications.

15.3. Delta reduction

Delta reduction is not one particular notion of reduction but a collection of these. They are all defined on an extension of the set Λ.

15.3.1. DEFINITION. (i) Let $\boldsymbol{\delta}$ be some constant. Then $\Lambda\boldsymbol{\delta}$ is the set of λ-terms built up from variables and $\boldsymbol{\delta}$ using application and abstraction in the usual way.

(ii) Similarly one defines $\Lambda\vec{\boldsymbol{\delta}}$, where $\vec{\boldsymbol{\delta}}$ is a sequence of constants.

Delta reduction serves to make some external function f on Λ internal by postulating

$$\boldsymbol{\delta}\vec{M} \to f(\vec{M}).$$

This is useful for applied (especially for computation oriented) λ-calculus.

The first example of δ-reduction introduces a test for equality on nf's.

15.3.2. DEFINITION (Church's $\boldsymbol{\delta}$). Let $\boldsymbol{\delta}_C$ be some constant. On $\Lambda\boldsymbol{\delta}_C$ define the following notion of reduction

$$\boldsymbol{\delta}_C\colon \begin{cases} \boldsymbol{\delta}_C MN \to \mathbf{T} & \text{if } M, N \in \beta\delta_C\text{-NF}^0,\ M \equiv N \\ \boldsymbol{\delta}_C MN \to \mathbf{F} & \text{if } M, N \in \beta\delta_C\text{-NF}^0,\ M \not\equiv N, \end{cases}$$

where $\beta\delta_C\text{-NF}^0 \subseteq \Lambda\boldsymbol{\delta}_C^0$ is the set of closed β-nf's not containing a subterm $\delta_C PQ$.

REMARKS. (i) Similar contraction rules which allow open nf's are not consistent:

$$(\lambda xy.\boldsymbol{\delta}xy)\mathbf{II} \twoheadrightarrow \delta\mathbf{II} \to \mathbf{T},$$

$$(\lambda xy.\boldsymbol{\delta}xy)\mathbf{II} \to (\lambda xy.\mathbf{F})\mathbf{II} \twoheadrightarrow \mathbf{F}.$$

Also, it is necessary that $\boldsymbol{\delta}$ acts on nf's. See, moreover, exercise 15.4.10.

(ii) If $\mathfrak{N} \subseteq \Lambda$ is a finite set of closed $\beta\eta$-nf's, then there is a term $D \in \Lambda^0$ such that for all $M, N \in \mathfrak{N}$

$$DMN \twoheadrightarrow \mathbf{T} \quad \text{if } M \equiv N,$$

$$DMN \twoheadrightarrow \mathbf{F} \quad \text{if } M \not\equiv N.$$

This follows from corollary 10.4.14. For infinite sets of closed $\beta\eta$-nf's this is generally false; see exercise 15.4.9.

That Church's $\beta\delta_C$-reduction is Church–Rosser follows easily from the following.

15.3.3. THEOREM (Mitschke [1976]). *Let* $\boldsymbol{\delta}$ *be some constant. Let* $R_1, \ldots, R_m \subseteq (\Lambda\boldsymbol{\delta})^n$ *be n-ary relations and let* $N_1, \ldots, N_m \in \Lambda\boldsymbol{\delta}$ *be arbitrary. Introduce the notion of reduction* $\boldsymbol{\delta}$ *by the following contraction rules:*

$$\boldsymbol{\delta}_M \begin{cases} \boldsymbol{\delta}\vec{M} \to N_1 & \text{if } R_1(\vec{M}), \\ \ldots & \\ \boldsymbol{\delta}\vec{M} \to N_m & \text{if } R_m(\vec{M}). \end{cases}$$

Then $\boldsymbol{\beta\delta}_M$ *is* CR *provided that*

(1) *The* R_i *are disjoint.*

(2) *The* R_i *are closed under* $\beta\delta_M$*-reduction and substitution (i.e.* $R_i(\vec{M}) \Rightarrow R_i(\vec{M}')$ *if* $\vec{M} \to_{\beta\delta_M} \vec{M}'$ *or* $\vec{M}'$ *is a substitution instance of* $\vec{M}$*).*

PROOF. First we show that $\boldsymbol{\delta}_M$ is CR. By lemma 3.2.2 it suffices to show that $\underset{=}{\to}_{\delta_M} \models \diamond$. This follows easily by some case distinction and the fact that the R_i are closed under δ_M-reduction. By the lemma of Hindley-Rosen (proposition 3.3.5) it suffices to show that $\boldsymbol{\beta}$ and $\boldsymbol{\delta}_M$ commute. One easily shows

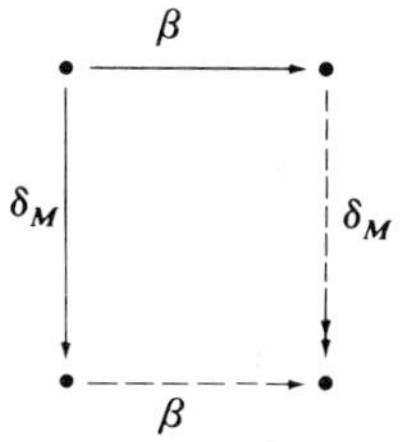

by considering the relative positions of the β- and δ-redexes; from this the commutation property follows by a diagram chase. □

15.3.4. COROLLARY. *Church's* $\beta\delta_C$*-reduction is* CR.

PROOF. Immediate. □

For some applications it is useful to have an analogue of theorem 15.3.3 not for a new constant δ but for the term $\boldsymbol{\Omega}$ which in β-reductions behaves as a constant.

15.3.5. THEOREM. *Let* $R_1, \ldots, R_m \subseteq \Lambda^n$ *be n-ary relations and let* $N_1, \ldots, N_m \in \Lambda$ *be arbitrary. Consider the notion of reduction* $\mathbf{\Omega}_\delta$ *defined by*

$$\mathbf{\Omega}_\delta : \begin{cases} \Omega \vec{M} \to N_1 & \textit{if } R_1(\vec{M}), \\ \cdots & \\ \Omega \vec{M} \to N_m & \textit{if } R_m(\vec{M}). \end{cases}$$

Then $\boldsymbol{\beta\Omega}_\delta$ is CR provided that
 (1) The R_i are disjoint
 (2) The R_i are closed under $\beta\Omega_\delta$-reduction and substitution.

PROOF. Analogous to the proof of theorem 15.3.3. □

15.3.6. COROLLARY. *Define on* Λ *the following notion of reduction*

$$\mathbf{\Omega}_1 : \mathbf{\Omega 1} \to \mathbf{T},\ \mathbf{\Omega I} \to \mathbf{F}.$$

Then $\boldsymbol{\beta\Omega}_1$ *is* CR.

PROOF. Immediate. □

15.3.7. COROLLARY. *There is a consistent* λ*-theory* $\mathfrak{T}$ *such that* $\mathfrak{T}\boldsymbol{\eta}$ *is inconsistent.*

PROOF. Let $\mathfrak{T}$ be axiomatized by $\boldsymbol{\lambda} + \mathbf{\Omega 1} = \mathbf{T} + \mathbf{\Omega I} = \mathbf{F}$. Since clearly

$$M =_{\beta\Omega_1} N \quad \text{iff} \quad \mathfrak{T} \vdash M = N$$

and $\boldsymbol{\beta\Omega}_1$ is CR it follows that $\mathfrak{T}$ is consistent. But

$$\mathfrak{T}\boldsymbol{\eta} \vdash \mathbf{T} = \mathbf{\Omega 1} = \mathbf{\Omega I} = \mathbf{F},$$

hence $\mathfrak{T}\boldsymbol{\eta}$ is inconsistent. □

15.3.8. DEFINITION (Jacopini, Venturini-Zilli). $M \in \Lambda$ is *easy* if

$$\forall N \in \Lambda \quad \text{Con}(M = N).$$

15.3.9. PROPOSITION. (Jacopini [1975]) $\mathbf{\Omega}$ *is easy.*

PROOF (Mitschke). Define the notion of reduction

$$\mathbf{\Omega}_M : \Omega \to M.$$

By theorem 15.3.5 for $n=0$ it follows that $\boldsymbol{\beta\Omega}_M$ is CR. Since clearly

$$P =_{\beta\Omega_M} Q \quad \text{iff} \quad \boldsymbol{\Omega} = M \vdash P = Q$$

it follows that $\mathrm{Con}(\boldsymbol{\Omega} = M)$. □

See also Baeten and Boerboom [1979] for a model theoretic proof of this result.

Other applications of Mitschke's method are in exercises 15.4.3 and 15.4.5. See Klop [1980] p. 225 for an extension of the method.

Non-Church–Rosser reduction

In 1972 C. Mann noticed that for the notion of reduction for "surjective pairing" (see also Barendregt [1974]) it is not clear how to prove the CR theorem. The system is obtained by adding to Λ new constants $\boldsymbol{\delta}$, $\boldsymbol{\delta}_1$, $\boldsymbol{\delta}_2$ and postulating for $M \in \Lambda\boldsymbol{\delta\delta}_1\boldsymbol{\delta}_2$

$$\mathrm{SP}\begin{cases} \boldsymbol{\delta}_i(\boldsymbol{\delta}M_1M_2) \to M_i, & i \in \{1,2\}, \\ \boldsymbol{\delta}(\boldsymbol{\delta}_1M)(\boldsymbol{\delta}_2M) \to M. \end{cases}$$

Hindley observed in 1973 that the difficulty is already in the system

$$\boldsymbol{\delta}_{\mathrm{H}}MM \to M.$$

Staples [1976] noted that even for the simplified system

$$\boldsymbol{\delta}_{\mathrm{S}}MM \to \boldsymbol{\varepsilon},$$

where $\boldsymbol{\varepsilon}$ is a new constant, the Church–Rosser property is not clear.

In Klop [1980] it is shown that $\boldsymbol{\beta\delta}_{\mathrm{S}}$ is in fact *not* Church–Rosser. It follows that $\boldsymbol{\beta\delta}_{\mathrm{H}}$ and $\boldsymbol{\beta SP}$ also are not Church–Rosser.

In the rest of this section we write $\boldsymbol{\delta}$ for $\boldsymbol{\delta}_{\mathrm{S}}$. The intuition behind Klop's counter-example is the following. For $M \in \Lambda\boldsymbol{\delta\varepsilon}$, define $\mathrm{BT}(M)$ by extending the usual definition by

$$\mathrm{BT}(\lambda\vec{x}.\boldsymbol{\delta}M_1,\ldots,M_n) = \begin{array}{c} \lambda\vec{x}.\boldsymbol{\delta} \\ \diagup \quad \diagdown \\ \mathrm{BT}(M_1) \quad \mathrm{BT}(M_n) \end{array}$$

and similarly for $\boldsymbol{\varepsilon}$. If $M \to_{\delta} N$, then $\mathrm{BT}(N)$ results from $\mathrm{BT}(M)$ by replacing a number of subtrees of the form

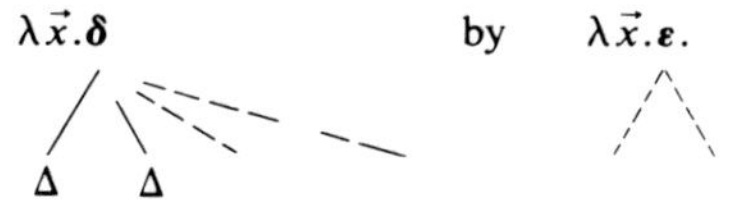

This number can even be infinite. E.g. take

$$M \equiv (\lambda z.zz)(\lambda a.x(\boldsymbol{\delta} bb)(aa)),$$

$$N \equiv (\lambda z.zz)(\lambda a.x\boldsymbol{\varepsilon}(aa)).$$

Then $M \to_{\delta} N$ and

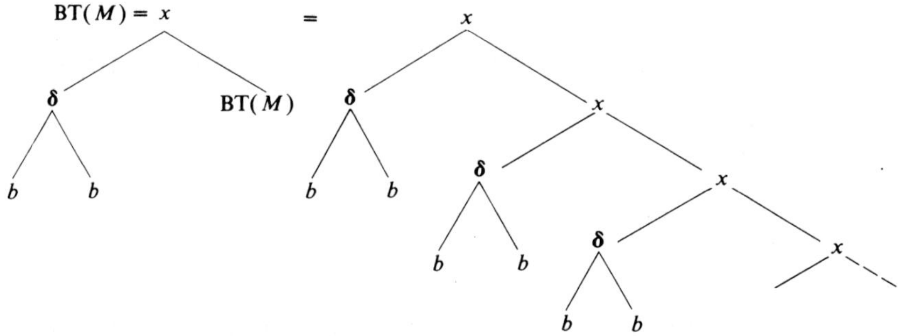

and

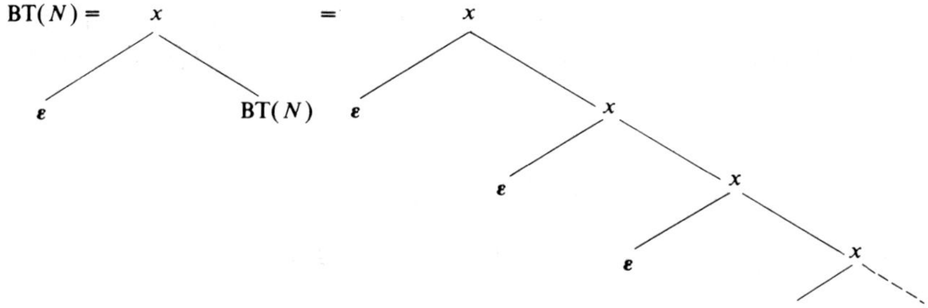

Now consider a term with tree

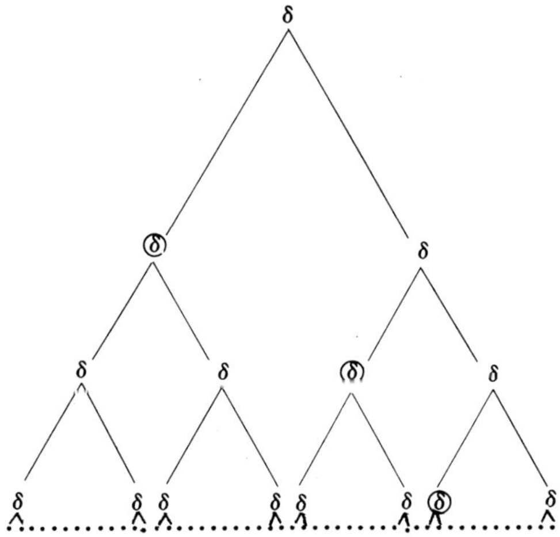

This tree may be reduced to $\boldsymbol{\varepsilon}$. But also to

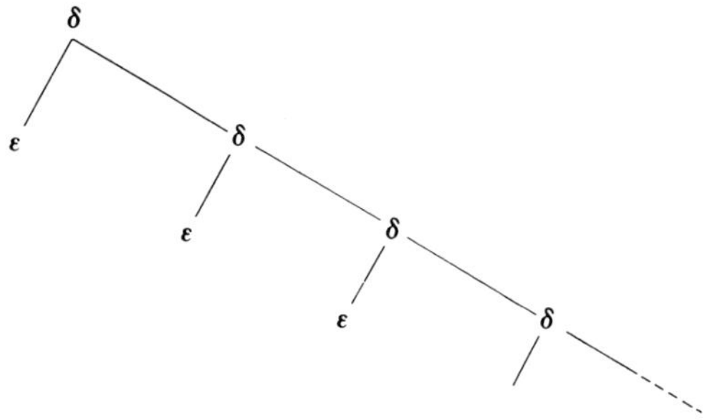

by contracting the subtrees whose top node are circled. And now there is no common reduct.

The following construction taken from Klop [1980] makes this precise.

15.3.10. DEFINITION. For the remainder of this section, let C and X be defined in $\Lambda\boldsymbol{\delta\varepsilon}$ by:

(i) $C \equiv \boldsymbol{\Theta}(\lambda cx.\boldsymbol{\delta}x(cx))$,

(ii) $X \equiv \boldsymbol{\Theta}C$.

By corollary 6.1.5 it follows that

$$Cx \twoheadrightarrow_\beta \boldsymbol{\delta}x(Cx) \quad \text{and} \quad X \twoheadrightarrow_\beta CX.$$

15.3.11. LEMMA. (i) $X \twoheadrightarrow_{\beta\delta} \boldsymbol{\varepsilon}$.

(ii) $X \twoheadrightarrow_{\beta\delta} C\boldsymbol{\varepsilon}$.

PROOF. $X \twoheadrightarrow_\beta CX \twoheadrightarrow_\beta \boldsymbol{\delta} X(CX) \twoheadrightarrow_\beta \boldsymbol{\delta}(CX)(CX) \to_\delta \boldsymbol{\varepsilon}$.
(ii) $X \twoheadrightarrow_\beta CX \twoheadrightarrow_{\beta\delta} C\boldsymbol{\varepsilon}$, by (i). □

15.3.12. LEMMA (Postponement of δ-reduction). *Let* $M, N \in \Lambda\boldsymbol{\delta\varepsilon}$. *Then*

$$M \twoheadrightarrow_{\beta\delta} N \Rightarrow \exists L \in \Lambda\boldsymbol{\delta\varepsilon} \;\; M \twoheadrightarrow_\beta L \twoheadrightarrow_\delta N.$$

PROOF. By a simple case distinction one shows

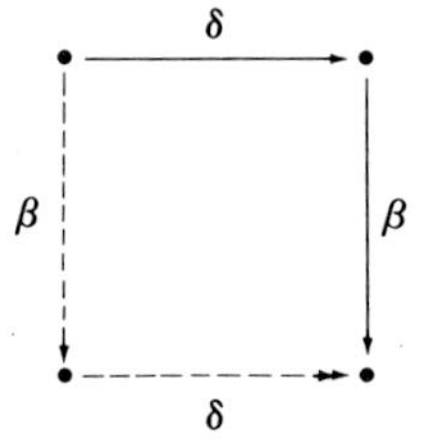

and the result follows by a diagram chase. □

15.3.13. LEMMA. *Suppose*

$$\sigma : \boldsymbol{\delta\varepsilon}(C\boldsymbol{\varepsilon}) \underset{\text{st}}{\twoheadrightarrow}_\beta L \twoheadrightarrow_\delta \boldsymbol{\varepsilon},$$

where $\underset{\text{st}}{\twoheadrightarrow}_\beta$ *denotes standard reduction. Then there is a* σ' *with* $\mathrm{lh}(\sigma') < \mathrm{lh}(\sigma)$ *and*

$$\sigma' : C\boldsymbol{\varepsilon} \underset{\text{st}}{\twoheadrightarrow}_\beta L' \twoheadrightarrow_\delta \boldsymbol{\varepsilon}.$$

PROOF. Clearly L is of the shape $L \equiv \boldsymbol{\delta\varepsilon} L'$ with $C\boldsymbol{\varepsilon} \twoheadrightarrow_\beta L'$. Therefore σ must go as follows

$$\sigma : \underbrace{\boldsymbol{\delta\varepsilon}(C\boldsymbol{\varepsilon}) \underset{\text{st}}{\twoheadrightarrow}_\beta \boldsymbol{\delta\varepsilon} L' \twoheadrightarrow_\delta \boldsymbol{\delta\varepsilon\varepsilon}}_{\sigma_1} \to_\delta \boldsymbol{\varepsilon}$$

Let σ_1 be σ with the last step omitted. Then σ' can be obtained from σ_1 by deleting in each term the initial $\boldsymbol{\delta\varepsilon}$.

15.3.14. MAIN LEMMA. *$C\boldsymbol{\varepsilon}$ and $\boldsymbol{\varepsilon}$ have no common βδ-reduct.*

PROOF. Otherwise $C\boldsymbol{\varepsilon} \twoheadrightarrow_{\beta\delta} \boldsymbol{\varepsilon}$. By lemma 15.3.12 and the standardization theorem it follows that for some σ one has

$$\sigma : C\boldsymbol{\varepsilon} \underset{\text{st}}{\twoheadrightarrow}_\beta L \twoheadrightarrow_\delta \boldsymbol{\varepsilon}.$$

Take σ of minimal length. Since the first part of σ is standard it follows that

$$\sigma : C\boldsymbol{\varepsilon} \underset{\text{st}\ \beta}{\twoheadrightarrow} \boldsymbol{\delta\varepsilon}(C\boldsymbol{\varepsilon}) \underset{\text{st}\ \beta}{\twoheadrightarrow} L \twoheadrightarrow_{\delta} \boldsymbol{\varepsilon}.$$

By lemma 15.3.13, for some σ' with $\mathrm{lh}(\sigma') < \mathrm{lh}(\sigma)$ one has

$$\sigma' : C\boldsymbol{\varepsilon} \underset{\text{st}\,\beta}{\twoheadrightarrow} L' \twoheadrightarrow_{\delta} \boldsymbol{\varepsilon},$$

contradicting the minimality of σ. □

15.3.15. THEOREM *The* λ*-calculus with constants* $\boldsymbol{\delta}, \boldsymbol{\varepsilon}$ *and extra contraction rule* $\boldsymbol{\delta} MM \to \boldsymbol{\varepsilon}$ *is not Church–Rosser.*

PROOF. Immediate by lemmas 15.3.11 and 15.3.14. □

Using that $\boldsymbol{\delta} MM \to \boldsymbol{\varepsilon}$ can be "imitated" by the $\boldsymbol{\delta}, \boldsymbol{\delta}_1, \boldsymbol{\delta}_2$ of surjective pairing, Klop [1980] shows that the latter system is also not Church–Rosser; see exercise 15.4.4.

15.4. Exercises

15.4.1. Show that every $M \in \Lambda$ is $\Omega\eta$-strongly normalizing.

15.4.2. (i) Let $A \equiv \omega\omega$ with $\omega \equiv \lambda axz.z(aa(x\boldsymbol{\Omega}))$. Then $Ax \twoheadrightarrow_{\beta} \langle A(x\boldsymbol{\Omega})\rangle$. Show that

$$x \in_{\beta\eta\Omega} Ax \text{ (see exercise 3.5.15 for the notation).}$$

[*Hint*. Using theorems 15.2.20 and 13.2.11 find a cofinal reduction path σ in $G_{\beta\eta\Omega}(Ax)$ such that for all M_i on σ one has $x \in \mathrm{FV}(M_i)$.]

(ii) Show that there is a natural choice of $O \in \Lambda^0$ such that

$$Ox \ulcorner n \urcorner z \twoheadrightarrow_{\beta} z\boldsymbol{\Omega}^{\sim n}(Ox \ulcorner n+1 \urcorner z)$$

and $x \in_{\beta\eta\Omega} Ox \ulcorner 0 \urcorner$.

(iii) Let $F \in \Lambda^0$. Show that there is a natural choice of $H \in \Lambda^0$ such that

$$Hcia \twoheadrightarrow_{\beta} [\mathsf{I}, Fca(Hcia^{+})]$$

and $x \in_{\beta\eta\Omega} Hcx \ulcorner 0 \urcorner$ where $a^{+} \equiv [\mathsf{F}, a]$ is the standard successor of a.

15.4.3 (Plotkin). Let $A \subseteq \mathbb{N}$. Define a notion of reduction Ω_A by

$$\Omega_A : \begin{cases} \Omega \ulcorner n \urcorner \to \mathsf{T} & \text{if } n \in A, \\ \Omega \ulcorner n \urcorner \to \mathsf{F} & \text{else.} \end{cases}$$

(i) Prove that $\boldsymbol{\beta\Omega}_A$ is CR.

(ii) Let $\mathfrak{T}_A$ be the theory $\boldsymbol{\lambda}$ extended with $\{\Omega \ulcorner n \urcorner = \mathsf{T} | n \in A\} \cup \{\Omega \ulcorner n \urcorner = \mathsf{F} | n \notin A\}$. Show that $\mathfrak{T}_A$ is consistent.

(iii) Conclude that there are $2^{\aleph_0}$ consistent extensions of the λ-calculus.

15.4.4 (Klop [1980]). Define on $\Lambda\boldsymbol{\delta}\boldsymbol{\delta}_1\boldsymbol{\delta}_2$ the notion of reduction $\boldsymbol{SP}$ (surjective pairing) by

$$\boldsymbol{SP}\begin{cases}\boldsymbol{\delta}_i(\boldsymbol{\delta}M_1M_2)\to M_i,\ i=1,2;\\ \boldsymbol{\delta}(\boldsymbol{\delta}_1M)(\boldsymbol{\delta}_2M)\to M.\end{cases}$$

Show that $\boldsymbol{\beta SP}$ is not Church–Rosser. [*Hint*. Define $\boldsymbol{\delta}_S=\lambda xy.\boldsymbol{\delta}(\boldsymbol{\delta}_1\langle x\rangle)(\boldsymbol{\delta}_2\langle y\rangle)(\mathbf{K}\boldsymbol{\delta})$. Then $\boldsymbol{\delta}_S MM \twoheadrightarrow \boldsymbol{\delta}$ and one can imitate the counter-example in theorem 15.3.15.]

15.4.5. (i) (Jacopini). Let $\mathfrak{T}$ be the extension of $\boldsymbol{\lambda}$ axiomatized by

$$\{\Omega\ulcorner 0\urcorner Z=\Omega\ulcorner 1\urcorner Z \mid Z\in\Lambda^0\}.$$

Show that $\mathfrak{T}\nvdash\Omega\ulcorner 0\urcorner=\Omega\ulcorner 1\urcorner$. [*Hint*. Use a Church–Rosser argument.]

(ii) Show that $\mathfrak{T}'=\mathfrak{T}+\Omega(\lambda x.\Omega\ulcorner 0\urcorner x)=\mathbf{T}+\Omega(\lambda x.\Omega\ulcorner 1\urcorner x)=\mathbf{F}$ is consistent, but $\mathfrak{T}'\omega$ not.

15.4.6 (Barendregt, Koymans). Show that there is a λ-algebra $\mathfrak{M}$ such that $\mathrm{Th}^{\mathrm{open}}(\mathfrak{M})$ is inconsistent. [*Hint*. Take $\mathfrak{M}=\mathfrak{M}^0(\mathfrak{T}')$, with $\mathfrak{T}'$ as in exercise 15.4.5.]

15.4.7. Show that for a notion of reduction $\boldsymbol{R}$ on Λ one does not have, in general, that WCR implies CR.

15.4.8 (van Daalen). Let $L\in\Lambda$. For $M\in\Lambda$ write $M^*=M[x:=L]$. If $\underset{\to}{x}$ is a free variable occurrence in M, then the *scope* of x is the maximal subterm of the form xP in M starting with the given x. E.g. in $M=\lambda y.y\underset{\to}{x}\mathbf{I}(\underset{\to}{x}\mathbf{IK})y$ the scope of the first x is x and of the second $x\mathbf{IK}$. Write $M\rightsquigarrow N$ if $M\equiv C[xP_1,\ldots,xP_n]$, where all outermost occurrences of x with corresponding scope are displayed, and $N\equiv C[Q_1,\ldots,Q_n]$ with $(xP_i)^*\twoheadrightarrow Q_i$, $1\leqslant i\leqslant n$.

(i) Show that M

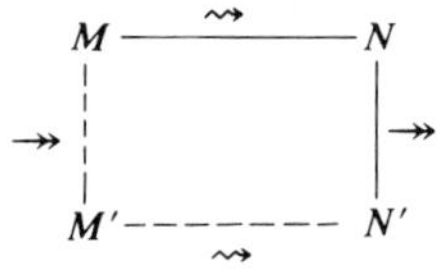

[*Hint*. If $M_i\rightsquigarrow N_i$, $i=1,2$, then $M_1[y:=N_1]\rightsquigarrow M_2[y:=N_2]$.]

(ii) Show that if $M^*\twoheadrightarrow N$, then $M\twoheadrightarrow M'\rightsquigarrow N$ for some M'.

(iii) Show that if $M^*\twoheadrightarrow\lambda y.P$, then either

$$M\twoheadrightarrow\lambda y.P_1 \quad\text{and}\quad P_1^*\twoheadrightarrow P$$

or

$$M\twoheadrightarrow x\vec{Q} \quad\text{and}\quad (x\vec{Q})^*\twoheadrightarrow\lambda y.P.$$

15.4.9 (Barendregt; Wadsworth). Define $\mathbf{0}=\mathbf{I}$, $\boldsymbol{n}+\mathbf{1}=\mathbf{K}\boldsymbol{n}$. Show that the function sg (sg(0) = 0, sg(n + 1) = 1) cannot be λ-defined w.r.t. $\mathbf{0}, \mathbf{1}, \ldots$. [*Hint*. Otherwise for some F one has $F\mathbf{0}=y$, $F\boldsymbol{n}+\mathbf{1}=z$; apply exercise 15.4.8 (ii) with $M\equiv Fx$, $L\equiv\boldsymbol{n}+\mathbf{1}$.] Conclude that Church's $\boldsymbol{\delta}$ is not definable in the λ-calculus.

15.4.10. Show that in the first order theory with a binary operation, equality, constants $\mathbf{k}$, $\mathbf{s}$, $\boldsymbol{\delta}$ and the axioms

$$\mathbf{k}xy=x,\quad \mathbf{s}xyz=xz(yz),\quad \boldsymbol{\delta}xx=\mathbf{k},\quad x\neq y\to\boldsymbol{\delta}xy=\mathbf{s}$$

one can derive $\forall xy\ x=y$.

PART IV

THEORIES

Barendregt (photo
by the author, 1977)

Visser (photo
by J. Visser, 1979)

CHAPTER 16

SENSIBLE THEORIES

A lambda theory $\mathcal{T}$ is a consistent extension of the λ-calculus. There are three reasons for studying such extensions.

(1) There is a good motivation for the new identifications in $\mathcal{T}$.

(2) $\mathcal{T}$ gives useful information about the λ-calculus itself.

(3) $\mathcal{T}$ is the theory of a model.

The theory $\mathcal{H}$ equating the unsolvables fits under (1) and (2). $\mathcal{H}$ has a unique Hilbert-Post completion $\mathcal{H}^*$, falling under all three points. It will be proved that there are $2^{\aleph_0}$ different sensible theories (extensions of $\mathcal{H}$). The theory $\mathcal{B}$ equating terms with equal Böhm tree is one among them.

16.1. The theory $\mathcal{H}$

In the discussion before proposal 2.2.14 it was argued that the unsolvable terms should be used to represent undefined. The genericity lemma 14.3.24 states that for unsolvable M,

$$\text{if } FM = P,\ P \text{ in nf, then } \forall N\ FN = P.$$

This shows the computational irrelevance of the unsolvable terms and also suggests that they may be identified.

Remember the following.

16.1.1. DEFINITION. (i) $\mathcal{H}_0 = \{M = N \mid M, N \in \Lambda^0 \text{ and are unsolvable}\}$.

(ii) $\mathcal{H} = \mathcal{H}_0^+$.

(iii) A λ-theory $\mathcal{T}$ is called *sensible* if $\mathcal{H} \subseteq \mathcal{T}$.

It will be shown that $\mathcal{H}$ is consistent, even in the presence of extensionality. Several consistency proofs will be given. In this section one via the CR property of $\boldsymbol{\beta\eta\Omega}$ and another one via the genericity lemma. In § 16.2 another proof theoretic consistency proof will be obtained while proving results about the HP-completion of $\mathcal{H}$. Finally in chapter 19 a model theoretic proof is presented: there it is shown that the λ-models $P\omega$ and D_∞ both satisfy $\mathcal{H}$.

Remember that if $\mathfrak{T}$ is a set of equations between λ-terms, then $\mathfrak{T}\boldsymbol{\eta}$ is $\{M = N \mid M, N \in \Lambda^0$ and $\boldsymbol{\lambda\eta} + \mathfrak{T} \vdash M = N\}$.

16.1.2. LEMMA. (i) *The notion of reduction* $\boldsymbol{\beta\Omega}$ *generates* $\mathcal{H}$, *i.e.*

$$\mathcal{H} \vdash M = N \Leftrightarrow M =_{\beta\Omega} N.$$

(ii) *The notion of reduction* $\boldsymbol{\beta\eta\Omega}$ *generates* $\mathcal{H}\boldsymbol{\eta}$, *i.e.*

$$\mathcal{H}\boldsymbol{\eta} \vdash M = N \Leftrightarrow M =_{\beta\eta\Omega} N.$$

PROOF. (i) (⇒) Note that if $M = N \in \mathcal{H}_0$, then $M =_{\Omega} N$ since M, N are unsolvable and hence $M \twoheadrightarrow_{\Omega} \boldsymbol{\Omega}$ and $N \twoheadrightarrow_{\Omega} \boldsymbol{\Omega}$. Therefore for all axioms $M = N$ of $\mathcal{H}$ one has $M =_{\beta\Omega} N$ and the result follows.

(⇐) Note that each $\boldsymbol{\beta}$ or $\boldsymbol{\Omega}$ one step reduction is a provable equality in $\mathcal{H}$. Hence the same holds for $\boldsymbol{\beta\Omega}$ convertibility.

(ii) Analogous to (i). □

16.1.3. THEOREM. Con($\mathcal{H}\boldsymbol{\eta}$).

PROOF. By lemma 16.1.2 and the CR property for $\boldsymbol{\beta\eta\Omega}$ it follows that $\mathcal{H}\boldsymbol{\eta} \nvdash \mathbf{I} = \mathbf{S}$. □

Now a proof of Con($\mathcal{H}\boldsymbol{\eta}$) will be given, using the genericity lemma. This method will yield some useful proof theoretic information.

The following conservative extension of $\mathcal{H}\boldsymbol{\eta}$ is needed.

16.1.4. DEFINITION. Let $\mathfrak{T}$ be the formal theory with as alphabet that of $\boldsymbol{\lambda}$ extended with the symbols "$\approx$" and "$\sim$". The terms of $\mathfrak{T}$ are exactly the λ-terms.

$\mathfrak{T}$ is axiomatized by the following axioms and rules (as usual M, M', N, L, Z denote arbitrary terms $\in \Lambda$).

(I.1) $M \approx M$,
(I.2) $(\lambda x.M)N \approx M[x := N]$, (β)
(I.3) $\lambda x.Mx \approx M$, (η)
(I.4) $M \approx M'$, if M, M' are unsolvable.

(II.1) $M \approx N \Rightarrow N \approx M$,
(II.2) $M \approx N \Rightarrow M \sim N$,
(II.3) $M \sim N \Rightarrow ZM \sim ZN$,
(II.4) $M \sim N \Rightarrow MZ \sim NZ$,
(II.5) $M \sim N \Rightarrow \lambda x.M \sim \lambda x.N$,
(II.6) $M \sim N \Rightarrow M = N$,
(II.7) $M = N, N = L \Rightarrow M = L$.

REMARK. $\approx$ is the reflexive symmetric relation corresponding to the axioms of $\mathcal{H}\boldsymbol{\eta}$.

$\sim$ is the compatible closure of $\approx$.

$=$ is the transitive closure of $\sim$.

In the rest of this section $\mathcal{T}$ denotes the theory of definition 16.1.4.

16.1.5. LEMMA. $\mathcal{T} \vdash M = N \Leftrightarrow \mathcal{H}\boldsymbol{\eta} \vdash M = N$.

PROOF. ($\Rightarrow$) By induction on the length of proof in $\mathcal{T}$ one shows that if

$$\mathcal{T} \vdash M \approx N, \qquad \mathcal{T} \vdash M \sim N \quad \text{or} \quad \mathcal{T} \vdash M = N,$$

then

$$\mathcal{H}\boldsymbol{\eta} \vdash M = N.$$

($\Leftarrow$) Note that provable equality in $\mathcal{T}$ is symmetric and compatible. Then it follows similarly that

$$\text{if } \boldsymbol{\lambda\eta} + \mathcal{H}_0 \vdash M = N, \text{ then } \mathcal{T} \vdash M = N. \quad \square$$

16.1.6. LEMMA. (i) $\mathcal{T} \vdash M = N \Leftrightarrow \exists n\ \exists M_1, \ldots, M_n$

$$\mathcal{T} \vdash M \sim M_1 \sim \cdots \sim M_n \equiv N.$$

(ii) $\mathcal{T} \vdash M \approx N \Leftrightarrow [M = N$ *or* $N = M$ *is an axiom of* $\boldsymbol{\lambda\eta}$ *or* $M = N \in \mathcal{H}_0]$.

PROOF. (i) ($\Rightarrow$) By induction on the length of proof of $M = N$.

($\Leftarrow$) By rules (II.6, 7).

(ii) Equally simple. $\square$

16.1.7. LEMMA. $\mathcal{T} \vdash M \sim N \Rightarrow$

$$\exists C[\ \ ]\ \exists M', N' [C[M'] \equiv M \wedge C[N'] \equiv N \wedge \mathcal{T} \vdash M \approx N].$$

PROOF. By induction on the length of proof of $M \sim N$.

If $M \sim N$ is a direct consequence of $M \approx N$, then take $C[\ \ ] \equiv [\ \ ]$, $M' \equiv M$, $N' \equiv N$.

If $M \sim N$ is $\lambda x.P \sim \lambda x\, Q$ and is a direct consequence of $P \sim Q$, then by the induction hypothesis for some $C_1[\ \ ]$, P', Q',

$$C_1[P'] \equiv P, \qquad C_1[Q'] \equiv Q \quad \text{and} \quad P' \approx Q'.$$

Now take $C[\ \ ] \equiv \lambda x.C_1[\ \ ]$, $M' \equiv P'$, $N' \equiv Q'$.

If $M \sim N$ is $ZP \sim ZQ$ or $PZ \sim QZ$ and is a direct consequence of $P \sim Q$, the argument is similar. $\square$

16.1.8. Main lemma. *Let N have a β-nf. Then*

$$\mathfrak{T} \vdash M = N \Rightarrow \boldsymbol{\lambda\eta} \vdash M = N.$$

Proof. Suppose $\mathfrak{T} \vdash M = N$. Then by lemma 16.1.6 (i) $\exists n\ M_1, \ldots, M_n$

$$(1) \qquad \mathfrak{T} \vdash M \sim M_1 \sim \cdots \sim M_n \equiv N.$$

By induction on n it will be shown that if (1) with N having a nf, then $\boldsymbol{\lambda\eta} \vdash M = N$.
If $n = 0$, then $M \equiv N$ and we are done. Now suppose

$$\mathfrak{T} \vdash M \sim M_1 \sim \cdots \sim M_n \sim M_{n+1} \equiv N.$$

By lemma 16.1.7 $\exists C[\ \ ]\ \exists M_n', M_{n+1}'$

$$\mathfrak{T} \vdash M_n' \approx M_{n+1}', \qquad C[M_n'] \equiv M_n \quad \text{and} \quad C[M_{n+1}'] \equiv M_{n+1}.$$

By lemma 16.1.6 (ii) there are two cases.

Case 1. $M_n' = M_{n+1}'$, say, is an axiom of $\boldsymbol{\lambda\eta}$. Then

$$M_n \equiv C[M_n'] =_{\beta\eta} C[M_{n+1}'] \equiv M_{n+1} \equiv N.$$

Hence by Corollary 15.1.5 M_n has a nf and therefore by the induction hypothesis

$$\boldsymbol{\lambda\eta} \vdash M = M_n = N.$$

Case 2. M_n', M_{n+1}' are unsolvable. Then, since

$$C[M_{n+1}'] \equiv M_{n+1} \equiv N$$

and N has a nf, say N', it follows by the genericity lemma 14.3.24 that $C[M_n'] = N'$. Therefore $M_n \equiv C[M_n'] = N'$ and hence by the induction hypothesis

$$\boldsymbol{\lambda\eta} \vdash M = M_n = N' = N. \quad \square$$

16.1.9. Theorem. *Let $N \in \Lambda$ have a β-nf. Then*

(i) $\mathcal{H}\boldsymbol{\eta} \vdash M = N \Rightarrow \boldsymbol{\lambda\eta} \vdash M = N$,

(ii) $\mathcal{H} \vdash M = N \Rightarrow \boldsymbol{\lambda} \vdash M = N$,

(iii) $\mathrm{Con}(\mathcal{H}\boldsymbol{\eta})$.

Proof. (i) Immediate by lemmas 16.1.5 and 16.1.8.

(ii) Similar to (i), introducing first an auxiliary theory $\mathfrak{T}$ not containing the scheme (I.3), i.e. (η).

(iii) By (i) e.g. $\mathbf{S}=\mathbf{I}$ is not provable in $\mathcal{H}\boldsymbol{\eta}$. □

Next it will be shown that the theory $\mathcal{H}$ is Σ_2^0-complete. The proof is taken from Barendregt et al. [1978].

16.1.10. LEMMA. *Let $R(\vec{n})$ be an* r.e. *predicate on* $\mathbb{N}$. *Then for some $F\in\Lambda^0$ one has in* $\mathcal{H}$

$$F\ulcorner\vec{n}\urcorner=\begin{cases}\mathbf{I} & \text{if } R(\vec{n}),\\ \Omega & \text{if } \neg R(\vec{n}).\end{cases}$$

PROOF. Let ψ be a partial recursive function such that $R(\vec{n})$ iff $\psi(\vec{n})\downarrow$. Let ψ be λ-defined by $G\in\Lambda^0$. Define $F=\lambda x.Gx\mathbf{KII}$. Then

$$\begin{aligned} R(\vec{n}) &\Rightarrow \psi(\vec{n})\downarrow,\\ &\Rightarrow G\ulcorner\vec{n}\urcorner=\ulcorner m\urcorner,\quad \text{for some } m,\\ &\Rightarrow F\ulcorner\vec{n}\urcorner=\ulcorner m\urcorner\mathbf{KII}=\mathbf{I};\\ \neg R(\vec{n}) &\Rightarrow \psi(\vec{n})\uparrow\\ &\Rightarrow G\ulcorner\vec{n}\urcorner \text{ unsolvable}\\ &\Rightarrow F\ulcorner\vec{n}\urcorner \text{ unsolvable}\\ &\Rightarrow F\ulcorner\vec{n}\urcorner=\Omega \text{ in } \mathcal{H}. \quad\square \end{aligned}$$

16.1.11. THEOREM. *The theory $\mathcal{H}$ is Σ_2^0-complete.*

PROOF. Clearly $\mathcal{H}_0=\{M=N\mid M,N\in\Lambda^0,\ M,N \text{ unsolvable})$ is Π_1^0. Therefore this set axiomatizes a Σ_2^0-theory.

Let $P(p)\equiv\exists n\,\forall m\,Q(n,m,p)$ be any Σ_2^0-predicate with recursive Q. By lemma 16.1.10 there is an $F\in\Lambda^0$ such that in $\mathcal{H}$

$$F\ulcorner p\urcorner\ulcorner n\urcorner=\begin{cases}\Omega & \text{if } \forall m\,Q(n,m,p),\\ \mathbf{I} & \text{else.}\end{cases}$$

Let $Hpzn \twoheadrightarrow [\mathbf{I}, Fpn(Hpz(S^+n))]$ and let x,y be different variables.

Claim. $\exists n\,\forall m\,Q(n,m,p)\Leftrightarrow\mathcal{H}\vdash H\ulcorner p\urcorner x\ulcorner 0\urcorner=H\ulcorner p\urcorner y\ulcorner 0\urcorner$. Indeed, if $\exists n\,\forall m\,Q(n,m,p)$, then $H\ulcorner p\urcorner z\ulcorner n\urcorner\twoheadrightarrow_{\beta\Omega}[\mathbf{I},\Omega]$, for such n, hence

$$\mathcal{H}\vdash H\ulcorner p\urcorner x\ulcorner 0\urcorner=[\mathbf{I},\mathbf{I},\ldots,\mathbf{I},\Omega]=H\ulcorner p\urcorner y\ulcorner 0\urcorner.$$

Conversely, if $\neg\exists n\ \forall m\ Q(n,m,p)$, then $\forall n\ F\ulcorner p\urcorner\ulcorner n\urcorner = \mathbf{I}$. By exercise 15.4.2 (iii) it follows that the natural choice for H is such that

$$H\ulcorner p\urcorner z\ulcorner 0\urcorner \twoheadrightarrow_{\beta\Omega} M \Rightarrow z \in \mathrm{FV}(M).$$

But then $\mathcal{H}\nvdash H\ulcorner p\urcorner x\ulcorner 0\urcorner = H\ulcorner p\urcorner y\ulcorner 0\urcorner$ by lemma 16.1.2 and the CR property for $\boldsymbol{\beta\Omega}$.

Therefore each Σ_2^0-predicate can be reduced to provability in $\mathcal{H}$. □

Similarly one shows that $\mathcal{H}\boldsymbol{\eta}$ is Σ_2^0-complete.

16.1.12. Remark. Relativizing to the I-case the definition of $\mathcal{H}$ becomes

$$\begin{aligned}\mathcal{H}_I &= \{M = N \mid M, M \in \Lambda_I^0\ I\text{-unsolvable}\}^+ \\ &= \{M = N \mid M, N \in \Lambda_I^0 \text{ without a nf}\}^+,\end{aligned}$$

by theorem 9.4.20.

16.1.13. Theorem. *In the* λI*-calculus (with extensionality) it is consistent to equate all terms without a* nf.

Proof. By relativizing theorem 16.1.9 (iii) to the I-case one obtains $\mathrm{Con}(\mathcal{H}_I\boldsymbol{\eta})$. (Note that M has a nf iff $\lambda\vec{x}.M$ has a nf.) □

In corollary 16.2.12 it will be shown that $\mathcal{H}_I\boldsymbol{\eta}$ is a HP-complete theory.

16.2. The theory $\mathcal{H}^*$

It turns out that the λ-theory $\mathcal{H}$ has a unique HP-complete (see definition 4.1.22) extension $\mathcal{H}^*$. The theory $\mathcal{H}^*$ was first introduced by Hyland and Wadsworth in connection with the λ-models D_∞, see theorem 19.2.12. The relation between $\mathcal{H}$ and $\mathcal{H}^*$ can, however, be examined without going into the model theoretic details.

16.2.1. Definition. Let $M, N \in \Lambda$. Remember that $M \sim_s N$ iff

$$\forall C[\ ]\ [C[M] \text{ is solvable} \Leftrightarrow C[N] \text{ is solvable}].$$

Define $\mathcal{H}^* = \{M = N \mid M, N \in \Lambda^0 \text{ and } M \sim_s N\}$.

16.2.2. Lemma. *$\mathcal{H}^*$ is an extensional λ-theory. More specifically*

(i) $\mathcal{H}^*\boldsymbol{\eta} \vdash M = N \Rightarrow M \sim_s N$;

in particular $\mathcal{H}^*\boldsymbol{\eta} = \mathcal{H}^*$.

(ii) $\mathrm{Con}(\mathcal{H}^*)$.

PROOF. (i) By induction on the length of proof of $\mathcal{H}^*\boldsymbol{\eta} \vdash M = N$.

If $M = N$ is an axiom of $\boldsymbol{\lambda\eta}$, then $M =_{\beta\eta} N$. Now

$$C[M] \text{ is solvable} \Rightarrow$$

$$\Rightarrow (\lambda\vec{x}.C[M])\vec{P} = \mathbf{I} \quad \text{for some } \vec{x}, \vec{P},$$

$$\Rightarrow (\lambda\vec{x}.C[N])\vec{P} =_{\beta\eta} \mathbf{I} \quad \text{since } M =_{\beta\eta} N,$$

$$\Rightarrow C[N] \text{ is } \beta\eta\text{-solvable}$$

$$\Rightarrow C[N] \text{ is solvable by proposition 15.1.7;}$$

and conversely. Hence $M \sim_s N$.

If $M = N$ is an axiom in $\mathcal{H}^*$, then we are done.

If $M = N$ is $\lambda x.P = \lambda x.Q$ and is a direct consequence of $P = Q$, then by the induction hypothesis for all contexts $C[\ ]$

$$C[P] \text{ solvable} \Leftrightarrow C[Q] \text{ solvable.}$$

Hence this holds for all contexts $C[\lambda x.[\ ]]$ and therefore $M \sim_s N$.

A similar argument applies if $M = N$ is $ZP = ZQ$ or $PZ = QZ$ and is a direct consequence of $P = Q$.

If $M = N$ is a direct consequence of $M = L$ and $L = N$, then by the induction hypothesis $M \sim_s L$ and $L \sim_s N$, hence for all contexts $C[\ ]$

$C[M]$ solvable $\Leftrightarrow C[L]$ solvable $\Leftrightarrow C[N]$ solvable, i.e. $M \sim_s N$.

(ii) Note that $\mathbf{I} \not\sim_s \mathbf{\Omega}$ since $\mathbf{I}$ is solvable and $\mathbf{\Omega}$ is not. Hence by (i) $\mathcal{H}^* \nvdash \mathbf{I} = \mathbf{\Omega}$. □

The following lemma yields a different consistency proof for $\mathcal{H}\boldsymbol{\eta}$.

16.2.3. LEMMA. (i) $\mathcal{H} \subseteq \mathcal{H}^*$.

(ii) Con($\mathcal{H}\boldsymbol{\eta}$).

PROOF. (i) Since $\mathcal{H}^*$ is a λ-theory it is sufficient to show that the axioms of $\mathcal{H}$, viz. $\mathcal{H}_0$, are part of $\mathcal{H}^*$.

Now let $M = N \in \mathcal{H}_0$, i.e. M, N unsolvable. Then for all $C[\ ]$

$$C[M] \text{ solvable} \Leftrightarrow$$

$$\Leftrightarrow \exists \vec{P}\, (\lambda\vec{x}.C[M])\vec{P} = \mathbf{I}$$

$$\Leftrightarrow \exists \vec{P}\, (\lambda\vec{x}.C[N])\vec{P} = \mathbf{I} \quad \text{by the genericity lemma 14.3.24,}$$

$$\Leftrightarrow C[N] \text{ solvable.}$$

Therefore $M \sim_s N$, i.e. $M = N \in \mathcal{H}^*$.

(ii) By (i) and lemma 16.2.2 (i)

$$\mathcal{H}\boldsymbol{\eta} \subseteq \mathcal{H}^*\boldsymbol{\eta} = \mathcal{H}^*.$$

Hence by lemma 16.2.2 (ii) Con($\mathcal{H}\eta$). □

16.2.4. MAIN LEMMA. Con ($\mathcal{H} + M = N) \Rightarrow M \sim_s N$.

PROOF. Suppose $M \not\sim_s N$; then for some context $C[\ \ ]$, say,

$$C[M] \text{ is solvable} \quad \text{and} \quad C[N] \text{ is unsolvable.}$$

Hence for some $\vec{x}$, $\vec{P}$

$$(\lambda\vec{x}.C[M])\vec{P} = \mathbf{I}$$

but $(\lambda\vec{x}.C[N])\vec{P}$ is unsolvable, by corollary 8.3.4. Now

$$\mathcal{H} + M = N \vdash \mathbf{I} = (\lambda\vec{x}.C[M])\vec{P} = (\lambda\vec{x}.C[N])\vec{P} = \boldsymbol{\Omega}_3.$$

where $\boldsymbol{\Omega}_3$ is as in lemma 4.1.8 and is unsolvable. Hence by that lemma $\neg$Con($\mathcal{H} + M = N$). □

16.2.5. COROLLARY. *Let $\mathcal{T}$ be a consistent set of closed equations between λ-terms extending $\mathcal{H}$. Then $\mathcal{T} \subseteq \mathcal{H}^*$.*

PROOF. Immediate from the lemma. □

16.2.6. THEOREM. *$\mathcal{H}^*$ is the unique HP-complete λ-theory extending $\mathcal{H}$.*

PROOF. Immediate from corollary 16.2.5 and lemma 16.2.2 (ii). □

The following result is borrowed from §19.2. Remember that $M \precsim_\eta N$ iff BT(M) $=_\eta$ BT(N).

16.2.7. THEOREM. *For $M, N \in \Lambda$*

$$\mathcal{H}^* \vdash M = N \Leftrightarrow M \precsim_\eta N.$$

PROOF. See theorem 19.2.12. The implication (⇒) follows by the Böhm-out technique; (⇐) by the HP-completeness of $\mathcal{H}^*$, provided we know that $\{M = N \mid M \precsim_\eta N\}(\supseteq \mathcal{H})$ is consistent. [The consistency of $\{M = N \mid M \precsim_\eta N\}$ follows model theoretically: $D_\infty \models M = N \Leftrightarrow M \precsim_\eta N$. As a consequence one has $\mathcal{H}^* = \text{Th}(D_\infty)$.] □

Next it will be shown that $\mathcal{H}^*$ is a Π^0_2-complete theory. The proof is due to Wadsworth.

16.2.8. LEMMA. *Let $M_n, N_n \in \Lambda$ be uniform sequences. Then* (*see definition* 8.2.3)

$$\forall n \quad \mathcal{H}^* \vdash M_n = N_n \Leftrightarrow \mathcal{H}^* \vdash [M_n] = [N_n].$$

PROOF. ($\Rightarrow$) The Böhm tree of $[M_n]$ is

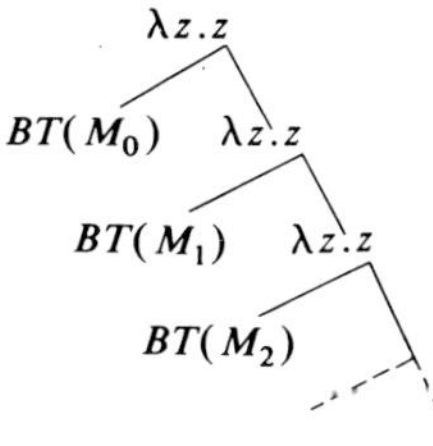

and similarly for $[N_n]$. Therefore, using theorem 16.2.7,

$$\forall n \quad \mathcal{H}^* \vdash M_n = N_n \Rightarrow$$

$$\Rightarrow \forall n\ M_n \precsim_\eta N_n$$

$$\Rightarrow [M_n] \precsim_\eta [N_n]$$

$$\Rightarrow \mathcal{H}^* \vdash [M_n] = [N_n].$$

($\Leftarrow$) By applying $\boldsymbol{\pi}_n$ of definition 8.2.3. □

16.2.9. THEOREM. *Let φ_n be the partial recursive function with index n. There are λ-terms $F_n \in \Lambda^0$ such that F_n λ-defines φ_n and*

$$\varphi_n \cong \varphi_m \Leftrightarrow \mathcal{H}^* \vdash F_n = F_m.$$

PROOF. By theorem 8.4.13 or 9.2.16 φ_n is λ-definable, say by G_n. let π be such that $\pi \ulcorner n \urcorner = \pi_n$ and define $F_n = \lambda x.\pi x[G_n \ulcorner 0 \urcorner, G_n \ulcorner 1 \urcorner, \ldots]$, see definition 8.2.3. Then clearly F_n λ-defines φ_n. Moreover if $\varphi_n \cong \varphi_m$, then

$$\forall p \in \mathbb{N} \quad \mathcal{H} \vdash G_n \ulcorner p \urcorner = G_m \ulcorner p \urcorner$$

(if $\varphi_n(p)\uparrow$, then $\varphi_m(p)\uparrow$ and both $G_n \ulcorner p \urcorner$, $G_m \ulcorner p \urcorner$ are unsolvable). Therefore

$$\mathcal{H}^* \vdash [G_n \ulcorner 0 \urcorner, \ldots] = [G_m \ulcorner 0 \urcorner, \ldots]$$

by lemma 16.2.8. It follows that $\mathcal{H}^* \vdash F_n = F_m$. The converse is trivial. □

16.2.10. COROLLARY. *$\mathcal{H}^*$ is Π_2^0-complete.*

PROOF. Clearly $\sim_s$ is a Π_2^0-predicate. Since the F_n can be found effectively from n and the relation $\varphi_n \cong \varphi_m$ is Π_2^0-complete, the result follows by the theorem. □

By relativizing to the λI-calculus one obtains the HP-complete theory $\mathcal{H}_I^*$. This theory can be described as follows.

16.2.11. PROPOSITION. *In the λI-calculus $\mathcal{H}^* = \mathcal{H}\boldsymbol{\eta}$, i.e.*

$$\mathcal{H}_I^* = \mathcal{H}_I\boldsymbol{\eta}.$$

PROOF. By lemmas 16.2.3 (i) and 16.2.2 (i)

$$\mathcal{H}_I\boldsymbol{\eta} \subseteq \mathcal{H}_I^*\boldsymbol{\eta} = \mathcal{H}_I^*.$$

Now suppose $M = N \in \mathcal{H}_I^*$ in order to show that

(1) $\qquad \mathcal{H}_I\boldsymbol{\eta} \vdash M = N$

By definition $M \sim_s N$ in the λI-calculus, i.e. for all contexts $C[\ ] \in \Lambda_I$

$$C[M] \text{ is } I\text{-solvable} \Leftrightarrow C[N] \text{ is } I\text{-solvable}.$$

Hence in particular

$$M \text{ is } I\text{-solvable} \Leftrightarrow N \text{ is } I\text{-solvable}.$$

Case 1. M, N are both I-unsolvable. Then $M = N \in \mathcal{H}_{0I}$, and therefore (1).

Case 2. M, N are both I-solvable. By corollaries 9.4.21 and 15.1.5 it follows that M, N both have $\beta\eta$-nf's, say M', N' respectively. If $M' \equiv N'$, then (1) follows:

$$\mathcal{H}_I\boldsymbol{\eta} \vdash M = M' \equiv N' = N.$$

If $M \not\equiv N'$, then $\neg\mathrm{Con}(M' = N')$ by Böhm's theorem 10.5.31 for $\boldsymbol{\lambda I}$, hence $\neg\mathrm{Con}(M = N)$, and so $\neg\mathrm{Con}(\mathcal{H}_I^*)$, a contradiction. □

16.2.12. COROLLARY. $\boldsymbol{\lambda I\eta} + \{M = N \mid M, N \in \Lambda_I^0$ *without a* nf$\}$ *is a* HP-*complete theory.*

PROOF. By proposition 16.2.11 and remark 16.1.12. □

Finally it will be shown that $\mathcal{H}_I^*$ and $\mathcal{H}_K^*(=\mathcal{H}^*)$ are overlapping sets of equations and therefore by their HP-completeness incompatible, i.e. $\mathcal{H}_I^* \cup \mathcal{H}_K^*$ is inconsistent.

16.2.13. REMARK. $\mathcal{H}_I^* \not\subset \mathcal{H}_K^*$ and $\mathcal{H}_K^* \not\subset \mathcal{H}_I^*$.

PROOF. Let $J = \boldsymbol{\Theta}(\lambda jxy.x(jy))$. Then $\mathsf{I} \simeq_\eta J$, see example 10.2.9, hence $\mathsf{I} = J \in \mathcal{H}_K^*$ by theorem 16.2.7. But $\mathsf{I} = J \notin \mathcal{H}_I^*$, since J has no nf and therefore is I-unsolvable.

On the other hand $\Omega = \lambda x.x\Omega \in \mathcal{H}_I^*$, since both terms have no nf; but $\Omega = \lambda x.x\Omega \notin \mathcal{H}_K^*$ since $\lambda x.x\Omega$ is K-solvable and Ω is not. □

16.3. $2^{\aleph_0}$ sensible theories

In this section continuum many sensible theories will be constructed. By taking closed term models it follows that also there are $2^{\aleph_0}$ non-isomorphic hard models. The result is taken from Barendregt et al. [1978].

16.3.1. DEFINITION. Let $\mathcal{T}$ be a λ-theory.

(i) A set $\mathcal{S}$ of equations between λ-terms is *independent over* $\mathcal{T}$ if for $M = N \in \mathcal{S}$

$$\mathcal{T} \cup \mathcal{S} - \{M = N\} \nvdash M = N.$$

(ii) A set $X \subseteq \Lambda$ is *independent over* $\mathcal{T}$ if for some $M_0 \in X$ the set

$$\mathcal{S}(X, M_0) = \{M = M_0 \mid M \in X, M \not\equiv M_0\}$$

is independent over $\mathcal{T}$.

16.3.2. LEMMA. *Let* $X = \{B_0, B_1, \dots\} \subseteq \Lambda^0$ *be a countable set independent over the* λ*-theory* $\mathcal{T}$. *Then there are* $2^{\aleph_0}$ *different* λ*-theories extending* $\mathcal{T}$.

PROOF. Assume that $\{B_n = B_0 \mid n \neq 0\}$ is independent over (and hence consistent with) $\mathcal{T}$. For $A \subseteq \mathbb{N}$, let

$$\mathcal{T}(A) = (\mathcal{T} + \{B_{n+1} = B_0 \mid n \in A\})^+.$$

Then clearly $\mathcal{T} \subseteq \mathcal{T}(A)$. Moreover for $A, A' \subseteq \mathbb{N}$

$$A \neq A' \Rightarrow \mathcal{T}(A) \neq \mathcal{T}(A'), \tag{1}$$

for if $n \in A$, $n \notin A'$, then

$$\mathcal{T}(A) \vdash B_{n+1} = B_0 \quad \text{while} \quad \mathcal{T}(A') \nvdash B_{n+1} = B_0.$$

By (1) there are $2^{\aleph_0}$ λ-theories extending $\mathcal{T}$. □

Next a uniform sequence $\{B^{\ulcorner 0 \urcorner}, B^{\ulcorner 1 \urcorner}, \dots\}$ will be constructed which forms a set independent over $\mathcal{H}\eta$.

16.3.3. NOTATION (for this section only). Let

$$\omega \equiv \lambda bxz.z(bbx) \quad \text{and} \quad B \equiv \omega\omega.$$

Note that

$$\Theta(\lambda bxz.z(bx)) \twoheadrightarrow B \quad \text{and} \quad B \twoheadrightarrow \lambda z.z(Bx).$$

In order to show that $\{B\ulcorner 0\urcorner, B\ulcorner 1\urcorner, \ldots\}$ is independent over $\mathcal{H}\eta$ one must show that for each $n \neq 0$

$$\mathcal{H}\boldsymbol{\eta} + \{B\ulcorner m\urcorner = B\ulcorner 0\urcorner \mid m \neq n\} \nvdash B\ulcorner n\urcorner = B\ulcorner 0\urcorner .$$

This will be done by introducing a notion of reduction $\boldsymbol{R}_n$ which generates equality in this theory.

16.3.4. Definition. (i) $\mathrm{Red}(Bx) = \{C(x) \mid Bx \twoheadrightarrow_\beta C(x)\}$.
(ii) $\boldsymbol{R}_n$ is the notion of reduction

$$\{\langle C(\ulcorner m\urcorner), C(\ulcorner 0\urcorner)\rangle \mid C(x) \in \mathrm{Red}(Bx), m \neq n\}.$$

(iii) $\boldsymbol{\beta\eta\Omega}_n$ is the notion of reduction

$$\boldsymbol{\beta\eta\Omega} \cup \boldsymbol{R}_n.$$

16.3.5. Lemma. *$\boldsymbol{\beta\eta\Omega}_n$ generates provable equality in*

$$\mathcal{H}\boldsymbol{\eta} + \{B\ulcorner m\urcorner = B\ulcorner 0\urcorner \mid m \neq n\}.$$

Proof. Obvious. □

The following notation is used in order to facilitate the computation of the reduction graph of Bx.

16.3.6. Notation. (i) $\square \equiv Bx \equiv (\lambda bxz.z(bbx))(\lambda bxz.z(bbx))x$
(ii) If Δ is a term, then

$$\Delta^0 \equiv \lambda z.z\Delta,$$

$$\Delta^1 \equiv (\lambda xz.z\Delta)x,$$

$$\Delta^{ij} \equiv (\Delta^i)^j \quad \text{for } i,j \in \{0,1\}.$$

16.3.7. Lemma. *$C(x) \in \mathrm{Red}(Bx)$ iff for some $n > 0$ and some $i_1, \ldots, i_n \in \{0, 1\}$*

$$(+) \qquad C(x) \equiv \square^{i_1 \cdots i_n}.$$

PROOF. Note that

(i) $\square \to_\beta M \Rightarrow M \equiv \square^1$,

(ii) $\Delta^0 \to_\beta M \Rightarrow M \equiv \blacktriangle^0$ where $\Delta \to \blacktriangle$,

(iii) $\Delta^1 \to_\beta M \Rightarrow M \equiv \Delta^0$, or $M \equiv \blacktriangle^1$ where $\Delta \to \blacktriangle$.

From (i)–(iii) it follows that all possible β-reducts of $\square$ are of the form (+). Moreover all terms of the form (+) are reducts of $\square$. $\square$

16.3.8. COROLLARY. *Let $C(x) \in \mathrm{Red}(Bx)$. Then*

(i) *$C(x)$ contains no η- or Ω-redex.*

(ii) *$C(x)$ has exactly one free variable occurrence. This variable is x and occurs as the rightmost symbol (not counting the parentheses) in $C(x)$.*

(iii) *$C(\ulcorner m \urcorner) \twoheadrightarrow_\beta M \Rightarrow M \equiv C'(\ulcorner m \urcorner)$ for some $C'(x)$ such that $C(x) \twoheadrightarrow C'(x)$.*

(iv) *$C(\ulcorner m \urcorner) \equiv \lambda c.M \Rightarrow M \equiv cC'(\ulcorner m \urcorner)$ for some $C'(x) \in \mathrm{Red}(Bx)$.*

(v) *Let $k = n$ or $k = 0$. Then $B\ulcorner k \urcorner \twoheadrightarrow_{\beta\eta\Omega_n} M \Rightarrow M \equiv C(\ulcorner k \urcorner)$ for some $C(x) \in Red(Bx)$.*

PROOF. (i) to (iv) are immediate, and (v) follows from (i) and (ii). $\square$

16.3.9. LEMMA. *For each $n \in \mathbb{N}$ the notion of reduction $\boldsymbol{R}_n$ is* CR.

PROOF. Let $M \to_{R_n} M_1$, $M \to_{R_n} M_2$. Then M_i is obtained from M by replacing some part $C_i(\ulcorner m_i \urcorner)$ by $C_i(\ulcorner 0 \urcorner)$. A common reduct M_3 can be found by making both changes in M. (If $C_1(\ulcorner m_1 \urcorner)$ and $C_2(\ulcorner m_2 \urcorner)$ are not disjoint, then by corollary 16.3.8 (ii) $m_1 = m_2$ and $C_1(\ulcorner m_1 \urcorner) \subset C_2(\ulcorner m_1 \urcorner)$, say. Then take M_3 to be M with $C_1(\ulcorner m_1 \urcorner)$ changed into $C_1(\ulcorner 0 \urcorner)$.) Hence $\to_{\underline{R}_n}$ satisfies the diamond property and therefore so does $\twoheadrightarrow_{R_n}$, i.e. $\boldsymbol{R}_n$ is CR. $\square$

16.3.10. PROPOSITION. *For each $n \in \mathbb{N}$ the notion of reduction $\boldsymbol{\beta\eta\Omega_n}$ is* CR.

PROOF. By theorem 15.2.15 (ii) and lemma 16.3.9 the notions of reduction $\boldsymbol{\beta\eta\Omega}$ and $\boldsymbol{R}_n$ are both CR. By the lemma of Hindley-Rosen it therefore suffices to show that they commute. For this it is sufficient to show that

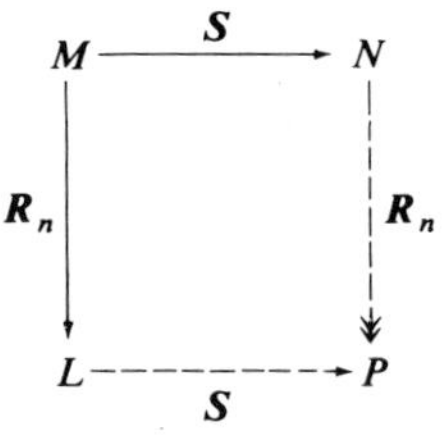

where $\boldsymbol{S}$ is the notion of reduction $\boldsymbol{\beta}$, $\boldsymbol{\eta}$, and $\boldsymbol{\Omega}$, respectively.

Case $\boldsymbol{S} = \boldsymbol{\beta}$. Let $R \equiv (\lambda z.V)W$ be the β-redex occurrence contracted in $M \to_\beta N$ and $C(\ulcorner m \urcorner)$ the R_n-redex in $M \to_{R_n} L$.

Case 1. $R \cap C(\ulcorner m \urcorner) = \emptyset$. Then P can be found easily.

Case 2. $R \subset C(\ulcorner m \urcorner)$. By corollary 16.3.8 (iii) P can be found.

Case 3. $C(\ulcorner m \urcorner) \subset R$.

Subcase 3.1. $C(\ulcorner m \urcorner) \subset W$. Then P can be found easily.

Subcase 3.2. $C(\ulcorner m \urcorner) \subset V$. Since $C(\ulcorner m \urcorner)$ is closed, nothing can be substituted in it and hence P can be found easily.

Subcase 3.3. $C(\ulcorner m \urcorner) \equiv \lambda z.V$. By corollary 16.3.8 (iv) $C(\ulcorner m \urcorner) \equiv \lambda z.zC'(\ulcorner m \urcorner)$ with $Bx \twoheadrightarrow_\beta C'(x)$. Hence $N \equiv \cdots WC'(\ulcorner m \urcorner) \cdots$, $L \equiv \cdots C(\ulcorner 0 \urcorner)W \cdots \equiv \cdots (\lambda z.zC'(\ulcorner 0 \urcorner))W \cdots$. Take $P \equiv \cdots WC'(\ulcorner 0 \urcorner) \cdots$.

Case $\boldsymbol{S} = \boldsymbol{\eta}$. Let $E \equiv \lambda y.Fy$ be the η-redex and $C(\ulcorner m \urcorner)$ the R_n redex constructed in M.

Case 1. $E \cap C(\ulcorner m \urcorner) = \emptyset$. Easy.

Case 2. $E \subset C(\ulcorner m \urcorner)$. This is impossible by corollary 16.3.8 (i).

Case 3. $C(\ulcorner m \urcorner) \subset E$.

Subcase 3.1. $C(\ulcorner m \urcorner) \subset F$. Easy.

Subcase 3.2. $C(\ulcorner m \urcorner) \equiv Fy$. This is impossible by corollary 16.3.8 (ii).

Case $\boldsymbol{S} = \boldsymbol{\Omega}$. Let H be the Ω-redex and $C(\ulcorner m \urcorner)$ the R_n redex contracted in M.

Case 1. $H \cap C(\ulcorner m \urcorner) = \emptyset$. Easy.

Case 2. $H \subset C(\ulcorner m \urcorner)$. This is impossible by corollary 16.3.8 (i).

Case 3. $C(\ulcorner m \urcorner) \subset H$. Then $H \equiv H'[C(\ulcorner m \urcorner)]$, $M \equiv \cdots H \cdots$, $N \equiv \cdots \boldsymbol{\Omega} \cdots$, $L \equiv \cdots H'[C(\ulcorner 0 \urcorner)] \cdots$.

Claim. $H'[C(\ulcorner 0 \urcorner)]$ is unsolvable. Indeed, notice that $C(\ulcorner m \urcorner)$ and $C(\ulcorner 0 \urcorner)$ have the same Böhm tree, hence by theorem 16.2.7 $C(\ulcorner m \urcorner) = C(\ulcorner 0 \urcorner) \in \mathcal{H}^*$. But then $C(\ulcorner m \urcorner) \sim_s C(\ulcorner 0 \urcorner)$ and since $H \equiv H'[C(\ulcorner m \urcorner)]$ is unsolvable, $H'[C(\ulcorner 0 \urcorner)]$ is unsolvable too.

By the claim one can take $P \equiv N$ to complete the diagram. □

16.3.11. Corollary. *$\{B\ulcorner 0 \urcorner, B\ulcorner 1 \urcorner, \ldots\}$ is an independent set over $\mathcal{H}\boldsymbol{\eta}$.*

Proof. One has to show that

$$\{B\ulcorner 1 \urcorner = B\ulcorner 0 \urcorner, B\ulcorner 2 \urcorner = B\ulcorner 0 \urcorner, \ldots\}$$

is independent over $\mathcal{H}\boldsymbol{\eta}$, i.e. for $n \neq 0$

$$\mathcal{H}\boldsymbol{\eta} + \{B\ulcorner m \urcorner = B\ulcorner 0 \urcorner \mid m \neq 0, m \neq n\} \nvdash B\ulcorner n \urcorner = B\ulcorner 0 \urcorner.$$

Suppose $B\ulcorner n \urcorner = B\ulcorner 0 \urcorner$ were provable in this theory. Then by lemma 16.3.5 and proposition 16.3.10 $B\ulcorner n \urcorner$ and $B\ulcorner 0 \urcorner$ would have a common $\beta\eta\Omega_n$-reduct. But this is impossible by corollary 16.3.8 (v) and (ii). □

16.3.12. Theorem. (i) *There are $2^{\aleph_0}$ sensible λ-theories between $\mathcal{H}\boldsymbol{\eta}$ and $\mathcal{H}^*$.*

(ii) *There are $2^{\aleph_0}$ sensible hard λ-algebras*

(iii) *There are $2^{\aleph_0}$ sensible extensional λ-models.*

PROOF. (i) By lemma 16.3.2 and corollary 16.3.11 there are $2^{\aleph_0}$ λ-theories extending $\mathcal{H}\eta$. These are all sensible and hence $\subseteq \mathcal{H}^*$ by corollary 16.2.5.

(ii), (iii) Note that for λ-theories $\mathfrak{T}$, $\mathfrak{T}'$

$$\mathfrak{T} = \mathfrak{T}' \Leftrightarrow \mathfrak{M}(\mathfrak{T}) = \mathfrak{M}(\mathfrak{T}')$$

and similarly for closed term models. Hence by taking closed term models of the theories in (i) one obtains $2^{\aleph_0}$ sensible hard λ-algebras. By taking open term models, one obtains $2^{\aleph_0}$ sensible extensional λ-models. □

16.4 The theory $\mathfrak{B}$

The theory $\mathfrak{B}$ equates all terms with the same Böhm tree. The continuity theorem is needed to show that $\mathfrak{B}$ is consistent. In § 19.1 it will be shown that for the graph model $P\omega$ one has $\text{Th}(P\omega) = \mathfrak{B}$.

Remember that $M \precsim\!\!\!\succsim N$ iff $\text{BT}(M) = \text{BT}(N)$.

16.4.1. DEFINITION. $\mathfrak{B} = \{M = N \mid M, N \in \Lambda^0 \text{ and } M \approx N\}$.

16.4.2. PROPOSITION. (i) $\mathfrak{B} \vdash M = N \Leftrightarrow M \approx N$.

(ii) *$\mathfrak{B}$ is a λ-theory with $\mathcal{H} \subseteq \mathfrak{B} \subseteq \mathcal{H}^*$.*

PROOF. (i) ($\Rightarrow$) First note that

$$M \approx N \Rightarrow C[M] \approx C[N],$$

for if $M \approx N$, then

$$BT(C[M]) = \cup_n BT(C[M^{(n)}]) = \cup_n BT(C[N^{(n)}])$$
$$= BT(C[N])$$

by corollary 14.3.20. Now by induction on the length of proof it follows that

$$\mathfrak{B} \vdash M = N \Rightarrow M \approx N.$$

$$(\Leftarrow) \quad M \approx N \Rightarrow \lambda\vec{x}.M \approx \lambda x.N$$

$$\Rightarrow \mathfrak{B} \vdash \lambda\vec{x}.M = \lambda\vec{x}.M$$

$$\Rightarrow \mathfrak{B} \vdash M = N.$$

(ii) By (i) one has $\mathfrak{B}^+ = \mathfrak{B}$. Since clearly $\mathbf{I} = \mathbf{S} \notin \mathfrak{B}$ it follows that $\mathfrak{B}$ is a λ-theory. The rest is easy, using theorem 16.2.6. □

16.4.3. LEMMA. *If* $M \rightarrow_\eta N$, *then* $\mathrm{BT}(M)$ *is obtained from* $\mathrm{BT}(N)$ *by replacing in the latter some*

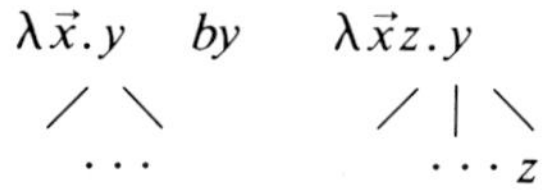

possibly infinitely often (but not changing the new variables z thus created).

PROOF. Obvious, after seeing the following examples. Let

$$M_0 \equiv \mathbf{\Theta}(\lambda mxy.x(\lambda z.yz)(mxy)),$$

$$N_0 \equiv \mathbf{\Theta}(\lambda mxy.xy(mxy))$$

Then $M_0 \rightarrow_\eta N_0$ and

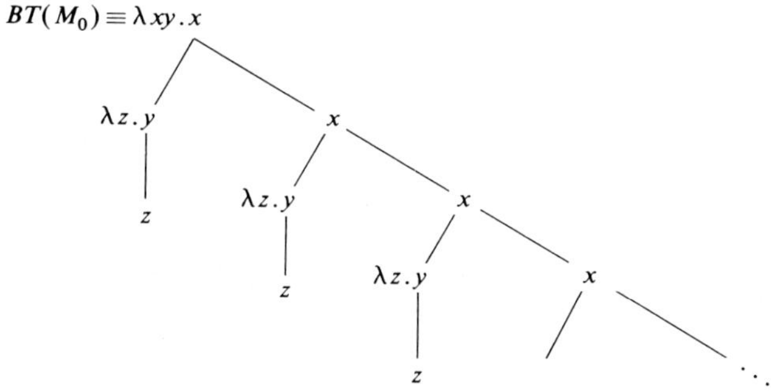

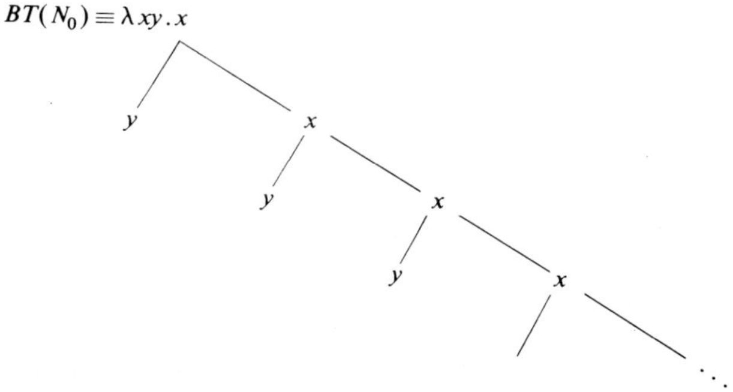

Note however that for M_1, N_1 corresponding to

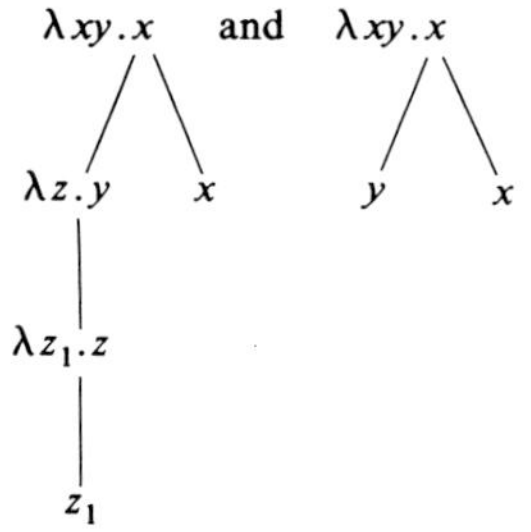

one has $M_1 \not\twoheadrightarrow_\eta N_1$. □

The following lemma is needed to show that $\mathfrak{B}\boldsymbol{\eta} \nvdash \omega$, see exercise 17.5.20.

16.4.4. LEMMA. *Let $\eta^n(x)$ be the tree*

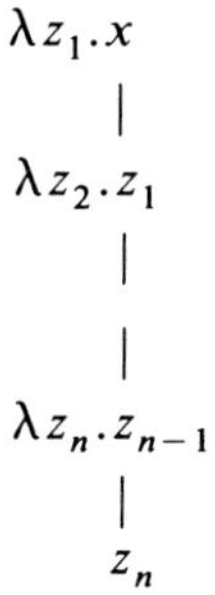

Let M, N have the following Böhm trees respectively:

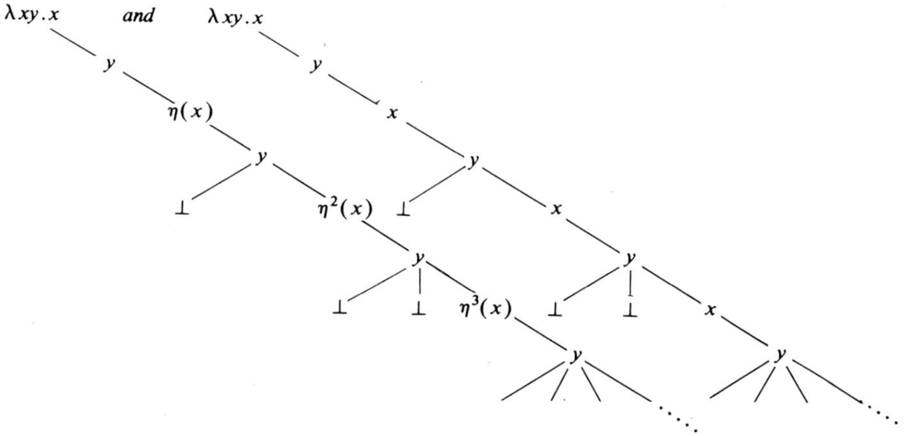

Then $\mathfrak{B}\boldsymbol{\eta} \nvdash M = N$.

PROOF. Suppose $\mathcal{B}\boldsymbol{\eta} \vdash M = N$. Then

$$M \equiv M_0 =_{\mathcal{B}} M_1 =_{\eta} M_2 =_{\mathcal{B}} \cdots =_{\eta} M_n \equiv N.$$

Hence only finitely often can a change described in lemma 16.4.3 occur. This is not enough to equate $\mathrm{BT}(M)$ and $\mathrm{BT}(N)$. □

The following way of defining λ-theories is inspired by Morris [1968].

16.4.5. DEFINITION. Let $\mathcal{P} \subset \Lambda$. Define

(i) $M \sqsubseteq_{\mathcal{P}} N \Leftrightarrow \forall C[\ \ ]\,[C[M] \in \mathcal{P} \Rightarrow C[N] \in \mathcal{P}]$;

(ii) $M \sim_{\mathcal{P}} N \Leftrightarrow M \sqsubseteq_{\mathcal{P}} N$ and $N \sqsubseteq_{\mathcal{P}} M$;

(iii) $\mathcal{T}_{\mathcal{P}} = \{M = N \,|\, M, N \in \Lambda^0$ and $M \sim_{\mathcal{P}} N\}$;

16.4.6. PROPOSITION. *Let* $\mathcal{P} \subseteq \Lambda$ *be non trivial* ($\neq \emptyset, \neq \Lambda$) *and closed under equality. Then*

(i) $\sim_{\mathcal{P}}$ *is a congruence relation.*

(ii) $\mathcal{T}_{\mathcal{P}}$ *is a λ-theory.*

PROOF. (i) Note that

$$M \sim_{\mathcal{P}} N \Leftrightarrow \forall C[\ \ ]\ [C[M] \in \mathcal{P} \Leftrightarrow C[M] \in \mathcal{P}].$$

Hence $\sim_{\mathcal{P}}$ is clearly an equivalence relation. Moreover,

$$M \sim_{\mathcal{P}} N \Rightarrow \forall C[\ \ ]\ [C[M] \sim_{\mathcal{P}} C[N]],$$

so $\sim_{\mathcal{P}}$ is a congruence relation.

(ii) By (i) $\mathcal{T}_{\mathcal{P}} \vdash M = N \Rightarrow M \sim_{\mathcal{P}} N$. Therefore $\mathcal{T}_{\mathcal{P}}^{+} = \mathcal{T}_{\mathcal{P}}$. Let $M \in \mathcal{P}$, $N \notin \mathcal{P}$. Then $M \not\sim_{\mathcal{P}} N$, hence $\mathcal{T}_{\mathcal{P}} \nvdash M = N$, i.e. $\mathcal{T}_{\mathcal{P}}$ is consistent. Since $\mathcal{P}$ is closed under equality, one has $\boldsymbol{\lambda} \subset \mathcal{T}_{\mathcal{P}}$. Therefore $\mathcal{T}_{\mathcal{P}}$ is a λ-theory. □

Note that for $\mathrm{SOL} = \{M \,|\, M$ is solvable$\}$ one has $\mathcal{T}_{\mathrm{SOL}} = \mathcal{H}^*$. Remember $\mathrm{NF} = \{M \in \Lambda \,|\, M$ has a nf$\}$. $\mathcal{T}_{\mathrm{NF}}$ is called *Morris' extensional theory*, see exercise 16.5.5.

16.4.7. PROPOSITION. (i) $\mathcal{B}\boldsymbol{\eta} \subseteq \mathcal{T}_{\mathrm{NF}} \subseteq \mathcal{H}^*$.

(ii) *The inclusions in* (i) *are proper.*

PROOF. (i) First we show $\mathbf{I} \sim_{\mathrm{NF}} \mathbf{1}$:

$$C[\mathbf{I}] \text{ has a nf} \Leftrightarrow C[\mathbf{I}] \text{ has a } \beta\eta\text{-nf by corollary 14.4.5,}$$

$$\Leftrightarrow C[\mathbf{1}] \text{ has a } \beta\eta\text{-nf}$$

$$\Leftrightarrow C[\mathbf{1}] \text{ has a nf.}$$

Therefore $\mathcal{T}_{\mathrm{NF}}$ is extensional.

Now let $\mathrm{BT}(M) = \mathrm{BT}(N)$ and assume $C[M] \in \mathrm{NF}$, say $C[M] = L$, L in nf. Since nf's are isolated in the tree topology, the continuity theorem implies

$$\exists k \ \forall M' \in O_{M,k} \quad C[M'] = L.$$

But then $C[N] = L$, i.e. $C[N] \in \mathrm{NF}$; By symmetry it follows that $M \sim_{\mathrm{NF}} N$.

So far we have $\mathcal{B}\eta \subset \mathcal{T}_{\mathrm{NF}}$. Since $\mathcal{H} \subset \mathcal{B}$ and $\mathcal{H}^*$ is the unique HP-completion of $\mathcal{H}$ one has $\mathcal{T}_{\mathrm{NF}} \subset \mathcal{H}^*$.

(ii) For $J = \boldsymbol{\Theta}(jxy.x(jy))$ one has $\mathbf{I} = J \in \mathcal{H}^*$ (use theorem 16.2.7) and clearly $\mathbf{I} = J \notin \mathcal{T}_{\mathrm{NF}}$ (J does not have a nf). Moreover for the M, N in lemma 16.4.4 one has $M = N \notin \mathcal{B}\eta$. But if $C[M]$ has a nf, then by continuity $C[M^{(k)}]$ has a nf, for some k. Note that there is an $N' \sqsupseteq M^{(k)}$ such that $N' =_{\beta\eta} N$. Hence $C[N] =_{\beta\eta} C[N']$ has a nf. By symmetry $M \sim_{\mathrm{NF}} N$ and therefore $M = N \in \mathcal{T}_{\mathrm{NF}}$. □

In the same way as for $\mathcal{H}^*$ it can be shown that the theory $\mathcal{B}$ is Π^0_2-complete.

16.5. Exercises

16.5.1. (i) Show that

$$\forall z \in \Lambda^0 \ \exists n \in \mathbb{N} \quad \mathcal{H} \vdash Z\Omega^{\sim n} = \Omega.$$

(ii) Let A be such that $Ax \twoheadrightarrow \lambda z.z(A(x\Omega))$. Show that

$$\forall Z, Z' \in \Lambda^0 \quad \mathcal{H} \vdash AZ = AZ';$$

$$\neg \forall Z, Z' \in \Lambda \quad \mathcal{H} \vdash AZ = AZ;$$

$$\forall Z, Z' \in \Lambda \quad \mathcal{H}^* \vdash AZ = A'Z.$$

16.5.2. Show that $\mathcal{H} \vdash \boldsymbol{ext}^0$ but $\mathcal{H} \nvdash \boldsymbol{ext}$.

16.5.3. Show directly that $\mathcal{H}^*$ is Π^0_2-complete. Similarly for $\mathcal{B}$.

16.5.4. Draw the reduction graph of Bx as defined in notation 16.3.3.

16.5.5 (Morris [1968]). Define

$$M \sqsubseteq_{m1} N \Leftrightarrow \forall C[\ ]\ [C[M] \text{ has a nf} \Rightarrow C[N] \text{ has the same nf}];$$

$$M \sqsubseteq_{m2} N \Leftrightarrow \forall C[\ ][C[M] \text{ has a } \beta\eta\text{-nf} \Rightarrow C[N] \text{ has the same } \beta\eta\text{-nf}];$$

$$M \sqsubseteq_{m3} N \Leftrightarrow \forall C[\ ]\ [C[M] \text{ has a nf} \Rightarrow C[N] \text{ has a nf}];$$

$$M \sqsubseteq_{m4} N \Leftrightarrow \forall C[\ ]\ [C[M] \text{ has a } \beta\eta\text{-nf} \Rightarrow C[N] \text{ has a } \beta\eta\text{-nf}].$$

Moreover let for $1 \leqslant i \leqslant 4$

$$M \sim_{mi} N \Leftrightarrow M \sqsubseteq_{mi} N \text{ and } N \sqsubseteq_{mi} M;$$

$$\mathfrak{T}_{mi} = \{M = N \mid M, N \in \Lambda^0 \text{ and } M \sim_{mi} M\}.$$

Show (i) $M \sqsubseteq_{m1} N \Rightarrow M \sqsubseteq N$.

(ii) $\mathfrak{B} \subsetneq \mathfrak{T}_{m1} \subsetneq \mathfrak{T}_{m2} = \mathfrak{T}_{m3} = \mathfrak{T}_{m4} \subsetneq \mathfrak{K}^*$.

[$\mathfrak{T}_{m2}$ is the original definition of Morris' extensional theory; $\mathfrak{T}_{m1}$ is called Morris' theory.]

16.5.6. Show that if $\mathcal{P} \subseteq \Lambda$ is a nontrivial open set, closed under equality, then $\mathfrak{T}_{\mathcal{P}} \supseteq \mathfrak{B}$.

16.5.7. Let $\mathfrak{T}_M = \mathfrak{T}\{N \mid N =_\beta M\}$. Show that

(i) $\boldsymbol{\lambda} \subsetneq \mathfrak{T}_{\boldsymbol{\Omega}}$,

(ii) $\mathfrak{B} \subsetneq \mathfrak{T}_{\mathsf{I}}$,

*(iii) $\mathfrak{T}_{\mathsf{I}} \subsetneq \mathfrak{T}_{\mathrm{NF}}$.

16.5.8. Show that the combinatory algebras do not form a Mal'cev variety, see remark 4.1.21. [*Hint*. Let $J = \boldsymbol{\lambda} + \mathsf{I} = \boldsymbol{\Omega}_3 \equiv \omega_3\omega_3$, with $\omega_3 = \lambda x.xxx$. Then $(\mathsf{I}, \boldsymbol{\Omega}_3) \in =_J \cdot =_{\mathfrak{K}}$ but $(\mathsf{I}, \boldsymbol{\Omega}_3) \notin =_{\mathfrak{K}} \cdot =_J$. (Use lemma 4.1.8 (ii), proposition 15.3.9 and theorem 16.1.9 (i).)] By a theorem of Mal'cev it follows that $\neg \exists F \in \Lambda^0\ Fxxy = y \wedge Fxyy = x$. Prove this corollary directly.

16.5.9. Show that $M \in \Lambda$ is solvable iff $\neg\mathrm{Con}(M = \mathbf{K}_\infty)$, where $\mathbf{K}_\infty = \boldsymbol{\Theta}\,\mathbf{K}$.

CHAPTER 17

OTHER LAMBDA THEORIES

In this chapter some λ-theories are studied that are not sensible. Usually, however, these theories are semi sensible, i.e. can be extended to a sensible theory. The reason for considering these also is that sensible theories are never recursively axiomatizable.

A result about recursively enumerable λ-theories states that they are dense (with respect to inclusion) and even complete for countable partial orderings.

Another group of theories are the ones closed under the ω-rule. The strength of adding the ω-rule will be examined. It turns out that both $\boldsymbol{\lambda\eta}$ and $\mathcal{H}\boldsymbol{\eta}$ are not closed under the ω-rule, but $\mathcal{H}^*$ is.

17.1. Semi sensible and r.e. theories

Remember that a λ-theory $\mathcal{T}$ is called semi sensible (s.s.) if $\mathcal{T} \nvdash M = N$ whenever M is solvable and N is unsolvable.

17.1.1. LEMMA. $\mathcal{T}$ *is* s.s.$\Leftrightarrow \mathcal{T} \subseteq \mathcal{H}^*$.

PROOF. (⇒) Let $M = N \in \mathcal{T}$. Suppose that $M = N \notin \mathcal{H}^*$, i.e. $M \not\sim_s N$, say for some context $C[M]$ is solvable, $C[N]$ is unsolvable. But $\mathcal{T} \vdash C[M] = C[N]$; contradicting that $\mathcal{T}$ is s.s.

(⇐) Let $\mathcal{T} \subseteq \mathcal{H}^*$ and $\mathcal{T} \vdash M = N$. Then $M \sim_s N$, hence M, N are both solvable or both unsolvable. □

Consequently $\boldsymbol{\lambda}$, $\boldsymbol{\lambda\eta}$, $\mathcal{H}$, $\mathcal{H}\boldsymbol{\eta}$ $\mathcal{B}$, $\mathcal{B}\boldsymbol{\eta}$, and $\mathcal{H}^*$ are all s.s. λ-theories.

17.1.2. COROLLARY. (i) $\mathcal{T}$ *is a* s.s. λ-*theory* $\Rightarrow \mathcal{T}\boldsymbol{\eta}$ *is a* s.s. λ-*theory*.
(ii) $\mathcal{T}_1$, $\mathcal{T}_2$ *are* s.s. λ-*theories* $\Rightarrow \mathcal{T}_1 \cup \mathcal{T}_2$ *is a* s.s. λ-*theory*.

PROOF. Immediate. □

In general the union of two λ-theories does not need to be a λ-theory. A nice example is due to M. Bel: there are three terms M, N, $L \in \Lambda^0$ such that

$$\text{Con}(M=N), \qquad \text{Con}(N=L), \qquad \text{Con}(L=M)$$

but $\neg\text{Con}(M=N=L)$ (see exercise 17.5.2).

One of the main features of s.s. λ-theories is that the concepts of solvability and separability are absolute.

17.1.3. DEFINITION. Let $\mathfrak{T}$ be a λ-theory.

(i) $M \in \Lambda^0$ is *$\mathfrak{T}$-solvable* if $\exists \vec{N}\ M\vec{N} =_{\mathfrak{T}} \mathbf{I}$. $M \in \Lambda$ is *$\mathfrak{T}$-solvable* if the closure $\lambda\vec{x}.M$ is $\mathfrak{T}$-solvable.

(ii) $F = \{M_1, \ldots, M_n\}$ is *$\mathfrak{T}$-separable* if

$$\forall N_1, \ldots, N_n\ \exists C[\ \ ]\quad C[M_1] =_{\mathfrak{T}} N_1 \wedge \cdots \wedge C[M_n] =_{\mathfrak{T}} N_n.$$

17.1.4. PROPOSITION. *Let $\mathfrak{T}$ be* s.s. *Then*

$$M \textit{ is } \mathfrak{T}\textit{-solvable} \Leftrightarrow M \textit{ is solvable}.$$

PROOF. It suffices to show this for closed M.

($\Rightarrow$) Let $M\vec{N} =_{\mathfrak{T}} \mathbf{I}$. Then by semi-sensibility $M\vec{N}$ is solvable, hence M is solvable.

($\Leftarrow$) Trivial. □

It is easy to see that proposition 17.1.4 characterizes s.s. λ-theories.

17.1.5. LEMMA. *Let $\mathcal{F} = \{M_1, \ldots, M_n\} \subseteq \Lambda$ be $\mathcal{H}^*$-separable. Then $\mathcal{F}$ is separable.*

PROOF. By assumption for some context

$$C[M_1] =_{\mathcal{H}^*} x_1, \ldots, C[M_n] =_{\mathcal{H}^*} x_n.$$

Then $C[M_i] \sim x_i$, by lemma 10.4.1, hence the $C[M_i]$ are all solvable with free head variables $x_1, x_2, \ldots$, respectively. But then by proposition 10.4.12 $\{C[M_1], \ldots\}$ is separable, hence so is $\mathcal{F}$. □

17.1.6. THEOREM. *Let $\mathfrak{T}$ be* s.s. *Then*

$$\mathcal{F} \textit{ is } \mathfrak{T}\textit{-separable} \Leftrightarrow \mathcal{F} \textit{ is separable}.$$

PROOF. Note that for λ-theories $\mathfrak{T}_1 \subseteq \mathfrak{T}_2$ one has

$$\mathfrak{T}_1\textit{-separability} \Rightarrow \mathfrak{T}_2\textit{-separability}.$$

Therefore one has

$$\mathscr{F} \text{ separable} \Rightarrow \mathscr{F}\ \mathfrak{T}\text{-separable}$$

$$\Rightarrow \mathscr{F}\ \mathcal{H}^*\text{-separable}$$

$$\Rightarrow \mathscr{F} \text{ separable},$$

by the previous lemma. □

Another characterization of semi-sensibility is topological:
$\mathfrak{T}$ is semi-sensible iff $\mathfrak{M}(\mathfrak{T})$ with the tree topology is not indiscrete. [The canonical topology on $\mathfrak{M}(\mathfrak{T})$ is the quotient topology via the canonical map $\varphi_{\mathfrak{T}}: \Lambda \to \mathfrak{M}(\mathfrak{T})$, with on Λ the tree topology defined in § 10.2.] This is shown in proposition 20.5.6

R.e. theories

Several results of this section are due to Visser. He has obtained them by considering term models as precomplete numbered sets in the sense of Ershov [1973]; see exercise 6.8.18. We present the results here without making reference to numbered sets.

17.1.8. LEMMA. *Let $\psi: \mathbb{N} \to \mathbb{N}$ be a partial recursive function. Then for some $n \in \mathbb{N}$*

$$\psi(n)\downarrow \Rightarrow \mathbf{E}\ulcorner n \urcorner = \mathbf{E}\ulcorner \psi(n) \urcorner .$$

PROOF. Let ψ be λ-defined by F. By the second fixed point theorem 6.5.9 for some $X \in \Lambda$, $X = \mathbf{E} \circ F \ulcorner X \urcorner$. Let $\ulcorner n \urcorner = \ulcorner X \urcorner$. Then

$$\mathbf{E}\ulcorner n \urcorner = \mathbf{E}\ulcorner X \urcorner = X \quad \text{by theorem 8.1.6,}$$

$$= \mathbf{E} \circ F \ulcorner X \urcorner = \mathbf{E}(F\ulcorner n \urcorner) = \mathbf{E}\ulcorner \psi(n) \urcorner . \quad \square$$

The following three results are taken from Visser [1980].

17.1.9. PROPOSITION. *Let $\mathfrak{T}$ be an* r.e. *λ-theory and let $M, N \in \Lambda$ be such that $\mathfrak{T} \nvdash M = N$. Then*

$$\exists P\ \forall Q \quad \mathfrak{T} + P = Q \nvdash M = N.$$

PROOF. Define $A_n = \{m \in \mathbb{N} | \mathfrak{T} + \mathbf{E}\ulcorner n \urcorner = \mathbf{E}\ulcorner m \urcorner \vdash M = N\}$. Then

(1) $\quad \forall n \quad n \notin A_n,$

(2) $\quad m \in A_n \Leftrightarrow \exists z\ R(n,m,z)$

for some recursive R. Consider

$$\psi(n) = (\mu z R(n, (z)_0, (z)_1))_0.$$

Then for all $n \in \mathbb{N}$

(3) $\psi(n)\downarrow \Leftrightarrow A_n \neq \emptyset,$

(4) $\psi(n)\downarrow \Rightarrow \psi(n) \in A_n.$

By the previous lemma there is some n_0 such that

(5) $\psi(n_0)\downarrow \Rightarrow \mathbf{E}\ulcorner n_0 \urcorner = \mathbf{E}\ulcorner \psi(n_0) \urcorner.$

Suppose $\psi(n_0)\downarrow$. Then $\psi(n_0) \in A_{n_0}$ by (4). But $\mathbf{E}\ulcorner n_0 \urcorner = \mathbf{E}\ulcorner \psi(n_0) \urcorner$ by (5), hence $\psi(n_0) \notin A_{n_0}$. Therefore $\psi(n_0)\uparrow$ and hence $A_{n_0} = \emptyset$ by (3). Now we can take $P = \mathbf{E}\ulcorner n_0 \urcorner$. □

A term P is $\mathfrak{T}$-*easy* if $\forall Q$ Con($\mathfrak{T} + P = Q$). Proposition 17.1.9 shows that for every r.e. λ-theory $\mathfrak{T}$, there is a $\mathfrak{T}$-easy term P.

The following theorem shows that the r.e. λ-theories are dense with respect to inclusion.

17.1.10. THEOREM. *Let* $\mathfrak{T} \subsetneq \mathfrak{T}'$ *be* r.e. λ-*theories. Then there exists an* r.e. λ-*theory* $\mathfrak{S}$ *such that* $\mathfrak{T} \subsetneq \mathfrak{S} \subsetneq \mathfrak{T}'$.

PROOF. Let $\mathfrak{T}' \vdash M = N$ and $\mathfrak{T} \nvdash M = N$. By the preceding proposition for some P

(1) $\forall Q \quad \mathfrak{T} + P = Q \nvdash M = N.$

Take $\mathfrak{S} = \mathfrak{T} + PM = PN$. Clearly $\mathfrak{S}$ is r.e. and $\mathfrak{T} \subseteq \mathfrak{S} \subseteq \mathfrak{T}'$.

Suppose $\mathfrak{T} = \mathfrak{S}$. Then

$$\mathfrak{T} + P = \mathbf{I} \;=\; \mathfrak{T} + PM = PN + P = \mathbf{I} \vdash M = N$$

contradicting (1).

Suppose $\mathfrak{T}' = \mathfrak{S}$. Then $\mathfrak{T} + PM = PN \vdash M = N$. Now $\mathfrak{T} + P = \mathbf{KI} \vdash PM = PN$. Hence $\mathfrak{T} + P = \mathbf{KI} \vdash M = N$, contradicting (1). □

17.1.11. COROLLARY. *There exists a family of* λ-*theories* $\{\mathfrak{T}_r\}_{r \in \mathbf{R}}$ *such that for real* r, r'

(1) $r < r' \Leftrightarrow \mathfrak{T}_r \subsetneq \mathfrak{T}_{r'}.$

PROOF. Using the preceding theorem one can embed the rationals into the r.e. λ-theories, i.e. construct a family $\{\mathfrak{T}_r\}_{r\in\mathbb{Q}}$ such that (1) holds for $r, r' \in \mathbb{Q}$. Now define, for $r \in \mathbb{R}$

$$\mathfrak{T}_r = \bigcup \left\{ \mathfrak{T}_q \,|\, q < r \text{ and } q \in \mathbb{Q} \right\}.$$

This clearly satisfies (1) for $r, r' \in \mathbb{R}$. □

In Visser [1980] it is proved also that every countable partial ordering can be inbedded into the r.e. λ-theories with inclusion.

Another kind of results on r.e. theories is the following "range theorem": If $\mathfrak{T}$ is an r.e. λ-theory, then the range of a definable map in the term model $\mathfrak{M}(\mathfrak{T})$ is either a singleton or infinite. This theorem was conjectured by Böhm and proved by Myhill and the author independently. In Visser [1980] it is pointed out that the proof can be given in a nice topological fashion. For the (shorter) original proof, see theorem 20.2.5.

17.1.12. DEFINITION. (i) The *Visser topology* on Λ is obtained by taking as basis open sets $O \subseteq \Lambda$ such that

(1) O is closed under β-equality

(2) O is (after coding) a Π_1^0 set.

(ii) Let $\mathfrak{T}$ be any λ-theory. The Visser topology on $\mathfrak{M}(\mathfrak{T})$ is the quotient topology for $\varphi_{\mathfrak{T}}$: $\Lambda \to \mathfrak{M}(\mathfrak{T})$, where $\varphi_{\mathfrak{T}}$ is the canonical map and Λ has the Visser topology.

For example the unsolvables form an open set in Λ. In $\mathfrak{M}(\mathfrak{H})$ the set $\{\Omega\}$ is open.

17.1.13. PROPOSITION. (i) *If f is some definable map on Λ (i.e. $f(M) = FM$ for some $F \in \Lambda$), then f is continuous w.r.t. the Visser topology.*

(ii) *Similarly for a definable map on $\mathfrak{M}(\mathfrak{T})$ (i.e. $f[M]_{\mathfrak{T}} = [FM]_{\mathfrak{T}}$).*

PROOF. (i) Let O be a basis open neighbourhood of FM. Let $O_M = \{N \,|\, FM \in O\}$. Then since O is Visser open, so is O_M and we are done.

(ii) By (i) and a diagram. □

A topological space is called *hyper-connected* iff any two non-empty open sets have a non-empty intersection. Such a space is clearly connected.

17.1.14. PROPOSITION. (i) *Λ with the Visser topology is hyper-connected.*

(ii) *$\mathfrak{M}(\mathfrak{T})$ with the Visser topology is hyper-connected for each λ-theory $\mathfrak{T}$.*

PROOF. (i) A set $A \subseteq \mathbb{N}$ is called *β-closed* if $[n \in A \wedge \mathbf{E}\ulcorner n \urcorner =_\beta \mathbf{E}\ulcorner m \urcorner] \Rightarrow m \in A$. We need the following

Sublemma. Let $A, B \subseteq \mathbb{N}$ be β-closed r.e. sets such that $A \cup B = \mathbb{N}$. Then $A = \mathbb{N}$ or $B = \mathbb{N}$.

Subproof. Suppose $A, B \neq \mathbb{N}$. Let $X, Y \subseteq \mathbb{N}$ be a pair of recursively inseparable disjoint r.e. sets. Let $n_A \in A - B$, $n_B \in B - A$. Define

$$\psi(n) = \begin{cases} n_A & \text{if } n \in X, \\ n_B & \text{if } n \in Y, \\ \uparrow & \text{else.} \end{cases}$$

Then ψ is partial recursive and hence can be λ-defined by say $F \in \Lambda$. Define

$$C = \{n \mid \sharp(F\ulcorner n \urcorner) \in A\}, \qquad D = \{n \mid \sharp(F\ulcorner n \urcorner) \in B\}.$$

Then C, D are r.e. and $C \cup D = \mathbb{N}$. Moreover

$$n \in X \Rightarrow \psi(n) = n_A \notin B$$

$$\Rightarrow \sharp F\ulcorner n \urcorner \notin B, \quad \text{since } F \text{ defines } \psi \text{ and } B \text{ is } \beta\text{-closed,}$$

$$\Rightarrow n \notin D.$$

Therefore $X \cap D = \emptyset$ and similarly $Y \cap C = \emptyset$.

By the reduction principle for r.e. sets there are r.e. sets $C' \subseteq C$, $D' \subseteq D$ with $C' \cup D' = C \cup D = \mathbb{N}$ and $C' \cap D' = \emptyset$. But then C' is recursive and separates X and Y contrary to the choice of X, Y. Sub□

Let $O_1, O_2 \subseteq \Lambda$ be open and suppose $O_1 \cap O_2 = \emptyset$. Define

$$A = \{n \mid \mathbf{E}\ulcorner n \urcorner \notin O_1\}, \qquad B = \{n \mid \mathbf{E}\ulcorner n \urcorner \notin O_2\}.$$

Then A, B satisfy the assumptions of the sublemma. Hence $A = \mathbb{N}$ or $B = \mathbb{N}$ and therefore $O_1 = \emptyset$ or $O_2 = \emptyset$.

(ii) $\mathfrak{M}(\mathfrak{T})$ is the image of the hyper-connected space Λ under the canonical map $\varphi_{\mathfrak{T}}$ which is by definition continuous. Therefore $\mathfrak{M}(\mathfrak{T})$ is hyper-connected. □

As an immediate corollary we have Scott's theorem: Every non-trivial set $\mathcal{A} \subseteq \Lambda$ closed under equality is non-recursive. Indeed, if $\mathcal{A}$ were recursive, then $\mathcal{A}$ and Λ-$\mathcal{A}$ would be Π_1^0, hence Visser-open, contradicting the connectedness of Λ.

17.1.15. Lemma. *Let* $\mathfrak{T}$ *be an* r.e. λ-*theory*.

(i) *Let* $\mathcal{A} \subseteq \mathfrak{M}(\mathfrak{T})$ *be finite. Then* w.r.t. *the Visser topology* $\mathcal{A}$ *is discrete.*

(ii) *Let* $\mathrm{BH}_{\mathfrak{T}} = \{[M]_{\mathfrak{T}} \mid M$ *is a* $\beta\eta$-nf$\} \subseteq \mathfrak{M}(\mathfrak{T})$. *Then also* $\mathrm{BH}_{\mathfrak{T}}$ *is discrete.*

PROOF. (i) Let $\mathcal{A} = \{[M_1]_{\mathfrak{T}}, \ldots, [M_n]_{\mathfrak{T}}\}$. Define

$$O_1 = \{[M]_{\mathfrak{T}} | M \neq_{\mathfrak{T}} M_2 \wedge \cdots \wedge M \neq_{\mathfrak{T}} M_n\}.$$

Then $[M_1]_{\mathfrak{T}} \in O_1$ and $O_1 \cap (\mathcal{A} - \{[M_1]_{\mathfrak{T}}\}) = \emptyset$. Moreover $\varphi_T^{-1}(O_1)$ is Π_1^0 and closed under equality, hence O_1 is Visser open. Therefore $[M_1]_{\mathfrak{T}}$ is an isolated point of $\mathcal{A}$. Since $[M_1]_{\mathfrak{T}}$ is arbitrary, $\mathcal{A}$ is discrete.

(ii) Let $[M_0]_{\mathfrak{T}} \in BH_{\mathfrak{T}}$; assume M_0 is in $\beta\eta$-nf. Define

$$O = \{[M]_{\mathfrak{T}} | \forall M' \text{ in } \beta\eta\text{-nf}[M' \not\equiv M_0 \Rightarrow M' \neq_{\mathfrak{T}} M]\}.$$

As before O is Visser open. By Böhm's theorem $[M_0]_{\mathfrak{T}} \in O$. Moreover $(\mathrm{BH}_{\mathfrak{T}} - \{[M_0]_{\mathfrak{T}}\}) \cap O = \emptyset$. Therefore $\{[M_0]_{\mathfrak{T}}\}$ is an isolated point of $\mathrm{BH}_{\mathfrak{T}}$ and so all of them are. □

17.1.16. RANGE THEOREM. *Let $\mathfrak{T}$ be an r.e. theory. Let f: $\mathfrak{M}(\mathfrak{T}) \to \mathfrak{M}(\mathfrak{T})$ be a definable map (i.e. $f([M]_{\mathfrak{T}}) = [FM]_{\mathfrak{T}}$ for some $F \in \Lambda$). Then the range of f is either a singleton or infinite. Similarly for f restricted to $\mathfrak{M}^0(\mathfrak{T})$.*

PROOF. Suppose range f is finite. Then by the preceding proposition it is discrete. On the other hand by propositions 17.1.13 (ii) and 17.1.14 (i), the range of f is the continuous image of a connected space hence connected. But the only connected discrete space is a singleton. As to the second statement, note that Λ^0 is open hence also hyper-connected. □

For several other models of the λ-calculus, e.g. $P\omega$, D_∞, the range theorem does hold, see theorem 20.2.6. It is an open problem whether the range theorem holds for $\mathfrak{M}^0(\mathcal{K})$.

17.1.17. COROLLARY. *Let $\mathfrak{T}$ be an* r.e. *theory. Let F be such that*

$$\forall M \in \Lambda \ \exists N \text{ in } \beta\eta\text{-nf} \quad FM =_{\mathfrak{T}} N.$$

Then F is constant modulo $\mathfrak{T}$ (i.e. $\forall M, N \ FM =_{\mathfrak{T}} FN$).

PROOF. Like the preceding proof. □

In exercise 20.6.12 the range theorem is interpreted in Ershov's theory of numerations.

17.2. Omega theories

The consistency of $\lambda\omega$ was shown in Barendregt [1971] by an ordinal analysis of proofs. Wadsworth [1976] and Nakajima [1975] showed that one has $D_\infty \models \omega$, that is, for $M, N \in \Lambda^0$

$$[\forall Z \in \Lambda^0\ D_\infty \models MZ = NZ] \Rightarrow D_\infty \models M = N.$$

Since $\text{Th}(D_\infty) = \mathcal{H}^*$ (see theorem 19.2.12) it follows that $\mathcal{H}^*$ must be closed under the ω-rule. An easy proof of this fact without reference to D_∞ will be presented. Nevertheless the consistency proof using ordinals will be given also, since it gives more proof theoretic information, culminating in theorem 17.2.17:

$$\mathcal{H}\omega \vdash M = \mathbf{I} \Rightarrow \boldsymbol{\lambda\eta} \vdash M = \mathbf{I}.$$

The proof that $\mathcal{H}^* \vdash \omega$ occupies 17.2.1–17.2.8. Use is made of ***CL***, since closed ***CL***-terms are presented without any variables. An auxiliary theory $\underline{\boldsymbol{CL}}$ is introduced in order to keep track of terms in a reduction.

17.2.1. DEFINITION. (i) The set $\underline{\mathcal{C}}^0$ (of closed *CL*-terms with underlining) is inductively defined as follows:

(1) $\boldsymbol{K}, \boldsymbol{S} \in \underline{\mathcal{C}}^0$,

(2) $P, Q \in \underline{\mathcal{C}}^0 \Rightarrow (PQ) \in \underline{\mathcal{C}}^0$,

(3) $P \in \mathcal{C}^0 \Rightarrow \underline{P} \in \underline{\mathcal{C}}^0$.

Note that by clause (3) only simple underlinings are present.

(ii) On $\underline{\mathcal{C}}^0$ the binary relations $\to_{\underline{w}}$ and $\twoheadrightarrow_{\underline{w}}$ are defined by the notion of reduction $\underline{\boldsymbol{w}}$, with as contraction rules

$$\boldsymbol{K}PQ \to P,$$

$$\boldsymbol{S}PQR \to PR(QR),$$

$$\underline{P}Q \to PQ \quad \text{for } P \in \mathcal{C}^0.$$

(iii) If $P \in \underline{\mathcal{C}}^0$, then $|P|$ is P without any underlining. $P \cong Q$ iff $|P| \equiv |Q|$ for $P, Q \in \underline{\mathcal{C}}^0$. $P \subset Q$ denotes that P is a subterm of Q, e.g. $K \subset \underline{KS}$, $\underline{K} \not\subset \underline{KS}$.

Note that $\mathcal{C}^0 \subseteq \underline{\mathcal{C}}^0$ and that on $\mathcal{C}^0$ the relations $\to_w$ and $\to_{\underline{w}}$ coincide, as do $\twoheadrightarrow_w$ and $\twoheadrightarrow_{\underline{w}}$.

17.2.2. LEMMA. (i) *Let* $P, P' \in \underline{\mathcal{C}}^0$. *Then*

$$[P \twoheadrightarrow_w P' \wedge \underline{Q}' \subset P'] \Rightarrow \exists Q \in \mathcal{C}^0\ [\underline{Q} \subset P \wedge Q \twoheadrightarrow_w Q'].$$

(ii) *Let* $F, P \cap \mathcal{C}^0$ *and* $P' \in \underline{\mathcal{C}}^0$. *Then*

$$[F\underline{P} \twoheadrightarrow_{\underline{w}} P' \wedge \underline{Q} \subset P'] \Rightarrow P \twoheadrightarrow_w Q.$$

PROOF. (i) By transitivity it suffices to show this for $P \to_{\underline{w}} P'$. This follows by induction on the generation of $\to_{\underline{w}}$; examples: $SPQ\underline{R} \to_{\underline{w}} P\underline{R}(Q\underline{R})$, $SPQ\underline{R} \to_{\underline{w}} SPQ\underline{R}'$.

(ii) Assume $F\underline{P} \twoheadrightarrow_{\underline{w}} P' \supset \underline{Q}$. By (i)

$$\exists Q_1 [\underline{Q}_1 \subset F\underline{P} \text{ and } Q_1 \twoheadrightarrow Q].$$

But then $Q_1 \equiv P$. □

17.2.3. LEMMA. *Let* $P, P' \in \mathcal{C}^0$ *and* $Q \in \underline{\mathcal{C}}^0$. *Then*

$$[P \cong Q \text{ and } P \twoheadrightarrow_w P'] \Rightarrow \exists Q' \in \underline{\mathcal{C}}^0 \; [P' \cong Q' \text{ and } Q \twoheadrightarrow_{\underline{w}} Q'].$$

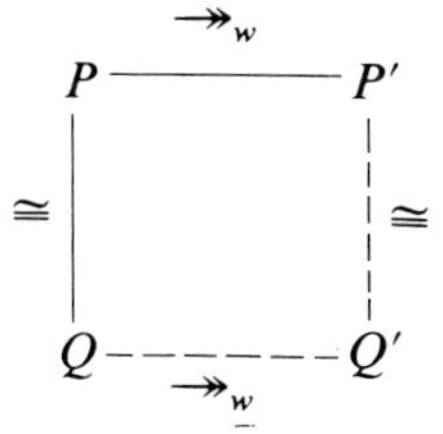

PROOF. Again it is sufficient to prove this for $\to_w$ on the LHS. This is easy to show. Note that rule $\underline{P}Q \to_{\underline{w}} PQ$ is needed. E.g. $\underline{\boldsymbol{K}}MN \cong \boldsymbol{K}MN \to_w M$. Then $\underline{\boldsymbol{K}}MN \to_{\underline{w}} \boldsymbol{K}MN \to_{\underline{w}} M$. □

17.2.4. DEFINITION. For $R \in \mathcal{C}^0$, define the map φ_R: $\underline{\mathcal{C}}^0 \to \mathcal{C}^0$ as follows:

$$\varphi_R(P) = P \quad \textit{if } P \in \mathcal{C}^0,$$

$$\varphi_R(\underline{P}) = R,$$

$$\varphi_R(PQ) = \varphi_R(P)\varphi_R(Q).$$

φ_R just replaces all underlined terms by R.

For $P, Q \in \mathcal{C}^0$ define

$$P \sim_s Q \Leftrightarrow \forall F \in \mathcal{C} \; [FP \text{ is } w\text{-solvable} \Leftrightarrow FQ \text{ is } w\text{-solvable}].$$

17.2.5. LEMMA. *Let* $M, N \in \Lambda^0$. *Then*

$$M \sim_s N \Leftrightarrow M_{CL} \sim_s N_{CL}.$$

PROOF. Immediate by proposition 8.3.22 and lemma 2.1.20. □

17.2.6. LEMMA. *Let* $P, Q \in \underline{\mathcal{C}}^0$, $R, R' \in \mathcal{C}^0$ *and* $\forall Z \in \mathcal{C}^0$ $RZ \sim_s R'Z$. *Then* $\varphi_{R'}(P) \sim_s \varphi_{R'}(Q)$ *under each of the following assumptions*:

(i) $P \to_{\underline{w}} Q$ *and* $\forall \underline{L} \subset P$ $L =_w R'$.

(ii) $P \twoheadrightarrow_{\underline{w}} Q$ *and* $\forall \underline{L} \subset P$ $L =_w R$.

(iii) $P \equiv F\underline{R} \twoheadrightarrow_{\underline{w}} Q$ *with* $F \in \mathcal{C}^0$.

PROOF. (i) By induction on the generation of $P \to_{\underline{w}} Q$. The only non-trivial case is $P \equiv \underline{C}D$, $Q \equiv CD$. Then $C =_w R$, hence

$$\varphi_{R'}(P) \equiv R' \varphi_{R'}(D) \sim_s R \varphi_{R'}(D) =_w C \varphi_{R'}(D) \equiv \varphi_{R'}(Q).$$

Now note that $X \sim_s Y =_w Z \Rightarrow X \sim_s Z$.

(ii) By (i) using transitivity and lemma 17.2.2 (i).

(iii) By (ii). □

17.2.7. PROPOSITION. *Let* $M, N \in \Lambda^0$ *and suppose* $\forall Z \in \Lambda^0 \ MZ \sim_s NZ$. *Then* $M \sim_s N$.

PROOF. Since M, N are closed, it suffices by lemma 2.1.20 to show

$$\forall F \quad [FM \text{ solvable} \Rightarrow FN \text{ solvable}].$$

Let F be given. Then

$$FM \text{ solvable} \Rightarrow$$

$$\Rightarrow F_{CL} M_{CL} \ w\text{-solvable}$$

$$\Rightarrow F_{CL} M_{CL} \vec{P} =_w \boldsymbol{S} \quad \text{for some } \vec{P} \in C^0,$$

$$\Rightarrow F_{CL} M_{CL} \vec{P} \twoheadrightarrow_w \boldsymbol{S} \quad \text{by CR for } \boldsymbol{w},$$

$$\Rightarrow F_{CL} \underline{M}_{CL} \vec{P} \twoheadrightarrow_{\underline{w}} S' \quad \text{with } S' \cong \boldsymbol{S}, \text{ by lemma 17.2.3.}$$

Case 1. $S' \equiv \boldsymbol{S}$. By assumption $\forall R \in C^0 \ M_{CL} R \sim_s N_{CL} R$; therefore by lemma 17.2.6 (iii) applied to $F' \equiv \lambda^* x. F_{CL} x \vec{P}$ and $\varphi_{N_{CL}}$

$$F_{CL} N_{CL} \vec{P} \sim_s S \Rightarrow F_{CL} N_{CL} \text{ is } CL\text{-solvable} \Rightarrow FN \text{ is solvable}.$$

Case 2. $S' \equiv \underline{\boldsymbol{S}}$. Then by lemma 17.2.2 (ii) $M_{CL} \twoheadrightarrow_w \boldsymbol{S}$ and by lemma 17.2.6 (iii)

$$F_{CL} N_{CL} \vec{P} \sim_s N_{CL}.$$

Since by lemma 17.2.5 and the assumption $M_{CL} \boldsymbol{I} \sim_s N_{CL} \boldsymbol{I}$, one has

$$F_{CL} N_{CL} \vec{\boldsymbol{P}} \boldsymbol{III} \sim_s N_{CL} \boldsymbol{III} \sim_s M_{CL} \boldsymbol{III} =_w \boldsymbol{SIII} =_w \boldsymbol{I}.$$

Hence $F_{CL} N_{CL}$ is solvable and so is FN. □

17.2.8. THEOREM. (i) $\mathcal{H}^* \vdash \omega$.

(ii) *If* $\mathcal{T}$ *is semi-sensible, then so is* $\mathcal{T}\omega$.

(iii) $\boldsymbol{\lambda}\omega \subseteq \mathcal{H}\omega \subseteq \mathcal{H}^*$.

PROOF. (i) By lemma 17.2.7 one has $\mathcal{H}^* \vdash \omega^0$. But then $\mathcal{H}^* \vdash \omega$, by lemma 4.1.15 (i).

(ii) $\mathcal{T}$ s.s. $\Rightarrow \mathcal{T} \subseteq \mathcal{H}^*$
$\Rightarrow \mathcal{T}\omega \subseteq \mathcal{H}^*\omega = \mathcal{H}^*$ by (i),
$\Rightarrow \mathcal{T}\omega$ s.s.
by lemma 17.1.1.

(iii) Since $\boldsymbol{\lambda}$, $\mathcal{H}$ are semi-sensible. □

Now the ordinal consistency proof of $\mathcal{H}\omega$ will be given. Since the ω-rule implies extensionality and $\boldsymbol{\lambda} + \boldsymbol{ext}$ and $\boldsymbol{CL} + \boldsymbol{ext}$ are equivalent the consistency of $\boldsymbol{\lambda}\mathcal{H}\omega$ is proved via the combinatory version $\boldsymbol{CL}\mathcal{H}\omega$. This is convenient since no (bound) variables are needed in $\boldsymbol{CL}$. The proof together with its proof-theoretic corollaries occupy 17.2.9–17.2.17.

17.2.9. DEFINITION. $\boldsymbol{CL}\mathcal{H}\omega'$ has the following language

$$\text{Alphabet}_{CL\mathcal{H}\omega'} = \text{Alphabet}_{CL} \cup \{\approx_\alpha, \sim_\alpha, =_\alpha\}_{\alpha\in\omega_1},$$

where ω_1 is the set of countable ordinals.

Terms. $\mathcal{C}^0$ is the set of terms for $\boldsymbol{CL}\mathcal{H}\omega'$.

Formulas. If $P, Q \in \mathcal{C}^0$, then $P =_\alpha Q$, $P \sim_\alpha Q$ and $P \approx_\alpha Q$ are formulas of $\boldsymbol{CL}\mathcal{H}\omega'$.

Axioms and rules:

(I.1) $\boldsymbol{CL}\mathcal{H} \vdash P = Q \Rightarrow P \approx_0 Q$ (where $\mathcal{H}$ is axiomatized by $\{P = Q \mid P, Q \in \mathcal{C}^0$ are unsolvable$\}$).
(I.2) $[\forall Z \in \mathcal{C}^0\ \exists \gamma < \alpha\ PZ =_\gamma QZ] \Rightarrow P \approx_\alpha Q$.
(II.1) $P \approx_\alpha Q \Rightarrow P \sim_\alpha Q$.
(II.2) $P \sim_\alpha Q \Rightarrow C[P] \sim_\alpha C[Q]$.
(III.1) $P \sim_\alpha Q \Rightarrow P =_\alpha Q$.
(III.2) $P =_\alpha Q, Q =_\alpha R \Rightarrow P =_\alpha R$.

REMARKS. The intuitive interpretation of
$P =_\alpha Q$ is that $P = Q$ is provable using the ω-rule at most α times, of
$P \sim_\alpha Q$ is that $P =_\alpha Q$ is provable without transitivity, and of
$P \approx_\alpha Q$ is that $P \sim_\alpha Q$ follows directly from the ω-rule (or is provable in $\boldsymbol{CL}\mathcal{H}$ in case $\alpha = 0$).

Note that

$$P \approx_\alpha Q \Rightarrow Q \approx_\alpha P$$

is a derived rule in $\boldsymbol{CL}\mathcal{H}\omega'$ and similarly for $\sim_\alpha$, $=_\alpha$. (Prove this simultaneously by induction on proofs in $\boldsymbol{CL}\mathcal{H}\omega'$.) Also one has

$$P \approx_\alpha Q,\ \alpha \leqslant \beta \Rightarrow P \approx_\beta Q$$

as a derived rule. Similarly, $\sim_\alpha$, $\alpha \leqslant \beta \Rightarrow \sim_\beta$ and $=_\alpha$, $\alpha \leqslant \beta \Rightarrow =_\beta$.

17.2.10. Lemma. (i) $CL\mathcal{H}\omega \vdash P = Q \Leftrightarrow \exists\alpha\ CL\mathcal{H}\omega' \vdash P =_\alpha Q$.

(ii) $CL\mathcal{H} \vdash P = Q \Leftrightarrow CL\mathcal{H}\omega' \vdash P =_0 Q$.

(iii) $CL\mathcal{H}\omega' \vdash P =_\alpha Q \Leftrightarrow \exists P_1 \cdots P_n\ CL\mathcal{H}\omega' \vdash P \sim_\alpha P_1 \sim_\alpha \cdots \sim_\alpha P_n \equiv Q$.

(iv) $CL\mathcal{H}\omega' \vdash P \sim_\alpha Q \Leftrightarrow$ *for some context* $C[\ \ ]$ *and some* $P', Q' \in \mathcal{C}$ *one has* $P \equiv C[P']$, $Q \equiv C[Q']$ *and* $CL\mathcal{H}\omega' \vdash P' \approx_\alpha Q'$.

(v) $CL\mathcal{H}\omega' \vdash P \approx_\alpha Q$ *and* $\alpha \neq 0 \Leftrightarrow \forall Z \in \mathcal{C}^0\ \exists\gamma < \alpha\ CL\mathcal{H}\omega' \vdash PZ =_\gamma QZ$.

Proof. Immediate. □

17.2.11. Lemma. *Let* $R, R' \in \mathcal{C}^0$ *and suppose* $CL\mathcal{H}\omega' \vdash R \approx_\alpha R'$ *for* $\alpha \neq 0$. *Let* $P, Q \in \underline{\mathcal{C}}^0$. *Then*

(i) $[P \to_{\underline{w}} Q \wedge \forall \underline{L} \subset P\ L =_w R] \Rightarrow \exists\gamma < \alpha\ CL\mathcal{H}\omega' \vdash \varphi_{R'}(P) =_\gamma \varphi_{R'}(Q)$.

(ii) *Similarly for* $\to_{\underline{w}}$ *replaced by* $\twoheadrightarrow_{\underline{w}}$

Proof. (i) By induction on the generation of $\to_{\underline{w}}$, the only non-trivial case being $\underline{L}B \to_{\underline{w}} LB$. But then for some $\gamma < \alpha$

$$CL\mathcal{H}\omega' \vdash \varphi_{R'}(\underline{L}B) \equiv R'\varphi_{R'}(B) =_\gamma R\varphi_{R'}(B) =_w L\varphi_{R'}(B),$$

since by assumption $L =_w R$. Since $=_w \Rightarrow\ \approx_0 \Rightarrow\ =_\gamma$ we are done.

(ii) By (i) using transitivity and lemma 17.2.2 (i). □

17.2.12. Corollary. *Let* $F, R, R' \in \mathcal{C}^0$. *Suppose*

$$FR \twoheadrightarrow_w \boldsymbol{I} \quad \textit{and} \quad CL\mathcal{H}\omega' \vdash R \approx_\alpha R' \qquad \textit{for } \alpha \neq 0.$$

Then $\exists\gamma < \alpha\ CL\mathcal{H}\omega' \vdash FR'\boldsymbol{I} =_\gamma \boldsymbol{I}$.

Proof. $FR \twoheadrightarrow_w \boldsymbol{I} \Rightarrow$

$\Rightarrow F\underline{R} \twoheadrightarrow_{\underline{w}} \boldsymbol{I}' \cong \boldsymbol{I}$ by lemma 17.2.3,

$\Rightarrow F\underline{R}\boldsymbol{I} \twoheadrightarrow_{\underline{w}} \boldsymbol{I}'\boldsymbol{I} \twoheadrightarrow_{\underline{w}} \boldsymbol{I}$ since $\boldsymbol{I}'$ can be $\underline{\boldsymbol{S}}\underline{\boldsymbol{K}}\underline{\boldsymbol{K}}$, $\underline{\boldsymbol{S}}\underline{\boldsymbol{K}}\boldsymbol{K}$, etcetera and in all cases $\boldsymbol{I}'\boldsymbol{I} \twoheadrightarrow_{\underline{w}} \boldsymbol{I}$,

$\Rightarrow \exists\gamma < \alpha\quad CL\mathcal{H}\omega' \vdash FR'\boldsymbol{I} =_\gamma \boldsymbol{I}$ by the preceding lemma. □

17.2.13. Lemma. *Let* $P \in \mathcal{C}^0$. *Then*

$$CL\mathcal{H}\omega' \vdash P =_\alpha \boldsymbol{I} \Rightarrow \exists n\ \ P\boldsymbol{I}^{\sim n} \twoheadrightarrow_w \boldsymbol{I}.$$

Proof. By induction on α. Because use will be made of a double induction, the induction hypothesis with respect to this induction is called the α-ind.hyp.

Case 1. $\alpha = 0$. Then

$$\begin{aligned}
&\boldsymbol{CL}\mathcal{H}\omega' \vdash P =_\alpha \boldsymbol{I} \Rightarrow \\
&\quad \Rightarrow \boldsymbol{CL}\mathcal{H} \vdash P = \boldsymbol{I} \quad \text{by lemma 17.2.10 (ii)}, \\
&\quad \Rightarrow \boldsymbol{CL} \vdash P = \boldsymbol{I} \quad \text{by theorem 15.1.9 (for } \boldsymbol{CL}\text{)}, \\
&\quad \Rightarrow P \twoheadrightarrow_w \boldsymbol{I} \quad \text{by CR for } \twoheadrightarrow_w .
\end{aligned}$$

Case 2. $\alpha > 0$. Assuming $\boldsymbol{CL}\mathcal{H}\omega' \vdash P =_\alpha \boldsymbol{I}$ it follows by lemma 17.2.10 (iii) that $\exists \vec{P}$

$$(1) \qquad \boldsymbol{CL}\mathcal{H}\omega' \vdash P \sim_\alpha P_1 \sim_\alpha \cdots \sim_\alpha P_k \twoheadrightarrow_w \boldsymbol{I}.$$

By induction on k it will be shown that $(1) \Rightarrow \exists n \; P\boldsymbol{I}^{\sim n} \twoheadrightarrow_w \boldsymbol{I}$. The induction hypothesis with respect to this induction is called the k-ind.hyp.

If $k = 0$, then we are done. Suppose $k > 0$. Then $\boldsymbol{CL}\mathcal{H}\omega' \vdash P_{k-1} \sim_\alpha P_k \twoheadrightarrow_w \boldsymbol{I}$. By lemma 17.2.10 (iv) for some context $C[\;\;]$ one has

$$P_{k-1} \equiv C[P'_{k-1}], \qquad P_k \equiv C[P'_k] \quad \text{and} \quad \boldsymbol{CL}\mathcal{H}\omega' \vdash P'_{k-1} \approx_\alpha P'_k.$$

Define $F \equiv \lambda^* x.C[x]$. Then $FP'_{k(-1)} =_w P_{k(-1)}$ and $FP'_k \twoheadrightarrow_w \boldsymbol{I}$. By corollary 17.2.12 it follows that

$$\exists \gamma < \alpha \quad \boldsymbol{CL}\mathcal{H}\omega' \vdash P_{k-1}\boldsymbol{I} =_0 FP'_{k-1}\boldsymbol{I} =_\gamma \boldsymbol{I}.$$

Hence by the α-ind.hyp.

$$\exists n \quad P_{k-1}\boldsymbol{I}\boldsymbol{I}^{\sim n} \twoheadrightarrow_w \boldsymbol{I},$$

thus

$$\exists n \quad \boldsymbol{CL}\mathcal{H}\omega' \vdash P\boldsymbol{I}\boldsymbol{I}^{\sim n} \sim_\alpha P_1\boldsymbol{I}\boldsymbol{I}^{\sim n} \sim_\alpha \cdots \sim_\alpha P_{k-1}\boldsymbol{I}\boldsymbol{I}^{\sim n} \twoheadrightarrow_w \boldsymbol{I}.$$

Therefore by the k-ind.hyp.

$$\exists n, n' \quad P\boldsymbol{I}\boldsymbol{I}^{\sim n}\boldsymbol{I}^{\sim n'} \twoheadrightarrow_w \boldsymbol{I},$$

i.e.

$$\exists n, n' \quad P\boldsymbol{I}^{\sim n+n'+1} \twoheadrightarrow_w \boldsymbol{I}. \quad \square$$

17.2.14. Corollary. *Let* $P \in \mathcal{C}^0$. *Then*

$$\boldsymbol{CL}\mathcal{H}\omega \vdash P = \boldsymbol{I} \Rightarrow \exists n \;\; \boldsymbol{CL} \vdash P\boldsymbol{I}^{\sim n} = \boldsymbol{I}.$$

Proof. By the previous lemma using lemma 17.2.10 (i). $\square$

17.2.15. THEOREM. (i) *Let* $M \in \Lambda$. *Then*

$$\mathcal{H}\omega \vdash M = \mathbf{I} \Rightarrow \exists n \ \lambda \vdash M\mathbf{I}^{\sim n} = \mathbf{I}.$$

(ii) $\mathcal{H}\omega$ *is consistent.*

PROOF. (i) First assume $M \in \Lambda^0$. Then the result follows by the preceding corollary and the standard translations between Λ and $\mathcal{C}$ (use theorems 7.3.12 and 7.3.10).

If M is open, let $F \equiv \lambda \vec{x}.M$ be its closure. Then

$$\begin{aligned} &\mathcal{H}\omega \vdash F\vec{x} = \mathbf{I} \Rightarrow \\ &\quad \Rightarrow \mathcal{H}\omega \vdash F\vec{\Omega} = \mathbf{I} \\ &\quad \Rightarrow \exists n \ \lambda \vdash F\vec{\Omega}\mathbf{I}^{\sim n} = \mathbf{I} \quad \text{since } F\vec{\Omega} \in \Lambda^0, \\ &\quad \Rightarrow \exists n \ \lambda \vdash F\vec{x}\mathbf{I}^{\sim n} = \mathbf{I} \quad \text{by proposition 14.3.24}, \\ &\quad \Rightarrow \exists n \ \lambda \vdash M\mathbf{I}^{\sim n} = \mathbf{I}. \end{aligned}$$

(ii) If $\mathcal{H}\omega$ were inconsistent, then $\mathcal{H}\omega \vdash \Omega = \mathbf{I}$. But then by (i) $\exists n$ $\Omega\mathbf{I}^{\sim n} = \mathbf{I}$, contradicting the Church-Rosser theorem. □

The following lemma will enable us to improve theorem 17.2.15. The method of proof is taken from Bergstra and Klop [1980], § 4.

17.2.16. LEMMA. *Let* $M \in \Lambda$ *and* $M \sim_s \mathbf{I}$. *Then*

$$M\mathbf{I} =_{\beta\eta} \mathbf{I} \Rightarrow M =_{\beta\eta} \mathbf{I}.$$

PROOF. By assumption and theorem 16.2.7 it follows that $M \gtrsim_\eta \mathbf{I}$. Hence BT($M$) is of the form

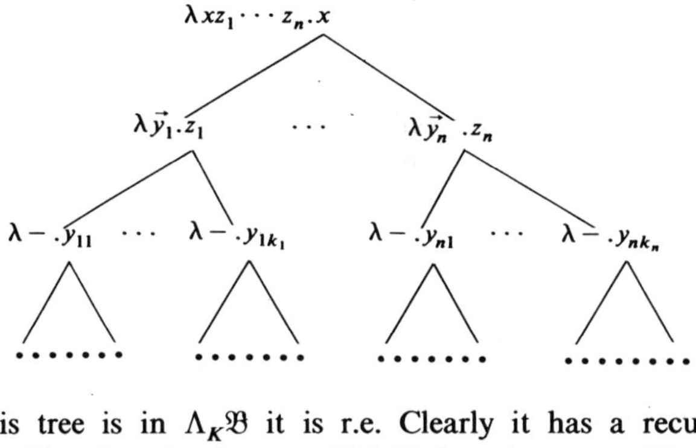

Since this tree is in $\Lambda_K\mathfrak{B}$ it is r.e. Clearly it has a recursive variable indicator. Therefore by theorem 10.1.25 there is a term $M_I \in \Lambda_I$ such that

(1) $\quad BT(M_I) = BT(M)$.

Then, since $\mathfrak{B}$ is a λ-theory,

(2) $BT(M_I\mathbf{I}) = BT(M\mathbf{I})$.

Remember that the remark before 10.1.18 states

(3) M has a nf $\Leftrightarrow BT(M)$ is finite and $\perp$-free.

Now we have $M\mathbf{I} =_{\beta\eta} \mathbf{I} \Rightarrow$
$\Rightarrow BT(M_I\mathbf{I}) = BT(M\mathbf{I})$ is finite and $\perp$-free, by (2), (3),
$\Rightarrow M_I\mathbf{I}$ has a nf, by (3),
$\Rightarrow M_I$ has a nf, by corollary 9.1.6,
$\Rightarrow BT(M) = BT(M_I)$ is finite and $\perp$-free, by (1), (3),
$\Rightarrow M$ has a nf, by (3),
$\Rightarrow M$ has a $\beta\eta$-nf, by corollary 15.1.5,
$\Rightarrow M =_{\beta\eta} \mathbf{I}$, since otherwise $M \not\sim_s \mathbf{I}$ by corollary 10.4.3. □

Combining the main results of this section one obtains the following.

17.2.17. THEOREM. *If $\mathcal{H}\omega \vdash M = \mathbf{I}$, then $\boldsymbol{\lambda\eta} \vdash M = \mathbf{I}$. In particular $\mathcal{H}\omega$ is consistent.*

PROOF. If $\mathcal{H}\omega \vdash M = \mathbf{I}$, then by theorems 17.2.8 and 17.2.15 one has $M \sim_s \mathbf{I}$ and $M\mathbf{I}^{\sim n} =_{\beta\eta} \mathbf{I}$ for some n. Now it follows by repeated use of lemma 17.2.16 that $M =_{\beta\eta} \mathbf{I}$. □

17.3. Partial validity of the ω-rule in $\boldsymbol{\lambda\eta}$

In this section it will be proved that in the theory $\boldsymbol{\lambda\eta}$ the ω-rule holds for terms M, N provided that one of them is not a $\beta\eta$-universal generator. The proof occupies 17.3.1–17.3.24 (subsection I). In general the ω-rule is however not valid in $\boldsymbol{\lambda\eta}$. This proof occupies 17.3.25–17.3.30 (subsection II). Similar results hold for the term rule in $\boldsymbol{\lambda}$.

I. Validity of the ω-rule in $\boldsymbol{\lambda\eta}$ for non-universal generators.

The validity in $\boldsymbol{\lambda\eta}$ of the ω-rule for non-universal generators was proved in Barendregt [1974a]. The idea is to use a closed term of order zero, like $\mathbf{\Omega}$: if $MZ = NZ$ for all closed Z, then also $M\mathbf{\Omega} = N\mathbf{\Omega}$. Because $\mathbf{\Omega}$ behaves almost like a variable, one is tempted to substitute for $\mathbf{\Omega}$ a fresh variable x obtaining $Mx = Nx$ and hence by extensionality $M = N$. However, there *is* a difference between a variable and $\mathbf{\Omega}$: in a reduction a fresh variable can never be created, whereas $\mathbf{\Omega}$ can. Therefore one should use a different term

Ξ of order zero, which will not be generated by M or N. If M or N is a universal generator there is not such a Ξ and the proof breaks down. In Plotkin [1974] two complicated universal generators are constructed for which the ω-rule is not valid.

17.3.1. DEFINITION. $\beta(\eta)$-$\mathfrak{UG} = \{M \in \Lambda | M$ is a $\beta(\eta)$-universal generator$\}$.

See proposition 8.2.8 for the construction of universal generators. In exercise 17.5.13 it is shown that

$$M \in \beta\text{-}\mathfrak{UG} \not\Leftarrow M \in \beta\eta\text{-}\mathfrak{UG}$$

The notion needed in this section is that of a $\beta\eta$-UG.

17.3.2. DEFINITION. Let $Z \in \Lambda$. Z is of *order* 0 (notation $Z \in 0$) if

$$\neg \exists P \in \Lambda \quad Z \twoheadrightarrow_{\beta} \lambda x.P.$$

EXAMPLES. $x \in 0$, $\Omega \in 0$; $\mathbf{K}^{\infty} \equiv \mathbf{\Theta}\,\mathbf{K} \notin 0$.

17.3.3. LEMMA. *Let* $Z \in 0$. *Then*

(i) $\neg \exists P \in \Lambda\ Z \twoheadrightarrow_{\beta\eta} \lambda x.P$,

(ii) $Z \twoheadrightarrow_{\beta\eta} Z' \Rightarrow Z' \in 0$,

(iii) $ZM \twoheadrightarrow_{\beta\eta} N \Rightarrow \exists Z', M'$ [$N \equiv Z'M'$ *and* $M \twoheadrightarrow_{\beta\eta} M'$ *and* $Z \twoheadrightarrow_{\beta\eta} Z'$],

(iv) $\forall M \in \Lambda\ ZM \in 0$.

PROOF. Note that a term is either a variable, an application (term) (of the form MN) or an abstraction (term) (of the form $\lambda x.M$).

(i) Suppose $Z \twoheadrightarrow_{\beta\eta} \lambda x.P$. Then by postponement of η-reduction, corollary 15.1.6, one has for some Z'

$$Z \twoheadrightarrow Z' \twoheadrightarrow_{\eta} \lambda x.P.$$

By assumption Z' is not an abstraction. Clearly Z' is not a variable, hence Z' is an application. But if $M \twoheadrightarrow_{\eta} N$ and M is an application, then so is N (by induction on the generation of $\twoheadrightarrow_{\eta}$), a contradiction.

(ii) Immediate by (i).

(iii) By induction on the length of reduction using (i).

(iv) By (iii) it follows that if $ZM \twoheadrightarrow N$, then N is an application. Hence $ZM \in 0$. □

In order to keep track of what happens in a reduction to a term of order 0, an auxiliary term system $\underline{\Lambda}$ is introduced.

17.3.4. DEFINITION. (i) The set $\underline{\Lambda}$ (of λ-terms with underlining) is inductively defined as follows:

$$M \in \Lambda \Rightarrow M \in \underline{\Lambda},$$

$$M \in \Lambda^0 \Rightarrow \underline{M} \in \underline{\Lambda},$$

$$M, N \in \underline{\Lambda} \Rightarrow (MN) \in \underline{\Lambda},$$

$$M \in \underline{\Lambda} \Rightarrow (\lambda x.M) \in \underline{\Lambda}.$$

(ii) The notions FV(M) and $M[x:=N]$ are extended to $\underline{\Lambda}$ in the obvious way. Note that $\mathrm{FV}(\underline{M}) = \emptyset$ and $\underline{M}[x:=N] = \underline{M}$.

(iii) On $\underline{\Lambda}$ the notion of reduction $\underline{\beta\eta}$ is defined by the following contraction rules:

$$(\lambda x.M)N \to M[x:=N],$$

$$\lambda x.Mx \to M \quad \textit{if } x \notin \mathrm{FV}(M).$$

As usual one has for the resulting relation $\to_{\underline{\beta\eta}}$ that for $C[\ \ ]$ with one hole

$$M \to_{\underline{\beta\eta}} M' \Rightarrow C[M] \to_{\underline{\beta\eta}} C[M'];$$

in particular for $M, M' \in \Lambda$

$$M \to_{\beta\eta} M' \Rightarrow \underline{M} \to_{\underline{\beta\eta}} \underline{M'}.$$

17.3.5. DEFINITION. (i) For $M, N \in \underline{\Lambda}$ the relation $M \subset N$ is defined in such a way that only $\underline{L}$ is a subterm of $\underline{L}$. To be explicit:

$$P \subset x \Leftrightarrow P \equiv x,$$

$$P \subset MN \Leftrightarrow P \subset M \text{ or } P \subset N \text{ or } P \equiv MN,$$

$$P \subset \lambda x.M \Leftrightarrow P \subset M \text{ or } P \equiv \lambda x.M,$$

$$P \subset \underline{M} \Leftrightarrow P \equiv \underline{M}.$$

(iii) If $M \in \underline{\Lambda}$, then $|M| \in \Lambda$ is M without underlining. $M \cong N$ iff $|M| = |N|$.

17.3.6. LEMMA. *Let* $M, N \in \Lambda$. *Then by*

(i) $M \twoheadrightarrow_{\beta\eta} N \Leftrightarrow M \twoheadrightarrow_{\underline{\beta\eta}} N$.

(ii) *If moreover* $M, N \in \Lambda^0$, *then* $M \twoheadrightarrow_{\beta\eta} N \Leftrightarrow \underline{M} \twoheadrightarrow_{\underline{\beta\eta}} \underline{N}$.

PROOF. By induction on the generation of $\twoheadrightarrow_{\beta\eta}$ and $\twoheadrightarrow_{\underline{\beta\eta}}$. □

17.3.7. LEMMA. *Let $M, N \in \underline{\Lambda}$ and $L, L' \in \Lambda$. Then*
(i) $\underline{L} \subset M[x:=N] \Rightarrow \underline{L} \subset M$ *or* $\underline{L} \subset N$,
(ii) $L \subset M[x:=\underline{L'}] \Rightarrow L \subset M$.

PROOF. By induction on the structure of M. □

17.3.8. LEMMA. (i) *Let $M, M' \in \underline{\Lambda}$ and $L' \in \Lambda$. Then*

$$[M \twoheadrightarrow_{\underline{\beta\eta}} M' \wedge \underline{L'} \subset M'] \Rightarrow \exists \underline{L} \subset M \ L \twoheadrightarrow_{\beta\eta} L'.$$

(ii) *Let $M, L, L' \in \Lambda$ and $M' \in \underline{\Lambda}$. Then*

$$[M\underline{L} \twoheadrightarrow_{\underline{\beta\eta}} M' \wedge \underline{L'} \subset M'] \Rightarrow L \twoheadrightarrow_{\beta\eta} L'.$$

PROOF. (i) By transitivity it is sufficient to prove this for $\rightarrow_{\underline{\beta\eta}}$ on the LHS. This is done by induction on the generation of $\rightarrow_{\underline{\beta\eta}}$ using (i) of the previous lemma.
(ii) Immediate by (i). □

17.3.9. LEMMA. *Let $M, Z, L \in \Lambda$ and $Z \in 0$. Then*

$$MZ \twoheadrightarrow_{\beta\eta} L \Rightarrow \exists L' \in \underline{\Lambda} \ \forall Z' \in \Lambda$$

$$[M\underline{Z} \twoheadrightarrow_{\underline{\beta\eta}} L' \cong L \wedge [\underline{Z'} \subset L' \Rightarrow Z \twoheadrightarrow_{\beta\eta} Z']].$$

PROOF. Call $P \in \underline{\Lambda}$ *proper* if $\underline{Q} \subset P \Rightarrow Q \in 0$. By induction on the generation of $\twoheadrightarrow_{\beta\eta}$ one can show that for all $M, N \in \Lambda$ and $M' \in \underline{\Lambda}$

$$[M \twoheadrightarrow_{\beta\eta} N,\ M \cong M' \text{ and } M' \text{ proper}] \Rightarrow$$
$$\Rightarrow \exists N' \in \underline{\Lambda} \quad [M' \twoheadrightarrow_{\underline{\beta\eta}} N',\ N \cong N' \text{ and } N' \text{ proper}].$$

Then the statement follows by (ii) of the preceding lemma. □

17.3.10. DEFINITION. Let x be any variable. A map φ_x: $\underline{\Lambda} \rightarrow \Lambda$ (which replaces all underlined terms by x) is defined as follows:

$$\varphi_x(y) \equiv y, \qquad \varphi_x(MN) \equiv \varphi_x(M)\varphi_x(N),$$

$$\varphi_x(\lambda y.M) \equiv \lambda y.\varphi_x(M), \qquad \varphi_x(\underline{M}) \equiv x.$$

17.3.11. LEMMA. *Let $M, N \in \underline{\Lambda}$ and $M \twoheadrightarrow_{\underline{\beta\eta}} N$. If x is a fresh variable, then $\varphi_x(M) \twoheadrightarrow_{\beta\eta} \varphi_x(N)$.*

PROOF. By induction on the generation of $\twoheadrightarrow_{\underline{\beta\eta}}$ using the following sublemma:

$$z \not\equiv y \Rightarrow \varphi_z(M[y:=N]) \equiv \varphi_z(M)[y:=\varphi_z(N)].$$

The sublemma is proved by induction on the structure of M. □

17.3.12. LEMMA. *Let* $M, N \in \Lambda$, $x \notin \mathrm{FV}(M)$ *and* $Mx \twoheadrightarrow_{\beta\eta} N$. *Then* $\exists M' \in \Lambda$ $[N \equiv M'x, x \notin \mathrm{FV}(M')$ *and* $M \twoheadrightarrow_{\beta\eta} M']$ *or* $M \twoheadrightarrow_{\beta\eta} \lambda x.N$.

PROOF. Trivial. □

Remember that for $M \in \Lambda$ its $\beta\eta$ family is

$$\mathcal{F}_{\beta\eta}(M) = \{N \in \Lambda \mid \exists M' M \twoheadrightarrow_{\beta\eta} M' \text{ and } N \subset M'\}.$$

17.3.13. LEMMA. *Let* $M, N, Z \in \Lambda$ *and* $L \in \underline{\Lambda}$. *Then*

$$[M\underline{N} \twoheadrightarrow_{\underline{\beta\eta}} L \text{ and } Z \subset L] \Rightarrow Z \in \mathcal{F}_{\beta\eta}(M).$$

PROOF. Without loss of generality we may assume that if $\underline{N}' \subset L$, then $\underline{N}' = \underline{N}$. Let x be a fresh variable. By lemma 17.3.11 it follows from the assumption that

$$Mx \twoheadrightarrow_{\beta\eta} \varphi_x(L).$$

By the preceding lemma there are two cases.

Case 1. $\varphi_x(L) \equiv M'x$ with $M \twoheadrightarrow_{\beta\eta} M'$ and $x \notin \mathrm{FV}(M')$. Then $L \equiv M'\underline{N}$. Now if $Z \subset L$, then $Z \subset M'$, hence $Z \in \mathcal{F}_{\beta\eta}(M)$.

Case 2. $M \twoheadrightarrow_{\beta\eta} \lambda x.\varphi_x(L)$. Now $Z \subset L \equiv \varphi_x(L)[x:=\underline{N}]$, hence by lemma 17.3.7 (ii) one has $Z \subset \varphi_x(L) \subset \lambda x.\varphi_x(L)$ and therefore also $Z \in \mathcal{F}_{\beta\eta}(M)$. □

17.3.14. DEFINITION. (i) $M \in \Lambda$ is called an **Ω**-*term* if M is of the form $\mathbf{\Omega} M'$.

(ii) A subterm occurrence Z of M is called *non-***Ω** *in* M if Z has no **Ω**-subterm and Z is not a subterm of an **Ω**-subterm of M.

(iii) $U \in \Lambda$ is a *hereditarily non-***Ω** UG if U is a closed β-UG such that $\forall U'[U \twoheadrightarrow_{\beta\eta} U' \Rightarrow \exists Z \subset U'$ $[Z \in \beta\text{-}\mathcal{UG}$ and occurs non-**Ω** in $U']]$

(iv) $\Xi \in \Lambda^0$ is called *variable-like* if Ξ is of the form $\mathbf{\Omega} U$, where U is a hereditarily non-**Ω** UG.

EXAMPLE. Only the second occurrence of Z in the term $x(\mathbf{\Omega}(MZ))Z$ is non-**Ω** (assuming that Z does not have an **Ω**-subterm).

17.3.15. LEMMA. (i) *A variable-like term is of order* 0.

(ii) *If* $\Xi \twoheadrightarrow_{\beta\eta} \Xi'$, *and* Ξ *is a variable-like term, then so is* Ξ'.

(iii) *There exists a variable-like term* $\Xi \in \Lambda^0$.

PROOF. (i), (ii) Obvious.

(iii) Let $\mathbf{E}$ be the enumerator of Λ^0 and define $F_x \equiv x\mathbf{TIIE'I}x$, where by exercise 6.8.8 $\mathbf{E}'$ is a nf such that

$$\mathbf{E'I} \twoheadrightarrow \mathbf{E}.$$

Then F_x is a nf and since $\ulcorner n \urcorner\, \mathbf{TII} \rightarrow \mathbf{I}$ one has

$$F_x[x := \ulcorner n \urcorner] \twoheadrightarrow \mathbf{E} \ulcorner n \urcorner .$$

Define

$$A \equiv \lambda bx.bb \ulcorner 0 \urcorner (bb[F, x])F_x, \qquad B \equiv AA.$$

Then

$$B \ulcorner n \urcorner \twoheadrightarrow B \ulcorner 0 \urcorner \, (B \ulcorner n+1 \urcorner)(E \ulcorner n \urcorner).$$

Hence as in proposition 8.2.8, $B\ulcorner 0 \urcorner$ is a UG. We claim that it is hereditarily non-Ω. Define

$$P \twoheadrightarrow_k Q \Leftrightarrow \exists P_1 \cdots P_k \;\; P \equiv P_1 \rightarrow_{\beta\eta} \cdots \rightarrow_{\beta\eta} P_k \equiv Q.$$

Suppose $B \ulcorner 0 \urcorner \twoheadrightarrow_{\beta\eta} U$. Then for some k one has $B \ulcorner 0 \urcorner \twoheadrightarrow_k U$. Since A is normal, U is of the form $B \ulcorner 0 \urcorner$, $(\lambda x.U'PQ) \ulcorner 0 \urcorner$ or $U'PQ$, where $B \ulcorner 0 \urcorner \twoheadrightarrow_r U'$ for some $r < k$. Now it follows by induction on k that U has a subterm which is a β-UG and non-Ω in U.

Finally take $\Xi \equiv \Omega(B \ulcorner 0 \urcorner)$. □

17.3.16. DEFINITION. Let $L \in \Lambda$, $L' \in \underline{\Lambda}$ and $L \cong L'$. Then L and L' are equal except for the underlining and we can give the following informal definitions.

(i) If Z' is a subterm occurrence of L', then there is a unique subterm occurrence Z of L which *corresponds to* Z', such that $Z \cong Z'$.

Instead of giving a formal definition we illustrate this definition by an example: let $L \equiv \mathbf{S(KS)(SKK)}$, $L' \equiv \mathbf{S}(\underline{\mathbf{KS}})(\underline{\mathbf{SKK}})$; then $L \cong L'$; $\mathbf{S}$ corresponds to $\mathbf{S}$, $\mathbf{KS}$ corresponds to $\underline{\mathbf{KS}}$ and $\mathbf{SKK}$ corresponds to $\underline{\mathbf{SKK}}$.

(ii) Let $L'' \in \underline{\Lambda}$ be another term with $L'' \cong L$. L'' *has more line than* L' (notation $L' \lhd L''$) if for all subterm occurrences $\underline{Z}'$ of L' there is a subterm occurrence $\underline{Z}''$ of L'' such that $Z' \subset Z''$, where Z', Z'' are the subterm occurrences of L corresponding to $\underline{Z}'$ and $\underline{Z}''$ respectively.

For example, let $L'' \equiv \mathbf{S}(\underline{\mathbf{KS}})(\underline{\mathbf{SKK}})$, then $L' \lhd L''$, where L' is as in the previous example.

(iii) Let Z be a subterm occurrence of L. Then Z is *exactly underlined* in L' if $\underline{Z}$ is a subterm occurrence of L' and Z corresponds to $\underline{Z}$; Z is *underlined in* L' iff $Z \subset Z_1 \subset L$ and Z_1 is exactly underlined in L'; Z has *some lines* in L' iff the corresponding subterm $Z' \subset L'$ is not element of Λ.

For instance in the above example $\mathbf{KS} \subset L$ is exactly underlined in L', the first $\mathbf{K}$ in L is underlined in L' and $\mathbf{SKK} \subset L$ has some line in L'.

17.3.17. LEMMA. *Let $L \in \Lambda$, $L', L'' \in \underline{\Lambda}$ and $L \cong L' \cong L''$.*

(i) *$L' \lhd L''$ and $L'' \lhd L' \Rightarrow L' \equiv L''$.*

(ii) *If for all subterm occurrences $\underline{Z}$ of L' the corresponding subterm occurrence Z of L is underlined in L'', then $L' \lhd L''$.*

PROOF. Immediate. □

17.3.18. LEMMA. (i) *Let $L \in \Lambda$, $L' \in \underline{\Lambda}$ and $L \cong L'$. Suppose that*

(1) *If Z is a subterm occurrence of L which is exactly underlined in L', then Z is an Ω-term.*

(2) *If Z is a subterm occurrence of L which is a UG, then Z has some lines in L'.*

Then every subterm occurrence Ξ of L which is a variable-like term is underlined in L'.

(ii) *Let $M \notin \beta\eta$-$\mathfrak{U}\mathfrak{G}$ and Ξ be a variable like term. Suppose $M\underline{\Xi} \twoheadrightarrow_{\beta\eta} L'$ and $L \equiv |L'|$. Then $U \subset L$ is exactly underlined in L' iff U is a maximal (with respect to $\subset$) variable-like subterm of L.*

PROOF. (i) One has $\Xi \equiv \Omega U$ with U a hereditary non-Ω UG. Hence there is a non-Ω subterm occurrence Z in U which is a UG (see figure 17.1).

By (2) Z has some lines in L'. The possibility that some subterm occurrence Z_1 of Z is exactly underlined in L' is excluded, since by (1) it would follow that Z_1 is an Ω-term, whereas Z is non-Ω subterm of L. Therefore Z is underlined in L', i.e. there is a subterm occurrence Z_2 such that $Z \subset Z_2 \subset L$ and which is exactly underlined in L'. We claim that $\Xi \equiv \Omega U \subset Z_2$ (see figure 17.1).

First it follows by (1) that Z_2 is an Ω-term. Since Z is a non-Ω subterm of U, it follows that Z_2 is not a subterm of U. Therefore U is a proper subterm of Z_2, since subterms are either disjoint or comparable with respect to the relation $\subset$. Hence indeed $\Omega U \subset Z_2$.

$$L \equiv \cdots(\underbrace{\Omega(\overbrace{\cdots Z \cdots}^{U}))}_{Z_2}\cdots$$

FIG. 17.1.

By the claim it follows that Ξ is underlined in L'.

(ii) We verify conditions (1) and (2) of (i) for L and L'.

(1) If $Z \subset L$ is exactly underlined in L', then $\underline{Z} \subset L'$, hence by lemma 17.3.8 (ii) one has $\Xi \twoheadrightarrow_{\beta\eta} Z$ and therefore Z is an $\mathbf{\Omega}$-term.

(2) If $Z \subset L$ is a UG, then $Z \notin \mathcal{F}_{\beta\eta}(M)$ (otherwise M would be a $\beta\eta$-UG). Let Z correspond to $Z' \subset L'$. If $Z' \in \Lambda$, then $Z \equiv Z'$ and by lemma 17.3.13 one has $Z' \in \mathcal{F}_{\beta\eta}(M)$, a contradiction. Therefore $Z' \in \underline{\Lambda} - \Lambda$, i.e. Z has some line in L'.

By (i) it follows that

$U \subset L$ is exactly underlined in L' iff

$U \subset L$ is maximally underlined in L' iff

$U \subset L$ is a maximal variable-like subterm. $\square$

17.3.19. PROPOSITION. *Let $M, N \in \Lambda$ be such that $M, N \notin \beta\eta\text{-}\mathfrak{UG}$. Let Ξ be a variable-like term. Then for some fresh x*

$$M\Xi =_{\beta\eta} N\Xi \Rightarrow Mx =_{\beta\eta} Nx.$$

PROOF. Assume $M\Xi =_{\beta\eta} N\Xi$. Then it follows by the CR property for $\boldsymbol{\beta\eta}$ that for some $L \in \Lambda$

$$M\Xi \twoheadrightarrow_{\beta\eta} L, \qquad N\Xi \twoheadrightarrow_{\beta\eta} L.$$

It follows by lemmas 17.3.9 and 17.3.15 (i) that there are $L', L'' \in \underline{\Lambda}$ such that $L \cong L' \cong L''$ and

$$M\underline{\Xi} \twoheadrightarrow_{\underline{\beta\eta}} L', \qquad N\underline{\Xi} \twoheadrightarrow_{\underline{\beta\eta}} L'', \qquad \text{(see figure 17.2).}$$

By lemma 17.3.18 (ii) it follows that for $Z \subset L$

Z is exactly underlined in L' iff
Z is a maximal variable-like subterm of L iff
Z is exactly underlined in L''.

It follows that $L' \equiv L''$.

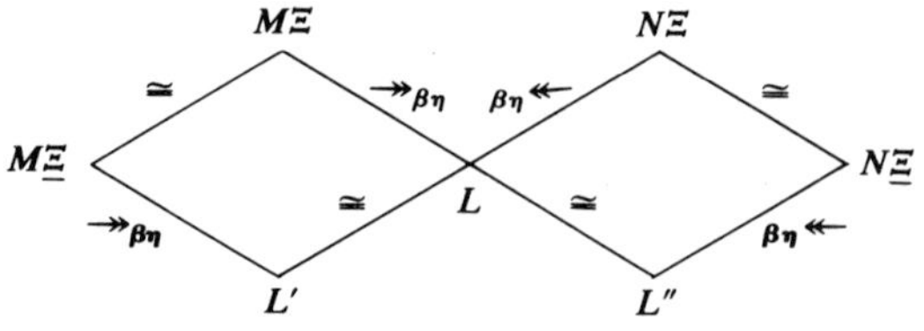

FIG. 17.2.

Let x be a fresh variable. Then by lemma 17.3.11

$$Mx \equiv \varphi_x(M\underline{\Xi}) \twoheadrightarrow_{\beta\eta} \varphi_x(L'), \qquad Nx \equiv \varphi_x(N\underline{\Xi}) \twoheadrightarrow_{\beta\eta} \varphi_x(L'').$$

Therefore $Mx =_{\beta\eta} Nx$. □

17.3.20. COROLLARY. *Let $M, N \notin \beta\eta$-$\mathfrak{UG}$. Then in $\boldsymbol{\lambda\eta}$ the ω-rule holds for M, N, i.e.*

$$\forall Z \in \Lambda^0 \; MZ =_{\beta\eta} NZ \Rightarrow M =_{\beta\eta} N.$$

PROOF. Immediate by the existence of variable like terms, the previous proposition and extensionality in $\boldsymbol{\lambda\eta}$. □

Plotkin has pointed out that in $\boldsymbol{\lambda\eta}$ the ω-rule is valid for M, N provided that only one of them is not a $\beta\eta$-universal generator. This is proved in 17.3.21–17.3.24.

17.3.21. LEMMA. *Let $M \in \Lambda$ and x be arbitrary. Then*

(i) $M\boldsymbol{\Omega} \in \beta\eta\text{-}\mathfrak{UG} \Rightarrow Mx \in \beta\eta\text{-}\mathfrak{UG}$,

(ii) $Mx \in \beta\eta\text{-}\mathfrak{UG} \Rightarrow M \in \beta\eta\text{-}\mathfrak{UG}$,

(iii) $M \in \beta\eta\text{-}\mathfrak{UG} \Rightarrow M[x := \boldsymbol{\Omega}] \in \beta\eta\text{-}\mathfrak{UG}$.

PROOF. Let $U \in \beta\eta\text{-}\mathfrak{UG} \cap \Lambda^0$ be such that $\Omega \not\subset U$. By the construction in proposition 8.2.8 or lemma 17.3.15 this is possible.

(i) If $M\boldsymbol{\Omega} \in \beta\eta\text{-}\mathfrak{UG}$, then by definition $M\boldsymbol{\Omega} \twoheadrightarrow_{\beta\eta} C[U] \equiv L$, say. But then by lemma 17.3.9

$$(1) \qquad M\underline{\boldsymbol{\Omega}} \twoheadrightarrow_{\underline{\beta\eta}} L' \cong L.$$

By lemma 17.3.8 (ii) it follows that

$$(2) \qquad \underline{P} \subset L' \Rightarrow \boldsymbol{\Omega} \twoheadrightarrow_{\beta\eta} P \Rightarrow \boldsymbol{\Omega} \equiv P.$$

On the other hand by lemma 17.3.11 and (1)

$$Mx \twoheadrightarrow_{\beta\eta} \varphi_x(L').$$

Since $\boldsymbol{\Omega} \not\subset U$ it follows by (2) that U in L has no line in L' and therefore $U \subset \varphi_x(L')$. But then $U \in \mathfrak{F}_{\beta\eta}(Mx)$, hence $Mx \in \beta\eta\text{-}\mathfrak{UG}$ itself.

(ii) By assumption

$$Mx \twoheadrightarrow_{\beta\eta} C[U] \equiv L.$$

By lemma 17.3.12 there are two cases.

Case 1. $L \equiv L'x$ and $M \twoheadrightarrow_{\beta\eta} L'$. Then $U \subset L' \in \mathfrak{F}_{\beta\eta}(M)$ and hence $M \in \beta\eta\text{-}\mathfrak{U}\mathfrak{G}$.

Case 2. $M \twoheadrightarrow_{\beta\eta} \lambda x.L$. Then also $U \in \mathfrak{F}_{\beta\eta}(M)$ and $M \in \beta\eta\text{-}\mathfrak{U}\mathfrak{G}$.

(iii) By assumption

$$M \twoheadrightarrow_{\beta\eta} C[U] \equiv L.$$

Hence $M[x:=\Omega] \twoheadrightarrow_{\beta\eta} L[x:=\Omega]$. Since $x \notin \mathrm{FV}(U)$ it follows that $U \in \mathfrak{F}_{\beta\eta}(M[x:=\Omega])$, hence the term in question is a $\beta\eta\text{-}\mathfrak{U}\mathfrak{G}$. □

17.3.22. LEMMA. (i) $M\Omega \twoheadrightarrow_{\beta\eta} L \notin \beta\eta\text{-}\mathfrak{U}\mathfrak{G} \Rightarrow \exists L'\ Mx \twoheadrightarrow_{\beta\eta} L' \notin \beta\eta\text{-}\mathfrak{U}\mathfrak{G}$.

(ii) $Mx \twoheadrightarrow_{\beta\eta} L' \notin \beta\eta\text{-}\mathfrak{U}\mathfrak{G} \Rightarrow \exists M'\ M \twoheadrightarrow_{\beta\eta} M' \notin \beta\eta\text{-}\mathfrak{U}\mathfrak{G}$.

PROOF. (i) $M\Omega \twoheadrightarrow_{\beta\eta} L \notin \beta\eta\text{-}\mathfrak{U}\mathfrak{G} \Rightarrow$

$\Rightarrow M\underline{\Omega} \twoheadrightarrow_{\beta\eta} L_1 \cong L$ by lemma 17.3.9,

$\Rightarrow Mx \twoheadrightarrow_{\beta\eta} \varphi_x(L_1) \equiv L'$ by lemma 17.3.11.

Now $L \equiv \varphi_x(L_1)[x:=\Omega]$. Therefore by (iii) of the previous lemma it follows that $L' \equiv \varphi_x(L_1) \notin \beta\eta\text{-}\mathfrak{U}\mathfrak{G}$.

(ii) Suppose $Mx \twoheadrightarrow_{\beta\eta} L' \notin \beta\eta\text{-}\mathfrak{U}\mathfrak{G}$. By lemma 17.3.12 there are two cases.

Case 1. $L' \equiv M'x$ and $M \twoheadrightarrow_{\beta\eta} M'$. Then $M' \notin \beta\eta\text{-}\mathfrak{U}\mathfrak{G}$ (otherwise $M'x \in \beta\eta\text{-}\mathfrak{U}\mathfrak{G}$) and we are done.

Case 2. $M \twoheadrightarrow_{\beta\eta} \lambda x.L'$. Then $\lambda x.L' \notin \beta\eta\text{-}\mathfrak{U}\mathfrak{G}$ (otherwise $L' \in \beta\eta\text{-}\mathfrak{U}\mathfrak{G}$) and we are also done. □

17.3.23. LEMMA. *If* $M\Omega =_{\beta\eta} N\Omega$ *and* $M \notin \beta\eta\text{-}\mathfrak{U}\mathfrak{G}$, *then* $\exists N'\ N \twoheadrightarrow_{\beta\eta} N' \notin \beta\eta\text{-}\mathfrak{U}\mathfrak{G}$.

PROOF. By the assumption and CR for $\beta\eta$ one has for some L

$$M\Omega \twoheadrightarrow_{\beta\eta} L_{\beta\eta}\twoheadleftarrow N\Omega.$$

By lemma 17.3.21 (i), (ii) one has $M\Omega \notin \beta\eta\text{-}\mathfrak{U}\mathfrak{G}$, hence $L \notin \beta\eta\text{-}\mathfrak{U}\mathfrak{G}$. But then the preceding lemma applies to $N\Omega \twoheadrightarrow_{\beta\eta} L \notin \beta\eta\text{-}\mathfrak{U}\mathfrak{G}$. □

17.3.24. THEOREM. *Let* $M, N \in \Lambda$ *and* $M \notin \beta\eta\text{-}\mathfrak{U}\mathfrak{G}$. *Then in* $\boldsymbol{\lambda\eta}$ *the* ω*-rule holds for* M, N, *i.e.*

$$\forall Z \in \Lambda^0 MZ =_{\beta\eta} NZ \Rightarrow M =_{\beta\eta} N.$$

PROOF. By assumption $M\Omega =_{\beta\eta} N\Omega$, hence by the preceding lemma $\exists N'\ N =_{\beta\eta} N' \notin \beta\eta\text{-}\mathfrak{U}\mathfrak{G}$. But then $M, N' \in \beta\eta\text{-}\mathfrak{U}\mathfrak{G}$ and $\forall Z \in \Lambda^0$ $MZ =_{\beta\eta} N'Z$. Therefore by corollary 17.3.20 $M =_{\beta\eta} N' =_{\beta\eta} N$. □

Similarly one can prove that in the theory $\boldsymbol{\lambda}$ the term rule

$$\forall Z \in \Lambda^0 \quad MZ = NZ \Rightarrow Mx = Nx \qquad (x \text{ fresh})$$

holds provided that $M \notin \beta\text{-}\mathfrak{UG}$; see exercise 17.5.11.

II. Invalidity of the ω-rule in $\boldsymbol{\lambda\eta}$ *in general.*

In this subsection a counterexample to the ω-rule in $\boldsymbol{\lambda\eta}$ due to Plotkin [1974] will be presented. Two closed terms Ξ, Ψ will be constructed such that

$$\forall Z \in \Lambda^0 \quad \Xi Z =_{\beta\eta} \Psi Z \qquad \text{but} \quad \Xi \neq_{\beta\eta} \Psi.$$

By the result in subsection I it follows that Ξ and Ψ must be complicated.

17.3.25. LEMMA. *There exist* F, $G \in \Lambda$ *such that*
(i) $Fxyz = Fx[Fx^+(Gx^+)zy](\mathbf{E}x)$,
(ii) $Gx = Fx^+(Gx^+)(\mathbf{E}x^+)(Gx)$,
where $x^+ \equiv [\mathbf{F}, x]$, *i.e. the successor of* x.

PROOF. Let

$$A \equiv \lambda fgxyz.fx[fx^+(gx^+)zy](\mathbf{E}x),$$

$$B \equiv \lambda fgx.fx^+(gx^+)(\mathbf{E}x^+)(gx).$$

By the double fixed point theorem 6.5.1 there are terms F, G such that

$$AFG = F, \qquad BFG = G.$$

One may assume $F, G \in \Lambda^0$ and the result follows. □

17.3.26. DEFINITION (Plotkin terms). Let $F, G \in \Lambda^0$ be determined by the proof of the previous lemma. Define

$$\Xi \equiv F\ulcorner 0 \urcorner(G\ulcorner 0 \urcorner), \qquad \Psi \equiv \lambda x.\Xi\mathbf{I}.$$

17.3.27. LEMMA. *Write* $F_n \equiv F\ulcorner n \urcorner$, $G_n \equiv G\ulcorner n \urcorner$ *and* $\mathbf{E}_n \equiv \mathbf{E}\ulcorner n \urcorner$. *Then*

$$\forall m \, \forall n \quad F_n G_n \mathbf{E}_n =_\beta F_n G_n \mathbf{E}_{n+m}.$$

PROOF. By induction on m. $m = 0$ is trivial, so suppose $m > 0$. Then

$$F_nG_n\mathbf{E}_n = F_n[F_{n+1}G_{n+1}\mathbf{E}_{n+1}G_n]\mathbf{E}_n$$

by lemma 17.3.25(ii),

$$= F_n[F_{n+1}G_{n+1}\mathbf{E}_{n+1+m-1}G_n]\mathbf{E}_n$$

by the induction hypothesis,

$$= F_nG_n\mathbf{E}_{n+m}$$

by lemma 17.3.25(i). □!

17.3.28. COROLLARY. $\forall Z \in \Lambda^0\ \Xi Z = \Psi Z$.

PROOF. By the lemma

$$\forall m \quad \Xi(\mathbf{E}\ulcorner 0\urcorner) = \Xi(\mathbf{E}\ulcorner m\urcorner).$$

Since $\mathbf{E}$ enumerates Λ^0 one has

$$\forall Z, Z' \in \Lambda^0 \quad \Xi Z = \Xi Z' \ \left(= \Xi(\mathbf{E}\ulcorner 0\urcorner)\right)$$

and therefore

$$\forall Z \in \Lambda^0 \quad \Xi Z = \Xi\mathbf{I} = \Psi Z. \quad \square$$

17.3.29. LEMMA. (i) *For any variable x one has $x \in_{\beta\eta} \Xi x$, i.e.*

$$\Xi x \twoheadrightarrow_{\beta\eta} M \Rightarrow x \in \mathrm{FV}(M)$$

(ii) $\Xi \neq_{\beta\eta} \Psi$.

PROOF. (i) After trying out some cases the reader will be convinced of this. For a precise proof using the standardization theorem, do exercise 17.5.10.

(ii) If $\Xi =_{\beta\eta} \Psi$, then $\Xi x = \Psi x = \Xi\mathbf{I}$ by CR for $\boldsymbol{\beta\eta}$ one has

$$\Xi x \twoheadrightarrow_{\beta\eta} M_{\beta\eta} \twoheadleftarrow \Xi\mathbf{I}.$$

But then $x \notin \mathrm{FV}(M)$, contradicting (i). □

17.3.30. THEOREM. (i) $\boldsymbol{\lambda\eta} \nvdash \omega$.
(ii) $\boldsymbol{\lambda} \nvdash \boldsymbol{tr}$.

PROOF. (i) By corollary 17.3.28 and lemma 17.3.29 (ii).
(ii) Similarly; do exercise 17.5.11. □

As a consequence of $\boldsymbol{\lambda\eta} \nvdash \omega$ and $\boldsymbol{\lambda} \nvdash \boldsymbol{tr}$ it follows that $\mathfrak{M}^0(\boldsymbol{\lambda\eta})$, $\mathfrak{M}^0(\boldsymbol{\lambda})$ are not weakly extensional λ-algebras, see § 20.1.

17.4. The ω-rule and $\mathcal{H}\eta$

In this section it is first proved that in $\mathcal{H}\eta$ the ω-rule is valid for M, N provided that one of these terms has a $\beta\eta\Omega$-nf. Then some counterexamples to the general ω-rule are given. These are much more natural than the counterexamples for $\boldsymbol{\lambda\eta}$. Finally some properties of $\mathcal{H}\omega$ are considered. It is proved that for some $\Pi \in \Lambda^0$ one has for closed F, G

$$\forall n \in \mathbb{N} \quad \mathcal{H}\omega \vdash F \ulcorner n \urcorner = G \ulcorner n \urcorner \Leftrightarrow \mathcal{H}\omega \vdash \Pi F = \Pi G.$$

Using this and a "representation" of the sequence numbers, it is conjectured that $\mathcal{H}\omega$ is a complete Π_1^1 set.

17.4.1. PROPOSITION. *Let M, N have $\beta\eta\Omega$-nf's. Then in $\mathcal{H}\eta$ the ω-rule is valid for M, N.*

PROOF. Without loss of generality it may be assumed that M, N are in $\beta\eta\Omega$-nf. Therefore

(1) $\quad$ BT(M), BT(N) are finite and in η-nf.

Suppose

$$\forall Z \in \Lambda^0 \quad \mathcal{H}\eta \vdash MZ = NZ.$$

Then by theorem 17.2.8 one has

$$M = N \in \mathcal{H}\omega \subseteq \mathcal{H}^*$$

and hence by theorem 16.2.7

(2) $\quad M \approx_\eta N.$

By (1), (2) it follows that BT(M) = BT(N) and hence $\mathcal{H}\eta \vdash M = N$.

17.4.2. LEMMA. *Assume*

(1) $\forall Z \in \Lambda^0\ \mathcal{H}\boldsymbol{\eta} \vdash MZ = NZ$,

(2) $\mathrm{BT}(M)$ *is finite.*

Then $\mathrm{BT}(N)$ *is finite.*

PROOF. Do exercise 17.5.14. □

17.4.3. COROLLARY. *In* $\mathcal{H}\boldsymbol{\eta}$ *the* ω*-rule is valid for* M, N *provided that* M *has a* $\beta\eta\Omega$-nf.

PROOF. By the preceding lemma and proposition, using M has a $\beta\eta\Omega$-nf $\Leftrightarrow$ $\mathrm{BT}(M)$ is finite. □

For results about $\mathcal{H}$ and the term rule, see exercise 17.5.15.

Now two examples from Barendregt et al. [1978] are presented which show that $\mathcal{H}\boldsymbol{\eta} \nvdash \omega$. As is the case with the Plotkin terms, the first one is asymmetrical. The second example is symmetrical; the idea of its construction is used in order to represent universal quantification over $\mathbb{N}$ in $\mathcal{H}\omega$.

17.4.4. LEMMA. $\forall Z \in \Lambda^0\ \exists n \in \mathbb{N}\ \mathcal{H} \vdash Z\Omega^{\sim n} = \Omega$.

PROOF. If M is unsolvable, then $\mathcal{H} \vdash Z = \Omega$. Otherwise M has a hnf $\lambda x_1 \ldots x_n . x_i M_1 \cdots M_m$. Then $\mathcal{H} \vdash Z\Omega^{\sim n} = \Omega$. □

17.4.5. PROPOSITION. *Let* $A \in \Lambda^0$ *be such that*

$$Ax \twoheadrightarrow \langle A(x\Omega)\rangle.$$

(*for example, let* $A \equiv \omega\omega$, *with* $\omega \equiv \lambda axz.z(aa(x\Omega))$.) *Then*

$$\forall Z \in \Lambda^0 \quad \mathcal{H} \vdash AZ = A\Omega \qquad \textit{but} \quad \mathcal{H}\boldsymbol{\eta} \nvdash Ax = A\Omega.$$

PROOF. Let $Z \in \Lambda^0$. Then

$$AZ \twoheadrightarrow \langle A(Z\Omega)\rangle \twoheadrightarrow \langle\langle A(Z\Omega^{\sim 2})\rangle\rangle \twoheadrightarrow \cdots \twoheadrightarrow \langle \cdots \langle A(Z\Omega^{\sim n})\rangle \cdots \rangle$$

$$=_{\mathcal{H}} \langle \cdots \langle A\Omega\rangle \cdots \rangle \quad \text{by lemma 17.4.4.}$$

On the other hand

$$A\Omega =_{\mathcal{H}} \langle A\Omega\rangle =_{\mathcal{H}} \cdots =_{\mathcal{H}} \langle \cdots \langle A\Omega\rangle \cdots \rangle.$$

If $\mathcal{H}\boldsymbol{\eta} \vdash Ax = A\Omega$, then by the CR theorem for $\boldsymbol{\beta\eta\Omega}$ one would have for some M

$$Ax \twoheadrightarrow_{\beta\eta\Omega} M\ {}_{\beta\eta\Omega}\!\twoheadleftarrow A\Omega.$$

Since $A\Omega \in \Lambda^0$, also $M \in \Lambda^0$. In exercise 15.4.2 (i) it is shown, however, that

$$Ax \twoheadrightarrow_{\beta\eta\Omega} M \Rightarrow x \in \mathrm{FV}(M)$$

and hence we have a contradiction. □

17.4.6. PROPOSITION. (i) *There exists a term* $O \in \Lambda^0$ *such that*

(1) $$Ox\ulcorner n \urcorner \twoheadrightarrow \lambda z.z\Omega^{\sim n}(Ox\ulcorner n+1\urcorner z).$$

(ii) *If* O *satisfies* (1), *then for all* x, y

$$\forall Z \in \Lambda^0 \quad \mathcal{H} \vdash Ox\ulcorner 0\urcorner Z = Oy\ulcorner 0\urcorner Z.$$

(iii) O *satisfying* (*i*) *can be chosen in such a way that for distinct* x, y *one has*

$$\mathcal{H} \nvdash Ox\ulcorner 0\urcorner = Oy\ulcorner 0\urcorner .$$

PROOF. (i) Using proposition 6.1.6 there exists F, $O \in \Lambda^0$ such that

$$Fzn \twoheadrightarrow \textit{If}\ \text{zero}\ n\ \textit{then}\ z\ \textit{else}\ Fzn^{-}\,\Omega,$$

$$Oxn \twoheadrightarrow \lambda z.\ Fzn(Oxn^{+}z),$$

where $n^{-} \equiv n\mathbf{F}$, $n^{+} \equiv [\mathbf{F}, n]$ are the predecessor and successor of n. Then for all $n \in \mathbb{N}$

$$Fz\ulcorner n\urcorner \twoheadrightarrow z\,\Omega^{\sim n}$$

and therefore (1).

(ii) Let $Z \in \Lambda^0$. Then in $\mathcal{H}$

$$\begin{aligned} Ox\ulcorner 0\urcorner Z &= Z(Ox\ulcorner 1\urcorner Z) \\ &= Z(Z\Omega(Ox\ulcorner 2\urcorner Z)) \\ &\quad \cdots \\ &= Z(Z\Omega(\cdots(Z\Omega^{\sim n}(Ox\ulcorner n+1\urcorner Z))\cdots)) \\ &= Z(Z\Omega(\cdots(\Omega)\cdots)) \quad \text{by lemma 17.4.4,} \\ &= Z(Z\Omega(\cdots(Z\Omega^{\sim n-3}(Z\Omega^{\sim n-1}))\cdots)) \end{aligned}$$

and similarly for $Oy\ulcorner 0\urcorner Z$ (if $Z=\Omega$, $Z\Omega=\Omega$ or $Z\Omega^{\sim 2}=\Omega$, then the computation is somewhat easier).

(iii) In exercise 15.4.2 (ii) it is shown that for the natural choice of O one has

$$(2)\qquad Ox\ulcorner 0\urcorner \twoheadrightarrow_{\beta\eta\Omega} M \Rightarrow x \in \mathrm{FV}(M).$$

Now assume $Ox\ulcorner 0\urcorner = Oy\ulcorner 0\urcorner$. By the CR theorem for $\boldsymbol{\beta\eta\Omega}$ one has

$$Ox\ulcorner 0\urcorner \twoheadrightarrow_{\beta\eta\Omega} M_{\beta\eta\Omega}\twoheadleftarrow Oy\ulcorner 0\urcorner,$$

contradicting (2). □

17.4.7. THEOREM. (i) $\mathcal{H}\boldsymbol{\eta} \nvdash \omega$.

(ii) $\mathcal{H} \nvdash \boldsymbol{tr}$.

PROOF. (i) Immediate by proposition 17.4.5 or 17.4.6.

(ii) Similarly. □

Using the idea behind the construction in proposition 17.4.6 one can construct a kind of universal quantifier for sensible ω-theories. Using this one can give a representation of arbitrary Π_1^1 sets in such theories. The method is again from Barendregt et al [1978].

17.4.8. DEFINITION. Let $A \in \Lambda^0$ be such that

$$Af\ulcorner n\urcorner \twoheadrightarrow \lambda y.[f\ulcorner n\urcorner, y\Omega^{\sim n}(Af\ulcorner n+1\urcorner y)]$$

Define $\Pi \in \Lambda^0$ by $\Pi \equiv \lambda f.Af\ulcorner 0\urcorner$.

17.4.9. THEOREM. *For all sensible λ-theories $\mathfrak{T}$ one has for arbitrary $F, G \in \Lambda^0$*

(i) $\forall n \in \mathbb{N}\ \mathfrak{T} \vdash F\ulcorner n\urcorner = G\ulcorner n\urcorner \Rightarrow \mathfrak{T}\omega \vdash \Pi F = \Pi G$,

(ii) $\forall n \in \mathbb{N}\ \mathfrak{T}\omega \vdash F\ulcorner n\urcorner = G\ulcorner n\urcorner \Leftrightarrow \mathfrak{T}\omega \vdash \Pi F = \Pi G$.

PROOF. (i) Suppose $\mathfrak{T} \vdash F\ulcorner n\urcorner = G\ulcorner n\urcorner$ for all n. *Claim*:

$$\forall Z \in \Lambda^0 \quad \mathfrak{T} \vdash \Pi FZ = \Pi GZ.$$

Indeed, given $Z \in \Lambda^0$, by lemma 17.4.4 for some n one has $\mathcal{H} \vdash Z\Omega^{\sim n} = \Omega$.

Take n the least such. Then in $\mathcal{T}$

$$\begin{aligned}\Pi FZ &= AF\ulcorner 0\urcorner Z\\ &= \big[F\ulcorner 0\urcorner, Z\big[F\ulcorner 1\urcorner, Z\Omega\cdots[F\ulcorner n\urcorner,\Omega]\cdots\big]\big]\\ &= \big[G\ulcorner 0\urcorner, Z\big[G\ulcorner 1\urcorner, Z\Omega\cdots[G\ulcorner n\urcorner,\Omega]..\big]\big]\\ &= AG\ulcorner 0\urcorner Z = \Pi GZ.\end{aligned}$$

Therefore by the ω-rule $\mathcal{T}\omega\vdash \Pi F = \Pi G$.

(ii) (⇐) By the Böhm out technique. Note that ΠF respectively ΠG have as Böhm trees

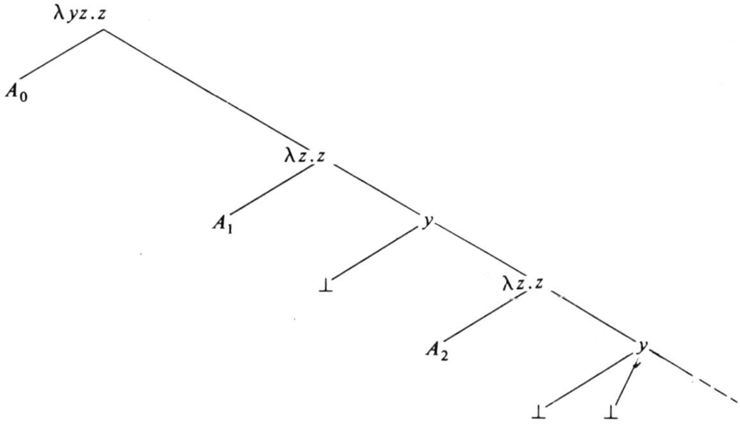

where A_n is BT$(F\ulcorner n\urcorner)$ or BT$(G\ulcorner n\urcorner)$ respectively. By proposition 10.3.7 and lemma 10.3.4 it follows that there are contexts $C_n[\ ]$ such that $C_n[\Pi F] = F\ulcorner n\urcorner$ and similarly for ΠG.
Therefore for all n

$$\mathcal{T}\omega\vdash F\ulcorner n\urcorner = C_n[\Pi F] = C_n[\Pi G] = G\ulcorner n\urcorner. \quad\square$$

In order to represent Π_1^1 predicates in $\mathcal{K}\omega$ first we construct a term that "codes" the Baire space $\mathbb{N}^{\mathbb{N}}$. For simplicity it will be assumed that the coding of finite sequences $\langle n_0,\ldots,n_k\rangle$ is such that Seq $=\mathbb{N}$. Let $\underline{*}\in\Lambda^0$ λ-define $*$, i.e. $\underline{*}\ulcorner s\urcorner\ulcorner s'\urcorner = \ulcorner s*s'\urcorner$ and write $M * N$ for $\underline{*}MN$. For $f\in\mathbb{N}^{\mathbb{N}}$ the sequence number $\langle f(0),\ldots,f(n-1)\rangle$ is denoted by $\bar{f}(n)$. In particular, $\bar{f}(0) = \langle\ \rangle$, the code of the empty sequence.

17.4.10. LEMMA. *There exists a* $B\in\Lambda^0$ *such that*

$$B\ulcorner s\urcorner \twoheadrightarrow [B\ulcorner s*0\urcorner, B\ulcorner s*1\urcorner,\ldots].$$

PROOF. The sequence $b\ulcorner s*0\urcorner, b\ulcorner s*1\urcorner, \ldots$ is uniform (via $\lambda n.b(\ulcorner s\urcorner * n)$). Hence we can take

$$B \equiv \mathbf{\Theta}(\lambda b.[b\ulcorner s*0\urcorner, b\ulcorner s*1\urcorner, \ldots]). \quad \square$$

Now $B\ulcorner\langle\ \rangle\urcorner$ represents the set of sequence numbers: if $B\ulcorner\langle n_1,\ldots,n_k\rangle)\urcorner$ is abbreviated by $Bn_1 \cdots n_k$, then

$$\begin{aligned} B\ulcorner\langle\ \rangle\urcorner &= \langle B0, B1, \ldots\rangle \\ &= \langle\langle B00, B01, \ldots\rangle, \langle B10, B11, \ldots\rangle, \ldots\rangle \\ &= \cdots \end{aligned}$$

Let $P(n)$ be a Π_1^1 predicate. Then

(1) $$P(n) \Leftrightarrow \forall f\ \exists m\ R(\bar{f}(m), n)$$

for some recursive R. A sequence number s is *n-secured* iff $\exists s' < s\ R(s', n)$, otherwise *n-unsecured*. Then $P(n)$ holds iff the n-unsecured sequence numbers are well-founded (i.e. not $s_0 < s_1 < s_2 < \cdots$ for some infinite sequence of n-unsecured sequence numbers).

Now the construction in lemma 17.4.10 will be modified in order to code the set of n-unsecured sequence numbers.

17.4.11. LEMMA. *There is a term* $\square$ *such that in* $\mathcal{H}$

$$\square\ulcorner n\urcorner\ulcorner s\urcorner = \begin{cases} \mathbf{I} & \textit{if } s \textit{ is } n\textit{-unsecured}, \\ \mathbf{\Omega} & \textit{else}. \end{cases}$$

PROOF. The notion "s is n-unsecured" is recursive, hence a fortiori r.e.. Therefore lemma 16.1.10 applies. $\square$

NOTATION. $\square^n$ denotes $\square\ulcorner n\urcorner$ and similarly for terms derived from $\square$.

17.4.12. LEMMA. *There is a* $B \in \Lambda^0$ *such that*

$$B^n\ulcorner s\urcorner \twoheadrightarrow \square^n\ulcorner s\urcorner[B^n\ulcorner s*0\urcorner, B^n\ulcorner s*1\urcorner, \ldots].$$

PROOF. As for lemma 17.4.10. □

Now $B^{n\ulcorner}\langle\ -\ \rangle^{\urcorner}$ represents in $\mathcal{H}$ the n-unsecured sequence numbers:

$$B^{n\ulcorner}\langle\ \ \rangle^{\urcorner}=[\,B^n0, B^n1,\dots\,]$$

$$=[\,[\,B^n00, \Omega, B^n02,\dots\,], [\,\Omega, B^n11,\dots\,],\dots\,]$$

$$=\dots$$

if e.g. $\langle 0,1\rangle$ and $\langle 1,0\rangle$ are n-secured.

17.4.13. DEFINITION. Given a Π_1^1 predicate $P(n)$ satisfying (1) above and the corresponding □, then as before one can construct a term $B\in\Lambda^0$ such that

$$Bixs \twoheadrightarrow \Box xs\,\Pi(\lambda a.\,Bix(s*a)).$$

Let $B_i^n\equiv B^{\ulcorner}i^{\urcorner\ulcorner}n^{\urcorner}$. Then

(2) $$B_i^n s\twoheadrightarrow \Box^n s\,\Pi(\lambda a.\,B_i^n(s*a)).$$

17.4.14. THEOREM. *Let $P(n)$ be Π_1^1 and satisfying* (1) *above and let $B\in\Lambda^0$ be the term satisfying* (2). *Then*

$$P(n)\Rightarrow \mathcal{H}\omega\vdash B_0^{n\ulcorner}\langle\ \ \rangle^{\urcorner}=B_1^{n\ulcorner}\langle\ \ \rangle^{\urcorner}.$$

PROOF. First we claim

(3) $$s \text{ is } n\text{-secured}\Rightarrow \mathcal{H}\omega\vdash B_0^{n\ulcorner}s^{\urcorner}=B_1^{n\ulcorner}s^{\urcorner}.$$

(4) $$[\forall m\ \mathcal{H}\omega\vdash B_0^{n\ulcorner}s*m^{\urcorner}=B_1^{n\ulcorner}s*m^{\urcorner}]\Rightarrow \mathcal{H}\omega\vdash B_0^{n\ulcorner}s^{\urcorner}=B_1^{n\ulcorner}s^{\urcorner}.$$

For by lemma 17.4.11 one has in $\mathcal{H}$

$$s \text{ is } n\text{-secured}\Rightarrow \Box^{n\ulcorner}s^{\urcorner}=\Omega$$

$$\Rightarrow B_0^{n\ulcorner}s^{\urcorner}=\Omega=B_1^{n\ulcorner}s^{\urcorner}.$$

And if s is n-secured, then (4) follows from (3). Otherwise $\Box^{n\ulcorner}s^{\urcorner}=\mathbf{I}$ and hence by (2),

$$B_0^{n\ulcorner}s^{\urcorner}=\Pi(\lambda a.B_0^n(^{\ulcorner}s^{\urcorner}*a)),$$

$$B_1^{n\ulcorner}s^{\urcorner}=\Pi(\lambda a.B_1^n(^{\ulcorner}s^{\urcorner}*a))$$

and (4) follows from theorem 17.4.9.

Now suppose $P(n)$. Then by (1)

(5) $\forall f\ \exists m\quad \bar{f}(m)$ is n-secured.

Now it follows from (3), (4), (5) and bar induction that $\mathcal{H}\omega \vdash B_0^n \ulcorner\langle\ \rangle\urcorner = B_1^n\ulcorner\langle\ \rangle\urcorner$. (The reader unfamiliar with bar induction may consult exercise 17.5.17.) □

From the proof of theorem 17.4.14 one gets the feeling that the well-foundedness of the n-unsecured sequence numbers is essential in order to show $\mathcal{H}\omega \vdash B_0^n\ulcorner\langle\ \rangle\urcorner = B_1^n\ulcorner\langle\ \rangle\urcorner$. Therefore

(6) $$P(n) \Leftrightarrow \mathcal{H}\omega \vdash B_0^n\ulcorner\langle\ \rangle\urcorner = B_1^n\ulcorner\langle\ \rangle\urcorner.$$

For a precise proof a deeper analysis of $\mathcal{H}\omega$ is needed.

17.4.15. Conjecture. $\mathcal{H}\omega$ is a Π_1^1-complete theory.

Motivation. As $\mathcal{H}\omega$ is given by an inductive definition, it is Π_1^1. Let $P(n)$ be an arbitrary Π_1^1 predicate. Then it follows from (6) that $P(n)$ can be reduced to provability in $\mathcal{H}\omega$. □

The following result shows how the various λ-theories are interrelated.

17.4.16. Theorem. *The following diagram indicates all possible inclusion relations of the λ-theories involved (if $\mathfrak{T}_1$ is above $\mathfrak{T}_2$, then $\mathfrak{T}_1 \subsetneq \mathfrak{T}_2$).*

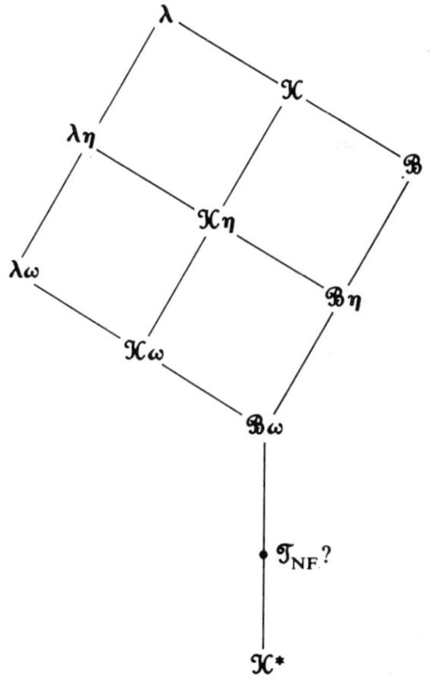

PROOF. Let $\mathfrak{T}$ be $\boldsymbol{\lambda}$, $\mathcal{H}$ or $\mathfrak{B}$. Then $\mathfrak{T} \subsetneq \mathfrak{T}\eta \subsetneq \mathfrak{T}\omega \subsetneq \mathcal{H}^*$ by § 17.3, § 17.4 § 16.4 and exercise 17.5.20. That $\mathfrak{B}\omega \subsetneq \mathfrak{T}_{\mathrm{NF}}$ is conjectured by Sallé. The other relations and incomparabilities are obvious. □

17.5. Exercises

17.5.1. Let $\mathfrak{T}$ be a sensible λ-theory. Show that $\mathfrak{T}$ is not r.e. [*Hint*. There is no $\mathfrak{T}$-easy term.]

17.5.2 (M.Bel). (i) A *magic triple* is a set of three terms $\{M, N, L\}$ such that $\mathrm{Con}(M = N)$, $(\mathrm{Con}(N = L)$, $\mathrm{Con}(L = M)$ but $\neg\mathrm{Con}(M = N = L)$. Construct a magic triple. [*Hint*. Take $\{\mathbf{I}, \Omega, \Omega\mathbf{S}\}$ and use proposition 14.5.9.]

(ii) There exists for $n \geqslant 3$ a *magic n-tuple*, i.e. a set of n-terms such that for each proper subset it is consistent to equate all terms in that subset, but not so for the set itself. [*Hint*. Using proposition 17.1.9 (ii) (or exercise 4.3.2 (iii)), construct terms $\Omega_1, \ldots, \Omega_k$ such that

$$\forall M_1, \ldots, M_k \quad \mathrm{Con}(\{\Omega_1 = M_1, \ldots, \Omega_k = M_k\}).$$

Then take $\{\mathbf{I}, \Omega_1, \Omega_1\Omega_2, \Omega_1(\Omega_2\Omega_3), \ldots, \Omega_1(\Omega_2(\cdots(\Omega_{k-1}\Omega_k)..)), \Omega_1(\Omega_2(\cdots(\Omega_k\mathbf{S})..))\}$.]

17.5.3. (i) Let $\mathfrak{T}$ be s.s and such that

$$(*) \qquad \mathfrak{B} \subseteq \mathfrak{T}.$$

Suppose that (1) $F\Omega =_{\mathfrak{T}} M$ and (2) M is Ω-free. Show that $\forall N\ FN =_{\mathfrak{T}} M$.

(ii) Show that in (i) condition (*) cannot be omitted, even not if (2) is replaced by (2′) M is a nf.

17.5.4. Show that every Visser open subset of Λ contains an unsolvable term.

17.5.5. Let $\mathfrak{T}$ be r.e. Show that $\mathfrak{M}(\mathfrak{T})$ with the Visser topology is a T_1-space but not a T_2-space.

17.5.6. Let $\mathfrak{T}$ be an arbitrary λ-theory. Show that there exists a term that is $\mathfrak{T}$-unsolvable.

17.5.7. Show that every r.e. λ-theory $\mathfrak{T}$ that is s.s. can be embedded in a finitely axiomatizable (over $\boldsymbol{\lambda}$) theory $\mathfrak{T}'$.

17.5.8. Let $\Omega_n = \Omega\ulcorner n \urcorner$.

(i) Show that $\exists F \in \Lambda^0\ F\Omega_1 = F\Omega_2 \neq Fx$.

(ii) Show that $\exists F, G \in \Lambda^0\ \{F\Omega_1 = G\Omega_1 \wedge F\Omega_2 = G\Omega_2 \wedge Fx \neq Gx\}$. [*Hint*. Simple terms can be found.]

17.5.9. (i) Let Ξ be Plotkin's term constructed in definition 17.3.26. Find a common reduct for $\Xi(\mathbf{E}\ulcorner 0 \urcorner)$ and $\Xi(\mathbf{E}\ulcorner 3 \urcorner)$.

(ii) Consider an applicative term system with constants $\{F_n, G_n, E_n\}_{n \in \mathbb{N}}$ and with the reduction rules

$$F_nMN \to F_n[F_{n+1}G_{n+1}NM]E_n,$$
$$G_n \to F_{n+1}G_{n+1}E_{n+1}G_n.$$

Construct in this system a common reduct for $F_0G_0E_0$ and $F_0G_0E_9$.

17.5.10 (Plotkin [1974]). Let F, G, Ξ be as in definition 17.3.26. The aim of this exercise is to prove lemma 17.3.29 (i), i.e.

$$(+) \qquad x \in_{\beta\eta} \Xi x$$

(i) Let $y \in \mathrm{FV}(N)$, $\sigma : FMNL \twoheadrightarrow_\beta Z$, $y \notin \mathrm{FV}(Z)$. Show that there is a reduction $\sigma' : N \underset{s}{\twoheadrightarrow}_\beta N'$ such that $y \notin \mathrm{FV}(N')$ and $\|\sigma'\| < \|\sigma\|$.

(ii) Let $y \in \mathrm{FV}(L)$, $\sigma : FMNL \underset{s}{\twoheadrightarrow}_\beta Z$, $y \notin \mathrm{FV}(Z)$. Show that $y \notin_{\beta\eta} L$.

(iii) Show that $(+)$ holds. [Use corollary 15.1.6.]

17.5.11. (i) Let M be not a β-UG and N be arbitrary. Show that in $\boldsymbol{\lambda}$ the term rule holds for M and N (i.e. $[\forall Z \in \Lambda^0\ MZ = NZ] \Rightarrow Mx = Nx$).
(ii) Show that $\boldsymbol{\lambda} \nvdash tr$.

17.5.12. Let $\boldsymbol{\lambda\eta} \vdash_k M = N$ mean that $M = N$ is derivable in $\boldsymbol{\lambda\eta}$ with a proof of length $\leqslant k$. Parikh's ω-rule for $\boldsymbol{\lambda\eta}$ is

$$[\exists k \in \mathbb{N}\ \forall Z \in \Lambda^0\ \boldsymbol{\lambda\eta} \vdash_k MZ = NZ] \Rightarrow \boldsymbol{\lambda\eta} \vdash M = N.$$

Show that this is derivable for arbitrary terms.

17.5.13 (Klop). (i) Show that there is a $\beta\eta$-UG which is not a β-UG [*Hint*. Let U be a β-UG; let U^η be U with all variable occurrences z that are passive (not occurring in a subterm (zN)) replaced by $\lambda x.zx$. Then U^η works.]
(ii) Let $M, N \notin \beta\text{-}\mathfrak{UG}$. Show that in $\boldsymbol{\lambda\eta}$ the ω-rule is generally not valid for M and N.

17.5.14. Show that if BT(M) is finite and $\forall Z \in \Lambda^0\ \mathfrak{K}\boldsymbol{\eta} \vdash MZ = NZ$, then BT($N$) is finite. [*Hint*. Use $Z \equiv \mathbf{P}_n \equiv \lambda x_0 \cdots x_n.\langle x_0, \ldots, x_n\rangle$, for large n.]

17.5.15. (i) Show that if M, N are $\beta\eta\Omega$-nf's, then in $\mathfrak{K}$ the term rule holds for M and N.
(ii) Show that if in (i) the notion "are $\beta\eta\Omega$-nf's" is replaced by "have $\beta\eta\Omega$-nf's", then the result is no longer valid.

17.5.16. Draw BT($B\ ^\ulcorner\langle\ \rangle^\urcorner$), where B is as in lemma 17.4.10.

17.5.17 (Classical bar induction). Let $P(s)$ be a predicate on sequence numbers. Suppose

$$(1) \qquad \forall f: \mathbb{N} \to \mathbb{N}\ \exists n \in \mathbb{N}\quad P(\bar{f}(n)),$$

$$(2) \qquad (\forall n \in \mathbb{N}\ P(s * \langle n\rangle)) \Rightarrow P(s), \text{ for all } s \in \text{Seq}.$$

Show that $P(\langle\ \rangle)$.

17.5.18. Show that $\boldsymbol{\lambda I\eta} \nvdash \omega$.

17.5.19. Show that there is no minimal λ-theory $\supsetneq \boldsymbol{\lambda}$.

17.5.20. Show that $\mathfrak{B}\eta \nvdash \omega$. [*Hint*. Use lemma 16.4.4.]

17.5.21. (i) Show that if $\mathfrak{T}$, $\mathfrak{T}'$ are λ-theories, then so is $\mathfrak{T} \cap \mathfrak{T}'$. (See also exercise 5.6.13.)
(ii) Consider the drawing in theorem 17.4.16. Show that

$$\boldsymbol{\lambda\eta} \cap \mathfrak{K} \neq \boldsymbol{\lambda}, \qquad \boldsymbol{\lambda\omega} \cap \mathfrak{K}\boldsymbol{\eta} \neq \boldsymbol{\lambda\eta},$$

$$\mathfrak{K}\boldsymbol{\eta} \cap \mathfrak{B} \neq \mathfrak{K}, \qquad \mathfrak{B}\boldsymbol{\eta} \cap \mathfrak{K}\omega \neq \mathfrak{K}\boldsymbol{\eta}.$$

PART V

MODELS

Scott (photo by
B. Obrecht, 1969)

Hyland (photo by
Mrs. D. van Dalen, 1981)

Koymans (1984)

Longo (photo by
Palamidessi Catuscia, 1983)

Plotkin (photo by
the author, 1979)

Wadsworth (1974)

CHAPTER 18

CONSTRUCTION OF MODELS

In chapters 4 and 5 the term models of consistent λ-theories were introduced. These were constructed starting from a set of equations to be satisfied in the model.

With the so-called "mathematical" models the situation is reversed. There one starts with a structure whose objects can be interpreted both as functions and arguments. Then later one may study the set of equation true in the model.

The first mathematical model was D_∞ constructed by Scott in 1969 as a projective limit of complete lattices. One of the reasons why his construction works is that complete lattices with appropriate continuous maps form a cartesian closed category with function spaces $[D \to D]$ of the same cardinality as D. And cartesian closedness corresponds to Schönfinkel's idea of reducing functions of several arguments to those of one.

Somewhat easier to construct than D_∞ is the graph model $P\omega$, due to Plotkin [1972] and Scott [1974], independently.

The constructions of D_∞ and $P\omega$ can be formulated also in the cartesian closed category **CPO**. We will do so, since cpo's are useful also for other models such as $\mathfrak{B}$ and $\mathbb{T}^\omega$; see Plotkin [1978] or Barendregt and Longo [1980] for the latter model.

The plan of this chapter is as follows. The general method for the construction of λ-models, described in § 5.4, is used in § 18.1 to construct the graph model $P\omega$ and in § 18.2 to construct the models D_∞. Finally in § 18.3 the Böhm tree model $\mathfrak{B}$ is introduced.

18.1. The graph model $P\omega$

In this section it will be shown that the powerset of the natural numbers is a reflexive cpo. Therefore, by § 5.4, this structure yields a λ-model.

18.1.1. DEFINITION. $P\omega = \{x \mid x \subseteq \mathbb{N}\}$ is the power set of $\mathbb{N}$, partially ordered by inclusion, $\subseteq$.

The construction of the graph model of Plotkin and Scott depends on the fact that a continuous function on $P\omega$ can be coded as a set. The same idea is used in Rogers [1967] §§ 9.7, 9.8. See Scott [1975], [1976] for discussion.

$P\omega$ is an algebraic cpo and will always be considered with its Scott topology. This topology is determined by finite *positive* information: the sets

$$O_e = \{x | e \subseteq x\}, \quad e \text{ finite},$$

form a base. By contrast the Cantor topology (the product topology on $P\omega \cong \{0,1\}^{\mathbb{N}}$ with $\{0,1\}$ discrete) is determined by finite *positive and negative* information. For example,

$$\{x \in P\omega | 7 \in x, 13 \notin x\}$$

is open in the Cantor topology, but not in the Scott topology.

18.1.2. PROPOSITION. *Let* $f: P\omega \to P\omega$.

(i) f *is continuous* $\Rightarrow f$ *is monotonic*

(ii) f *is continuous* $\Leftrightarrow f(x) = \cup\{f(e) | e \subseteq x, e$ *finite*$\}$.

PROOF. (i) By corollary 1.2.7,

(ii) By propositions 1.2.24 and 1.2.31. □

18.1.3. DEFINITION. (Coding of ordered pairs and finite sets.)

(i) For $n, m \in \mathbb{N}$, let

$$(n, m) = \tfrac{1}{2}(n+m)(n+m+1) + m$$

(ii) For $n \in \mathbb{N}$, define the finite set e_n as follows.

$$e_n = \{k_0, \ldots, k_{m-1}\} \text{ with } k_0 < k_1 < \cdots < k_{m-1} \Leftrightarrow n = \sum_{i<m} 2^{k_i}.$$

EXAMPLE. To calculate e_{13}, write 13 in binary notation: 1101. This gives $e_{13} = \{0, 2, 3\}$. To calculate n, m such that $(n, m) = 13$, realize that

14				
9	13			
5	8	12		
2	4	7	11	
0	1	3	6	10

is the picture corresponding to the coding (n, m). Hence $(1, 3) = 13$.

Note that $(0, 0) = 0$, $e_0 = \emptyset$ and $e_1 = \{0\}$.

18.1.4. PROPOSITION. (i) $\lambda nm.(n, m)$ *is a bijection mapping* $\mathbb{N}^2$ *onto* $\mathbb{N}$.

(ii) $\lambda n.e_n$ *is a bijection mapping* $\mathbb{N}$ *onto* $\{x \in P\omega | x$ *finite*$\}$.

PROOF. Standard. □

The construction of $P\omega$ can be carried out for arbitrary bijective codings (n, m) and e_n. However, for the structure of $P\omega$ the specific coding is essential. See exercise 19.4.7.

Since by proposition 18.1.2 a continuous $f: P\omega \to P\omega$ is determined by its values on the finite sets, f can be coded as an element of $P\omega$. This gives a continuous map

$$\text{graph}: [P\omega \to P\omega] \to P\omega$$

with an obvious "inverse" and the result of § 5.4 can be applied. Recall that $[P\omega \to P\omega]$ is an algebraic cpo with pointwise inclusion and has the corresponding Scott topology.

18.1.5. DEFINITION. (i) For $f \in [P\omega \to P\omega]$, let

$$\text{graph}(f) = \{(n, m) | m \in f(e_n)\}.$$

(ii) Let $u \in P\omega$. Define $\text{fun}(u) \in [P\omega \to P\omega]$ by

$$\text{fun}(u)(x) = \{m | \exists e_n \subseteq x (n, m) \in u\}.$$

18.1.6. PROPOSITION. (i) $\text{graph}: [P\omega \to P\omega] \to P\omega$ *is continuous.*

(ii) $\forall u \in P\omega\, \text{fun}(u) \in [P\omega \to P\omega]$.

(iii) $\text{fun}: P\omega \to [P\omega \to P\omega]$ *is continuous.*

(iv) $\forall f \in [P\omega \to P\omega]\, \text{fun}(\text{graph}(f)) = f$.

(v) $\forall u \in P\omega\, \text{graph}(\text{fun}(u)) \supseteq u$.

PROOF. (i) Let $F \subseteq [P\omega \to P\omega]$. Then

$$\begin{aligned}\text{graph}(\sqcup F) &= \{(n, m) | m \in (\sqcup F)(e_n)\} \\ &= \Big\{(n, m) | m \in \bigcup_{f \in F} f(e_n)\Big\} \\ &= \bigcup_{f \in F} \{(n, m) | m \in f(e_n)\} \\ &= \bigcup_{f \in F} \text{graph}(f).\end{aligned}$$

Hence graph is continuous by proposition 1.2.6.

(ii) Let $g = \text{fun}(u)$ and let $X \subseteq P\omega$ be directed. Then

$$\begin{aligned}g(\cup X) &= \{m | \exists e_n \subseteq \cup X (n, m) \in u\} \\ &= \bigcup_{x \in X} \{m | \exists e_n \subseteq x (n, m) \in u\} \\ &= \bigcup_{x \in X} g(x)\end{aligned}$$

(the middle equation holds since X is directed), and proposition 1.2.6 applies.

(iii) Let $U \subseteq P\omega$. Then

$$\begin{aligned}\mathrm{fun}(\cup U)(x) &= \{m \mid \exists e_n \subseteq x\,(n,m) \in \cup U\}\\ &= \bigcup_{u \in U} \{m \mid \exists e_n \subseteq x\,(n,m) \in u\}\\ &= \bigcup_{u \in U} (\mathrm{fun}(u)(x))\\ &= \Big(\bigsqcup_{u \in U} \mathrm{fun}(u)\Big)(x).\end{aligned}$$

Hence $\mathrm{fun}(\cup U) = \bigsqcup_{u \in U} \mathrm{fun}(u)$ and therefore fun is continuous.

(iv) Let $f \in [P\omega \to P\omega]$. Then

$$\begin{aligned}\mathrm{fun}(\mathrm{graph}(f))(x) &= \{m \mid \exists e_n \subseteq x\,(n,m) \in \mathrm{graph}(f)\}\\ &= \{m \mid \exists e_n \subseteq x\, m \in f(e_n)\}\\ &= \cup\{f(e_n) \mid e_n \subseteq x\} = f(x)\end{aligned}$$

by proposition 18.1.2(ii). Therefore $\mathrm{fun}(\mathrm{graph}(f)) = f$.

(v)
$$\begin{aligned}\mathrm{graph}(\mathrm{fun}(u)) &= \{(n,m) \mid m \in \mathrm{fun}(u)(e_n)\}\\ &= \{(n,m) \mid \exists e_k \subseteq e_n\,(k,m) \in u\}.\end{aligned}$$

Now let $p \in u$ and say $p = (n, m)$. Then $p \in \mathrm{graph}(\mathrm{fun}(u))$, since $e_n \subseteq e_n$ and $(n, m) = p \in u$. Therefore $u \subseteq \mathrm{graph}(\mathrm{fun}(u))$. □

It now follows from the results of § 5.4 that $P\omega$ can be considered as a λ-model. To make this model more explicit, the following notation is introduced.

18.1.7. DEFINITION. (i) For $x, y \in P\omega$ let

$$x \cdot y = \mathrm{fun}(x)(y) = \{m \mid \exists e_n \subseteq y\,(n,m) \in x\}$$

(ii) For $f \in [P\omega^{k+1} \to P\omega]$ let

$$\begin{aligned}\lambda^G x.f(x,\vec{y}) &= \mathrm{graph}(\boldsymbol{\lambda} x.f(x,\vec{y}))\\ &= \{(n,m) \mid m \in f(e_n,\vec{y})\}.\end{aligned}$$

18.1.8. COROLLARY. (i) *$P\omega = (P\omega, \cdot)$ is a λ-model.*

(ii) *The representable functions on $P\omega$ are exactly the continuous ones.*

(iii) *The interpretation of λ-terms in $P\omega$ is inductively defined as follows. Let ρ be a valuation in $P\omega$.*

$$[\![x]\!]_\rho^{P\omega} = \rho(x),$$

$$[\![MN]\!]_\rho^{P\omega} = [\![M]\!]_\rho^{P\omega} \cdot [\![N]\!]_\rho^{P\omega} = \left\{ m \mid \exists e_n \subseteq [\![N]\!]_\rho^{P\omega} (n, m) \in [\![M]\!]_\rho^{P\omega} \right\},$$

$$[\![\lambda x.M]\!]_\rho^{P\omega} = \lambda^G a.[\![M]\!]_{\rho(x:=a)}^{P\omega} = \left\{ (n, m) \mid m \in [\![M]\!]_{\rho(x:=e_n)}^{P\omega} \right\}.$$

PROOF. By proposition 18.1.6 $F=$ fun and $G=$ graph is a retraction pair showing that P is a reflexive cpo. Hence definition 5.4.2 and theorem 5.4.4 apply. □

Following convention 5.3.8 we write e.g.: "in $P\omega$ one has

$$xa = \{ m \mid \exists e_n \subseteq a (n, m) \in x \},$$

$$\lambda x.xa = \{ (n, m) \mid m \in e_n a \}$$

$$= \{ (n, m) \mid \exists e_{n'} \subseteq a (n', m) \in e_n \}".$$

18.1.9. PROPOSITION. *Let $a, b \in P\omega$ and let $A, B \in \mathcal{T}(P\omega)$. Then in $P\omega$ one has*

(i) $a \subseteq \lambda x.ax = \text{graph}(\text{fun}(a))$.

(ii) $a \subseteq a', x \subseteq x' \Rightarrow ax \subseteq a'x'$.

(iii) $\forall x\ A \subseteq B \Leftrightarrow \lambda x.A \subseteq \lambda x.B$.

PROOF. (i) $\lambda x.ax = \text{graph}(\boldsymbol{\lambda} x.ax)$

$= \text{graph}(\text{fun}(a))$

$\supseteq a$ by proposition 18.1.6 (v).

(ii) Application is continuous and hence monotonic.

(iii) ($\Leftarrow$) Suppose $\lambda x.A \subseteq \lambda x.B$. Then

$$A = (\lambda^G x.A)x$$

$$\subseteq (\lambda x.B)x \quad \text{by (ii)},$$

$$= B.$$

($\Rightarrow$) Suppose $\forall x\ A \subseteq B$. Then

$$\lambda x.A = \{ (n, m) \mid m \in A[x:=e_n] \}$$

$$\subseteq \{ (n, m) \mid m \in B[x:=e_n] \} = \lambda x.B. \quad \square$$

It is easy to show that $P\omega$ is not extensional, hence in general $a \neq \lambda x.ax$; see exercise 18.4.1.

18.1.10. COROLLARY. *Let $f \in [P\omega \to P\omega]$ and let $a = graph(f)$. Then in $P\omega$*

$$a = \lambda x.ax.$$

PROOF.

$$\begin{aligned}\lambda x.ax &= \text{graph} \circ \text{fun} \circ \text{graph}(f)\\ &= \text{graph}(f) \quad \text{by proposition 18.1.6(iv)},\\ &= a. \quad \square\end{aligned}$$

18.1.11. COROLLARY. *Let $M, M' \in \Lambda$ and $C[\ ] \in \Lambda[\ ]$. Then*

$$P\omega \models M \subseteq M' \Rightarrow P\omega \models C[M] \subseteq C[M'].$$

PROOF. By induction on the structure of $C[\ ]$. $\square$

The following definition and lemmas are useful for the analysis of the structure of $P\omega$. At first reading the rest of this section may be omitted.

18.1.12. DEFINITION. For $a \in P\omega$ and $n \in \mathbb{N}$, let

$$(a)_n = \{m \in a \mid m \leqslant n\}.$$

Clearly $a = \cup_n (a)_n$.

18.1.13. LEMMA. *The coding of the finite sets e_k and the ordered pairs (n, m) is such that*

(i) $m \in e_k \Rightarrow m < k$,
(ii) $m \leqslant (n, m)$; $n \leqslant (n, m)$,
(iii) $m = (n, m) \Leftrightarrow m = n = 0$,
(iv) $n = (n, m) \Leftrightarrow m = 0 \wedge n \in \{0, 1\}$.

PROOF. Easy. $\square$

18.1.14. COROLLARY (Basic equations for $P\omega$).
(i) $d = \cup_n (d)_n$; $((d)_n)_m = (d)_{\min(n,m)}$.
(ii) $\emptyset d = \lambda d.\emptyset = \emptyset = (\emptyset)_n$.
(iii) $(d)_0 c = (d)_0 \emptyset = ((d)_0 \emptyset)_0 = (d\emptyset)_0 = (d)_0$;
$(d)_{n+1} c = (d)_{n+1}(c)_n = ((d)_{n+1}(c)_n)_n \subseteq (d(c)_n)_n$.

PROOF. Easy. $\square$

Lemma 18.1.13 and therefore its corollary depend essentially on the coding of finite sets and ordered pairs. Cf. exercise 19.4.7.

18.1.15. COROLLARY. *In $P\omega$ one has $\mathbf{I} \neq \emptyset$.*

PROOF. If $\mathbf{I} = \emptyset$, then

$$d = \mathbf{I}d = \emptyset d = \emptyset \quad \text{for all } d \in P\omega. \quad \square$$

Since $P\omega$ is not extensional, an $f \in [P\omega^p \to P\omega]$ can be represented by several elements. It will be shown that there is a least representing element. This will be useful for the characterization of equality in $P\omega$.

18.1.16. DEFINITION. (i) Let $a_1, \ldots, a_p, b_1, \ldots, b_p \in P\omega$. Say

$$\vec{a} \subseteq \vec{b} \quad \textit{iff} \quad a_i \subseteq b_i \quad \textit{for } 1 \leqslant i \leqslant n.$$

(ii) Let $X \subseteq P\omega^p$. Then $\vec{a}$ is a *minimal element* of X iff $\vec{a} \in X$ and $\forall \vec{b} \in X[\vec{b} \subseteq \vec{a} \Rightarrow \vec{b} = \vec{a}]$.

18.1.17. LEMMA. *Let $f \in [P\omega^p \to P\omega]$. Then there exists a minimal $a \in P\omega$ such that*

$$\forall \vec{x} \in P\omega^p \quad a\vec{x} = f(\vec{x})$$

PROOF. Write $\langle n_1 \rangle = n_1$ and $\langle n_1, n_2, \ldots, n_{k+1} \rangle = (n_1, \langle n_2, \ldots, n_{k+1} \rangle)$ for $n_1, n_2, \ldots, \in \mathbb{N}$. Define

$$a = \Big\{ \langle k_1, \ldots, k_p, m \rangle | m \in f\big(e_{k_1}, \ldots, e_{k_p}\big) \text{ and}$$
$$\vec{e}_k \text{ is a minimal such } p\text{-tuple} \Big\}.$$

Then an easy computation shows that a minimally represents f. $\square$

18.1.18. NOTATION. (i) $\lambda^- \vec{x}.f(\vec{x})$ denotes the element a constructed in the previous lemma.

(ii) $\mathbf{P}_n^- \equiv \lambda^- x_0 \cdots x_{n+1}.x_{n+1}x_0 \cdots x_n$, i.e. the minimal version of the term $\mathbf{P}_n$ needed for the Böhm out technique.

18.1.19. COROLLARY. $P\omega \models \mathbf{P}_n^- a_0 a_1 \cdots a_{n+1} = a_{n+1} a_0 \cdots a_n$. $\square$

18.1.20. LEMMA. *Let $A_0, \ldots, A_p, A'_0, \ldots, A'_{p'} \in \mathfrak{T}(P\omega)$. Then*

$$P\omega \models \lambda x_0 \cdots x_q \cdot \mathbf{P}_n^- A_0 \cdots A_p \not\subseteq \mathbf{P}_n^- A'_0 \cdots A'_{p'},$$

for $q \geqslant 0$, $p, p' \leqslant n$.

PROOF. An easy calculation shows, in the notation of the proof of lemma 18.1.17, that for $p \leqslant n$

(1) $$\mathbf{P}_n^- x_0 \cdots x_p = \Big\{\langle k_{p+1},\ldots,k_{n+1}, m\rangle \mid \exists s_0 \cdots s_p \Big[\vec{e}_s, \vec{e}_k \text{ is a minimal } n+2\text{-tuple satisfying } e_{s_0} \subseteq x_0,\ldots,e_{s_p} \subseteq x_p \text{ and } m \in e_{k_{n+1}} e_{s_0} \cdots e_{s_p} e_{k_{p+1}} \cdots e_{k_n}\Big]\Big\}.$$

Now we show for $a_0,\ldots,a_p \in P\omega$, $p \leqslant n$,

(2) $$\mathbf{P}_n^- a_0 \cdots a_p \neq \emptyset.$$

Indeed by (1) $\langle 0,0,\ldots,0,1,0\rangle \in \mathbf{P}_n^- a_0 \cdots a_p$, since $e_1 = \{0\}$ and $\forall x\{0\}x = \{0\}$.

Moreover if $A \in \mathfrak{T}(P\omega)$, then

(3) $$P\omega \vDash (\lambda x.A)\emptyset = \emptyset \Rightarrow \exists m_0\, \forall k (k, m_0) \in \lambda x.A.$$

Indeed, let $m_0 \in (\lambda x.A)\emptyset$. Then by monotonicity

$$m_0 \in (\lambda x.A)e_k = A[x := e_k] \text{ for all } k.$$

Since $\lambda x.A = \{(k, m) \mid m \in A[x := e_k])$ we have $\forall k\ (k, m_0) \in \lambda x.A$.

Similarly one shows

(4) $$P\omega \vDash (\lambda \vec{x}.A)\vec{\emptyset} \neq \emptyset \Rightarrow \exists m_0\, \forall k \quad (k, m_0) \in \lambda \vec{x}.A,$$

where $\vec{x} = x_0,\ldots,x_q, \vec{\emptyset} = \emptyset,\ldots,\emptyset$. By (2) it follows that for $p \leqslant n$

$$(\lambda \vec{x}.\mathbf{P}_n^- A_0 \cdots A_p)\vec{\emptyset} = \mathbf{P}_n^- A_0^* \cdots A_p^* \neq \emptyset,$$

hence by (4)

(5) $$\exists m_0\, \forall k \quad (k, m_0) \in \lambda \vec{x}.\mathbf{P}_n^- A_0 \cdots A_p.$$

On the other hand it follows from the minimality condition in (1) that

(6) $$(k, m) \in \mathbf{P}_n^- A_0' \cdots A_p' \text{ and } e_k \not\subseteq e_k \;\Rightarrow\; (k', m) \notin \mathbf{P}_n^- A_1' \cdots A_p'.$$

Now the statement of the lemma follows from (5) and (6). □

18.2. The models D_∞

Scott [1969] and [1972] showed that each complete lattice D can be embedded in a complete lattice D_∞ such that

$$(+) \qquad D_\infty \cong [D_\infty \to D_\infty].$$

Moreover various other recursive domain equations like $(+)$ can be solved in a similar way; see exercises 18.4.19 and 18.4.26. By the result of § 5.4 it then follows that D_∞ is an extensional λ-model.

The construction can be done also for cpo's rather than complete lattices. Following this approach, in this section $D, D', \ldots$ will range over cpo's equipped with the Scott topology.

18.2.1. DEFINITION. A pair of mappings (φ, ψ) is a *projection* of D' on D if
(i) $\varphi : D \to D'$, $\psi : D' \to D$ are continuous,
(ii) $\psi \circ \varphi = \mathrm{id}_D (= \lambda x \in D.x)$,
(iii) $\varphi \circ \psi \sqsubseteq \mathrm{id}_{D'}$, i.e. $\forall x \in D'\ \varphi(\psi(x)) \sqsubseteq x$.

Clearly if (φ, ψ) is a projection of D' on D, then D is isomorphic to a retract of D' with retraction map $\varphi \circ \psi$. Then, up to isomorphism, $D \subseteq D'$.

18.2.2. LEMMA. *Let (φ, ψ) be a projection of D' on D. Then there exists a projection (φ^*, ψ^*) of $[D' \to D']$ on $[D \to D]$ defined as follows: for $f \in [D \to D]$, $g \in [D' \to D']$*

$$\varphi^*(f) = \varphi \circ f \circ \psi, \qquad \psi^*(g) = \psi \circ g \circ \varphi.$$

(see figure 18.1).

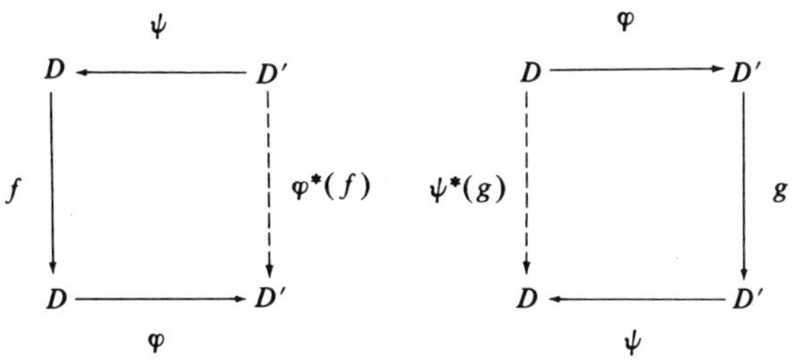

FIG. 18.1.

PROOF. One has

$$\begin{aligned}\varphi^*(f) &= \lambda x' \in D'.\varphi(f(\psi(x)))\\ &= \lambda x' \in D'.\varphi(Ap(f, \psi(x)))\end{aligned}$$

and hence the continuity of φ^* follows by propositions 1.2.13 and 1.2.14; similarly ψ^* is continuous. Moreover

$$\psi^*(\varphi^*(f)) = \psi \circ \varphi \circ f \circ \psi \circ \varphi = f$$

and similarly

$$\varphi^*(\psi^*(f)) \sqsubseteq f. \quad \Box$$

Lemma 18.2.2 shows in fact that in the category **CPO*** with as objects cpo's and as arrows projection pairs the $\boldsymbol{F}$ defined by

$$\boldsymbol{F}D = [D \to D]$$

can be considered as a functor, see exercise 18.4.26.

In order to construct D_∞ isomorphic to its own function space one has to find a fixed point of $\boldsymbol{F}$. Try $D_\infty = \lim_n \boldsymbol{F}^n D$. But in what sense does one take the limit? Well, let $p = (\varphi_0, \psi_0)$ be a given projection of $\boldsymbol{F}D$ on D. Then $(\boldsymbol{F}^n D, \boldsymbol{F}^n p)$ is an inverse system in **CPO** and one can define the inverse limit

$$D_\infty = \underset{\leftarrow}{\lim}\,(\boldsymbol{F}^n D, \boldsymbol{F}^n p).$$

Then

$$\begin{aligned}[D_\infty \to D_\infty] &= \boldsymbol{F}D_\infty \\ &= \underset{\leftarrow}{\lim}\,(\boldsymbol{F}^{n+1} D, \boldsymbol{F}^{n+1} p) \cong D_\infty .\end{aligned}$$

This is the motivation behind the construction that follows.

18.2.3. LEMMA. *Let D be given. Define maps $\varphi_0 : D \to [D \to D]$, $\psi_0 : [D \to D] \to D$ by*

$$\varphi_0(x) = \boldsymbol{\lambda} y \in D.x,$$

$$\psi_0(f) = f(\bot).$$

Then (φ_0, ψ_0) is a projection of $[D \to D]$ on D, the so-called standard projection.

PROOF. φ_0 is continuous: for directed X one has

$$\begin{aligned}\varphi_0(\sqcup X) &= \boldsymbol{\lambda} y.\sqcup X \\ &= \bigsqcup_{x \in X} \boldsymbol{\lambda} y.x \quad \text{by definition of } \sqcup \text{ in a function space,} \\ &= \sqcup \varphi_0(X),\end{aligned}$$

and similarly ψ_0 is continuous. Moreover

$$\varphi_0(\psi_0(f)) = \varphi_0(f(\perp)) = \lambda x.f(\perp)$$

$$\sqsubseteq \lambda x.f(x) \quad \text{since f is monotonic,}$$

$$= f;$$

trivially $\psi_0 \circ \varphi_0 = \text{id}_D$. $\square$

18.2.4. DEFINITION (Construction of D_∞). Let D be given and let $\langle \varphi_0, \psi_0 \rangle$ be the standard projection of $[D \to D]$ on D. Define

$$D_0 = D,$$

$$D_{n+1} = [D_n \to D_n],$$

$$(\varphi_{n+1}, \psi_{n+1}) = (\varphi_n^*, \psi_n^*),$$

the projection of D_{n+1} on D_n defined from (φ_n, ψ_n) in lemma 18.2.2. Then

$$D_0 \underset{\psi_0}{\overset{\varphi_0}{\rightleftarrows}} D_1 \underset{\psi_1}{\overset{\varphi_1}{\rightleftarrows}} D_2 \quad \cdots$$

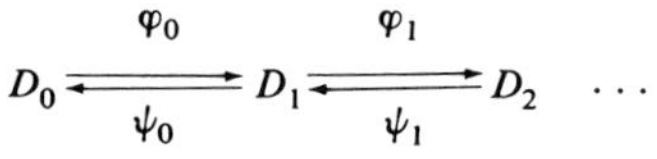

FIG. 18.2.

Hence $(D_n, \psi_n)_{n \in \mathbb{N}}$ is an inverse system of cpo's. Finally define

$$D_\infty = \varprojlim (D_n, \psi_n).$$

In the rest of this section D is a fixed cpo and D_n, D_∞ are the resulting cpo's constructed as above.

NOTATION. For $D_\infty \subseteq \Pi_{n \in \mathbb{N}} D_n$ the following conventions will be used. Let $x \in D_\infty$. Then

$$x_n = x(n),$$

$$x = \langle x_0, x_1, \ldots \rangle = \langle x_n \rangle_{n \in \mathbb{N}} = \langle x_n \rangle.$$

18.2.5. DEFINITION. (i) For $n, m \in \mathbb{N}$ define $\Phi_{nm}: D_n \to D_m$ (by following the arrows in figure 18.2) as follows.

If $n \leqslant m$, say $m = n + k$, then Φ_{nm} is defined by induction on k:

$$\Phi_{nn} = \lambda x \in D_n.x,$$

$$\Phi_{n(m+1)} = \varphi_m \circ \Phi_{nm}.$$

If $m \leqslant n$, say $n = m + k$, then Φ_{nm} is again defined by induction on k:

$$\Phi_{(n+1)m} = \Phi_{nm} \circ \psi_n.$$

(ii) $\Phi_{\infty n} : D_\infty \to D_n$ is defined by $\Phi_{\infty n}(x) = x_n$.
(iii) $\Phi_{n\infty} : D_n \to D_\infty$ is defined by $\Phi_{n\infty}(x) = \langle \Phi_{ni}(x) \rangle_{i \in \mathbb{N}}$.

18.2.6. LEMMA. (i) *For* $0 \leqslant n \leqslant m \leqslant \infty$, $\langle \Phi_{nm}, \Phi_{mn} \rangle$ *is a projection of* D_m *on* D_n.
(ii) *For* $0 \leqslant n \leqslant m \leqslant l \leqslant \infty$

$$\Phi_{ml} \circ \Phi_{nm} = \Phi_{nl}.$$

PROOF. Standard. $\square$

By the remark following definition 18.2.1 it follows that up to isomorphism

$$D_0 \subseteq D_1 \subseteq \cdots \subseteq D_\infty.$$

In fact in the category **CPO**, D_∞ is not only an inverse limit $\lim\limits_{\leftarrow}(D_n, \psi_n)$ but also a direct limit

$$D_\infty \cong \lim_{\rightarrow}(D_n, \varphi_n);$$

see exercise 18.4.17.

Henceforth each element $x \in D_n$ will be identified with $\Phi_{n\infty}(x) \in D_\infty$, as is customary for direct limits. This makes properties of D_∞ more elegant to formulate.

18.2.7. LEMMA. (i) *If* $x \in D_n$, *then* $x_n = x$.
(ii) *If* $x \in D_n$, *then* $\varphi_n(x) = x$
(iii) *If* $x \in D_{n+1}$, *then* $\psi_n(x) \sqsubseteq x$.

PROOF. (i) x in D_∞ is $\langle \ldots, \psi_{n-1}(x), x, \varphi_n(x), \ldots \rangle$. Hence $x_n = x$.
(ii) $\varphi_n(x)$ in D_∞ is $\langle \ldots, \psi_n(\varphi_n(x)), \varphi_n(x), \varphi_{n+1}(\varphi_n(x)), \ldots \rangle$. Since $\psi_n(\varphi_n(x)) = x$, this is the same as x in D_∞.
(iii) Analogous, using $\varphi_n(\psi_n(x)) \sqsubseteq x$. $\square$

18.2.8. LEMMA. *In* D_∞
(i) $(x_n)_m = x_{\min(n,m)}$,
(ii) $n \leqslant m \Rightarrow x_n \sqsubseteq x_m \sqsubseteq x$,
(iii) $x = \bigsqcup_{n \in \mathbb{N}} x_n$,
(iv) $\bot_n$ *is the bottom element of* D_n,
(v) $\bot_n = \bot$.

PROOF. (i) If $m < n$, then

$$(x_n)_m = \Phi_{nm} x_n = \psi_{m+1} \circ \cdots \circ \psi_{n-1}(x_n) = x_m,$$

since $x \in D_\infty$. If $m \geqslant n$, then by lemma 18.2.7(ii)

$$(x_n)_m = \varphi_{m-1} \circ \cdots \circ \varphi_n(x_n) = x_n.$$

(ii) By lemma 18.2.7(iii)

$$x_m = \psi_m(x_{m+1}) \sqsubseteq x_{m+1}$$

Hence $x_0 \sqsubseteq x_1 \sqsubseteq \cdots$. Furthermore $x_n \sqsubseteq x$ since

$$\forall i (x_n)_i = x_{\min(i,n)} \sqsubseteq x_i.$$

(iii) By (ii) the set $X = \{x_n | n \in \mathbb{N}\}$ is directed. Hence by proposition 1.2.19

$$\begin{aligned} \sqcup X &= \langle \sqcup_n (x_n)_i \rangle_{i \in \mathbb{N}} \\ &= \langle \bigsqcup_n x_{\min(n,i)} \rangle i \in \mathbb{N} \quad \text{by (i)}, \\ &= \langle x_i \rangle_{i \in \mathbb{N}} \quad \text{by (ii)}, \\ &= x. \end{aligned}$$

(iv) Let $\perp_n'$ be the bottom element of D_n. Then again by proposition 1.2.19

$$\perp = \sqcup \emptyset = \langle \sqcup \emptyset \rangle_{n \in \mathbb{N}} = \langle \perp_n' \rangle_{n \in \mathbb{N}}.$$

Hence $\perp_n = \perp_n'$.
(v) By (ii) $\perp_n \sqsubseteq \perp \sqsubseteq \perp_n$, hence $\perp = \perp_n$. □

The following lemma is useful for determining the applicative behavior of x_n for $x \in D_\infty$.

18.2.9. LEMMA. *Let $x, y \in D_\infty$. Then for all $n, k \in \mathbb{N}$ with $n \leqslant k$*
(i) $x_{n+1}(y_n) \sqsubseteq x_{k+1}(y_k)$,
(ii) $(x_{n+1})_{k+1}(y_k) = x_{n+1}(y_n)$,
(iii) $(x_{k+1}(y_n)_k)_n = x_{n+1}(y_n)$.

PROOF. (i) It is sufficient to prove this for $k = n+1$.

$$\begin{aligned} x_{n+1}(y_n) &= (\psi_{n+1}(x_{n+2}))(\psi_n(y_{n+1})) \quad \text{since } x, y \in D_\infty, \\ &= \psi_n \circ x_{n+2} \circ \varphi_n(\psi_n(y_{n+1})) \\ &= \psi_n(x_{n+2}(\varphi_n \circ \psi_n(y_{n+1}))) \\ &\sqsubseteq \psi_n(x_{n+2}(y_{n+1})) \quad \text{since } (\varphi_n, \psi_n) \text{ is a projection,} \\ &\sqsubseteq x_{n+2}(y_{n+1}) \quad \text{by lemma 18.2.7(iii).} \end{aligned}$$

(ii) By induction on $k \geqslant n$. If $k = n$, this is trivial, so consider $k+1$.

$$\begin{aligned} (x_{n+1})_{k+2}(y_{k+1}) &= \varphi_{k+1}((x_{n+1})_{k+1})(y_{k+1}) \\ &= \varphi_k \circ (x_{n+1})_{k+1} \circ \psi_k(y_{k+1}) \\ &= \varphi_k((x_{n+1})_{k+1}(y_k)) \\ &= (x_{n+1})_{k+1}(y_k) \quad \text{by lemma 18.2.7(ii),} \\ &= x_{n+1}(y_n) \quad \text{by the induction hypothesis.} \end{aligned}$$

(iii) By induction on $k \geqslant n$. The case $k = n$ is trivial, so consider $k+1$.

$$\begin{aligned} (x_{k+2}(y_n)_{k+1})_n &= \Phi_{k+1n}(x_{k+2}(\varphi_k((y_n)_k))) \\ &= \Phi_{kn} \circ \psi_k \circ x_{k+2} \circ \varphi_k((y_n)_k) \\ &= \Phi_{kn}((\psi_{k+1}(x_{k+2}))((y_n)_k)) \\ &= \Phi_{kn}(x_{k+1}(y_n)_k) \\ &= (x_{k+1}(y_n)_k)_n \\ &= x_{n+1}(y_n) \quad \text{by the induction hypothesis.} \quad \square \end{aligned}$$

Now we can define a binary operation which will make D_∞ into an extensional λ-model.

18.2.10. DEFINITION. A binary operation application is defined on D_∞ as follows:

$$(1) \qquad x \cdot y = \bigsqcup_n x_{n+1}(y_n).$$

That is, if $x, y \in D$, then

(2) $$x \cdot y = \bigsqcup_n \Phi_{n\infty}(\mathrm{Ap}_n(\Phi_{\infty n+1}(x), \Phi_{\infty n}(y)))$$

where $\mathrm{Ap}_n : [D_{n+1} \times D_n] \to D_n$ is the canonical application, see proposition 1.2.13.

By convention this definition will be written down simply as (1). The full meaning of (1) is formulated in (2).

18.2.11. PROPOSITION. *Application on D_∞ is continuous.*

PROOF. By definition 18.2.10 in its form (2) and the continuity of the Φ_{ij} and Ap_k using lemmas 1.2.10 and 18.2.9(i). □

18.2.12. PROPOSITION. *Application in D_∞ is well-defined, in the sense that if $x \in D_{n+1}$, $y \in_n$, then*

$$x \cdot y = x(y).$$

PROOF.

$$\begin{aligned} x \cdot y &= x_{n+1} \cdot y_n \quad \text{by lemma 18.2.7(i)},\\ &= \bigsqcup_{i=0}^{\infty} (x_{n+1})_{i+1}((y_n)_i)\\ &= \bigsqcup_{i=0}^{n} x_{i+1}(y_i) \quad \text{by lemma 18.2.8(i)},\\ &= x_{n+1}(y_n) \quad \text{by lemma 18.2.9(i)}. \quad \square \end{aligned}$$

The following equations are important for determining the structure of D_∞.

18.2.13. PROPOSITION. *For $x, y \in D_\infty$ and $n \in \mathbb{N}$*

(i) $x_{n+1} \cdot y = x_{n+1} \cdot y_n = (x \cdot y_n)_n$,

(ii) $x_0 \cdot y = x_0 = (x \cdot \bot)_0$.

PROOF. (i)

$$\begin{aligned} x_{n+1} \cdot y &= \bigsqcup_{i=0}^{\infty} (x_{n+1})_{i+1}(y_i)\\ &= \bigsqcup_{i=n}^{\infty} (x_{n+1})_{i+1}(y_i) \quad \text{by lemma 18.2.9(i)},\\ &= \bigsqcup_{i=n}^{\infty} x_{n+1}(y_n) \quad \text{by lemma 18.2.9(ii)},\\ &= x_{n+1} \cdot y_n \quad \text{by proposition 18.2.12}. \end{aligned}$$

On the other hand

$$\begin{aligned}(x\cdot y_n)_n &= \Big(\bigsqcup_{i=0}^{\infty}(x_{i+1}\cdot(y_n)_i)\Big)_n\\ &= \bigsqcup_{i=0}^{\infty}(x_{i+1}\cdot(y_n)_i)_n \quad \text{by continuity,}\\ &= \bigsqcup_{i=n}^{\infty}(x_{i+1}((y_n)_i))_n \quad \text{by lemma 18.2.9(i),}\\ &= \bigsqcup_{i} x_{n+1}(y_n) \quad \text{by lemma 18.2.9(iii),}\\ &= x_{n+1}\cdot y_n.\end{aligned}$$

(ii)

$$\begin{aligned}x_0\cdot y &= (x_0)_1\cdot y\\ &= (x_0)_1(y_0) \quad \text{by (i) and proposition 18.2.12,}\\ &= \varphi_0(x_0)(y_0) = x_0.\end{aligned}$$

Moreover:

$$\begin{aligned}x_0 &= \psi_0(x_1) = x_1(\perp)\\ &= x_1(\perp_0) = (x\cdot\perp)_0, \text{ by (i).} \quad \square\end{aligned}$$

18.2.14. THEOREM (Extensionality). *For* $x, y \in D_\infty$
(i) $x \sqsubseteq y \Leftrightarrow \forall z \in D_\infty\, x\cdot z \sqsubseteq y\cdot z$,
(ii) $x = y \Leftrightarrow \forall z \in D_\infty\, x\cdot z = y\cdot z$.

PROOF. (i) ($\Rightarrow$) By the monotonicity of $\lambda\!\!\!\lambda x(x\cdot z)$.
($\Leftarrow$) Suppose $\forall z\ x\cdot z \sqsubseteq y\cdot z$. Then $x\cdot\perp \sqsubseteq y\cdot\perp$, hence by proposition 18.2.13(ii)

$$x_0 = (x\cdot\perp)_0 \sqsubseteq (y\cdot\perp)_0 = y_0.$$

Moreover $x\cdot z_n \sqsubseteq y\cdot z_n$. Hence by propositions 18.2.12 and 18.2.13(i)

$$x_{n+1}(z_n) = (x\cdot z_n)_n \sqsubseteq (y\cdot z_n)_n = y_{n+1}(z_n).$$

It follows that

$$\forall n\,\forall z\in D_n \quad x_{n+1}(z)\sqsubseteq y_{n+1}(z),$$

hence $\forall n\ x_{n+1} \sqsubseteq y_{n+1}$, i.e. $x \sqsubseteq y$.
(ii) Immediate by (i). $\square$

18.2.15. THEOREM (Completeness). *Define for* $f \in [D_\infty \to D_\infty]$

$$\Box f = \bigsqcup_n (\lambda y \in D_n.(f(y))_n).$$

Then

$$\forall y \in D_\infty \quad f(y) = \Box f \cdot y.$$

PROOF. Note that the supremum defining $\Box f$ is directed. Also note that if for a_{ij} in a cpo

$$\forall i, j \exists k \quad a_{ij} \sqsubseteq a_{kk},$$

then

$$\bigsqcup_{i,j} a_{ij} = \bigsqcup_k a_{kk}.$$

Now

$$\begin{aligned}
\Box f \cdot y &= \bigsqcup_m (\Box f)_{m+1}(y_m) = \bigsqcup_m (\Box f \cdot y_m)_m \\
&= \bigsqcup_m \left(\left(\bigsqcup_n \lambda y \in D_n.(f(y))_n \right) \cdot y_m \right)_m \\
&= \bigsqcup_{m,n} ((\lambda y \in D_n.(f(y))_n) \cdot y_m)_m \\
&= \bigsqcup_m ((\lambda y \in D_m.(f(y))_m)(y_m))_m \\
&= \bigsqcup_m (f(y_m))_m = \bigsqcup_{k,l} (f(y_k))_l \\
&= \bigsqcup_k f(y_k) = f(y).
\end{aligned}$$

These equations follow easily from the continuity (monotonicity) of the functions involved and the remarks above. □

18.2.16. THEOREM. $D_\infty = [D_\infty \to D_\infty]$ *up to isomorphism* (*in fact homeomorphism, hence partial order isomorphism*).

PROOF. For $x \in D_\infty$, let $F(x) = \lambda y \in D_\infty.x.y$. F is surjective by theorem 18.2.15, injective by theorem 18.2.14(ii) and continuous by proposition 18.2.11. The inverse of F is by theorem 18.2.15

$$G = \lambda f. \bigsqcup_n \Phi_{n\infty}(\lambda y \in D_n.\Phi_{\infty n}(f(\Phi_{n\infty}(y))))$$

which is continuous by lemma 1.2.10. Since continuous maps are also monotonic, the spaces are isomorphic cpo's. □

18.2.17. Corollary. (i) *$(D_\infty, \cdot)$ is an extensional λ-model in which the representable functions are exactly the continuous ones.*

(ii) *The interpretation of λ-terms in $(D_\infty, \cdot)$ is given as follows. Let ρ be a valuation in D_∞, then*

$$[\![x]\!]_\rho = \rho(x),$$
$$[\![MN]\!]_\rho = [\![M]\!]_\rho [\![N]\!]_\rho,$$
$$[\![\lambda x.M]\!]_\rho = \lambda^G d \in D_\infty . [\![M]\!]_{\rho(x:=d)},$$

where

$$\lambda^G d \in D_\infty . [\![M]\!]_{\rho(x:=d)} = G(\lambda\!\!\!\lambda\, d \in D_\infty . [\![M]\!]_{\rho(x:=d)}).$$

Proof. By § 5.4. □

Again one uses convention 5.3.8. E.g. in D_∞

$$\lambda x.x = \bigsqcup_n (\lambda\!\!\!\lambda\, x \in D_n . x).$$

18.3. The model $\mathfrak{B}$

The set of Böhm-like trees $\mathfrak{B}$ will be made into a λ-model. The continuity theorem plays an important role in the construction. For the resulting model $\mathfrak{B}$ one will have

$$\mathfrak{B} \models M = N \;\Leftrightarrow\; \mathrm{BT}(M) = \mathrm{BT}(N).$$

18.3.1. Definition. (i) Let $A_n, A \in \mathfrak{B}$. Then $\lim_{n\to\infty} \uparrow A_n = A$ if $A_0 \subseteq A_1 \subseteq A_2 \subseteq \cdots$ and $\cup_n A_n = A$.

(ii) Let $M_n \in \Lambda$, $A \in \mathfrak{B}$. Then $\lim_{n\to\infty} \uparrow M_n = A$ if $\lim_{n\to\infty} \uparrow \mathrm{BT}(M_n) = A$.

(iii) Let $M_n, M \in \Lambda$. Then $\lim_{n\to\infty} \uparrow M_n = M$ if $\lim_{n\to\infty} \uparrow \mathrm{BT}(M_n) = \mathrm{BT}(M)$.

18.3.2. Definition. Let $A, B \in \mathfrak{B}$. Define

(i) $A \cdot B = AB = \lim_{n\to\infty} \uparrow (M_{A^n} M_{B^n})$, see definition 10.1.16.

(ii) $\lambda x.A = \lim_{n\to\infty} \uparrow (\lambda x.M_{A^n})$.

(iii) $A(x := B) = \lim_{n\to\infty} \uparrow (M_{A^n}[x := M_{B^n}])$.

18.3.3. Lemma. *The increasing limits in definition* 18.3.2 *exist.*

Proof. (i) Since $A^n \subseteq A^{n+1}$ one has $M_{A^n} \underset{\sim}{\sqsubseteq} M_{A^{n+1}}$ and similarly for the B_n. Hence by corollary 14.3.20(iii)

$$M_{A^n} M_{B^n} \underset{\sim}{\sqsubseteq} M_{A^{n+1}} M_{B^{n+1}}.$$

Therefore $\lim_{n\to\infty} \uparrow (M_{A^n} M_{B^n})$ exists.

(ii), (iii) Similarly. □

Note that $A(x:=B)$ is the result of "substituting B for x in A and then working out the resulting tree labelled tree". For example

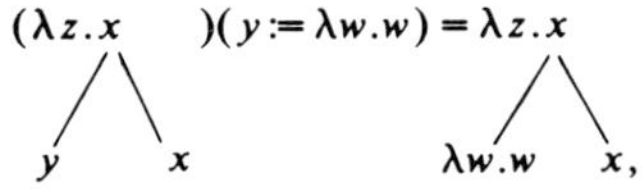

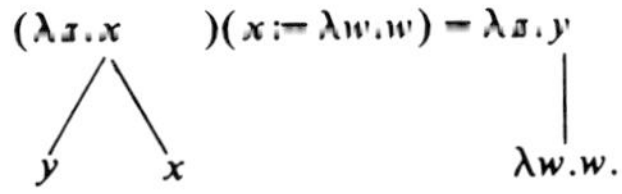

18.3.4. Proposition. (i) *Let* $M, N \in \Lambda$. *Then*

$$\mathrm{BT}(MN) = \mathrm{BT}(M)\mathrm{BT}(N),$$
$$\mathrm{BT}(\lambda x.M) = \lambda x.\mathrm{BT}(M),$$
$$\mathrm{BT}(M[x:=N]) = \mathrm{BT}(M)(x:=\mathrm{BT}(N)).$$

(ii) *The operations* $\lambda\!\!\lambda AB.AB, \lambda\!\!\lambda A.(\lambda x.A)$ *and* $\lambda\!\!\lambda AB.A(x:=B)$ *are continuous on* $\mathfrak{B}$.

Proof. (i) Since $M^{(n)} \sqsubseteq M$, $M^{(n)}N^{(n)} \sqsubseteq MN$, that is $\mathrm{BT}(M^{(n)}N^{(n)}) \subseteq \mathrm{BT}(MN)$; it follows that

$$\begin{aligned}\mathrm{BT}(M)\mathrm{BT}(N) &= \bigcup_n \mathrm{BT}(M_{\mathrm{BT}^n(M)} M_{\mathrm{BT}^n(N)}) \\ &= \bigcup_n \mathrm{BT}(M^{(n)}N^{(n)}) \quad \text{by definition 10.1.18,} \\ &\subseteq \mathrm{BT}(MN).\end{aligned}$$

The converse inclusion follows from

(1) $\qquad \forall k\, \exists n \quad \mathrm{BT}^k(MN) \subseteq \mathrm{BT}(M^{(n)}N^{(n)}),$

since then

$$\begin{aligned}\mathrm{BT}(MN) &= \bigcup_k \mathrm{BT}^k(MN) \\ &\subseteq \bigcup_n \mathrm{BT}(M^{(n)}N^{(n)}) \\ &= \mathrm{BT}(M)\mathrm{BT}(N).\end{aligned}$$

To show (1), recall that

$$O_{M,k} = \{N \in \Lambda | M^{(k)} \underset{\sim}{\sqsubset} N\}$$

is a basis neighborhood of M. Given k one has $MN \in O_{MN,k}$. Hence by the continuity theorem for some k_1, k_2

$$O_{M,k_1} O_{N,k_2} \subseteq O_{MN,k}.$$

Let $n \geqslant k_1, k_2$. Then

$$M^{(n)} \in O_{M,k_1}, N^{(n)} \in O_{N,k_2}$$

$$\Rightarrow M^{(n)}N^{(n)} \in O_{MN,k} \;\Rightarrow\; (MN)^{(k)} \underset{\sim}{\sqsubset} M^{(n)}N^{(n)}$$

This proves (1).

The proofs of the other statements are similar.

(ii) We show that $A \cdot B$ is continuous in A. Let $A = \cup_k A_k$ be a directed union. Then

$$AB = \bigcup_n \mathrm{BT}(M_{A^n} M_{B^n}),$$

$$\bigcup_k (A_k B) = \bigcup_{k,n} \mathrm{BT}(M_{A_k^n} M_{B^n}).$$

Clearly $\cup_k (A_k B) \subseteq AB$. To show the converse inclusion, note that

$$A^n \subseteq \bigcup_k A_k^n.$$

Since A^n is a compact element of $\mathfrak{B}$ it follows that $A^n \subseteq A_k^n$ for some k. Therefore

$$M_{A^n} \underset{\sim}{\sqsubset} M_{A_k^n} \;\Rightarrow\; M_{A^n} M_{B^n} \underset{\sim}{\sqsubset} M_{A_k^n} M_{B^n} \;\Rightarrow\; \mathrm{BT}(M_{A^n} M_{B^n}) \subseteq \mathrm{BT}(M_{A_k^n} M_{B^n})$$

and it follows that $AB \subseteq \cup_k (A_k B)$. This shows $AB = \cup_k (A_k B)$ and the continuity in A follows from proposition 1.2.6. The continuity in B is proved similarly. By lemma 1.2.12 we are done.

In the same way the other operators are proved to be continuous. ☐

18.3.5. LEMMA. *Let* $\lim_{n\to\infty} \uparrow M_n = A$ *and* $\lim_{n\to\infty} \uparrow N_n = B$. *Then*

(i) $AB = \lim_{n\to\infty} \uparrow M_n N_n$,

(ii) $\lambda x.A = \lim_{n\to\infty} \uparrow \lambda x.M_n$,

(iii) $A(x := B) = \lim_{n\to\infty} \uparrow M_n[x := N_n]$.

PROOF. (i)

$$AB = \bigcup_n \mathrm{BT}(M_n) \cdot \bigcup_{n'} \mathrm{BT}(N_{n'})$$

$$= \bigcup_{n,n'} \mathrm{BT}(M_n)\mathrm{BT}(N_{n'}) \quad \text{by continuity of } \cdot,$$

$$= \bigcup_n \mathrm{BT}(M_n)\mathrm{BT}(N_n) \quad \text{since the } M_n, N_n \text{ are linearly ordered by } \sqsubseteq,$$

$$= \bigcup_n \mathrm{BT}(M_n N_n) \quad \text{by proposition 18.3.4(i).}$$

Therefore $AB = \lim_{n\to\infty} \uparrow M_n N_n$.
(ii), (iii) Similarly. □

Substitution of trees and operations on them interact as expected.

18.3.6. LEMMA. (i) $x(x{:=}C) = C$.
(ii) $y(x{:=}C) = y$.
(iii) $(AB)(x{:=}C) = (A(x{:=}C))(B(x{:=}C))$.
(iv) $(\lambda y.A)(x{:=}C) = \lambda y.A$ if $x \equiv y$,
$= \lambda y.A(x{:=}C)$ if $x \not\equiv y$.

PROOF. In (i) x stands of course for $\mathrm{BT}(x)$. Since all cases are similar we show only (iii).

$$(AB)(x{:=}C) = \lim_{n\to\infty} \uparrow M_{A^n} M_{B^n}[x{:=}M_{C^n}]$$

$$= \lim_{n\to\infty} \uparrow M_{A^n}[x{:=}M_{C^n}] M_{B^n}[x{:=}M_{C^n}]$$

$$= \Big(\lim_{n\to\infty} \uparrow M_{A^n}[x{:=}M_{C^n}]\Big)\Big(\lim_{n\to\infty} \uparrow M_{B^n}[x{:=}M_{C^n}]\Big)$$

$$= A(x{:=}C)B(x{:=}C),$$

using several times lemma 18.3.5. □

18.3.7. LEMMA. (i) $(\lambda x.A)x = A$.
(ii) $(\lambda x.A)B = A(x{:=}B)$.

PROOF. (i)

$$(\lambda x.A)x = \lim_{n\to\infty} \uparrow (\lambda x.M_{A^n})x = \lim_{n\to\infty} \uparrow M_{A^n} = A.$$

(ii) By (i), substituting B for x and lemma 18.3.6. □

Now it will be shown that $\mathfrak{B}$ can be turned into a λ-model.

18.3.8. DEFINITION. For a valuation ρ in $\mathfrak{B}$ define $[\![M]\!]_\rho$ inductively as follows:

$$[\![x]\!]_\rho = \rho(x),$$

$$[\![c_A]\!]_\rho = A,$$

$$[\![PQ]\!]_\rho = [\![P]\!]_\rho [\![Q]\!]_\rho,$$

$$[\![\lambda x.P]\!]_\rho = \lambda x.[\![P]\!]_{\rho(x:=BT(x))}.$$

18.3.9. LEMMA. *Let $M \in \Lambda(\mathfrak{B})$. Write $M \equiv M(\vec{x}, \vec{c}_A) \equiv M(\vec{x}, \vec{y})[\vec{y}:=\vec{c}_A]$ with all constants and free variables displayed. Then in $\mathfrak{B}$*

$$[\![M]\!]_\rho = BT(M(\vec{x}, \vec{y}))(\vec{x}, \vec{y}:=\overrightarrow{\rho(x)}, \vec{A}),$$

where $(\vec{x}, \vec{y}:=\overrightarrow{\rho(x)}, \vec{A})$ denotes simultaneous substitution.

PROOF. Induction on the structure of M, using $\mathrm{BT}(P)(z:=\mathrm{BT}(z)) = \mathrm{BT}(P)$ by proposition 18.3.4. $\square$

18.3.10. THEOREM. *Let $\mathfrak{B} = (\mathfrak{B}, \cdot, [\![\ ]\!])$.*
(i) *$\mathfrak{B}$ is a λ-model*
(ii) $\mathfrak{B} \vDash M = N \Leftrightarrow \mathrm{BT}(M) = \mathrm{BT}(N)$.

PROOF. (i) The only non-trivial things to show are conditions 4 and ξ of definitions 5.3.1 and 5.3.2 respectively.

As to 4, let $P \in \Lambda(\mathfrak{B})$. For notational simplicity assume that P does not contain constants. Let (—) denote the substitution $(\vec{y}:=\overrightarrow{\rho(y)})$ for $\vec{y} = \mathrm{FV}(P)$. Then

$$\begin{aligned}
[\![\lambda x.P]\!]_\rho . A &= \mathrm{BT}(\lambda x.P)(—).A, && \text{by lemma 18.3.9,}\\
&= (\lambda x.\mathrm{BT}(P)(—)).A, && \text{by proposition 18.3.4,}\\
&= \mathrm{BT}(P)(x:=A)(—), && \text{by lemma 18.3.7(ii),}\\
&= [\![P]\!]_{\rho(x:=A)}, && \text{by lemma 18.3.9.}
\end{aligned}$$

As to ξ, use a similar notation as above.

$$\begin{aligned}
&\forall A \in \mathfrak{B} [\![M]\!]_{\rho(x:=A)} = [\![N]\!]_{\rho(x:=B)}\\
&\quad\Rightarrow \forall A \in \mathfrak{B}\, \mathrm{BT}(M)(x:=A)(—) = \mathrm{BT}(N)(x:=A)(—)\\
&\quad\Rightarrow \mathrm{BT}(M)(—) = \mathrm{BT}(N)(—), \quad \text{by taking } A = \mathrm{BT}(x),\\
&\quad\Rightarrow \lambda x.\mathrm{BT}(M)(—) = \lambda x.\mathrm{BT}(N)(—)\\
&\quad\Rightarrow \mathrm{BT}(\lambda x.M)(—) = \mathrm{BT}(\lambda x.N)(—)\\
&\quad\Rightarrow [\![\lambda x.M]\!]_\rho = [\![\lambda x.N]\!]_\rho.
\end{aligned}$$

(ii) $\mathfrak{B} \models M = N \Rightarrow \forall\rho [\![M]\!]_\rho = [\![N]\!]_\rho$
$\Rightarrow \mathrm{BT}(M) = \mathrm{BT}(N)$

taking $\rho(y) = \mathrm{BT}(y)$. Conversely

$$\begin{aligned}\mathrm{BT}(M) = \mathrm{BT}(N) &\Rightarrow \mathrm{BT}(M)(-) = \mathrm{BT}(N)(-)\\ &\Rightarrow [\![M]\!]_\rho = [\![N]\!]_\rho\\ &\Rightarrow \mathfrak{B} \models M = N. \quad \square\end{aligned}$$

18.3.11. COROLLARY. $\mathrm{Th}(\mathfrak{B}) = \mathcal{B}$. $\square$

REMARK. Although $(\mathfrak{B}, \cdot)$ is a λ-model with continuous $\cdot$ (with respect to the topology on $\mathfrak{B}$), not all continuous functions are representable. See exercise 18.4.25.

18.4. Exercises

18.4.1. Show that $P\omega$ is not an extensional λ-algebra. In particular $P\omega \models \mathbf{1} = \mathbf{I}$, where $\mathbf{1} = \lambda xy.xy$.

18.4.2. Let $\top = \mathbb{N}$ and $\bot = \emptyset$ be top and bottom of $P\omega$. Show that in $P\omega$

(i) $\top x = \top = \lambda x.\top$,

(ii) $\bot x = \bot = \lambda x.\bot$.

Exercises 18.4.3–18.4.9 are due to Scott [1975, 1976]:

18.4.3. Define

$$\boldsymbol{F} = \{ a \in P\omega \mid a = \mathbf{1}a \} \text{ (functions)},$$

$$\boldsymbol{R} = \{ a \in P\omega \mid a = a \circ a \} \text{ (retraction maps)},$$

$$\boldsymbol{C} = \{ a \in P\omega \mid \mathbf{I} \subseteq a = a \circ a \} \text{ (closure operations)}.$$

Then $F \supseteq R \supseteq C$. For $a \in P\omega$ define

$$\breve{a} = \{ x \in P\omega \mid ax = x \}.$$

(i) Show that

(1) $a \in F \Rightarrow \breve{a}$ is a complete lattice.

(2) $a \in R \Rightarrow \breve{a}$ is a continuous lattice.

(3) $a \in C \Rightarrow \hat{a}$ is an algebraic lattice.

(ii) As a converse to (i), show that

(1) If D is a complete lattice and D has a countable base for its Scott topology, then $\exists a \in F$ $\breve{a} \cong D$.

(2) If D is a continuous lattice and D has a countable base for its Scott topology, then $\exists a \in R$ $\breve{a} \cong D$.

(3) If D is an algebraic lattice and D has at most countably many compact points, then $\exists a \in C$ $\breve{a} \cong D$.

18.4.4. For $a, b \in P\omega$ define $a \circ\!\!\rightarrow b = \lambda x.b \circ x \circ a$.

(i) Show that if $f \in (a \circ\!\!\rightarrow b)\breve{}$ and $x \in \breve{a}$, then $f \cdot x \in \breve{b}$.

(ii) For $X = F, R, C$ show that $\forall a, b \in X a \circ\!\!\rightarrow b \in X$.

(iii) Prove $\forall a, b \in R (a \circ\!\!\rightarrow b)\breve{} \cong [\breve{a} \rightarrow \breve{b}]$.

[*Hint*. Define for $f \in [\breve{a} \rightarrow \breve{b}]$, $\psi(f) = \text{graph } \lambda\!\!\lambda x.f(a.x)$ and, for $x \in (a \circ\!\!\rightarrow b)\breve{}$, $\varphi(x) = \mathrm{fun}(x) \upharpoonright \breve{a}$.]

18.4.5. Show that $\exists a \in P\omega$ $C = \breve{a}$. Hence $(C, \subseteq)$ is a complete lattice. [*Hint*. $x \in C \Leftrightarrow x = x \circ x \cup \mathbf{I}$].

18.4.6. Define for $a, b \in R$

$$a \circ\!\leqslant b \Leftrightarrow a = a \circ b = b \circ a.$$

Clearly if $a \circ\!\leqslant b$, then $\check{a}$ is a retract of $\check{b}$. Show that $\circ\!\leqslant$ is a partial ordering on R (or even on $P\omega$).

18.4.7. Show

(i) $\exists a \in C\ F = \check{a}$,

(ii) $\exists a \in F\ R = \check{a}$ (see also exercise 18.4.10).

18.4.8. Show $\exists a \in C\ C = \check{a}$, hence is an algebraic lattice. [*Hint*. Define $V = \lambda ax. Y_T(\lambda y. x \cup a \cdot y)$, where Y_T is the least fixed point operator on $P\omega$. Then

(i) $\forall x \in P\omega\ Vx \in C$.

(ii) $x \in C \Leftrightarrow Vx = x$. Hence $\check{V} = C$.

(iii) $V \in C$.]

18.4.9. (i) Show $\exists c \in C\ [c = c \circ\!\!\rightarrow c \wedge \operatorname{card}(\check{c}) > 1]$. [*Hint*. Consider $f = \lambda\!\!\!\lambda c \in C. c \circ\!\!\rightarrow c$ and $\mathbf{I}_n = f^n(\mathbf{I})$. Show $\mathbf{I}_1 \subseteq \mathbf{I}_2 \subseteq \cdots$; $\mathbf{I}_1 \circ\!\leqslant \mathbf{I}_2 \circ\!\leqslant \cdots$. The least fixed point of f in the lattice $(C, \subseteq)$ is $c = \cup_{n \in \mathbb{N}} \mathbf{I}_n$. Conclude that $\top, \bot \in \check{C}$.]

(ii) Conclude from (i) using exercise 18.4.4(iii) that there is a complete sublattice D of $P\omega$ such that $D \cong [D \rightarrow D]$ and $\operatorname{Card}(D) > 1$. By theorem 5.4.4 this D yields an extensional λ-algebra.

18.4.10 (Ershov). Show that $\neg \exists a \in R\ R = \check{a}$. [*Hint*. Let $a \in R$; a is called *nonextensive* iff for all finite $e \neq \emptyset$ one has $e \subsetneq a.e$. a is called *finite* iff $\forall x \in \check{a}\ x$ is finite. Let $\sqcup$ and $\sqcap$ be the sup and inf operations on R.

(i) Show that for $a, b \in R$, if a is nonextensive and b finite, then $a \sqcap b = \bot\ (= \emptyset)$.

(ii) Show that there exists a nonextensive $a \in R$ such that $a \neq \bot$. [Define $f(x) = \{m \mid \exists n \in x\ m \ll n\}$ where $\ll$ is a linear ordering of $\mathbb{N}$ of order type $\mathbb{Q}$ (the rationals). Then $f \in [P\omega \rightarrow P\omega]$. Take $a = \operatorname{graph}(f)$.]

(iii) The operation $\sqcap$ on R is not continuous. [Let $b_n = \lambda x. e_n$. Then $\cup_n b_n = \lambda x. \top = \top$. If $\sqcap$ were continuous, then for nonextensive a one has

$$a = a \sqcup \top = a \sqcap \bigcup_n b_n = \bigcup_n a \sqcap b_n = \bot,$$

contradicting (ii).]

(iv) Conclude from (iii) that $(R, \subseteq)$ is not a continuous lattice. The statement now follows from exercise 18.4.3(i).

18.4.11. Let $\langle n \rangle = n$, $\langle n_1, \ldots, n_{k+1} \rangle = (n_1, \langle n_2, \ldots, n_{k+1} \rangle)$, where $(\ldots,\ldots)$ is the pairing of $\mathbb{N}$. Show that in $P\omega$

(i) $xy_1 \cdots y_k = \{m \mid \exists e_{n_1} \subseteq y_1 \cdots \exists e_{n_k} \subseteq y_k \langle n_1, \ldots, n_k, m \rangle \in x\}$

(ii) $\lambda x_1 \cdots x_k \cdot f(x_1, \ldots, x_k) = \{\langle n_1, \ldots, n_k, m \rangle \mid m \in f(e_{n_1}, \ldots, e_{n_k})\}$ where $f \in [P\omega^k \rightarrow P\omega]$.

18.4.12 (de Vrijer). Show that the theory λ + surjective pairing (cf. exercise 15.3.4) is consistent by finding in $P\omega$ elements d, d_1, d_2 such that $d_i(dx_1x_2) = x_i$, $i = 1, 2$, and $d(d_1x)(d_2x) = x$. [*Hint*. Show that $f(x_1, x_2) = \{2m \mid m \in x_1\} \cup \{2m+1 \mid m \in x_2\}$ is continuous and has continuous projections.] See also exercise 18.4.19.

18.4.13. (i) Let $I^{n+1} = \lambda\!\!\!\lambda x \in D_n . x$. Show that in D_∞

$$\mathbf{I} = \langle \bot, I^1, I^2, \ldots \rangle.$$

(ii) Let $K^{n+2} = \lambda\!\!\!\lambda x \in D_{n+1} \lambda\!\!\!\lambda y \in D_n . \psi_n(x)$. Show that in D_∞

$$\mathbf{K} = \langle \bot, I^1, K^2, K^3, \ldots \rangle.$$

(iii) Let $S^{n+3} = \lambda\!\!\!\lambda x \in D_{n+2} \lambda\!\!\!\lambda y \in D_{n+1} \lambda\!\!\!\lambda z \in D_n . x(\varphi_n z)(yz)$,

$$S^2 = \lambda\!\!\!\lambda x \in D_1 \lambda\!\!\!\lambda y \in D_0 . x \bot.$$

Show that in D_∞

$$\mathbf{S} = \langle \perp, I^1, S^2, S^3, \ldots \rangle.$$

18.4.14. Let $\omega^{n+1} = \lambda x \in D_n . \varphi_n(x)(x)$. Show that in D

$$\lambda x . xx = \langle \perp, \omega^1, \omega^2, \ldots \rangle.$$

Conclude that in D_∞

$$\mathbf{\Omega} = \perp .$$

18.4.15 (Wadsworth). Show that in general in D_∞

$$(x \cdot y)_n \neq x_{n+1}(y_n).$$

[*Hint* Take $x = \lambda a . aa$, $y = \mathbf{I}$.]
18.4.16 (Scott). Let $(x^n)_{n \in \mathbb{N}}$ be a sequence of elements of D_∞ and let $x = \sqcup_n x^n$. Show that

$$\forall n\, x_n = x^n \Leftrightarrow \forall n \left[x^n \in D_n \text{ and } \psi_n(x^{n+1}) = x^n \right].$$

18.4.17 (Scott). (i) Show that in the category **CPO** D_∞ is isomorphic to the direct limit $\varinjlim(D_n, \varphi_n)$.
(ii) Show that in general $D_\infty \neq \cup_n D_n$. [*Hint.* $I \notin \cup D_n$.] Conclude that in the category of partial ordered sets with directed sup preserving maps, $D_\infty \neq \varinjlim(D_n, \varphi_n)$.
18.4.18 (Scott). Show that in D_∞

$$x \in D_0 \Leftrightarrow \forall y \in D_\infty x \cdot y = x$$

18.4.19 (Scott). (i) Construct a cpo E such that $E \cong E \times E$. [Take $E = D^\omega$].
(ii) Let $E \in$ **CPO**. Construct a $D \in$ **CPO** such that $D \cong [D \to E]$. [Define an appropriate inverse limit.]
(iii) Let D, $E \in$ **CPO** be such that $E \times E \cong E$ and $D \cong [D \to E]$. Show that $D \cong D \times D \cong [D \to D]$. Conclude that the theory $\boldsymbol{\lambda\eta}$ + surjective pairing is consistent.
18.4.20 (Park). Let Y_{Tarski} be the minimal fixed point operator for the cpo D_∞ defined in theorem 1.2.17. Let Y_{Curry} be the image in D_∞ of $\lambda f.(\lambda x. f(xx))(\lambda x. f(xx))$. Show that in D_∞ one has

$$Y_{\text{Tarski}} = Y_{\text{Curry}},$$

(when Y_{Tarski} is considered as an element of D_∞). See also the next exercise and theorem 19.3.4 for an alternative proof.
[*Hint.* Clearly $Y_{\text{Tarski}} \sqsubseteq Y_{\text{Curry}}$. Let $f \in D_\infty$, $y = \lambda x. f(xx)$. Show that in D_∞
(i) $y_{n+1} y_n = f_{n+1}(y_n y_{n-1})$
(ii) $y_1 y_0 = f_1(f_0 \perp)$. Conclude that

$$y_{n+1} y_n = f_{n+1}(f_n(\cdots(f_1(f_0))\cdots)) \sqsubseteq f^{n+1}(\perp).$$

Hence $Y_{\text{Curry}} \cdot f \sqsubseteq Y_{\text{Tarski}} \cdot f$.]
18.4.21 (Park). (i) Let $a \in D_0$ be a compact element $\neq \perp$. Define $\varphi_0' \colon D_0 \to D_1$, $\psi_0' \colon D_1 \to D_0$ by

$$\varphi_0'(x) = f_{a,x}, \qquad \psi_0'(x) = x(a)$$

where $f_{a,x}(y) =$ if $y \sqsupseteq a$ then x else $\perp$.
Show that (φ_0', ψ_0') is a projection of D_1 on D_0.
(ii) Show that the construction of D_∞ can be done using the initial projection (φ_0', ψ_0') instead of (φ_0, ψ_0). This yields model D_∞^a. Show that all results in § 18.2 go through D_∞^a except lemma 18.2.8(v). In particular D_∞^a is an extensional λ-model.

(iii) Show that $Y_{\text{Tarski}} \neq Y_{\text{Curry}}$ in D_∞^a.
[*Hint*. In D_∞^a one has $Y_{\text{Curry}}\mathbf{I} = a$, but $Y_{\text{Tarski}}\mathbf{I} = \bot$.]
(iv) Let $M \in \Lambda^0$. Show that $M \sqsupseteq a$ in D_∞^a.
18.4.22* (Sanchis [1979]). For $x, y \in P\omega$ define

$$x!y = \{ m \mid \forall \alpha\, \exists k\, \exists e_n \subseteq y \langle \bar{\alpha}(k), n, m \rangle \in x \}.$$

Here α ranges over $\mathbb{N}^{\mathbb{N}}$, m, k, n range over $\mathbb{N}$ and $\bar{\alpha}(k) = \langle \alpha(0), \ldots, \alpha(k-1) \rangle$. It will be shown that $(P\omega, !)$ is a combinatory algebra.
Notation. $[xy_1 \cdots y_n] = (\cdots((x!y_1)!y_2) \cdots !y_n)$
$(xy_1 \cdots y_n) = (\cdots((x \cdot y_1) \cdot y_2) \cdots \cdot y_n)$,
where $\cdot$ denotes the usual application in $P\omega$.
Consider relations $R(x_1, \ldots, x_p, m_1, \ldots, m_q)$ with the x's ranging over $P\omega$, the m's over $\mathbb{N}$. Such a relation is an *H-relation* if it is in the inductive class defined as follows.
(1) $m \in x$ is an H-relation. $R(m_1, \ldots, m_p)$ is an H-relation if R is r.e.
(2) H-relations are closed under conjunction, disjunction and numerical quantification.
(3) If $R(\vec{x}, m, \vec{n})$ is an H-relation, so is $\forall \alpha\, \exists k\, R(\vec{x}, \bar{\alpha}(k), \vec{n})$.
(i) Show that for all $k \in \mathbb{N}$

$$\forall x \in P\omega\, \exists x' \in P\omega\, \forall y_1 \cdots y_k \quad (xy_1 \ldots y_k) = [x'xy_1 \cdots y_k].$$

(ii) If $R(\vec{y}, z, \vec{m})$, with $\vec{y}, z \in P\omega$, $\vec{m} \in \mathbb{N}$, is an H-relation, then for some $x \in P\omega$

$$[(x\vec{y})z] = \{ \langle \vec{m} \rangle \mid R(\vec{y}, z, \vec{m}) \},$$

where $\langle \vec{m} \rangle$ is defined as in exercise 18.4.11.
(iii) If $R(\vec{y}, \vec{m})$ is an H-relation, then for some $x \in P\omega$

$$[x\vec{y}] = \{ \langle \vec{m} \rangle \mid R(\vec{y}, \vec{m}) \}.$$

(iv) Conclude that $(P\omega, !)$ is a combinatory algebra. Is it a λ-algebra? Is it weakly extensional? [In Koymans [1984] it is shown that $(P\omega, !)$ is not a λ-model.]
18.4.23. Let $q > q'$ and $p, p' \leqslant n$. Show

$$P\omega \models \lambda x_0 \cdots x_q . \mathbf{P}_n^- \sigma_0 \cdots \sigma_p \subsetneq \lambda x_0 \cdots x_q . \mathbf{P}_n^- \sigma_0' \cdots \sigma_p'.$$

18.4.24. Show that not all continuous $f: \mathfrak{B} \to \mathfrak{B}$ are representable. [*Hint*. Let $f(A) =$ *If* $A = \bot$ *then* $\bot$ *else* $\lambda x.x$].
18.4.25. Show that $(P\omega, \cdot, \lambda^-)$ is not a λ-algebra.
18.4.26 (Scott; Plotkin and Smyth [1978]). (i) Define **CPO*** as the subcategory of **CPO** with the same objects and as arrows

$$\text{Hom}(D, D') = \{ f \in [D \to D'] \mid (f, g) \text{ is a projection of } D' \text{ on } D \text{ for some } g \}.$$

Show that if f is a morphism in **CPO***, then the corresponding g is unique and may be denoted by f^R.
(ii) Show that **CPO*** has direct limits and that

$$\varinjlim (D_i, f_i) = \varprojlim (D_i, f_i^R)$$

where the direct limit is taken in **CPO*** and the inverse in **CPO**.
(iii) A functor F: **CPO*** $\to$ **CPO*** is called locally continuous if

$$F(\cup f_n) = \sqcup F(f_n),$$

where the $f_n \in [D \to D']$ are directed. Assume
(1) F is a locally continuous functor on **CPO***.
(2) $\exists D_0 \in \mathbf{CPO^*}\, \exists ff \in \text{Hom}_{\mathbf{CPO^*}}(D_0, FD_0)$.

Show that then $D_\infty = FD_\infty$ for some $D_\infty \in \mathbf{CPO}^{(*)}$.

(iv) Show that Scott's construction of D_∞ can be seen as an application of (iii) by considering the map $\boldsymbol{F}(D) = [D \to D]$ as a $\mathbf{CPO}^*$ functor.

(v) Define for $D, D' \in \mathbf{CPO}$ the sum $D + D'$ by the following picture:

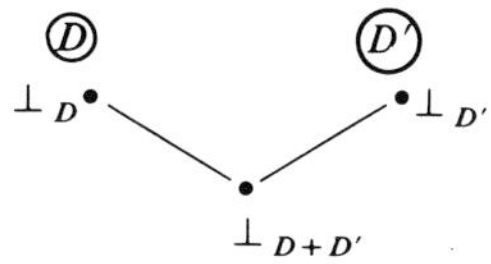

i.e. take disjoint copies and add a new $\perp$.

Construct in **CPO** solutions of the following "recursive domain equations": $D = D_0 + [D \to D]$, $D = D \times ([D_0 \to D] + D)$, where D_0 is given.

18.4.27 (Scott [1976]). Extend the set Λ to the set LAMBDA by adding a constant 0, unary operations $+1, -1$ and a ternary operation $- \supset -, -$. The semantics in $P\omega$ of these new symbols is defined as follows.

$$\begin{aligned} 0 &= \{0\}, \\ x + 1 &= \{n + 1 \mid n \in x\}, \\ x - 1 &= \{n \mid n + 1 \in x\}, \\ z \supset x, y &= \{n \in x \mid 0 \in z\} \cup \{m \in y \mid \exists k\; k + 1 \in z\}. \end{aligned}$$

Show that the interpreation of the LAMBDA terms in $P\omega$ is exactly the collection of r.e. sets.

18.4.28. Let $D \in \mathbf{CPO}$ be isomorphic to $\{f: D \to D \mid f \text{ monotonic}\}$, with the pointwise partial ordering. Show that then D is trivial.

18.4.29 (Engeler [1981]). Let $\mathfrak{M} = \langle A, \cdot \rangle$ be an applicative structure. Show that $\mathfrak{M}$ can be embedded into a λ-model. See also exercises 5.8.5 and 18.4.31. [*Hint*. Consider the λ-model D_A introduced in § 5.4. Define $f_n, f: A \to D_A$ by $f_0(a) = \{a\}$; $f_{n+1}(a) = f_n(a) \cup \{(\{a'\}, b) \mid a' \in A \wedge b \in f_n(a \cdot a')\}$; $f(a) = \cup_n f_n(a)$. Show that f embeds $\mathfrak{M}$ into D_A.]

18.4.30 (M. Boffa). It is known that in Zermelo-Fraenkel set theory the axiom of foundation may be consistently replaced by its extreme opposite, claiming that for each model $\langle A, R \rangle$ of the axiom of extensionality there is a transitive set T such that $\langle A, R \rangle \cong \langle T, \in \rangle$. This replacement does not affect the mathematical strength of set theory. Show that in the new theory the following is provable: every extensional applicative structure $\langle X, \cdot \rangle$ is isomorphic to one in which $\cdot$ coincides with actual set theoretic function application (i.e. $x.y = x(y)$).

18.4.31 (Scott). Show that every applicative structure $(A, *)$ can be embedded into an extensional λ-model. (See also exercise 5.8.5.) [*Hint*. Define $D_0 = A \cup \{\perp\}$ partially ordered such that $\perp \sqsubseteq a$ for $a \in A$ and no other relations hold. Construct D_∞ with D_0 a retract of D_∞: $p: D_\infty \to D_0$, $q: D_0 \to D_\infty$, $p \circ q = \mathrm{id}_{D_0}$ and moreover $q(a)x = q(a)$ for all $x \in D_0$ (see proposition 18.2.13(ii)). Assume that A contains at least three distinct elements $0, 1, 2$. Show that there is a map $e: A \to D_\infty$ satisfying

$$\begin{aligned} e(a)x &= q(a) && \text{if } p \circ x \circ q(1) = 0, \\ &= q(2) && \text{if } p \circ x \circ q(1) = 1, \\ &= e(a * p \circ x \circ q(0)) && \text{if } p \circ x \circ q(1) = 2, \\ &= 1 && \text{else.} \end{aligned}$$

Then $e(a)e(b) = e(a * b)$ and e is injective.]

CHAPTER 19

LOCAL STRUCTURE OF MODELS

In this and the next chapter the structure of several λ-algebras will be investigated. There are two aspects of this structure, the local and the global.

The *local structure* of a λ-algebra $\mathfrak{M}$ is

$$\mathrm{Th}(\mathfrak{M}) = \{M = N \mid \mathfrak{M} \models M = N,\ M, N \in \Lambda^0\}.$$

For the models $P\omega$ and D_∞ the local structure will be determined. The local structure of the term model of a λ-theory $\mathfrak{T}$ is simply

$$\mathrm{Th}(\mathfrak{M}(\mathfrak{T})) = \mathfrak{T};$$

for the model $\mathfrak{B}$ the local structure is $\mathcal{B}$.

The *global structure* of a model consists of properties true in $\mathfrak{M}$ like extensionality and other ones (not necessarily first order). Some of these global properties will be examined in the next chapter.

19.1. The local structure of $P\omega$

The local structure of $P\omega$ can be characterized nicely as follows:

$$P\omega \models M = N \Leftrightarrow \mathrm{BT}(M) = \mathrm{BT}(N),$$

$$P\omega \models M \subseteq N \Leftrightarrow \mathrm{BT}(M)^\eta \subseteq \mathrm{BT}(N).$$

This is a reformulation in terms of Böhm trees of results due to Hyland [1976].

Wadsworth's $\lambda\bot$-calculus will be a useful tool for examining the value of terms in $P\omega$.

19.1.1. DEFINITION. Let ρ be a valuation in $P\omega$. The semantic function $[\![\ \ ]\!]_\rho : \Lambda \to P\omega$ is extended to $\Lambda\bot$ by adding $[\![\bot]\!]_\rho = \emptyset$ to the clauses of corollary 18.2.8 (iii).

Note that by this definition the $\perp$-reductions $\perp x \to \perp$ and $\lambda x.\perp \to \perp$ correspond to the valid equations $\emptyset x = \lambda x.\emptyset = \emptyset$. Therefore

$$M =_{\beta\perp} N \Rightarrow P\omega \models M = N.$$

The term $\perp$ does not add to the expressive power of the λ-calculus, since also $[\![\Omega]\!] = \emptyset$, as will be shown below.

The reader should recall the notions $N \sqsubseteq M$, $\mathscr{A}(M)$ and $M^{[k]}$ for $M, N \in \Lambda\perp$ introduced in § 14.3.

19.1.2. LEMMA. $N \in \mathscr{A}(M) \Rightarrow P\omega \models N \subseteq M$.

PROOF. Notice that M results (up to β-equality) from N by replacing some $\perp$'s by other terms. Hence the result. Example: let $M \twoheadrightarrow_\beta \lambda x.xM$. Then $\lambda x.x\perp \in \mathscr{A}(M)$ and $P\omega \models \lambda x.x\perp \subseteq \lambda x.xM = M$. □

One also has

$$M \sqsubseteq N \Rightarrow P\omega \models M \subseteq N$$

for all $M, N \in \Lambda\perp$, see lemma 19.1.11. But if M has no $\beta\perp$-nf, this does not follow as easily as in the previous lemma.

The following approximation theorem is an important step towards the characterization of (in)equality in $P\omega$:

$$M = \bigcup \{N \mid N \in \mathscr{A}(M)\}.$$

This theorem was conjectured by Scott, proved by Hyland and improved by Wadsworth. The proof will make use of the normalization theorem for the $\lambda\perp^{\mathbb{N}}$-calculus.

19.1.3. DEFINITION. The semantic function $[\![\ ]\!]_\rho : \Lambda\perp \to P\omega$ is extended to $\Lambda\perp^{\mathbb{N}}$ by setting

$$[\![M^n]\!]_\rho = ([\![M]\!]_\rho)_n,$$

cf. definition 18.1.12.

19.1.4. DEFINITION. Let $M \in \Lambda\perp$. An *indexing* for M is a mapping I that assigns to each subterm of M an element of $\mathbb{N}$. M^I is the resulting completely indexed term.

19.1.5. LEMMA. *Let* $M \in \Lambda\perp$. *Then in* $P\omega$

$$M = \bigcup \{M^I \mid I \text{ indexing for } M\}.$$

PROOF. Induction on the structure of M, using $x = \bigcup_n (x)_n$. □

19.1.6. LEMMA. *Let* $M, N \in \Lambda\bot^{\mathbb{N}}$ *with* $M \twoheadrightarrow_{\text{lab}.\beta} N$. *Then*
(i) $P\omega \models M \subseteq N$,
(ii) $N \underset{\sim}{\sqsubset} M$.
(Note the different order in (i), (ii).)

PROOF. (i) The basic equations, corollary 18.1.14, show that after a lab.β-reduction the value of a term is the same or increased.
(ii) The approximation comes in at contractions like

$$(\lambda x.P)^0 Q \to (P[x := \bot])^0.$$

By corollary 14.3.20 $C[\bot] \underset{\sim}{\sqsubset} C[Q]$ for all Q. Therefore

$$(P[x := \bot])^0 \underset{\sim}{\sqsubset} P[x := Q] \approx (\lambda x.P)Q. \quad \square$$

19.1.7. LEMMA. *Let* $M \in \Lambda\bot^{\mathbb{N}}$. *Then there exists an* $N \in \Lambda\bot^{\mathbb{N}}$ *such that*
(1) $P\omega \models M \subseteq N$,
(2) $|N| \in \mathcal{Q}(|M|)$.

PROOF. Given M, let N be its lab.β-nf. N exists by theorem 14.1.12. Then by the previous lemma $P\omega \models M \subseteq N$ and $N \underset{\sim}{\sqsubset} M$, hence $|N| \in \mathcal{Q}(|M|)$. □

19.1.8. APPROXIMATION THEOREM. *In* $P\omega$ *one has for* $M \in \Lambda\bot$

$$M = \bigcup \{N \mid N \in \mathcal{Q}(M)\}.$$

PROOF. In $P\omega$ one has

$$\begin{aligned} M &= \bigcup \{M^I \mid I \text{ indexing for } M\} \quad \text{by lemma 19.1.5,} \\ &\subseteq \bigcup \{L \in \Lambda\bot^{\mathbb{N}} \mid |L| \in \mathcal{Q}(M)\} \quad \text{by lemma 19.1.7,} \\ &\subseteq \bigcup \{N \in \Lambda\bot \mid N \in \mathcal{Q}(M)\} \quad \text{since } P\omega \models L \subseteq |L|, \\ &\subseteq M \quad \text{by lemma 19.1.2.} \quad \square \end{aligned}$$

19.1.9. COROLLARY. *In* $P\omega$ *one has for* $M \in \Lambda\bot$,

$$M = \bigcup_k M^{[k]}.$$

PROOF. Let $N \in \mathcal{A}(M)$. Let all nodes in BT(N) have depth $< k$. Then $N \sqsubseteq M^{[k]}$, hence $P\omega \models N \subseteq M^{[k]}$ by lemma 19.1.2, and the result follows. □

Next a model theoretic proof of the consistency of $\mathcal{H}$ can be given.

19.1.10. THEOREM. (i) *Let* $M \in \Lambda$. *Then*

$$M \text{ is unsolvable} \Leftrightarrow P\omega \models M = \emptyset.$$

(ii) $P\omega \models \mathcal{H}$, *i.e.* $P\omega$ *is sensible.*

PROOF. (i) ($\Rightarrow$) If M is unsolvable, then $\mathcal{A}(M) = \{\perp\}$, and hence $[\![M]\!] = \bigcup \{[\![\perp]\!]\} = \emptyset$.

($\Leftarrow$) If M were solvable, then for some $\vec{x}$, $\vec{N}$ (using corollary 18.1.14),

$$P\omega \models \mathbf{I} = (\lambda\vec{x}.M)\vec{N} = (\lambda\vec{x}.\emptyset)\vec{N} = \emptyset\vec{N} = \emptyset,$$

contradicting corollary 18.1.15.

(ii) Immediate by (i). □

Now we can prove a general version of lemma 19.1.2.

19.1.11. LEMMA. *Let* $M, N \in \Lambda\perp$. *Then*

$$M \sqsubseteq N \Rightarrow P\omega \models M \subseteq N.$$

PROOF.

$$M \sqsubseteq N \Rightarrow \forall k\ M^{[k]} \sqsubseteq N$$

$$\Rightarrow \forall k\ P\omega \models M^{[k]} \subseteq N \quad \text{by lemma 19.1.2,}$$

$$\Rightarrow P\omega \models M = \bigcup_k M^{[k]} \subseteq N$$

by the (corollary to the) approximation theorem. □

Remember how relations on Böhm trees are translated to terms. For example,

$$M \lesssim_\eta N \Leftrightarrow \mathrm{BT}(M) \leqslant_\eta \mathrm{BT}(N).$$

The definitions are extended to $\Lambda\perp^{\mathbf{N}}$ in the obvious way.

19.1.12. LEMMA. *Let* $M \in \Lambda\bot$ *and* $x \lesssim_\eta M$. *Then*

$$P\omega \models x \subseteq M.$$

PROOF. If M is a finite η-expansion of x, then this follows directly from

$$(1) \qquad P\omega \models a \subseteq \lambda z.az,$$

proposition 18.1.9 (i). In the general case one has by assumption

$$M = \lambda a_1 \cdots a_n.xM_1 \cdots M_n.$$

By induction on k it will be shown that

$$P\omega \models (x)_k \subseteq M;$$

then the result follows since $x = \bigcup_k (x)_k$. Let $k = 0$. Then

$$\begin{aligned}(x)_0 &\subseteq \lambda a_1 \cdots a_n.(x)_0 a_1 \cdots a_n \\ &= \lambda a_1 \cdots a_n.(x)_0 \bot \cdots \bot \\ &\subseteq \lambda a_1 \cdots a_n.xM_1 \cdots M_n = M\end{aligned}$$

by (1) and the basic equations (corollary 18.1.14). For the case $k+1$ it follows again by the basic equations that

$$\begin{aligned}(x)_{k+1} &\subseteq \lambda a_1 \cdots a_n.(x)_{k+1} a_1 \cdots a_n \\ &\subseteq \lambda a_1 \cdots a_n.(x)_{k+1}(a_1)_k(a_2)_{k-1} \cdots (a_n)_{k+1-n}.\end{aligned}$$

Since $x \lesssim_\eta M$, we have

$$a_i \lesssim_\eta M_i, \quad 1 \leqslant i \leqslant n$$

hence by the induction hypothesis

$$P\omega \models (a_i)_{k-i+1} \subseteq M_i, \quad 1 \leqslant i \leqslant n$$

and therefore

$$P\omega \models (x)_{k+1} \subseteq \lambda a_1 \cdots a_n.xM_1 \cdots M_n = M. \quad \square$$

19.1.13. LEMMA. *Let* $M, N \in \Lambda\bot$.
(i) *If* M *is in* $\beta\bot$*-nf and* $M \lesssim_\eta N$, *then* $P\omega \models M \subseteq N$.
(ii) $M \lesssim_\eta N \Rightarrow P\omega \models M \subseteq N$.

PROOF. (i) By induction on the structure of M. If $M \equiv x$, this is just lemma 19.1.12, so suppose $M \equiv \lambda \vec{x}.yM_1 \cdots M_n$. By assumption

$$N = \lambda \vec{x}\vec{a}.yN_1 \cdots N_n\vec{L}$$

with $\vec{M} \lesssim_\eta \vec{N}$ and $\vec{a} \lesssim_\eta \vec{L}$. Then by the induction hypothesis and the previous lemma one has in $P\omega$

$$M = \lambda \vec{x}.y\vec{M} \subseteq \lambda \vec{x}\vec{a}.y\vec{M}\vec{a} \subseteq \lambda \vec{x}\vec{a}.y\vec{N}\vec{L} = N.$$

(ii) This follows from (i) by the approximation theorem (see the proof of lemma 19.1.11). □

19.1.14. PROPOSITION. *Let* $M, N \in \Lambda\bot$. *Then*

$$M^\eta \mathrel{\underset{\sim}{\sqsubseteq}} N \Rightarrow P\omega \vDash M \subseteq N.$$

PROOF.

$$M^\eta \mathrel{\underset{\sim}{\sqsubseteq}} N \Rightarrow M \lesssim_\eta M' \mathrel{\underset{\sim}{\sqsubseteq}} N, \quad \text{for some } M',$$

$$\Rightarrow P\omega \vDash M \subseteq M' \subseteq N,$$

by lemma 19.1.11 and 19.1.13 (ii). □

Next the converse of proposition 19.1.14 will be shown. The proof occupies 19.1.15–19.1.18.

19.1.15. DEFINITION. Let M, $N \in \Lambda$, $\sigma \in \mathrm{Seq}$.

(i) Write M $\sup_\alpha$ N if $\mathrm{BT}(M)$ $\sup_\alpha$ $\mathrm{BT}(N)$ (see definition 10.2.28 (ii)).

(ii) p is *large enough* for α-M-N if p is larger than the number of successor nodes of any node $\beta \leqslant \alpha$ in $\mathrm{BT}(M)$ or $\mathrm{BT}(N)$.

(iii) An α-M-N *substitutor* is a map $+ : \Lambda \to \mathfrak{T}(P\omega)$ such that for some variables $y_0, \ldots, y_n$ and some p large enough for α-M-N one has for all $Q \in \Lambda$

$$Q^+ \equiv Q[y_0 := \mathbf{P}_p^- y_0] \cdots [y_n := \mathbf{P}_p^- y_n].$$

where the $\mathbf{P}_p^- \in P\omega$ are defined in definition 18.1.18.

NOTATION. Write $+ \in \alpha$-M-N iff $+$ is an α-M-N substitutor.

19.1.16. LEMMA. *Let* A, $B \in \mathfrak{T}(P\omega)$ *with*

$$A \equiv xA_1 \cdots A_n, \qquad B \equiv yB_1 \cdots B_m.$$

Then $P\omega \nvDash A \subseteq B$ *if* $x \not\equiv y$ *or* $n \neq m$.

PROOF. *Case* 1. $x \not\equiv y$. Let $a, b \in P\omega$ be such that $a \not\subseteq b$. Take $\rho(x) = \lambda a_1 \cdots a_n.a$, $\rho(y) = \lambda b_1 \cdots b_m.b$. Then $P\omega, \rho \not\models A \subseteq B$.

Case 2. $x \equiv y$ and $n \neq m$, say $n = m + 2$ for simplicity. Suppose $P\omega \models A \subseteq B$. Then

$$P\omega \models xA_1 \cdots A_{m+2}zzw = xB_1 \cdots B_m zzw$$

Substitute $x := \lambda a_1 \cdots a_{m+3}.a_{m+3}$. Then it follows that

$$P\omega \models zzw \subseteq w$$

contradicting case 1. □

19.1.17. LEMMA. *Let* α *be a minimal node in* $BT(N)$ *such that* $M \sup_\alpha N$. *Then*

$$\forall + \in \alpha\text{-}M\text{-}N \quad P\omega \not\models M^+ \subseteq N^+.$$

PROOF. By induction on the length k of α. The most involved case is $k = 0$, i.e. $\alpha = \langle\ \rangle$. Let $+ \in \langle\ \rangle\text{-}M\text{-}N$ substitute $\mathbf{P}_p^-$. Suppose

(1) $\quad P\omega \models M^+ \subseteq N^+$

towards a contradiction. By assumption $M \sup_{\langle\ \rangle} N$, i.e. BT($M$) does not fit in BT($N$). Therefore M is solvable and has a hnf, say,

(2) $\quad M = \lambda x_1 \cdots x_n.yM_1 \cdots M_m.$

Case 1. N is unsolvable. Then by theorem 19.1.10 one has $P\omega \models N^+ = \emptyset$ and hence by (1) it follows that $P\omega \models M^+ = \emptyset$. Then (by applying both sides to $x_1, \ldots, x_n$ and, if it was not done already, making the substitution $[y := \mathbf{P}_p^- y]$) one obtains

$$P\omega \models \mathbf{P}_p^- yM_1^+ \cdots M_m^+ = \emptyset x_1 \cdots x_n = \emptyset.$$

Therefore

$$P\omega \models \mathbf{P}_p^- yM_1^+ \cdots M_m^+ z_{m+1} \cdots z_{p+1} = \emptyset,$$

hence

$$P\omega \models z_{p+1} yM_1^+ \cdots M_m^+ z_{m+1} \cdots z_p = \emptyset$$

by corollary 18.1.19. Since z_{p+1} can be interpreted arbitrarily, this is false.

Case 2. N is solvable, say with hnf

(3) $\quad N = \lambda x_1 \cdots x_{n'}.y' N_1 \cdots N_{m'}.$

By assumption $M \operatorname{sup}_{\langle\ \rangle} N$, that is

$$\langle \lambda x_1 \cdots x_n . y, m \rangle \quad \text{does not fit in} \quad \langle \lambda x_1 \cdots x_{n'} . y', m' \rangle .$$

Hence

$$y \not\equiv y' \quad \text{or} \quad m - n \neq m' - n' \quad \text{or} \quad n > n'.$$

Case 2.1. $y \not\equiv y'$. Let $n \geqslant n'$. By applying both sides of (1) to $x_1 \ldots, x_n$ and making possibly (if it was not done already) the substitutions $[y := \mathbf{P}_p^- y]$, $[y' := \mathbf{P}_p^- y']$ one obtains

$$P\omega \vDash \mathbf{P}_p^- y M_1^+ \cdots M_m^+ \subseteq \mathbf{P}_p^- y' N_1^+ \cdots N_{m'}^+ x_{n'+1} \cdots x_n.$$

By substituting $\mathbf{I}$ for $x_{n'+1}, \ldots, x_n$ in this formula and applying both sides to enough $\mathbf{I}$'s, it follows that

$$P\omega \vDash \mathbf{P}_p^- y M_1^{+\mathrm{I}} \cdots M_m^{+\mathrm{I}} \mathbf{I}^{\sim k} \subseteq \mathbf{P}_p^- y' N_1^{+\mathrm{I}} \cdots N_{m'}^{+\mathrm{I}} \mathbf{I}^{\sim k'}$$

for some large k, k'. Since $p > m, m'$ (because $+ \in \alpha\text{-}M\text{-}N$) it follows by corollary 18.1.19

$$P\omega \vDash \mathbf{I} y M_1^{+\mathrm{I}} \cdots M_m^{+\mathrm{I}} \mathbf{I}^{\sim k-1} \subseteq \mathbf{I} y' N_1^{+\mathrm{I}} \cdots N_{m'}^{+\mathrm{I}} \mathbf{I}^{\sim k'-1},$$

contradicting lemma 19.1.16.

Case 2.2. $y \equiv y'$ and $n - m \neq n' - m'$. Now applying both sides of (1) to $x^{\sim k}$, with large k, (and possibly performing the substitution $[y := \mathbf{P}_p^- y]$) yields

$$P\omega \vDash \mathbf{P}_p^- y M_1^+ \cdots M_m^+ x^{\sim (k-n)} \subseteq \mathbf{P}_p^- y N_1^+ \cdots N_{m'}^+ x^{\sim (k-n')}$$

Hence by corollary 18.1.19

$$P\omega \vDash xy M_1 \cdots M_m^+ x^{\sim (k-n-1)} \subseteq xy N_1^+ \cdots N_{m'}^+ x^{\sim (k-n'-1)}$$

contradicting lemma 19.1.16 ($m + k - n - 1 \neq m' + k - n' - 1$ by the case assumption).

Case 2.3. $y \equiv y'$ and $n > n'$. By applying both sides of (1) to $x_1, \ldots, x_{n'}$, (and possibly making a substitution) one obtains

$$P\omega \vDash \lambda x_{n'+1} \cdots x_n . \mathbf{P}_p^- y M_1^+ \cdots M_m^+ \subseteq \mathbf{P}_p^- y N_1^+ \cdots N_m^+,$$

contradicting lemma 18.1.20. The proof for $k = 0$ is now complete.

If $k > 0$, then $\alpha = \langle i \rangle * \beta$ and BT(M) fits in BT(N). Since $M \operatorname{sup}_\alpha N$ it follows that M, N are solvable and for the hnf's (2) and (3) one has

$$y \equiv y', \quad n \leqslant n' \quad \text{and} \quad m - n = m' - n' \quad (\text{hence } m \leqslant m').$$

Let $+\in\alpha$-M-N and assume again (1). By the induction hypothesis one has

(4) $\quad \forall +\in\beta\text{-}M_i\text{-}N_i \quad P\omega \nvDash M_i^+ \subseteq N_i^+.$

From (1) it follows in the by now familiar way that

$$P\omega\vDash \mathbf{P}_p^- yM_1^+ \cdots M_m^+ x^{\sim n'-n} z^{\sim k} \subseteq \mathbf{P}_p^- yN_1^+ \cdots N_{m'} z^{\sim k}.$$

Hence

$$P\omega\vDash zyM_1^+ \cdots M_m^+ x^{\sim n'-n} z^{\sim k-1} \subseteq zyN_1^+ \cdots N_{m'}^+ z^{\sim k-1}.$$

By interpreting z as $\lambda a_0 a_1 \cdots a_{k-1+m'}.a_i$ one obtains

$$P\omega\vDash M_i^+ \subseteq N_i^+.$$

Since $+\in\alpha$-M-N, a fortiori $+\in\beta$-M_i-N_i and this contradicts (4). □

19.1.18. Proposition. $M^\eta \not\subseteq N \Rightarrow P\omega \nvDash M \subseteq N$.

Proof. By assumption and lemma 10.2.30 $M \operatorname{sup}_\alpha N$ for some $\alpha\in \mathrm{BT}(N)$. Take α of minimal length. Then by lemma 19.1.17 it follows (take the empty substitution) that $P\omega \nvDash M \subseteq N$. □

Finally we have the characterization theorem due to Hyland [1976].

19.1.19. Characterization Theorem for $P\omega$. *Let* $M, N \in \Lambda$. *Then*
(i) $P\omega\vDash M \subseteq N \Leftrightarrow \mathrm{BT}(M)^\eta \subseteq \mathrm{BT}(N)$,
(ii) $P\omega\vDash M = N \Leftrightarrow \mathrm{BT}(M) = \mathrm{BT}(N)$.

Proof. (i) By propositions 19.1.14 and 19.1.18.
(ii) By (i) and lemma 10.2.24 (i). □

19.2. The local structure of D_∞

The local structure of D_∞ can be characterized nicely as follows. For all cpo's D

(i) $D_\infty \vDash M = N \Leftrightarrow \mathcal{H}^* \vdash M = N$
$\Leftrightarrow \mathrm{BT}(M) =_\eta \mathrm{BT}(N)$.
(ii) $D_\infty \vDash M \sqsubseteq N \Leftrightarrow \forall C[\;]\,[C[M] \text{ solvable} \Rightarrow C[N] \text{ solvable}]$
$\Leftrightarrow \mathrm{BT}(M)^\eta \subseteq^\eta \mathrm{BT}(N)$.

It follows that the local structure of D_∞ is independent of D.

The proof is along the same lines as that for the analysis of $P\omega$. The above is a reformulation in terms of Böhm trees of results, obtained independently in 1972, of Hyland [1976] and Wadsworth [1976]. Hyland's analysis of $P\omega$ was given later in 1973. The formulation in terms of Böhm trees is taken from Barendregt [1977]. See also Nakajima [1975], cf. exercise 19.4.4.

19.2.1. DEFINITION. Let ρ be a valuation in D_∞. The semantic function $[\![\ \ ]\!]_\rho : \Lambda \to D_\infty$ is extended to $\Lambda\bot$ and $\Lambda\bot^{\mathbb{N}}$ by setting

$$[\![\bot]\!]_\rho = \bot, \qquad [\![M^n]\!]_\rho = ([\![M]\!]_\rho)_n.$$

19.2.2. APPROXIMATION THEOREM FOR D_∞. *Let $M \in \Lambda\bot$. Then in D_∞*

$$M = \bigsqcup\{N \mid N \in \mathcal{A}(M)\}.$$

PROOF. Analogous to the proof of the approximation theorem for $P\omega$. One shows that in D_∞ for $M \in \Lambda\bot$

$$M = \bigsqcup\{M^I \mid I \text{ an indexing for } M\}.$$

Similarly lemmas corresponding to 19.1.2, 19.1.6 and 19.1.7 can be proved and the result follows. □

19.2.3. COROLLARY. *In D_∞ one has for $M \in \Lambda\bot$*

$$M = \bigsqcup_k M^{[k]}.$$

PROOF. As for corollary 19.1.9. □

19.2.4. THEOREM. (i) *Let $M \in \Lambda$. Then*

$$M \text{ is unsolvable} \Leftrightarrow D_\infty \models M = \bot.$$

(ii) *$D_\infty \models \mathcal{H}\eta$; in particular D_∞ is sensible and $\mathcal{H}\eta$ is consistent.*

PROOF. (i) As for theorem 19.1.10 using $\bot x = \lambda x.\bot = \bot$.

(ii) By (i) and the fact that $D_\infty \models$ extensionality (theorem 18.2.14 (ii)). □

19.2.5. COROLLARY. *Let $M, N \in \Lambda$. Then*

$$D_\infty \models M \sqsubseteq N \Rightarrow \forall C[\ \ ]\, [C[M] \text{ solvable} \Rightarrow C[N] \text{ solvable}].$$

PROOF. Suppose that $M \sqsubseteq N$ in D_∞ and choose $C[\ ] \in \Lambda$. If $C[N]$ were unsolvable, then in D_∞

$$\perp = C[N] \sqsupseteq C[M]$$

hence $C[M] = \perp$ and therefore $C[M]$ is unsolvable. □

19.2.6. LEMMA. *Let* $M, N \in \Lambda\perp$. *Then*

(i) $M \underset{\sim}{\sqsubseteq} N \Rightarrow D_\infty \vDash M \sqsubseteq N$

(ii) $M \lesssim_\eta N \Rightarrow D_\infty \vDash M \sqsubseteq N$

(iii) $M \lesssim_\eta N \Rightarrow D_\infty \vDash M = N$.

PROOF. (i), (ii) As for $P\omega$ one shows this first for M in $\beta\perp$-nf. Then the approximation theorem applies.

(iii) $M \lesssim_\eta N \Rightarrow \forall k\ \exists M_0\ M_0 \twoheadrightarrow_\eta M$ and $M_0^{(k)} = N^{(k)}$ by lemma 10.2.26,

$$\Rightarrow \forall k\ D_\infty \vDash N^{(k)} = M_0^{(k)} \sqsubseteq M_0 = M$$

$$\Rightarrow D_\infty \vDash N = \bigsqcup_k N^{(k)} \sqsubseteq M,$$

hence the result follows from (ii). □

19.2.7. PROPOSITION. $M\,{}^\eta\!\underset{\sim}{\sqsubseteq}{}^\eta N \Rightarrow D_\infty \vDash M \sqsubseteq N$.

PROOF.

$$M\,{}^\eta\!\underset{\sim}{\sqsubseteq}{}^\eta N \Rightarrow M \lesssim_\eta M' \underset{\sim}{\sqsubseteq} N'\,{}_\eta\!\gtrsim N \quad \text{for some } M', N'$$

$$\Rightarrow D_\infty \vDash M = M' \sqsubseteq N' = N$$

by the previous lemma. □

19.2.8. PROPOSITION.

$$\forall C[\ ]\ [C[M]\ \textit{solvable} \Rightarrow C[N]\ \textit{solvable}] \Rightarrow M\,{}^\eta\!\underset{\sim}{\sqsubseteq}{}^\eta N.$$

PROOF. If $M\,{}^\eta\!\underset{\sim}{\not\sqsubseteq}{}^\eta N$, then $\mathrm{BT}(M)^\eta \not\subseteq {}^\eta\mathrm{BT}(N)$ and hence by lemma 10.2.30 $M \not\sim_\alpha N$ and $M|\alpha\downarrow$ for some $\alpha \in \mathrm{Seq}$. By taking α of minimal length it follows that $\mathfrak{F} = \{M, N\}$ agrees along α. By proposition 10.3.13 there is a Böhm transformation π which is α-$\mathfrak{F}$-faithful; that is $M^\pi \not\sim N^\pi$ and M^π is solvable. But then by lemma 10.4.1 (ii) for some π' one has

$$M^{\pi'} \text{ solvable} \quad \text{and} \quad N^{\pi'} \text{ unsolvable.}$$

Therefore

$$C_{\pi'}[M] \text{ solvable} \quad \text{and} \quad C_{\pi'}[N] \text{ unsolvable},$$

by lemma 10.3.4. □

Now we are able to prove the characterization theorem for D_∞ of Hyland and Wadsworth.

19.2.9. CHARACTERIZATION THEOREM FOR D_∞. *Let $M, N \in \Lambda$. Then for each cpo D*

(i) $D_\infty \models M \sqsubseteq N \Leftrightarrow \forall C[\;\;]\,[C[M] \text{ solvable} \rightarrow C[N] \text{ solvable}]$
$\Leftrightarrow \mathrm{BT}(M)^\eta \subseteq^\eta \mathrm{BT}(N)$

(ii) $D_\infty \models M = N \Leftrightarrow \mathcal{H}^* \vdash M = N$
$\Leftrightarrow \mathrm{BT}(M) =_\eta \mathrm{BT}(N)$.

PROOF. (i) By corollary 19.2.5 and propositions 19.2.7, 19.2.8.

(ii) By (i) one has

$$\begin{aligned} D_\infty \models M = N &\Leftrightarrow \forall C[\;\;][C[M] \text{ solvable} \Leftrightarrow C[N] \text{ solvable}] \\ &\Leftrightarrow \mathcal{H}^* \vdash M = N \quad \text{by lemma 16.2.2,} \\ &\Leftrightarrow \mathrm{BT}(M)^\eta \subseteq^\eta \mathrm{BT}(N)^\eta \subseteq^\eta \mathrm{BT}(M) \\ &\Leftrightarrow \mathrm{BT}(M) =_\eta \mathrm{BT}(N), \end{aligned}$$

by definition of $=_\eta$. □

In terms of Böhm like trees the characterization theorem can be put this way. Remember that for $A \in \mathfrak{B}$ the tree $\infty\eta A$ is its infinite η-nf; see proposition 10.2.15. It is not necessarily the case that $\infty\eta\mathrm{BT}(M) \in \mathfrak{B}\Lambda$.

19.2.10. COROLLARY.

$$D_\infty \models M = N \Leftrightarrow \infty\eta\mathrm{BT}(M) = \infty\eta\mathrm{BT}(N).$$

PROOF. By theorem 10.2.31. □

A corresponding statement for $\sqsubseteq$ is not true; see exercise 19.4.8.

From the characterization theorem it follows that $D_\infty \models \mathsf{I} = J$, with $J = \mathbf{\Theta}(\lambda jxy.x(jy))$; see example 10.2.9. This valid equation was found by Wadsworth [1971], using an ad hoc computation.

The following consequence of the proof of the characterization theorem had been noticed by Wadsworth [1976] and Nakajima [1975].

19.2.14. COROLLARY. *$D_\infty \models \omega$, i.e. let $M, N \in \Lambda$, then*

$$[\forall Z \in \Lambda^0 \; D_\infty \models MZ = NZ] \Rightarrow D_\infty \models M = N.$$

PROOF. Let $M, N \in \Lambda^0$. Reason in D_∞. Suppose $\forall Z \in \Lambda^0 \; MZ = NZ$ but $M \neq N$, say $M \not\sqsubseteq N$. Then by the theorem

$$\exists C[\;\;] \quad C[M] \text{ solvable, } C[N] \text{ unsolvable.}$$

This statement is proved by the Böhm out technique. Since M, N are closed one therefore has (see lemma 10.3.4 (ii)):

$$C[M] = MP_1 \cdots P_m \text{ is solvable,}$$

$$C[N] = NP_1 \cdots P_m \text{ is unsolvable.}$$

Without loss of generality one may assume that the $\vec{P}$ are closed (otherwise substitute something in them). By assumption $M\vec{P} = N\vec{P}$, hence

$$\bot \neq M\vec{P} = N\vec{P} = \bot,$$

by theorem 19.2.4 (i), a contradiction.

We have shown now that $D_\infty \models \omega^0$. By proposition 5.3.20 it follows that $D_\infty \models \omega$. □

In exercise 19.4.6 it is shown that $D_\infty \not\models \omega$-ax.

In view of the characterization theorems for $P\omega$ and D_∞ one may wonder whether there is a cpo λ-model $\mathfrak{M}$ such that

$$\mathfrak{M} \models M \sqsubseteq N \Leftrightarrow \mathrm{BT}(M) \subseteq \mathrm{BT}(N).$$

This is the case for Plotkin's model $\mathbb{T}^\omega$; see Barendregt and Longo [1980].

19.3. Continuous λ-models

The approximation theorem is an important feature of $P\omega$ and D_∞. Welch [1975] therefore introduced the notion of a "continuous semantics," which is essentially as follows.

19.3.1. DEFINITION. A *continuous λ-model* is a structure $\mathfrak{M} = (X, \cdot, \sqsubseteq)$ such that

(1) $\mathfrak{M} = (X, \sqsubseteq)$ is a cpo.

(2) $\mathfrak{M} = (X, \cdot)$ is a λ-model in which the operation $\cdot$ is continuous (w.r.t. the Scott topology induced by $\sqsubseteq$).

(3) For $M \in \Lambda$ the set $\{M^{[n]} | n \in \mathbb{N}\}$ is directed and in $\mathfrak{M}$ one has $M = \bigsqcup_n M^{[n]}$. Here $\bigsqcup$ is the supremum operator in $\mathfrak{M}$ and the constants $\perp$ in $M^{[n]}$ are to be interpreted as the least element of $\mathfrak{M}$.

By (2) it follows that in a continuous λ-model all representable functions are continuous.

19.3.2. FACT. $P\omega$, D_∞ and $\mathfrak{B}$ are continuous λ-models.

PROOF. For $P\omega$, D_∞ properties (1) and (2) are the main theorem in § 18.1, 18.2. Property (3) is the approximation theorem for these models (corollaries 19.1.9, 19.2.3). For $\mathfrak{B}$ properties (1), (2) and (3) are the main theorems of § 18.3. Property (2) is the nontrivial one and expresses the continuity of Böhm tree application. □

It is not required that in a continuous λ-model all continuous functions are representable. In fact this is not the case for $\mathfrak{B}$; see exercise 18.4.24.

19.3.3. PROPOSITION. *Let $\mathfrak{M}$ be a continuous λ-model and $M, N \in \Lambda$. Then*

$$\mathrm{BT}(M) = \mathrm{BT}(N) \Rightarrow \mathfrak{M} \models M = N.$$

In particular $\mathfrak{M}$ is sensible.

PROOF. Immediate since the $M^{[n]}$ are the truncated Böhm trees. □

Remember that $Y \in \Lambda$ is a fixed point combinator iff $\forall F \in \Lambda\ YF = F(YF)$. For $f \in \mathfrak{M}$ define $Y^*(f) = \bigsqcup_n f^n(\perp)$. Then Y^* is the least fixed point operator, see theorem 1.2.17.

The following theorem of Welch [1975] smoothly generalizes results of Morris [1968] and Park [1976]. The original proofs require some computations, see exercise 18.4.20.

19.3.4. THEOREM. *Let $\mathfrak{M}$ be a continuous λ-model. All fixed point operators in Λ are equal in $\mathfrak{M}$ and represent the least fixed point combinator Y^*.*

PROOF. Suppose $Y \in \Lambda$ is a fixed point combinator. Then

$$Yf = f(Yf).$$

As in the proof of lemma 6.5.3 it follows that

$$Y = \lambda f.Yf = \lambda f.f(Yf).$$

Hence BT(Y) is

$$\begin{array}{c}\lambda f.f\\ |\\ f\\ |\\ \vdots\end{array}$$

By the previous proposition it now follows that all fixed point combinators are equal in $\mathfrak{M}$. Moreover for $f \in \mathfrak{M}$ one has in $\mathfrak{M}$

$$Yf = (\bigsqcup_n Y^{[n]})f = \bigsqcup_n (Y^{[n]}f) = \bigsqcup_n f^n(\bot) = Y^*(f).$$

Hence Y represents Y^*. □

In general a continuous map $\varphi : \mathfrak{M} \to \mathfrak{M}$ is not representable. The theorem says that $Y^* \in [\mathfrak{M} \to \mathfrak{M}]$ is even definable.

19.3.5. Corollary (Morris [1968]). *Let $Y \in \Lambda$ be a fixed point combinator. Then*

$$\forall F, M \in \Lambda \left[FM = M \Rightarrow YF \underset{\sim}{\sqsubset} M \right],$$

i.e. YF is the $\underset{\sim}{\sqsubset}$-least fixed point of F.

Proof. Take $\mathfrak{M} = \mathfrak{B}$ in the theorem. □

See exercise 16.5.5 for the original version of Morris' theorem.

19.3.6. Corollary (Park [1976]). *Let $\mathfrak{M}$ be $P\omega$ or D_∞. Let $Y_{\text{Tarski}} \in \mathfrak{M}$ be the element representing the least fixed point operator Y^*. Let Y_{Curry} be the image in $\mathfrak{M}$ of a fixed point combinator $\in \Lambda$. Then*

$$Y_{\text{Curry}} = Y_{\text{Tarski}}.$$

Proof. (For $P\omega$; for D_∞ the proof is easier.) By the theorem

$$\forall f \quad Y_{\text{Tarski}} f = Y^*(f) = Y_{\text{Curry}} f$$

hence by weak extensionality

$$\lambda f.Y_{\text{Curry}} f = \lambda f.Y_{\text{Tarski}} f$$

and therefore

$$Y_{\mathrm{Curry}} = Y_{\mathrm{Tarski}}$$

(Note that for Y equal Y_{Curry} or Y_{Tarski} one has $Y = \lambda f.Yf$: for the first one this is because $Y = \lambda f.f(Yf)$; for the second because $Y = \mathrm{graph}(Y^*)$.) □

19.4. Exercises

19.4.1. For $M \in \Lambda^0$ show directly

$$M \text{ unsolvable} \Rightarrow M = \emptyset \text{ in } P\omega.$$

19.4.2 (Wadsworth). Let $J = \boldsymbol{\Theta}(\lambda jxy.x(jy))$. Show that $D_\infty \models \mathbf{I} = J$. Conclude that for no subset $E \subseteq D_\infty$ one has for $M \in \Lambda^0$

$$[\![M]\!]^{D_\infty} \in E \Leftrightarrow M \text{ has a nf.}$$

19.4.3 (Wadsworth). (i) Let $M \in \Lambda^0$ be solvable. Show that there is a sequence $M_n \in \Lambda^0$ such that in D_∞ (1) $M_0 \sqsubseteq M_1 \sqsubseteq \cdots$; (2) $M = \bigsqcup_n M_n$; (3) $\forall n\, M \neq M_n$.
[*Hint*. Let N be an infinite η-expansion of M. Take $M_n = N^{(n)}$.]

(ii) Let $M, N \in \Lambda^0$. Suppose $D_\infty \models \bot \neq M \sqsubseteq N$. Show that there exists a sequence $N_n \in \Lambda^0$ such that in D_∞ one has:

$$(1) \quad N_0 \sqsubseteq N_1 \sqsubseteq \cdots; \quad (2)\ N = \sqcup_n N_n; \quad (3)\ \forall n\, M \not\sqsubseteq N_n.$$

(iii) Show that for $M, N \in \Lambda^0$ one has in D_∞

$$M \ll N \Rightarrow M = \bot.$$

Conclude that D_∞^0 is never a continuous lattice.

19.4.4 (Nakajima [1975]). Define the Nakajima tree for $M \in \Lambda$, a labelled tree which is infinitely branching, as follows.

$$\mathrm{NT}(M) = \bot \quad \text{if } M \text{ is unsolvable,}$$

$$\mathrm{NT}(M) = \lambda \vec{x} z_0 z_1 \cdots .y \quad \text{if } M \text{ has hnf } \lambda \vec{x}.yM_1 \cdots M_m.$$

$$\mathrm{NT}(M_1) \cdots \mathrm{NT}(M_m)\ \mathrm{NT}(z_0)\ \mathrm{NT}(z_1) \cdots$$

where $z_0, z_1, \ldots$ is an infinite list of fresh variables. $\mathrm{NT}(M)$ is, so to speak, the maximal infinite η-expansion of $\mathrm{BT}(M)$. As with λ-terms and Böhm trees, Nakajima trees are considered modulo a change of bound variables.
Define $\subseteq$ as for Böhm trees. Show

(i) $D_\infty \models M \sqsubseteq N \Leftrightarrow \mathrm{NT}(M) \subseteq \mathrm{NT}(N)$,
(ii) $D_\infty \models M = N \Leftrightarrow \mathrm{NT}(M) = \mathrm{NT}(N)$.

19.4.5. Show that $\bot$ is the only definable element of D_∞ in D_0. [*Hint*. Use exercise 18.4.18.]

19.4.6. (i) Show $D_\infty \nvDash \omega$-ax, i.e. for $M, N \in \Lambda$ in general *not*

$$D_\infty \vDash \Big[\bigwedge\!\!\!\bigwedge_{Z \in \Lambda^0} MZ = NZ \Big] \rightarrow M = N.$$

[*Hint*. Consider $x = \lambda z.(z_0)$ and $y = \lambda z.\bot$.]

19.4.7 (Baeten, Boerboom). The model $(P\omega, \cdot)$ depends on the coding (n, m) of pairs and e_k of finite sets. Let $C : \mathbb{N}^2 \rightarrow \mathbb{N}$ be an arbitrary bijection.

(i) Show that using C as pairing and the same e_k's one can define a graph model $P\omega_C$. Let $[\![M]\!]_C$ be the value of a closed term in $P\omega_C$.

(ii) Show

$$a \in [\![\Omega]\!]_C \Rightarrow \exists k \;\; C(k, a) \in e_k,$$

$$e_k = \{C(k, a)\} \Rightarrow a \in [\![\Omega]\!]_C.$$

(iii) Show that for all $x \in P\omega$ there is a pairing C such that in

$P\omega_C$ one has $\Omega = x$.

[Baeten en Boerboom [1979] have shown something stronger, namely

$$\forall M \in \Lambda^0 \; \exists C \quad P\omega_C \vDash \Omega = M;$$

hence $\forall M \in \Lambda^0$ Con$(\Omega = M)$. Cf. proposition 15.3.9.]

19.4.8. Show that

$$\infty\eta(\mathrm{BT}(M)) \subseteq \infty\eta(\mathrm{BT}(N)) \Rightarrow D_\infty \vDash M \sqsubseteq N,$$

but not conversely.

19.4.9. (i) Show that $[\![M]\!]^{P\omega}$ for $M \in \Lambda^0$ is always recursively enumerable.

(ii) (Giannini–Longo [1983]). Show that for closed terms M having a normal form $[\![M]\!]^{P\omega}$ is recursive.

(iii) Construct a closed term M such that $[\![M]\!]^{P\omega}$ is not recursive.

19.4.10. (i) (Barendregt–Longo [1983]). For $A = (x, y) \in P\omega^2$, write $A_- = x$, $A_+ = y$. Let $E_n = (e_{(n)_0}, e_{(n)_1})$ be an enumeration of the finite elements of $P\omega^2$. For $A, B \in P\omega^2$ let $A \subseteq B \Leftrightarrow A_- \subseteq B_-$ and $A_+ \subseteq B_+$. For $A \in P\omega^2$ and Scott continuous $f: P\omega^2 \rightarrow P\omega^2$, define

$$F(A) = \lambda\!\!\lambda B \in P\omega^2.\, AB,$$

where

$$AB = (\{m \mid \exists E_n \in B\; (n, m) \in A_-\}, \{m \mid \exists E_n \in B\; (n, m) \in A_+\});$$

$$G(f) = (\{(n, m) \mid m \in f(E_n)_-\}, \{(n, m) \mid m \in f(E_n)_+\}).$$

Show that F, G make $P\omega^2$ into a λ-model.

(ii) (Scott). Show that there is a pairing $C: \omega^2 \rightarrow \omega$, such that $P\omega_C \cong P\omega^2$, see exercise 19.4.7. [*Hint*. Define

$$C(n, 2m) = 2(n, m), \quad \text{where } (n, m) \text{ is the usual coding of pairs;}$$

$$C(n, 2m+1) = 2(n, m) + 1;$$

$$\phi(x) = (\{n \mid 2n \in x\}, \{n \mid 2n+1 \in x\})].$$

CHAPTER 20

GLOBAL STRUCTURE OF MODELS

The global structure of a λ-algebra $\mathfrak{M}$ consists of properties true in $\mathfrak{M}$ other than equations. Some of these properties are treated in this chapter.

20.1. Extensionality; categoricity

Several results on extensionality of term models are corollaries of proof theoretic considerations in part IV. For example, one has $\mathfrak{M}^0(\mathfrak{T})$ is extensional iff $\mathfrak{M}^0(\mathfrak{T}) \models \boldsymbol{\omega}$ iff $\mathfrak{T} \vdash \boldsymbol{\omega}$. Since $\boldsymbol{\lambda\eta} \nvdash \boldsymbol{\omega}$ it follows that $\mathfrak{M}^0(\boldsymbol{\lambda\eta})$ is not (weakly) extensional. Similarly $\boldsymbol{\lambda} \nvdash \boldsymbol{tr}$ implies that $\mathfrak{M}^0(\boldsymbol{\lambda})$ is not weakly extensional.

20.1.1. THEOREM. (i) $\mathfrak{M}(\boldsymbol{\lambda\eta}) \models \boldsymbol{ext}$ and $\mathfrak{M}^0(\boldsymbol{\lambda\eta}) \not\models \boldsymbol{ext}$.
(ii) $\mathfrak{M}(\mathcal{H}\boldsymbol{\eta}) \models \boldsymbol{ext}$ *and* $\mathfrak{M}^0(\mathcal{H}\boldsymbol{\eta}) \not\models \boldsymbol{ext}$.

PROOF. (i) Immediate by corollary 5.3.25, theorem 17.3.30 and proposition 4.1.18 (iii).
(ii) Similarly using theorem 17.4.7. □

20.1.2. COROLLARY. (i) $\mathfrak{M}^0(\boldsymbol{\lambda\eta}) \not\models$ w.e.; $\mathfrak{M}^0(\boldsymbol{\lambda}) \not\models$ w.e.
(ii) $\mathfrak{M}^0(\mathcal{H}\boldsymbol{\eta}) \not\models$ w.e.; $\mathfrak{M}^0(\mathcal{H}) \not\models$ w.e.

PROOF. (i)

$$\begin{aligned}\mathfrak{M}(\boldsymbol{\lambda\eta}) \models \boldsymbol{ext} &\Rightarrow \mathfrak{M}(\boldsymbol{\lambda\eta}) \models \mathbf{1} = \mathbf{I} \quad \text{by theorem 5.2.10,}\\ &\Rightarrow \mathfrak{M}^0(\boldsymbol{\lambda\eta}) \models \mathbf{1} = \mathbf{I}\\ &\Rightarrow \mathfrak{M}^0(\boldsymbol{\lambda\eta}) \not\models \text{w.e.}\end{aligned}$$

since otherwise $\mathfrak{M}^0(\boldsymbol{\lambda\eta}) \models \boldsymbol{ext}$.
By theorem 17.3.30 (ii) one has $\boldsymbol{\lambda} \nvdash \boldsymbol{tr}$. That is

$$\exists M, N \in \Lambda^0 \quad [\forall Z \in \Lambda^0\ \boldsymbol{\lambda} \vdash MZ = NZ \text{ and } \boldsymbol{\lambda} \nvdash Mx = Nx].$$

Hence $\mathfrak{M}^0(\boldsymbol{\lambda}) \models \forall x\ Mx = Nx$ but $\mathfrak{M}^0(\boldsymbol{\lambda}) \not\models \lambda x.Mx = \lambda x.Nx$.
(ii) Similarly using theorem 17.4.7. □

20.1.3. LEMMA. (i) $P\omega^0 \models \eta$, *i.e.* $P\omega^0 \models \forall x\ x = \lambda z.xz$.
(ii) $P\omega^0 \nvDash \mathbf{1} = \mathbf{I}$.
(iii) $P\omega^0 \nvDash$ w.e.

PROOF. (i) Let $M \in \Lambda^0$. If M is solvable, then by theorem 8.3.14 M has a hnf, and so $\lambda z.Mz = M$.

If M is unsolvable, then $P\omega \models M = \emptyset$ and the statement follows from $P\omega \models \emptyset = \lambda z.\emptyset z$ by corollary 18.1.14 (ii).

(ii) By corollary 18.1.8 (i) and exercise 18.4.1 $P\omega \models$ w.e. and $P\omega \nvDash$ ***ext***. Hence by theorem 5.2.10 one has $\mathbf{1} \neq \mathbf{I}$ in $P\omega$ hence in $P\omega^0$.

(iii) By (i)

$$P\omega^0 \models \forall x\ x = \lambda y.xy.$$

By (ii)

$$P\omega^0 \nvDash \lambda x.x = \lambda xy.xy.$$

Hence $P\omega^0 \nvDash$ w.e. □

20.1.4. COROLLARY. *$P\omega$ and $P\omega^0$ both fail to be extensional, but for different reasons*:
(i) $P\omega \models$ w.e. *and* $P\omega \nvDash \eta$,
(ii) $P\omega^0 \nvDash$ w.e. *and* $P\omega^0 \models \eta$.

PROOF. Immediate. □

The situation for the D_∞ models is as follows.

20.1.5. THEOREM. *Let D be a* cpo. *Then*
(i) $D_\infty \models$ ***ext***, $D_\infty \models \omega$ *but* $D_\infty \nvDash \omega$-ax.
(ii) $D_\infty^0 \models$ ***ext***.

PROOF. (i) By theorem 18.2.14, corollary 19.2.14 and exercise 19.4.6.
(ii) By (i) and proposition 5.3.23 (iii). □

Finally some other negative results.

20.1.6. FACT. (i) In general (as one would expect)

$$\mathfrak{M}^0 \models \boldsymbol{ext} \not\Rightarrow \mathfrak{M} \models \boldsymbol{ext}.$$

(ii) There exists a hard λ-algebra $\mathfrak{M}$ such that
(1) $\mathfrak{M}$ cannot be mapped homomorphically onto an extensional λ-algebra.
(2) $\mathfrak{M}$ cannot be embedded into an extensional λ-algebra.

PROOF. Do exercises 20.6.3 and 20.6.5. □

For the typed λ-calculus the situation is different. See proposition A.1.15 in the appendix.

Now some results about the categoricity of models. Extensional λ-models (λ-algebras, combinatory algebras) are trivially categorical. The following results are taken from Longo [1983], where they are proved in a more general setting.

20.1.7. THEOREM. (i) (Bruce, Longo). *$P\omega$ is a categorical λ-model.*

(ii) *$P\omega$ is not a categorical combinatory algebra.*

PROOF. (i) Define $x \in P\omega$ to be *saturated* if $(n, m) \in x \wedge e_n \subseteq e_{n'} \to (n', m) \in x$.

Step 1. Assume x, x' are saturated and $\forall y\; xy = x'y$. Then $x = x'$.

Proof. $(n, m) \in x \Rightarrow m \in xe_n = x'e_n$

$$\Rightarrow \exists e_{n'} \subseteq e_n (n', m) \in x'$$

$$\Rightarrow (n, m) \in x', \qquad \text{by saturation.}$$

Therefore $x \subseteq x'$; hence $x = x'$ by symmetry. $\square_1$

Now let G satisfy 1,2 of theorem 5.6.8 for $P\omega$.

Step 2. (i) $a = \{(n, m)\} \Rightarrow a \subseteq G(F(a))$.

(ii) $\forall x f(x) \subseteq g(x) \Rightarrow G(f) \subseteq G(g)$.

Proof. (i) $G(F(a))e_n = ae_n = \{m\}$

$$\Rightarrow \exists e_{n'} \subseteq e_n\; (n', m) \in G(F(a))$$

$$\Rightarrow m \in G(F(a))e_{n'} = ae_{n'}$$

$$\Rightarrow n = n', \quad \text{since } \exists e_{n''} \subseteq e_{n'} (n'', m) \in a, \text{ hence } n = n'' = n',$$

$$\Rightarrow (n, m) \in G(F(a)).$$

(ii) Assume $\forall x\, f(x) \subseteq g(x)$. Note that

$$G(f) = 1_G \text{ graph } (f).$$

where graph $(f) = \{(n, m) | m \in f(e_n)\}$ is the standard graph for $P\omega$. Therefore

$$G(f) = 1_G \text{ graph } (f) \subseteq 1_G \text{ graph } (g) = G(g). \quad \square_2$$

Step 3. $G(f)$ is saturated.
Proof. Assume $(n, m) \in G(f)$ and $e_n \subseteq e_{n'}$. Then

$$\begin{aligned}(n', m) &\in G \circ F(\{(n', m)\}), &&\text{by 2(i)},\\ &\subseteq G \circ F(\{(n, m)\}), &&\text{by 2(ii)},\\ &\subseteq G \circ F(G(f)), &&\text{by 2(ii)},\\ &= G(f). \quad \square_3\end{aligned}$$

Finally, let G, G' satisfy 1,2 of theorem 5.6.8. Then

$$\begin{aligned}&G(f)(x) = f(x) = G'(f)(x)\\ \Rightarrow\ &G(f) = G'(f), \qquad \text{by steps 3 and 1},\\ \Rightarrow\ &G = G'.\end{aligned}$$

Therefore by theorem 5.6.8 (iii) $P\omega$ is a categorical λ-model.

(ii) By (ii) step 3, $k = [\![K]\!]^{P\omega}$ is saturated. Clearly $k \neq \emptyset$, say $(n, m) \in k$. Let $e_n \subsetneqq e_{n'}$. Then $(n', m) \in k$ and $k' = k - \{(n', m)\}$ acts extensionally the same as k. Hence k is not unique. $\square$

20.1.8. THEOREM. (i) *D_A is not a categorical λ-model.*
(ii) *As combinatory algebras $P\omega$ and D_A are not isomorphic.*

PROOF. (i) In D_A the map G is defined by $G(f) = \{(\beta, b) \mid b \in f(\beta)\}$. But $G'(f) = G(f) \cup A$ also works.
(ii) By (i) and theorem 20.1.7 (ii). $\square$

In Longo [1983] it is also shown that as applicative structures $P\omega$ and D_A are for countable A mutually embeddable into each other.

20.2. The range property

The results of this section are taken from Barendregt et al. [1976a].

20.2.1. DEFINITION. Let $\mathfrak{M}$ be a λ-algebra. An external map

$$\varphi : \mathfrak{M}^k \to \mathfrak{M}$$

is *representable* by $a \in \mathfrak{M}$ if $\forall \vec{b} \in \mathfrak{M}\ \varphi(\vec{b}) = a\vec{b}$. Moreover f is *definable* if φ is representable by some $F \in \mathfrak{M}^0$.

20.2.2. DEFINITION. Let $\mathfrak{M}$ be a λ-algebra.

(i) Let $\varphi : \mathfrak{M} \to \mathfrak{M}$. The *range* of φ is

$$\mathrm{Ra}(\varphi) = \{\varphi(a) | a \in \mathfrak{M}\}.$$

(ii) $\mathfrak{M}$ satisfies the *range property* if for all definable $\varphi : \mathfrak{M} \to \mathfrak{M}$ the cardinality of $\mathrm{Ra}(\varphi)$ is either 1 or $\mathrm{Card}(\mathfrak{M})$.

(iii) If $F \in \Lambda^0$, then $\mathrm{Ra}^{\mathfrak{M}}(F)$, or just $\mathrm{Ra}(F)$, denotes $\mathrm{Ra}(\varphi)$ where $\varphi : \mathfrak{M} \to \mathfrak{M}$ is the function defined by F.

First it will be shown that the range property holds in open term models. Remember that if $\mathfrak{T}$ is a λ-theory, then $x \in_{\mathfrak{T}} M$ iff $\forall N[N =_{\mathfrak{T}} M \Rightarrow x \in \mathrm{FV}(N)]$.

20.2.3. LEMMA. *Let $F \in \Lambda^0$ and $x \in_{\mathfrak{T}} Fx$. Then $y \in_{\mathfrak{T}} Fy$ for all variables y.*

PROOF. Suppose $y \notin_{\mathfrak{T}} Fy$, i.e. $\mathfrak{T} \vdash Fy = M$ and $y \notin \mathrm{FV}(M)$. We may suppose that $x \notin \mathrm{FV}(M)$. [Let $M' \equiv M[x := \mathbf{I}]$. Then by proposition 4.1.3 $\mathfrak{T} \vdash Fy = M'$ and moreover $y \notin \mathrm{FV}(M')$, $x \notin \mathrm{FV}(M')$.] Now

$$\mathfrak{T} \vdash Fx = Fy[y := x] = M[y := x] = M.$$

Since $x \notin \mathrm{FV}(M)$, this contradicts $x \in_{\mathfrak{T}} Fx$. □

20.2.4. PROPOSITION. *Let $\mathfrak{T}$ be a λ-theory. Then $\mathfrak{M}(\mathfrak{T})$ satisfies the range property.*

PROOF. Let $F \in \Lambda^0$. Consider Fx for some variable x.

Case 1. $x \notin_{\mathfrak{T}} Fx$. *Claim*. $\mathrm{Ra}(F)$ is a singleton. Indeed, let $\mathfrak{T} \vdash Fx = M$ with $x \notin \mathrm{FV}(M)$. Then by proposition 4.1.3

$$\mathfrak{T} \vdash FZ = M \quad \text{for all } Z \in \Lambda.$$

Hence F is constant.

Case 2. $x \in_{\mathfrak{T}} Fx$. *Claim*. $\mathrm{Ra}(F)$ is infinite. Indeed, by lemma 20.2.3 one has $y \in_{\mathfrak{T}} Fy$ for all variables y. But then $\mathfrak{T} \nvdash Fy = Fy'$ for $y \not\equiv y'$, for otherwise $y \in \mathrm{FV}(Fy')$. Therefore range F contains the infinite set

$$\{Fx | x \text{ is a variable}\}. \quad \square$$

Now we restate the range theorem 17.1.16 with its original proof (not mentioning topologies).

20.2.5. THEOREM. *Let $\mathfrak{T}$ be an* r.e. *λ-theory. Then $\mathfrak{M}^0(\mathfrak{T})$ satisfies the range property.*

PROOF. Let $F \in \Lambda^0$. Suppose in $\mathfrak{M}^0(\mathcal{T})$

$$\mathrm{Ra}(F) = \{M_1, \ldots, M_n\}, \quad n > 1.$$

Define

$$\Lambda_i^0 = \{M \in \Lambda^0 \mid FM = M_i \text{ in } \mathfrak{M}^0(\mathcal{T})\}, \quad 1 \leqslant i \leqslant n.$$

Then Λ^0 is the disjoint union of the Λ_i^0. Moreover each Λ_i^0 is r.e. ($M \in \Lambda_i^0$ iff $\mathcal{T} \vdash FM = M_i$). But then

$$\Lambda^0 - \Lambda_1^0 = \Lambda_2^0 \cup \cdots \cup \Lambda_n^0$$

is also r.e., hence Λ_1^0 is recursive. As Λ_1^0 is clearly closed under equality this contradicts Scott's theorem 6.6.2. It follows that Ra(F) is infinite. Since Card ($\mathfrak{M}^0(\mathcal{T})$) = $\aleph_0$, we are done. □

The theorem applies e.g. to $\mathfrak{M}^0(\boldsymbol{\lambda})$ and $\mathfrak{M}^0(\boldsymbol{\lambda\eta})$.
The next result is due to Wadsworth.

20.2.6. THEOREM. *Let $\mathfrak{M}$ be a continuous λ-model. Then $\mathfrak{M}$ and $\mathfrak{M}^0$ satisfy the range property.*

PROOF. Let $f : \mathfrak{M} \to \mathfrak{M}$ be definable by $F \in \Lambda^0$. Consider BT(Fx).

Case 1. $x \notin \mathrm{BT}(Fx)$. Then $\mathrm{BT}(Fx) = \mathrm{BT}(Fy)$, hence by proposition 19.3.3 $\mathfrak{M} \models Fx = Fy$, i.e. Ra($f$) has cardinality 1.

Case 2. $x \in \mathrm{BT}(Fx)$. Then by corollary 10.3.9 for some $\vec{P}, \vec{Q} \in \Lambda$

$$Fx\vec{P} = x\vec{Q}.$$

Since $a\vec{Q}$ can take arbitrary values in $\mathfrak{M}$ when a ranges over $\mathfrak{M}$, it follows that Ra(f) has cardinality Card($\mathfrak{M}$).

The proof for $\mathfrak{M}^0$ is the same. □

In the formulation of the range property it is essential that $\varphi : \mathfrak{M} \to \mathfrak{M}$ is definable, not just representable.

20.2.7. PROPOSITION. *Let $\mathfrak{M} = P\omega$. Then there is a representable $\varphi : \mathfrak{M} \to \mathfrak{M}$ such that* Card(Ra(φ)) = 2.

PROOF. Define

$$\varphi(a) = \begin{cases} \mathbb{N} & \text{if } a \neq \emptyset, \\ \emptyset & \text{else.} \end{cases}$$

Then (since $\{a \in P\omega \mid a \neq \emptyset\}$ is open) φ is continuous and hence representable. Clearly Ra(φ) = $\{\emptyset, \mathbb{N}\}$. □

20.2.8. CONJECTURE. $\mathfrak{M}^0(\mathcal{H})$ *satisfies the range property*.

See exercises 20.6.9–20.6.11 for some evidence for this conjecture.

20.3. Nondefinability results

This section considers some nondefinability results for $\mathfrak{M}^0(\boldsymbol{\lambda})$ and also for $\mathfrak{M}^0(\boldsymbol{\lambda\eta})$. It is proved that there is no discriminator for closed nf's.

20.3.1. DEFINITION. Let $\mathfrak{N} \subseteq \Lambda^0$ be a set of nf's.

(i) A discriminator for $\mathfrak{N}$ is a function $\delta_{\mathfrak{N}}: \mathfrak{M}^0(\boldsymbol{\lambda}) \to \mathfrak{M}^0(\boldsymbol{\lambda})$ such that for all $M_1, M_2 \in \mathfrak{N}$

$$\delta_{\mathfrak{N}}(M_1, M_2) = \begin{cases} \mathsf{T} & \text{if } M_1 \equiv M_2, \\ \mathsf{F} & \text{else.} \end{cases}$$

(ii) Church's δ is $\delta_{\mathfrak{N}}$ where $\mathfrak{N}$ is the set of all closed nf's.

By the generalized Böhm theorem it follows that for each finite $\mathfrak{N} \subseteq \{M \in \Lambda^0 | M$ in $\beta\eta$-nf$\}$, $\delta_{\mathfrak{N}}$ is definable. It will be shown below that Church's δ is not definable (not even $\delta_{\mathfrak{N}}$ with $\mathfrak{N} = \{M \in \Lambda^0 | M$ in $\beta\eta$-nf$\}$). For a different proof of the following lemma see exercise 15.4.9.

20.3.2. LEMMA. *Let* $\boldsymbol{0} = \mathsf{I}$, $\boldsymbol{n+1} = \mathsf{K}\boldsymbol{n}$. *Then* $\boldsymbol{0}, \boldsymbol{1}, \ldots$ *is not an adequate system of numerals.*

PROOF. It will be shown that the function sg is not λ-definable, i.e. for no $F \in \Lambda^0$

$$(1) \qquad F\boldsymbol{n} = \begin{cases} \boldsymbol{0} & \text{if } n = 0, \\ \boldsymbol{1} & \text{if } n > 0. \end{cases}$$

Indeed if F satisfies (1), then F is not constant, hence by corollary 10.3.9 and exercise 10.6.13 for some $\vec{P}, \vec{Q} \in \Lambda$

$$Fx\vec{P} = xQ_1 \cdots Q_q.$$

But then for all $n \geqslant q+1$

$$\boldsymbol{1}\vec{P} = F\boldsymbol{n}\vec{P} = \boldsymbol{n}\vec{Q} = \boldsymbol{n-q},$$

i.e. $\boldsymbol{n} = \boldsymbol{m}$ for sufficiently large n, m contradicting the fact that the $\boldsymbol{n}$ are different nf's and hence not convertible. □

The following corollary is due independently to Wadsworth and the author.

20.3.3. COROLLARY. *Church's δ is not λ-definable.*

PROOF. If $\delta \in \Lambda$ satisfies for all nf's $M, N \in \Lambda^0$

$$\delta MN = \begin{cases} \mathbf{T} & \text{if } M \equiv N, \\ \mathbf{F} & \text{if } M \not\equiv N, \end{cases}$$

then $\lambda x.\delta x\mathbf{0}\mathbf{0}\mathbf{1}$ would represent the function sg w.r.t. the numerals $\mathbf{0}, \mathbf{1}, \ldots,$ a contradiction. □

See section 15.3, where it is shown that Church's δ can be added to $\boldsymbol{\lambda}$ consistently. It is also shown that if the axioms for δ are not formulated carefully, then the resulting system is inconsistent.

20.3.4. PROPOSITION. *Let $\mathfrak{T}$ be an* r.e. *λ-theory and let $\mathbf{0}, \mathbf{1}, \ldots$ be some adequate set of numerals. Let $\varphi : \mathfrak{M}^0(\mathfrak{T}) \rightarrow \mathfrak{M}^0(\mathfrak{T})$ be the characteristic function of $\{\mathbf{n} | n \in \mathbb{N}\}$, i.e.*

$$\varphi(M) = \begin{cases} \mathbf{T} & \textit{if } M = \mathbf{n} \textit{ for some } \mathbf{n}, \\ \mathbf{F} & \textit{else}. \end{cases}$$

Then φ is not definable in $\mathfrak{M}^0(\mathfrak{T})$.

PROOF. By the range theorem 20.2.5. □

In exercises 20.6.13 and 20.6.14 this is sharpened to the following. There is no $F \in \Lambda^0$ such that for $M \in \Lambda^0$

FM has a nf	if $M = \mathbf{n}$ for some $\mathbf{n}$,
FM has no nf	else

or

FM is solvable	if $M = \mathbf{n}$ for some $\mathbf{n}$,
FM is unsolvable	else.

20.4. Local vs. global representability

The results of this section are taken from Barendregt et al. [1978]. The introduction of the following concepts was inspired by notions in Volken [1978]. See addendum 3 at the end of the book.

20.4.1. DEFINITION. (i) Let $\varphi : \mathfrak{M} \rightarrow \mathfrak{M}$. Then φ is called *locally representable* if for each $b \in \mathfrak{M}$ the function $\psi_b : \mathfrak{M} \rightarrow \mathfrak{M}$ defined by

$$\psi_b(a) = \varphi(a).b$$

is representable. That is, for some element $\psi(b) \in \mathfrak{M}$ one has for all $a \in \mathfrak{M}$

(1) $\varphi(a).b = \psi(b).a.$

If (1) holds for all $a, b \in \mathfrak{M}$, then ψ is called a *dual* to φ.

(ii) $\mathfrak{M}$ is called *rich* if all locally representable functions $\varphi : \mathfrak{M} \to \mathfrak{M}$ are representable.

20.4.2. LEMMA. *Let* $\varphi : \mathfrak{M} \to \mathfrak{M}$.

(i) φ *is locally representable iff* φ *has a dual* ψ.

(ii) *If* φ *is representable, then* φ *has a dual which is also representable.*

(iii) *Let* $\mathfrak{M} \vDash$ **ext**. *Then* φ *has at most one dual.*

PROOF. (i) ($\Leftarrow$) Trivial. ($\Rightarrow$) By the axiom of choice.

(ii) Let $\varphi(x) = ax$ for all $x \in \mathfrak{M}$. Take $\psi(y) = \lambda x.axy$. Then for all $x, y \in \mathfrak{M}$

$$\varphi(x)y = axy = \psi(y)x.$$

Hence ψ is dual to φ and ψ is representable by $\lambda yx.axy$.

(iii) Let ψ, ψ' be both dual to φ. Then for all $x, y \in \mathfrak{M}$

$$\psi(y)x = \varphi(x)y = \psi'(y)x$$

hence by extensionality $\psi(y) = \psi'(y)$, i.e. $\psi = \psi'$. □

20.4.3. PROPOSITION. *If* $\mathfrak{M}$ *is rich, then* $\mathfrak{M}$ *is extensional.*

PROOF. Suppose $\mathfrak{M}$ is not extensional. Then there exists $c, c' \in \mathfrak{M}$ such that for all $x \in \mathfrak{M}$ $cx = c'x$ and $c \neq c'$. Define $\varphi : \psi : \mathfrak{M} \to \mathfrak{M}$ by

$$\varphi(a) = \begin{cases} c' & \text{if } a = c, \\ c & \text{else.} \end{cases}$$

and $\psi(b) = \mathbf{K}(cb)$. Then for all $a, b \in \mathfrak{M}$

$$\varphi(a)b = cb = \psi(b)a.$$

Hence ψ is dual to φ. But φ cannot be represented since it has no fixed point. □

By the results in § 20.1 it follows that e.g. $\mathfrak{M}(\boldsymbol{\lambda})$, $\mathfrak{M}^0(\boldsymbol{\lambda\eta})$, $P\omega$, $P\omega^0$ are not rich.

20.4.4. THEOREM. D_∞ *is rich.*

PROOF. Let $\varphi : D_\infty \to D_\infty$ be locally representable. Then φ has a dual ψ. In order to show that φ is representable, by theorem 19.3.15 it suffices to show that φ is continuous. Let $X \subseteq D_\infty$ be directed. Then for all $b \in D_\infty$

$$\begin{aligned}\varphi(\bigsqcup X)b &= \psi(b)\bigsqcup X \\ &= \bigsqcup_{a \in X} \psi(b)a = \bigsqcup_{a \in X} \varphi(a)b \\ &= \Big(\bigsqcup_{a \in X} \varphi(a)\Big)b = (\bigsqcup \varphi(X))b;\end{aligned}$$

therefore by extensionality of D_∞ one has $\varphi(\bigsqcup X) = \bigsqcup\varphi(X)$ for all directed $X \subseteq D_\infty$, i.e. φ is continuous. □

20.4.5. THEOREM. *If $\mathfrak{M}$ is a hard λ-algebra with $\mathfrak{M} \models \mathcal{B}$, then $\mathfrak{M}$ is not rich.*

PROOF. Let $\chi : \mathbb{N} \to \mathbb{N}$ be a map that is not representable in $\mathfrak{M}$, i.e. for no $H \in \Lambda^0$ one has

$$\forall n \in \mathbb{N} \quad \mathfrak{M} \models H \ulcorner n \urcorner = \ulcorner \chi(n) \urcorner .$$

Since hard models are countable such a χ exists. Let $A_n(x, y)$ be the term

$$x\Omega^{\sim n}\big(y\Omega^{\sim n}(\ulcorner \chi(n) \urcorner)\big).$$

Definition. A sequence of terms $\{A_n\}_n$ is *uniform* w.r.t. $\mathfrak{M}$ if for some $F \in \Lambda$

$$\forall n \in \mathbb{N} \quad \mathfrak{M} \models F \ulcorner n \urcorner = A_n .$$

In that case one can code as in definition 8.2.3 the A_n as a term $[A_n]_{n \in \mathbb{N}}$ such that

$$\forall m \in \mathbb{N} \quad \mathfrak{M} \models \boldsymbol{\pi}_m([A_n]_{n \in \mathbb{N}}) = A_m .$$

Although the sequence $\{A_n(x,y)\}_n$ is not uniform, for each $M \in \Lambda^0$ the sequence $\{A_n(M,y)\}_n$ is uniform w.r.t. $\mathfrak{M}$. This is so because $\mathfrak{M}$ is sensible, hence by lemma 17.4.4

$$\forall M \in \Lambda^0 \ \exists k \in \mathbb{N} \quad \mathfrak{M} \models M\Omega^{\sim k} = \Omega;$$

therefore in $\mathfrak{M}$ the sequence $\{A_n(M,y)\}_n$ is

$$\Big\{M\big(y(\ulcorner \chi(0) \urcorner)\big), M\Omega\big(y\Omega(\ulcorner \chi(1) \urcorner)\big), \ldots,$$
$$M\Omega^{\sim k-1}\big(y\Omega^{\sim k-1}(\ulcorner \chi(k-1) \urcorner)\big), \Omega, \Omega, \ldots\Big\}$$

and an almost constant sequence is clearly uniform. Similarly for all $N \in \Lambda^0$ the sequence $\{A_n(x, N\}_n$ is uniform w.r.t. $\mathfrak{M}$. Now let for $M, N \in \Lambda^0$

$$\varphi(M) = \lambda y.[A_n(M,y)]_n, \qquad \psi(N) = \lambda x.[A_n(x,N)]_n .$$

Since $\mathfrak{M}$ is hard, one has $\varphi, \psi : \mathfrak{M} \to \mathfrak{M}$. Note that φ and ψ are dual

$$\varphi(M)N = [A_n(M,N)]_n = \psi(N)M.$$

Therefore f is locally representable. Suppose $\mathfrak{M}$ is rich, then for some $F \in \Lambda^0$ one has in $\mathfrak{M}$

$$FMN = \varphi(M)N = [A_n(M,N)]_n .$$

But then

$$\pi_n(F(\mathbf{K}^n\mathbf{I})(\mathbf{K}^n\mathbf{I})) = \ulcorner \chi(n) \urcorner$$

and it would follow that χ were representable in $\mathfrak{M}$, a contradiction. □

It follows that e.g. D_∞^0 is not rich.

Now a condition on $\mathfrak{T}$ will be introduced which ensures that $\mathfrak{M}(\mathfrak{T})$ is rich. The notion is due to H. Lub and Visser.

20.4.6. DEFINITION. A λ-theory $\mathfrak{T}$ is *decent* if for all variables x,y and all $M \in \Lambda$

$$x \in_{\mathfrak{T}} M \Rightarrow x \in_{\mathfrak{T}} My.$$

20.4.7. LEMMA. *Let* $\mathfrak{T}$ *be decent.*

(i) *Let* x,y *be different variables. Then*

$$x \in_{\mathfrak{T}} M \Leftrightarrow x \in_{\mathfrak{T}} My.$$

(ii) *Let* φ, ψ *be dual functions on* $\mathfrak{M}(\mathfrak{T})$. *Let* $x \not\equiv y$, $x \not\equiv y'$. *Then*

$$x \in_{\mathfrak{T}} \varphi(y) \Leftrightarrow x \in_{\mathfrak{T}} \psi(y').$$

(*Of course* $\varphi(y)$ *denotes* $\varphi([y]_{\mathfrak{T}})$ *and* $x \in_{\mathfrak{T}} [M]_{\mathfrak{T}}$ *iff* $x \in_{\mathfrak{T}} M$.)

PROOF. (i) ($\Leftarrow$) Suppose $x \notin_{\mathfrak{T}} M$. Then $\exists M' =_{\mathfrak{T}} M$ $x \notin \mathrm{FV}(M')$. But then $x \notin \mathrm{FV}(M'y)$ and $M'y =_{\mathfrak{T}} My$. Hence $x \notin_{\mathfrak{T}} My$.

(ii) $x \in_{\mathfrak{T}} \varphi(y) \Leftrightarrow x \in_{\mathfrak{T}} \varphi(y)y'$ by (1)
$\Leftrightarrow x \in_{\mathfrak{T}} \psi(y')y$ by duality
$\Leftrightarrow x \in_{\mathfrak{T}} \psi(y')$ by (i). □

20.4.8. THEOREM. *Let* $\mathfrak{T}$ *be an extensional and decent λ-theory. Then* $\mathfrak{M}(\mathfrak{T})$ *is rich.*

PROOF. Let $\varphi: \mathfrak{M}(\mathfrak{T}) \to \mathfrak{M}(\mathfrak{T})$ be locally representable and let ψ be the dual of φ. *Claim*. For some variable x and for all $M \in \Lambda$ one has in $\mathfrak{T}$

(1) $\quad \varphi(x)[x:=M] = \varphi(M).$

Indeed, let v be any variable and let $x \not\equiv v$ and $x \notin_{\mathfrak{T}} \varphi(v)$. Then by lemma 20.4.7 (ii)

(2) $\quad x \not\equiv z \Rightarrow x \notin_{\mathfrak{T}} \psi(z).$

Given M, one can find a variable y such that

$$y \notin_{\mathfrak{T}} M, \varphi(M), x, \varphi(x).$$

Then

(3) $\qquad x \not\equiv y$ and $x \notin_{\sigma} \psi(y)$

by (2). Now by (3)

$$\begin{aligned}(\varphi(x)[x:=M])y &= (\varphi(x)y)[x:=M]\\ &= (\psi(y)x)[x:=M]\\ &= \psi(y)M = \varphi(M)y;\end{aligned}$$

hence (1) follows by extensionality.

By (1) it follows that

$$\varphi(M) = (\lambda x.\varphi(x))M,$$

i.e. φ is representable. □

20.4.9. LEMMA. $\boldsymbol{\lambda\eta}$ *and* $\mathcal{H}\boldsymbol{\eta}$ *are decent.*

PROOF. The proof is done for $\boldsymbol{\lambda\eta}$. For $\mathcal{H}\boldsymbol{\eta}$ the proof is similar (using the notion of reduction $\boldsymbol{\beta\Omega\eta}$).

Step 1. $x \in_{\lambda\eta} M \Leftrightarrow \forall N \in \Lambda\ [M \twoheadrightarrow_{\beta\eta} N \Rightarrow x \in \mathrm{FV}(N)]$

Proof. By the Church-Rosser theorem. $\square_1$

Step 2. Let $M' \equiv M[z:=x]$ and $M' \twoheadrightarrow_{\beta\eta} N'$. Then $\exists N\ [M \twoheadrightarrow_{\beta\eta} N$ and $N' \equiv N[z:=x]]$.

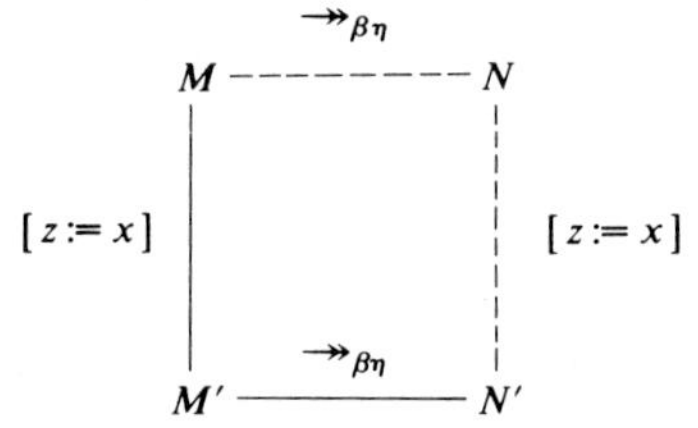

Proof. By induction on the length of reduction $M' \twoheadrightarrow N'$. $\square_2$

Step 3. $x \in_{\lambda\eta} M \Rightarrow x \in_{\lambda\eta} M[z:=y]$ for $z \not\equiv x$.

Proof. By steps 1, 2. $\square_3$

Step 4. $x \in_{\lambda\eta} \lambda y.P \Rightarrow x \in_{\lambda\eta} P$ and $x \not\equiv y$.

Proof. Clearly $x \not\equiv y$. Suppose $P =_{\beta\eta} N$. Then $\lambda y.P =_{\beta\eta} \lambda y.N$, hence by assumption $x \in \mathrm{FV}(\lambda y.N) \subseteq \mathrm{FV}(N)$. Therefore $x \in_{\lambda\eta} P$. $\square_4$

Step 5. $x \in_{\lambda\eta} M \Rightarrow x \in_{\lambda\eta} My$.

Proof. Assume $x \in_{\lambda\eta} M$ and $My \twoheadrightarrow_{\beta\eta} N$. We wish to prove $x \in \mathrm{FV}(N)$.

Case 1. $N \equiv M'y$ with $M \twoheadrightarrow_{\beta\eta} M'$. Since $x \in_{\lambda\eta} M$ also $x \in \mathrm{FV}(M') \subseteq \mathrm{FV}(N)$.

Case 2. $M \twoheadrightarrow \lambda z.M'$ and $My \twoheadrightarrow (\lambda z.M')y \to M'[z:=y] \twoheadrightarrow N$. Since $x \in_{\lambda\eta} M$, also $x \in_{\lambda\eta} \lambda z.M'$ hence $x \in_{\lambda\eta} M'$ by step 4 and $x \not\equiv z$. So $x \in_{\lambda\eta} M'[z:=y]$ by step 3 and therefore $x \in \mathrm{FV}(N)$. $\square_5$ □

20.4.10. COROLLARY. *$\mathfrak{M}(\boldsymbol{\lambda\eta})$, $\mathfrak{M}(\mathcal{H}\boldsymbol{\eta})$ are rich.*

It is open whether there are hard models that are rich. The only candidates so far are $\mathfrak{M}^0(\boldsymbol{\lambda\omega})$ and $\mathfrak{M}^0(\mathcal{H}\boldsymbol{\omega})$.

20.5. The tree topology on models

Remember how the tree topology on Λ is defined. First $\mathfrak{B} = (\mathfrak{B}, \subseteq)$ is given the Scott topology. Then Λ is given the least topology such that the map $\mathrm{BT} : \Lambda \to \mathfrak{B}$ is continuous. Similarly the tree topology on Λ^0 is defined. Obviously Λ^0 is a subspace of Λ.

For a term model $\mathfrak{M}(\mathfrak{T})$ of a λ-theory $\mathfrak{T}$ the canonical map $\varphi : \Lambda \to \mathfrak{M}(\mathfrak{T})$ is defined by $\varphi(M) = [M]_{\mathfrak{T}}$. For a λ-algebra $\mathfrak{M}$ the canonical map $\varphi : \Lambda^0 \to \mathfrak{M}^0$ is defined by $\varphi(M) = [\![M]\!]^{\mathfrak{M}}$.

20.5.1. DEFINITION. (i) Let $\mathfrak{T}$ be a λ-theory. Let $\varphi : \Lambda \to \mathfrak{M}(\mathfrak{T})$ be the canonical map. The *tree topology* on $\mathfrak{M}(\mathfrak{T})$ is the quotient of the tree topology on Λ w.r.t. the map φ, i.e. $O \subseteq \mathfrak{M}(\mathfrak{T})$ is open if $\varphi^{-1}(O) \subseteq \Lambda$ is open.

(ii) Let $\mathfrak{M}^0$ be a hard λ-algebra. Let $\varphi : \Lambda^0 \to \mathfrak{M}^0$ be the canonical map. The *tree topology* on $\mathfrak{M}^0$ is the quotient of the tree topology on Λ^0 w.r.t. the map φ.

Note that if $\mathfrak{T} \subseteq \mathfrak{T}'$ are λ-theories, then the canonical map $\varphi_{\mathfrak{T}\mathfrak{T}'} : \mathfrak{M}(\mathfrak{T}) \to \mathfrak{M}(\mathfrak{T}')$ is continuous by lemma 4.1.20.

There are two ways to define the tree topology on $\mathfrak{M}^0(\mathfrak{T})$: as a subspace of $\mathfrak{M}(\mathfrak{T})$ or as a hard λ-algebra. However both definitions coincide by the following lemma.

20.5.2. LEMMA. The tree topology on $\mathfrak{M}^0(\mathfrak{T})$ is the tree topology on $\mathfrak{M}(\mathfrak{T})$ relativized to $\mathfrak{M}^0(\mathfrak{T})$.

PROOF. This follows from the fact that topologically Λ^0 is a subspace of Λ. $\square$

20.5.3. LEMMA. (i) (Wadsworth) *In D^0_∞ the element* $\mathbf{I}$ *is not isolated* w.r.t. *either the Scott or the tree topology.*

(ii) *In $P\omega^0$ the element* $\mathbf{I}$ *is not isolated* w.r.t. *the Scott topology.*

PROOF. Suppose $\{\mathbf{I}\}$ were Scott open. Since in D_∞ one has $\mathbf{I} = J = \bigsqcup_n J^{(n)}$ (see example 10.2.9.) it would follow that $\exists n\ J^{(n)} \in \{\mathbf{I}\}$, a contradiction. Similarly one shows that $\{\mathbf{I}\}$ is not open w.r.t. the tree topology.

(ii) If $\{\mathbf{I}\}$ in $P\omega^0$ were Scott open, then since $\mathbf{I} \subseteq J$ also $J \in \{\mathbf{I}\}$; contradiction. $\square$

In $P\omega^0$ the element $\mathbf{I}$ is isolated w.r.t. the tree topology, see proposition 20.5.8.

20.5.4. PROPOSITION. (i) *Let* $\mathcal{T} = \boldsymbol{\lambda}, \boldsymbol{\lambda\eta}, \mathcal{H}, \mathcal{H}\boldsymbol{\eta}, \mathcal{B}$ *or* $\mathcal{B}\boldsymbol{\eta}$. *Then the canonical map* $\varphi : \Lambda \to \mathfrak{M}(\mathcal{T})$ *is open.*

(ii) *The canonical map* $\varphi : \Lambda^0 \to P\omega^0$ *is open (with respect to the tree topology on* $P\omega^0$*).*

(iii) *The canonical map* $\varphi : \Lambda^0 \to D_\infty^0$ *is not open (with respect to the tree topology on* D_∞^0*).*

PROOF. *Claim.* Let $\mathcal{T} = \boldsymbol{\lambda}, \boldsymbol{\lambda\eta}, \mathcal{H}, \mathcal{H}\boldsymbol{\eta}, \mathcal{B}$ or $\mathcal{B}\boldsymbol{\eta}$. Then

(1) $M =_{\mathcal{T}} M'$ and $M' \underset{\sim}{\sqsubset} N' \Rightarrow \exists N\; N =_{\mathcal{T}} N'$ and $M \underset{\sim}{\sqsubset} N$.

(2) $M =_{\mathcal{T}} M'$ and $M' = \bigsqcup_i M_i$, then

$$\exists N_i \quad N_i = M_i \quad \text{for all } i \text{ and } M = \bigsqcup_i N_i.$$

For $\mathcal{T} = \boldsymbol{\lambda}, \mathcal{H}$ or $\mathcal{B}$ this is trivial, since then

$$M =_{\mathcal{T}} N \Rightarrow \mathrm{BT}(M) = \mathrm{BT}(N).$$

If $\boldsymbol{\eta}$ is added, this is not difficult either (do exercise 20.6.16).

(i) Suppose $O \subseteq \Lambda$ is open. Then $\varphi(O) \subseteq \mathfrak{M}(\mathcal{T})$ is open iff $O' = \varphi^{-1}(\varphi(O)) \subseteq \Lambda$ is open. By (1) and (2) O' is indeed open.

(ii) Similarly.

(iii) $\{\mathbf{I}\} \subseteq \Lambda$ is open. But by the previous lemma $\{[\![\mathbf{I}]\!]^{D_\infty}\}$ is not. □

If $\mathfrak{M} = P\omega$ or D_∞ then the canonical map $\varphi : \Lambda^0 \to \mathfrak{M}^0$ is not open w.r.t. the Scott topology on $\mathfrak{M}$. Again, this is because $\mathbf{I}$ is isolated in Λ but not in $P\omega^0$ or D_∞^0.

20.5.5. COROLLARY. *Let* $\mathfrak{M} = \mathfrak{M}(\mathcal{T})$ *with* $\mathcal{T}$ *as in the previous proposition or* $\mathfrak{M} = P\omega^0$. *Then application (and hence any definable function) is continuous* w.r.t. *the tree topology.*

PROOF. Let φ be the canonical map onto $\mathfrak{M}$. Let $a_1, a_2 \in \mathfrak{M}$, say $\varphi(M_i) = a_i$. Let $a_1 a_2 \in O \subseteq \mathfrak{M}$, O open. Then $\varphi^{-1}(O) \subseteq \Lambda$ is open and contains $M_1 M_2$. Since application is continuous on Λ, theorem 14.3.22, there are open sets $O_1 \ni M_1$, $O_2 \ni M_2$ such that $O_1 O_2 \subseteq \varphi^{-1}(O)$. But then $\varphi(O_1)\varphi(O_2) \subseteq O$ and moreover by the proposition $\varphi(O_i)$ is a neighbourhood of a_i. □

20.5.6. PROPOSITION. *Let* $\mathfrak{M}$ *be a hard* λ*-algebra or a term model* $\mathfrak{M}(\mathcal{T})$ *equipped with the tree topology. Then*

$$\mathfrak{M} \textit{ is semi-sensible} \Leftrightarrow \mathfrak{M} \textit{ is not indiscrete}.$$

PROOF. The proof is given for the hard λ-algebra; for $\mathfrak{M}(\mathfrak{T})$ it is analogous. Let $\varphi : \Lambda^0 \to \mathfrak{M}$ be the canonical map.

($\Rightarrow$) Since $\mathfrak{M}$ is semi-sensible one has for $\mathrm{SOL}^0 = \{M \in \Lambda^0 \mid M \text{ solvable}\}$

$$\varphi^{-1}(\varphi(\mathrm{SOL}^0)) = \mathrm{SOL}^0.$$

Hence by example 10.2.5 $\varphi(\mathrm{SOL}^0) \subseteq \mathfrak{M}$ is open and is neither $\emptyset$ nor $\mathfrak{M}$

($\Leftarrow$) Assume $\mathfrak{M}$ is not indiscrete and not semi-sensible in order to derive a contradiction. Then

(1) $$\exists O \subseteq \mathfrak{M} \quad \emptyset \neq O \neq \mathfrak{M}, \quad O \text{ open}.$$

(2) $$\exists M \in \mathrm{SOL}^0, \exists N \in \Lambda^0 - \mathrm{SOL}^0 \quad \mathfrak{M} \models M = N.$$

By (2)

$$\exists \vec{Q} \quad M\vec{Q} = \mathbf{I}, \; N\vec{Q} \text{ unsolvable}.$$

Hence

$$\forall P \in \Lambda^0 \quad M\vec{Q}P = P, \; N\vec{Q}P \text{ unsolvable}.$$

Therefore

(3) $$\forall P \in \Lambda^0 \; \exists Q \in \Lambda^0 - \mathrm{SOL}^0 \quad \mathfrak{M} \models P = Q.$$

By (1) the set $\varphi^{-1}(O) \neq \emptyset$ is open in Λ^0. Let $P \in \varphi^{-1}(O)$. Then by (3) for some unsolvable P' one has $P' \in \varphi^{-1}(O)$. But then by lemma 10.2.11 $\varphi^{-1}(O) = \Lambda^0$ since for all $R \in \Lambda^0$ one has $P' \underset{\sim}{\sqsubseteq} R$. Hence $O = \mathfrak{M}$, a contradiction. □

A point x in a topological space X is called a *compactification point* if the only neighbourhood of x is the space X itself.

20.5.7. COROLLARY. *Let $\mathfrak{M}$ be a hard λ-algebra or a term model equipped with the tree topology. If $\mathfrak{M}$ is semi-sensible, then for a λ-term M*

$$M \textit{ is unsolvable} \Leftrightarrow M \textit{ is a compactification of } \mathfrak{M}.$$

PROOF. Suppose $\mathfrak{M}$ is a hard λ-algebra; the other case is analogous. Let $\varphi : \Lambda^0 \to \mathfrak{M}$ be the canonical map.

($\Rightarrow$) Let M be unsolvable and $\varphi(M) \in O \subseteq \mathfrak{M}$, O open. Then $M \in \varphi^{-1}(O)$, $\varphi^{-1}(O)$ open in Λ^0. Then $\varphi^{-1}(O) = \Lambda^0$ by lemma 10.2.6 and therefore $O = \mathfrak{M}$.

($\Leftarrow$) Suppose M were solvable. Then $M \in \mathrm{SOL}^0$ and

$$\varphi(M) \in \varphi(\mathrm{SOL}^0) \neq \mathfrak{M}$$

and as in the previous proof the set $\varphi(\mathrm{SOL}^0)$ is open. □

20.5.8. PROPOSITION. *Let* $\mathfrak{T} = \boldsymbol{\lambda}, \boldsymbol{\lambda\eta}, \mathcal{H}, \mathcal{H}\boldsymbol{\eta}, \mathfrak{B}$ *or* $\mathfrak{B}\boldsymbol{\eta}$. *Let* $\mathfrak{M}$ *be* $\mathfrak{M}(\mathfrak{T})$ *or* $\mathfrak{M}^0(\mathfrak{T})$, *equipped with the tree topology. Then*

$$M \text{ has a nf} \Leftrightarrow M \text{ in } \mathfrak{M} \text{ is isolated}.$$

PROOF. The following properties of $\mathfrak{M}$ are used
(1) $\mathfrak{M}$ is semi-sensible.
(2) $\mathfrak{M} \models M = N \Rightarrow \mathrm{BT}(M)$, $\mathrm{BT}(N)$ are both finite or both infinite. Clearly this is satisfied by all $\mathfrak{M}$ as described. To fix the ideas let $\mathfrak{M} = \mathfrak{M}(\mathfrak{T})$ with $\mathfrak{T}$ as above. Let $\varphi : \Lambda \to \mathfrak{M}$ be the canonical map and let $O = \varphi^{-1}(\varphi(M)) \subseteq \Lambda$.

($\Rightarrow$) Suppose M has a nf. We verify the two conditions of lemma 10.2.6 to show that O is open.

Suppose $M' \in O$, $M' \underset{\sim}{\sqsubset} N$ in order to show $N \in O$.

Claim. $\mathrm{BT}(M')$ is $\bot$-free. If not, then by the Böhm out technique one has for some context $C[\ ]$

$$C[M'] \text{ is unsolvable}, \quad C[M] \text{ is solvable},$$

(since M has a nf), contradicting (1). By the claim and $M' \underset{\sim}{\sqsubset} N$ one has $N \approx M'$. Since $\mathrm{BT}(M)$ is finite it follows by (2) that $\mathrm{BT}(N) = \mathrm{BT}(M')$ is finite, therefore $M' =_\beta N$ and hence $\mathfrak{M} \models N = M$, i.e. $N \in O$.

Suppose $M' \in O$ and $\mathrm{BT}(M') = \cup_i \mathrm{BT}(M_i)$ (directed sup), in order to show $\exists i\ M_i \in O$. Again $\mathrm{BT}(M')$ is finite, hence a compact point in $\mathfrak{B}$. Therefore for some i one has $\mathrm{BT}(M') = \mathrm{BT}(M_i)$. Again $\mathrm{BT}(M')$ is $\bot$-free, hence $M' =_\beta M_i$ and therefore $M_i \in O$.

($\Leftarrow$) Suppose M is isolated in $\mathfrak{M}$. Then $O \subseteq \Lambda$ is open. We claim:
(3) $\mathrm{BT}(M)$ is finite.
(4) $\mathrm{BT}(M)$ is $\bot$-free.

As to (3), $\mathrm{BT}(M) = \cup_n \mathrm{BT}(M^{(n)})$. Since $(M \in)\ O$ is open it follows that $\exists n\ \mathrm{BT}(M) = \mathrm{BT}(M^{(n)})$, i.e. the tree is finite. As to (4), suppose the contrary. Then $\exists M^*\ M \underset{\sim}{\sqsubset} M^*$ and $\mathrm{BT}(M^*)$ is infinite. But then $M^* \in O$, hence $\mathfrak{M} \models M = M^*$ contradicting (2) and (3).

By (3), (4) M has a finite $\bot$-free Böhm tree, i.e. a nf. □

By lemma 20.5.3 proposition 20.5.8 is false for D_∞^0.

As an application one has the following generalization of the genericity lemma 14.3.24.

20.5.9. COROLLARY. *Let $\mathfrak{M}$ be one of the models in proposition* 20.5.8. *Suppose $F \in \Lambda^0$, M is unsolvable and N has a* nf. *Then*

$$\mathfrak{M} \models FM = N \Rightarrow \mathfrak{M} \models \forall x\ Fx = N.$$

PROOF. By the proposition N is in $\mathfrak{M}$ an isolated point. Hence by the continuity of F (corollary 20.5.5) there is a neighbourhood O of M such that $F(O) = \{N\}$. But M is a compactification point by corollary 20.5.7; hence O is the whole model. □

20.6. Exercises

20.6.1. Show that, if $\mathfrak{M}$ is a hard sensible λ-algebra, then $\mathfrak{M} \models \boldsymbol{\eta}$.

20.6.2. Show $P\omega \not\models \boldsymbol{tr}$. [*Hint*. Consider $F = \lambda xz.zxx$ and $F' = \lambda xz.zx(\lambda v.xv)$.]

20.6.3. Show that in general $\mathfrak{M}^0 \models \boldsymbol{ext} \not\Rightarrow \mathfrak{M} \models \boldsymbol{ext}$.

20.6.4. Show that if $\mathfrak{T} \neq \mathfrak{T}\boldsymbol{\eta}$, then $\mathfrak{M}(\mathfrak{T})$ cannot be embedded into an extensional λ-algebra.

20.6.5. Show that there exists a λ-algebra $\mathfrak{M}$ that cannot be embedded into nor be projected on an extensional λ-algebra. [*Hint*. Use corollary 15.3.7.]

20.6.6. Let φ be a definable map on $\mathfrak{M}^0(\lambda)$, such that $\varphi(M)$ has a nf for all M. Show that φ is constant.

20.6.7. (i) (Church). Add to the λ-calculus a new constant $\boldsymbol{\delta}$ and the axioms

$$(1) \qquad \boldsymbol{\delta}MN = \mathbf{T} \quad \text{if } M \equiv N,$$
$$= \mathbf{F} \quad \text{if } M \not\equiv N$$

where M, N range over closed β-nf's not having a subterm of the form $\boldsymbol{\delta}PQ$. Show that this extension, the so-called $\lambda\delta$-calculus, is consistent.

(ii) Show that if in (1) M, N are not required to be closed terms, then the resulting system is inconsistent.

(iii) Show that there is no consistent extension $\mathfrak{T}$ of $\boldsymbol{\lambda}$ such that for some constant $\boldsymbol{\delta}$ one has for $M, N \in \Lambda^0$

$$\mathfrak{T} \vdash \boldsymbol{\delta}MN = \mathbf{T} \quad \text{if } \mathfrak{T} \vdash M = N,$$

$$\mathfrak{T} \vdash \boldsymbol{\delta}MN = \mathbf{F} \quad \text{if } \mathfrak{T} \nvdash M = N.$$

20.6.8 (de Jongh). Let $\mathfrak{M}$ satisfy the range property and let φ be a definable map on $\mathfrak{M}^k$. Show that the range of φ is either infinite or a singleton.

20.6.9. For $F \in \Lambda^0$ and $\mathfrak{M}$ a λ-algebra, define

$$F``\mathfrak{M} = \{Fa \in \mathfrak{M} \mid a \in \mathfrak{M}\}.$$

Construct terms F such that

(i) $F``\mathfrak{M}^0(\boldsymbol{\lambda})$ is infinite, but $F``\mathfrak{M}^0(\mathcal{K})$ is a singleton.

(ii) $F``\mathfrak{M}^0(\mathcal{K})$ is infinite, but $F``\mathfrak{M}^0(\mathcal{K}^*)$ is a singleton.

20.6.10. Show that there is no $F \in \Lambda^0$ such that in $\mathcal{K}$

$$FM = \begin{cases} \mathbf{I} & \text{if } M \in \Lambda^0 \text{ is solvable,} \\ \mathbf{\Omega} & \text{if } M \in \Lambda^0 \text{ is unsolvable.} \end{cases}$$

[*Hint*. Use the range property for D_∞^0].

20.6.11 (i) Let M_n be a sequence uniform in n. Construct an $F \in \Lambda^0$ such that

$$F \ulcorner n \urcorner x \twoheadrightarrow \langle F \ulcorner n+1 \urcorner (xM_n) \rangle$$

(remember $\langle P \rangle = \lambda z.zP$). Let $G = F \ulcorner 0 \urcorner$.

(ii) If $M_n \equiv \mathbf{\Omega}$ for all n, what is the cardinality of $\mathrm{Ra}(G)$ in $\mathfrak{M}^0(\mathcal{K})$?

(iii) Same question with $M_n \equiv \mathbf{I}$ for all n.

(iv) Same question with M_n is the sequence $\mathbf{\Omega}$, $\mathbf{I}$, $\mathbf{\Omega}$, $\mathbf{I}$, ...

(v) Same question with M_n is the sequence $\mathbf{\Omega}$, x, $\mathbf{\Omega}$, x, ...

(vi) Same question with M_n is the sequence $\mathbf{\Omega}$, $x\mathbf{I}\mathbf{\Omega}$, $\mathbf{\Omega}$, $x\mathbf{I}\mathbf{\Omega}^{\sim 2}$, $\mathbf{\Omega}$, $x\mathbf{I}\mathbf{\Omega}^{\sim 3}$, ...

(vii) Same question with $M_n \equiv \mathbf{E} \ulcorner n \urcorner$.

For the next exercise, see the definitions just before exercise 6.8.18. A numbered set $\gamma = (S, \nu)$ is *positive* if $\{(n, m) | \nu(n) = \nu(m)\}$ is r.e.; γ is *complete* with *special element* a if

$$\forall \psi \in \boldsymbol{P} \quad \exists f \in \boldsymbol{F} \quad [\forall x \in \mathrm{Dom}(\psi)\ \nu(f(x)) = \nu(\psi(x)) \wedge$$
$$\forall x \notin \mathrm{Dom}(\psi)\ \nu(f(x)) = a].$$

20.6.12. (i) Show that $(\mathfrak{M}^0(\boldsymbol{\lambda}), \nu_{\mathbf{E}})$ with $\nu_{\mathbf{E}}(n) = \mathbf{E} \ulcorner n \urcorner$ is a positive, precomplete numbered set.

(ii) Show that $(\mathfrak{M}^0(\mathcal{K}), \nu_{\mathbf{E}})$ is a complete numbered set with special element $\mathbf{\Omega}$.

(iii) Let γ, γ' be numbered sets with γ positive and precomplete. Let $\mu \in \mathrm{Mor}(\gamma, \gamma')$. Then the range of μ is either infinite or a singleton.

20.6.13. (i) Show that there is no $F \in \Lambda^0$ such that for all $M \in \Lambda^0$

FM has a nf	if $M = \ulcorner n \urcorner$ for some n,
FM has no nf	else.

(ii) Prove (i) for any adequate system of numerals. [*Hint*. It follows from the proof of lemma 20.3.2 that $\mathbf{K}^n\mathbf{I}$, for some n, is not in the given system.]

20.6.14. (i) Show that there is no $F \in \Lambda^0$ such that for all $M \in \Lambda^0$

FM is solvable	if $M = \ulcorner n \urcorner$ for some n,
FM is unsolvable	else.

(ii) Prove (i) for any adequate system of numerals.

20.6.15. Show that

(i) M has a finite Böhm tree $\Leftrightarrow M$ in $\mathfrak{B}$ is compact.

(ii) M has an $\perp$-free Böhm tree $\Leftrightarrow M$ in $\mathfrak{B}$ is maximal $\Leftrightarrow M$ in D_∞^0 is maximal.

(iii) $\mathbf{I}$ is not maximal in $P\omega^0$, nor in D_∞.

20.6.16. For $\mathfrak{T} = \boldsymbol{\lambda\eta}$, $\mathcal{K}\boldsymbol{\eta}$ or $\mathfrak{B}\boldsymbol{\eta}$, show the conditions (1), (2) in the proof of proposition 20.4.4.

20.6.17. (i) Show that not all continuous $\varphi: \mathfrak{M}^0(\boldsymbol{\lambda}) \to \mathfrak{M}^0(\boldsymbol{\lambda})$ are representable. [*Hint*. See the hint for exercise 18.4.24.]

(ii) Show the same for $\mathfrak{M}(\boldsymbol{\lambda})$.

20.6.18. Show that on $\mathfrak{B}^0$ the Scott and tree topologies coincide.

20.6.19. Investigate the relationship between the Scott and the tree topology on $P\omega^0$ and D_∞^0.

20.6.20. Show that $\mathfrak{M}(\mathfrak{B}\boldsymbol{\eta})$ is rich.

20.6.21. Show that $\mathfrak{M}^0(\mathcal{K}) \models$ ***ext***-rule, but $\mathfrak{M}^0(\mathcal{K}) \not\models$ ***ext***-ax.

20.6.22 (Longo [1983]). (i) Show that if $A \neq \emptyset$, then $P\omega \hookrightarrow D_A$ (as applicative structures). [*Hint*. For $n \in \omega$ write $n = (n_1, n_2, \ldots, n_k, 0) = (n_1, (n_2, \ldots (n_k, 0) \ldots))$ with $k \geqslant 0$ and $n_k \neq 0$. Similarly in the model D_A write $(\beta_1, \beta_2, \ldots, \beta_n, b)$ for $(\beta_1, (\beta_2, \ldots (\beta_n, b) \ldots))$. Let $a \in A$. Define maps

$$[\ \ ]: \omega \to D_A,$$

$$f: \{e \subseteq \omega \mid e \text{ finite}\} \to \{\beta \subseteq B \mid \beta \text{ finite}\},$$

$$h: \omega \to B,$$

as follows:

$$[0] = \{a, (\emptyset, a), (\emptyset, \emptyset, a), \ldots\},$$

$$f(\emptyset) = \emptyset,$$

$$h(0) = a,$$

$$[(n_1, \ldots, n_k, 0)] = \{(f(e_{n_1}), \ldots, f(e_{n_k}), b) \mid b \in [0]\},$$

$$f(e_n) = \{h(m_1), \ldots, h(m_q)\}, \quad \text{if } e_n = \{m_1, \ldots, m_q\},$$

$$h(n_1, \ldots, n_k, 0) = (f(e_{n_1}), \ldots, f(e_{n_k}), a).$$

Finally define $\phi: P\omega \to D_A$ by

$$\phi(x) = \{[n] \mid n \in x\}.]$$

(ii) Show that if A is countable, then $D_A \hookrightarrow P\omega$ (as applicative structures). [*Hint*. Let $A = \{a_0, a_1, a_2, \ldots\}$. Define $m: B \to \omega$ by

$$m(a_n) = (1, n),$$

$$m(\beta; b) = \left(\sum \{2^{m(b')} \mid b' \in \beta\}, m(b)\right),$$

$\psi: D_A \to P\omega$ is defined by $\psi(d) = \{m(b) \mid b \in d\}$.]

CHAPTER 21

COMBINATORY GROUPS

The operation composition $x \circ y = \lambda z.x(yz)$ is associative. With this operation every combinatory algebra $\mathfrak{M}$ becomes a semigroup. If moreover $\mathfrak{M} \models \eta$, then the semigroup has $\mathbf{I}$ as unit element. The combinatory group of $\mathfrak{M}$ consists of the invertible elements of this monoid. For several λ-algebras the structure of its combinatory group will be determined. See addendum 4 at the end of the book.

21.1 Combinatory semigroups

Given a λ-algebra $\mathfrak{M}$ with $\mathfrak{M} \models \boldsymbol{\eta}$, one can define the following semigroup and group.

21.1.1. Definition. Let $\mathfrak{M} = \langle X, \cdot \rangle$ be a λ-algebra satisfying $\boldsymbol{\eta}$.

(i) The *semigroup of* $\mathfrak{M}$ is the structure

$$S(\mathfrak{M}) = \langle X, \circ, \mathbf{I} \rangle,$$

where in $\mathfrak{M}$ one has $a \circ b = \lambda z.a(bz)$ and $\mathbf{I} = \lambda z.z$. Clearly $\circ$ is associative and $\boldsymbol{\eta}$ implies that $\mathbf{I}$ is a (two sided) unit element.

(ii) The *group of* $\mathfrak{M}$ is the subgroup of $S(\mathfrak{M})$ consisting of invertible elements:

$$G(\mathfrak{M}) = \langle \{ a \in S(\mathfrak{M}) | \exists b \in S(\mathfrak{M}) a \circ b = b \circ a = \mathbf{I} \}, \circ \rangle,$$

Clearly $G(\mathfrak{M})$ is the largest subgroup contained in $S(\mathfrak{M})$.

(iii) Let $\mathcal{T}$ be a λ-theory with $\mathcal{T} \vdash \boldsymbol{\eta}$. Then $\mathfrak{M}(\mathcal{T}) \models \boldsymbol{\eta}$ and $\mathfrak{M}^0(\mathcal{T}) \models \boldsymbol{\eta}$ and we define

$$S(\mathcal{T}) = S(\mathfrak{M}(\mathcal{T})), \qquad G(\mathcal{T}) = G(\mathfrak{M}(\mathcal{T})),$$

$$S^0(\mathcal{T}) = S(\mathfrak{M}^0(\mathcal{T})), \qquad G^0(\mathcal{T}) = G(\mathfrak{M}^0(\mathcal{T})).$$

Remark. Clearly every homomorphism $\varphi : \mathfrak{M} \to \mathfrak{M}'$ induces homomorphisms $\varphi_S : S(\mathfrak{M}) \to S(\mathfrak{M}')$ and $\varphi_G : G(\mathfrak{M}) \to G(\mathfrak{M}')$. If φ is surjective, then so is φ_S, but not necessarily φ_G. An element $\varphi_S(a) \in S(\mathfrak{M}')$ may be invertible but not $a \in S(\mathfrak{M})$.

An example is $G(\mathcal{H}^*)$ which turns out to be a proper extension (of the canonical image) of $G(\boldsymbol{\lambda\eta})$.

Following Church [1937], the structures $S(\mathfrak{M})$ are called *combinatory semigroups*, and the structures $G(\mathfrak{M})$ *combinatory groups*. For several $\mathfrak{M} \models \boldsymbol{\eta}$ the structure of $G(\mathfrak{M})$ will be determined. For all known hard $\mathfrak{M}$, $G(\mathfrak{M})$ turns out to be a decidable group. By contrast, the $S(\mathfrak{M})$ are never decidable.

21.1.2. THEOREM (Church [1937]). *$S^0(\boldsymbol{\lambda\eta})$ is a recursively presented semigroup having four generators with an unsolvable word problem.*

PROOF. Define

$$\mathbf{C}_* \equiv \lambda xy.yx, \qquad \mathbf{B} \equiv \lambda xyz.x(yz).$$

Then the following is provable in $\boldsymbol{\lambda\eta}$

(1) $\quad \mathbf{C}_*(xy) = \mathbf{C}_*y \circ \mathbf{C}_*x \circ \mathbf{B},$

(2) $\quad \mathbf{C}_*x \circ \mathbf{C}_* = x.$

Consider

$$\mathcal{X} = \{\mathbf{C}_*\mathbf{K}, \mathbf{C}_*\mathbf{S}, \mathbf{B}, \mathbf{C}_*\} \subseteq S^0(\boldsymbol{\lambda\eta}).$$

Since $\{\mathbf{K}, \mathbf{S}\}$ is a basis for Λ^0, it follows by (1) that for each $M \in S^0(\boldsymbol{\lambda\eta})$

$$\mathbf{C}_*M \in \{\mathbf{C}_*\mathbf{K}, \mathbf{C}_*\mathbf{S}, \mathbf{B}\}^+$$

(see footnote*). Hence by (2) one has $S^0(\boldsymbol{\lambda\eta}) \subseteq \mathcal{X}^+$. Therefore $S^0(\boldsymbol{\lambda\eta})$ is finitely generated.

Now a relation $A = B$ holds in $S^0(\boldsymbol{\lambda\eta})$ if it is provable in $\boldsymbol{\lambda\eta}$. Therefore $S^0(\boldsymbol{\lambda\eta})$ is recursively presented.

Conversely for $M_1, M_2 \in \Lambda^0$ one has

$$\boldsymbol{\lambda\eta} \vdash M_1 = M_2 \Leftrightarrow S^0(\boldsymbol{\lambda\eta}) \models M_1^* = M_2^*,$$

where M_i^* is M_i written in terms of the set of generators with composition (e.g. $\mathbf{KS}^* \equiv \mathbf{C}_*\mathbf{S} \circ \mathbf{C}_*\mathbf{K} \circ \mathbf{B} \circ \mathbf{C}_* = \mathbf{KS}$, by (1) and (2)). Since $\boldsymbol{\lambda\eta}$ is undecidable, theorem 6.6.6, the word problem for $S^0(\boldsymbol{\lambda\eta})$ is unsolvable. □

*$\mathcal{X}^+$ stands for the set generated by $\mathcal{X}$; see definition 8.1.1.

It is not known whether $S^0(\boldsymbol{\lambda\eta})$ can be finitely presented. However by the analogon of Higman's theorem for semigroups, see Murskii [1967], $S^0(\boldsymbol{\lambda\eta})$ can be embedded in a finitely presented semigroup.

21.1.3. COROLLARY. *Let $\mathfrak{M} \vDash \boldsymbol{\eta}$. Then $S(\mathfrak{M})$ is not decidable. Moreover, if $\mathfrak{M}$ is hard, then $S(\mathfrak{M})$ is finitely generated.*

PROOF. Given $\mathfrak{M}$, then for $M_1, M_2 \in \Lambda^0$

$$\mathfrak{M} \vDash M_1 = M_2 \Leftrightarrow S(\mathfrak{M}) \vDash M_1^* = M_2^*.$$

Since $\mathrm{Th}(\mathfrak{M})$ is undecidable, theorem 6.6.6, so is $S(\mathfrak{M})$.

If $\mathfrak{M}$ is hard, then $S(\mathfrak{M})$ is a homomorphic image of $S^0(\boldsymbol{\lambda\eta})$ and hence generated by the image of $\mathfrak{X}$. □

The following is proved by Böhm.

21.1.4. COROLLARY. *$S^0(\boldsymbol{\lambda\eta})$ can be generated by two elements. The same is true for each $S(\mathfrak{M}^0)$.*

PROOF. Note that in $\boldsymbol{\lambda\eta}$

(3) $\qquad \mathbf{B} = \mathbf{S} \circ \mathbf{K},$

(4) $\qquad \mathbf{C}_* x \circ \mathbf{K} = \mathbf{I}.$

Define $\mathbf{H} \equiv \mathbf{C}_*\mathbf{S} \circ (\mathbf{C}_*(\mathbf{K} \circ \mathbf{C}_*\mathbf{K}))$. Then

(5) $\qquad \mathbf{H} \circ \mathbf{C}_* = \mathbf{C}_*\mathbf{S} \circ (\mathbf{C}_*(\mathbf{K} \circ \mathbf{C}_*\mathbf{K})) \circ \mathbf{C}_*$

$\qquad\qquad = \mathbf{C}_*\mathbf{S} \circ \mathbf{K} \circ \mathbf{C}_*\mathbf{K}$ by (2) in theorem 21.1.2,

$\qquad\qquad = \mathbf{C}_*\mathbf{K}$ by (4).

Moreover

$$\mathbf{H} \circ \mathbf{K} = \mathbf{C}_*\mathbf{S} \circ (\mathbf{C}_*(\cdots)) \circ \mathbf{K}$$

$\qquad\qquad = \mathbf{C}_*\mathbf{S} \circ \mathbf{I}$ by (4),

$\qquad\qquad = \mathbf{C}_*\mathbf{S}.$

Hence

(6) $\qquad \mathbf{C}_*\mathbf{S} = \mathbf{H} \circ \mathbf{K}$

$\qquad\qquad = \mathbf{H} \circ \mathbf{C}_*\mathbf{K} \circ \mathbf{C}_*$ by (2),

$\qquad\qquad = \mathbf{H} \circ \mathbf{H} \circ \mathbf{C}_* \circ \mathbf{C}_*$ by (5).

Also

$$\begin{aligned}\mathbf{B} &= \mathbf{S} \circ \mathbf{K} \quad \text{by (3)},\\ &= \mathbf{C_*S} \circ \mathbf{C_*} \circ \mathbf{C_*K} \circ \mathbf{C_*} \quad \text{by (2)},\\ &= \mathbf{H}^2 \circ \mathbf{C}_*^3 \circ \mathbf{H} \circ \mathbf{C}_*^2 \quad \text{by (6), (5)}.\end{aligned}$$

Therefore

$$\{\mathbf{C_*K}, \mathbf{C_*S}, \mathbf{B}, \mathbf{C_*}\} \subseteq \{\mathbf{H}, \mathbf{C_*}\}^+$$

and hence by the proof of theorem 21.1.2 $S^0(\boldsymbol{\lambda\eta})$ is generated by $\mathbf{H}$ and $\mathbf{C_*}$.

As before it follows that $S(\mathfrak{M}^0)$ is generated by $\{[\![\mathbf{H}]\!]^{\mathfrak{M}}, [\![\mathbf{C_*}]\!]^{\mathfrak{M}}\}$. □

21.2. Characterization of invertibility

In order to investigate the structure of several combinatory groups the notion of invertibility is examined.

21.2.1. DEFINITION. Let $\mathfrak{T}$ be a λ-theory. Then $M \in \Lambda$ is *$\mathfrak{T}$-invertible* if $\exists N \in \Lambda\ \mathfrak{T} \vdash M \circ N = N \circ M = \mathbf{I}$.

In Dezani [1976] a characterization of $\boldsymbol{\lambda\eta}$-invertibility is given for terms having a nf. Bergstra and Klop [1980] show that the assumption of normality can be dropped. This is done by characterizing first the notion of $\mathcal{H}^*$-invertibility in terms of Böhm trees. We follow their treatment, which uses several ideas of Dezani.

21.2.2. DEFINITION. Let $M \in \Lambda$.

(i) M is *head free* if M has a hnf with free head variable. This free head variable is called the *free head* of M.

(ii) A *head free* (*substitution*) *instance* of M is

$$M^\bullet \equiv M[\vec{y} := \vec{N}]$$

where the $\vec{N}$ are all head free.

(iii) $M^\bullet, M^\blacksquare, \ldots$ range over head free instances of M.

21.2.3. LEMMA (i) *If M has the free head u and N has the free head v, then $M[u:=N]$ has the free head v.*

(ii) *M is head free $\Rightarrow M^\bullet$ is head free.*

PROOF. (i) Let $M = \lambda\vec{x}.u\vec{P}$, $N = \lambda\vec{y}.v\vec{Q}$. Then

$$M[u{:=}N] = \lambda\vec{x}.(\lambda\vec{y}.v\vec{Q})\vec{P} = \lambda\vec{x}\cdots.v\cdots.$$

(ii) If no substitution is made in the free head of M we are done. Otherwise use (i). □

21.2.4. LEMMA. (i) *Suppose*

$$\mathcal{H}^* \vdash \lambda z x_1 \cdots x_n.z(P_1x_1)\cdots(P_nx_n) = \mathbf{I}$$

and $x_i \notin FV(P_i)$ *for* $1 \leqslant i \leqslant n$. *Then*

$$\mathcal{H}^* \vdash P_i = \mathbf{I}, \quad 1 \leqslant i \leqslant n.$$

(ii) *Suppose*

$$\mathcal{H}^* \vdash \lambda z x_1 \cdots x_n.yQ_1 \cdots Q_m = \mathbf{I}.$$

Then $y \equiv z$, $m = n$ *and* $\mathcal{H}^* \vdash Q_i = x_i$.

PROOF. (i) By assumption and theorem 19.2.12

$$\mathbf{I} \precsim_\eta \lambda z x_1 \cdots x_n.z(P_1x_1)\cdots(P_nx_n).$$

Hence

$$\lambda z x_1 \cdots x_n.z x_1 \cdots x_n \precsim_\eta \lambda z x_1 \cdots x_n.z(P_1x_1)\cdots(P_nx_n)$$

and therefore

$$x_i \precsim_\eta P_i x_i, \quad 1 \leqslant i \leqslant n.$$

Again by theorem 19.2.12 it follows that

$$\mathcal{H}^* \vdash x_i = P_i x_i$$

hence

$$\mathcal{H}^* \vdash \mathbf{I} = \lambda x_i.x_i = \lambda x_i.P_i x_i = P_i, \quad 1 \leqslant i \leqslant n.$$

(ii) Similarly. □

21.2.5. DEFINITION. (i) $\mathcal{H}^*(M,N)$ if $\mathcal{H}^* \vdash M \circ N = N \circ M = \mathbf{I}$.

(ii) M is *of type* $\mathbf{I}$ if M has the hnf

$$\lambda z x_1 \cdots x_n.zP_1 \cdots P_m, \quad n, m \geqslant 0.$$

(iii) $\mathcal{H}^*(M,N)^\bullet$ if M,N are of type I and for some head free instances one has

$$\mathcal{H}^* \vdash M^\bullet \circ N^\bullet = N^\blacksquare \circ M^\blacksquare = \mathsf{I}.$$

21.2.6. LEMMA. $\mathcal{H}^*(M, N) \Rightarrow \mathcal{H}^*(M, N)^\bullet$.

PROOF. Suppose $\mathcal{H}^*(M,N)$. First we claim that M,N are solvable. Indeed in $\mathcal{H}^*$ one has $M \circ N = \mathsf{I}$, hence $M(N\mathsf{I}) = \mathsf{I}$. Thus M is $\mathcal{H}^*$-solvable and therefore by proposition 17.1.4 solvable; and similarly for N.

Next we claim that M,N are of type I. For by theorem 8.3.14 M has a hnf, say

$$M = \lambda x_1 \cdots x_n . v M_1 \cdots M_m .$$

If $v \not\equiv x_1$, then

$$\mathcal{H}^* \vdash \mathsf{I} = M \circ N = \lambda z . M(Nz) = \lambda z x_2 \cdots x_n . v M_1^* \cdots M_m^* .$$

contradicting lemma 21.2.4(ii). Hence $v \equiv x_1$ and M is of type I; and similarly for N.

The last condition for $\mathcal{H}^*(M, N)^\bullet$ is trivially satisfied, since $\mathcal{H}^*(M, N)$. □

21.2.7. DEFINITION. Let S_n be the permutation group on n elements and let $\pi \in S_n$. Then $\langle \pi | M_1, \ldots, M_n \rangle$ denotes

$$\lambda z x_1 \cdots x_n . z(M_1 x_{\pi 1}) \cdots (M_n x_{\pi n}).$$

21.2.8. MAIN LEMMA. *Suppose* $\mathcal{H}^*(M,N)^\bullet$. *Then for some* $n \in \mathbb{N}$, *some* π, $\sigma \in S_n$ *and some* $M_1, \ldots, M_n$, $N_1, \ldots, N_n \in \Lambda$ *one has*

(i) $M =_{\beta\eta} \langle \pi | M_1, \ldots, M_n \rangle$, $N =_{\beta\eta} \langle \sigma | N_1, \ldots, N_n \rangle$.

(ii) $\pi = \sigma^{-1}$.

(iii) $\mathcal{H}^*(M_i, N_{\pi i})^\bullet$ for $1 \leqslant i \leqslant n$.

PROOF. By assumption M,N are of type I. Hence by taking, if necessary, some η-expansions one has

$$\begin{aligned} M &=_{\beta\eta} \lambda z x_1 \cdots x_n . z P_1 \cdots P_{m_1} \\ N &=_{\beta\eta} \lambda z y_1 \cdots y_n . z Q_1 \cdots Q_{m_2} \end{aligned} \qquad (1)$$

for some n, m_1, m_2.

Claim 1. All P_i, Q_i are solvable. Moreover $n = \frac{1}{2}(m_1 + m_2)$.

Proof. Indeed, for some instances $M^\bullet$, $N^\bullet$

$$\mathcal{H}^* \vdash \mathsf{I} = M^\bullet \circ N^\bullet$$

$$= \lambda z x_1 \cdots x_n . N^\bullet z P_1^{\bullet\,\blacksquare} \cdots P_{m_1}^{\bullet\,\blacksquare}$$

(2) $$= \begin{cases} \lambda z x_1 \cdots x_n . z Q_1^{\bullet\,*} \cdots Q_{m_2}^{\bullet\,*} P_{n+1}^{\bullet\,\blacksquare} \cdots P_{m_1}^{\bullet\,\blacksquare} & \text{if } m_1 \geqslant n, \\ \lambda z x_1 \cdots x_n y_{m_1+1} \cdots y_n . z Q_1^{\bullet\,\blacktriangle} \cdots Q_{m_2}^{\bullet\,\blacktriangle} & \text{if } m_1 \leqslant n, \end{cases}$$

where

(3) $$(\ \ )^* = (\ \ )[y_1, \ldots, y_n := P_1^{\bullet\,\blacksquare}, \ldots, P_n^{\bullet\,\blacksquare}]$$

and similarly for $(\ \ )^\blacktriangle$.

Let, say, $m_1 \geqslant n$. By lemma 21.2.4 (ii) one has $n = m_2 + m_1 - n$, i.e. $n = \frac{1}{2}(m_1 + m_2)$ and

(4) $$\mathcal{H}^* \vdash Q_i^{\bullet\,*} = x_i \quad \text{for } 1 \leqslant i \leqslant m_2.$$

Hence each Q_i is ($\mathcal{H}^*$-) solvable, by lemma 8.3.3 and proposition 17.1.4. Similarly the P_i are solvable. $\square_1$

By claim 1 and theorem 8.3.14 it follows that the P_i, Q_i have a hnf, say

(5) $$\begin{aligned} P_i &= \lambda \vec{p}_i . u_i \cdots & 1 \leqslant i \leqslant m_1, \\ Q_i &= \lambda \vec{q}_i . v_i \cdots & 1 \leqslant i \leqslant m_2, \end{aligned}$$

and hence (1) becomes

(6) $$\begin{aligned} M &=_{\beta\eta} \lambda z x_1 \cdots x_n . z(\lambda \vec{p}_1 . u_1 \cdots) \cdots (\lambda \vec{p}_{m_1} . u_{m_1} \cdots), \\ N &=_{\beta\eta} \lambda z y_1 \cdots y_n . z(\lambda \vec{q}_1 . v_1 \cdots) \cdots (\lambda \vec{q}_{m_2} . v_{m_2} \cdots). \end{aligned}$$

By the variable convention one has $\{\vec{x}\} \cap \{\vec{v}\} = \{\vec{y}\} \cap \{\vec{u}\} = \emptyset$.

Claim 2. In (6) one has

(i) $\{u_1, \ldots, u_{m_1}\} \subseteq \{x_1, \ldots, x_n\}$,

(ii) $\{v_1, \ldots, v_{m_2}\} \subseteq \{y_1, \ldots, y_n\}$.

Proof. (ii) One has in $\mathcal{H}^*$ (if $m_1 \geqslant n$) for $1 \leqslant i \leqslant m_2$

(7) $$\begin{aligned} x_i &= Q_i^{\bullet\,*} \quad \text{by (4)}, \\ &= (\lambda \vec{q}_i . v_i \cdots)^\bullet [\vec{y} := \vec{P}^{\bullet\,\blacksquare}] \quad \text{by (3), (5).} \end{aligned}$$

First we show that the free head of $Q_i^\bullet$ is v_i. If not, let it be a_i; by the variable convention one has $a_i \notin \{\vec{x},\vec{y}\}$. But then by (7)

$$x_i = \lambda \vec{r}_i . a_i \cdots$$

contradicting lemma 21.2.4 (ii).

Therefore (7) becomes

$$x_i = (\lambda \vec{s}_i . v_i \cdots)[\vec{y} := \cdots].$$

Since $v_i \not\equiv x_i$, it follows that $v_i \in \{\vec{y}\}$. If $m_1 \leqslant n$ the reasoning is similar.

(ii) Similarly. $\square_2$

By claim 2 there are maps

$$\pi : \{1, \ldots, m_1\} \to \{1, \ldots, n\},$$

$$\sigma : \{1, \ldots, m_2\} \to \{1, \ldots, n\}$$

such that $u_i \equiv x_{\pi i}$, $v_i \equiv y_{\sigma i}$ for all relevant i.

Claim 3. (i) $m_1 = m_2 = n$.

(ii) $\pi \circ \sigma = \sigma \circ \pi = \mathrm{id}$ on $\{1, \ldots, n\}$. Hence π, σ are permutations and $\pi = \sigma^{-1}$.

Proof. (i), (ii). Let $\mathcal{H}^* \vdash M^\bullet \circ N^\bullet = \mathsf{I}$. By claim 2 and (6)

$$M^\bullet =_{\beta\eta} \lambda z x_1 \cdots x_n . z(\lambda \cdots . x_{\pi 1} \cdots) \cdots (\lambda \cdots . x_{\pi m_1} \cdots),$$

$$N^\bullet =_{\beta\eta} \lambda z y_1 \cdots y_n . z(\lambda \cdots . y_{\sigma 1} \cdots) \cdots (\lambda \cdots . y_{\sigma m_2} \cdots).$$

Assume $m_1 < n$. Then $m_2 > n$, by claim 1, and hence $\sigma i = \sigma j \leqslant n$, for some $i, j \leqslant m_2$. Now in $\mathcal{H}^*$

$$\begin{aligned}\mathsf{I} &= M^\bullet \circ N^\bullet \\ &= \lambda z x_1 \cdots x_n . N^\bullet z(\lambda \cdots . x_{\pi 1} \cdots) \cdots (\lambda \cdots . x_{\pi m_1} \cdots) \\ &= \lambda z x_1 \cdots x_n y_{m_1+1} \cdots y_n . z(\lambda \cdots . y^*_{\sigma 1} \cdots) \cdots (\lambda \cdots . y^*_{\sigma m_2} \cdots),\end{aligned}$$

where

$$y^*_{\sigma i} \equiv \begin{cases} x_{\pi\sigma i} & \text{if } \sigma i \leqslant m_1; \\ y_{\sigma i} & \text{else.} \end{cases}$$

By lemma 21.2.4 (ii) the sequence $x_1, \ldots, x_n, y_{m_1+1}, \ldots, y_n$ equals $y^*_{\sigma 1}, \ldots, y^*_{\sigma m_2}$, but since $\sigma i = \sigma j$ this is impossible.

Therefore $m_1 \geqslant n$. Now one has in $\mathcal{H}^*$

$$\mathbf{I} = M^{\bullet} \circ N^{\bullet}$$

$$= \lambda z x_1 \cdots x_n . z(\lambda \cdots . y^*_{\sigma 1} \cdots) \cdots$$

$$\cdots (\lambda \cdots . y^*_{\sigma m_2} \cdots)(\lambda \cdots . x_{\pi(n+1)} \cdots) \cdots (\lambda \cdots . x_{\pi m_1} \cdots),$$

where $y^*_{\sigma i} \equiv x_{\pi\sigma i}$. Hence by lemma 21.2.4 (ii) the sequence $x_1, \ldots, x_n$ equals $x_{\pi\sigma 1}, \ldots, x_{\pi\sigma m_2}, x_{\pi(n+1)}, \ldots, x_{\pi m_1}$.

It follows that $\pi\sigma i = i$ for $1 \leqslant i \leqslant m_2$.

We have proved, now assuming $\mathcal{H}^* \vdash M^{\bullet} \circ N^{\bullet} = \mathbf{I}$, that $m_1 \geqslant n$ and $\pi\sigma i = i$ for $1 \leqslant i \leqslant m_2$.

Similarly one can prove, assuming $\mathcal{H}^* \vdash N^{\blacksquare} \circ M^{\blacksquare} = \mathbf{I}$, that $m_2 \geqslant n$ and $\sigma\pi i = i$ for $1 \leqslant i \leqslant m_1$.

Since by claim (i) one has $n = \frac{1}{2}(m_1 + m_2)$, it follows that $m_1 = m_2 = n$ and that $\sigma \circ \pi = \pi \circ \sigma = \mathrm{id}$ on $\{1, \ldots, n\}$. $\square_3$

Define

$$M_i = \lambda x_{\pi i} . P_i, \qquad N_i = \lambda y_{\sigma i} . Q_i$$

for $1 \leqslant i \leqslant n$. By claim 3 it follows that $x_{\pi i}$ is the free head of P_i, hence each M_i is of type $\mathbf{I}$. Similarly for the N_i.

Claim 4. (i) $M =_{\eta} \langle \pi | M_1, \ldots, M_n \rangle$, $N =_{\eta} \langle \sigma | N_1, \ldots, N_n \rangle$.

(ii) $\mathcal{H}^*(M_i, N_{\pi i})^{\bullet}$ for $1 \leqslant i \leqslant n$.

Proof. (i)

$$\langle \pi | M_1, \ldots M_n \rangle = \lambda z x_1 \ldots x_n . z(M_1 x_{\pi 1}) \cdots (M_n x_{\pi n})$$

$$= \lambda z x_1 \ldots x_n . z P_1 \cdots P_n =_{\beta\eta} M.$$

Similarly $\langle \sigma | N_1, \ldots, N_n \rangle =_{\beta\eta} N$.

(ii) By assumption one has for some head free instances $M^{\bullet}, N^{\bullet}$

$$\mathbf{I} = M^{\bullet} \circ N^{\bullet}$$

$$= \lambda z x_1 \cdots x_n . N^{\bullet} z(M_1^{\bullet\blacksquare} x_{\pi 1}) \cdots (M_n^{\bullet\blacksquare} x_{\pi n})$$

$$= \lambda z x_1 \cdots x_n . z(N_1^{\bullet}(M_{\sigma 1}^{\bullet\blacksquare} x_{\pi\sigma 1})) \cdots (N_n^{\bullet}(M_{\sigma n}^{\bullet\blacksquare} x_{\pi\sigma n}))$$

$$= \lambda z x_1 \cdots x_n . z((N_1^{\bullet} \circ M_{\sigma 1}^{\bullet\blacksquare}) x_1) \cdots ((N_n^{\bullet} \circ M_{\sigma n}^{\bullet\blacksquare}) x_n)$$

(since $\pi \circ \sigma = \mathrm{id}$), where $X^{\blacksquare} \equiv X[z := N^{\bullet} z]$ is a head free instance. Hence by lemma 21.2.4 (i) for all i

$$\mathcal{H}^* \vdash N_i^{\bullet} \circ M_{\sigma i}^{\bullet\blacksquare} = \mathbf{I}$$

but since $\pi = \sigma^{-1}$ this is the same as

$$(8) \qquad \mathcal{H}^* \vdash N^{\bullet}_{\pi i} \circ M_i^{\bullet\blacksquare} = I.$$

Similarly it follows from $\mathcal{H}^* \vdash N^* \circ M^* = \mathbf{I}$, that

$$(9) \qquad \mathcal{H}^* \vdash M_i^* \circ N_{\pi i}^{*\blacktriangle} = I$$

for some head free instances $*$, $*\blacktriangle$. Since the M_i, N_i are of type $\mathbf{I}$ it follows that $\mathcal{H}^*(M_i, N_{\pi i})^{\bullet}$ for all i. $\square_4$

Now the statement of the main lemma follows from claims 3 and 4. $\square$

21.2.9. Definition. (i) A Böhm-like tree A is a *hereditary permutation* (notation $A \in \mathcal{HP}$) if A is of the form

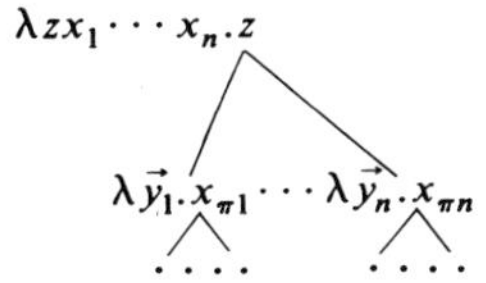

i.e. every abstracted variable occurs exactly once and except for the head variable z, every abstracted variable occurs at one level lower than the place where it is abstracted.

(ii) A is a finite *hereditary permutation* (notation $A \in \mathcal{FHP}$) if $A \in \mathcal{HP}$ and A is finite.

(iii) $\mathrm{HP} = \{M \in \Lambda \mid \mathrm{BT}(M) \in \mathcal{HP}\}$ and FHP is defined similarly.

21.2.10. Examples. (i) The following tree is in $\mathcal{FHP}$:

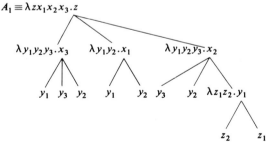

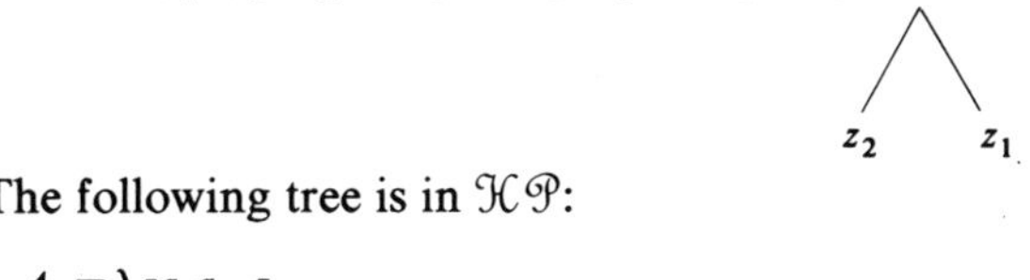

(ii) The following tree is in $\mathcal{HP}$:

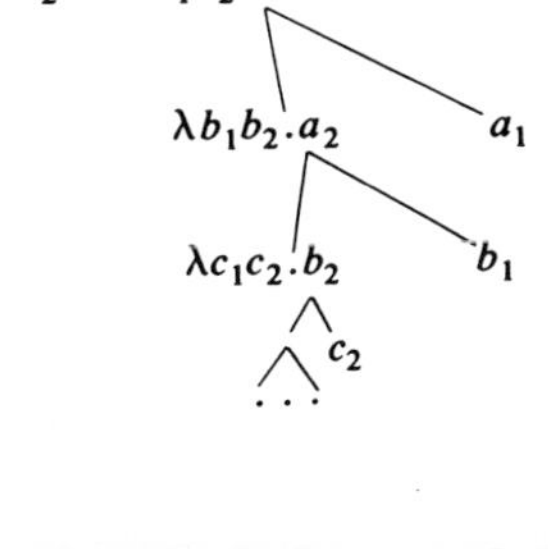

21.2.11. DEFINITION. (i) A is up to level k in $\mathcal{HP}$ (notation $A \in_k \mathcal{HP}$) if $\exists B \in \mathcal{HP}\ A =_k B$ (i.e. the trees are equal for level $<k$).

(ii) $M \in_k \mathrm{HP}$ if $\mathrm{BT}(M) \in_k \mathcal{HP}$.

EXAMPLE. Let

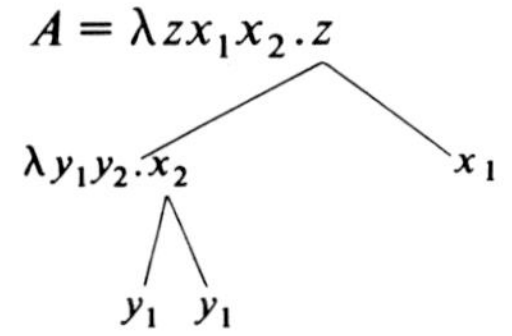

Then $A \in_2 \mathcal{HP}$ but $A \notin_3 \mathcal{HP}$.

21.2.12. LEMMA. *Let* $\pi \in S_n$. *Then*

$$M_1, \ldots, M_n \in_k \mathrm{HP} \Rightarrow \langle \pi | M_1, \ldots, M_n \rangle \in_{k+1} \mathrm{HP}.$$

PROOF. Note that

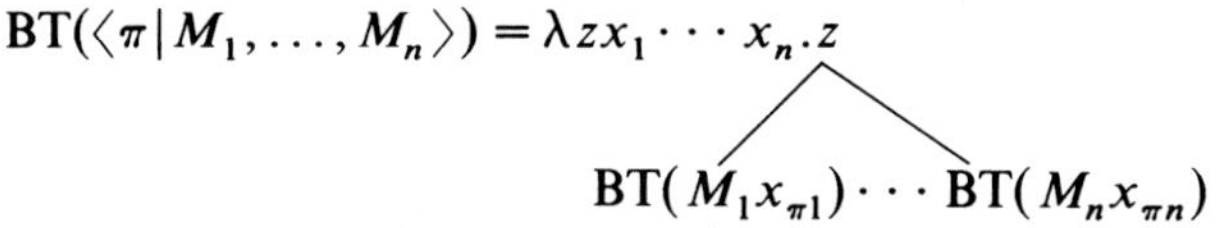

□

21.2.13. PROPOSITION. $\mathcal{H}^*(M, N) \Rightarrow M \in \mathrm{HP}$.

PROOF. By induction on k it will be shown that

(1) $\qquad \mathcal{H}^*(M, N)^\bullet \Rightarrow M \in_k \mathrm{HP}.$

The case $k=0$ is trivial since always $A =_0 B$. Let $k>0$ and suppose $\mathcal{H}^*(M, N)^\bullet$. Then by the main lemma 21.2.8 one has $M =_{\beta\eta} \langle \pi | M_1, \ldots, M_n \rangle$, $N =_{\beta\eta} \langle \sigma | N_1, \ldots, N_n \rangle$ and $\mathcal{H}^*(M_i, N_{\pi i})^\bullet$ for $1 \leqslant i \leqslant n$. Hence by the induction hypothesis $M_i \in_k$ HP for $1 \leqslant i \leqslant n$. Therefore $M \in_{k+1}$ HP by the preceding lemma.

Now one has

$$\begin{aligned} \mathcal{H}^*(M, N) &\Rightarrow \mathcal{H}^*(M, N)^\bullet \quad \text{by lemma 21.2.6,} \\ &\Rightarrow \forall k\ M \in_k \mathrm{HP} \quad \text{by (1),} \\ &\Rightarrow M \in \mathrm{HP}. \ \square \end{aligned}$$

21.2.14. LEMMA. (i) *Let* $\pi \in S_n$. *Then*

$$\langle \pi | M_1, \ldots, M_n \rangle =_{\beta\eta} \langle \pi^* | M_1, \ldots, M_n, \mathbf{I}_1, \ldots, \mathbf{I}_k \rangle,$$

where $\mathbf{I}_1 \equiv \cdots \equiv \mathbf{I}_k \equiv \mathbf{I}$ *and* $\pi^* \in S_{n+k}$ *is the extension of* π *such that* $\pi^*(n+i) = n+i$ *for* $1 \leqslant i \leqslant k$.

(ii) *Let* $\pi, \sigma \in S_n$. *Then*

$$\langle \pi | M_1, \ldots, M_n \rangle \circ \langle \sigma | N_1, \ldots, N_n \rangle = \langle \pi \circ \sigma | N_1 \circ M_{\sigma 1}, \ldots, N_n \circ M_{\sigma n} \rangle .$$

PROOF. (i)

$$\begin{aligned}
&\langle \pi | M_1, \ldots, M_n \rangle \\
&\quad = \lambda z x_1 \cdots x_n . z (M_1 x_{\pi 1}) \cdots (M_n x_{\pi n}) \\
&\quad =_{\beta\eta} \lambda z x_1 \cdots x_n x_{n+1} \cdots x_{n+k} . z (M_1 x_{\pi 1}) \cdots \\
&\qquad \cdots (M_n x_{\pi n}) x_{n+1} \cdots x_{n+k} \\
&\quad = \langle \pi^* | M_1, \ldots, M_n, \mathbf{I}, \ldots, \mathbf{I} \rangle .
\end{aligned}$$

(ii)

$$\begin{aligned}
&\langle \pi | M_1, \ldots, M_n \rangle \circ \langle \sigma | N_1, \ldots, N_n \rangle = \\
&\quad = \lambda z . \langle \pi | M_1, \ldots \rangle (\langle \sigma | N_1, \ldots \rangle z) \\
&\quad = \lambda z . (\lambda z \vec{x} . z (M_1 x_{\pi 1}) \cdots)(\langle \sigma | N_1, \ldots \rangle z) \\
&\quad = \lambda z \vec{x} . \langle \sigma | N_1, \ldots \rangle z (M_1 x_{\pi 1}) \cdots (M_n x_{\pi n}) \\
&\quad = \lambda z \vec{x} . (\lambda z \vec{y} . z (N_1 y_{\sigma 1}) \cdots) z (M_1 x_{\pi 1}) \cdots \\
&\quad = \lambda z \vec{x} . z (N_1 (M_{\sigma 1} x_{\pi \sigma 1})) \cdots (N_n (M_{\sigma n} x_{\pi \sigma n})) \\
&\quad = \langle \pi \circ \sigma | N_1 \circ M_{\sigma 1}, \ldots, N_n \circ M_{\sigma n} \rangle . \quad \square
\end{aligned}$$

The sets $\mathcal{HP}$ and HP can be determined as follows in the style of the informal definition 10.1.3 of Böhm trees.

21.2.15. REMARK. (i) Let $B_1, \ldots, B_n \in \mathfrak{B}$ and $\pi \in S_n$. Define $\langle \pi | B_1, \ldots, B_n \rangle \in \mathfrak{B}$ by

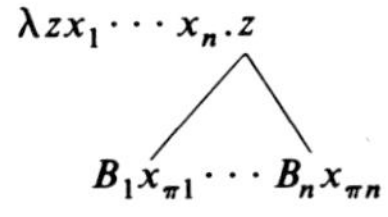

Then one has for $A \in \mathfrak{B}$

$$A \in \mathcal{HP} \Leftrightarrow \exists n \geqslant 0 \ \exists \pi \in S_n \ \exists B_1, \ldots, B_n \in \mathcal{HP} \ A = \langle \pi | B_1, \ldots, B_n \rangle .$$

(To be consistent one can put $\langle \emptyset | \ \rangle = \lambda x . x$.)

(ii) Similarly for $M \in \Lambda$

$$M \in \mathrm{HP} \Leftrightarrow \exists n \geqslant 0\ \exists \pi \in S_n\ \exists M_1, \ldots, M_n \in \mathrm{HP}\quad M = \langle \pi | M_1, \ldots, M_n \rangle.$$

Now for each tree in $\mathcal{HP}$ a "formal inverse" will be defined. The definition is informal but can be made precise in exactly the same way as the informal definition of 10.1.3 of Böhm trees is made precise in definition 10.1.4.

21.2.16. DEFINITION. (i) Let $A \in \mathcal{HP}$. The *formal inverse* of A (notation A^{-1}) is defined as follows. If $A = \langle \pi | B_1, \ldots, B_n \rangle$, then

$$A^{-1} = \langle \pi^{-1} | B^{-1}_{\pi^{-1}1}, \ldots, B^{-1}_{\pi^{-1}n} \rangle.$$

in particular

$$(\lambda x.x)^{-1} = \langle \emptyset |\ \rangle^{-1} = \langle \emptyset |\ \rangle = \lambda x.x.$$

(ii) Let $M \in \mathrm{HP}$. Then a formal inverse of M (notation M^{-1}) is a term such that

$$\mathrm{BT}(M^{-1}) = \mathrm{BT}(M)^{-1}.$$

Note that $\mathrm{BT}(M)$ and therefore $\mathrm{BT}(M)^{-1}$ is an r.e. tree without free variables. Therefore by theorem 10.1.23 such a term M^{-1} exists.

Clearly for $M = \langle \pi | M_1, \ldots, M_n \rangle \in \mathrm{HP}$ one has

$$M^{-1} = \langle \pi^{-1} | M^{-1}_{\pi^{-1}1}, \ldots, M^{-1}_{\pi^{-1}n} \rangle.$$

21.2.17. EXAMPLE. Referring to example 21.2.10 one has the following

(i) $A_1^{-1} = \lambda z x_1 x_2 x_3.$

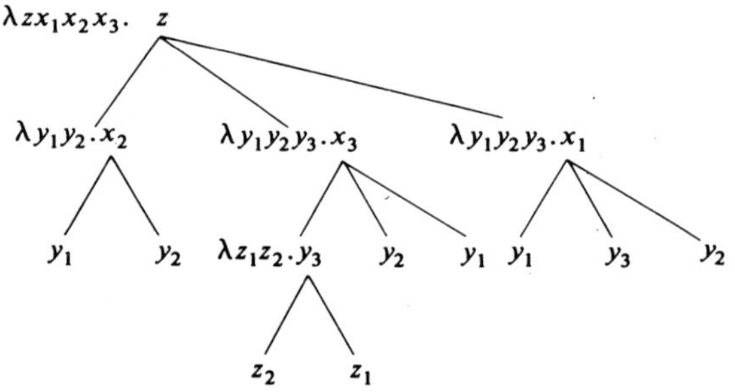

(ii) $A_2^{-1} \neq A_2$.

21.2.18. PROPOSITION. *Let* $M \in \mathrm{HP}$. *Then* $\mathcal{H}^*(M, M^{-1})$.

PROOF. Define for $N \in \Lambda$

$$N =_k \mathbf{I} \Leftrightarrow \exists \mathbf{I}' \ \mathrm{BT}(N) =_k \mathrm{BT}(\mathbf{I}') =_\eta \mathrm{BT}(\mathbf{I}).$$

Then

(1) $$\forall k \ N =_k \mathbf{I} \Rightarrow \mathrm{BT}(N) =_\eta \mathrm{BT}(\mathbf{I}).$$

By induction on k we will show

(2) $$M \circ M^{-1} =_k \mathbf{I} \quad \text{and} \quad M^{-1} \circ M =_k \mathbf{I}.$$

If $k = 0$, this is trivial, so consider $k+1$. Let $M = \langle \pi | M_1, \ldots, M_n \rangle$. Then $\langle \pi^{-1} | M^{-1}_{\pi^{-1}1}, \ldots \rangle$. Hence by lemma 21.2.14 (ii)

$$M \circ M^{-1} = \langle \mathrm{id}_n | M^{-1}_{\pi^{-1}1} \circ M_{\pi^{-1}1}, \ldots \rangle.$$

By the induction hypothesis $M_j^{-1} \circ M_j = k\mathbf{I}$ for $1 \leqslant j \leqslant n$. Therefore $M \circ M^{-1} =_{k+1} \mathbf{I}$. Similarly for $M^{-1} \circ M$.

By (1) and (2) one has

$$\mathrm{BT}(M \circ M^{-1}) =_\eta \mathrm{BT}(\mathbf{I}) =_\eta \mathrm{BT}(M^{-1} \circ M);$$

hence by theorem 19.2.12 it follows that

$$\mathcal{H}^* \vdash M \circ M^{-1} = M^{-1} \circ M = \mathbf{I}. \quad \square$$

Thus we obtain the characterization of $\mathcal{H}^*$-invertibility due to Bergstra and Klop [1980].

21.2.19. THEOREM. *$M \in \Lambda$ is $\mathcal{H}^*$-invertible iff $M \in \mathrm{HP}$.*

PROOF. By propositions 21.2.13 and 21.2.18. $\square$

Now we want to investigate $\mathcal{T}$-invertibility for different λ-theories $\mathcal{T}$.

Remember that the depth of a Böhm-like tree A is $d(A) = \sup\{\mathrm{lh}(\alpha) | \alpha \in A\}$ and that $d(M) = d(\mathrm{BT}(M))$.

21.2.20. LEMMA. (i) *$d(\langle \pi | M_1, \ldots, M_n \rangle) \geqslant m+1 \Leftrightarrow d(M_i) \geqslant m$ for some i.*

Let $M, N \in \mathrm{HP}$. Then

(ii) *$d(M) \geqslant m \Rightarrow d(M \circ N) \geqslant m$, $d(N \circ M) \geqslant m$.*

(iii) *$d(M) = \infty \Rightarrow d(M \circ N) = d(N \circ M) = \infty$.*

PROOF. (i) By definition.

(ii) By induction on m. If $m = 0$, this is trivial, so consider $m+1$.

Suppose $d(M) \geqslant m+1$. Then $M = \langle \pi | M_1, \ldots, M_n \rangle$ with $M_i \in \mathrm{HP}$ for $1 \leqslant i \leqslant n$. By (i) one has $d(M_{i_0}) \geqslant m$ for some i_0. Let $N = \langle \sigma | N_1, \ldots, N_{n'} \rangle$. By lemma 21.2.14 it may be assumed that $n = n'$ and

$$N \circ M = \langle \sigma \circ \pi | M_1 \circ N_{\pi 1}, \ldots, M_n \circ N_{\pi n} \rangle.$$

By the induction hypothesis

$$d(M_{i_0} \circ N_{i_0}) \geqslant m,$$

hence $d(N \circ M) \geqslant m+1$ by (i) and similarly for $d(M \circ N)$.

(iii) Immediate by (ii). □

The characterization of $\boldsymbol{\lambda\eta}$-invertibility due to Dezani and Bergstra, Klop is given next.

21.2.21. THEOREM. *M is $\boldsymbol{\lambda\eta}$-invertible $\Leftrightarrow M \in$ FHP.*

PROOF. ($\Rightarrow$) If M is $\boldsymbol{\lambda\eta}$-invertible, then M is $\mathcal{H}^*$-invertible and by theorem 21.2.19 one has $M \in \mathrm{HP}$. Suppose $M \notin \mathrm{FHP}$. Then $d(M) = \infty$ and hence by lemma 21.2.20 (iii)

(1) $\quad d(M \circ N) = \infty \quad$ for $N \in \mathrm{HP}$.

On the other hand, for some $N \in \Lambda$ one has in $\boldsymbol{\lambda\eta}$

$$M \circ N = N \circ M = \mathbf{I}.$$

Then also $N \in \mathrm{HP}$. By corollary 15.1.5 $M \circ N$ has a β-nf, so $\mathrm{BT}(M \circ N)$ is finite contradicting (1).

($\Leftarrow$) If $M \in \mathrm{FHP}$, then $k = d(M) < \infty$. By induction on k it will be shown that in $\boldsymbol{\lambda\eta}$

$$M \circ M^{-1} = M^{-1} \circ M = \mathbf{I}$$

and we are done. If $k = 0$, then $M = \mathbf{I}$ and $M^{-1} = \mathbf{I}$. Consider $k+1$. Then $M = \langle \pi | M_1, \ldots, M_n \rangle$ with $d(M_i) \leqslant k$ for $1 \leqslant i \leqslant n$ and $M^{-1} = \langle \pi^{-1} | M^{-1}_{\pi^{-1}1}, \ldots, M^{-1}_{\pi^{-1}n} \rangle$. We have in $\boldsymbol{\lambda\eta}$

$$\begin{aligned} M \circ M^{-1} &= \langle \pi \circ \pi^{-1} | M^{-1}_{\pi^{-1}1} \circ M_{\pi^{-1}1}, \ldots \rangle && \text{by lemma 21.2.14 (ii),} \\ &= \langle \mathrm{id} | \mathbf{I}, \ldots, \mathbf{I} \rangle && \text{by the induction hypothesis,} \\ &= \langle \emptyset | \ \rangle = \mathbf{I} && \text{by lemma 21.2.14 (i).} \end{aligned}$$

Similarly $M^{-1} \circ M =_{\beta\eta} \mathbf{I}$. □

Using the proof-theoretic analysis of $\mathcal{H}\omega$ one obtains the following consequences. Result (ii) probably also holds for $\mathcal{B}\eta$ and $\mathcal{B}\omega$.

21.2.22. COROLLARY. (i) *Let* $\mathcal{T}$ *be* $\boldsymbol{\lambda}$, $\mathcal{H}$ *or* $\mathcal{B}$. *Then*

$$M \in \Lambda \text{ is } \mathcal{T}\text{-invertible} \Leftrightarrow M =_{\mathcal{T}} \mathsf{I}.$$

(ii) Let $\mathcal{T}$ be $\boldsymbol{\lambda\eta}$, $\boldsymbol{\lambda}\omega$, $\mathcal{H}\boldsymbol{\eta}$, $\mathcal{H}\omega$. Then

$$M \in \Lambda \text{ is } \mathcal{T}\text{-invertible} \Leftrightarrow M \in \text{FHP}.$$

PROOF. (i) ($\Leftarrow$) Trivial. ($\Rightarrow$) Note that

(1) $\mathcal{T} \vdash M = N \Rightarrow \text{BT}(M) = \text{BT}(N).$

If M is $\mathcal{T}$-invertible, then M is $\mathcal{H}^*$-invertible and hence $M \in \text{HP}$. Suppose $M \neq_{\mathcal{T}} \mathsf{I}$. Then $M = \langle \pi | M_1, \ldots, M_n \rangle$ with $n > 0$. But then for N the inverse of M one has in $\mathcal{T}$

$$\begin{aligned} \mathsf{I} &= M \circ N \\ &= \lambda z.M(Nz) \\ &= \lambda z\vec{x}.Nz(M_1 x_{\pi 1}) \cdots \end{aligned}$$

contradicting (1).

(ii) ($\Leftarrow$) If $M \in \text{FHP}$, then by the theorem M is $\lambda\eta$-invertible, hence $\mathcal{T}$-invertible.

($\Rightarrow$) If M is $\mathcal{T}$-invertible, then for some $N \in \Lambda$ one has in $\mathcal{T} \subseteq \mathcal{H}\omega$

$$M \circ N = N \circ M = \mathsf{I}$$

But then by theorem 17.2.17 the same is true in $\boldsymbol{\lambda\eta}$, i.e. M is $\lambda\eta$-invertible. Hence by the theorem $M \in \text{FHP}$. □

REMARK. If a term M is $\mathcal{T}$-invertible, then M is $\mathcal{T}$-bijective (in the obvious sense). It is open whether the converse holds (on $\mathfrak{M}^0(\mathcal{T})$). See also exercises 21.4.2, 21.4.3.

21.3. The groups $G(\boldsymbol{\lambda\eta})$ and $G(\mathcal{H}^*)$

From corollary 21.2.22 it follows that

$$\begin{aligned} &G(\boldsymbol{\lambda}) = G(\mathcal{H}) = G(\mathcal{B}) = \{e\}, \quad \text{the trivial group}, \\ &G(\boldsymbol{\lambda\eta}) = G(\boldsymbol{\lambda}\omega) = G(\mathcal{H}\boldsymbol{\eta}) = G(\mathcal{H}\omega), \\ &G(\mathcal{H}^*) \supseteq G(\boldsymbol{\lambda\eta}). \end{aligned}$$

In this section the group theoretic structure of $G(\boldsymbol{\lambda\eta})$ and $G(\mathcal{H}^*)$ will be determined. First the following group theoretic notions are reviewed.

21.3.1. DEFINITION. (i) S_ω is the group of all permutations on $\mathbb{N}$ (i.e. bijections $\pi : \mathbb{N} \to \mathbb{N}$).

$$\underset{\smile}{S_\omega} = \{\pi \in S_\omega \mid \pi(k) = k \text{ for all but finitely many } k \in \mathbb{N}\}$$

(ii) If H is a group with unit e, then H^ω is the group of all infinite sequences $\{\langle h_0, h_1, \ldots \rangle \mid h_k \in H\}$, with coordinatewise multiplication.

$$H^{\underset{\smile}{\omega}} = \{\vec{h} \in H^\omega \mid h_k = e \text{ for all but finitely many } k \in \mathbb{N}\}.$$

(iii) Each $\pi \in \underset{\smile}{S_\omega}$ induces an automorphism on $H^{\underset{\smile}{\omega}}$ as follows

$$\pi\langle h_0, h_1 \cdots \rangle = \langle h_{\pi 0}, h_{\pi 1}, \ldots \rangle .$$

Notation: for $\vec{h} \in H^{\underset{\smile}{\omega}}$ write $\vec{h}^\pi = \pi\vec{h}$.

(iv) The *semidirect product* of $\underset{\smile}{S_\omega}$ and $H^{\underset{\smile}{\omega}}$ (notation $\underset{\smile}{S_\omega} \otimes H^{\underset{\smile}{\omega}}$) is

$$\{\langle \pi, \vec{h} \rangle \mid \pi \in \underset{\smile}{S_\omega}, \vec{h} \in H^{\underset{\smile}{\omega}}\}$$

with as multiplication*

$$\langle \pi, \vec{h} \rangle \langle \sigma, \vec{g} \rangle = \langle \pi\sigma, \vec{g}\vec{h}^\sigma \rangle .$$

(v) A *direct* (respectively *inverse*) *system* of groups is a sequence $(H_n, f_n)_{n \in \mathbb{N}}$ such that each H_n is a group and $f_n : H_n \to H_{n+1}$ (respectively $f_n : H_{n+1} \to H_n$) is a homomorphism

(vi) If (H_n, f_n) is a direct system of groups, define

$$f_{n,n+k} = f_{n+k-1} \circ \cdots \circ f_{n+1} \circ f_n : H_n \to H_{n+k}$$

($f_{n,n}$ is the identity on H_n).

For $a, b \in \bigcup H_n$, say $a \in H_{n_1}, b \in H_{n_2}$,

define

$$a \sim b \Leftrightarrow \exists m \geqslant n_1, n_2 \quad f_{n_1, m}(a) = f_{n_2, m}(b).$$

Then $\sim$ is an equivalence relation. $[a]$ is the equivalence class of a in $\bigcup H_n$.

*Usually one takes for the product $\langle \pi\sigma, \vec{h}^\sigma\vec{g} \rangle$, but since a group X with multiplication $\cdot$ is isomorphic to X with multiplication $x \odot y = y \cdot x$ (via the map $\boldsymbol{\lambda} z.z^{-1}$) this is the same.

The *direct limit* of the system (H_n, f_n) (notation $\varinjlim (H_n, f_n)$ or $\varinjlim H_n$) is the group

$$\bigcup H_n/\sim$$

with multiplication

$$[a][b] = \left[f_{n_1,m}(a) f_{n_2,m}(b) \right]$$

for some $m \geqslant n_1, n_2$.

(vii) The *inverse* or *projective limit* of an inverse system (H_n, f_n) (notation $\varprojlim (H_n, f_n)$ or $\varprojlim H_n$) is

$$\{\langle h_0, h_1, \dots \rangle | \forall k \in \mathbb{N} [h_k \in H_k \text{ and } f_k(h_{k+1}) = h_k]\},$$

with coordinatewise multiplication.

21.3.2. DEFINITION. (i) A group $\langle H, \cdot, ^{-1} \rangle$ is *recursive* if there is a partial surjection $\nu : \mathbb{N} \to H$ and there are total recursive functions m, i such that

$$\nu(m(n_1, n_2)) \simeq \nu(n_1) \cdot \nu(n_2),$$

$$\nu(i(n)) \simeq \nu(n)^{-1}$$

(in the sense that if one of the two sides is defined, then so is the other and the two sides are equal).

(ii) A direct (or inverse) system (H_n, f_n) of groups is *uniformly recursive* if each H_n is a recursive group via the maps ν_n, m_n, i_n and

(1) $\lambda nxy.m_n(x, y)$ and $\lambda nx.i_n(x)$ are recursive

(2) there exists a total recursive function $\lambda nx.\psi_n(x)$ such that for all $n, x \in \mathbb{N}$

$$f_n(\nu_n(x)) \simeq \nu_{n+1}(\psi_n(x))$$

(respectively $f_n \circ \nu_{n+1} = \nu_n \circ \psi_n$).

(iii) Let (H_n, f_n) be a uniformly recursive inverse system of groups. Then the *recursive inverse limit* of (H_n, f_n) (notation $\varprojlim^{\mathrm{r}} (H_n, f_n)$ or $\varprojlim^{\mathrm{r}} H_n$) consists of

$$\left\{ \langle h_n \rangle \in \varprojlim H_n | \forall n\ \nu_n(g(n)) = h_n \text{ for some recursive } g \right\},$$

with coordinatewise multiplication. $\varprojlim^{\mathrm{r}} H_n$ is clearly a subgroup of $\varprojlim H_n$.

21.3.3. Proposition. (i) *Let* (H_n, f_n) *be a uniformly recursive direct system of groups. Then* $\lim\limits_{\rightarrow} H_n$ *is recursive.*

(ii) *Let* (H_n, f_n) *be a uniformly recursive inverse system of groups. Then* $\lim\limits_{\leftarrow}{}^{\mathrm{r}} H_n$ *is recursive.*

Proof. Let (H_n, f_n) be uniformly recursive via the functions $\nu_n, m_n(x,y)$, $i_n(x)$ and $\psi_n(x)$.

(i) Define $\nu(\langle x, n\rangle) \simeq [\nu_n(x)]$ where $\langle\ ,\ \rangle$ is the standard pairing of the integers. Then $\nu : \mathbb{N} \to \lim\limits_{\rightarrow} H_n$ is surjective. Define

$$m(\langle x, n_x\rangle, \langle y, n_y\rangle) = \langle m_n\big(\psi_{n_x, n-1}(x), \psi_{n_y, n-1}(y)\big), n\rangle$$

where $n = \max\{n_x, n_y\}$ and the $\psi_{n,m}$ are defined from the ψ_n as the $f_{n,m}$ from the f_n. Then clearly m is recursive and satisfies the required property. Similarly i can be found.

(ii) Define

$$\begin{aligned} \nu(n) &= \langle \{n\}(k)\rangle_{k\in\mathbb{N}} && \text{if this is in } \lim\nolimits^{\mathrm{r}} H_n, \\ &= \uparrow && \text{else.} \end{aligned}$$

Then ν is a partial surjection. Define

$$m(n_1, n_2) = \Lambda k. m_k(\{n_1\}(k), \{n_2\}(k))$$

where $\Lambda k. \cdots$ is the (canonically constructed) Gödel number of the partial recursive function $\lambda k. \cdots$. Then m is total recursive and represents multiplication in $\lim\limits_{\leftarrow}{}^{\mathrm{r}} H_n$. Similarly i can be constructed. □

21.3.4. Definition. (i) By induction on n define the groups G_n as follows.

$$G_0 = \{e\}, \quad \text{the trivial group,}$$

$$G_{n+1} = S_{\underset{\smile}{\omega}} \otimes G_n^{\underset{\smile}{\omega}}.$$

(ii) For each n there is a canonical homomorphism $f_n : G_n \to G_{n+1}$ defined by

$$f_0(e) = e_1, \quad \text{the unit element of } G_1,$$

$$f_{n+1}(\langle \pi, \vec{x}\rangle) = \langle \pi, \langle f_n(x_i)\rangle_i\rangle,$$

where $\langle \pi, \vec{x}\rangle = \langle \pi, \langle x_i\rangle_i\rangle$ is an arbitrary element of G_{n+1}.

(iii) For each n there is a canonical homomorphism $g_n : G_{n+1} \to G_n$ defined by

$$g_0 = \lambda x.e,$$

$$g_{n+1}(\langle \pi, \vec{x} \rangle) = \langle \pi, \langle g_n(x_i) \rangle_i \rangle.$$

Note that (G_n, f_n) is a direct system and (G_n, g_n) is an inverse system such that $g_n \circ f_n$ is for all n the identity on G_n.

21.3.5. PROPOSITION. (i) *$S_{\underset{\smile}{\omega}}$ is recursive.*
(ii) *If H is a recursive group, then so are $H^{\underset{\smile}{\omega}}$ and $S_{\underset{\smile}{\omega}} \otimes H^{\underset{\smile}{\omega}}$.*
(iii) *(G_n, f_n) and (G_n, g_n) are uniformly recursive systems.*

PROOF. (i) Define $\nu : \mathbb{N} \to S_{\underset{\smile}{\omega}}$ by

$$\nu(n) = \begin{cases} \pi_n & \text{if } n \text{ is the sequence number } \langle n_0, \ldots, n_{k-1} \rangle \\ & \text{and } \pi_n(i) = \begin{cases} n_i & \text{if } i < k, \\ i & \text{else;} \end{cases} \text{ is a bijection;} \\ \uparrow & \text{else.} \end{cases}$$

Clearly ν is surjective. By Church's thesis appropriate m and i can be found.

(ii) Suppose H is recursive. Similarly to (i) $H^{\underset{\smile}{\omega}}$ is recursive. For $S_{\underset{\smile}{\omega}} \otimes H^{\underset{\smile}{\omega}}$ define

$$\nu(n) \cong \langle \nu_1((n)_0), \nu_2((n)_1) \rangle$$

where ν_1, ν_2 are the enumerators of $S_{\underset{\smile}{\omega}}$ and $H^{\underset{\smile}{\omega}}$. Then $\nu : \mathbb{N} \to S_{\underset{\smile}{\omega}} \otimes H^{\underset{\smile}{\omega}}$ is a partial surjection and again by Church's thesis appropriate m and i can be constructed.

(iii) Since G_n, f_n and g_n are defined inductively the (G_n, f_n) and (G_n, g_n) are uniformly recursive. □

21.3.6. DEFINITION. (i) $\vec{G} = \lim\limits_{\rightarrow} G_n$.
(ii) $\overleftarrow{G} = \lim\limits_{\leftarrow} G_n$.
(iii) $\overleftarrow{G}^{\mathrm{r}} = \lim\limits_{\leftarrow}{}^{\mathrm{r}} G_n$.

It will be shown that for $\mathcal{T} = \lambda\eta$, $\lambda\omega$, $\mathcal{H}\eta$, $\mathcal{H}\omega$; one has $G(\mathcal{T}) \cong \vec{G}$. Moreover $G(\mathcal{H}^*) \cong \overleftarrow{G}^{\mathrm{r}}$.

21.3.7. DEFINITION. Define the following sets $F_k \subseteq G(\lambda\eta)$:

$$F_0 = \{\mathbf{I}\},$$

$$F_{k+1} = \{\langle \pi | M_1, \ldots, M_n \rangle | n \in \mathbb{N}, \pi \in S_n, M_1, \ldots, M_n \in F_k\}.$$

21.3.8. LEMMA. (i) $F_k = (F_k, \circ)$ *is a subgroup of* $G(\boldsymbol{\lambda\eta})$.
(ii) $G(\boldsymbol{\lambda\eta}) = \bigcup_k F_k$.
(iii) $\forall k\ F_k \subseteq F_{k+1}$.

PROOF. (i) By induction on k it follows that the terms defining F_k are in FHP, hence $F_k \subseteq G(\boldsymbol{\lambda\eta})$. By lemma 21.2.14 the F_k are closed under $\circ$ and by definition 21.2.16 under ${}^{-1}$. Therefore $(F_k, \circ)$ is a subgroup of $G(\boldsymbol{\lambda\eta})$.
(ii) For each $M \in$ FHP one has $M \in F_k$ where $k = d(M)$.
(iii) Again by induction on k, using $\mathbf{I} =_{\beta\eta} \langle \mathrm{id} | \mathbf{I} \rangle$ for the base. □

21.3.9. LEMMA. *Let* (G_k, f_k) *be as in definition* 21.3.4 *and let* i_k *be the embedding* $F_k \subseteq F_{k+1}$. *Then the direct systems* (G_k, f_k) *and* (F_k, i_k) *are isomorphic.*

PROOF. Define by induction on k maps $h_k : F_k \to G_k$

$$h_0(\mathbf{I}) = e_0,$$

$$h_{k+1}(\langle \pi | M_1, \ldots, M_n \rangle)$$

$$= \langle \pi^\infty, \langle h_k(M_1), \ldots, h_k(M_n), e_k, e_{k+1}, \ldots \rangle \rangle$$

where π^∞ is the canonical embedding of π into S_ω and e_k is the unit element of G_k. By a routine argument one shows that the h_k are isomorphisms (use lemma 21.2.14) such that $h_{k+1} \circ i_k = f_k \circ h_k$ for all k. □

21.3.10. PROPOSITION. $G(\boldsymbol{\lambda\eta}) \cong \vec{G}$.

PROOF.

$$G(\boldsymbol{\lambda\eta}) \cong \lim_{\rightarrow} (F_k, i_k) \quad \text{by lemma 21.3.8,}$$

$$= \lim_{\rightarrow} (G_k, f_k) \quad \text{by lemma 21.3.9,}$$

$$= \vec{G}. \quad \square$$

21.3.11. THEOREM. (i) *Let* $\mathfrak{T} = \boldsymbol{\lambda\eta}, \boldsymbol{\lambda\omega}, \mathcal{H}\boldsymbol{\eta}, \mathcal{H}\boldsymbol{\omega}$. *Then* $G(\mathfrak{T}) \cong \vec{G}$.
(ii) *Let* $\mathfrak{T} = \boldsymbol{\lambda}, \mathcal{H}$ *or* $\mathfrak{B}$. *Then* $G(\mathfrak{T}) = \{e\}$, *the trivial group.*

PROOF. (i) By corollary 21.2.22 (ii)

$$G(\mathfrak{T}) = \mathrm{FHP}/=_{\mathfrak{T}}$$

But for $M, N \in$ FHP one has

$$M =_{\boldsymbol{\lambda\eta}} N \Rightarrow M =_{\mathfrak{T}} N \Rightarrow M =_{\mathcal{H}^*} N \Rightarrow M \approx_\eta N \Rightarrow M =_{\boldsymbol{\lambda\eta}} N$$

since M, N have finite Böhm trees. Therefore

$$G(\mathcal{T}) = \mathrm{FHP}/=_{\lambda\eta} = G(\lambda\eta)$$

and the result follows by the preceding proposition.

(ii) Similarly, using corollary 21.2.22 (i). □

Now it will be proved that $G(\mathcal{H}^*) \cong \overleftarrow{G}^{\mathrm{r}}$. The proof occupies 21.3.12–21.3.16.

21.3.12. Definition. By induction on k the following homomorphisms $j_k : F_{k+1} \to F_k$ are defined

$$j_0(x) = \mathbf{I},$$

$$j_{k+1}(\langle \pi | M_1, \ldots, M_n \rangle) = \langle \pi | j_k(M_1), \ldots, j_k(M_n) \rangle .$$

It is routine to show that the j_k are well defined and indeed homomorphisms.

21.3.13. Lemma. (F_k, j_k) *is an inverse system of groups, isomorphic to* (G_k, g_k).

Proof. By the same maps h_k as in the proof of lemma 21.3.9. □

21.3.14. Definition. Define

$$p_k : \mathrm{HP} \to \mathrm{HP} \quad \text{and} \quad q_k : G(\mathcal{H}^*) \to F_k .$$

by

$$p_0(M) = \mathbf{I},$$

$$p_{k+1}(\langle \pi | M_1, \ldots, M_n \rangle) = \langle \pi | p_k(M_1), \ldots, p_k(M_n) \rangle ,$$

$$q_k([M]_{\mathcal{H}^*}) = [p_k(M)]_{\lambda\eta} .$$

Example. If

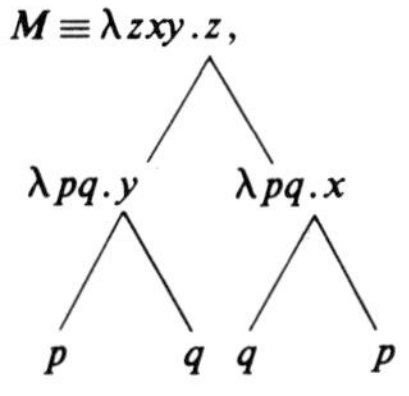

then

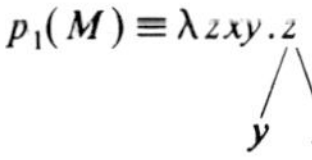

21.3.15. LEMMA. (i) *The* p_k, q_k *are well defined.*

(ii) *The* q_k *are homomorphisms such that* $j_k \circ q_{k+1} = q_k$ *for all* k.

PROOF. (i) Routine. For the p_k, use remark 21.2.15 (ii). For the q_k, show by induction on k that

$$M =_{\mathcal{H}^*} N \Rightarrow p_k(M) =_{\lambda\eta} p_k(N).$$

(ii) Entirely routine. □

21.3.16. THEOREM. $G(\mathcal{H}^*) \cong \overleftarrow{G}^{\mathrm{r}}$.

PROOF. Define a map

$$l : G(\mathcal{H}^*) \to \underleftarrow{\lim}^{\mathrm{r}}(F_k, j_k)$$

by

$$l(a) = \langle q_0(a), q_1(a), \ldots \rangle .$$

By lemma 21.3.15 (ii) and Church's thesis l is a well defined homomorphism.

If $a \neq a'$, then this is noticable at a finite level of the trees corresponding to a, a'. Hence $q_k(a) \neq q_k(a')$ for some k. Therefore l is injective.

By the existence theorem for recursive trees, theorem 10.1.23, l is surjective.

Therefore l is an isomorphism and

$$G(\mathcal{H}^*) \cong \underleftarrow{\lim}^{\mathrm{r}} F_k \cong \underleftarrow{\lim}^{\mathrm{r}} G_k = \overleftarrow{G}^{\mathrm{r}},$$

by lemma 21.3.13. □

It follows that $\overleftarrow{G}^{\mathrm{r}} \hookrightarrow G(D_\infty)$. In exercise 21.4.5 is shown that even $\overleftarrow{G} \hookrightarrow G(D_\infty)$. In general the inclusion is strict.

21.4. Exercises

21.4.1. Show that $S(\mathfrak{M})$ cannot be generated by one element.

21.4.2 (Klop). Show that $\lambda zab.z(\lambda f.fab)$ in $\mathfrak{M}(\boldsymbol{\lambda\eta})$ is surjective but not injective.

21.4.3* (Klop). Let $M_1 \equiv \lambda za.z(\lambda f.a(f(aa)))$ and $M_2 \equiv \lambda zab.z(ba)(ab)$. Show that M_1 is surjective but not injective and that M_2 is injective but not surjective, all in $\mathfrak{M}(\boldsymbol{\lambda\eta})$.

21.4.4 (Klop). (i) Show that $G(\boldsymbol{\lambda\eta})$ is locally finite (i.e. every finitely generated subgroup is finite).

(ii) Show that $G(\mathcal{H}^*)$ has elements of infinite order.

21.4.5. (i) Show that $\overleftarrow{G}$ can be embedded into $G(D_\infty)$.

(ii) (Scott). Show that Aut(D) (i.e. the group of automorphisms of the cpo D) can be embedded into $G(D_\infty)$.

(iii) Show that in general the subgroup of $G(D_\infty)$ generated by $\overleftarrow{G}$ and Aut(D) is not the whole group.

(iv) Let D be the cpo with two elements. Is $G(D_\infty) \cong \overleftarrow{G}$?

21.4.6. (i) Show that the canonical topology on $\mathfrak{M}(\mathcal{K}^*)$ induces on $G(\mathcal{K}^*)$ a topology which makes it a totally disconnected topological group.

(ii) Show that for each $a \in G(\mathcal{K}^*)$ the sequence $a, a^2, a^3, \ldots$ has a subsequence which converges to e (the unit element).

21.4.8 (Böhm and Dezani [1974]). (i) Show that if $F \in \Lambda^0$ has a left inverse in $S(\boldsymbol{\lambda})$, then F is injective on $\mathfrak{M}(\boldsymbol{\lambda})$ and $\mathfrak{M}^0(\boldsymbol{\lambda})$ but not conversely.

(ii) Show that $F \in \Lambda^0$ has a right inverse in $S(\boldsymbol{\lambda})$ iff F is surjective on $\mathfrak{M}(\boldsymbol{\lambda})$. The same holds for $\mathfrak{M}^0(\boldsymbol{\lambda})$.

(iii) Show that $F \in \Lambda^0$ has a right inverse in $S(\boldsymbol{\lambda})$ iff F is of the form $\lambda x.xN$.

(iv) Show that $F \in \Lambda^0$ has a left inverse in $S(\boldsymbol{\lambda})$ iff some terminal node α in BT(Fx) has label with free head variable x and for no $\beta < \alpha$ this is the case.

(v) Conclude that F is invertible in $S(\boldsymbol{\lambda})$ iff F is bijective on $\mathfrak{M}(\boldsymbol{\lambda})$ or $\mathfrak{M}^0(\boldsymbol{\lambda})$ iff $F = \mathbf{I}$.

21.4.9. Show that $F \in \Lambda^0$ defines a bijective function on $\mathfrak{M}(\boldsymbol{\lambda\eta})$ iff F is $\lambda\eta$-invertible. [For $\mathfrak{M}^0(\boldsymbol{\lambda\eta})$ this is an open problem.]

21.4.10* (A. Batenburg, J. Velmans). Let $F = \lambda xz.x(\lambda p.z(zp))$. Show that F is injective but has no left inverse in $\mathfrak{M}^0(\lambda\eta)$. [*Hint*. Use underlining.]

APPENDICES

Friedman (photo by
the author, 1978)

Seldin (photo by
R.I.P. Bulkeley, 1979)

Statman (photo by
the author, 1976)

Tait (photo by
J.-Y. Girard, 1972)

Appendices A and B give a short introduction to two topics not treated in this book, viz. the *typed lambda calculus* and *illative combinatory logic*. Appendix C deals with variables and gives a justification for the variable convention 2.1.13. Few proofs are given; the reader is often referred to the literature.

APPENDIX A

TYPED LAMBDA CALCULUS

A.1. The pure typed lambda calculus

A.1.1. Definition. Typ, the set of *types*, is inductively defined as follows.

(1) $0 \in \text{Typ}$.

(2) $\sigma, \tau \in \text{Typ} \Rightarrow (\sigma \rightarrow \tau) \in \text{Typ}$.

The following gives the intended interpretation of types.

A.1.2. Definition. Let X be any set. By induction on $\sigma \in \text{Typ}$ sets X_σ are defined.

$$X_0 = X,$$

$$X_{\sigma \rightarrow \tau} = X_\tau^{X_\sigma}, \quad \text{the collection of set theoretic functions from } X_\sigma \text{ to } X_\tau.$$

A.1.3. Remarks. (i) Other notations in the literature for $(\sigma \rightarrow \tau)$ are $(\sigma\tau)$, $(\sigma)\tau$, $\sigma(\tau)$ or $F\sigma\tau$.

(ii) 0 is the so called *ground type*.

Sometimes more than one ground type is allowed.

(iii) $\sigma_1 \rightarrow \sigma_2 \rightarrow \cdots \rightarrow \sigma_n$ is a shorthand for $(\sigma_1 \rightarrow (\sigma_2 \rightarrow (\cdots \rightarrow \sigma_n)))$. Note that each type is of the form $\sigma = \sigma_1 \rightarrow \cdots \rightarrow \sigma_n \rightarrow 0$ with $n \geqslant 0$.

(iv) Sometimes rule 2 in the formation of types is replaced by

$$\sigma_1, \ldots, \sigma_n, \tau \in \text{Typ} \Rightarrow (\sigma_1, \ldots, \sigma_n; \tau) \in \text{Typ}.$$

The interpretation is

$$X_{(\sigma_1, \ldots, \sigma_n; \tau)} = X_\tau^{X_{\sigma_1} \times \cdots \times X_{\sigma_n}}$$

($\times$ denotes the cartesian product). In view of Schönfinkel's reduction of functions of more arguments to unary ones the type $(\sigma_1, \ldots, \sigma_n; \tau)$ may be replaced by $\sigma_1 \rightarrow \sigma_2 \rightarrow \cdots \rightarrow \sigma_n \rightarrow \tau$ and therefore one does not always postulate these types.

A.1.4. Definition. The *typed λ-calculus* (notation $\boldsymbol{\lambda}^\tau$) is the theory defined as follows.

(i) $\boldsymbol{\lambda}^\tau$ has the following alphabet.
$v_0^\sigma, v_1^\sigma, \ldots$ variables for each $\sigma \in \mathrm{Typ}$,
λ, (,) auxiliary symbols.

(ii) The set of *terms* of $\boldsymbol{\lambda}^\tau$ of *type* σ (notation Λ_σ) is inductively defined as follows.

$$v_i^\sigma \in \Lambda_\sigma,$$

$$M \in \Lambda_{\sigma\to\tau},\ N \in \Lambda_\sigma \Rightarrow (MN) \in \Lambda_\tau,$$

$$M \in \Lambda_\tau,\ x \in \Lambda_\sigma \Rightarrow (\lambda x.M) \in \Lambda_{\sigma\to\tau}$$

where x ranges over the variables. Often we write $M \in \sigma$ for $M \in \Lambda_\sigma$.

The set of typed λ-terms (notation Λ^τ) is $\cup\{\Lambda_\sigma | \sigma \in \mathrm{Typ}\}$.

(iii) Formulas of $\boldsymbol{\lambda}^\tau$ consist of equations $M = N$ with $M, N \in \Lambda_\sigma$ and $\sigma \in \mathrm{Typ}$ arbitrary.

(iv) The notions of free and bound variables, closed terms and substitution are defined in the obvious way. Λ_σ^0 denotes the set of closed terms of type σ.

(v) $\boldsymbol{\lambda}^\tau$ is axiomatized by the equality axioms and rules (including rule ξ; see definition 2.1.4) and the axiom scheme

$$(\beta) \qquad (\lambda x.M)N = M[x := N]$$

(where the types are such that the terms make sense).

(vi) $\boldsymbol{\lambda\eta}^\tau$ is $\boldsymbol{\lambda}^\tau$ extended by the scheme

$$(\eta) \qquad \lambda x.Mx = M \quad \text{if } x \notin \mathrm{FV}(M).$$

A.1.5. Remarks. (i) *Typed combinatory logic* (notation $\boldsymbol{CL}^\tau$) is a combinatory version of $\boldsymbol{\lambda}^\tau$ which has the primitive constants

$$\boldsymbol{K}_{\sigma\tau} \in \sigma \to (\tau \to \sigma),$$

$$\boldsymbol{S}_{\sigma\tau\rho} \in (\sigma \to (\tau \to \rho)) \to ((\sigma \to \tau) \to (\sigma \to \rho))$$

for every $\sigma, \tau, \rho \in \mathrm{Typ}$ and the axiom schemes

$$\boldsymbol{K}_{\sigma\tau} MN = M,$$

$$\boldsymbol{S}_{\sigma\tau\rho} MNL = ML(NL)$$

where M, N, L are of appropriate type.

(ii) Note that the types of $\boldsymbol{K}$ and $\boldsymbol{S}$ become valid proposition if $\to$ is interpreted as implication. See § A.3 for an expansion of this idea.

(iii) In the presence of extensionality the theories $\boldsymbol{\lambda}^\tau$ and $\boldsymbol{CL}^\tau$ become equivalent. Also there is a combinatory version of $\boldsymbol{CL} + \boldsymbol{A}_\beta$ (see theorem 7.3.10) which is equivalent to $\boldsymbol{\lambda}^\tau$; see Sanchis [1967].

(iv) There are also the theories $\boldsymbol{\lambda I}^\tau$ and $\boldsymbol{CL}_I^\tau$.

Provable equality in the theories $\boldsymbol{\lambda}$ and $\boldsymbol{\lambda\eta}$ can be analyzed by the notions of reduction $\boldsymbol{\beta}$ and $\boldsymbol{\beta\eta}$ respectively. Something similar is true for $\boldsymbol{\lambda}^\tau$ and $\boldsymbol{\lambda\eta}^\tau$.

A.1.6. PROPOSITION. (i) *There is a notion of reduction* $\boldsymbol{\beta}(\boldsymbol{\eta})$ *adequate for* $\boldsymbol{\lambda}(\boldsymbol{\eta})^\tau$ *that is Church–Rosser.*

PROOF. Exercise. □

The following theorem indicates an essential difference between $\boldsymbol{\lambda}^\tau$ and $\boldsymbol{\lambda}$.

A.1.7. THEOREM. (i) *Every* $M \in \Lambda^\tau$ *has a* nf.

(ii) $\boldsymbol{\lambda}(\boldsymbol{\eta})^\tau$ *is strongly normalizing, i.e. every* $\beta(\eta)$*-reduction of a* λ^τ*-term terminates.*

PROOF. (i) This was first proved by Turing, see Gandy [1980].

(ii) This follows from the analogous statement for the stronger system $\mathfrak{T}$ (see theorem A.2.3). □

In particular, no fixed point operators exist in $\boldsymbol{\lambda}^\tau$.

A.1.8. COROLLARY. *Provable equality in* $\boldsymbol{\lambda}(\boldsymbol{\eta})^\tau$ *is decidable.*

PROOF. $\boldsymbol{\lambda}(\boldsymbol{\eta})^\tau \vdash M = N$ if M, N have the same $\beta(\eta)$-nf's. Moreover the nf's can be found effectively by the theorem. In Statman [1979] it is proved that the decision method is not Kalmar elementary. □

Some type free λ-terms like $\lambda x.x$ can be given a type: $\lambda x^\sigma.x^\sigma \in \sigma \to \sigma$. This is possible for every σ. One says that $\sigma \to \sigma$ is a possible type for $\lambda x.x \in \Lambda$. Other λ-terms do not have a type, e.g. $\lambda x.xx$.

A.1.9. DEFINITION. (i) Let $M \in \Lambda_\sigma$. Then $|M| \in \Lambda$ is M with all type symbols erased. One says that $|M|$ is *typable* and that σ is a possible type for $|M|$.

(ii) If $\sigma \in$ Typ, then an *instance* σ^* of σ is the result of replacing the 0's is σ by some other type. E.g. $\sigma \to \sigma$ is an instance of $0 \to 0$ and also of 0.

A.1.10. PROPOSITION. (i) *The set of typable* λ*-terms is recursive.*

(ii) *If* $M \in \Lambda$ *is typable, then one can find effectively a unique* $\sigma \in$ Typ *such that every possible type for M is an instance of* σ. [*This type* σ *is called the* principal type scheme *for M.*]

PROOF. See Hindley [1969]. □

The Church numerals $c_n \equiv \lambda fx.f^n x$ have as type $(0\to 0)\to 0\to 0$. Therefore the c_n can be considered in Λ^τ. It is a natural question to ask what numeric functions are definable on these numerals in $\boldsymbol{\lambda}^\tau$.

The *extended polynomials* consist of the least class of numeric functions containing the projections, the constant functions, the *sg* function ($sg(0) = 0$, $sg(n+1) = 1$) and is closed under sum and product of functions.

The following is independently due to Schwichtenberg and Statman.

A.1.11. PROPOSITION. *Exactly the extended polynomials are $\boldsymbol{\lambda}^\tau$-definable on the Church numerals.*

PROOF. See Schwichtenberg [1975/76]. □

As to models of the typed theory, for sake of simplicity only typed combinatory algebras and typed extensional λ-algebras are considered.

A.1.12. DEFINITION. Let $\mathfrak{M} = \langle\{A_\sigma | \sigma \in \text{Typ}\}, \{\cdot_{\sigma\tau} | \sigma, \tau \in \text{Typ}\}\rangle$ where the A_σ are sets and $\cdot_{\sigma\tau} : A_{\sigma\to\tau} \times A_\sigma \to A_\tau$ is a map (application).

Write $x \in \mathfrak{M}$ if $x \in A_\sigma$ for some σ; in that case we write also $x \in \mathfrak{M}_\sigma$ and say that x is of type σ.

(i) $\mathfrak{M}$ is a *combinatory type structure* if A_0 has more than one element and for each $\sigma, \tau, \rho \in \text{Typ}$ there are elements

$$k_{\sigma\tau}, s_{\sigma\tau\rho} \in \mathfrak{M} \text{ satisfying for all } x, y, z \text{ of appropriate types}$$

$$k_{\sigma\tau}xy = x, \qquad s_{\sigma\tau\rho}xyz = xz(yz).$$

(ii) $\mathfrak{M}$ is an *extensional type structure* if for $x, x' \in \mathfrak{M}_{\sigma\to\tau}$ one has also

$$[\forall z \in \mathfrak{M}\ x.z = x'.z] \Rightarrow x = x'.$$

If M is a combinatory (extensional) type structure, then for typed combinatory terms M, N (respectively $M, N \in \Lambda^\tau$) of the same type one can define

$$\mathfrak{M} \models M = N.$$

One has for a combinatory type structure

$$\boldsymbol{CL}^\tau \vdash M = N \Rightarrow \mathfrak{M} \models M = N$$

and for an extensional one

$$\boldsymbol{\lambda\eta}^\tau \vdash M = N \Rightarrow \mathfrak{M} \models M = N.$$

It is easier to find models for $\boldsymbol{\lambda}^\tau$ than for $\boldsymbol{\lambda}$.

A.1.13. DEFINITION. Let X be a set with more than one element. The *full type structure* over X is

$$\mathfrak{M}(X)=\langle\{X_\sigma|\sigma\in\mathrm{Typ}\},\{\cdot_{\sigma\tau}|\sigma,\tau\in\mathrm{Typ}\}\rangle$$

where the X_σ are introduced in definition A.1.2 and $\cdot_{\sigma\tau}$ is the obvious application map.

Clearly $\mathfrak{M}(X)$ is an extensional type structure.

A.1.14. REMARK. Definition A.1.13 can be relativized to any cartesian closed category $\boldsymbol{C}$ with object X such that $\mathrm{Hom}_{\boldsymbol{C}}(X, X)$ has more than one element. The resulting type structure is denoted by $\mathfrak{M}_{\boldsymbol{C}}(X)$. It does not need to be extensional.

The following proposition is due to Zucker; see Troelstra [1973], 2.4.5. It states that every combinatory type structure can be collapsed onto an extensional one. This is in contrast with the untyped structures, see exercise 20.6.5.

A.1.15. PROPOSITION. *There is a uniform way of constructing from a combinatory type structure $\mathfrak{M}$ an extensional type structure $\mathfrak{M}^{\mathrm{E}}$ such that*

(1) $\qquad \mathfrak{M}\models M = N \Rightarrow \mathfrak{M}^{\mathrm{E}}\models M = N.$

$\mathfrak{M}^{\mathrm{E}}$ is called the *extensional collapse* of $\mathfrak{M}$.

PROOF SKETCH. Define for $x, y\in\mathfrak{M}_\sigma$ a relation $=_\sigma$ by induction on σ:

$$x=_0 y\Leftrightarrow x=y,$$

$$x=_{\sigma\to\tau}y\Leftrightarrow\forall z, z'\in\mathfrak{M}_\sigma\ \left[z=_\sigma z'\Rightarrow xz=_\tau yz'\right].$$

Define

$$\mathfrak{N}_\sigma=\{x\in\mathfrak{M}_\sigma|x=_\sigma x\},\qquad \mathfrak{M}^{\mathrm{E}}_\sigma=\mathfrak{N}_\sigma \text{ modulo} =_\sigma.$$

Then the $\mathfrak{M}^{\mathrm{E}}_\sigma$ form an extensional type structure satisfying (1). □

Other type structures are the heriditarily recursive operations HRO and the heriditarily effective operations HEO defined in Troelstra [1973], § 2.4.

A.1.16. DEFINITION. (i) For $n, m\in\mathbb{N}$ let $\{n\}(m)$ be the nth partial recursive function applied to m. Write $n\cdot m$ for $\{n\}(m)$. Define

$$A_0=\mathbb{N},$$

$$A_{\sigma\to\tau}=\{n\in\mathbb{N}|\forall m\in A_\sigma\ n\cdot m\in A_\tau \text{ (and is defined)}\}.$$

Then HRO $= \langle \{A_\sigma\}, \{\cdot_{\sigma\tau}\}\rangle$, where $\cdot_{\sigma\tau}$ is $\cdot$ for each σ, τ.
(ii) HEO $=$ HRO^{E}.

A.1.17. PROPOSITION. (i) HRO *is a combinatory type structure.*
(ii) HEO *is an extensional type structure.*

PROOF SKETCH. (i) Elements $k_{\sigma\tau}$ and $s_{\sigma\tau\rho}$ can be found independently of σ, τ, ρ by the *s-m-n*-theorem.
(ii) By proposition A.1.15. □

REMARK. The above definition of HEO is not exactly the same as the original one; see Troelstra [1973], theorem 2.4.12, but M. Bezem has proved the isomorphy (J. Symbolic Logic, to appear).

Finally there are the term models.

A.1.18. DEFINITION. $\mathfrak{M}(\boldsymbol{CL}^\tau)$, $\mathfrak{M}(\boldsymbol{\lambda}^\tau)$ and $\mathfrak{M}(\boldsymbol{\lambda\eta}^\tau)$ are the open term models defined in the obvious way. [Closed term models do not exist since there are no closed terms of type 0.]

Obviously $\mathfrak{M}(\boldsymbol{CL}^\tau)$ and $\mathfrak{M}(\boldsymbol{\lambda}^\tau)$ are combinatory type structures. $\mathfrak{M}(\boldsymbol{\lambda\eta}^\tau)$ is an extensional type structure.

One has the following completeness results by Friedman and Statman.

A.1.19. THEOREM *Let M, N be terms of the same type. Then*
(i) $\boldsymbol{\lambda\eta}^\tau \vdash M = N \Leftrightarrow \mathfrak{M}(\mathbb{N}) \models M = N$.
(ii) *For every $M, N \in \Lambda^\tau$ there is an $n \in \mathbb{N}$ such that*

$$\boldsymbol{\lambda\eta}^\tau \vdash M = N \Leftrightarrow \mathfrak{M}(\{0, \ldots, n\}) \models M = N.$$

PROOF. (i) See Friedman [1975], p. 27.
(ii) See Statman [1982], thm. 2. The number n depends only on M. □

A.1.20. COROLLARY. *Let M, N range over λ^τ-terms. Then*

$$\mathfrak{M}(\mathbb{N}) \models M = N$$

is decidable.

PROOF. By theorem A.1.19 and corollary A.1.8. □

By contrast, Friedman [1975], thm. 5, shows the following.

A.1.21. THEOREM. *Let M, N range over (open) λ^τ-terms. Then*

$$\mathfrak{M}(\mathbb{N}) \models M \neq N$$

is not an arithmetical predicate.

The following is taken from Statman [1982].

A.1.22. DEFINITION. Let X be a set of variables (with at least two of type 0). Then

(i) $\mathfrak{F}_0(X)$ is the substructure of $\mathfrak{M}(\boldsymbol{\lambda\eta}^\tau)$ consisting of those $[M]$ with $\mathrm{FV}(M) \subseteq X$.

(ii) $\mathfrak{F}(X) = \mathfrak{F}_0(X)^{\mathrm{E}}$.

A.1.23. THEOREM. (i) *If X is a set of typed variables containing at least one variable of the types* 0, $0 \to 0$, $0 \to 0 \to 0, \ldots,$ *then* $\mathfrak{F}(X) = \mathfrak{F}_0(X)$ *up to isomorphism, hence for all* $M, N \in \Lambda^\tau$

$$\boldsymbol{\lambda\eta}^\tau \vdash M = N \Leftrightarrow \mathfrak{F}(X) \models M = N.$$

(ii) *If X contains only type 0 variables and at least two of them, then*

$$\mathrm{Con}(\boldsymbol{\lambda\eta}^\tau + M = N) \Leftrightarrow \mathfrak{F}(X) \models M = N.$$

PROOF. See Statman [1982], propositions 5 and 8. □

It follows that e.g. $\mathfrak{F}(\{x^0, y^0\})$ is an extensional type structure in which no more identifications between closed terms can be made. This is the counterpart in the typed λ-calculus of the type free model $\mathfrak{M}(\mathcal{H}^*)$.

Finally a result on pairing functions is mentioned.

A.1.24. DEFINITION. (i) A *pairing* in $\boldsymbol{\lambda}^\tau$ for types σ, τ is a triple D, D_1, D_2 with for some type ρ

(1) $D \in \sigma \to \tau \to \rho$, $D_1 \in \rho \to \sigma$ and $D_2 \in \rho \to \tau$.

(2) $D_i(DM_1M_2) = M_i$, for all $M_1 \in \sigma$, $M_2 \in \tau$.

(ii) The pairing is *surjective* if moreover

$$D(D_1M)(D_2M) = M \quad \text{for all } M \in \rho.$$

A.1.25. PROPOSITION. (i) *In $\boldsymbol{\lambda}^\tau$ there is in general no pairing for types σ and τ.*

(ii) *In $\boldsymbol{\lambda\eta}^\tau$ there is a pairing for all types σ and τ.*

(iii) *In $\boldsymbol{\lambda\eta}^\tau$ there is no surjective pairing for any types.*

PROOF. See Barendregt [1974]. □

The proof of (iii) above is a typical application of the type-free λ-calculus to the typed λ-calculus: if D, D_1, D_2 work for $\boldsymbol{\lambda\eta}^\tau$, then these terms without type work for $\boldsymbol{\lambda\eta}$; but then $\boldsymbol{\Omega}$ gives a contradiction.

A.2. Primitive recursive functionals

In Gödel [1958] a consistency proof of arithmetic is given that makes use of functionals of higher type. The central idea is to replace in an arithmetical formula a quantifier change

$$\forall x \; \exists y \quad P(x,y)$$

into

$$\exists f \; \forall x \quad P(x,fx).$$

If this is iterated, then one needs higher type functionals. In this way Gödel translated every arithmetical formula A into

$$A^D = \exists \vec{x} \; \forall \vec{y} \; A_D(\vec{x},\vec{y})$$

where A_D is quantifier free. He showed that if A is provable in intuitionistic arithmetic, then A^D becomes valid when the $\vec{x}, \vec{y}$ range over a class of "constructive functionals". (See Troelstra [1973] Ch. III § 5, and Hindley et al. [1972], Ch. 11 for an exposition). Later on it was realized that this class of functionals can be described by extending $\boldsymbol{\lambda}^\tau$ with numerals, a successor and recursion operators. The resulting system is called Gödel's $\mathfrak{T}$ of primitive recursive functionals.

A.2.1. DEFINITION. Gödel's $\mathfrak{T}$ is the extension of $\boldsymbol{\lambda}^\tau$ defined as follows.

(i) The set of terms of $\mathfrak{T}$, notation $\Lambda\mathfrak{T} = \bigcup \{\Lambda\mathfrak{T}_\sigma | \sigma \in \mathrm{Typ}\}$ is defined by adding to Λ^τ constants

$$\boldsymbol{0} \in \Lambda\mathfrak{T}_0, \qquad \mathbf{S}^+ \in \Lambda\mathfrak{T}_{0\to 0},$$

$$\mathbf{R}_\sigma \in \Lambda\mathfrak{T}_{\sigma\to(\sigma\to 0\to\sigma)\to 0\to\sigma}.$$

and closing under application and abstraction.

(ii) Formulas of $\mathfrak{T}$ are equations between elements of $\Lambda\mathfrak{T}$. The theory $\mathfrak{T}$ is axiomatized by equality axioms and rules, β-conversion and a scheme for primitive recursion of higher type

$$\boldsymbol{R}_\sigma MN\mathbf{0} = M$$

$$\boldsymbol{R}_\sigma MN(\boldsymbol{S}^+x) = N(\boldsymbol{R}_\sigma MNx)x$$

where $M, N \in \Lambda\mathfrak{T}$ are of appropriate type and x is a variable of type 0.

(iii) $\mathfrak{T}\boldsymbol{\eta}$ is the extension of $\mathfrak{T}$ by η-conversion.

A.2.2. PROPOSITION. *There are on $\Lambda\mathfrak{T}$ notions of reduction $\boldsymbol{\beta}\mathfrak{T}$ and $\boldsymbol{\beta\eta}\mathfrak{T}$ that correspond to provable equality in $\mathfrak{T}$ and $\mathfrak{T}\boldsymbol{\eta}$ respectively and are both Church-Rosser.*

The following is proved independently by Dragalin [1968], Hinata [1967], Hinatani [1966], Sanchis [1967], Shoenfield [1967] and Tait [1967] (!).

A.2.3. THEOREM (Strong normalization for $\mathfrak{T}$). *For $M \in \Lambda\mathfrak{T}$ every $\beta\eta\mathfrak{T}$-reduction terminates.*

PROOF. Define the following classes of terms:

$$C_0 = \{M \in \Lambda\mathfrak{T}_0^0 | \beta\eta\mathfrak{T}\text{-SN}(M)\},$$

$$C_{\sigma\to\tau} = \{M \in \Lambda\mathfrak{T}_{\sigma\to\tau}^0 | \forall N \in C_\sigma\ MN \in C_\tau\},$$

$$C = \bigcup \{C_\sigma | \sigma \in \text{Typ}\},$$

$$C_\sigma^* = \{M \in \Lambda\mathfrak{T}_\sigma | \text{every instance of } M \text{ with elements in } C \text{ is in } C\}.$$

Then one shows by simultaneous induction on σ that

(1) $\qquad M \in C_\sigma \Rightarrow \beta\eta\mathfrak{T}\text{-SN}(M)$

(2) $\qquad \lambda x_1^{\sigma_1} \cdots x_n^{\sigma_n}.\boldsymbol{0} \in C_\sigma \quad \textit{if } \sigma = \sigma_1 \to \cdots \to \sigma_n \to 0.$

Finally one shows by induction on M that

(3) $\qquad M \in \Lambda\mathfrak{T}_\sigma \Rightarrow M \in C_\sigma^*.$

By (1) and (3) every term of $\mathfrak{T}$ strongly normalizes. □

The terms $\boldsymbol{0}$, $\boldsymbol{1} \equiv \boldsymbol{S}^+\boldsymbol{0}$, $\boldsymbol{2} \equiv \boldsymbol{S}^+\boldsymbol{1}, \ldots$ serve as numerals in $\mathfrak{T}$. The $\boldsymbol{R}_\sigma$ are introduced to define primitive recursion. Clearly all the primitive recursive functions are $\mathfrak{T}$-definable on the numerals $\boldsymbol{0}, \boldsymbol{1}, \ldots$. But since the σ in $\boldsymbol{R}_\sigma$ are arbitrary types, more than the primitive recursive functions are $\mathfrak{T}$-definable.

A.2.4. EXAMPLE. In Péter [1967] the following example of a function that is not primitive recursive is given (a simplification of the Ackermann function):

$$\psi(0, n) = n + 1,$$

$$\psi(m + 1, 0) = \psi(m, 1),$$

$$\psi(m + 1, n + 1) = \psi(m, \psi(m + 1, n)).$$

It is easy to represent ψ in $\mathfrak{T}$. Write

$$\psi_m(n) = \psi(m, n).$$

If ψ_m is represented by $\boldsymbol{Fm}$, then ψ_{m+1} is represented by $\boldsymbol{R}(\boldsymbol{Fm1})(\lambda ab.\boldsymbol{Fm}(a)) = G(\boldsymbol{Fm})$ say. Therefore $F \equiv \boldsymbol{RS}^+(\lambda ab.G(a))$ represents ψ.

The following result exactly characterizes the $\mathfrak{T}$-definable functions. For α an ordinal $\leqslant \varepsilon_0$, the α-recursive functions on $\mathbb{N}$ are those functions definable using transfinite recursion up to α. The $<\alpha$-recursive functions are the set of all β-recursive functions for some $\beta < \alpha$.

A.2.5. THEOREM. *The $\mathfrak{T}$-definable numeric functions are exactly the $<\varepsilon_0$-recursive functions.*

PROOF. See Kreisel [1959], Schwichtenberg [1975] and also Terlouw [198+]. □

A remarkable fact on higher type definability in $\mathfrak{T}$ is exhibited in the final exercise 2. Now we turn to models of $\mathfrak{T}$.

A.2.6. DEFINITION. (i) A *model* of $\mathfrak{T}$ is a combinatory type structure $\mathfrak{M}$ such that there are $0, s^+, r_\sigma \in \mathfrak{M}$ satisfying the axioms for $\mathbf{R}_\sigma$.

(ii) An *extensional* model of $\mathfrak{T}$ is in addition an extensional type structure.

(iii) An *ω-model* of $\mathfrak{T}$ is a model $\mathfrak{M}$ of $\mathfrak{T}$ such that $\mathfrak{M}_0 = \{[\![\boldsymbol{n}]\!] \mid n \in \mathbb{N}\}$.

Note that since in $\mathfrak{T}$ there are closed terms of any type, it makes sense to define for a model $\mathfrak{M}$ the interior $\mathfrak{M}^0$.

A.2.7. PROPOSITION. (i) *$\mathfrak{M}(\mathfrak{T}\boldsymbol{\eta})$ is an extensional model of $\mathfrak{T}$.*

(ii) HRO, *$\mathfrak{M}^0(\mathfrak{T}\boldsymbol{\eta})$ and $\mathfrak{M}^0(\mathbb{N})$ are non-extensional ω-models of $\mathfrak{T}$.*

(iii) HEO *and $\mathfrak{M}(\mathbb{N})$ are extensional ω-models of $\mathfrak{T}$.*

PROOF. (i) Easy, cf. corollary 5.3.25.

(ii) Clearly these structures are ω-models. HRO is not extensional because there are different recursive indices of say the function $\lambda x.\mathbf{0}.\mathfrak{M}^0(\mathfrak{T}\boldsymbol{\eta})$ is not extensional: consider $\lambda x.\mathbf{0}$ and $\lambda x.x \dot{-} x$. That $\mathfrak{M}^0(\mathbb{N})$ is not extensional is proved in the final exercises.

(iii) Obvious. □

In contrast to corollary A.1.20 one has the following.

A.2.8. THEOREM. *For $M, N \in \Lambda\mathfrak{T}$ the relation $\mathfrak{M}(\mathbb{N}) \models M = N$ is complete Π^1_1.*

PROOF. See Friedman [1975]. □

Finally we discuss briefly some extensions of $\mathfrak{T}$.

Bar recursion

Spector [1962] extended Gödel's consistency proof of arithmetic to analysis. For this the "bar recursive" functionals were needed. These functionals can be described by extending $\mathfrak{T}$ with the so-called bar recursor to obtain the theory $\mathfrak{T}\mathfrak{B}$.

$\mathfrak{M}(\mathbb{N})$ is not a model of $\mathfrak{T}\mathfrak{B}$ since bar recursion presupposes that the functionals are continuous (in a specific sense). Also HRO and HEO are not models of $\mathfrak{T}\mathfrak{B}$ as was shown by Kreisel [1959].

Tait [1971] showed that the weak normalization theorem also holds for $\mathfrak{T}\mathfrak{B}$. Therefore $\mathfrak{M}^0(\mathfrak{T}\mathfrak{B})$ is an ω-model of $\mathfrak{T}\mathfrak{B}$. Another model of $\mathfrak{T}\mathfrak{B}$ are the countable functionals of Kleene and Kreisel. This model can be described as $\mathfrak{M}_C(\mathbb{N})$, when C is the cartesian closed category of limit spaces, see Hyland [1975].

For information about bar recursion see also Howard [1968], Scarpellini [1971], Luckhardt [1973], Ershov [1973/75], Diller and Vogel [1975] and Vogel [1976].

Infinite terms

$\mathfrak{T}^\infty$ is obtained by adding to term formation the following rule: if $t_0, t_1, \ldots$ are terms of type σ, then $\langle t_0, t_1, \ldots \rangle$ is a term of type $0 \to \sigma$. For these new terms the following axioms are postulated:

$$\langle \vec{t} \rangle \boldsymbol{n} = t_n, \qquad \langle \vec{t} \rangle MN = \langle \vec{t}\, N \rangle M.$$

Using ordinals up to ε_0 Tait [1965] shows that terms in $\mathfrak{T}$ normalize and relates this with the consistency proof of arithmetic using the ω-rule and cut elimination.

Intuitionistic arithmetic in all finite types

HA^ω is the theory obtained by adding to $\mathfrak{T}$ logic and the Peano axioms. This theory is called *intuitionistic arithmetic in all finite types* and is studied in Troelstra [1973].

LCF

The theory "Logic for Computable Functions" originated with Scott. Milner and collaborators extended this in several stages to a computer system LCF which has the capacity to prove properties of programs (like correctness) in a semi-automatic way.

One part of LCF consists of a theory PPλ which essentially consists of $\mathfrak{T}$ extended as follows:

(1) There are more types (formation of direct product $\sigma \times \tau$ and disjoint sum $\sigma \oplus \tau$).

(2) For each type σ there is a fixed point combinator $\boldsymbol{Y}_\sigma \in (\sigma \to \sigma) \to \sigma$ such that $\boldsymbol{Y}_\sigma M = M(\boldsymbol{Y}_\sigma M)$. (This creates terms without nf.)

(3) The theory is embedded into predicate logic. Models of PPλ are easy to construct: start with an arbitrary cpo X and form $X_0 = X$, $X_{\sigma\to\tau} = X_\sigma \to X_\tau$ etc. By proposition 0.2.17 (ii) an interpretation for the $\boldsymbol{Y}_\sigma$ can be given.

The system LCF is designed to prove theorems about programs in an interactive way. The program and its properties are formulated in PPλ. The interaction consists of proof strategies given by the human user and computations (like conversion) by the machine. A special part of LCF consists of a formal metalanguage ML in which the proof strategies can be formulated. See Gordon et al. [1980] for an introduction and references.

A.3. Formulae as types

In Curry et al. [1958], it was noticed that the types of $\boldsymbol{K}_{\sigma\tau}$ and $\boldsymbol{S}_{\sigma\tau\rho}$ (see Remark A.1.5 (i)) are valid formulas of proposition logic if $\to$ is interpreted as implication. Tait [1965] indicated a close connection between β-reduction of typed terms and cut elimination in derivations. These observations inspired Howard in 1969, [1980], to give a correspondence between typed terms and derivations, via the so-called *formulae-as-types* notion: the end formula of a derivation Π is considered as the type of Π; application corresponds to modus ponens and abstraction to the discharging of assumptions (in natural deduction).

Independently de Bruijn [1970] introduced a language Automath as a tool for verifying mathematical proofs by machine. Automath is a typed λ-calculus where the types are again (typed) λ-terms. The formulae-as-types notion plays an essential role in the translation of actual proofs in this language. For more information see de Bruijn [1980] (survey), Zucker [1977] and van Benthem Jutting [1979] (translating actual mathematics) and van Daalen [1980] (theoretical aspects of Automath and related languages). Seldin [1979] introduces a system called generalized functionality. This is essentially the same as one of the languages in the Automath family.

Again another independent approach to formulae-as-types is the work of Girard [1971]. He considers a typed λ-calculus with operations on the types such as λ-abstraction. (By contrast the Automath languages have only free variables in the terms that function as types.) This corresponds to predicate quantification in second order logic. By showing in an ingenious way strong normalization for the terms in question, Girard obtained a proof of the cut elimination theorem for analysis and type theory.

The formulae-as-types idea gave rise to several investigations connecting typed λ-calculus, proof theory and some category theory, see Lambek [1980], Mann [1975], and Szabo [1978]. See also Pottinger [1977]. Another direction is the connection between subsystems of logic and restricted versions of the typed λ-calculus (e.g. relevance logic and the typed λI-calculus), see Helman [1977].

APPENDIX B

ILLATIVE COMBINATORY LOGIC

As was mentioned in chapter 1, one of the aims of the founders of the λ-calculus and combinatory logic was to provide a basis for mathematics. We want to show in some detail that if one is not careful, this may lead to inconsistencies. The derivation of the so called Curry paradox is of interest in its own, since it is closely related to the theorem of Löb [1955] (in the same way as the Liar's paradox is related to Gödel's incompleteness theorem), see van Benthem [1978].

B.1. DEFINITION. (i) An *illative combinatory logic* (notation $\boldsymbol{ICL}$) is a theory with as alphabet that of $\boldsymbol{CL}$ extended with a set of *logical constants*.

(ii) Terms of $\boldsymbol{ICL}$ are defined inductively:

(1) Every variable or constant is a term.

(2) If M, N are terms, then so in (MN).

(iii) Formulas of $\boldsymbol{ICL}$ are defined as follows:

(1) If M, N are terms of $\boldsymbol{ICL}$, then $M = N$ is a formula.

(2) If M is a term of $\boldsymbol{ICL}$, then M is a formula.

B.2. REMARKS. (i) In Curry's school the formula M is written as $\vdash M$. Since this does not imply that M is provable we prefer our notation. The intended interpretation of M is "M is true".

(ii) An illative theory could be based also on the λ-calculus.

B.3. DEFINITION. (i) $\boldsymbol{ICL}_0$ is an illative combinatory logic based on the following set of logical constants.

$$\{\boldsymbol{K}, \boldsymbol{S}, \boldsymbol{F}, \boldsymbol{Q}, \boldsymbol{E}, \boldsymbol{\Xi}, \boldsymbol{\Pi}, \boldsymbol{P}\}$$

(ii) The following abbreviations give some idea of the intended interpretation of these constants.

$M \in N$ is NM, $\qquad M \to N$ is $\boldsymbol{P}MN$,

$M \subseteq N$ is $\boldsymbol{\Xi}MN$, $\qquad N^M$ is $\boldsymbol{F}MN$,

$\forall x\ M$ is $\boldsymbol{\Pi}(\lambda^* x.M)$.

(iii) The theory $\boldsymbol{ICL}_0$ is axiomatized by the following axioms and rules.
(1) Equality axioms and rules including:

$$\frac{M \quad M = N}{N}$$

(2) Combinatory axioms:

$$\boldsymbol{K}MN = M, \qquad \boldsymbol{S}MNL = ML(ML).$$

(3) The following introduction and elimination rules for each logical constant ($\not\equiv \boldsymbol{E}$) in the style of natural deduction (see Gentzen [1969]); in the introduction rules for $\boldsymbol{F}$, $\boldsymbol{\Xi}$ and $\boldsymbol{P}$ some of the assumptions have to be discharged.

	Elimination	Introduction
$\boldsymbol{Q}$	$\dfrac{\boldsymbol{Q}MN}{M = N}$	$\dfrac{M = N}{\boldsymbol{Q}MN}$
$\boldsymbol{P}$	$\dfrac{M \to N, M}{N}$	$[M]$ $\vdots$ $\dfrac{N}{M \to N}$
$\boldsymbol{\Xi}$	$\dfrac{M \subseteq N \quad Z \in M}{Z \in N}$	$[x \in M]$ $\vdots$ $\dfrac{x \in N}{M \subseteq N}$, x fresh
$\boldsymbol{\Pi}$	$\dfrac{M \in \boldsymbol{\Pi}}{N \in M}$	$\dfrac{x \in M}{M \in \boldsymbol{\Pi}}$, x fresh
$\boldsymbol{F}$	$\dfrac{Z \in N^M \quad U \in M}{ZU \in N}$	$[x \in M]$ $\vdots$ $\dfrac{Zx \in N}{Z \in N^M}$, x fresh
$\boldsymbol{E}$	$M \in \boldsymbol{E}$	

B.4. PROPOSITION. *The constants* $\boldsymbol{E}$, $\boldsymbol{F}$, $\boldsymbol{P}$ *and* $\boldsymbol{\Pi}$ *can be defined from the others* $(\boldsymbol{K}, \boldsymbol{S}, \boldsymbol{Q}, \boldsymbol{\Xi})$ *such that the rules becomes derivable.*

PROOF. Define $\boldsymbol{E} \equiv \lambda^* x.\boldsymbol{Q}xx$, $\boldsymbol{F} \equiv \lambda^* xyz.\boldsymbol{\Xi}x(y \circ z)$, $\boldsymbol{P} \equiv \lambda^* xy.\boldsymbol{\Xi}(\boldsymbol{K}x)(\boldsymbol{K}y)$ and $\boldsymbol{\Pi} \equiv \boldsymbol{\Xi}\boldsymbol{E}$. Then the rules for these defined constants follow easily. For example, for $\boldsymbol{F}$:

elimination

$$\dfrac{\dfrac{\dfrac{\dfrac{Z\in N^{M}}{Z\in FMN}}{\Xi M(N\circ Z)}}{M\subseteq N\circ Z}\qquad\qquad U\in M}{\dfrac{\dfrac{U\in N\circ Z}{N(ZU)}}{ZU\in N}}$$

introduction

$$\begin{array}{l}[x\in M]\qquad (1)\\ \quad\vdots\\ \dfrac{\dfrac{\dfrac{Zx\in N}{x\in N\circ Z}}{M\subseteq(N\circ Z)}\,(1)}{Z\in N^{M}}\end{array}$$ □

REMARK. *Also* Ξ *is definable from* $\boldsymbol{F}$. *For example, taking* $\Xi\equiv\lambda^{*}xy.\boldsymbol{F}xy\boldsymbol{I}$ *or alternatively* $\Xi\equiv\lambda^{*}xy.\boldsymbol{F}x\boldsymbol{I}y$ *the rules for* Ξ *are satisfied.*

An ***ICL*** is called inconsistent if every M can be derived. The following is known as Curry's paradox.

B.5. PROPOSITION. $\boldsymbol{ICL}_0$ *is inconsistent. In fact one only needs the rule* $\boldsymbol{P}$ *to derive the inconsistency.*

PROOF. Let M be an arbitrary term. By the fixed point theorem construct an X such that

$$X=X\to M$$

Then the following is a derivation of M

$$\dfrac{\dfrac{\dfrac{[X](1)\quad \dfrac{[X](1)}{X\to M}}{\dfrac{M}{X\to M}\,(1)}}{X\quad X\to M}}{M}$$

[Taking $M\equiv\boldsymbol{Q}P\boldsymbol{Q}$ one can also derive every equation $P=Q$.]. □

Curry and his school proposed to avoid the paradox by introducing a constant $\boldsymbol{H}$ with for $X \in \boldsymbol{H}$ the intended interpretation "X is a proposition" and restricting the rules for the logical constants in an appropriate way to the class $\boldsymbol{H}$. The above inconsistency then disappears since for $X = X \rightarrow M$ one cannot show that X is a proposition. Unfortunately several of the resulting systems are still not free from contradictions; see for example Bunder [1974]. On the other hand those systems in e.g. Curry et al. [1972] that are provably consistent are all too weak to be a foundation for logic.

Also Aczel [1980] proposes to avoid the paradoxes by introducing a class of propositions. Since his approach is semantical (based on arbitrary λ-models) his theory is consistent.

Another approach is the work of Feferman [1975], [1980] where application is a partially defined operator. Then the paradoxes are avoided since the paradoxical object does not need to be defined.

APPENDIX C

VARIABLES

This appendix discusses free and bound variables. A theoretical background is given for considering terms modulo α-congruence. This is done following two methods: one of Curry and one of de Bruijn. The latter approach has the advantage of being also useful for implementing λ-conversions on a computer.

In ancient mathematics (formal) variables were hardly used. Under the influence of Vieta at the end 16th century variables became a standard tool in the subject. There was however much confusion about the nature of variables: an integer variable was a "changing magnitude" that was sometimes even, sometimes odd and that could be "kept constant" during a proof. Such entities do not exist, however.

Frege and Peirce clarified the precise nature of variables: they are syntactic objects and distinction should be made between *free* and *bound* variables.

A free variable is a syntactic object, usually occurring in some context, in which other syntactic objects may be substituted. When a term containing free variables is to be interpreted in a structure $\mathfrak{M}$, a choice is needed of how to interpret these variables as elements in the domain of $\mathfrak{M}$.

Bound variables on the other hand do not admit substitution or a choice of interpretation. In the following examples x is a bound variable

$$\int_0^1 x^2 + 1\,\mathrm{d}x; \qquad \sum_{x=0}^{10} x^2 + 1; \qquad \exists x\, x^2 + 1 = 0; \qquad \lambda x.x^2 + 1.$$

If a term t is substituted (naively) in the free occurrences of a variable y in an expression $A \equiv A(y)$, then some variables in t may become bound. Let $A(y)$ be the correct formula

$$\int_0^1 x^2 + y\,\mathrm{d}x = y + \frac{1}{3}$$

and let $t \equiv x$, then $A(x)$ is the incorrect

$$\int_0^1 x^2 + x\,\mathrm{d}x = x + \frac{1}{3}.$$

This is called *confusion of variables*.

A term t is *substitutible* for y in A, notation t-y-A if no free variable of t becomes bound after substituting t for (the free occurrences of) y in A. Clearly not

$$x - y - \int_0^1 x^2 + y\,\mathrm{d}x = y + \frac{1}{3};$$

this caused the mentioned confusion of variables. By changing bound variables in A one always can avoid collision of variables. For example

$$x - y - \int_0^1 u^2 + y\,\mathrm{d}u = y + \frac{1}{3}.$$

In the λ-calculus substitution is a fundamental operation. To insure substitutability, terms are considered modulo change of bound variables, that is modulo $\equiv_\alpha$ (see definition 2.1.11). Therefore λ-terms themselves are representatives of the objects we are interested in. Thus it becomes necessary to show that the operations on terms determine well defined operations on the $\equiv_\alpha$-equivalence classes. For application and abstraction this is obvious. For substitution one has to show

$$M \equiv_\alpha M',\ N \equiv_\alpha N' \Rightarrow M[x:=N] \equiv_\alpha M'[x:=N'].$$

But in the definition 2.1.15 of substitution the variable convention was already used. This is circular and hence we must have a fresh look at λ-terms and the definition of substitution. Two different approaches will be described. The first one is taken from Curry e.a. [1958], the second one from de Bruijn [1972].

Curry defined substitution as follows.

C.1. Definition. Let $M, N \in \Lambda$. Then $M[x:=N]$ is defined inductively as follows (even if the variable convention is not observed).

M	$M[x:=N]$
x	N
$y \not\equiv x$	y
M_1M_2	$M_1[x:=N]M_2[x:=N]$
$\lambda x.M_1$	$\lambda x.M_1$
$\lambda y.M_1, y \not\equiv x$	$\lambda z.M_1[y:=z][x:=N]$ where $z \equiv y$ if $x \notin \mathrm{FV}(M_1)$ or $y \notin \mathrm{FV}(N)$, else z is the first variable in the sequence $v_0, v_1, v_2, \ldots$ not in M_1 or N.

It is easy to see that this definition is a proper one by induction on $\|M\|$ (note that $\|M_1[y:=z]\| = \|M_1\|$). Using this notion of substitution the equivalence relation $\equiv_\alpha$ is defined.

C.2. PROPOSITION. *For the notions of substitution and α-congruence defined as above, one has*

$$M \equiv_\alpha M' \text{ and } N \equiv_\alpha N' \Rightarrow M[x:=N] \equiv_\alpha M'[x:=N'].$$

PROOF. See Curry et al [1958] pp. 94–104. □

If one observes the variable convention, then $M[x:=N]$ as in definition 2.1.15 is the same substitution as in Curry's definition C.1. Therefore in that case one may work with ordinary λ-terms as representatives of $\equiv_\alpha$-classes and work with these terms in the naive way.

In de Bruijn [1972] a different approach is given. It was introduced for the automatic manipulation of terms needed in the implementation of Automath (See § A.3). The relation $\equiv_\alpha$ is relatively involved for the machine. Therefore a different notation is given for λ-terms, obtaining the so-called *nameless terms*. A nameless λ-term is a syntactic object such that no names are given to bound variables. These objects are introduced in such a way that an α-congruence class of ordinary λ-terms correspond exactly to one nameless term. The definition is as follows.

C.3. DEFINITION. (i) The set of nameless terms, notation Λ^*, has the following alphabet:

$$\lambda, (,), 1, 2, 3, \ldots$$

(ii) Λ^* is defined inductively as follows

$$n \in \Lambda^* \quad \text{for } n \in \mathbb{N} - \{0\},$$

$$A, B \in \Lambda^* \Rightarrow (AB) \in \Lambda^*,$$

$$A \in \Lambda^* \Rightarrow \lambda A \in \Lambda^*.$$

The intuitive meaning of name free terms becomes clear from the following examples. Consider the term $M \equiv \lambda x.x(\lambda y.xyy)$. In tree form this term may be represented as

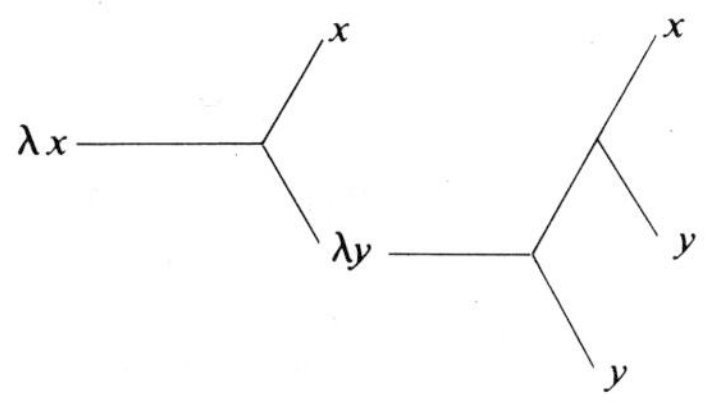

M corresponds to the nameless term M with tree

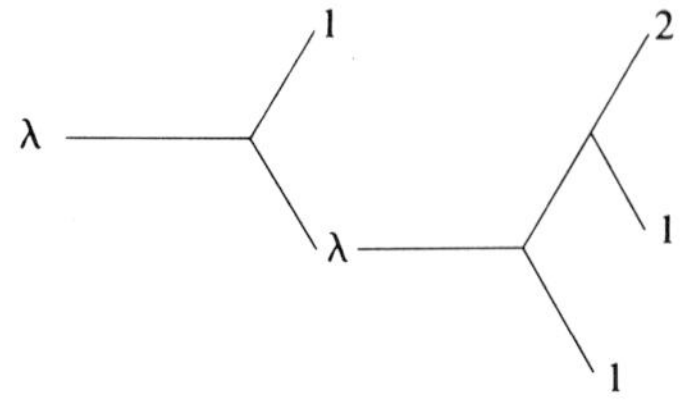

i.e. to $M^* \equiv \lambda 1(\lambda 211)$, using the same brackets convention as for λ-terms. A number occurrence n in M^* corresponds to the fact that the variable in the corresponding place in M is bound by the λ at a distance n (along a path in the tree) of that place.

If a number occurrence n in a nameless term is larger than the number of λ's, say k, down the tree from it, then this n refers to the free variable $v_{n\text{-}k\text{-}1}$. For example consider $N \equiv \lambda x.x(\lambda y.xv_2y)$. In nameless notation this becomes $N^* \equiv \lambda 1(\lambda 251)$. The meaning of this nameless term can be found easily by writing it as

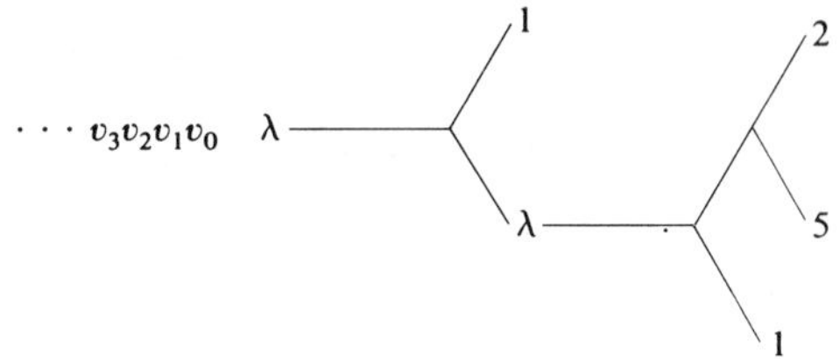

and counting also the free variables at the root of the tree. In this way one sees that $\lambda x.xv_3(\lambda y.xyv_2)$ corresponds to $\lambda 15(\lambda 215)$. Note that $\lambda x.xv_2$ and $\lambda y.yv_2$ both correspond to $\lambda 14$: it is not necessary in Λ^* to give a name to the bound variables.

C.4. PROPOSITION. *There is a canonical map* $*: \Lambda \to \Lambda^*$ *such that*

$$*(M) \equiv *(N) \Leftrightarrow M \equiv_\alpha N.$$

PROOF. Implicit in de Bruijn [1972]. See the examples above. □

Therefore Λ^* is isomorphic to $\Lambda/\equiv_\alpha$ and nameless terms are considered as the "real" terms. The difference with Curry's approach is that elements of Λ^* have a concrete notation and that substitution on Λ^* can be defined directly (rather than via substitution on Λ).

C.5. PROPOSITION. *There is an operation substitution* $A[x:=B]$ *for* $A, B \in \Lambda^*$ *such that for* $M, N \in \Lambda$

$$*(M[x:=N]) \equiv *(M)[x:=*(N)],$$

where the first $[x{:=}\ \ ]$ *is naive substitution as in definition* 2.1.15 *with* M, N *satisfying the variable convention.*

PROOF. Implicit in de Bruijn [1972]. □

C.6. COMMENT. Some shifting is needed for substitution on Λ^*. E.g. $\lambda 12[v_0{:=}\lambda 13]\equiv\lambda 1(\lambda 14)$, that is $\lambda 13$ becomes after substitution $\lambda 14$. This example corresponds to $\lambda x.xv_0[v_0{:=}\lambda y.yv_2]\equiv\lambda x.x(\lambda y.yv_2)$.

The moral of all this is that the nameless terms are good for machine manipulation and metamathematical reasoning; for the human user they are not very convenient. Therefore the best is to work with ordinary λ-terms, and to consider them tacitly as representatives of the corresponding terms in Λ^*. Provided one observes the variable convention, substitution can be done naively on the level of the representatives. The same is true for application and abstraction.

Final Exercises

1. (Kreisel). The aim is to show that $\mathfrak{M}^0(\mathbb{N})$, the substructure of $\mathfrak{T}$-definable elements in $\mathfrak{M}(\mathbb{N})$, is not extensional.

(i) Let $1=0\to 0$, $2=1\to 0$ and $3=2\to 0$ be types. Define $d_n, d_\infty\in\mathfrak{M}^0(\mathbb{N})_1$ and $f\in\mathfrak{M}^0(\mathbb{N})_{2\to 1}$ as follows:

$$d_n(x)=\begin{cases}0 & \text{if } x<n,\\ 1 & \text{else.}\end{cases}$$

$$d_\infty(x)=0.$$

$$f_F(x)=\begin{cases}0 & \text{if } \neg\,\exists y<x+1\ F(d_\infty)=F(d_y),\\ 1 & \text{else.}\end{cases}$$

Show that if $F\in\mathfrak{M}(\mathbb{N})_2$ is continuous with respect to the Baire topology, then

$$F(d_0)\neq F(d_\infty)\Rightarrow F(f_F)\neq F(d_\infty),$$

and for discontinuous F this is false in general. [*Hint*. Note that $\lim_{n\to\infty}d_n=d_\infty$; consider $\mu m[F(d_m)=F(d_\infty)]$.]

(ii) Construct an element $\Phi\in\mathfrak{M}^0(\mathbb{N})_3$ that is not constant, but such that for continuous $F\in\mathfrak{M}(\mathbb{N})_2$ one has $\Phi F=0$.

(iii) Show that if $F\in\mathfrak{M}^0(\mathbb{N})_2$, then F is continuous.

(iv) Conclude that $\mathfrak{M}^0(\mathbb{N})$ is not extensional.

2. (Bergstra). Let F range over $\mathfrak{M}(\mathbb{N})_2$ and let d_n be as in 1 above. Show that the predicate

$$\exists n\in\mathbb{N}\quad Fd_n=0$$

is primitive recursive (i.e. definable in $\mathfrak{T}$). [*Hint* (J. Terlouw). Construct primitive recursive Φ, Ψ such that

$$\Phi Fn=\ \text{ if } \exists k<n\ Fd_k=0 \text{ then 1 else 0},$$

$$\Psi Fn=\ \text{ if } \exists k<n+1\ Fd_k=0 \text{ then 1 else 0}.$$

By considering $n_0=\mu n[Fd_n=0]$, show that

$$\exists n\ Fd_n=0\ \Leftrightarrow\ [F(\Phi F)\neq F(\Psi F)\vee Fd_0=0].]$$

3. Try to solve open problems in the λ-calculus; see Problems [1975], [1980].

ADDENDA

1. Some interesting information about partial versus total combinatory algebras has been obtained by Klop [1982].

DEFINITION. (i) A *partial combinatory algebra* is a structure $\mathfrak{A} = \langle X, \cdot, k, s \rangle$ with $\cdot : X^2 \hookrightarrow X$ a partial map, satisfying for all x, y

$$kxy \simeq x, \qquad sxyz \simeq xz(yx),$$

$$kx\downarrow, \qquad sx\downarrow, \qquad sxy\downarrow.$$

[Here $t\downarrow$ denotes that t is defined; $t \simeq s$ denotes ($t\downarrow \Leftrightarrow s\downarrow$ and $t\downarrow \Rightarrow t = s$).]

$\mathfrak{A}$ is *total* if xy is always defined.

(ii) $\mathfrak{A}$ *can be completed* if there is a total combinatory algebra $\mathfrak{A}'$ such that $\mathfrak{A} \hookrightarrow \mathfrak{A}'$.

(iii) $\mathfrak{A}$ *has unique head normal forms* if for all x, y the elements k, s, kx, sx, sxy are pairwise distinct and

$$sxy = sx'y' \;\Rightarrow\; x = x' \text{ and } y = y'.$$

THEOREM. (i) *Not every partial combinatory algebra can be completed.*

(ii) *If $\mathfrak{A}$ has unique head normal forms, then $\mathfrak{A}$ can be completed.*

(iii) *If $\mathfrak{A} \models s(kk)k = s(ks)(s(kk)k)$, in particular if $\mathfrak{A}$ is a partial λ-algebra, then $\mathfrak{A}$ is already total.*

PARTIAL PROOF. (i) Let $1 = s(sk)$. Klop showed that the theory of partial combinatory algebras is consistent with

$$(*) \qquad AC \neq BC \quad \text{and} \quad 1A = 1B,$$

where A, B, C are some constants. Note that $1Ax = Ax$ only if $x(Ax)\downarrow$. A partial combinatory algebra $\mathfrak{A}$ with some elements a, b, c satisfying $(*)$ cannot be made total since $1A = 1B \Rightarrow AC = BC$ if the operation $\cdot$ is total.

(iii) Note that $s(kk)kxyz = x$ always, but $s(ks)(s(kk)k)xyz \simeq kx(yz)$. Hence $yz\downarrow$ for all y, z. Therefore $\mathfrak{A}$ is total. □

2. In Longo [1983] it is proved that

$$D_A \models M \subseteq N \;\Leftrightarrow\; \mathrm{BT}(M) \subseteq \mathrm{BT}(N)$$

and hence

$$D_A \models M = N \;\Leftrightarrow\; \mathrm{BT}(M) = \mathrm{BT}(N).$$

Let $\mathfrak{F}$ be the filter model of Barendregt et al. [1983], see also exercise 5.8.8. In Ronchi [1982] it is shown that

$$\mathfrak{F} \models M \subseteq N \;\Leftrightarrow\; M \underset{\sim}{\sqsubseteq}^{\eta} N, \quad \text{i.e.}$$

$$\Leftrightarrow\; \exists N' \in \Lambda \;\; M \underset{\sim}{\sqsubseteq} N' \geqslant_{\eta} N$$

and hence again $\mathrm{Th}(\mathfrak{F}) = \mathfrak{B}$.

3. The notion of rich model is improved by Koymans as follows. Let $\phi: \mathfrak{M}^2 \to \mathfrak{M}$, where $\mathfrak{M}$ is a λ-algebra. ϕ is *representable in its variables separately* if $\lambda\!\!\!\lambda\, b.\phi(a_0, b)$ and $\lambda\!\!\!\lambda\, a.\phi(a, b_0)$ are representable for all $a_0, b_0 \in \mathfrak{M}$. Then $\mathfrak{M}$ is called *affluent* if separate representability implies representability. Then one has

$$\mathfrak{M} \text{ is rich} \;\Leftrightarrow\; \mathfrak{M} \text{ is affluent and extensional.}$$

By the methods of § 20.4 one can show

$$\mathfrak{M}^0(\mathfrak{B}) \text{ is not affluent,}$$

$$\mathfrak{M}(\lambda) \text{ is affluent.}$$

4. Instead of defining $S(\mathfrak{M})$ for $\mathfrak{M} \models \eta$ (i.e. $\mathfrak{M} \models \forall x \quad x = \lambda y.xy$) one can define these groups for arbitrary $\mathfrak{M}$ as follows. Let $\mathfrak{M}$ be a λ-algebra. Define

$$\mathfrak{M}^{\eta} = \{a \in \mathfrak{M} \mid 1a = a\}$$

$$S(\mathfrak{M}) = \langle \mathfrak{M}^{\eta}, \circ, I \rangle,$$

$$G(\mathfrak{M}) = \{a \in S(\mathfrak{M}) \mid a \text{ invertible}\}.$$

This is a monoid (semigroup with two sided unit). Then it makes sense to define $S(\mathcal{T})$ and $G(\mathcal{T})$ also for non extensional $\mathcal{T}$. In this sense

$$G(\lambda) = G(\mathcal{H}) = G(\mathcal{B}) = \{e\},$$

the trivial group, as remarked in the beginning of § 21.3.

5. New references are added in this edition. The ones that are not mentioned in the text fall on the borderline (sometimes a wide one) of lambda calculus and the following subjects.

(i) *Computer science*	
non determinism	Ashcroft et al. [1980]
functional programming	Berkling et al. [1982]
	Turner [1979]
rewrite systems	Bergstra et al. [1982]
	Dershowitz [1982]
	Huet [1977]
	Huet et al. [1980]
denotational semantics	Scott [1982]
(ii) *Types*	
semantics of types	Barendregt et al. [1983]
	Coppo et al. [1983]
	Coppo [198–]
	Donahue [1979]
	Hindley [1982], [1983]
cartesian closed categories	Lambek et al. [1982]
second order typed λ-calculus	Fortune et al. [1980]
typed λ-calculus	Schwichtenberg [1982]
	Statman [1980], [1981]
(iii) *Logic and mathematics*	
	Beeson [198–]
	Bunder [1980], [1981]
	Chauvin [1979]
	Fitch [1980]
	Feferman [1982]
	Kuzichev [1980], [1983]
	Martin-Löf [1982]
	Rezus [1982a]
(iv) *Numbered sets and recursion theory*	
	Barendregt et al. [1983]
	Giannini et al. [1983]

Still more references can be found in Rezus [1982].

REFERENCES

ACZEL, P.,
[1980] Frege structures and the notions of proposition, truth and set, in: BARWISE et al. [1980], pp. 31–60.

ARBIB, M. A. and MANES, E. G.,
[1975] *Arrows, Structures and Functors* (Academic Press, New York).

ASHCROFT, E. A. and HENNESSY, M. C. B.,
[1980] A mathematical semantics for a nondeterministic typed lambda calculus, *Theor. Comput. Sci.* 11, pp. 227–245.

AUSIELLO, G. and BÖHM, C. (eds.),
[1978] *Automata, Languages and Programming*, Fifth Colloquium, Udine, Italy, July 1978, Lecture Notes in Computer Science 62 (Springer-Verlag, Berlin).

BAETEN, J. and BOERBOOM, B.,
[1979] Ω can be anything it shouldn't be, *Indag. Math.* 41, pp. 111–120.

BARENDREGT, H.P.,
[1971] Some Extensional Term Models for Combinatory Logics and λ-calculi, Dissertation, University of Utrecht.
[1973] Combinatory logic and the axiom of choice, *Indag. Math.* 35, pp. 203–221.
[1973a] A characterization of terms of the λ-I-calculus having a normal form, *J. Symbolic Logic*, 38, pp. 441–445.
[1974] Pairing without conventional restraints, *Z. Math. Logik Grundlag. Math.* 20, pp. 289–306.
[1974a] Combinatory logic and the ω-rule, *Fundamenta Math.* 82, pp. 199–2155.
[1975] Normed uniformly reflexive structures, in: BÖHM [1975], pp. 272–286.
[1976] A global representation of the recursive functions in the lambda calculus, *Theor. Comput. Sci.* 3, pp. 225–242.
[1977] The type free lambda calculus, in: BARWISE [1977], pp. 1092–1132.

BARENDREGT, H. P. et al. (= BARENDREGT, H.P.; BERGSTRA, J.; KLOP, J. W., and VOLKEN, H.),
[1976] Some notes on lambda reduction, in: Degrees, reductions and representability in the lambda calculus. Preprint no. 22, University of Utrecht, Department of mathematics, pp. 13–53.
[1976a] Representability in lambda algebras, *Indag. Math.* 38, pp. 377–387.
[1978] Degrees of sensible lambda theories, *J. Symbolic Logic* 43, p. 45–55.

BARENDREGT, H. P., COPPO, M. and DEZANI-CIANCAGLINI, M.,
[198–] A filter lambda model and the completeness of type assignment, *J. Symbolic Logic*, to appear.

BARENDREGT, H. P. and KOYMANS, K.,
[1980] Comparing some classes of lambda calculus models, in: HINDLEY and SELDIN [1980], pp. 287–302.

BARENDREGT, H. P. and LONGO, G.,
[1980] Equality of λ-terms in the model $\mathbb{T}^\omega$, in: HINDLEY and SELDIN [1980], pp. 303–339.
[198–] Recursion theoretic operators and morphisms on numbered sets, *Fund. Math.* CXIX, to appear.

BARWISE, J. (ed.),
[1977] *Handbook of Mathematical Logic*, Studies in Logic 90 (North-Holland, Amsterdam).

BARWISE, J.,
[1977a] An introduction to first order logic, in: BARWISE [1977], pp. 5–46.

BARWISE, J. et al. (= BARWISE, J.; KEISLER, H. J., and KUNEN, K. (eds.)),
[1980] *The Kleene Symposium*, Studies in Logic 101 (North-Holland, Amsterdam).

BEESON, M.,
[198–] *Foundations of Constructive Mathematics. Metamathematical Studies* (Springer-Verlag, Berlin, to appear).

BEHMANN, H.,
[1922] Beiträge zur Algebra der Logik, insbesondere zum Entscheidungsproblem, *Math. Annalen* 86, pp. 163–229.

BEL, M.,
[1977] An intuitionistic combinatory theory not closed under the rule of choice *Indag. Math.* 39, pp. 69–72.

VAN BENTHEM, J. F. A. K.,
[1978] Four paradoxes, *J. Philos. Logic* 7, pp. 49–72.

VAN BENTHEM JUTTING, L. S.,
[1979] Checking Landau's "Grundlagen" in the Automath System, Mathematical Centre Tracts, Mathematical Centre, Amsterdam.

BERGSTRA, J. A. and KLOP, J. W.,
[1979] Church-Rosser strategies in the lambda calculus, *Theor. Comput. Sci.* 9, pp. 27–38.
[1980] Invertible terms in the lambda calculus, *Theor. Comput. Sci.* 11, pp. 19–37.
[1982] Strong normalization and perpetual reductions in the lambda calculus , *J. Inform. Process. Cybernet.* 18 (718), pp. 403–417. see BARENDREGT et al. [1976], [1976a], [1978].
[1982] Conditional rewrite rules: confluency and termination, preprint, Mathematical Centre, Kruislaan 413, 1098 SJ Amsterdam, The Netherlands.

BERKLING, K. J. and FEHR, E.,
[1982] A modification of the lambda calculus as a base for functional programming languages, in: NIELSEN and SCHMIDT [1982], pp. 35–47.

BERRY, G.,
[1978] Séquentialité de l'évaluation formelle des λ-expressions, in: *Proc. 3-e Colloque International sur la Programmation, Paris*, mars 1978 (Dunod, Paris).

BOERBOOM, B.,
see BAETEN and BOERBOOM [1979].

BOFFA, M. et al. (= BOFFA, M.; VAN DALEN, D. and MCALOON, K. (eds.)),
[1980] *Logic Colloquium* '78, Studies in Logic 97 (North-Holland, Amsterdam).

BÖHM, C.,
[1968] Alcune proprietà delle forme β-η-normali nel λ-K-calcolo, Pubblicazioni dell' Istituto per le Applicazioni del Calcolo.n. 696, Roma (19 pp.).

BÖHM, C. (ed.),
[1975] *λ-calculus and Computer Science Theory*, Proceedings of the Symposium held in Rome, March 25–27, 1975, Lecture Notes in Computer Science 37 (Springer-Verlag, Berlin).

BÖHM, C. and DEZANI-CIANCAGLINI, M.,
[1972] Can syntax be ignored during translation?, in: NIVAT [1972], pp. 197–207.
[1974] Combinatorial problems, combinator equations and normal forms, in: LOECKX [1974], pp. 185–199.
[1975] λ-Terms as total or partial functions on normal forms, in: BÖHM [1975], pp. 96–121.
see AUSIELLO and BÖHM [1978].

BOLLOBÁS, B.,
[1979] *Graph Theory* (Springer-Verlag, Berlin).

DE BRUIJN, N. G.,
[1970] The mathematical language Automath, its usage and some of its extensions, in: *Symposium on Automatic Demonstration*, IRIA, Versailles, Dec. 1968, Lecture Notes in Mathematics 125 (Springer-Verlag, Berlin), pp. 29–61.
[1972] Lambda calculus notation with nameless dummies, a tool for automatic formula manipulation, *Indag. Math.* 34, pp. 381–392.
[1980] A survey of the project Automath, in: HINDLEY and SELDIN [1980], pp. 579–607.

BUNDER, M. W.,
[1974] Some inconsistencies in illative combinatory logic, *Z. Math. Logik Grundlag. Math.* 20, pp. 71–73.
[1980] The naturalness of illative combinatory logic as a basis for mathematics, in: HINDLEY and SELDIN [1980], pp. 55–64.
[1981] Predicate calculus and naive set theory based on pure combinatory logic, *Arch. Math. Logik Grundlagenforsch.* 21, p. 169–177.

BURGE, W.,
[1978] *Recursive Programming Techniques* (Addison-Wesley, Reading, MA).

CHAUVIN, A.,
[1979] Theory of objects and set theory: introduction and semantics, *Notre Dame J. Formal Logic* 20, pp. 37–54.

CHURCH, A.,
[1932/3] A set of postulates for the foundation of logic, *Annals of Math.* (2) 33, pp. 346–366 and 34, pp. 839–864.
[1936] An unsolvable problem of elementary number theory, *Amer. J. Math.* 58, pp. 354–363.
[1936a] A note on the Entscheidungsproblem. A correction, *J. Symbolic Logic* 1, pp. 40–41, 101–102.
[1937] Combinatory logic as a semigroup (abstract), *Bull. Amer. Math. Soc.* 43, pp. 333.
[1941] *The Calculi of Lambda Conversion* (Princeton University Press, Princeton).
[1956] *Introduction to Mathematical Logic* (Princeton University Press, Princeton).

CHURCH, A. and KLEENE, S. C.,
[1937] Formal definitions in the theory of ordinal numbers, *Fund. Math.* 28, pp. 11–21.

CHURCH, A. and ROSSER, J. B.,
[1936] Some properties of conversion, *Trans. Amer. Math. Soc.* 39, pp. 472–482.

COHEN, L. J., LOS, J., PFEIFFER, H. and PODEWSKI, K.-P. (eds.),
[1982] *Logic, Methodology and Philosophy of Science VI (North-Holland, Amsterdam).*

COPPO, M.,
[198–] Completeness of type assignment in continuous lambda models, *Theor. Comput. Sci.*, to appear.

COPPO, M. et al. (= COPPO, M.,: DEZANI-CIANCAGLINI, M. and RONCHI DELLA ROCCA, S.),
[1978] (Semi-)separability of finite sets of terms in Scott's D_∞-models of the λ-calculus, in: AUSIELLO and BÖHM [1978], pp. 142–164.

COPPO, M. et al. (= COPPO, M., DEZANI-CIANCAGLINI, M. and VENNERI, B.),
[1980] Principal type schemes and λ-calculus semantics, in: HINDLEY and SELDIN [1980], pp. 535–560.

COPPO, M., DEZANI-CIANCAGLINI, M., HONSELL, F. and LONGO, G.,
[1983] Extended type structures and filter lambda models, in: LONGO, LOLLI and MARCIJA [1983], to appear.

CROSSLEY, J. N. (ed.),
[1975] *Algebra and Logic*, Lecture Notes in Mathematics 450 (Springer-Verlag, Berlin).

CROSSLEY, J. N. and DUMMETT, M. A. E. (eds.),
[1965] *Formal Systems and Recursive Functions*, Proc. 8th Logic Colloquium, Oxford, July 1963 (North-Holland, Amsterdam).

CURRY, H. B.,
[1930] Grundlagen der kombinatorischen Logik, *Amer. J. Math.* 52, pp. 509–536, 789–834.

CURRY, H. B. et al. (= CURRY, H. B. and FEYS, R.),
[1958] *Combinatory Logic, Vol. I* (North-Holland, Amsterdam).

CURRY, H. B. et al. (= CURRY, H. B.; HINDLEY, J. R. and SELDIN, J. P.),
[1972] *Combinatory Logic, Vol. II*, Studies in Logic 65 (North-Holland, Amsterdam).

VAN DAALEN, D. T.,
[1980] The Language Theory of Automath, Dissertation, Technological University Eindhoven.

VAN DALEN, D. ET AL. (= VAN DALEN, D., DOETS, H. C. and DE SWART, H. C. M.),
[1978] *Sets. Naive, Axiomatic and Applied* (Pergamon Press, New York).
see BOFFA et al. [1980].

DEBUSSY, C.,
[1903] Consideration sur le prix de Rome au point de vue musical, *Musica* (mai).

DEKKER, J. C. E. (ed.),
[1962] *Recursive Function Theory*, Proceedings of Symposia in Pure Mathematics, Vol. V (*Amer. Math. Soc., Providence, RI*).

DEZANI-CIANCAGLINI, M.,
[1976] Characterization of normal forms possessing inverse in the λ-β-η calculus, *Theor. Comput. Sci.* 2, pp. 323–337.
see BÖHM and DEZANI-CIANCAGLINI, M. [1972].
see COPPO et al. [1978].

DEZANI-CIANCAGLINI, M. and MONTANARI, U. (eds.),
[1982] *International Symposium on Programming*, Lecture Notes in Computer Science 137 (Springer-Verlag, Berlin).

DERSHOWITZ, N.,
[1982] Oderings for term rewriting systems *Theor. Comput. Sci.*, 17, pp. 279–301.

DILLER, J. and MÜLLER, G. H. (eds.),
[1975] *ISILC. Proof Theory Symposium*. Dedicated to Kurt Schütte on the Occasion of His 65-th Birthday. Proceedings of the International Summer Institute and Logic Colloquium, Kiel, 1974. Lecture Notes in Mathematics 500 (Springer-Verlag, Berlin).

DILLER, J. and VOGEL, H.,
[1975] Intensionale Funktionalinterpretation der Analysis, in: DILLER and MÜLLER [1975], pp. 56–72.

DOETS, H. C.,
see VAN DALEN et al. [1977].

DONAHUE, J.,
[1979] On the semantics of "data type", *SIAM J. Comput.* 8, pp. 546–560.

DRAGALIN, A. G.,
[1968] The computation of primitive recursive terms of finite type, and primitive recursive realization, Zap. Naucń. Sem. Leningrad, Otdel Mat. Inst. Steklov 8, pp. 32–45.

DUMMETT, M. A. E.,
see CROSSLEY and DUMMETT [1965].

ENDERTON, H. B.,
[1972] *A Mathematical Introduction to Logic* (Academic Press, New York and London).

ENGELER, E.,
[1981] Algebras and combinators, *Algebra Universalis* 13(3), pp. 389–392.

ERSHOV, IU. L.,
[1973/1975/1977] Theorie der Numerierungen, *Z. Math. Logik Grundlag. Math.* 19 (1973), pp. 289–388; 21 (1975), pp. 473–584 and 23 (1977), pp. 289–371.

FEFERMAN, S.,
[1975] A language and axioms for explicit mathematics, in: CROSSLEY [1975], pp. 87–139.
[1980] Constructive theories of functions and classes in: BOFFA et al. [1980], pp. 159–224.
[1982] Towards useful type-free theories I, preprint, Dept. Mathematics, Stanford, CA 94305, USA.

FENSTAD, J. E. (ed.),
[1971] *Proceedings of the Second Scandinavian Logic Symposium*, Studies in Logic 63 (North-Holland, Amsterdam).

FEYS, R.,
see CURRY et al. [1958].

FITCH, F. B.,
[1974] *Elements of Combinatory Logic* (Yale University Press, New Haven and London).
[1980] An extension of a system of combinatory logic, in: HINDLEY and SELDIN [1980], pp. 125–140.

FORTUNE. S., LEIVANT, D. and O'DONNELL, M.,
[1980] The expressiveness of simple and second order type structures, Research Report RC8542, IBM Research Center, Yorktown Heights, NY 10598, USA.

FREGE, G.,
[1893/1903] Grundgesetze der Arithmetik, begriffschriftlich abgeleitet (Jena; reprint: Olms, Hildesheim, 1962).

FRIEDMAN, H.,
[1975] Equality between functionals, in: PARIKH [1975], pp. 22–37.

GANDY, R. O.,
[1980] An early proof of normalisation by A. M. TURING, in: HINDLEY and SELDIN [1980], pp. 453–456.

GANDY, R. O. and YATES, C. M. E. (eds.),
[1971] *Logic Colloquium* '69, Studies in Logic 61 (North-Holland, Amsterdam).

GENTZEN, G.,
[1969] *The Collected Papers of Gerhard Gentzen*, Edited by M. E. Szabo (North-Holland, Amsterdam).

GIANNINI, P., and LONGO, G.,
[1983] Effectively given domains and lambda calculus semantics, Preprint, Dipt. Informatica, Corso Italia 40, 56100 Pisa, Italy.

GIERZ, G. et al. (= GIERZ, G.; LAWSON, J. D.; HOFMANN, K. H.; MISLOVE, M.; KEIMEL, K. and SCOTT, D. S.),
[1980] *A Compendium of Continuous Lattices* (Springer-Verlag, Berlin).

GIRARD, J.-Y.,

[1971] Une extension de l'interprétation de Gödel à l'analyse et son application à l'élimination des coupures dans l'analyse et la théorie des types, in: FENSTAD [1971], pp. 63–92.

GÖDEL, K.,

[1958] Über eine bisher noch nicht benützte Erweiterung des finiten Standpunktes, *Dialectica* 12, pp. 280–287.

GORDON, M. J. C.,

[1973] Evaluation and Denotation of Pure LISP, a Worked Example in Semantics, Dissertation, University of Edinburgh.

[1979] *The Denotational Description of Programming Languages* (Springer-Verlag, Berlin).

GORDON, M. J. C. et al. (= GORDON, M. J. C.; MILNER, R. and WADSWORTH, C.),

[1979] *Edinburgh LCF. A Mechanical Logic of Computation*, Lecture Notes in Computer Science 78 (Springer-Verlag, Berlin).

GUILLAUME, M. (ed.),

[1977] *Colloque International de Logique*, Clermont-Ferrand, 18–25 Juillet, 1975 (CNRS. Paris).

HALMOS, P. R.,

[1960] *Naive Set Theory* (D. van Nostrand, Princeton).

HARARY, F.,

[1969] *Graph Theory* (Addison-Wesley, Reading, MA), 3rd Ed. 1977.

HELMAN, G.,

[1977] Restricted Lambda-abstraction and the Interpretation of Some Non-classical Logics, Dissertation, University of Pittsburgh.

HENDERSON, P.,

[1980] *Functional Programming, Application and Implementation* (Prentice-Hall, London).

HEYTING, A. (ed.),

[1959] *Constructivity in Mathematics* (North-Holland, Amsterdam).

HINATA, S.,

[1967] Calculability of primitive recursive functionals of finite type, Science Reports of the Tokyo Kyoiku Daigaku, A, 9, pp. 218–235.

HINATANI, Y.,

[1966] Calculabilité des fonctionnels recursives primitives de type fini sur les nombres naturels, *Ann. Japan, Assoc. Philos. Sci.* 3, pp. 19–30.

HINDLEY, J. R.,

[1964] The Church-Rosser Property and a Result in Combinatory Logic, Dissertation, University of Newcastle-upon-Tyne.

[1967] Axioms for strong reduction in combinatory logic, *J. Symbolic Logic* 32, pp. 224–236.

[1969] The principal type scheme of an object in combinatory logic, *Trans. Amer. Math. Soc.* 146, pp. 29–60.

[1977] Combinatory reductions and lambda-reductions compared, *Z. Math. Logik Grundlag Math.* 23, pp. 169–180.

[1978] Reductions of residuals are finite, *Trans. Amer. Math. Soc.* 240, pp. 345–361.

HINDLEY, R.,

[1982] The simple semantics for Coppo-Dezani-Sallé type assignment, in: DEZANI-CIANCAGLINI and MONTANARI [1982], pp. 212–226.

[1983] The completeness for typing lambda terms, *Theor. Comput. Sci.* 22, pp. 1–17.

HINDLEY, J. R. et al. (= HINDLEY, J. R.; LERCHER, B. and SELDIN, J. P.),

[1972] *Introduction to Combinatory Logic* (Cambridge University Press, London).

HINDLEY, J. R. and LONGO, G.,
[1980] Lambda calculus models and extensionality, *Z. Math. Logik Grundlag. Math.* 26, pp. 289–310.

HINDLEY, J. R. and SELDIN, J. P. (eds.),
[1980] *To H. B. Curry: Essays on Combinatory Logic, Lambda-Calculus and Formalism* (Academic Press, New York and London).
see CURRY et al. [1972].

HOFMANN, K.-H.,
see GIERZ et al. [1980].

HOWARD, W.,
[1968] Functional interpretation of bar induction by bar recursion, *Comp. Math.* 20, pp. 107–124.
[1980] The formulae-as-types notion of construction, in: HINDLEY and SELDIN [1980], pp. 479–490.

HUET, G.,
[1977] Confluent reductions: abstract properties and applications to term rewriting systems, *18th IEEE Symposium on Foundations of Computer Science*, pp. 30–45.

HUET, G. and OPPEN, D. C.,
[1980] Equations and rewrite rules, a survey, Technical Report CSL-111, SRI International.

HYLAND, J. M. E.,
[1973] A simple proof of the Church-Rosser theorem, Typescript, Oxford University, 7 pp.
[1975] Recursion Theory on the Countable Functionals, Dissertation, Oxford University.
[1975a] A survey of some useful partial order relations on terms of the lambda calculus, in: BÖHM [1975], pp. 83–95.
[1976] A syntactic characterization of the equality in some models of the λ-calculus, *J. London Math. Soc.* (2), 12, pp. 361–370.

JACOPINI, G.,
[1975] A condition for identifying two elements of whatever model of combinatory logic, in: BÖHM [1975], pp. 213–219.

KALMÁR, L.,
[1937] Zurückführung des Entscheidungsproblem auf den Fall von Formeln mit einer einzigen binären Funktionsvariablen, *Compt. Math.* 4, pp. 137–144.

KANGER, S. (ed.),
[1975] *Proceedings of the Third Scandinavian Logic Symposium*, Studies in Logic 82 (North-Holland, Amsterdam).

KEIMEL, K.,
see GIERZ et al. [1980].

KEISLER, H. J.,
see BARWISE et al. [1980].

KELLEY, J. L.,
[1955] *General Topology* (D. van Nostrand, Princeton).

KLEENE, S. C.,
[1936] λ-definability and recursiveness, *Duke Math. J.* 2, pp. 340–353.
[1952] *Introduction to Metamathematics* (P. Noordhof N. V., Groningen).
[1961/1962] Lambda definable functionals of finite types, *Fundamenta Math.* 50, pp. 281–303.

KLEENE, S. C. and ROSSER, J. B.,
[1935] The inconsistency of certain formal logics, *Annals of Math.* (2) 36, pp. 630–636
see CHURCH and KLEENE [1937].

KLOP, J. W.,
[1975] On solvability by λ-*I*-terms, in: BÖHM [1975], pp. 342–345.
[1980] Combinatory reduction systems, Mathematical Center Tracts 129, Amsterdam.
[1980a] Reduction cycles in combinatory logic, in: HINDLEY and SELDIN [1980], pp. 193–214.
see BARENDREGT et al. [1976], [1976a], [1978].
see BERGSTRA and KLOP [1979], [1980], [1980a].
[1982] Extending partial combinatory algebras, *Bull. Europ. Ass. Theor. Comput. Sci.* 16, pp. 30–34.

KNASTER, B.,
[1928] Un thèoréme sur les fonctions d'ensembles, *Annales Soc. Pol. Math.* 6, pp. 133–134.

KNUTH, D. E.,
[1970] Examples of formal semantics, in: ENGELER, E. (ed.). *Symposium on Semantics and Algorithmic Languages*, Lecture Notes in Mathematics 188. (Springer-Verlag, Berlin) pp. 212–235.

KOYMANS, K.,
see BARENDREGT and KOYMANS [1980].
[1982] Models of the lambda calculus, *Inform. Control*, 52, pp. 306–332.
[1984] Models of the Lambda Calculus, Ph.D. dissertation, Mathematical Center Tracts, Amsterdam.

KREISEL, G.,
[1959] Interpretation of analysis by means of constructive functionals of finite types, in: HEYTING [1959], pp. 101–128.
[1971] Some reasons for generalizing recursion theory, in: GANDY and YATES [1971], pp. 139–198.

KUNEN, K.,
see BARWISE et al. [1980].

KUZICHEV, A. S.,
[1980] Sequential systems of lambda conversion and of combinatory logic, in: HINDLEY and SELDIN [1980], pp. 141–155.
[1983] Arithmetically consistent lambda theories of the type free logic, *Dokl. Akad. Nauk. SSSR* 268, pp. 288–292.

LAMBEK, J.,
[1980] From λ-calculus to cartesian closed categories, in: HINDLEY and SELDIN [1980], pp. 375–402.

LAMBEK, J., and SCOTT, P. J.,
[1982] Cartesian closed categories and lambda calculus, preprint, Dept. Mathematics, McGill University, Montreal, Canada.

LANDIN, P. J.,
[1965] A correspondence between ALGOL 60 and Church's lambda notation, *Comm. Assoc. Comput. Mach.* 8, pp. 89–101, 158–165.
[1966] A λ-calculus approach, in: *Advances in Programming and Nonnumerical Computation* (Pergamon Press, New York) pp. 97–141.
[1966a] The next 700 programming languages, *Comm. Assoc. Comput. Mach.* 9, pp. 157–164.

LAWVERE, F. W., (ed.),
[1972] *Toposes, Algebraic Geometry and Logic*, Lecture Notes in Mathematics 274 (Springer-Verlag, Berlin).

LAWSON, J. D.,
see GIERZ et al. [1980].

LERCHER, B.,
[1963] Strong Reduction and Recursion in Combinatory Logic, Dissertation, The Pennsylvania State University.

[1967] The decidability of Hindley's axioms for strong reduction, *J. Symbolic Logic* 32, pp. 237–239.
see HINDLEY et al. [1972].

LÉVY, J.-J.,
[1975] An algebraic interpretation of the λ-β-K-calculus and a labelled λ-calculus, in: BÖHM [1975], pp. 147–165.
[1978] Réductions correctes et optimales dans le lambda calcul, Thèse de doctorat d'état, Université Paris VII.
[1980] Optimal reductions in the lambda calculus, in: HINDLEY and SELDIN [1980], pp. 159–192.

LÖB, M. H.,
[1955] A solution of a problem of Henkin, *J. Symbolic Logic* 20, pp. 115–118.

LOECKX, J., (ed.),
[1974] *Automata, Languages and Programming*, 2nd Colloquium, University of Saarbrücken, 1974, Lecture Notes in Computer Science 14 (Springer-Verlag, Berlin).

LONGO, G.,
see BARENDREGT and LONGO [1980].
see HINDLEY and LONGO [1980].
[1983] Set-theoretical models of λ-calculus: theories, expansions, isomorphisms, *Ann. Pure Appl. Logic*, 24, pp. 153–188.

LONGO, G., LOLLI, G. and MARCJA, A. (eds.),
[198–] *Logic Colloquium '82* (North-Holland, Amsterdam).

LUCKHARDT, M.,
[1973] *Extensional Gödel Functional Interpretation. A Consistency Proof of Classical Analysis* Lecture Notes in Mathematics 306 (Springer-Verlag, Berlin).

MACLANE, S.,
[1972] *Categories for the Working Mathematician*, (Springer-Verlag, Berlin).

MANES, E. G.,
see ARBIB and MANES [1975].

MANN, C. R.,
[1975] The connection between equivalence of proofs and cartesian closed categories, *Proc. London Math. Soc.* (3) 31, pp. 289–310.

MARTIN-LÖF, P.,
[1982] Constructive mathematics and computer programming, in: COHEN et al. [1982], pp. 153–178.

MCALOON, K.,
see BOFFA et al. [1980].

MCCARTHY, J.,
[1962] *The LISP* 1.5 *Programmers' Manual* (MIT Press, Cambridge, MA).

MEREDITH, C. A. and PRIOR, A. N.,
[1963] Notes on the axiomatics of propositional calculus, *Notre Dame J. Formal Logic* 4, pp. 172–187.

VAN DER MEY, G.,
see VAN DER POEL et al. [1980].

MEYER, A.,
[1982] What is a model of the lambda calculus?, *Inform. Control* 52, pp. 87–122.

MILNE, R. E. and STRACHEY, C.,
[1976] *A Theory of Programming Language Semantics*, 2 vols. (Chapman and Hall, London; Wiley, New York).

MILNER, R.,
see GORDON et al [1980].

MISLOVE, M.,
see GIERZ et al. [1980].

MITSCHKE, G.,
[1976] λ-Kalkül, δ-Konversion und axiomatische Rekursionstheorie, Preprint Nr. 274, Technische Hochschule, Darmstadt. Fachbereit Mathematik, 77 pp.
[1979] The standardization theorem for the λ-calculus, *Z. Math. Logik Grundlag. Math.* 25, pp. 29–31.

MORRIS, J.-H.,
[1968] Lambda Calculus Models of Programming Languages, Dissertation, M.I.T.

MÜLLER, G. H.,
see DILLER and MÜLLER [1975].

MURSKII, V. L.,
[1967] Isomorphic embeddability of semigroups with countable sets of defining relations in finitely presented semigroups, *Mat. Zametki* 1, pp. 217–224.

NAKAJIMA, R.,
[1975] Infinite normal forms for the λ-calculus, in: BÖHM [1975], pp. 62–82.

NEWMAN, M. H. A.,
[1942] On theories with a combinatorial definition of "equivalence," *Ann. of Math.* (2) 43, pp. 223–243.

NIELSEN, M. and SCHMIDT, E. M. (eds.),
[1982] *Automata, Languages and Programming*, Lecture Notes in Computer Science 140 (Springer-Verlag, Berlin).

NIVAT, M. (ed.),
[1972] *Automata, Languages and Programming* (North-Holland, Amsterdam).

O'DONNELL, M. J.,
[1977] *Computing in Systems Described by Equations*, Lecture Notes in Computer Science 58 (Springer-Verlag, Berlin).

OLLONGREN, A.,
[1975] *A Definition of Programming Languages by Interpreting Automata* (Academic Press, New York and London).

PARIKH, R. (ed.),
[1975] *Logic Colloquium*, Symposium on Logic Held at Boston, 1972–1973, Lecture Notes in Mathematics 453 (Springer-Verlag, Berlin).

PARK, D.,
[1976] The *Y*-combinator in Scott's Lambda Calculus Models (revised version), Theory of Computation Report No. 13; University of Warwick, Dept. of Comput. Sci.

PÉTÈR, R.,
[1967] *Recursive Functions* (Academic Press, New York and London).

PLOTKIN, G. D.,
[1972] A Set-Theoretical Definition of Application, School of Artificial Intelligence, Memo MIP-R-95, University of Edinburgh.
[1974] The λ-calculus is ω-incomplete, *J. Symbolic Logic* 39, pp. 313–317.
[1975] Call-by-name, call-by-value and the λ-calculus, *Theor. Comput. Sci.* 1, pp. 125–159.
[1976] A powderdomain construction, *SIAM J. Comput.* 5, pp. 452–487.
[1977] LCF as a programming language, *Theor. Comput. Sci.* 5, pp. 223–257.
[1978] $\mathbb{T}^{\omega}$ as a universal domain, *J. Comput. Syst. Sci.* 17, pp. 209–236.

PLOTKIN, G. D. and SMYTH, M. B.,
[1978] The category-theoretic solution of recursive domain equations, DAI Research Report 60, University of Edinburgh.

VAN DER POEL, W. L. et al. (= VAN DER POEL, W. L.; SCHAAP, C. E. and VAN DER MEY, G.),
[1980] New Arithmetical Operators in the theory of Combinators, *Indag. Math.* 42 (to appear).

POTTINGER, G.,
[1977] Normalization as a homomorphic image of cut elimination, *Ann. Math. Logic* 12, pp. 323–357.

PRIOR, A. N.,
see MEREDITH and PRIOR [1963].

PROBLEMS,
[1975] Open problems, in: BÖHM [1975], pp. 367–370.
[1980] Open problems, *Bull. European Ass. Theor. Comp. Sci.* 10, pp. 136–140.

REYNOLDS, J. C.,
[1970] GEDANKEN—A simple typeless language based on principle of completeness and reference concept, *Comm. Assoc. Comput. Mach.* 13 (5), pp. 308–319.

REZUS, A.,
[1982] *A Bibliography of Lambda Calculi, Combinatory Logics and Related Topics*, Mathematical Center Tracts, Amsterdam.
[1982a] On a theorem of Tarski, *Libertas Math.* 2, pp. 63–97.

ROGERS, H.,
[1967] *Theory of Recursive Functions and Effective Operations* (McGraw Hill, New York)

RONCHI DELLA ROCCA, S.,
see COPPO et al. [1978].
[1982] Characterization theorem for the filter lambda model, preprint Dip. Informatica, Corso M. d'Azeglio 42, 10125 Torino, Italy.

ROSE, H. E. and SHEPERDSON, J. C. (eds.),
[1975] *Logic Colloquium* '73, Studies in Logic 80 (North-Holland, Amsterdam).

ROSEN, B. K.,
[1973] Tree manipulation systems and Church-Rosser theorems, *J. Assoc. Comput. Mach.* 20, pp. 160–187.

ROSSER, J. B.,
[1935] A mathematical logic without variables, *Annals of Math.* (2) 36, pp. 127–150; *Duke. Math. J.* 1, pp. 328–355.
see CHURCH and ROSSER [1936].
see KLEENE and ROSSER [1935].

SANCHIS, L. E.,
[1967] Functionals defined by recursion, *Notre Dame J. Formal Logic* 8, p. 161–174.
[1979] Reducibilities in two models for combinatory logic, *J. Symbolic Logic* 44, pp. 221–234.

SCARPELLINI, B.,
[1971] A model for bar recursion of higher types, *Comp. Math.* 23, pp. 123–153.

SCHAAP, C. E.,
see VAN DER POEL et al. [1980].

SCHÖNFINKEL, M.,
[1924] Über die Bausteine der mathematischen Logik, *Math. Annalen* 92, pp. 305–316.

SCHROER, D. E.,
[1965] The Church-Rosser Theorem, Dissertation, Cornell University, Ithaca, NY.

SCHWICHTENBERG, H.,
[1975] Elimination of higher type levels in definitions of primitive recursive functions by means of transfinite recursion, in: ROSE and SHEPERDSON [1975], pp. 279–303.
[1975/6] Definierbare Funktionen im λ-Kalkül mit Typen, *Arch. Math. Logik Grundlagenforsch.* 17, (3–4), pp. 113–114.
[1982] Complexity of normalizations in the pure typed lambda calculus, in: TROELSTRA and VAN DALEN [1982], pp. 453–458.

SCOTT, D. S.,
[1963] A system of functional abstraction (unpublished).
[1969] Models for the λ-calculus, Manuscript (unpublished), 53 pp.
[1972] Continuous lattices in: LAWVERE [1972], pp. 97–136.
[1973] Models for various type free calculi, in: SUPPES et al. [1973], pp. 157–187,
[1974] The language LAMBDA (abstract), *J. Symbolic Logic* 39, pp. 425–427.
[1975] Lambda calculus and recursion theory, in: KANGER [1975], pp. 154–193.
[1975a] Combinators and classes, in: BÖHM [1975], pp. 1–26.
[1975b] Some philosophical issues concerning theories of combinators, in: BÖHM [1975], pp. 346–366.
[1976] Data types as lattices, *SIAM J. Comput.* 5, pp. 522–587.
[1980] Lambda calculus: some models, some philosophy, in: BARWISE et al. [1980], pp. 223–266.
[1980a] Relating theories of the λ-calculus, in: HINDLEY and SELDIN [1980], p. 403–450.
see GIERZ et al. [1980].
[1982] Domains for denotational semantics, in: NIELSEN and SCHMIDT [1982], pp. 577–613.

SCOTT, D. S. and STRACHEY, C.,
[1971] Toward a mathematical semantics for computer languages, Proc. Symp. on Computers and Automata, Polytechnic Institute of Brooklyn, 21, pp. 19–46.

SELDIN, J. P.,
[1976/7] Recent advances in Curry's program, *Rend. Sem. Mat. Univers. Politecn. Torino* 35, pp. 77–88.
[1979] Progress report on generalized functionality, *Ann. Math. Logic* 17, pp. 29–59.
see CURRY et al. [1972].
see HINDLEY et al. [1972].
see HINDLEY and SELDIN [1980].

SHEPERDSON, J. C.,
see ROSE and SHEPERDSON [1975].

SHOENFIELD, J. R.,
[1967] *Mathematical Logic* (Addison-Wesley, Reading, MA).

SPECTOR, C.,
[1962] Provably recursive functionals of analysis: a consistency proof of analysis by an extension of principles formulated in current intuitionistic mathematics, in: DEKKER [1962], pp. 1–27.

STAPLES, J.,
[1975] Church-Rosser Theorems for replacement systems, in: CROSSLEY [1975], pp. 291–307.

STATMAN, R.,
[1979] The typed λ-calculus is not elementary recursive, *Theor. Comput. Sci.* 9, pp. 73–81
[1980] On the existence of closed terms in the typed lambda calculus I, in: HINDLEY and SELDIN [1980], pp. 511–534.
[1981] On the existence of closed terms in the typed lambda calculus II: transformations of unification problems, *Theor. Comput. Sci.* 15, pp. 329–338.
[1982] Completeness, invariance and λ-definability, *J. Symbolic Logic* 47(1), pp. 17–26.

STOY, J. E.,
[1977] *Denotational Semantics. The Scott-Strachey Approach to Programming Languages* (MIT Press, Cambridge).

STRACHEY, C.,
see MILNE and STRACHEY [1976].
see SCOTT and STRACHEY [1971].

STRONG, H.,
[1968] Algebraically generalized recursive function theory, *IBM J. Research Develop.* 12, pp. 465–475.

SUPPES, P. et al. (= SUPPES, P.; HENKIN, L.; JOJA, A.; MOISIL, GR. C. (eds.)),
[1973] *Logic, Methodology and Philosophy of Science IV*, Studies in Logic 74 (North-Holland, Amsterdam).

DE SWART, H. C. M.,
see VAN DALEN et al. [1977].

SZABO, M. E.,
[1978] *Algebra of Proofs*, Studies in Logic 88 (North-Holland, Amsterdam).

TAIT, W.,
[1965] Infinitely long terms of transfinite type, in: CROSSLEY and DUMMETT [1965], pp. 176–185.
[1967] Intensional Interpretations of functionals of finite type I, *J. Symbolic Logic* 32, pp. 198–212.
[1971] Normal form theorem for barrecursive functions of finite type, in: FENSTAD [1971], pp. 393–367.

TARSKI, A.,
[1955] A lattice-theoretical fixed point theorem and its applications, *Pacific J. Math.* 5, pp. 285–309.

TERLOUW, J.,
[1982] On definition trees of ordinal recursive functionals: reduction of the recursion orders by means of type level raisings, *J. Symbolic Logic* 47(2), pp. 395–403

TROELSTRA, A. S. (ed.),
[1973] *Metamathematical Investigations of Intuitionistic Arithmetic and Analysis*, Lecture Notes in Mathematics 344 (Springer-Verlag, Berlin).

TROELSTRA, A. S.,
[1975] Nonextensional equality, *Fundamenta Math.* 82, pp. 307–322.

TROELSTRA, A. S. and VAN DALEN, D. (eds.),
[1982] *The L. E. J. Brouwer Centenary Symposium* (North-Holland, Amsterdam).

TURING, A. M.,
[1936] On computable numbers with an application to the Entscheidungsproblem, *Proc. London Math. Soc.* 42, pp. 230–265.
[1937] Computability and λ-definability *J. Symbolic Logic* 2, pp. 153–163.
[1937a] The $\mathfrak{p}$-functions in λ-*K*-conversion *J. Symbolic Logic* 2, pp. 164.

TURNER, D. A.,
[1979] A new implementation technique for applicative languages, *Software-practice and Experience* 9, pp. 31–49.

VENNERI, B.,
see COPPO et al. [1980].

VISSER, A.,
[1980] Numerations, λ-calculus and arithmetic, in: HINDLEY and SELDIN [1980], pp. 259–284.

VOGEL, H.,
[1967] Ein starker Normalisationssatz für die Bar-rekursiven Funktionale, *Arch. Math. Logik* 18, pp. 81–84.
see DILLER and VOGEL [1975].

VOLKEN, H.,
[1978] Formale Stetigkeit und Modelle des Lambda-Kalküls, Dissertation, Eidgen. Technische Hochschule, Zürich.
see BARENDREGT et al. [1976], [1976a], [1978].

WADSWORTH, C. P.,
[1971] Semantics and Pragmatics of the Lambda-calculus, Dissertation. Oxford University.
[1976] The relation between computational and denotational properties for Scott's D_∞-models of the lambda-calculus, *SIAM J. Comput.* 5, pp. 488–521.
[1980] Some unusual λ-calculus numeral systems, in: HINDLEY and SELDIN [1980], pp. 215–230.
see GORDON et al. [1980].

WAGNER, E.,
[1969] Uniform reflexive structures: on the nature of Gödelizations and relative computability, *Trans. Amer. Math. Soc.* 144, pp. 1–41.

WEGNER, P.,
[1972] *The Vienna Definition Language*, AGM Computing Surveys 4.

WELCH, P. H.,
[1975] Continuous semantics and inside out reductions, in: BÖHM [1975], pp. 122–146.

YATES, C. M. E.,
see GANDY and YATES [1971].

ZUCKER, J.,
[1975] Formalization of classical mathematics in Automath, in: GUILLAUME [1977], pp. 135–145.

INDEX OF NAMES

INDEX OF DEFINITIONS

INDEX OF SYMBOLS

The symbols are classified in the following categories: *terms*, *sets of terms*, *operations on terms*, *relations between terms*, *reduction*, *trees*, *theories*, *models* and *other symbols*.

For most symbols the definition is given, or else they are used in a typical context.

Terms

λ-terms

$\mathbf{I}$	$\equiv \lambda x.x$	31
$\mathbf{K}$	$\equiv \lambda xy.x$	31
$\mathbf{S}$	$\equiv \lambda xyz.xz(yz)$	31
$\mathbf{B}$	$\equiv \lambda xyz.x(yz)$	194
$\mathbf{C}$	$\equiv \lambda xyz.xzy$	194
$\mathbf{1}$	$\equiv \lambda xy.xy$	77
$\mathbf{1}_n$	"$\lambda x_1 \cdots x_n.x_1 \cdots x_n$"	116
$\mathbf{\Omega}$	$\equiv (\lambda x.xx)(\lambda x.xx)$	133
$\mathbf{Y}$	$\equiv \lambda f.(\lambda x.f(xx))(\lambda x.f(xx))$ $\mathbf{Y}f = f(\mathbf{Y}f)$	131
$\mathbf{\Theta}$	$\equiv (\lambda xy.y(xxy))(\lambda xy.y(xxy))$ $\mathbf{\Theta}f \twoheadrightarrow f(\mathbf{\Theta}f)$	132
$\mathbf{T}$	$\equiv \lambda xy.x (\equiv \mathbf{K})$ (true)	133
$\mathbf{F}$	$\equiv \lambda xy.y$ (false)	133
$\mathbf{U}_i^n$	$\equiv \lambda x_0 \cdots x_n.x_i$	134
π_i^n	$\pi_i^n[M_0, \ldots, M_n] = M_i \ (1 \leqslant i \leqslant n)$	134
$\mathbf{P}_i^n$	$\mathbf{P}_i^n\langle M_0, \ldots, M_n\rangle = M_i \ (1 \leqslant i \leqslant n)$	134
$\ulcorner n \urcorner$	the nth numeral	134
$\mathbf{S}^+$	$\mathbf{S}^+ \ulcorner n \urcorner = \ulcorner n+1 \urcorner$	134
$\mathbf{P}^-$	$\mathbf{P}^- \ulcorner n+1 \urcorner = \ulcorner n \urcorner$	134
Zero	**Zero** $x = \mathbf{T}$ if $x = \ulcorner 0 \urcorner$ $= \mathbf{F}$ if $x = \ulcorner n+1 \urcorner$	134

CL-terms

λI-terms

Sets of Terms

Operations on Terms

Relations between Terms

Reduction

Notions of reduction

On Λ

On Λ'

On $\Lambda\bot$

On $\Lambda\bot^{\mathbf{N}}$

Reduction strategies

Other concepts related with reductions

Trees

Models